You May Ask Yourself

AN INTRODUCTION TO THINKING LIKE A SOCIOLOGIST

Seventh Edition

You May Ask Yourself

AN INTRODUCTION TO THINKING LIKE A SOCIOLOGIST

Dalton Conley

PRINCETON UNIVERSITY

W. W. NORTON
NEW YORK | LONDON

W. W. Norton & Company has been independent since its founding in 1923, when William Warder Norton and Mary D. Herter Norton first published lectures delivered at the People's Institute, the adult education division of New York City's Cooper Union. The firm soon expanded its program beyond the Institute, publishing books by celebrated academics from America and abroad. By mid-century, the two major pillars of Norton's publishing program—trade books and college texts—were firmly established. In the 1950s, the Norton family transferred control of the company to its employees, and today—with a staff of five hundred and hundreds of trade, college, and professional titles published each year—W. W. Norton & Company stands as the largest and oldest publishing house owned wholly by its employees.

Editor: Michael Moss
Project Editor: Michael Fauver
Assistant Editor: Angie Merila
Managing Editor, College: Marian Johnson
Managing Editor, College Digital Media: Kim Yi
Production Manager: Sean Mintus
Media Editor: Eileen Connell
Media Project Editor: Danielle Belfiore
Associate Media Editor: Ariel Eaton
Media Editorial Assistant: Alexandra Park
Marketing Director, Sociology: Julia Hall
Book Designer: Kiss Me I'm Polish LLC, New York
Design Director: Rubina Yeh
Director of College Permissions: Megan Schindel
Photo Editor: Melinda Patelli
College Permissions Associate: Patricia Wong
Composition: Six Red Marbles
Manufacturing: Transcontinental

ISBN: 978-0-393-42829-2

Library of Congress Cataloging-in-Publication Data
Names: Conley, Dalton, 1969- author.
Title: You may ask yourself : an introduction to thinking like a sociologist /
    Dalton Conley, Princeton University.
Description: Seventh edition. | New York : W.W. Norton, [2021] | Includes bibliographical
    references and index.
Identifiers: LCCN 2020053655 | ISBN 9780393428292 (paperback) | ISBN
    9780393537611 (epub)
Subjects: LCSH: Sociology—Methodology. | Sociology—Study and teaching.
Classification: LCC HM511 .C664 2021 | DDC 301.01—dc23
LC record available at https://lccn.loc.gov/2020053655

W. W. Norton & Company, Inc., 500 Fifth Avenue, New York, NY 10110
wwnorton.com
W. W. Norton & Company, Ltd., 15 Carlisle Street, London W1D 3BS

3 4 5 6 7 8 9 0

Brief Contents

Contents

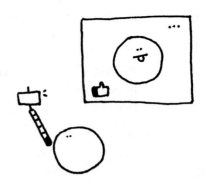

202 CHAPTER 6: SOCIAL CONTROL AND DEVIANCE

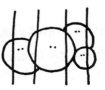

732 CHAPTER 17: SCIENCE, THE ENVIRONMENT, AND SOCIETY

Preface

I came to sociology by accident, so to speak. During the 1980s, there were no sociology courses at the high-school level, so I entered college with only the vaguest notion of what sociology—or even social science—was. Instead, I headed straight for the pre-med courses. But there was no such thing as a pre-med major, so I ended up specializing in the now defunct "humanities field major." This un-major major was really the result of my becoming a junior and realizing that I was not any closer to a declared field of study than I had been when arriving two years earlier. So I scanned a list of all the electives I had taken until then—philosophy of aesthetics, history of technology, and so on—and marched right into my adviser's office, declaring that it had always been my lifelong dream to study "art and technology in the twentieth century." I wrote this up convincingly enough, apparently, because the college allowed me to write a senior thesis about how the evolution of Warner Brothers' cartoon characters—from the stuttering, insecure Porky Pig to the militant Daffy Duck to the cool, collected, and confident Bugs Bunny—reflected the self-image of the United States on the world stage during the Depression, World War II, and the postwar period, respectively. Little did I know, I was already becoming a sociologist.

After college, I worked as a journalist but then decided that I wanted to continue my schooling. I was drawn to the critical stance and reflexivity that I had learned in my humanities classes, but I knew that I didn't want to devote my life to arcane texts. What I wanted to do was take those skills—that critical stance—and apply them to everyday life, to the here and now. I also was rather skeptical of the methods that humanists used. What texts they chose to analyze always seemed so arbitrary. I wanted to systematize the inquiry a bit more; I found myself trying to apply the scientific method that I had gotten a taste of in my biology classes. But I didn't want to do science in a lab. I wanted to be out in the proverbial real world. So when I flipped through a course catalog with these latent preferences somewhere in the back of my head, my finger landed on the sociology courses.

Once I became a card-carrying sociologist, the very first course I taught was Introduction to Sociology. I had big shoes to fill in teaching this course at Yale. Kai Erikson, the world-renowned author of *Wayward Puritans* and

Everything in Its Path and the son of psychologist Erik Erikson, was stepping down from his popular course, The Human Universe, and I, a first-year assistant professor, was expected to replace him.

I had a lot of sociology to learn. After all, graduate training in sociology is spotty at best. And there is no single theory of society to study in the same way that one might learn, for example, the biochemistry of DNA transcription and translation as the central dogma of molecular biology. We talk about the sociological imagination as an organizing principle. But even that is almost a poetic notion, not so easily articulated. Think of sociology as more like driving a car than learning calculus. You can read the manual all you want, but that isn't going to teach you how to do it. Only by seeing sociology in action and then trying it yourself will you eventually say, "Hey, I've got the hang of this!" The great Chinese philosopher Confucius said about learning: "By three methods we may learn wisdom: First, by reflection, which is noblest; second, by imitation, which is easiest; and third by experience, which is the bitterest." Hopefully you can skip the bitterness, but you get the general idea. For example, by trying to fix a local problem through appealing to your elected officials, you might better grasp sociological theories of the state.

Hence the title of this book. In *You May Ask Yourself*, I show readers how sociologists question what most others take for granted about society, and I give readers opportunities to apply sociological ways of thinking to their own experiences. I've tried to jettison the arcane academic debates that become the guiding light of so many intro books in favor of a series of contemporary empirical (gold) nuggets that show off sociology (and empirical social science more generally) in its finest hour. Most students who take an introductory sociology class in college will not end up being sociology majors, let alone professional sociologists. Yet I aim to speak to both the aspiring major and the student who is merely fulfilling a requirement. So rather than having pages filled with statistics and theories that will go out of date rather quickly, *You May Ask Yourself* tries to instill in the reader a way of thinking—a scientific approach to human affairs that is portable, one that students will find useful when they study anything else, whether history or medicine.

To achieve this ambitious goal, I tried to write a book that was as "un-textbook"-like as possible, while covering all the material that a student in sociology needs to know. In this vein, each chapter is organized around a motivating paradox, meant to serve as the first chilling line of a mystery novel that motivates the reader to read on to find out (or rather, figure out, because this book is not about spoon-feeding facts) the nugget, the debate, the fundamentally new way of looking at the world that illuminates the paradox. Along with a paradox, each chapter begins with a profile of a relevant person who speaks to the core theme of the chapter. These range from myself to Angelina Jolie to a guy who wore a rainbow-colored clown wig to try and get media attention to share his Christian message. In addition, to show the usefulness of sociological knowledge in shaping the world around us, each chapter culminates in a Policy discussion and a Practice activity for students.

WHAT'S NEW IN THE SEVENTH EDITION

Higher education is in rapid transition, with online instruction expanding in traditional institutions, in the expanding for-profit sector, and in the new open-courseware movement. The industry is still very much in flux, with massive open online courses (MOOCs) failing to displace traditional classroom education (so far). With these changes, textbooks must also reinvent and reorient themselves. Students now expect, I believe, an entire multimedia experience when they purchase a textbook.

To that end, the Third Edition included animations of the associated chapter Paradoxes. For the Fourth Edition, in addition to a new round of interviews with sociologists, we filmed Sociology on the Street assignment videos. To illustrate a "breaching experiment," for example, I went on camera to perform one myself. It has been years since I have been as nervous speaking on camera as I was the day I walked—barefoot but dressed in a suit—into W. W. Norton's conference room filled with unsuspecting volunteers and proceeded to clip my toenails while I explained the plan for the day and we surreptitiously filmed their (surprisingly unflinching) response. In the Fifth Edition, we brought the streets into the classroom. Along with new Q&A videos with professional sociologists, we added videos (and text) from folks outside the ivory tower who are doing sociology in their work. These interviews help students understand the real-world relevance of sociology and reflect the applied turn in the field.

Further reflecting the increasing emphasis on applications within the discipline, the Sixth Edition featured a revamping of the fourth "P" in each chapter (the first three being the Paradox, Person, and Policy). Rather than just answering review questions, Practice activities send students out into the proverbial "streets" (sometimes just metaphorically), where they get to learn by doing—whether that's discovering the true price of unpaid labor in our personal economies, analyzing the structural forces that contribute to one's own carbon emissions, better managing competing roles and statuses in one's life, or, failing that, figuring out how to completely disappear in today's totally connected society. The other major change to the Sixth Edition was an overhaul of the Gender chapter. Perhaps no domain of social life in US society has changed more dramatically in the past few years than that of gender. So with extensive help from experts in the fields of sex, gender, and sexuality, I really tried to dig into the concept of gender, turning it inside out, in the service of conveying an understanding of gender and the sex—gender system as something processual and fluid.

The graying of America is of increasing social importance, so the Seventh Edition features new coverage of aging-related topics throughout the book. Several new interviews with sociologists and gerontologists focus on inequalities in the aging experience and the social determinants of health and aging. Other new "sociological conversation" interviews explore intergroup race relations, immigration, and indoctrination in public education. While working on the Seventh Edition, we witnessed the devastation of the coronavirus pandemic as well as the widespread protests for racial justice that followed the killing of George Floyd. These events get covered in multiple chapters, including an expanded treatment of the Black Lives Matter movement in the Collective Action, Social Movements, and Social Change chapter, a new section on COVID-19 health inequalities in the Health and Society chapter, and my own experience contracting the coronavirus disease as the Person example in the opener to the Health and Society chapter.

Finally, we have changed the conventions regarding capitalization of racial/ethnic categories. Specifically, in this edition, racial and ethnic categorizations are considered proper nouns and thus are capitalized. As Temple University journalism professor Lori Tharps notes, "Black with a capital B refers to people of the African diaspora. Lowercase black is simply a color" (Tharps, 2014). In the same way, "White" as a racial category acknowledges the functions of this label in society. Racial designations are not neutral markers of skin tone, but socially constructed categories whose meanings and boundaries shift over time and place. Treating these categories as proper nouns recognizes them as such (Appiah, 2020).

There is an alternative school of thought that claims that capitalization leads to reification of those somewhat arbitrary and historically contingent categories and thus argues for capitalizing neither label. Indeed, some languages do not even capitalize nationalities. Yet another line of reasoning says that Black should be capitalized but white should not be on the grounds that there is a common experience of structural racism among the African diaspora while there is no unifying experience of white people and that capitalizing it only lends legitimacy to those who seek a "white nationalism." But this, in turn, denies the commonness of White privilege, for example, as a shared referent. Of course, it also denies the folk usage of White as a socially constructed term that conveys a tacit understanding of membership in a particular identity group. To those who say the White experience is too diverse to deserve such a label, the same can be said for the Black experience.

Then there is the issue of how to call those who might be referred to as Hispanic or of Hispanic origin or Latino. Over the last couple of decades, Latino has become a preferred way to reference the diverse category of people that includes those of Cuban, Puerto Rican, Mexican, Guatemalan, and Colombian descent—to name a few. It also includes those from Latin America who hail from non-Spanish-speaking countries, such as people of Brazilian descent (who typically speak Portuguese) or those from Belize (where English is an official language). Meanwhile, the term *Hispanic* is a language-based category that also included people from Spain but excluded those whose origin was in Latin American countries that were not Spanish-speaking (e.g., Brazil). Never mind that significant populations from some "Spanish-speaking" countries speak indigenous languages (and not Spanish) such as Quechua.

While most people who would fit into either of these categories actually prefer to use their specific national origin to denote their identity (such as Mexican or Mexican American), the terms remain in common usage for a variety of reasons—not least of which is that Hispanic has been an official US government category since 1977 (a development that was pursued thanks to the wishes of some [pro-assimilationist, conservative] Mexican American political groups). The term *Latino*, meanwhile, gained usage currency starting in the 1990s. Today, however, there is increasing recognition that—as for terms in other Latin-derived languages—the male designation stands in for a mixed-gendered category. Some activists see its assimilation into English as an opportunity to change that gender dynamic and prefer to use the term *Latinx*—the "x" removing any gendered connotation from the group. This is the term that is used in the present edition. Some readers may object to this choice on the basis that strong majorities of Latinx individuals, when surveyed, reject the term. However, linguistic innovations often start among a highly engaged, highly informed minority to whom the issue is of paramount importance. Such is the case with Latinx. Of course, like all terms for social groups, this one may fade or further evolve, in which case, look out for new usage in the future editions! (This is, of course, true for all the categories discussed herein.) All of these decisions are highly political and sociological, and my own subject position as a cis-White male should be acknowledged in my role as the author who has had to make these decisions (in conjunction with, of course, the editor/publisher and in consideration of reviewer/reader feedback).

In addition, we revised every chapter in the book to include updated data, research, and examples. Here are some of the highlights:

WHAT'S NEW CHAPTER BY CHAPTER

CHAPTER 1: THE SOCIOLOGICAL IMAGINATION: AN INTRODUCTION

By reviewer request, the discussion of the merits of a college degree has been condensed and edited for clarity. It also includes updated data on the cost of college and earnings by degree holders. The discussion of the history of sociology now includes the key terms **positivism** and **interpretive sociology**. The section on modern sociological theories has been reorganized to group together the theories of functionalism, conflict theory, and symbolic interactionism to make it easier for students to understand these foundational theories in relation to one another. A completely new section, Doing Theory, addresses how sociologists use theory in practice. It also includes a new table that shows how different theory perspectives approach the same topic, in this case using household division of labor as the example.

CHAPTER 2: METHODS

To help illustrate how sociologists conduct research, a more detailed discussion of how danah boyd uses both qualitative and quantitative methods in her research has been added. A new Policy feature addresses the 2020 Census and the controversy over the attempt by Wilbur Ross (secretary of commerce under President Trump) to add a question about citizenship to the census questionnaire.

CHAPTER 3: CULTURE AND MEDIA

By reviewer request, the discussion on Goth culture now references Peter Hodkinson's historical overview of the subculture. The section on the history of media includes updated data on the percentage of Americans with broadband internet access at home as well as those who use smartphones as their main source of internet access. The section on stereotypes features new coverage of the underrepresentation of Black professionals in the media and publishing industries. In the section on the political economy of the media, a new discussion concerning how and why the internet often reinforces prejudices has been added.

CHAPTER 4: SOCIALIZATION AND THE CONSTRUCTION OF REALITY

The section on family socialization features research from Amy Hsin on whether the amount of time parents spend at home with their children affects children's cognitive outcomes. This section also features new research that Thomas Laidley and I conducted on how weather patterns affect children's performance in school. The section on peer socialization has been updated with a newer study on where adolescents learn about dating and sex. The section on adult socialization has been thoroughly revised and now covers Erik Erikson's eight stages of human development as well as agents of socialization for older adults. The section on social interaction has a new discussion of gender reveal parties and expanded coverage of adolescent socialization and gender roles.

CHAPTER 5: GROUPS AND NETWORKS

The section on networks includes a new "sociological conversation" interview with Stacy Torres that introduces the concept of elastic social ties, which she developed while researching aging in place among older adults living in cities. A video of the interview is embedded in the ebook. The section on social capital has been condensed and edited for clarity.

CHAPTER 6: SOCIAL CONTROL AND DEVIANCE

The section on the US criminal justice system includes a new analysis of explanations for the declining crime rate that began in the 1990s. It also covers the First Step Act of 2018 in the discussion of federal prison reforms. A new "sociological conversation" interview with Jacqueline Stevens addresses controversial ICE detention practices of undocumented immigrants. A video of the interview is embedded in the ebook. Figures and data throughout the chapter have been updated with the most recently available information about crime and homicide rates, prison population and demographics, executions, and death row exonerations.

CHAPTER 7: STRATIFICATION

A new section on modern theories of inequality has been added. This new section discusses the emergence of structural functionalism and conflict theory as interpretive lenses through which to view inequality. The section on the elite–mass stratification dichotomy includes new data on financial elites in high-ranking political positions. The chapter includes updated data on how much CEOs of America's largest companies make compared to the average worker, the proportion of high-school graduates who attend college, and the poverty line for a family of four in 2020. In the section on global inequality, a new figure has been added that shows GDP per capita for countries around the world.

CHAPTER 8: GENDER

In the section on conflict theories, Marilyn Frye's metaphor of a birdcage has been added to illustrate the concepts of intersectionality and gender inequality. The overall discussion of theory has also been simplified and edited for clarity. By reviewer request, the section on inequality at work features a new discussion of holistic approaches to harassment and includes findings from a recent National Academies of Science report. The section on sociology in the bedroom features recent research from Lisa Wade in her book, *American Hookup: The New Culture of Sex on Campus*. A new subsection on sex and aging has been added that covers research on relationships and sexual activity among the 65+ population. Data and figures throughout the chapter have been updated with the most recently available information, including the percentage of US children living in households with married parents, college enrollment numbers by gender, the prevalence of violent crime victimization by gender, gender- and race-based pay disparities, the average age of marriage, and sexual activity among high-school students.

CHAPTER 9: RACE

This chapter includes a new "sociological conversation" interview with Maria Abascal on the declining White majority in the United States and how that affects inter-group relations. To help students understand the concepts of race and ethnicity, I've added a story about the personal experience of an individual who is Korean-born, Italian-raised, and now living in the United States. The section that was previously called "Ethnic Groups in the United States" has been reframed around racial groups to help clarify the distinctions between race and ethnicity. Throughout the racial groups section, US population data by group have been updated with the most recently available information. Data on unemployment rates by race and racial wealth disparities have also been updated. Near the end of the chapter, a new "sociological conversation" interview with Kevin Lewis discusses his research on dating apps and how racial barriers can be either reinforced or broken down in an online dating environment.

CHAPTER 10: POVERTY

By reviewer request, the section on the culture of poverty has been condensed and edited for clarity. A discussion about universal basic income and its recent appearance in American politics has been added. The section on the war on poverty has an extended treatment of evictions in the United States, including a more detailed look at Matthew Desmond's research. The section on absolute and relative poverty features a more thorough explanation of income inequality and relative poverty. Figures and data have been updated throughout the chapter with the most recently available information, including the US poverty rate, cost of living, median net worth of Americans, and global poverty rates by country.

CHAPTER 11: HEALTH AND SOCIETY

A new chapter opener tells the story of my own experience contracting the coronavirus disease. The section on the social determinants of health and illness features a new "sociological conversation" interview with Morgan Levine on how our social environments age us in uneven ways. To make room for new content, the section on the relationship between height and health has been removed. The section on postnatal health inequalities includes a new discussion of my own research on health outcome disparities among siblings with different skin colors. This section also features a new "sociological conversation" interview with Daniel Belsky about sex differences in health and mortality rates. A new section on aging and health continues the discussion of Daniel Belsky's research on aging and inequality and analyzes various methods for determining a person's health level and biological age. A new section on health care for older Americans includes a discussion of the aging US population and long-term care for older adults, and a new "sociological conversation" interview with Corey Abramson concerning his research on inequality in the aging experience. Following this, a new section explores the "Black–White mortality cross-over" concept, in which it is thought that even though Black Americans live shorter lives on average than White Americans, Black Americans who make it to a certain age then tend to live longer than their White American counterparts. A new section on the COVID-19 pandemic and health inequalities related to it has been added. It also includes a new figure on infection and mortality rates by race. Throughout the chapter, data and figures have been updated with the most recently available information.

CHAPTER 12: FAMILY

A new chapter opener explores changing family patters through my own experience becoming a new parent again two decades after having my first child. The section on Malinowski and the traditional family has a new discussion of the creation and dominance of the nuclear family model as a norm in post–World War II America. The discussion of cross-cultural variations in family structure has been expanded to help clarify that the nuclear family as a norm is far from universal. This section also expands its coverage of the Na people in southwestern China and how family structures there impact gendered behavior. Data and figures throughout the chapter have been updated with the most recently available information, including marriage and divorce rates, median age for marriage, birthrate and adoption rates, labor force participation among women, family structure variations by race and socioeconomic status, and opinions on same-sex marriage.

CHAPTER 13: EDUCATION

A new "sociological conversation" interview with Tamara Pavasović Trošt discusses the "hidden curriculum" in the United States and abroad. Amanda Lewis and John Diamond's research from their book, *Despite the Best Intentions: How Racial Inequality Thrives in Good Schools*, has been added. A new section on adult learning covers the impact of lifelong learning on older adults, citing research from Slovenia, Finland, and England. The section on class-based inequalities in schooling now addresses how the COVID-19 pandemic has exacerbated socioeconomic disparities. The section on race-based inequalities in schooling offers new research on how the differential between punishment of Black and White students may account for Black-White test score gaps. This section also now features research from Patrick Sharkey on how neighborhood violence has negatively impacted Black children's test scores relative to their White peers.

The section on the gene movement has been expanded to cover and critique Charles Murray's 2020 book, *Human Diversity: The Biology of Gender, Race, and Class.* Data and figure updates include more recent information on functional illiteracy and mathematical illiteracy, the percentage of the US population with a college degree, educational attainment and poverty rates by race and ethnicity, and the gender pay gap.

CHAPTER 14: CAPITALISM AND THE ECONOMY

The section on the service sector now discusses how the COVID-19 pandemic has impacted service sector workers. A new section on how the aging population and workforce impacts the economy has been added. It also introduces the Horndal effect and how research in Sweden has shown that older workforces can be quite productive. The feature on the gig economy has been updated to address how gig workers have been affected by the COVID-19 pandemic. The section on globalization has been updated to include the 2020 USMCA trade agreement between the United States, Mexico, and Canada. Data and figures throughout the chapter have been updated with the most recently available information, including gender pay gap data, the proportion of US married families that are either single- or dual-income, paid family leave trends, global wealth disparities, global hunger rates, and unionization rates.

CHAPTER 15: AUTHORITY AND THE STATE

The section on authority, legitimacy, and the state has been updated to discuss the killing of George Floyd. In the section on the international system of states, the discussion of African states has been revised and expanded to address how European colonial powers created borders as a proxy struggle against other European powers rather than taking into consideration local populations. A new Policy feature prompts students to think critically about how age relates to voting power, including the overrepresentation of older adults in American politics and arguments for lowering the voting age.

CHAPTER 16: RELIGION

This chapter includes a new discussion about the changing global composition of Christianity. The section on social solidarity includes a new example about millennials' health outcomes and religious affiliation rates. The section on secularization has been updated with recent data on religious affiliation and participation trends among Americans. The section on the commercialization of religious life has been updated to include the use of social media in religious marketing. The Policy feature on teaching the Bible in schools now includes Indiana representative Dennis Kruse's 2019 bill to teach alternative theories of the origin of life.

CHAPTER 17: SCIENCE, THE ENVIRONMENT, AND SOCIETY

The section on science and politics now includes a discussion of the COVID-19 pandemic and funding for the massive research endeavors to study and battle it. The section on global warming and climate change includes updated data on global greenhouse gas emissions, variations over time in the surface temperate of the earth, and the contributions of air travel to global warming. The section on biotechnology and the human genome now discusses the use of DNA fingerprinting by law enforcement and considers the example of the Golden State Killer's capture via identification by a distant relative's DNA.

CHAPTER 18: COLLECTIVE ACTION, SOCIAL MOVEMENTS, AND SOCIAL CHANGE

This chapter includes a new key term, **value-added theory**. In the section on types of social movements, the discussion of #NeverAgain has been updated to consider how political resistance and lobbying pressure have resulted in the group being less successful than similar type groups facing less political resistance. This section also discusses how the COVID-19 pandemic has given the Critical Mass movement the political opportunity to advance its agenda for increased protection of cyclists on city streets. A new section on frame alignment has been added. It discusses the George Floyd killing and the Black Lives Matter movement's recent success in reframing the issues concerning policing and racial injustice. It also considers how the movement has impacted other reforms, such as the recent name change of the Washington football team. The discussion of Black Lives Matter also addresses the rise of counterprotest movements. The section on causes of social change now includes a discussion of mask wearing during the COVID-19 pandemic.

ACKNOWLEDGMENTS

You May Ask Yourself originated in the Introduction to Sociology course that I have taught on and off since the mid-1990s at New York University, Yale University, and Columbia University. However, the process of writing it made me feel as if I were learning to be a sociologist all over again. For example, I never taught religion, methodology, or the sociology of education. But instructors who reviewed the manuscript requested that these topics be covered, so with the assistance of an army of graduate students who really ought to be recognized as coauthors, I got to work. The experience was invaluable, and in a way, I finally feel like a card-carrying sociologist, having acquired at last a bird's-eye view of my colleagues' work. I consider it a great honor to be able to put my little spin (or filter) on the field in this way, to be able not just to influence the few hundred intro students I teach each year, but to excite (I hope) and instill the enthusiasm I didn't get to experience until graduate school in students who may be just a few months out of high school (if that).

I mentioned that the graduate students who helped me create this book were really more like coauthors, ghostwriters, or perhaps law clerks. Law clerks do much of the writing of legal opinions for judges, but only a judge's name graces a decision. I asked Norton to allow more coauthors, but they declined—perhaps understandably, given how long such a list would be—so I will take this opportunity to thank my students and hope that you are still reading this preface.

The original transcription of my lectures that formed the basis of this text was completed by Carse Ramos, who also worked on assembling the glossary and drafted some parts of various chapters, such as sections in the economic sociology chapter, as well as some text in the chapters on authority and deviance. She also served as an all-around editor. Ashley Mears did the heavy lifting on the race, gender, family, and religion chapters. Amy LeClair took the lead on methods, culture, groups and networks, socialization, and health. Jennifer Heerwig cobbled together the chapter on authority and the state and deviance (a nice combo), while her officemate Brian McCabe whipped up the chapter on science, technology, and the environment and the one on social movements. Melissa Velez wrote the first draft of the education chapter (and a fine one at that). Michael McCarthy did the same for the stratification chapter. Devyani Prabhat helped revise the social movements chapter. My administrative assistant, Amelia Branigan, served as fact-checker, editor, and box drafter while running a department, taking the GREs, and writing and submitting her own graduate applications. When Amelia had to decamp for Northwestern University to pursue her own doctorate, Lauren Marten took over the job of chasing down obscure references, fact-checking, and proofreading. Alexandre Frenette drafted the questions and activities in the practice sections at the end of each chapter.

For the Second Edition, much of the work to integrate the interview transcripts and update material based on reviewer feedback fell to a great extent on the shoulders of Laura Norén, a fantastic New York University graduate student who has worked on topics as far-ranging as public toilets (with my colleague Harvey Molotch) and how symphonies and designers collaborate (as part of her dissertation). I hope Laura will find her crash-course overview of sociology useful at some point in what promises to be a productive and exciting scholarly career.

When it was time to begin the Third Edition, the updating of all the statistics, fact-checking, and so on that is the bread and butter of a revision fell upon the capable shoulders of Emi Nakazato who, although trained as a social worker in graduate school, adeptly pivoted to that field's cousin, sociology.

For the Fourth and Fifth Editions, Laura Norén returned as the research assistant. With her prior experience she picked up the task ably without dropping a beat. Finally, for the Sixth and Seventh Editions, I turned to then–graduate student Thomas Laidley, who did a more-than-thorough job of not only updating facts and figures but questioning them as well.

In addition to the students who have worked with me on the book, I need to give shout-outs to all the top-notch scholars who found time in their busy schedules to sit down with me and do on-camera interviews: Julia Adams, Andy Bichlbaum, danah boyd, Andrew Cherlin, Nitsan Chorev, Susan Crawford, Adam Davidson, Matthew Desmond, Stephen Duncombe, Mitchell Duneier, Paula England, John Evans, Michael Gaddis, David Grusky, Fadi Haddad, Michael Hout, Jennifer Jacquet, Shamus Khan, Annette Lareau, Jennifer Lee, Ka Liu, Amos Mac, Douglas McAdam, Ashley Mears, Steven Morgan, Alondra Nelson, Devah Pager, Nathan Palmer, C. J. Pascoe, Frances Fox Piven, Allison Pugh, Adeel Qalbani, Marc Ramirez, Asha Rangappa, Jen'nan Read, Victor Rios, Jeffrey Sachs, Jennifer Senior, Mario Luis Small, Zephyr Teachout, Duncan Watts, and Robb Willer.

For the interview videos, the filmmaking, editing, and postproduction were done in earlier editions by Erica Rothman at Nightlight Productions with the assistance of Jim Haverkamp, Kevin Wells, Saul Rouda, Dimitriy Khavin, and Arkadiy Ugorskiy, and then in this new Seventh Edition by Elizabeth Audley and Ragnar Freidank. This was no easy task, because we wanted a bunch of cuts ranging from 30-second sound bites to television-show-length segments of 22 minutes. Although a bunch of interviews with academic social scientists on topics ranging from estimating the effects of Catholic schools on student outcomes to the political economy of global trade to the social contagion of autism are not likely to win any Emmys or rock the Nielsens (with the possible exception of the one on college sex), it has certainly been one of the most exciting highlights in my sociological career to host this makeshift talk show on such a wide range of interesting topics. (If only more of our public discourse would dig into issues in the way that we did in these interviews, our society and governance would be in better shape—if I do say so myself!)

When I began work on the Seventh Edition's updates and revisions, I knew I could use some expert help. I relied on a number of scholars who generously read chapters of this book and offered valuable feedback, criticisms, and suggestions:

REVIEWERS FOR THE SEVENTH EDITION

Edward Avery-Natale, Mercer County Community College

Brandi M. Barnes, The University of Memphis

Sherri Chandler, Muskegon Community College

Brittany Chozinski, Our Lady of the Lake University

Patricia Neff Claster, Edinboro University

Vy T. Dao, Columbus State University

Corina Diaz, Cerritos College

Cindy Epperson, St. Louis Community College—Meramec Campus

Mary Beth Finch, Northwestern University

Christopher Hamilton, St. Louis University

Devin A. Heyward, Saint Peter's University

Rachel Howard, East Central College

Marla H. Kohlman, Kenyon College

Molly Monahan Lang, Penn State Erie, The Behrend College

Bridget Cowan Longoria, University of Nevada, Las Vegas

Hayley Pierce, Brigham Young University

Derek Roberts, Monroe County Community College

Sandra M. Rogers, North Carolina Central University

Teal Rothschild, Roger Williams University

Jeffrey O. Sacha, American River College

Sahar Sadeghi, Muhlenberg College

Kevin Shafer, Brigham Young University

Beth Simmert, Adrian College

Jeremy N. Thomas, Idaho State University

Mark Tromans, Broward College

Adria Welcher, Morehouse College

Elena Windsong, Colorado State University

As you can see, it took a village to raise this child. But that's not all. At Norton, I need to thank, first and foremost, Michael Moss, the editor into whose lap this project landed (after having passed through the hands of Justin Cahill, Steve Dunn, Melea Seward, and most notably Karl Bakeman, who got promoted onward and upward). Michael deserves great credit for bringing a fresh set of eyes and a powerful brain to help me sociologically question my own assumptions about the book, which, in turn, led to this edition's overhaul. In addition, I am grateful to assistant editor Angie Merila, project editor Michael Fauver, and production manager Sean Mintus, who handled every stage of the manuscript and managed to keep the innumerable pieces of the book moving through production. Agnieszka Gasparska and her team at Kiss Me I'm Polish are responsible for the terrific book design.

I also must thank Norton's sociology marketing director Julia Hall and the social science sales and market development specialists Julie Sindel, Courtney Brandt, and Janise Turso. Much of *You May Ask Yourself*'s success is due to their boundless energy and enthusiasm. Finally, I owe a special thanks to Eileen Connell, Ariel Eaton, and Alexandra Park. They are responsible for putting together all of the video and electronic resources that accompany *You May Ask Yourself*. Those who develop new digital products to help instructors teach in the classroom or teach online are the most creative and resourceful folks working in college publishing today.

CORRELATION WITH PSYCHOLOGICAL, SOCIAL, AND BIOLOGICAL FOUNDATIONS OF BEHAVIOR SECTION OF THE MCAT®

In 2015, the Association of American Medical Colleges revised the Medical College Admissions Test (MCAT) to include fundamental concepts from sociology. To help students prepare for the test, here is a correlation guide for *You May Ask Yourself*, Seventh Edition.

FOUNDATIONAL CONCEPT 7

Biological, psychological, and sociocultural factors influence behavior and behavior change.

FOUNDATIONAL CONCEPT 8

Psychological, sociocultural, and biological factors influence the way we think about ourselves and others as well as how we interact with others.

CHAPTER	HEADING/DESCRIPTION	PAGE
3	Ethnocentrism	86
3	Cultural relativism	92
4	Me, Myself, and I: Development of the Self and the Other	127
4	Agents of Socialization	131
4	Social Interaction	141
4	Dramaturgical Theory	150
5	Social Groups	166
5	From Groups to Networks	176
5	Network Analysis in Practice	189
5	Organizations	194
6	Stigma	227
9	Inter-Group Relations	377
9	Prejudice, Discrimination, and the New Racism	388
9	Institutional Racism	393
13	Stereotypes	584
15	Legal-Rational Authority	641
15	Characteristics of Bureaucracies	643

FOUNDATIONAL CONCEPT 9

Cultural and social differences influence well-being.

FOUNDATIONAL CONCEPT 10

Social stratification and access to resources influence well-being.

Seventh Edition

You May Ask Yourself

AN INTRODUCTION TO THINKING LIKE A SOCIOLOGIST

USING YOUR SOCIOLOGICAL IMAGINATION

Every January, the group Improv Everywhere organizes the No Pants Subway Ride in New York and cities around the world. In this picture who is violating social norms: the people with pants, or those without?

PARADOX

1

A SUCCESSFUL SOCIOLOGIST
MAKES THE FAMILIAR STRANGE.

Animation at digital.wwnorton.com/youmayask7

The Sociological Imagination: An Introduction

If you want to understand sociology, why don't we start with you. Why are you taking this class and reading this textbook? It's as good a place to start as any—after all, sociology is the study of human society, and there is the sociology of sports, of religion, of music, of medicine, even a sociology of sociologists. So why not start, by way of example, with the sociology of an introduction to sociology?

For example, why are you bent over this page? Take a moment to write down the reasons. Maybe you have heard of sociology and want to learn about it. Maybe you are merely following the suggestion of a parent, guidance counselor, or academic adviser. The course syllabus probably indicates that for the first week of class, you are required to read this chapter. So there are at least two good reasons to be reading this introduction to sociology text.

Let's take the first response, "I want to educate myself about sociology." That's a fairly good reason, but may I then ask why you are taking the class rather than simply reading the book on your own? Furthermore, assuming that you're paying tuition, why are you doing so? If you really are here for the education, let me suggest an alternative: Grab one of the course schedules at your college, decide which courses to take, and just show up! Most introductory classes are so large that nobody notices if an extra student attends. If it is a smaller, more advanced seminar, ask the professor if you

SOCIOLOGY

the study of human society.

can audit it. I have never known a faculty member who checks that all class attendees are legitimate students at the college—in fact, we're happy when students *do* show up to class. An auditor, someone who is there for the sake of pure learning, and who won't be grade grubbing or submitting papers to be marked, is pure gold to any professor interested in imparting knowledge for learning's sake.

You know the rest of the drill: Do all the reading (you can usually access the required texts for free at the library), do your homework, and participate in class discussion. About the only thing you won't get at the end of the course is a grade. So give yourself one. As a matter of fact, once you have compiled enough credits and written a senior thesis, award yourself a diploma. Why not? You will probably have received a better education than most students—certainly better than I did in college.

But what are you going to do with a homemade diploma? You are not here just to learn; you wish to obtain an actual college degree. Why exactly do you want a college degree? Students typically answer that they have to get one in order to earn more money. Others may say that they need credentials to get the job they want. And some students are in college because they don't know what else to do. Whatever your answer, the fact that you asked yourself a question about something you may have previously taken for granted is the first step in thinking like a sociologist. "Thinking like a sociologist" means applying analytical tools to something you have always done without much conscious thought—like opening this book or taking this class. It requires you to reconsider your assumptions about society and question what you have taken for granted in order to better understand the world around you. In other words, thinking like a sociologist means *making the familiar strange*.

This chapter introduces you to the sociological approach to the world. Specifically, you will learn about the *sociological imagination*, a term coined by C. Wright Mills. We'll return to the question "Why go to college?" and apply our sociological imaginations to it. You will also learn what a social institution is. The chapter concludes by looking at the sociology of sociology— that is, the history of sociology and where it fits within the social sciences.

SOCIOLOGICAL IMAGINATION

the ability to connect the most basic, intimate aspects of an individual's life to seemingly impersonal and remote historical forces.

The Sociological Imagination

More than 50 years ago, sociologist C. Wright Mills argued that in the effort to think critically about the social world around us, we need to use our sociological imagination, the ability to see the connections between our personal experience and the larger forces of history. This is just what we are doing when we question this textbook, this course, and college in general. In *The Sociological Imagination* (1959), Mills describes it this way: "The first fruit of this imagination—and the first lesson of the social science that embodies it—is the idea that the individual can understand his own experience and gauge his own fate only by locating himself within his period, that he can know his own chances in life only by becoming aware of those of all individuals in his circumstances. In many ways it is a terrible lesson; in many ways a magnificent one." The terrible part of the lesson is to make our own lives ordinary— that is, to see our intensely personal, private experience of life as typical of the period and place in which we live. This can also serve as a source of comfort, however, helping us realize we are not alone in our experiences, whether they

Sociologist C. Wright Mills smoking his pipe in his office at Columbia University. How does Mills's concept of sociological imagination help us make the familiar strange?

involve our alienation from the increasingly dog-eat-dog capitalism of modern America, the peculiar combination of intimacy and dissociation that we may experience on the internet, or the ways that nationality or geography affect our life choices. The sociological imagination does not just leave us hanging with these feelings of recognition, however. Mills writes that it also "enables [us] to take into account how individuals, in the welter of their daily experience, often become falsely conscious of their social positions." The sociological imagination thus allows us to see the veneer of social life for what it is and to step outside the "trap" of rapid historical change in order to comprehend what is occurring in our world and the social foundations that may be shifting right under our feet. As Mills wrote after World War II, a time of enormous political, social, and technological change, "The sociological imagination enables us to grasp history and biography and the relations between the two within society. That is its task and its promise. To recognize this task and this promise is the mark of the classic social analyst."

Mills offered his readers a way to stop and take stock of their lives in light of all that had happened in the previous decade. Of course, we almost always feel that social change is fairly rapid and continually getting ahead of us. Think of the 1960s or even today, with the rise of the internet and global terror threats. In retrospect, we consider the 1950s, the decade when Mills wrote his seminal work, to be a relatively placid time, when Americans experienced some relief from the change and strife of World War II and the Great Depression. But Mills believed the profound sense of alienation experienced by many during the postwar period was a result of the change that had immediately preceded it.

HOW TO BE A SOCIOLOGIST ACCORDING TO QUENTIN TARANTINO: A SCENE FROM *PULP FICTION*

Have you ever been to a foreign country, noticed how many little things were different, and wondered why? Have you ever been to a church of a different denomination—or a different religion altogether—from your own? Or have you been a fish out of water in some other way? The only guy attending a social event for women, perhaps? Or the only person from out of state in your dorm? If you have experienced that fish-out-of-water feeling, then you have, however briefly, engaged your sociological imagination. By shifting your social environment enough to be in a position where you are not able to take everything for granted, you are forced to see the connections between particular historical paths taken (and not taken) and how you live your daily life. You may, for instance, wonder why there are bidets in most European bathrooms and not in American ones. Or why people waiting in lines in the Middle East typically stand closer to each other than they do in Europe or America. Or why, in some rural Chinese societies, many generations of a family sleep in the same bed. If you are able to resist your initial impulses toward xenophobia (feelings that may result from the discomfort of facing a different reality), then you are halfway to understanding other people's lifestyles as no more or less sensible than your own. Once you have truly adopted the sociological imagination, you can start questioning the links between your personal experience and the particulars of a given society without ever leaving home.

In the following excerpt of dialogue from Quentin Tarantino's 1994 film *Pulp Fiction*, the character Vincent tells Jules about the "little differences" between life in the United States and life in Europe.

VINCENT: It's the little differences. A lotta the same shit we got here, they got there, but there they're a little different.

JULES: Example?

VINCENT: Well, in Amsterdam, you can buy beer in a movie theater. And I don't mean in a paper cup either. They give you a glass of beer, like in a bar.

Vincent Vega (John Travolta) describes his visit to a McDonald's in Amsterdam to Jules Winnfield (Samuel L. Jackson).

In Paris, you can buy beer at McDonald's. Also, you know what they call a Quarter Pounder with Cheese in Paris?

JULES: They don't call it a Quarter Pounder with Cheese?

VINCENT: No, they got the metric system there, they wouldn't know what the fuck a Quarter Pounder is.

JULES: What'd they call it?

VINCENT: Royale with Cheese.

VINCENT: [Y]ou know what they put on french fries in Holland instead of ketchup?

JULES: What?

VINCENT: Mayonnaise. [. . .] And I don't mean a little bit on the side of the plate, they fuckin' drown 'em in it.

JULES: Uucccch!

Your job as a sociologist is to get into the mind-set that mayonnaise on french fries, though it might seem disgusting at first, is not strange after all, certainly no more so than ketchup.

Another way to think about the sociological imagination is to ask ourselves what we take to be natural that actually isn't. For example, let's return to the question "Why go to college?" Sociologists and economists have shown that the financial benefits of education—particularly higher education—appear to be increasing. They refer to this as the "returns to schooling." In today's economy, the median (i.e., typical) annual income for full-time workers ages 25 to 37 with a high-school degree is $31,000; for those with a bachelor's degree, it is $56,000 (Pew Research, 2019). That $25,000 annual advantage seems like a good deal, but is it really? Let's shift gears and do a little math.

WHAT ARE THE TRUE COSTS AND RETURNS OF COLLEGE?

Now that you are thinking like a sociologist, let's compare the true cost of going to college for four or five years to calling the whole thing off and taking a full-time job right after high school. First, there is the tuition to consider. Let's assume for the sake of argument that you are paying $10,116 per year for tuition (Powell & Kerr, 2019). That's a lot less than what most private four-year colleges cost, but about average for in-state tuition at a state school.

Using a standard formula to adjust for inflation and bring future amounts into current dollars, we can determine that paying out $10,116 this year and slightly higher amounts over the next three years (assuming a 3.3 percent annual rise in tuition and a corresponding discount rate) is equivalent to paying about $40,500 in one lump sum today; this would be the direct cost of attending college. Indirect costs—so-called opportunity costs—exist as well, such as the costs associated with the amount of time you are devoting to school. Taking into account the typical wage for a high-school graduate, we can calculate that if you worked full-time instead of going to college, you would make $30,000 this year. Thus we find that the present value of the total wages lost over the next four years by choosing full-time school over full-time work is about $144,000. Add these opportunity costs to the direct costs of tuition, and we get $184,500.

Next we need to calculate the "returns to schooling." For the sake of simplicity, we will regard the $56,000 annual earnings figure for recent college graduates as fixed for the first 10 years past college graduation. We will use a higher estimate for annual earnings after that, to take into account the fact that mid-career workers make more. But remember, those who start working right out of high school begin earning about five years earlier than those who spend that time in college (the average time it takes to complete a bachelor's degree at a public university is 5.2 years [Shapiro et al., 2016]). Assuming you retire at age 65, you will have worked 42 years (high-school grads will be in the workforce for 47 years because of that 5-year head start). However, given your higher average earnings per year of work, when we

Two famous college dropouts. Facebook CEO Mark Zuckerberg (left) attended Harvard but dropped out before graduating. Oprah Winfrey (right) left Tennessee State University as a sophomore to begin a career in media.

compare your lifetime earnings to the lifetime earnings of someone who has only a high-school education, we find that with a college degree you will make about $1,500,000 more than someone who went straight to work after high school (Figure 1.1). On top of this substantial financial return to schooling, research also shows that earning a high-school and/or college degree makes us healthier and less likely to engage in unhealthy behaviors like smoking, even after accounting for other factors like income (Heckman et al., 2016).

But wait a minute: How do we know for sure that college really mattered in the equation? Individuals who finish college might earn more because they actually learned something and obtained a degree, or—a big OR—they might earn more regardless of the college experience because people who stay in school (1) are innately smarter, (2) know how to work the system, (3) come from wealthier families, (4) can delay gratification, (5) are more efficient at managing their time, or (6) all of the above—take your pick. In other words, State U. graduates might not have needed to go to college to earn higher wages; they might have been successful anyway.

Maybe, then, the success stories of Mark Zuckerberg, Steve Jobs, Lady Gaga, and other college dropouts don't cut against the grain so sharply after

FIGURE 1.1 Returns to Schooling

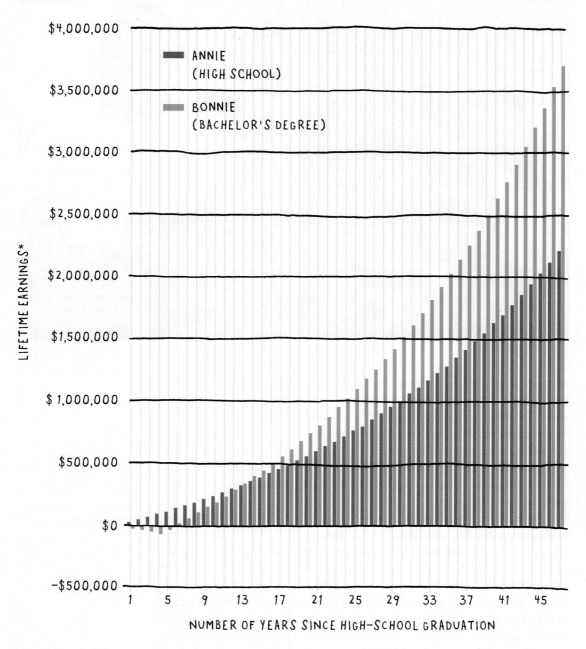

*This set of hypothetical women—Annie and Bonnie—live in a world that is not quite like reality. We did not flatten Annie's trajectory to account for the fact that high-school diploma holders are more likely to experience periods of forced part-time work and/or unemployment. We also assumed the same rate of income increase over time (i.e., raises) for these two, although high-school diploma holders are more likely to experience wage stagnation than college diploma holders.

SOURCE: Carnevale et al., 2014.

all. Maybe they were the savvy ones: Convinced of their ability to make it on their own, thanks to the social cues they received (including the fact that they had been admitted to college), they decided that they wouldn't wait four years to try to achieve success. They opted to just go for it right then and there. College's "value added," they might have concluded, was marginal at best.

GETTING THAT "PIECE OF PAPER"

Even if college turns out to matter in the end, does it make a difference because of the learning that takes place there or because of our credentialist society that it aids and abets? The answer to this question has enormous implications for what education means in our society. Imagine, for example, a society in which people become doctors not by doing well on the SATs, going to college, taking premed courses, acing the MCATs, and then spending more time in the classroom. Instead, the route to becoming a doctor—among the most prestigious and highly paid occupations in our society—starts with emptying bedpans as a nurse's aide and working your way up through the

ranks of registered nurse, apprentice physician, and so forth; finally, after years of on-the-job training, you achieve the title of doctor. Social theorist Randall Collins has proposed just such a medical education system in the controversial *The Credential Society: A Historical Sociology of Education and Stratification* (1979), which argues that the expansion of higher education has merely resulted in a ratcheting up of credentialism and expenditures on formal education rather than reflecting any true societal need for more formal education or opening up opportunities to more people.

College bulletin boards are covered with advertisements like this one promoting websites that generate diplomas. Why are these fake diplomas not worth it?

If Collins is correct and credentials are what matter most, then isn't there a cheaper, faster way to get them? In fact, all you need are $29.95 and a little guts, and you can receive a diploma from one of the many online sites that promise either legitimate degrees from nonaccredited colleges or a faux college diploma from any school of your choosing. Thus why not save four years and lots of money and obtain your credentials immediately?

Obviously, universities have incentives to prevent such websites from undermining their exclusive authority over conferring degrees. They rely on a number of other social institutions, ranging from copyright law to magazines that publish rankings to protect their status. Despite universities' interest in protecting their reputations, I had never had a university employer verify my education claims when applying to teach until 2015 when I moved to Princeton. Every other employer, including NYU, accepted my résumé without calling my graduate or undergraduate universities. NYU does check to make sure student applicants have completed high school, however. Are universities too lazy to care? Probably not.

There are strong informal mechanisms by which universities protect their status. First, there is the university's alumni network. Potential

TABLE 1.1 Overcredentialed? Workers with Bachelor's Degrees in 1970 and 2015

JOB TITLE	PERCENTAGE OF WORKFORCE, AGES 25–64, WITH BACHELOR'S DEGREE		
	1970	2015	% CHANGE
Bartenders	3%	20%	567%
Photographers	10%	50%	400%
Electricians	2%	7%	250%
Accountants and auditors	42%	78%	86%
Actors, directors, and producers	41%	74%	80%
Writers and authors	47%	84%	79%
Military personnel	24%	37%	54%
Dental hygienists	29%	36%	24%
Primary-school teachers	84%	94%	12%
Doctors	96%	99%	3%
Preschool teachers	53%	48%	−9%
Human-resource clerks	40%	29%	−28%
Machine programmers	27%	7%	−74%

A recent article in *The Economist* found that since the 1970s, more American workers in most professions have earned a bachelor's degree. In half of these professions, the authors found that real wages have actually fallen. Do these examples support Collins's argument about overcredentialism? Have these jobs gotten more demanding or technologically complex over time, or are there just more people doing them with a diploma?

SOURCES: University of Minnesota IPUMS; *The Economist* (2018a).

employers rarely call a university's registrar to make sure you graduated, but they will expect you to talk a bit about your college experience. If your interviewer is an alumnus/alumna or otherwise familiar with the institution, you might also be expected to talk about what dorm you lived in, reminisce about a particularly dramatic homecoming game, or gripe about an especially unreasonable professor. If you slip up on any of this information, suspicions will grow, and then people might call to check on your graduation status. Perhaps there are some good reasons not to opt for that $29.95 degree and to pay the costs of college after all.

On a more serious note, the role of credentialism in our society means that getting in—especially to a wealthy school with plenty of need-based aid available—can make a huge difference for lower-income students. I sat down with Asha Rangappa, the dean of admissions at Yale Law School (and former FBI agent), who explained that by the time students are old enough to apply to law school, middle-class and upper-class students have already been granted all sorts of opportunities that make them appear to be stronger candidates even if they do not have better moral character or a stronger aptitude for law than their less affluent counterparts in the same applicant pool:

> I read anywhere from three thousand, four thousand applications a year, and I do a kind of character and personality assessment. I decide who gets in. . . . I think that there's a meritocracy at the point where I'm doing it, but I think accessing the good opportunities that allow you to take advantage of the meritocracy is limited.

I think that's the problem, I think that's what somebody like me in my position works very hard to correct for. When twenty-two to twenty-five years of someone's life are behind them, it is too late to correct the disparity in access that really needed to have been corrected from like zero to five years, zero to ten years.

Do I think that people who have had access to more resources and opportunities and money are going to do better in the admissions process? Yeah. Because they're just going to have the

DIGITAL.WWNORTON.COM/YOUMAYASK7

To see my interview with Asha Rangappa, go to digital.wwnorton.com/youmayask7 richer background. And [admissions counselors] have to be able to be in a position where [we] can afford to account for that and take the risk. (Conley, 2015a)

What's more, law schools' rankings in magazines like *US News and World Report* are impacted by the average LSAT scores of their incoming classes. Rangappa's school, Yale, is so elite that it is able to maintain its ranking even if its average LSAT score drops a little. But for other schools, a drop in LSAT scores will cause their ranking to drop, leading to a decline in high-quality applicants and a further drop in rankings. From Rangappa's perspective:

I've now read over ten years, over thirty thousand admission files. To me, the LSAT is one number, and I can look at the rest of the file. There may very well be somebody who has a crappy LSAT score, but . . . I can tell in the totality of the application that the applicant is going to be a better person at the school. I have the luxury of taking that person because it's Yale Law School and the way the *US News* formula is created, we're not going to suffer a consequence if our median LSAT drops one point.

Rangappa's account shows that elite educational institutions perform a balancing act whereby they often seek to broaden the population who gains from the opportunities and status they provide while at the same time maintaining their own rank in the hierarchy of similar institutions. That is, even when such institutions do want to level the playing field, they themselves are trapped in a highly competitive environment that does not allow them to fully counteract preexisting inequalities. Social institutions thus have a tendency to reinforce existing social structures and the inequalities therein. College (and graduate school) is no exception.

What Is a Social Institution?

The university, then, is more than just a printing press that churns out diplomas, and, for that matter, it does not merely impart formal knowledge. It fulfills a variety of roles and provides links to many other societal institutions. For example, a college is an institution that acts as a gatekeeper to what are considered legitimate forms of educational advantage by certifying what is legitimate knowledge. It is an institution that segregates great swaths of the population by age. (You won't find a more age-segregated environment than a four-year college; it even beats a retirement home in having the smallest amount of age variation in its client population.) A college is a proprietary brand that is marketed on sweatshirts and mugs and through televised sporting events. Last but not least, it is an informal set of stories told within a social network of students, faculty, administrators, alumni, and other relevant individuals.

This last part of the definition is key to understanding one of sociology's most important concepts, the social institution. A social institution is a complex group of interdependent positions that, together, perform a social role and reproduce themselves over time. A way to think of these social positions is as a set of stories we tell ourselves: Social relations are a network of ties, and the social role is a grand narrative that unifies these stories within the network. In order to think sociologically about social institutions, you need to think of them not as monolithic, uniform, stable entities—things that "just are"—but as institutions constructed within a dense network of other social institutions and meanings. Sound confusing? Bear with me as I provide an example: I teach at Princeton University. What exactly is the social institution known as Princeton? It is not the collection of buildings I frequent. It certainly cannot be the people who work there, or even the students, because they change over time, shifting in and out through recruitment and retirement, admission and graduation. We might thus conclude that a social institution is just a name. However, an institution can change its name and still retain its social identity. Duke University was once called Normal College and then Trinity College, yet it remains the same institution.

Of course, all such transitions involving a change of name, location, mission, and so on require a great deal of effort and agreement among interested parties. In some cases, changes in personnel, function, or location may be too much for a social institution to sustain, causing it to die out and be replaced by something that is considered new. Sometimes institutions even try to rupture their identity intentionally. Tobacco company Philip Morris had received such bad press as a cigarette manufacturer for so long that it

SOCIAL INSTITUTION

a complex group of interdependent positions that, together, perform a social role and reproduce themselves over time; also defined in a narrow sense as any institution in a society that works to shape the behavior of the groups or people within it.

Tobacco company Philip Morris changed its name to Altria at a stockholders' meeting in January 2003.

changed its name to Altria, hoping to start fresh and shake off the negative connotations of its previous embodiment. For that effort to succeed, the narrative of Philip Morris circulating in social networks had to die out without being connected to Altria.

This grand narrative that constitutes social identity is nothing more than the sum of individual stories told between pairs of individuals. Think about your relationship to your parents. You have a particular story that you tell if asked to describe your relationship with your mother. She also has a story. Your story may change slightly, depending on whom you are talking to; you may add some details or leave out others. Your other relatives have stories about your mother and her relationship to you. So do her friends and yours. Anyone who knows her contributes to her social identity. The sum total of stories about your mom is the grand narrative of who she is.

All of this may seem like a fairly flimsy notion of how things operate in the social world, but even though any social identity boils down to a set of stories within a social network, that narrative is still hearty and robust. Imagine what it would take to change an identity. Let's say your mom is 50 years old. You want to make her 40 instead. You would not only have to convince her to refer constantly to herself as 10 years younger; you would also have to get your other relatives and her friends to abide by this change. And it wouldn't stop there. You'd have to change official documents as well—her driver's license, passport, and so on. This is not so easily done. Even though your mother's identity (in this case her age, although the same logic can be extended to her name, ethnicity, and many other aspects of her identity) could be described as nothing more than an understanding among her, everyone who knows her, and the formal authorities, the matter is a fairly complicated one. Just think about trying to change the identity of a major institution such as your university. You'd have to convince the board of directors, alumni, faculty, students, and everyone else who has a relationship to the school of the need for a change. Altering an identity is fairly difficult, even though it is ultimately nothing more than an idea.

I mentioned that if you wanted to change your mother's age, name, or race, you'd have to convince not only her friends but also the formal authorities, which are social institutions with their own logics and inertias. Let's take the example of college once again. Other than the informal ties of people who have a relationship to the grand narrative of a particular college, a number of social structures exist that make colleges, which are themselves made up of a series of stories within social networks, possible:

1. The *legal system* enforces copyright law, making fake diplomas illegitimate.

2. The *primary and secondary educational system* (i.e., K–12 schooling) prepares students both academically and culturally for college as

well as acting as an extended screening and sorting mechanism to help determine who goes to college and to which one.

3. The *Educational Testing Service* and *ACT* are private companies that have a duopoly on the standardized tests that screen for college admission.

4. The *wage labor market* encompasses the entire economy that allows your teacher to be paid, not to mention the administrators, staff, and other outside contractors who maintain the intellectual, fiscal, and physical infrastructure of the school you attend.

5. *English*, although not the official language of the United States (there isn't one!), is the language in which instruction takes place at the majority of US colleges. Language itself is a social phenomenon; some would argue that it is the basis for all of social life. But a given language is a particular outcome of political boundaries and historical struggles among various populations in the world. It is often said that the only difference between a language and a dialect is that a language has an army to back it up. In other words, deciding whether a spoken tongue is a language or merely a dialect is a question of power and legitimacy.

Trying to understand social institutions such as the legal system, the labor market, or language itself is at the heart of sociological inquiry. Although social institutions shape every aspect of our behavior, they are not monolithic. In fact, every day we construct and change social institutions through ordinary interactions and the meanings we ascribe to them. By becoming aware of the intersections between social institutions and your life, you are already thinking like a sociologist.

The Sociology of Sociology

Now that we have an idea of how sociologists approach their analysis of the world, let's turn that lens, the sociological imagination, to sociology itself. As a formal field, sociology is a relatively young discipline. Numerous fields of inquiry exist, such as molecular genetics, radio astronomy, and computer science, that could not emerge until a certain technology was invented. Sociology might seem to fall outside this category, but to study society, we need not only a curious mind and a certain willingness but also the specific frame of reference—the lens—of the sociological imagination. The sociological imagination is a technology of sorts, a technology that could have developed only during a certain time. That time was, arguably, the nineteenth century, when French scholar Auguste Comte (1798–1857) invented what he called "social physics" or positivism.

AUGUSTE COMTE AND THE CREATION OF SOCIOLOGY

According to Comte, positivism arose out of a need to make moral sense of the social order in a time of declining religious authority. Comte claimed that a secular basis for morality did indeed exist—that is, we could determine right and wrong without reference to higher powers or other religious concepts. And that was the job of the sociologist: to develop a secular morality. Comte further argued that human society had gone through three historical stages with respect to our understanding of morality. In the first, which he

POSITIVISM

the approach to sociology that emphasizes the scientific method as an approach to studying the objectively observable behavior of individuals irrespective of the meanings those actions have for the subjects themselves.

TWO CENTURIES OF SOCIOLOGY

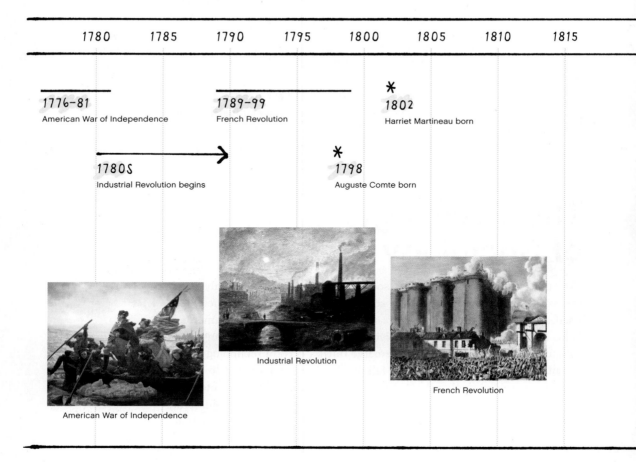

| 1780 | 1785 | 1790 | 1795 | 1800 | 1805 | 1810 | 1815 |

1776–81
American War of Independence

1789–99
French Revolution

*
1802
Harriet Martineau born

1780S
Industrial Revolution begins

*
1798
Auguste Comte born

Industrial Revolution

American War of Independence

French Revolution

referred to as the theological stage, society seemed to be the result of divine will. If you wanted to understand why kings ruled, why Europe used a feudal and guild system of labor, or why colonialism took root, the answer was that it was God's plan. To better understand God's plan and thus comprehend the logic of social life, scholars of the theological period might consult the Bible or other ecclesiastical texts. During stage two, which Comte called the metaphysical stage, Enlightenment thinkers such as Jean-Jacques Rousseau, John Stuart Mill, and Thomas Hobbes saw humankind's behavior as governed by natural, biological instincts. To understand the nature of society—why things were the way they were—we needed to strip away the layers of society to better comprehend how our basic drives and natural instincts governed and established the foundation for the surrounding world. Comte called the third and final stage of historical development the scientific stage. In

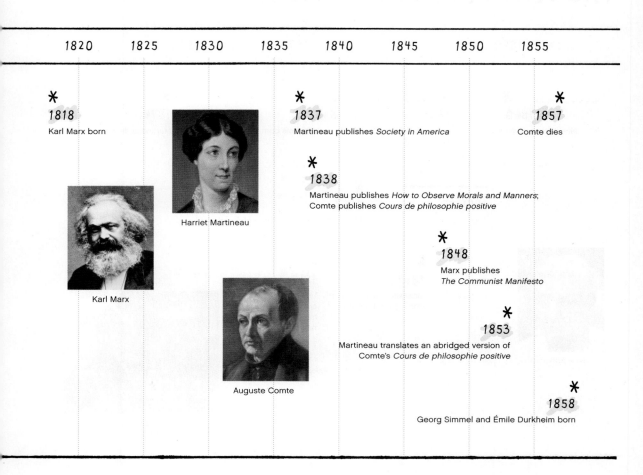

| 1820 | 1825 | 1830 | 1835 | 1840 | 1845 | 1850 | 1855 |

1818
Karl Marx born

Harriet Martineau

Karl Marx

Auguste Comte

1837
Martineau publishes *Society in America*

1838
Martineau publishes *How to Observe Morals and Manners*; Comte publishes *Cours de philosophie positive*

1848
Marx publishes *The Communist Manifesto*

1853
Martineau translates an abridged version of Comte's *Cours de philosophie positive*

1857
Comte dies

1858
Georg Simmel and Émile Durkheim born

this era, he claimed, we would develop a social physics of sorts in order to identify the scientific laws that govern human behavior. The analogy here is not theology or biology but rather physics. Comte was convinced we could understand how social institutions worked (and didn't work), how we relate to one another (whether on an individual or group level), and the overall structure of societies if we merely ascertained their "equations" or underlying logic. Needless to say, most sociologists today are not so optimistic.

Harriet Martineau Harriet Martineau (1802–1876), an English social theorist, was the first to translate Comte into English. In fact, Comte assigned his students to read her translations, claiming that they were better than the original. She also wrote important works of her own, including *Society in America* (1837), in which she describes our nation's physical and social aspects.

TWO CENTURIES OF SOCIOLOGY

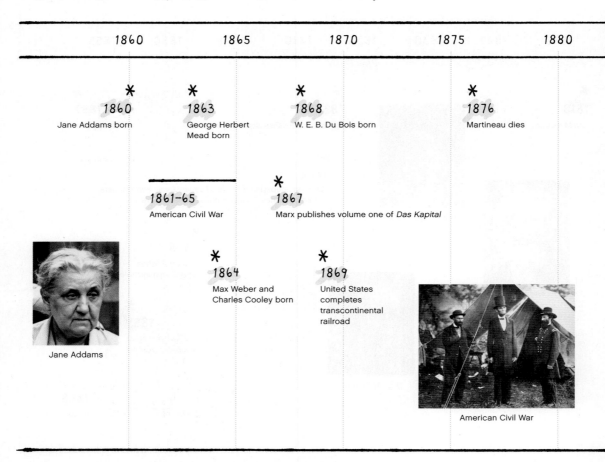

| 1860 | 1865 | 1870 | 1875 | 1880 |

✳ 1860
Jane Addams born

✳ 1863
George Herbert Mead born

✳ 1868
W. E. B. Du Bois born

✳ 1876
Martineau dies

1861–65
American Civil War

✳ 1867
Marx publishes volume one of *Das Kapital*

✳ 1864
Max Weber and Charles Cooley born

✳ 1869
United States completes transcontinental railroad

Jane Addams

American Civil War

She addressed topics ranging from the way we educate children (which, she attests, affords parents too much control and doesn't ensure quality) to the relationship between the federal and state governments. She was also the author of the first methods book in the area of sociology, *How to Observe Morals and Manners* (1838), in which she took on the institution of marriage, claiming that it was based on an assumption of the inferiority of women. This critique, among other writings, suggests that Martineau should be considered one of the earliest feminist social scientists writing in the English language.

CLASSICAL SOCIOLOGICAL THEORY

Although Comte and Martineau preceded them, Karl Marx, Max Weber, and Émile Durkheim are often credited as the founding fathers of the sociological

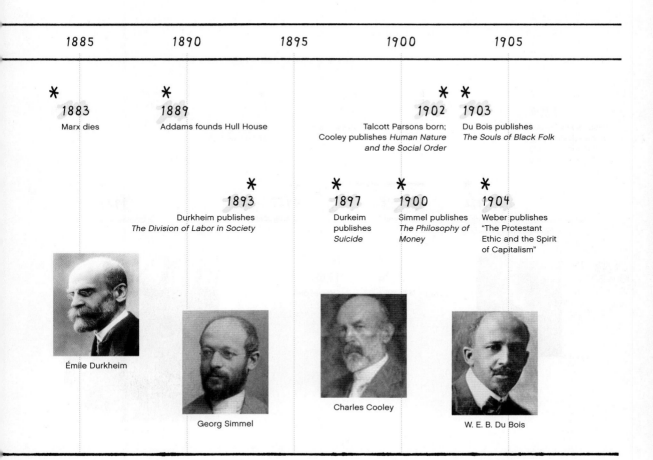

| 1885 | 1890 | 1895 | 1900 | 1905 |

* 1883
Marx dies

* 1889
Addams founds Hull House

* 1902
Talcott Parsons born;
Cooley publishes *Human Nature and the Social Order*

* 1903
Du Bois publishes
The Souls of Black Folk

* 1893
Durkheim publishes
The Division of Labor in Society

* 1897
Durkeim
publishes
Suicide

* 1900
Simmel publishes
The Philosophy of Money

* 1904
Weber publishes
"The Protestant Ethic and the Spirit of Capitalism"

Émile Durkheim

Georg Simmel

Charles Cooley

W. E. B. Du Bois

discipline. Some would add a fourth classical sociological theorist, Georg Simmel, to the triumvirate. A brief overview of each of their paradigms follows. We will return to the work of these thinkers throughout the book.

Karl Marx Karl Marx (1818–1883) is probably the most famous of the three early sociologists; from his surname the term *Marxism* (an ideological alternative to capitalism) derives, and his writings provided the theoretical basis for Communism. When Marx was a young man, he edited a newspaper that was suppressed by the Prussian government for its radicalism. Forced into exile, Marx settled in London, where he wrote his most important works. Marx was essentially a historian, but he did more than just chronicle events. He elaborated a theory of what drives history, now called historical materialism. Marx believed that it was primarily the conflicts between classes

TWO CENTURIES OF SOCIOLOGY

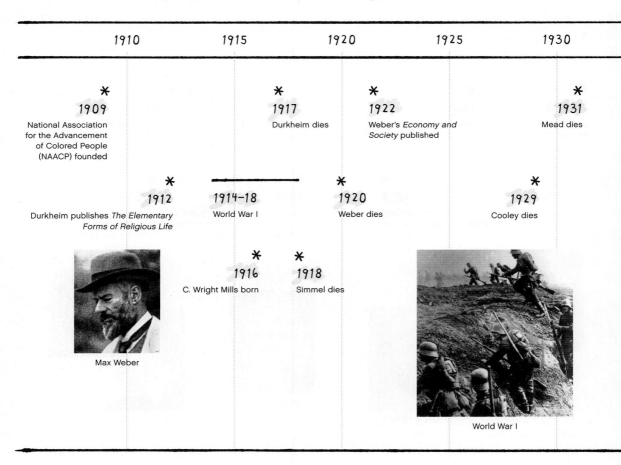

1910	1915	1920	1925	1930

✻
1909
National Association for the Advancement of Colored People (NAACP) founded

✻
1917
Durkheim dies

✻
1922
Weber's *Economy and Society* published

✻
1931
Mead dies

✻
1912
Durkheim publishes *The Elementary Forms of Religious Life*

1914–18
World War I

✻
1920
Weber dies

✻
1929
Cooley dies

✻
1916
C. Wright Mills born

✻
1918
Simmel dies

Max Weber

World War I

that drove social change throughout history. Marx saw history as an account of man's struggle to gain control of and later dominate his natural environment. However, at a certain point—with the Industrial Revolution and the emergence of modern capitalism—the very tools and processes that humans embraced to survive and to manage their surroundings came to dominate humans. Instead of using technology to master the natural world, people became slaves to industrial technology in order to make a living. In Marx's version of history, each economic system, whether small-scale farming or factory capitalism, had its own fault lines of conflict. In the current epoch, that fault line divided society into a small number of capitalists and a large number of workers (the proletariat) whose interests were opposed. The political struggle, along with escalating crises within the economic system itself, would produce social change through a Communist revolution. In

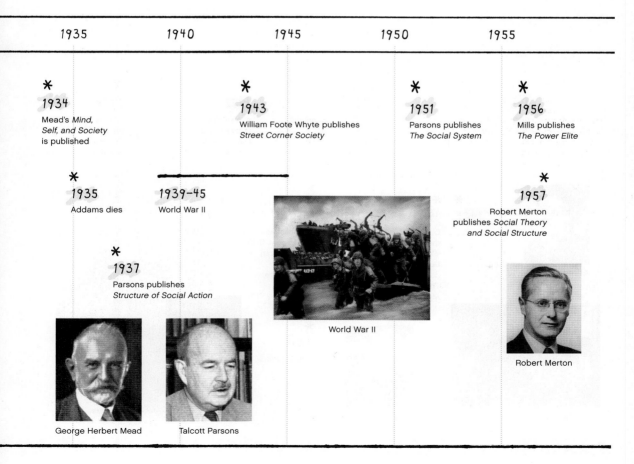

1935 1940 1945 1950 1955

1934
Mead's *Mind, Self, and Society* is published

1943
William Foote Whyte publishes *Street Corner Society*

1951
Parsons publishes *The Social System*

1956
Mills publishes *The Power Elite*

1935
Addams dies

1939–45
World War II

1957
Robert Merton publishes *Social Theory and Social Structure*

1937
Parsons publishes *Structure of Social Action*

World War II

Robert Merton

George Herbert Mead

Talcott Parsons

the ensuing Communist society, private property would be abolished and the resulting ideology governing the new economy would be "from each according to his abilities, to each according to his needs" (Marx & Engels, 1848/1998). We will explore Marx's theories on social stratification in depth in Chapter 7.

Max Weber If Karl Marx brought the material world back into history, which had been thought of as mostly idea-driven until then, Max Weber (1864–1920), writing shortly after Marx, is said to have brought ideas back into history. Weber and others believed Marx went too far in seeing culture, ideas, religion, and the like as merely an effect and not a cause of how societies evolve. Specifically, Weber criticized Marx for his exclusive focus on the economy and social class, advocating sociological analysis to accommodate

TWO CENTURIES OF SOCIOLOGY

1960	1965	1970	1975	1980

1959
Erving Goffman publishes *The Presentation of Self in Everyday Life*; Mills publishes *The Sociological Imagination*

1966
Equality of Educational Opportunity (the Coleman Report) is published.

1972
Ann Oakley publishes *Sex, Gender, and Society*

1978
William Julius Wilson publishes *The Declining Significance of Race*

Erving Goffman

1962
Mills dies

1963
Du Bois dies; the March on Washington; Betty Friedan publishes *The Feminine Mystique*

1967
Elliot Liebow publishes *Tally's Corner*; Peter M. Blau and Otis Dudley Duncan publish *The American Occupational Structure*

1973
Daniel Bell publishes *The Coming of the Post-Industrial Society*

1977
Paul Willis publishes *Learning to Labor*

1969
Woodstock

Ann Oakley

1979
Parsons dies

March on Washington

C. Wright Mills

the multiple influences of culture, economics, and politics. Weber is most famous for his two-volume work *Economy and Society* (published post-humously in 1922) as well as for a lengthy essay titled "The Protestant Ethic and the Spirit of Capitalism" (1904/2003). In the latter, he argued that the religious transformation that occurred during the Protestant Reformation in the sixteenth and early seventeenth centuries laid the groundwork for modern capitalism by upending the medieval ethic of virtuous poverty and replacing it with an ideology that saw riches as a sign of divine providence. *Economy and Society* also provided the theories of authority, rationality, the state (i.e., government), and status, and a host of other concepts that sociologists still use today.

One of Weber's most important contributions was the concept of *Verstehen* ("understanding" in German). By emphasizing *Verstehen*, Weber

VERSTEHEN

German for "understanding." The concept of *Verstehen* comes from Max Weber and is the basis of interpretive sociology.

| 1985 | 1990 | 1995 | 2000 | 2005 | 2010 | 2015 |

✳
1984
Pierre Bourdieu publishes *Distinction*; Anthony Giddens publishes *The Constitution of Society*

Anthony Giddens

✳
1999
Duncan Watts publishes *Small Worlds*; Mary Pattillo publishes *Black Picket Fences*

✳
2016
Matthew Desmond publishes *Evicted: Poverty and Profit in the American City*

✳
1989
Arlie Hochschild publishes *The Second Shift: Working Parents and the Revolution at Home*

Duncan Watts

Matthew Desmond

Arlie Hochschild

✳
1991
James Coleman publishes *Foundations of Social Theory*

William Julius Wilson

✳
1993
Douglas S. Massey and Nancy A. Denton publish *American Apartheid*

James Coleman

Mary Pattillo

a type of scholarship
in which researchers
imagine themselves
experiencing the life
positions of the social
actors they want to
understand rather than
treating those people as
objects to be examined.

ANOMIE

a sense of aimlessness
or despair that arises
when we can no longer
reasonably expect life
to be predictable; too
little social regulation;
normlessness.

POSITIVIST
SOCIOLOGY

the approach to sociology
that emphasizes the
scientific method
as an approach to
studying the objectively
observable behavior of
individuals irrespective
of the meanings of those
actions for the subjects
themselves.

was suggesting that sociologists approach social behavior from the perspective of those engaging in it. In other words, to truly understand why people act the way they do, a sociologist must understand the meanings people attach to their actions. Weber's emphasis on subjectivity is the foundation of interpretive sociology, the study of social meaning.

Émile Durkheim Across the Rhine in France, the work of Émile Durkheim (1858–1917) focused on themes similar to those studied by his German colleagues. He wished to understand how society holds together and how modern capitalism and industrialization have transformed the ways people relate to one another. Durkheim's sociological writing began with *The Division of Labor in Society* (1893/1997). The division of labor refers to the degree to which jobs are specialized. A society of hunter-gatherers or small-scale farmers has a low division of labor (each household essentially carries out the same tasks to survive); today the United States has a high degree of division of labor, with many highly specialized occupations. What made the substance of Durkheim's sociology of work, in addition to economics, was the fact that the division of labor didn't just affect work and productivity but had social and moral consequences as well. Specifically, the division of labor in a given society helps determine its form of social solidarity—that is, the way social cohesion among individuals is maintained. Durkheim followed this work with *Suicide* (1897/1951), in which he shows how this individual act is, in reality, conditioned by social forces: the degree to which we are integrated into group life (or not) and the degree to which our lives follow routines. Durkheim argues that one of the main social forces leading to suicide is the sense of normlessness resulting from drastic changes in living conditions or arrangements, which he calls anomie. He also wrote about the methods of social science as well as religion in *The Elementary Forms of Religious Life* (1917/1995). Although the concept originated with Comte, Durkheim is often considered the founding practitioner of positivist sociology, a strain within sociology that believes the social world can be described and predicted by certain observable relationships.

Georg Simmel Until recently, Georg Simmel (1858–1918) has historically received less credit as one of the founders of sociology. In a series of important lectures and essays, Simmel established what we today refer to as formal sociology—that is, a sociology of pure numbers. For example, among the issues he addressed were the fundamental differences between a group of two and a group of three or more (independent of the reasons for the group or who belongs to it). His work was influential in the development of urban sociology and cultural sociology, and his work with small-group interactions served as an intellectual precedent for later sociologists who came to study microinteractions. He provided formal definitions for small and large groups, a party, a stranger, and the poor. (These are antecedents of network theory, which emerged in the latter half of the twentieth century.)

AMERICAN SOCIOLOGY

Throughout the history of sociology, the pendulum has tended to swing back and forth between a focus on big, sweeping theories and on more focused empirical research. The emergence of American sociology was characterized by the latter, an applied perspective best embodied by what came to be referred to as the Chicago School, named for many of its proponents' affiliation with the University of Chicago. If the Chicago School had a basic premise, it was that humans' behaviors and personalities are shaped by their social and physical environments, a concept known as social ecology.

Chicago, which had grown from a midsize city of 109,260 in 1860 to a major metropolis by the beginning of the twentieth century, when these scholars were writing, served as the main laboratory for the Chicago School's studies. Chicago proved to be fertile ground for studying urbanism and its many discontents. Immigration, race and ethnicity, politics, and family life all became topics of study, primarily through a community-based approach (i.e., interviewing people and spending time with them). Robert Park (1864–1944), for example, exhorted scholars to "go and get the seat of [their] pants dirty in real research." The early twentieth century was a time of rapid growth in urban America thanks to a high rate of foreign immigration as well as the Great Migration of African Americans from the rural South to the urban North. The researchers of the Chicago School were concerned with how race and ethnic divisions played out in cities: how Polish peasants and African American sharecroppers adapted to life in a new, industrialized world, or how the anonymity of the city itself contributed to creativity and freedom on the one hand and to the breakdown of traditional communities and higher rates of social problems on the other. For example, in the classic Chicago School essay "Urbanism as a Way of Life" (1938), Louis Wirth—himself an immigrant from a small village in Germany—described how the city broke down traditional forms of social solidarity while promoting tolerance, rationality (which led to scientific advances), and individual freedom. Much of the work was what would today be called cultural sociology. For example, in their studies of ethnicity, Park and others challenged the notion inherited from Europe that ethnicity was about bloodlines and instead showed ethnicity "in practice" to be more about the maintenance of cultural practices passed down through generations. Likewise, the stages of immigrant assimilation into American society (contact, then competition, and finally assimilation), which are today regarded as common knowledge and indeed part of our national ideology, were first described by Park.

If there was a theoretical paradigm that undergirded much of the research of the Chicago School, it would be the theory of the "social self" that emerged from the work of the social psychologists Charles Horton Cooley (1864–1929) and George Herbert Mead (1863–1931). Cooley and Mead adapted the Chicago School's theme of how the social environment shapes the individual to incorporate some of the key ideas of the pragmatist school of philosophy (which argues that inquiry and truth cannot be understood outside their environment—i.e., that environment affects meaning). Cooley, who taught at the University of Michigan, is best known for the concept of the "looking-glass self." He argued that the self emerges from an interactive social process. We envision how others perceive us; then we gauge the responses of other individuals to our presentation of self. By refining our vision of how others perceive us, we develop a self-concept that is in constant interaction with the surrounding social world. Much of Cooley's work described the important role that group dynamics played in this process. (See Chapter 5 on groups and networks.)

In his book *Mind, Self, and Society* (1934) Mead described how the "self" itself (i.e., the perception of consciousness as an object) develops over the course of childhood as the individual learns to take the point of view of specific others in specific contexts (such as games) and eventually internalizes what Mead calls the "generalized other"—our view of the views of society as a whole that transcends individuals or particular situations. (Mead's theories are discussed in depth in Chapter 4 on socialization.) Key to both Cooley's and Mead's work is the notion that meaning emerges through social interaction. This theoretical paradigm is perhaps best summarized by another Chicago scholar, W. I. Thomas, who stated that "if men define situations as real they are real in their consequences" (Thomas & Thomas, 1928, p. 572). This statement was an important precursor to the notion of the social construction of reality.

W. E. B. Du Bois However, even as the Chicago School questioned essentialist notions of race and ethnicity (and even the self), the community of scholars was still dominated by White men. The most important Black sociologist of the time, and the first African American to receive a PhD from Harvard, W. E. B. Du Bois (1868–1963) failed to gain the renown he deserved. (For a discussion on the capitalization of racial and ethnic terms, see the preface.) The first sociologist to undertake ethnography in the African American community, Du Bois made manifold contributions to scholarship and social causes. He developed the concept of double consciousness, a process in which African Americans constantly maintain two behavioral scripts. The first is the script that any American would have for moving through the world; the second is the script that takes the external opinions of an often racially prejudiced onlooker into consideration. The double consciousness is a "sense of always looking at one's self through the eyes

DOUBLE CONSCIOUSNESS

a concept conceived by W. E. B. Du Bois to describe the behavioral scripts, one for moving through the world and the other incorporating the external opinions of prejudiced onlookers, which are constantly maintained by African Americans.

of others, of measuring one's soul by the tape of a world that looks on in amused contempt and pity" (1903, p. 2). Without a double consciousness, a person shopping for groceries moves through the store trying to remember everything on the list, maybe taste-testing the grapes, impatiently scolding children begging for the latest sugary treat, or snacking on some cookies before paying for them at the register. With a double consciousness, an African American shopping for groceries is aware that he or she might be watched carefully by store security and makes an effort to get in and out quickly. He or she does not linger in back corners out of the gaze of shop-keepers and remembers not to reach into a pocket lest this motion be perceived as evidence of shoplifting. Snacking on a bag of chips before reaching the register or sampling a tasty morsel from the bulk bins is totally out of the question. Those operating with a double consciousness risk conforming so closely to others' perceptions that they are fully constrained to the behaviors predicted of them. Du Bois was also interested in criminology, using Durkheim's theory of anomie to explain crime rates among African Americans. Specifically, Du Bois theorized that the breakdown of norms resulting from the former slaves' sudden and newfound freedom caused high crime rates among Blacks (at least in the South). He also analyzed the social stratification among Philadelphia's Black population and argued that such class inequality was necessary for progress in the Black community. African Americans, he argued, would be led by what he coined "the talented tenth," an elite of highly educated professionals. In addition to being a major academic sociologist, Du Bois worked to advance a civil rights agenda in the United States. To this end, he co-founded the National Association for the Advancement of Colored People (NAACP) in 1909.

W. E. B. Du Bois (second from right) at the office of the NAACP's *Crisis* magazine.

Jane Addams Women, much like African Americans, didn't always receive the respect they deserved among sociologists. Jane Addams (1860–1935), for example, was considered a marginal member of the Chicago School, yet many of the movement's thinkers drew some of their insights from her applied work. In Chicago, Addams founded Hull House, the first American settlement house that attempted to link the ideas of the university to the poor through a full-service community center, staffed by students and professionals, which offered educational services and aid and promoted sports and the arts. It was at Hull House that the ideas of the Chicago School were put into practice and tested. Although many of Addams's observations and experiences at Hull House were influential in the development of the Chicago School's theories and Addams herself was a prolific author on both the substance and methodology of community studies, she was regarded as a social worker by the majority of her contemporaries. This label, which she rejected, partly resulted from the applied nature of her work, but undoubtedly gender also played a role in her marginalization: Many of the men of the Chicago School also engaged in social activism yet retained their academic prestige.

MODERN SOCIOLOGICAL THEORIES

Talcott Parsons Although American sociology was born in a tradition of community studies that avoided grand theory and drew its insights from the careful observation of people in their environments, it was largely characterized by the concept of functionalism for much of the twentieth century. Drawing on the ideas of Durkheim and best embodied by the work of Talcott Parsons (1902–1979), functionalism derived its name from the notion that the best way to analyze society was to identify the roles that different aspects or phenomena play. These functions may be manifest (explicit) or latent (hidden). This lens is really just an extension of a nineteenth-century theory called *organicism*, the notion that society is like a living organism, each part of which serves an important role in keeping society together. The state or government was seen to be the brain, industry was the muscular system, media and mass communications were the nervous system, and so on.

Twentieth-century sociologists had moved beyond such simplistic biological metaphors, yet the essential notion that social institutions were present for a reason persisted. Hence analysis by Parsons and others sought to describe how the various parts of the whole were integrated with, but articulated against, one another. Almost every social phenomenon was subjected to functionalist analysis: What is the function of schooling? The health care system? Even crime and the Mafia were seen to play a role in a functioning society. For example, functionalists view social inequality as a "device by which societies ensure that the most important positions are conscientiously filled by the most qualified persons" (Davis & Moore, 1944).

FUNCTIONALISM

the theory that various social institutions and processes in society exist to serve some important (or necessary) function to keep society running.

Although associated with mid-twentieth-century sociology, the functionalist impulse originated in the nineteenth century, most notably in the work of Durkheim, who in 1893 (1972) wrote, "For, if there is nothing which either unduly hinders or favours the chances of those competing for occupations, it is inevitable that only those who are most capable at each type of activity will move into it. The only factor which then determines the manner in which work is divided is the diversity of capacities." Functionalism was still being applied into the late twentieth century by Richard J. Herrnstein and Charles Murray, who argued in *The Bell Curve* that "no one decreed that occupations should sort us out by our cognitive abilities, and no one enforces the process. It goes on beneath the surface, guided by its own invisible hand" (1994, p. 52).

Conflict Theory Even though functionalism continues to reappear in many guises, its fundamental assertions have not gone unchallenged. Sociologists such as C. Wright Mills, writing from 1948 through 1962, criticized Parsons and functionalist theory for reinforcing the status quo and the dominant economic system with its class structures and inequalities instead of challenging how such systems evolved and offering alternatives. Functionalism also took a beating in the turbulent 1960s, when its place was usurped by a number of theories frequently subsumed under the label Marxist theory or conflict theory. Whereas functionalists painted a picture of social harmony as the well-oiled parts of a societal machine working together (with some friction and the occasional breakdown), conflict theorists viewed society from exactly the opposite perspective. Drawing on the ideas of Marx, the theory—as expressed by Ralf Dahrendorf, Lewis Coser, and others—stated that conflict among competing interests is the basic, animating force of any society. Competition, not consensus, is the essential nature, and this conflict at all levels of analysis (from the individual to the family to the tribe to the nation-state), in turn, drives social change. And such social change occurs only through revolution and war, not evolution or baby steps.

According to conflict theorists, inequality exists as a result of political struggles among different groups (classes) in a particular society. Although functionalists theorize that inequality is a necessary and beneficial aspect of society, conflict theorists argue that it is unfair and exists at the expense of less powerful groups. Today most sociologists see societies as demonstrating characteristics of both consensus and conflict and believe that social change does result from both revolution and evolution.

Symbolic Interactionism A strain of thought that developed in the 1960s was symbolic interactionism, which eschewed big theories of society (macrosociology) and instead focused on how face-to-face interactions create the social world (microsociology). Exemplified most notably

CONFLICT THEORY

the idea that conflict between competing interests is the basic, animating force of social change and society in general.

SYMBOLIC INTERACTIONISM

a micro-level theory in which shared meanings, orientations, and assumptions form the basic motivations behind people's actions.

Female textile workers struggle with a national guardsman during a 1929 strike in Gastonia, North Carolina. How might a conflict theorist interpret labor unrest?

by the work of Herbert Blumer, one of George Herbert Mead's students, this paradigm operates on the basic premise of a cycle of meaning—namely, the idea that people act in response to the meaning that signs and social signals hold for them (e.g., a red light means stop). By acting on perceptions of the social world in this way and regarding these meanings as *sui generis* (i.e., appearing to be self-constituting rather than flimsily constructed by ourselves or others), we then collectively assign them meaning that defines their existence. For instance, there is no intrinsic reason for red to signify "stop" and green "go," but over time we have come to assign these meanings based on a collective thinking and practice; we (tacitly) have come to a social agreement on what these things signify in the context of driving. We then act in ways that reify, or make consequential, this consensus and arrive at our calculations based on the supposed objectivity of this "fact."

The groundwork for symbolic interactionism was laid by Erving Goffman's dramaturgical theory of social interaction. Goffman had used the language of theater to describe the social facade we create through devices such as tact, gestures, front-stage (versus backstage) behavior, props, and scripts. For example, in *The Presentation of Self in Everyday Life* (1959), Goffman explored how our everyday personal encounters shape and reinforce our notions about class and social status. According to Goffman, we make judgments about class and social status based on how people speak, what they wear, and the other tiny details of how they present themselves to others, and at the same time, they rely on the same information from our everyday interactions with them to classify us too.

POSTMODERNISM

a condition characterized by the questioning of the notion of progress and history, the replacement of narrative with pastiche (i.e., a collage of existing ideas) or imitation of other work in the service of satire or subversion, and multiple, perhaps even conflicting, identities resulting from unconnected affiliations.

Postmodernism If symbolic interactionism emphasizes the meanings negotiated through the interaction of individuals, postmodernism can perhaps be summarized succinctly as the notion that these shared meanings have eroded. A red light, for instance, may have multiple meanings to different groups or individuals in society. There is no longer one version of history that is correct. Everything is interpretable within this framework; even "facts" are up for debate. It's as if everyone has become a symbolic interactionist and decided that seemingly objective phenomena are

Las Vegas, the ultimate postmodern city, borrows from various regions, times, and cultures to shape its constantly changing landscape.

social constructions, so that all organizing narratives break down. Postmodernists may not feel compelled to act on these shared meanings as seemingly objective, because the meanings aren't, in fact, objective. The term itself derives from the idea that the grand narratives of history are over (hence, "after" modernism, *postmodernism*).

Midrange Theory Although many sociologists have taken to the postmodernist project of deconstructing social phenomena (i.e., showing how they are created arbitrarily by social actors with varying degrees of power), most sociologists have returned, as the pendulum swings yet again, to what sociologist Robert Merton called for in the middle of the last century: midrange theory.

Midrange theory is neither macrosociology (it doesn't try to explain all of society) nor microsociology. Rather, midrange theory attempts to predict how certain social institutions tend to function. For example, a midrange theorist might develop a theory of democracy (under what political or demographic conditions does it arise?), a theory of the household (when do households expand to include extended kin or non-kin, and when do they contract to the nuclear family unit or the individual?), or a theory explaining the relationship between the educational system and the labor market. The key to midrange theory is

SOCIAL CONSTRUCTION

an entity that exists because people behave as if it exists and whose existence is perpetuated as people and social institutions act in accordance with widely agreed-on formal rules or informal norms of behavior associated with that entity.

MIDRANGE THEORY

a theory that attempts to predict how certain social institutions tend to function.

that it generates falsifiable hypotheses—predictions that can be tested by analyzing the real world. (Hypothesis generation is covered in Chapter 2.)

Feminist Theory Emerging from the women's movement of the 1960s and 1970s, feminist theory shares many ideas with Marxist theory—in particular, the Marxist emphasis on conflict and political reform. Feminism is not one idea but a catchall term for many theories. What they all have in common is an emphasis on women's experiences and a belief that sociology and society in general subordinate women. Feminist theorists emphasize equality between men and women and want to see women's lives and experiences represented in sociological studies. Early feminist theory focused on defining concepts such as sex and gender, and on challenging conventional wisdom by questioning the meanings usually assigned to these concepts. In *Sex, Gender, and Society* (1972), sociologist Ann Oakley argued that much of what we attribute to biological sex differences can be traced to behaviors that are learned and internalized through socialization (see Chapter 8 on gender).

In addition to defining sex and gender, much feminist research focuses on inequalities based on gender categories. Feminist theorists have studied women's experiences at home and in the workplace. They have also researched gender inequality in social institutions such as schools, the family, and the government. In each case, feminist sociologists remain interested in how power relationships are defined, shaped, and reproduced on the basis of gender differences.

DOING THEORY

Theories are not something to which sociologists should be beholden. That is, a sociologist might find a Marxian approach fruitful in understanding and analyzing a particular problem around immigration but then turn to feminist theory when attempting to explain Filipino politics. Rather than being one-size-fits-all grand narratives, theories should be useful lenses through which to view puzzles out there in the world. Think of them as different tints that you can overlay onto your sociological goggles. Sometimes when we approach a problem they bring social dynamics into sharp relief. At other times we may see things through the lens of a given theory that we had not noticed before. They help make the familiar strange. Table 1.2 provides a particular example of how a few foundational social theories may address the same phenomenon. Theories are like the ancient Indian parable of the blind men and the elephant: One thinks the beast is like a fan because he is touching its ear; another a snake, for he is grasping its trunk; a third a rope, for he is feeling the tail; and so on. Theories alone cannot tell us the whole story, but they are helpful pieces of the puzzle.

TABLE 1.2	Applying Theory to the Question of the Gendered Division of Household Labor (Or: Who Works Outside the Home and Who Does Unpaid Household Work)

FUNCTIONALISM	CONFLICT THEORY	SYMBOLIC INTERACTIONISM
Posits that clearly defined positions within a complex society—i.e., breadwinner and housewife—may help reduce strain and confusion by assigning complementary roles within households.	Would study the shift in gender expectations and roles in families resulting from the political struggles of women to challenge an inherently oppressive division of labor that leaves them dependent on male breadwinners and exploited for nonwage household work.	Would take as a given that these roles are arbitrary and not dictated by any natural laws and thus would ask how social actors (i.e., people) play (or rather improvise/construct) the roles of "housewife," "house husband," "primary breadwinner," and so on.

Sociology and Its Cousins

We have already noted that a sociology of sports exists, as can a sociology of music, of organizations, of economies, of science, and even of sociology itself. What then, if anything, distinguishes sociology from other disciplines? Certainly overlap with other fields does occur, but at the same time, there is something distinctive about sociology as a discipline that transcends the sociological imagination discussed earlier. All of sociology boils down to comparisons across cases of some form or another, and perhaps the best way to conceptualize its role in the landscape of knowledge is to compare it with other fields.

HISTORY

Let's start with history. History is concerned with the *idiographic* (from the Greek *idio*, "unique," and *graphic*, "depicting"), meaning that historians have traditionally been concerned with explaining unique cases. Why did Adolf Hitler rise to power? What conditions led to the Haitian slave revolt 200 years ago (the first such rebellion against European chattel slavery)? How did the Counter-Reformation affect the practices of lay Catholics in France? What was the impact of the railroad on civilization's sense of time? How did adolescence arise as a meaningful stage of life? Historians' research questions center on the notion that by understanding

Italian dictator Benito Mussolini (on the left) and Nazi despot Adolf Hitler at a 1937 rally in Munich. How do different disciplines provide various tools to analyze the rise of fascism under these leaders?

the particularity of certain past events, individual people, or intellectual concepts, we can better understand the world in which we live.

Sometimes historians use comparative frameworks to situate their analysis—for example, comparing how Hitler and Mussolini rose to power in order to examine why the Third Reich pursued a genocidal agenda, whereas the Italian fascists had no such agenda and, in fact, somewhat resisted cooperating with Germany's deportation of Jews. Another strategy historians often use, although it is sometimes frowned on, is the notion of the counterfactual: What would have happened had Hitler been killed rather than wounded in World War I? Would World War II have been inevitable even if the victors in World War I had not pursued such a punitive reparations policy after defeating Germany?

The preceding description is, of course, an oversimplification of a diverse field. History runs the gamut from "great man" theories (a focus on figures like Hitler) to people's histories (a focus on the lives of anonymous, disempowered people in various epochs, or on groups traditionally given short shrift in historical scholarship, such as women, African Americans, and subaltern [i.e., historically marginalized and disempowered] colonials) to historiography (in essence, metahistory examining the intellectual assumptions and constraints on knowledge entailed by the subjects and methods historians choose), in which historians rely on archival material and primary resources.

Sociology, by contrast, is generally concerned not with the uniqueness of phenomena but rather with commonalities that can be abstracted across cases. Whereas the unique case is the staple of the historian, the comparative method is the staple of sociologists. Historical comparative sociologist Julia Adams explained what makes her work different from what a historian would do: "If you define the difference according to whether one is engaged in primary archival research or not, I would . . . also be an historian as well as a sociologist," but the big difference is that historical sociologists are "consciously theoretical" and "very keen to explain and illuminate" historical patterns (Conley, 2013a). Whether looking at contemporary American life, the formation of city-states in medieval Europe, or the origins of unequal economic development thousands of years ago, sociologists formulate hypotheses and theorems about how social life works or worked.

Instead of inquiring why Hitler rose to power, the sociologist might ask what common element allowed fascism to arise during the early to mid-twentieth century in Germany, Italy, Spain, and Japan but not in other countries such as France, Great Britain, or the Scandinavian nations. Of course, sociologists recognize that there is no one-size-fits-all hypothesis that will explain all these cases perfectly, but the exercise of considering competing explanations is illuminating in and of itself. Instead of asking what specific conditions led to the Haitian slave revolt in 1791, the sociologist might ask under what general conditions uprisings have occurred among indentured populations. Instead of asking how the Counter-Reformation affected the practices of lay Catholics in one region of Europe, the sociologist might ask what aspects of the conditions in various regions of Europe made the reaction to the Catholic Church's reforms different. This is a subtle but important difference in focus. Instead of examining the impact of the railroad on our sense of time, the sociologist might compare the railroad to other forms of transportation that both collapsed distances and opened up the possibility of more frequent and longer migrations. And finally, instead of asking how adolescence arose as a meaningful stage of life, the sociologist might compare various societies that have distinct roles for individuals aged 13 to 20 to examine how those labor markets, educational systems, family arrangements, life expectancies, and so on lead to different experiences for that age group.

DIGITAL.WWNORTON.COM/YOUMAYASK7

To see my interview with Julia Adams, go to
digital.wwnorton.com/youmayask7

Whether sociologists are comparing two tribes that died out 400 years ago, two countries today, siblings within the same family, or even changes in the same person over the course of his or her life, they are always seeking a variation in some outcome that can be explained by variation in some input. This holds true, I would argue, whether the methods are interviews, research using historical archives, community-based observation studies of participants, or statistical analyses of data from the US Census. Sociologists are always at least implicitly drawing comparisons to identify abstractable patterns.

ANTHROPOLOGY

The field of anthropology is split between physical anthropologists, who resemble biologists more than sociologists, and cultural anthropologists, who study human relations similarly to the way sociologists do.

How does anthropologist Natasha Dow Schüll's research on slot-machine gamblers challenge the traditional boundaries between anthropology and sociology?

Traditionally, the distinction was that sociologists studied "us" (Western society and culture), whereas anthropologists studied "them" (other societies or cultures). This distinction was helpful in the early to mid-twentieth century, when anthropologist Margaret Mead studied rites of passage in Samoa and sociologists interviewed Chicago residents, but it is less salient today. Sociologists increasingly study non-Western social relations, and anthropologists do not hesitate to tackle domestic social issues.

Take two recent examples that confound this division from either side of the metaphorical aisle: Caitlin Zaloom is a cultural anthropologist whose "tribe" (she likes to joke) is the group of commodities traders who work on the floor of the Chicago Mercantile Exchange. Natasha Dow Schüll, another anthropologist, has studied gamblers in Las Vegas and how they lose themselves and their money in the machine zone. Meanwhile, recent sociological scholarship includes Stephen Morgan's study of African status attainment and patronage relations. Another project, spearheaded by business school professor Doug Guthrie in 2006, investigated the way informal social connections facilitate business in China. Given the era of globalization we have entered, it is appropriate that division on the basis of "us" and "them" has diminished. Many scholars now question the legitimacy of such a division in the first place, asking whether it served a colonial agenda of dividing up the world and reproducing social relations of domination and exclusion—accomplishing on the intellectual front what European imperialism did on the military, political, and economic fronts.

What then distinguishes sociology from cultural anthropology? Nothing, some would argue. However, although certain aspects of sociology are almost indistinguishable from those of cultural anthropology, sociology as a whole has a wider array of methods to answer questions, such as experimentation and statistical data analysis. Sociology also tends more toward comparative case study, whereas anthropology is more like history in its focus on particular circumstances. This does not necessarily imply that sociology is superior; a wider range of methods can be a weakness as well as a strength because it can lead to irreconcilable differences within the field. For example, demographic and ethnographic studies of the family may employ different definitions of what a household is. This makes meaningful dialogue between the two subfields challenging.

THE PSYCHOLOGICAL AND BIOLOGICAL SCIENCES

Social, developmental, and cognitive psychology often address many of the same questions that sociologists do: How do people react to stereotypes? What explains racial differences in educational performance? How do individuals respond to authority in various circumstances? Ultimately, however, psychologists focus on the individual, whereas sociologists focus on the supra-individual (above or beyond the individual) level. In other words, psychologists focus on the individual to explain the phenomenon under consideration, examining how urges, drives, instincts, and the mind can account for human behavior, whereas sociologists examine group-level dynamics and social structures.

Biology, especially evolutionary biology, increasingly attempts to explain phenomena that once would have seemed the exclusive dominion of social scientists. There are now biological (evolutionary) theories of many aspects of gender relations—even rape and high-heeled shoes (Posner, 1992). Medical science has claimed to identify genes that explain some aspects of social behavior, such as aggressiveness, shyness, and even thrill seeking. Increasingly, social differences have been medicalized through diagnoses such as attention-deficit hyperactivity disorder (ADHD) and disorders on the autism spectrum. The distinction between these areas of biology and the social sciences lies not so much in the topic of study (or even the scientific methods in some cases), but rather in the underlying variation or causal mechanisms with which the disciplines are concerned. Sociology addresses supra-individual-level dynamics that affect our behavior; psychology addresses individual-level dynamics;

and biology typically deals with the intra-individual-level factors (those within the individual) that affect our lives, such as biochemistry, genetic makeup, and cellular activity. So if a group of biologists attempted to explain differences in culture across continents, they would typically analyze something like local ecological effects or the distribution of genes across subpopulations.

ECONOMICS AND POLITICAL SCIENCE

The quantitative side of sociology shares many methodological and substantive features with economics and political science. Economics traditionally has focused on market exchange relations (or, simply, money). More recently, however, economics has expanded to include social realms such as culture, religion, and the family—the traditional stomping ground of sociologists. What distinguishes economics from sociology in these contexts is the underlying view of human behavior. Economics assumes that people are rational utility maximizers: They are out to get the best deal for themselves. Sociology, on the other hand, has a more open view of human motivation that includes selfishness, altruism, and simple irrationality. (New branches of economics are moving, however, into the realm of the irrational.) Another difference is methodological: Economics is a fundamentally quantitative discipline, meaning that it is based on numerical data.

Similarly, political science is almost a subsector of sociology that focuses on only one aspect of social relations—power. Of course, power relations take many forms. Political scientists study state relations, legal structure, and the nature of civic life. Like sociologists, political scientists deploy a variety of methods, ranging from historical case studies to abstract statistical models. Increasingly, political science has adopted the rational actor model implicit in economics in an attempt to explain everything from how lobbyists influence legislators to the recruitment of suicide bombers by terrorist groups.

Having examined all of these distinctions, we should keep in mind that disciplinary boundaries are in a constant state of flux. For example, Stanford English professor Franco Moretti argues that books should be counted, mapped, and graphed. In his research, Moretti statistically analyzes thousands of books by thematic and linguistic patterns. Economist Steven Levitt has explored how teachers teach to the test (and sometimes cheat) and how stereotypically African American names may or may not disadvantage their holders. Historian Zvi Ben-Dor Benite has assembled a global, comparative history of how different societies execute criminals. It all sounds like sociology to me! For now, let's just say that significant overlap exists between various arenas of scholarship, so that any divisions are simultaneously meaningful and arbitrary.

Divisions within Sociology

Even if sociologists tend to leverage comparisons of some sort, significant fault lines still persist within sociology. Often, the major division is perceived to exist between those who deal in numbers (statistical or quantitative researchers) and those who deal in words (qualitative sociologists). Another split exists between theorists and empiricists. These are false dichotomies, however; they merely act as shorthand for deeper intellectual divisions for which they are poor proxies. A much more significant cleavage exists between interpretive and positivist sociology. Positivist sociology is born from the mission of Comte—that mission being to reveal the "social facts" (to use the term Durkheim later coined) that affect, if not govern, social life. It is akin to uncovering the laws of "social physics," although most sociologists today would shun Comte's phrase because it implies an overly deterministic sense of unwavering, time-transcendent laws.

To this end, the standard practice is to form a theory about how the social world works—for instance, that members of minorities have a high degree of group solidarity. The next task is to generate a hypothesis that derives from this theory, perhaps that minority groups should demonstrate a lower level of intragroup violence than majority groups. Next, we make predictions based on our hypotheses. Both the hypotheses and predictions have to be falsifiable by an empirical, or experimental, test; in this case, it might involve examining homicide rates among different groups in a given society or in multiple societies. And last comes the acceptance or rejection of the hypothesis and the revision (or extension) of the theory (in the face of contradictory or confirming evidence). These scientific methods are the same as in any basic science. For that reason, positivism is often called the "normal science" model of sociology.

Normal science stands in contrast to interpretive sociology, which is much more concerned with the meaning of social phenomena to individuals (remember Weber's *Verstehen*). Rather than make a prediction about homicide rates, the interpretive sociologist will likely seek to understand the experience of solidarity among minority groups in various contexts. An interpretive sociologist might object to the notion that we can make worthwhile predictions about human behavior—or more precisely, might question whether such an endeavor is worth the time and effort. It is a sociology predicated on the idea that situation matters so much that the search for social facts that transcend time and place may be futile. Why measure the number of friends we have by the number of people we see face-to-face every day, given the existence of the internet and how it has redefined the meaning of social interaction so thoroughly?

MICROSOCIOLOGY AND MACROSOCIOLOGY

A similar cleavage involves the distinction between *microsociology* and *macrosociology*. Microsociology seeks to understand local interactional contexts—for example, why people stare at the numbers in an elevator and are reluctant to make eye contact in this setting. Microsociologists focus on face-to-face encounters and the types of interactions between individuals. They rely on data gathered through participant observations and other qualitative methodologies (for more on these methods, see Chapter 2).

Macrosociology is generally concerned with social dynamics at a higher level of analysis—across the breadth of a society (or at least a swath of it). A macrosociologist might investigate immigration policy or gender norms or how the educational system interacts with the labor market. Statistical analysis is the most typical manifestation of this kind of research, but by no means the only one. Macrosociologists also use qualitative methods such as historical comparison and in-depth interviewing. They may also resort to large-scale experimentation. That said, a perfect overlap does not exist between methodological divisions and level of analysis. For example, microsociologists might use an experimental method such as varying the context of an elevator to see how people react. Or they might use statistical methods such as conversation analysis, which analyzes turn-taking, pausing, and other quantifiable aspects of social interaction in localized settings.

Conclusion

The bottom line is that anything goes; as long as you use your sociological imagination, you will be asking important questions and seeking the best way to answer them. As you read the subsequent chapters, keep in mind that a sociologist "makes the familiar strange." I have divided this book into three parts. The first six chapters introduce the methodological and theoretical tools that you need in order to think like a sociologist. The second part, Chapters 7 through 11, asks you to study the inequalities and differences that divide people in our society. The third part, Chapters 12 through 18, gives you an overview of the social institutions that are the building blocks of our society.

QUESTIONS FOR REVIEW

1. Some people accuse sociologists of observing conditions that are obvious. How does looking at sociology as "making the familiar strange" help counter this claim? How does sociology differ from simple commonsense reasoning?

2. What is the sociological imagination, and how do history and personal biography affect it? If a sociologist studies the challenges experienced by students earning a college degree, how could the lessons gained be described as "terrible" as well as "magnificent"?

3. What is a social institution, and how does it relate to social identity? Choose a sports team or another social institution to illustrate your answer.

4. A sociologist studies the way a group of fast-food restaurant employees do their work. From what you read in this chapter, how would Max Weber and Émile Durkheim differ in their study of these workers?

5. Compare functionalism and conflict theory. How would the two differ in their understanding of inequality?

6. You tell a friend that you're taking a class in sociology. There's a chance she knows about sociology and is quite jealous. There's also a chance she's confusing sociology with the other social sciences. How would you describe sociology? How does sociology differ from history and psychology?

7. Sociology, like any discipline, features some divisions. What are some of the cleavages in the field, and why might these be described as false dichotomies?

8. Why do people go to college, and how does Randall Collins's book *The Credential Society* make the familiar reality of college education seem strange?

PRACTICE

SEEING
SOCIOLOGICALLY

TRY IT!

Much of what we accept as "natural" in our daily lives is actually agreed-on social norms. Identify all the mistakes here. For example, notice that the shopping cart has square wheels. Which are violating laws of nature, and which are sociological?

Now do it for real: Go out and about today with your sociological notebook and note how many "rules" of social life you have been taking for granted.

SOCIAL NORM	WHERE YOU SAW IT
LINING UP AT THE CASHIER	GROCERY STORE
STRANGER NODDING HELLO	ELEVATOR AT WORK
STAYING QUIET IN A STUDY SPACE	CAMPUS LIBRARY

THINK ABOUT IT

What was the most surprising aspect of daily life that you now realize is social in origin rather than natural? Is this social norm unique to your community or does it apply pretty much anywhere? Is it a recent development (like smartphone etiquette) or has it been around since humans tamed fire? What is a specific annoying social norm you wish would go away, and why?

SOCIOLOGY ON THE STREET

The neighborhood where you grow up exerts a significant effect on the rest of your life. How did your house, neighbors, street, and town influence you? Watch the Sociology on the Street video to find out more: digital.wwnorton.com/youmayask7.

WANT MORE PRACTICE?

Complete the InQuizitive activity for this chapter at digital.wwnorton.com /youmayask7

PARADOX

2

IF WE SUCCESSFULLY ANSWER ONE QUESTION, IT ONLY SPAWNS OTHERS. THERE IS NO MOMENT WHEN A SOCIAL SCIENTIST'S WORK IS DONE.

Animation at digital.wwnorton.com/youmayask7

Methods

danah boyd (yes, all lowercase) grew up in Lancaster, Pennsylvania, during a period in which the region was trying to adapt to the decline of the farming economy by reinventing itself as an industrial center. The bad news for central Pennsylvania was that factory employment in the United States had already had its heyday, so by the time Lancaster tried to invigorate its economy with manufacturing, the odds were stacked against it. Though Lancaster would later find its economic footing, other towns in the region would not be as lucky.

Raised by a single mother, danah saw her own financial fortunes ebb and flow with the transformation of the American economic landscape. For example, her mother supported herself by running a local franchise of the direct-mail coupon company Valpak. Of course, direct mail has also now been largely displaced by online marketing.

danah's own intellectual trajectory reflects all the subtleties of this background. Though she was taught some computer programming as a young child in school, her interest in this new technology really took off thanks to her brother's hogging of the home phone line. Back in the days of dial-up connections, her brother would take over the family phone line to communicate with other users on various online bulletin boards. Little is more annoying to a teenage girl, danah says, than a younger brother bogarting the telephone, but when she realized that there were actually other people whose computers were deciphering the clicks, beeps, and screeches emanating from her line, that's when the die was cast. Computing was social. And it was cool.

At Brown University danah combined her varied interests by concocting a hybrid concentration: computational gender studies. Her senior thesis research involved studying how sex hormones affect depth-cue prioritization in virtual reality spaces by investigating the changes experienced by transgender people undergoing hormone therapy. Evidently, the retina of the eye is the place in the body with the most sex hormone receptors outside of our

DIGITAL.WWNORTON.COM/YOUMAYASK7

To see my interview with danah boyd, go to
digital.wwnorton.com/youmayask7

reproductive system (who knew?), so how we see the world—quite literally—is shaped by sex.

danah continued her cross-disciplinary studies at MIT's Media Lab, where she showed how to graph the social networks of individuals without ever seeing their electronic communications, but rather, only observing those of their friends. It was during a gap year between completing her master's degree and starting her PhD studies at the University of California that she bluffed her way into conducting her first real independent qualitative study. Her subject was early Friendster adopters. (Friendster was among the first social network sites, followed later by Myspace and more recently Facebook and Instagram.)

As an early adopter herself, she managed to gain incredible access to both Friendster and Myspace. Although many researchers study youth culture ethnographically by talking to kids and hanging out in spaces where teen-agers congregate, and others perform "content analysis" of online interactions such as Twitter feeds, blogs, and so on, few have combined the two so deftly as danah. Access to online social networks allows her to draw samples of users to contact both online and offline in order to make sure that her interviews and participant observation are not only deep but also broad. She can cover not only different groups based on race, class, gender, and sexuality, but also different cliques that are not so easily categorized by demographers. This dual online—offline approach makes her work more generalizable than the typical approach that solely studies online data or offline socializing.

ETHNOGRAPHY

a qualitative method of studying people or a social setting that uses observation, interaction, and sometimes formal interviewing to document behaviors, customs, experiences, social ties, and so on.

The face-to-face ethnography that danah does is critical to understanding the social lives of teens. This is because teens often speak in code online to avoid being understood by their parents or other adult figures who may be observing them. At other times, what teens say face-to-face is belied by what danah observes online. For example, although some teens talk about racial integration and cross-race friendships, online she observes very segregated social networks. Understanding who is left out of social networks can be just as important as mapping who is included in them.

As more and more social life takes place across platforms, we need more researchers like danah who carefully stitch together the domains of our fragmented lives and help us make sense of them.

As scientists, we follow the scientific method: That is, we observe the world, form a theory about an aspect of it, generate hypotheses (testable predictions based on that theory) about our subject matter, and set up an experiment or systematic observations to test those hypotheses. After conducting our analysis, we accept or reject our hypotheses and revise our theory, if necessary. Rinse and repeat. This has been the approach of science since the Enlightenment in the seventeenth century, and it has worked remarkably well.

In everyday speech we use the word *theory* as a synonym for "idea" or "hunch." But in science, a theory is a systematic, generalized model of how some aspect of the world works. It is more abstract and general than a specific hypothesis, and in fact, may generate multiple, testable hypotheses. A theory articulates a system of relationships between facts and suggests causes and effects emerging out of those relationships. One scientific theory you may be familiar with is Darwin's theory of evolution by natural selection. Now fundamental to the way evolutionary biologists see the world, this theory wasn't just an idea that popped into Darwin's head. It was the product of many years of hypothesis, revision, and further hypothesis: the scientific method at work.

As social scientists, we sociologists have a set of standard approaches that we follow in investigating our questions. We call these rules research methods. They're the tools we use to describe, explore, and explain various social phenomena in an ethical fashion. There are two general categories of methods for gathering sociological data: quantitative and qualitative.

Quantitative methods seek to obtain information about the social world that is already in or can be converted to numeric form. These methods then use statistical analysis to describe the social world that those data represent. Some of this analysis attempts to mimic the scientific method of using treatment and control (or placebo) groups to determine how changes in one factor affect another social outcome, while factoring out every other simultaneous event. Such information is often acquired through surveys but may also include data collected by other means, ranging from sampling bank records to weighing people on a scale to hanging out with teens at the mall. For example, had danah boyd coded her field notes and then tested whether the frequency of references to social media varied to a statistically significant extent whether she was observing her subjects in a mall or a private setting (such as someone's home), she would have been deploying quantitative methods.

Qualitative methods, of which there are many, attempt to collect information about the social world that cannot be readily converted to numeric form. The information gathered with this approach is often used to document the meanings that actions engender in social participants or to describe the mechanisms by which social processes occur. Qualitative data are collected in a host of ways, from spending time with people and recording what they say and do (participant observation) to interviewing them in an open-ended

SCIENTIFIC METHOD

a procedure involving the formulation, testing, and modification of hypotheses based on systematic observation, measurement, and/or experiments.

THEORY

an abstracted, systematic model of how some aspect of the world works.

RESEARCH METHODS

approaches that social scientists use for investigating the answers to questions.

QUANTITATIVE METHODS

methods that seek to obtain information about the social world that is already in or can be converted to numeric form.

QUALITATIVE METHODS

methods that attempt to collect information about the social world that cannot be readily converted to numeric form.

manner to reviewing archives. danah did, in fact, rely on qualitative methods in her study—she interviewed her subjects on occasion, but mostly she hung out and took notes, which she later analyzed to draw out patterns and themes without resorting to counting them explicitly.

Both quantitative and qualitative research approaches provide ways to establish a causal relationship between social elements. Researchers using quantitative approaches, by eliminating all other possibilities through their study's design, hope to state with some certainty that one condition causes another. Qualitative methodology describes social processes in such detail as to rule out competing possibilities.

This chapter gives examples of sociological research conducted using different methods, starting with the various theoretical viewpoints from which social scientists approach research. We'll then examine some techniques used by researchers to tell causal stories and give examples of specific studies that have employed these methods. Finally, we'll talk about the ways that social research can be used for ends other than filling textbooks and keeping sociologists busy.

Research 101

The general goal of sociology is to allow us to see how our individual lives are intimately related to (and, in turn, affect) the social forces that exist beyond us. Good sociological research begins with a puzzle or paradox and asks, "What causes such and such a thing to happen?" Once you pick a question to investigate, there are two ways to approach research: *deductively* and

CAUSAL RELATIONSHIP

the idea that one factor influences another through a chain of events; such a dynamic is different from two factors being merely associated or correlated, in which case they may appear to vary together but that could be due to chance or a third factor causing both.

FIGURE 2.1 The Research Cycle

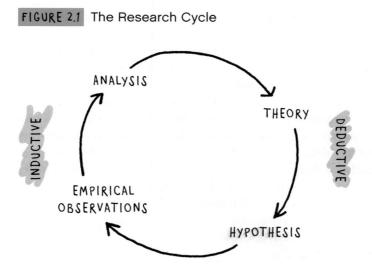

inductively. A deductive approach starts with a theory, forms a hypothesis, makes empirical observations, and then analyzes the data to confirm, reject, or modify the original theory. Conversely, an inductive approach starts with empirical observations and then works to form a theory. These different approaches are represented in the research cycle shown in Figure 2.1.

CAUSALITY VERSUS CORRELATION

Regardless of which method we use, social research is about telling a story. The goal is to recount the story as completely as possible so we're fairly certain it can't be told any other way. Let's take an example of something we'll examine more closely in Chapter 11: the relationship between income and health. We know that a correlation (or association) exists between income and health—that is, they tend to vary together. For example, people with higher levels of income tend to enjoy better overall health. But to say that two things are correlated is very different from stating that one causes the other. In fact, there are three possible causal stories about the relationship between income and health. We might reasonably assert that bad health causes you to have a lower income—because when you get sick you can't work, you lose your job, and so forth. If we drew a diagram of such a scenario, it would look like this:

POORER HEALTH   ⟶   LOWER INCOME

However, we could just as easily tell the opposite story—that higher income leads to better health because you can afford better doctors; you have access to fresh, healthful foods in your upscale neighborhood; and there's a gym at the office. The diagram of this story would look like this:

POORER HEALTH   ⟵   LOWER INCOME

Finally, we could conclude that a third factor causes both income and health to vary in the same direction. For the sake of argument, we will call this factor "reckless tendencies"—a love of fast cars, wine, and late nights. Such shortsighted behavior could negatively affect our health (especially the wine). And it could also affect our income. Maybe we are unable to get to work on time or are spending too much money on those fast cars instead of investing it in the stock market. In that case, the causal diagram would look like this:

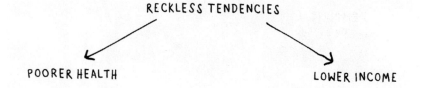

RECKLESS TENDENCIES

POORER HEALTH   LOWER INCOME

DEDUCTIVE APPROACH

a research approach that starts with a theory, forms a hypothesis, makes empirical observations, and then analyzes the data to confirm, reject, or modify the original theory.

INDUCTIVE APPROACH

a research approach that starts with empirical observations and then works to form a theory.

CORRELATION OR ASSOCIATION

when two variables tend to track each other positively or negatively.

In this scenario, if we merely observe health and income, it may appear as if one causes the other, but the truth of the matter is that they are not related in the slightest apart from being connected through a third factor.

How can we arrive at any conclusions with respect to the health–income correlation? We can't randomly assign people to different jobs at various pay levels and see what happens, nor can we independently affect people's health and (ethically) observe what happens to their income, and it is certainly difficult to curb or instill reckless tendencies on a random basis. Thus we can't really rule out any of the arrows, but we can confirm some of them. We can rule out many third factors by measuring them and then comparing individuals who are similar in that particular respect (like education level) but differ in other key regards (say, income). Other factors may not be so easy to measure, and in these cases we might look for a natural experiment—that is, an event or change in the real world that affects the factor we believe causes an outcome but does not affect the outcome in any way other than through that factor. For example, some researchers have used lottery winnings as a natural experiment, comparing the health of winners who won a significant sum with those who won only a token amount. The assumption, based on how lotteries work, is that the amount won is not determined by the winner's health, but that subsequent changes in health may well be driven by the money won.

Although few certain answers exist in social science, we can safely conclude that low income does contribute to poor health, at least to some extent in specific contexts. (We can also be fairly sure that bad health has a negative effect on income.) However, our case would be stronger if we knew exactly what effect low income has on health. In other words, we don't know the causal mechanism. Is it that low-wage jobs are stressful? (It is well known that certain types of chronic stress are bad for you.) If so, does such stress

NATURAL EXPERIMENT

something that takes place in the world that affects people in a way that is unrelated to any other preexisting factors or their characteristics, thereby approximating random assignment to treatment or control groups.

How did studying lottery winners help sociologists understand the relationship between income and health?

cause low-wage workers' behavior to change, perhaps by increasing their consumption of fast food, smoking rates, or alcohol intake? Or is there a more direct, psychobiological pathway—say, the stress of a verbally abusive boss that can cause higher corticosteroid levels in the bloodstream? Or is it all of these factors and more? The more dots we can connect, the stronger our causal story becomes and the better prepared we are to intervene.

Remember, it is very difficult, especially in social science, to assert causality—that change in one factor causes a change in another. It's much easier to say two things are correlated, which just means that we observe change in both. For example, as race varies (across individuals), so does average life expectancy. Likewise, as nutrition changes across or within populations, so does average height, but can we say that better nutrition causes some populations to be taller? Maybe, but maybe not. Let's further examine this.

To establish causality, three factors are needed: correlation, time order, and ruling out alternative explanations. We've already covered correlation. We notice variations in nutrition across countries and simultaneously observe different average heights across the same countries that tend to correspond statistically to those differences in nutrition. Now we need to establish time order. Have people in country A always been taller than those in country B (a bad sign for the "better nutrition causes height" case)? Did changes in nutrition occur before increases (or decreases) in height? imagine a situation where a drought, flood, frost, or some other ental factor destroyed a main food source in country B, leading changes in people's diet and altering average heights in that we have to rule out alternative explanations for the variboth nutrition and height. Is a third factor responsible he groundwater supply perhaps? Groundwater supply tion through higher crop yields (which turns out say), but it could also lead to cleaner drinking hich turns out to matter for height, again for

CAUSALITY

the notion that a change in one factor results in a corresponding change in another.

busness

→ HEIGHT

GHT

you should
u are trying to
e measured fac-
variable. Because
e, we will call the
ference between the
ge in your dependent
iable. Knowing which
ndates for establishing

n and height spurious?

the sake of argument). If this were the case, then the relationship between nutrition and height would be termed spurious or false, whereas the relationship between infection and height might be described as a "true" causal relationship. Figure 2.2 illustrates this possibility.

REVERSE CAUSALITY

a situation in which the researcher believes that A results in a change in B, but B, in fact, is causing A.

The Problem of Reverse Causality Reverse causality is just what it sounds like: You think A is causing B when, in fact, B is causing A. Let's look at the relationship between income and health. We know that people who are sick often have less income. But which one is causing the other to happen? Is it that when you're sick, you miss lots of school, don't receive as much education, must take off more time from work, are passed over for promotions, and ultimately remain stuck in a lower-level job and therefore have a lower income than your comparatively healthy neighbor? Or is it that when you're employed in a lower-paying job, you may experience more on-the-job stress and more stress as a result of worrying about money, which has a negative impact on your health by putting you at higher risk for cardiovascular disease? On top of that, you can't afford good health care, a gym membership, or fresh, nutritious food. The problem of reverse causality is what makes it so important to establish time order. If a person's income drops only after getting sick sick, we can be surer that it was sickness that led to the decline in income.

However, we should also note that time order is no guarantee by itself. People may alter their current behavior based on future expectations. Perhaps, for example, I choose to save less today because I assume that my children will become rich adults on their own and support me in my old age. Strict reliance on time order—observing current savings behavior and children's income 30 years later—would lead me to the wrong conclusion: A the things I bought for my kids that put me into debt caused my childre success later in life, when it was actually the other way around. Their fut success caused me to spend wantonly, assuming that they would bail m once they got their six-figure salaries. One way to fix this, of course, be to directly measure my expectations for my children's future inc resolve the matter of time order.

VARIABLES

In research we talk a great deal about variables. Simply pu always have one dependent variable, which is the outcome y explain, and one or more independent variables, which are t tors that you believe have a causal impact on the dependent it's possible to have more than one independent variab most important one the *key independent variable*. The dif independent and the dependent variables is that chan variable depends on change in your independent va variable is which is important for complying with m

DEPENDENT VARIABLE

the outcome the researcher is trying to explain.

INDEPENDENT VARIABLE

a measured factor that the researcher believes has a causal impact on the dependent variable.

causality. Often, when we establish correlation but can't do the same for causality, it's because we don't know which variable is causing change in the other—we can't establish time order, for example, so we don't know which variable is the independent and which is the dependent.

In high-school science class, you may have learned that a hypothesis is an educated guess. In social research, we use the term *hypothesis* to refer to a proposed relationship between two variables, usually with a stated direction. The *direction* of the relationship refers to whether your variables move in the same direction (positive) or in opposite directions (negative).

Let's take some examples. We know that income is positively related to education: As people's education increases, usually so too does their income. Overt prejudice, on the other hand, is negatively related to education: As people's educational levels increase, generally their levels of expressed prejudice decrease.

HYPOTHESIS

a proposed relationship between two variables, usually with a stated direction.

HYPOTHESIS TESTING

Are you starting to see how the pieces fit together in the design of a research project? Perhaps we have a special interest in one concept, say, poverty. Poverty is a broad concept, so we need to specify what we mean by poverty in this particular study. The process of assigning a precise definition for measuring a concept being examined in a particular study is called operationalization. When you read a study, it's important to understand how the author is operationalizing his or her concept. If I do a study on poverty among Americans who fall below the official US poverty line, and someone else completes a study that examines poverty using the United Nations' definition of it— namely, subsistence on less than $1.25 per day—we're discussing two very different concepts of poverty. As the old adage says, we're comparing apples and oranges. Once I decide how I'm defining poverty, I can begin to consider all the variables related to my concept. In the case of poverty, we might take a look at education, employment status, race, or gender.

OPERATIONALIZA-TION

how a concept gets defined and measured in a given study.

It's time to make some decisions. First of all, is poverty my dependent or independent variable? Am I thinking about poverty as the cause of something else (poor health) or its result (lack of formal education)? Let's say I want to examine the factors that cause poverty, and I'm especially interested in the effect of parental education on children's poverty levels, because theory tells me that a link exists. Assuming that I've defined educational level (Number of years in school? Grades or degrees completed? Scores on a certain test? Prestige of any college attended?), now I'm ready to pose my research question: What effect do parents' educational levels have on children's chances of living in poverty as adults? And I can form a hypothesis:

> Hypothesis: The lower the educational level of the parents, the greater the chance that their children will be poor as adults.

Also for each hypothesis, an equal and opposite alternative hypothesis exists:

> Alternative hypothesis: There is a positive relationship between parental education and children's likelihood of living in poverty as adults.

Parental education is my key independent variable, but I also believe that race and family structure may affect how my independent variable matters. In this example, race and family structure would be moderating variables—that is, they affect the relationship between my independent and my dependent variables. (Children's education or test scores in this example would be mediating variables that are positioned between the independent and dependent variables but do not interact with either to affect the relationship between them.)

I am not quite ready to test my hypotheses, however. First, I need to tell stories—that is, causal stories about why I would expect the hypotheses to be true. In support of the hypotheses, I might say that parents who are more educated have acquired more confidence and skills for succeeding in our economy and that they are then more likely to pass on some of this knowledge and positive outlook to their kids at home. In support of my alternative hypothesis, parents who have spent a great deal of money on their own education may have less left over to help their children. Establishing the groundwork for a reasonably "fair fight" between main and alternative hypotheses is important so we do not spend time discovering trivialities that are already well known (e.g., low-income individuals tend to be poor). So how good were my guesses or hypotheses?

VALIDITY, RELIABILITY, AND GENERALIZABILITY

VALIDITY

the extent to which an instrument measures what it is intended to measure.

RELIABILITY

the likelihood of obtaining consistent results using the same measure.

Validity, reliability, and generalizability are simple but important concepts. To say a measure has validity means that it measures what you intend it to. So if you step on a scale and it measures your height, it's not valid. Likewise, if I ask you how happy you are with your life in general, and you tell me how happy you are with school in particular, at this exact moment my question isn't a valid measure of your life satisfaction. Reliability refers to how likely you are to obtain the same result using the same measure the next time. A scale that's off by 10 pounds might not be totally valid—it will not give me my actual weight—but the scale is reliable if every time I step on it, it reads exactly 10 pounds less than my true weight. Likewise, a clock that's five minutes fast is reliable but not valid. But if I ask you to rate your overall satisfaction with your life so far, and you honestly tell me you would give yourself a 10 out of 10, and then a week from now I ask you to rate your overall satisfaction with life so far, and you honestly tell me you'd give yourself a 7 out of 10 (because that first time you had just found $10 on the floor), then that measure (my question) is valid but not reliable. Ideally, we'd like our measures to be both valid and reliable, but sometimes we have to make trade-offs between the two. Keep this in mind as we discuss the various methods of data collection.

Finally, generalizability is the extent to which we can claim that our findings inform us about a group larger than the one we studied. Can we generalize our findings to a larger population? And how do we determine whether we can?

ROLE OF THE RESEARCHER

Experimenter Effects As if social research weren't hard enough already, there are also "white coat" effects—that is, the effects that researchers have on the very processes and relationships they are studying by virtue of being there. Often, subjects change their behavior, consciously or not, just because they are part of a study. Have you ever been in a classroom when the teacher is being observed? It might prove to be the best class the teacher has ever taught, even if she didn't mean to put on the charm for the observer.

When we do qualitative fieldwork (interviews, ethnography, or participant observation), we talk about reflexivity, which means analyzing and critically considering the white coat effects you may be inspiring with your research process. What is your relationship to your research subjects? Frequently, research focuses on groups that are disadvantaged relative to the researcher in one way or another. Researchers might have more money, more education, or more resources in general. How does that shape the interactions between researcher and study participants, and ultimately, the findings?

Sociologist Shamus Khan, now a faculty member at Columbia University, attended an exclusive, private boarding school called St. Paul's. Khan has used his alumnus status to gain access to the institution in order to study how elites are groomed and trained (and whether kids on scholarships end up doing just as well as everyone else). He notes that the degree of privilege in his upbringing is not "so rare" among sociologists working in elite sociology departments like his. He admits, "A lot of sociologists . . . obscure their class

● ● ●

DIGITAL.WWNORTON.COM/YOUMAYASK7

To see my interview with Shamus Khan, go to
digital.wwnorton.com/youmayask7

backgrounds. They tend [to act] as if they were middle class, but if you looked at the backgrounds of a lot of the people at elite departments, they would be from relatively advantaged class backgrounds" (Conley, 2014b). We will hear more from Khan in Chapter 13, where he talks about what it was like to go back and research the imbuing of social status at St. Paul's. For now, think about how researchers' class backgrounds might (unintentionally) influence what they choose to study and how they present their findings.

In a completely different setting, urban ethnographer Mitchell Duneier spent five years hanging out with booksellers in Manhattan's Greenwich Village. He wanted to understand how these street vendors and their groups of friends, many of them homeless, functioned in the community. During the course of his research, Duneier became friends with many of his participants, which was apparent when he and I talked about how he made sure he was not exploiting them. Duneier's firm belief in the researcher's responsibility to his or her participants is not always easy for him. He told me, "In the process of doing my research, before I publish my work, I make an effort to try to show the research that I'm going to publish to the people who are depicted in it. . . . Doing this is a very stressful process. Sometimes you have to read people things that are very unflattering to them. And for me, it has taken a lot of courage to sit in a room with someone, with a manuscript, and to read those things to them. Sometimes I can be shaking when I do it because I'm so afraid of the way people are going to respond. But I feel that if I am going to be writing something about people, and I'm going to be putting it out there for the public to read, whether it's with their name on it or not, then they deserve the basic respect of hearing it from me in advance." Even after the private reading and scrutiny of the work for its most important audience—the subject—Duneier notes that the researcher must show ongoing respect for subjects:

> One of the most basic things that one can do, is to try really hard, to make sure that people don't feel used by you, after you leave the field. It's very easy given the constraints of our lives and the academy, and the great pressures we are under within our own universities, running departments, engaging in teaching, supervising students in research, it's very possible that given those demands that when we leave the field site that we can walk away from our subjects' lives and not stay in touch with them. Not ever send them any acknowledgment of the time that they spent with us. Not ever send them the results of the research. Especially if we end up moving to other parts of the country from where they live, and it's hard to stay in touch with them. It's very easy for them to get the impression that we have just walked away, benefited at their expense. They have given us their emotions, we have appropriated their lives for our sociological purposes, and then have gone on with ours. (Conley, 2009a)

As researchers, we're supposed to remain objective, but even if you want to (and some people may not want to remain impartial in certain situations), it's not always possible. One day an incident occurred between the police and the street vendors when Duneier was there (with his tape recorder running in his shirt pocket, unbeknownst to the police). He defended his friends to the officers. Because he was a White, well-spoken, and highly educated professional, his interactions with the police probably differed significantly from those between African American street vendors and the police. Duneier could speak his mind with a bit less fear of arrest and with the knowledge that he could afford a competent lawyer to defend himself. How did Duneier's presence change the interaction that transpired? Most social scientists would argue that once subjects become accustomed to the researcher's presence, they again behave as normal, but we don't have any real way to determine this. When we're engaged in qualitative research, we may find ourselves in situations where we have to choose whether objectivity and distance are more important than standing up for what we believe is right. At these times, we need to take a step back and think about our own role as both researcher and participant, because it is our perception and experience of events that eventually become the data from which we make our claims. Duneier acknowledges that ethnographers are not perfect

How is the white coat effect in play here? Sociologist Mitch Duneier (center), who studied sidewalk booksellers for his book *Sidewalk* (1999), talks with a police officer. To see an interview with Duneier, go to digital.wwnorton.com /youmayask7.

observer-reporters whose presence has absolutely no effect on subjects' attitudes and behavior. The ethnographer, like any other scientist, has a responsibility to readers to make his or her data collection methods public. Furthermore, readers "have to have a sense for how the conclusions were drawn . . . by [researchers] making the lens through which the reality is being refracted apparent. That means telling them something about who we are, not only our race, not only our class or our gender, but a number of other fundamental things."

Power: In the Eyes of the Researcher, We're Not All Equal Along these lines, it is worth asking the following: What role does power play in research? As social researchers, we're not supposed to make value judgments; we should put aside our personal biases, strive for neutrality, and remain impartial and objective. The truth, however, is that we make judgments all the time, beginning at the most basic level of deciding what to study. What does the field in general deem worthy of scholarly attention? What topics am I sufficiently interested in to spend 2, 5, or 10 years, or my entire career, studying? What research do grant-making institutions regard as important enough to fund? What does the social scientific community more broadly view as problematic or interesting and in need of explanation?

Historically, sociology, like most sciences, has been male dominated. But it's also a discipline founded on the idea of making the natural seem unnatural, so it's a good place from which change can percolate. Following the second-wave feminist movement of the late 1960s, a growing stream of thought within sociology sought to turn a critical feminist lens on the discipline itself. Because research ultimately forms the foundation of our work, methods became a key site of debate, and thus the concept of feminist methodology was born. What do feminist research methods look like? First, it's important to understand that there is no one feminist research method, just as there is no single school of feminism. Feminist researchers use the same techniques for gathering data as other sociologists, but they employ those techniques in ways that differ significantly from traditional methods. As Sandra Harding (1987) explains it, feminist researchers

> listen carefully to how women informants think about their lives and men's lives, and critically to how traditional social scientists conceptualize women's and men's lives. They observe behaviors of women and men that traditional social scientists have not thought significant. They seek examples of newly recognized patterns in historical data. (p. 2)

The feminist part doesn't lie in the method per se, or necessarily in having women as subjects. Rather, Harding proposes three ways to make research distinctly feminist. First, treat women's experiences as legitimate empirical and theoretical resources. Second, engage in social science that may bring

---

FEMINIST METHODOLOGY

a set of systems or methods that treat women's experiences as legitimate empirical and theoretical resources, that promote social science for women (think public sociology, but for a specific half of the public), and that take into account the researcher as much as the overt subject matter.

about policy changes to help improve women's lives. Third, take into account the researcher as much as the overt subject matter. When we enter a research situation, an imbalance of power usually exists between the researcher and the research subjects, and we need to take this power dimension seriously. The point of adopting feminist methods isn't to exclude men or male perspectives: It's not *instead of*; it's *in addition to*. It means taking all subjects seriously rather than privileging one type of data, experience, or worldview over another.

CHOOSING YOUR METHOD

In Chapter 1, I described the differences between positivist and interpretive sociology. As distinct as they are in their focus, they also lend themselves to different methodological approaches to research. Because positivists are concerned with the factors that influence social life, they tend to rely more heavily on quantitative measures. If, however, you're more concerned with the meanings actors attach to their behavior, as interpretive sociologists are, then you'll likely be drawn to more qualitative measures.

Ultimately, the distinction between quantitative and qualitative methods is a false dichotomy: The most important thing is to determine what you want to learn and then contemplate the best possible way to collect the empirical data that would answer your question—that is, deploy whatever tool or set of tools is called for by the present research problem. That's why getting the research question right is so important to the entire endeavor. Once the question is precisely operationalized, the method to answer the question should be obvious. If the question still could be approached in several ways, then you probably haven't refined it enough. Figure 2.3 gives an overview of the entire process.

DATA COLLECTION

Remember that social science research is largely about collecting empirical evidence to generate or test empirical claims. So how do we go about collecting the evidence needed to support our claims? Let's use case studies—that is, particular examples of good research—and see what these researchers wanted to know, how they obtained their data, and what they found.

Participant Observation Neighborhoods rise and fall and (sometimes) rise again. Often these changes in fortune are accompanied by racially tinged dynamics: White flight in one direction and, when the tides turn again, (White) gentrification. But sometimes neighborhoods are reshaped by class dynamics within racial groups. With the rise of a Black professional class since the civil rights era, gentrification—the movement of higher-income individuals into once-distressed inner-city neighborhoods—can be an

FIGURE 2.3 The Research Process

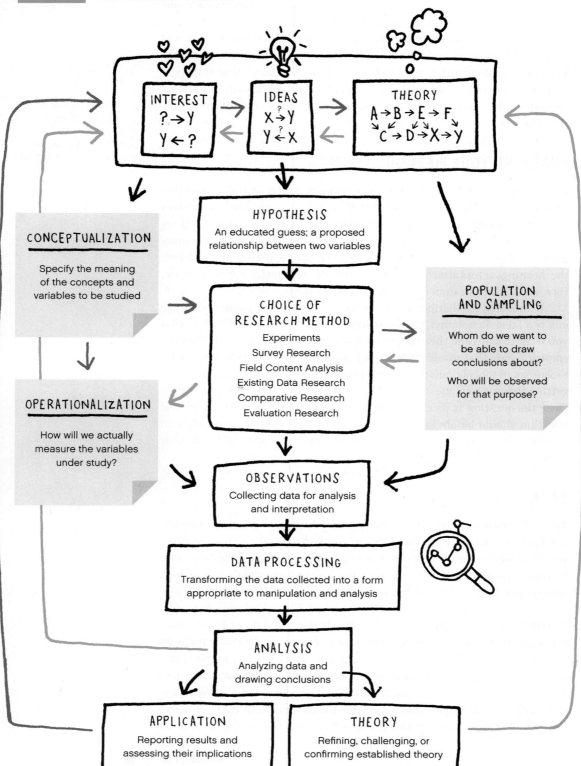

entirely Black affair. But does that create the same tensions as cross-race urban transitions? Or does it provide its own set of unique problems?

To answer this (and other) questions, sociologist Mary Pattillo (2007) studied the Chicago neighborhood of North Kenwood–Oakland, using the method called participant observation. This approach aims to uncover the meanings people give to their own social actions (and those of others) by observing their behavior in practice, in contrast to just asking them about it after the fact. This strategy is predicated on the notion that surveys, interviews, and other approaches are more easily "managed" by the respondents. That is, studying racial attitudes by surveying respondents, for instance, may lead to subjects telling the researcher what they think is the "right" answer and what the researcher wants to hear. But by hanging out in a given community over a long period, integrating into its daily fabric, and letting the dramas of everyday life unfold with minimal intrusion, participant observers are more likely to capture what folks actually think, feel, and do rather than what they would like to think they do.

This type of sociology typically involves a significant time investment because the participant observer must gain access to a given community, learn its local norms and logic of behavior, and then watch social dynamics unfold. Often it can take years to do an ethnographic study of this nature. In Pattillo's case, she moved into the community right when other professional Blacks were moving in. She attended local community board meetings, went to block parties, socialized with neighbors—basically she hung out like everyone else. But the difference was that she was engaging her sociological imagination and took extensive field notes about what was unfolding around her.

What she found was that unlike in typical cross-race situations of gentrification, the middle-class Blacks who moved in and revitalized the area occupied a "middleman" status. They offered social resources to their lower-class neighbors—helping them navigate city politics and bureaucracy, for example. But the role came with costs and conflicts as well: Residents of different classes disagreed about the proper use of space, such as whether the front porch was a proper hangout or where barbecuing should take place (in the front yard or back yard). There were also more consequential struggles, such as those over local schools. In the end, Pattillo's combination of historical analysis and time spent "hanging out" in the neighborhood painted a rich portrait of class and race as it plays out in Chicago's South Side.

Interviews Want to know how and why someone does something? Why not just ask them to tell you all about it? Interviews are one common form of gathering qualitative data. For her book *Money, Morals, and Manners* (1992), sociologist Michèle Lamont interviewed upper-middle-class men in France and the United States about their tastes. She chose the men in her sample based on their social status—they were employed as managers,

---

PARTICIPANT OBSERVATION

a qualitative research method that seeks to uncover the meanings people give their social actions by observing their behavior in practice.

professionals, and entrepreneurs—arguing that these people hold enormous power in their jobs and communities, and consequently their tastes are influential in shaping the culture around them. Lamont (1992) conducted more than 160 interviews, trying to determine how the people in her sample defined what it means to be a "worthy person" and analyzing "the relative importance attached to religion, honesty, low moral standards, cosmopolitanism, high culture, money, [and] power." The comparative aspect of her research design allowed her to identify some of the cultural differences between American and French tastes. For example, she ascertained that the French men valued art more than their American counterparts, whereas the Americans cared more about money than their French counterparts.

By using unstructured, open-ended interviews, Lamont allowed her subjects to go off on tangents, to vent, and to share intimacies that might not appear at first glance to be related to the study. But she also did probe—that is, she pushed subjects past their initial, comfortable answers on somewhat delicate, controversial issues. Knowing how and when to probe and when to back off is part of the art of interviewing that results from practice. Other researchers may rely on semistructured or structured interviews—that is, interviews in which the researchers have more than just a set of topics to cover in no preset order; rather, the researchers develop a specific set of questions to address with all respondents in a relatively fixed sequence. If an interview becomes very structured, it falls into the next category: survey research.

Survey Research Chances are you've filled out a survey at some point. One customarily receives them from the manufacturers and retailers of electronics and from restaurants and hotels. Surveys are an ordered series of questions intended to elicit information from respondents, and they can be powerful methods of data collection. Surveys may be done anonymously and distributed widely, so you can reach a much larger sample than if you relied solely on interviews. At the same time, however, you have to pay attention to your response rate. Out of all the surveys you distributed, how many were actually completed and returned to you? Lately, we have been bombarded with more and more surveys soliciting our opinions about everything from what soap we prefer to how to stop global warming. It has become increasingly difficult for researchers to get their surveys answered amid the din of our information society, and response rates, in general, continue to fall.

Why does this matter? If those who answered your survey or tore it up were truly random, then the only concern would be the cost in time and money to obtain, say, 200 completed surveys. But, as it turns out, who responds and who doesn't is not random. As a researcher, you need to consider the ways that selection bias can enter your sample. Are the people who completed the survey different in some significant way from

SURVEY

an ordered series of questions intended to elicit information from respondents.

the people who didn't complete it? If your survey is about the sacrifices respondents would be willing to make to slow global warming and the only folks who bother to respond are environmentalists, your results will likely indicate that the population is willing to sacrifice far more than it actually would. In fact, the nonrespondents were not even willing to sacrifice the 10 minutes to take the survey. Surveys can also be done in person or over the phone. This method of survey design differs from interviews in that a set questionnaire exists. Surveys are generally converted into quantitative data for statistical analysis—everything from simple estimates (How many gay policemen are there in America?) to comparisons of averages across groups (What proportion of gay policemen support abortion rights, and what proportion of retired female plumbers do?) to complex techniques such as multiple regression, where one measured factor (such as education level) is held constant, or statistically removed from the picture, to pin down the effect of another factor (such as total family income) on, say, reported levels of happiness.

The General Social Survey (GSS) run by the National Opinion Research Center of the University of Chicago is one of the premier surveys in the United States. Since 1972, the GSS has asked a nationally representative sample of respondents a battery of questions about their social and demographic characteristics and their opinions on a wide range of subjects. Conducted every other year, the GSS includes some new questions, but many are the same from one survey to the next. This consistency has allowed researchers to track American attitudes about a range of important issues, from race relations to abortion politics to beliefs about sexual orientation, and to see how the beliefs of different demographic subgroups have converged or diverged over four decades. The GSS is an example of a repeated cross-sectional survey. That is, it samples a new group of approximately 2,000 Americans in each yearly survey wave. Each sample should represent a cross section of the US population of that particular survey year.

A cross-sectional study stands in contrast to a panel survey, also known as a longitudinal study, which tracks the same individuals, households, or other social units over time. One such survey, the Panel Study of Income Dynamics (PSID), run by the Institute for Social Research at the University of Michigan, has followed 5,000 American families each year since 1968. (Recently, the PSID had to trim back to every other year because of budget cutbacks.) It even tracks family members who have split off and formed their own households and families. In this way, the survey has taken on the structure of a family tree. The PSID has contributed to important research on questions about how families transition in and out of poverty, what predicts whether marriages will last, and how much economic mobility exists in the United States across generations—just to name a few of the topics that PSID analysis has illuminated.

REPRESENTATIVE SAMPLE

the idea that a particular slice of social observation—a sample of survey respondents, an ethnographic research site such as an organization, or a batch of social media posts—captures in an accurate way the larger set (or universe) of those phenomena that it is meant to stand in for.

SAMPLES:
THEY'RE NOT JUST THE FREE TASTES
AT THE SUPERMARKET

? !

POPULATION

an entire group of individual persons, objects, or items from which samples may be drawn.

SAMPLE

the subset of the population from which you are actually collecting data.

Volunteer Phyllis Evans (center) questions a homeless man about his living situation and encourages him to seek help while conducting a survey with team members in New York City.

People use the word *sample* in many different ways, but in social research it has a very specific and important meaning. You are always studying a population. It could be the entire US population, gay fathers, public schools in the rural South, science textbooks, gangs, Fortune 500 companies, or middle-class, Caucasian, single mothers. Most of the time it's too time-consuming and expensive to collect information about the entire population you want to study, so instead you focus on a sample. Your sample, then, is the subset of the population from which you are actually collecting data. (If you do collect information on the entire population, it's called a *census*.)

How you go about collecting your sample is probably one of the most important steps of your research. Let's say I want to study attitudes toward underage drinking in the United States and hand out a survey to your sociology class. Based on the findings of that survey, I make claims about how the entire US population feels about underage drinking: They're in favor of it. Would you believe my claims? I hope not! Your sociology class is probably

not representative of the US population as a whole. Age would be the most important factor, but differences in socioeconomic status, education, race, and the like would exist. In other words, the results I would obtain from a survey of a college sociology class would not be generalizable to the US population and probably not to college students as a whole—maybe not even to students at your school (the students next door in organic chemistry might have very different thoughts about underage drinking). I would be "speaking beyond my data."

Although the issues of generalizability are always at play, they become particularly acute when social scientists use case studies. A case study, often used in qualitative research, is an in-depth look at a specific phenomenon in a particular social setting. If we wanted to understand the interaction among parents, teachers, and administrators in the American public school system, we might do a case study of your high school. How representative of all US high schools do you think your school is?

Census conductor talking with Charles F. Piper as he works on his car.

Does your town have a higher or lower average household income than the United States as a whole? Is the PTA particularly vocal? Is yours a regional high school whose students travel long distances to attend? All of these factors—these variables—are important, and if your town isn't typical (statistically speaking), we'd question the usefulness of the findings. This is perhaps the main drawback of the case study method. The findings have very low generalizability. One benefit, however, is that we typically obtain very detailed information. So there is often a trade-off between breadth (i.e., generalizability) and depth (i.e., amount of information and nuanced detail). A case study can serve as a useful starting point for exploring new topics. For example, researchers often use case studies to develop hypotheses and to generate and refine survey questions that the researchers will then administer to a much larger sample. Likewise, qualitative case studies are sometimes used to try to understand causal mechanisms that have been indicated in large-scale survey studies.

CASE STUDY

an intensive investigation of one particular unit of analysis in order to describe it or uncover its mechanisms.

HISTORICAL METHODS

research that collects data written from reports, newspaper articles, journals, transcripts, television programs, diaries, artwork, and other artifacts that date back to the period under study.

Children of a plantation sharecropper preparing food on a woodstove in a sparsely furnished shack in 1936. How did Jill Quadagno use historical methods to analyze the ways in which people like these children were excluded from the benefits of the New Deal?

Historical Methods, Comparative Research, and Content Analysis

How do we study the past? We can't interview or survey dead people, and we certainly can't observe institutions or social settings that no longer exist. What researchers employing historical methods do is collect data from written reports, newspaper articles, journals, transcripts, television programs, diaries, artwork, and other artifacts that date back to the period they want to study. Researchers often study social movements using historical methods, because the full import of the movement may not be apparent until after it has ended.

How did America end up with a relatively weak welfare state and a high tolerance for inequality, particularly in the context of race, compared with other industrialized democracies? To answer this question, sociologist Jill Quadagno (1996) went back to the archives to research what had been said officially (in regulations and other government documents) and unofficially (in the press) about the passage and implementation of the New Deal in the 1930s and the War on Poverty in the 1960s.

Quadagno took into account many different explanations: timing (the United States industrialized early, before the adequate development of protective political institutions), institutions (the United States has one of the most fragmented political systems in the developed world, making it comparatively difficult to marshal large-scale government programs), and "American exceptionalism" (the notion that our culture, lacking a history of feudalism, was uniquely individualistic and nonpaternalistic).

Finally, the issue on which Quadagno focused her research was the looming shadow of racism in America. According to Quadagno, in order to prevent Blacks from participating fully in the American social contract, authority devolved from the federal government to state and local authorities, which could then exclude Blacks overtly or covertly. The result was a much weaker safety net and one that, for a long time, excluded minorities disproportionately. For example, to ensure that congressional committees controlled by racist Southern Democrats passed Social Security, President Franklin D. Roosevelt had to agree to exclude agricultural and domestic workers when the system was established in 1935. This exception was made purposely to exclude African Americans, who were disproportionately employed in these two sectors. Thus by conducting historical, archival research, Quadagno and others have been able to show the relevance of race in explaining the particularities of the social safety net in the United States.

Whereas the example just discussed focuses on one case, sometimes sociologists compare two or more historical societies; we call this "comparative historical" research. For example, Rogers Brubaker (1992) compared the conceptions of citizenship and nationhood in France and Germany. Comparative research is a methodology by which a researcher compares two or more entities with the intent of learning more about the factors that differ between them. By examining official documents and important texts written over a period of many years leading up to, during, and after the formation of the German and French states, Brubaker showed that their historical circumstances led to very different visions of citizenship in each nation. France was formed from a loosely knit group of powerful duchies and principalities. There was no preexisting French nation or nationality before the creation of the French government. The idea of nationhood—that is, of French identity—had to be forged by the state itself, and this led to a very inclusive notion of citizenship. Germany, by contrast, grew out of an already well-refined, tribal sense of Prussian nationality. Thus Germany's citizenship policy was based on excluding others rather than including them.

The general approach to comparative research is to find cases that match on many potentially relevant dimensions but vary on just one, allowing researchers to observe the effect of that particular dimension. Although all social science research makes inferences based on implicit or explicit comparison, comparative research usually refers to cross-national studies. For example, in studying the effects of gun ownership rates on deaths from firearms, it would be better to compare the United States (which has one of the most hands-off approaches to gun regulations and a high degree of gun ownership) with Australia (which was very much like the United States with respect to gun culture—as well as other aspects of culture—but which changed its policy drastically in 1996 in response to a massacre) than to compare Yemen (which, like the United States, has heavily armed populations) with Sweden (which doesn't), because the latter two countries are so different from each other geographically and culturally.

One distinct subtype of historical methods research, content analysis, is a systematic analysis of the content in written or recorded material. Race scholar Ann Morning (2004) used content analysis to investigate depictions

Greek miners seeking work in the German Ruhr Basin in 1960 after West Germany began a guest-worker program. What did Rogers Brubaker's comparative research about European immigration policies reveal about definitions of citizenship?

COMPARATIVE RESEARCH

a methodology by which two or more entities (such as countries), which are similar in many dimensions but differ on the one in question, are compared to learn about the dimension that differs between them.

CONTENT ANALYSIS

a systematic analysis of the content rather than the structure of a communication, such as a written work, speech, or film.

Fans line up outside a bookstore in Tel Aviv, Israel, in anticipation of the release of the final book in the Harry Potter series by J. K. Rowling. Using Duncan Watts's ideas, how can we explain the massive success of this cultural product?

and discussions of race in American textbooks across academic disciplines over time. Morning analyzed both manifest and latent content on race in a sample of 92 high-school textbooks published in the United States between 1952 and 2002 in the fields of biology, anthropology, psychology, sociology, world culture, and world geography. *Manifest content* refers to what we can observe; Morning's study included overt discussions and definitions of race and images of different races. *Latent content* refers to what is implied but not stated outright; Morning looked for sections of the texts where race was directly implied, even if the word *race* wasn't used.

Ultimately, Morning's analysis disputed earlier findings that biology textbooks no longer discuss race. Her findings showed that only social sciences texts employed constructivist approaches (i.e., the belief that race is a social construct), whereas biology books reinforced essentialist conceptualizations (i.e., the belief that race is innate and genetically determined). However, contrary to her original hypotheses, social sciences textbooks also used biological components in their definitions of race, and only the fields of anthropology and sociology critiqued the traditional concept of race. Why does all this matter? As Morning points out, if textbooks aren't changing, how are students supposed to learn new concepts or viewpoints? Anthropology and sociology aren't widely taught at the high-school level, whereas biology is mandatory in most public school systems.

EXPERIMENTAL METHODS

methods that seek to alter the social landscape in a very specific way for a given sample of individuals and then track what results that change yields; they often involve comparisons to a control group that did not experience such an intervention.

Experimentation Because social scientists deal with people, the controlled environment of a laboratory-based experiment is not always an option. For example, I dream of randomly assigning the students in one of my classes to married or single life in order to examine marital status on some dimension. Assuming seating is random, I'd just draw a line straight down the middle of the lecture hall; all the students on one side would have to marry, while those on the other side would have to remain single. Think of the possibilities! For better or worse, however, I'm not allowed to perform such experiments.

Some sociologists do use experimental methods, however. For instance, sociologist Duncan Watts conducted an experiment to find out the extent to which taste in cultural products like music and movies is determined by what other people think. Watts speculated: "When we look at cultural markets it's very clear that the successful ones are many times more successful than average, so you see things like Harry Potter books have sold probably about 400 million copies around the world. . . . What was puzzling to us about this fact, is that nobody seems to be able to predict which movies, books, albums, etc., are going to be these massive hits" (Conley, 2009b). Watts hypothesized that it was not just the innate cultural quality of a product but the luck of catching on through peer-to-peer influence that determined success in film, music, or publishing. Along with his co-researchers Matthew Salganik and Peter Dodds, Watts

DIGITAL.WWNORTON.COM/YOUMAYASK7

MUSIC LAB

COLUMBIA UNIVERSITY

CLICK HERE TO START

FREE MUSIC DOWNLOADS

To learn more about Duncan Watts's Music Lab experiment, you can watch my interview with him at digital.wwnorton.com/youmayask7

tested his hypothesis by creating an online site called Music Lab where they posted mp3s from unknown bands (Salganik et al., 2006). Visitors to the site could download songs and rate how much they liked the music. Some of the 14,341 downloaders saw how many times these previously unheard-of songs from unknown bands had been downloaded by the previous downloaders, some were unable to see download traffic, and still others could see the song rankings but they had been altered, unbeknownst to the subjects. The researchers found that the best songs in one condition rarely did poorly in another condition and the worst rarely did well, but that the songs in the middle could be heavily influenced by how they were rated (if, that is, the downloaders could see those ratings). I asked Watts if his Music Lab experiment could explain other social phenomena. He explained that we can see the same kinds of social influence in the housing bubble and the Great Recession that followed in 2008. According to Watts, "If you look at the recent financial crisis many things went wrong, right? But the big things that went wrong on the way up were this belief that housing prices could not go down, and on the way down a real collapse of our trust in the financial system. Both of them are driven by people thinking whatever they think because of what other people think. These are not fundamentally financial phenomena or economic phenomena even, they're really social phenomena" (Conley, 2009b).

Ethics of Social Research

Earlier in this chapter, I mentioned the contributions feminists made to research methods with their emphasis on examining relationships between power and the process of knowledge generation. Today, we have more codified standards that must be met by all researchers. Many professional associations have their own ethical standards; doctors, lawyers, journalists, psychologists, and sociologists all do, just to name a few. Colleges and universities, too, often have guidelines for research conducted with humans (as well as with animals, particularly vertebrates). As a professional sociologist, I am beholden to the ethical guidelines established by my peers and by the American Sociological Association. As a professor, I am also responsible to my home institution. And as a researcher, I am ultimately responsible to my research subjects. I work with already-collected statistical information (or secondary data) for the most part, which makes the process a little easier, but that doesn't mean I don't have to pay careful attention to the ethical standards of my discipline.

A few golden rules exist in research. The first is "Do no harm." This may seem obvious; you don't want to cause physical harm to your subjects. But what about psychological or emotional harm? What if you want to interview men and women on their attitudes toward abortion, and a respondent becomes very upset because he or she cares deeply about the subject? The initial charge not to do harm gets complicated quickly. Often, we try to design research projects so that subjects will encounter no more risk than that associated with everyday life.

The second rule is to get informed consent. Subjects have a right to know they are part of a study, what they are expected to do, and how the results will be used. If you're interviewing people or asking them to complete a survey, this makes sense. But how far do you take the rule of informed consent in participant observation? Generally, you have to obtain permission to be at your chosen site, but do you remind every person you bump into that you're doing research? What's more, sometimes mild forms of deception are necessary for the sake of research. In Duncan Watts's research about the way a song's rating influenced the way a new listener would rate it, he could not tell his subjects if the ratings they saw were fake. This small amount of deception is usually considered ethically acceptable, but because deception is a slippery slope, panels of academic peers review all research designs to ensure that subjects are protected. If researchers deceive subjects, the deception must be absolutely necessary to the study, and above all else, the subjects better be safe.

The third rule is to ensure voluntary participation, which usually goes hand in hand with informed consent. People have a right to decide if they want to participate in your study. They are allowed to drop out at any point with no penalty. If you're interviewing someone who doesn't want to answer a question, he or she can skip questions; if the interviewee wants to stop for whatever reason or no reason, that's his or her prerogative. Ethically, the researcher cannot badger respondents into participating in the study or completing it once they have started. There are also certain protected populations—minors, prisoners and other institutionalized individuals, pregnant women and their unborn fetuses, people with disabilities—whom you need additional approval to study. As danah boyd's research with teens shows, it's not impossible to study these populations; it just requires additional effort and caution.

Find out if your college or university has an institutional review board and what the requirements are to gain approval for a research project before you start your budding career as a sociologist. And then you are all set to question everything and make the familiar strange. Good luck!

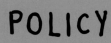

POLICY

 ## THE POLITICAL BATTLE OVER THE CITIZENSHIP QUESTION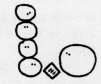

You might think that whether or not a question should be added to the US Census is an arcane and unsexy concern of nerdy researchers trying to eke out as much data on the population as they can. In most cases, you would be right. Survey length is an important concern when it comes to response rates. If a survey starts to get tedious, respondents tend to stop answering, or worse, they may just fill in random answers to speed through, thereby generating misleading data. If the people who choose not to answer a question are systematically different from those who do, that can also bias results.

In the case of the 2020 Census, there was no more hot-button, politically charged issue than whether to add a question about citizenship status. In 2018, Wilbur Ross, the secretary of commerce in the Trump administration, ordered the

The battle over whether or not questions regarding citizenship status should be added to the US Census show that the Census is far from being apolitical.

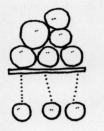

question "Is this person a citizen of the United States?" to be added to the household roster (the listing of everyone living in a given abode). Ross claimed that he needed to restore this question (the last time it was asked was in the 1950 Census) in order to gather information to help the Department of Justice better enforce the 1965 Voting Rights Act. However, the American Community Survey, an ongoing survey of the US population that replaced the long-form census, has already asked about citizenship status since 2005, so the US government already has those figures.

As it turned out, the Justice Department never asked for this change to be implemented as Ross had testified. Investigation revealed that this rationale was a fig leaf for the true reason: to provide a political advantage to the Republican Party when the time came to redistrict based on the census results. This strategy was the brainchild of Republican strategist Thomas Hofeller. Households that do have an undocumented alien would be much more reluctant to share information for fear of deportation and thus not fill out the form. This is not an unfounded fear, as it turns out, since Ross

testified before Congress in 2017 that he wanted to share census data so that they could be "strategically reused" by other government agencies and even private sector organizations. Indeed, in 2004, the Department of Homeland Security was able to locate Americans of Arab descent based on census data. And back in 1940, census data were used to round up 120,000 citizens of Japanese descent for internment into detention camps, a crime for which the government later apologized and paid reparations.

Households with immigrants tend to be located in Democratic-leaning areas like big cities, and thus any reduction in response rates due to the citizenship question would hurt Democrats disproportionately when it came time to redistrict. In addition, even those who answered the census but checked noncitizen could be excluded for the purposes of redistricting when it came time to apportion seats if the state legislatures chose to base maps on citizen-only population counts. This, too, would help Republicans and hurt Democrats.

It might seem obvious that the census should only count citizens; however, the purpose of the decennial census, as laid out in the Constitution, is to "enumerate" (i.e., count) the people living in the United States—citizen or not, documented or undocumented. Thus, when it was revealed that the Commerce Department was motivated by political ends and had misrepresented the real reasons for the change—in combination with the fact that it did not follow the proper procedure for instituting such a change (including providing a period for public comment) in violation of the Administrative Procedure Act—the Supreme Court blocked the administration's attempt to add the question and in July of 2019, as the deadline for printing the census forms was fast approaching, the Trump administration gave up.

This is probably not the last time a question being added to or subtracted from the census will end up in a political fight. Sociologists have long known that data are far from being apolitical, even if they are often portrayed as value-neutral.

Conclusion

Sociology is a field that deploys a variety of methodologies from survey research to participant observation to historical approaches. Therefore, we sociologists often feel that we have to defend our very identity as scientists. Indeed, even some sociologists would argue that sociology is not a science. I would argue, however, that sociology is among the most difficult sciences of all. Sociology is a science in which you can't complete the controlled experiments that are the staple of most bench science. Perhaps zoology and paleontology are other examples of fields in which the scientist is called on to piece together observational data without the ability to run experiments. Nonetheless, sociologists also must face the task of imputing causal processes, not just describing or classifying the world.

How does one assess causality with only observational data to go by, especially when there are multiple factors to analyze—factors that may all interact with one another? And add to that this complication: Reality changes as you study it and by virtue of the fact that you study it. Our basic units of analysis, such as the family, and our conceptual frameworks, such as race and class, are always shifting as we study them. On top of that, the fact remains that many of the topics we study, such as gender and sexuality, race and class, family life, politics, and so on, are, by design, the most politically charged and most personally sensitive topics in our society. This doesn't make research easy. So what we sociologists are trying to do in this difficult field is to inch our way toward causality.

QUESTIONS FOR REVIEW

1. What is the difference between causality and correlation? Use the example from early in the chapter, on the link between health and income, to illustrate this difference.

2. Describe one of the studies discussed in this chapter, its methodology (e.g., interviews), and its general findings. Then imagine how an additional study using a different methodology (e.g., comparative research) might build on these findings and generate new questions.

3. A sociologist observes the work-seeking habits of welfare recipients. After weeks of observation, trends emerge and the researcher forms a theory about the behaviors of this group. Is the sociologist in this example using a deductive or inductive approach? How would the sociologist study this phenomenon using the other approach?

4. Participant observation research is often long, painstaking, and personally demanding for the sociologist. Why bother with this data collection method? Use the example of Mary Pattillo's research to support your answer.

5. Surveys are complicated to design, costly to administer, and potentially suffer from response bias with respect to who answers them. Why use this data collection method? Draw on the case of the General Social Survey to support your answer.

6. Why do sociologists have to run their projects by institutional review boards? What are the "golden rules" sociologists should keep in mind when conducting research?

PRACTICE

SOCIOLOGY, WHAT IS IT GOOD FOR?

You may think this chapter (indeed, this book) won't have much application to your life after the semester is over. But think again! The research methods described in this chapter—the tools of a social scientist—are the same ones used in many different jobs and careers.

TRY IT!

Let's say you're a brand-new marketing assistant at a cable company. You are given this draft of a survey for customers. Don't forget your research question: You are hoping to figure out why an increasing number of consumers are dropping their cable subscription service, i.e., "cutting the cord." Putting your sociology cap on, see if you can identify and fix some issues:

Age: _____ **Gender:** _____ **Race/ethnicity:** _____

....

Do you currently subscribe to cable? ☐ Yes ☐ No

....

If yes:

Have you considered "cutting the cord"?

☐ Yes ☐ No

Do you agree that cable programming is superior to free video available on the internet?

☐ Yes ☐ No

If no:

Do you not subscribe to cable because you can't afford it?

☐ Yes ☐ No ☐ refuse to answer

Do you watch cable programming illegally?

☐ Yes ☐ No ☐ refuse to answer

THINK ABOUT IT

Customer surveys are just one area of the economy that uses sociological tools. Using the pairings below, describe how each sociological method might be useful in the career it's matched with.

SOCIOLOGICAL SKILL	CAREER
Goffman's front stage (dramaturgical analysis)	Policy analyst for education department
Survey	Human resources manager
Participant observation	FAA crash site investigator
Mills's method of difference	Real estate agent
Social network analysis	Marketer for pharmaceutical company
Experimental methods	Family therapist or social worker

SOCIOLOGY ON THE STREET

There are many ways to research a sociological issue. How might your choice of research methods, subjects, and even your perspective alter your results? Watch the Sociology on the Street video to find out more: **digital.wwnorton.com /youmayask7**.

WANT MORE PRACTICE?

Complete the InQuizitive activity for this chapter at digital.wwnorton.com /youmayask7

PARADOX

3

DO MASS MEDIA CREATE SOCIAL NORMS
OR MERELY REFLECT THEM?
CULTURE IS LIKE TWO MIRRORS
FACING EACH OTHER:
IT SIMULTANEOUSLY REFLECTS AND
CREATES THE WORLD WE LIVE IN.

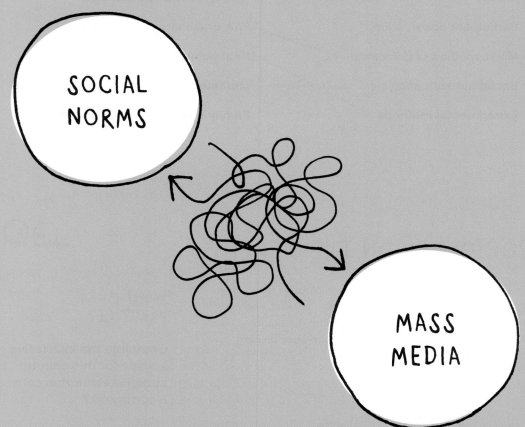

SOCIAL
NORMS

MASS
MEDIA

Culture and Media

The year: 1977. The place: a Portland Trail Blazers basketball game. The star was not on the court but in the audience—Rollen Stewart, aka Rockin' Rollen, aka Rainbow Man. Caught on camera at the game in a rainbow-colored clown's wig, Rockin' Rollen began his 15 minutes of fame. His plan: First, create a celebrity image; then, cash in on that notoriety by landing roles on TV or in the movies. After that first appearance in Portland, Rollen became a fixture at sports events, from Super Bowls to the 1984 Olympics in Sarajevo. He was featured in a beer commercial, was invited to glamorous parties, and lived the Hollywood high life.

After a few years of the extravagant lifestyle, however, he found it "shallow and unhappy." Watching a television program called *Today in Bible Prophecy* following a Super Bowl game, he experienced a religious epiphany and became a born-again Christian. Retaining his colorful wig, he decided to use major sporting events to garner media attention and share a Christian message. He sold everything he owned, lived in his car, and used his money for tickets to key sporting events. He wore shirts and signs quoting John 3:16: "For God so loved the world that he gave his one and only Son, that whoever believes in him shall not perish but have eternal life." He would even carry a small TV set with him into the stands so that he could best position himself to be captured on the cameras, much to the chagrin and annoyance of TV stations. Some members of the media threatened him, so frustrated were they by his co-optation of their precious airtime to spread a religious message for free.

In the mid-1980s Rollen came to believe that Judgment Day was nearing. He decided to focus on the message, discarding the wig so it wouldn't

be a distraction. To get out the final message, he decided to use negative press. He set off a series of stink bombs, mainly in Christian bookstores, and soon the FBI was hunting for him. He claimed that he was trying to direct people's attention to religious scholars. In a dangerous and emotional media-hungry escalation, he held a maid hostage in a hotel room for nine hours, posting religious messages in the hotel window for the media. In the end, the former Rainbow Man admitted that he wasn't receiving the press he wanted—he had lost control of the final presentation. He received three life sentences in prison.

What do we make of the story of Rollen Stewart? We might describe him as a crazy zealot. Alternatively, we might describe him as a media-savvy cultural icon. It's this second definition we're interested in, for the sake of this chapter, at least. What does it mean to be media-savvy? What does it mean to be a cultural icon? Before we can answer these questions, we need to back up and take a look at two key concepts: culture and media.

How did Rockin' Rollen manipulate the media to spread his own message?

Definitions of Culture

Culture is a vague term we use to rationalize many behaviors and describe all sorts of peoples and patterns. We talk about a culture of poverty in the United States (see Chapter 10). We hear about corporate cultures and subcultures, culture wars, the clash of cultures, culture shock, and even cultural conflicts on a global scale. Culture is casually used as shorthand for many things, ranging in meaning from innate biological tendencies to social institutions, and everything in between.

CULTURE

the sum of the social categories and concepts we embrace in addition to beliefs, behaviors (except institutional ones), and practices; everything but the natural environment around us.

CULTURE = HUMAN – NATURE

We might say that culture is the sum of the social categories and concepts we recognize in addition to our beliefs, behaviors (except the instinctual ones), and practices. In other words, culture is everything but nature.

The last sentence captures exactly how culture has been defined through the ages—in opposition to nature. The word *culture* derives from the Latin verb *colere* ("to cultivate or till"), suggesting the refinement of crops to meet human needs. (We still use *culture* as a verb in a similar sense, as when we culture bacteria in a petri dish.) The more common meaning of *culture* as a noun developed from the same kind of human control and domination over nature. We could say that culture began when humans started acting as the architects of nature by growing crops rather than hunting and gathering, hence the terms *agriculture* and *aquaculture* (growing fish and other aquatic organisms for human consumption). Dating back centuries, the term *culture* has referred to the distinction between what is natural—what comes directly from the earth and follows the laws of physics—and what is modified or created by humans and follows (or breaks) the laws of the state. That said, culture is both the technology by which humans have come to dominate nature and the belief systems, ideologies, and symbolic representations that constitute human existence.

In the fifteenth century, when European nations organized expeditions to extend commerce and establish colonies in North America, Africa, and Asia, Western peoples confronted non-Western natives. The beliefs and behaviors of these peoples served as a foil to modern European culture. Today, we recognize that culture is always relative. We cannot talk about culture without reference to the global world, but the definitions, practices, and concepts that we use in this chapter largely emanate from a Western viewpoint. It may also be easier to identify cultural elements when they are different from our own. The challenge in this chapter will be to take what we see as natural and view it as a product of culture. We'll also explore the media and the role they play in the birth and dissemination of culture.

CULTURE = (SUPERIOR) MAN – (INFERIOR) MAN

As colonialism led to increased interaction with non-Westerners, Europeans came to recognize that much of what they took for granted as natural was not. Alternative ways of living existed, as manifested in a variety of living arrangements and marital rules, different styles of dress (or lack thereof), other ways of building cities, and other kinds of foodstuffs. Take, for example, the fact that American architecture of the nineteenth and twentieth centuries tended to use the three major Greek styles of columns: Doric, Ionic, and Corinthian. This was merely a product of tradition: There's nothing natural about these columnar styles that made them the dominant choices in the American architecture of those centuries. And if you traveled to non-Western cities, you would encounter examples of other columnar styles—for instance, the massive fluted columns in the Blue Mosque in Istanbul, Turkey, or the Toltec columns in Tula, Mexico. Such differences may not seem so striking to us now, but think about what it was like for Westerners who rarely came into contact with non-Westerners.

Clockwise from top left: US Capitol, Washington, D.C.; Lincoln Memorial, Washington, D.C.; Blue Mosque, Istanbul, Turkey; and Toltec columns, Tula, Mexico.

ETHNOCENTRISM

the belief that one's own culture or group is superior to others, and the tendency to view all other cultures from the perspective of one's own.

In the wake of these colonial encounters with the New World, philosophers began to define culture in contrast not just to nature but also to what other peoples did, realizing that the way they performed tasks or lived life was a historical product of specific cultural influences. People started to contemplate why their traditions, beliefs, styles of art, and other ways of living arose. There was nothing inevitable about them, and valid alternative approaches to interacting with the world existed. Coming face-to-face with these alternative ways of living caused Westerners to question the culture that they had so far taken for granted. Philosophers such as Jean-Jacques Rousseau idealized non-Western "savages" in contrast to corrupt and debased Europeans; others declared their own culture superior, going so far as to claim that non-Western peoples didn't have culture. Ethnocentrism is a term that encapsulates the sense of taken-for-granted superiority in the context of cultural practices and attitudes. It is both the belief that one's own culture or group is superior to others and the tendency to view all other cultures from the perspective of one's own. Some even believed that non-Westerners did not have souls and weren't human, and this notion was used to justify slavery, violence, and oppression. Such claims obviously weren't true (and we owe a lot to anthropologists for disproving them), but the long history of racism with which we still struggle does have some of its roots in these ideas.

CULTURE = MAN - MACHINE

Not long after European empires began to emerge and spread, new technologies and forms of business upended European definitions of culture at home. Beginning in the eighteenth and nineteenth centuries, goods that were previously expensive and handcrafted began to be mass-produced and priced within the reach of the average European. New industries and a growing middle class of merchants and industrialists started to transform the political and social climate of Europe, particularly in Great Britain. In response to these rapid social changes, the poet and cultural critic Matthew Arnold (1822–1888) redefined culture as the pursuit of perfection and broad knowledge of the world in contrast to narrow self-centeredness and material gain. Intellectual refinement was the "pursuit of our natural perfection by means of getting to know, on all the matters which most concern us, the best which has been thought and said in the world." Arnold's definition of culture in his book *Culture and Anarchy* (1869) elevates it beyond dull, middle-class institutions such as religion, liberal economics, and political bureaucracy.

A sixteenth-century Aztec's drawing of the conquistador Hernán Cortés. Why did Western definitions of culture change during the Age of Exploration?

Arnold's definition of culture was an extension of views advanced in Plato's *Republic*, which argues that culture is an ideal, standing in opposition to the real world. Plato argues that God is the ideal form of anything. A carpenter, for example, tries to construct a material embodiment of that ideal form. He starts with a vision, the divine vision of what a chair or table should look like, and he works his hardest to bring that vision to fruition. Of course, it can never be perfect; it can never approximate the platonic ideal.

The artist's job, in contrast, is to *represent* the ideal within the realm of the real. In fact, there's a long history of artists attempting to represent the ideal female in sculpture and painting, but in reality, no woman could ever exist as a flawless object, content to be gazed upon. Jean Auguste Dominique Ingres's *La Grande Odalisque* has an unrealistically long spine, allowing her to appear smooth, supple, and gracefully elegant as she shows us her backside but turns her face to meet the viewer's gaze with a hint of a smile. In this conception of art—and this understanding of culture—there is a single,

Jean Auguste Dominique Ingres's *La Grande Odalisque* (1814).

best example of any element in the world, from the ideal woman to the ideal form of government to the ideal citizen, which humanity ought to emulate. Furthermore, we see that the ideal woman (and meal and family and governmental structure) is a fluid notion, changing from one place to another and across time periods. Can an ideal be discovered, as Plato believed, or is it constructed?

Material versus Nonmaterial Culture

Today, we tend to think that everything is a component of culture. Culture is a way of life created by humans, whatever is not natural. We can divide culture into nonmaterial culture, which includes values, beliefs, behaviors, and social norms, and material culture, which is everything that is a part of our constructed, physical environment, including technology. Well-known monuments, such as the Statue of Liberty or Mount Rushmore, are part of our culture, but so are modern furniture, books, movies, food, magazines, cars, and fashion. Of course, a relationship exists between nonmaterial culture and material culture, and that can take many forms. When someone conjures up a concept like a portable computer, such an invention flows directly from an idea into a material good. Other times, however, it is technology that generates ideas and concepts, values and beliefs. Before phones with cameras and apps such as Instagram, the word *selfie* did not exist, and before selfies there were no selfie sticks. When it takes time for culture to catch up with technological innovations, there is a cultural lag.

LANGUAGE, MEANING, AND CONCEPTS

Another way to contemplate culture is the following: It is what feels normal or natural to us but is, in fact, socially produced, like saying "Bless you" when someone—even a stranger—sneezes. Another way to put it is this: Culture is what we do not notice at home but would spot in a foreign context (although remember, the sociologist's job is to notice these things at home too). In France, no one says "*Santé*" when a stranger sneezes in the grocery store. When meeting someone for the first time, if you are holding packages in your right hand, have you instead extended your left in greeting? In Saudi Arabia, this action would be construed as highly disrespectful. Have you ever taken public transportation during rush hour? Do the passengers waiting to board generally move aside to let people off the train first? In Moscow, nobody steps aside; in Japan, people wait so long that they practically miss the train! Even your sociology class probably has a different culture—language, meanings, symbols—from a biology or dance class.

Another way to think about culture is that it is a way of organizing our experience. Take our symbols, for example. What does a red light mean? It could mean that an alarm is sounding. It could mean that something is X-rated (the "red-light" district in Amsterdam, for instance). It could also mean "stop." There is nothing inherent about the meaning of the red light. It is embedded within our larger culture and therefore is part of a web of meanings. You cannot change one without affecting the others. Moving from one culture to another can induce feelings of culture shock—that is, confusion and anxiety caused by not knowing what words, signs, and other symbols mean. People who move fluidly from one cultural setting to another learn to code switch by swapping out one set of meanings, values, and/or languages on the fly. Elijah Anderson (1999) and others have pointed out how many minority groups, such as African Americans, learn to code switch in their daily lives by going back and forth between standard English and African American English as they move between predominantly White social contexts (perhaps their workplace) to environments in which they form the majority (such as at home or in church).

Language is an important part of culture. According to the Sapir-Whorf Hypothesis in linguistics, the language we speak directly influences (and reflects) the way we think about and experience the world. On a more concrete level, if you speak another language, you understand how certain meanings can become lost in translation—you can't always say exactly what you want. Many English words have been adopted in other languages, often as slang, such as *hamburger* and *le weekend* in French. Some staunch traditionalists are opposed to such borrowing because they regard it as a threat to their culture. How many words do we have for college? How central does that make higher education to our society? Many words describe the state of being intoxicated. What does that say about our culture?

CULTURE SHOCK

doubt, confusion, or anxiety arising from immersion in an unfamiliar culture.

CODE SWITCH

to flip fluidly between two or more languages and sets of cultural norms to fit different cultural contexts.

There are no inherent meanings behind a red light; its symbolism varies depending on context.

Concepts such as race, gender, class, and inequality are part of our culture as well. If you try to explain the American understanding of racial differences to someone from another country, you might get frustrated because it may not resonate with him or her. That's because meanings are embedded in a wider sense of cultural understanding; you cannot just extract concepts from their context and assume that their meanings will retain a life of their own. In some cases, when opposing concepts come into contact, one will necessarily supplant the other. For example, when European colonization first hit the Americas, Native Americans believed that owning land was similar to the way Americans now feel about owning air—a resource that was very difficult to put a price on and best understood as a collective responsibility. From a real estate perspective, the Europeans must have been very excited. ("All this land and *nobody* owns it?") The issue was not a language barrier: Native Americans had a social order that had nothing to do with assigning ownership to pieces of the earth. Acting on their concepts of ownership, Europeans thus began the process of displacing native peoples from their homelands and attacking them when they resisted.

IDEOLOGY

IDEOLOGY

a system of concepts and relationships; an understanding of cause and effect.

Nonmaterial culture, in its most abstract guise, takes the form of ideology. Ideology is a system of concepts and relationships, an understanding of cause and effect. For example, generally on airplanes you're not allowed to use the toilets in the first-class cabin if you have a coach-class ticket. Why not? It's not as if the lavatories in first class are that much better. What's the big deal? We subscribe to an ideology that the purchase of an airline ticket at the coach, business, or first-class fare brings with it certain service expectations—that an expensive first-class ticket entitles a passenger to priority access to the lavatory, more leg room, and greater amenities, such as warm face towels. The ideology is embedded within an entire series of suppositions and, if you cast aside some of them, they will no longer hold together as a whole. If everyone flying coach started to hang out in first class, chatting with the flight attendants and using the first-class toilets, the system of class stratification (in airplanes at least) would break down.

People would not be willing to pay extra for a first-class ticket; more airlines might go bankrupt, and the industry itself would erode.

Even science and religion, which may seem like polar opposites, are both ideological frameworks. People once believed that the sun circled around the earth, and then, in the late fifteenth and early sixteenth centuries, along came Copernicus, Kepler, and Galileo, and this system of beliefs was turned inside out. The earth no longer lay at the center of the universe but orbited the sun. This understanding represented a major shift in ideology, and it was not an easy one to make. In a geocentric universe, humans living on earth stand at its center, and this idea corresponds to popular Christian notions at the time that humans are the lords of the earth and the chosen children of God. However, when we view the earth as a rock orbiting the sun, just like seven other planets and countless subplanetary bodies, we may feel significantly less special and have to adjust our notion of humanity's special role in the universe. People invest a lot in their belief systems, and those who go against the status quo and question the prevailing ideology may be severely punished, as was Galileo.

More recently, the 2016 presidential election had the potential to shatter the ideology of democracy—that is, the belief that the candidate who receives the most votes ascends to power. The winner of the popular vote, Hillary Clinton, was in fact defeated by Donald Trump, who accumulated the requisite number of Electoral College votes. This was the second time in the last five elections that the winner lost the popular vote, challenging the idea that the United States is a true democracy. That faith was further tested by the proliferation of fake news during the election, Russian meddling through social media, and leaks of stolen e-mails. Many norms of how we have practiced government have shattered (such as the need for 60 votes to end a filibustered nominee to the Supreme Court or the tradition that presidential candidates release their taxes to the public before the election); and yet the institutions of government and the democratic ideology behind them have soldiered on without collapsing.

Of course, on occasion ideologies do shatter. The fall of the former Soviet Union, for example, marked not just a transition in government but the shattering of a particular brand of Communist ideology. Similarly, when apartheid was abolished in South Africa, more than just a few laws changed; a total reorganization of ideas, beliefs, and social relations followed. Often, ideological change comes more slowly. The fight for women's rights, including equal pay, is ongoing even today, but women won the right to vote way back in 1920.

STUDYING CULTURE

In the United States, the scholarly study of culture began in the field of anthropology. Franz Boas founded the first PhD program in anthropology at Columbia University in the early 1930s and developed the concept of

CULTURAL RELATIVISM

taking into account the differences across cultures without passing judgment or assigning value.

CULTURAL SCRIPTS

modes of behavior and understanding that are not universal or natural.

Margaret Mead with two Samoan women, 1926.

cultural relativity. Ruth Benedict, following Boas, her teacher and mentor, coined the term *cultural relativism* in her book *Patterns of Culture* (1934). Cultural relativism means taking into account the differences across cultures without passing judgment or assigning value. For example, in the United States you are expected to look someone in the eye when you talk to him or her, but in China this is considered rude, and you generally divert your gaze as a sign of respect. Neither practice is inherently right or wrong. By employing the concept of cultural relativism, we can understand difference for the sake of increasing our knowledge about the world. Cultural relativism is also important for businesses that operate on a global scale.

But what should one's position be when local traditions conflict with universally recognized human rights? For example, should Western businesspeople condone the cutting of the clitoris in young girls as a local cultural practice, something to be respected, as they go about their business in parts of Africa? There are, of course, limits to cultural relativism. In some countries, it is both legal and socially acceptable for a man to beat his wife. Should we accept that wife beating is part of the local culture and therefore conclude that we are not in a position to judge those involved? In the United States, some Jehovah's Witnesses reject blood transfusions because they believe blood is sacred and not for "consumption" by Christians. If parents refuse a potentially lifesaving surgery for their child because it will require a transfusion, do we respect their right to religious freedom or arrest them for neglect? Where we draw the lines is a difficult matter to decide and sparks a great deal of political debate on topics such as domestic violence, female genital mutilation, and medical practices versus religious beliefs in treating the critically ill.

Margaret Mead, Benedict's student, further developed ideas about cultural relativism when she wrote *Coming of Age in Samoa* (1928), which has become part of the canon of anthropology and cultural studies. Based on her ethnographic fieldwork among a small group of Samoans, she concluded that women there did not experience the same emotional and psychological turmoil as their American counterparts in the transition from adolescence to adulthood. She found that young women engaged in and enjoyed casual sex before they married and reared children. The book, published in 1928, caused an uproar in the United States and eventually contributed to the feminist movement. The validity of Mead's findings has been disputed, but her work continues to be a landmark of early anthropology for introducing the idea that cultural scripts, modes of behavior and understanding that are not universal or natural, shape our notions of gender. This concept stands in opposition to the belief that such ideas derive from biological programming.

Cockfighting and Symbolic Culture Clifford Geertz, another American anthropologist, was well known for his studies of and writings on culture, one of which concerned the meaning of cockfighting in Bali. Cockfighting

A cockfight in Bali, Indonesia. How are roosters central to Bali's symbolic culture?

involves placing two roosters together in a cockpit, a ring especially designed for the event, and watching them fight. The meaning of cockfighting varies, however. Some see it as one of the basest forms of cruelty to animals. Others attach religious and spiritual meaning to the event. In the Balinese village where Geertz lived, cockfighting was primarily a vehicle for gambling, but it was also an important cultural event. Very few men are allowed to referee these fights, and their decisions are treated with more regard than the law. People bet a lot of money, often forming teams that pool their resources. Bettors profess themselves to be "cock crazy."

The owners of the prized cocks expend an enormous amount of time caring for them. They feed them special diets, bathe them with herbs and flowers, and insert hot peppers in their anuses to give them "spirit." The cock takes on larger symbolic meaning within Balinese society. According to Geertz (1973),

> The language of everyday moralism is shot through, on the male side of it, with roosterish imagery. *Sabung*, the word for cock, is used metaphorically to mean "hero," "warrior," "champion," "man of parts," "political candidate," "bachelor," "dandy," "lady-killer," or "tough guy." . . . Court trials, wars, political contests, inheritance disputes, and street arguments are all compared to cockfights. Even the very island itself is perceived from its shape as a small, proud cock, poised, neck extended, back taut, tail raised, in eternal challenge to large, feckless, shapeless Java. (pp. 412, 454)

In the United States, cocks do not have much symbolic meaning. A more central metaphor in American society is baseball. According to anthropologist Bradd Shore (1998), baseball's function in the United States is similar to cockfighting's function in Bali. We call baseball America's favorite pastime and regularly use baseball metaphors in our daily conversations. If your parents inquire about how you're doing in school this semester, you might say you're "batting a thousand." If you ask your friend how it went the other night at a party when she spoke to the smart guy from your sociology class, and she says she "struck out," you know not to ask, "So when's your first date?" We could learn a lot about American culture by studying baseball, how people watch the game, and what symbolic meanings they attach to it, just as Geertz learned such things about the Balinese by using cockfights as the center of his analysis.

In *The Interpretation of Cultures* (1973), perhaps his most famous book, Geertz wrote, "Culture is a system of inherited conceptions expressed in symbolic forms by means of which people communicate, perpetuate, and develop their knowledge about and attitudes toward life" (p. 89). He was trying to get away from a monolithic definition of culture. So for some, culture is watching players hit a small, hard ball into a field and run around a diamond; for others, it's squatting down in the dust beside a ring and watching two roosters brawl. Putting aside the issue that one is cruel to chickens and one uses cowhide to construct the balls, Geertz argues that one pastime isn't inherently better than the other. They're both interesting in their own right, and by understanding the significance of these events for the local people, we can better understand their lives.

SUBCULTURE

SUBCULTURE

the distinct cultural values and behavioral patterns of a particular group in society; a group united by sets of concepts, values, symbols, and shared meaning specific to the members of that group and distinctive enough to distinguish it from others within the same culture or society.

Like culture, subculture as a concept can be a moving target: It's hard to lock into one specific definition of the term. Historically, subcultures have been defined as groups united by sets of concepts, values, symbols, and shared meaning specific to the members of that group. Accordingly, they frequently are seen as vulgar or deviant and are often marginalized. Part of the original impetus behind subculture studies was to gain a deeper understanding of individuals and groups who traditionally have been dismissed as weirdos at best and deviants at worst.

For example, many music genres have affiliated subcultures: hip-hop, hardcore, punk, Christian rock. High-school cliques may verge on subcultures—the jocks, the band kids, the geeks—although these groups don't really go against the dominant society, because athleticism, musical ambition, and academic diligence are fairly conventional values. But what about the group of kids who dress in black and wear heavy eyeliner? Maybe teachers simply see them as moody teenagers, with a penchant for dark fashion and extreme makeup, just seeking to annoy the adults in their life, but perhaps their style of self-presentation means more to them.

Goths in Germany (left) and Japan. What characteristics of goth culture make it a subculture?

Goth culture has its roots in the United Kingdom of the 1980s, yet remains one of the most durable subcultures in a world where subcultures tend to come and go, according to Peter Hodkinson, author of *Goth: Identity, Style and Subculture*. Goth originally emerged as an offshoot of post-punk music. Typified by a distinctive style of dress—namely, black clothing with a Victorian flair—and a general affinity for gothic and death rock, goth culture has evolved over the last three decades, with many internal subdivisions. Some goths are more drawn to magical or religious aspects of the subculture, whereas others focus mainly on the music. Even the term *goth* has different meanings to people within the subculture: Some see it as derogatory; some appropriate it for their own personal meaning. An internal struggle has grown over who has the right to claim and define the label.

What makes today's goths a subculture? They are not just a random group of people dressed in black listening to music (for example, classical musicians usually wear black when they perform, but we don't consider them goth). Certain words and phrases are unique to goth communities, such as *baby bat* (young goth poseur) and *weekend goth* (someone who dresses up and enters the subculture only on the weekends). Goths in Germany may look very different from those in the United Kingdom, and norms even differ among US cities, so each is a distinct branch of the subculture. Yet as a whole, goths do have their own shared symbols, especially with regard to fashion, so they are visible as a subculture. Not all subcultures, however, adopt characteristic dress or other easily identifiable features. For example, Black men on the down low (secretly seeking sex with men) by definition do not want to be identifiable.

CULTURAL EFFECTS: GIVE AND TAKE

How does culture affect us? As we've discussed, culture may be embedded in ideologies. Our understanding of the world is based on the various ideologies we embrace, and ideologies tend to be culturally specific. Culture also affects us by shaping our values, our moral beliefs. The concept of equal opportunity is a good example of this. The majority of us have been taught that everybody should have an equal shot at the "American dream": going to college, obtaining a job, and becoming economically self-sufficient. This is a relatively recent cultural conception. In England 600 years ago, there was no such culture of equal opportunity but rather a feudal system. If you had asked someone in the government of that period, a social elite, if he (and it would definitely have been a man) believed that everyone should have equal opportunity, he would probably have rejected such a claim. He would likely have insisted that the elite, the nobles, should have more rights, privileges, and opportunities than everybody else. Class mobility simply wasn't a concept that existed. Similarly, the way that the concept of equal opportunity is expressed in the contemporary United States has a particularly American flavor. We have a very individualistic culture, meaning that we hold dear the idea that everyone should have the opportunity to advance, but we believe that people should do it on their own—"pull yourself up by your bootstraps," as we say. Americans hold tightly to the rags-to-riches dream of triumph over adversity, of coming from nothing and becoming a success despite hardship. The problem with this cultural trope is that, as sociologists like to point out, the larger, structural, macro-level forces—general social stratification, racial segregation, sexism, differential access to health care, and education—keep the concept of equal opportunity more fiction than reality. As a culture, Americans tend to suffer a bit from historical amnesia. Slavery was abolished in 1863, and legal segregation lasted until the 1960s. Historically speaking, this is not very long ago. Our notion of equal opportunity often fails to take into account the very unequal starting positions from which people set out to achieve their goals.

If values are abstract cultural beliefs, norms are how values are put into play. We value hygiene in our society, so it is a norm that you wash your hands after going to the bathroom. When you are little, your parents and teachers must remind you, because chances are you haven't yet fully internalized this norm. Once you're an adult, however, you are in charge of your own actions, yet others may still remind you of this norm by giving you a dirty look if you walk from a stall straight past the sinks and out the door of a public restroom. In an office, people might gossip about the guy who doesn't wash his hands—they are shaming him for not following this norm. When you arrive at college, you enter a new culture with different norms and values, and you must adjust to that new environment. If you're attending a school with a major emphasis on partying, you might be reading this textbook secretly because the cultural norm in that kind of environment is not to buy the assigned books or even go to class on a regular basis. If you are enrolled at a community college, commuting may be the main cultural practice. You go there for class and then leave shortly thereafter.

REFLECTION THEORY

Culture affects us. It's transmitted to us through different processes, with socialization—our internalization of society's values, beliefs, and norms—being the main one. But how do we affect culture? Let's start with reflection theory, which states that culture is a projection of social structures and relationships into the public sphere, a screen onto which the film of the underlying reality or social structures of our society is shown. For example, some people claim that there is too much violence in song lyrics, particularly in rap music. How do hip-hop artists often respond? "I live in a violent world, and I'm like a reporter. I'm telling it like it is; so if you want to fix that, then fix the problems of violence in my community. I'm just the messenger." They are invoking reflection theory.

A different version of reflection theory derives from the Marxist tradition (see Chapter 1), which says that cultural objects reflect the material labor and relationships of production that went into them. Earlier in this chapter, we discussed the distinction between material and nonmaterial culture. Karl Marx asserted that it is a one-way street—from technology and the means of production to belief systems and ideologies. According to Marx's view of reflection theory, our norms, values, sanctions, ideologies, laws, and even language are outgrowths of the technology and economic means and modes of production. Likewise, for Marx, ideology has a very specific definition: culture that justifies given relations in production.

By way of example, consider the creation of limited liability partnerships. The concept of limited liability emerged in the nineteenth century during the Industrial Revolution, when new technologies enabled the growth of factories and long-distance travel. At the same time, European countries such as Great Britain were colonizing regions all over the world and establishing large global trade networks. As merchants and factory owners tried to expand, they needed more capital from investors. To attract the most money, they came up with the idea of limited liability partnerships. Limited liability means that when you invest money in a publicly traded corporation, you are not responsible for its debt (you can't lose more than what you paid for your shares) or its actions (unless you are on the board of directors). So if you have stock in a cereal company and it goes bankrupt, the farmers who supply the grain can't hit you up for unpaid bills. Likewise, if several small children choke on the prize included in their boxes of cereal, you cannot be held personally responsible for this tragedy. All you lose is the money you invested in the shares. Even if you didn't know what limited liability meant before you read this paragraph, the legal concept is something we take for granted as part of our common understanding of how capitalism works. Historically, however, it arose from a choice made in England in a specific context. Marx would argue that the combination of factory labor and global

SOCIALIZATION

the process by which individuals internalize the values, beliefs, and norms of a given society and learn to function as members of that society.

REFLECTION THEORY

the idea that culture is a projection of social structures and relationships into the public sphere, a screen onto which the film of the underlying reality of social structures of a society is projected.

How has the cultural significance of Shakespeare's plays changed over the last 400 years? Compare the poster for an 1884 performance of Macbeth (left) with the poster for the 2015 movie starring Michael Fassbender and Marion Cotillard (right).

trade relations between England and its colonies necessitated and inevitably led to these kinds of legal structures.

Like most theories, reflection theory has its limitations. It does not explain why some cultural products have staying power, whereas others fall by the wayside. Why is it that *The Cuckoo's Calling* (2013) by Robert Galbraith had terrible sales until it was leaked that the actual author was J. K. Rowling, who wrote the Harry Potter series? Conversely, Wolfgang Amadeus Mozart was a popular composer in his own day. Why is he still so popular today? Clearly, the relations of production and underlying social structures—indeed, Western society as a whole—have drastically changed since the late eighteenth century, yet the appeal of Mozart's music is as strong as ever. If culture is just a reflection of the state of society in a given epoch, then Mozart should have fallen completely out of favor and we would no longer be interested in him or his music, but this doesn't seem to be the case.

Likewise, if reflection theory is true, why do some products change their meaning over time? Shakespeare is a good example. In nineteenth-century America, Shakespeare was the poet of the people, the playwright for the common man. Scenes from various Shakespearean plays were performed during the intermissions of other events. Conversely, during the intermissions for a full-length Shakespearean play, carnival-like entertainment for the masses, called spectacles, would be presented. Shakespeare was the most widely performed playwright in England's former colonies, but not revered in terms of high culture. This is not quite what we associate Shakespeare with today, correct? It's just the opposite, in fact: His work is now considered high art. In this instance, the same product changed its meaning over time, and reflection theory doesn't help us understand that change.

Most important, reflection theory has been rejected largely because it is unidirectional—that is, it basically buys the rappers' defense that culture has no impact on society. Do we really believe that the media have no impact on the way we live or think? Do we really believe that ideologies have no effect on the choices we make? No. Most people now understand that an interactive process exists between culture and social structure. Most would agree that culture has an impact on society and it is not just a unidirectional phenomenon.

Media

Among the most pervasive and visible forms of culture in modern societies are those produced by the mass media. We might define media as any formats or vehicles that carry, present, or communicate information. This definition would, of course, include newspapers, periodicals, magazines, books, pamphlets, and posters. But it would also include wax tablets, sky writing, web pages, and the children's game of telephone. We'll first discuss the history of the media and then tackle theory and empirical studies.

FROM THE TOWN CRIER TO THE FACEBOOK WALL: A BRIEF HISTORY

When we talk about the media, we're generally talking about the mass media. The first form of mass media was the book. Before the invention of the printing press, the media did exist—the town crier brought news, and royal messengers traveled by horseback, every now and then hopping off to read a scroll—but they did not exactly reach the masses. People passed along most information by word of mouth. After the 1440s, when Johannes Gutenberg developed movable type for the printing press, text could be printed

MEDIA

any formats, platforms, or vehicles that carry, present, or communicate information.

Innovations in mass media include the invention of the printing press and movable type in the fifteenth century, the creation of moving pictures at the turn of the twentieth century, and the adoption of the scrolling ticker by today's 24-hour news channels.

much more easily. Books and periodicals were produced and circulated at much greater rates and began to reach mass audiences. Since that time the terms *media* and *mass media* have become virtually synonymous.

The innovations didn't stop there, however. In the 1880s along came another invention: the moving picture or silent film. Its quality was not the best at first, but it improved over time. In the 1920s sound was added to films. For many, this represented an improvement over the radio, which had come along about the same time as the silent film. Television was invented in the 1930s, although this technology didn't make its way into most American homes until after World War II. During the postwar period, new forms of media technology quickly hit the market, and the demand for media exploded: glossy magazines; color televisions; blockbuster movies; Betamax videos, then VHS videos, then DVDs; vinyl records, then 8-track tapes, then cassette tapes, then CDs—and once the internet came along, the sky was the limit! In 2019, 73 percent of the American population had broadband internet at home, with access clustered among the younger, wealthier, and better educated, while 17 percent used their smartphones in place of high-speed internet service (Pew Research Center, 2019).

You're well aware of all the forms the media come in, but let's stop for a minute and contemplate the impact certain forms, such as television, have had on society. Again, televisions didn't become household items in the United States until after World War II. From 1950, the year President Harry S Truman first sent military advisers to South Vietnam, to 1964, when Congress approved the Gulf of Tonkin Resolution calling for victory by any means necessary, the share of American households with television

In 1963, for the first time, televisions beamed images such as this photo of police officers attacking a student in Birmingham, Alabama. How did television influence the reaction to events such as the civil rights movement?

sets increased from 9 to 92 percent. During the Vietnam War, the American public witnessed military conflict in a way they never had before, and these images helped fuel the antiwar movement. Likewise, television played a large role in the civil rights movement of the 1950s and 1960s. It was one thing to hear of discrimination secondhand, but quite another to sit with your family in the living room and watch images of police setting attack dogs on peaceful protesters and turning fire hoses on little African American girls dressed up in their Sunday best.

HEGEMONY: THE MOTHER OF ALL MEDIA TERMS

All of us might be willing to agree that, on some level, the media both reflect culture and work to produce the very culture they represent. How does this dynamic work? Antonio Gramsci, an Italian political theorist and activist, came up with the concept of hegemony to describe just that. Gramsci, a Marxist, was imprisoned by the Fascists in the 1920s and 1930s; while in jail, he attempted to explain why the working-class revolution Marx had predicted never came to pass. He published his findings in his "prison notebooks" of 1929–35 (Gramsci, 1971). In this vein, then, hegemony "refers to a historical process in which a dominant group exercises 'moral and intellectual leadership' throughout society by winning the voluntary 'consent' of popular masses" (Kim, 2001). This concept of hegemony stands in contrast to another of Gramsci's ideas, *domination*. If domination means getting people to do what you want through the use of force, hegemony means getting them to go along with the status quo because it seems like the best course or the natural order of things. Although domination generally involves an action by the state (such as the Fascist leaders who imprisoned those who disagreed with them), "hegemony takes place in the realm of private institutions . . . such as families, churches, trade unions, and the media" (Kim, 2001). For example, if free-market capitalism is the hegemonic economic ideology of a given society, then the state does not have to explicitly work to inculcate that set of principles into its citizenry. Rather, private institutions, such as families, do most of the heavy lifting in this regard. Ever wonder why children receive an allowance for taking out the trash and doing other household chores? Gramsci might argue that this is the way capitalist free-market ideology is instilled in the individual within the private realm of the family.

The concept of hegemony is important for understanding the impact of the media. It also raises questions about the tension between structure and agency. Are people molded by the culture in which they live, or do they actively participate in shaping the world around them? As we discussed earlier in the chapter, it's not an either/or question. Later in the chapter we'll talk about some of the debates between structure and agency in regard to the media, look at some examples of hegemony in practice, and discuss the possibilities for countercultural resistance.

HEGEMONY

a condition by which a dominant group uses its power to elicit the voluntary "consent" of the masses.

The Media Life Cycle

We live in a media-saturated society, but one of the most exciting aspects of studying the media is that it allows us to explore the tensions and contradictions created when large social forces conflict with individual identity and free will. We see how people create media, how the media shape the culture in which people live, how the media reflect the culture in which they exist, and how individuals and groups use the media as their own means to shape, redefine, and change culture.

TEXTS

Why do the adventures in a fairy tale often begin once a mother dies? Are Blacks more often portrayed as professionals or criminals in television sitcoms? How often are Asians the lead characters in mainstream films? Who generally initiates conversation, men or women, in US (or Mexican) soap operas? These questions are all examples of textual analysis, analysis of the content of media in its various forms, one of the important strands of study to materialize in the wake of Gramsci's work.

During the 1960s and 1970s, academic studies focused almost solely on texts—television talk shows, newspapers, and magazine pages. Finally, scholars recognized the importance of finding out how people read and interpret, and are affected by, these texts: Audience studies were born. The field of psychology has expended a lot of time investigating claims about the effects of television on children, and the debate continues. Sociologists have explored the way women read romance novels or how teenage girls interpret images of super-thin models in magazines. For example, in *Reading the Romance: Women, Patriarchy, and Popular Literature* (1987), Janice Radway argues that women exhibit a great deal of individual agency when reading romance novels, which help them cope with their daily lives in a patriarchal society by providing both escapes from the drudgery of everyday life and alternative scripts. We are not just passive receptors of media; as readers or viewers, we experience texts through the lens of our own critical, interpretive, and analytical processes.

BACK TO THE BEGINNING: CULTURAL PRODUCTION

The media don't just spontaneously spring into being. They aren't organic; they're produced. You may have heard the expression "History is written by the winners." Well before something becomes history, it has to happen in the present. Who decides what's news? How are decisions made about the content of television shows? To write his classic *Deciding What's News* (1979a), Herbert Gans went inside the newsrooms at *CBS Evening News, NBC Nightly*

News, Newsweek, and *Time* in the late 1970s. He paid careful attention to the processes by which these news outlets made their decisions on editorial content, "writing down the unwritten rules of journalism," because rules, sociologists know, contain values. Journalists are supposed to be objective, but Gans illustrated the ways in which the mainstream American values journalists had internalized biased the finished product—the news. The notion of "the facts, just the facts, and nothing but the facts" is a worthy idea but to a large degree a farce. Powerful boards of directors regulate the various media; writers, casting agents, directors, and producers decide what goes into sitcoms, soap operas, and after-school specials. Even the huge cache of secret government documents made available on the internet by WikiLeaks in 2010 (and in other dumps since then) was prescreened by individual hackers and researchers. The media are produced by human beings often working for organizations within which they can be influenced by market pressures to publish "fresh" stories rather than follow situations unfolding slowly over time (Usher, 2014).

Increasingly, however, humans are only indirectly "deciding" what's news by designing the artificial intelligence algorithms that figure out which stories to put before our eyes (based on our past browsing behavior). These algorithms were gamed by the campaigns (and Russian operatives) in the 2016 election, causing Facebook to alter its own software to try to better protect users against "fake news." Computers are even writing the news sometimes: Software is able to write simple stories like the recap of a sporting event, based on data from the game itself, and the bots are getting better and better with each passing day. Online activist and entrepreneur Eli Pariser (CEO of Upworthy) and others have become worried about what he calls the "filter bubble" or online echo chamber (Pariser, 2011). Since what we are shown in our newsfeed depends on what we clicked through before (or what our friends liked), we risk never seeing new information that conflicts with our preexisting views—not a healthy algorithm for a robust, democratic society.

Media Effects

In considering the media, mass culture, and subcultures, we can plot the media's effects in a two-dimensional diagram, as shown in Figure 3.1. The vertical dimension indicates whether the effect is intended (i.e., deliberate) or unintended. The horizontal axis depicts whether it is a short- or long-term effect. A short-term, deliberate media effect (section A in the illustration) would be advertising. As a kid, you may have watched Saturday morning cartoons; watch them now and keep track of the number of advertisements for children's food. A child today might see an ad for Cocoa Puffs

FIGURE 3.1 Media Effects

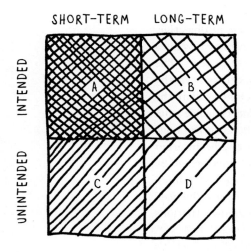

and that same afternoon go grocery shopping with his or her parents. That child is possibly on a sugar crash from an early-morning bowl of Super Frosted Mega Marshmallow Crackle Blasts and might really be clamoring for a box of Cocoa Puffs. The advertisers timed it just right, with the pressure on Mom or Dad to buy that cereal.

Section B of Figure 3.1, on the other hand, represents a deliberate, long-term media campaign. Here, a single theme is reinforced through repeated exposure, as in public service announcements or when *Sesame Street* repeats counting and spelling to help educate children. *Sesame Street* was created with the intent of providing educational programming for low-income children who didn't have the same opportunities for day care and preschool as their wealthier peers, and it works! This type of campaign is generally used by not-for-profit organizations to educate the public. Other examples include Smokey the Bear (created in 1944, "Only you can prevent forest fires"), Woodsy Owl (created in 1970, "Give a hoot, don't pollute"), and the "This is your brain on drugs" commercials from the Partnership for a Drug-Free America (the original fried egg aired in 1987, and the sequel frying-pan smash aired a decade later). In a new public service announcement from the Ad Council—the nonprofit behind ad campaigns like Smokey the Bear—the advertisement reads, "You don't want them responding to your text" next to an ambulance (Ad Council, 2018). Other recent campaigns focus on sexual harassment, suicide prevention, and health problems like type 2 diabetes.

Of course, not all attempts at deliberate, long-term effects are a success. Often, an issue must be framed as a problem before solutions can be advocated, and that can take a long time in a media campaign. For instance, various environmental groups have advocated for taking measurable action to reduce the release of greenhouse gases. However, only in 2013 did the Environmental Protection Agency feel it had enough support in Congress to propose greenhouse gas emission limits for power plants.

Section C of Figure 3.1 represents media with short-term, unintended consequences. An example might be when teenagers play violent video games and then go out and commit crimes almost identical to those portrayed in the game, or when a kid listens to heavy metal music with violent lyrics and then commits a school shooting. You hear of such events every so often, and sometimes the media's creator will use the defense that the short-term response was not intended. In an interview, for example, the software producer or musician might be asked, "Did you know that your music is causing teenage boys to commit violent crimes?" And the response will be, "That is not my intention at all. I use violence as a metaphor."

Scientific research hasn't yet ruled definitively one way or the other on this controversial subject, but many believe that the media occasionally have short-term, unintended effects.

Finally, section D of the illustration represents the long-term, unintended effects of the media. Many people, not just cultural conservatives, argue that we have been desensitized to violence, sexual imagery, and other content that some people consider inappropriate for mass audiences. In the film industry, for example, the Production Code, also known as the Hays Code, was a set of standards created in 1930 (although it wasn't officially enforced until 1934) to protect the moral fabric of society. The guidelines were fairly strict, and they were a testament to the mainstream ideologies of the time (see the box on pages 106–7). Slowly, however, the power of the code began to erode because of the influence of television and foreign films and the fact that being condemned as immoral didn't prevent a film from becoming a success. In 1967 the code was abandoned for the movie rating system. Over time, we have grown accustomed to seeing sexually explicit material in films, on television, and on the internet. Those who lament this desensitization seek to reinstitute controls over media content.

Mommy, Where Do Stereotypes Come From?

On December 22, 1941, two weeks after the Japanese attack on Pearl Harbor, *Time* magazine ran an article with the headline "How to Tell Your Friends from the Japs." There were annotated photographs to help readers identify characteristics that would distinguish, for instance, friendly Chinese from the Japanese, America's enemies during World War II. The magazine offered the following rules of thumb, although it admitted that they were "not always reliable":

- Some Chinese are tall (average: 5 ft. 5 in.). Virtually all Japanese are short (average: 5 ft. 2-1/2 in.).

- Japanese are likely to be stockier and broader-hipped than short Chinese.

- Japanese—except for wrestlers—are seldom fat; they often dry up and grow lean as they age. The Chinese often put on weight, particularly if they are prosperous (in China, with its frequent famines, being fat is esteemed as a sign of being a solid citizen).

THE RACE AND GENDER POLITICS OF MAKING OUT

"When I'm good, I'm very good, but when I'm bad, I'm better." —ACTRESS MAE WEST

The movie industry's Production Code (1930) enumerated three "general principles":

1. No picture shall be produced that will lower the moral standards of those who see it. Hence the sympathy of the audience should never be thrown to the side of crime, wrongdoing, evil, or sin.
2. Correct standards of life, subject only to the requirements of drama and entertainment, shall be presented.
3. Law, natural or human, shall not be ridiculed, nor shall sympathy be created for its violation.

Specific restrictions were spelled out as "particular applications" of these principles:

- Nudity and suggestive dances were prohibited.

- The ridicule of religion was forbidden, and ministers of religion were not to be represented as comic characters or villains.
- The depiction of illegal drug use was forbidden, as well as the use of liquor, "when not required by the plot or for proper characterization."
- Methods of crime (e.g., safecracking, arson, smuggling) were not to be explicitly presented.
- References to "sex perversion" (such as homosexuality) and venereal disease were forbidden, as were depictions of childbirth.
- The language section banned various words and phrases considered to be offensive.
- Murder scenes had to be filmed in a way that would not inspire imitation in real life, and brutal killings could not be shown in detail. "Revenge in modern times" was not to be justified.
- The sanctity of marriage and the home had to be upheld. "Pictures shall not infer that low forms of sex relationship are the accepted or common thing." Adultery and illicit sex, although recognized as sometimes necessary to the plot, could not be explicit or justified; they were never to be presented as an attractive option.

Lucille Ball and Desi Arnaz in the 1950s hit television comedy *I Love Lucy*. Even though their characters were married, they still did not share a bed.

- Portrayals of interracial relationships were forbidden.
- "Scenes of passion" were not to be introduced when not essential to the plot. "Excessive and lustful kissing" was to be avoided, along with any other physical interaction that might "stimulate the lower and baser element."
- The flag of the United States was to be treated respectfully, as were the people and history of other nations.
- "Vulgarity," defined as "low, disgusting, unpleasant, though not necessarily evil, subjects," must be treated "subject to the dictates of good taste." Capital punishment, "third-degree methods," cruelty to children and animals, prostitution, and surgical operations were to be depicted with similar sensitivity and discretion.

"Rules were made to be broken," the old saying goes, and the film industry did its best to prove the maxim true. Filmmakers like Alfred Hitchcock pushed the boundaries of a 10-second time limit for kisses by filming a lip-lock for the maximum allotted time, panning away, and then returning

to the couple still passionately embracing. Rules such as this were slow to change, but not as slow as others. For one thing, you can be sure that the people kissing were a man and a woman, and they were both White. In fact, in the beginning they would have been married, too, but that ideology—the sanctity of marriage—fell away more quickly on the silver screen than did notions about racial and gender hierarchies and stereotypes. The first on-screen interracial kiss, between Sidney Poitier and Katharine Houghton in *Guess Who's Coming to Dinner*, didn't occur until 1967, the same year the US Supreme Court ruled that state laws preventing interracial marriage were unconstitutional. And in a 1968 episode of *Star Trek*, William Shatner and Nichelle Nichols boldly ventured where no one had gone before with the first Black–White lip-lock televised in the United States. The first homosexual kiss between two women hit prime time in 1991 (on the TV show *L.A. Law*, which received backlash from advertisers), while the first same-sex kiss between two men did not happen until 2001 on *Will and Grace*. Change in the media takes time; as society's ideologies about what constitutes good and bad love change, the media will reflect those changes by portraying more positive images of people loving whomever they choose.

Tituss Burgess and Mike Carlsen portray a gay couple on Netflix's *Unbreakable Kimmy Schmidt*.

- Chinese, not as hairy as Japanese, seldom grow an impressive mustache.

- Most Chinese avoid horn-rimmed spectacles.

- Although both have the typical epicanthic fold of the upper eyelid (which makes them look almond-eyed), Japanese eyes are usually set closer together.

- Those who know them best often rely on facial expression to tell them apart: the Chinese expression is likely to be more placid, kindly, open; the Japanese more positive, dogmatic, arrogant.

How can Gramsci's concept of hegemony help us understand this piece from *Time*? Does this article tell us more about the physical differences between Japanese and Chinese, or about the state of mind of the American public at the time? What values are reflected and projected? Are the descriptors empirical (based on fact) or normative (based on opinion)? This is what racism looks like on paper, and it clearly illustrates America's fear and hatred of the Japanese at that time.

RACISM IN THE MEDIA

The media continue to reflect and perpetuate racist ideologies, even if such examples are not usually as blatant as those in the 1941 article in *Time*. Sometimes the racism is obvious, and these instances present us with the opportunity to discuss racism in the media. In early September 2005, just days after Hurricane Katrina had devastated the areas surrounding the Mississippi River basin, two photos quickly began to circulate on the internet amid discussion of racism and the role it played in the reaction (or inadequate government response) to the catastrophe. The first photo, published by the Associated Press, showed a young African American wading through chest-high water toting groceries; the caption proclaimed that the man had just been "looting a grocery store." The second pictured a White couple doing the same thing; the caption stated that the two were photographed "after finding bread and soda at a local grocery store" (Ralli, 2005). The conclusion these images and their captions conveyed was this: White looters, in their struggle to survive the catastrophe, were not committing a crime, whereas Blacks resorting to the same behavior were. Indeed, much of the coverage in the wake of Katrina focused on the looting, vandalism, and other criminal acts that took place. What critics have pointed out, however, is that these people did what most of us would logically do—try to obtain food and water for our suffering families in the absence of competent government assistance and disaster relief. Because the city of New Orleans, which received the majority of the media attention, was 78 percent nonwhite, the victims were frequently portrayed as criminals.

The controversial O. J. Simpson arrest photo. *Time* magazine was accused of darkening his features for its cover.

The photo above, published by the Associated Press, shows a young Black man wading through chest-high water toting groceries; the caption proclaimed that the man had just been "looting a grocery store." The photo on the right pictures a White couple doing the same thing; the caption stated that the two were photographed "after finding bread and soda at a local grocery store."

The coverage of Hurricane Katrina, which was exceptional in the amount of criticism that was publicly levied against such racially charged portrayals (unlike, for example, the December 1941 *Time* piece), supports the main thesis of Barry Glassner's *The Culture of Fear: Why Americans Are Afraid of the Wrong Things* (1999). Glassner asserts that, as a culture, we grossly exaggerate the frequency of rarely occurring events, often through amplification of a single instance through media repetition. We tend to divert or redirect our attention from political, economic, and cultural issues that are either taboo or simply too difficult to talk about, toward sensational, but rare, events like school shootings and terrorist attacks. The media are the main vehicles through which this process occurs. In the case of Katrina, we blame the victims, the poorest of the poor, for not leaving the city, rather than ask how the government could leave its own citizens stranded like refugees without access to life's basic necessities.

It is not just major events like Hurricane Katrina that reflect racial bias in the media. The skin tone of Black models is routinely lightened in post-production, for example. What can be done about such practices? One issue is who makes up the population of media professionals. According to a survey by *Publisher's Weekly* (an industry magazine), the percentage of Whites in the publishing industry has ranged from 86 to 89 percent. If White people are the decision makers, it may come as no surprise that Black media producers are not adequately represented. Looking at the top 500 books used as "comps" over the period from 2013 to 2019, Stanford University researchers Laura McGrath and Jonathan Morales found that only 22 were written by nonwhite authors (10 were Black authors). "Comps" are the successful books that agents and authors and publishers use to compare their books to in order to make a case that they will sell, as in "It's *Harry Potter* meets *Lord of the Rings*." So, within book publishing at least, overwhelmingly White editors are making decisions on whether to publish books that are predominantly compared to other books by White writers. No wonder it may be hard for a minority author to get a book out there.

SEXISM IN THE MEDIA

A frequent critique of the media centers on the representation of women. American media in particular, and Western media more generally, are charged with glamorizing and perpetuating unrealistic ideals of feminine beauty. Some argue that repetitive bombardment by these images decreases girls' self-esteem and contributes to eating disorders. Women's magazines have been heavily criticized, although some researchers (such as Angela McRobbie from the United Kingdom) have taken care to show that women who are active, critical readers still enjoy reading women's magazines. However, as the Canadian sociologist Dawn Currie (1999) points out, although girls can choose which magazines, if any, to read and how to read them critically, they can't control the images available to them in those and other texts.

Another focus of feminist media critiques has been images of violence against women. Jean Kilbourne has become one of the most popular lecturers at college and university campuses across America. In 1979 she released a film titled *Killing Us Softly: Advertising's Image of Women*, in which she examines the ways in which women are maimed, sliced, raped, and otherwise deformed in advertising images. One classic example is a photo that shows the image of a woman's body in a garbage can, with only her legs and a fantastic pair of high heels on her feet visible. The message is clear: These shoes are, literally, to die for. Kilbourne's point is clear, too: Such images help sustain a kind of symbolic violence against women. In this critique, advertising does not just reflect the underlying culture that produced it but also creates desires and narratives that enter women's (and men's) lives with causal force.

Of course, there's always room for innovation. Some girls (with the help of their parents) have responded by creating their own magazines that focus on topics other than makeup, clothing, and boys, as mainstream teenage magazines do. For example, *New Moon Girls* is written and edited by girls aged 8 to 13 and contains no advertisements. Likewise, magazines exist for adult women that have more pro-woman messages; *Ms.* magazine was founded in 1971 during the feminist movement to give voice to women and explore women's issues. Because such magazines don't accept advertising from huge makeup companies and designer fashion houses, however, they are often less economically viable than mainstream women's magazines, which carry ads on as many as 50 percent of their pages. *Bitch* magazine ("It's a noun; it's a verb; it's a magazine"), which has been around since 1996, is a self-declared feminist response to pop culture. It is supported by advertisers but is a not-for-profit publication.

Some advertisers have responded to feminist critiques of the media with new approaches. In 2005 Dove, a manufacturer of skin-care products, launched a new series of ads backed by a social awareness program called the Campaign for Real Beauty. Instead of models, the ads featured "real" women complete with freckles, frizzy hair, wrinkles, and cellulite. The images were intentionally meant to offer a contrast to the images we're accustomed to seeing. And, as Dove's advertisers have said, "firming the thighs of a size 2 supermodel is no challenge" (Triester, 2005). The latest version of Dove's Real Beauty campaign shows side-by-side sketches of the same woman as drawn by a sketch artist. The first image is drawn based on the woman's description of herself and is always less attractive than the second image, which is drawn based on someone else's description of the woman, revealing women's inner negative body images. But can calling attention to the way women describe themselves change this inner dialogue? Or will it simply point out another unattractive flaw—low self-esteem?

A 2005 billboard from Dove's Real Beauty advertising campaign, featuring women who are not professional models.

On the one hand, a pessimist might point out that these "real beauty" ads use nontraditional models merely as a way to be novel; typical models are all so uniformly perfect, they've become boring. Also, Dove isn't telling women that they're beautiful whether or not they have dimpled thighs and therefore they don't need firming lotion. Rather, the manufacturer's message is that it's okay to need firming lotion because you're not the only one who does. Furthermore, the women in the campaign are never overweight, yet 70.7 percent of adult Americans *are* overweight or obese (Centers for Disease Control and Prevention, 2017). An optimist, on the other hand, might view this ad campaign as Dove's effort to be socially responsible and to provide alternative images of beauty that aren't based on the stick-thin, perfect bone structure, wrinkle-free, supermodel ideal. Because you're an active, critical reader, and not a passive receptor of the media, I'll let you decide.

Political Economy of the Media

In the United States, we (politicians especially) spend a lot of time talking about freedom, particularly freedom of the press. The freedom to say whatever you want is often upheld as one of the great markers of the "land of the free." The press, however, is hardly free. Most broadcasting companies are privately owned in the United States, are supported financially by advertising, and are therefore likely to reflect the biases of their owners and backers. (Compare this model with the United Kingdom's, where the British Broadcasting Company [BBC] cannot accept private funding; households must pay fees for owning television sets; and these fees help cover the BBC's operating costs. This system is beginning to change, however, because of increasing economic pressures, such as competition from satellite television.)

In 2017, just two corporations—Alphabet, the parent company of Google, and Facebook—generated 20 percent of global advertising revenue (Zenith USA, 2018). Ownership alone does not equal censorship, but when the majority of the media lie in the hands of a few players, it is easier to ignore or purposely suppress messages that the owners of the media don't agree with or support. For example, Apple's App Store is the dominant player in the sales of apps for smartphones. Apple demands to review every app to ensure that the content is not something that they "believe is over the line," which they go on to explain is something developers will just know when they cross it. This type of vague policy tends to promote a "chilling effect" whereby developers—not knowing where this mystical "line" is—choose to avoid any content they think might be at all objectionable. Receiving Apple's approval is important because once developers have made an app for Apple's iOS platform, they cannot sell it anywhere but the App Store. Is Apple protecting its shoppers, or ruling the app developers through a combination of monopoly power and shadowy threats? As corporate control of the media becomes more and more centralized (owned by fewer and fewer groups), the concern is that the range of opinions available will decrease and that corporate censorship (the act of suppressing information that may reflect negatively on certain companies and/or their affiliates) will further compromise the already-tarnished integrity of the mainstream media.

The internet, to some extent, has balanced out communications monopolies. But only somewhat. It's much easier to put up a website expressing alternative views than it is to broadcast a television or radio program suggesting the same. The Center for Civic Media at MIT, led by Ethan Zuckerman, works to leverage the internet for the promotion of local activism. One of the MIT projects—VGAZA or Virtual Gaza—allowed Palestinians in the Gaza Strip to document crises and share local stories globally while under embargo. But the internet is not beyond the realm of political economy. Yelp.com, for example, reports that updates to Google's search algorithm place Google+ reviews higher in Google's search results than reviews for the same venues on other sites, shifting web traffic to Google+ at the expense of competing review sites like Yelp and Thrillist (Leswing, 2015). Moreover, the internet often acts as a force for reinforcing our prejudices—including extremist views—by creating a "filter bubble" in the words of Eli Pariser, author of a book by that title. That is, the major corporations that own the backbones of how we interact with the internet, such as Alphabet, Facebook, and so on, have a profit incentive to feed us news, posts, and so on that confirm our preexisting desires, beliefs, and viewpoints since we are more likely to click on such links. Sometimes the internet can act as so much of an echo chamber that it encourages violent actions on the part of users, as was the case for a mass shooter in El Paso, Texas, in 2019, who found his violent views reinforced on the controversial forum 8chan.

DIGITAL.WWNORTON.COM/YOUMAYASK7

To see my interview with Allison Pugh, go to
digital.wwnorton.com/youmayask7

CONSUMER CULTURE

America is often described as a consumer culture, and rightly so. In my interview with sociologist Allison Pugh, she pointed out that "corporate marketing to children is a 22 billion dollar industry." She then added, "Children 8 to 11 ask for between two and four toys [for Christmas], and they receive eleven on average!" (Conley, 2011a). Sales on major patriotic holidays (Veterans Day, Memorial Day, Presidents' Day) thrive as a result of the notion that it is our duty as American citizens to be good shoppers. As Sharon Zukin points out in her book on shopping culture, *Point of Purchase: How Shopping Changed American Culture* (2003), 24 hours after the terrorist attacks of September 11, 2001, Mayor Rudy Giuliani urged New Yorkers to take the day off and go shopping. It's the tie that binds our society; everyone's got to shop. The term consumerism, however, refers to more than just buying merchandise; it refers to the belief that happiness and fulfillment can be achieved through the acquisition of material possessions. Versace, J. Crew, and real estate agents in certain hip neighborhoods are not just peddling shoes, jeans, and apartments. They are also selling a self-image, a lifestyle, and a sense of belonging and self-worth. The media, and advertising in particular, play a large role in the creation and maintenance of consumerism.

CONSUMERISM
the steady acquisition of material possessions, often with the belief that happiness and fulfillment can thus be achieved.

ADVERTISING AND CHILDREN

The rise of the consumer-citizen has been met with increasing criticism, but how does our society produce these consumer-citizens? Canadian author and activist Naomi Klein published *No Logo: Taking Aim at the Brand Bullies* in 2000. In this book Klein analyzes the growth of advertising in

These third-grade students at an elementary school in San Clemente, California, seem to be very concentrated on their Google Chromebook laptops. Do you think Google is doing a good thing by providing low-cost technology to school districts, or is it creating millions of consumer-citizens?

schools. Pepsi and Coca-Cola now bargain for exclusive rights to sell their products within schools, and brand-name fast foods are often sold in cafeterias. The logos of companies that sponsor athletic fields are displayed prominently. This has been commonplace in many colleges and universities for some time now, but the increasing presence of advertising in middle and high schools should also be noted.

One striking example is Google Classroom. Google gives out its low-cost Chromebook laptop computers to many schools and school districts, charging only a $30 annual management fee. The computers include a suite of web-based software applications ranging from Google Docs to Google Classroom (a learning management system). Going from basically nothing in 2012, Google had shipped almost 8 million devices to schools by 2016, with the trend line showing no signs of flattening out anytime soon. For example, the city of Chicago, the third-largest school district in the country, saved about $1.6 million per year in technology costs by switching to Google (Singer, 2017). Sounds like a win for everyone from the company whose motto was "Don't be evil," right? Well it is, in many ways, but some parents worry about the data their children are providing the company whose financial model is based almost solely on advertising revenue. Since students will migrate their educational accounts over to their noneducational Google accounts, the company will have "watched" the developmental trajectory of these students throughout most of their childhood and now be able to better target them with ads.

The result of all of this advertising is the creation of a self-sustaining consumer culture among children—albeit one that plays out differently for low-income and high-income families. Let's hear Pugh discuss her research with me again on this point:

> I found, for low-income parents, a practice of what I ended up calling "symbolic indulgence." They couldn't afford everything that a middle-class family might consider part of an adequate resource to childhood. So, they might not have blocks, or a bike. They might not have those basics, but they would have the thing that kind of gave the child something to talk about at school [such as a Gameboy]. And so it would be these highly [socially] resonant items [that parents would purchase]. (Conley, 2011a)

In other words, these highly symbolic purchases of "in" toys or devices gave low-resource families an avenue to feel as though they were able to participate in the broader American consumer culture. Meanwhile, ironically, middle-class parents downplayed their consumerism:

> "I'm not materialistic. I'm not one of those bad parents you read about on TV . . . never being able to say no to my kids," [they would say]. So what I found for them is the systematic practice of "symbolic deprivation." The kid would have an enormous amount of stuff. There would be mostly yeses in that child's life. But there would be particular things that that child didn't have, so that they [the parents] could really kind of convince me, and convince themselves, that they were honorable people. (Conley, 2011a)

Pugh emphasizes that these dynamics are not just about corporate advertising but about the local social systems in which kids and their families find themselves. So to fix the problem, we have to change that dynamic by (somehow) making people less afraid of being different, or perhaps more realistically by diminishing difference itself through sameness—by students wearing school uniforms, for example.

CULTURE JAMS: HEY CALVIN, HOW 'BOUT GIVING THAT GIRL A SANDWICH?

People can take back the media or use the media for their own ends. In that sense, Rockin' Rollen, whom we met at the beginning of the chapter, was hacking media coverage with pro-Christian messages to override the lack of attention to Christianity he found on TV. Culture jamming (a term that evolved from radio jamming, another form of guerrilla cultural resistance that involves seizing control of the frequency of a radio station) is the act of co-opting media in spite of themselves. Part of a larger movement against consumer culture and consumerism, it's based on the notion that advertisements are basically propaganda. Culture jamming differs from appropriating advertisements for the sake of art and sheer vandalism (where the sole goal is the destruction of property), although advertisers probably don't care too much about this latter distinction. Numerous anticonsumerist activist groups have sprung up, such as *Adbusters*, a Canadian magazine that specializes in spoofs of popular advertising campaigns. For example, it parodied a real Calvin Klein campaign (which advanced the career of Kate Moss and ushered in an age of ultra-thin, waiflike models) with a presumably bulimic woman vomiting into a toilet. *Adbusters* also sponsors an annual Buy Nothing Day (held, with great irony, on the day after Thanksgiving, known in retail as "Black Friday," the busiest shopping day of the year), which encourages people to do just that—buy nothing on this specific day of the year—so

CULTURE JAMMING

the act of turning media against themselves.

Two satirical ads from *Adbusters* magazine. How do these ads critique or subvert the tobacco and fashion industries?

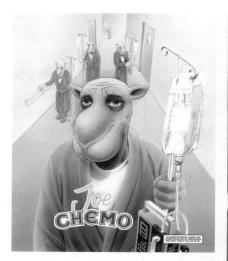

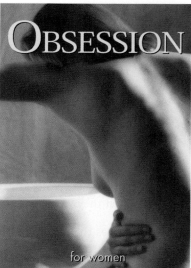

that they can reclaim their buying power and focus on the noncommercial aspects of the holiday, such as spending time with family and friends.

Another *Adbusters* spoof caricatured the legendary Joe Camel, the anthropomorphic advertising icon of Camel cigarettes from 1987 until 1997, when R. J. Reynolds, the tobacco firm that conjured up the character, voluntarily stopped using his image after receiving complaints from Congress and various public-interest groups that its ads primarily targeted children. (In 1991, a *Journal of the American Medical Association* study found that more five- and six-year-old kids recognized Joe Camel than they did Mickey Mouse or Fred Flintstone [Fischer et al., 1991].) In the *Adbusters* spoof, "Joe Chemo" is walking down a hospital hallway with an IV, presumably dying of cancer caused by smoking.

Conclusion

The chapter opened with a description of Rockin' Rollen, the Rainbow Man. Now perhaps you can see how he fits into a discussion of culture and media. He began his 15 minutes of fame by acting the role of an enthusiastic fan at a sporting event. He was ahead of his time in terms of being famous for absolutely nothing. (Note the rise in reality show stars—the ultimate paradox, as the participants are selected because they're "normal" and we then get hooked on watching their "real" lives.) After Rollen's religious conversion, he was almost a genius in the way he co-opted the media for his own ends—namely, the promotion of his religious messages. That Rollen was ultimately sentenced to three life sentences (a little harsh for a nine-hour standoff

POLICY

WHAT'S IN A NAME?

I named my kids E and Yo Xing Heyno Augustus Eisner Alexander Weiser Knuckles, so forgive me if I didn't see what all the fuss was about when Kanye West and Kim Kardashian West named their kids North, Chicago, and Saint. After all, unlike in countries such as France or Japan, there is no US law that constrains what we can name our offspring; only names that would be considered abusive can be stopped. Names present a unique measure of culture: There are few rules, and no institutions attempt to directly influence our choices, unlike almost every other aspect of culture from food to film to fashion. Thus trends in names are as close to a pure, unmediated, reflective mirror of societal culture as we can get.

In that light, one could say it was almost inevitable that West and Kardashian West chose unique names for their children. On the one hand, there's a long tradition of celebrities marking their status by giving atypical names to their children. Remember Moon Unit Zappa? Born in 1967, she was perhaps one of the first notable celebrity offspring given a "weird" moniker. The 1960s was the Age of Aquarius, after all. Besides her own siblings, she was followed by uncapitalized "america," the child of Abbie Hoffman; and Free, the spawn of Barbara Hershey and David Carradine, just to mention a few. Fast-forward to Gwyneth Paltrow's daughter, Apple Martin, and it should come as no surprise that celebrities do things differently.

The more interesting sociological phenomenon that North West embodies, as the daughter of a Black man, is the rise of unique Black names.

Around the same time celebrities started thinking up names that otherwise served as nouns, verbs, or adjectives, African Americans began to abandon long-standing naming patterns. Until the civil rights movement, a typical Black name might have been Franklin or Florence. But then Black Power happened. Blacks wanted to assert their individuality and break ties from the dominant society, so the proportion of unique names—those that appear in birth records only once for that year—shot up.

Kim Kardashian West and Kanye West's decision to name their daughter "North" represents a larger sociological trend of parents giving their children unique names.

Until about 1960, the proportion of unique names for White Americans hovered around 20 percent for girls. For Blacks it had always been higher—around 30 percent. During the 1960s, the number of White girls with unique names started to inch up to about 25 percent, but for Blacks, it literally skyrocketed, peaking around 1979 at more than 60 percent for girls and reaching almost 40 percent for boys in 1975 (based on Illinois data). Harvard sociologists Stanley Lieberson and Kelly S. Mikelson, who examined this trend in a 1995 paper, followed it only through the 1980s. But I'd be willing to guess that the practice has continued at a similar rate.

You might think that all this name coinage would lead to gender confusion in kindergartens. Though I am not advocating gender rigidity, there is some evidence that gender-ambiguous names can cause problems for boys. Economist David Figlio (2007) found that "boys named Sue" tend to get into more trouble at school around sixth grade, when puberty hits.

But it turns out that even unique names are gendered. When Lieberson and Mikelson gave a list of unique names they found in the Illinois database to respondents, the vast majority identified the gender of the actual child—for example, Cagdas (boy) or Shameki (girl)—correctly. My own experience mirrors this. Nobody mistakes Yo for a girl's name. Meanwhile, three other Es, who heard about my daughter's name from my public musings, wrote to me. (So much for unique . . .) Two of them were female, bringing the total to 75 percent female. I only wish I had 25 other kids so I could test the gender of every letter in the alphabet. If you think I'm crazy, move to Paris.

with the police after he took a hostage) perhaps speaks to the fundamental nature of media and culture in our society. Remember that one job of the sociologist is to see what is usually taken for granted as actually socially constructed. In a way, Rollen committed the crime of disrupting our status quo and violating the unspoken norms of our culture. Religious fanatics are often seen as freaks or terrorists in our culture—in other cultures, they may be viewed quite differently. We rarely question the media's right to control what we see (to be fair, they are for-profit businesses). Did Rollen have a right to position himself strategically behind home plate at major league baseball games? How was his John 3:16 sign different from an "I ♥ MOM" or a "Reverse the Curse" sign?

This chapter has presented some new ways of looking at culture: how we construct it, how it affects us, and what this means for understanding ourselves and the world in which we live. Do you now have a new understanding of culture? Can you now see your own culture through a critical lens? What have you previously taken for granted that you can now view as a product of our culture? Can you now look at the media in a different way? Don your critical thinking cap and put some of the stuff you've just learned into practice.

QUESTIONS FOR REVIEW

1. Thinking about "reality" television shows and people who are well known primarily on social media platforms, define *celebrity* and *cultural icon*. Are people celebrities because they are talented, or can anyone achieve this status? How might this question parallel debates about high culture versus low culture?

2. How does Herbert Gans's *Deciding What's News* (1979a) help us understand the way that cultural production simultaneously reflects and creates our world?

3. Goths are visible as a subculture, in part because of their taste in music and fashion. Using these criteria, identify another subculture. In which ways might this group's values oppose the dominant culture?

4. A student holds the widespread cultural belief in upward social mobility through education and therefore studies thoroughly before an upcoming sociology exam. How might this represent an example of hegemony?

5. The term *culture* is complex, in part because it is used in numerous (sometimes contradictory) ways. Use three of the definitions of culture from this chapter to illustrate how a Shakespearean play might be considered "culture."

6. Let's consider how we are part of a consumer culture. Think about a consumer good you recently acquired and care about, such as an item of clothing. Does this item in any way help establish or demonstrate who you are, what you are about, and how you perceive yourself? How so?

7. How do social media platforms such as Instagram and YouTube potentially change the dynamics of media coverage in the context of a system controlled by a few large companies? Could Instagrammers and YouTubers be considered culture jammers? Explain your answer.

PRACTICE

SUBCULTURE WARS

Some observers think the internet has been a homogenizing force that drives all eyeballs to the latest meme and creates winner-take-all cultural markets. Others suggest that by allowing geographically dispersed individuals to organize around common interests, the internet and social media create a cultural garden where a thousand flowers can bloom. Maybe it's both.

TRY IT!

How do subcultures appropriate and reinterpret mainstream cultural memes? Pick an interest from the list below and two subcultures. Search these combinations and see how these subcultures form unique communities and practices around that hacked theme—for example, Goth Cats versus Emo Cats. You're welcome to go to Google, YouTube, Reddit, Pinterest, or other online sites to research the combinations.

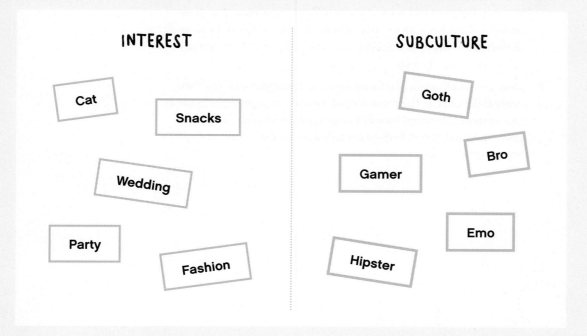

INTEREST

Cat

Snacks

Wedding

Party

Fashion

SUBCULTURE

Goth

Bro

Gamer

Emo

Hipster

THINK ABOUT IT

How do the two subcultures put their unique stamps on something otherwise generic and mainstream? What do you think are the chances that the subcultural interpretation will go viral and influence the mainstream?

SOCIOLOGY ON THE STREET

How can we make assumptions about people before we even meet them? What assumptions do you make if you know a person's name? Watch the Sociology on the Street video to find out more: **digital.wwnorton.com/youmayask7**.

WANT MORE PRACTICE?

Complete the InQuizitive activity for this chapter at digital.wwnorton.com /youmayask7

PARADOX

4

THE MOST IMPORTANT ASPECTS OF SOCIAL LIFE ARE THOSE CONCEPTS WE LEARN WITHOUT ANYONE TEACHING US.

Socialization and the Construction of Reality

Think back to your first day of college. What did you do upon arriving at the classroom? Presumably, you sat in a chair. You probably opened a notebook and took out either a pen or a pencil, or maybe you fired up a laptop. When the professor walked in and called the class to attention, you stopped talking to the person next to you (or, if you didn't, you at least knew that you should). When handed a stack of syllabi, you took one and passed along the rest. You did not sit on anyone's lap. A million dollars says that you were wearing clothes. Another safe bet is that you did not physically assault anyone. Is all of this an accurate description of what occurred?

Congratulations! You've been properly socialized. So how did I know what you did, and more important, how did you know what to do? Why did you sit in a chair and not on the floor? What if no furniture had been in the room? If a blackboard hung on one wall, you probably sat facing it in the absence of desks. Why? How did you know to bring paper and something with which to write? Did you receive an e-mail earlier in the week with explicit instructions telling you to do so? Why did you put on clothes this morning? When someone hands you a stack of papers, he or she might say, "Take one and pass them along," but even if that person doesn't, you still know what to do. You've internalized many unwritten rules about social

the process by which
individuals internalize
the values, beliefs, and
norms of a given society
and learn to function as
members of that society.

behavior and public interaction. We call the process by which you learn how to become a functioning member of society socialization.

Imagine Mr. Spock, Tarzan, or an android trying to disguise himself as a college freshman. The droid would have to be programmed in minute detail with an endless list of possible reactions to potential situations. Think for a moment about the differences between your knowledge of how to respond to the following situations versus the responses of our droid: knowing how to answer when someone asks "What's up?"; knowing to shift one's knees when someone else needs to slip in or out of a row of seats in the lecture hall; knowing to wait your turn when asking a question in the lecture or discussion section; knowing how to react when someone yells "Fire!" during class and then screams, versus a student shouting the same word during a final exam and then laughing. Consider the difference between these two possible scenarios at a pizzeria: (1) Someone asks for dough, holding out a $5 bill to the cashier; (2) someone asks for dough, pointing a gun at the same cashier. You know that in the second scenario it is not a wheat-based product to which that person refers. The droid doesn't. He hasn't been socialized. Think how much you have needed to learn, how much knowledge you have internalized and processed, in order to understand that making direct eye contact with someone in a crowded elevator is inappropriate, whereas such behavior at a crowded party might be acceptable. The former might be considered creepy; the latter, flirting.

One famous test in the computer science field of artificial intelligence is the Turing Test, in which a subject is asked to have two parallel conversations. One exchange occurs with an actual human, the other with a computer. Both are conducted by instant messaging or some other text-based platform. If the subject can't reliably distinguish the computer from the living human, then the computer is said to have passed the Turing Test (named for the scientist Alan Turing, who first proposed the test in a 1950 research paper). It was not until 2014 that a computer passed this simple test (fooling 33 percent of judges for five minutes—Turing had seen the threshold at 30 percent) (*Guardian*, 2014). Now imagine adding facial expressions, body language, and other nonverbal communication cues to the test criteria. It quickly becomes clear why to be human is to be socialized and that true artificial intelligence is still a long way off.

Interestingly, while the field of artificial intelligence gets better and better at Turing Tests, psychiatrist Fadi Haddad worries that humans may be getting less socially nuanced. Working in New York City surrounded by people who often avoid interacting with one another, he wonders whether "soon we are all going to be autistic." He remembers riding the subway "ten years ago [when] people used to look at each other and say hi sometimes if you clicked eyes with a stranger. . . . [T]oday nobody does that. Everybody has a cell phone or does something like this [his face goes blank and he stares off at nobody in particular], and that's very autistic behavior . . . that's what we see in New York. I think everybody here is autistic." Sociologist Erving

Goffman, though, would call politely ignoring fellow subway and elevator riders "civil inattention" and argue that those who exercise civil inattention on the subway are well socialized. So how do we decide when interaction or inattention is the socially optimal option? If we choose to interact, how do we know which interactions are acceptable? We know how to behave because we are socialized. But what is socialization and how does it work?

Socialization: The Concept

Socialization, then, as defined by Craig Calhoun in the *Dictionary of the Social Sciences* (2002, p. 47), is "the process through which individuals internalize the values, beliefs, and norms of a society and learn to function as its members." Starting from when you were born, the interactions between you and the rest of the world have shaped who you are. Presumably, as a baby, you were wrapped in either a pink or a blue blanket to signify your being a girl or a boy. At some point, you were potty trained—a critical expectation of our society. For babies, the primary unit of socialization is generally the family. As children grow older and enter the educational system, school becomes a key location in their socialization. This is where you probably learned to sit facing the front of the classroom. You learned to raise your hand before asking or answering a question. You learned not to talk when the teacher was speaking and what the punishment would be if you failed to follow this rule. By the time you entered college, you did not have to be told explicitly to do these things because you had *internalized* the rules that govern situations in which the people we designate students and teachers operate. As the examples that open this chapter illustrate, however, we learn more than explicit sets of rules. We learn how to interact on myriad levels in an endless number of situations.

You recognize the limits of your socialization when you find yourself in a new situation and aren't quite sure how to behave. If you've been shy and bookish in high school and you find yourself among a new set of party-going friends at a raucous fraternity party in college, you may not know just what to wear or how to behave. You may take as your model what you've seen on television and in the movies, but the party you are attending may not be quite the same. If, on the other hand, you've been going to similar parties, maybe even at the very same fraternity, with an older brother or sister for the past year or two, this particular party will not present any sort of anxiety. You'll know what to wear, which bathroom to use, whether or not it is cool to post photos to Instagram, what music to like, and which songs deserve an eye-roll. Your previous experience as a tagalong may now make you a leader among your freshman peers.

Early in elementary school you were taught to raise your hand to speak in class. Can you think of other examples of internalized behavior?

Limits of Socialization

Although socialization is necessary for people to function in society, individuals are not simply blank slates onto which society transcribes its norms and values. Twins are often used to support one or the other side of the nature-versus-nurture debate, because they allow us to factor out genetics. Twins living hundreds or even thousands of miles apart may simultaneously experience the same pain in their right arms—score one point for nature. Take another set of twins, however, who were separated at birth in the early 1900s. One of them was raised as a Jew and the other became a Nazi—score one for nurture. So which theory is correct? Both and neither. In sociology, we tend to think less about right and wrong and more about which theories are more or less helpful in explaining and understanding our social world. The concept of socialization is useful for understanding how people become functioning members of society. Like most concepts, however, socialization can be limited in its explanatory power. Have you ever heard someone discussing a "problem child"? The conversation might go something like this: "I just don't know what's wrong with him. He comes from such a nice family. And his older brothers are such nice, respectful boys." How did this child go astray? The primary unit of socialization, the family, seems to have been functional. The other children went on to lead happy and productive lives. What else might explain the youngest son's delinquency? For starters, human beings have agency. This means that while we operate within limits that largely are not of our own making (e.g., we cannot choose our parents or siblings, and US law requires that all children receive schooling), we also make choices about how to interact with our environment. We can physically walk out of the school, fall asleep in class, or run away from home.

"HUMAN" NATURE

Is there such a thing as human nature? It's physiology that prompts you to urinate, but it's socialization that tells you where and when to do so. We are largely shaped by interaction, such that without society the human part of human nature would not develop. We can observe this in children raised by animals or denied human contact. Take the case of "Anna," a young girl whose true age was unknown but estimated at about five years and who had been found in torturous conditions, bound to a chair in an attic, where she had been left almost completely alone in the dark since birth. Her nutritional requirements had been minimally met, and it is believed that her only regular human contact was when her mother delivered these small meals. She could not properly speak or use her limbs, or even walk, when she was discovered. She did not respond to light or sounds the way children normally do. With some care and attention, the nurses at the treating hospital were able to provoke some giggles and coos by tickling her. Eventually, she was able to make speech-like sounds and gain more control of her body, but she never developed to the level of most children her age and died a few years later. Some of the doctors examining her wondered if she had been born mentally disabled, but ultimately, they opined that she could not have survived such an environment unless she had been healthy at birth.

The professionals who cared for Anna and followed her case reached five general conclusions:

1. Her inability to develop past an "idiot level of mentality . . . is largely the result of social isolation."

2. "It seems almost impossible for any child to learn to speak, think, and act like a normal person after a long period of isolation."

3. When she is compared with other cases of isolated children, the similarities "seem to indicate that the stages of socialization are to some extent necessarily related to the stages of organic development."

4. "Anna's history . . . seems to demonstrate that human nature is determined by the child's communicative social contacts as much as by his organic equipment and that the system of communicative symbols is a highly complex business acquired early in life as the result of long and intimate training."

5. Theories of socialization are neither right nor wrong in this case "but simply inapplicable." (Davis, 1940, pp. 554–65)

What this case illustrates is that "human nature" is a blend of "organic equipment," the raw materials we are physically made of, and social interaction, the environment in which we are raised. In what other ways can we look at the role of socialization and social structures in shaping our behaviors?

Theories of Socialization

Now that we have identified this process called socialization, we can turn to some of the theories about how it works.

ME, MYSELF, AND I: DEVELOPMENT OF THE SELF AND THE OTHER

Have you ever seen a little girl cover her eyes with her hands and declare, "You can't see me now!"? She does not realize that just because she cannot see you doesn't mean you cannot see her. She is incapable of distinguishing between

How does a small child playing peekaboo demonstrate the social process of creating the self?

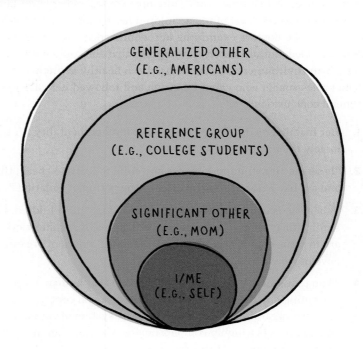

FIGURE 4.1 Mead's Stages of Social Development

GENERALIZED OTHER
(E.G., AMERICANS)

REFERENCE GROUP
(E.G., COLLEGE STUDENTS)

SIGNIFICANT OTHER
(E.G., MOM)

I/ME
(E.G., SELF)

SELF

the individual identity of
a person as perceived by
that same person.

I

one's subjective sense of
having consciousness,
agency, action, or power.

ME

the self perceived as an
object by the "I"; the self
as one imagines others
perceive one.

I and *you* and has not yet formed an idea of her individual self. How does the concept of the self develop? Sociologists would argue that it emerges through a social process. Perhaps the first full theory of the social self was developed by Charles Horton Cooley, who coined the term *the looking-glass self*. According to Cooley in *Human Nature and the Social Order* (1922), the self emerges from our ability to assume the point of view of others and thereby imagine how they see us. We then test this "theory" of how we are perceived by gauging others' reactions and revise our theory by fine-tuning our "self concept."

In the 1930s, George Herbert Mead further elaborated the process by which the social self develops (Figure 4.1). Infants only know the I—that is, one's sense of agency, action, or power. Through social interaction, however, they learn the me—that is, the self as a distinct object to be perceived by others (and by the I). Imagine, for example, that you are taking care of your two-year-old cousin Joey. He wants a cookie. You explain to him that you will happily give him a cookie just as soon as you go to the bathroom. He starts shouting, "I want cookie! I want cookie!" And you are ready to scream, "But I have to pee!" In a more rational moment, you might argue with your adorable cousin: "How would you feel if I demanded a cookie immediately when you entered the house after a six-hour car ride with no rest stops along the way and your bladder was about to explode?" Although such a line of logic might work with your cousin's seven-year-old sister, it will not work with little Joey because he has yet to develop a sense of the other—that is, someone or something outside of oneself. In Joey's mind, there is no *other*, the *you* who hasn't seen a toilet in six hours; there is only the *self* who wants a cookie. This is why we allow children a certain amount of leeway. If your best friend behaved like this, however, you would accuse him or her of being childish, and you would be correct.

How do we move beyond the self? To function as fully adult members of society, we need to be able to recognize that other people have wants, needs, and desires that are sometimes similar to and sometimes different from our own. Thus, imitation, play, and games are important components of childhood development. When a child imitates, he or she is just starting to learn to recognize an other. That's what peekaboo is all about. Eventually, kids understand that you are still there when they cover their eyes. They can then advance to play, according to Mead. During play, children are able to make a distinction between the self and the other. Suppose that you are playing with your cousin Joey, who is now five years old, and he says, "Let's play school. I'll be the teacher and you be the student." He's recognizing you as the other, the student, who has a different set of motives, responses, and actions from the teacher. Eventually, children move beyond play to formal games.

Games involve a more complex understanding of multiple roles; indeed, you must be able to recognize and anticipate what many other players are going to do in a given situation. Have you ever watched a swarm of toddlers try to play soccer? It's a mess. They're content to kick the ball; that's enough for them. They can't pass, let alone coordinate an offensive attack on an empty goal. It takes an understanding of the other to coordinate passing: You have to consider where to place the ball and calculate whether your teammate can make it to that spot in time for the pass to occur. Games such as soccer involve more than just hand—eye (or foot—eye) coordination. They involve a sophisticated understanding of the various positions others can occupy—that is, they require a theory of social behavior, knowing how others are likely to react to different situations. The goalie is not likely to leave the box in front of the goal, even if I tempt him or her with the ball. But a defender or midfielder is likely to pursue me if I am not controlling the ball very well. We have learned to anticipate these

OTHER
someone or something outside of oneself.

Why are games an important part of child development? What do team sports like soccer teach us about multiple roles?

Theories of Socialization   129

behaviors from repeated experience in the context of a particular sort of constrained social interaction—namely, a soccer game.

As our parents, siblings, friends, teachers, and soccer coaches socialize us, we learn to think beyond the self to the other. According to Mead, however, that brings us only halfway to being socialized. The final step is developing a concept of the generalized other, which represents an internalized sense of the total expectations of others in a variety of settings—regardless of whether we've encountered those people or places before. In this way, we should be able to function with complete strangers in a wide range of social settings. For example, it is the perception of the generalized other that keeps you from taking off your pants to lounge more comfortably in the park on hot summer days, that (it's hoped) keeps you from singing on the bus no matter how much you are enjoying the song on Spotify, and that keeps you from picking a wedgie in public. We can, and do, continually update our internal sense of the generalized other as we gather new information about norms and expectations in different contexts.

For instance, as a child, you may have been chided by your parents not to pick your nose. You have to be taught that this is unacceptable behavior, because otherwise it might seem perfectly reasonable. You have something in your nose, it's bothering you, you want to remove whatever is stuck there, and, lo and behold, your finger is just the right size. It's remarkably convenient. However, you learn not to pick your nose because it's a socially unacceptable action. But wait! Sometimes you might catch your dad picking his nose in the bathroom at home. Now you revise the original lesson and realize what is most important: not to pick your nose in public. You may even have been taught explicitly that certain activities that are acceptable in private are unacceptable in public. The concept of the generalized other shapes our actions by our internalization of what is, and is not, acceptable in different social situations. Some of us may have internalized the notion that nose picking is inherently disgusting and should never be done anywhere. Some of us may have internalized the notion that nose picking is a little gross but believe it's okay when done in private; the action should just not be performed in public. If you walked outside right now and saw a child picking his nose, you might think, "Ew" but laugh because he is, after all, a child. On the other hand, if his mom was picking her nose too, you might give her a look of disapproval for violating an established social norm.

People may also intentionally violate established norms. It is not uncommon for children to touch their genitalia in public (watch any group of four- or five-year-olds and you will quickly spot who needs to go to the bathroom). As a society, however, not touching or exposing your genitals in public is a well-established norm (a law, in fact). The exhibitionist who exposes himself or masturbates in public does so not because he was poorly

GENERALIZED OTHER

an internalized sense of the total expectations of others in a variety of settings—regardless of whether we've encountered those people or places before.

socialized. He has a keen understanding of the generalized other and violates the norm with the explicit purpose of soliciting a reaction from a generalized other (or a very specific other, in some cases).

Agents of Socialization

FAMILIES

For most individuals, the family is the original source of significant others and the primary unit of socialization. If you have siblings, you may develop the sense that older and younger children are treated differently. The general impression is that the younger siblings get away with more. Parents, having already gone through the experience of child rearing, may relax their attitudes and behaviors toward later children (even if unconsciously). Note, too, that socialization can be a two-way street. Information doesn't always flow from the older to the younger family members. For example, the children of immigrants—who are immersed in the US school system while their parents may maintain less contact with mainstream American communities—are likely to take on the role of an agent of socialization instead of the other way around, teaching their parents the language and other tools of cultural assimilation. In a similar vein, a study by economist Ebonya Washington (2008) showed that members of Congress who had daughters were more likely to vote for feminist measures. Perhaps daughters socialize their parents into being more sensitive to women's concerns. Alternatively, it could be that when legislators have their own daughters' future to worry about, they vote for legislative changes that will help them (and, by extension, women in general). So it's hard to say whether this is really socialization at work or merely a change in rational, selfish calculations. Meanwhile, sociologist Emily Rauscher and I found that for the average American, daughters made parents more politically conservative, specifically with respect to views about sexuality (Conley & Rauscher, 2013).

The socialization that occurs within the family can be affected by various demographics. Parents of different social classes socialize their children differently. For example, when asked what values they want their children to have, middle-class parents are more likely to stress independence and self-direction, whereas working-class parents prioritize obedience to external authority (Kohn & Schooler, 1983). Indeed, sociologists have long recognized that parents' social class matters, but how exactly this privilege is transmitted to children (beyond strictly monetary benefits) has been less clear. To better understand this process, ethnographer Annette Lareau spent time in both Black and White households with children approximately 10 years of

According to Annette Lareau, how do working-class and middle-class families structure their children's free time differently? What are the results of these different socializing behaviors?

age. She found that middle-class parents, both Black and White, are more likely to engage in what she calls "concerted cultivation." They structure their children's leisure time with formal activities (such as soccer leagues and piano lessons) and reason with them over decisions in an effort to foster their kids' talents.

Working-class and poor parents, in contrast, focus on the "accomplishment of natural growth." They give their children the room and resources to develop but leave it up to the kids to decide how they want to structure their free time. A greater division between the social life of children and that of the adults exists in such households (Lareau, 2002). Whereas middle-class parents send their kids off to soccer practice, music lessons, and myriad other after-school activities, kids in poor families spend a disproportionate amount of time "hanging out," as has been observed by Jason DeParle in *American Dream* (2004), his chronicle of three families on public assistance struggling through the era of welfare reform in Milwaukee. Likewise, a 2006 study by Annette Lareau, Eliot Weingarter, and this author shows the same statistical results: Outside of school, disadvantaged children spend 40 percent more time in unstructured activities than their middle-class counterparts.

Middle-class kids, on the other hand, spend their days learning how to interact with adult authority figures, how to talk to strangers, and how to follow rules and manage schedules. From a very young age, they are taught to use logic and reason to support their choices by mirroring their parents' explanations of why they can or cannot get what they want. Low-income parents, Lareau found, were more likely to answer their children with "Because I said so," instilling respect for authority but missing an opportunity to help their children develop logical reasoning skills commonly used in adult interactions. Middle-class kids discover the confidence that comes with achievements such as learning to play the piano or mastering a foreign language. Whether they actually have fun is unknown, but they are certainly socialized into the same kind of lifestyles that their parents hope them to have as adult professionals. In fact, it should be no surprise that the rise of the "overscheduled" child comes during a period when, for the first time in history, higher-income Americans work more hours than lower-income Americans. If we flip the equation and look at leisure time, it seems that getting lots of education might limit your fun time. Those with advanced degrees reported the fewest hours of weekly leisure time (31.3) while those who didn't graduate high school reported the most (44.38; Bureau of Labor Statistics, 2019), though half of the leisure gap is due to the difficulty less-educated men and women have finding full-time jobs (Attanasio et al., 2013). Professional parents familiarize their children with the kind of lives they expect them to lead as adults.

An important question, however, is how these different parenting strategies may or may not affect the long-term outcomes of kids. Indeed, work by Amy Hsin (2009), for example, has shown that the amount of time parents spend with their children—while highly correlated with social class—did not predict children's cognitive outcomes. Later work found that perhaps intensive parenting did have a delinquency-protective effect, but only in adolescence (Milkie et al., 2015). The problem with much of the work on parenting and how kids spend their time is that many parenting behaviors and decisions regarding the child's activities may be in response to how a child is faring. For example, a kid at risk of failing in school may garner extra attention and more intensive parenting than her sibling who is doing fine. This reactive nature of parenting, then, may obscure what is a true effect since kids who are worse off may get more intensive attention, thereby canceling out a positive effect of such parenting when studied through mere correlations. To try to address this concern, Thomas Laidley and I used random variation in weather patterns to study whether how kids spent their time affected their cognitive performance. We found that physical, outdoor activity had a positive influence on math test scores while indoor, sedentary behavior had the opposite effect. There may be something said, then, for the 1970s style of parenting of just sending your kids outside to play (without phones) all day as compared to having them sit inside on screens.

On the issue of even longer-term effects of different child-rearing patterns, I was able to speak to Annette Lareau upon the publication of her updated edition of *Unequal Childhoods* (2011), for which she went back and followed up with many of the families she had originally studied. Here's what she told me:

> There really were no surprises. I would say it was sad. Many of the working-class and poor children had wanted to do well, their parents had wanted them to do well, but things had not worked out. Not one was in the professional sector. [For] the middle-class families, it wasn't always easy sailing [either]. Garrett Talinger got his heart broken. Melanie Hamlin had a friend killed in a car accident. It's not that bad things don't happen to middle-class kids; they do. But in terms of being launched, in terms of their life chances, they were much more likely to go to college, and their parents helped them and supervised them in college. So their parents helped them choose their college classes, they gave them advice on their majors, and so the parents continued to provide guidance and help as they went into adulthood. Alexander Williams, the middle-class African American boy, is now going to become a doctor. Garrett Talinger became a high-level manager. He has a suit and tie, his face is shining. (Conley, 2011b)

This was interesting, so I probed further: What exactly happened in the poor and working-class families' lives that caused the kids, despite their high aspirations, to drop out of high school or go no further than a high-school diploma?

DIGITAL.WWNORTON.COM/YOUMAYASK7

To see my interview with Annette Lareau about *Unequal Childhoods*, go to digital.wwnorton.com/youmayask7

To apply to college involves many, many, many steps. If they wanted to go to college, did you take, say, advanced algebra? Did you take the [other] classes you needed to apply to college? Then did they take the SAT and the ACT? Did they apply to college? And if they got in, did they go? And so by the end you have these diversions in pathways between the parents who are middle class and the parents who are working class, despite the aspirations.

Lareau went on to provide a concrete example of these hurdles in the case of a working-class girl who was not included in the book due to space reasons:

> She applied to colleges, but she applied to colleges that were two and three hundred points above her SAT. Now, if she had been my daughter, could I have gotten her into a school? Probably. I would have found a school that would have taken a child who had a learning disability, or had low scores, and I could have placed her in college. It would have taken a lot of work. But in her system, her mother depended on the [high] school to help her daughter go to college. So the mother didn't see the applications, and the mother had a car, but she didn't go on college tours. It was up to her daughter and the school. And that is a reasonable decision. Her daughter was rejected everywhere, and she ended up going to community college for a semester and dropping out. And [her experience follows] a very typical pattern for working-class families.

Though Lareau can't definitively discern cause and effect here—What if Tara's SAT scores had been higher? Or if she had lucked out with a fabulous guidance counselor?—things might have turned out differently for Tara, despite the "natural growth" strategy her mother followed. But by showing how social stratification actually worked on the ground, Lareau tells a pretty convincing—if depressing—story.

SCHOOL

When children enter school, the primary locus of socialization shifts to include reference groups such as peers and teachers. In addition to helping you learn the three Rs, one of the teacher's main goals is to properly socialize you—teaching you to share, take turns, resolve conflict with words, be quiet when necessary, and speak when appropriate. Walk into any kindergarten classroom and compare it with a third-grade class. What are the main differences? For starters, there is probably a lot more order, and less noise, among the third-graders. When you were young and needed to leave the classroom as a group (whether for recess, gym, or music class), you probably had to line up and follow your teacher. Did you have to do this in high school? Highly unlikely, because teenagers are able to get themselves from one classroom to the next, whereas five-year-olds are not.

When students resist classroom behavior norms, many parents and teachers turn to medication. Psychiatrist Fadi Haddad, whom we heard from in the chapter opener, treats kids who have been referred to him because their parents or teachers think they have attention-deficit hyperactivity disorder (ADHD). He has identified four factors leading to the uptick in ADHD cases

DIGITAL.WWNORTON.COM/YOUMAYASK7

To see my interview with Fadi Haddad, go to
digital.wwnorton.com/youmayask7

in the United States. Only one of them is the mental health of the kid; the rest are rooted in the broader social context. He sees that "the demands of the schools are built on certain curricul[a]" that are "not very flexible . . . they want the kid to behave in a certain way." If a kid does not behave, "it's easy to say this kid has ADHD and that's why he is not successful in school rather than, oh, well, maybe this kid, his brain is functioning a little bit different, and if we change the curriculum, he will be a brilliant kid and he will succeed."

A compounding parallel issue is that American culture is "work, work, work, work. So parents start work at 8:00 in the morning. They don't come home before 5:00 or 6:00 in the evening . . . and they want kids to do their homework. If the kid is not able because of many different reasons. . . . This kid might have symptoms of depression, and that's why he's not able to concentrate on his work. It's much easier for the parents to say, 'Well, my son has ADHD and he needs medication' rather than dealing with other issues that [are] affecting them." The school structure and the long work hours parents face run into a third concern. Haddad is a psychiatrist specializing in children's mental health, but, as he says:

> [A]ny doctor can prescribe medications for ADHD, and many people, because [of] the difficulty of accessing child psychiatrists and the expense—because child psychiatrists are very expensive— say, "well, I cannot afford going to a child psychiatrist. I will go to my pediatrician." And they'll sit with the pediatrician for five minutes, and the pediatrician gets convinced, "all right, you have ADHD, so let me give you medications for ADHD." So we see half of the kids taking ADHD medications, [although] many of them would benefit from something else. (Conley, 2014c)

Ultimately, Haddad says, it is easier to medicate the children to fit with the socialization norms than to change society. As he sums up the standardizing impact of socialization: "[A]nybody who's different, anybody who's functioning on [a] different level, we do not accommodate them." For active young kids, "we just claim that, 'okay, *you* have a problem. You need help.' And the easiest problem to have is ADHD because the medications are easy to prescribe." Socialization may not come easily for anyone, but it is especially difficult for those who find conformity a challenge.

Schools, however, teach us more than how to show up prepared for class, and all schools are not created equal. In *Preparing for Power* (1985), Peter W. Cookson Jr. and Caroline Hodges Persell explore how private prep schools indoctrinate the students who attend them into a world of social status and privilege. The researchers "document how the philosophies, programs, and lifestyles of boarding schools help transmit power and privilege and how elite families use these schools to maintain their social class." Admission to these schools is highly competitive and far from democratic. "Legacies" (children who come from families where at least one other member has attended the same school) make up more than half (54 percent) of the attendees on average and as many as 75 percent at some schools. The non-academic part of the curriculum ranges from upper-class sports such as crew and sailing to cultural education in the form of study abroad and smaller field trips overseas. Probably the most important aspect of prep-school education is that it links students into social networks—helping them get into the top colleges and hobnob with students from wealthy and powerful families—that they will have access to and benefit from for the rest of their lives.

PEERS

Once we reach school age, peers become an important part of our lives and function as agents of socialization. Adolescents, in particular, spend a great deal of their free time in the company of peers. Peers can reinforce messages taught in the home (even the most liberal of friends will probably expect you to wear clothing when you hang out with them after school) or contradict them. Either way, conformity is generally expected; hence the term *peer pressure*. Walk into any high-school cafeteria and you'll observe the power of conformity among peer groups. If you have ever tried drugs or alcohol, did you do so by yourself? Probably not. Even when we are being deviant, we often do so in the company (and often at the suggestion) of others. This is why parents express concern about their children hanging out with the "wrong crowd." They're not just being paranoid.

Adolescents do tend to glean as much (or more) information on sex and dating from their peers and even the media compared to their parents. A 2018 study of young adolescents aged 14–17 (by Bleakley et al.) found, on the one hand, that friends were a major source of information on dating and sex. This makes sense. No matter how cool your parents are (or try to be), when you're 15, you probably don't want to talk to them about your love life. On the other hand, most research tends to show that adolescents who communicate more with their parents about sex tend to engage in safer sex behaviors than their peers (i.e., using contraceptives; Widman et al., 2016). It seems as if most adolescents have already learned that they shouldn't believe everything they hear from their peers or the media.

ADULT SOCIALIZATION

The socialization we receive as children can never fully prepare us for the demands that we will face as adults. *Adult socialization* simply refers to the ways in which you are socialized as an adult. When you work at a restaurant, you learn, for instance, what your job responsibilities are, how to take orders and place them in the kitchen, and how to carry a tray full of drinks. As a result of your prior socialization, you probably already knew that you should not talk back to customers. Similarly, your plans upon graduation from college might include moving out of your parents' house, finding a job, and maybe starting a family. Right now, you may not know everything you need to in order to function in each of those situations, but you will learn. Some roles, like some jobs, take more preparation than others—you have to go to law school to become an attorney and medical school to become a doctor. Did you ever wonder why parenting schools don't exist?

Resocialization is a more drastic form of adult socialization. When you change your environment, you may need some resocialization. If you plan to live in another country, you may have to learn a new language and new ways of eating, speaking, talking, listening, or dressing. If you went to a single-sex high school and are attending a co-ed college or university, this change will probably require some resocialization, depending on the extent to which you interacted with the opposite sex during your high-school years. The most drastic case of resocialization would be necessary if you had suffered a terrible accident and lost all of your memory. You would need to relearn everything—how to hold a fork and knife, how to tie your shoes, how to engage in conversation. You would be completely childlike once again—and any inappropriate nose picking would be forgiven.

Adult socialization doesn't just occur when we move out of our parents' home or join the military or go to prison. As we navigate new challenges that come with each stage of development we are influenced by the people and institutions in our life. Of psychologist Erik Erikson's eight stages of human development (and their associated struggles), only the first five take place during childhood. The final three stages all take place in adulthood.

Key to Erikson's theory is the notion that if we do not successfully navigate the tension inherent to a particular stage of development, we are headed for problems later on thanks to our "unresolved issues." Each stage has a virtue that is acquired if the tension of that stage is successfully overcome; likewise, each period has a key social relationship. For example, in the first stage, the salient connection is to the mother. During this first stage, Erikson

---

RESOCIALIZATION

the process by which one's sense of social values, beliefs, and norms are reengineered, often deliberately, through an intense social process.

claimed that the infant is learning how much they should trust people (generalized from the mother). If the baby is cared for and responded to when, for example, they are hungry, then that person will emerge with the virtue of hope. The next stage, from ages 2 to 4, is about autonomy—learning to exert control over oneself through mastery of toilet training and dressing oneself among other skills. Here the parents are the key social actors and the emergent virtue is "will."

The next phase of childhood (ages 5–8) is characterized by a struggle between initiative and feelings of guilt. The child is exploring the world and makes "mistakes" or takes action against the wishes of the family. If successful, the child emerges from this phase with a sense of "purpose." In middle childhood (9–12 years old), the question driving the individual is how they stack up in the world. School, for instance, becomes a primary social milieu where the child is judging themself; does the child end up with the virtue of "competence" or do they end up feeling inferior? The final childhood stage is, of course, adolescence (ages 13–19), during which the individual is finding their identity among their peers (and with respect to role models). The fundamental question here is "Who am I?" A well-adjusted adolescent emerges with a sense of "fidelity"—that is, a true inner self that serves as a lodestar to guide the person going forward into adulthood.

Erikson located the ages between the 20s and the 40s as the prime time when we struggle with making connections with others—friends and spouses. Indeed, research shows that the average age at which lifelong friends are made is 21. However, Erikson claimed that if we hadn't developed a clear sense of self during adolescence, we might have trouble developing intimate relationships and experience, instead, loneliness and emotional isolation. (Most people experience loneliness from time to time, but a successful navigation of this stage means that emotional isolation does not become our predominant experience.)

Meanwhile, middle adulthood—the period from the 40s to 50s—is a period when people struggle to avoid stagnation and achieve "generativity," which means a feeling that one is productively contributing to society and leaving a small mark. Often this is tied to both child raising and how one's work career plays out. The final social-psychological stage begins around age 60 according to Erikson. In this phase of life, we either feel a sense of "integrity"—that is, a pride in our accomplishments in life—or we may "despair" in the face of too many "could haves" and "should haves" as we reflect backwards on our life.

Erikson's model has been revised and critiqued in the decades since it was first proposed. For example, Joan Erikson, his wife and collaborator on the theory, added a ninth stage, where the first eight are reexperienced in reverse order. Others have claimed that the struggles of each stage do not necessarily happen sequentially. Finally, some claim that the theory is not as universally applicable as it is intended to be but rather describes an idealized life progression for European American males, ignoring the experiences of women and minorities.

Whether the theory needs tweaking or not, the question arises as to the social influences during these stages. Let's take early adulthood—the period when we seek intimate love and companionship. It has long been known that people tend to pick spouses that are like themselves on a wide range of attributes from height to political ideology. However, it is also true that spouses are an important socializing agent for each other; for example, often one spouse will convert to the other's religion.

With respect to middle adulthood, research has shown that socialization effects between parents and offspring are not a one-way street. That is, children can affect their parents' attitudes and beliefs just as parents try to instill values in their little 'uns. For example, some research has examined whether the gender of children affects their parents' political beliefs. It has been shown that judges and congressmen and women tend to vote more liberally when they have daughters. Evidence for the general population is more mixed, however.

Finally, a study on the effect of "trash television" shows that its effects are strongest among the youngest (under age 10) and oldest (age 55 plus) of us. In order to deal with the fact that very different people may be attracted to watching lots of lowbrow programming on TV, the authors used the fact that in Italy, a new network called Mediaset was rolled out gradually across the country, so some communities were exposed to its light fare of movies and entertainment (without as much news as the preexisting channels) for longer than others. In this natural experiment, young kids suffered in terms of their test scores due to increased Mediaset exposure—which then had a number of other effects on voting, trust, and so on. The elderly didn't suffer cognitively like the youngest group did, but they became more populist and angry in their voting patterns. A similar effect was seen in Indonesia, among 606 villages that got TV at different times: Those who were more exposed to broadcasts became more distrustful and participated in civic life less.

The point is that we are not done being socialized at 18 or even 25 years old, like a Jell-O mold that has set. Our social environments— spouses, children, peers, media, work, and so on—continue to shape who we are as we transition through life's stages.

TOTAL INSTITUTIONS

The term total institution refers to an institution that controls all the basics of day-to-day life. Members of the institution eat, sleep, study, play, and perhaps even bathe and pray together. Boarding schools, colleges, monasteries, the army, and prisons are all total institutions to varying degrees— prisons being the most extreme (see Chapter 6). Sociologist Gwynne Dyer's

TOTAL INSTITUTION

an institution in which one is totally immersed and that controls all the basics of day-to-day life; no barriers exist between the usual sphere of daily life, and all activity occurs in the same place and under the same single authority.

War (1985) provides some insight into the total institution of the US Marine Corps. Marine boot camp strips down much of the prior socialization of recruits and resocializes them to become Marines. Think about how boot camp treats new enlistees: Certain parts of their identity are erased. Uniforms are handed to them and males' heads are shaved. Enlistees live, eat, sleep, bathe, exercise, and study together. Their every move is watched and critiqued, from how they hold a weapon to how they tuck in the corners of their bedsheets. New Marines—and recruits in all branches of the armed forces—also must be resocialized to accept the notion that it is okay, even necessary, to kill. Most of us have learned quite the opposite, of course—that under no circumstances should we kill another person. Basic training is not only about teaching recruits new skills; it's about changing them so that they can perform tasks they wouldn't have dreamed of doing otherwise. It works by applying enormous physical and mental pressure on men and women who have been isolated from their normal civilian environment and constantly placed in situations where the only right way to think and behave is that espoused by the Marine Corps. For people to be effective soldiers, they must learn a new set of rules about when it is okay and/or necessary to kill (that is, when they are on active duty, not on leave and at the pizza parlor with their family).

Marines training at Parris Island. How is Marine boot camp an example of a total institution?

Social Interaction

To talk about how institutions and society as a whole socialize us, we need a language to describe social interaction. Robert Merton's role theory provides just such a vocabulary. The first key concept for an understanding of role theory is status, which refers to a recognizable social position that an individual occupies. The person who runs your class and is responsible for grading each student has the status of professor. Roles, then, refer to the duties and behaviors associated with a particular status. You can reasonably expect your professor to show up on time, clothed, and prepared for class. You can also expect that he or she has a fair amount of education, often a PhD, and is knowledgeable about the material. This may not always be true, but it is a fairly standard set of role expectations for someone with the status of

STATUS

a recognizable social position that an individual occupies.

ROLE

the duties and behaviors expected of someone who holds a particular status.

ROLE STRAIN

the incompatibility among
roles corresponding to a
single status.

professor. Roles are complicated, however, and relatively few of them materialize with handbooks and clear sets of expectations. Sometimes we experience role strain, the incompatibility among roles corresponding to a single status. An example of this is the old dictum for university faculty, particularly young professors, to "publish or perish." On the one hand, they need to stay on top of their research, write articles, give lectures, and attend conferences to stay abreast of current topics and remain active in the academic world. On the other hand, they have to teach and perform all the teaching roles that come with the status of professor—preparing lectures, running class sections, meeting with students, grading papers, and writing letters of recommendation.

When your professor arrives at class tomorrow morning with bags under her eyes and a look on her face that seems to say, "No amount of coffee will help me at this point," you may be tempted to conclude, "Oh, she's experiencing role strain." But what if her exhaustion results not from the time demands of simultaneously grading her midterms and preparing for an upcoming research conference, but rather from the turmoil that ensued last night when the family dog destroyed her daughter's biology project and she had to stay up all night helping her daughter redo it? In this case, role conflict is the culprit. It is not the roles within her status as professor that are the root of her problems, but rather the tensions between her role as professor and her role as mother. Whereas *role strain* refers to conflicting demands within the same status, *role conflict* describes the tension caused by competing demands between two or more roles within different statuses. Each one of us, at any given time, enjoys numerous statuses. These statuses (and their corresponding roles) can and do change over time and between places. When you started college, how did your status change? The obvious answer is that you went from being either a high-school student or perhaps an unskilled worker to becoming a college student. If you graduated from high school and went straight to college, you traded in one status for another. If you still maintain a full- or part-time job, you have added another status. The term status set refers to all the statuses you have at any given time.

To obtain a better sense of how roles and statuses function, try the following experiment: Write down as many answers to the question "Who am I?" as you can. Compare your answers with your classmates'. With remarkable similarity, the lists will include statuses such as brother, sister, daughter, boyfriend, student, lifeguard, babysitter, roommate, and so forth. This occurs because we know ourselves in our social roles, in the ways in which we relate to others. You most likely will have listed the key components of your status set.

There are some other key terms that you must learn to understand role theory. Sociologists often make a distinction between an ascribed status and an achieved status, which basically amounts to what you are born with versus what you become. Another way to think about it is in terms of

ROLE CONFLICT

the tension caused by
competing demands
between two or more
roles pertaining to
different statuses.

STATUS SET

all the statuses one holds
simultaneously.

involuntary versus voluntary status. Your age, race, and sex are all largely ascribed statuses, whereas your status as a juggler, drug dealer, peace activist, or reality television aficionado is an achieved status. Sometimes, one status within our status set stands out or overwhelms all the others. This is called a master status. Examples might include being unemployed, being lesbian, being disabled, or any status that overshadows other statuses. Master status roles can be ascribed, like disability, or achieved, like being a celebrity. The key characteristic of a master status is that people tend to interact with you on the basis of that one status alone.

GENDER ROLES

One of the most popular lines of thought to evolve from role theory has been the concept of gender roles, sets of behavioral norms assumed to accompany one's identity as masculine, feminine, or other. In their critiques of role theory, gender theorists such as Candace West and Don Zimmerman (1987) have argued that the statuses of male/female have distinct power and significance that role theory doesn't adequately capture (you can read more about this in Chapter 8 on sex and gender). We can see how gender fits into larger theories of socialization. Sometimes the gendering starts before birth: One recent tradition is the gender reveal party, where a baker is given

ASCRIBED STATUS

a status into which one is born; involuntary status.

ACHIEVED STATUS

a status into which one enters; voluntary status.

MASTER STATUS

one status within a set that stands out or overrides all others.

GENDER ROLES

sets of behavioral norms assumed to accompany one's status as masculine, feminine, or other.

Who are you? What are the different roles in your status set? For example, singer Beyoncé's statuses include mother, daughter, and partner.

How do the displays at this New York City toy store serve as an example of the ways that we learn gender roles through socialization?

the results of a sonogram or other test that reveals the biological sex of the fetus and then bakes a cake or cupcakes with either pink or blue filling. The family gathers around to celebrate the revealed sex by eating the sweet. Knowing the sex of a baby may influence how parents talk to it—i.e., the tone of voice and what they say—even before it leaves the womb.

More often, from the moment they are born, babies may be dressed in either pink or blue to designate their sex if their parents want to signal to the wider society that they should be treated as one gender (although many hospitals now offer gender-neutral blankets, hats, and so on to patients). These seemingly silly differences—babies don't care if they wear blue or pink—create a context for older kids and adults to treat babies not as an undifferentiated group of babbling incoherents but as boys and girls. Studies (Lewis et al., 1992) have shown that people interact with babies differently based on whether they are boys or girls, commenting on how "big" and "strong" baby boys are and how "pretty" baby girls may be, or closely snuggling with female babies rather than holding them facing outward, as with male babies, so that they might see the world.

Not just family members but people in the larger social world interact with boys and girls very differently and, consequently, socialize them into different roles and into the schema of a gender binary itself (the idea that one has to pick between two genders). Take a stroll through your local toy store, and you will glimpse the function of toys and play—both very important to the development of children—in creating and maintaining gender roles. The toys for playing house will likely be displayed in boxes showing images of little girls pushing and pulling pink irons and purple vacuum cleaners. The boxes for toy stoves will depict girls cooking. Baby dolls will be wrapped in pastel colors, and their packaging will show little girls cradling them. Now meander through the section of the store displaying tool sets, workbenches, and toys related to outdoor activities. On the packages, you will note little boys dressed in bright primary colors, wielding hammers and fishing poles. The action-figure aisle will be similarly gendered (think Barbie versus G.I. Joe). (Admittedly, these are generalizations. Some images will show boys playing house and girls constructing a bridge, but the vast majority will adhere to what we perceive as traditional gender roles.)

In high school, gender-role socialization continues as peers police each other. Sociologist C. J. Pascoe spent a year in a working-class high school in California finding out just how teens enforce gender norms on one another. She discovered what she calls "fag discourse," a term that describes the near-continuous use of the term *fag* or *faggot* as an insult teenage boys use against one another to curtail improper behavior. She explained in a recent interview how it worked. Someone could get called a fag if, as she said, "you danced, if you cared about your clothing, if you were too emotional, or if you were incompetent." What's more, actually being gay turned out to be beside the point. As Pascoe explained: "What I came to realize was that they used *fag* as an insult to police the boundaries of masculinity. It wasn't about same-sex desire. In fact, when I asked them about same-sex desire, one boy said, 'Well being gay is just a lifestyle; you can still throw a football around and be gay.'" This "masculinity policing" is no joking matter. A boy she called Ricky was "targeted so relentlessly that he dropped out of school" (Conley, 2009c).

DIGITAL.WWNORTON.COM/YOUMAYASK7

To see my interview with C. J. Pascoe about *Dude, You're a Fag*, go to digital.wwnorton.com/youmayask7

If boys are constantly policing the boundaries of masculinity with homophobic insults, how are girls being socialized into their gender roles? At the school in Pascoe's study, girls did not insult each other. Instead they had to put up with constant sexual harassment from the boys. As the boys looked for behaviors that would prove they were not fags, they used girls as unwitting resources with which to perform aggressive sexuality by describing to one another either how they could "get" girls or the outlandish and often violent sexual escapades that would then follow. Further, they engaged in rituals of forceful touching, often physically constraining girls' movements. Pascoe describes one hallway scene in which she "watched one boy walk down the hallway jabbing a girl in the crotch with his drumstick yelling, 'Get raped, get raped'" (Conley, 2009c). In this case, gender socialization looks a lot like gender-based bullying. Do these scenes remind you of high school? Was your gender performance policed by your peers?

For some, constant gender-boundary policing has catastrophic effects. Ricky was subject to the steadiest, most virulent fag discourse in Pascoe's study and he dropped out. An 11-year-old in Massachusetts committed suicide after being relentlessly teased; many of the insults he received were part of fag discourse. And Pascoe points out that 90 percent of school shooters who go on rampage school shootings have been subject to homophobic harassment and teasing (Conley, 2009c). Even when it does not end so tragically, such gender socialization during childhood may form the roots of adult gender performances—ranging from the fact that men are more likely to sexually harass women in the workplace than the reverse, to the simple fact that men are 33 percent more likely to talk over or interrupt a woman than they are a man (Shore, 2017).

Recent evidence on adolescent socialization contains good and bad news. Ninety-two percent of respondents to a recent poll of 10-to-18-year-olds believed in gender equality as a principle, and a majority agreed that sexism still persists and equality has yet to be achieved. Life goals were the same, overall, by gender, and girls were as represented as boys in school leadership positions and were as likely to aspire to leadership positions in life as well as to value a career. Moreover, the survey found that it is now more acceptable for girls to violate traditional gender norms by adopting "male" interests, styles, and manners. That said, boys still felt very constrained by expectations for them to be stoic, strong, and athletic. Girls, by contrast, were discomforted by how much emphasis was placed on their looks (a finding that is echoed by adult women) by society and how sexualized they were by the boys. Finally, 3 percent of respondents identified as transgender, illustrating the breaking down of the entire gender-binary system to a certain extent (see Chapter 8 for more on gender fluidity). So, while the next generation (and women in particular) may view (and adopt) gender roles in a more fluid manner, there are still deeply ingrained ways of behaving with respect to sexuality and gender that persist. We should keep in mind that these overall numbers obscure significant variation by race, class, and region. Indeed, most roles are better thought of through an intersectional lens—that is, related to the specific subject's position of being, for example, a White woman from a wealthy, rural family—rather than based on single categories. More on intersectionality in Chapter 8.

The Social Construction of Reality

In a February 19, 2006, *New York Times* op-ed essay titled "Mind over Splatter," Vassar professor Don Foster commented on the debate surrounding a Jackson Pollock painting that was recently alleged to be a fake. Is the painting

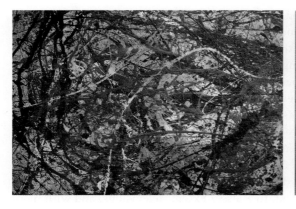
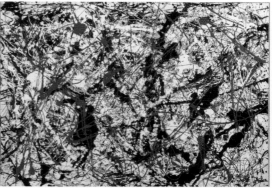

any less artistic for not being a real Pollock when it was, after all, good enough to fool so many people for so long? In a similar vein, Shakespeare's Juliet once inquired, "What's in a name? That which we call a rose by any other name would smell as sweet." The implication is that something is what it is, apart from what we call it or who made it. But do we agree? This question speaks less to the essential nature of things and more to the social construction of reality. Something is real, meaningful, or valuable when society tells us it is.

Which one of these paintings is a "real" Jackson Pollock? Does it matter? (For the record, the real one is on the right.) How is the controversy over the Pollock paintings an example of the social construction of reality?

So what does it mean to say that something is socially constructed? This question is less a debate about what is real versus fake and more an explanation of how we give meanings to things or ideas through social interaction. Two good ways of understanding how we socially construct our reality are to compare one society over different time periods and to compare two contemporary societies. Let's look at some examples.

In US society we take for granted that childhood is a critical and unique stage of life. It wasn't always considered so, however; this view came about through a series of cultural, political, and economic changes. In preindustrial times children were expected to care for younger siblings and contribute to the household in other ways as soon as they were physically capable. Toys specifically for children, one of the cultural markers of childhood, did not exist. The early years of one's life were not regarded as a time for play and education. They represented a time of work and responsibility, like most of life's course. However, the development of the industrial factory led to the need for schools, a place where children might spend their days, because parents now left home to go to work. This change in parents' lifestyles meant that a separate sphere had to be created for children. People's lives became more segregated by age, and because of this separation, childhood began to be taken seriously and protected. For example, child labor laws sprang up to protect children from hazardous working conditions.

Adolescence has had a similar history. The notion that a distinct phase exists between childhood and adulthood is relatively new. This important change evolved during the 1950s. After decades of financial hardship and war, America's booming economy led to a new freedom in the popular culture. Access to higher education broadened as well. For many Americans, this extension of educational opportunity delayed the onset of adult responsibilities—such as employment and raising families. With the possibility of an extended adolescence, teenagers (biologically able to reproduce but delayed in their assumption of adult sexual roles) emerged as a discrete social category. Concurrently, cultural changes were marked by the advent of rock and roll, doo-wop, and other popular forms of music. With more access to radios and, to a lesser extent, televisions, and with more free hours after school, teens found the time and means to consume this emerging music culture. Today we can see the life course becoming even further subdivided, with the advent of terms such as *tween*, which refers to the time between childhood and one's teenage years (roughly, ages 10 to 12) and *emerging adulthood*, which is between age 18 and the late 20s.

As an example of cross-cultural differences in the social construction of reality, consider the following question: What constitutes food? We tend to think of insects as interesting, necessary to the ecosystem, annoying, or maybe simply gross. However, we generally do not regard them as food. In other cultures, dishes such as fried grasshoppers and chocolate-covered ants are considered a delicacy. Which perspective is "right"? In fact, Americans may be an exception in not eating insects, which, I am told, are delicious. Insects are nutritious (high in protein, low in fat and calories, and a good

Lunch? Cicadas, grasshoppers, and other insects on skewers for sale in Donghuamen Night Market in Beijing, China.

source of many vitamins and minerals) and economical, but they are inherently neither gross nor delicious. The point is that foods, which we take for granted as natural or self-evident, are assigned meanings and values in different cultural contexts.

We might call the process by which things—ideas, concepts, values—are socially constructed symbolic interactionism (see Chapter 1), which suggests that we interact with others using words and behaviors that have symbolic meanings. This theory has three basic tenets:

1. Human beings act toward ideas, concepts, and values on the basis of the meaning that those things have for them.

2. These meanings are the products of social interaction in human society.

3. These meanings are modified and filtered through an interpretive process that each individual uses in dealing with outward signs.

Symbolic interactionism can be very useful in understanding cultural differences in styles of social interaction. A classic example of this would be the distance two people stand from one another when conversing. Just because these boundaries are often symbolic does not mean that they aren't real. In an interaction between a tourist and a local, standing too close or too far away may make one of the parties feel uncomfortable, but in an international business meeting or in peace talks between nations, symbolic interactions take on a greater level of importance. And, of course, during periods of pandemic, how much social distance one maintains in face-to-face interaction transcends the symbolic and becomes a matter of, perhaps, life and death. However, even in such circumstances where there are serious biological consequences to how far apart people stand from each other, there is no escaping the social and cultural signaling that becomes encoded with such choices on a daily level. In the United States, for example, wearing protective masks and keeping six feet apart have been highly charged political issues, showing that the symbolic nature of interactional choices persists in both low-stakes and high-stakes scenarios.

In another example, in the United States we generally believe that looking someone in the eye while talking to them indicates respect and sincerity. In some other cultures, however, it is considered extremely rude to look someone directly in the eye. When you raise your glass in a toast with others and say, "Cheers," you can generally focus your eyes wherever you want. In many European countries, however, it is highly impolite and may be regarded as a sign of dishonesty not to establish eye contact while touching glasses.

Comprehending the three basic tenets of symbolic interactionism listed earlier is key to seeing how the process of social construction is both ongoing and embedded in our everyday interactions. Symbolic interactionism as a

SYMBOLIC INTERACTIONISM

a micro-level theory in which shared meanings, orientations, and assumptions form the basic motivations behind people's actions.

How does symbolic interactionism help us understand the differences in greetings among various cultures? Pictured here (clockwise from bottom) are Bedouins touching noses, Malian men with their arms around each other, and the Belgian royal family celebrating the prince's eighteenth birthday.

theory is a useful tool for understanding the meanings of symbols and signs and the way shared meanings—or a lack thereof—facilitate or impede routine interactions. Let's look at another theory of human interaction, Erving Goffman's dramaturgical theory of society, which laid the groundwork for symbolic interactionism by using the language of theater as a paradigm to formally describe the ways in which we interact to maintain social order.

DRAMATURGICAL THEORY

All the world's a stage,
And all the men and women merely players.

—William Shakespeare, *As You Like It*

We might say that the dramaturgical theory of society has its roots in William Shakespeare, but we generally credit Goffman with expounding this theory in *The Presentation of Self in Everyday Life* (1959). He argued that life is essentially a play—a play with a moral, of sorts. And this moral is what Goffman and social psychologists call "impression management." That is, all of us actors on the metaphorical social stage are struggling to make a good impression on our audience (who also happen to be actors). What's more, the goal is not just to make the best impression on others; we often actively work to ensure that others will believe they are making a good impression as well. This helps keep society and social relations rolling along smoothly (without the need for too many retakes).

Because we are all actors with roles, according to Goffman's dramaturgical theory, we also need scripts, costumes, and sets. Think again about your first day in this college classroom. You knew your role was student, and presumably the professor understood his or her role as well. The professor handed out the syllabus (a prop), talked about the general outline of the class for the semester (a script), and maybe gave a short lecture (a performance). What if he had instead started talking about his love for Batman and all things related to Batman? You might have indulged him briefly, thinking that he seemed a bit loony but would eventually relate this tangent to sociology. If your professor, however, had spent the entire lecture talking about Batman, how would you feel? Shocked? Confused? The professor would have deviated from the script generally followed in a college classroom. Was anyone wearing a tuxedo or dressed like an action hero? Probably not, because those are not the costumes we wear to a sociology lecture. Think back to your status set for a minute and ask yourself what the stages, costumes, scripts, and other props associated with each of your roles are. For some, the answer is fairly clear.

We act out some of our roles much more intentionally than others, such as when we are a member of a sports team. If you are on the basketball team, you play on a basketball court (the stage or set), wear a uniform (the costume), follow the rules (the script), and play with a ball (a prop). Often, we play several roles simultaneously, and if we have been properly socialized and don't suffer from too much role conflict, we can transition in and out of roles with a certain amount of ease. Presumably, you understand that the classroom is not the appropriate stage on which to act out an intimate scene with your partner. If you did, one of your classmates might heckle you to "get a room." In dramaturgical theory, the translation would be "This is the wrong stage. Find the right one."

Another important part of Goffman's theory is the distinction between front-stage and backstage arenas. If you've ever participated in a school play or some other type of performance, you know all about front stage and backstage. Here the meanings are quite literal—a curtain separates these areas, so the border between the front stage and the backstage is clearly delineated. If you've ever worked in a restaurant, you see very clearly a similar line of demarcation. As a waiter you are all smiles out in the dining room. Whenever the customer asks for something, you reply politely with a "Yes, ma'am" or "Right away, sir." Back in the kitchen, however, you might complain loudly to the rest of the staff, criticizing your customer's atrocious taste for ordering escargot with his cheeseburger.

For people in certain professions, the distinction between front stage and backstage is more literal. In the news we sometimes hear about celebrities who have been caught saying something inappropriate because they thought the camera or microphone was off—they believed they were comfortably backstage. Whoops! The higher your profile, particularly if you have a master status such as a celebrity or politician, the greater the portion of your daily world that takes on the designation of front stage. You are always under close scrutiny, so you are always expected to perform your role. In other situations, the lines between front stage and backstage become more blurred. Has a professor ever caught you off guard while you were talking with friends about her class? You might have thought that you were backstage when joking with your friends in the student union, but the unfortunate, unexpected appearance of your professor turned the situation into a front-stage experience.

FACE

the esteem in which an individual is held by others.

Face, according to Goffman, is the esteem in which an individual is held by others. We take this notion very seriously; hence the idea of saving face, which is essentially the most important goal of impression management. If your best friend walked into the classroom right now and sat down beside you with a big smear of chocolate on his face, you would tell him. If the professor walked in sporting the same chocolate smear, however, you might not say anything. Because of the difference in status, and therefore power, between you and the professor, you might decide it's not your place, your role, to say something. If few students are in the class and the professor is your adviser with whom you have a fairly amicable relationship, you might indicate to him that he's got a little something on his cheek. Have you ever encountered a stranger with toilet paper stuck to the bottom of her shoe or with the fly of his pants unzipped? Did you say something? If you did, you were probably motivated by the thought that, if it were you, you would want someone to say something. If you didn't, perhaps you thought calling attention to the toilet paper or exposed underwear would embarrass the person. Or maybe you just simply felt it wasn't any of your business to interfere with a stranger. So you can see how no absolute, fixed scripts exist. (That said, one common rule of thumb is to speak up if the person can do something about it. For example, you would tell a man that he has chocolate on his face because he can wipe his face and remove the chocolate. On the other hand, you would not tell him that his shirt is ugly, because he probably cannot change his shirt at that moment.)

Similarly, if your professor walked in tomorrow with a black eye, you might ask him what happened. Not wanting to admit he fell asleep grading papers and smacked his face on the desk, he might simply say, "You should see the other guy." This is a common joke people make to save face in light of injuries about which they do not wish to speak. There are many subtleties to learn in life, and nobody explicitly teaches us all of these things. Like driving a car, we generally learn by doing and by sometimes making mistakes.

Indeed, mistakes, called breaches, are themselves an important part of the game. When there's a breach in an established script, we work hard to repair it and move forward. Humor is a useful tool in getting the script back in place. So if your professor lets out an enormous belch in the middle of a lecture, how would you react? You might be horrified; you might laugh nervously. You might delight a little because she has been so arrogant all semester and you are pleased to see her off script, not the perfectly polished professor. If the professor manages to recover and says, "Note to self: Skip the Mountain Dew before lecture next time!" it may smooth over the situation a little (but just a little, because let's face it, what happened was funny) and allow class to continue without a hitch. If the same thing happens during your next class, however, you are just going to assume that your professor is either poorly socialized and extremely uncouth, has severe gastrointestinal problems, or needs to scale back on carbonation.

After Sony Pictures Entertainment's internal computer system was hacked, executive Amy Pascal suffered from scandal when her e-mails and other personal information were released and her backstage life became public.

Sometimes, the stakes are so high or the situation is so new that we seek explicit guidance. People can and do make careers out of negotiating social scripts and methods for saving face—think about Miss Manners, Emily Post, or Dear Abby. Not wanting to act inappropriately but unsure of how to behave in situations where we lack a script, we may appeal to professional etiquette experts to coach us through a scene and give stage directions. The truth is, however, that human social interaction is too complex for a single script to work universally.

The art of tact even involves, on occasion, breaking the rules to make others feel comfortable. One particular fable tells the story of a peasant who is invited to the palace for dinner. Unknowingly, she picks up the bowl of water meant for handwashing and begins to drink from it. Many of the nobles at the table chuckle and mutter disparaging comments under their breath. But the queen, who invited the poor woman to dine with her, instead picks up her own silver finger bowl and drinks the water from it. She breaks a formal rule to preserve the face of the invited guest. Moreover, the social situation dictates that only the queen herself, as the most powerful figure at the table, can do that to repair the situation and save face for everyone.

There are some ways to generalize, however. For example, we almost always need to begin our scripts in specific ways; we generally can't just plunge into our lines. (Imagine a colleague getting on the elevator, not saying hello or even looking directly at you, but launching straight into the story of what happened to her on the way to work that day while staring up at the floor number indicators.) Goffman uses the term *opening* to signal the start of an encounter—that is, the first bracket. The closing bracket marks the end of an encounter. Sometimes, we need a nonverbal bracket to commence an encounter, a signal to cease our civil inattention. *Civil inattention* means refraining from directly interacting with someone, even someone you know, until an opening bracket has been issued. For example, you might clear your throat before speaking to somebody. You might catch his or her eye. You might stand up. You might purposely go to the bathroom first, so you can pass that person on the way back and start a conversation. You hope that you will bump into the person and catch his or her eye. We have to signal to people; we have to warn them that we are going to break civil inattention and initiate an encounter.

Openings can be awkward, but it may be even more difficult to end situations. How many times have you gotten off the phone saying, "I should get going." Where? To do what? Or you may say, "Well, I should let you go." Maybe you do hear sirens and screams in the background and you are genuinely concerned that your conversation is keeping the person on the phone from more pressing matters. Under less extreme circumstances, you may be phrasing your desire to end the conversation as a kind gesture to your interlocutor. Sometimes, we resort to formal closings. A ringing bell often indicates the end of a class period. In the absence of a bell, or even prior to its ringing, however, you may close your notebook, start to pack your books, and pick up your coat to signal to the professor that, although the lecture on socialization is fascinating, you have another class in 10 minutes that is a 15-minute walk away. There are *given gestures* that signal a closing, such as putting on your coat. Or, at the end of a meal, you may rub your stomach and say, "Boy, that was delicious. I'm stuffed!" to indicate that you have finished eating but did very much enjoy the food. However, *given-off gestures* also exist, unconscious signals of our true feelings. If you grimace every time your fork reaches your mouth, you communicate something else entirely regarding your thoughts about the meal. Many of our gestures and brackets are nonverbal. This is why it is often more difficult to end a conversation on the phone than in person: Much of our toolbox is not available to us.

ETHNOMETHODOLOGY

At this point, you should be thinking more critically about the everyday interactions that we often (necessarily) take for granted. In the 1950s and 1960s Harold Garfinkel (1967) developed a method for studying social interactions, ethnomethodology, that involves *acting* critically about them. Ethnomethodology literally means "the methods of the people" (from *ethnos*, the Greek word for "people"). Garfinkel and his followers became famous for their "breaching experiments." They would send their students into the social world to see what happened when they breached social norms. In one example, Garfinkel sent his students home for the weekend and told them to behave as if their parents' home were a rooming house where they paid rent. Imagine what would happen if you sat down at the kitchen table and demanded to know when dinner was typically served and what days of the week the bed linens were changed. Similarly, a New York City professor instructed his students to ask people on the subway for their seats without offering any reason. Some students simply could not take this action. Others did it, but lied and said that they were not feeling well when they asked for the seat. Try your own breaching experiments. What do you normally do when you get in an elevator? You face forward and watch the numbers above the door. Next time you get into an elevator, face backward. See how the other people in the elevator react. A few weeks into the semester, students tend to sit in the same seats in the same class, particularly if it's a small group, even if they do not have assigned seats. The next time you are in such a situation, take someone else's usual seat and see how he or she reacts. (Come on, that's an easy one!)

Let's think through some of the reactions to breaches. Take the example of the student on the subway asking a stranger to give up his seat. What would you do if this happened to you? Would you give up your seat to the student? You might just get up and offer it to him, because you assume he would not ask for it unless he had a good reason (even if you don't see a cast on his leg). If the stranger were elderly, on crutches, or pregnant or had a small child, you might be more willing to get up—in fact, on most forms of public transportation, seats are marked as reserved for exactly these kinds of people. When this class assignment was originally handed out, note that some of the students simply could not bring themselves to do it. Others lied, saying they were sick, because being ill provides a valid excuse to sit down. Why is that? What's the big deal in asking someone to give you a seat? Well, you might decide, you just don't typically do such a thing. It's not normal behavior. But note that as a society, we construct rules and meanings for what constitutes normal.

Now contemplate the previously mentioned elevator scenario. How would you react if you stepped into an elevator and the only other person inside was

A scene from the film *Borat*. What established scripts did Sacha Baron Cohen's character Borat violate by going on an elevator naked? How did the unsuspecting woman on the elevator try to cope with the breach?

facing away from the door (assuming the elevator only opens on one side)? You might look at the wall to see if something is there at which the person is looking and that you can't see. You might try to stand farther away from that person. If someone else got on the elevator, maybe you would gauge her reaction. If she gave you a look that said, "What's this guy doing?" you might give a sympathetic look, even the hint of a smile, to indicate your agreement: "Yeah, crazy, huh?" Then you could breathe a little easier, knowing that the guy facing backward in the elevator is abnormal, and you, the other passenger, and anyone else who steps inside and faces forward are normal, although there's no social imperative to face forward rather than backward in an elevator.

If you walked into the classroom today and someone was sitting in the seat you consider "yours," how would you feel? Maybe you wouldn't think twice about it, but chances are you would notice, have an emotional reaction—be it annoyance, confusion, even anger—and get to class earlier the next time to claim what's rightfully yours.

NEW TECHNOLOGIES: WHAT HAS THE INTERNET DONE TO INTERACTION?

What happens when we are faced with entirely new situations? We have no rules, no scripts, no established social norms. How do people know what to do or what constitutes appropriate behavior? Usually, some continuity exists between situations, so we can draw on our previous knowledge (just as you could anticipate the norms of a college classroom even though you had never been in one before). But what about something like the internet, something that humans created, which in turn creates social situations never before possible? Let's think about what happens.

Take social media, for example. Tinder, Reddit, Second Life, and other online forums provide an interesting test of the dramaturgical model. The potential anonymity of the internet allows us to portray ourselves however we choose. Online I can play the role of a 57-year-old stay-at-home mom who was an international college badminton champ and who enters semi-annual pesto-making competitions. Is that who I am? Some online dating and networking websites allow us to craft our own presentation of self, alter our identities, and thereby create new "realities." We've largely removed the stage, costumes, props, vocal inflections, and other nonverbal cues, so we must depend entirely on the scripts with which we are presented. We even develop new ways of communicating—for example, by using emojis to substitute for nonverbal cues to indicate tone (e.g., that we're joking in a text). 😊 😢

The internet has changed society in other ways, such as forcing us to develop new technologies to prevent identity theft and to create secure online transactions for shopping and banking. Certain aspects of the internet have also altered the nature and details of crime. Software that allows for music sharing necessitates the development of a new set of ethics. Is it okay to download music free from the internet? It's illegal in most cases, for sure, but is it unethical? Are there certain circumstances in which it might be okay? For example, when Radiohead made its album *In Rainbows* available for download and left the amount of payment up to customers, should folks have paid, or was it just fine to download without donating? The new technologies are changing what we as a society mean by the term *stealing*. Other websites, such as eBay, allow for the sale of stolen goods in ways previously unforeseen. Intentionally or not, people may foster underground economies by purchasing stolen goods in a way not possible before the advent of online auctions. Clicking on an item and entering your credit card number is a completely different social interaction than walking into a dark alley and buying something that literally fell off the back of a truck.

ROOMMATES WITH BENEFITS

Eager to throw off my nerdy past and reinvent myself at college, I wrote "party animal" on my roommate application form where it asked incoming freshmen whether they wanted to bunk with a smoker or a nonsmoker. When I told my mother about this later, she laughed and bought me a T-shirt that sported the image of Spuds MacKenzie, the 1980s Budweiser beer mascot, under the words "The original party animal."

I ended up with Tony from Sacramento, a very quiet, Republican son of a judge. (I suppose it's good policy to separate the party animals from those who request them.) I learned to appreciate his taste in music (U2 and the Smiths, as opposed to my predilection for reggae and jazz), and we agreed to disagree about politics during the reelection campaign of Alan Cranston, then one of the most liberal members of the US Senate. I had never met anyone like Tony. And I'm pretty sure he hadn't come across many half-Jewish, Democratic children of New York artists. We learned to get along that first year at Berkeley, and every now and then even tried on each other's values and beliefs, just to see how they fit.

Today I am sad that most of my students will not experience what I did back when Facebook CEO Mark Zuckerberg was in diapers. While the internet has made it easy to reconnect with the lost Tonys of our lives, it has made it a lot more difficult to meet them in the first place, by taking a lot of randomness out of life. We tend to value order and control over randomness, but when we lose randomness, we also lose serendipity.

As soon as today's students receive their proverbial fat envelope from their top-choice college, they are on Facebook meeting other potential freshmen. By the time the roommate application forms arrive, many like-minded students with similar backgrounds have already connected and agreed to request one another as roommates.

It's just one of many ways in which digital technologies now spill over into non-screen-based aspects of social experience. I know certain people who can't bear to eat in a restaurant they haven't researched on Yelp. And Google and Facebook, of course, tailor content to exactly what they think you want to find.

But this loss of randomness is particularly unfortunate for college-age students, who should be trying on new hats and getting exposed to new and different ideas. Which students end up bunking with whom may seem trivial at first glance. But research on the phenomenon of peer influence—and the influences of roommates in particular—has found that there are, in fact, long-lasting effects based on whom you end up living with your first year.

David R. Harris, a sociologist at Cornell, studied roommates and found that White students who were assigned a roommate of a different race ended up more open-minded about race (Harris & Sim, 2002). In an earlier study, the economist Bruce Sacerdote (2001) found that randomly assigned roommates at Dartmouth affected each other's GPAs.

(Of course, influences can sometimes be negative. Roommates can drive each other's

Patti Kilroy, right, and Bliss Baek in their dorm room at NYU after first contacting each other through Facebook. Does this process of connecting online reduce the diversity and randomness of the college experience?

grades up or down. In 2003, researchers at four colleges discovered that male students who reported binge drinking in high school drank much more throughout college if their first-year roommate also reported binge drinking in high school [Duncan et al., 2005; Eisenberg et al., 2013; Kremer & Levy, 2008].)

These studies are important because we know that much education takes place outside the formal classroom curriculum and in the peer-to-peer learning that occurs in places like dorm rooms.

Other than prison and the military, there are not many other institutions outside of college that shove two people into a 100-square-foot space and expect them to get along for nine months. Can you think of any better training for marriage? In fact, in my research with Jennifer A. Heerwig, we found that Vietnam-era military service actually lowers the risk of subsequent divorce (Conley & Heerwig, 2011). It's possible that the military

teaches you how to subsume your individual desires for the good of the collective—in other words, how to get along well with others.

The drive to tame randomness into controllable order is a noble impulse, but letting a little serendipity flourish isn't such a bad thing. Nor is getting to know someone different from yourself. All colleges should follow the lead of Hamilton College in New York, where roommate choice is not allowed. And if you end up with the roommate from hell? You'll survive, and someday have great stories to tell your future spouse, with whom you'll probably get along better.

Conclusion

In the nature-versus-nurture debate, sociologists have generally fallen firmly on the side of nurture. At least that's what most of us study. Socialization helps us understand and explain how it is that babies—those wrinkled, sometimes alien-looking creatures newly emerged from their mothers' wombs—become people who attend college. How much stake do we put in preserving normality, the status quo? We already talked about tact. Little children are tactless all the time. I once handed my grandfather a wrapped present and said, "Happy Father's Day! It's a shirt!" It was cute because I was 5, but what if I had done the same thing at 15? Would it have been cute? Somewhere along the way, we learn the unwritten rules.

On May 23, 1999, the World Wrestling Federation (WWF) aired a live pay-per-view event called *Over the Edge*. When a harness malfunctioned, wrestler Owen Hart, who was being lowered into the ring, fell 78 feet to his death. Although television viewers did not see the live footage of his death, once Hart was removed and sent to the hospital (he was pronounced dead on arrival), the program continued. The decision to go forward with the event sparked conversation and criticism far beyond the wrestling world. Some were shocked, even outraged, that the producers did not cancel the program, whereas others stood by the old adage "The show must go on." Why the radically different reactions? Well, for starters, we do not have a social script for this type of incident. Death is a serious matter, to be sure, but how should death be handled when it occurs on live television? We tend to seek a return to normalcy when things do not go as planned. Trying to quickly transition the situation back to normal (and probably to keep its paying customers happy), the WWF continued the live event. Others were disgusted by this seeming insensitivity. The following night the association aired a two-hour tribute to the fallen wrestler.

This is an extreme example and a tragic one, but we witness more mundane, even comical, breaches on a fairly regular basis. When someone important commits them, they draw yet more attention. The point is that we all have a stake in things going a certain way. When things don't go according to plan, depending on the severity,

Paramedics try to resuscitate professional wrestler Owen Hart after a deadly fall in Kansas City, Missouri.

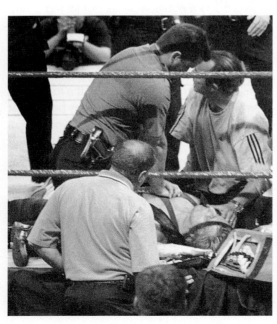

nature, and context of the deviation, we must find some way to recover, and recover we usually do. Whether it is a small breach in our shared understanding of turn-taking etiquette or a major rupture to the fabric of society, people work hard to broker consensus with respect to shared meaning. The alternative is nothing less than chaos and social insanity.

QUESTIONS FOR REVIEW

1. How does George Herbert Mead's concept of "generalized other" explain why, at the beginning of class, you became silent when your professor started speaking?

2. How does the case of "Anna" affect your assessment of early-socialization programs like Head Start?

3. School plays an important role in our socialization. Think about the way socialization works: What are some of the things we learn from schooling (e.g., the first years in elementary school), and how does this learning differ from what we are taught by our teacher? How are things like gender performance shaped in school?

4. Parents of different social classes socialize children differently. For example, middle-class parents are more likely to stress independence and self-direction, whereas working-class parents prioritize obedience to external authority. Using this example, how do you think socialization through families potentially reproduces social inequality?

5. You are a university student, but you also wait tables at a restaurant. One evening, one of your professors happens to come in for a meal (awkwardly, on a first date!). Use role theory to describe the interaction (and possible role conflict) that ensues.

6. What do sociologists mean by "social construction of reality"? How does the idea of social construction bring into question certain elements of everyday life, like gender roles?

7. Let's imagine you use file-sharing networks to download music and discuss your favorite music subgenres with people throughout the world. How does this differ from, for example, speaking only with employees at your local music store? Think about the way technology affects how you interact, the characteristics of the people with whom you're interacting, and how different ways of interacting might affect socialization.

PRACTICE

ROLE CONFLICT AND ROLE STRAIN

Part of modern social life involves seamlessly managing the inevitable conflicts and strains that arise due to the many hats we wear. Sociologist Robert Merton identified two forms of this phenomenon: (1) role strain, where the tension is between two roles (i.e., duties or scripts) associated with a particular status; and (2) role conflict, which stems from competing demands arising from different statuses.

TRY IT!

Make a list of a few of your statuses, e.g., student, roommate, waitress. For each of the statuses, list three roles that each entails. Here's one example:

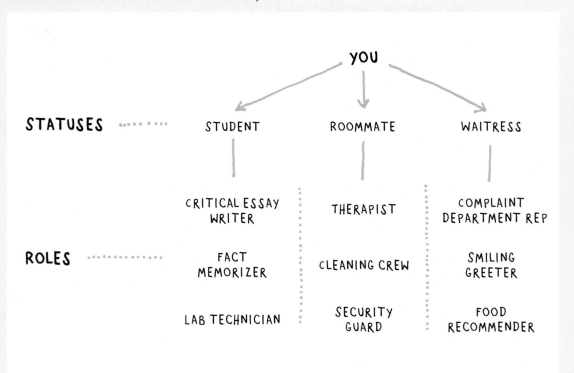

YOU

STATUSES · · · · · · · · · · · STUDENT   ROOMMATE   WAITRESS

	STUDENT	ROOMMATE	WAITRESS
	CRITICAL ESSAY WRITER	THERAPIST	COMPLAINT DEPARTMENT REP
ROLES	FACT MEMORIZER	CLEANING CREW	SMILING GREETER
	LAB TECHNICIAN	SECURITY GUARD	FOOD RECOMMENDER

When you lay out these various roles, you can see that the role of "complaint department rep" is in conflict with the role of "food recommender." You have to upsell the food and make it sound appealing—but then you have to take seriously complaints about the undercooked burger you just recommended.

ROLE STRAIN: COMPLAINT DEPARTMENT REP ⟷ FOOD RECOMMENDER

We can also see evidence of role strain. Let's say your essay is due by midnight. You've made some progress, but the door to your dorm room springs open and your roommate is weeping because her boyfriend just dumped her. What do you do?

ROLE CONFLICT: CRITICAL ESSAY WRITER ⟷ THERAPIST

How do you manage the role strains and conflicts that you've identified? Merton talked about compartmentalization, for example, in which you create a firewall between two conflicting statuses.

SOCIOLOGY ON THE STREET

Why does breaking social norms make others uncomfortable or even hostile? Watch the Sociology on the Street video to find out more: **digital.wwnorton.com/youmayask7**.

WANT MORE PRACTICE?

Complete the InQuizitive activity for this chapter at digital.wwnorton.com /youmayask7

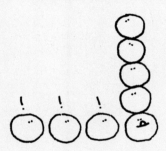

THE STRENGTH OF WEAK TIES:
IT IS THE PEOPLE WITH
WHOM WE ARE THE LEAST
CONNECTED WHO OFFER US
THE MOST OPPORTUNITIES.

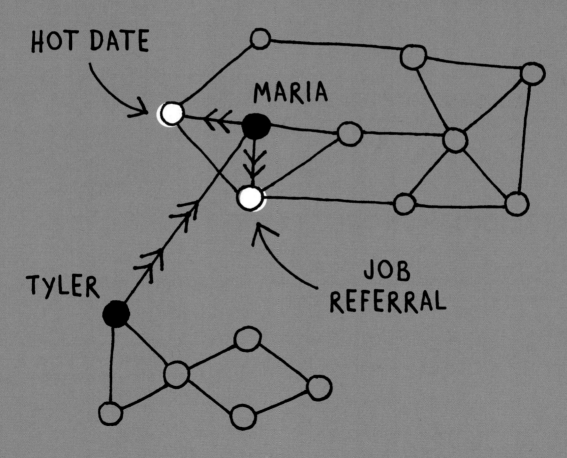

HOT DATE

MARIA

TYLER

JOB
REFERRAL

Groups and Networks

Who is Satoshi Nakamoto? Nobody really knows for sure. Candidates have included a deceased extropian cryptographer on the West Coast of the United States named Hal Finney (extropians are a group of people dedicated to finding a way to live forever), a Hungarian American recluse, an Australian academic, and others. What is for sure is that whoever uses the pseudonym Satoshi Nakamoto is one of the richest people in the world, due to the value of the bitcoin that person possesses (worth about $9 billion at the time of this writing). In late 2008, someone using the name Satoshi Nakamoto published a white paper online titled "Bitcoin: A Peer-to-Peer Electronic Cash System." The idea was bold: Instead of keeping financial records in a central system, like a bank, all financial transactions would appear on a public shared ledger, the "blockchain." It wasn't until January 2009, at the depths of the financial crisis and the Great Recession, that Nakamoto released the software to make operational the concept of a peer-to-peer anonymous form of currency. In the first "block" issued in the blockchain, Nakamoto embedded the following message: "The Times 3 January 2009 Chancellor on brink of second bailout for banks." And, voilà, the first major cryptocurrency was born.

Since the launch of bitcoin, the number of cryptocurrencies has skyrocketed. New ones include ethereum, litecoin, and zcash. Once mainly used for the "dark web," or online trade in illegal goods, bitcoin, as well as other electronic currency, is now accepted as payment by a rapidly growing number of mainstream businesses. Many residents of countries with unstable currencies who may have once tried to shift their assets to dollars or euros now use bitcoin to avoid the possibility that runaway inflation will decimate their savings. The CEO of America's largest bank, JPMorgan Chase, once scoffed at

bitcoin, claiming that he would fire anyone who traded in it, but he now admits the power of the blockchain concept. Cryptocurrencies represent an amazing feat of technical savvy—specifically the use of digital signatures and hash functions—to make sure all transactions are on the up-and-up. (For a great overview on how they work from a technical perspective, see **youtube.com /watch?v=bBC-nXj3Ng4**). But they also represent the triumph of social networks.

↑

In Seoul, South Korea, monitors display exchange rates of cryptocurrencies including bitcoin (top left), ethereum, and litecoin.

All currencies rely on trust within a social network to some extent (see Chapter 14). After all, if everyone suddenly decided not to accept British pounds sterling or Swiss francs, the value of these fancy pieces of paper would evaporate. But traditional currencies are all backed by a government—usually a central bank—that regulates the amount in circulation and "guarantees" their authenticity. Even pseudo-currencies like airline points (which exceeded the total value of dollars or euros or pounds back in 2005 [Clark, 2005]) require a central authority to lend them value—namely the airline. What's unique about bitcoin and other cryptocurrencies is that their authority and value is not centralized at all but rests in the social network itself by virtue of the fact that a coin is merely an entry into a public ledger (or blockchain) that is recorded multiple times across the entire network of users' computers. Yet the owners (and miners) of bitcoin can remain completely anonymous, like our protagonist, Satoshi Nakamoto. Welcome to the power of social networks.

This chapter explores some of the basic theories about group interaction and how it shapes our social world. We'll look at the connections between groups: how size and shape matter, what roles group members play, and how the power of groups works in comparison to that of individuals and other institutions. We'll also discuss organizations and how they both react to and create social structure.

Social Groups

Unless you live alone in the woods, and perhaps even then, you are a member of many social groups. Social groups form the building blocks of society and most social interaction. In fact, even the self evolves from groups. Let's start by talking about the various types and sizes of groups. In his classic work "Quantitative Aspects of the Group," sociologist Georg Simmel (1950) argues that without knowing anything about the group members' individual psychology or the cultural or social context in which they are embedded, we can make predictions about the ways people behave based solely on the number of members, or "social actors," in that group. This theory applies not just to groups of people but also to states, countries, firms, corporations, bureaucracies, and any number of other social forms.

JUST THE TWO OF US

Simmel advances the notion that the most important distinction is that between a relationship of two, which he calls a dyad, and a group of three, which he calls a triad. This is the fundamental distinction between most social relations, he argues, and it holds regardless of the individual characteristics of the group's members. Of course, personality differences do influence social relations, but there are numerous social dynamics about which we can make predictions that have nothing to do with the content of the social relations themselves.

DYAD
a group of two.

TRIAD
a group of three.

Dyads are the foundation of all social relationships. Why are they the most intimate relationship, according to Georg Simmel?

The dyad has several unique characteristics. For starters, it is the most intimate form of social life, partly because the two members of the dyad are mutually dependent on each other. That is, the continued existence of the group is entirely contingent on the willingness of both parties to participate in the group; if either person leaves, the dyad ceases to be. This intimacy is enhanced by the fact that no third person exists to buffer the situation or mediate between the two. Meanwhile, the two members of a dyad don't need to be concerned about how their relationship will be perceived by a third party within the group since there is no third party.

For example, we might consider a couple the most intimate social arrangement in our society. Both people must remain committed to being in the dyad for it to exist, and if one partner leaves, the couple no longer exists. There can be no secrets—if the last piece of chocolate cake disappears and you didn't eat it, you know who did. You could withhold a secret from your dyadic partner, but in terms of the actions of the group itself, no mystery lingers about who performs which role or who did what. Either you did it, or the other person did.

In a dyad, symmetry must be maintained. There might be unequal power relations within a group of two to a certain extent, but Simmel would argue that in a group of two an inherent

symmetry exists because of the earlier stipulation of mutual dependence: The group survives only if both members remain. Even in relationships where the power seems so clearly unequal—think of a master and a servant or a prisoner and his captor—Simmel argues that there's an inherent symmetry. Yes, the servant may be completely dependent on the master for his or her wages, sustenance, food, and shelter, but what happens to the master who becomes dependent on the labor that the servant performs? Of course, forcible relationships might develop in which one of two parties is forced to stay in the dyad, but to be considered a pure dyad, the relationship has to be voluntary. Because a dyad could fall apart at any moment, the underlying social relation is heightened.

The dyad is also unique in other ways. Because the group exists only as long as the individuals choose to maintain it in a voluntary fashion, the group itself exerts no collective influence over the individuals involved. For example, whereas a child might claim, "She made me do it" and shamelessly tell on her older sister, a member of a dyad is less likely to say, "I was just following orders" or "The whole group decided to go see *Mission: Impossible 7*, and I really didn't want to, but I went anyway." The force of a group is much stronger when three or more individuals are part of the group.

Let's take a real-life example of how the characteristics of a dyad play out and see why they matter. Think about divorce. One point in a marriage at which the divorce rate is especially high is when a first child is born (and not just because of the parental sleep deprivation that arrives with a newborn). The nature of the relationship between the two adults changes. They have gone from being a dyad to becoming a triad. Perhaps the parents feel a sudden lack of intimacy, even though the baby is not yet a fully developed social actor. On the flip side, a husband or wife might begin to feel trapped in a marriage specifically because of a child. All of a sudden, group power exists—a couple has evolved into a family, and with that comes the power of numbers in a group.

AND THEN THERE WERE THREE

This brings us to the triad, distinguished by characteristics you can probably infer by now. In a triad, the group itself holds a degree of collective power. In other words, in a group of three or four, I can say, "I'm really unhappy, I hate this place, I hate you, and I'm leaving," but the group will go on. The husband may walk out on his wife and children, but the family he's abandoning still exists. He's ending his participation in the group, but the group will outlast his decision to leave it. Therefore, the group is not dependent on any one particular member.

What's more, in a triad, secrets can exist. Who left the cap off the toothpaste? If more than two people live under the same roof, you can't be sure. Politics is another aspect inherent in a group of three or more. Instead of generating consensus between two individuals, now you have multiple points of view and preferences that need to be balanced. This allows for power politics among the group's members. Simmel refers to three basic forms of political relations that can evolve within a triad depending on what role the entering third party assumes (Figure 5.1). The first role is that of mediator, the person who tries to resolve conflict between the other two and is sometimes brought in for that explicit purpose. A good example would be a marriage counselor. Rather than

go to therapy, couples having marital problems often start a family because they believe a baby will bring them back together. Unfortunately, as most couples come to realize sooner rather than later, a baby cannot play the role of a mediator. Rather, the dynamics of the unhappy family may turn into a game of chicken: Which parent is more devoted to the child? Which dyad forms the core of the group, and which person will be left out or can walk away more easily?

A second possible role for the incoming third member of a triad is that of *tertius gaudens* (Latin for "the third that rejoices"). This individual profits from the disagreement of the other two, essentially playing a role opposite from the mediator's. Someone in this position might have multiple roles. In the previous example, the marriage counselor plays the part of the mediator, but she is also earning her wages from the conflict between the couple. Maybe she encourages continued therapy even after the couple appear to have resolved all their issues, or perhaps she promotes their staying together even though they've already decided to get a divorce.

The third possible role that Simmel identifies for a third party is *divide et impera* (Latin for "divide and conquer"). This person intentionally drives a wedge between the other two parties. This third role is similar to *tertius gaudens*, the difference between the two being a question of intent and whether the rift preexisted. (If you've ever seen or read Shakespeare's *Othello*, there is no better example of *divide et impera* than the way Iago, counselor to Othello, uses the Moor's insecurities to foster a rift between him and his wife, Desdemona, in order to strengthen Iago's own hand in court politics. The play ends tragically, of course.)

To take an example with which millions of Americans are familiar, let's return to the case of the triad formed when a romantic couple has a child but experiences strife and separates. What happens when the couple

In what ways are triads more complex than dyads? What are the possible roles of triad members?

MEDIATOR

the member of a triad who attempts to resolve conflict between the two other actors in the group.

TERTIUS GAUDENS

the member of a triad who benefits from conflict between the other two members of the group.

DIVIDE ET IMPERA

the role of a member of a triad who intentionally drives a wedge between the other two actors in the group.

FIGURE 5.1 Political Relations within a Triad

MEDIATOR

The mediator attempts to resolve conflict between the other two members of the triad and is sometimes brought in for that explicit purpose.

TERTIUS GAUDENS

Latin for "the third that rejoices." This individual profits from the disagreement of the other two actors, essentially playing the opposite role from the mediator.

DIVIDE ET IMPERA

Latin for "divide and conquer." This person intentionally drives a wedge between the other two parties.

divorces? What role does the child play? A child could play any of the roles mentioned above. In the original dyad of the biological parents, the child can be a mediator, forcing his or her parents to work together on certain issues pertaining to his or her care. A child can be "the third who rejoices" from the disagreement of the two, profiting from the fact that he or she might receive two allowances or extra birthday presents because each parent is trying to prove that he or she loves the child more. A complicated *divide et impera* situation could develop if one of the child's parents enters into a second marriage, in which the kid remains the biological child of one parent and becomes the stepchild of the other. In this case, all sorts of politics arise because of the biological connection between the one parent and the child versus the marital-love relationship between the two adults. The relationship between the nonbiological parent and the stepchild, who have the weakest bond, may be difficult. The situation could unfold in any number of ways. Many domestic comedies (think *The Parent Trap*) are based on the premise of a young, angst-ridden prankster playing the role of *divide et impera* between his or her parent and the new stepmother or stepfather.

When contemplating how these theoretical concepts work within actual social interaction, keep in mind that these groups—dyads and triads—don't exist in a vacuum in real life. In discussing the politics of a stepfamily, we're talking about a household where there's a stepparent, a biological parent, and a child. Beyond our textbook example, in real life, this triad probably doesn't function so independently. There is likely another biological parent living elsewhere, maybe another stepparent, maybe siblings. Most social groups are very complex, and we need to take that into consideration when we attempt to determine how they operate. This is why we start with Simmel's purest forms. The interactions that take place in groups of two and three become the building blocks for those in much larger groups.

SIZE MATTERS: WHY SOCIAL LIFE IS COMPLICATED

One key insight is that as the number of people (nodes) in the group increases geometrically ($2 + 1 = 3$; $3 + 1 = 4$; $4 + 1 = 5$), the complexity of analyzing that group's ties (edges) increases exponentially ($2 \cdot 2 = 4$; $4 \cdot 4 = 16$; $16 \cdot 16 = 256$). A two-person group has only one possible and necessary relationship; a tie must exist between the two people for there to be a group. In a triad, a sum of three relationships exists, with each person within the group having two ties. And again, for it to be a group of three, we're not talking about possible connections but actual ones. Each person in the triad has to have two ties—breaking a single tie turns the triad into two dyads. Even if one of the ties between two members is weaker, it is so well reinforced by the remaining two ties that it is unlikely to fade away, a feature known as the "iron law" of the triad, or more technically, "triadic closure." When you move beyond triads to groups of four or more, something different happens. To create a group of four, there must be at least four relationships, but you can have as many as six. Figure 5.2 shows this exponential rise in possible relationships graphically.

In a diagram with four people (A, B, C, and D), we can cross out the diagonals and the group will still exist. Everyone may have only two relationships as opposed to three (the number of possible relationships). A and D might never have spoken to each other, but the group will continue to function. The tendency, however, is for these possible relationships to become actual relationships. You and your roommate are in separate chemistry classes, but your lab partners happen to be roommates. If you both become friendly with your lab partners outside of class, chances are that you will meet your roommate's lab partner and vice versa. Such social ties between friends of the same friend tend to form. This can be good or bad. You may form a study group and, if your roommate's lab partner's boyfriend is a chemist, you (and everyone else) may benefit from his help. On the other hand, if the two break up and you start dating the chemist, it might make future labs a little uncomfortable for your roommate.

FIGURE 5.2 Relationship between Group Size and Complexity

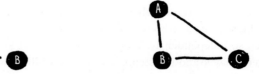

ONE POSSIBLE RELATIONSHIP

THREE POSSIBLE RELATIONSHIPS

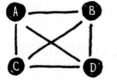

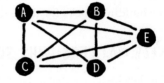

SIX POSSIBLE RELATIONSHIPS

TEN POSSIBLE RELATIONSHIPS

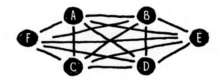

FIFTEEN POSSIBLE RELATIONSHIPS

LET'S GET THIS PARTY STARTED: SMALL GROUPS, PARTIES, AND LARGE GROUPS

SMALL GROUP

a group characterized by face-to-face interaction, a unifocal perspective, lack of formal arrangements or roles, and a certain level of equality.

Groups larger than a dyad or triad, according to Simmel, can be classified into one of three types: small groups, parties, and large groups. A small group is characterized by four factors. The first is *face-to-face interaction*; all the members of the group at any given time are present and interact with one another. They are not spread out geographically. Second, a small group is *unifocal*, meaning that there's one center of attention at any given time. Turn-taking among speakers occurs. A classroom, unless it's divided and engaged in group work, should be unifocal.

Classes usually don't qualify as small groups because a third characteristic of small groups is a *lack of formal arrangements* or *roles*. A study group, though, might qualify if you decide shortly before an exam to meet with some of your classmates. You need to agree on a place and time to meet, but otherwise there is no formal arrangement. In the classroom, however, a professor is in attendance, as are teaching assistants and students—all of whom play official roles in the group. The roles generally encountered in classes also contradict the fourth defining characteristic of a small group,

equality. After all, you won't be giving your professor a grade, nor will she get into trouble, as you might, for arriving late at a planned lecture. Yours isn't a reciprocal and equal relationship. Within a small group, as in a dyad, there is a certain level of equality. Only in a dyad can pure equality exist, because both members hold veto power over the group. However, in a small group, even if the group will continue to exist beyond the membership of any particular member, no particular member has greater sway than the others. No one member can dissolve the group. If someone in your study group gets tired and falls asleep on his book, you and your classmates can continue to study without him.

When does a small group become a party? If you have ever hosted a party, you know that the worst phase is the beginning. You're worried that people might not show up: The party has started, only three people are there (everyone, after all, tends to arrive fashionably late), and you start to wonder, "Is this going to be it?" You have to keep a conversation going among three people; you refill their glasses as soon as they take one sip. If you're drinking alcohol (only if you're of legal drinking age, of course), you may consume more at the beginning of the party because you are nervous about it not going well. When does your small gathering officially evolve into a party, so that you can relax and enjoy yourself? Simmel would say that a party, like a small group, is characterized by face-to-face interaction but differs in that it is *multifocal*. Going back to the example of your sociology study group, if two people begin to talk about Margaret Mead's theory of the self while the rest of you discuss the differences between role conflict and role strain, then it is bifocal; if another subgroup splits off to deliberate on reference groups, then it has become multifocal. According to Simmel, you've got yourself a party! So when you're hosting your next party, you'll recognize when it has officially started.

What makes the study group on the left a small group, and how is it different from the cocktail party on the right?

PARTY

a group that is similar to a small group but is multifocal.

↑

How is this classroom an example of a large group?

LARGE GROUP

a group characterized by the presence of a formal structure that mediates interaction and, consequently, status differentiation.

PRIMARY GROUPS

social groups, such as family or friends, composed of enduring, intimate face-to-face relationships that strongly influence the attitudes and ideals of those involved.

The last type of group to which Simmel makes reference is the large group. The primary characteristic of a large group is the presence of a *formal structure* that mediates interaction and, consequently, *status differentiation*. When you enter a classroom, it should be clear who the teacher is, and you comprehend that she has a higher status than you have in that specific social context.

The professor is an employee of the university, knows more than you know about the subject being taught, and is responsible for assigning you a grade based on your performance in the course. You might be asked to complete a teacher evaluation form at the end of the semester, but it's not the same thing as grading a student. You and your professor aren't equals. The point is that the inherent characteristics of a group are determined not just by its size but also by other aspects of its form, including its formal, bureaucratic structures (if it has any). Whether a group stays small, becomes a party, or evolves into a large group may depend on numbers, but it also may depend on the size and configuration of the physical space or technological platform that mediates interactions between and among group members, preexisting social relationships, expectations, and the larger social context in which the group is embedded.

PRIMARY AND SECONDARY GROUPS

Simmel wasn't the only one who tried to describe the basic types of groups. Sociologist Charles Horton Cooley (1909) emphasized a distinction between what he called primary and secondary groups. Primary groups are *limited in the number of members*, allowing for face-to-face interaction. The group is an end unto itself, rather than a means to an end. This is what makes your family different from a sports team or small business: Sure, you want the family to function well, but you're not trying to compete with other families or manufacture a product. Meanwhile, primary groups are *key agents of socialization*. Most people's first social group is their family, which is a primary group. Your immediate family (parents and siblings) is probably small enough to sit down at the same dinner table or at least gather in the same room at the same time. Loyalty is the primary ethic here. Members of a primary group are *noninterchangeable*—you can't replace your mother or father. And while you have strong allegiances to your friends, your primary loyalty is likely to be to your family. Finally, the relationships within a primary group are *enduring*. Your sister will always be your sister. Another example of a primary group might be the group of your closest friends, especially if you've known each other since your sandbox years.

The characteristics of secondary groups, such as a labor union, stand in contrast to those of primary groups. The group is *impersonal*; you may or may not know all of the members of your union. It's also *instrumental*; the group exists as a means to an end, in this case for organizing workers and representing their interests. In a secondary group, affiliation is *contingent*. You are only a member of your union so long as you hold a certain job and pay your dues. If you change jobs or join another union, your membership in that earlier group ends. Because the members of a secondary group change, the roles are more important than the individuals who fill them. The shop steward, the person chosen to interact with the company's management, may be a different person every year, but that position carries the same responsibilities within the group regardless of who fills it. A sports team is another example of a secondary group, although if you're also close friends with your teammates and socialize with them when you're not playing sports, the line between a primary and secondary group can become blurred.

GROUP CONFORMITY

Although we tend to put a high value on individuality in American culture, our lives are marked by high levels of conformity. That is, groups have strong influences over individual behavior. In the late 1940s the social psychologist Solomon Asch carried out a now-famous series of experiments to demonstrate the power of norms of group conformity. He gathered subjects in a room under the pretense that they were participating in a vision test, showed them two images of lines, and asked which ones were longer than the others and which were the same length (Figure 5.3).

The trick was that only one person in each room was really a research subject; the rest of the people had been told ahead of time to give the same wrong answer. While a majority of subjects answered correctly even after they listened to others give the wrong answer, about one-third expressed serious discomfort—they clearly struggled with what they thought was right in light of what everyone else was saying. Subjects were the most confused when the entire group offered an incorrect answer. When the group members gave a range of responses, the research subjects had no trouble answering correctly. This experiment demonstrates the power of conformity within a group. More troubling instances of group

SECONDARY GROUPS

groups marked by impersonal, instrumental relationships (those existing as a means to an end).

FIGURE 5.3 The Asch Test

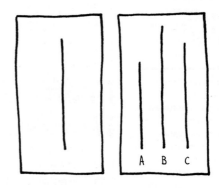

SOURCE: Asch, 1956.

conformity may be seen in cases of collective violence such as gang rape, which tends to occur among tightly knit groups like sports teams or fraternities (Sanday, 1990).

IN-GROUPS AND OUT-GROUPS

IN-GROUP

another term for the powerful group, most often the majority.

OUT-GROUP

another term for the stigmatized or less powerful group, the minority.

In-groups and out-groups are another broad way of categorizing people. The in-group is the powerful group, most often the majority, whereas the out-group is the stigmatized or less powerful group, usually the minority (though the numbers don't have to break down this way). For example, in the United States, heterosexuals are the in-group in terms of sexuality (both more powerful and numerically greater), whereas homosexuals, bisexuals, and those who have other nonnormative sexual identities fall into the out-group. However, in South Africa, despite being a minority group, Whites are the in-group because of their enormous political and economic power (the legacy of colonialism and apartheid), whereas Blacks are the out-group despite their greater numbers. The significance of in-groups and out-groups lies in their relative power to define what constitutes normal versus abnormal thoughts and behavior.

REFERENCE GROUPS

REFERENCE GROUP

a group that helps us understand or make sense of our position in society relative to other groups.

SOCIAL NETWORK

a set of relations— essentially, a set of dyads—held together by ties between individuals.

We often compare ourselves to other groups of people we do not know directly in order to make comparisons. For example, your class might compare itself to another introduction to sociology class, which has a take-home midterm and an optional final. If your class has a 20-page term paper and a two-hour comprehensive final exam, you might feel as if you face an unfair amount of work. If your class has no external assignments, however, and your final grades are based on self-assessment, you might feel comparatively lucky. In either case, the other class serves as a reference group. Reference groups help us understand or make sense of our position in society relative to other groups. The neighboring town's high school or even another socioeconomic class can serve as a reference group. In the first instance, you might compare access to sporting facilities; in the second, you might compare voting patterns.

TIE

the connection between two people in a relationship that varies in strength from one relationship to the next; a story that explains our relationship with another member of our network.

From Groups to Networks

Dyads, triads, and groups are the components of social networks. A social network is a set of relations—a set of dyads, essentially—held together by *ties* between individuals. A tie is the content of a particular relationship.

One way to think about "the ties that bind" is as a set of stories we tell each other that explain a particular relationship. If I ask you how you know a specific person, and you explain that she was your brother's girlfriend in the eighth grade, and the two of you remained close even after her relationship with your brother ended, that story is your tie to that person. For every person in your life, you have a story. To explain some ties, the story is very simple: "That's the guy I buy my coffee from each morning." This is a uniplex tie. Other ties have many layers. They are multiplex: "She's my girlfriend. We have a romantic relationship. We also are tennis and bridge partners. And now that you mention it, we are classmates at school and also fiercely competitive opponents in Trivial Pursuit."

A narrative is the sum of stories contained in a set of ties. Your university or college is a narrative, for example. Every person with whom you have a relationship at your university forms part of that network. For all your college-based relationships—those shared with a professor, your teaching assistant, or classmates—your school is a large part of the story, of the tie. Without the school, in fact, you probably wouldn't share a tie at all. When you add up the stories of all the actors involved in the social network of your school—between you and your classmates, between the professors and their colleagues, between the school and the vendors with whom it contracts—the result is a narrative of what your college is. Of course, you may have other friends, from high school or elsewhere, who have no relationship to your school, so your college is a more minor aspect of those relationships.

In Chapter 4 we talked about the power of symbols. What would you need to do if you wanted to change the name of your school? You and your friends could just start calling it something else. But you'd probably have to hire a legal team to alter the contracts (a form of tie that is spelled out explicitly in a written "story") that the school maintains with all its vendors. You would need to alert alumni and advise the departments and staff at school to change their stationery, their websites, and any marketing materials. You would have to advise faculty to use the new name when citing their professional affiliation. You would need to contact legacy families (let's say a family whose last seven generations have attended this college) and inform them of the name change. Do you now have a sense of how complicated it would be to change this narrative? If you try to make a change that involves a large network, the social structure becomes very powerful. Ironically, something abstract like a name can be more robust than most of the physical infrastructure around us.

EMBEDDEDNESS: THE STRENGTH OF WEAK TIES

One important dimension of social networks is the extent to which they are embedded. Embeddedness refers to the degree to which a social relationship is reinforced through indirect paths (i.e., friends of friends) within a

NARRATIVE
the sum of stories contained in a set of ties.

EMBEDDEDNESS
the degree to which social relationships are reinforced through indirect ties (i.e., friends of friends).

network. The more embedded a tie is, the stronger it is. That is, compared to a relationship with someone whom only you yourself know, a tie to someone who also knows your mother, your best friend, and your teacher's daughter is more likely to last. It may feel less dramatic and intimate, but it's robust and more likely to endure simply by virtue of the fact that it's difficult to escape. You will always be connected to that person—if not directly, then through your "mutual" friends. However, the counterpoint to this dynamic lies in what sociologist Mark Granovetter (1973) calls the strength of weak ties, referring to the fact that relatively weak ties—those not reinforced through indirect paths—often turn out to be quite valuable because they bring novel information. Let's say you're on the track team and that's your primary social group. Occasionally you now see an old classmate from high school whom you didn't really know (or run in the same circles with) back then, because he also attends your college, but he's on the volleyball team. If the track team isn't doing anything on Friday night but the volleyball team is having a party, you've got an "in" through this relationship that's much weaker than the ones you've got with the other members of the track team. That is the strength of the weak tie you maintain with the classmate from home. If you end up taking your friends from the track team to the volleyball party and they become friends with your old friend, the tie between you and your old classmate is no longer weak because it is now reinforced by the ties between your old friend and your new track friends—regardless of whether you are actually more intimate with him or not. This example helps explain why the structure of the network is more complicated than the tie from one individual to another. Even though your friendships did not change at the volleyball party, the fact that people in your social network befriended others in your social network strengthens the ties between you and both of the individuals.

STRENGTH OF WEAK TIES

the notion that relatively weak ties often turn out to be quite valuable because they yield new information.

Small business owners exchanging business cards at a speed networking event. In a limited amount of time, participants hope that making as many weak ties as they can will eventually help them expand and improve their businesses.

The strength of weak ties—as compared to strong, multi-reinforced ties—has been found especially useful in job searches (Granovetter, 1974). In a highly embedded network of strong ties, all the individuals probably know the same people, hear of the same job openings, maintain the same contacts, and so on. However, your grandparents' neighbor, whom you see every so often, probably has a completely different set of connections. The paradox is that this weak tie provides the most opportunities. When Granovetter (1973) interviewed professionals in Boston, he determined that among the 54 respondents who found their employment through personal network ties, more than half saw their contact person "occasionally" (less than once a week but more than once a year). Perhaps even more surprising was the fact that the runners-up in this category were not people whom the respondents saw "often" (once a week or more); it was those they saw "rarely" (once a year or less), by a factor of almost two to one. Additional research finds that weak ties offer the greatest benefits to job seekers who already have high-status jobs, suggesting that social networks combine with credentials to sort job applicants, and that strong ties may be more useful in low-status, low-credential job markets (Wegener, 1991).

As seen in Figure 5.4, by linking two otherwise separate social networks, the weak tie between Natalie and Emily provides new opportunities for dating—not only for them but for their friends as well. Their tie bridges what we call a structural hole between the two cliques, a gap between network clusters, where a possible tie could become an actual tie or where an intermediary could control the communication between the two groups on either side of the hole. In the figure, Jenny is a social entrepreneur bridging a structural hole because the people on the left side of the network diagram (Emily and Jason) have no direct ties with the people on the right (Michael, Doug, and Jeff). Their ties are only indirect, through Jenny. Assuming that the two sides have resources (romantic or otherwise) that would complement each other's, Jenny is in a position to mediate by acting as a go-between for the groups. When a third party connects two groups or individuals

STRUCTURAL HOLE

a gap between network clusters, or even two individuals, if those individuals (or clusters) have complementary resources.

FIGURE 5.4 The Strength of Weak Ties

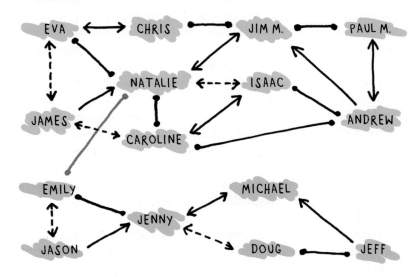

Natalie and Emily are social entrepreneurs; they command information to which the rest of their respective networks do not have access.

DIGITAL.WWNORTON.COM/YOUMAYASK7

To see my interview with Stacy Torres about elastic ties,
go to digital.wwnorton.com/youmayask7

who would be better off in contact with each other, that third party is an "entrepreneur," and he or she can profit from the gap. (Sounds like the *tertius gaudens* in the triad? It should.)

When sociologist Ronald Burt (1992) studied managers in a large corporation, he found that those with the most structural holes in their social networks were the ones who rose through the company ranks the fastest and farthest. This notion can be expanded to explain how a great deal of profit making occurs in today's economy. At one extreme is the totally free market, in which there are no structural holes; no restriction on information exists, and all buyers and sellers can reach one another—think eBay. At the other extreme is the monopoly, in which one firm provides necessary information or resources to a multitude of people (i.e., maintains and profits from a gaping structural hole). And then there is everything in between these extremes: everyone from shipping magnates to spice traders to mortgage brokers to multilevel marketers. Take real estate agents as an example. They earn their money by contractually maintaining (or creating) a structural hole. By signing up sellers, the real estate agents prevent the sellers from directly engaging in a transaction with potential buyers. Recently, the social network possibilities facilitated by the internet (discussed later in this chapter) have done much to erode the power of brokers—for example, by driving once-powerful travel agents into near extinction (ditto for stockbrokers).

Sociologist Stacy Torres noticed a third kind of tie in her ethnography of a New York City elderly population that was "aging in place" (that is, growing old where they had lived for most of their adult lives rather than moving to a retirement destination or some form of supportive housing). These ties that her subjects cultivated were not quite strong, but nor were they weak, exactly. She called them "elastic ties." Here's Torres:

I noticed that there were these relationships [that] filled many of the criteria we associate with these [strong] close ties—that these people spent a lot of time with each other. They helped each other when certain crises emerged, they cared about each other. But when I started to interview people about their relationships with each

ELASTIC TIES

social connections that display the repeated interactions characteristic of strong ties while maintaining a degree of protective social distance (i.e., not knowing more than a first name, if that).

other at the bakery and outside of the neighborhood with family, they often didn't name each other as friends. A lot of times they didn't even know each other's names. They saw each other multiple times a week, multiple times a day, and it took a long time for them to learn each other's names if ever and they didn't know each other's last names. They didn't have a lot of information about each other.

But they would notice if somebody didn't show up to this bakery for a couple of days and they would want to check in on them, or if somebody was in the hospital or had to go to a nursing home, they would visit them. I found that these elastic ties were kind of outside [the framework of] close and weak, and it was a way for these people and this place to meet their needs for connection and closeness and support while maintaining some distance and not having to feel that they were getting overinvolved with people who now were their best friends and they had to visit every day and take care of (Conley, 2019a).

SIX DEGREES

You have probably heard the term *six degrees of separation* and wondered if it is really true that each one of us is connected to every other person by social chains of no more than six people. The evidence supporting the six degree theory came out of research undertaken in the 1960s by Stanley Milgram, whose colleagues were pestering him about why it always seemed like the strangers they met at cocktail parties turned out to be friends of a friend. Milgram decided to test the reach of social networks by asking a stockbroker in Boston to receive chain letters from a bunch of folks living in Lincoln, Nebraska. The Lincolnites could send letters only to friends or relatives whom they believed would be likely to know someone who might know someone who might know the guy in Boston. About 20 percent of the letters eventually made it to Boston, and the average trip length was just over five people, hence the idea that in the United States there are no more than five people between any set of strangers, or six degrees of separation.

DIGITAL.WWNORTON.COM/YOUMAYASK7

To see my interview with Duncan Watts about six degree theory, go to digital.wwnorton.com/youmayask7

Duncan Watts (2003) noticed that Milgram's findings applied only to the letters that made it to their final destination. What about the letters that did not complete the journey? Were their chains quite a bit longer than six steps, thus making our six degree theory more like a twelve degree theory? Watts set up a similar—this time worldwide—experiment using e-mail and statistical models to estimate global connectedness and found that Milgram was not quite right. In Watts's words, "It's not true that everyone is connected to everyone else, but at least half the people in the world are connected to each other through six steps, which is actually kind of surprising" (Conley, 2009b). Furthermore, Watts was able to test the commonsense notion that there are some people out there who just seem to know everyone and that it must be through these superconnected people that the rest of us are able to say we're only six degrees from Kevin Bacon (or whomever). But instead he found that when it comes to whom we know, "the world's remarkably egalitarian," and that superconnectors played almost no role in getting the e-mail forwarded all the way to its destination (Conley, 2009b).

SOCIAL CAPITAL

Having many weak ties is one form of what sociologists call *social capital*. Like human capital, the training and skills that make individuals more productive and valuable to employers, social capital is the information, knowledge of people or things, and connections that help individuals enter preexisting networks or gain power in them. Consider the importance of networking in endeavors such as preventing neighborhood crime or obtaining a good job. As it turns out, the cliché holds a lot of truth: It's not just what you know but whom you know. Weak ties may be the most advantageous for an individual; however, for a community, many dense, embedded ties are generally a sign of high levels of social capital.

This concept makes sense when you think about it. Dense social capital means that people are linked to one another through a thick web of connections. As a result of these connections, they will feel inclined—perhaps even impelled—to help each other, to return favors, to keep an eye on one another's property. The more connections there are, the more norms of reciprocity, values, and trust are shared. After all, there is no such thing as total anonymity: Even if

Neighbors in the Central City section of New Orleans gather for their weekly domino game. Communities with thick webs of connection tend to thrive, with lower crime rates and more volunteer involvement.

you don't know someone directly, chances are that you are only one or two degrees removed from him or her.

In this way, strong social capital binds people together; it weaves them into a tight social fabric that can help a community thrive. "You tell me how many choral societies there are in an Italian region," notes social capital scholar Robert Putnam, "and I will tell you plus or minus three days how long it will take you to get your health bills reimbursed by its regional government" (Edgerton, 1995). After years of research in Italy, Putnam determined that different regions of the country varied widely in their levels of participation in voluntary associations. As it turns out, the strength of participation in a region was a fairly good predictor of the quality and efficiency of its regional government (and, in turn, its economic growth).

The United States and Social Capital If it's true that social capital is correlated with economic and political health, some critics would say that the United States may be in trouble, especially when we compare our recent past with what some see as America's golden age of joining.

In the 1830s, Alexis de Tocqueville wrote *Democracy in America* based on his visit to the United States from France. Tocqueville was surprised to find that America was, in his words, a "land of joiners." By this, Tocqueville meant that Americans frequently came together to join voluntary associations. "Americans of all ages, all conditions, all minds constantly unite," Tocqueville wrote. "Not only do they have commercial and industrial associations in which all take part, but they also have a thousand other kinds: religious, moral, grave, futile, very general and very particular, immense and very small." Tocqueville observed that in democratic societies such as the United States, citizens enjoyed greater equality than citizens in aristocratic societies. Although Tocqueville praised this equality, he also believed that it made democratic citizens independent and weak, so organizations made citizens politically stronger. After all, what good is one vote? He wrote that democratic citizens "can do almost nothing by themselves, and none of them can oblige those like themselves to lend them their cooperation. They therefore all fall into impotence if they do not learn to aid each other freely" (Tocqueville, 1835). Voluntary associations in Tocqueville's land of joiners were a way for independent citizens to assist one another.

The propensity of Americans to join voluntary groups—the Parent Teacher Association at your high school, the local softball league, or a knitting club—has puzzled sociologists, historians, and political scientists since Tocqueville first wrote about America as a land of joiners. Why are Americans so likely to join groups? Our participation in elections and formal political processes is one of the lowest in the world, which makes the question all the more intriguing. Some, like Tocqueville, suggest that the uniquely egalitarian nature of American democracy has made Americans more likely than Europeans to enlist in voluntary organizations (Doyle, 1977). Other

Bowling alone? Although the overall number of bowlers has increased, the number of people bowling in groups has dropped. Are we seeing a decline in social engagement?

scholars suggest that America's unique pattern of settlement is responsible for high levels of voluntary organizations. In particular, the town square culture of early New England, in which people came together in town squares to discuss and debate current civic issues, created a long-lasting culture of voluntary association (Baker, 1997). Still others point to America's identity as a land of immigrants who formed voluntary organizations to unite with other immigrants who shared similar cultural or political values (Gamm & Putnam, 1999).

In recent years, however, voluntary participation in civic life has taken a turn for the worse, and as a result, the nation's stock of social capital is at risk. In his best seller *Bowling Alone: The Collapse and Revival of American Community* (2000), Putnam traces the decline of civic engagement in the last third of the twentieth century. We are more loosely connected today than ever before, he says, experiencing less family togetherness, taking fewer group vacations, and demonstrating little civic engagement.

Indeed, more and more people are bowling alone. Actual bowling activity was on the rise at the end of the twentieth century, when Putnam was writing—the total number of bowlers in America increased by 10 percent from 1988 to 1993—but *league* bowling dropped a whopping 40 percent in the same time frame. Putnam argued that bowling alone is part of a more general trend of civic disengagement and a decline in social capital. It's happening in PTAs, the Red Cross, local elections, community cleanups, and labor unions. Even membership in the Boy Scouts has decreased by 26 percent since the 1970s. More people live alone (Klinenberg, 2012). Some go so far as to say that friendships have become shallower, and the phenomenon of deep, enduring friendships is an increasing rarity (Flora, 2013; Wuthnow, 1998). As civic participation withers, activities once performed by communities have moved toward private markets.

Who's to blame for America's fading civic life? The social entrepreneur who has too many structural holes to maintain? Helicopter parents? Our school systems? The internet? A combination of all these and other factors works in conjunction with broad social trends, creating an increasingly differentiated, specialized, urbanized, and modern world. Social institutions must adjust to the flexibility, sometimes called the liquidity, of modernity by becoming more fragmented, less rigid, and more "porous" (Wuthnow, 1998). It becomes easier to come and go, to pass through multiple social groups such as churches, friends, jobs, and even families. Gone is the rigid fixity of finding and holding on to a lifelong "calling." Similarly, a majority of graduating college students (60 percent) attend more than one school before receiving a degree (Zernike, 2006).

This mobility and flexibility take a toll on people's lives. More than in previous eras, people report feeling rushed, disconnected, and harried, so it's no surprise that civic responsibilities are pushed aside. It's not that Americans don't care. In fact, they join more organizations and donate more money than ever before. They just don't give their time or engage in face-to-face activities (Skocpol, 2004). One possible explanation for this trend is the rise of online associations. We may be showing up less because the internet makes it easy to form new groups whenever we feel the need. It also allows for social connection (of some form) without requiring face-to-face contact. Political activism has moved online as well, with the Donald Trump and Bernie Sanders campaigns leading successful web-based fund-raising efforts that brought new donors into the political process. What's more, after the devastating 2010 Haitian earthquake, the American Red Cross was able to raise more than $22 million through text messaging alone (Strom, 2010); meanwhile, the website gofundme.com has allowed folks to raise a total of $5 billion.

↑

Anthony Fitz poses in front of the historic Malek Theater in Independence, Iowa. Decades after his mother was forced to close the theater in 1996, Fitz created a GoFundMe campaign to raise $150,000 for repairs. Why might crowdfunding— that is, requesting small amounts of money from a large number of people— be more effective than asking face-to-face?

Lastly, before we blame the internet for a decline in social capital and civic life, we should note that the trend toward giving more but showing up less predates the web. It is probably more a result of increased work hours and other pressures to keep up in an age of rising inequality.

The social pendulum swinging between loneliness and unity may be starting to turn back toward togetherness, with slightly different characteristics than we are used to seeing. Sociologist Eric Klinenberg (2013) set out to study people who live alone, trying to understand the costs and benefits of leaving some of the ties that bind dangling free. He found that being old and living alone is indeed a lonely reality and a growing problem for women, who have always tended to outlive their husbands but are now aging alone in neighborhoods that their children have left for jobs and lives elsewhere. But for young and middle-aged people, living alone is a lifestyle frequently filled with friends, dates, coworkers, volunteer work, and plenty of socializing. People who live alone are more likely to volunteer than people the same age who are living with partners or families. Maybe civic participation is not dying, after all.

CASE STUDY:
SURVIVAL OF THE AMISH

Pennsylvania's Lancaster County attracts more than 5 million visitors a year with its Pennsylvania Dutch country charm. Horse-drawn wagons carry visitors over covered bridges toward historic museums, colonial homes, and restaurants. Lancaster thrives on tourists' curiosity about the Amish, who first settled the land in 1693. Today about 59,350 Amish live in nearby homogenous farm communities. As far as appearances go, they certainly meet tourists' expectations.

Wearing straw hats and black bonnets, riding in horse-drawn buggies, the Amish provide great photo opportunities. Children are taught in private schoolhouses, typically one room, only until the eighth grade, at which point they work full-time on the family farm. The lives of the Amish revolve around going to church, tilling the earth, and working for the collective good. They value simplicity

and solidarity. How, visitors wonder, have Amish communities in Pennsylvania and other states survived in our fast-paced society?

The Amish certainly appear to be relics of the past, but looks can be deceiving. Although the Amish place primary importance on agriculture, they do so in anything but a premodern fashion. The Amish, especially those living close to urban areas, have adopted farming innovations such as the use of insecticides and chemically enhanced fertilizers. Their homes are stylishly modern, with sleek kitchens and natural gas–powered appliances.

Because Lancaster County has experienced a certain degree of urban growth and sprawl, the Amish are not immune to the hustle and bustle of commerce. In fact, many Amish are savvy business owners. The number of Amish-owned micro-enterprises more than quadrupled between 1970 and 1990. By 1993 more than one in four Amish homes had at least one nonfarm business owner (Kraybill & Nolt, 1995). The result of this economic growth is a curious mix of profit-seeking entrepreneurship with a traditional lifestyle. Imagine finding out that your local rabbi, priest, or imam doubled as a high-rolling stock trader during the week.

How can these seemingly incompatible spheres of religious tradition and commerce coexist? This is the question Donald Kraybill set out to answer when he studied 150 Amish business entrepreneurs in Lancaster County (1993; in 1995 with Nolt). Not only do the Amish trade with outsiders, Kraybill documented, but they do so

An Amish barn raising in Tollesboro, Kentucky.

quite successfully: About 15 percent of the businesses he studied had annual sales exceeding half a million dollars. Their success rate is phenomenal: Just 4 percent of Amish start-ups fail within a decade, compared with the 75 percent of all new American firms that fail within three years of opening. That is, in a time when the majority of new American business ventures flop, virtually all Amish businesses succeed. Are the Amish just naturally better at conducting commerce? Is it something in their faith, or self-discipline? Perhaps the answer lies in the community's hand-pumped water?

The answer is, none of the above. The secret to Amish success turns out to be the way they strategically combine their traditions with the rest of the modern world. As the Amish have become increasingly entangled in the economic web of contemporary capitalism, they have held on to their cultural traditions by maintaining an ideologically integrated and homogenous community. They are distinctly premodern and un-American in that they believe in the subordination of the individual to the community. They have rejected the prevalent American culture of rugged individualism, the notion of "every man for himself," often said to be the basis for successful entrepreneurship, in favor of "every man for the greater good." Individuals are expected to submit not only to God but also to teachers, elders, and community leaders. Their social fabric firmly binds people together. Whereas fashion for many people is a means of self-expression, the dark, simple clothing of the Amish signals membership in and subordination to the community. They have no bureaucratic forms of government or business; rather, they operate in a decentralized, loose federation of church districts. They reject mass media and automobiles and limit their exposure to diverse ideas and lands. The outcome is homogeneity of belief, unified values, and not surprisingly, dense social capital. Amish businesses, like

Kimberly Hamme works on billing for her online business, Plainly Dressed, in her Paradise Town, Pennsylvania, home office. Hamme sells what most people would call Amish clothing. She does most of her business over the internet.

the people themselves, are tightly enmeshed in social networks, such as church and kinship systems, that provide economic support. The typical Amish person has more than 75 first cousins, most of whom shop in the same neighborhood. Add to that the taboo on bankruptcy within the community, and Amish businesses would be a dream come true for investors—that is, if the Amish were to accept outside capital (they don't).

Rather than marvel at how this culture maintains its centuries-old traditions while functioning in the business world, we should look at how they succeed in business regardless of being Amish. Kraybill and Nolt found that the cultural restraints of being Amish do indeed thwart business opportunity to some extent. Amish business owners aren't allowed to accept financial capital from outsiders or to prosecute shoplifters (to do so would single out lawbreakers and go against community solidarity). The success of Amish entrepreneurship is a telling example of the power of social capital.

Volunteers build an elementary school playground in New Orleans. After Hurricane Katrina devastated the Gulf Coast in 2005, thousands of college volunteers participated in the rebuilding efforts.

Understandably, Putnam's claims have ignited much controversy. Some researchers have noted that even if an increase in participation occurred after 9/11, it was short-lived among adults (Sander & Putnam, 2010). Others claim the opposite, insisting that social capital never declined as Putnam declared. Rather, it has simply become more informal. Wuthnow, for example, argues that modernization brings about new forms of "loose connection" but hardly a disappearance of all connection. Nor does it necessarily follow that modern Americans are any worse off than when connections were tight. Things change, but that does not always mean they change for the worse. Though Putnam laments the loss of face-to-face communal ties, in the past three decades we've witnessed an explosion of non-place-based connections: Think of the rich social life occurring on social media, including Twitter, blogs, and Facebook.

With the exit of the old (such as the Elks, Rotary, and other fraternal and civic organizations), new kinds of clubs have come in—large national groups, including netroots political groups such as MoveOn.org, which one can join by mail or online, and informal support groups like WW (formerly Weight Watchers) and hybrids like Meetup.com, where interest groups form online but then meet face-to-face. Furthermore, the trend of declining social capital is falsely described as linear, as if from the 1970s to today civic society has moved in one simple direction (downhill). It is more probable that civic engagement moves like a pendulum, swinging back and forth between privatism (as in the 1920s) and heightened public consciousness (as in the 1930s). Right now it may feel like the end of social capital, but perhaps we're just at a low point on a constantly shifting trend line. The calls to save social capital may be a form of projected nostalgia, a misplaced romanticizing of the past.

Sociologist Michael Gaddis has been using network structure to look at another challenging aspect of social capital: Even for people with a healthy number of ties to friends, family, and community, not all social capital is equal. As Gaddis points out, "Everyone knows friends, coworkers, family members, but the important part of social capital . . . is the resources that are linked to you through these networks. Do I know someone who knows someone who has a job opening and could refer me? Can I access those resources?" He looked at kids growing up in "low-income families, one-parent families" who applied to the Big Brothers Big Sisters program, where they hoped to be assigned an adult mentor with whom to spend time. Because of high demand, only some students got

DIGITAL.WWNORTON.COM/YOUMAYASK7

To see my interview with Michael Gaddis about the impact of social networks on low-income children, go to digital.wwnorton.com/youmayask7

to participate, making it possible for Gaddis to compare students who got mentors with those who wanted them but were not able to get them. It turned out that "mentors with higher education levels, higher income" were "able to make greater changes" among the little brothers and sisters (Conley, 2013b). It is not how many people you know that gives you greater social capital but the resources associated with the people you know, and their willingness to share those resources with you.

The picture we've arrived at is that of a complex social world where the decay of some forms of civic life is accompanied by the eventual emergence of new ways of building communities. Americans living in modern, urban, anonymous, and loosely connected communities carve out new social spaces, in turn creating a different kind of social fabric that holds together our republic. People adapt to what's new, retain what they can of the old, and negotiate within global forces and local communities.

Network Analysis in Practice

Researchers take the concepts we've discussed so far—embeddedness, the iron law of the triad, and network position—and apply them to real-world contexts in order to understand how group life shapes individual behavior. Network analysts also map out social relationships to better understand transmission phenomena such as the spread of disease, the rise and fall of particular fads, the genesis of social movements, and even the evolution of language itself.

THE SOCIAL STRUCTURE OF TEENAGE SEX

According to sociologists Lisa Wade (2017) and Kathleen Bogle (2008), "hooking up" has replaced going steady on campus; "friends with benefits" are preferred over girlfriends and boyfriends, with all their attendant demands and the corresponding commitment (see Chapter 8). On the other hand, Wade also reports that about one-third of college students do not (or cannot) participate in this romantic culture on campus. In fact, the proportion of teens and young adults who are not having sex at all has risen across the globe in recent years (*Economist*, 2018b).

Here are some nationally representative numbers for the United States: About 50 percent of American teenagers over the age of 15, when interviewed by researchers, have admitted to engaging in sexual intercourse. (Boys probably tend to exaggerate their sexual experience, and girls probably downplay it.) A good number of those who have not yet had intercourse are still sexually active in other ways: Approximately one-third have "had genital contact with a partner resulting in an orgasm in the past year." Bluntly put, what this means is that a good two-thirds of American teens are having sex or participating in some form of sexual activity. Teenagers' romantic relationships tend to be short-term compared with adults', averaging about 15 months, so there is a fair amount of partner trading. Survey research among students in college, where hook-up culture is prevalent, found that 70 percent use condoms when they engage in vaginal/penile intercourse. That 70 percent is "a lot less than a hundred, but a lot more than zero," notes principal investigator Paula England (Conley, 2009d). To top that off, most adolescents with a sexually transmitted infection "have no idea that they are infected." All of these factors combine to make American teenagers a breeding ground for sexually transmitted infections, which have increased dramatically in this age group in the last decade.

So what's a public health officer to do? During the administration of George W. Bush, the religious right and conservative policy makers suggested the "virginity pledge" and other abstinence policies as a solution. As it turns out, the pledge does delay the onset of sexual activity on average, but when the teenagers who take it

Despite sensational media reports about teenage hook-ups, monogamous couples such as the one featured below are more typical. What else does research reveal about high-school sexual relationships?

FIGURE 5.5 Analysis of High-School Sexual Relationships

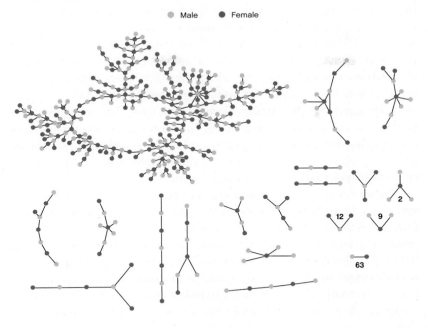

○ Male   ● Female

SOURCE: Bearman et al., 2004.

eventually do have sex, they are much more likely to practice unsafe sex (Bearman & Brückner, 2001; Brückner & Bearman, 2005). Among the many problems in designing safe-sex or other programs to reduce the rate of STIs among teenagers is the fact that we knew very little about the sexual networks of American adolescents until quite recently. It would not be far off to say that we knew more about the sexual networks of Aboriginal tribes on Groote Eylandt than we did about those of American teenagers.

One component of the National Longitudinal Survey of Adolescent Health, conducted by J. Richard Udry, Peter Bearman, and others from 1994 to 1996, investigated the complete sexual network at 12 high schools across the nation, including the pseudonymous Jefferson High School, whose 1,000-person student body is depicted in Figure 5.5 (Bearman et al., 2004). They focused their analysis on Jefferson because its demographic makeup, although almost all White, is fairly representative of most American public high schools and, more important, it is in a fairly isolated town, so less chance exists of the sexual networks spilling over to other schools.

The pink dots represent girls and the green ones boys. The dyad in the lower right-hand corner tells us that there are 63 couples in which the partners have only had sex with each other. There are small, comparatively isolated networks consisting of 10 or fewer people, and then one large ring that encompasses hundreds of students. Preventing the transmission of infection in the small networks is much simpler than preventing the spread in the large ring. One young man in the ring has had nine partners, but even if you persuaded him to use condoms or practice abstinence, you still wouldn't address most of the network. Your action might positively impact the people immediately around him. But to the extent other origin points of infection exist within the network, it is going to be very difficult to stop transmission. One practice that would slow the spread of STIs is lengthening the gap between partners: Sleeping with more than one person at a time increases the rate of transmission. The fuzzy ring structure represents a type of network called a circular spanning tree—a spanning tree being one of four ideal types of sex networks hypothesized by Bearman and other epidemiologists (scientists who study the spread of diseases).

Figure 5.6 illustrates the four different possible models of contact and spread for STIs. Panel A shows a core infection model, where the dark, filled-in circles representing infected people are all connected to this core group. Therefore, the infection circulates through everyone in the group, but they're also connected outward to other partners. If you mapped out a sexual network like this, with the objective of stopping diseases from being sexually transmitted, you would try to isolate that core network and either cut them off from sexual relations with others or at least ensure that when they came into contact with uninfected partners, they practiced safe sex. Panel B shows a possible structural hole. Imagine an infected group and an uninfected group, but one person bridges them. Theoretically, such a

FIGURE 5.6 Models for Spread of Sexually Transmitted Infections

Panel A: core infection model

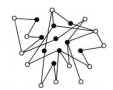

Panel C: inverse core model

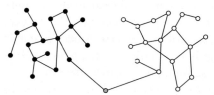

Panel B: bridge between
disjointed populations

Panel D: spanning tree

SOURCE: Bearman et al., 2004.

circumstance is fairly easy to address, in that all you have to do is cut the tie or persuade that one person to engage in safe sex, and you will have protected the uninfected population. Panel C depicts an inverse core model, representing the way much of AIDS transmission occurs in populations where men routinely spend long periods of time away from their families, such as long-haul truckers and some men from African villages. The traveling men visit prostitutes in the city or at truck stops, acquire the virus from one, transmit it to another, and then bring the virus back home. The infected members are not connected directly with one another (i.e., the prostitutes are not having sex with each other); rather, the individuals at the periphery of the core (the men who solicit the prostitutes) connect the core members to each other and possibly beyond the group to other populations. The last network model, illustrated in panel D, is the spanning tree model, in linear rather than circular form. This is essentially how power grids are laid out: There's a main line, and branches develop off of that line. It is difficult to completely stop transmission along a spanning tree model. That's why we design electrical grids to be a series of spanning trees so that if one circuit fails the power can continue to flow around it, although as anyone who has experienced a blackout knows, specific sections can be left without power if they are severed from the rest of the tree. In terms of STI transmission, you could initiate some breaks that would split the tree into two groups, but that's not going to completely isolate the infection. If you attack something on a branch, you're not doing anything to the rest of the network. There's no key focal point that allows you to stop the spread.

ROMANTIC LEFTOVERS

When Bearman and his colleagues analyzed the sexual habits of teenagers, they uncovered another rule that governed this social network. They found lots of examples of triads, where partners are traded within groups. But the main rule that seemed to govern these relationships was "no cycles of four," which means you do not date the ex of your ex's current boyfriend or girlfriend. The most interesting aspect of the rule, sociologically speaking, is that no one was consciously aware of this pattern. The researchers interviewed many students and not one of them directly stated, "Of course not, you don't date the ex of your ex's new flame." Yet it's the single taboo that governs everyone. Figure 5.7 illustrates this rule of thumb graphically.

At time 1, Matt and Jennifer are dating, as are Jareem and Maya. At time 2, Jennifer and Jareem date. The rule suggests that Matt and Maya will never date. Why is that? Once Jennifer and Jareem start dating, if Matt and Maya decide to date each other, they are relegating themselves to secondary social status, as if they were "leftovers." The practical, take-home lesson in all of this is that if you want to date the ex of your ex's new crush, act before your ex does. If you're Jennifer and you wish to prevent your old boyfriend Matt

FIGURE 5.7 Romantic "Leftovers"

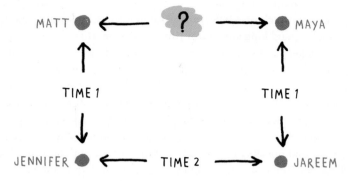

SOURCE: Bearman et al., 2004.

from going out with Maya, quickly start dating Jareem, because then Maya and Matt will never date. But extend the "no seconds" rule to thirds or more, and the taboo erodes. The fact that no students in the high school studied were aware of the rule is what makes this kind of social norm possible: It's not conscious. This is a good example of how social structures govern individual-level behavior, and it speaks to some of the limitations of interpretive sociology. If the researchers had taken a more Weberian approach and asked students how they choose partners and, more important, why they don't date certain people, they probably wouldn't have discovered this rule. The researchers could see it only by taking a bird's-eye view and analyzing this structure with mathematical tools.

Organizations

I've mentioned several times that sociology—here network analysis—can be applied not just to individuals but to all social actors, which may include school systems, teams, states, and countries. In the contemporary United States, companies and organizations are important social actors. In fact, thanks to the Fourteenth Amendment, they have identities as legal persons: They sponsor charitable causes; they can sue and be sued; they even have birthdays.

Organization is an all-purpose term that can describe any social network—from a club to a Little League baseball team to a secret society to your local church to General Motors to the US government—that is defined by a common purpose and has a boundary between its membership and the rest of the social world. *Formal* organizations have a set of governing structures and rules for their internal arrangements (the US Army, with its ranks and rules), whereas *informal* organizations do not (the local

ORGANIZATION

any social network that is defined by a common purpose and has a boundary between its membership and the rest of the social world.

Meetup.com group for ambidextrous tennis players [an actual group!]). Of course, a continuum exists, because no organization has absolutely no rules, and no organization has a rule for absolutely everything. Therefore, the study of organizations focuses mainly on the social factors that affect organizational structure and the people in those organizations.

ORGANIZATIONAL STRUCTURE AND CULTURE

Have you ever heard the phrase *the old boys' club*? The term is used to refer to exclusive social groups and derives from fraternities, businesses, and country clubs that allow only men—specifically, certain groups of elite men—to join. These groups have their own customs, traditions, and histories that make it difficult for others to join and feel as if they belong, even when the "boys" aren't being deliberately hostile. The term organizational culture refers to the shared beliefs and behaviors within a social group and is often used interchangeably with *corporate culture*. The organizational culture at a slaughterhouse—where pay is low, employees must wear protective gear, the environment is dangerous, and animals are continuously being killed—is probably very different from the organizational culture at a small, not-for-profit community law center. The term organizational structure refers to how power and authority are distributed within an organization. The slaughterhouse probably has a hierarchical structure, with a clear ranking of managers and supervisors who oversee the people working the lines. The law center, however, might be more decentralized and cooperative, with five partners equally co-owning the business and collaborating on decisions. How an organization is structured often affects the type of culture that results. If a business grants both parents leave when a new child enters the home, allows for flextime or telecommuting, or has an on-site child-care center, those structural arrangements will be much more conducive to creating a family-friendly organizational culture than those of a company that doesn't offer such benefits.

The growth of large multinational corporations over the course of the last 100 years has affected organizational structure. One example of this impact can be seen in *interlocking directorates*, the phenomenon whereby the members of corporate boards often sit on the board of directors for multiple companies. In 2013, for example, the boards of insurance companies such as AIG, Humana, MetLife, and Travelers frequently had board members who also served on the board of drug and medical device makers such as Johnson & Johnson, DuPont, Abbott Laboratories, and Dow Chemical. (The website theyrule.net allows you to create an interactive map of companies' and institutions' boards of directors.) Does it matter that these people sit together on the same boards? The problem, critics argue, is that we then allow a select group of people—predominantly rich, White men—to control the decisions made in thousands of companies. Such people also have ties to research institutions and elected officials that may compromise their objectivity and create conflicts of

ORGANIZATIONAL CULTURE

the shared beliefs and behaviors within a social group; often used interchangeably with *corporate culture*.

ORGANIZATIONAL STRUCTURE

the ways in which power and authority are distributed within an organization.

interest. Capitalism, after all, is based on competition, but if board members on interlocking directorates favor the other companies to which they are connected, suppliers may not be competing on a level playing field when bidding for contracts. Or worse, take the situation that might develop when a board member of a drug maker asks his friend and fellow board member at a health insurance company to give preferential coverage to his company's drugs over a competitor's drugs. This can lead to higher prices for consumers who need to purchase the competitor's drugs. Another situation might arise in which one of these two board members knows a former member of Congress through board service together whom they can use as a lobbyist to see that federal health programs like Medicare and Medicaid also give preferential treatment to a particular drug, costing taxpayers more than they would have paid without the pressure arising from these relationships. This type of situation can lead to what sociologist C. Wright Mills called a "power elite" or aristocracy. (Concern over the consolidation of control in the media industry, for example, is discussed in Chapter 3.)

INSTITUTIONAL ISOMORPHISM: EVERYBODY'S DOING IT

Networks can be very useful. They provide information, a sense of security and community, resources, and opportunities, as we saw illustrated by Granovetter's concept of weak ties. Networks can also be constraining, however. Paul DiMaggio and Walter Powell (1983), focusing on businesses, coined the phrase *institutional isomorphism* to explain why so many businesses that evolve in very different ways still end up with such similar organizational structures. Isomorphism, then, is a "constraining process that forces one unit in a population to resemble other units that face the same set of environmental conditions" (Hawley, 1968). In regard to organizations, this means that those facing the same conditions (say, in industry, the law, or politics) tend to end up like one another.

ISOMORPHISM

a constraining process that forces one unit in a population to resemble other units that face the same set of environmental conditions.

Let's consider a hypothetical case: A new organization enters a fairly established industry but wants to approach it differently. Perhaps it is a bank that wants to distinguish itself from other banks by being more casual or more community-oriented. The theory of isomorphism suggests that such a bank, when all is said and done, will wind up operating as most other banks do. It's locked into a network of other organizations and therefore will be heavily influenced by the environment of that network. The same is true for new networks of organizations. A group of not-for-profits might spring up in a specific area. Because all will face the same environmental conditions, they will likely be, in the final analysis, more similar than different, no matter how diverse their origins. DiMaggio and Powell are part of a school of social theory referred to as the new institutionalism, which essentially tries to develop a sociological view of institutions (as opposed to, say, an economic view). In this vein, networks of connections among institutions are key to understanding how the institutions look and behave. These theorists would argue that all airlines raise and lower their fares at the same time, for example, not because they are independently reacting to pure market forces but because symmetry, peer pressure, social signaling, and network laws all govern the organizational behavior of these Fortune 500 companies to the same extent that these forces affect the sex lives of seniors at Jefferson High School. Pretty scary, huh?

POLICY

RIGHT TO BE FORGOTTEN

When I was in high school, I thought I would try to be cool and up my social status by swiping a bottle of my father's booze and bringing it along on a school trip. I had little experience with this sort of activity, so I just grabbed whatever I saw. My plan backfired: It turned out that I had stolen dry vermouth, typically used only in minute amounts for mixing martinis or Manhattans. I had no idea that vermouth was not something generally drunk straight. (Though, in an ironic twist, it turns out that it is actually quite sophisticated to have it alone with an orange peel, I have since learned.) The moment after I whispered conspiratorially to one of the cool kids that I had booze and showed him the bottle in my possession, laughter spread across the chartered bus. For the rest of my high-school career, I was labeled "vermouth man."

Thankfully for me, I went to college 3,000 miles away where almost no others from my high school attended, so I was able to reinvent myself. Today, however, with social media, almost everything teenagers do is recorded for posterity, leaving digital traces. (This is one of the main changes to adolescent social life documented by danah boyd; see my interview with her in Chapter 2.) College counselors tell students to set their privacy settings on the most strict level when it's application season. Students themselves often use "senior names" on social media to disguise their real identities. These solutions to the privacy problem don't always work. Just ask the 10 students who had their admissions to Harvard revoked when it was revealed that they had shared sexually explicit and racially offensive memes within their "Harvard memes for horny bourgeois teens" Facebook group (Natanson, 2017).

But even if these short-term fixes work, what about the rest of their lives? A dumb or offensive comment that makes it onto a website or an embarrassing party photo that tags you might trail you like a digital ball and chain each time you try to apply for a new job or date a new suitor. Is there a right to be forgotten just like the right to free speech or the right to a trial by one's peers?

The European Commission seems to think so. The EU has drafted regulations guaranteeing the right to "obtain from the controller [i.e., the data collector or manager, such as a search engine or online database] the erasure of personal data relating to them and the abstention from further dissemination of such data, especially in relation to personal data which are made available by the data subject while he or she was a child or where the data is no longer necessary for the purpose it was collected for, the subject withdraws consent, the storage period has expired, the data subject objects to the processing of personal data or the processing of data does not comply with other regulation." What this—and the results of a lawsuit against Google in Spanish court—essentially means is that search engine firms now provide

Should there be a universal "right to be forgotten"? What are some arguments for, and some arguments against, data erasure on social networking websites?

Europeans with a form they can fill out to request removal of links to information they'd rather not have out there, so to speak. The "right to be forgotten" is now considered a fundamental human right in some jurisdictions.

Sounds reasonable, no? Why should this generation enjoy any less privacy than prior ones just because technology has changed? Well, not so fast. As with almost any "right," there are competing interests. Does your right to be forgotten trump my right to know about you as a potential employer, neighbor, or boyfriend? Where does it end if we allow whitewashing of historical records? While we might all agree that revenge porn should be banned, what about links to bad reviews? Or even tags by former flames in photos that are searchable but might upset our new partners? The line is hard to draw. Perhaps, like sealed criminal records, the age of maturity should be used to wipe the slate clean? What about material that is moved to jurisdictions that have looser laws (like the United States, which privileges free speech to a greater extent than Europe does)? The global reach of the internet's many-headed hydra makes it hard to slice off one head of information without another popping up elsewhere.

While this battle between privacy advocates and free-speech diehards is likely to be fought out for many years on multiple fronts, one thing is certain: The changing nature of social media and online networks means it's probably better to think more carefully about swiping a bottle of booze than I did back in the dark ages of 1985.

Conclusion

What do we learn from the formal analysis of group characteristics and social networks? Simply knowing the formal characteristics of a group helps us understand much of the social dynamics within it. Is it a dyad or a triad? What is the proper reference group for a particular social process? Is this group a primary or secondary group—and what does that mean for my obligations to it? Likewise, we can use network analysis in micro- and macro-level studies. You could carefully weigh the potential consequences of dating your best friend's ex by mapping out your social network and anticipating shifts in ties that might transpire. Or you could analyze President Richard Nixon's strategy of "triangulation" of the Soviet Union and Communist China during the early 1970s using the iron law of the triad. Sociologists use network analysis to study everything from migration to social movements to cultural fads to global politics.

QUESTIONS FOR REVIEW

1. Cryptocurrencies such as bitcoin rely on a technology called "blockchain": every transaction between any two individuals is recorded in a public ledger. How does this illustrate the concept of embeddedness?

2. What are some of the benefits, problems, and obstacles to implementing a right to be forgotten on the web?

3. If getting a job is all about connections, how does the work on the strength of weak ties round out our understanding of this phenomenon? How does nepotism (hiring family members) fit into this discussion?

4. An undecided voter who knows little about the political candidates reads the result of the latest poll on voting day and sees that other voters seem inclined to choose one of the candidates. According to Asch's work on conformity, how might the poll affect the voter's behavior? Do you think media sources should release polls shortly before an election?

5. If you could choose your position in a social network, would you want to bridge a structural gap? Why might the manager of a company try to prevent the development of structural gaps between the company's various departments? Would a high-school nurse be more likely to encourage or discourage structural gap formation?

6. What is an organizational structure? Describe the organizational structure at your school or workplace and determine how this structure might affect the organizational culture.

7. A new coffee shop opens in your neighborhood, which already has two other coffee shops. The new coffee shop offers free internet access to customers. Within a few weeks, the two other shops offer free internet access as well. Explain how this example might illustrate Paul DiMaggio and Walter Powell's concept of institutional isomorphism.

8. You live in an apartment in a medium-sized city. There is a blackout that lasts for weeks. When, how, and why do you call on your strong, weak, and elastic ties?

PRACTICE

HOW TO DISAPPEAR

In 1995, on a red eye to Poland, I fell asleep and had my passport stolen. For all I know, there is another Dalton Conley with my papers who is still off drinking vodka and eating kielbasa. That happened before RFID chips, computerized global databases, and biometrics. Today, it would be a lot harder for me to mimic what my thief did—that is, either disappear or assume a new identity. Back then, records of documents were more easily falsified and one didn't leave digital traces with every trip to the supermarket. Before 9/11, you could even check into a hotel with no ID. But in today's hyperconnected world, it's much harder to fall off the grid.

TRY IT!

Let's say you wanted to disappear. What are the steps you'd take to drop off the face of the earth—at least according to the social networks in which you're embedded? Here are the steps I would take:

Sell all my worldly possessions for cash on Craig's List

↓

Buy a burner phone

↓

**Hitchhike to Mexico (certain border crossings
don't check ID in that direction)**

↓

Learn Spanish

↓

Find a job picking fruit

↓

Never contact anyone from my prior life ever again

THINK ABOUT IT

Disappearing doesn't just mean shutting down your social media and saying good-bye to your friends. How would you actually function in society if you had to be completely on the DL—invisible to banks, the government, and every other institution?

SOCIOLOGY ON THE STREET

How have social media significantly changed the number and strength of our weak ties? Watch the Sociology on the Street video to find out more: **digital.wwnorton.com/youmayask7**.

WANT MORE PRACTICE?

Complete the InQuizitive activity for this chapter at digital.wwnorton.com /youmayask7

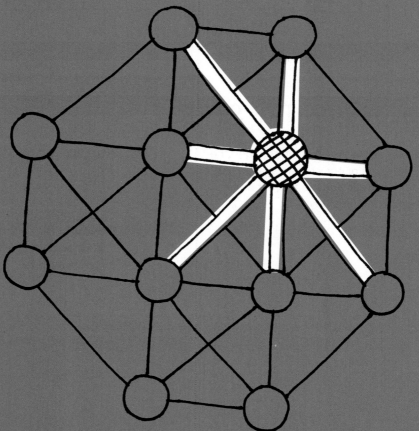

PARADOX

6

IT IS THE DEVIANTS AMONG US WHO HOLD SOCIETY TOGETHER.

Animation at digital.wwnorton.com/youmayask7

Social Control and Deviance

Smiley got his nickname because he always smiled at the most improbable times. When teachers yelled at him because he had trouble paying attention, he smiled. When his smile upset the teachers and incited more yelling, he kept smiling. When he and a friend broke into a car for a place to sleep after his abusive parents kicked him out, he smiled. He was surely smiling at the pretty girls with lipstick-reddened lips and pompadours whom he and a couple of homies decided to visit in the neighborhood of a rival gang. He was likely still smiling when eight rival gang members showed up, bringing guns to what might have been a fistfight. Smiley was shot in the head. His homie Victor scooped him off the pavement, bits of fresh brain matter clinging to his new sneakers. Victor cradled the dying Smiley in the backseat on the way to the emergency room; there was no time to wait for an ambulance that might never show up at their ghetto address.

When the police arrived at the hospital, they assigned partial blame to Victor, threatening to charge him as an accessory to murder for being present at the scene. Victor, in anger and disbelief, instead demanded that the police find the real shooter. "What for?" one of them replied. "We want you to kill each other off."

Homeboy Victor is now Associate Professor Victor Rios at the University of California, Santa Barbara. The other 67 homies from the original gang have not had Victor's success: 4 were murdered; 9 were permanently injured, most with handguns; 12 became addicted to drugs, sometimes living on the streets and panhandling to survive. Just 2 graduated from high school; only Victor went on to college. If it is surprising that Victor, a gang-member son of a single mother on welfare in an impoverished neighborhood, made it into one of the most heavily credentialed occupations, what does that tell us about the relationship between deviance and social mobility?

Because Victor is now a sociologist, I asked him what he has to say about getting out of the ghetto and into the ivory tower. "A lot of times people say to me, 'Oh, Professor Rios, you're so unique. You have all these qualities, you made it out. You pulled yourself up by the bootstrap. You made it out of the ghetto and now you are here.' And my response is, 'Well, part of it is hard work, but everyone works hard.' For example, my mom, she's washed dishes 30 years of her life, working 10 hours a day, and she still makes 10, 11 dollars an hour. That's hard work. But she never progressed." He argues that hard work is not enough; there must be an opportunity trajectory leading out of poverty.

Victor clearly recalls when he started to recognize systemwide short-comings: "I was fortunate to find a teacher that cared, and she heard what happened [to Smiley], and she reached out to me and got me mentors from the university—students, college students, that wanted to go help the ghetto kids." These students provided enlightenment through the sociological imagination; they helped Victor see that there was a system at work larger than himself, larger even than his community: "I was actually living in a world of poverty that wasn't necessarily just produced by the way that people in my community acted, but it was also produced by a larger system of racism, classism, and segregation" (Conley, 2009e).

In his book *Punished: Policing the Lives of Black and Latino Boys* (2011), Rios examines the way the current aggressive policing strategies have effectively criminalized young boys in poor neighborhoods. Police and parole officers are stationed in schools and community centers, the spaces in which education and mentoring traditionally occur, creating a self-fulfilling prophecy where teens are assumed to be criminals, treated with suspicion bordering on aggression, and watched closely until caught in some criminal act. Is flooding crime-ridden neighborhoods with aggressive policing the right thing to do? Or does sending more police to a neighborhood where criminal activity is concentrated simply increase the number of people who get caught, closing routes out of that neighborhood by saddling its residents with criminal records?

The goal of this chapter is to examine how society coheres and why some people transgress the boundaries of normality. For starters, how do people who presumably started life as innocent little kids end up in prison? How did Rios, an impoverished gang member growing up amid

DIGITAL.WWNORTON.COM/YOUMAYASK7

To see my interview with Victor Rios, author of *Punished*, go to **digital.wwnorton.com/youmayask7**

violence and theft, end up getting a PhD and becoming a professor? We can then turn to broader questions: Why doesn't society at large look like the violence-ridden Oakland, California, neighborhood of Victor's youth? Why do most of us choose to sacrifice some of our personal interests for the sake of the social whole? How can we explain how society achieves predictable order, and what role does the criminal justice system play? Theorists of social deviance have produced various answers to these questions.

What Is Social Deviance?

Social deviance, loosely understood, can be taken to mean any transgression of socially established norms. It can be as minor as farting in church or as serious as murder, so long as it consists of breaking the rules by which most people abide. Minor violations are acts of informal deviance, such as picking your nose. Even if no one will punish you, you sense it is somehow wrong. At the other end of the continuum, we have formal deviance, or crime, which is the violation of laws enacted by society. When deviant persons are caught in deviant acts, depending on the seriousness of the offense, they are subject to punishment. For instance, farting in church might result in glares from your fellow churchgoers, whereas a crime like theft may result in formal state-sanctioned punishments such as fines or community service, or for more severe violations, imprisonment, death, or even torture.

Because social norms and rules are fluid and subject to change, the definitions of what counts as deviance are likely to vary across contexts. Even seemingly obvious cases of deviance, such as killing another person, may not be so clear upon further investigation. When a soldier kills an enemy combatant, that act is considered heroic. But if the same soldier kills his or her spouse, the act is considered heinous and punishable by a long prison sentence. Persons and behaviors have been variously called deviant, depending on what culture and historical period they happen to fall in. When women engaged in premarital sex in the Puritan colonies, they were subject to social exile; when women do so today in some Islamic countries, they risk public execution by stoning. In contemporary American society, however, sex outside of marriage is common and largely accepted. Similarly, 50 years ago, it was a crime for African Americans to share water fountains and swimming pools with White citizens; most people would consider such legislation unthinkable bigotry today. Just four decades ago, homosexuality was illegal nationwide. Gay bars were frequent targets of police raids, and sexual orientation was grounds for excluding immigrants (a rule that held until the Immigration Act of 1990; Foss, 1994). As recently as 2003, the US Supreme Court struck down Texas's criminalization of homosexual sex in *Lawrence v. Texas*; before the ruling, it was punishable by arrest and a $500

SOCIAL DEVIANCE

any transgression of socially established norms.

CRIME

the violation of laws enacted by society.

fine. Changes in laws signal shifting social values and changes in social norms, such as increased tolerance of sexual and racial diversity.

In the popular conception, deviance typically takes the form of blatant rule-breaking or lawlessness. But deviance does not necessarily require outlandish activity on the part of social misfits. Deviance is a broad concept covering everything from answering your cell phone during a lecture to murder. Both formal deviance and informal deviance are collectively defined and often subject to a range of punishments. For example, transgender persons—those who do not have a categorical masculine or feminine identity—are often subject to informal and formal punishments for their gender deviance, although most are perfectly law-abiding citizens. The same goes for ethnic minorities, people who bike down crowded city streets, and those who sing along with their smartphones on the subway or bus. Even reserved, soft-spoken people, if they find themselves in a noisy crowd, may learn that because their behavior goes against the grain, they become, for the moment, social deviants. Yet deviance is sticky; it cannot be turned off and on so easily. Deviance can be a powerful label, capable of reproducing the entrenched social inequalities that punishment is often supposed to correct.

Functionalist Approaches to Deviance and Social Control

Imagine that society is a single, complex organism with many internal organs that perform specific tasks. The state is society's brain, its decision-making center where legislators contemplate the morality of laws and communicate legislative decisions to other social organs charged with implementation.

All of society's organs are necessary to keep the social organism alive and healthy, and these organs are composed of groups of individuals, or cells. A functionalist approach explains the existence of social phenomena by the functions they perform. In this framework, the state develops because society needs a decision-making center to help organize and direct social life. All of society's various parts, or organs, are defined by their functions and are arranged according to the needs of the social organism.

Émile Durkheim, author of *The Division of Labor in Society* (1893/1997), used such a functionalist approach to explain social cohesion—the way people form social bonds, relate to each other, and get along on a day-to-day basis. Durkheim's thesis is that there are two basic ways society can hold together, or cohere, which he called mechanical and organic solidarity. Mechanical or segmental solidarity—which characterized premodern society—was based on the sameness of the individual parts. In this model, the functional units are like cargo containers; each container is like all the others and can perform the same function as the next. Cohesion stems from the reliable similarity of the parts. In a state of organic solidarity—which characterizes modern society—social cohesion is based on interdependence, because the members in this type of social body perform different, specialized functions, and this increased mutual dependence among the parts is what allows for the smooth functioning of the whole. The physical analogy here is a machine in which each part is different and none would be so meaningful outside the context of the machine.

In premodern society, people were held together by sameness. A peasant farmer in feudal times might have eked out a living by tilling a small plot of land, planting seeds, and then harvesting crops. The peasant next door also eked out a living by tilling, planting, and harvesting. Slight variations existed from one farm to the next, but the farmers' life conditions, and particularly their day-to-day experiences in the field, were roughly the same. The farmers' conversations probably would not have been strained or awkward; the two neighbors would have had plenty of advice and commiseration to share. Such a situation would be an example of mechanical solidarity.

SOCIAL COHESION

social bonds; how well people relate to each other and get along on a day-to-day basis.

MECHANICAL OR SEGMENTAL SOLIDARITY

social cohesion based on sameness.

ORGANIC SOLIDARITY

social cohesion based on difference and interdependence of the parts.

Social norms and the punishments for violating them change over time and from place to place. Whether it was executing women as witches in the seventeenth century, enforcing Jim Crow laws in the segregated South, or prosecuting John Geddes Lawrence and Tyron Garner for engaging in a same-sex relationship, our definitions of what constitutes deviance change.

Farmers in premodern society would not have struggled to relate to one another; their sense of sameness bred mechanical solidarity. In contrast, most workers in the industrial and postindustrial economy perform such specialized tasks that they relate to one another through organic solidarity.

As Western society became more industrialized in the late eighteenth and nineteenth centuries, however, workers developed specialized skills, allowing them to perform particular tasks better and more quickly. This division of labor resulted in a dramatic increase in productivity, but with the efficiency and high productivity of specialization have come some negative consequences. Specialized workers have less and less in common with one another, and they may be less able to understand each other. For example, if you held a highly specialized position within the economy as, say, a techno-artist punk rocker, you might find yourself thinking that no one understands what it's like to be you. As a techno-artist punk rocker, you are isolated and alienated because your highly specialized position—your role within the economy and society more generally—makes it difficult to find common ground with others. If you sit down on a commuter train next to an investment banker and try to talk with her, an awkward conversation might ensue, in which each of you tries to comprehend the daily activities of the other. You may share your morning commute and nothing more. Labor specialization divides us by making it more difficult to form social bonds. However, specialization of tasks enables everyone to do something best. Maybe you are *the best* Japanese humane-certified chicken farm sex determiner (actually called a chick sexer, and yes, they make six figures), because, among other reasons, you don't really have much competition. This high degree of labor specialization makes us all interdependent, creating organic cohesion.

Distinguishing between these two types of social solidarity leads us to our first insight into social deviance. When individuals commit acts of deviance, they offend what Durkheim calls the collective conscience, meaning the common faith or set of social norms by which a society and its members abide. Without a collective conscience—a set of common assumptions about how the world works—there would be no sense of moral unity, and society would quickly dissolve into chaos. So when individuals break from the collectively produced moral fabric, societies are faced with the task of repairing the tear in the fabric by realigning the deviant individual through either punishment or rehabilitation.

The way in which social realignment is achieved, Durkheim concludes, depends on the type of solidarity holding that particular society together. Premodern societies, where people are united by sameness, tend to be characterized by punitive justice: making the offender suffer and thus defining the boundaries of acceptable behavior. Such punishment might involve collective vengeance. If someone in a medieval village committed adultery, stole vegetables, or murdered someone, the villagers would gather together, perhaps in a rowdy, pitchfork-wielding mob, to punish the criminal who had offended the collective conscience. The act of collective group punishment might have culminated in storming the offender's house or hanging the poor sap in public. In either case, the group punishes the criminal in an act of collective vengeance. The collective probably wasn't interested in hearing the criminal's side of the story: the facts of his personal life, his possible motivations for committing the crime, or the details of his regrettable childhood. Mechanical social sanctions both reinforce the boundaries of acceptable behavior and unite collectivity through actions such as hanging, stoning, or publicly chastising a former member of the community. It is important to note that it is this collective, vengeful action that, by uniting the group through its perpetration and associated emotions of revenge, guilt, and so on, is key to the production of cohesion and unity. (Of course, there are always exceptions, such as the premodern Amish [see Chapter 5] who don't even bother to prosecute shoplifters.)

Two women accused of collaborating with the Nazis are marched through the streets of Paris in the summer of 1944. The mob ripped the women's clothes, then painted swastikas on their shorn heads in order to punish them. How is this an example of a mechanical social sanction?

A similar form of justice can be administered by the state through a more formal process. When the infamous Oklahoma City bomber, Timothy McVeigh, was put to death, he was, in effect, murdered by the collectivity, by the citizenry of the United States. To opponents of the death penalty, McVeigh's execution amounted to state-sponsored murder. To others, however, his death signaled that killing innocent people is not acceptable behavior. Although only a small team actually carried out McVeigh's execution, his death was an act in which—theoretically at least—we all participated. When we collectively and publicly put McVeigh to death, we were united in our reinforcement of social norms: Paradoxically, his deviance helped keep our society together.

Organic solidarity, in contrast, by differentiating individuals, produces social sanctions that focus on the individual—that is, they are tailored to the specific conditions and circumstances of the perpetrator. This response to deviance is rehabilitative, meaning that the response is designed to transform the offender into a productive member of society. In the modern mind-set, we care about the rapist's or murderer's motivations and regrettable childhood. We treat the criminal as an individual who can be "fixed" if we can root out the causes of, and triggers for, his or her criminality. For example, what happens if a drug addict steals car radios to support her cocaine habit? The court may order the addict into rehab in hopes of reintegrating her into the productive mainstream.

Punishments may also be restitutive—that is, they may attempt to restore the status quo that existed before an offense or event. Tort law is an example of restitutive social sanctions. For instance, let's say a negligent contractor doesn't bother to install grating at the bottom of a swimming

Eric Todaro (left) and Richard Grooms, inmates at a state penitentiary in Oregon, work on a General Education Diploma (GED) test. According to Durkheim, why would prisons provide educational programs and other rehabilitative tools?

pool. A little girl playing at the edge of the pool is sucked into the drain, almost drowns, and ends up with brain damage. Restitutive social sanctions, or tort law, force the contractor (or his insurance company) to pay millions of dollars to the parents of the little girl. The money attempts to reestablish social equilibrium by repaying the parents for what they have lost. (Of course, in this case at least, money is a wholly inadequate salve.)

In the United States, we consider ourselves a modern society, yet both forms of social sanctions, mechanical and organic, still lurk within the US justice system. We don't only try to rehabilitate our criminals and reimburse victims. We also still employ the death penalty in many states. Does Texas, where approximately one-third of the executions in the United States have taken place, have a more premodern division of labor than Wisconsin, which does not punish crimes with the death penalty? Probably not. Did the division of labor revert to primitive, subsistence levels all of a sudden in 1976, when the Supreme Court reinstated the legality of the death penalty? Of course not. Furthermore, some traditionally liberal states such as California and Oregon still have the death penalty on their books. At the same time, we also have a signature form of modern, organic social sanctions as embodied by our elaborate court system. Durkheim doesn't argue that these forms of social sanctions are mutually exclusive—that they can't exist together. In fact, he would expect to find much more of one form of social sanction, but not only one form. Both forms, however, help hold us together by reinforcing the boundaries of normal, socially acceptable behavior.

To make his case, Durkheim analyzed different historical penal and moral codes to discern the ratio of premodern sanctions to modern sanctions throughout history. He examined the Code of Hammurabi in Babylon dating back to 1750 B.C.E. as well as the Pentateuch, the first five books of the Old Testament. He studied more recent sanctions in the Magna Carta, the Napoleonic Code in France, and the South American Drago Doctrine. He argued that, as history progressed and the division of labor developed, the ratio of premodern to modern sanctions changed to favor modern, less punitive sanctions. So although the United States may still permit its states to apply the death penalty, Durkheim would hypothesize that as our labor market changes to favor even more specialization, we might expect the death penalty to fizzle out. In fact, approximately a dozen states have repealed the death penalty in recent decades, but we should be cautious in drawing overall conclusions about the relationship between division of labor and forms of punishment by focusing on one particular form of sanction.

SOCIAL CONTROL

We have explored the paradox of deviance in Durkheim's *The Division of Labor in Society*—the idea that deviance, and specifically the act of collective punishment, holds us together. But what makes us good law-abiding

SOCIAL CONTROL

mechanisms that create normative compliance in individuals.

FORMAL SOCIAL SANCTIONS

mechanisms of social control by which rules or laws prohibit deviant criminal behavior.

INFORMAL SOCIAL SANCTIONS

the usually unexpressed but widely known rules of group membership; the unspoken rules of social life.

citizens in the first place? Social control is what sociologists refer to as the set of mechanisms that create normative compliance, the act of abiding by society's norms or simply following the rules of group life. Other sociologists have tried to explain how social control works on individuals to induce compliance to social norms.

Sociologists classify mechanisms of social control into two categories. The first are called formal social sanctions. In most modern societies, these formal sanctions would be rules or laws prohibiting deviant criminal behavior such as murder, rape, and theft. These sanctions are formal, overt "expressions of official group sentiment" (Meier, 1982). Informal social sanctions are based on the usually unexpressed but widely known rules of group membership. Have you ever heard someone use the expression "an unwritten rule"? Informal social sanctions are the unwritten rules of social life. So, hypothetically, if you loudly belch in public, you will probably be the object of scowls of disgust. These gestures of contempt at your socially unacceptable behavior are examples of informal social sanctions, the ways we keep each other in check by watching and judging those around us. As discussed in Chapter 4, the process of socialization is largely responsible for our acquisition and understanding of these unspoken rules of group social life. Through years of trial and error, we have internalized the rules of the social game.

The idea behind informal social sanctions is that we are all simultaneously enforcing the rules of society and having them enforced on us. How does this work? At the same time we are watching or observing others, others are watching us, too. All of us are both spectators and objects of spectacle. We are all the agents of a diffuse, watchful gaze, as in the 1881 painting *Luncheon of the Boating Party* by Pierre-Auguste Renoir, where everyone is gazing at someone else, but no two people make direct eye contact. And beyond watching, all of us can grant rewards for others' good behavior in the form of smiles and encouragement, but we can also sanction with dirty looks, snide comments, and worse. In this way, we are all chipping in our small contributions to the construction of the social whole.

Think about the neighborhood watch groups that preceded the widespread adoption of electronic home security systems. People in a community banded together and agreed to keep an eye out for trespassers, burglars, and suspicious strangers. The idea behind these groups was that neighborhoods could maintain social order by overtly declaring their intention to visually monitor their turf. Sometimes such groups issued signs or decals for doors and windows to signal to unsavory characters that the neighborhood was being "protected" by watchful eyes. But this kind of activity doesn't have to be so formalized. The urban theorist Jane Jacobs (1961) coined the term *the eyes and ears of the street* to describe the fact that, ideally, in mixed-use (i.e., commercial and residential) neighborhoods, the thread of social control is implicitly woven into daily life. Through their windows, grandmothers watch children playing baseball on the street below, on the alert for any trouble. During the course of a busy weekday, a shopkeeper might notice a group of teenagers, who should be at school, loitering outside his store and report this to their parents or the school.

In any society, many agents of both formal and informal social control exist. Our local neighbors act as the primary agents of informal social control, whereas the state, or the government, often has a hand in the construction of formal social sanctions by making laws.

Pierre-Auguste Renoir's *Luncheon of the Boating Party* (1881).

The police are an obvious example of an agent of state social control formed for the protection of the public. The police patrol public parks and neighborhoods after nightfall and contain public protests to ensure social order.

Informal social control is the bedrock on which formal social control must rest. If the police go on strike, for example, whether chaos will ensue depends on the degree of social cohesion in a given community. Likewise, without strong informal social norms, the police are relatively helpless. Consider the difficulty police officers have in tracking down and arresting those who loot and commit acts of vandalism during an urban riot. Or the difficulty in solving or prosecuting a crime if witnesses are not willing to step forward and testify. If an entire community relaxes its informal social control, formal social control inevitably fails. Lately, the boundary between informal and formal social control is perhaps blurring a bit with the proliferation of surveillance cameras installed by private and public entities.

A NORMATIVE THEORY OF SUICIDE

After making his observations on social solidarity and social control in *The Division of Labor in Society*, Durkheim next applied his ideas to the sociological study of suicide, perhaps the most individual act of deviance. Or is it? If you were asked to explain what causes a person to die by suicide, you might say mental illness, depression, drug addiction, or perhaps a catastrophic event. These accounts reflect our perception of suicide as something intensely personal, mediated by individual life circumstances or caused by chemical imbalances and emotional disorders. And these explanations may contain a piece of the answer. However, Durkheim believed these individualistic accounts of suicide were inadequate.

FIGURE 6.1 A Normative Theory of Suicide

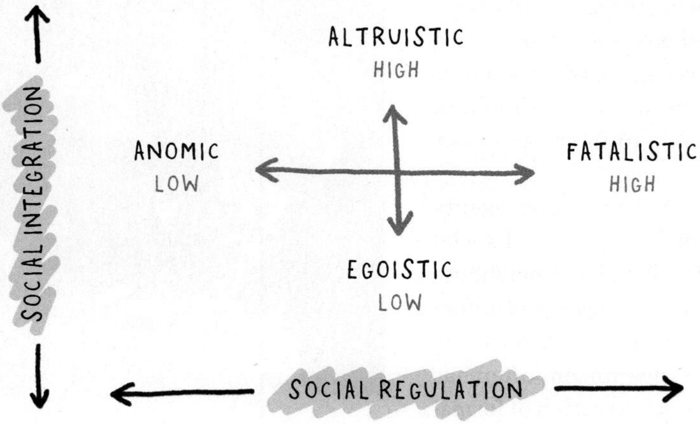

In his 1897 book *Suicide*, Durkheim sought to explain how social forces beyond the individual shaped suicide rates. According to Durkheim, suicide is, at its root, an instance of social deviance. By observing patterns in suicide rates across Europe (just as he had previously discerned patterns in penal codes), Durkheim developed a normative theory of suicide.

Durkheim proposed that by plotting "social integration" on the *y*-axis and "social regulation" on the *x*-axis of a Cartesian coordinate system, we can better see how social forces influence suicide rates (Figure 6.1). Social integration refers to the degree to which you are one with your social group or community. A tightly knit community in which members interact with each other in a number of different capacities—say the coach of your child's Little League team is also your dentist and you are the dentist's mechanic—is more socially integrated than one in which people do not interact at all or interact in only one role. Social regulation refers to how many rules guide your daily life and what you can reasonably expect from the world on a day-to-day basis—the degree to which tomorrow will look like today, which looks like yesterday. To be at low risk for suicide (and other deviant behavior), you need to be somewhere in the middle: integrated into your community with a reasonable (not oppressive) set of guidelines to structure your life. If you go too far in either direction along either axis, you have either too much or too little of some important facet of "normal" life.

Let's say you drop down the *y*-axis significantly in the direction of egoism. You are not very well integrated into your group. And Durkheim argues that, because others give your life meaning, you would feel hopeless. You wouldn't be part of some larger long-term project, would feel insignificant, and would be at risk of committing egoistic suicide. We all need to feel as

SOCIAL INTEGRATION

the extent to which you are integrated into your social group or community.

SOCIAL REGULATION

the number of rules guiding your daily life and, more specifically, what you can reasonably expect from the world on a day-to-day basis.

EGOISTIC SUICIDE

suicide that occurs when one is not well integrated into a social group.

if we have made a difference in other people's lives or produced something for their good that will endure after we have died.

Durkheim demonstrated the prevalence of this phenomenon by using statistics about suicide rates across different religious groups. Although many Western religions formally prohibit suicide, rates varied substantially across religious affiliations. Durkheim found that throughout Europe, Protestants killed themselves most often, followed by Catholics and then Jews. Why? Protestantism is premised on individualism. In most Protestant denominations, there isn't an elaborate church hierarchy as there is in the Catholic Church, and Protestants are encouraged to maintain a direct personal relationship with God. By changing the individual's relationship to God (and therefore the individual's relationship to the church), Protestantism also stripped away many of the integrative structures of Catholicism, putting its members at greater risk for egoistic suicide. (More recent research shows that today the greater distinction is between people who are religiously affiliated and those who are not, the latter experiencing significantly higher levels of suicide.)

But why did Jews have the lowest suicide rate of any major European religious group if all these religions prohibited suicide? Judaism may be less structured than Catholicism, but historically speaking, Jews have remained a persecuted minority group. When a social group is persecuted or rejected by the so-called mainstream, its members often band together for protection from persecution. For example, in the United States today, African Americans have one of the lowest suicide rates, probably as a result of their bonding as a minority group, united in a common struggle against a history of oppression.

Too little social integration increases the risk of suicide, but too much social integration can also be dangerous. A person who strays too far up the *y*-axis might commit altruistic suicide, because a group dominates the life of that individual to such a degree that he or she feels meaningless aside from this social recognition. Think about Japanese ritual suicide, sometimes called seppuku (and sometimes colloquially known as hara-kiri). In this scenario, samurai warriors who had failed their group in battle would disembowel themselves with a sword rather than continue to live with disgrace in the community. Durkheim uses the example of Hindu widows in some castes and regions of India, who were expected to throw themselves on their husbands' funeral pyre to prove their devotion. This practice, called suttee or sati, symbolized that a woman properly recognized that her life was meaningless outside her social role as a wife. Official efforts to ban suttee commenced as early as the sixteenth century, and it is now illegal and extremely rare in India.

Altruistic suicide can be a more personal, less ritualistic, choice, as well. For example, do you think that suicide rates in the military are higher

ALTRUISTIC SUICIDE

suicide that occurs when one experiences too much social integration.

A Japanese man performs hara-kiri in this staged photograph from the 1880s. What makes this action altruistic suicide?

↑

ANOMIE

a sense of aimlessness or despair that arises when we can no longer reasonably expect life to be predictable; too little social regulation; normlessness.

ANOMIC SUICIDE

suicide that occurs as a result of insufficient social regulation.

among enlisted soldiers or officers? Enlisted soldiers might be the obvious choice because they experience a lower standard of living and less social prestige, but statistics show that the suicide rate is, in fact, higher among officers. Why? Too much social integration. The identity of officers—their sense of honor and self-worth—is more completely linked to their role in the military. Enlisted soldiers, in contrast, are not as responsible for group performance. More likely, these soldiers perceive their military service as a job and still identify strongly with their other, civilian roles, so they have a lower risk of altruistic suicide.

As we move to the x-axis, social regulation, why or how would social regulation influence the suicide rate? Imagine you commute to school every day. You rise at approximately 7:00 A.M., leave the house by 8:00, and take the 8:10 bus to school. But now imagine that some days the bus is late, some days the bus is early, and sometimes it just doesn't come at all. You have no way of knowing when or if the bus will come. You get tired of standing on a cold, lonely corner waiting for a bus that may never come, and after a while you might just stop trying to get to class at all. What's the point of waking up if you won't make it to class on time despite your effort? You have developed a sense of learned helplessness, a depressed outlook in which sufferers lack the will to take action to improve their lives, even when obvious avenues are present.

At the heart of learned helplessness is the sense that we are unable to stave off the sources of our pain, that we have no control over our own well-being. Durkheim studied a similar condition, which he termed *anomie*. Literally meaning "without norms," anomie is a sense of aimlessness or despair that arises when we can no longer reasonably expect life to be more or less meaningful. Our sense of connection between our actions and values is eroded, because too little social regulation exists. Durkheim labeled suicide that resulted from insufficient social regulation anomic suicide. For example, after the stock market crashed in 1929, many businessmen jumped out of skyscraper windows to their deaths. These stockbrokers and investors may have felt that they did everything right and still ended up destitute. For them, the connection between what they thought was the right thing to do—work hard on Wall Street—and just rewards was severed. They had no idea how to cope with the changes.

Durkheim's argument about anomic suicide seems intuitive when it refers to negative events rupturing our everyday lives, but the same principle also holds for positive life events. For example, many lottery winners report spells of severe depression after winning millions of dollars, displaying another case of anomie (Nissle & Bshor, 2002). If a very poor, frugal man wins the lottery, all of his money-saving habits instantaneously become irrelevant, unnecessary, or even a bit silly. Maybe he previously structured his Sundays this way: Walk down to the corner store just as it's about to close to pick up a castoff of the Sunday paper, painstakingly cut coupons from the circulars for hours, and then plan a visit to each of three local grocery stores to find the best deals throughout the week. Maybe he always took lunch to work in reused brown paper bags to save money. Now he has $5 million in his checking account and no behavioral template (something that social processes yield) for life as a wealthy man. His difficulties do not revolve around the quantity of material resources or standard of living suddenly available to him. They rest in how meaningless the rules he previously used to give meaning to his life now seem.

The final coordinate is fatalistic suicide, which occurs when a person experiences too much social regulation. Instead of floundering in a state of anomie with no guiding rules, you find yourself doing the same thing day after day, with no variation and no surprises. In 10 years, what will you be doing? The same thing. In 20 years? The same thing. You have nothing to look forward to because you reasonably expect that nothing better than this will ever happen for you. This type of suicide usually occurs among slaves and prisoners. You might imagine that slaves and prisoners would commit suicide because of their physical hardships, but Durkheim's research suggested that it is more accurate to understand their suicidal deaths as resulting from the suffocating tyranny of monotony.

Early feminists wrote of the "problem that has no name": that life as a 1950s suburban stay-at-home mother was a stifling routine, the same every day, for as long as the imagination could conjure. Sylvia Plath, a feminist poet and writer, committed suicide in 1963 shortly after the publication of her novel *The Bell Jar*, in which the semiautobiographical character Esther's fatalism is palpable: "I saw the days of the year stretching ahead like a series of bright white boxes, and separating one box from another was sleep, like a black shade. Only for me, the long perspective of shades that set off one box from the next had suddenly snapped up, and I could see day after day after day glaring ahead of me like a white, broad, infinitely desolate avenue" (1971, p. 143). Women's roles in society were tightly controlled, and thus they were at higher risk for fatalistic suicide.

According to many theories of deviance, what happens at the group level affects what happens at the individual level. For example, Durkheim hypothesized that members of minority groups were more socially integrated within their group, and therefore Jews in Europe had lower suicide

FATALISTIC SUICIDE
suicide that occurs as a result of too much social regulation.

rates. Perhaps minority solidarity inspires feelings of belonging and love between family and nonfamily alike within the group. Because feeling loved and wanted is generally regarded as a good thing, we could say that this solidarity makes group members happy or at least staves off depression. Less depressed, happier people commit suicide less often than those who feel unimportant, worthless, and hopeless. Group dissimilarities start at the macro level (group solidarity), filter down to the individual level (feelings of depression or happiness), and can be detected again in the aggregate (differential suicide rates).

SOCIAL FORCES AND DEVIANCE

In keeping with Durkheim's attempt to discover the social roots of suicide and other forms of deviance, sociologist Robert Merton pioneered a complementary theory of social deviance. Instead of stressing the way sudden social changes lead to feelings of helplessness, Merton argued that the real problem behind anomie occurs when a society holds out the same goals to all its members but does not give them equal ability to achieve these goals. Merton's strain theory, advanced in 1938, explains how society gives us certain templates for acting correctly or appropriately. More specifically, we learn what society considers appropriate goals and appropriate means of achieving them. The *strain* in strain theory arises when the means don't match up to those ends; hence, Merton's theory is also called the "means-ends theory of deviance." When someone fails to recognize and accept either socially appropriate goals or socially appropriate means (or both), he or she becomes a social deviant.

If you have decided to pursue a college education to land a decent job, you are probably what Merton terms a conformist. A conformist accepts both the goals and strategies to achieve those goals that are considered socially acceptable. Your goal is to earn a good living, maybe start a family, and take long, exotic vacations where you will take photos with a fancy camera and then post them online to impress your friends. You've decided to pursue this lifestyle through a better education, deliberate cultivation of the right social network, and hard work.

Now let's say that you go to class every day, take minimal notes, and read just enough to earn a passing grade. All you want is to get by and be left alone. You don't care how much money you will earn, as long as it's enough to pay for your studio apartment and other small monthly bills. You've accepted society's acceptable means (you're still going to college, after all), but you've rejected society's goals (the big house, the 2.3 kids, and the new car). You've rejected the idea of getting ahead through hard work, the American dream. You are a ritualist, a person who rejects socially defined goals but not the means.

STRAIN THEORY

Robert Merton's theory that deviance occurs when a society does not give all of its members equal ability to achieve socially acceptable goals.

CONFORMIST

an individual who accepts both the goals and the strategies that are considered socially acceptable to achieve those goals.

RITUALIST

an individual who rejects socially defined goals but not the means.

INNOVATOR

social deviant who accepts socially acceptable goals but rejects socially acceptable means to achieve them.

If, however, you yearn to be rich and famous but don't have the scruples, patience, or economic resources to get there by using socially acceptable means, you may be an innovator. Let's say you are particularly interested in buying a mansion and expensive jewelry, and marrying a gorgeous husband or wife. Instead of slaving away on Wall Street for years, you sell drugs, fence stolen goods, and make a few friends in the Mafia.

Among those who reject *both* means and goals are retreatists and rebels, although the boundaries between the two are not always so cut-and-dried. Retreatists completely stop participating in society. This type is perhaps illustrated by adventurer Christopher Johnson McCandless, the subject of Jon Krakauer's best-selling 1996 book *Into the Wild*, who simply decided not to play the game and moved to the Alaskan woods, where he lived without running water or electricity. (I won't tell you what happens to him in case you want to read the book or watch the 2007 film adaptation.) A rebel also rejects both traditional goals and traditional means but wants to change

RETREATIST

one who rejects both socially acceptable means and goals by completely retreating from, or not participating in, society.

REBEL

an individual who rejects both traditional goals and traditional means and wants to alter or destroy the social institutions from which he or she is alienated.

Conformist

Ritualist

Innovator

Retreatist

Rebel

Which type are you? Do you follow socially accepted means and goals? According to Robert Merton, you're a conformist. Doing the bare minimum? You're probably a ritualist. If you're like the late WorldCom CEO Bernard Ebbers and want to earn big rewards but have few scruples about how you reach them, you're an innovator. You're a retreatist if, like members of a self-supporting commune, you reject all means and goals of society. You're a rebel, like Che Guevara, if you not only reject social means and goals but also want to change society itself.

(or destroy) the social institutions from which he or she is alienated. One example is Ernesto "Che" Guevara, the Argentine Marxist who famously fought for communism in Cuba. His disgust at the impoverished conditions he encountered as a doctor traveling through Latin America led to the formation of a guerrilla group. Che chose to fight the government rather than, say, propose new legislation or raise money for a new hospital.

Symbolic Interactionist Theories of Deviance

Whereas Durkheim and Merton focused on the ways different parts of the organic social body function together, another school of sociologists in the 1960s and 1970s took a different approach to the study of deviance. Working in the tradition of symbolic interactionism (see Chapters 1 and 4), a term coined by Herbert Blumer (1969), these sociologists stressed the particular meanings individuals bring to their actions, rather than the broader social structures of which they are unwittingly a part. To determine why people commit crimes, or to seek the root causes of deviance in a given society, a symbolic interactionist would look at the small and subtle particulars of a social context, and the beliefs and assumptions people carry into their everyday interactions. Functionalist theories, such as Durkheim's and Merton's, are sometimes called macro theories because they seek to paint the social world in wide brushstrokes: generalizable trends, global or national forces, and broad social structures. At the opposite end of the spectrum, micro theories such as symbolic interactionism zoom in on the individual. Symbolic interactionism takes seriously our inner thoughts and everyday interactions with one another, including how others see us and how we respond to our surroundings.

LABELING THEORY

As a child, did you ever shoplift, trespass, or forge a document? If you were slow and tactless enough to get caught, your parents probably gave you a stern lecture and maybe grounded you. Chances are, however, that over time the incident slowly faded into the background and you stopped feeling guilty. You probably never came to think of yourself as a shoplifter or trespasser, as a criminal or social deviant. You simply made a stupid mistake, never to be repeated. Let me give you an example from my own past. One afternoon when I was in junior high school, a friend and I decided to play "fireman, waterman," a game that required one person (the fireman) to flick lit matches into the air, while the waterman tried to extinguish them with a plant mister. To make a long story short, I was the fireman and I won. As you might expect, the incident ended badly—specifically, one of the stray, airborne matches set my friend's apartment on fire. After extinguishing the blaze, fire department officials questioned me about my role in starting the fire, but ultimately, I was absolved from blame and the fire was declared an accident. My parents, although obviously shaken and disappointed, never formally punished me. The trauma of the incident, they said, was lesson enough. Now imagine that, instead of being pardoned, I was held accountable for my role in starting the fire and sent to a juvenile corrections facility. Do you think I still would have followed the same life trajectory, eventually going to college and graduate school, and becoming a sociology professor and textbook author?

The labeling theory of social deviance offers insight into how people become deviants. According to this theory, individuals subconsciously notice how others see or label them, and their reactions to those labels over time form the basis of their self-identity. It is only through the social process of labeling that we create deviance by assigning shared meanings to acts. We all know that stealing, trespassing, and vandalizing are wrong, abnormal, and criminal behavior, but these acts are considered deviant only because of our shared meanings about the sanctity of private property and our rules about respecting that property. Although the fire caused by my unfortunate stint in pyrotechnics was labeled an accident, it might have been termed a crime just as easily. There was and is nothing inherently deviant about setting an apartment on fire, accidentally or otherwise. In 1963, Howard S. Becker, a proponent of labeling theory, made precisely this point, arguing that individuals don't commit crimes in a vacuum. Rather, social groups create deviance, first by setting the rules for what's right and wrong, and second by labeling wrongdoers as outsiders. Offenders are not born; they are made. They are a consequence of how other people apply rules and sanctions to them.

Social groups create rules about the correct or standard mode of conduct for social actors. When these rules are broken, society's reaction to the act determines if the offense counts as deviance. Take, for example, the case of opioid use. When opioid use was dominated by heroin and disproportionately afflicted Black Americans, it was criminalized. However, when such drug addiction soared among Whites, it was seen more as a health issue than one of crime or deviancy, and was referred to in medical terms such as "epidemic." Becker also argues that not only are deviant acts created by a process of labeling but *deviants* are also created by a process of labeling. If you break a rule—say, accidentally burn down an apartment—but your violation is not labeled a crime or otherwise recognized as deviant, then *you* are not recognized as a criminal or deviant. We become (or don't become) deviant only in interaction with other social actors. It is this social reaction to an act, and the subsequent labeling of that act and offender, that create social deviance.

LABELING THEORY

the belief that individuals subconsciously notice how others see or label them, and their reactions to those labels over time form the basis of their self-identity.

↑

How did Howard Becker apply labeling theory to the use of marijuana?

To illustrate this process of becoming deviant, Becker interviewed 50 marijuana users in "Becoming a Marihuana User" (1953)—in a period when not only was marijuana illegal in all states, but it was quite socially stigmatized. He began his study with a simple inquiry: Are marijuana users different from nonusers? Is there something about the individual psychology of marijuana users that causes them to smoke marijuana? The answer given by most scientists, politicians, and parents in the 1950s was a hearty *yes*. But Becker argues that chronic marijuana use results from a process of social learning. Before people light up, they must first learn how to smoke marijuana. More important, they must then redefine the sensations of marijuana use as "fun" and desirable. Just as setting an apartment on fire is not inherently a crime, getting high is not "automatically or necessarily pleasurable" (Becker, 1963). In fact, one user he spoke with never could learn to enjoy pot:

> It [marijuana] was offered to me, and I tried it. I'll tell you one thing. I never did enjoy it at all. I mean it was just nothing that I could enjoy. [Becker: Well, did you get high when you turned on?] Oh, yeah, I got definite feelings from it. But I didn't enjoy them. I mean I got plenty of reactions, but they were mostly reactions of fear. [You were frightened?] Yes. I didn't enjoy it. I couldn't seem to relax with it, you know. (p. 240)

A person trying marijuana is usually able to redefine the experience when smoking with long-term users who assure the novice that the physical effects are normal, even enjoyable. One of Becker's interviewees, a veteran smoker, recalled how a beginner "became frightened and hysterical" after smoking for the first time. An older user told the newbie, "I'd give anything to get that high myself" (Becker, 1963). This comment and others like it apply new meaning to the sensations of getting high. For some, marijuana smoking becomes pleasant only through a social process. How objects and sensations become meaningful (or pleasant) through social processes is the focus of Becker's study, in contrast to explanations that focus on what objects *are*. Similarly, the taste of alcohol probably didn't appeal to your palate when you first tried it; however, because alcohol had a certain social allure, being associated with either adulthood or rebellion, you may have learned to appreciate its taste (perhaps before you reached the legal drinking age).

Another example of a social process may help illustrate the power of labeling theory. As part of a psychology experiment, a group of eight adults with steady employment and no history of mental illness presented themselves at different psychiatric inpatient hospitals and complained of hearing voices (Rosenhan, 1973). Each of the pseudo-patients was admitted after describing the alleged voices, which spoke words like "thud," "empty," and "hollow." In all cases, the pseudo-patients were admitted with a diagnosis of schizophrenia. The researchers instructed the pseudo-patients, once they were hospitalized, to stop "simulating any symptoms of abnormality." Each pseudo-patient "behaved on the ward as he 'normally' behaved." Still, the doctors and staff did not suspect that the pseudo-patients were imposters. Instead, the treating psychiatrists changed their diagnosis of schizophrenia to "schizophrenia in remission." Something even more troubling than the misdiagnosis occurred. Once the pseudo-patients had been labeled insane, all their subsequent behavior was interpreted accordingly. One male pseudo-patient, for example, gave the hospital staff a truthful account of his personal history. During his childhood he had been close to his mother but not his father. Later in life, he became close with his father and more distant from his mother. His marriage was "characteristically close and warm," with no persistent problems. He reported rarely spanking his children. Sounds like a fairly typical guy, right? This is how the hospital record described the pseudo-patient's personal history:

> This white 39-year-old male . . . manifests a long history of con-
> siderable ambivalence in close relationships, which begins in early

In experiments such as David L. Rosenhan's or films like *Shock Corridor* (left), people with no history of mental illness are admitted into psychiatric hospitals. These examples raise questions about the stickiness of labels. What are some of the consequences of being labeled a deviant?

THE STANFORD PRISON EXPERIMENT AND ABU GHRAIB

The force of labels and roles can affect us very quickly. The Stanford Prison Experiment, conducted by Philip Zimbardo in 1971, provides insight into the power of such social labels and how they might explain the incredibly inhumane acts of torture, most involving violence and humiliation, committed at Abu Ghraib, the American-run prison in Iraq. Zimbardo, a psychology professor at Stanford, rounded up some college undergraduate men to participate in an experiment about "the psychology of prison life." Half the undergraduates were assigned the role of prisoner, and half were assigned the role of prison guard. These roles were randomly assigned, so there was nothing about the inherent personalities of either group that predisposed them to prefer one role over the other.

A film still from *The Stanford Prison Experiment*, which reenacted Philip Zimbardo's now infamous study.

To simulate the arrest and incarceration process, the soon-to-be prisoners were taken from their homes, handcuffed, and searched by actual city police. Then all the prisoners were taken to "prison"—the basement of the Stanford psychology department set up with cells and a special solitary confinement closet. The guards awaited their prisoners in makeshift uniforms and dark sunglasses to render their eyes invisible to inmates. Upon arrival at the prison, all the criminals were stripped, searched, and issued inmate uniforms, which were like short hospital gowns. The first day passed without incident, as prisoners and guards settled into their new roles. But on the morning of the second day, prisoners revolted, barricading themselves in their mock cells and sparking a violent confrontation between the fictitious guards and prisoners that would ensue for the next four days. From physical abuse, such as hour-long counts of push-ups, to psychological violence, such as degradation and humiliation, the guards' behavior verged on sadism, although just days before, these same young men were normal Stanford undergrads. The prisoners quickly began "withdrawing and behaving in pathological ways," while some of the guards seemed to relish their abuse. The original plan was for the experiment to last 14 days, but after only 6 days it spiraled out of control and had to be aborted.

The lesson, claims Zimbardo, is that good people can do terrible things, depending on their social surroundings and on expectations. When thrown into a social context of unchecked authority, anonymity, and high stress, average

This Iraqi detainee in Abu Ghraib prison was hooked up to wires after American soldiers made him stand on a box. How can Zimbardo's experiments help us to understand the torture at Abu Ghraib?

people can become exceptional monsters. It's a phenomenon Zimbardo calls the "Lucifer effect," and it offers insights into how the atrocities at Abu Ghraib prison in Iraq became possible (Zimbardo, 2007). In 2005, when the media made public the horrifying images of Iraqi prisoners being degraded and abused—some naked and on their knees inches from barking dogs; some wearing hoods and restrained in painful, grotesque positions; some forced to lie atop a pile of other naked prisoners—with grinning American soldiers looking on, many commentators (and military officials) sought to explain the abuses as a case of "bad apples" among otherwise good soldiers. Bad apples don't just arise out of nowhere, however, nor are people inherently malicious or brutal by nature. Zimbardo's experiment, it seemed, offered a viable explanation.

In 2018, however, the Stanford Prison Experiment was again in the news when journalist Ben Blum published an article calling the experiment a "sham," questioning its ethical and methodological basis. Blum claimed the study was engineered to encourage the "guards" to humiliate and abuse the "prisoners." In response, Zimbardo forcefully defended his experiment, insisting that its goal was not to faithfully re-create the conditions of a prison, but rather to provide a "cautionary tale of what might happen to any of us if we underestimate the extent to which the power of social roles and external pressures can influence our actions" (2018). Sounds pretty sociological to me.

Wherever we stand on this debate, Zimbardo's quote confirms what we already know about socialization: when given limitless power under high stakes and in an environment of extreme uncertainty—as happened to the soldiers at Abu Ghraib—abuse can become the norm, and people who are otherwise good can do evil things.

childhood. A warm relationship with his mother cools during adolescence. A distant relationship to his father is described as becoming very intense. Affective stability is absent. His attempts to control emotionality with his wife and children are punctuated by angry outbursts and, in the case of his children, spankings. And while he says that he has several good friends, one senses considerable ambivalence embedded in those relationships also. (Rosenhan, 1973, p. 253)

Even though the pseudo-patient was acting "normally" shortly after his admission, the "abnormal" label stuck and continued to color the staff's perceptions and diagnoses. Just in case you are curious, the pseudo-patients were kept by the hospitals for 7 to 52 days, with an average stay of 19 days. Sticky label, indeed.

Labeling theorists believe that the fact that deviant labels stick, no matter what the circumstances, has important consequences for behavior. If, after committing a crime or hearing voices, you were labeled deviant and people treated and thought about you differently, how would you feel? Like the same person but just someone who, say, was arrested for possessing drugs? Or would the criminal label become part of the way you thought about yourself? Labeling theorists call the first act of rule breaking (which can include experiences or actions such as hearing voices, breaking windows, or dyeing one's hair neon orange) primary deviance. After you are labeled a deviant (a criminal, a drug addict, a shoplifter, even a prostitute), you might begin behaving differently as a result of the way people think about and act toward you. Others' expectations about how you *will* act affect how you *do* act. Secondary deviance refers to deviant acts that occur after primary deviance and as a result of your new deviant label. For example, a deviance researcher interviewed a woman in her sixties who had been under psychiatric care for some 20 years (Glassner, 1999). This is how she recalls the process of becoming mentally ill:

> The first time I was taken to a psychiatrist for help was when I was getting depressed over a miscarriage. I had tried for many years to have that baby, and finally I was pregnant and planning to be a mother and all, and then I lost it. Anyhow, they told me I was "deeply depressed," but it didn't really mean much to me. I figured I'd get over it once I got pregnant again or something. But when I went home, everybody treated me differently. My husband and my mother had met with the social worker, who explained that I had this problem, with depression and all. From then on I was a depressive. I mean, that's the way everyone treated me, and I thought of myself in the same way after a while. Maybe I am that way, maybe

PRIMARY DEVIANCE

the first act of rule breaking that may be given a label of "deviant" and thus influence how people think about and act toward you.

SECONDARY DEVIANCE

subsequent acts of rule breaking that occur after primary deviance and as a result of your new deviant label and people's expectations of you.

I was born that way or grew up like that, but anyhow, that's what I am now. (p. 73)

First, the woman sees her experience with depression as a passing phase, something she will recover from in time. Then a psychiatrist labels her "deeply depressed." When she arrives home, family members treat her differently, and "from then on" she is "a depressive." You can see how the woman's initial experience is redefined by her interaction with the psychiatrist and how the psychiatrist's label eventually becomes an integral part of the woman's identity. Of course, these labels themselves are socially structured by group stereotypes that can often serve as default cognitive categories.

STIGMA

We've seen how primary deviance can snowball into secondary deviance, whereby a few initial wrong steps or unlucky breaks can define a person's future actions and reactions. It doesn't end there. Secondary deviance can quickly become social stigma. A stigma is a negative social label that not only changes others' behavior toward a person but also alters that person's self-concept and social identity. We frequently say that certain behaviors, groups, identities, and even objects are stigmatized. Mental illness still carries a stigma in our society. Pedophilia carries a bigger one.

Having a criminal record can also carry a stigma, as can a person's race. In 2001 the late sociologist Devah Pager, then a graduate student in sociology, conducted a study to determine the effects of race and a criminal record on employment opportunities. She dispatched potential job candidates (African American and White male college students who had volunteered for the experiment) with similar résumés to apply for entry-level service positions. Half the participants of each race were told to indicate a prior felony conviction on their job applications. Pager (2003) found that of those with no criminal record, the White applicants were more likely to get a response (34 percent compared with 14 percent) but also that the White men with a supposed felony conviction were more likely to be called back than the Black men who did not report a criminal record (17 percent compared with 14 percent). The employers in Pager's study were slightly more willing to consider a White applicant with a felony record than a Black applicant with a clean history. So not only is a criminal record a stigma that deters potential employers, but the race of a job applicant continues to matter. One possible explanation, reasoned Pager, is that

> employers are attempting to select the best candidate for the job, but are affected by all kinds of pervasive and largely unconscious

STIGMA
a negative social label that not only changes others' behavior toward a person but also alters that person's own self-concept and social identity.

To see my interview with Devah Pager, author of *Marked*, go to
digital.wwnorton.com/youmayask7

stereotypes that result in privileging or preferring a White candidate to a Black candidate. . . . Employers have these negative stereotypes based on really pervasive media imagery, for example, of young Black men involved with the criminal justice system or acting out in some negative way. There's lots of information we get about all of the negative characteristics that we might attribute to the African American population. . . . They talked about Black men as being lazy and dangerous and criminal and dressing poorly; they were very candid about all of these negative characteristics that they attributed to Black men. But then, right after that, when I asked them about their experiences over the past year with Black applicants or Black employees, they had a much harder time coming up with concrete examples of those general attitudes, and for the most part, employers reported having very similar kinds of experiences with their Black and White employees. (Conley, 2009f)

Pager's research reveals how stigmas have real consequences, shaping the map of opportunities for men with criminal records, and illuminates the challenges faced by Black men, whose skin carries a stigma of deviance into the labor market whether they've been in prison or not. Of course, in this case, because the testers were trained with a script, the issue of internalized self-stigma doesn't come up to influence their interactions. But such internalized stigma is itself an important source of disadvantage and stress for marginalized groups. (See discussion of stereotype threat on page 584.)

BROKEN WINDOWS THEORY OF DEVIANCE

As labeling theory predicts, the ways other people see you affect your behavior and overall life chances. So, too, does the way you see your social surroundings, according to the broken windows theory. In 1969 Zimbardo conducted another experiment in which he and his graduate students abandoned two cars, leaving them without license plates and with their hoods propped up, in two different neighborhoods (Wilson & Kelling, 1982). The first car was abandoned in a seemingly safe neighborhood in Palo Alto, California, where Stanford University is located. The second car was left in the South Bronx in New York City, then one of the most dangerous urban ghettos in the country. Unsurprisingly, the abandoned car in Palo Alto remained untouched, whereas the car deposited in the South Bronx lost its hubcaps, battery, and any other usable parts almost immediately. However, it was the next stage in the experiment that offers valuable insight into how social context affects social deviance. Zimbardo went back to the untouched car in Palo Alto and smashed it with a sledgehammer. He and his graduate students shattered the windshield, put some dents in the car's sides, and again fled the scene. What do you think happened to the smashed and dented car in the "safe," rich neighborhood? Passersby began stopping their cars and getting out to further smash the wreck or tag it with graffiti. The social cues, or social context, influenced the way people, even in a rich neighborhood, treated the car.

In the South Bronx, the overall social context—involving many broken windows, graffiti, and dilapidated buildings—encouraged deviant acts at the outset because the neighborhood setting of decay and disorder signaled to residents that an abandoned car was fair game for abuse. In Palo Alto, where neighborhood conditions were clean and orderly, people were unlikely to vandalize an abandoned car. However, when the vehicle was already mangled, that cue of turmoil signaled to people that it was okay to engage in the otherwise deviant act of vandalism. The broken windows theory of deviance explains how social context and social cues impact the way individuals act—specifically, whether local, informal social norms allow such acts. When signals seem to tell us that it's okay to do the otherwise unthinkable, sometimes we do. The broken windows theory of deviance has inspired some politicians to institute policies that target the catalysts for inappropriate behavior (vandalism, burglary, and so forth). In fact, one of Zimbardo's graduate students who participated in the car experiment, George Kelling, later worked as a consultant for the New York City Transit Authority in 1984, devising a plan to crack down on graffiti. The underlying assumption of the plan was that the continued presence of graffiti-covered cars served as a green light for more graffiti and perhaps even violent crimes. The Transit Authority then launched a massive campaign to clean up graffiti, car by car, to erase the signs of urban disorder, in the hope of reducing subway crime. In the mid-1990s New York City mayor Rudy Giuliani also initiated a campaign of "zero tolerance" for petty crimes such as turnstile jumping, public urination, the drinking of alcohol in public, and graffiti. Today, the city's newer subway cars are "graffiti-proof," meaning that spray

BROKEN WINDOWS THEORY OF DEVIANCE

theory explaining how social cues impact whether individuals act deviantly—specifically, whether local, informal social norms allow deviant acts.

paint doesn't adhere to the metal exterior of the cars. Indeed, both petty and serious crimes have dropped dramatically in New York City since the 1990s (Kelling & Sousa, 2001), although some criminologists dispute the causal impact of the Giuliani strategy.

Crime

As noted earlier, crime is a more formal sort of deviance, not only subject to social sanction but also punishable by law. Sometimes an act falls clearly at one end of the spectrum or the other. Situations of self-defense aside, killing a person is generally agreed to be criminal; nose picking, however unpalatable, isn't. In other cases, though, the distinction is not so clear. Whereas you might get strange looks for wearing aluminum-foil hot pants to class, if you show up with no clothes on at all, you will likely be sent to a mental health care provider for assessment or arrested and thrown in jail for indecent exposure. But what if your hot pants weren't foil at all but just silver paint? Would this be indecent exposure?

Crime runs the gamut in type and degree. Most of us think of violence or drugs when we contemplate crime, but there are many other ways of breaking the law.

STREET CRIME

You don't make up for your sins in church. You do it in the streets.
—"Johnny Boy" Civello in *Mean Streets*

STREET CRIME

crime committed in public and often associated with violence, gangs, and poverty.

Street crime generally refers to crime committed in public. The term invokes specific images, however, of violent crime, typically perpetrated in an urban landscape. Both historically and today, street crime is often associated with gangs, and currently it is also associated with both disadvantaged minority groups and poverty. Just why people are drawn to a career of street crime has long been a favorite question of social scientists and is still a matter of heated debate. Explanations for the fluctuations and trends in violent crime rates also vary widely. One theory, for example, posits that street crime rises and falls in relation to the availability of opportunity within the legitimate economy. When this is lacking, people turn elsewhere. A wrinkle on this theory is provided by "differential opportunity theory" (Cloward & Ohlin, 1960). Differential opportunity theory states that in addition to the legitimate economic structure, an illegitimate opportunity structure also exists that is unequally distributed across social classes. That is, some groups have more opportunities than others in the illicit economy, and it is really the ratio of risks and rewards in the formal and black market economies that influences participation in crime (rather than just the opportunities in the mainstream economy alone).

One way, then, to reduce crime would be to raise the costs of working in the illegitimate economy, thereby lowering the net returns. Such a strategy lies behind tougher sentencing policies, such as "three strikes" laws (if you are convicted of three felony crimes, you are imprisoned for life), which aim simultaneously to deter criminals and to incarcerate habitual offenders. The focus of such policies tends to be violent crime; lately, however, such laws have been extended to nonviolent crimes, such as drug dealing. Another strategy would be to increase the returns to entry-level opportunities in the legitimate economy; raising the minimum wage is one way to do this. Either strategy—decreasing the returns to the illegitimate economy or increasing the returns to the legitimate economy—shortens the distance, or differential, between the two economies.

Many people attribute the decrease in crime rates over the past few decades to the adoption of a community policing ideology, in which police officers are viewed (and view themselves) as members of the community they serve, and not to the punitive nature of prison life. Rather than enforce laws from the outside in, as community members walking the streets, police can work to develop reliable relationships and bonds of trust with community residents. On a practical level, this means that greater police presence is felt in areas where community policing is in effect. (However, convincing evidence on this causal claim is still lacking; that said, community policing probably doesn't make crime rates any worse.)

WHITE-COLLAR CRIME

Bernard L. Madoff rose through the social ranks of wealth on Long Island, then Manhattan, and then London, and eventually became the chairman of the NASDAQ exchange, which was based on technology his privately held firm had developed. In 2009, he was sentenced to 150 years in prison—a life sentence for the then-71-year-old. His crime was taking money from investors and fabricating great rates of return to pump up his reputation and keep money coming in when, in fact, his funds were losing money. Returns to investors were paid not from any actual gains their initial investments were accruing, but from the new money coming in the door. Madoff lived an opulent lifestyle, employing well-connected friends and family to keep a steady stream of new investments coming in. During the economic downturn in 2008, Madoff could not keep up with investors' demands to cash out. An investigation by the Federal Bureau of Investigation (FBI) led to his arrest. Madoff estimated that he had lost $50 billion, making his the largest fraud in American history.

Bernie Madoff.

WHITE-COLLAR CRIME

offense commited by a professional (or professionals) against a corporation, agency, or other institution.

Infractions such as fraud are called white-collar crime, a term coined by sociologist Edwin Sutherland in 1939. It is typically committed by a professional (or professionals) in his or her (or their) capacity in the professional world against a corporation, agency, or other professional entity. According to the FBI (2003),

> [w]hite-collar crimes are categorized by deceit, concealment, or violation of trust and are not dependent on the application or threat of physical force or violence. Such acts are committed by individuals and organizations to obtain money, property, or services, to avoid the payment or loss of money or services, or to secure a personal or business advantage.

Although street crime is the most prevalent type of crime, looking strictly at the numbers, white-collar crime has greater financial impact. In 2018, just two individual prosecutions of financial crimes—the bankruptcy of Theranos, Inc., and multistate, systematic medical billing fraud—amounted to nearly $4 billion in damages to investors and other victims (Dodge, 2019). In contrast, the FBI estimates that in 2018, the total estimated losses of all property crimes in the United States, which include robbery, larceny, and motor vehicle theft, amounted to $16.4 billion (FBI, 2018a).

CORPORATE CRIME

a particular type of white-collar crime committed by the officers (CEOs and other executives) of a corporation.

A particular type of white-collar crime is corporate crime, offenses committed by the officers (CEOs and other executives) of a corporation. In the late spring of 2012, JPMorgan Chase trader Bruno Iksil (also known as the London Whale) placed a giant risky trade and ended up losing $6.2 billion for the bank. Losing billions on a trade is deviant but not illegal. Iksil was fired, but he avoided arrest. US federal prosecutors have indicted his boss and his assistant for conspiring to cover up the losses by filing false reports. Penalties for their crimes include a $920 million fine for JPMorgan, but no individuals did time (Stewart, 2015). On a broader level, although the 2007–8 meltdown of the banking system was the worst financial crisis since the Great Depression, nobody went to jail for the shady practices that caused it.

INTERPRETING THE CRIME RATE

Although it may seem, after a glance at the gruesome headlines in today's newspapers, that crime is getting worse, the truth is that deviance has always been present. Kai Erikson, in *Wayward Puritans* (2005), demonstrates how even America's seemingly most upstanding and God-fearing community, the Puritans, produced some bad apples—drunkards, adulterers, and thieves. Erikson's point, however, was that while what is defined as deviant may change over time, deviance is forever with us. For example, Erikson found "crimes against the Church," particularly by Quakers in the late 1650s, to be of central concern to the Puritan community. Religious or moral offenses,

FIGURE 6.2 Total US Violent Crime Rate, 1960–2018

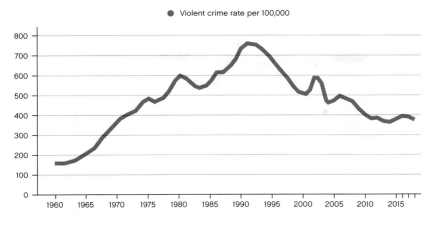

● Violent crime rate per 100,000

SOURCE: FBI, 2018b.

such as drunkenness and adultery, were of primary concern over economic or political ones—at least those were the crimes taken most seriously and probably reported most frequently during the Puritan era. Erikson's central thesis is that a relatively stable amount of deviance may be expected in a given community, but what counts as deviance evolves depending on the type of society or historical period we examine. Think back to our early definition of social deviance: It is, after all, a social construct and subject to change over time and across cultural values.

If the definitions of deviance and crime are always changing, how can we discern if the crime rate is going up or down? In 1960, the total crime rate was around 160.9 per 100,000 people. By 1992, that number had soared to a little over 757, but it has now fallen back to around 370. Figure 6.2 shows the violent crime rate in the United States from 1960 to 2018.

How can so much change occur in the crime rate in so little time? Is the situation really rapidly degenerating into complete chaos? Probably not. To make a statement about the crime rate going up or down, we have to know what is factored into the crime rate. For instance, the definition of assault may change to include more minor offenses. Recently, one local government proposed including brawls at sporting events in the assault category. And if the classifications of violent crimes are changing, it's difficult to compare the crime rate over time. It is also possible that levels of crime reporting by victims fluctuate. In times of economic recession, people might be less likely to report crime because they feel helpless, depressed, or apathetic. Alternatively, a presidential address on fighting terrorism or injustice might make us more diligent in defending the social order.

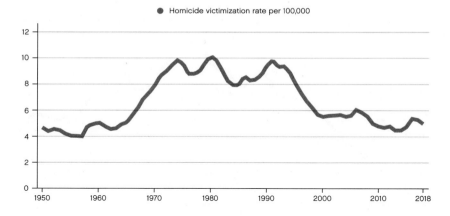

FIGURE 6.3 Homicide Victimization Rate, 1950–2018

● Homicide victimization rate per 100,000

SOURCES: FBI, 2018b.

The point is that the crime rate changes in response to fluctuations in how society classifies and reacts to deviance. In fact, reporting bias may work in the opposite direction from the actual crime rate. Imagine a neighborhood where crime is common. People might be reluctant to report being pickpocketed on the subway when they have just read about three murders the same day. Conversely, in a situation where crime rates are perceived to be low, such as at the opera house, you might be more likely to report a missing wallet. In this way, the reporting of petty crimes may vary inversely to the rate of serious crimes. For these reasons, criminologists (experts trained in studying crime) usually reject the overall crime rate as a reliable indicator of trends in crime. Instead, criminologists use the murder rate to make statements about the overall health of society. Why do they use these statistics instead of violent crime rates? For one thing, it's difficult to fake a murder—either there is a body or there isn't. The murder rate is the best indicator we have of crime in general (Figure 6.3), but even it is not immune to broader changes in society.

For example, if you were shot today in the United States, you would have a much better chance of surviving the gunshot injury than you would have had in 1960. It could be that many more people are arriving at the hospital with bullet wounds, but far fewer of those victims are dying on the operating table thanks to advances in medical technology. The greater survival rate complicates our interpretation of the murder rate (Harris et al., 2002). Has there been a decline in the number of murder attempts, or are doctors just better able to treat bullet wounds? It's difficult to say definitively. We can use the murder rate as a gauge to gain a general sense of crime fluctuations, but precise statistics are practically impossible to gather.

Crime Reduction

Thus far, we have studied some of the functions and social origins of criminal behavior, as well as the prevalent methods of measuring crime. So how do crime fighters fight crime?

DETERRENCE THEORY OF CRIME CONTROL

In 1971 President Richard M. Nixon ushered in America's first War on Drugs. Linking drug use to violent crimes and the decay of social order, the federal and state governments instituted an array of harsher penalties for the possession or sale of illegal substances. The philosophy of deterrence, or deterrence theory, suggests that "crime results from a rational calculation of the costs and benefits of criminal activity" (Spohn & Holleran, 2002). If you know you can make a quick buck by selling cocaine (maybe enough to pay your rent, say, or put food on the table), you might be tempted to engage in such illicit activities. But what if, instead of getting a slap on the wrist, a person caught with small quantities of cocaine is sentenced to a minimum of 15 years in prison? The temptation to sell cocaine might be reduced because you know that the cost of getting caught is higher than the potential benefits of selling drugs. Let's say you are arrested and wind up in prison for 15 years. Would you choose to sell cocaine again? How might the criminal justice system prevent you from doing so?

There are two types of deterrence. Specific deterrence is what the system attempts when it monitors and tries to prevent known criminals from committing more crimes. An example would be the prison parole system, because the criminal remains under supervision and is being specifically deterred from committing another crime. An example of general deterrence would be if, from word on the street, you learn that dealing cocaine carries a prison sentence of 15 years and decide not to risk it. Deterrence theory suggests that crime in general can be reduced through general deterrence, and recidivism in particular can be reduced through specific deterrence. Recidivism is the "reversion of an individual to criminal behavior" after involvement with the criminal justice system (Maltz, 2001).

However, deterrence theory—in practice—has other, unintended consequences that may lead to more crime. For one thing, increased supervision and stricter parole codes have made it more likely that offenders will commit technical violations against their parole terms. Because the system has increased its surveillance of former prisoners, requiring time-consuming meetings with parole officers, the system creates better odds for technical slipups and for catching and punishing them. This is suggested by studies showing that rates of new criminal offenses (as opposed to technical violations) for parolees tend to resemble those of people with comparable

DETERRENCE THEORY

philosophy of criminal justice arising from the notion that crime results from a rational calculation of its costs and benefits.

RECIDIVISM

when an individual who has been involved with the criminal justice system reverts to criminal behavior.

sociodemographic characteristics who have never been incarcerated. In addition, the prison experience might not have the intended rehabilitative effect. Could prisons make it more difficult for offenders to return to the straight and narrow?

Let's first think back to Durkheim and his theory of anomie, which affirms that when our normal lives are disrupted and we can no longer rely on things being relatively stable, we are more likely to commit suicide or engage in other deviant acts. Going to prison for 10 or 15 years might have just this effect; it would be very difficult to "find stable employment, secure suitable housing, or reconcile with . . . family" afterward. Also, reintegration into a community after release from prison is extremely difficult because of "the absence of . . . informal social controls and strong social bonds" (Spohn & Holleran, 2002). Furthermore, while in prison, drug offenders rarely receive the kind of substance abuse treatment that addicts need. They are thus more likely to revert to drug use upon release. Therefore, imprisonment may be particularly counterproductive for drug offenders, and getting tough on crime may inadvertently breed criminals. In addition, as low-level offenders interact daily with serious criminals in prison, they may become socialized by these new peers, adopting their attitudes and behaviors.

Ex-convict turned prison reentry social worker (and later lawyer) Marc Ramirez has an insider's perspective on the system, arguing that the violent, punitive culture of incarceration is counterproductive to rehabilitating prisoners, socializing them productively, and preparing them to give back to society.

> We're paying top dollar to incarcerate people when there are cheaper alternatives. There's been study after study on the [rehabilitative] effects of education, but yet we take Pell Grants and education programs out of prison. Family, having a family base [is critically important for successful reentry], but then these people in prisons are so far away from their families, that they lose ties. We make visiting so difficult for families, you know, it's hard to maintain the family. The cost of making a phone call from a lot of prisons is prohibitive. (Conley, 2014d)

Ramirez is angry that the options facing newly released prisoners are suffocatingly limited. He remembers seeing prisoners "terrified to leave prison because they have not prepared, they have no support system. They don't know what they're going to do . . . there were so many people who would come back. And my thing was always like wow, so many of you guys have had breaks your way and I can't get a break. You gotta do better. You gotta want better. But you're not really given the tools to do better . . . the system is kind of designed to fail." Ramirez's story suggests that providing more housing, employment, and counseling to former convicts as they reenter society may help reduce the number of former prisoners who commit more crime upon release.

Sociologists and geographers have also examined the impact of incarceration on the communities prison inmates call home (Fagan et al., 2003; Williams, 2005). In New York City the incarcerated population is disproportionately drawn from a small handful of neighborhoods, a pattern that is sustained even as crime rates have dropped dramatically. While they are in prison, inmates cannot make positive contributions to the community in terms of providing steady incomes, starting families, or building up social networks that lead to employment in legitimate industries. At the community level, high rates of incarceration among community members create conditions for continued poverty, as those left behind must support families on fewer salaries both during and after incarceration. From Pager's research earlier in this chapter, we know that former felons have a difficult time finding employment. Blocked access to legitimate employment creates conditions for sustained poverty. At the same time, historical crime rates are used to determine current police involvement, which means that once-crime-ridden neighborhoods will continue to receive disproportionate formal surveillance and their residents will be more likely to be arrested.

DIGITAL.WWNORTON.COM/YOUMAYASK7

To see my interview with Marc Ramirez, go to digital.wwnorton.com/youmayask7

GOFFMAN'S TOTAL INSTITUTION

The high rates of recidivism in the United States bring us back to labeling theory, which suggests that the process of becoming a deviant often involves contact with, even absorption into, a special institution such as a prison or mental health institution. And as labeling theorists have shown, our interaction with others very significantly impacts the formation of our personal identity. Erving Goffman, writing in the symbolic interactionist tradition, theorized about how institutions such as prisons and mental health hospitals often become breeding grounds for secondary deviance, providing an important link in the reproduction of deviance through their effects on inmates and patients (Goffman, 1961).

TOTAL
INSTITUTION

an institution in which
one is totally immersed
and that controls all the
basics of day-to-day life;
no barriers exist between
the usual spheres of daily
life, and all activity occurs
in the same place and
under the same single
authority.

Presumably, most of us sleep, play, and work in different places, with different people and rules structuring our interactions at each location. For example, you probably spend the evening in your home or dorm, relatively undisturbed, and leave in the morning for class, where you are expected to dress appropriately and respect your professors. Total institutions are distinguished by "a breakdown of the barriers separating" these "three spheres of life" (sleep, work, play). In total institutions, "all aspects of life are conducted in the same place and under the same single authority" (Goffman, 1961). In total institutions such as prisons and mental hospitals, life is highly regimented, and the inmates take part in all scheduled activities together. The inmates have no control over the form or flow of activities, which are chosen by the institutional authorities to "fulfill the official aims of the institution." Thus, if the official aim of prisons is rehabilitation, prisoners might be required to attend at least one self-improvement class a day or engage in some sort of productive labor. All of these activities occur in the same place with the same group of people every day.

In Chapter 4 we examined the various theories of socialization and the development of the self through our interactions with other social actors. All your life you have been slowly accumulating knowledge about who you are in the world. Once you enter a total institution such as a prison, a process that strips away your sense of self begins. As Goffman puts it, "a series of abasements, degradations, humiliations, and profanations" quickly commences. Once people enter a prison or a mental institution, they are closed off from their normal routines and cease to fulfill their usual social roles. Because the roles people play are important to the way they perceive themselves,

Inmates in an Arizona jail. The local sheriff requires all of the county's inmates to work seven days a week. They are fed only twice a day, are denied recreation, and receive no coffee, cigarettes, salt, pepper, or ketchup.

this separation from the world erodes that sense of identity. In the Stanford Prison Experiment, what first occurred when the "inmates" arrived at the "prison" in the basement of the psychology department? They were issued uniforms and given numbers in place of names. The mandated homogeneity of prisoners (and patients) results in an erasure of self. The total institution simultaneously strips away clothes, personal belongings, nicknames, hairstyles, cosmetics, and toiletries—all the tools that people use to identify themselves. The inmates no longer have control over their environment, peer group, daily activities, or personal possessions. It's not hard to see how this process leads to a sense of helplessness. The total institution rapidly destroys a prisoner's sense of self-determination, self-control, and freedom.

The authorities in these total institutions are given the unenviable duty of "showing the prisoners who's boss" and expediting the process of prisoner degradation to ensure "co-operativeness" (Goffman, 1961). Wardens must "socialize" inmates into compliance through informal "obedience test[s]" or "will-breaking contest[s]" until the inmate "who shows defiance receives immediate visible punishment, which increases until he openly 'cries uncle' and humbles himself." When Zimbardo locked a group of seemingly normal college kids into the basement of a Stanford building (discussed in the box on pages 224–25), he found that not only were the inmates affected but the guards also felt impelled to use increasingly violent and inhumane means to solidify their authority and keep the prisoners in check. We can see these patterns in everyday life, too. When given the responsibility of watching younger siblings, have you ever secretly (or not so secretly) delighted in bossing them around? Because the roles we play are important to how we think about ourselves, it is hardly possible for the self-images of both guards and prisoners to remain unaffected by the prison environment.

FOUCAULT ON PUNISHMENT

On March 2, 1757, Damiens the regicide was condemned "to make the amende honorable [a kind of ritual abasement] before the main door of the Church of Paris," where he was to be "taken and conveyed in a cart, wearing nothing but a shirt, holding a torch of burning wax weighing two pounds"; then, "in the said cart, to the Place de Greve, where, on a scaffold that will be erected there, the flesh will be torn from his breasts, arms, thighs, and calves with red-hot pincers, his right hand, holding the knife with which he committed the said parricide, burnt with sulfur, and, on those places where the flesh will be torn away, poured molten lead, burning oil, burning resin, wax and sulfur melted together and then his body drawn and quartered by four horses and his limbs and body consumed by fire, reduced to ashes and his ashes thrown to the winds" (Foucault, 1977, p. 1).

The execution of Robert-François Damiens, a French servant who attempted to assassinate King Louis XV at Versailles in 1757.

Besides possibly turning your stomach, the above passage vividly illustrates the dramatic shift in penal practices from the eighteenth century to the present day. How do we conceive of punishment nowadays? We usually think of prisons, juvenile detention centers, and probation. In *Discipline and Punish* (1977), the French theorist Michel Foucault examines the emergence of the modern penal system and how this system represents a transformation in social control. How did the modern prison system emerge? And what functions does it serve in the disciplining of modern life?

When Robert-François Damiens was publicly tortured and then eventually drawn and quartered for trying to kill King Louis XV, the target of punishment was Damiens's body. The entire public spectacle revolved around Damiens suffering for his wrongdoing, culminating in his death. Damiens was even put to death holding the same knife he used to attack the king. According to Foucault (1977), this gruesome "violence against the body" exemplifies a premodern form of punishment, which is concentrated on the body and associated with the crime committed. So, for example, if you kill someone, you are publicly executed. If you steal something, perhaps your fingers or hand will be cut off. This "eye for an eye" mentality is similar to that represented by Durkheim's mechanical social sanctions.

We might like to believe that modern punishment came about because prison reformers lobbied for more humane penal tactics that aimed to reform the criminal through rehabilitation. We no longer (with the exception of the death penalty) publicly violate the criminal's flesh by, for example, pouring molten lead on his excoriated body. Punishment takes place in private, away from the public eye, and it leaves the criminal's body intact. (Although much violence, including rape, does occur inside prison walls, the state does not formally sanction it and is supposed to protect prisoners from such attacks.)

Foucault claims that modern punishment has as its target what he calls "the soul" of the prisoner. The soul, for Foucault, is the sum of an individual's unique habits and peculiarities: what makes me *me* and you *you*. Such a penal system tries to understand the individual and his or her abnormalities to correct or reform bad habits. (Again, this is a highly stylized view of the history of criminal justice, given that in the United States, some jurisdictions still impose the death penalty and our government has even tortured political detainees. At the very least, we have witnessed an incomplete Foucaultian transformation.)

By "reforming the soul," Foucault means the use of experts such as social workers, psychologists, and criminologists to analyze and correct individual behavior. How does a prisoner become eligible for parole? The *New York State Parole Handbook* (New York State Division of Parole, 2007) indicates that "parole 'readiness'" depends on the inmate's "good prison behavior," involvement in "prison programming" for education and skills acquisition, and substance abuse counseling, all to "make important strides in self-improvement." After a criminal leaves prison on parole, the newly released prisoner is assigned a field parole officer who is in charge of monitoring the whereabouts of the parolee and guiding his or her reentry into community life. The handbook also indicates that a parole officer must help parolees "develop positive attitudes and behavior" and "encourage participation in programs for self-improvement." Parolees are, in principle, scrupulously supervised by parole officers and sometimes subject to unscheduled visits at work or home. This is all part of what Foucault would consider the modern face of penal practices.

How did the transformation in penal practice, from punishment targeted at the body to reform of the soul, take place? Foucault believes that this transformation is linked to changes in how social control operates more generally, which in turn led to innovations in penal practices. Foucault uses the following example to illustrate the way modern punishment is organized and its implications for modern social control:

> The prisoners' day will begin at six in the morning in winter and at five in the summer. They will work for nine hours a day throughout the year. Two hours a day will be devoted to instruction. Work and the day will end at nine o'clock in winter and at eight in summer. . . . At the first drum-roll, the prisoners must rise and dress in silence, as the supervisor opens the cell doors. At the second drum-roll, they must be dressed and make their beds. (Foucault, 1977, p. 6)

Foucault's example, extracted from a contemporary prisoners' timetable in France, contrasts strikingly with the way poor Damiens was punished several centuries earlier. Foucault's point, however, is that this sort of regimentation happens not only in prisons but also in society at large. Penal

PANOPTICON

a circular building composed of an inner ring and an outer ring designed to serve as a prison in which the guards, housed in the inner ring, can observe the prisoners without the detainees knowing whether they are being watched.

The Stateville Penitentiary in Illinois was built along the principles of Bentham's panopticon, a model for a prison in which inmates would always be visible.

practices are indicative of how social control is exercised outside prison walls. Disciplinary techniques are modes of monitoring, examining, and regimenting individuals that are diffused throughout society. Foucault gives many examples of where and how this discipline takes place both in and out of prisons—in the military, in schools, in medical institutions, and so forth. For example, when you first entered school, perhaps even when you entered college, you were probably required to take a series of standardized tests. You were also required to visit your pediatrician for shots and a checkup in which he or she meticulously documented your growth and health. Once in school, you were made to sit in straight, orderly rows (so the teacher could see all students at all times) and then were issued a report card every term. If you were chronically disruptive or inattentive in class, you might have been sent for special testing by experts to determine if you had a learning or behavioral disorder. These are all examples of how you have been subjected to various modes of discipline that monitor, examine, and regiment individuals.

Foucault used the imagined architectural design of the panopticon as a metaphor for this march toward total surveillance and control. Jeremy Bentham, an English philosopher, devised the panopticon as a prison design. The panopticon is a circular building composed of an inner ring and an outer ring. Prisoners' cells are located in the outer ring, and large windows compose the front and back of each cell, allowing ample natural light to flood the rooms. The inner ring is a guards' tower, which also has large windows, that open onto the windows of prisoners' cells. The guards can always see the prisoners, regardless of where they are in their cells, but the prisoners do not know when they are being watched (although the visibility of the central tower serves as a reminder that they are always under scrutiny). Foucault (1977) asserts that the "power" of the guards is both "visible and unverifiable."

Foucault uses the panopticon as a metaphor for the general functioning of disciplinary techniques in society. Therefore, when the modern prison system emerged, based on monitoring, examining, and regimenting individual prisoners, there was a "gradual extension of the mechanisms of discipline," and they "spread throughout the whole social body," which led to "the formation of what might be called in general the disciplinary society." Remember all the steps you had to go through to gain entrance to kindergarten? The tests and checkups? And then the report cards, the parent–teacher conferences, the tidy rows of desks? These are the sorts of panoptic (literally, "all-seeing") disciplinary techniques diffused throughout the social body. In Foucault's words, "our society is one not of spectacle, but of surveillance."

THE US CRIMINAL JUSTICE SYSTEM

At various points in history, the US criminal justice system has fluctuated between two approaches to handling criminals: rehabilitation and punishment. Since the 1890s, argues Frank Allen (1981), the rehabilitative ideal has lost most of its significance and appeal because of shifting cultural values among Americans. Despite what Durkheim predicted, the concept of punishment ("lock 'em up and throw away the key") has largely replaced rehabilitation, winning political and popular favor and influencing criminal justice policy. The result? In late 2016, about 6.6 million people were on probation, on parole, or in state/federal prison, about 2.6 percent of US adults or 1 in every 38 (Kaeble & Cowhig, 2018; Figure 6.4). We are in an era of what sociologists call "mass incarceration."

Not all Americans have been affected equally by the policy of mass incarceration, however. While Black adults have experienced the largest declines in incarceration over the past decade among any racial category, in 2017 Black men were still imprisoned almost six times as much as White men, and more

FIGURE 6.4 Size of US Prison Population, 1980–2016

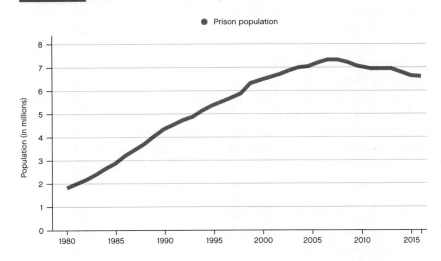

SOURCE: Kaeble & Cowhig, 2018.

than twice as much as Hispanic men (BJS, 2019). A similar pattern holds among women, although far fewer women are incarcerated overall—about 8 percent of state and federal prisoners. Black women are about 90 percent more likely to be incarcerated compared to White women, and 40 percent more likely than Hispanic women (BJS, 2019). If current incarceration rates were not to change (but see below on prison reform), a whopping 32 percent of Black males would be predicted to serve time in a state or federal prison during their lifetime, compared with 17 percent of Hispanic men and 5.9 percent of White men. These numbers of prisoners are strikingly high for an industrialized democracy. Also, the United States is the only industrialized nation in the world to use capital punishment (US Department of Justice, 2007).

Some advocates for deterrence theory claim that the tough-on-crime policies that led to the era of mass incarceration are responsible for the dramatic drop in violent crime the United States has experienced since the early 1990s (Levitt, 2004; Corman & Mocan, 2005). Others point to factors as varied as the elimination of lead in gasoline and the passage of the Clean Air Act (reducing exposure to toxins that can induce behavioral problems and cognitive deficits; Reyes, 2002), the legalization of abortion in the early 1970s (leading to a reduction in unwanted children who might be more likely to commit crime; Berk et al., 2003), an aging population (retirees are less likely to mug someone; Perkins, 1997), the stabilization of the crack epidemic (which had spurred turf wars when it first arrived on the scene; Johnson et al., 2005), the growing ubiquity of surveillance cameras (which act as a deterrent by making it harder to get away with property or violent crime; Welsh & Farrington, 2004); and even the digitization of the economy (since it's easier to scam people for their social security numbers online than it is to break into their houses and steal their TV sets). Indeed, it seems like the pendulum in US policy is finally swinging back to a more rehabilitative stance, as one of the major pieces of legislation enacted by Donald Trump was federal prison reform, the First Step Act of 2018, which is likely to reduce the number of prisoners under lock and key. Many states are passing similar sentencing reforms, reducing terms for nonviolent crimes. Such state-level changes are actually more critical to the size of the incarcerated population, since the vast majority of detainees are held by states (about 1.3 million) and not by the national government (about 220,000; Sawyer & Wagner, 2019).

One area where the federal government is detaining a lot of people is in the immigration domain. While those migrants (or suspected migrants) being detained by US Immigration and Customs Enforcement (ICE) are officially civil and not criminal detainees, they have been treated in many cases worse than some criminal offenders. The separation of children from their parents at the border received much press attention, as did the terrible conditions of some detention centers; however, there are other aspects of ICE detention practices that have garnered less attention. For instance, since these are not criminal detainees, they should be paid minimum wage when doing work. But instead, they are paid only a dollar per day, as if they were criminally incarcerated. There is also a lack of proper due process, which has led to a large number of US citizens being deported! Many of these practices are driven by the private prison industry, which profits off the detention of migrants and which is "promised" a certain number of filled beds per federal law. Political scientist Jacqueline Stevens has not only spent much time writing about the conditions of ICE detention but has initiated a number of lawsuits to change them (Conley, 2019b).

DIGITAL.WWNORTON.COM/YOUMAYASK7

To see my interview with Jacqueline Stevens about the conditions of ICE detention, go to digital.wwnorton.com/youmayask7

Similar to both criminal and civil imprisonment rates and conditions, justice on death row is not color-blind (see Figure 6.5). In 1998 a study of Philadelphia death penalty cases revealed ample evidence of some form of racial discrimination: Either the race of the defendant or the race of the victim came to bear on the outcome of the case (Baldus et al., 1998). First, the race of the murder victim matters. For example, in a study of the North Carolina justice system, researchers found that the odds of a murderer receiving a death sentence rose 3.5 times if the victim was White, holding constant other relevant factors (Unah & Boger, 2001). Second and more obviously, the race of the accused matters. Contrary to popular belief about Black-on-White violence, interracial murders are fairly rare. As of 2019, out of 1,512 executions carried out in the United States since 1976 (when the Supreme Court reinstated the death penalty), 294 involved cases of Black-on-White homicide, but only 21 involved executions arising from cases of White-on-Black murder (Death Penalty Information Center, 2020a). One hypothesis would assert that these statistics could result from African Americans committing disproportionately more crime than Whites while receiving, on average, appropriate penalties for their criminal behaviors. To make this sort of claim, we would need to have faith in the criminal justice system as a sound entity that generally delivers fair and accurate punishment. However, more than enough data to the contrary exist. Between 1973 and December 31, 2018, 167 people were exonerated from death row: Of these, 87 were Black, 62 White, and 15 Latinx (Death Penalty Information Center, 2020b). In 2017 and 2018 alone, five persons were released from death sentences, after an average of 30 years behind bars, their careers and families having been permanently altered (Death Penalty Information Center, 2020c). Some

DOES PRISON WORK BETTER AS PUNISHMENT OR REHAB?

With prison overcrowding resulting from our extremely high incarceration rate (see page 243), one of the questions running through criminal justice research is the proper role of time behind bars. Does going to prison give inmates access to services and treatment that make them better equipped to be productive members of society, thereby reducing the number of crimes they might commit in the future? Is it plausible to think that individuals who are incarcerated may spend their time kicking drug habits, gaining religion, avoiding negative influences in their community, and obtaining an education, and emerge less likely to commit crime when they are released?

Or perhaps the very thought of serving hard time works to deter crime? If so, we might expect the strongest deterrent effect to be among those who have already dealt with the harsh realities of prison life. After all, who would want to go back to jail after being released and tasting the freedom that most of us take for granted? This is the principle behind "scared straight" programs for youth who are teetering on the path of righteousness. By showing teenagers in trouble what prison is "really" like, such interventions hope to take any glamorous shine off a life of crime.

But it could also be the case that prison ends up being like "college for criminals"—a chance to network with other convicts, learn new illicit skills, and harden oneself to mainstream social norms, all while missing out on work experience and educational opportunities and acquiring the stigma of having done time. In other words, perhaps prison actually creates crime by increasing recidivism.

At first blush it would seem that prison does indeed breed crime. After all, one of the best predictors of future arrest is past incarceration. However, it could obviously be the case that those criminals sent up the river, so to speak, are the ones most beyond hope of reform. That is, they would have committed more crimes regardless of whether they went to prison, received probation, or were let off completely. We could, of course, look at offenders who commit the same crime, comparing those who go to prison and those who don't, to see how they fare afterward. But the problem is that there may be subtle differences in the two groups that judges knew about but that we cannot hope to adequately measure from administrative records.

A solution to this problem comes from the fact that some states and localities randomly

Inmates at San Quentin State Prison in an adult education class. Why do prisons spend taxpayer money to fund educational opportunities for inmates?

assign judges to cases. Like anyone else, judges are human beings with certain tendencies. Specifically, some judges are harsher in their sentencing than others. So it's like assigning convicts to a randomized medical treatment: Some get the "treatment" (the harsh judge who sends them to prison) and some get the "placebo" (the more lenient judge who gives them probation). By examining variability in outcomes among convicted criminals based on the type of judge they were assigned (not on the prisoners' own characteristics), we can identify the effects of incarceration—and, by extension, the effects of the massive investment we've made in the prison system.

As it turns out, for adults, it doesn't make much difference to their probability of committing a future crime (and getting caught) whether or not they go to prison. (This lack of a difference suggests that taxpayers could get roughly the same crime rate but save a bunch of money on

prison overhead by sentencing most criminals to house arrest. Of course, for this to work we have to assume that the deterrent effect against first-time offenses is minimal as well.)

For youth, the story is even starker: Across the United States, more than 130,000 juveniles are detained each year, and on any given day 70,000 minors are in formal detention. But as it turns out, locking these kids up makes them less likely to complete high school and more likely to commit crimes as adults (as evidenced from the random assignment to judges). In other words, far from being "scared straight," kids sent to detention are simply prepped for criminal life. Of course, this means that not only is locking kids up expensive, but it generates future costs in the form of more crime to deal with when they grow up.

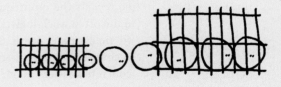

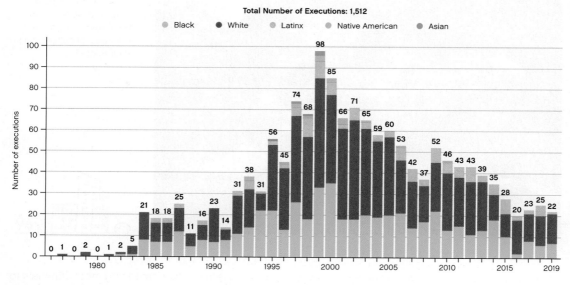

FIGURE 6.5 Number of Executions by Race, 1976–2019

Total Number of Executions: 1,512

● Black ● White ● Latinx ● Native American ● Asian

SOURCE: Death Penalty Information Center, 2020a.

of these exonerations resulted from new DNA evidence. In a sense, the new technology has shed light on the flaws in the system, raising the question "How many cases were wrongly judged before the deployment of DNA testing?" This evidence of injustice has led to the abolition of the death penalty in Illinois, Connecticut, New Jersey, New York, New Mexico, Maryland, Delaware, New Hampshire, and Nebraska since 2007.

Conclusion

Training a sociological lens on deviance requires a careful and thorough review of not only the immediate causes and effects of deviance but also the broader social forces that undergird and define it. Sometimes, doing so takes us to paradoxical places, such as Émile Durkheim's finding that some degree of crime is healthy for a society, insofar as crime unites the social body by allowing us all to rally against a common enemy. Sometimes, doing so reveals the unintended consequences of labels such as "deviant." And quite often, sociologists study tragedies in order to seek the social answers to violence and death. Sociology does not hope to provide comprehensive accounts of criminal acts or injustice, but it does seek to dig deeper for concrete answers in our social world.

QUESTIONS FOR REVIEW

1. How does Philip Zimbardo's Stanford Prison Experiment help explain the behavior documented at Abu Ghraib prison?

2. Describe two potential functions—as punishment or rehab—that prisons could play in society. What evidence from this chapter suggests that prisons "work" to rehabilitate people? To scare or punish people?

3. Explain the difference between mechanical and organic solidarity. How do deviants hold us together in both types of society?

4. We usually think of suicide as solely the result of an intensely personal decision. What is Émile Durkheim's explanation for suicide? Define egoistic suicide and describe why, according to Durkheim, more Protestants commit suicide than Catholics.

5. A student wants to achieve good grades but is not interested in studying for exams; instead, the student finds various ways to cheat. How does Robert Merton's strain theory explain this behavior, and which "type" does the student exemplify?

6. How does the broken windows theory of deviance support the claim that the definition of *deviant* depends on social context? What happened to social control mechanisms like formal and informal social sanctions in Philip Zimbardo's study involving cars?

7. Why don't criminologists use the crime rate as an indicator of crime trends? What do they use instead, and why?

8. Describe Émile Durkheim's theory of the collective conscience and explain how it is related to punishment. How does Michel Foucault's focus in *Discipline and Punish* (1977) differ from Durkheim's work regarding punishment in premodern and modern societies?

9. Explain how a fraternity house could be considered a total institution.

EVERYDAY DEVIANCE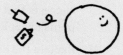

One legal scholar has claimed that the average American citizen commits three felonies a day (Silverglate, 2011). This may sound like a gross overestimate, but underneath lies a provocative argument: that our society has become overcriminalized by federal prosecutors who take vague laws and misconstrue seemingly ordinary activity as criminal. Regardless of what you think of this argument, I hope this chapter has helped convince you that crime and deviance are part of the fabric of our society and that breaking the rules is more common than some care to admit.

TRY IT!

Write a list of what petty crimes you commit on a regular basis. I'll start us off.

ON A TYPICAL DAY, I MAY (OR MAY NOT) HAVE:

JAYWALKED

_____

SPED WHILE DRIVING (AND BROKEN OTHER MOTOR VEHICLE RULES)

_____

STREAMED A TV SHOW ON A SKETCHY WEBSITE

_____

LOITERED

_____

ROBBED A BANK (JUST KIDDING)

_____

_____

_____

_____

_____

THINK ABOUT IT

Have you ever been cited or arrested for any of your activities? If not, why not? If so, did it affect your future behavior?

Do you think everyone (i.e., people in different demographics) could get away with the same things you do? Why or why not? How do informal social norms and formal laws mesh or clash?

SOCIOLOGY ON THE STREET

Formal and informal social sanctions allow people to coexist with strangers in crowded public spaces. When do people break these sanctions, and how do others enforce sanctions? Watch the Sociology on the Street video to find out more: **digital.wwnorton.com/youmayask7.**

WANT MORE PRACTICE?

Complete the InQuizitive activity for this chapter at digital.wwnorton.com /youmayask7

Part 2

FAULT LINES...
SOCIAL DIVISION AND
INEQUALITY

In 2004 photographer Tuca Vieira captured this now-iconic view of São Paulo, Brazil: the favela (or shantytown) of Paraisópolis next to the wealthy community of Morumbi.

7

INEQUALITY IS THE RESULT
OF ABUNDANCE.

Stratification

Sarah Katz, meet Jeff Rutgers. While it turns out that first names probably don't predict success all that well, last names not only tell us about our chances for success today, but also link us to the successes (or lack thereof) of our distant ancestors. By analyzing the distribution of last names in the professional directories of lawyers and doctors, economic historian Gregory Clark (2014) is able to assess the degree to which societies demonstrate social mobility or its opposite, social reproduction.

As it turns out, by being an Ashkenazi Jew (those who populated Europe), Sarah Katz enjoys about an eightfold greater chance of being a medical doctor today than does Jessica Smith (Smith being the most common surname in the United States). Jeff Rutgers, meanwhile, by virtue of being descended from a male ancestor who attended an Ivy League or similarly old university sometime between 1650 and 1850, enjoys an approximate threefold advantage. Also of advantaged pedigree are Hiro Suzuki, by virtue of having a Japanese surname, and Patricia Winthrop, who shares a name with a rich family of the 1920s.

Perhaps unsurprisingly, the actor Denzel Washington does not hail from a family of doctors and lawyers. Washington is among the most common African American surnames and displays the mark of racial inequality such that Black Washingtons are two-thirds less likely to be represented among the directory of physicians than they should be based on overall numbers in the population. Ditto for Annie Begay and John Yazzie, who have the two most common Native American names and are 94 percent less likely to be doctors compared with the US average! While racial inequality for these groups is well known, I'd like to introduce you to Ralph Gagnon, who I bet you didn't know was also disadvantaged even though he is White.

According to Clark, the descendants of New France settlers—that is, the mostly French people who came through Québec, Canada, and other northern areas—have 40 percent lower odds of becoming a doctor. Though this is, of course, less than the disadvantage of being Black, Latinx, or Native American, it is also perhaps more surprising because we think of the French as not only White but a relatively high-status group. Indeed, some of our most snooty words come from French (Hors d'oeuvres, anyone?). What's more, people of French origin have been associated with an elite status since the time of the Norman conquest of England in 1066.

More than figuring out what your name says about your postgraduation chances, Clark's analysis is interesting because it challenges some of our most cherished assumptions about social mobility. Through his analysis of names in Sweden, India, medieval Europe, the modern United Kingdom, the United States, Chile, and other societies, Clark finds that the intergenerational correlation in status is much higher than we had previously thought. Typically, sociologists and economists examine the extent to which parent-and-child measures of social class, such as income, are correlated. Zero would mean that it makes no difference whatsoever to your income what your parent earned. One would mean that there was an absolutely rigid caste system where each generation perfectly reflects the success of the prior one. Most societies obviously fall in the middle somewhere. The latest research on income, for example, has busted the myth that the United States, despite being more unequal than most European societies, has higher rates of economic mobility. Indeed, the United States consistently ranks as the least mobile rich country in the world when it comes to income.

But Clark's analysis tells us that the US parent–child correlation in "social class" overall is about .84, compared to .3 to .6 in income depending on the study. To explain the discrepancy, he suggests that earlier work focused on one measure of social class, making it look like there's a lot more mobility than there actually is. Take Microsoft founder Bill Gates Jr., for example. He dropped out of college even though his father graduated from law school, so by education measures Gates Jr. would seem to be downwardly mobile. But measure income or wealth, of course, and he is upwardly mobile in a huge way. However, Clark's contention is that in some underlying, summary measure of class or status, most of us reflect our parents' social position a lot more than we may care to believe. This, he argues, is the only reason he would see the effects of what your ancestors did 15 generations ago on what you might be doing for a living now.

Perhaps even more surprising than the fact that the rates of social mobility are lower than we thought they were is that, according to Clark, they don't vary all that much across time and place. Medieval Europe with its feudal system had more or less the same degree of social exchange between classes as does modern Britain today. The unequal, deregulated United States enjoys more or less the same fluidity as social democratic Sweden on the one hand, and on the other hand is not significantly more mobile than India, whose caste system is thought to be the most rigid social structure of all. (Though discrimination based on castes has been outlawed in India since 1950, there are still enormous inequalities by caste membership.) Even conscious efforts to totally remodel society, including the slaughtering of elites, can only temper slightly the degree of social inheritance. Despite the purges of the Cultural Revolution, massive land redistribution, and complete political transformation, Communist China under Mao Zedong reduced its intergenerational persistence to only about .7, down from .8.

So if we value social mobility, what's a poor old sociologist to do in light of Clark's analysis? Maybe we should all give up and just change our last names to Potros, a Coptic Christian name from Egypt. As it turns out, in the United States at least, Copts are the most successful group of all. One version of Coptic lore claims that they are the true descendants of the pharaohs. If that's right, then maybe the long arm of social history is even stronger than Clark imagined.

Views of Inequality

To answer questions about stratification, we need a conceptual framework through which to view inequality. In the following section, I present three possible frameworks and leave it to you to decide which you think is most appropriate to explain the intersection of various dimensions of stratification. We'll start with the Enlightenment in the eighteenth century and move forward from there.

JEAN-JACQUES ROUSSEAU

Writing prolifically from 1750 to 1782, Jean-Jacques Rousseau greatly influenced the political ideas of the French Revolution and the development of socialist thought. Seeing humankind as naturally pure and good, Rousseau appealed to biology and human instincts to explain social outcomes. For Rousseau, it is only through the process of building society and repressing this pure natural character that social problems develop. Specifically, Rousseau sees the emergence of private property, the idea that a person has the right to own something, as the primary source of social ills. If we were to strip away the elements of society that result from the institution of private property— the competition, isolation, aggression, and hierarchical organization—only social equality, a condition in which no differences in wealth, power, prestige, or status based on nonnatural bases exist, would remain. According to Rousseau (2004), there are two forms of inequality: physical (or natural), which "consists in a difference of age, health, bodily strength, and the qualities of the mind or of the soul," and social (or political), which

> depends on a kind of conventional inequality and is established or
> at least authorized by the consent of men. This latter consists of

STRATIFICATION

the hierarchical organization of a society into groups with differing levels of power, social prestige, or status and economic resources.

SOCIAL EQUALITY

a condition in which no differences in wealth, power, prestige, or status based on nonnatural conventions exist.

Jean-Jacques Rousseau.

the different privileges which some men enjoy to the prejudice of others, such as that of being more rich, more honored, more powerful, or even in a position to exact obedience. (p. 15)

Rousseau acknowledges that a certain amount of natural inequality will always exist among people: Someone is always going to be better than someone else at kicking a ball, hunting large game, doing math, or seeing long distances. Some of these inequalities are a simple result of aging, as a basketball player in her twenties will almost certainly have greater physical abilities than a basketball player in her eighties. In contrast, social inequality is a result of privileges and uneven access to resources (i.e., private property) and will eventually lead to social ills. There are only so many resources available in any society and, more broadly, in the world as a whole.

Imagine that all the resources available in a given society are represented in a single pizza, cut into 10 slices, and 10 hungry people are sitting around the pie. In Rousseau's ideal natural world, where people are inherently good and lack any notion of personal ownership, each individual would get one slice. But in a world where private property is the norm, the division is likely to be significantly less equitable. For whatever reason—maybe some of the 10 have more guile, maybe some paid more than others, maybe one person's family owns the pizza parlor—the pie is distributed unevenly among the group. Rousseau sees such inequality as ultimately detrimental and as a catalyst for social conflict.

Imagine yourself as one of the people who get no pizza, even though there are 10 of you and 10 slices. Imagine further that you have a hungry family who would certainly have appreciated that slice of pizza. Now imagine watching the person sitting across from you slowly enjoying 5 steaming slices, one by one. Would this make you jealous? Would it make you spiteful? Would it make you subvert your essentially good nature in trying to steal a slice? Might you even be willing to hurt the pizza hoarder to feed yourself and your family? Might the pizza hoarder then defend his personal property and maybe even hurt you to keep your hands off it? According to Rousseau, he might also buy off the biggest and strongest of those who have no pizza with two slices in order to protect his rights.

THE SCOTTISH ENLIGHTENMENT AND THOMAS MALTHUS

Rousseau saw the move away from the pure state of nature as an extremely negative historical development, complaining that "man was born free, and he is everywhere in chains." But thinkers of the later Enlightenment, including Adam Ferguson and John Millar of Scotland and Thomas Malthus of England, saw inequality as good—or at least necessary. These three agreed that inequality arises when private property emerges and that private property emerges when resources can be preserved, because it is only through surpluses that some people are able to conserve and increase their bounty. This leads to the paradox of this chapter: Inequality is a result of surplus.

When individuals or groups in society become more efficient and productive, they can gather, hunt, or grow more than they themselves can consume at a given time. They can then conserve such a surplus, whether that means turning milk into cheese, making berries into preserves, or putting their money into a hedge fund. In whatever way they choose, they can preserve current resources and transform them into assets, a form of wealth that can be stored for the future. (In fact, the word *asset* comes from the French legal expression *aver assetz*, meaning "to have enough.") Whereas previously the incentive might have been to share the wealth when you couldn't store it—to generate reciprocal goodwill for the rainy day when you don't have enough to eat and your neighbor does—now, when property can be preserved, the incentive is for individuals to hoard all of it, so that when a rainy day comes along, personal savings are available. Alternatively, if a resource-rich individual decides to distribute surplus wealth, he or she might decide to extract power, promises, and rewards in return for what he or she provides.

For Ferguson and Millar, such social developments resulting from the establishment of private property represent a huge improvement in society, because private property leads to higher degrees of social organization and efficiency: If an individual can preserve and accumulate resources and become more powerful by storing up assets (private property), he or she will have much more incentive to work. Thanks to personal incentives, people won't just slack off after they have accumulated what they need for the day's survival, but will instead work to build up society, and as a by-product they will improve civilization. For the Scottish Enlightenment thinkers, inequality was a prerequisite for social progress, and social progress was a prerequisite for the development of civilization—the greatest goal toward which humankind could strive.

Malthus also had a positive view of inequality, but for a different reason. In 1798, Malthus published an anonymous treatise titled "An Essay on the Principle of Population as It Affects the Future Improvement of Society," arguing that human populations grow geometrically (multiplicatively, like rabbits), while our ability to produce food increases only arithmetically (much more slowly). Simply put, his theory suggests that a rising number of people on the planet will eventually use up all the available resources and bring about mass starvation and conflict. Take the pizza example from above: With 10 people and 10 slices, the pie could be divided so that everyone got enough to eat. But what if there were 20 people or 50 people? Or 100 people? As the number of people increases, each person gets less and less, even if the pie is divided evenly. Humankind, Malthus believed, was similarly destined to live in a state of constant near-death misery, as population growth always pushed society to the limits of food availability.

Because of these dire trends, Malthus believed inequality was good, or at least necessary, for avoiding the problem of massive overpopulation and hence starvation. Inequality, from his perspective, kept the population in check. After all, for Malthus, the main problem with the world—especially with England—was the number of people in it, and anything that tended to restrain population growth was supremely good. In this vein, he denounced soup kitchens and early marriages while defending the effects of smallpox, slavery, and child murder (Heilbroner, 1999). Malthus believed that overpopulation would create more and more human misery, and therefore the most logical solution would be to allow the population to thin itself out naturally rather than to exacerbate the problem by reducing the levels of inequality, a measure that would "temporarily" ease the condition of the "masses," thereby causing their numbers to swell even more. Such a condition is today called a Malthusian population trap—a situation in which population growth leads not to abundance but to increased poverty.

In an interview for this book, I asked Jeffrey Sachs of the Earth Institute at Columbia University if he thought that sub-Saharan Africa might be facing a Malthusian trap as the per capita land available for farming dwindles, and if so, what can be done to get out of the trap. Sachs captured the complexity of the big picture, so I'll let him speak for himself:

In Africa there's been a partial transition from high mortality to low mortality, from maybe 600 of every 1,000 children dying before their fifth birthday to a situation where it's perhaps around 150 per 1,000 dying. Still remarkably high by global standards, but way down from what it was. But the fertility rates especially in the rural areas remain high—as many as five or six, sometimes even seven per woman. That means rapid population growth. The woman that has six children, [of whom] two die, has on average four children who grow up to adulthood. Two of those will be daughters. Each woman is replacing herself with two daughters in the next generation. That's a doubling of the population from one generation to the next, called a gross population number. That's extraordinary. You can't keep ahead of that in terms of economic development, and certainly not in ecology. So what do you do about that? What do you do to accelerate the reduction of fertility? Save the children. It seems paradoxical. But when the children are staying alive, the families say, "Ah! It's safe to have fewer children. I don't need to have six for insurance. My children will survive."

Make sure the girls stay in school, especially secondary school. A girl who has a chance to go to secondary school will get married several years later. By then she will be more empowered, have a market value in the economy, [and] say, "I'm gonna go out and get a job. I don't want to get married, and also I'm not gonna let my father choose to marry me at age 12," which is how it might be normally.

Farmworker Stella Machara and her sons Kudakwachi and Simbaracha in front of their home in Zimbabwe. According to Jeffrey Sachs, why is sub-Saharan Africa stuck in a Malthusian population trap? To see more of the conversation with Sachs, visit **digital.wwnorton .com/youmayask7**.

Make sure there are contraceptives available. Family planning is not a freebie. It absolutely requires training, skilled community work, health workers, the physical availability of contraception; and that's more than an impoverished woman, in a patriarchal setting, with lots of children dying in a rural area, is going to somehow find her way to on her own. She may have zero cash. History has shown free availability of family planning and contraceptive services is part of the set of things that are necessary to lower fertility that also includes child survival, girls' education, women's awareness, and community health workers. That can lead to a remarkably accelerated demographic transition, and that's the kind of holistic approach that successful societies have done. (Conley, 2009g)

GEORG WILHELM FRIEDRICH HEGEL

A third view of inequality comes from the German philosopher Georg Wilhelm Friedrich Hegel, who viewed history in terms of a master–slave (sometimes called a master–servant) dialectic. The word dialectic means a two-directional relationship—one that goes both ways, like a conversation between two people. One person talks, putting out an idea or thesis. Then the other responds, pointing out some problems with the thesis or posing a counterposition, an antithesis. Then the original speaker responds, and it is hoped, the two arrive at a synthetic arrangement constructed from elements of the original position and the strongest counterpoints.

In Hegel's master–slave dialectic, the slave is dependent on the master because the master provides food, shelter, and protection. In this way, the

DIALECTIC

a two-directional relationship, following a pattern in which an original statement or thesis is countered with an antithesis, leading to a conclusion that unites the strengths of the original position and the counterarguments.

slave is akin to a child raised by the master. However, as Hegel observed, the master is also dependent on the slave, who performs the basic duties of survival until the master can no longer function on his own. He doesn't remember how to grow his own food, prepare meals, or even get dressed without help. Basically, the master would not be able to function if left to fend for himself. Thus the master–slave nexus becomes a relationship of mutual dependency.

But Hegel was writing in the early nineteenth century. There really aren't masters and slaves today, are there? In fact, while we think of slavery as a dreadful practice left on the ash heap of the past, researchers of modern human trafficking believe that there are actually more enslaved people now—estimates suggest 40.3 million people (Global Slavery Index, 2020)—than there were at the height of the transatlantic slave trade (Bales, 2016). These slaves often toil in ecologically devastating industries like brick making, charcoal production, and strip-mining, according to Kevin Bales, author of *Blood and Earth* (2016).

What's more, according to the CIA, the United States is no exception to this phenomenon, with forced laborers constituting tens of thousands of entrants to the country each year. Modern human trafficking often involves females who are kept as domestic workers and/or sex workers in cities around the world, but some tomato pickers in Florida and construction workers in Dubai have also been considered part of the modern trade in humans (Ehrenreich & Hochschild, 2004; Estabrook, 2009; Human Rights Watch, 2006).

Florencia Molina, a victim of human trafficking, became virtually enslaved at a dressmaking shop on the outskirts of Los Angeles, where she worked up to 17 hours a day, seven days a week, and lived there too, without the option of showering or washing her clothes.

The path to becoming a slave is often paved with a mixture of deceit and desperation. Poor families in rural areas are perhaps too eager to believe the promises of men traveling through their villages, who offer to find good, safe work for their daughters in the city. Once the girls arrive, they are often raped by these men to "teach" them how to serve clients, given a meager room, watched over to prevent escape, and told they must work to repay the cost of their travel and lodging. Some end up staying this way for life, because the stigma of prostitution is something they cannot bear to take back to their families and they have no other way to make money.

In the case of the tomato pickers, the story has a more optimistic ending. After pressure from the Coalition of Immokalee Workers, 30,000 tomato pickers in Florida now receive an extra penny per pound and are better protected from verbal and sexual abuse following a three-year campaign. The campaign started with a boycott of Taco Bell and has now won support from Taco Bell's parent company, Yum! Brands, as well as Burger King, Trader Joe's, Chipotle, Whole Foods, Subway, and Walmart (Greenhouse, 2014). In this sense, it took a coalition of determined outsiders to break the dependencies between the exploited people who needed their abusers for lodging and the abusers who thought they could not stay in business if they charged their corporate purchasers that extra penny per pound.

Hegel views history as marching steadily forward from a situation of few masters and many servants or slaves—such as monarchies and empires, not to mention the entire feudal system—to a society with more and more free men and women, a situation of democracy and equality. His was an optimistic view of history, to say the least. According to Hegel, notions of inequality are constantly evolving in a larger historical arc. He saw this as a trajectory that would eventually lead to equality for all (or very nearly all). We will see that many sociologists have had a bone or two to pick with this position, as well as with those laid out by Rousseau, Ferguson, Millar, and Malthus.

MODERN THEORIES OF INEQUALITY

Karl Marx has been said to have stood Hegel on his head by challenging his notion of an automatic march to greater freedom (and equality). Marx's theory of history emphasized class conflict and struggle that would only end with a Communist revolution wherein private property (what the Enlightenment thinkers praised as the seed of innovation) was eliminated. Marx's theory of history—dialectic materialism—put group struggles for control of economic resources at the center of social change. Hegel, according to Marx, had focused too much on cognitive states (i.e., the mind) and not enough on real-world material struggles for survival.

In the twentieth century, however, in most Western societies, history did not play out as Marx's theory of conflict and violent revolution had predicted. Capitalism did not collapse under its own contradictions. Indeed, moderating forces like the welfare state (social insurance) and labor unions emerged, and a tacit peace between capital and labor—Marx's two great oppositional forces in the capitalist phase—developed. The proletariat did not get poorer and poorer and rise up in revolt. In order to explain this turn of events, a new group of theories emerged to explain this economic and social cohesion. Stemming from Durkheim's notions of organic solidarity (Durkheim, 1893 [1997]; see Chapter 6) and Herbert Spencer's metaphor of society as an organism (Spencer, 1898 [1967]), the school of thought called "structural functionalism" emphasized the economy and society as an organized system that—though it occasionally faced strains—for the most part efficiently allocated individuals to their most suitable occupations. Most famously described in a 1945 article by Kingsley Davis and Wilbur Moore (Davis and Moore, 1945), inequality in

DIALECTIC MATERIALISM

a notion of history that privileges conflict over economic, material resources as the central struggle and driver of change in society.

STRUCTURAL FUNCTIONALISM

a theory in which society's many parts—institutions, norms, traditions, and so on—mesh to produce a stable, working whole that evolved over time. Best embodied by Talcott Parsons.

this rendering was necessary to induce the most talented people to fill the most demanding positions that require the highest skills and dedication. That is, medical doctors are paid a lot because they are much needed within society, while also being members of a profession that demands great talent and sacrifice. This theory was critiqued on many grounds—notably the fact that there is no reason to assume that high rewards go to people or positions that are "needed" by society (whatever that means).

Conflict theory emerged to reconcile the view of Marx and the functionalists. As embodied by the work of Ralf Dahrendorf (1958), this paradigm suggested that while the world did not turn out as Marx had predicted, there were constant struggles between interest groups in society for authority. These conflicts drove societal change. To the extent that there was order, it was imposed from the top, not part of a natural state of being as presupposed by the functionalists. Another strand of the theory—as offered by Lewis Coser (1957)—suggested that conflict itself could serve a cohesive role in society. For example, when conflict was against an external enemy (or out-group), it served to unify individuals in the in-group. Conflict also served a communication function, by making various interests and points of view known to the various parties. The bottom line was that conflict among groups for limited resources was a perennial feature of human societies and this conflict, in turn, drove historical change. To the extent there appeared to be consensus in a given moment, it was a veneer that was maintained by top-down coercive authority that sought to tamp down claims for resources on the part of less powerful groups.

CONFLICT THEORY

the idea that conflict between competing interests is the basic, animating force of social change and society in general.

Standards of Equality

Assuming for the moment that we do value equality in society, what kind of equality do we want? There are different ideologies or belief systems regarding equality, so it's important to recognize that when various groups use the rhetoric of equality, particularly in the political sphere, they may be talking past each other or jostling for advantage. What did Thomas Jefferson mean when he proclaimed in the Declaration of Independence that "all men are created equal"? And what exactly do we mean by equality in the twenty-first century?

EQUALITY OF OPPORTUNITY

the idea that everyone has an equal chance to achieve wealth, social prestige, and power because the rules of the game, so to speak, are the same for everyone.

EQUALITY OF OPPORTUNITY

One standard of equality is termed equality of opportunity. Let's think of society as a game of Monopoly, in which all of the players try to maximize their holdings of wealth (the game's houses and hotels) and their income (the rent collected from other players who land on built-up properties after an unfortunate roll of the dice). In this game, the person with the most money in the end is the winner. Monopoly follows the rules of equality of opportunity. Sure, one player may wind up flat broke and another player may control 95 percent of the wealth, but the rules were fair, right? Everyone had an equal chance at the start. Assuming nobody cheated, any differences were a result of luck (the dice) and skill (the players' choices). The same goes for society. The mere existence of inequality is not at issue here. Some people have more wealth and income than others, and some people enjoy greater social prestige or power than others, but the rules of the game are still fair. We all go into the game of society, as we do into a game of Monopoly, knowing the rules, and therefore any existing inequality is fair as long as everyone plays by the rules.

Civil rights activists in San Francisco demonstrate against Jim Crow laws in 1964. Why did the demand for equal opportunity resonate with most Americans?

This is the standard model for what equality means in a bourgeois society, such as modern capitalist society. Although the word *bourgeois* is often used pejoratively, here I mean it as a neutral description—a society of commerce in which the maximization of profit is the primary business incentive. Almost all modern capitalist societies purport to follow an ideology of equal opportunity. The equal opportunity ideology was adopted by civil rights activists in the 1960s, who argued that the rules were unfair. For instance, the segregation of public spaces and other Jim Crow laws (a rigid set of anti-Black statutes that relegated African Americans to the status of second-class citizens through educational, economic, and political exclusion) were seen as incompatible with the bourgeois notion of fairness or equality of opportunity.

BOURGEOIS SOCIETY

a society of commerce (modern capitalist society, for example) in which the maximization of profit is the primary business incentive.

The rallying cry for equality of opportunity resonates with our overall capitalist ideology. Unequal opportunity clearly stifles meritocracy, a system in which advancement is based on individual achievement or ability. For example, if you were to have a heart transplant, would you not want the most knowledgeable heart surgeon with the most dexterous hands? Or would you settle for the one born to rich parents who finagled their child's way into medical school? Under a system of equal opportunity, everyone who is willing can compete to become a heart surgeon, and eventually the most talented will rise to fill the most demanding, important positions.

EQUALITY OF CONDITION

the idea that everyone should have an equal starting point.

EQUALITY OF CONDITION

A second standard of equality is a bit more progressive and is termed equality of condition. Going back to our Monopoly analogy, imagine if at the beginning of the game, two players started out with an extra $5,000 and already owned hotels on Boardwalk and Park Place, and Pennsylvania and North Carolina Avenues, respectively, while the other two players started out with a $5,000 deficit and owned no property. Some would argue that the rules of the game need to be altered in order to compensate for inequalities in the relative starting positions. This is the ideology behind equality of condition. An example of this ideology is affirmative action, which involves preferential selection to increase the representation of women, racial and ethnic minorities, and/or people from less privileged social classes in areas of employment, education, and business from which they have historically been excluded (see the policy discussion at the end of this chapter). Affirmative action occurs when a person or group in a gatekeeper position, such as a college admissions office or the human resources department in charge of hiring new workers, actively selects some applicants who have faced the steep slope of an uneven playing field, often due to racism or sexism in society. Sometimes these policies can enhance efficiency if they result in fairer competition; other times they may result in a trade-off between efficiency and equality in favor of the latter. We may accept that certain groups with slightly lower SAT scores are admitted to colleges because they faced much greater obstacles to attain those SAT scores than other groups of test takers who enjoyed more advantages. Such "social engineering" may be based on race, class, gender, or any other social sorting category, as long as the proponents can make a justifiable claim that the existing playing field is tilted against them.

Middlebury College student Laura Blackman received help from the Posse Foundation, which recruits inner-city kids for elite colleges. How are affirmative action policies an example of equality of condition?

EQUALITY OF OUTCOME

The final and most radical (or rather most antibourgeois and anticapitalist) form of equality is equality of outcome, the position that each Monopoly player should end up with the same amount regardless of the fairness of the "game." This admittedly would make for a dull round of Monopoly: In this scenario, the players on Baltic Avenue would make just as much as those on Boardwalk, and some mechanism in the game—say, a central banker or all the players pooling their resources—would ensure game play that lived up to Karl Marx's maxim in the *Critique of the Gotha Programme* (1999), "From each according to his ability, to each according to his needs." This standard is concerned less with the rules of the game than with the distribution of resources; it is essentially a Marxist (or Communist) ideology. Like Rousseau's idea that there will always be physical inequalities—some will be better at math, others will be better at physical work, and so on—equality of outcome is the idea that everyone contributes to society and to the economy according to what they do best. For instance, someone who is naturally gifted at math might become an engineer or a mathematician, whereas someone better at physical work might build infrastructure such as roads and bridges. A centrally organized society calls on its citizens to contribute to the best of their ability, yet everyone receives the same rewards. The median income is everyone's income regardless of occupation or position.

Under equality of outcome, or equality of result, the individual incentives touted by the Scottish Enlightenment thinkers are eliminated. Nobody earns more power, prestige, and wealth by working harder. In this system, the only incentive is altruistic; you are giving to society for the sake of its progress and not merely for your own betterment (although arguably, it may be in the self-interest of the individual to see society progress as a whole). Facebook founder Mark Zuckerberg and his wife, Priscilla Chan, would probably have to give up 99.99 percent of their wealth rather than the "mere" 99 percent they have pledged to charity to help equalize outcomes (Brandon, 2015), whereas a single mother working two jobs in order to provide food, shelter, and day care for her children is likely to take a bit of a step up. Critics worry that without the selfish incentives of capitalism, all progress would halt, and sloth might take over. Unless an oppressive rule emanated from some central agency, collective endeavors would be doomed to failure on account of the free rider problem, the notion that when more than one person is responsible for getting something done, the incentive is for each individual to shirk responsibility and hope others will pull the extra weight. (You might have encountered this sort of situation while collaborating on group projects for school.) Critics of this system argue that even when there is a relatively strong central planning agency to assign each worker a task and enforce productivity, such an administrative mechanism cannot make decisions and allocate resources as efficiently as a more free-market approach does.

EQUALITY OF OUTCOME

the idea that each player must end up with the same amount regardless of the fairness of the "game."

FREE RIDER PROBLEM

the notion that when more than one person is responsible for getting something done, the incentive is for each individual to shirk responsibility and hope others will pull the extra weight.

Forms of Stratification

Thus far we have discussed standards of equality and inequality only in general terms, but there are many dimensions and forms by which this equality or inequality can emerge in a given society. For example, a society can be stratified based on age. In many tribes, for instance, age determines the social prestige and honor that the group accords an individual. (By contrast, some argue that in the youth-obsessed culture of the United States, age is a source of dishonor.) Those younger than you would place great weight on your words and in some cases treat them as commands. Furthermore, birth order can be the basis of inequality. Such a system was prevalent as late as the nineteenth century in European society, where the firstborn male typically inherited the family estate; however, in certain parts of the world, birth order still plays a role in resource distribution. Gender or race and ethnicity also can be the predominant forms social stratification takes. Ultimately, many dimensions exist within which inequality can emerge, and often these dimensions overlap significantly.

↑

In Western Australia, Aboriginal elder Brandy Tjungurrayi wears a pencil through his nose—a sign of his senior status.

Stratified societies are those where human groups within them are ranked hierarchically into strata, along one or more social dimensions. Many sociologists and philosophers believe that there are four ideal types of social stratification—estate system, caste system, class system, and status hierarchy system—although all societies have some combinations of these forms and no type ever occurs in its pure form. In addition to these, some sociologists propose a fifth ideal type, an elite—mass dichotomy. Each system has its own ideology that attempts to legitimate the inequality within it.

ESTATE SYSTEM

ESTATE SYSTEM

a politically based system of stratification characterized by limited social mobility.

The first ideal type of social stratification is the estate system. Primarily found in feudal Europe from the medieval era through the eighteenth century, and in the American South before the Civil War, social stratification in estate systems has a political basis. That is, laws are written in a language in which rights and duties separate individuals and distribute power unequally.

For example, in the antebellum American South, many states required land ownership for voting privileges. Europe also historically restricted voting rights to landowners. Before reforms, political participation depended on the social group (the estate) to which you belonged. There was limited mobility among the three general estates—the clergy, the nobility, and the common-ers (the commoners were typically further divided into peasants and city dwellers)—and each group enjoyed certain rights, privileges, and duties. In certain eras, it was possible for a rich commoner to buy a title and become a member of the nobility. And often, one son or daughter of a noble family would join the clergy and become part of that estate. Therefore, there was some mobility, but social reproduction—you are what your parents were and what your children will be—generally prevailed. (We'll examine the concept of social mobility more closely below.)

CASTE SYSTEM

A second type of stratification is a caste system. As opposed to having a political basis, the caste system is religious in nature. That is, caste societies are stratified on the basis of hereditary notions of religious purity. Today the caste system is primarily found in South Asia, particularly in India. The historical legacy of the caste system still dominates rural India despite its constitutional abolition almost 70 years ago and despite affirmative action policies to help those of lower caste origins. Although contradictory opin-ions exist, origins of the caste system are rooted in Hinduism and a division of labor predetermined by birth. Social hierarchy was further entrenched by preferential treatment of upper caste members during British colonial-ism. The result was rigid social stratification of four main castes or *varnas*: Brahman (priests and scholars), Kshatriya (soldiers), Vaishya (merchants and farmers), and Shudra (servants class). Excluded completely from the caste system are both Adivasi (India's indigenous people) and Dalit or "Untouch-ables," who are considered the least pure of all class distinctions. Over time, the caste system in India has evolved into a complex matrix of thousands of subcastes. Each of the major castes is allowed to engage in certain ritual practices from which the others are excluded. For instance, the Shudra caste is not permitted to study ancient Hindu texts, while Dalits are prohibited from entering temples or performing *any* rituals that confer purity. This places them at the bottom of the social hierarchy and typically leaves them with occupations seen as impure, such as the cremation of corpses or dis-posal of sewage, reinforcing their "untouchable" social status.

There has historically been little mobility between caste ranks in India. This is in part because castes are largely endogamous—communities in which members generally marry within the group. Because of the result-ing problems with classifying children born from intercaste marriages,

CASTE SYSTEM

a religion-based system of stratification characterized by no social mobility.

Islamic law prohibits Muslims from serving or imbibing alcohol, so the Christian Vaishya handle beer distribution in Pakistan. This employee inspects a bottle of vodka at the Murree Brewery Company, Pakistan's oldest public company and only brewery.

the caste system would simply fall apart if high levels of exogamy (marriage between castes) occurred. The strict divisions would begin to look more like a spectrum and would eventually fade away. Practicing endogamy is an example of *social closure,* a powerful method of maintaining the caste hierarchy within Indian society. For example, if you are born into the Dalit or "Untouchable" caste, you will likely marry a Dalit and your children will be Dalits. An increase in exogamy is creeping in, but social mobility remains low, especially for Dalits.

Although there is little to no individual mobility in caste systems, one unique fact of the system is that an entire caste could obtain a higher position in the hierarchy by adopting practices and behaviors of the upper castes. This process is called sanskritization. Typically practices that are adopted are those that pertain to a higher degree of religious purity (vegetarianism or fasting, for example). At the same time, a caste will eschew aspects of its own traditions that are considered impure (animal sacrifice or the consumption of alcohol). In this way, an entire group of people can rise in social status in one to two generations. Sometimes such an attempt works, and sometimes it doesn't. During the colonial period, when the British governed South Asia, the Vaishya, the second-lowest caste in Pakistan, adopted Christianity, the religion of the British, in an attempt to jump ahead in the hierarchy. Their attempt was not successful. However, by becoming Christian, the Vaishya caste did enjoy a unique fate after the partition of Pakistan from India. Pakistan became a Muslim state in which Islamic law (the shar'ia) was enforced. One of the rules of the shar'ia is that Muslims are forbidden from imbibing or serving alcohol (or any mind-altering substances). So who got the jobs serving foreigners in the hotel bars? The Vaishya, who were now Christian. Their efforts to jump ahead in the caste system may have failed, but they ended up with fairly decent jobs in a relatively impoverished country by capitalizing on westernization.

CLASS SYSTEM

A third type of stratification is the class system, an economically based hierarchical system characterized by cohesive oppositional groups and somewhat loose social mobility. Class means different things to different people, and there is no consensus among sociologists as to the term's precise definition.

For instance, some might define class primarily in terms of money, whereas others see it as a function of culture or taste. Some people barely even notice it (consciously at least), whereas others feel its powerful effects in their daily lives. So what is class? Is it related to lifestyle? Consumption patterns? Interests? Attitudes? Or is it just another pecking order similar to the caste system? Some controversy has existed about whether class is a real category or a category that exists in name only. As in the caste and estate systems, the lines that separate class categories in theory should be clearly demarcated, but there have been problems in drawing boundaries around class categories— for instance, upper class, middle class, and so on. Some scholars have even argued that class should be abandoned as a sociological concept altogether. So let's try to clear up some of the misconceptions.

Why is the concept of class problematic? For example, Oseola McCarty, of Hattiesburg, Mississippi, worked as a washerwoman and had only a sixth-grade education. However, she donated $150,000 to the University of Southern Mississippi from her savings.

Unlike other systems, a class system implies an economic basis for the fundamental cleavages in society. That is, class is related to position in the economic market. Notions of class in sociological analysis are heavily influenced by two theorists, Karl Marx and Max Weber. In Marxist sociological analyses, every mode of production—from subsistence farming to small-scale cottage industries to modern factory production to the open-source information economy—has its own unique social relations of production, basically the rules of the game for various players in the process. Who controls the use of capital and natural resources? How are the tasks of making and distributing products divided up and allocated? And how are participants compensated for their roles? In tips? Hourly wages? In-kind goods? Profit or rent? Thus, to talk about class in this Marxist language is to place an individual into a particular group that has a particular set of interests that often stand opposite to those of another group. For example, workers want higher wages; employers (specifically, capitalists) wish to depress wages, which come largely out of profits.

In this sense, class is a relational concept. That is, one can't gain information about a person's class by simply looking at his or her income (as in, "That person made only $13,000 last year; therefore, she is working-class"). Class identity, in fact, does not correspond to an individual at all but rather corresponds to a role. A person may pull in a six-figure salary, but as long as he owns no capital (i.e., stock or other forms of firm ownership) and earns his salary by selling his labor to someone else, he finds himself in the same category as the lowest-paid wage laborer and antagonistic to "owners," who may net a lot less income than he does. And an individual may, over the course of her career, change class positions as she changes jobs. Class positions of jobs themselves—that is, their roles with respect to the production process—do not change, however.

Indeed, for Marx, it all boils down to two antagonistic classes in a fully mature capitalist society: the employing class (the bourgeoisie or capitalist class) and the working class (the proletariat). The proletariat sells its labor to the bourgeoisie in order to receive wages and thereby survive. But, according to Marx, the bourgeoisie extract surplus value from the proletariat, even when a few of the proletarians make high incomes. As this is a fixed-pie or zero-sum view of economic production, an exploitative and hence inherently conflict-ridden relationship exists between the two classes. The central aspect of Marxist class analysis is this exploitation—capitalists taking more of the value of the work of laborers than they repay in wages.

Because the two-class model does not appear to adequately describe the social world as we find it in most modern capitalist economies, more recent Marxist theorists such as Erik Olin Wright have elaborated this basic model with the concept of contradictory class locations. Wright suggests that people can occupy locations in the class structure that fall between the two "pure" classes. For instance, managers might be perceived as part of both working class and capitalist class: They are part of the working class insofar as they sell their labor to capitalists in order to live (and don't own the means of production), yet they are in the capitalist class insofar as they control (or dominate) workers within the production process. Conversely, the petit bourgeoisie, a group including professionals, craftsmen, and other self-employed individuals or small-business owners, according to Wright, occupy a capitalist position in that they own capital in the form of businesses, but they aren't fully capitalist because they don't control other people's labor. The issue of class definition could also be further complicated by multiple class locations (multiple jobs), mediated class locations (the impact of relationships with family members, such as spouses, who are in different class locations), and temporally distinct class locations (for instance, many corporations require that all their managers spend a couple of years as a shop floor worker before becoming a manager). Marxists use these distinctions to analyze how various classes rise and fall under the capitalist system.

Max Weber takes an alternative view of class. He argues that a class is a group that has as its basis the common life chances or opportunities available to it in the marketplace. In other words, what distinguishes members of a class is that they have similar value in the commercial marketplace in terms of selling their own property and labor. Thus, for Weber, property and lack of property are the basic categories for all class situations. If you have just graduated from law school, you may have no current income or wealth, but you enjoy a great deal of "human capital" (skills and certification)

PROLETARIAT

the working class.

BOURGEOISIE

the capitalist class.

CONTRADICTORY CLASS LOCATIONS

the idea that people can occupy locations in the class structure that fall between the two "pure" classes.

to sell in the labor market, so you would clearly be in a different class from someone with little education but a similar current economic profile. But if you owned a company that you inherited, for instance, you would belong to yet another (higher) class. Weber's paradigm is distinct from the Marxist class framework, where the basic framework is antagonistic and exploitative; rather, for Weber, class is gradated, not relational. Put another way, your class as a newly minted attorney does not affect or determine my class as an accountant, computer programmer, or day laborer.

STATUS HIERARCHY SYSTEM

The fourth type of stratification system, a status hierarchy system, has its basis in social prestige, not in political, religious, or economic factors. In classical sociology, Weber contributed most heavily to the modern-day sociologist's understanding of status. For Weber, status groups are communities united by either a positive or negative social estimation of their honor. Put more simply, status is determined by what society as a whole thinks of the particular lifestyle of the community to which you belong. In this sense, those with and without property can belong to the same status group if they are seen to live the same lifestyle. Let's use the example of professors. There are certain things that professors typically do in common: They attend conferences to discuss scholarly issues, they teach college courses, and they tend to read a lot. This leads society as a whole to confer a certain status on professors, without placing the sole focus on income, which can vary widely among professors.

But even this lumping of professors (or other occupational categories) into one group can obscure huge status distinctions within that particular group. Some faculty are lucky enough to be on what's called the tenure track, a system designed to protect academic freedom. Once tenure-track faculty achieve tenure, they obtain a level of job security that is similar to that of civil servants and others who cannot easily be fired. Unless an entire school goes bankrupt, they can lose their jobs only if they grossly violate the terms of their employment by, say, not showing up to teach or sexually harassing students or falsifying their research. Compare that level of security to that of the growing ranks of adjunct professors, who

these days are the workhorses of academia. They get paid by course taught, typically without benefits; usually have to teach many more courses than full-time or tenured professors; and often do not know whether they will have enough work until right before a semester starts. Though they are also professors—usually with the same credentials as their tenured peers—their lifestyle shares some similarities with that of itinerant laborers, salespeople who work on commission, or others who enjoy only a minimal level of predictability in their income flows. Of course, the converse can also hold true. Namely, various individuals in a society who earn similar incomes may not have much in common in terms of lifestyles (and therefore status). Think again of a professor and, say, a plumber, who may earn the same annual incomes but have very different day-to-day experiences of work and orientations to the world.

Although a status group can be defined by something other than occupation, such as a claim to a specific lifestyle of leisure (skate punks) or membership in an exclusive organization that defines one's identity (the Daughters of the American Revolution), much work by sociologists has been related to occupational status. After all, work is one of the most centrally defining aspects of our lifestyle. In the 1960s, for example, Peter M. Blau and Otis Dudley Duncan (1967) created the Index of Occupational Status by polling the general public about the prestige of certain occupations (an abbreviated version based on more recent data appears in Table 7.1). Many folks have since refined this rank ordering, but the story is much the same. What is particularly interesting is that the hierarchy is largely stable over time and across place. Occasionally, new jobs need to be slotted in (there were no web designers in the 1960s), but they generally are slotted in fairly predictable ways based on the status of similar occupations and do not create much upheaval within the overall rank ordering. The scores on the Duncan scale (as it is known) range from 0 to 96, with 0 being the least prestigious and 96 the most prestigious.

Table 7.1 shows that occupations with very different characteristics may have similar prestige scores. For instance, actors and firefighters enjoy roughly the same amount of prestige despite being very different in both their daily labor and their job security (firefighters are usually civil servants with job protection, while actors often piece together a living through gig work). Blau and Duncan observed that five-sixths (just over 83 percent) of the explanation for people's status ratings of occupations was attributed to the education necessary for the position and not the income corresponding to that position.

Although we have emphasized that status may have its basis in occupation, it can also be formed through consumption and lifestyle, though these factors are often closely linked with occupation. This means that there should be a tendency for status differences between groups to be finely

TABLE 7.1 The Relative Social Prestige of Selected U.S. Occupations

Occupation	Blue-collar occupation / White-collar occupation — Prestige Score	↓	↓	Occupation	Blue-collar occupation / White-collar occupation — Prestige Score	↓	↓
Physician/surgeon	86	X		Welder	41		X
Lawyer	74	X		Data entry operator	41	X	
Architect	72	X		Farmer/rancher	40		X
Dentist	72	X		Carpenter	39		X
Member of the clergy	68	X		File clerk	36	X	
Registered nurse	66	X		Child-care worker	35		X
Secondary-school teacher	66	X		Auto body repairperson	32		X
Veterinarian	62	X		Retail salesperson	31	X	
Sociologist	61	X		Truck driver	31		X
Police officer	58		X	Aircraft mechanic	31		X
Actor	55	X		Cashier	30	X	
Firefighter	53		X	Taxi driver/chauffeur	29		X
Realtor	48	X		Waiter/waitress	28		X
Machinist	47		X	Bartender	25		X
Musician/singer	47	X		Door-to-door salesperson	23		X
Construction equipment operator	46		X	Janitor	22		X

SOURCE: Frederick, 2010.

gradated and not relational: Fundamentally antagonistic status groups such as capitalists and laborers or owners and renters do not exist. Rather, people exist along a status ladder, so to speak, on which there is a lot of social mobility. Often, individuals seek to assert their status or increase their status not just through their occupation but also through their consumption, memberships, and other aspects of how they live. They might try to generate social prestige by driving a fancy car, living in a gated community, wearing stylish clothes, or using a certain kind of language.

ELITE—MASS DICHOTOMY SYSTEM

The fifth and final stratification system is the elite—mass dichotomy system, with a governing elite, a few leaders who broadly hold the power in society. Vilfredo Pareto, in *The Mind and Society* (1983), took a positive view of elite—mass dichotomies, whereas C. Wright Mills saw much to dislike in such systems. For Pareto, when a select few elite leaders hold power—as long as the elites are the most able individuals and know what they are doing—the masses are all the better for it. This imbalance, where a small number of people (say 20 percent) cause a disproportionately large effect (more like 80 percent), has come to be known as the Pareto Principle or the 80/20 rule. The basis for Pareto's argument is that individuals are unequal physically, intellectually, and morally. He suggests that those who are the most capable in particular groups and societies should lead. In this way, Pareto believes in a meritocracy, a society where status and mobility are based on individual attributes, ability, and achievement. Pareto opposed caste systems of stratification that create systematic inequality on the basis of birth into a specific group. He criticized societies based on strict military, religious, and aristocratic stratification, arguing that these systems naturally tend to collapse. Concerning such systems, he argued that aristocracies do not last, and that, in fact, history is a "graveyard of aristocracies" (Pareto & Finer, 1966).

Along these lines, the ideal governing elite for Pareto is a combination of foxes and lions—that is, individuals who are cunning, unscrupulous, and innovative along with individuals who are purposeful and decisive, using action and force. This applies not only to the political realm but also to the economic realm, and the masses will be better off for it. The whole system works over time, in Pareto's view, when there is enough opportunity and social mobility to ensure that the most talented individuals end up in the elite and that it does not become a rusty aristocracy.

Mills takes a much more negative view of the elite—mass dichotomy, arguing that it is neither natural nor beneficial for society. In Mills's view, the elite do not govern the way Pareto claims they do. Mills argues in *The Power Elite* (2000) that there are three major institutional forces in modern American society where the power of decision making has become centralized: *economic institutions* (with a few hundred giant corporations holding the keys to economic decisions), the *political order* (the increasing concentration of power in the federal government and away from the states and localities, leading to a centralized executive establishment that affects every cranny of society), and the *military order* (the largest and most expensive feature of government). According to Mills, "families and churches and schools adapt to modern life; governments and armies and corporations shape it; and, as they do so, they turn these lesser institutions into means for their ends." The elite for Mills are simply those who have most of what there is to possess: money, power, and prestige. But they would not have the most were it not for their positions within society's great institutions. Whereas Pareto views elite status as the reward for the talent that helped certain individuals rise through the ranks of society, Mills sees the unequal power and rewards as determining the positions. And whereas Pareto sees a benefit in hav-

2016 presidential candidate Hillary Clinton, former president Bill Clinton, and their daughter, Chelsea Clinton, who has worked as an NBC news correspondent and management consultant. How do the Clintons represent modern power elites?

ing power centralized in a large, otherwise ungovernable society, Mills warns of the dangers. For Mills, such a system hurts democracy by consolidating the power to make major decisions into the hands (and interests) of the few.

The power elite is further stratified for Mills; at the inner core of the power elite are those individuals who interchange commanding roles at the top of one dominant institutional order with those in another. In Mills's view, as the interactions among the big three power elites increase, so does the interchange of personnel among them. For example, after serving as President Barack Obama's budget director, Peter Orszag took a top management position at Citigroup, a firm that benefited substantially from the government bailout after the 2008 financial crisis. Who replaced him in the White House? Jacob Lew, who was budget director under President Bill Clinton and later worked for Citigroup himself. Likewise, back in 1961, Robert McNamara left the presidency of Ford Motor Company to serve as secretary of defense under President John F. Kennedy. More recently, business elites like President Donald Trump and his son-in-law, Jared Kushner, have been running our political affairs. Three members of the presidential cabinet at the time of this writing have nine-figure net worths or more from careers in business or as part of family businesses: Secretary of the Treasury Steven Mnuchin, Commerce Secretary Wilbur Ross, and Education Secretary Betsy DeVos (Alexander et al., 2019). Such exchange across domains is of central importance to Mills, because as the elite increasingly assume positions in one another's domains, the coordination among the elite becomes more and more entrenched.

The inner core also includes the professional go-betweens of economic, political, and military affairs. These include individuals at powerful legal firms and financial institutions, such as corporate lawyers and investment

INCOME VERSUS WEALTH

Most people, when they consider economic status, think of income: money received by a person for work, from transfers (gifts, inheritances, or government assistance), or from returns on investments. Recent trends in earnings in the United States suggest that there is an increasing divergence or inequality between the bulk of the people and the rich, but especially between the super-rich and the merely rich. For instance, from 1950 to 1970, for every dollar earned by the bottom 90 percent of the American population, those in the top 0.01 percent earned an additional $162. If that sounds like a big distinction, that's nothing compared with more recent data. Between 1990 and 2002, for every dollar earned by those in the bottom 90 percent, each taxpayer at the top (and this would include Bill Gates) took home $18,000 (Johnston, 2005).

A recent trend in sociological analysis, however, is to analyze stratification in terms of wealth ownership. What is *wealth* in relation to income? Wealth is a family's or individual's net worth (total assets minus total debts). For the majority of American families, assets include a home, cars, other real estate, and business assets, along with financial forms of wealth such as stocks, bonds, and mutual funds. Put simply, wealth is everything you own minus debts such as mortgages on a home, credit card debt, and, as most of you will probably have, debt from student loans. One way to think about the difference between income and wealth is to imagine income as a stream or river of money flowing through a family's hands. Wealth, by contrast, is a pool of collected resources that can be drawn on at specific times, a financial reservoir. In 2015, half of the world's wealth was held by just 1 percent of its residents (Kersley & Stierli, 2015).

bankers. The outer fringes of the power elite, which change more readily than the core, are individuals who count in the decisions that affect all of us but who don't actually make those decisions.

Let's take, for example, the business sector in America. More than 80 percent of the 1,000 largest corporations shared at least one director with another large company, and on average any two of the corporations were connected by fewer than four degrees of separation (Davis, 2003). Wall Street is particularly densely connected. Most troubling is the fact that many US Treasury secretaries, including the current one, Steven Mnuchin, have worked at a single firm: the investment bank Goldman Sachs. As a result of these networks, which Mills both saw and predicted, decisions by various companies become increasingly similar. Many studies have suggested that these elite networks share practices, principles, and information that account for some of the surprising conformity in approaches to corporate governance and ethics. For example, the response to the 2008 financial crisis was evidently mapped out in a room with a dozen or so top bankers and the president of the New York Federal Reserve, Tim Geithner, who later became Treasury secretary in the Obama administration.

How Is America Stratified Today?

Sociologists often use the phrase socioeconomic status to describe an individual's position in a stratified social order. When sociologists talk about socioeconomic status, they are referring to any measure that attempts to classify groups, individuals, families, or households in terms of indicators such as occupation, income, wealth, and education. Although the boundaries between socioeconomic categories are not sharply defined, the lay public generally divides society into the upper class, the middle class, the working class, and the poor. Because these are common terms, we need to take them seriously, even if they are not of scientific origin and lack sufficient rigor.

THE UPPER CLASS

Generally, the upper class refers to the group of individuals at the top of the socioeconomic food chain. In practice, however, the term is used to describe diverse and complex concepts. Historically, the upper class was often distinguished by not having to work. (The economist and social critic Thorstein Veblen dubbed this group "the leisure class.") Its members were able to maintain their lifestyle by collecting rent and/or other investment returns. They were the aristocracy, the wealthy, the elite, the landowners. The only way to join this sphere was by birth or (occasionally) marriage. The upper class was the basis for Marx's capitalist class.

In the United States, "upper class" is associated with income, wealth, power, and prestige. According to some sources, the primary distinguishing characteristic of upper-class individuals is their source of income—generally

SOCIOECONOMIC STATUS

an individual's position in a stratified social order.

INCOME

money received by a person for work, from transfers (gifts, inheritances, or government assistance), or from returns on investments.

WEALTH

a family's or individual's net worth (i.e., total assets minus total debts).

UPPER CLASS

a term for the economic elite.

more from returns on investments rather than wages. Although estimates vary, approximately 1 percent of the US population is considered to fall into this stratum (Figure 7.1). From 1980 to 2014, the average income in the bottom half of earnings remained $16,000 (adjusted for inflation). Over the same period, the average earnings of the 1 percent tripled—from $420,000 to $1.3 million (Piketty et al., 2018). By 2012, the top 0.1 percent owned 22 percent of the total wealth in the United States, up from 7 percent in the late 1970s (Saez & Zucman, 2016). In 2018 the CEOs of America's largest companies made 278 times that of the typical worker, compared to 59 times the average in 1989 (Mischel & Schieder, 2019). In the period between 2009 and 2012, the top 1 percent of Americans saw their income grow by 31.4 percent, but the income of all other Americans barely grew at all, increasing just 0.4 percent (Saez, 2013). Over and above income levels, the upper class is also distinguished by prestige and power, which can be used to promote personal agendas and influence everything from political decisions to consumer trends. This is of particular importance because, as noted earlier, members of the upper class often wear many hats. As Dennis Gilbert states in *The American Class Structure in an Age of Growing Inequality* (1998):

> The members of the tiny capitalist class at the top of the hierarchy have an influence on economy and society far beyond their numbers. They make investment decisions that open or close employment opportunities for millions of others. They contribute money

FIGURE 7.1 Distribution of Net Worth in the United States, 2016

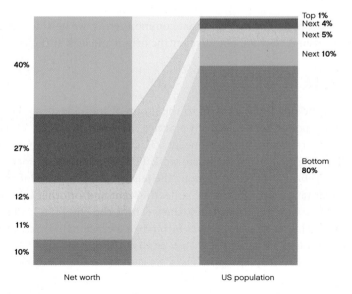

SOURCE: Wolff, 2017.

to political parties, and they often own media enterprises that allow them influence over the thinking of other classes. (p. 286)

THE MIDDLE CLASS

Although those in the upper class have very real influence and control, the effects of this are sometimes limited in the public perception. In the 2007 article "The American People: Social Classes" published in the online magazine *Life in the USA* (a "complete web guide to American life for immigrants and Americans"), Elliot Essman speaks for much of the mainstream media when he asserts that the implications of such power are not far-reaching in our daily lives. "The very rich control corporations and have some political power, but the lifestyle and values of the very wealthy do not have much impact on the country in general," he states. "America is a middle class nation."

The United States is often thought of as a middle-class nation—so much so that depending on how the question is phrased, almost 90 percent of Americans have self-identified with this stratum. That said, there is no consensus on what the term middle class really means. Sociologists, economists, policy makers, think tank analysts, and even the public at large all work with different operating assumptions about the term. The categories become particularly blurry when we attempt to separate the middle class from the working class (or "working families," to use the political campaign euphemism).

So what is the middle class? If you look up the term in various dictionaries, you'll encounter lots of definitions. Some refer explicitly to position (i.e., below upper class, above lower class); others speak to shared vocational characteristics and values. Still others mention principles. One of the most interesting comes from *Merriam-Webster's Collegiate Dictionary,* which indicates that the middle class is "characterized by a high material standard of living, sexual morality, and respect for property."

MIDDLE CLASS

a term commonly used to describe those individuals with nonmanual jobs that pay significantly more than the poverty line— though this is a highly debated and expansive category, particularly in the United States, where broad swaths of the population consider themselves middle-class.

The Middle Class and Working Class: Expansion and Retrenchment In the United States, the middle class has historically been composed of white-collar workers (office workers), and the working class composed of those individuals who work manually (using their hands or bodies). However, this distinction eroded with two trends. First, the post–World War II boom led to the enrichment of many manual workers. In those days, most working-class Whites, ranging from factory workers to firemen to plumbers, were able to buy their own homes, afford college for their children, and retire comfortably. The working class became the newly expanded middle class.

From the post–World War II era of the late 1940s through the oil crisis of 1973, this middle class was a large and fairly stable group, maintained by corporate social norms emphasizing equality in pay and salary increases (Krugman, 2005). From 1947 through 1979, the average salary increase was fairly stable across all household income levels—in fact, the lowest-earning 20 percent of households showed the highest average earnings increase, 116 percent.

A second, countervailing trend has also eroded the traditional manual–nonmanual distinction between the working and middle classes: the rise of the low-wage service sector. Since 1973, manufacturing has steadily declined in the United States, and the service jobs replacing factory work have generally been either very high-skilled (and rewarded) or relatively low-skilled (and therefore not paid very well). This new and expanding group of low-wage service workers challenges the notion that working-class status arises from physical labor. Data-entry clerks, cashiers, paralegals, and similar occupations are technically white-collar jobs, yet they pull in working-class wages.

Over the past three decades, the income gap between a corporate CEO and a single-mother waitress has grown exponentially, and the relatively stable middle class of previous decades has become increasingly stratified (Figure 7.2). For example, a CEO who makes at least $200,000 is in the top 5 percent of households, and his or her average expected salary increase since 1979 (adjusted for inflation) is about 50 percent. On the other end of the scale, a waitress who makes only $22,000 is in the bottom 20 percent of households, and her income will have increased by 27 percent over

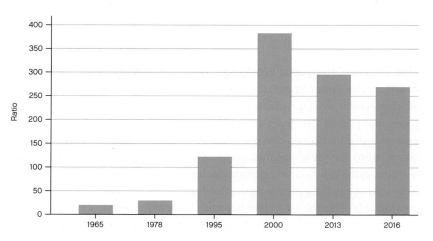

FIGURE 7.2 Ratio of US CEO Pay to Average Worker Pay, 1965–2016

SOURCES: Davis & Mishel, 2014; Mishel & Schieder, 2017.

the same period. And if we consider an average family—say, a two-parent household with two kids and a middle-range annual income of $52,000—then this family would probably have experienced an income increase of only 14 percent since 1979, a sign of what some call the shrinking middle class (Gould, 2014). (Go to **wealthinequality.org** for more information.)

How and why has this differential income growth happened? One factor may be the changing nature of available employment. As the technological sector expands, the majority of jobs are being created either at very high skill levels with correspondingly high salaries (engineers and hedge fund managers) or at very low levels with little room for upward mobility (baristas at Starbucks who serve lattes to those hedge fund managers). And the fastest-growing job category for those with no more than a high-school education is food preparation and service.

DIGITAL.WWNORTON.COM/YOUMAYASK7

To see sociologist Michael Hout discuss the benefits of a college education, see digital.wwnorton.com/youmayask7

Furthermore, this bifurcated job growth is reflected in the change in educational expectations of potential employers. Whereas for much of the post–World War II period, a high-school diploma could earn a person (a White man, specifically) enough to support a family, a college degree is now often a minimum requirement for decent employment. (We'll examine the phenomenon of credentialism in Chapter 13 on education.) But although the number of high-school graduates going to college has increased (to roughly 70 percent in 2018; Bureau of Labor Statistics, 2019), bachelor's degree completion rates still stand at approximately 59 percent nationally (i.e., lots of students are not finishing) (National Center for Education Statistics, 2019). If a college education is the gateway to becoming middle-class and only about a third of the American population has at least a four-year degree, we can expect the percentage of middle-class Americans to shrink.

In an interview for this book, sociologist Michael Hout helped explain that even though there has been stagnation in the number of people receiving bachelor's degrees, the value of those degrees is increasing. Hout pointed out that part of what is holding students back from getting their degree is that the cost of college is increasing and a larger proportion of the cost is borne by individuals and families rather than states. For example, due to state budget shortfalls, the University of California system—one of the biggest and best—announced a tuition hike of 32 percent for the academic year starting in 2010 that was swiftly followed by another 9.6 percent rise in 2011 and was slated to increase another 28 percent by 2019 (McMillan, 2011; Pickert, 2014). Hout goes on to describe the way that sacrificing to pay for college plays out differently across social classes.

> There is a class-specific preference for these kinds of risks. The sons and daughters of college graduates see the benefit of a college education more clearly. They have had it drummed into them since they could talk. . . . Sons and daughters of people who haven't been to college can exercise a certain skepticism about it, and they see in their neighborhoods evidence that it might not pay off. Who leaves the neighborhood? Somebody who has reaped the full benefit of the college education. They're out of sight and out of mind. Who's back in the neighborhood? That kid who maybe dropped out after three years, with a three-figure loan debt, [or] six-figure loan debt. And the presence of those people makes it look like college doesn't pay off. (Conley, 2009h)

Some argue that along with income inequality, income insecurity (or volatility) has also increased for the middle classes. In *The Great Risk Shift* (2006), Jacob Hacker asserts that the chances of an American family experiencing a 50 percent drop in their annual income from one year to the next were 17 percent in 2002, up from around 7 percent in 1970. A 50 percent salary cut would still leave the CEO mentioned earlier in the top 40 percent of household incomes, but how about our waitress and our middle-income family? Cutting their salary by half would send either into a major financial crisis, maybe even bankruptcy. However, other researchers argue that income instability is not the result of fluctuating earnings or job insecurity but rather stems from two major changes in family dynamics. First, there are more changes to household structure today because of divorce and remarriage; second, women now play a greater role in breadwinning (even exceeding men as a proportion of the workforce at one point during the recent recession), but they also enter and exit the workforce with greater frequency than men. (See Chapters 8 and 14 for more about women in the workforce.)

THE POOR

Unlike the fuzzy definitions of other classes, poverty (which gets its own, entire chapter in this book, Chapter 10) has an official, government definition. In 2018, the poverty line for a family of four was $26,200 (US Department of Health and Human Services, 2020). The poor are, ironically, often said to resemble the rich in being more oriented toward the present and therefore less worried about the future than their middle-class and working-class counterparts (although this is highly debated). Day-to-day survival keeps the poor clearly planted in the present. Of course, like any class, the poor are not a unified group. In fact, one distinction often made in political speeches is that between the "working poor" (those who deserve our assistance) and the "nonworking poor" (those who can work but don't and therefore have a weaker moral claim on assistance). This latter group is sometimes called the "underclass." Of course, even these two categories obscure huge distinctions within either group; in fact, poverty is a state that families usually shift in and out of throughout their history, and often a clear distinction does not exist between the working class and the poor.

Global Inequality

One of the main reasons cited for rising income and wealth inequality in the United States is globalization—the rise in the trade of goods and services across national boundaries, as well as the increased mobility of multinational businesses and migrant labor. (See Chapter 14 for an extended discussion of globalization.) If the effect of globalization in the United States has been to bifurcate labor into high-skilled and low-skilled jobs, what has been the effect on worldwide inequality? The answer to that question depends on how you frame the analysis. In the long view, there is no question that global income inequality has been steadily rising over the last few centuries. At the start of the agricultural and industrial revolutions, almost the entire population of the world lived in poverty and misery (see the discussion of Malthus earlier in the chapter). Birthrates were high, but so was mortality. Most people barely survived, no matter where they lived.

But then, thanks to technological innovations, food production started to increase dramatically in some areas of Europe (see Chapter 14 on the economy). Soon after—during the Industrial Revolution—large-scale factory production took the place of small cottage industries, resulting in the creation of vast, unequally distributed wealth. Simultaneously, European powers began to explore, conquer, and extract resources from other areas of the globe. Fast-forward a few hundred years to the mid-twentieth century, when the world and most of its wealth were carved up and ruled by major Western powers. Enormous global inequalities had emerged through the combination of colonialism and unequal development. Since around 1950, many of these former colonies have gained political independence, but they have lagged well behind the West in terms of income per capita.

Scholars have long been trying to figure out why Europe developed first. Early explanations, dating back to the French essayist Montesquieu (1748/1750), focused on geographic differences between the peoples of Europe and the global

South (as the less developed regions of the world are sometimes called). Perhaps because of the South's heat or humidity, Montesquieu associated virtue and rationality with the North; the South he associated with vice and passion. Montesquieu's views are now discarded as a racist account of uneven development, but more recent versions of the geographical explanation focus on differences in the length of growing seasons, the higher variability of water supply (because of more frequent droughts), the types of cereal crops that can grow in temperate zones compared with tropical and subtropical regions, the lack of coal deposits (the first fuel that drove industrialization, long before oil), and perhaps most important, the disease burden in warmer climates (Sachs, 2001).

Economist Jeffrey Sachs explains that Africa's geography made it much more difficult for an agricultural revolution to occur. He prods us to understand the complexity of the constraints on Africa's development before pointing fingers:

> Africa is a continent largely of that rain-fed agriculture, whereas the Green Revolution was based first and foremost on irrigation agriculture. Now is that bad governance that Africa does not have vast river systems? Or is that a matter of the Himalayan Tibetan plateau, which creates the Indus, the Punjab (meaning five rivers, after all), the Ganges, the Yangtze, and so forth? These are functions of physical geography. Africa has a savannah region, which means a long dry season together with a single wet season typically. (Conley, 2009g)

DIGITAL.WWNORTON.COM/YOUMAYASK7

Watch an interview with economist Jeffrey Sachs about overcoming poverty in Africa at **digital.wwnorton.com/youmayask7**

So Africa was not fortunate when it came to physical geography, and it missed out on the Green Revolution because it could not easily implement irrigation agriculture. But that's not all. If you recall from our discussion of Malthus, Africa also carried a higher disease burden because of the way malaria is transmitted through animal hosts—more deadly in Africa than in Asia. Even with that, Sachs is not through explaining just how Africa came to be so disadvantaged compared with other regions of the world. Important impacts of colonialism would be easy to overlook if we focused only on geography and infectious disease transmission, he says.

Tremendous global inequalities have emerged through the combination of colonialism and unequal development. What are some of the ways that social scientists explain the gap between rich and poor regions of the world?

Was the atrocious treatment by colonial powers somehow the fault of African leaders? Does this ever-so-brief primer on the history of African development help you understand that the sociological imagination cannot function properly without a wide array of information about everything from epidemiology to history to geography and beyond?

Others argue that geography doesn't matter as much as social institutions do. In one version of this line of reasoning, it is a strong foundation of property rights, incorruptible judiciaries, and the rule of law in general that predicts economic development (Easterly & Levine, 2002). These, in turn, were institutions "native" to Europe and were transferred to the areas where European colonists settled and lived in significant numbers (Acemoglu et al., 2001), spurring later development in areas such as India and Latin America (compared with much of Africa, where Europeans did not settle, and which has lagged in development). Other scholars argue that the types of relationships different colonized regions had with the European powers largely determined their fate today: For example, under the rule of the British Raj, India was endowed with a huge network of railways to move cotton, tea, and other products to market. This network, in turn, helped spur economic growth once India got over the rocky transition to self-government after gaining its independence. By contrast, because of the disease burden in most sub-Saharan African countries, Europeans didn't stay and invest but rather focused on extractive industries, building railways that ran just to and from mines instead of extensive networks of roads and train tracks.

Today that legacy of unequal starting places and economic potentials means that the latest spurt of globalization has engendered an even greater

FIGURE 7.3 Gross Domestic Product (GDP) per Capita, 2017

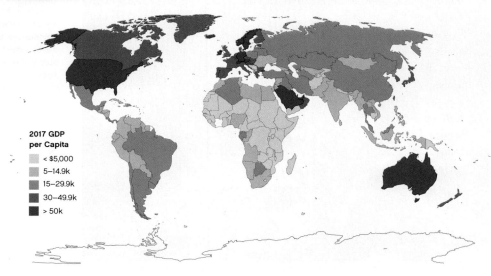

2017 GDP
per Capita

- < $5,000
- 5–14.9k
- 15–29.9k
- 30–49.9k
- > 50k

SOURCE: CIA, 2020.

level of income inequality across the North–South divide while creating huge differences within developing countries. Indeed, some regions, such as sub-Saharan Africa and eastern Europe, have become poorer over the last 25 years, whereas in some previously poor regions, such as South and East Asia, income levels have risen. Considering the net change, economist Xavier Salai-i-Martin estimates that there were around half a billion fewer poor people in the world by the turn of the twenty-first century than there were in the 1970s (Salai-i-Martin, 2002). Likewise, he claims, "all indexes show a reduction in global income inequality between 1980 and 1998." There have indeed been global reductions in population-weighted between-country differences, which can largely be attributed to the rapid growth of the Chinese and Indian economies over this period. Within individual countries, however, inequality has generally risen over the same time frame. The story of globalization and inequality is thus a complex and constantly changing one.

Social Reproduction versus Social Mobility

Once we begin to understand the basics of stratification—how members of a society are hierarchically organized along different lines—the next issue is the possibility of those members changing their social position in the hierarchy. This is generally referred to as social mobility, the movement between different positions within a system of social stratification in any given society. Pitirim A. Sorokin (1959) emphasized the importance of not just looking at the mobility of individuals but also examining group mobility. For example, rather than just asking why Ugo, a cashier at Sears, was promoted to regional manager, thereby increasing his income and status, Sorokin suggests we also look at why the group Ugo belongs to—Black males of Nigerian descent in their mid-twenties—does or does not appear to be generally mobile.

Sorokin noted that social mobility can be either horizontal or vertical. *Horizontal social mobility* means a group or individual transitioning from one social status to another situated more or less on the same rung of the ladder. Examples of this might be a secretary who changes firms but retains her occupational status, a Methodist person who converts to Lutheranism, a family that migrates to one city from another, or an ethnic group that shifts its typical job category from one form of unskilled labor to another. *Vertical social mobility*, in contrast, refers to the rise or fall of an individual (or group) from one social stratum to another. We can further distinguish two types of vertical mobility: *ascending* and *descending* (more commonly termed *upward* and *downward*). An individual who experiences ascending vertical mobility either rises from a lower stratum into a higher one or creates an entirely new group that exists at a higher stratum. Ugo's promotion to regional manager at Sears is an example of rising from a lower stratum to a higher one. By becoming a manager, he has changed his class position, a change that confers both a higher salary and more prestige. Conversely, imagine that for some reason there was an immediate need for translators of Igbo (or Ibo, the language spoken by the Igbo people based in southeast Nigeria) in the United States. Ugo, who speaks Igbo, along with many other Nigerians who speak the language, would then find better jobs and thereby enjoy higher social status. This would be an example of a new group, Igbo translators, existing in a higher stratum.

Descending vertical mobility can similarly take either of two forms: individual or group. One way to think of these forms is as the distinction between a particular person falling overboard from a ship and the whole ship sinking. Sorokin (1959) asserted that "channels of vertical circulation necessarily exist in any stratified society and are as necessary as channels for blood circulation in the body."

Most sociologists concerned with studying mobility focus on the process of individual mobility. These studies generally fall into two types: mobility tables (or matrices) and status attainment models. Constructing a mobility table is easy, although making sense of it is much more difficult (see Table 7.2 for an example). Along the left-most column of a grid, list a number of occupations for people's fathers (it was traditionally done for males only). Across the top, list the same occupational categories for the sons (the

---

SOCIAL MOBILITY

the movement between different positions within a system of social stratification in any given society.

TABLE 7.2 Mobility Table: Father's Occupation by Son's First Occupation

FATHER'S OCCUPATION	SON'S OCCUPATION					
	UPPER NONMANUAL	LOWER NONMANUAL	UPPER MANUAL	LOWER MANUAL	FARM	TOTAL
Upper nonmanual	1,414	521	302	643	40	2,920
Lower nonmanual	724	524	254	703	48	2,253
Upper manual	798	648	856	1,676	108	4,086
Lower manual	756	914	771	3,325	237	6,003
Farm	409	357	441	1,611	1,832	4,650
TOTAL	4,101	2,964	2,624	7,958	2,265	19,912

SOURCE: Hout, 1983.

respondents). There can be as many or as few categories as you see fit, so long as they are consistent for the parental and child generations. For example, a five-category analysis might include upper nonmanual occupations (managers and professionals), lower nonmanual occupations (administrative and clerical workers, low-level entrepreneurs, and retail salespeople), upper manual occupations (skilled workers who primarily use physical labor, such as plumbers and electricians), lower manual occupations (unskilled physical laborers), and farmworkers. The number of categories can be expanded, and it is not uncommon to see seven-, nine-, or even fourteen-category tables. The key is filling in the boxes. Probably not many people fall into the cell where the father is upper nonmanual and the son is a farmer. However, because of the decline in the agricultural workforce over the course of the twentieth century, you are likely to observe (at least in the United States) a fair bit of movement from farmwork in the parental generation to other occupations in the children's generation. Changes in the distribution of jobs lead to what sociologists call structural mobility, mobility that is inevitable given changes in the economy. With the decline of farmwork because of technology, the sons and daughters of farmers are by definition going to

STRUCTURAL MOBILITY

mobility that is inevitable from changes in the economy.

have to find other kinds of work. This type of mobility stands in contrast to exchange mobility, in which, if we hold fixed the changing distribution of jobs, individuals trade jobs such that if one person is upwardly mobile it necessarily entails someone else being downwardly mobile.

EXCHANGE
MOBILITY

mobility resulting from the swapping of jobs.

As most measures of economic inequality have risen each year since the 1960s, Americans have comforted themselves with the thought that they still live in the land of opportunity. Rates of occupational (and income) mobility in the United States have long been thought to have dwarfed those of European societies with their royalty, aristocracies, and long histories. However, recent research suggests that this may be cold comfort: Some economists have argued that US mobility rates have declined significantly since the 1960s. Others go so far as to say that Americans now enjoy less mobility than their European counterparts. A fierce debate has ensued, because many of these studies compare apples and oranges—different measures, different data, different years. However, a consensus seems to be slowly emerging that mobility rates should be broken down into the two components discussed above, structural and exchange mobility. When we do this, it turns out that rates of "trading places" are fairly fixed across developed societies. By contrast, historically, the United States has enjoyed an advantage in growth-induced upward mobility; as the farm and blue-collar sectors withered and white-collar jobs expanded, sons and daughters of manual workers experienced, by necessity, a degree of upward occupational mobility. However, sociologists and economists debate whether economic growth still drives upward mobility, or whether bifurcated job growth means intergenerational stagnation.

Another common methodology for studying social mobility is the status-attainment model. This approach ranks individuals by socioeconomic status, including income and educational attainment, and seeks to specify the attributes characteristic of people who end up in more desirable occupations. The occupational status research of Peter M. Blau and Otis Dudley Duncan (1967), who ranked occupations into a status hierarchy to study social attainment processes, is generally seen as the paradigmatic work in this tradition. Unlike mobility tables, the status-attainment model allows sociologists to study some of the intervening processes. For example, how important is education in facilitating upward occupational shifts in status? How critical is the prestige of a person's first job out of school? How does IQ relate to the chances for upward or downward mobility? The status-attainment model is an elastic one that allows researchers to throw in new factors as they arise and see how they affect the relationships between existing ones, generally ordered chronologically over a typical life course. For the most part, it is thought that education is the primary mediating variable between parents' and children's occupational prestige. That said, research shows that parental education and net worth, not occupation or income,

STATUS-
ATTAINMENT
MODEL

approach that ranks individuals by socioeconomic status, including income and educational attainment, and seeks to specify the attributes characteristic of people who end up in more desirable occupations.

best predict children's educational and other outcomes (Conley, 1999). Blau and Duncan didn't measure net worth, but by now it has become a fairly standard factor in many socioeconomic surveys.

Although there is increasing consensus on what aspects of class background matter (and how much they do), there is relatively little understanding of the multiple mechanisms by which class is reproduced (or how mobility happens). For instance, families with a higher socioeconomic status are likely to have more success in preparing their children for school, entry exams, and ultimately the job market because they have greater access to resources that promote and support their children's development. These might include educational toys when the children are very young, tutors in grade school, and expensive test-preparation courses for exams such as the SAT, GRE, LSAT, and MCAT. Once again, let us compare the CEO of a large, profitable US corporation with a single mother working as a waitress at the local diner. The status of the CEO's occupation and his disproportionate income and wealth in relation to the waitress's easily put his socioeconomic status leaps and bounds ahead of hers. Because of this disparity, he can send his children to the top private schools, where they will be funneled toward highly paid positions. In contrast, assuming that the single mother has no other source of income, her children are likely to get a public education without all the extras. This by no means mandates that they are destined for lower-level occupations, but it certainly suggests that if this were a race, the CEO's children started several miles ahead. (See Chapters 10, 11, and 13 on the various ways in which these factors act as agents of class reproduction.)

POLICY

CLASS-BASED AFFIRMATIVE ACTION

The push for class-based affirmative action (for lack of a better term) is partly a response to the slow decline of race-based affirmative action, as evidenced by the Supreme Court's 2014 ruling to uphold the decision of Michigan's voters to ban race-based affirmative action across the University of Michigan system. In addition to the (legally) declining significance of race in admissions, the call for economic considerations in the college admissions process arises from mounting evidence that class has become an increasingly salient driver of academic opportunity (and success).

The statistics about increasing class stratification on American campuses are alarming: "The college-completion rate among children from high-income families has grown sharply in the last few decades, whereas the completion rate for students from low-income families has barely moved" (Bailey & Dynarski, 2011). Moreover, high-income students make up an increasing share of the enrollment at the most selective colleges and universities (Reardon et al., 2012), even when compared with low-income students with similar test scores and academic records (Bailey & Dynarski, 2011; Belley & Lochner, 2007; Karen, 2002).

Class-based admissions policies, then, offer a way to redress unequal access to selective institutions of higher education while also indirectly tackling racial disparities. In addition, class-based policies, if well designed, can help address some of the criticisms of traditional, race-based affirmative action.

One of the most common criticisms of race-based affirmative action is that as currently designed, it typically helps those minorities who least need it. Whereas before the 1970s race was seen to trump class in determining the life chances for success for the vast majority of African Americans, today it is the reverse pattern that predominates (Reardon et al., 2012). Back in 1967, Peter M. Blau and Otis Dudley Duncan described the process of stratification in the United States in their landmark book *The American Occupational Structure*. In this study, they found that class background mattered little for African Americans compared with Whites. Instead, they described a dynamic called "perverse equality": No matter what the occupation of the father of a Black man (this was a period of low labor-force participation for women overall, even if Black women did work at significant rates), the son himself was most likely to end up in the lower, manual sector of the labor market. Meanwhile, in each generation a small, new cadre of professional Blacks would emerge seemingly randomly through a dynamic they described as "tokenism"—that is, family background mattered little in predicting who emerged into the small, Black professional class.

By the mid-1970s, however, this dynamic had changed. In 1978, sociologist William Julius Wilson described a Black community where class stratification was increasingly rearing its head. Later work confirmed intergenerationally what Wilson observed cross-sectionally: There were

What challenges
do colleges face in
promoting diversity
through admissions
policies?

increasing class divisions within the Black (and Latinx) communities, and class background was an increasingly salient predictor of economic success, not just for Whites but for minorities as well (Conley, 1999; Killewald, 2013).

Sean Reardon (2013) goes so far as to argue that class disparities have eclipsed racial ones, at least in terms of achievement: "The Black-White achievement gap was considerably larger than the income achievement gap among cohorts born in the 1950s and 1960s, but now it is considerably smaller than the income achievement gap. This change is the result of both the substantial progress made in reducing racial inequality in the 1960s and 1970s and the sharp increase in economic inequality in education outcomes in more recent decades." Economist Roland Fryer Jr. (2010) sums this up nicely: "Relative to the 20th century, the significance of discrimination as an explanation for racial inequality across economic and social indicators has declined."

In short, although class divisions within historically underrepresented minority groups are increasing, 1960s identity-group policies treat disadvantaged groups uniformly. The result of such a homogenizing admissions policy is that the most disadvantaged minorities are not being helped today, and intraracial stratification is enhanced. Thus, either in lieu of, or in combination with, race-based policies, class-based affirmative action could address these inequalities within minority (and majority) communities.

If one were to decide to design a class-based admissions policy, how would one implement such a scheme? Can we just ask students' parents to self-report their "class" or socioeconomic status by disclosing their income, education, and wealth? Here's where the devil lies in the details. Parental income is the most easily verifiable, because colleges can ask for tax returns. But analysis shows that it matters the least in predicting college enrollment and completion. In other words, by designing admissions policies around income, we would be doing less well in helping those who need it most. Parental education is actually the strongest predictor but the least verifiable. (How can you check that someone has *more* education than they report on a form?) Parental wealth, meanwhile, is the most unequal by race—getting us the most racial bang for the buck, so to speak. The typical African American family has about 10 percent of the net worth of the typical White family. Wealth also predicts college outcomes (though not as strongly as parental education). So it would seem to be an ideal measure for balancing concerns about race and class diversity on campus.

However, parental wealth faces an even greater problem of verification, potential gaming, and perverse incentives against savings. For example, because Medicaid has strict asset limits, many families shift assets from one individual to another (or even get divorced) in anticipation of needing Medicaid's long-term care insurance component. Similar shell games may emerge in response to offspring approaching their senior year of high school. Unlike the case of education, however, where self-reporting is the only metric to go by for parental wealth, we can infer a lot based on a few factors that are less apt to be gamed.

First, we can measure the median housing value of a community in which a student was raised. This has been shown to be a very good proxy for individual wealth level. If it were measured for all years from birth, the incentive to move to a poor-value neighborhood in the period just preceding college applications would be minimized. Second, other forms of wealth can be ascertained or imputed through property tax records, estate tax records, and schedules A through D of the federal income tax return. While these individual-level measures could theoretically be gamed, the fact that they are measured over multiple years (as with the address of the applicant) minimizes such potential threats, and when combined with the neighborhood-level measures, such risk is further minimized.

Or, when all is said and done, if we want to maintain or increase diversity on campus, we can do what we are already doing: just asking applicants to check a box on the race question on their application (never asking for verification), while hoping that people are honest and the courts are sympathetic.

Conclusion

This Horatio Alger Jr. novel features a newsboy who rises to newspaper editor. Are most Americans today likely to achieve upward mobility?

Horatio Alger Jr. (1832–1899) was an American author of dime novels that told rags-to-riches stories. The narratives typically depicted a plucky young downtrodden boy who eventually achieved the American dream of success and fortune through tenacious hard work while maintaining a genuine concern for the well-being of others. Alger wrote more than 130 novels with titles such as *Sink or Swim* (1870), *Up the Ladder* (1873), *From Boy to President* (1881), *Making His Way* (1901), *A New Path to Fortune* (1903), and *Finding a Fortune* (1904). Works like these contributed to the national ideology that all Americans could make it if they only pulled themselves up by their own bootstraps.

Although more than 100 years old, Alger's novels still resonate with a faith in mobility that is woven into the national fabric and self-image of Americans. Today the majority of Americans are no longer optimistic about the possibility of upward mobility. A 2013 poll by the Pew Charitable Trusts

found that only 37 percent of Americans thought that their children would be better off than they were (Stokes, 2017), and in 2017 only 36 percent of Americans believed that they themselves had achieved the American dream (Pew Research Center, 2017b). What is so striking is that more and more Americans are buying into the Alger myth—more Americans than 20 years ago believe it possible to start at the bottom and work your way to the top. People generally believe that hard work and education are more important than social connections or a wealthy background. Are Americans overly optimistic or are sociologists just being naysayers? Only more research will tell us for sure.

QUESTIONS FOR REVIEW

1. How does the number of doctors with last names from particular ethnic groups demonstrate the lasting influence of history on intergenerational mobility?

2. How does class-based affirmative action continue to help some racial minority students? What does this tell you about the status of various categories of stratification in America?

3. Whereas inequality is the result of abundance, how does the relationship between the bourgeoisie and proletariat suggest that abundance is the result of inequality?

4. To talk about the rich, the poor, and the way society is economically stratified sounds like the job of economists. Why should sociologists be interested in stratification? How does a better understanding of stratification potentially contribute to the well-being of society?

5. Why, according to Adam Ferguson and John Millar, is inequality necessary? In what way does their argument anticipate the "free rider problem"?

6. What is "equality of condition," and why did Thomas Malthus argue against striving for this form of equality?

7. What are the ideal types of social stratification and how do they differ? Which one, in your opinion, best describes stratification in the United States?

8. What is the difference between income and wealth? Why might certain sociologists prefer to measure inequality based on wealth instead of income?

9. What is structural mobility, and how does this concept describe the decline of manufacturing jobs in the United States since the late 1970s?

10. According to Max Weber, what do being a teacher, having a cool car, and being a member of a prestigious association have in common?

THE $5,000 TOOTHBRUSH

Scholars from Weber to Bourdieu have talked about lifestyle and consumption choices as an important part of the stratification system. It tends to be the most extreme examples that remind us of so-called conspicuous consumption, a term first coined in 1899 by sociologist Thorstein Veblen in his book *The Theory of the Leisure Class*. For example, in a video for *GQ*'s series "Most Expensivest Shit," rapper 2 Chainz tries out a $5,000 luxury toothbrush, one of the most costly toothbrushes in the world. (His reaction? "Tastes like titanium" [*GQ*, 2014].)

TRY IT!

Pick an object you frequently use—an article of clothing, a toothbrush, your phone. Then choose a service you take advantage of, such as getting your hair cut, getting around town, or eating out. Research the most and least expensive of each of these goods and services, and provide specific examples.

Where do your consumption practices fall in relation to these extremes? Where do your practices fall compared to those of your friends?

FREQUENTLY USED OBJECT

_____

MOST EXPENSIVE

$ _____

LEAST EXPENSIVE

$ _____

FREQUENTLY USED SERVICE

_____

MOST EXPENSIVE	LEAST EXPENSIVE
_____	_____
$	$

THINK ABOUT IT

What geographic areas tend to have more narrow ranges of inequality, with most products priced similarly, and what areas tend to have wider ranges, with extremes on both ends? What do these differences imply about income inequality in the United States?

If rich people are spending their money on titanium toothbrushes, does that mean inequality is harmless or even good because it stimulates the economy? Along these lines, is it better or worse for society as a whole if one rich person buys a $5,000 toothbrush meant to last a lifetime, or buys a 10-cent toothbrush for every day of the year, keeping the difference in the bank?

SOCIOLOGY ON THE STREET

Some people you would consider rich may not think of themselves that way. If the label "rich" is relative, what does it mean to be rich? Watch the Sociology on the Street video to find out more: **digital.wwnorton.com/youmayask7**.

WANT MORE PRACTICE?

Complete the InQuizitive activity for this chapter at digital.wwnorton.com /youmayask7

HOW DO WE INVESTIGATE INEQUALITY
BETWEEN MEN AND WOMEN
WITHOUT REINFORCING BINARY
THINKING ABOUT GENDER?

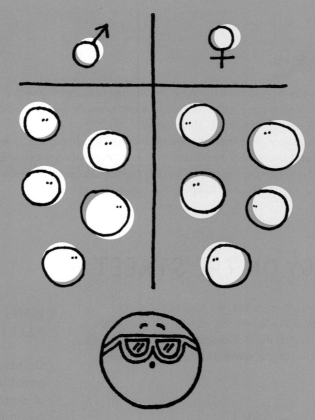

Animation at digital.wwnorton.com/youmayask7

Gender

When most people go to the bathroom, it's because they need to pee. But for one student in Bentonville, Arkansas, nature calling wasn't such a simple affair:

> I got followed into a women's bathroom today at school.
>
> The man who followed me, a teacher, called, "Young man!" in a shocked voice.
>
> I turned, and immediately realized what had happened. Several people, men and women alike, have confronted me in bathrooms at this point. Most apologize after they hear my voice; I look fairly androgynous, but I sound like a Disney princess.
>
> I am a trans man, but in situations like this, people assume that I am a trans woman, which can be dangerous for me.
>
> In most cases, I back down quickly when someone confronts me, for my own safety. Today, though, I saw an opening to fight back a little. I'm on my period, and I was heading into the bathroom to change my pad. I had a new, unopened one in my pocket.
>
> "Sorry," I said to the teacher in my highest pitched voice. I pulled out the pad and held it up. "I was just going to change my pad."
>
> He muttered something about me looking like a boy and backed up a little.
>
> I was secretly flattered, because I *want* to look like a boy, but obviously that isn't a good reason to chase someone into a bathroom. "No worries," I said in my sugarplum fairy voice. "Sometimes it's easy to forget that there are a lot of ways to look like a girl." Then I marched into a stall and shut the door.

The boy's name is Elliot Jackson. In this story, the teacher makes a key assumption: that because Elliot looks like a boy, he shouldn't be going into

A protester expresses concern over North Carolina's House Bill 2, also known as the "Bathroom Bill," which requires transgender people to use public restrooms that match the sex on their birth certificate.

a girl's bathroom. But when Elliot turns up the volume on his self-described "sugarplum fairy" voice and brandishes a feminine hygiene product, the teacher becomes confused—Elliot is blurring lines that many often take for granted.

The teacher isn't unlike many Americans, who in recent years have been increasingly exposed to the visibility of transgender people in our society. Television and film are depicting more transgender characters; two notable TV shows are *Pose* and *Orange Is the New Black*. Transgender rights issues are also in the news, for the very reason Elliot experienced so much discomfort: A series of "bathroom bills," passed in states like North Carolina and considered in others ranging from Florida to Washington, have made the bathroom the site of gender policing.

But the bathroom is just one of the many places where gender matters. Gender is a powerful force in our lives, determining everything from the toys we play with to our opportunities in school and at work. A key idea we'll encounter throughout this chapter is that gender is composed of a set of traditions, assumptions, and expectations—and that together, these norms are a key building block of society. As Elliot opened the door to the girls' restroom he violated one of these unspoken rules.

We'll hear more from Elliot later in this chapter, but first we have an important sociological task at hand. What is the difference between gender, sex, and sexuality? While intertwined, these concepts are analytically distinct.

Let's Talk about ~~Sex~~ Gender

Sex is typically used to describe socially accepted, perceived biological differences that distinguish males from females. There are many biological differences between humans; society gives some of those biological differences gendered labels that, in turn, come to define sex categories such as "male" and "female." The categories are seemingly rooted in biological reality, since these biological differences tend to cluster into two groups according to sex chromosomes a person has. Gender denotes a social position— namely, the set of social arrangements that are built around normative sex categories. Sexuality, meanwhile, refers to desire, sexual preference, and sexual identity and behavior.

No one disputes that many biological differences exist between those who typically identify as men and those who see themselves as women—nor that many of those distinctions can be traced to the difference between having two copies of the X chromosome (XX, female) versus one X and one Y (XY, male). However, what we make of those differences—which themselves are a matter of averages, not absolutes—does not inevitably arise out of the biological. Like many social categories we've discussed, gender is one set of stories we tell each other to get by in the world. It's a collectively defined guidebook that humans use to make distinctions among themselves, to comprehend an otherwise fuzzy mass of individuals. But the gender story can change, and we'll see how it has done so throughout history and across cultures.

And if gender is a human invention, we have to take it as seriously as we would any other institution, as Judith Lorber argues. In *Paradoxes of Gender* (1994), Lorber claims that gender is a social structure that "establishes patterns of expectations for individuals, orders the social processes of everyday life, is built into the major social organizations of society, such as the economy, ideology, the family, and politics, and is also an entity in and of itself." Although gender is a social construction, it matters in the real world, organizing our day-to-day experiences and having profound and unequal consequences for the life chances of people—effects that themselves vary by the other social categories to which an individual belongs. Gender is not just about people—institutions, occupations, and even nouns (in some languages) can all be gendered. In this way gender ultimately embodies power struggles and how they organize daily life, from household economies and wage labor to birth control and babies' names.

Sex: A Process in the Making

We make sense of much variation between men and women by referring to their assumed biological differences. Such differences can range from the behavioral consequences of hormones (such as premenstrual syndrome), relative physical strength of bodies (for example, women's gymnastics emphasizes balance, and men's upper-body strength), brain architecture (men supposedly being more left-brain dominant), and chromosomes (XX or XY). But in so doing, we tend to miss a crucial link between nature and nurture. The study of gender boils down to seeing how the two spheres, nature and nurture, overlap, penetrate, and shape each other. The biological

GENDER

a social position; behaviors and a set of attributes that are associated with sex identities.

SEXUALITY

desire, sexual preference, and sexual identity and behavior.

world of sex and bodies does not exist outside of a social world, and the social world of human beings is always made up of human bodies. Studying the links between the two allows us to see the social construction of both gender and sex.

SEEING SEX AS SOCIAL: THE CASE OF NONBINARY INDIVIDUALS

Bodies are, so we often think, natural, God- (or evolution-) given, sacred, hardwired. Human babies come equipped with a set of male or female organs, hormones, and chromosomes—what we might call "the plumbing" determined by our DNA. We usually think of sex as an either/or binary. You're either male or female. But in fact, there are some exceptions and blurred lines that have led sociologists to view this model of "natural" sex as more of an approximation than an absolute.

Take, for example, people who are born with both male and female genitalia, neither, or ambiguous ones that do not conform to the gender binary (also included in this category are those whose sex chromosomes do not match up in the normative way to outward sexual appearance). The medical industry used to refer to such children as "intersex"; these days, they refer to a "disorder of sex development." Most doctors today still typically recommend secretive surgery during infancy to make nonbinary children conform to a preconceived notion of what "unambiguous" genitalia should look like. About 90 percent of these surgeries reassign an ambiguous male anatomy into a female one because, in the disquieting (and offensive) phrase of the surgical world, "It's easier to make a hole than build a pole" (Hendricks, 1993).

These practices have lately come under scrutiny, however. Founded in 1993, the Intersex Society of North America (ISNA) was succeeded in 2008 by the Accord Alliance, which has the same mission: to reduce embarrassment and secrecy over intersex conditions. Sociologist Georgiann Davis (2015), who herself learned only as an adolescent that she had male sex chromosomes, has documented rifts within the intersex community. Some members find comfort in the scientific, medicalizing label of "disorder of sex development," while many resist the assertion that their identity is a pathology rather than just part of natural human variation.

In 2017, three former surgeons general of the United States coauthored a report advocating the reconsideration of sex-reassignment surgeries (Elders et al., 2017). They wrote about the emerging medical consensus that "children born with atypical genitalia should not have genitoplasty performed on them absent a need to ensure physical functioning." They also point out that such surgeries became commonplace in the United States only as of the 1950s, and that many other governments and the World Health Organization have already called for a moratorium.

Most people think—if they think about it at all—that the medical construction of sex applies only to a handful of individuals. However, Brown University biology researcher Anne Fausto-Sterling (2000) estimates that the number of deviations from the binary of male or female bodies may be as high as 2 percent of live births, and the number of people receiving "corrective" genital surgery runs between 1 and 2 in every 1,000 births. Just to give you an idea of what 2 in 1,000 looks like, there are now about 2 in 1,000 children born with trisomy 21 (also known as Down syndrome), a biological condition that is more visible than nonbinary sexual identity. Activists argue that social discomfort and fear of difference, rather than medical necessity, may be what pushes parents and surgeons to the operating table.

SEXED BODIES IN THE PREMODERN WORLD

Whereas today we often operate on a mutually exclusive two-sex model of human body types, a lesser known but equally plausible "one-sex" model dominated Western biological thought from the ancient Greeks until the mid-eighteenth century (Laqueur, 1990). In the old one-sex way of thinking, there was only one body (a male body) and the female body was regarded as its inversion—that is, as a male body whose parts were flipped inside rather than hanging on the outside. People believed that women were a lesser but not so radically different version of men—an illustration of how social power relationships can shape scientific belief.

Not until the two-sex model of human bodies gained ground did women and men become such radically different creatures in the popular conception. Incidentally, historian Thomas Laqueur shows us that this differentiation of bodies prompted changes in ideas about the female orgasm. In the one-sex model, it was believed that both a man's orgasm and a woman's were requirements for conception. (There is new medical evidence, in fact, that dual orgasms do increase the chance of conception.) But in the mid-1800s, around the time the two-sex model was gaining ground, female orgasm was considered unnecessary. Whereas seventeenth-century (female) midwives advised would-be mothers that the trick to conceiving lay in an orgasm, nineteenth-century (male) doctors debated whether female orgasm was even possible.

CONTEMPORARY CONCEPTS OF SEX AND THE PARADOXES OF GENDER

The point of all this sex talk is to challenge our tendency to think of bodies as wholly deterministic. That is, to acknowledge that our understandings of, categorizations of, and behavior toward bodies are not set in stone. We're pushing back against essentialist arguments, which explain social phenomena in terms of natural ones. Essentialist thought often relies on biological

ESSENTIALIST

arguments explaining social phenomena in terms of natural, biological, or evolutionary inevitabilities.

determinism—which assumes that what you do in the social world is a direct result of who you are in the natural world. If you are born with male parts, essentialists believe, you are essentially and absolutely a man, and you will be sexually attracted to women only, as preordained by nature. As we've seen, medical experts have maintained the ideal of a dimorphic or binary (either male or female) model of sex by tweaking babies who blur the boundaries. The trick is to recognize that the very boundaries separating male and female bodies are themselves contested.

This is not to say that there is no reality to biology. Simply put, rather than believing biology comes before or dictates behavior, sociologists now think of the nature–behavior relationship as a two-way street. Feminist philosopher Elizabeth Grosz (1994) proposes that we view the relationship between the natural and the social (in this case, sex and gender) as akin to a Möbius strip. The Möbius strip is an old math puzzle that looks like a twisted ribbon loop, yet it has just one side and one boundary. Biological sex makes up the inside of the strip, whereas the social world—culture, experience, and gender—make up the outside. But as happens in the contours of gender, the inside and outside surfaces are inseparable. In thinking or talking about sex and gender, we often switch from one to the other without even noticing that we've changed our focus (Fausto-Sterling, 2000).

Gender: What Does It Take to Be Feminine or Masculine?

I hope you can now see that biological sex does not exist in the world in some fixed, natural state—medically or historically. Our next step is to trace the different social meanings that humans have taken from sex. There are many historical and cross-cultural meanings, roles, and scripts for behavior that we like to think correspond to more or less fixed biological categories. This complete set of scripts is what sociologists refer to as gender, which, broadly speaking, has divided people, behaviors, and institutions into two categories: masculine and feminine.

Much like sex difference, people tend to think that gender difference is a natural cleavage between two static groups. Why do men tend to fight one another, dominate the natural sciences, and outnumber women in the top political and executive offices? Why do women tend to stay more connected with their families and outnumber men in occupations that involve caring for others? The short (essentialist) answer is that men and women are naturally (that is, biologically) different, so they behave differently.

The longer, sociological answer is that gender differences are much more fluid and ambiguous than we may care to admit. Take Elliot, for example. He called himself androgynous—that is, his gender presentation didn't seem obviously masculine or feminine. Elliot's gender cannot be easily explained by appeals to natural differences between the sexes, because it doesn't neatly sync up to a clearly male or clearly female outward appearance or biology (remember the pad he was waving?). And it's not just Elliot who challenges the essentialist argument: There are plenty of people whose behaviors, occupations, and roles don't correspond neatly to essentialist expectations.

ANDROGYNOUS

neither masculine nor feminine.

But just because gender isn't tied to some fixed biological reality doesn't mean it doesn't have real consequences. Gender establishes patterns of expectations for people, orders our daily lives, and is one of the fundamental building blocks of society—law, family, education, the economy, everything. The process of forming a gendered identity starts before a person is even born, as soon as the sex of a fetus is estimated or even earlier in the case of in vitro fertilization (IVF), where the sex chromosomes can be identified before implantation into the uterus. Through socialization and personality development—such as being steered to certain games or ways of dressing, and even how they are named—many children acquire a gendered identity that, in most cases, reproduces the attitudes and values of their society. We impose rigid boundaries to maintain a gender order, but if we look at how gender systems vary, we can expose those boundaries as social constructions. Our challenge is to identify those systems and inequalities without unwittingly reproducing the binary thinking we wanted to investigate in the first place.

MAKING GENDER

To start seeing gender sociologically, it helps to look at other cultures. While many Western cultures divide the world neatly between men and women with correspondingly clear male and female bodies, that's not so for the Navajo society of Native Americans. In Navajo tribes, there are not two but three genders: masculine men, feminine women, and the *nadle*. The *nadle* might be born with ambiguous genitalia or they may declare a *nadle* identity later on regardless of genitalia. The *nadle* perform both masculine and feminine tasks and dress for the moment, according to whatever activity they're doing. Although they are often treated like women, they have the freedom to marry people of any gender, "with no loss of status" (Kimmel, 2000).

Nadles are not the only examples of nonbinary gender configurations. Serena Nanda (1990) and Gayatri Reddy (2005) studied *hijras* in India, a group that is often included in textbooks like this one as proof that a

Would a member of the *hijra* community define their identity in terms of gender, or something else?

binary either/or gender system is not so natural after all. From Reddy we know that "hijras are phenotypic men who wear female clothing and ideally, renounce sexual desire and practice by undergoing a sacrificial emasculation—that is, an excision of the penis and testicles." To our Western ears, then, these men who renounce manhood but who are not women are actively staking a claim for a third gender. But Reddy goes on to develop the definition of what it means to be a *hijra*, which includes behaviors that may have little to do with gender: dedication to the goddess Bedhraj Mata, conferring fertility to newlyweds and newborns; a sometimes reluctant, sometimes quite dedicated entry into prostitution; communal living; self-sacrifice; and poverty. Thus *hijra* identity is a master status, but it is not experienced by the *hijras* as a fight for turf between gender categories. Like the Brazilian *travesti* described by Don Kulick (see page 335), the *hijras* may have few qualms about the balance they've struck between gender and sexuality but more fears about the way their poverty and stigmatization will shape their chances in life.

And as the chapter-opening story about Elliot shows, the growing prominence and social awareness of transgender people in our own society helps us break out of binary thinking about gender, since we tend to assume everyone is cisgender. Amos Mac, a man who was raised as a girl, came to talk to my class about his experience and the magazine *Original Plumbing* he publishes for a transgender audience. When I asked Mac whether he felt more like a man now than he had before he transitioned, he politely corrected my assumptions about a before—after binary gender narrative: "I actually don't even know like what is a man supposed to feel like. You

TRANSGENDER

describes people whose gender does not correspond to their birth sex.

CISGENDER

describes people whose gender corresponds to their birth sex.

know, I don't really know what a woman is supposed to feel like. . . . I feel comfortable in my skin right now, and I feel comfortable the way people are perceiving me, like strangers on the street. I don't care if people know my history" (Conley, 2014e). He allows that some of his friends may have been "born knowing something [was] terribly wrong . . . or that they [didn't] feel comfortable in their body," but that there is no common narrative that encompasses what being transgender is like. Mac explained, "I don't think there's a right or wrong way to have this experience, and I don't think it's

DIGITAL.WWNORTON.COM/YOUMAYASK7

To see my interview with Amos Mac, go to
digital.wwnorton.com/youmayask7

necessarily a fun one that you would want to go out of your way to have." The search or space for a third gender may be limited by our assumption that gender should be a fixed category. Rather, gender is a spectrum that is constantly changing, along which individuals may change positions over their lifetimes.

GENDER DIFFERENCES OVER TIME

Within a two-gender system, there is enormous variation in what counts as a "good" or "bad" man or woman. For example, how the ideal man or woman looks is itself historically contingent. Specifically, ideal feminine beauty has been a continuous site of change and contestation. Look at the seventeenth-century Rubenesque women, the voluptuous beauties who by today's high-fashion standards are simply overweight. In traditional economies where food was scarce, a plump woman was a sign of good health, wealth, and attractiveness. The long-standing preference for a robust female body has changed as industrialized societies moved from relative scarcity of food to plenitude. Today the cheaper foods are the fattening ones, and only people with enough disposable income can afford gym memberships and healthy diets. So we can see that dominant or "emphasized" definitions of femininity—as embodied by looks—are always undergoing change, from the hysterical Victorian housewife to the sporty working girl of the 1980s to today's heroically perfect-in-all-ways supermom.

WELCOME TO ZE COLLEGE, ZE

In recent years, colleges have been at the forefront of a startling reconfiguration in our society: to acknowledge difference in sex/gender identities. For example, the State University of New York, one of the nation's largest state university systems, is now allowing students to choose among seven gender identities, including "trans man," "questioning," and "genderqueer." Harvard University and other colleges now have spaces to allow students to choose gender-neutral pronouns such as "they" or "ze." Other schools are sure to follow.

Some activists and scholars advocate a brand-new pronoun like "ze" or "hir," noting that "Ms." seemed strange when first proposed but now is commonly accepted. Others suggest "they" as a non-gender-binary pronoun since it is already readily used informally when English speakers want to avoid gendering the person to whom they are referring. That's the easy part: Just like choosing how we want someone to address us—by our formal name or nickname or initials—it seems pretty straightforward to allow individuals to select their own pronouns. Elliot Jackson, for example, whose story opened this chapter, asked that I use "he" and "him" pronouns. Easy enough!

But implementing a fluid notion of sex/gender identity for all aspects of the life in the institution we call campus gets trickier. Take campus sports. The policy of Bates College—which is fairly typical of the NCAA—is the following: "A transgender student athlete should be allowed to participate in any sports activity so long as that athlete's use of hormone therapy, if any, is consistent with the National College Athletic Association (NCAA) existing policies on banned medications." So, a female transitioning to male via hormone therapy is no longer allowed to

---

HEGEMONIC MASCULINITY

the condition in which men are dominant and privileged, and this dominance and privilege is invisible.

This might be an easy point to grasp about femininity, but most people think that masculinity is less subject to such trends and fashions. It is always harder to denaturalize the dominant category; being the norm, it often is invisible. Among social categories, those who go unquestioned tend to be most privileged. In *Manhood in America* (1996), Michael Kimmel traces the development of hegemonic masculinity in the West and finds that in the eighteenth century, the ideal man was not associated with physical fitness,

compete on women's teams but is eligible for men's sports. Ditto in reverse. The NCAA does not have a mandatory policy for transgender inclusion, but the association claims that inclusion is an "NCAA value" (Kanno-Youngs, 2015).

The final frontier—on college campuses and beyond—has been locker room and bathroom policy (as illustrated by Elliot's story at the start of the chapter). Under the Obama administration, federal agencies ruled that Title VII of the Civil Rights Act bars discrimination based on gender identity (i.e., not just sex), and this includes locker room segregation. The Office of Civil Rights of the US Department of Education rejected the argument that female students needed to be protected from being seen naked by an individual who was biologically still male. Separate facilities for transgender individuals were seen to be akin to the now unacceptable "separate but equal" racial policy of Jim Crow (Phillips et al., 2015).

Harvard University student Schuyler Bailar became the first openly transgender swimmer to compete in the NCAA.

However, as political winds shift, this is likely not the final word on the matter. For example, the Obama administration interpreted Title IX of the Education Amendments of 1972 as applicable to discrimination based on gender identity, not just gender. This meant that schools that received federal funding (i.e., almost all) were required to make nonseparate restrooms accessible to transgender individuals based on their self-identified gender. However, the Trump administration withdrew that guideline in its first year in office. (To be continued . . .)

money-making endeavors, or sports. Business endeavors were the boorish concerns of the rude trade classes, and physical strength undermined one's gentlemanly dispositions. Ideal masculinity in the 1700s went hand in hand with kindness and intellect, and preferably a little poetry, a very different image from the modern-day ideal of the "man's man."

Erving Goffman (1963) describes the masculine ideal of mid-twentieth-century America as a young man who is "married, white, urban, northern, heterosexual, Protestant, father, of college education, fully employed, of good complexion, weight and height, and [with] a decent record in sports." Today that definition has blossomed to include more forms of dominant masculine identity, including, for example, the metrosexual male, who, as described by sociologist Kristen Barber (2016), is typically White and wealthy and spends a large amount on grooming activities, such as manicures, that would have been considered feminine in the days Goffman was writing. Likewise, many men take on what Tristan Bridges and C. J. Pascoe (2014) call "hybrid masculinities," in which, for example, young White men may try to distance themselves from hegemonic masculinity and instead adopt aspects of, say, African American masculinity. They argue, however, that this cultural practice can often serve to conceal inequalities. That is, when White adolescent males emulate the masculine practices of marginalized groups, this dynamic serves to mitigate the real power differences and inequalities between the groups, as if race and class were just a style one can adopt or shed as one likes (Aboim, 2016, p. 56; Bridges & Pascoe, 2014).

Over time and from place to place, our ideas about gender are fluid, changing, and context-specific. Many of the differences we observe between men and women do not have much to do with individual gender differences at all; instead, the behaviors arise as a result of the different positions men and women occupy. Sociologist Cynthia Fuchs Epstein (1988) calls these "deceptive distinctions" that grossly exaggerate the actual differences between men and women. To illustrate her idea, here's a quick thought experiment: Imagine a doctor and a nurse. Did you assume the doctor was a man and the nurse a woman? Tied up in these expectations are other ideas, such as the stereotypes that women are nurturing and men are analytical. The main difference between the doctor and nurse isn't gender, but power and social status.

Baby names provide another striking example of the power of gender. Analysis by Stanley Lieberson, Susan Dumais, and Shyon Baumann (2000)

Kristen Barber would probably call the man on the left "metrosexual": He's getting his eyebrows trimmed in a new men-only section of a beauty salon. The White men on the right exemplify what Tristan Bridges and C. J. Pascoe call "hybrid masculinities": By emulating Black hip-hop culture, they erase their own privilege.

↓

shows that names flow from male to androgynous to female but never in reverse. If you know, for example, a male named Kim, chances are he was born before 1958, the year that Hitchcock's movie *Vertigo* was released, making the actress Kim Novak a household name. The number of boys named Kim dropped to almost zero the next year. Carol, Aubrey, and Lindsay (and many others) started as male names and became feminized. The fact that there is a one-way flow from male to female in terms of child naming tells us something about gender norms and inequality—namely, that masculinity dictates culture more than femininity does, or that femininity seeks to emulate masculinity while the masculine sees the feminine as corrupting.

While gender norms can be fluid, one constant across time and culture is that men have held more power than women—a question that has preoccupied social thinkers for a long time.

Theories of Gender Inequality

In applying our sociological imaginations to sex and gender, we will come across many feminist strands of thought. Feminism was at first embraced as a social movement to advocate for women's right to vote; it later became a consciousness-raising movement to get people to understand that gender is an organizing principle of life. One of the central ideas of this "second-wave" feminism is that gender is important because it structures relations between people. Further, as gender shapes social relations, it does this on unequal ground, meaning gender is not just an identifying characteristic (I'm a guy, you're a girl), but embodies real powers and privileges. Regardless of which "wave" we are talking about, the basic idea behind feminism is that women and men (and other-gendered people) should be accorded equal opportunities and respect.

At the start of the second wave of the feminist movement in the 1960s, theorists scrambled to find an answer to the "woman question": What explains the nearly universal dominance of men over women? What is the root of patriarchy, a system involving the subordination of femininity to masculinity?

RUBIN'S SEX/GENDER SYSTEM

Anthropologist Gayle Rubin was one of the first in a long string of thinkers to argue that the nearly universal oppression of women was in need of an explanation. In the field of anthropology, most scholars studying societies

FEMINISM

a social movement to get people to understand that gender is an organizing principle in society and to address gender-based inequalities that intersect with other forms of social identity.

PATRIARCHY

a nearly universal system involving the subordination of femininity to masculinity.

A "new feminist bookstore" in 1970. Feminist theorists since the 1960s have attempted to explain the "woman question"—why, in nearly every society across history, do men hold power over women?

around the world had previously assumed that, since women's subordination occurred everywhere, it must be fulfilling some societal function, and therefore was less interesting than other possible research questions.

Rubin (1975) challenged this notion and proposed the "sex/gender system." In this system, the raw materials of biological sex are transformed through kinship relations into asymmetrical gender statuses. She used the structural perspective of Claude Lévi-Strauss, a French anthropologist, to suggest that because of the universal taboo against incest—fathers and brothers cannot sleep with their daughters and sisters—women who start out belonging to one man (their father, or their brother if Dad dies) must leave their families of origin and go belong to another man (their husband). Women are treated like valuable property whose trade patterns strengthen relations between families headed by men. Indeed, traditional wedding vows in the West involve a commitment to "obey" only on the part of the wife. This "traffic in women" gives men certain rights over their female kin. The resulting sex/gender system, Rubin argued, was not a given; it was the result of human interaction.

Rubin's theories made waves. Feminist thinkers widely agreed that the task at hand was to explain universal male dominance. Why were women—despite a few token examples of matrifocal or women-led tribes in the anthropology books—typically on the bottom of stratification systems? That is, why did women in almost every society seem to get short shrift? Anthropologist Michelle Rosaldo (1974) answered that it must be women's universal association with the private sphere. Because women give birth and then rear children, they become identified with domestic life, which universally is accorded less prestige, value, and rewards than men's public sphere of work and politics. Meanwhile, anthropologist Sherry Ortner (1974) claimed that women are identified with something that every culture defines as lower than itself—nature. A woman, she reasoned, comes to be identified with the chaos and danger of nature because of bodily functions like lactation and menstruation (what feminist philosopher Simone de Beauvoir [1952] poetically described as "woman's enslavement to the species").

PARSONS'S SEX ROLE THEORY

Ortner's answer to the woman question sounds like a plausible one. But note the binary logic at work in these anthropological accounts: culture versus nature, private versus public, man versus woman. The world is less rigid, more nuanced, and certainly less easily molded into binary categories than these theories suggest. What underlies these theoretical approaches is structural functionalism. This theoretical tradition dominated early anthropological thought, and it assumed that every society had certain structures (such as the family, the division of labor, or gender) that existed to fulfill some set of necessary functions. Talcott Parsons, an influential American sociologist of the 1950s, offered a widely accepted functionalist account of gender relations. According to Parsons's (1951) sex role theory, the heterosexual nuclear family is the ideal arrangement in modern societies because it fulfills the function of reproducing workers. With a work-oriented father in the public sphere and a domestic-oriented mother in the private sphere, children are most effectively reared to be people who can meet the labor demands of a capitalist system. Sex, sexuality, and gender are taken to be stable and dichotomous, meaning that each has two categories. Each category is assigned a role and a given script that actors carry out according to the expectations of those roles, which are enforced by social sanctions to ensure that the actors do not forget their lines. Women and men play distinctive roles that are functional for the whole of society; a healthy, harmonious society exists when actors stick to their normal roles. Generally speaking, according to Parsons, social structures such as gender and the division of labor are held in place because they work to ensure a stable society.

Functionalism was a hit in the 1950s; after all, it makes intuitive sense (and feels very satisfying) that there must be a good reason for the way things happen to be, some internal logic—at least to those who benefit from those arrangements. But Parsons's sex role theory falls short on several points. For starters, the argument is tautological—that is, it explains the existence of a structure in terms of its function, essentially claiming that things work the way they do because they work. In explaining a phenomenon in terms of its function, functionalists relied on the presumption that the need for the function preexists the phenomenon, a tricky leap of logical faith. Furthermore, they glossed over the possibility that other ways of organizing society than the structures of gender, race, and so on that we currently have could fulfill the same functions, and the question of whether those

STRUCTURAL FUNCTIONALISM

a theory in which society's many parts—institutions, norms, traditions, and so on—mesh to produce a stable, working whole that evolves over time. Best embodied by Talcott Parsons.

SEX ROLE THEORY

Talcott Parsons's theory that men and women perform their sex roles as breadwinners and wives/mothers, respectively, because the nuclear family is the ideal arrangement in modern societies, fulfilling the function of reproducing workers.

In the 1950s, Talcott Parsons advanced the idea that the nuclear family effectively reared children to meet the labor demands of a capitalist system.

"functions" are themselves legitimate or ultimately desirable. The end result is a theory that tends to justify or "naturalize" existing forms of social relationships—such as gender wage gaps and the unequal division of labor in housework.

The functionalist sex role story also does not explain how and why structures change throughout history. If traditional husband-and-wife sex roles were so functional, why did they change drastically in the 1970s? In Parsons's account, gender roles appear to be a matter of voluntarism, as if women and men choose, independently of external power constraints, to be housewives and breadwinners, respectively. Of course, this is a myopic view of roles since women of color and immigrant women had always worked outside the home at high rates. Finally—and this is a problem with much early feminist thinking as well—sex and gender are regarded as being composed of dichotomous roles, when these categories are, in fact, fuzzy, flexible, and variable in combination with other social positions, such as race and class.

PSYCHOANALYTIC THEORIES

Where functionalism focuses too much, perhaps, on society as a whole, Freudian theorists have provided an overly individualistic, psychoanalytic account of sex roles. The father of psychoanalysis, Sigmund Freud (1856–1939), famously quipped, "Anatomy is destiny." Although biological determinism plays a major role in Freudian theory, so does the idea that gender develops through family socialization.

According to Freud's developmental psychology, girls and boys develop masculine and feminine personality structures through early interactions with their parents. Boys, so the story goes, have a tormented time achieving masculinity because they must resolve the Oedipal complex. In this stage of development, around age three, every normal boy experiences heterosexual love for his maternal figure. But he soon realizes that he will be castrated (psychologically, not literally) by his father if he continues to fancy his mother. To resolve this Oedipal conflict, the boy rejects his mother, in turn emulating his emotionally distant father and developing rigid ego boundaries.

In Freud's view, girls do not experience quite the same resolution to their analogous "penis envy." When a little girl realizes that she lacks the plumbing to have sexual relations with her mother, she experiences penis envy toward her father, according to Freud. However, she ultimately realizes that one day she too can have a baby, thus providing feminine gratification.

Girls end up identifying with their mothers, growing up with less rigid ego boundaries and more easily connecting with others than boys do.

Many thinkers have picked up and used Freudian ideas to theorize differences between men and women. For example, feminist psychoanalyst Nancy Chodorow (1978) modified Freud's theory to answer a particular version of the woman question: Why are women predominantly the caregivers? She reasoned that parents' unequal involvement in child rearing was a partial cause of the universal oppression of women. Her answer was that mothering by women is reproduced in a cycle of role socialization, in which little girls learn to identify as mothers and little boys as fathers (and workers outside the home). Chodorow concluded that egalitarian relations between the sexes would be possible if men shared the mothering.

Before you see a psychoanalyst to discuss your own penis envy, consider the assumptions underlying these psychological accounts. For starters, Freud's theories lacked empirical evidence and assumed a heterosexual, two-parent nuclear family. Since only about 64 percent of American children live in households headed by two married parents (NCES, 2019a), many of you reading this probably did not grow up in the nuclear family setting that Freud and Chodorow describe. Sociologist Carol Stack underscored this point in her ethnography of a poor Black community. In *All Our Kin* (1974), she finds that the division between male and female roles and attitudes is not as clear-cut as Freud or Chodorow would have us think. In the community Stack studied, caregiving was a valued responsibility for both men and women. Moreover, these early psychoanalytic theorists took for granted a binary sex/gender system, whereas we now know that those categories are much more fluid in real life.

CONFLICT THEORIES

By the 1980s, another wave of thinkers began to tackle an issue missing from earlier discussions of the woman question: power. Conflict theorists mixed old-school Marxism with feminism to claim that gender, not class, was the driving force of history. Socialist feminists, also known as radical feminists, claimed that the root of all social relations, including relations of production, stemmed from unequal gender relations.

Economist Heidi Hartmann (1981) and legal theorist Catharine MacKinnon (1983), for example, both analyzed how capitalism combines with patriarchy to make women economically dependent on a man's income. This means that in a capitalist society, women have a disadvantaged position in the job market and within the family. Capitalists (predominantly men), in turn, reap all the benefits of women's subordination. When women are subordinate, men benefit. To radical feminists, gender inequality is first and foremost about power inequalities, and gender differences (as in personality development) emerge from there. A useful metaphor for the

Many conflict theorists argue that patriarchal capitalists benefit through systems that subordinate women. For instance, many cotton mills in the nineteenth and early twentieth centuries hired young, unmarried women and required them to live in company boarding houses in order to regulate their behavior.

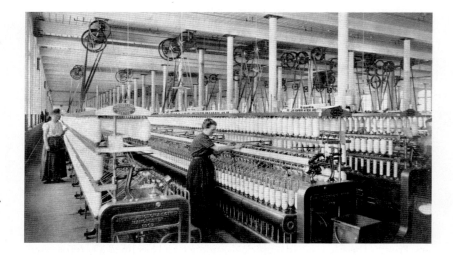

pervasiveness of gender oppression has been offered by Marilyn Frye: the birdcage. Women, she argued in 1983, find themselves like birds trapped in a cage. One can focus on one of the wires of sexism up close, but then we cannot see the other wires that complete the cage. It is the combination of the many strands (bars of the cage) of sexism that oppress women—not any single one in isolation. A bar can be workplace discrimination, unequal housework burdens, and so on.

"DOING GENDER": INTERACTIONIST THEORIES

A social theory is useful only if it helps you understand the social world in which you live. For example, Candace West and Don H. Zimmerman argue in their influential article "Doing Gender" (1987) that gender is not a fixed identity or role that we take with us into our interactions. Rather, it is the product of those interactions. In this framework, gender is a matter of active doing, not simply a matter of natural being. To be a man or a woman, they argue, is to perform masculinity or femininity constantly. In this social constructionist theory, gender is a process, not a static category.

The "doing gender" perspective is rooted in Erving Goffman's dramaturgical theory, symbolic interactionism, and ethnomethodology. (See discussion of these terms in Chapter 4.) That is, West and Zimmerman argue that people create their social realities and identities through interactions with one another. Unlike the structural functionalists, psychoanalysts, and conflict theorists, however, social constructionists view gender roles as having open-ended scripts. Perhaps individuals come to the stage situated differently according to their place in power hierarchies or personality development, but their lines and gestures are far from being predetermined. Regardless of social location, individuals are always free to act, sometimes in unexpected ways that change the course of the play. For example, the presence of openly transgender people has been said to "undo" or "redo" gender by subverting the binary norms (Connell, 2010; Sawyer et al., 2016). But by and large, as a result of doing gender, people contribute to, reaffirm, and reproduce masculine dominance and feminine submissiveness in the bedroom, kitchen, workplace, and so on.

BLACK FEMINISM AND INTERSECTIONALITY

If gender is a performance, it is much more than a set of neutral scripts that we "voluntarily" follow. Our actions are influenced by structural forces that we might not even be aware of, such as class or race privilege. As Patricia Hill Collins (1990) claims, we "do" a lot more than gender; gender intersects with race, class, nationality, religion, and so forth. Black feminists have made the case that early liberal feminism was largely by, about, and for White middle-class women. In trying to answer the woman question and explain women's oppression, early feminists assumed that all women were in the same oppressed boat. In so doing, they effaced multiple lines of fragmentation and difference into one simple category: woman. For example, by championing women's rights to work outside the home in *The Feminine Mystique* (1997), leading second-wave feminist Betty Friedan ignored the experiences of thousands of working-class women and women of color who were already working, sometimes holding down two jobs to support their families. Indeed, a third wave of feminism focuses on how the identities surrounding gender, sex, and sexuality intersect with other meaningful social categories like race or class in a process called intersectionality, as articulated by critical race theorist Kimberlé Williams Crenshaw (1989) and sociologist Beatrice Potter Webb back in 1913.

As illustrated by the concept of intersectionality, "woman" is not a stable or obvious category of identity. Rather, women are differentially located in what Collins calls a matrix of domination. A 40-year-old poor, Black, straight, single mother living in rural Georgia will not have the same conception of what it means to be a woman as a 25-year-old professional, White, single, lesbian in Chicago. More fundamentally, Collins (1990) argues, Black women face unique oppressions that White women don't. For instance, Black women experience motherhood in ways that differ from the White masculinist ideal of the family, as "bloodmothers," "othermothers," and "community othermothers," thus revealing that White masculine notions of the world do not capture the daily lived experiences of many Black women.

Gender, sexual orientation, race, class, nationality, ability, and other factors all intersect. Just as some women enjoy privilege by virtue of their wealth, class, education, and skin color, some men are disadvantaged by their lack of these same assets. As bell hooks (1984) noted, if women's liberation is aimed at making women the social equals of men, women should

INTERSECTION-ALITY

the idea that it is critical to understand the interplay between social identities such as race, class, gender, ability status, and sexual orientation, even though many social systems and institutions (such as the law) try to treat each category on its own.

MATRIX OF DOMINATION

intersecting domains of oppression that create a social space of domination and, by extension, a unique position within that space based on someone's intersectional identity along the multiple dimensions of gender, age, race, class, sexuality, location, and so on.

Patricia Hill Collins criticized feminist leaders such as Betty Friedan (pictured in the red dress), Billie Jean King (in tan pants and a blue shirt on the left), and Bella Abzug (in the gray dress, with the hat) for ignoring the experiences of thousands of working-class women and women of color.

first stop and consider which men they would like to equal. Certainly, not all men are privileged over all women. Making universal comparisons of men to women misses these nuances and implicitly excludes marginally positioned people from the discussion. For example, men of color certainly experience oppression that intersects with their gender identities (for example, Black men bearing the brunt of police harassment). Even going beyond demographic groups, men who do not embody or perform the dominant form of masculine behavior often suffer for it, occupying a subordinate status (Connell, 1987). Power comes from many different angles; it doesn't sit evenly on a plane for all women. When the Black activist Sojourner Truth (1797–1883) asked, "Ain't I a woman?" (1851), she summed up some elusive philosophical questions: What is a woman? Who counts as a woman and why?

POSTMODERN AND GLOBAL PERSPECTIVES

As perspectives have expanded and previously rigid categories have begun to crumble, the validity of the woman question is itself now in question. For instance, anthropologist Oyèrónkẹ́ Oyěwùmí argues that the woman question is a product of uniquely Western thought and cannot be applied to African societies. In *The Invention of Women* (1997), she presents ethnographic research on Yoruban society in West Africa, which she claims was once a genderless society. Among the Yoruba, before the arrival of anthropologists, villagers did not group themselves as men or women or use body markers at all. Rather, they ranked themselves into strata by seniority. When Western feminist scholars arrived on the scene, presuming the preexistence of gender relations, they, of course, found a system of gender. But this system of categories—distinct males and females—indicates a Western cultural logic, what Oyěwùmí has termed *bio-logic*.

Bio-logic runs deep in our cultural experiences and understandings of gender. It acts as a sort of filter through which all knowledge of the world runs, though there may be different ways of knowing outside such a paradigm. But if "woman" is such an unstable, fragmented category—one that is merely "performed" through discourse, as postmodern and queer theorist Judith Butler (2006) suggests—how are we supposed to study it? Feminists must have some sturdy ground on which to unite, build coalitions, and tackle injustice. Philosopher Susan Bordo (1990) provides a pragmatic buoy by arguing that there are hierarchical and binary power structures out there that do still oppress women and are handy when it comes to addressing issues such as the wage gap, eating disorders, or rape.

Growing Up, Getting Ahead, and Falling Behind

In summer 2017, a Google employee named James Damore circulated a memo to his colleagues questioning the pursuit of gender diversity at the company, in which he claimed the real reason that women were underrepresented among coders and in management was due to "biological causes." Perhaps understandably, the memo caused an uproar within the firm, and once it was leaked to the press, it went viral. Upper-level management at Google disavowed the statement, Damore was forced out of the company, and critics referred to the memo as a blatant example of workplace sexism, while others defended his right to air "un-PC" views on free speech grounds.

Damore's memo shone a light on the underrepresentation of women at Google and companies like it, but the tech industry is just the tip of the iceberg when it comes to gender inequality. About 57 percent of college students in 2017 were women (National Center for Education Statistics, 2018c; Figure 8.1). However, despite their increased enrollment, women remain overrepresented in traditionally feminine fields of study: the arts and the humanities. Men also outnumber women at elite colleges, where they are groomed for high-power professions in finance, law, or politics.

Do men disproportionately become computer scientists and financiers and women kindergarten teachers and dental hygienists because they are hardwired to do so? Putting aside Damore's controversial argument, we do know that cis-men and cis-women vary in thousands of major and minor measures. Let's start at the beginning.

SEXISM

occurs when a person's sex or gender is the basis for judgment, discrimination, or other differential treatment against that person.

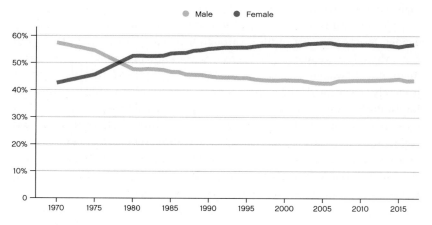

FIGURE 8.1 College Enrollment by Gender, 1970–2018

SOURCE: National Center for Education Statistics, 2018c.

GROWING UP WITH GENDER

Gender socialization begins at birth (see Chapter 4) when parents dress their children differently by sex. It continues through school—where boys and girls are treated differently (see Chapter 13) such that boys are called on by teachers more often (Sadker & Sadker, 1994; Sadker et al., 2009). And it is apparent in family life, where even though women's roles have expanded in the formal labor force, men's have only slightly budged toward more involvement in the domestic sphere (see Chapter 12).

The average male newborn weighs two ounces more than the average female newborn. For infant death rates, however, the disadvantage is tilted against males, who are at higher risk of death than females. Psychologist Carol Gilligan (1982) contends that by adolescence, the disadvantages are stacked against girls, who "lose their voices" as they suffer blows to their self-confidence. Depending on the study, eating disorders may be up to twice as likely to affect adolescent and teen girls compared with their male peers (Pisetsky et al., 2008). More than half of teenage girls are on diets or think they should be. What's more, girls more frequently report low self-esteem, more girls attempt suicide, and more girls report experiencing some form of sexual harassment in school (Johnson et al., 2016).

Psychologist Christina Hoff Sommers challenges this "girl crisis" in *The War against Boys: How Misguided Feminism Is Harming Our Young Men* (2000). She finds that because they are inadvertently penalized for the shortchanging of girls, boys are the ones suffering in education and adolescent health. For example, although females in general attempt suicide twice as frequently as males, boys ages 15 to 19 succeed in killing themselves four times more often than girls. (That's not to mention transgender people, who unfortunately suffer from extraordinarily high rates of suicide. Researchers estimate that between one-third and one-half of trans people attempt suicide at some point in their lives [Virupaksha et al., 2016].) Teenage girls may sneak more cigarettes than boys, but boys are more likely to be involved in crime, alcohol, and drugs and to be suspended from school or drop out. High-school-aged male teens are also 28 percent more likely to be victimized by violent crime, and that's even taking rape into account (Child Trends Data Bank, 2018).

What accounts for the wide range of statistical differences that exist between men and women? Essentialists might refer to natural sex differences, but as we saw earlier, sociologists are apt to call these same differences "deceptive distinctions," those that arise because of the particular roles individuals come to occupy (Epstein, 1988). Why might some people believe men to be more capable of logic, abstraction, and rationality? Perhaps because their employment possibilities are more likely to include jobs with these demands—a circular argument. Why do women seem to be so good at parenting? Maybe because their weaker employment prospects encourage them to accept domestic roles and rely on a male's salary. Who is more relational and who is more rational? Anthropologists Jean O'Barr and William O'Barr find that the true test of what type of language an individual uses during testimony in court is the witness's occupation, not gender (O'Barr, 1995; Kimmel, 2000). Physicists tend to speak in more abstract terms, teachers in more relational ones, regardless of gender. Once such deceptive distinctions are revealed, it is easy to flip the essentialist rhetoric to see that gender differences may be a product of gender expectations, rather than the cause. Physicists speak in more abstract terms and teachers in more relational ones because their jobs demand it. The question then shifts to: How and why does gender inequality exist? We need to peel back another layer of the gender onion.

INEQUALITY AT WORK

The past few decades have brought arguably the biggest change in American gender relations—in the world of paid work. Compared to the 1970s, almost 43 million more women are in the labor force, an increase from 31.5 million in 1970 to 75.2 million in 2017 (Figure 8.2). Of course, the overall population has increased by 50 percent in that period as well, accounting for part of the rise, but the percentage of women ages 16 to 64 who are in the workforce has risen from approximately 43 percent in 1970 to 57 percent in 2017. Because the Great Recession of 2008–9 hit male-dominated industries the hardest (such as construction), it helped accelerate the trend toward gender equality in labor force participation; in fact, there was a brief period at the depth of the economic crisis during which women's totals exceeded those of men in the workforce. However, men have since caught up and reclaimed their

FIGURE 8.2 Increase of Women in the Workforce, 1970–2017

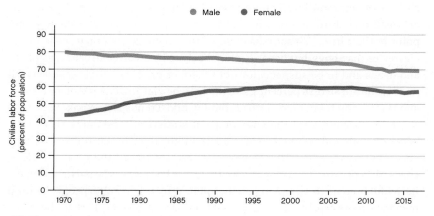

SOURCE: Bureau of Labor Statistics, 2018d.

majority position: men's labor force participation is at 69 percent compared to women's 57 percent. Because women are disproportionately employed in the public sector, and state governments have yet to recover from the twin challenges of economic woes and ballooning budgets, it may be some time before women once again approach parity (Covert, 2011).

The greater number of women entering the labor force has not catapulted them to equality with their male peers in the workplace (see Chapter 14). Despite the passage of Title VII of the 1964 Civil Rights Act, which declared it unlawful for employers to discriminate on the basis of a person's race, nationality, creed, or sex, women have continued to fare much worse than their male counterparts in the workforce. Although legally entitled to enter all lines of work, women routinely face sexual harassment, an illegal form of discrimination that runs the gamut from inappropriate jokes on the job to outright sexual assault to sexual "barter," in which sexual favors are extracted from victims under the threat of punishment (Kimmel, 2000). Intended to make people feel uncomfortable and unwelcome, sexual harassment occurs across many settings and in all kinds of relationships; walking down the street and having to listen to "Whooo, baby!" is just one annoying everyday example. In the workplace, some argue, sexual harassment is one of the chief ways in which men resist gender equality. In 1982, the US Court of Appeals ruled that sexual harassment is a violation of the Civil Rights Act, because it is a form of discrimination against an individual on the basis of sex. But even though sexual harassment is illegal, it often takes insidious forms not easily detected by everyone or verifiable in court. Most commonly, sexual harassment takes the form of "hostile environments" in which individuals feel unsafe, excluded, singled out, and mocked.

SEXUAL HARASSMENT

an illegal form of discrimination revolving around sexuality that can involve everything from inappropriate jokes to sexual "barter" (where victims feel the need to comply with sexual requests for fear of losing their job) to outright sexual assault.

A recent report by the National Academies of Science on harassment suggests that organizations (in science and academia but also outside) need to take a holistic approach, addressing three forms of harassment: (1) gender harassment (sexist hostility and crude behavior), "(2) unwanted sexual attention (unwelcome verbal or physical sexual advances), and (3) sexual coercion (when favorable professional or educational treatment is conditioned on sexual activity)." (Gender harassment is, in fact, the most common form.) The report further argues that it is not enough to just directly address the so-called bad apples. Better work environments will be fostered only if structural conditions that breed harassment are altered. These include: "male-dominated work settings; hierarchies that concentrate power in individuals and make . . . others dependent on them for . . . career advancement; symbolic legal compliance policies and procedures that are ineffective at preventing harassment; and uninformed leadership at all levels lacking the tools, intention, and/or focus needed to undertake the key actions necessary to reduce and prevent sexual harassment."

In addition to sometimes having to work in hostile environments, women have consistently been paid less than their male peers, earning about 81 cents to every $1 of a man's wage (Bureau of Labor Statistics, 2019d; Figure 8.3). This overall gap obscures stark racial differences, however. Black women earn 94 cents to the Black male dollar (but only 70 cents to the White male dollar). Meanwhile, White women have similar earnings to those of Black men, yet only earn 80 cents to the dollar of White men (Bureau of Labor Statistics, 2019d). (In some large, economically successful cities, however, the gender gap may be shrinking or even reversing among young adults [Bacolod, 2017]). The media touted women's gains in the 1970s and 1980s, when masses of women entered the US labor force. Yet women

It takes a special kind of girl
to inspire this kind of trust

As a Stewardess with British Airways, European Division, you'll be in a very responsible position. Our passengers—some very young, some a little apprehensive—will look to you for the attention and reassurance that is such a vital part of your job. A great deal of trust will be placed in you, as the member of the aircrew most in the public eye.

It takes a special kind of girl—perhaps you? You must be aged 19 to 30 and be 5'3" to 5'9" tall. Looks are important and you must be physically fit. Adaptability and friendliness are called for as is patience and the ability to work happily with the rest of the crew of a modern airliner.

If you feel you can match these requirements we would like to hear from you—training for these **London** based vacancies starts in early 1975. You'll enjoy an initial

salary of £1517 rising to £1732 after 3 months, but with generous allowances whilst flying, average earnings are in excess of £2200. (Threshold payments are additional to salaries quoted.) The job may be more demanding than most, but offers travel and the freedom from a 9 to 5 rut.

Send us a postcard for an application form to: Assistant Personnel Officer (NV1) (Cabin Services), British Airways European Division PO Box 6, Heathrow Airport London, Hounslow, Middlesex.

(Local interviews will be held at selected centres throughout the UK).

British airways

This British Airways recruiting ad from the 1970s seeks a "very special kind of girl" for a stewardess position: "You must be aged 19 to 30 and be 5' 3" to 5' 9" tall. Looks are important and you must be physically fit. Adaptability and friendliness are called for as is patience and the ability to work happily with the rest of the crew of a modern airliner."

FIGURE 8.3 Pay Discrepancy Based on Gender

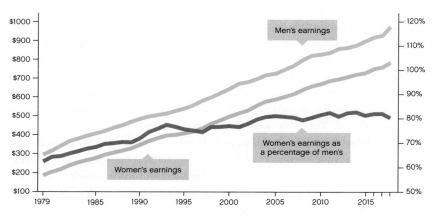

SOURCE: Bureau of Labor Statistics, 2019d.

disproportionately entered the lower rungs of the occupational hierarchy. These feminized jobs, what Louise Howe (1977) calls "pink-collar" jobs, are low-paid service industry jobs. Cleaning buildings, filing papers, and making coffee are hardly what women imagine when they dream of independence. Caring work tends to be feminized as well—think home health aides, nurses, or child-care workers. Meanwhile, "purple-collar" labor—a name given to occupational niches typically filled by transgender individuals— often involves trans women performing emotional work to reduce tensions in high-stress environments, such as one Philippine call center that was studied by Emmanuel David (2015).

How does this occupational segregation happen? Many new women workers find themselves shuffled into occupations dominated by other women, and women who go into a male-dominated field often find that, soon enough, they are surrounded by women. Like names, jobs become feminized when too many more women hit the scene. This has happened in fields such as real estate sales, clerical work, pharmaceuticals, public relations, bartending, bank telling, and more recently, the academic disciplines of sociology and biology. In *Job Queues, Gender Queues* (1990), sociologists Barbara Reskin and Patricia Roos argue that women end up in lower-paid jobs because these occupations lose (or have lost) their attractiveness for White men. When a job becomes deskilled and less autonomous—such as secretarial work, which way back when was men's work—earnings decline, routes of upward mobility close off, work conditions in general deteriorate, and men flee to better positions, leaving (typically White) women next in line to shuffle into the ranks of men's cast-off work.

Take book editing, which changed from a "gentlemen's profession" for most of its history to a virtual female ghetto by the end of the twentieth century (Reskin & Roos, 1990). Formerly the high-cultural mission of men with elite academic records, book editing evolved into a more commercial enterprise in the 1960s and 1970s. The result was that editorial work took a downturn in autonomy, job security, and importance. As the job lost its attractiveness to male candidates, the female labor supply was increasing on the crest of second-wave feminism. Thus book-editing jobs, like the other fields that optimists point to as women's inroads into traditionally male-dominated work, became resegregated and ghettoized as women's work. And anything categorized as women's work tends to yield lower pay, prestige, and benefits such as health coverage than men's.

That's not to say that gender norms do not exact a cost on workers in male-dominated jobs as well. Take for example, the construction industry: In an era of weak worker protections and declining male job prospects, one study has found that men who work in construction feel a need to demonstrate their masculinity through sexist, homophobic, and racist comments and through displays of physical strength. The consequences are not just cultural, however. Such displays of masculinity often involve bodily risk-taking with respect to occupational safety that serves to prove workers are "man enough" to perform and keep their jobs in this era of stiff worker competition. The end result is higher rates of worker accidents (and disability), acceleration of the decline of union power, and an overall loss of social status for the workers themselves (Landsbergis et al., 2014).

Glass Ceilings When women do enter more prestigious corporate worlds, they often encounter gendered barriers to reaching the very top: the so-called glass ceiling, which effectively is an invisible limit on women's climb up the occupational ladder. Sociologist Rosabeth Moss Kanter argues in her classic study *Men and Women of the Corporation* (1977) that the dearth of women in top corporate positions results from a cultural conflation of authority with masculinity. In Indesco, the fictitious name of the corporation Kanter studied, she found that most people believed that men and women come to occupy the kinds of jobs for which they are naturally best suited. To the contrary, Kanter showed, the job often makes the person; the person doesn't make the job.

Employee behavior tends to be determined by job requirements and the constraints of the organizational structure of the company. At Indesco, secretarial positions (98.6 percent

GLASS CEILING
an invisible limit on women's climb up the occupational ladder.

Betty Dukes (right) was a longtime greeter for Walmart and became the lead plaintiff in a class-action gender discrimination lawsuit against the discount retailer. She and her counterparts claimed that they were passed over for promotions and paid less than men for the same work. In 2011 the Supreme Court dismissed the case in a controversial 5–4 decision.

female) were based on "principled arbitrariness," meaning there were no limits to the (male) boss's discretion as to what his secretary should do (type, fax, pick up his dry cleaning, look after his dog when he's away). Furthermore, secretarial work was characterized by fealty, the demand of personal loyalty and devotion of secretary to boss. Under these conditions, secretaries adopted certain behaviors to get through a day's work, including timidity and self-effacement, addiction to praise, and displays of emotion—all qualities that Indesco bosses tended to think of as just the way women are.

But what happens when a woman breaks into a top managerial position at Indesco? She becomes a numerical minority, what Kanter calls a token, a stand-in for all women. Because tokens have heightened visibility, they experience greater surveillance and thus performance pressures. Male peers tend to rely on gender stereotypes when interpreting a token's behavior, seeing female managers as "seductresses, mothers, pets," or tough "iron maidens." When a token female manager botches the job, it just goes to show that women can't handle the corporate world and should be kept out of it.

Similarly, Jennifer L. Pierce's (1995) study of law firms showed that sexual stereotypes, as much as organizational structure, are underlying causes of job segregation. Paralegals—who are 86 percent female—are expected to be deferential (that is, they should not stick up for themselves), caring, and even motherly toward the trial lawyers for whom they work. Given the adversarial model of the US legal system, trial lawyers, in contrast, perform what Pierce calls masculine emotional labor. To excel in the job takes aggression, intimidation, and manipulation. Even though almost half of law school graduates are female, women make up only 16 percent of partners at firms (Scharf & Flom, 2010). When a woman joins the higher ranks of trial lawyering, she's likely to face exclusion from informal socializing with her colleagues (no drinks after work), deflation of her job status (frequently being mistaken for a secretary), and difficulty bringing clients into the firm.

Thus female litigators find themselves in a double bind not experienced by their male counterparts. When deploying courtroom tactics of aggression and intimidation—the very qualities that make a male lawyer successful and respected—women litigators find themselves being called "bitches," "obnoxious," and "shrill." But when they fail to act like proper "Rambo litigators" in the courtroom, women are equally chided for being "too nice" and "too bashful." The trade-off between being a good woman and being a successful lawyer adds yet another obstacle for women to make it to the top in male-dominated jobs—and that's not even taking into account the added burden of sexual harassment in the workplace (which women bear the brunt of; see the #MeThree Policy feature on page 342).

Glass Escalators Just as the odds are stacked against female tokens, they tilt in favor of men in female-dominated jobs. In *Still a Man's World* (1995), Christine Williams found that male nurses, elementary school teachers, librarians, and social workers inadvertently maintain masculine power and privilege. Specifically, when token men enter feminized jobs, they enjoy a quicker rise to leadership positions on the aptly named glass escalator. These escalators also operate in law firms, where male paralegals, themselves tokens in the overwhelmingly female semi-profession, reap benefits from their heightened visibility (Pierce, 1995). Male paralegals are said to enjoy preferential treatment over their female peers, such as promotions and even the simple (but substantial) benefit of being invited to happy hour with the litigators. Recent research finds, however, that the glass escalator is racialized: men of color do not ascend within their occupations at the same rates as their White counterparts (Dill et al., 2016; Wingfield, 2009).

GLASS ESCALATOR

the accelerated promotion of men to the top of a work organization, especially in feminized jobs.

Williams's (2013) new research suggests that women are holding a more equitable share of the top spots in nursing, elementary schools, and libraries, but that a larger problem is emerging that hits both men and women, and their families' overall well-being: Wages in these careers have not kept pace with the cost of living. Careers that have traditionally been associated with women are not the only ones that have seen declining wages. Manufacturing, trucking, and warehouse jobs—traditionally dominated by male workers—are also paying less (Mishel & Shierholz, 2013).

In the fashion industry, the escalator reverses the gender filter Williams originally found for women-dominated fields. Aspiring male models are forced off at the second floor while a small number of women models can continue to top model status. I talked with sociologists (and former model) Ashley Mears about the wage structure in the modeling industry. She confirmed that "you see a complete inverse" where "women outearn men by two to one, sometimes much more" and that "there are just more jobs and opportunities for women models." She explained that there are two reasons for this, one cultural and one structural. From a cultural perspective, "for a man to do the work of showing his body, displaying his body, it's read as being less than what we fully expect in a hegemonically masculine way. It's read as being effeminate work." From a structural perspective there simply are no stepping-stones to managerial positions or other promotions for models. According to Mears, on the models' job escalator, "there's no place to go" because career positions in the fashion industry

DIGITAL.WWNORTON.COM/YOUMAYASK7

Go to digital.wwnorton.com/youmayask7 to see more of my interview with Ashley Mears.

go to experienced businesspeople and designers who, surprise, tend to be men (Conley, 2013c; Reimer, 2016). So even though male *models* don't enjoy a glass escalator, the wider industry ends up dominated by men all the same.

Sociology in the Bedroom

Sex. You think it's the most personal, intimate act. The bedroom is surely the one place where the sociological imagination is the last thing you'll need. But just as we've untangled the terms *sex* and *gender*, we'll take a sociological look at sex, which can reveal some startling insights. Connections may be found between the sheets and history, desire and science, how we do it and how it in turn organizes what we do, as well as with whom and with what meanings. As expected, an excavation into the social construction of sexuality divulges a surprising amount of variation in what is considered normal bedroom behavior. By exposing different social patterns of sexuality, throughout history and across cultures, the sociologist can trace unequal gender relations and show how sexuality expresses, represses, and elucidates those relations.

SEX: FROM PLATO TO NATO

Among the ancient Greeks, relationships between two men were accepted as normal. Engaging in same-sex acts did not confer a particular identity, because the practice varied in frequency across the population among those who did and those who did not also participate in opposite-sex sexual relations. Rather, the socially important distinction revolved around an active/passive dichotomy (although historians have shown that many exceptions existed). The active partner was supposed to be older or higher in status than the passive partner. To flip the rules was a violation, and it was considered shameful for a master or noble to be penetrated by a younger man. A more extreme and brutal example of sexual relations founded on power relations can be found today in the social orders in US prisons, where it is easy to see that rape is about power: who is in charge, who is being penetrated, and who is normal versus deviant. Prison rape, like any rape, may not be primarily about seeking sexual gratification; indeed, it is reported that few prison rapists climax during the act. In prison, the same-sex sex act is often seen as something altogether distinct from gay identity.

Or, consider sexual normality among the Sambia, a mountain people in Papua New Guinea. Anthropologist Gilbert Herdt (1981) reported that fellatio played a significant role in a boy's transition into manhood. Young boys are initiated into manhood by a daily ritual of fellatio on older boys and men. By taking in the vital life liquid (semen) of older men, boys prepare themselves to be warriors and sexual partners with women. Fellatio, for Sambia boys, then, is the only way to become "real" men.

Other cultures' attitudes toward male homosexuality are on a whole different level. Both the Siwans of North Africa and the Keraki, also in New Guinea, prefer homosexuality to heterosexuality, for fairly straightforward, practical reasons (Kimmel, 2000). Because every male is homosexual during his adolescence and then bisexual after heterosexual marriage, limiting straight sex keeps down the birthrate. In these cultures with scant resources, homosexuality makes practical sense to limit the chances of teen pregnancy and overpopulation.

There is enormous variation in how humans have sex and what it means to them. Mouth-to-mouth kissing, common in Western cultures, is unthinkable among the Thonga and Sirono cultures: "But that's where you put food!" (Kimmel, 2000). American, heterosexual middle-class couples have sex a few nights a week for about 15 minutes a pop; the people of Yapese cultures near Guam engage in sex once a month. Marquesan men of French Polynesia are said to have anywhere from 10 to 30 orgasms a night! Which of these is "normal"?

An ancient Greek image of two male lovers. How can comparing social patterns of sexuality across cultures and throughout history help sociologists understand modern sexuality?

THE SOCIAL CONSTRUCTION OF SEXUALITY

By treating sexuality as a social construction—that is, as always shaped by social factors—the sociologist would argue that the notion of normal, especially pertaining to what happens behind closed bedroom (or bathroom or car) doors, is always contested. In other words, there is no natural way of doing it. If an essentially right way existed, we wouldn't be able to find such wild and woolly variation throughout history and across cultures. Starting from the view that sex itself is a social creation, sociologists tend to argue that humans have sexual plumbing but no sexuality until they are located in a social environment. The range of normal and abnormal is itself a construction, a production of society. The study of this range can lead the willing sociologist into an exploration of the social relations on which sex is built.

Sexuality and Power Marxist feminists, for instance, argue that sexuality in America is an expression of the unequal power balance between men and women. Catharine MacKinnon (1983) argued that in male-dominated

BISEXUAL

an individual who is sexually attracted to both genders/sexes.

societies, sexuality is constructed as a gender binary, with men on top and women on the bottom (literally and figuratively). To MacKinnon, sexuality is the linchpin of gender inequality, an expression of male control. Some feminists also argue that our experiences of what is titillating are shaped by the fetishization of male power. So being "taken" is exciting and pleasurable to women, revealing that even those things we think of as the most personal of experiences are shaped by social power arrangements.

Adrienne Rich (1980) called sexuality in America a "compulsory heterosexuality." This "political institution," at least for some, is not a preference but something that has been imposed, managed, organized, and enforced to serve a male-dominated capitalist system in which women's unpaid domestic work is required to support men's paid work outside of the home. Because her work is unpaid, the woman in this situation is unable to leave a bad husband. According to Rich, people come to see heterosexuality as the norm, when it is, in fact, a mechanism integral to sustaining women's social subordination.

HOMOSEXUAL

the social identity of a person who has sexual attraction to and/or relations with people of the same sex.

Same-Sex Sexuality The connections between sex and power are best exemplified in the social construction of the homosexual in the current West, the social identity of a person who has sexual attraction to and/or relations with people of the same sex. For most of the past century, the dominant view has been that individuals are born either homosexual or heterosexual, gay or straight, queer or normal. Sexual orientation was thought of as a kind of personhood automatically acquired at birth or something carried in our genes (despite documented cases of identical twins in which one is straight and the other gay). But recall the ancient Greeks' homosexual love, the Sambian rites of manhood, or prison rape. Jane Ward (2015), for example, studied straight men who have sex with other men in the contemporary United States, including fraternity members, or military personnel who engage in sex acts with their compatriots as part of hazing, or men who answer ads to find other men to masturbate with. Men in these examples engage in homosexual acts without adopting a homosexual identity (Silva, 2017). When do acts, behaviors, or desires crystallize into identities?

Before 1850, there was no such thing as a homosexual. Sure, people engaged in same-sex sexual behaviors—but it was not yet an identity in the way we now know it. French philosopher Michel Foucault (1926–1984) led the way to poststructuralist notions of the body and sexuality as historical productions. In *The History of Sexuality* (1978), Foucault made the case that the body is "in the grip" of cultural practices. That is, there is no pre-social or natural body; instead, culture is always already inscribed on our bodies. Foucault further argued that the way in which we know our bodies is linked to power, and knowledge and power go hand in hand. As the population expanded in nineteenth-century Europe, newly formed states and their administrators developed a concern for population management.

The rise of scientific ways of thinking at the time led to the creation of what Foucault calls "bio-power," the control of populations by influencing patterns in births, deaths, and illnesses.

Discourses on sexuality had by then surfaced. People talked about sex, scientists studied it, and government officials tried to regulate it, whereas a century before, all this sex talk did not exist. With the development of the biological and human sciences in the nineteenth century, doctors wanted to know which kinds of sex were normal and which were deviant, and new attention was paid to policing those differences. By the late 1800s, "Homosexuality appeared as one of the forms of sexuality when it was transposed from the practice of sodomy onto a kind of interior [identity]" (Foucault, 1978). In Foucault's account, the category of homosexuality arises from the efforts of government bureaucrats trying to assert their power (that of the state) over human populations.

Meanwhile, the American Psychiatric Association and the American Psychological Association listed homosexuality on their list of mental disorders until 1973. Homosexuals were regarded as needing to be regulated, observed, studied, and most important, controlled. Because everyone was capable of, or in danger of, sexual deviance, the urgency to confess one's sexuality grew, as did the scientific need for public surveillance. Who was gay? How could a homosexual be detected? Anyone could be a pervert—your professor, your roommate, even you!

Sexual acts became synonymous with the person who performed them. Even our language reflects the way sexual behavior becomes more than a single event among the many other behaviors that make up an individual's life—it often becomes a master status. Here's what I mean. If a man roasts a whole pig—a serious, time-consuming undertaking that requires research, dedication, and planning—he is not known ever after as a "pig roaster" or even as a gourmand. He's still just Bob from down the block who hosted one heck of a barbecue. But if a man has anal sex with another man—something that takes less time and probably less dedication and research than roasting a pig—he becomes a sodomite, a homosexual, gay, or whatever terminology might fit the context.

This was not always so. At one point, what happened in the bedroom (or car or motel or . . .) stayed there. But over the last century what happened behind closed doors was outed, and a whole new person was produced. Today our society places a huge emphasis—our entire selfhood, according to Foucault—on sexuality. Sexuality, in other words, is a prime factor that goes into the

Homosexuality was considered a mental disorder by the American Psychological Association until 1973. Here, in 1967, Dr. Joseph Wolpe treats a homosexual patient by showing a series of risqué images intended to elicit arousal.

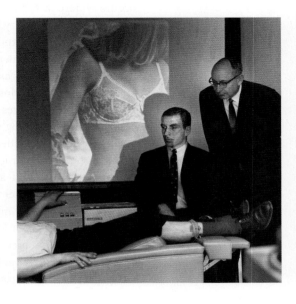

Thousands participate in a pride parade in 2018. How does Foucault show that the rise of the "homosexual" as an identity was a historical process? How might he respond to pride parades and other contemporary assertions of gay identity?

construction of gender—a dynamic that may not have been as important in days gone by. Now, what you do (and with whom) defines who you are: not just how others see you, but how you experience yourself.

Consider a widely used argument against lesbian and gay couplings: "It's unnatural," meaning that sex is supposed to be about reproduction. This is a popular argument against same-sex marriages, but it also stigmatizes straight couples who can't or don't have children. Besides, homosexuality occurs widely in nature; one of our closest primate cousins, the bonobo, practices homosexuality (Parker, 2007). Though based on questionable data, Alfred Kinsey's 1948 study *Sexual Behavior in the Human Male* suggested that at least 10 percent of men were homosexual. He challenged the psychiatric model of homosexuals as perverse and abnormal and instead viewed sexuality as a continuum. Most people, he claimed, experience both heterosexual and homosexual desires and behaviors. Kinsey's figures have since been disputed—his sampling was not representative of the US population as a whole—but the basic idea holds. Across the globe and throughout history, there has been more or less the same degree of homosexual behavior.

What is different across time and place, however, is how sexuality is perceived. Gender often plays a large role. For example, Yale historian George Chauncey makes the case in *Gay New York* (1994) that in early twentieth-century New York, an emerging working-class gay world was split between masculine men (tops) and the effeminate men who solicited them (bottoms). As long as men stuck to their masculine gender scripts, no matter how often they engaged in gay sex, they were not considered abnormal like the more feminine men, who were derided for their effeminacy.

The reverse is true among the *travesti*, transgender prostitutes in Brazil. Anthropologist Don Kulick (1998) conducted an ethnography of the *travesti*, males who adopt female names, clothing styles, hairstyles, cosmetic practices, and linguistic pronouns; ingest female hormones; and inject industrial silicone directly into their bodies to give themselves breasts and round buttocks or *bunda*. They display stereotypically feminine traits, yet they do not self-identify as women. In fact, they think it is both repugnant and impossible for men to try to become women. Kulick argues that in Brazil, gender is determined by sexual practice: "What one does in bed has immediate and lasting consequences for the way one is perceived (and the way one can perceive oneself) as a gendered being. If one penetrates, in this particular configuration of sexuality and gender, one is a 'man.' If one expresses interest in the penis of a male, and especially if one 'gives'—allows oneself to be penetrated by a male—then one is no longer a man." However, the *travesti* do not think they are women; they think of themselves as *travesti*, men who emulate women but are not women. The primacy of penetration as a determinant of gender is common across cultures and challenges Americans to look beyond chromosomes and hormones to practices and cultural context.

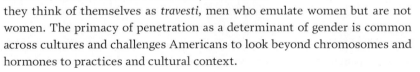

How do *travesti* challenge common binary models of understanding gender and sexuality?

CONTEMPORARY SEXUALITIES: THE Q WORD

But it is not just straight men who have sex with other men or bisexuals who complicate the sexuality (and/or gender) binary. There's a reason the term LGBTQIA has seemed to add letters lately—there's a growing recognition that if we look closely and without judgment, we see many forms of gender/sexuality identity that do not conform to categories that dominated discussion since, roughly, the 1850 period that Foucault marked as the start of the era of the "homosexual."

We have already discussed L (lesbian), G (gay [male]), B (bisexual), and T (trans). We have also discussed I (intersex). So let's skip to the last letter in the acronym, "A." Asexuality has, of late, become a more visible sexual identity. Many individuals do not feel sexual attraction; these individuals may identify as asexual (often "ace" for short). They may not experience sexuality-related bodily feelings or actions, but others who identify as asexual may, for example, masturbate to fantasies of fictional characters. The American Psychiatric Association has defined asexuality as a paraphilia—which is an atypical sexual attraction. This lumps it in with medical disorders, whether or not asexuality results in significant distress for the individual or others, such as a partner. Sociologists challenge this definition, pointing out that many ace individuals enjoy sexual fantasies that involve others or involve themselves in a completely fictional way (that is, younger, kinkier, or even a superhero) (Scherrer & Pfeffer, 2017). A better way to think about asexuality is as an identity based on membership in a shared sexual community. Hence the "A" was added to the LGBT alphabet as asexual activists have sought to be included in nondominant gender/ sexuality social movements, protests, and so on.

What about the Q-word? *Queer* is a derogatory term, reclaimed by those it was originally intended to wound, to become a broader, encompassing term for nonheteronormative sexual behaviors/identities. That is, when someone self-identifies as queer, they may be a lesbian looking for a broader, more inclusive umbrella that is not already overly associated with, say, White middle-class people. Or they may be someone who participates in what might be called "kinky" sexual practices, such as BDSM (a term meant to capture bondage/discipline/submission/sadomasochism and related practices). Or they may simply be someone who does not feel comfortable with and wishes to reject other aspects of heteronormativity. For instance, some queer people reject the notion of same-sex marriage. They reject what they see as assimilation into heteronormative culture, and instead prefer to organize their lives differently in terms of kinship, sexuality, and so on.

One form of nonheteronormativity that has garnered a lot of attention of late is non-monogamy. Non-monogamy is not just having sex with multiple people (because, for example, people can be in monogamous relationships and cheat on their partners). Rather, it is the practice of having multiple sexual (or intimate) relationships (or merely the desire to) with the full knowledge and consent of all the people involved. Polyamory is a particular form of non-monogamy (Sheff, 2014). While there is no agreed on, universal definition of polyamory, it usually involves *intimate* relationships with more than one partner (again, with the knowledge and consent of all involved). So a couple who agree that they can have one-night stands with other people are non-monogamous but not polyamorous. Mimi Schippers (2016) finds that some forms of polyamory subvert gender/sexuality norms more than others. For example, a relationship including a woman and two men challenges heterosexual norms and gender power relations more than a relationship among one man and two women, since the latter more easily allows for male dominance and because female bisexuality is more socially acceptable than male bisexuality.

Fluid notions of acceptable sexual relationships aren't only limited to those under the LGBTQIA umbrella: Indeed, how we think about sex among teen and college-aged people is rapidly changing.

HETERO- NORMATIVITY

the idea that heterosexuality is the default or normal sexual orientation from which other sexualities deviate.

"HEY": TEEN SEX, FROM HOOKING UP TO VIRGINITY PLEDGES

Sometimes the policies meant to achieve one end backfire and cause the opposite outcome, despite the best intentions. Government efforts to influence healthy teen sexuality provide one example. Recent studies have described the blasé attitude that contemporary American teenagers supposedly bring to their love lives. When sociologist Paula England surveyed students at one midwestern university about their sex lives, half reported that their previous sexual partner was someone they had slept with only once. Here's how she explained hook-up culture, which has replaced dating as the route to romance on college campuses around the country. She did her first surveys at Northwestern, where "before people ever go on a date, they hook up." Lest there be any confusion: a hook-up is not sex . . . unless it is. (According to sociologist Lisa Wade, 40 percent of hook-ups involve intercourse.) A hook-up means "something sexual happens, that 'something sexual' is not always intercourse, often in fact [in] the majority of cases it isn't, and there is no necessary implication that anybody's interested in a relationship, but they *might* be interested." Why so many short-lived hook-ups instead of longer-term relationships? For one thing, it turns out there are not "so many" hook-ups. The average in Lisa Wade's study was eight over four years. Moreover, a third of students never hooked up. Meanwhile, dating is infrequent, but it is not completely dead. It is "charged with more meaning now, and it's more likely to be leading to a relationship." Furthermore, "there's a strong norm that relationships should be monogamous and marriages should be monogamous and that people eventually want to get to monogamy and a marriage. They're just putting it off a lot longer. That's really what's changed, I think" (Conley, 2009d).

That is, most students are not looking to begin families anytime soon. For another, relationships are just more work—for the men, at least. England found that heterosexual males are not necessarily expected to sexually satisfy the women they hook up with, but the opposite is true when they are in relationships (Armstrong et al., 2012). This has led to what they call "the orgasm gap." England and coauthors' analysis shows "that specific

DIGITAL.WWNORTON.COM/YOUMAYASK7

To see an interview with Paula England about hook-up culture, go to digital.wwnorton.com/youmayask7

sexual practices [such as oral sex or genital stimulation], experience with a particular partner, and commitment all predict women's orgasm and sexual enjoyment"—all conditions less present in hook-ups than in relationships. For example, with respect to oral sex, England explains that in a hook-up "it's much more likely that the woman is servicing the guy than vice versa. So it seems like the hook-ups are prioritizing male pleasure" (Conley, 2009d).

In a hook-up culture, what might determine whether a pair continues to hook up or moves on to new partners? England has a theory that goes like this:

> Partner-specific investment may well be important. In other words, . . . our ability to please partners may not just be generally what have we learned from a lifetime of experience but what have we actually learned about this particular partner and what works for them and what they like and what they need. . . . If it's hook-up number two, she's more likely to have an orgasm than if it's one, and if it's three more likely, and if it's four even more likely. (Conley, 2009d)

She also noted that these hook-ups rarely produce babies—but nearly 14 percent of students still did not use any method to prevent pregnancy the last time they had sex.

Here are more numbers: Fewer than 40 percent of American high-school students tell surveyors that they have had sexual intercourse (Figure 8.4), but this rate is not growing; it has remained more or less steady since 2003 (Centers for Disease Control and Prevention, 2018a). Boys probably lie more often about the extent of their sexual experience (citing the proverbial girl-friend in a different state), and girls possibly downplay their sexual activity. Many of those who have not had intercourse are still sexually active in other ways. Teenagers' romantic interludes last about 15 months on average, leaving them plenty of time before marriage (median age of 28.0 for women and 29.8 for men in 2019) to have many partners (US Census Bureau, 2019b). To top it off, most adolescents with a sexually transmitted disease (STD) don't know that they are infected. All of these factors combine to put American teenagers at high risk for STDs, which have been increasing dramatically since the 1970s.

So what's a public health officer to do? During its years in office, the Bush administration (2001–9) advocated a "virginity pledge" and other abstinence policies, and the abstinence advocacy group True Love Waits says that 2.5 million young people have made the virginity pledge since 1993 (Herbert, 2011). As it turns out, the pledge does, on average, delay the onset of sexual activity as well as reduce a teenager's number of sexual partners, according to the National Longitudinal Study of Adolescent Health (Brückner & Bearman, 2005)—particularly when it occurs in a school context where a sizable number of students take the pledge, creating a meaningful

FIGURE 8.4 Percentage of High-School Students Who Have Had Sex, 1991–2017

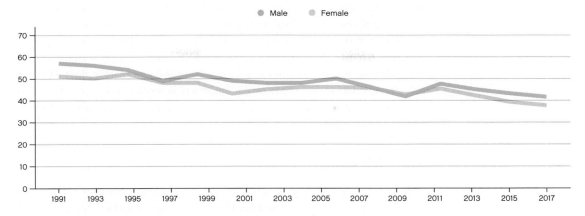

SOURCE: Centers for Disease Control and Prevention, 2018a.

identity of sorts through collective abstinence (Bearman & Brückner, 2001). That said, most pledgers (about 60 percent) break their pledge. And when sex happens, it's much more likely to come in a rush of surprisingly strong, unfettered desire. Among the pledgers, only 40 percent ended up using a condom during sex—why would they have a condom if they were planning to be virgins until marriage?—compared with 60 percent of teens who had not pledged. The end result was a net higher rate of HPV infection and pregnancy among the pledgers (Paik et al., 2016).

What is for certain is that teens—like their adult counterparts—are navigating new terrain in terms of romantic and sexual relations thanks to technology. One way we can see this is in the debate over opening lines in online dating apps. Three million messages per day on the Tinder app begin with "Hey." Does such a generic approach represent laziness (that is, not having read someone's profile in order to say something specific)? Or is it just a universal human way to say "hi" without concocting some phony pickup line (even if it is not as vulnerable online as it would be in person at a party or a bar)? One thing is for sure—it probably beats the most searched GIF on Tinder: Joey from the show *Friends*, asking "How you doing?" (Verdier, 2016).

Figuring out the right way to approach someone online is not the only challenge that teens and adults have in the evolving world of Tinder, Grindr, and OkCupid. A new phenomenon of the "define-the-relationship" (DTR) conversation is emerging. In a world where a new potential partner is only a swipe away, and where people are inventing new ways of being romantic or sexual, and where one cannot assume a single narrative arc of how such relationships are meant to progress, the DTR talk is a way that people can clarify expectations, hopes, fears, and so on after getting to know each other. Will we be monogamous, or friends with benefits? If monogamous, do we delete our dating apps? Will we be public on Facebook as a couple? Is this just something fun for now, or do we mutually envision a longer-term relationship between us? These are just some of the questions the DTR conversation may address. As to when to have (or avoid) that conversation, just as there are myriad relationship types nowadays, there is no clear norm on what's too soon (or too late) to discuss or define one's relationship. Stay tuned: Norms can evolve fast in the face of technological innovation.

SEX AND AGING

Sex, as it turns out, isn't just for teenagers. It may come as a surprise to many college students that sex continues to be an important life issue well after retirement age. Moreover, like most important aspects of life, sex at older ages displays inequalities that match patterns in other domains like work and family.

Specifically, the discrepancy in life expectancy between men and women colors many aspects of social life at older ages, but perhaps no domain as much as sexuality. In fact, the life expectancy difference comes on top of the typical age difference in married, heterosexual couples—the man is typically almost three years older than the woman in such unions. The result is the starkly different sociosexual positions in which older adults find themselves. For example, among men age 65 or older, over 71 percent are currently married, whereas the corresponding figure for women is a mere 43 percent. Indeed, there are as many widowed women over 65 as there are married women. (Meanwhile, a mere 14 percent of men in this age bracket are widowed.)

Such a disparity translates into a gender gap in sexual activity as well since most sex takes place within an ongoing relationship. So while there is much attention to the so-called sex recession among youth and the orgasm gap on college campuses, it may be at older ages where we can more frequently see social patterning of sexual behavior. For instance, among those 70 or older, men were about twice as likely to have had sexual intercourse as compared to women in the past year (43 percent to 22 percent). That disparity carries over to other forms of sexual activity such as oral sex, mutual masturbation, and anal sex. Curiously, when asked about masturbating alone, despite their greater access to sexual partners, men also reported having engaged in that activity more frequently than women did (46 percent to 33 percent). All else equal, we might expect older women to masturbate more often than men given their relative lack of other options. However, social norms about sexuality are often formed early in life, and many older individuals surveyed today came of age before the sexual revolution of the

1960s. It will be interesting to see if that gap closes among later cohorts where female masturbation was more socially accepted. It may even be the case that part of the current difference is due to social desirability bias. That is, given discomfort around discussing female masturbation, perhaps more older women are doing it than admit to doing it to the interviewers of the National Survey of Sexual Health and Behavior.

Of course, these differences in masturbation rates tell us that a lot more than rates of survivorship and widowhood influence sexuality among older adults. In both sexes, production of sex hormones (estrogen for women and testosterone for men) declines with age; however, the pattern of decline is starkly different. For men there is a gradual drift downward while for women there is a steep drop at menopause (the period when women stop ovulating and experiencing menses). Menopause has an additional social effect for some women: Menopause marks the end of the potential link between sex and reproduction, so this changes the psychological dynamic of heterosexual intercourse.

Yet the causation does not stop with biology, of course. As paradoxical as the masturbation figures are by gender, so too are those regarding chronic diseases that affect sexual activity. Among those 75 and older, only 13 percent of women report experiencing a health condition that restricts sexual activity—the single largest cause being arthritis. But a full 45 percent of men report such biological impediments—most frequently due to prostate cancer or high blood pressure. But of course, older men are still having more sex! Why? Because there is a pill for men—developed by big pharma—and there isn't one for women.

By age 70, only 10 percent of men report "always or almost always" being able to get and maintain an erection adequate for satisfactory intercourse, while 38 percent report never being able to. Into this epidemic of erectile dysfunction (or ED) has stepped big pharma with drugs such as Viagra, Cialas, and Levitra, all of which treat ED to great success.

Meanwhile, while Viagra was approved by the FDA in 1998, it wasn't until 17 years later that Addyi, a drug for women with hypoactive sexual desire disorder (HSSD), was approved. It works completely differently—whereas the male drugs work on the blood vessels of the penis and surrounding area to promote flow, the female-targeted drugs work on the brain, altering the balance between the neurotransmitters serotonin, on the one hand, and dopamine and norepinephrine, on the other hand, in order to increase sex drive. During clinical trials Addyi generated a 10 percent positive response in the treatment group when adjusted for the placebo effect and also had much more frequent adverse side effects, including dizziness, fainting, nausea, and insomnia. So, all in all, not a great deal for women. Until the pharmaceutical industry invents a female sex pill that generates the kind of global response that Viagra and its kin have, some women have decided to take the men's drugs themselves. Evidence is mixed on how well they work; so, the search continues for the blockbuster female sex pill.

POLICY

#METHREE

The #MeToo moment that began in 2017 unleashed a tsunami of sexual harassment and assault allegations that had built up over decades while predatory behavior went on unabated. It has prompted many policy makers to ask what can be done to prevent such a buildup of allegations in the future. That is, how do we get harassment or assault victims to step forward in real time? Or better still, get perpetrators fearful enough of being called out with consequences for bad behavior so that they don't perpetrate it in the first place! One thing is for sure: What organizations from colleges to corporations to Congress are doing presently does not work. Namely, watching videos or even engaging in live training with HR professionals does not seem to have the effects on actual workplace or school harassment and assault that it is intended to. It can even backfire by reinforcing gendered roles, according to sociologist Justine Tinkler (2013), by depicting men exclusively as harassers and women only as victims. But all this doesn't mean nothing works and we should give up hope of a civil public space where individuals can feel safe and respected.

The ideas that have been offered include rewarding managers when reports of harassment increase, focusing training on getting bystanders (as opposed to the victims themselves) to intervene in some way, and promoting more women into leadership roles (which often changes the norms of what is acceptable behavior). One particularly novel notion is the formation of "information escrows"—secret repositories where complaints can be reported anonymously. The idea is this:

Many people want to give others the benefit of the doubt. They don't want to start a huge stir and possibly ruin someone's career if it is truly a case of a one-off mistake or a misunderstanding. They also don't want to risk the cost to their own reputation (or career) in coming forward in what may end up being a he said–she said (or he said–he said, or . . .) situation that ends up inconclusive and uncomfortable for all involved. But if the action—say a misplaced hand or inappropriate humor or a refusal to take no for an answer when asking out a coworker—is part of a larger pattern of behavior, then as most would agree, it should have consequences. That's where the information escrow comes into the picture.

The escrow is managed by someone in human resources or could even be set up to be totally computerized. If I experience something that may qualify as harassment, I can lodge a complaint confidentially, detailing the alleged infraction. But I can then specify the conditions under which I want my grievance to trigger action. For example, I might say, as long as nobody else has complained about our shift manager pinching them, my allegation should remain secret and dormant. But the moment someone else also files a report to the information escrow of inappropriate touching (or perhaps other infractions), my testimony becomes an official complaint too. That way, it is no longer one person's word against another's but an established pattern of behavior documented independently—in other words, a much more powerful case. Likewise, if the behavior was a one-off and never occurred again, I might choose to let it go. Of course, the presence of the information escrow option doesn't (and isn't meant to) preclude someone from reporting someone else's misbehavior straightaway through formal channels.

As proposed by Ian Ayres and Cait Unkovic (2012), such allegation escrows work best when infractions are underreported and when they typically involve more than one victim. Such harassment escrows are a particular case of a broader class of possible information escrows that can cover everything from bids in a trade (where the trade occurs and bids are revealed only if the seller and buyer overlap in price) to a revelation of mutual romantic crushes. In fact, some modern dating apps like Tinder and Bumble essentially act as escrows: Only if we both swipe right does our mutual interest get revealed. Imagine a similar app for deterring harassers. In an era where one camp is worried about the potential for false accusations to ruin someone's life without due process while the other side is concerned with victims who fear going public alone, it may be worth a try.

Conclusion

Starting with our friend Elliot, we've learned that what seems to be normal or natural often turns out to be fluid and contingent. The stuff we build up around biological plumbing—roles, expectations, psyches, institutions—is not essential. These are socially constructed facts, built less on the biological and more on the existing social structures of power.

We've learned a lot about how these norms of gender can create inequality, but what happens when gender can become something empowering? Elliot concludes his story on an uplifting note:

Today, I felt gender euphoria.

Euphoria is the opposite of dysphoria. I see my reflection, and I love the guy I see. No matter what I'm wearing, I feel nothing but confidence in how I look and who I am. I am brave enough to confront rude people who follow me into bathrooms, to wave menstrual hygiene products at them. I feel like myself. I feel like an Elliot.

Days like today were almost nonexistent before I realized I was trans and began socially transitioning. When I was pretending to be a girl, even the highest joys and deepest sadnesses in my life were missing something, a certain depth, a certain extra grounding in reality. I'm not a girl. No matter how I try, dressing like a girl, acting like one, will always ring hollow, always feel wrong. That isn't who I am.

I'm a boy. Maybe nobody but me sees or feels a difference when I present male, but I feel better. I feel real, alive. I feel every bit of emotion the world has to offer me.

That, no matter how many self-appointed bathroom guardians I have to face, will always be worth it.

We've traced how our intricate system of sexes, genders, and sexualities has evolved. Can we "undo gender," or are we stuck in the paradox of reproducing the binaries we started with, even if we recognize their inequalities? If we humans have constructed gender as a way to organize, simplify, and control a messy social world, then indeed we can deconstruct it. As Judith Lorber (1994) argued, only when we stop using gender as a basis for dividing up the world—in terms of which jobs people hold, what rights they exercise, how much money they earn, how much control they have over their bodies, with whom they can have sex, and yes, what bathroom they use—will we find true equality.

QUESTIONS FOR REVIEW

1. What is binary thinking about sex and gender? How do individuals who challenge these binaries (such as transgender or intersex people) help us understand that sex and gender are social, not natural, categories?

2. Women represent a minority group in the military. Men are in the minority as nurses and paralegals. How are women and men treated differently in these positions, and what does this difference suggest about the way gender structures social relations?

3. How do the cases of the *hijras* and the *travesti*, as described in this chapter, challenge our understanding of sex and gender?

4. What might the idealized man of the mid-twentieth century as described by Erving Goffman think of more recent forms of masculinity, such as Kristen Barber's metrosexual male or the "hybrid masculinities" described by Tristan Bridges and C. J. Pascoe? Despite these differences, how are most forms of dominant masculine identity similar?

5. Names such as Carol and Aubrey used to be boys' names but today are almost exclusively female. Nursing and secretarial work used to be associated with men but these days are overwhelmingly performed by women. Why do names or careers become feminized, and what does this say about masculinity?

6. How does Talcott Parsons describe the role of men and women in his "sex role theory"? Explain how conflict theories can be seen as a critique of structural functionalism, and describe some limitations of each approach.

7. What is the difference between homosexual "acts" and a homosexual "identity"? How did the historical development of the latter, according to Michel Foucault, affect how one sees oneself?

8. More differences seem to exist among boys and girls than between them. Nonetheless, we tend to think of boys and girls as different. What are "deceptive distinctions," and how do they create gender differences? Use an example from Rosabeth Moss Kanter's work to support your answer.

PRACTICE

MEASURING MANSPLAINING

Sites like **arementalkingtoomuch.com**, the "Time to Talk" app, and others have sprung up recently after it became widely reported that men tend to dominate conversations and talk over women. This is something that sociologists have known since Carol Stack and Don Zimmerman famously found that men overwhelmingly interrupt women in everyday conversations (1975). More recent research has continued to support this finding. For example, a recent study by the *Harvard Business Review* used 15 years of oral argument transcripts to show that male Supreme Court justices interrupt each other three times less often than they interrupt their female peers (Jacobi & Schweers, 2017). And it's not just interrupting: Compared to women, men also tend to take up more conversational airtime in social settings from the classroom to the boardroom.

TRY IT!

Observe a class discussion and measure how much time men speak versus how much time women speak. You can try any of the apps or websites mentioned above, or simply use a stopwatch. It would be ideal to sit in on a class you're not taking (but be sure to check with the instructor first). And don't spill the beans about your project—if your research subjects know what you're measuring, you'll probably get lousy results.

While you're measuring female versus male airtime, also note how many times a male student interrupts a female student and vice versa.

THINK ABOUT IT

Once you have your results, compare the amount of airtime to the proportion of men and women in the class. Did men disproportionately dominate the conversation? Did men interrupt women more often than women interrupted men? Did these gender dynamics vary intersectionally—that is, for example, by the race of the would-be speakers?

   Whether or not the results of your study support the finding that men are socialized to talk over women, reflect on the assumptions you made in performing the experiment. Did a two-category scorecard force you to make any assumptions about the gender of individuals—assumptions that you might not have made without discrete categories?

SOCIOLOGy ON THE STREET

Internet dating is a major resource for people looking for potential partners, with a seemingly unlimited pool. What are the similarities and differences between dating online and dating in person? Watch the Sociology on the Street video to find out more: **digital.wwnorton.com/youmayask7**.

WANT MORE PRACTICE?

Complete the InQuizitive activity for this chapter at digital.wwnorton.com /youmayask7

9

RACE AS WE KNOW IT HAS NO DETERMINISTIC BIOLOGICAL BASIS: ALL THE SAME, RACE IS SO POWERFUL THAT IT CAN HAVE LIFE-OR-DEATH CONSEQUENCES.

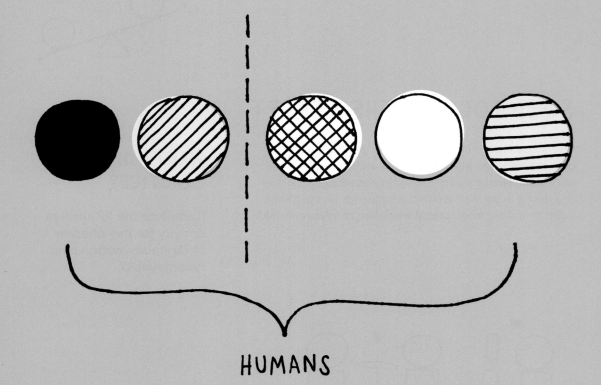

HUMANS

Race

"I found my baby sister!" I declared to my mother, wheeling a carriage around for her to see the newest member of our family, whom I had just kidnapped. I was not quite three years old, and the toddler was only a few months younger than that, with cornrows braided so tightly on her little head that they pulled the brown skin of her face tautly upward. I remember that she was smiling up at me, and I must have taken her smile as permission to swipe the unattended stroller from the courtyard of our housing complex.

"No, you haven't!" my mother gasped, putting a hand over her open mouth. The child was quickly returned to her frantically searching mother, despite my tearful protests.

This story fascinates me today: I wanted a baby sister so badly that I kidnapped a Black child, not realizing that race is a primary way we divide families. How could I be so oblivious to the meaning of race—something that years later feels so natural, so innate? To my childhood self, race was neither a meaningful category nor a too obvious one. In the largely minority housing project where I grew up in the 1970s, race was not something mutable, like a freckle or hairstyle; it defined who looked like whom, who was allowed to be in the group and who wasn't. But for my sister and me, as Whites, race was turned inside out. We had no idea that we belonged to the majority group, the privileged one. We just thought we didn't belong.

Is race real? You might consider this a paradoxical question. After all, how is a huge part of your identity *not* real? The sociological study of race treats it as a social phenomenon that seems natural but isn't. That is, race is a real social distinction, and people around the world and throughout history have drawn sharp lines between "us" and "them" on the basis of race. But as a biological, genetic, geographic, or cultural category, race has fluid and changeable boundaries. In this sense, race is constructed in the interests of groups that wish to maintain power and social exclusion. To the sociologist, understanding racial differences—including by income, educational attainment, crime rates, and teen pregnancy—means treating differences not just as personal matters but as pieces of a larger social picture. Having grown up as a "honky" in the housing projects of New York City's Lower East Side, a fish out of water, I've been looking at race with the sociological imagination ever since my failed kidnapping. Now it's your turn.

The Myth of Race

Perhaps you have heard claims that race is fake, that it's "just a myth." Race refers to a group of people who share a set of characteristics—typically, but not always, physical ones—and are said to share a common bloodline. People obviously have different physical appearances, including eye color, hair texture, and skin color, so it's perhaps puzzling to hear that (biological) racial differences somehow do not exist. To speak of the myth of race is to say that it is largely a social construction, a set of stories we tell ourselves to organize reality and make sense of the world, rather than a fixed biological or natural reality. In this sense, it resembles the socially constructed notions of childhood and adolescence that we discussed in Chapter 4. We tell the set of stories over and over and, collectively, believe in it and act on it, therefore making it real through practices such as largely separate marriage and reproductive communities. But we could organize our social distinctions a different way (for example, based on foot size or hair color), and indeed, throughout history, we have told this set of stories in myriad ways.

Take, for example, the following passage from an 1851 issue of *Harper's Weekly Magazine*, in which the author attempts to assess the character of a certain racial group based on facial features or expressions—a pseudoscience known as physiognomy. Try to guess which race the author is describing:

> [They are] distinctly marked—the small and somewhat upturned nose, the Black tint of the skin. . . . [They] are ignorant, and as a consequence thereof, are idle, thriftless, poor, intemperate, and barbarian. . . . Of course they will violate our laws, these wild bisons leaping over the fences which easily restrain the civilized domestic cattle, will commit great crimes of violence, even capital offences, which certainly have increased as of late.

Most people would guess that the minority group in question here is African Americans. This passage was written, in fact, about Irish immigrants, who in late-nineteenth-century America struggled to assimilate amid fierce and widespread racism (Knobel, 1986). It was believed that the Irish were a distinct category of people who carried innate differences in their blood, differences that made them permanently inferior to their White American neighbors.

When the term *race* comes up in America today, we usually think in two colors: Black and White. But, at the turn of the twentieth century, Americans categorized themselves into anywhere from 36 to 75 different races that they organized into hierarchies, with Anglo-Saxon at the top followed by Slav, Mediterranean, Hebrew, and so on down the list (Jacobson, 1998). Even though the United States was a nation of immigrants, many Americans doubted whether "ethnic stock," such as the Irish, were fit for self-governance in the new democracy.

In 1790, Congress passed the first naturalization law, limiting the rights of citizenship to "free White persons." This law strikes us today as both restrictive and inclusive. It was restrictive because it granted naturalization only to free Whites, thereby coloring American citizenship. Yet it also set up an initially broad understanding of "Whiteness," an umbrella term that in common parlance could include not just Anglo but also Slavic, Celtic, and Teutonic (German) Europeans. However, as millions of immigrants surged to the shores of America—25 million European immigrants arrived between 1880 and World War I—the notion of "free White persons" was reconsidered. With an Irish-born population of more than 1 million in 1860, Americans began to theorize racial differences within the White populace. Questions arose in the popular press and imagination, such as "Who should count as White?" "Whom do we want to be future generations of Americans?" "Who is fit for self-governance?" The inclusiveness of "White persons" splintered into a range of Anglos and "barbarous" others, and Americans began to distinguish among Teutons, Slavs, Celtics, and even the "swarthy" Swedes. The Immigration Act of 1924 formalized the exclusive definition of Whiteness by imposing immigration restrictions based on a quota system that limited the yearly number of immigrants from each country. The law set an annual ceiling of 18,439 immigrants from eastern and southern Europe, following the recommendation of a report stating that northern and western Europeans were of "higher intelligence" and thus ideal "material for American citizenship" (Jacobson, 1998).

A racist ideology can be seen in this early line of thinking about Whiteness. Racism is the belief that members of separate races possess different and unequal traits coupled with the power to restrict freedoms based on those differences. Racist thinking is characterized by three key beliefs: that humans are divided into distinct bloodlines and/or physical types; that these bloodlines or physical traits are linked to distinct cultures, behaviors,

THE USUAL IRISH WAY OF DOING THINGS.

An anti-immigration cartoon from an 1871 issue of *Harper's Weekly.* How have attitudes about race changed over the course of American history?

RACISM

the belief that members of separate races possess different and unequal traits.

personalities, and intellectual abilities; and that certain groups are superior to others.

European immigration slowed during World War I and essentially came to a halt as a result of the 1924 National Origins Act, while internal African American migration from the rural South to the industrial North skyrocketed. These shifts, along with the solidification of the one-drop rule (see later in the chapter), shifted national attention away from White–nonwhite relations toward White–Black relations. Whites of "ethnic stock" were drawn back into the earlier, broad category of White, thereby reuniting Anglos and other Europeans. Public horror at Nazi crimes following the conclusion of World War II further strengthened the idea of Whiteness as an inclusive racial category.

Today, being of Irish descent is a matter of ethnic—not racial—identification, a reason to celebrate on St. Patrick's Day. I know this first-hand: Being one-eighth Irish and having an Irish-WASP (White Anglo-Saxon Protestant) name like Dalton Conley entitles me to free drinks on the Irish holiday. Irish American is no longer considered a restrictive racial category, as once was the case. Whiteness today is something we take for granted, a natural part of the landscape. But dig back just a hundred years into the unnatural history of race, and you might not even recognize it. Not only have groups of people been categorized differently over time, showing that there is nothing natural about how we classify groups into races today, but the very concept of what a race is has changed over time.

We may be undergoing a similar shift today given the demographic changes that are occurring. Professor Maria Abascal and I discussed how intergroup relations are changing and how racial groups are even being redefined in the context of the anticipated decline of the White majority over the next few decades. In our discussion, she points out that Latinx individuals are fluid in terms of their racial identification (and with whom they intermarry), making it tough to predict just how big the "White" and "non-White" populations will be in the coming years.

Moreover, in her research, Abascal found that when faced with a growing Latinx population, Whites and Blacks reacted very differently in a game of

DIGITAL.WWNORTON.COM/YOUMAYASK7

To see my interview with Maria Abascal, go to
digital.wwnorton.com/youmayask7

altruism. She experimentally primed some respondents to hear about the growing numbers of Latinx Americans while a control group did not get this "reminder." She then administered a "dictator game" to each subject. Abascal explains what this game entails:

> In a dictator game, it's a very simple experiment in which you give somebody some amount of money. I gave people $10 and I said, "You can split this money however you want with a stranger." And that stranger was either someone who had a distinctively White name or someone who had a distinctively Black name. They could give zero of those $10, they could give all $10 to the other person (Conley, 2020c).

Among Whites, those who were informed about the growing Latinx population became less charitable to African Americans, while Blacks actually became more equal in their treatment of African Americans and Whites. That is, when perceiving a demographic threat, Whites circled the wagons, so to speak, treating all minority groups less charitably—i.e., not just the group that was growing. By contrast, when African Americans were confronted with a trend toward a more multiracial society, their own, in-group preferences declined—that is, they become more charitable to Whites. In this way, Abascal's results suggest that the social categories of race will change and that interracial relations will evolve in a complex way that makes it difficult to predict trends in race relations in the decades ahead.

The Concept of Race from the Ancients to Alleles

The idea of race, some scholars have claimed, did not exist in the ancient world (Fredrickson, 2002; Hannaford, 1996; Smedley, 1999; Snowden, 1983). Well, it did and it didn't. It did in the sense that the ancients recognized physical differences and grouped people accordingly. In ancient Egypt, for example, physical markers were linked to geography. Believing that people who looked a certain way came from a certain part of the world, the Egyptians spoke, for instance, of the "pale, degraded race of Arvad," whereas their darker-skinned neighbors were designated the "evil race of Ish." The Chinese also linked physical variation to geography, as laid out in a Chinese creation myth. As the ancient tale goes, a goddess cooked human beings in an oven. Some humans were burned Black and sent to live in Africa. The underdone ones turned out White and were sent to Europe. Those humans cooked just right, a perfect golden brown, were the Chinese.

However, in the ancient worlds of Greece, Rome, and early Christendom, the idea of race did not exist as we know it today, as a biological package of traits carried in the bloodlines of distinct groups, each with a separate way of being (culture), acting (behavior), thinking (intelligence), and looking (appearance). The Greek philosopher Hippocrates, for instance, believed that physical markers such as skin color were the result of different environmental factors, much as the surface of a plant reflects the constitution of its soil and the amount of sunlight and water it receives. To be sure, the Greeks liked the looks of their fellow Greeks the best, but the very notion of race goes against Aristotle's principle of civic association, on which Greek society was based. The true test of a person was to be found in his (women were excluded) civic actions. Similarly, the Romans maintained a brutal system of slavery, but their slaves, as well as their citizens, represented various skin colors and geographic origins. The ancients may have used skin color to tell one person from the next—they weren't color-blind—but they didn't discriminate in the sense of making judgments about people on the basis of their racial category without regard to their individual merit (Hannaford, 1996). The notion has been so thoroughly displaced by racialized thinking that to us moderns, it is impossibly idealistic to imagine a society without our race concept.

RACE IN THE EARLY MODERN WORLD

Modern racial thinking developed in the mid-seventeenth century in parallel with global changes such as the Protestant Reformation in Europe, the Age of Exploration, and the rise of capitalism. For example, European colonizers, confronted with people living in newly discovered lands, interpreted human physical differences first with biblical and later with scientific explanations, and race proved to be a rather handy organizing principle to legitimate the imperial adventure of conquest, exploitation, and colonialism. To make sense of what they considered the "primitive" and "degraded" races of Africa, Europeans turned to a biblical story in the book of Genesis, the curse of Ham. According to this obscure passage, when Noah had safely navigated his ark over the flood, he got drunk and passed out naked in his tent. When he woke from his stupor, Noah learned that his youngest son, Ham, had seen him naked, whereas his other sons had respectfully refused to behold the spectacle. Noah decided to curse Ham's descendants, saying, "A slave of slaves shall he be to his brothers" (Gourevitch, 1998). European Christians and scientists interpreted this tale to mean that Ham was the original Black man, and all Black people were his unfortunate, degraded descendants. For an expanding Europe and America, the Hamitic myth justified colonialism and slavery.

When the divine right of conquest lost its sway, science led the way as an authority behind racial thinking, legitimating race by scientific mandate. Scientific racism, what today we call the nineteenth-century theories of race, brought a period of feverish investigation into the origins, explanations, and classifications of race. In 1684, François Bernier (1625–1688) proposed a new geography based not on topography or even political borders but on the body, from facial lineaments to bodily configurations. Bernier devised a scheme of four or five races based on the following geographic regions:

- *Europe* (excluding Lapland), *South Asia, North Africa,* and *America:* people who shared climates and complexions

- *Africa proper:* people who had thick lips, flat noses, Black skin, and a scanty beard

- *Asia proper:* people who had White skin, broad shoulders, flat faces, little eyes, and no beard

- *Lapps* (small traditional communities living around the northern regions of Finland and Russia): people who were ugly, squat, small, and animal-like

Scientific racism sought to make sense of people who were different from White Europeans—who constituted the norm, according to the French scientist Comte de Buffon (1707–1788). This way of thinking, called ethnocentrism, the judgment of other groups by one's own standards and values, has plagued scientific studies of "otherness." In Buffon's classification schemes, anyone different from Europeans was a deviation from the norm. His pseudoscientific research, like all racial thinking of the time, justified imperial exploits by automatically classifying nonwhites as abnormal, improper, and inferior.

With the publication of *On the Natural Varieties of Mankind* in 1775, Johann Friedrich Blumenbach (1752–1840), widely considered the founder of anthropology, cataloged variation by race, including differences in head formation, a pseudoscience called phrenology. Blumenbach's aim was to classify the world based on the different types of bumps he could measure on people's skulls. Based on these skull measurements, he came up with five principal varieties of humans: Caucasian, Mongoloid, Ethiopian, American, and Malay. Caucasians (named after the people who live on the southern slopes of the Georgian region of eastern Europe), he decided, were the superlatives of the races based on their excellent skull qualities.

Another eighteenth-century thinker, the Swiss theologian Johann Caspar Lavater (1741–1801), popularized physiognomy, which correlated outside appearances with inner virtues. Not surprisingly, light skin and

SCIENTIFIC RACISM

nineteenth-century theories of race that characterize a period of feverish investigation into the origins, explanations, and classifications of race.

ETHNOCENTRISM

the belief that one's own culture or group is superior to others and the tendency to view all other cultures from the perspective of one's own.

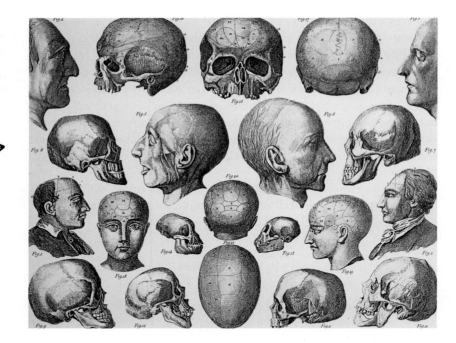

Charts like this one helped phrenologists interpret the shapes of human skulls. How did nineteenth-century theorists use this sort of pseudoscience to justify racism?

small features signified high intellect and worthy character. Political philosophers were also on board with racial thinking. Charles de Secondat, Baron de Montesquieu, had already made the connection between climate and certain forms of government in *The Spirit of the Laws* (1748/1750).

Race was now considered not just a set of physical traits but something that comes with social implications. Immanuel Kant (1724–1804) argued for a link between inner character and outer physiognomy and further claimed that these individual markers were also imprinted on an entire nation's moral life.

However, racial differences were still believed by many to be the product of climate (and therefore not immutable or innate to the soul). In fact, in 1787 the Reverend Minister Samuel Stanhope Smith, who was president of what is now Princeton University, wrote an essay in which he proposed that dark skin should be thought of as a "universal freckle." Differences in skin shade, he maintained, were really just like different levels of suntans. It was his belief that if an African from the sub-Sahara were transplanted to Scandinavia, his dark-brown skin would turn lighter over the course of generations (and perhaps the underlying social and cognitive characteristics associated with race would change as well). Notice how Smith's pliable view of race captures a spirit of ontological equality: We are all born the same deep beneath our skin; it just so happens that some of us have been out in the sun a bit longer than others. Ontological equality is the philosophical and religious notion that all people are created equal.

ONTOLOGICAL EQUALITY

the philosophical and religious notion that all people are created equal.

The Reverend Smith's line of thinking also demonstrates the scientific influence of Lamarckism, now a discredited footnote in the history of scientific thought. The basic tenet of Lamarckism is that acquired traits can be passed down across generations. For example, an acquired attribute such as flexibility, language skill, or sun exposure can be passed down to a person's offspring, affecting generations to come.

Lamarckism was debunked by Charles Darwin, who in 1859 published his theory of natural selection. Darwin argued that acquired attributes could not be transmitted; instead, change can occur only through the positive selection of mutations. Darwin's theory had an enormous impact on how people thought of race. In effect, it called into question the popular belief that climate influenced racial difference and instead offered an account in which racial lineages were much more deeply rooted and long-standing. What's more, humankind was now seen as being on a trajectory in which some groups have advanced (or evolved) more than others. The popular nineteenth-century notion of social Darwinism was the application of Darwinian ideas to society—namely, the evolutionary "survival of the fittest." Social theorist Herbert Spencer (1820–1903) promulgated the idea that some people, defined by their race, are better fit for survival than others and are therefore intended by nature to dominate inferior races. A new puzzle arose with Darwinian ideas: What, if not inherited climate change, could explain the development of humans along such radically different lines?

SOCIAL DARWINISM

the application of Darwinian ideas to society—namely, the evolutionary "survival of the fittest."

EUGENICS

Scientists now had to arrive at a new explanation of physical difference among humans, and the scientific community confronted a growing debate: monogenism versus polygenism. The debate turned on the origins of the various races of humans. Were humans a united species, or did we come from separate origins? Monogenists, including religious traditionalists, believed that humans were one species, united under God. Polygenists believed that different races were, in fact, distinct species. Darwin sided with the monogenists, claiming that the notion of different species was absurd. (Politics, it is said, makes for strange bedfellows. It certainly did in this case, as Darwinists and religious traditionalists, usually opposed, became allies in arguing that all humans were one species.)

Even though the monogenists won the debate, the notion of separate roots and distinct reproductive genetic histories has had a lasting impact on how we think of human difference. Under the model of natural selection, human difference must have evolved over tens or hundreds of thousands of years (if not millions), not just over a few generations in relative sun or shade. Such a vast time frame was used as evidence that races were very different (and not simply superficially so).

Herbert Spencer coined the term "survival of the fittest." How did Spencer draw from the work of Darwin to justify racism?

Howard Knox (center), assistant surgeon at Ellis Island from 1912 to 1916, examined immigrants for diseases and disabilities, including mental illnesses.

EUGENICS

literally meaning "well born"; a pseudoscience that postulates that controlling the fertility of populations could influence inheritable traits passed on from generation to generation.

NATIVISM

the movement to protect and preserve indigenous land or culture from the allegedly dangerous and polluting effects of new immigrants.

A new movement, eugenics, took the idea of very distant origins and ran with it. Eugenicists, led by Sir Francis Galton (1822—1911), claimed that each race had a separate package of social and psychological traits transmitted through bloodlines. Eugenics literally means "well born"; it is the pseudoscience of genetic lines and the inheritable traits they pass on from generation to generation. Everything from criminality and feeblemindedness to disease and intelligence, Galton asserted, could be traced through bloodlines and selectively bred out of or into populations. One of his followers, the American psychologist H. H. Goddard (1866—1957), applied eugenic thinking to generalize findings from his intelligence tests in America. He tested a handful of immigrants arriving at Ellis Island in the early twentieth century and generalized their test scores to whole populations, claiming—and garnering many believers too—that around 70 percent of the immigrants sailing from eastern and southern Europe were, in his phraseology, "morons" who posed a serious threat to the good of the nation. Goddard supported the immigration exclusion acts that in 1924 largely blocked non-Anglos from immigrating and were intended to improve the "stock" of the nation. This concern about the new and objectionable stock of immigrants, as opposed to "native," more desirable immigrants of an earlier epoch, was the crux of nativism, the movement to protect and preserve indigenous land or culture from the allegedly dangerous and polluting effects of new immigrants. Madison Grant (1865—1937), an influential writer, epitomized the spirit of nativism when he argued that not restricting the immigration of southern and eastern Europeans meant "race suicide" for the White race (1916/1936).

The problem with race, for eugenicists, scientists, and politicians, has always been that if race is such an obvious, natural means of dividing the world, why does no foolproof way of determining racial boundaries exist? According to the social historian Ian Haney López (1995), the US Supreme Court grappled with this question in the late nineteenth and early twentieth centuries. In a landmark case in 1923, for example, Dr. Bhagat Singh Thind, a Sikh from India, was denied American citizenship. The Supreme Court ruled that he did not qualify as a "free White person," despite being the first Indian Sikh to be inducted into the US Army in World War I. In previous cases, the Court relied on a combination of scientific evidence and "common knowledge" to decide who counted as White. But the Thind case posed a particular challenge because leading anthropologists at the time uniformly classified Asian Indians as members of the "Caucasian" race. The very notion of Whiteness was at stake: If the anthropologists were right, then the commonly accepted conception of Whiteness would be radically changed to include dark-skinned immigrants like Thind. The Court therefore decried science as failing to distinguish human difference sufficiently, relying on common knowledge alone to deny Thind's claims to Whiteness. As the Court put it, "The words 'free White persons' are words of common speech, to be interpreted in accordance with the understandings of the common man" (Haney López, 1995).

Bhagat Singh Thind.

TWENTIETH-CENTURY CONCEPTS OF RACE

The judges in the Thind case were not the only people who attempted to define Whiteness and nonwhiteness in the absence of a stable scientific taxonomy of race. In Nazi Germany, for example, race posed certain key questions: How can Jewishness be detected? Are Jews a race or a religious group? Both, actually: They are a religious group that has been racialized. Scholars have pointed out that the seeds of racism may be traced to anti-Judaism among early Christians, who forced Jews to convert. Anti-Semitism grew in the eleventh century and was based on the belief that getting rid of Jews was preferable to converting them. But Jewishness was still a social identity at this point—a matter of having religious beliefs that differed from the norm. Anti-Semitism did not turn into racism until the idea took hold that Jews were intrinsically inferior, having innate differences that separated them from their Christian neighbors (Fredrickson, 2002; Smedley, 1999). In Nazi Germany, where Jews were believed to have such innate and inherited differences, the problem remained: How can a person be identified as Jewish? This became an obsession during the Nazis' program of racial purification. They devised a "scientific" way to detect Jewishness by measuring ratios of forehead to nose size to face length, but they had little luck in nailing down a reliable method for making such a determination (hence, Jews in Nazi-occupied countries were forced to wear a yellow Star of David as a marker of their identity).

In the 1960s, many Whites in rural parts of America similarly failed in trying to distinguish themselves from their neighbors who had a mix of European, Indigenous, and African ancestry (known as "tri-racial isolates") by searching for distinguishing signs on the body, such as differences in fingernails, feet, gums, and lines on the palm of a hand. In exasperation, some Whites reported having to rely on good, old-fashioned "instinct" to distinguish themselves from nonwhites (Berry, 1963).

One means (but still not foolproof) of drawing sharp racial boundaries in America was the one-drop rule, asserting that just "one drop" of Black blood makes a person Black. The rule developed out of the laws passed in many US states forbidding miscegenation, or interracial marriage. By 1910, most Whites in the United States had accepted this doctrine. The one-drop rule was integral in maintaining the Jim Crow system of segregation upheld in the 1896 Supreme Court decision in *Plessy v. Ferguson*. In the American South, it was clear that anyone of Black lineage fell on the unfortunate side of the racial divide, and the rule essentially cleaved America into two societies: one Black, one White. This meant again clumping together all "White ethnics" into one united category. As F. James Davis notes (1991), the one-drop rule was highly efficient, not least because it completely erased stratification *within* the Black community that had previously been based on skin tone.

Scientific racial thought slowly passed out of vogue as theories of cultural difference gained momentum among American intellectuals from the 1920s to the 1940s. Anthropologist Franz Boas dismissed the claims of the biological basis of discrete races, and sociologists such as Robert Park advanced new ideas about culture's importance in determining human behavior. Race, these thinkers argued, was less about fixed inherited traits than about particular social circumstances. Furthermore, when World War II exposed the kind of atrocities to which scientific racism could lead, it became socially and scientifically inappropriate to discuss race in biological terms, and eugenics came to be considered a dangerous way of thinking. With the decline of scientific racism and the shift toward cultural theories of race and ethnicity, the Immigration Act of 1924 was gradually chipped away at starting in 1959 and then completely repealed in 1965. Don't let the formal denunciation of racial thinking fool you, however. Cultural explanations of race often reflect a disguised racist ideology just as much as biological ones do.

Despite the ideas of scholars such as Boas and Park, the old idea of fixed, biological racial differences remains alive and well today, although in modified form. The search for racial boundaries continues in the twenty-first century with the rise of molecular genetics. DNA research now allows us to look deeper than the bumps on our heads, deeper than skin tone or palm lines. Today you can find a number of DNA testing companies offering you an inside look at your heritage. For as little as $70 or so, a testing kit arrives in the mail, you swab your mouth according to the directions, and then send the swab to the company. Your "real" identity comes back from the lab in about seven weeks. (See Chapter 17 for more on race and genetics.)

Wayne Joseph, a 53-year-old Louisiana high-school principal with Creole roots, did just that. Born and raised Black, but having light skin, Joseph was mildly curious about the ancestry in his veins. He received some unexpected results: His genetic makeup is 57 percent Indo-European, 39 percent Native American, 4 percent East Asian, and zero percent African (Kaplan, 2003). Despite the findings, Joseph continues to embrace his identity as Black. As he put it to reporters, "The question ultimately is, are you who you say you are, or are you who you are genetically?"

Marion West (center) embraces Vy Higgensen (right). The distant cousins discovered their relationship after the results of separate DNA tests were entered into a database.

Cells, alleles, and gene sequences have become the new tools of science that promise to reveal our racial truths, but the old idea hasn't much changed—that there is a biological and social package of traits inside our bodies that can be traced through our lineage—despite our knowledge that humans are biologically one species. There is no doubt that there exists genetic variation that corresponds to the general geographic origins of what we call race, but the amount of variation is nowhere near as great as most people believe. Further, the relationship between genes and complex social behavior (e.g., intelligence) is not very well understood. Yet when the 2018 General Social Survey (GSS) asked respondents why, on average, African Americans have worse jobs, income, and housing than White people, about 8 percent responded that Blacks "have less in-born ability to learn." (Moreover, a whopping 36 percent of respondents believed that Blacks are worse off because they "just don't have the motivation or will power to pull themselves up out of poverty" [National Opinion Research Center, 2019].) The historical search for difference affects our belief system today.

Racial Realities

The biological validity of discrete racial categories—be it the bumps on your skull or the DNA in your blood—may be debatable, but in social life, race is real, with real consequences. Just ask someone of the Burakumin race in Japan. Today making up anywhere from 1 to 3 percent of the Japanese population, depending on the estimate, the Burakumin originated as a group of displaced people during fourteenth-century feudal wars (Hankins, 2014). With no connection other than being Japanese, the Burakumin suddenly shared something undesirable—they were homeless, destitute, and forced to wander the countryside together. Imagine all the homeless people today in Miami or Los Angeles suddenly uniting. The Burakumin formed a distinct social category, with complete social closure, their own reproductive pool, their own occupational pool, and so on, although they were not a distinct group genetically. Today, however, it is commonly believed that the Burakumin "are descendants of a less human 'race' than the stock that fathered the Japanese nation as a whole" (De Vos & Wagatsuma, 1966). Six hundred years later, the Burakumin still display no physical distinctions from their fellow Japanese citizens. For those people in Japan wishing to avoid interrelations with the Burakumin, this lack of distinctiveness poses a dilemma. So for a hefty price, there are private investigators for hire who will confirm the pedigree of your prospective employee, tenant, or future son-in-law.

In Japan, the Burakumin live in ghettos, called *burakus*, and score lower on health, educational achievement, and income compared with their fellow Japanese citizens. Yet when Japanese and Burakumin emigrate to America, the scoring gap narrows dramatically. The distinction between Burakumin and other Japanese is meaningless outside of the significance bestowed on it in their home country. Again, we see that race is not necessarily just about physical or biological differences.

The Burakumin are a minority who can be distinguished from the rest of the Japanese population only by genealogical detectives. Prejudice against this group often leads to homelessness.

To take an example of racial realities closer to home, consider the consequences of being Arab—or perhaps I should say being perceived as Muslim—in post-9/11 America. In an interview for this book, Jen'nan Read used the image of a Venn diagram to explain that "Arab is an ethnicity; being a Muslim is a religious categorization. In the US context a lot of Muslims and Arabs seem to be the same group. In fact, most Arabs in the United States are Christians who immigrated prior to World War One. And most Muslims are actually not Arab . . . one-third are South Asian, one-third are Arab, and about a quarter are African Americans who have converted to the religion" (Conley, 2009i). In the United States, Muslims are often identified with Islamic terrorists. Followers of Islam these days are often lumped into a fixed racial category as a dangerous and undemocratic "other," seen as separate from, and inferior and hostile to, Christians.

In the first year after the events of 9/11, the number of anti-Muslim hate crimes shot up

1,600 percent (Read, 2008). And though reported crimes dropped over the following decade and a half, such backlash has resurged after the 2016 presidential campaign of Donald Trump, which some see as linked to his tendency to retweet incendiary remarks or memes. In the first year of his administration, anti-Islamic hate crimes rose by 17 percent from the prior year (marking the third year of rise, which suggests that Trump's behavior may be more of a reflection than a cause) (Birnbaum, 2018). Most notable were mosque torchings, cemetery vandalism, and an incident in Bloomington,

To see my interview with Jen'nan Read, go to
digital.wwnorton.com/youmayask7

Minnesota, when a bomb was thrown into a mosque in an act Governor Mark Dayton called terrorism (Bromwich, 2017). The following year total hate crimes were down slightly, but the number of violent incidents rose (Treisman, 2019).

In the wake of anxiety about terrorists, and several years into the war on terror, Muslims in America have undergone what scholars call racialization, the formation of a new racial identity by drawing ideological boundaries of difference around a formerly unnoticed group of people. These days, any brown-skinned man with a beard or woman with a headscarf is subject to threats, violence, and harassment. And men with turbans bear some of the worst discrimination, although nearly all men who wear turbans in the United States are Sikh, members of one of the world's largest religious groups, which originated in India. Four days after 9/11, Balbir Singh Sodhi, a Sikh living in Mesa, Arizona, was shot five times and killed in the gas station he owned. He was the first victim of an anti-Muslim epidemic, and he wasn't even Muslim. In one Harvard study, 83 percent of Sikhs interviewed said that they or someone they knew personally had experienced a hate crime or incident, and another 64 percent felt fear or danger for their family and themselves (Han, 2006). Even more striking is what happens to White Americans who convert to Islam. One woman, despite having fair skin and green eyes, has been categorized by people as Palestinian when she wears the Muslim headscarf, called the *hijab*. She's even been told, "Go back to your own country," although she was born and raised in California (Kuruvil, 2006; Spurlock, 2005). The frequency of such incidents is likely to increase as more people convert to Islam in the United States (Read, 2008).

RACIALIZATION

the formation of a new racial identity by drawing ideological boundaries of difference around a formerly unnoticed group of people.

A group of Sikhs protest after the murder of Balbir Singh Sodhi.

The racialization of Muslims operates on several flawed assumptions. First, people make stereotyped assumptions based on appearance (turban = Osama bin Laden), even if in their own personal experience they know better (most people wearing turbans in the United States are Sikhs, not Muslim extremists). Second, making snap judgments about Muslims requires a gross caricaturization of Islam's followers. Remember, two-thirds of Arabs in the United States are not Muslim but Christian (Pew Research Center, 2011a).

As it turns out, American Muslims are both a highly diverse population and a very mainstream one. Muslims have been in North America since the seventeenth century, when they were transported from Africa as slaves, and about 37 percent of Muslims were born in America (Pew Research Center, 2011a). As a group, they are assimilated with the mainstream, having income and education levels similar to those of the rest of the population. By and large, they hold fast to the ideas that education is important and that hard work pays off in a successful career. Doesn't sound too radical, does it? That's because the overwhelming majority of Muslims in America and throughout the world strongly disagree with Islamic extremism (Pew Research Center, 2011a). Of course, no racial boundaries are drawn along accurate lines or real differences, but again, once racialized, a group faces real social consequences.

Race versus Ethnicity

What's the difference between race and ethnicity anyway? Some books use the terms interchangeably; most subsume *race* under the umbrella label of "ethnicity." Today's understanding of race is that it is

- *Externally imposed:* Someone *else* defines you as Black, White, or other.

- *Involuntary:* It's not up to you to decide to which category you belong; someone else puts you there.

- *Usually based on physical differences:* Those unreliable bumps on your head.

- *Hierarchical:* Not White? Take a number down the ranks.

- *Exclusive:* You don't get to check more than one box.

- *Unequal:* It's about power conflicts and struggles.

This last point is important for making sense of the Burakumin and Muslim Americans. Racial groupings are about domination and struggles for power. They are organizing principles for social inequality and a means of legitimating exclusion and harassment.

Ethnicity, one's ethnic affiliation, is by contrast

- *Voluntary:* I choose to identify with my one-eighth Irish background (it makes me feel special, so why not?).

- *Self-defined:* It is embraced by group members from within.

- *Nonhierarchical:* Hey, I'm Irish, you're German. *Great!*

- *Fluid and multiple:* I'm Irish *and* German. *Even better!*

- *Cultural:* It is based on differences in practices such as language, food, music, and so on.

- *Planar:* It is much less about unequal power than race is.

Ethnicity can be thought of as a nationality, not in the sense of carrying the rights and duties of citizenship but in the sense of identifying with a past or future nationality. (There is, for example, a Kurdish ethnicity even though there has yet to be a Kurdistan.) The story of a friend of mine might help clarify the distinction between race and ethnicity: She was born in Korea to Korean parents, but she was adopted shortly after birth by an Italian couple who brought her back to Italy and raised her there. She never learned to speak Korean and does not enjoy Korean cuisine. She is, in fact, an excellent cook of Italian food and an Italian film maven. She is an Italian citizen with an Italian last name who self-identifies as Italian. At one point in her life, she came to the United States to study. By living in the country of her citizenship, she had developed an Italian identity that became her ethnic identity. She bonded with fellow Italian speakers in the United States, for example, and went to Italian restaurants to watch when big soccer games were broadcast. However, here in the United States, she was swept up into the race system we have constructed. Whites and Blacks and Asians treated her as Asian based on how she looked. She had no control over this. It was externally imposed. She was racially "Asian" even though she felt ethnically "Italian."

For Americans, Herbert Gans (1979b) called the voluntary, chosen form of ethnic identification "symbolic ethnicity." While asserting symbolic

ETHNICITY

one's ethnic quality or affiliation. It is voluntary, self-defined, nonhierarchical, fluid and multiple, and based on cultural differences, not physical ones per se.

SYMBOLIC ETHNICITY

a nationality, not in the sense of carrying the rights and duties of citizenship but in the sense of identifying with a past or future nationality. For later generations of White ethnics, it is something not constraining but easily expressed, with no risks of stigma and all the pleasures of feeling like an individual.

ethnic identity was particularly difficult for my Italian friend, for most White middle-class Americans today symbolic ethnicity is largely a matter of choice. It has no risk of stigma and confers the pleasures of feeling like an individual.

In this way, the differences between race and ethnicity underscore the privileged position of Whites in America, who have the freedom to pick and choose their identities, to wave a flag in a parade, or to whip up Grandma's traditional recipe and freely show their ethnic backgrounds. The surge of ethnic pride among White Americans today implies a false belief that all ethnic groups are the same, but in the very way that symbolic ethnicity is voluntary for White ethnics, it is not so for nonwhite Americans such as African Americans, Latinxs, and Asians (like my friend). As soon as someone classifies you as racially different on the basis of your physical features, you lose the ability to choose your ethnic identity. It becomes racialized—subsumed under a forced identifier, label, or racial marker of "otherness" that you cannot escape. Thus, although it is common to use the term *ethnicity* across the board to refer to Latinx, Black, Asian, or Irish backgrounds, being Irish in America is something that a person can turn on or off at will. You can never *not* be Asian or Black: Your body gives away your otherness, no matter how much you want to blend in.

To be Black in America is to be just that—Black. Some scholars argue that this is the fundamental issue about race in America. Blacks were considered, until recently, a monolithic group. They were unique among racial groups in that their ethnic (tribal, language group, and national) distinctions were deliberately wiped out during the slave trade in order to prevent social organization and revolt (Eyerman, 2001), resulting in the stripping of "ethnic honor." Alex Haley's landmark novel *Roots* (1976) raised an awareness among African Americans about tracing their ethnic rather than racial identity. This is changing now as more African Americans trace their roots to specific places in Africa through genealogical research or DNA testing. Likewise, immigration from Africa and the Caribbean has created distinctly recognizable national groups of origin among the US Black population. Finally, the presidential campaign of Barack Obama led, perhaps, to a symbolic expansion of who counts as Black within the African American community: even the son of a White, Kansan mother and a Kenyan father

Crowds line the street at the St. Patrick's Day Parade in New York City. How is this an example of symbolic ethnicity?

who has half-Asian and fully African half-siblings. Though some African Americans were initially uncomfortable with embracing Obama and his mixed racial heritage as "Black like us," their attitudes would have had little impact on the wider perception of Obama as a Black man because of the continuing significance of the one-drop rule in America. Indeed, the White nationalist backlash that followed Obama's inauguration, which has continued through the campaign and election of Donald Trump, suggests that the one-drop rule is alive and well. That is, the fact that Obama was biracial and not a descendant of US slaves did not seem to matter to Americans who cheered his ascent or those who wished for his downfall.

Racial Groups in the United States

The United States is home to numerous racial groups today. It has such a heterogeneous population, in fact, that it is on its way to having no single numerically dominant group. Until the mid-nineteenth century, racial diversity was minimal because immigration rates were relatively low until about 1820. Early in the country's formation, White Anglo-Saxon Protestants dominated over Native Americans as well as Black slaves. From that point forward, Anglos secured their place at the top of the cultural, political, and economic hierarchy, prevailing over other immigrant populations. As exemplified in the following snapshot of racial groups in America today, these historical hierarchies have remained relatively stable and intact despite drastically changing demographics.

NATIVE AMERICANS

According to archaeological findings, the original settlers of the North American continent arrived anywhere between 12,000 and 50,000 years ago from northeast Asia, traveling by foot on glaciers. This is disputed by some tribes, such as the Ojibwe, who believe that their ancestors came from the east, not the west. Before European explorers arrived in significant numbers for extended periods in the fifteenth century (there is evidence that the Vikings had reached North America before then), the Indigenous population was anywhere between 10 and 100 million. The tribes living here when Europeans showed up were geographically, culturally, and physically diverse, but they were categorically viewed as a single uncivilized group by arriving Spanish, French, and British explorers. Even today, "Indians" in America are part of 280 distinct cultural groups (Gray & Nye, 2001). Foreshadowing

The Oglala Nation Powwow and Rodeo parade is a bright spot for the Pine Ridge Indian Reservation, which, like many federal reservations, is plagued by problems linked to low socioeconomic status.

the lack of respect to come, Columbus called all of the people he met Indians, despite their clear cultural differences, because he thought he was in India. Confronted with foreign diseases and unfamiliar military technology, the Indians were quickly dominated by White invaders. In Central and South America, the Spanish brutally enslaved them as labor for the mining industry. In the northern parts of North America, French colonialists nurtured their relationships with the Indians in order to cultivate a profitable fur trade. The British, chiefly concerned with acquiring land, settled colonies with the long-term goal of expanding the British state, dispossessing and "civilizing" America's Indigenous population in the process (Cornell, 1988).

American Indians' way of life was completely obliterated by the European settlements, as vital land was taken from them and their communal infrastructure was disrupted. Most devastating were the newly imported diseases, such as smallpox and cholera, against which the Indians, having no native immunity, were virtually defenseless. There were also grueling forced marches from native lands to dedicated reservations. By the end of the 1800s, the Native American population had dwindled to approximately 250,000 (US Census Bureau, 1993). The Indian Bureau (later called the Bureau of Indian Affairs) was established as part of the War Department in 1824 to deal with the remaining "Indian problem," and its chief means was "forced assimilation." This involved removing Indian children from their families and putting them in government-run boarding schools that taught the superiority of Anglo culture over "primitive" Native culture and religion. Children who refused to adopt Western dress, language, and religion met with harsh physical and emotional punishment (Cornell, 1988). (A similar project was undertaken in British-ruled Australia with the native Aboriginal tribes.) Despite this poor treatment, Navajo men served the United States in World War II, in which 29 "code talkers" used the Navajo language in lieu of cryptography to protect the secrecy of American communications. The work of the code talkers was critically instrumental in the American victory at Iwo Jima and many other battles throughout the war (Bixler, 1992).

In 2018, people claiming at least some Native American ancestry number about 5.6 million (US Census Bureau, 2020c). Only about one-fifth of Native Americans live in a designated American Indian area. The largest reservation, Navajoland or Diné Bikéyah, covers approximately 16 million acres of Arizona, New Mexico, and Utah. Reservations are generally impoverished and rife with health problems, domestic abuse, substance abuse, poor infrastructure, and crime. In fact, Native Americans as a whole are plagued by the lowest average socioeconomic status in the United States. They rank among the worst in terms of high-school dropout rates and unemployment, which go hand in hand with poor health outcomes such as alcoholism, suicide, and premature death. Suicide rates are more than double that of the general population and are the second-leading cause of death for Native Americans from ages 15 to 34 (Centers for Disease Control and Prevention, 2012a). Around 33 percent of Native Americans die before age 45, compared with 11 percent of the US population as a whole (Garrett, 1994).

Though facing many social problems, Native Americans are becoming more politically organized and active as a bloc. For example, sustained protests against the Dakota Access Pipeline crossing sacred ground—and the reservation's water source—in North Dakota led to a delay and rerouting of the oil conduit (McKenna, 2016). And recent lawsuits brought by Native Americans in Colorado have successfully challenged the gerrymandering that had concentrated their numbers into a single state district, thereby diluting their power (Turkewitz, 2018).

AFRICAN AMERICANS

The first Black people in North America arrived not as slaves but as indentured servants contracted by White colonialists for set periods. They were in the same circumstances as poor, unfree Whites such as those from Ireland or Scotland (Franklin, 1980). The system of slavery, however, evolved to meet colonial labor needs, and the slave trade was a fixed institution by the end of the seventeenth century. African Americans have been, all in all, on the bottom of the racial hierarchy ever since.

Just before the American Revolution, slaves made up more than 20 percent of the colonial population (Dinnerstein et al., 1996). As of 2018, about 12.7 percent of the American population is Black (US Census Bureau, 2020c). Like the Japanese Burakumin, this minority group has high rates of poverty, health problems, unemployment, and crime. According to the US Census Bureau, the median income of African Americans as a group is roughly 62.8 percent that of Whites (US Census Bureau, 2017c, 2017d). In 2015, more than 6.7 million people in the United States were on probation or parole, in jail, or in prison—that's 2.7 percent of all US adult residents, or 1 in every 37 adults (Kaeble & Glaze, 2016). Among men ages 25 to 39, Blacks are imprisoned 2.5 times and 6 times as often as Hispanics and Whites, respectively; overall, just 0.5 percent of White men are imprisoned (Carson, 2014).

Sociologists and demographers today are beginning to study how new Black immigrants are fracturing the holistic conception of "African American." For the first time, more Africans are entering the country

Wiley College student body president Kabamba Kiboko dances at a pep rally. Her family came to the United States from the Congo. For the first time, more Africans are entering the country than during the slave trade.

than during the slave trade. About 10.2 percent of the Black population is foreign-born (US Census Bureau, 2020m). Afro-Caribbeans such as Cubans, Haitians, and Jamaicans resent being unilaterally categorized as African American, because each of these immigrant groups enjoys a unique history, culture, and language that do not correspond to the American stereotypes of people with Black skin. For this reason, new Black immigrant groups would rather not assimilate, but instead retain their distinctive immigrant status, setting themselves apart from the lowest status group in America, Blacks (Greer, 2006).

LATINXS

Latinx (the gender-neutral construction of Latino) means individuals who trace their ancestry back to Latin America. So in theory, this group includes Brazilians who speak Portuguese and Belizeans who speak English. *Hispanic* means descended from (or identifying with) Spanish-speaking populations (including from Spain itself). So, while they are not technically the same groups, the terms are often used interchangeably in practice. In 2018, the majority of Latinxs in the United States were from Mexico (about 61.9 percent), Puerto Rico (about 9.7 percent), Cuba (4 percent), and the Dominican Republic (3.5 percent) (US Census Bureau, 2020f). (Figure 9.1 provides a breakdown of the US Hispanic population by region of origin.) They are a huge and rapidly expanding segment of the American population; in 2018 they made up approximately 18 percent of the population, surpassing African

FIGURE 9.1 US Hispanic Population by Region of Origin, 2018

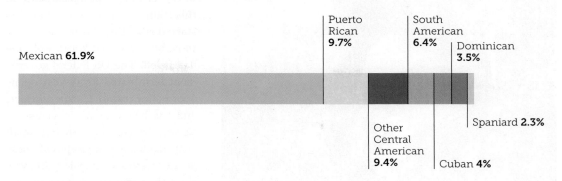

SOURCE: US Census Bureau, 2020f.

Americans (US Census Bureau 2020f). Latinxs also live in a wide array of locations, although they have clustered in the West Coast and Southwest regions (US Census Bureau, 2020g).

Hispanics are often called an "in between" racial group because of their intermediate status, sandwiched between Whites and African Americans. Unlike African Americans, the majority of Latinxs in America today have come by way of voluntary immigration, particularly during the last four decades of heavy, second-wave immigration. Puerto Ricans are the exception, because they have been able to travel freely to the United States since 1917, when Puerto Rico became an American territory and its inhabitants US citizens. The chief motivation for Latinx immigration is economic because of America's high demand for labor in the service, agriculture, and construction industries.

Mexicans, Puerto Ricans, and Cubans all have diverse phenotypical traits that make racial distinctions of a unified Latinx type nearly impossible. Mexicans are generally classified as "mestizos," a term referring to a racially mixed heritage that combines Native American and European traits. And for instance, Puerto Ricans are often a mixture of African, European, and Indian backgrounds. So ambiguous is the Latinx label that at various times the US Census has classified them as part of the White race and as a separate race. At the moment, being Hispanic or Latinx is considered by the US government to be an ethnic identity, not a racial identity, although, as I mentioned above, many researchers consider Latinxs a racialized group.

This is, of course, complicated. Take Cubans. Most Cubans consider themselves Hispanic Whites, although their immigration status has changed drastically in recent years. Following the Communist revolution led by Fidel Castro, the first large wave of Cuban immigrants arrived in southern Florida in the 1960s. These immigrants were of the upper or middle class, were educated, and were perceived as the victims of a Communist regime that came to power

A crowd gathers for a Cinco de Mayo parade in Southwest Detroit. How do the boundaries between race and ethnicity overlap in the Latinx community?

during the Cold War. As such, they were welcomed enthusiastically to this country, and their assimilation started smoothly (Portes, 1969). By 1995, however, that warm welcome had faded. The US federal government terminated its 35-year open-door policy toward Cuban refugees, and the heavy media coverage of Cubans arriving since then in small boats has led to stereotypes of a desperate "wetback" invasion. Arrivals since the 1970s—who generally are from lower socioeconomic backgrounds in Cuban society—have met more resistance from their host society, consequently experiencing higher rates of unemployment, low-wage work, and dependence on welfare and charity than native Whites and previous Cuban émigrés (Portes et al., 1985). More recently, with the normalization of relations between the United States and Cuba, the special status that Cubans had with respect to immigration (essentially a fast track to American citizenship) has been terminated, and as a result, deportations have increased. Some 37,000 Cubans face deportation orders as of 2018 (Torres, 2017). The Trump administration revised Obama's policies, so limbo and uncertainty may continue for a while.

ASIAN AMERICANS

Like *Latinx*, the term *Asian American* is very broad, encompassing diverse and sometimes clashing peoples from China, Korea, Japan, and Southeast Asia. The first wave of Asians to arrive in the United States in the mid-nineteenth century were predominantly laborers of Chinese, then Japanese, then Korean and Filipino origin. A second large wave of immigration is currently under way, mostly made up of well-educated and highly skilled people from all over Asia.

Early Asian immigrants were perceived as a labor threat and therefore met with extreme hostility. The Chinese Exclusion Act of 1882, which led to a ban against the Chinese in 1902, marked the first time in American history in which a group was singled out and barred entry. Urban "Chinatowns" developed out of ghettos in which marginalized Chinese workers, mostly men, were forced to live. Japanese immigrants faced similar hostilities and were formally barred entry by the Oriental Exclusion Act of 1924. By 2018, Asian and mixed-Asian US residents amounted to 6.7 percent of the population. This was a 28 percent increase since 2010, making Asian Americans the fastest-growing racial group (US Census Bureau, 2020n). They are most heavily concentrated in California, Hawaii, New York, Illinois, and Washington.

Asian Americans are unique among racial minorities because of their high average socioeconomic status, surpassing that of most other minority groups as well as most Whites in terms of educational attainment. For example, the median household income for the US population as a whole in 2018 was $61,937, whereas for Asian Americans it was $87,243 (US Census Bureau, 2020i). That said, despite the overall success of Asian Americans, certain groups—notably Cambodians and Hmong (from Laos and Vietnam)—experience very high poverty rates.

Furthermore, Asian Americans overall find it a bit more difficult to be reemployed once they lose a job. In the first quarter of 2020, the Asian American unemployment rate for those with bachelor's degrees or higher was 0.9 percentage point higher than the rate for Whites (Bureau of Labor Statistics, 2020e), and Asian Americans and Blacks suffer from the longest average duration of unemployment spells. In March 2020, unemployed Asian Americans experienced a median 6.6 weeks before they found work again. For Blacks that year, the figure was 8.8 weeks. (Whites and Latinxs had 6.5- and 5-week median durations between jobs, respectively, in 2020 [Bureau of Labor Statistics, 2020f].) However, these Black–Asian and White–Latinx similarities obscure different reasons for the long duration of unemployment for the various groups. Whereas Blacks typically face barriers to employment, Asians have more family support and savings and thus are able to wait out a bad labor market for the best possible job.

In recent years, Asians have been applauded for their smooth assimilation as the "model minority," the implication being that if only other racial groups could assimilate so well, America would have fewer social problems. Such a view, however, effaces the rather unsmooth history Asian immigrants have faced in this country as well as the continuing poverty and discrimination faced by some Asians. Furthermore, "positive" stereotypes of high achievement are not always beneficial and can place enormous pressure on Asian youths to measure up to an impossibly high ideal.

Not only can the model minority myth be damaging to Asians themselves, but it can be used by those with an extremist agenda. For example, Richard Spencer, the president of the National Policy Institute, a White supremacist think tank, routinely cites data claiming that East Asians have the highest IQs on average, followed by those of European descent. This placement of Whites second to another group paints a patina of scientific objectivity onto the claims that so-called alt-right race rabble-rousers like himself are merely "race realists." How biased can he be, after all, if he's not even listing his own group first? Of course, the real point is to pave the way for claims that other nonwhite groups are intellectually inferior. Even back in the 1960s, the case of Asian American assimilation and upward mobility was used to blame other groups for their failures to achieve success—ignoring the circumstances minority groups faced and inherited (Lim, 2018).

MIDDLE EASTERN AMERICANS

Middle Easterners are a group that are in the middle of a process of becoming racialized in the US context. They come from places as diverse as the Arabian Peninsula, North Africa, Iran, Iraq, and the Palestinian territories. Middle Easterners established communities in the United States as far back as the late 1800s, but their numbers have swelled since the 1970s as part of the rising tide of non-European immigration. Middle Easterners in this second wave of immigration often arrive from politically tumultuous areas to seek refuge in the United States—such as the many refugees who have recently fled from war-torn Syria.

Today about 2.1 million Americans report Arab ancestry, and even more Americans have a Middle Eastern heritage, because not all Middle Easterners are Arab (US Census Bureau, 2020j) despite the fact that most Americans regard anyone from the Middle East as Arab and Muslim. In fact, the largest Middle Eastern population in the United States today is from Iran, and they are Persians, not ethnic Arabs, and do not generally speak Arabic. Similarly, although the majority of new Middle Eastern Americans are Muslim, many of them are Christian, and a small number are Jewish (Bozorgmehr et al., 1996).

Widespread misunderstandings about Middle Easterners derive, in part, from their negative stereotyping in the mainstream media. In one study of television portrayals of Arabs, researchers found four basic myths that continue to surround this group. First, they are often depicted as fabulously wealthy—as sultans and oil tycoons. Second, they are shown as uncivilized and barbaric. Third, they are portrayed as sex-crazed, especially for underage White sex slaves. Fourth, they are said to revel in acts of terrorism, desiring to destroy all things American (Shaheen, 1984). Little has changed since this study came out over 30 years ago, although after 9/11, the emphasis shifted away from stereotypes of Arabs as extremely rich and toward one of Middle Easterners as terrorists.

The Importance of Being White

We've seen some of the trajectories of various ethnic and racial groups in America, but what about the largest racial population, Whites? Scholars have begun to pay more attention to what it means to be a White person. Every year on the first day of my Introduction to Sociology class, I ask my 200 or so students to write down the five social categories that best describe who they are. Black students almost always put their race at or near the top of the list. Latinx and Asian American students usually list their ethnicity as well. Until recently, I could be fairly confident that Whites would not list their race. Some might identify Polish, German, or another ethnic or national origin, but not one White student would write down Caucasian, White, or even Euro-American. And that was the point of my experiment.

We have already seen how the category of Whiteness is socially constructed—first inclusively defined as all "free White persons" in 1790, then restrictively defined as only northern and western European Whites in the early twentieth century, and reformulated back to an umbrella category by the mid-twentieth century. We know now that this category, which seems so natural and innate, is actually a flexible label that has expanded over time to include many formerly nonwhite groups such as Jews, Irish, and Italians. Today most White people have little awareness of the meaning of Whiteness as a category. As Nell Irvin Painter, the author of *The History of White People*, says, "The foundation of White identity is that there isn't any. You're just an individual" (Schackner, 2002).

Whiteness, argues Peggy McIntosh (1988), is an "invisible knapsack of privileges" that puts White people at an advantage, just as racism places nonwhites at a disadvantage. In her now classic essay "White Privilege: Unpacking the Invisible Knapsack" (1989), McIntosh catalogs more than 50 "Daily Effects of White Privilege," ranging from the mundane to the major. Here are just a few that McIntosh notices:

- I can log into Netflix and count on finding movies and TV featuring people of my race represented, go into a supermarket and find the staple foods which fit with my cultural traditions, and walk into a hairdresser's shop and find someone who can cut my hair.

- I can arrange to protect my children most of the time from people who might not like them.

- I do not have to educate my children to be aware of systemic racism for their own daily physical protection.

- I am never asked to speak for all the people of my racial group.

- I am not made acutely aware that my shape, bearing, or body odor will be taken as a reflection on my race.

- I can choose blemish cover or bandages in "flesh" color and have them more or less match my skin. (pp. 3–5)

Whiteness, then, is about not feeling the weight of representing an entire population with one's successes or failures. It's about not having to think about race much at all.

In recent years, however, awareness of Whiteness has been on the rise, as evidenced by the profusion of scholarship on Whiteness, the goal of which is to call attention to the social construction and ensuing privilege

Former Klansman David Duke stands under a Confederate battle flag. How was Duke able to cast the NAAWP as a pro-White movement instead of a racist organization?

of the category. Calling attention to Whiteness helps Whites understand how slanted the playing field really is. It also helps rectify something wrong with the way we study race in America: By traditionally focusing on minority groups, the implicit message that scholarship projects is that nonwhites are "deviant," to borrow from the Comte de Buffon, and that's why we study them. Even popular culture has caught on with memes like "stuff White people like," "columbusing," and "if Black people said the stuff White people say," which offer humorous yet pointed critiques of privileges that affluent White people tend to have in America.

But White consciousness may have another, more troubling side. In 1980, before White studies got under way in universities, the White supremacist David Duke left his position as the grand wizard of the Knights of the Ku Klux Klan and founded the National Association for the Advancement of White People (NAAWP), attempting to sugarcoat his racist movement with a seemingly more politically correct approach. In this new framework, Duke presented Whites as a besieged minority, writes sociologist Mitch Berbrier (2000), defining the NAAWP's mission as a pro-White heritage movement as opposed to an anti-Black one. Sociologist Abby Ferber has analyzed the clever appropriation of civil rights language in Duke's White supremacist discourse. For example, in an article by Duke in the *White Patriot,* Ferber finds the rhetoric of reverse discrimination, victimhood, and the right to cultural difference:

> [O]ur race and all others should have the right to determine their own destiny through self-determination and rule. . . . [E]very people on this planet must have the right to life: the continued existence of its unique racial fabric and resulting culture. (*White Patriot*, no. 56, p. 6, quoted in Ferber, 1999)

Sounds reasonable, right? That's because the new language of White supremacy allows racists to move away from explicitly racist language (of biological inferiority, for example). Duke's NAAWP also co-opts civil rights discourse, as in the organization's original mission statement: "The NAAWP is a not for profit, nonviolent, civil rights educational organization, demanding equal rights for Whites and special privileges for none."

Such examples demonstrate one possible outcome of the emergence of White studies: to politically empower extremists by giving them a legitimate language for their racist ends. Note, however, that this rhetoric does not acknowledge the advantages Whites typically enjoy. The power of White-ness studies is that it exposes the social construction of a seemingly natural (and neutral) category, giving a sense of the unequal footing beneath the labels "White" and "Black." (That is, Whites can embrace ethnic identity, but Blacks are stuck in a racial category.) But like any new "technology," such discourse can be used for many ends.

Inter-Group Relations

What are the *social* consequences of race? Scholars have defined four broad forms that inter-group relations can take: assimilation, pluralism, segregation, and conflict.

In the 1920s, sociologist Robert Park began to wonder what, on the one hand, held together the diverse populations in major American cities and, on the other hand, sustained their cultural differences. He came up with a race relations cycle of stages: contact, competition, accommodation, and assimilation. His model, called straight-line assimilation, was at first accepted as the universally progressive pattern in which immigrants arrive, settle in, mimic the practices and behaviors of the people who are already there, and achieve full assimilation in a newly homogenous country.

Milton Gordon (1964) tweaked Park's model by suggesting multiple kinds of assimilation outcomes. For Gordon, an immigrant population can pass through (or stall in) seven stages of assimilation: cultural, structural, marital, identification, attitude reception, behavior reception, and civic assimilation (Table 9.1).

STRAIGHT-LINE ASSIMILATION

Robert Park's 1920s universal and linear model for how immigrants assimilate: they first arrive, then settle in, and achieve full assimilation in a newly homogenous country.

TABLE 9.1 Gordon's Stages of Assimilation

STAGES OF ASSIMILATION	CHARACTERISTIC
Cultural assimilation	Change of cultural patterns to those of host society
Structural assimilation	Large-scale entrance into cliques
Marital assimilation	Large-scale intermarriage
Identification assimilation	Development of sense of collective identity based exclusively on host society
Attitude reception assimilation	Absence of prejudice
Behavior reception assimilation	Absence of discrimination
Civic assimilation	Absence of value and power conflict

With Park and Gordon in mind, let's do a thought experiment. Imagine yourself as a Polish immigrant arriving at Ellis Island in 1900. You don't have much money, and you've come to America in search of opportunity; this is the land of plenty, so you've been told. You settle into a Polish enclave of Manhattan, where you connect with friends and maybe some family. You do your best to learn English. You buy a pair of riveted denim pants, popular among American workmen. You secure work in a factory thanks to your connections in the Polish community. After an initial period of tension and conflict stemming from job competition and housing constraints, you eventually are accepted by your Anglo-American neighbors, first by being allowed to join the workers' union and then—and this probably only happens to your children—by being allowed to marry into an Anglo family. By this time, you think of yourself as an American. Congratulations, you have reached Milton Gordon's final stage of civic assimilation.

Harold Isaacs (1975) noticed something that these theories of assimilation could not explain: People did not so easily shed their ethnic ties. Ethnic identification, among White ethnics and everyone else, persisted even after a group attained certain levels of structural assimilation. Clifford Geertz (1973) explained this persistence as a matter of primordialism—that is, the strength of ethnic ties resides in deeply felt or primordial ties to one's culture. Ethnicity is, in a word, *fixed*. If not biologically rooted, it's rooted in some other intractable source that Geertz reasoned must be culture.

PRIMORDIALISM

Clifford Geertz's term to explain the strength of ethnic ties because they are fixed and deeply felt or primordial ties to one's homeland culture.

The flip side of this argument came from Nathan Glazer and Daniel P. Moynihan in *Beyond the Melting Pot* (1963). Far from being a deeply rooted structure that kept people bonded to their culture, ethnic identification, they reasoned, persisted because it was in an individual's best interest to maintain it. They saw ethnic groups as miniature interest groups—individuals uniting for instrumental purposes, such as fending off job competition. Glazer and Moynihan believed that ethnicity was fluid and circumstantial. More recently, scholars have posited that ethnic identification is both a deeply felt attachment and an instrumental position that can change according to circumstance (Cornell & Hartmann, 1998).

PLURALISM

For most people, however, assimilation into American society is not so easy, and acceptance varies systematically. At times a pressure cooker has been invoked as a more appropriate metaphor than a melting pot. Park's model was useful in shifting attention away from essentialist explanations of the so-called innate differences among immigrants, but it suffers from several shortcomings. Most obviously, it does not apply to nonwhite immigrants, many of whom are not fully accepted into all areas of American society. Park's model also does not apply to involuntary immigrants, notably African Americans and some refugees. Ernest Barth and Donald Noel (1972) noted that assimilation is not necessarily the end result for immigrants. On the contrary, other outcomes such as exclusion, pluralism, and stratification are possibilities. And as others point out (Lieberson, 1961; Massey, 1995; Portes & Zhou, 1993), some immigrants assimilate more easily than others, depending on a variety of structural factors, like migration patterns; differences in contact with the dominant or majority groups; demographics including fertility, mortality rates, and age structure; and ultimately, power differentials among groups. This is the case for the "new immigration," which, in comparison with the earlier era of European immigration (1901–30), is a large-scale influx of non-European immigration that began in the late 1960s and continues to the present (Figure 9.2).

The new immigrants, largely from Hispanic and Asian countries, are racialized as nonwhites—even though Asians are widely considered a "model minority." They therefore are subject to a different set of conditions for assimilating and face greater obstacles to their upward mobility (Massey, 1995). For example, Portes and Zhou (1993) report that the children of Haitian immigrants living in Miami's Little Haiti are at high risk for downward mobility because they face social ostracism from their own ethnic community if they choose to adopt the outlook and cultural ways of native-born Americans. Among Haitian youth, a common message is the devaluation of mainstream norms, and anyone who excels at school or abides by mainstream rules runs the risk of being shunned for "acting White." This picture of assimilation is much more complex than Park's initial formulation.

A society with several distinct ethnic or racial groups is said to exhibit pluralism, meaning that a low degree of assimilation exists. A culturally pluralistic society has one large sociocultural framework with a diversity of cultures functioning within it. This is the premise of multiculturalism in America. Statistically speaking, in a pluralist country, no single group commands numerical majority status. Switzerland, with its three linguistic groups—German, French, and Italian—is a striking example of ethnic autonomy and balance. Demographic projections suggest that Whites will make up about 46 percent of the US population by 2065 (Pew Research Center, 2015c). A broader definition of pluralism, however, is a society in which minority groups live separately but equally. Imagine America with no substantial stratification, no oppression, and no domination. In Switzerland, despite slight income differences among ethnic groups (with the exception of recent immigrant groups like the Turkish), no one group dominates politically, but the same cannot be said for America.

PLURALISM

the presence and engaged coexistence of numerous distinct groups in one society.

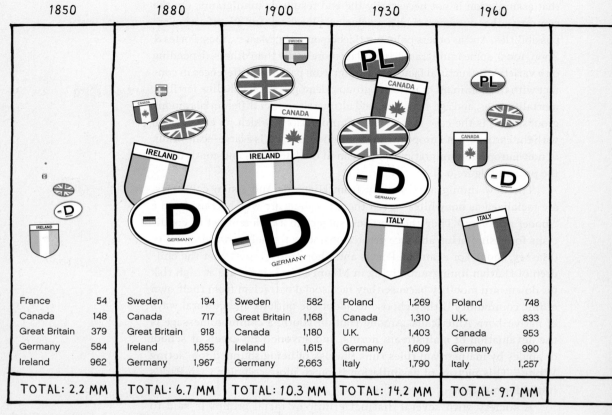

FIGURE 9.2 Five Largest Foreign-Born Populations in the United States, 1850 to 2018 (in thousands)

1850		1880		1900		1930		1960	
France	54	Sweden	194	Sweden	582	Poland	1,269	Poland	748
Canada	148	Canada	717	Great Britain	1,168	Canada	1,310	U.K.	833
Great Britain	379	Great Britain	918	Canada	1,180	U.K.	1,403	Canada	953
Germany	584	Ireland	1,855	Ireland	1,615	Germany	1,609	Germany	990
Ireland	962	Germany	1,967	Germany	2,663	Italy	1,790	Italy	1,257
TOTAL: 2.2 MM		**TOTAL: 6.7 MM**		**TOTAL: 10.3 MM**		**TOTAL: 14.2 MM**		**TOTAL: 9.7 MM**	

NOTE: The total numbers include all foreign-born populations, not just those in the top five.
SOURCES: Gibson & Jung, 2006; US Census Bureau, 2020k.

SEGREGATION AND DISCRIMINATION

SEGREGATION

the legal or social practice of separating people on the basis of their race or ethnicity.

A third paradigm for inter-group relations is segregation, the legal or social practice of separating people on the basis of their race or ethnicity. An extreme case of segregation was the southern United States before the civil rights movement. Under the Jim Crow system of segregation, reinforced by the Supreme Court's 1896 ruling in *Plessy v. Ferguson*, a "separate but equal" doctrine ruled the South. Strictly enforced separation existed between Blacks and Whites in most areas of public life—from residence to health facilities to bus seats, classroom seats, and even toilet seats.

Although the *Plessy* decision ruled that separate facilities for Blacks and Whites were constitutional as long as they were equal, in real life the doctrine legalized unequal facilities for Blacks. The NAACP has long recognized

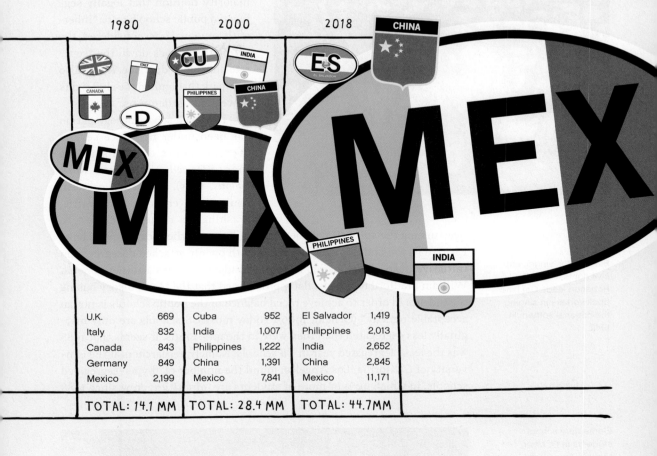

1980		2000		2018	
U.K.	669	Cuba	952	El Salvador	1,419
Italy	832	India	1,007	Philippines	2,013
Canada	843	Philippines	1,222	India	2,652
Germany	849	China	1,391	China	2,845
Mexico	2,199	Mexico	7,841	Mexico	11,171
TOTAL: 14.1 MM		TOTAL: 28.4 MM		TOTAL: 44.7MM	

that segregation and discrimination are inescapably linked. Nowhere is this clearer than in the case of education. Social science data consistently show that an integrated educational experience for minority children produces advantages over a nonintegrated school experience. School segregation almost always entails fewer educational resources and lower quality for minority students. (See Chapter 13 for more on racial inequalities in schooling.)

As Anthony Marx (1998) has noted, concern over segregation grew during World War II as America was caught in the embarrassing contradiction of espousing antiracist rhetoric against its Nazi foes while upholding an egregiously racist doctrine at home. America emerged from the war as a global force with heightened stakes for its world reputation; this new status, along with growing public dissent, perhaps helped motivate the Supreme Court's

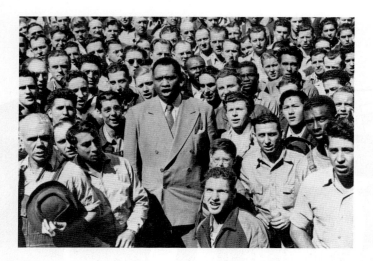

landmark 1954 decision in *Brown v. Board of Education*. The Court's majority opinion that legally segregated public schools were "inherently unequal" is considered the ruling that struck down the "separate but equal" doctrine. It was also the spark that ignited the civil rights movement of the 1960s.

However, school desegregation has been under fire since several Supreme Court decisions in the 1990s (*Dowell*, 1991; *Pitts*, 1992; *Jenkins*, 1995). Two 2007 cases in Louisville, Kentucky, and Seattle, Washington, came the closest to overturning the spirit (if not the letter) of *Brown*. Earlier, former presidents Richard Nixon and Ronald Reagan had both openly attacked desegregation initiatives, especially busing. In 1981, President Reagan's attorney general, William Bradford Reynolds, flatly proclaimed that the "compulsory busing of students in order to achieve racial balance in the public schools is not an acceptable remedy" (Orfield, 1996). Today most US schools are only marginally less segregated than they were in the mid-1960s. It seems that 1988 was the least segregated year in US schools. Namely, researchers at the University of California, Los Angeles, found the number of "hyper-segregated schools, in which 90% or more of students are minorities, grew since 1988

Black actor, singer, and civil rights leader Paul Robeson leads Oakland dockworkers in singing the national anthem in 1942.

Elementary school students in Ft. Myer, Virginia, face each other on the first day of desegregation.

from 5.7% to 18.4%" (Orfield et al., 2016). School segregation is invariably linked to poverty, which is perpetuated by residential segregation, and perhaps this issue is the one we should be addressing if we are concerned about mitigating racial disparities.

In 1968, under President Lyndon B. Johnson's initiative, the Kerner Commission reported that despite the civil rights movement sweeping the nation, America was split into two societies: "one Black, one White—separate and unequal." The main reason for the fissure was

In 1942, a race riot broke out in Detroit, Michigan, during an attempt by White residents to force African Americans out of the neighborhood.

residential segregation, what sociologist Lawrence Bobo (1989) has termed the "structural linchpin of American racial inequality." Residential segregation, scholars argue, maintains an urban underclass in perpetual poverty by limiting its ties to upwardly mobile social networks, which connect people to jobs and other opportunities. When you live in the ghetto, your chances of landing a good job through your social network are indeed slim (Wilson, 1987).

It has also been suggested that residential segregation inflicts poverty through a "culture of segregation" (Massey & Denton, 1993). According to this argument, you live in a ghetto that's extremely isolated from the outside world—no family restaurants like the Olive Garden, no mainstream bank branches, not even a chain grocery store that sells fresh vegetables. You're surrounded daily by the ills that accompany poverty: poor health, joblessness, out-of-wedlock children, welfare, educational failure, a drug economy, crime and violence, and in general, social and physical deterioration. In the ghetto, the most extreme form of residential segregation, you come to believe that this is all there is to life; the social ills become normative. It's no big deal to sell drugs, drop out of school, depend on welfare, or run with a gang. You slide into the very behaviors that, in turn, reproduce the spiral of decline of your neighborhood.

Whether you buy this line of thought or not (and this viewpoint has been criticized as being overly deterministic), consider how a segregated neighborhood got that way in the first place. It didn't just pop up out of nowhere, nor was it always there. As Douglas Massey and Nancy Denton (1993) have argued, the ghetto was deliberately and systematically constructed by Whites to keep Blacks locked into their (unequal) place. Before 1900, Blacks faced job discrimination but relatively little residential segregation. Blacks and Whites lived side by side in urban centers, as the index

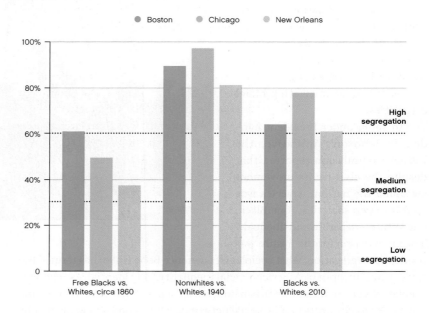

FIGURE 9.3 Index of Racial Dissimilarity

● Boston ● Chicago ● New Orleans

High
segregation

Medium
segregation

Low
segregation

Free Blacks vs.
Whites, circa 1860

Nonwhites vs.
Whites, 1940

Blacks vs.
Whites, 2010

NOTE: The index of dissimilarity measures the degree of segregation in a given city. A value under 30 is low, one between 30 and 60 is medium, and one over 60 is high.
SOURCES: Massey & Denton, 1993; Brookings Institution, 2010.

of dissimilarity numbers in Figure 9.3 show. The index of dissimilarity, the standard measure of segregation, captures the degree to which Blacks and Whites are evenly spread among neighborhoods in a given city. The index tells you the percentage of nonwhites who would have to move in order to achieve residential integration.

Various structural changes—industrialization, urbanization, the influx to the North of Southern Blacks who competed with huge waves of European immigrants—led to increased hostility and violence toward Blacks, who found themselves shut out of both White jobs and White neighborhoods. The color line, previously more flexible and fuzzy, hardened into a rigid boundary between Black and White.

The Black ghetto was manufactured by Whites through a set of deliberate, conscious practices. Boundaries separating Black neighborhoods were policed by Whites, first with the threat of violence and periphery bombings in the 1920s and then with "neighborhood associations" that institutionalized housing discrimination. Property owners signed secret agreements promising not to allow Blacks into their domain. When a Black family did move to a neighboring block, Whites often adopted the strategy of flight instead of fight, and this process of racial turnover yielded the same result: Black isolation. Even today, when a Black family moves into a White neighborhood, the property value declines slightly, in subtle anticipation of the process of White flight, which leaves behind a run-down, undesirable Black neighborhood—a veritable vicious circle. On the other hand, the formerly Black neighborhood of Harlem in New York City is now no longer majority Black, a consequence of the recent in-migration of Whites and Hispanics (Roberts, 2010).

Also helping create the Black ghetto have been specific government policies, such as those of the Home Owners' Loan Corporation (HOLC), which in the early 1930s granted loans to homeowners who were in financial trouble. The HOLC also instituted the practice of "redlining," which declared inner-city, Black neighborhoods too much of a liability and ineligible for aid. Following the HOLC's lead, the US Federal Housing Administration and the Veterans Administration—both of which were designed to make home ownership a reality for struggling Americans—funneled funds away from Black areas and predominantly into White suburbs. Finally, by the 1950s, urban slums were being razed in the name of "urban renewal," which essentially became a program of removal, as African Americans were relocated to concentrated public housing projects (Massey & Denton, 1993). These deliberately discriminatory policies are perpetuated today by de facto segregation in the form of continued suburban White flight and the splintering of school districts along racial lines.

Some scholars argue that a new form of segregation has emerged in America: the criminal justice system. During the 1960s, Blacks were slightly over-represented in the nation's prisons, but in absolute numbers there were many more White felons, because Whites made up a larger percentage of the total US population. Today the racial distribution in jails and prisons is the reverse. Blacks and Latinxs now make up the majority of incarcerated people. Recent studies estimate that nearly half of all Black men will be arrested before the age of 23 (Brame et al., 2014). Is imprisonment just another means of confining the Black population away from Whites? Several scholars make this case, based on changes in drug laws that affect minorities disproportionately.

RACIAL CONFLICT

The final paradigm of race relations is conflict relations, when antagonistic groups within a society live integrated in the same neighborhoods, hold the same jobs, and go to the same schools. This was the volatile scenario in Rwanda in 1994, when roughly 800,000 Tutsi were murdered by Hutu, mostly by machete, in the span of 100 days. That's well over 300 killings per hour (Gourevitch, 1998). The killings, as well as the maiming and systematic rape of Tutsi women, were the culmination of more than a century of racial hostility that began with the Belgian colonization of Rwanda.

Belgian explorers, immersed in discourses of scientific racism, confronted two Rwandan tribes, the Hutu and the Tutsi, who for ages had been living and working together and intermarrying. Because of all their shared

social, cultural, and genetic heritages, scientists today cannot distinguish Hutu and Tutsi into separate biological populations. But in the late nineteenth century, the Belgians gave preferential treatment to the Tutsi, whom they believed to be superior to the Hutu. What followed was a brutal system of oppression in which the Tutsi dominated the Hutu. In other words, the Belgian imperialists racialized what was once an ethnic distinction by creating inequality and thus hardening the inter-group boundaries.

When Rwanda was granted independence in 1962, after a century of hatred brewing between the two groups, the Hutu took power under a dictatorship masked as a democracy, and their long-standing animosity simmered into an explosion in April 1994 after three years of failed crops. The result was genocide, the mass killing of a particular population based on racial, ethnic, or religious traits. The genocide, backed by the government and media, turned neighbors into murderers overnight: Friends killed friends, teachers killed students, and professionals killed coworkers. The Rwandan genocide was a stark reminder that when we speak of the myth or fiction of race, we cannot deny its reality in social life.

Tutsi troops overlook a pile of skulls that will be reburied in a memorial to approximately 12,000 Tutsi massacred by Hutu militias.

GENOCIDE

the mass killing of a group of people based on racial, ethnic, or religious traits.

Group Responses to Domination

There are several forms of response to oppression, four of which are briefly outlined in this section: withdrawal, passing, acceptance, and resistance. Although we tend to think of minority groups as being oppressed by majority groups, keep in mind that sometimes the majority are the oppressed group, as in South African apartheid, where 4.5 million White Afrikaners and British dominated 19 million Indigenous people.

WITHDRAWAL

An oppressed group may withdraw, as the Jewish population did after Nazi persecution in Poland. Before World War II, Jews in Poland numbered 3.3 million, the second-largest Jewish population in the world. Eighty-five percent of Polish Jews died in the Holocaust, leaving roughly 500,000. After World War II, violence against Jews continued, and many moved. These conditions, plus the bitter taste of Polish complicity in the Holocaust itself, caused many Jews to leave for good. By 1947, Poland was home to just 100,000 Jews.

Another case of withdrawal was the Great Migration of the mid-twentieth century in the United States. Blacks streamed from the Jim Crow rural South in search of jobs and equality in the industrialized urban North and West; an estimated 1.5 million African Americans left per decade between 1940 and 1970. The North opened opportunities to Blacks that previously had been violently denied them in the South, including economic and educational gains as well as the cultural freedom manifested in the Harlem Renaissance. But leaving the South did not always lead to immediate improvements. In their search for a better life, many African Americans found cramped shantytowns on the edge of urban centers, exploitation by factory owners looking for cheap Black labor, and increasing hostility from White workers. Racialized competition for housing and employment some-times led to violent clashes, such as the East St. Louis riots in the summer of 1917. The riots, principally involving White violence against Blacks, raged for nearly a week, leaving nine Whites and hundreds of African Americans dead. An estimated 6,000 Black citizens, fearing for their lives, fled the city, another stark example of withdrawal.

PASSING

Another response to racial oppression is passing, or blending in with the dominant group. For example, during his early adulthood, Malcolm X attempted to look more like White men through the painful process of chem-ically straightening or "conking" his hair. A more recent example was the pop star Michael Jackson, who underwent plastic surgery on his nose and repeated skin-lightening procedures. And an even more recent, interesting case is that of Rachel Dolezal, who was of White, European ancestry but tried to (and did for a while) pass as African American by altering her hair and skin tone. Her efforts were so successful for a time that she became president of the Spokane, Washington, chapter of the National Association for the Advancement of Colored People (NAACP). Once it was revealed that she did not have any African ancestry, she was dubbed the "undisputed heavyweight champion of racial appropriation" (Vestal, 2017). She then lost her leadership position in the Spokane chapter of the NAACP as well as her job teaching in the Africana Studies department at Eastern Washington University (Samuels, 2015).

Passing is not necessarily about physical changes, though. One of the most common ways people have tried to pass has been to change their surnames. The single largest ethnic group in the United States today is German Americans. Not English, but German. Where, do you ask, are all the Schmidts and Muellers? They now go by Smith and Miller, after a huge wave of name changing among German Americans during the world wars—if not during the first one, then often by the time of the second.

ACCEPTANCE VERSUS RESISTANCE

Another response is acceptance, whereby the oppressed group feigns compliance and hides its true feelings of resentment. In Erving Goffman's (1959) terms, members of this group construct a front stage of acceptance, often using stereotypes to their own advantage to "play the part" in the presence of the dominant group (see Chapter 4). Backstage, however, privately among their subaltern or oppressed group, they present a very different self. Sociologist Elijah Anderson refers to this as "code-switching," a strategy used by African Americans in the presence of dominant White society. In Anderson's ethnography of a Black neighborhood in Philadelphia, Blacks learn two languages, one of the street and one of mainstream society, and daily survival becomes a matter of knowing which one to speak at the right time. For an inner-city youth, an act of code-switching could be as simple as putting on a leather jacket and concealing his textbook beneath it for the walk home from school (Anderson, 1999). (Code-switching is akin to the double consciousness that W. E. B. Du Bois ascribed to African Americans who maintain two behavioral scripts; see Chapter 1.)

A more overt form of resistance, the fourth paradigm of group responses to domination, would be collective resistance through a movement such as revolution or genocide or through nonviolent protest as in the US civil rights movement (see Chapter 18 for a discussion of social movements).

Prejudice, Discrimination, and the New Racism

On the individual level, racism can manifest itself as prejudice or discrimination. Prejudice refers to thoughts and feelings about an ethnic or racial group, whereas discrimination is an act. Robert Merton (1949a) developed a diagram for thinking about the intersections of prejudice and discrimination (Figure 9.4). One who holds prejudice and discriminates is an "active bigot." This is the prototypical racist who puts his money (or burning cross) where his (or her) mouth is. Those who are neither prejudiced nor discriminatory are "all-weather liberals," not only espousing ideologies of racial equality or talking the talk, but also walking the walk when faced with real choices.

SUBALTERN

a subordinate, oppressed group of people.

COLLECTIVE RESISTANCE

an organized effort to change a power hierarchy on the part of a less powerful group in a society.

PREJUDICE

thoughts and feelings about an ethnic or racial group, which lead to preconceived notions and judgments (often negative) about the group.

DISCRIMINATION

harmful or negative acts (not mere thoughts) against people deemed inferior on the basis of their racial category, without regard to their individual merit.

FIGURE 9.4 Merton's Chart of Prejudice and Discrimination

ACTIVE BIGOT (PREJUDICED-DISCRIMINATES)	TIMID BIGOT (PREJUDICED)
FAIR-WEATHER LIBERAL (DISCRIMINATES)	ALL-WEATHER LIBERAL

SOURCE: Merton, 1949a.

Many people fall between these two stances. A "timid bigot" is one who is prejudiced but does not discriminate—a closet racist perhaps, who backs down when confronted with an opportunity for racist action. Conversely, one who is not prejudiced but does discriminate is termed a "fair-weather liberal." Despite the fair-weather liberal's inner ideological stance in favor of racial equality, he or she still discriminates, perhaps without knowing it. For instance, a couple who consider themselves open-minded about race relations may feel compelled to sell their home as soon as they are confronted with new Black neighbors (White flight, as discussed earlier). Of course, they do not cite residential integration as their motivation for leaving, but instead offer an excuse that has embedded racist reasons, such as the differences in school districts. In fact, the prime time for families to move out of integrated neighborhoods happens to be around the time when the eldest child of the family turns five and begins school.

Active bigots are rarer to come by, because prejudicial viewpoints are largely unacceptable in most of the ostensibly antiracist West. But don't be fooled into thinking that race doesn't matter anymore. It does, and racism is still alive and going strong, although it's veiled in different terms. You just have to know how to look for it. Old-fashioned, overt racism tended to convey three basic ideas: Humans are separable into distinct types; they have essential traits that cannot be changed; and some types of people are just better than others. Not many people openly make such claims in America today, as they tend to be frowned on.

As this old kind of racism declines, race scholars are beginning to find traces of a new kind of racism gaining ground. Eduardo Bonilla-Silva calls this "color-blind racism." According to Howard Winant (2001), such new racial hegemony comes with "race-neutral" rhetoric and relies more on culture and nationality to explain differences between nonwhites and Whites than

COLOR-BLIND RACISM

the view that racial inequality is perpetuated by a supposedly color-blind stance that ends up reinforcing historical and contemporary inequities, disparate impact, and institutional bias by "ignoring" them in favor of a technically neutral approach.

Right-wing National Democratic Party members protest immigration and refugee policies in Germany. How is this an example of cultural racism?

immutable physical traits. The new line of thinking replaces biology with culture and presumes that there is something fixed, innate, and inferior about nonwhite cultural values. In America, this kinder, gentler anti-Black ideology is characterized by the persistence of negative stereotyping, the tendency to blame nonwhites for their own problems, and resistance to affirmative action policy (Bobo et al., 1997). (Remember the policy on class-based affirmative action in Chapter 7? This is a good time to refresh your memory.) The irony is that since the civil rights triumphs of the 1960s, the official stance of formal equality has brought about subtler forms of prejudice and discrimination, making it harder to tackle racism and inequality. When a state proclaims racial equality, White privilege is let off the hook and goes unnoticed.

Likewise, in the new color-blind Europe, argues Neil MacMaster (2001), a "differentialist" or "cultural" racism has taken hold. Characteristic of cultural racism is the call to protect national (White) identity from "criminal" and polluting cultural outsiders, constructing an image of "fortress Europe." Antirefugee commentary is one example of the new racist ideology. For example, in a televised speech in 1978, Margaret Thatcher made the following appeal to cultural purity in regard to 4 million immigrants from recently decolonized countries: "Now that is an awful lot, and I think it means that people are really rather afraid that this country might be swamped by people with a different culture" (MacMaster, 2001). In France, for example, the government does not collect information about race, but social scientists have conducted experiments by sending in job applications with identical résumés other than the names being changed. They show that, with all else equal, those with Arab- (Adida et al., 2010) or North African- (Pierné, 2013) sounding names get fewer callbacks. Racism can exist even when race does not officially exist.

How Race Matters: The Case of Wealth

Nonwhites, especially African Americans, Latinxs, and Native Americans, lag behind Whites on a number of social outcomes, from income and educational attainment to crime rates and infant mortality rates. For example, Blacks are half as likely as Whites to graduate from college or hold a professional or managerial job and are twice as likely to be unemployed and to die before their first year of life. As striking as the figures are, if there is one statistic that captures the persistence of racial inequality in the United States, it is net worth. If you want to determine your net worth, all you have to do is add up everything you own and subtract from this figure the total amount of your outstanding debt. When you do this for nonwhite and White families, the differences are glaring. So while most of America felt the impact of the housing market crash and 2008–9 recession, African Americans and Latinxs felt the blow far more sharply than Whites. Median wealth for Whites fell 16 percent, yet African Americans and Latinxs experienced 53 and 66 percent losses, respectively (Pew Research Center, 2011b).

Latinxs are a varied group, but their wealth measures are largely similar to those of African Americans, who had an average household net worth of $17,100 in 2016. The median Latinx family in 2016 had about $20,600 in net assets, and about one-third of both Black and Latinx households had zero or negative net worth. Compare those figures to the $171,000 in household wealth of the average White family (Kochhar & Cilluffo, 2017). We know considerably less about Native Americans because reliable data are lacking, but given that they have a poverty rate of 23.7 percent (compared with just 10.9 percent for Whites), their wealth is not likely to be high (US Census Bureau, 2020l). Asian Americans, however, have low rates of poverty (10.8 percent) (US Census Bureau, 2017h) and high rates of home ownership, at about 59 percent (US Census Bureau, 2020d).

This "equity inequality" has grown in the decades since the civil rights progress of the 1960s. What's more, the wealth gap cannot be explained by income differences alone. That is, the asset gap remains large even when we compare Black and White families at the same income levels. For many among the growing Black and Latinx middle classes, the lack of assets may mean living from paycheck to paycheck, being trapped in a job or neighborhood that is less beneficial in the long run, and not being able to send one's kids to college. Parents' wealth is also a strong predictor of children's teenage and young adult outcomes—everything from teenage premarital childbearing to educational attainment to welfare dependency (Conley, 1999).

Equity inequality captures the historical disadvantage of minority groups and the way those disadvantages accrue over time. The institutional barriers to Blacks acquiring property, discussed earlier, were only one such mechanism. These included redlining by banks (whereby loans, especially mortgages, were not given in predominantly Black neighborhoods seen as higher-risk), racially restrictive covenants (whereby owners had to agree to sell their homes to only Whites), and Blacks' disproportionate exclusion from government benefits such as FHA and VA mortgages and Social Security retirement pensions (agricultural and domestic workers, who were largely Black, were initially excluded from these programs; Truman corrected this).

Similar processes and policies have decimated the wealth of Native Americans, who went from living off the land (the entire US territory) to being disproportionately impoverished and dispossessed over the course of a century by exploitative US policies. One of the most telling examples of this sort of institutionalized dispossession happened to Japanese Americans. As skilled farmers, Japanese immigrants accrued enough wealth in the early twentieth century to attract resentment, culminating in the 1924 Alien Land Act, which prohibited noncitizens from owning land. Japanese immigrants then found success in business, running nurseries and selling cut flowers, and amassed considerable wealth by 1941, about $140 million cumulatively (Lui, 2004). When World War II broke out and panic spread over the possibility of a treacherous Japanese population in America, the Roosevelt administration mandated a program of internment by Executive Order 9066. Japanese American citizens were placed into camps in the western part of the United States. They were given only a week to dispose of all their assets, forcing them to sell their homes and businesses to Whites at scandalously low prices (Lui, 2004). The result was a huge forced transfer of wealth from Japanese to Whites under discriminatory government policy.

What were the consequences of the Japanese internment camps? How are they an example of equity inequality?

Japanese Americans still alive at the time were paid reparations in 1988. Some have argued for a similar policy to compensate African Americans for the institution of slavery (and racially unequal asset policies since Emancipation). Each year, until his retirement in 2017, Congressman John Conyers introduced a bill to study the issue; so far, even the creation of a commission to assess the issue has been blocked. Meanwhile, the tax reform bill known as the Tax Cuts and Jobs Act of 2017 raised the amount of an estate not subject to taxes to 11.2 million dollars. Because the number of African Americans and Hispanics who would benefit is extremely small, it will serve to widen the already large racial wealth gap.

In summary, policies intending to address disparities between nonwhites and Whites must take into account the extreme wealth gap and its historical trajectory. Affirmative action that is aimed at improving wages and increasing job openings for Blacks, Hispanics, and Native Americans can address only a piece of a larger cycle of wealth inequality. Income from work provides for the day-to-day, week-to-week expenses; wealth is the stuff long-term upward mobility is made of.

INSTITUTIONAL RACISM

Another cause of the asset inequality discussed in this chapter is the simple fact that property in Black neighborhoods doesn't accrue value at the same rate as that in mostly White areas. Property reflects only the value accorded to it in the marketplace. In this vein, when a neighborhood's housing values precipitously decline as the proportion of Black residents rises, the price changes provide a record of the economic value of "Blackness." And it does not take any "active bigots" or otherwise racist individuals to generate this phenomenon. Namely, aside from any personal ideology, Whites have an economic incentive to sell when they sense a neighborhood starting to integrate, as evidence shows that once a neighborhood reaches somewhere between 5 and 20 percent Black, it quickly becomes predominantly Black due to a rash of selling (with an accompanying drop in values) (Card et al., 2008). This expectation means that it is rational for Whites to be the first to sell as Blacks increase in numbers in a given area in order to prevent a loss of equity. This, of course, becomes a self-fulfilling prophecy and a vicious circle linking race and property values—to the disadvantage of Blacks. (Meanwhile, property value does not follow the same clear-cut pattern for other ethnic minorities, although minority enclaves generally have lower real estate values than exclusively White neighborhoods.)

The case of race and property values is an example of institutional racism—institutions and social dynamics that may seem race-neutral but actually end up disadvantaging minority groups. Another example is provided by sentencing laws for dealing or consuming cocaine. At the height of a period of panic over crack cocaine infiltrating neighborhoods, the United States passed the Anti–Drug Abuse Act of 1986. This law declared that for sentencing purposes, 1 gram of crack cocaine was equivalent to 100 grams of powdered cocaine. The result was a mandatory minimum sentence of five years for a first-time possession charge for a typical crack user. Because crack was cheaper and more prevalent in low-income, predominantly Black communities, the result was a huge racial disparity in drug sentences by race. President Obama addressed this issue in 2010 by signing the Fair Sentencing Act, which reduced the sentencing ratio between powder cocaine and crack from 100-to-1 to 18-to-1. This ratio, while an improvement, still leaves a significantly disparate impact by race (Davis, 2011).

Given the role of drug prosecutions as a lynchpin of institutional racism in the criminal justice system, one might think that legalization would be a way to

INSTITUTIONAL RACISM

institutions and social dynamics that may seem race-neutral but actually disadvantage minority groups.

eliminate such disparate impact. However, if we look at the case of marijuana, we can see that institutional racism can even color decriminalization efforts. Blacks and Whites use marijuana at similar rates, but Blacks are up to eight times more likely to be arrested for possession thanks to who gets targeted by police and where and how the drug is consumed (American Civil Liberties Union, 2013). Such disparities continue into an age of semi-legalization. That is, to be legal, marijuana must be consumed in your home. But those who live in public housing or rental apartments that do not permit it tend to consume the drug outside, where they are vulnerable to arrest. In fact, in Washington, D.C., arrests for possession of marijuana almost tripled in the year after it was legalized there. Ditto for arrests for selling: Those affected are primarily Black residents. Meanwhile, when licenses were awarded to legal growers in nearby Maryland, Black companies were shut out since the commission awarding the contracts sought "geographic diversity." So the profits in what is likely to become a massive industry will be unequally distributed by race too (Milloy, 2017).

Yet another example of institutional racism can be found in the case of hiring patterns by employers. With limited information about job applicants, employers may be rational to use social networks to recruit employees since informal ties (i.e., references) can provide more reliable information about individuals than can be gleaned from paper job applications. And because Whites tend to hold more managerial positions, and social networks tend to be segregated by race, this need for additional information on the part of employers also perpetuates racial disparities with no racially explicit motivation.

A related dynamic is called statistical discrimination, where firms use race as a shorthand proxy for having attended poorer schools and having experienced other disadvantages that would lead to less productive performance. Although this dynamic is not completely color-blind, it is different from overt

FIGURE 9.5 An Ethnic Snapshot of America in 2018

White, not Hispanic
61.1%

racism in that the motivation is not about race per se but about underlying characteristics that tend to be associated with race. Finally, institutional racism can even be encoded into the educational system through test construction. There has been much debate about cultural bias in testing. Beyond this issue, however, is the effect of stereotypes on performance. The psychologists Claude Steele and Joshua Aronson, for example, have shown that they can drive Black students' test scores down just by priming them with negative stereotypes before they sit for the exam (Steele & Aronson, 1998). These are just a few of the ways race can continue to disadvantage certain groups even in an age when overt racial animus may have waned in significance.

The Future of Race

This brief overview of the history of race and its present-day ramifications allows us to make some guesses about the future of race. For starters, racial and ethnic diversity in America will tend to increase. The 2010 Census data show a 134 percent increase in Americans who identify as multiracial—that is, 9 million people (Pew Research Center, 2011). The number of foreign-born people in the United States surpassed 37 million (US Census Bureau, 2010a). And according to National Research Council projections, by the year 2060, largely thanks to the most recent wave of immigration (along with differential fertility rates), America's Latinx and Asian populations will triple, making up about 28.6 percent and 11.7 percent of the US population, respectively (Colby & Ortman, 2015). No longer Black and White, America is now a society composed of multiple ethnic and racial groups with an ever-shifting color line marking fuzzy boundaries (Figure 9.5).

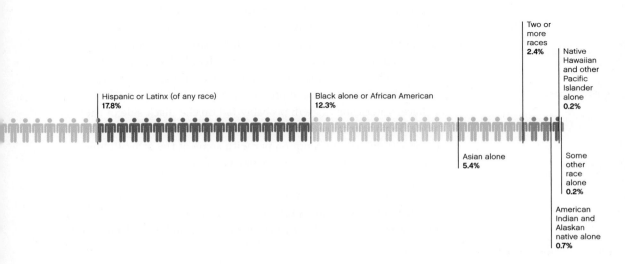

Hispanic or Latinx (of any race)
17.8%

Black alone or African American
12.3%

Asian alone
5.4%

Two or more races
2.4%

Native Hawaiian and other Pacific Islander alone
0.2%

Some other race alone
0.2%

American Indian and Alaskan native alone
0.7%

FIGURE 9.6 Race Questions from the 2010 US Census

9. What is Person 1's race? Mark ☒ one or more boxes.

☐ White
☐ Black, African Am., or Negro
☐ American Indian or Alaska Native—Print name of enrolled or principal tribe. ↘

[ ][ ][ ][ ][ ][ ][ ][ ][ ][ ][ ][ ][ ][ ][ ][ ]

☐ Asian Indian   ☐ Japanese   ☐ Native Hawaiian
☐ Chinese   ☐ Korean   ☐ Guamanian or Chamorro
☐ Filipino   ☐ Vietnamese   ☐ Samoan
☐ Other Asian—Print race. for example, Hmong, Laotian, Thai, Pakistani, Cambodian, and so on. ↘   ☐ Other Pacific Islander—Print race, for example, Fijian, Tongan, and so on. ↘

[ ][ ][ ][ ][ ][ ][ ][ ][ ][ ][ ][ ][ ][ ][ ][ ]

☐ Some other race—Print race. ↘

[ ][ ][ ][ ][ ][ ][ ][ ][ ][ ][ ][ ][ ][ ][ ][ ]

In 1996, there was a Multiracial March on Washington in which multiracial activists demanded a separate census category to bolster their political claims and recognition. Although the movement did not result in a multiracial identity category, for the first time ever, the 2000 Census allowed respondents to check off more than one box for racial identity. The resulting multiracial population is currently estimated to be about 9 million, and those are just the self-identified people who checked more than one race box in 2010. The 2010 census also asked separate questions about race and ethnicity, which means that census data can now be used to examine some of the racial diversity within the Hispanic population, as well as some ethnic diversity among African American and White populations (Figure 9.6).

This so-called browning of America brings us to a new crossroads. The White–Black divide may become the White–nonwhite divide or the Black–nonblack divide. Sociologist Jennifer Lee has looked at just this question, and her research shows that the experience of first- and especially second-generation Asians and Latinxs indicates the new color line is Black–nonblack. What does this mean? In the simplest terms, it means that the biggest differences in demographic characteristics like income, educational attainment, and interracial marriage will be between Blacks and all other groups, while the distinctions between these other groups continue to narrow. Lee notes,

> If you look at rates of educational attainment or interracial marriage or multiracial reporting among Asians and Latinos, their disadvantage stems from their immigrant histories, and so with each generation you see outcomes improving. For African Americans, you see there's some progress, but it's not nearly at the same speed, and so what I see is [that] the divide is really Blacks and everyone else. . . . The one caveat I would add is that those Latinos who have darker skin, who are more mistaken for African Americans or Black Americans . . . will probably fall on the Black side of the divide. In part because of their skin color, but also because their socioeconomic status is not on par with some of the other lighter skin Latino groups like Cubans. (Conley, 2009j)

Lee points out that the biggest losers in this new configuration of race in America are likely to be—no surprise—Blacks, who may be blamed for their own poverty when compared with successful Latinx and Asian immigrants.

Lee cautions, "Someone will look at African Americans who have been here longer and who aren't attaining certain levels of mobility and say, why can't they make it? If race isn't an issue for Asians and Latinos, it shouldn't matter for Blacks. What I argue is that the stigma attached to Blackness because of the history of Blackness is so different; they are not immigrants. To compare African Americans to immigrants is never fair."

How close are we to this new Black–nonblack color line? At least four states (California, Texas, Hawaii, and New Mexico) are deemed "majority minority" states, where Whites are not the majority of the population within major metropolitan areas (US Census Bureau, 2010b). But let's not forget that racial categories are social constructions, not static entities. To claim a multiracial identity presupposes the existence of a monoracial identity, when we know no scientifically pure or distinct race of people exists. Similarly, the notion of a White minority presumes that Whiteness is a fixed racial category, whereas Whiteness has expanded to include groups that were considered nonwhite in the past and may continue to fold Asians and Latinxs into a kind of Whiteness that emphasizes symbolic ethnicity. Indeed, as Warren and Twine (1997) point out, as long as Blacks are present, a back door is open for nonblacks to slip under the White umbrella. For example, the Asian success story as the "model minority" is made possible by Asians' ability to blend in with Whites, because they are unequivocally not Black. We are at a point in American history when Whiteness may be expanding again, with Blacks, as always, serving as the counterweight.

Another consequence of the "browning of America" is the adoption by White nationalists of the rhetoric of minority status. Though it will not be until 2044 that Whites are no longer a majority—at which time they will still be the single biggest racial group at 49.9 percent of the population (Colby & Ortman, 2015)—that has not stopped many alt-right politicos from using the fears of being lost in the melting pot to bolster their political power very effectively. Once we actually do arrive at a population distribution in which Whites are a minority—though if history holds, likely a wealthy and politically

DIGITAL.WWNORTON.COM/YOUMAYASK7

To see my interview with Jennifer Lee, go to
digital.wwnorton.com/youmayask7

DIGITAL.WWNORTON.COM/YOUMAYASK7

To see my interview with Kevin Lewis, go to
digital.wwnorton.com/youmayask7

powerful one—it will be interesting to observe what kind of dynamics emerge. There are cases worldwide of what Amy Chua (1998) calls "market dominant minorities," such as Whites in South Africa, Chinese in Indonesia, and Indians in some Caribbean nations. When the minority group is the economically and socially dominant group, it is a delicate situation because blame and backlash can flare up when that country's economic prospects falter. For the time being, however, it is (some) Whites themselves who seem to be playing the part of aggrieved, oppressed minority group—at least at the ballot box.

That said, the changing nature of how we interact—or in this case, date—is also affecting race relations. Back in the day, so to speak, we were limited in our dating pool by who was in our local neighborhood or our social networks, whom we worked with, and so on. That is, we had to meet someone in person to be able to date them. Today, dating apps have, essentially, lifted those structural constraints on whom we can meet and date. As a result, it appears that interracial romantic contact has risen (though there is still segregation online). Sociologist Kevin Lewis found this to be the case when analyzing data from a major online dating site: "The punchline of that particular paper is essentially that people are a lot more open to interracial interaction than we might think—so long as the other person goes first. If someone from a different racial background reaches out to me, not only am I more likely to reply to them than you would guess based on my initiation behavior, I'm actually more likely, in the short term future, to reach out to other people from a different background." While Lewis notes that people are prone to reproduce the same fences in a digital space as they put up offline, his findings provide justification for the optimistic take that those structures need not be permanent (Conley, 2019c).

DNA DATABASES

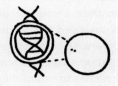

The #BlackLivesMatter social movement is a product of many social forces. There is, of course, explicit and implicit racial bias among law enforcement officers that causes racialized police violence. But there is an important role of technology in explaining how the issue of police violence became so big so quickly. First, there is the social media that allow what might have been local incidents to be strung together into a national awareness—not to mention acting as an organizing tool for actual protests. Perhaps the most important technological innovation contributing to the concern about racialized police brutality, however, is the cell phone camera. Urban theorist Jane Jacobs (1961) once talked about the "eyes on the street" as the primary means by which order was kept in cities. That is, there simply were not enough police to enforce good behavior at all times in all places. Informal watching of our neighbors along with social sanctions is what really kept order, according to Jacobs. But today it is more likely that the cell phones on the street matter most—at least when it comes to policing the policers. Has racialized police violence gotten worse or are we simply more aware of it now that almost every citizen has a handy-dandy camera at hand? Technology reveals—and may ultimately help resolve—a racial problem. One of the most debated policies around police behavior is the implementation of body cameras on police to keep records of interactions.

Seems like a no-brainer, right? But what might be the racialized consequences of this technological fix? Police, for instance, may avoid interactions with African American residents, fearful that any misstep might cost them their career if caught on camera. The potential result? Even less attention might be paid to segregated Black communities on the part of police. Some have argued that the huge spike in murders among African Americans in Baltimore in the two months after the anti-police riots of 2015 was the result of a police pullback reaction.

The point is that as long as race matters, seemingly "neutral" technology will be inflected with racialized power relations. Take another example: forensic DNA databases—the stuff of TV courtroom drama. Today, when people are taken into custody by law enforcement in most jurisdictions, a sample of DNA is taken from them. This DNA is then available to compare with all other criminal cases that contain DNA data. Many of the stories in the media are about DNA exonerating—often years later—wrongly convicted individuals. The Innocence Project—started in 1992 at Cardozo Law School—pioneered the movement to initiate appeals of flimsy convictions based on often-overlooked biological samples. And the success of the Innocence Project—along with its heart-wrenching tales of wrongful imprisonment—seems to suggest that civil libertarians should welcome this new era of forensic science. This would seem to have a racial-equality-producing effect by countering other forms of bias (say by juries) in the criminal justice system.

On the side of prosecutors, DNA has also been a boon where it has been available at a crime scene or obtained from a rape kit. Now suspects can be definitively matched to the scene of the crime via blood or semen, for instance. At first blush, then, it seems that DNA in the courtroom is an unalloyed good: It reduces the error term in an otherwise error-ridden system that relies on fallible human testimony and other less "scientific" approaches to establishing perpetrator identities.

But like most technologies, forensic genetics has a tendency to reproduce existing inequalities. If you are caught because you have a prior conviction and your bodily fluids at the scene of a new crime match those that are on file, that is unfortunate for you, but it is hard to make a case that it is inherently or systematically unfair. People who have committed prior crimes are more likely to be caught than those who are not in the system. However, if your brother or mother has been genotyped by law enforcement—even if you have led a squeaky-clean life until now—then you are also more likely to be fingered by your genetic fingerprint. That is, your DNA will identify you as a first-degree relative of your sibling. And that information, plus a little detective work, is almost as good as you, yourself, appearing in the data set. DNA fingerprinting can even identify cousins or grandchildren—although with less certainty. So if your relatives are more likely to have been registered in the database, you are more likely to be located, even if you yourself have no priors. Of course, in this case, the unfairness lies not in the fact that you were tripped up by your DNA but rather in the fact that the person who committed a crime who comes from a more advantaged background and thus does not have relatives in the database gets away with murder (literally or figuratively). Add in the sort of class or race stratification in the criminal justice system that is thought to exist, and you have a perfect storm by which DNA amplifies existing inequalities. In the United Kingdom, for example, 1 in 4 Black children over the age of 10 have their DNA in a database, while only 1 in 10 White children do (Doward, 2009). Multiply that out to their relatives, and boom, a technology that gets a lot of press for exonerating wrongly convicted minorities suddenly does more to add to the disproportionality in the system.

Conclusion

When you look at race using the sociological imagination, you'll recognize that it's hardly a cut-and-dried issue. You'll see the historical social construction of ideas and identities. You'll see the present-day realities—sometimes monstrosities—of an aspect of our lives so often called a myth or fiction. And you'll be equipped to look at the changing nature of race and race relations that will affect your future.

QUESTIONS FOR REVIEW

1. What does the childhood anecdote from the beginning of the chapter, about not yet having learned the meaning of race, teach us regarding the nature of race? Would a nonwhite three-year-old have brought home a White "baby sister"? How does this question bring up the "invisible knapsack of privileges" that puts White people at an advantage?

2. What does real estate value have to do with school segregation? With this link in mind, how have inequalities in wealth contributed to long-term inequality between Blacks and Whites in the United States?

3. Although the validity of "race" is debatable, why do sociologists study race as it relates, for example, to the likelihood of going to prison? What does this mean about what is "real," the way people understand the world, and what sociologists should study?

4. How has science been informed by culture (including racist beliefs), and in turn, how has science fueled racism?

5. As the saying goes, "You can't judge a book by its cover." How do eugenics and physiognomy contradict this saying (in regard to people)? Are the principles behind these pseudosciences still with us today? If so, in what capacity?

6. What is "racialization," and how has it differed between Muslims and the Irish?

7. How is stating your ethnicity more similar to stating that you like the Beatles than describing your race?

8. Which of the four forms of minority—majority group relations has recently been most prevalent in the United States and Rwanda, respectively? How have the minority groups in these countries responded quite differently to domination?

9. Thinking about the history of race, what do you predict for the future of "race" and "ethnicity" as social categories? Will they stay the same? What do demographic trends and history lessons suggest might happen in the coming decades in the United States?

PRACTICE

HOW SEGREGATED ARE YOU?

In recent decades, the United States has undergone what some scholars call "the Big Sort," whereby we have segregated ourselves by political views (think red state versus blue state) and are now clustered into communities of like-minded people. But as we separate into different communities by lifestyle and belief systems, does that mean that we are also living in more racially homogenous social worlds? There is some debate about the overall trends when it comes to racial segregation. By some measures, America today is actually less integrated across racial lines than it was 30 years ago; by others it is more so. It all depends on how we measure the phenomenon.

TRY IT!

Put your hometown's zip code into American Fact Finder at **data.census.gov**. (If you aren't from the United States, use the zip code where your college is based or pick your favorite five-digit number.) From the list of data sets, choose a recent estimate of racial and ethnic origin—a good one is the American Community Survey's "Demographic and Housing Estimates."

   Then compare the racial/ethnic diversity of your community to that of the country overall. Follow the same instructions above, except instead of your zip code, search for "United States" and pull up the same data set you used to measure the diversity in your community. I'll plug in my NYC zip code:

RACE / ETHNICITY	PERCENTAGE
WHITE	65.0
BLACK OR AFRICAN AMERICAN	9.0
AMERICAN INDIAN AND ALASKA NATIVE	0.4
ASIAN	16.8
NATIVE HAWAIIAN AND OTHER PACIFIC ISLANDER	0.0

RACE / ETHNICITY	PERCENTAGE
SOME OTHER RACE	5.0
TWO OR MORE RACES	3.8
HISPANIC OR LATINX (OF ANY RACE)*	17.3

*Remember that the US Census Bureau does not consider "Hispanic" or "Latinx" as racial categories. That's why most data sets include a breakdown of racial origin (e.g., White, African American, Asian), and a separate breakdown of Latinx or Hispanic origin.

THINK ABOUT IT

Is your hometown more racially homogenous than the national average? How do you think the results would change if you zoomed into your specific neighborhood or zoomed out to a wider view such as your metropolitan area or state?

The American Community Survey includes data over five years. Compare the diversity of your community today and five years ago. Is yours a community in transition?

SOCIOLOGY ON THE STREET

Decades after real estate segregation (or "redlining") became illegal, many Americans still live in communities that are highly segregated by race and/or socioeconomic status. How does unofficial segregation occur? Watch the Sociology on the Street video to find out more: **digital.wwnorton.com/youmayask7**.

WANT MORE PRACTICE?

Complete the InQuizitive activity for this chapter at digital.wwnorton.com /youmayask7

10

HOW DO WE HELP THE POOR WITHOUT CREATING PERVERSE INCENTIVES THAT INDUCE MORE POVERTY IN THE LONG RUN?

RICH IN RESOURCES

LIMITED RESOURCES

Poverty

Around the time President Lyndon B. Johnson delivered his first State of the Union address on January 8, 1964, declaring a War on Poverty in the United States, Marlin Card was conceived in a "real nice ride, parked at the top of a hill in Roslyn Heights in Long Island, New York." The car was parked behind Linden Court, one of a handful of public housing projects that pepper Nassau County's north shore. As Marlin's 19-year-old mother was experiencing the most intense period of morning sickness, toward the end of her first trimester, Johnson addressed a special session of Congress. On March 16, he declared, "Because it is right, because it is wise, and because, for the first time in our history, it is possible to conquer poverty, I submit, for the consideration of the Congress and the country, the Economic Opportunity Act of 1964." Johnson forcefully called for his economically progressive policy: "It charts a new course. It strikes at the causes, not just the consequences of poverty."

Poverty can be defined as a condition of deprivation due to economic circumstances; this deprivation may be absolute or relative but is generally thought to be severe enough that the individual in this condition cannot live with dignity in his or her society. Intended to combat such deprivation, Johnson's legislation added new programs to old ones and brought them all under a single umbrella, the new Office of Economic Opportunity. This 1964 legislation introduced Head Start, College Work Study, and the Job Corps, to name just a few of its many programs. It wasn't merely a reshuffling of existing government programs, the new president argued: "Rather, it is a commitment. It is a total commitment by this President, and this Congress, and this nation, to pursue victory over the most ancient of mankind's enemies" (Johnson, 1998). Nearly 50 years later, Johnson's words seem quaintly naive—and yet somehow still moving.

Which brings us to a question that is so deceptively simple at first glance as to appear silly: Does poverty matter? More accurately, would raising the incomes of the least well-off in the United States have any payback in terms

of breaking the intergenerational cycle of poverty, making the American dream possible for more of our citizens and, in turn, saving society money in the long run? Or are such endeavors just a waste of money? Even worse, does aiding the poor create more problems than it solves through unintended consequences? In other words, is poverty cause or effect? Some would argue that we still don't know the answer to these questions long after Johnson promised to eradicate poverty as if it were smallpox. But perhaps poverty is neither cause nor effect but rather a reflec-

↑

President Lyndon B. Johnson visits Inez, Kentucky, in 1964 to promote his War on Poverty and listen to resident Tom Fletcher describe some of the town's problems.

tion of an underlying social disease—namely, inequality and economic segregation. Significant new research suggests that this may, in fact, be the case.

This debate about whether poverty really hinders the life chances of low-income families or whether, instead, America is a land of opportunity and the poor are their own worst enemies, has continued to rage through Republican and Democratic administrations, through welfare expansion and retrenchment, and through research study after research study. This debate has brought us such terms as the "culture of poverty," "welfare queens," and the "underclass"; it led Ronald Reagan to wave a copy of the help-wanted section of the *Washington Post* during the recession of 1983, asking why welfare recipients couldn't find work when there were so many job listings; it led to Bill Clinton's "end to welfare as we know it" in 1996, which prompted his assistant secretary of health and human services to resign in protest; and it led to George W. Bush's strategy of promoting marriage as economic policy.

After six decades, it seems appropriate to reflect on the impact of the War on Poverty and on the science that undergirded it, then and now. Usually, such evaluations are performed through objective analyses of statistics and economics. But there is also value in mapping onto social policy a human life—particularly one that has been directly affected by the policy. In many concrete ways, Marlin's life has reflected American social policy since his time in the womb: He was fed by food stamps, housed by the Department of Housing and Urban Development (HUD), and shuttled through the low end of the educational system before being shuttled into the ever-expanding prison-industrial complex. Faces like Marlin's appear on right-wing literature advocating lock-'em-up-and-throw-away-the-key sentencing policies. It's life histories like Marlin's that liberals prefer to ignore in favor of talking about "working families," but such histories must be confronted to illuminate the nature of poverty in America. Like the rest of us, Marlin is a complicated character whose life both challenges and fulfills many of the presumptions of both the left and the right.

On August 20, 1964, the Economic Opportunity Act of 1964 was born (about nine weeks before Marlin). Thirty-eight years and much social policy later, I interviewed him for a book about sibling differences in economic success. He volunteered to participate in my study as a way to gain some intellectual stimulation beyond the legal research he was doing in the prison library for his upcoming parole hearing.

When I met Marlin, he was finishing a five-year sentence for burglary. He had been caught stealing from a stereo shop in Long Island. He has never carried a gun, never even hurt anyone, but has been a serial offender since his teens. Although born in rural Alabama, Marlin grew up in the public housing projects of New York City and neighboring Long Island. He had a younger sister who died days after her birth and a brother who died at 14 months. Marlin would have had an older sibling, too, if not for the back-woods abortion that he claims made his mother go crazy from infection at age 16. According to Marlin, his mother, Annie, spent most of her days man hunting, sipping homemade hooch from a mayonnaise jar, and waiting in line in a welfare office. She had one other surviving child—a girl she bore in her mid-twenties, despite the pain of the rheumatoid arthritis that she had already developed (made worse by her drinking). In short, Marlin is the product of the worst stereotypes of the urban American lower classes. Despite the fact that he suffered from a self-diagnosed case of attention-deficit hyperactivity disorder (ADHD), he always received high praise in school and the neighborhood for his abilities. "Marlin, you're real smart," he was often told, "but you're bad as hell and C-R-A-Z-Y." Those same admirers would be quick to add that it was not his fault but his mother's.

Regardless of who was to blame, as Marlin grew older, the combination of his keen intellect and self-assessed attention-deficit tendencies caused him to become bored and restless in his low-achievement school environment, he explained. The "crazy" part overtook the "smart" side. The result of Marlin's erratic behavior was that rather than being placed in a gifted program or given medication to treat his hyperactivity, he was transferred to what was known as a "600" school, a special education program for problem kids. He eventually worked his way back to the regular education system, albeit to the lowest tracks in some of the worst-performing schools in New York, but by then the damage was done.

Before Marlin had entered middle school, he had cultivated his own taste for alcohol. By high school he had started using cocaine. He had lots of reasons to escape, plenty of direct emotional trauma apart from the daily stressors of poverty. In addition to his mother's debilitating illness, his baby brother, Lew, had just died.

To support his growing drug habit, Marlin took to stealing, something he had learned from his mother. One Christmas, she told her kids to put on their winter coats and come shopping with her. Marlin wore a blue parka whose hood was trimmed with synthetic dog fur. The pockets had been torn out, which offered him easy access to the space between the outer shell and the inner lining. His assignment then was to appropriate the sugar, ketchup, and Kool-Aid needed for the family's Christmas meal. His brother, who wore a brown tweed three-quarter-length coat, also with synthetic fur lining, was to steal a family-size can of Spam. Their mother meanwhile had two dollars of food stamps to her name, with which she purchased a bag of onions and a sack of potatoes, providing her two sons with a smooth exit in the process. That Christmas, she also announced that because of budgetary constraints, she had decided they would become Jehovah's Witnesses, who, as a matter of doctrine, don't believe in exchanging presents.

Stealing, Marlin learned from a young age, was what you did to eat on Christmas—or any other time you didn't have a dime to your name. He never wanted to get shot or hurt anyone, so he robbed businesses rather than residences; he did not want to confront someone in his or her own home. "I don't want to wake up some Clint Eastwood in the middle of the night," he explained. Furthermore, because he believed that most businesses carried insurance, his victims seemed less real and personalized to Marlin—after all, he claimed, "They all got insurance to the max. Hell, I thought I was helping them out when sales were slow." Even after he kicked his drug habit during a prison bid in New Jersey, Marlin continued to steal electronics equipment and similar items, fencing them on 125th Street in Harlem. It was hard for him to stop. Certainly, as he was a felon without much formal schooling, it would have been difficult for him to get a legitimate job, but he also liked the thrill—the rush of putting on black sweats and a mask, sneaking into a store in the middle of the night, running from the cops, and negotiating for the best prices when he sold his successful scores to other shops that didn't hesitate to do business with him.

Marlin's case puts the central question of poverty up front: If society had increased his mother's income, would he have fared any better? Could he have been lifted out of a life of crime if his mother's financial struggle had been any easier? Or would such an effort have been throwing good money after bad? Was poverty a cause or an effect in Marlin's life?

The Culture of Poverty

In 1966, when Marlin was two years old, anthropologist Oscar Lewis published an article titled "The Culture of Poverty," which served as the capstone to a long career devoted to studying the lives of poor Mexicans (as well as some Puerto Ricans on the island and in New York City). The lives of Mexican peasants during the 1950s would have seemed to have little relevance to poverty in the United States, by then one of the richest nations in the world. But suddenly, the phrase *culture of poverty*, which Lewis had used to describe a supposedly self-defeating set of practices of a few Mexican families, took root in the American public consciousness. The culture of poverty argument was that poor people adopt certain practices that differ from those of middle-class, "mainstream" society in order to adapt and survive in difficult economic circumstances. In the US context, these practices might include illegal work, multigenerational living arrangements, multifamily households, serial relationships in place of marriage, and the pooling of community resources as a form of informal social insurance (otherwise known as "swapping"). Each of these cultural practices seems to be a rational response to a shaky financial situation; according to the culture of poverty theory, once these survival adaptations are in place, they take on a life of their own, and in the long run they hold poor people back when they are no longer advantageous.

Let's take swapping as an example of an informal social safety net meant to make up for the sizable holes in the official one. Neighbors, friends, and relatives exchange time, money, and other resources when needed to make up for temporary shortfalls. If I have a job interview, you might watch my kids for a couple of hours, but I'll owe you one. Or when you're short on food at the end of the month, I might give you some of my food stamps if I have come into some extra cash that week. Swapping works when times are tough but also may hold people back from making it, because this practice enmeshes people in many cross-cutting obligations of reciprocity from which they cannot escape. If I finally secure a steady job, I will probably find many people coming to my door in need. So why strive to outdo the Joneses? I would just have to support them anyway.

Lewis's hypothesis of a self-perpetuating cycle of poverty played right into the already raging debate over the ambitious social programs started in the 1960s—dubbed "The Great Society" by President Lyndon Johnson and his supporters. It seems that Lyndon Johnson's War on Poverty had in a short time engendered a sizable backlash. Researchers who felt that poverty was the cause, not the effect, of the poor's ills spent much of the next few years rebutting contrary claims implicit in the culture of poverty thesis. During this time, Marlin was tagging along with his mother to various welfare offices in downtown Brooklyn for her "face-to-faces"—the humiliating rituals that public assistance recipients have to go through in order to stay on the welfare rolls. The two would have to get an early start the morning of their appointment day because, by then, Marlin's

CULTURE OF POVERTY

the argument that poor people adopt certain practices that differ from those of middle-class, "mainstream" society in order to adapt and survive in difficult economic circumstances.

How did Oscar Lewis's study of Mexican peasants during the 1950s influence Americans' consciousness regarding poverty?

Becky De La Rosa (far left, on couch) and her best friend Malinda Puga (far right) sometimes watch several children, including their own, during the day to help out their friends and siblings. How is this an example of an informal safety net?

mother suffered from a severe case of rheumatoid arthritis. Marlin had to dress her before dawn so that they could secure a good spot in line. Even with such a jump start, they often spent many hours standing in various lines to comply with regulations. These obstacles aside, their mood would lift dramatically once she had "busted her digit"—that is, cashed her check. Busting a digit meant the end of the preceding week of "hard times," as they called the last week of the month, when the previous check had long since run out and the only provisions remaining in the house were typically a box of Quaker Oats grits, a light-bulb, and a gallon jug of ice water.

Welfare dependence was one of the supposedly self-defeating cultural practices of the poor. The notion was that reliance on the government created a sense of helplessness and dependency, and hindered entry into the formal labor market when the economy picked up. It is fairly obvious that welfare did hinder work, but perhaps not through any complicated social-psychological dynamic of "learned helplessness" or the like. Rather, it could simply be that once you are on the dole, you have to spend considerable time and energy jumping through the hoops that the bureaucracy requires of you—not to mention making those Quaker Oats grits last through the week while attending to the full-time rigors of child care and housework. So it's not so easy to secure a decent job (even if there is one to be had) when you have to spend entire days keeping appointments to get your kids' food stamps that month. In addition, the government offices administering food stamps or the Special Supplemental Nutrition Program for Women, Infants, and Children (better known as WIC) are open for only limited hours and often are not located optimally to serve the poorest areas. This lack of accessibility could partly explain why the 42.1 million participants in the food stamp program (now renamed the Supplemental Nutrition Assistance Program, or SNAP; US Department of Agriculture, 2018b) does not include another 17 percent of people who are eligible to apply (Gray & Cunnyngham, 2017).

Recently, I interviewed sociologist Mario Luis Small and asked him about the culture of poverty thesis. He has studied urban poverty for decades, enough time to consider the drawbacks and benefits of the culture of poverty argument. He notes that "this argument was rejected both empirically and theoretically . . . because there were a lot of empirical problems with it, conceptual problems as well," including a widespread concern that it made it easy to blame the victims of poverty for their inability to escape it. But, he argues, these problems should not have resulted in sociologists ignoring culture as an explanatory tool for research on poverty. When he teaches, he uses "a notion of culture as frames" that he derived from Erving Goffman. It goes like this: "Imagine a world in which everybody wears glasses. Nobody can see without glasses, and in addition, it's a world in which all glasses are tinted some color. Nobody has transparent glasses" (Conley, 2013d).

DIGITAL.WWNORTON.COM/YOUMAYASK7

You can watch my interview with Mario Luis Small at
digital.wwnorton.com/youmayask7

NEGATIVE INCOME TAX

Minimizing the stigma and hassle of welfare was among the many rationales behind the next idea in social policy: the negative income tax experiment. In the late 1960s and early 1970s, around the time Marlin was dressing his mother to wait in line at public assistance offices, the United States conducted its most ambitious social experiment to date. At several sites around the country, scientists enrolled poor people in treatment and control groups. The control group stood in line and got their welfare checks or their wages as before, whereas the treatment group received a guaranteed check, as in social democracies such as Sweden. In this *negative income tax* experiment, the government wrote checks to low-earning households in order to ensure that they had a certain minimum amount of income available. Once the households crossed the predetermined earning threshold, they were expected to start paying "positive" taxes. The research study began in 1968 across multiple sites in the state of New Jersey and then moved to Seattle and Denver in the early 1970s after some retooling.

The study's results confirmed the worst political fears of the left: In the treatment group, women left their marriages in droves because they were no longer financially dependent on a man, and unemployment spells increased in duration. (Of course, a number of feminists argued that providing some women with economic independence so they could escape bad or abusive marriages was a good thing; however, a policy that discourages marriage doesn't generally go over well in the United States.) For example, the

Stanford Research Institute found that in Seattle and Denver, the treatment groups experienced an average work reduction of 9 percent for men and 18 percent for women. According to analyst Jodie T. Allen, who wrote about the program in "Designing Income Maintenance Systems" (1973), these statistics suggested that as much as 50 to 60 percent of the money paid to two-parent families under a negative income tax would replace earnings so that people would work less. We might not be able to lift families out of poverty, but we could give them a lot more leisure time.

Recently, the idea of a universal basic income (a close cousin of the negative income tax) has made a resurgence in some progressive political quarters—in the United States most notably through the campaign of Andrew Yang who went from being unknown to becoming a top-tier candidate for the Democratic nomination for president by pushing a guaranteed $1,000 per month for every American adult (see discussion later in this chapter).

THE UNDERCLASS

For the next decade or so, as Marlin made his way through various public schools, there was silence from most poverty experts. In the meantime, however, real incomes had begun to stagnate (because of the 1973 energy crisis and a variety of other forces). By the late 1970s, inequality was sharply on the rise, welfare rolls swelled, and the crime rate had also turned sharply upward. By the 1980s, as Marlin started using crack cocaine, two more versions of the culture of poverty thesis had emerged. Writing in the *New Yorker* in 1981, journalist Ken Auletta inaugurated the concept of the underclass— the culture of poverty supersized for the 1980s. The underclass thesis states that not only are the poor different from the mainstream in their inability to take advantage of what society has to offer, but they also are increasingly deviant and even dangerous to the rest of us.

Poverty researchers were slow to respond. In the meantime, social critic Charles Murray argued that the underclass thesis was flawed: The poor are no different from the rest of us; they respond rationally to economic incentives. According to Murray, poverty per se is not the culprit, nor is the so-called culture. The poor, he argued in *Losing Ground* (1984), were the victims of an ever-expanding welfare state that provided the wrong long-term incentives. Welfare regulations made work and marriage less attractive and rising welfare benefits more attractive. To make his case, Murray pointed to the expansion of welfare over the same period that showed a rise in crime, the proportion of out-of-wedlock births, and the duration of unemployment. To bolster his claim, he rolled out the results of the negative income tax experiment. (See Chapter 15 for more on the modern welfare state.)

Social scientists who disagreed with both arguments found themselves trapped. To argue against the underclass concept, they had to show that the

UNDERCLASS

the notion, building on the culture of poverty argument, that the poor not only are different from mainstream society in their inability to take advantage of what society has to offer but also are increasingly deviant and even dangerous to the rest of us.

poor were no different from the rest of us but were merely responding to a lack of opportunity. But that view played right into Murray's thesis about the perverse incentives of welfare. My conversation with Professor David Grusky, director of Stanford University's Center for the Study of Poverty and Inequality, illustrates this dilemma (along with the opportunity that the 1996 welfare reform law provided):

> A long-standing argument against building a bigger safety net has been that it creates perverse incentives: that if we had an attractive alternative to the labor market, in the form of very substantial safety net resources, people would opt for the safety net instead of the labor market. It strikes me as highly implausible that anyone in a country like the United States that so values work would choose the nonwork alternative. I think that's implausible in the extreme. Now there were some situations in the old thinking of the past in which perverse incentives were created, and perhaps one could apply logic of that sort. But . . . for whatever you think of them, the Clinton Welfare Reforms eliminated most of those perverse incentives. And so I think it would be very old-fashioned at this point in time to worry about perverse incentives built into the safety net. (Conley, 2011c)

To pose an alternative to both positions—poor as deviant, and poor as rational followers of perverse incentives—prominent sociologists such as William Julius Wilson argued that welfare was really a minor consideration with respect to the labor and marriage markets in inner cities. Deindustrialization, globalization, suburbanization, discrimination, gentrification, and other factors were the real culprits, according to Wilson (1978, 1996) and his supporters, and the lack of jobs created by these factors led to a dearth of employed men for women to marry.

In the wake of Wilson's research, many poverty policy experts wanted to "make work pay." Hence the abandonment of dreams of a Swedish-style

PERVERSE INCENTIVES
reward structures that lead to suboptimal outcomes by stimulating counterproductive behavior; for example, it is argued that welfare—to the extent that it discourages work efforts—has perverse incentives.

DIGITAL.WWNORTON.COM/YOUMAYASK7

To watch more of my conversation with David Grusky, visit digital.wwnorton.com/youmayask7

welfare state in favor of targeted, work-friendly policies such as the expansion of the earned income tax credit, which eliminates some of the taxes that low-income workers have to pay. Politicians also pushed to raise the income limits on Medicaid, so that the poor would not lose their health insurance as they left welfare for the low-wage labor market. Finally, there was the 1996 Personal Responsibility and Work Opportunity Reconciliation Act (PRWORA), otherwise referred to as "the end of welfare as we know it." The PRWORA shifted more of the responsibilities of running welfare programs onto individual states, limited the number of months that a person can receive aid, and added other components to encourage two-parent families and discourage out-of-wedlock births.

One of the biggest changes in PRWORA was the implementation of work requirements for the receipt of welfare. After a certain period of receiving no-strings-attached assistance, welfare recipients would be required to perform so-called workfare. This work requirement came in the form of "make-work jobs," which get their name because their main purpose is not to provide the government with economic benefits but instead to provide recipients with the dignity and routine associated with holding a job. If you can work a make-work job, proponents reasoned, you'd have a better chance of getting a "real" job without depending on welfare. However, such workfare never really materialized because make-work jobs are costly to administer and states aren't mandated to implement them. Instead, work requirements in effect became a way to enforce much stricter time limits than the full

Workfare recipients build a fence in Los Angeles in 1997. Why do policy makers want to put welfare recipients to work?

five years recipients are supposed to have under PRWORA. It's a catch-22: Individuals who cannot find a job need to do workfare to keep their benefits, but the state does not offer any workfare slots. The result is that individuals get kicked off the rolls. Workfare—which as we've seen really boils down to a time limit—is also required of those who receive SNAP (food stamps), and the Trump administration tried to impose such work requirements on the Medicaid program as well (Super, 2018), though presently the policy is being challenged in the federal court system (Goodnough, 2020).

Through these changes to welfare and other benefits, all but forsaking poor adults in favor of the "deserving poor" or children, Democrats seemed to blunt the conservative critiques of perverse incentives in welfare. In lieu of universal health insurance, progressives pushed successfully for the Children's Health Insurance Program, or CHIP (a precursor to the Affordable Care Act, aka Obamacare). Instead of more income support for families, Democrats proposed establishing children's savings accounts that parents couldn't touch. As late as the 2000 presidential campaign, Al Gore argued for universal day care, the idea of making Head Start available to all American families, as was Social Security, and thus removing the stigma that derives from income requirements. After all, children shouldn't be held responsible for their parents' poor choices. Or should they?

About the same time that welfare reform went into effect, a new, almost fatal blow was dealt to leftists' arguments for an expanded safety net and a renewed focus on the well-being of poor children. It came from Susan Mayer, a sociologist who wrote *What Money Can't Buy: Family Income and Children's Life Chances* (1997). In it, she argued that the effects of income poverty on

Deindustrialization and globalization hit cities such as Detroit hard. There are about 18,000 abandoned homes in the Detroit area, a by-product of the rapid depopulation of the city since the 1950s (City of Detroit, 2019).

children have been vastly overstated. Study after study had showed that a childhood spent in poverty was associated with poor health, behavioral problems, bad grades, teenage pregnancy, and dropping out of school, and ultimately continued poverty as an adult. The correlation between family income and children's outcomes is indeed huge. But documenting an *association* (i.e., correlation) between two factors is different from showing that poverty *caused* all these social ills (see Chapter 2). This logic was exactly what social scientists had used to debunk Murray a few years earlier: Just because you can draw a correlation between welfare expenditures and out-of-wedlock childbearing doesn't mean that one is driving the other. Rather, it may be a coincidence, or both may be caused jointly by something else, like the underlying skills of the parents that lead them to earn more money and teach their kids well. (In the case of the welfare—marriage link, some scholars have argued that good jobs are the missing third factor.)

Mayer used a variety of approaches to distinguish correlation from causation when it came to the effect of family income. For example, she reasoned that if income really mattered in terms of school dropout rates, it should be family income before the age of dropping out that matters, not parental income afterward. But in her analysis, parents' income when a kid was in his or her twenties seemed to matter almost as much as parental income when that child was an adolescent, when he or she was at risk of leaving high school. Mayer smelled something fishy here. Likewise, when she compared different sources of income—from welfare, from earnings, and from investments—she found that earnings, the source most linked to successful parents, were more highly associated with positive outcomes for children, such as higher test scores and pro-social behavior. If it were truly the dollars that mattered for children, then investment income, gifts, and welfare dollars should have a positive effect, too, but they didn't seem to in her data. She also examined the association between parental income and certain purchases that are supposed to matter for young children. She found a relatively weak relationship between income and the standard measures that psychologists have used to rate the educational environment of the home, such as the presence of books, educational toys, and so on. Meanwhile, the household conditions that are highly responsive to income—such as money spent

According to sociologist Susan Mayer, how does poverty affect children?

on food, eating out, more spacious residences, and car ownership—were also weakly related to children's outcomes. In other words, what appears to matter for children is not money itself. Thus giving money to poor parents would seem like an illogical policy prescription.

Mayer didn't begin this endeavor with a political agenda. She had assumed her research would document that poverty mattered for children, not that the data would provide evidence to the contrary. She herself had been poor. As Mayer writes in the introduction of her book, "I've been poor and I've been not poor, and believe me, being not poor is much better."

THE BELL CURVE THESIS

In their best-selling book *The Bell Curve: Intelligence and Class Structure in American Life* (1994), Richard Herrnstein and Charles Murray came to policy conclusions similar to Mayer's—that the same traits that make adults economically successful make them good parents—in a more controversial and less nuanced fashion. Mayer focused on the likelihood that the same skills both lead to higher incomes and make for good parenting; Herrnstein and Murray went a step further, arguing that what really matters is good genes. In an interview in *Skeptic*, Murray explained what he meant, using the example of child neglect:

> Well, as every parent knows without reading anything about I.Q., there is a plausible relationship between intelligence and child abuse. Which is to say, any parent knows if a child has had a fever for 24 hours and hasn't been taking in liquids, you make a calculation that this has gone on too long and we've got to get this kid to a doctor, etc. Any parent knows that childproofing a home takes foresight and thoughtfulness—it takes a certain amount of I.Q. With that plausible relationship in mind, the failure of social science and politicians alike to confront the possibility that low I.Q. is an important risk factor in child neglect is scandalous. Every single bit of evidence that does bear on this says that I.Q. is a great big factor in child neglect. (Miele, 1995)

And where does a low IQ come from? Genes, of course.

According to Herrnstein and Murray, successful parents have fortunate genes and pass them on to their kids—whether or not they buy books or educational toys or stream Mozart throughout the house. Herrnstein and Murray also claim that as the United States has become more meritocratic over the last half century, fewer people with bad genes have risen to the top, and fewer with good ones have gotten stuck at the bottom. Thus the poor are increasingly hopeless because it is increasingly their genes' fault that they remain at the bottom of the ladder. So why waste any money helping them climb out of poverty, as it's bound to be futile? If either Murray and Herrnstein or Mayer is correct, it means that the advocates for prenatal care, child care, and reductions in child poverty, who argue that a dollar spent on early-childhood services yields several dollars of savings in the long run, are way off the mark.

The poverty research community once again found itself on the ropes. Just showing an association between growing up poor and any adverse outcome was no longer good enough. The ultimate gauntlet had been thrown down: Was poverty just a side effect of biological conditions or did it actually cause limited opportunities for children? Some sociologists and economists have responded by conducting experiments. The last time researchers ventured into the world of socially engineered experiments, the result was disastrous for progressive arguments for expanded aid to the poor. Why would this time be different?

MOVING TO OPPORTUNITY

In 1966, when Marlin was two years old, Dorothy Gautreaux, a resident in a project on Chicago's South Side, took part in a class-action lawsuit that alleged public housing was serving as de facto government-sponsored segregation. *Gautreaux v. Chicago Housing Authority* dragged on for 10 years in federal courts, finally working its way up to the Supreme Court. Before the Court could rule, attorneys for the residents settled the suit with HUD. As a result of the lawsuit, the government undertook a new social experiment of sorts: a housing voucher plan to help 7,100 families in public housing secure homes in the private rental market in the more affluent Chicago suburbs. The goal was to disperse at least 75 percent of the families into neighborhoods with less than 30 percent minority residents. In addition to the vouchers, the participants received counseling and rental referral services to help them locate available units. Essentially, it represented an end run to the years-long waiting list for the regular Section 8 program that provided poor families with subsidies in the private rental market.

The results of a study done decades later by Northwestern University sociologist James Rosenbaum (2000) found that those who moved out of the ghetto and into low-poverty areas had better employment situations, and their children improved on a number of indicators. The problem was that the Gautreaux Assisted Housing Program wasn't really an experiment: Families self-selected into the moving group, so there wasn't a fair comparison to a real control group. Furthermore, at the time of the second interview in 1989, researchers tracked down only 60 percent of the original group who had relocated, so some suggested that the better outcomes might be attributable to the fact that the people interviewed were those most successful in their new homes.

A subsequent study, "Moving to Opportunity" (MTO), attempted to pick up where Gautreaux left off. The sample of families was randomly assigned to move to a low-poverty area or, for the control group, to wherever they wanted (usually a high-poverty neighborhood). All efforts were made to track them down whether they stayed put or continued to move. In 1994, HUD secretary Henry Cisneros picked Baltimore, Boston, Chicago, Los Angeles, and New York as the sites where this experiment would be carried out. Seventy million dollars was authorized for the study, and more funds would become available for a 10-year evaluation.

Of the families that agreed to participate, one-third received no housing voucher at all, another third received vouchers with no restrictions on where they moved, and the final group—the treatment group—received the vouchers and assistance in relocating to rental units in areas with less than 10 percent poverty rates plus tutorials in basic life skills ranging from balancing a checkbook to yard work to lease negotiation. It turned out that those in the treatment group reported experiencing less stress from violence and other factors and were generally happier and healthier. Among children, the effects were the most dramatic: Test scores increased, school truancy dropped, and health improved; most notably, the incidence of injuries and asthma episodes decreased. The bad news was that there was little in the way of short-run changes in welfare use between the treatment and control groups (although overall welfare rates did begin to drop in the late 1990s) or in employment and earnings, which also improved for all groups thanks

The Cabrini-Green public housing complex in Chicago was infamous for both its high crime rates and close proximity to Chicago's Gold Coast and Magnificent Mile. Changing real estate values and public housing policies led to the demolition of Cabrini-Green, which was replaced by retail stores and mixed-income buildings.

to the economic boom of the 1990s. One limitation of the study was that it yielded findings only for families who had enrolled in the original study. We will never know about those families who would have been eligible for MTO but had either no knowledge of the program or no interest in it. Getting out of the ghetto may help only those poor families who want to leave and have the resources to remain informed about such opportunities.

When researchers revisited the families much later, they found that while the teenagers who had moved out as part of the experiment did not experience substantially brighter futures, their younger siblings often did. Kids who moved to lower-poverty neighborhoods in early childhood revealed huge opportunity bonuses while it actually hurt teenagers to move. Those who moved to low-poverty areas before their teen years were more likely to go to college and earned 31 percent more as adults as compared to their counterparts who did not win the "lottery." Meanwhile, teens in the treatment group (i.e., the lower-poverty group) suffered from incomes 13 to 15 percent *lower* than those who were in the control group. Moving during adolescence may be so disruptive that any positive effects of richer neighborhoods were more than made up for by the trauma of moving (Chetty et al., 2015). These findings about the importance of age differences in exposure to high-poverty neighborhoods were reinforced by a massive analysis of tax records that compared siblings among families who moved—the sibling who spent more years in a higher-income area did better on average than the sibling who spent more of his or her childhood in a higher-poverty zone (Chetty & Hendren, 2015).

Unfortunately, however, MTO also didn't answer the poverty question, because incomes were held constant and the social environment had changed. So it really was the converse study to the negative income tax experiment of 25 years earlier, in which social conditions were not altered but incomes changed. In fact, MTO may be viewed as a direct test of the culture of poverty thesis. Better outcomes among those living in low-poverty neighborhoods can come about because of more opportunity or more tranquility or both. The results of MTO appear to suggest that uprooting families from high-poverty, high-risk neighborhoods produces greater tranquility, if not greater opportunity (at least initially). That is, the main return on investment seems to be the outcomes that are the most sensitive to social or cultural conditions and the behavior of peers: violence, fear, stress, and child development measures. The outcomes related to economic opportunity, such as parents' success in the labor force, seem less responsive. Read as a whole, the results suggest that when poor people live together, each family's risk of adverse outcomes increases. Isn't that the culture of poverty argument made more empirical? After all, what's so bad about living with poor people if not their own behavior? It's hard to argue that cleaner streets, better garbage service, backyards, lawns, and better-funded schools made the difference. Probably more important is not having to worry about your neighbors shooting you when you step outside your front door. MTO's results serve as an indictment both of the social problems rampant in poor neighborhoods and of the larger society that has invested in gated communities, suburban sprawl, and other forms of economic (and racial) segregation. MTO seems to imply that if income is not the main problem, social division is.

As for income itself, there has been a series of smaller-scale experiments such as providing the poor with matching funds for savings accounts or offering private school vouchers through a lottery system. The best evidence about the impact of income comes not from purposive social experimentation but rather from accidental science—natural experiments that some researchers have exploited to examine the impact of income. Several recent studies that together form the best evidence on the impact of income concern gambling. Economists Guido Imbens, Donald Rubin, and Bruce Sacerdote (2001) surveyed lottery players in the mid-1980s and found that a modest prize ($15,000 a year for 20 years) did not have much effect on work behavior. A larger prize (around $80,000 per year) did reduce work hours by about 20 percent (reproducing the negative income tax's results). Perhaps the most interesting results were those showing that people with zero earnings, who were not in the workforce at all before winning, increased their commitment to work after receiving their prize, even if it was modest. This could mean that those at the very bottom face significant financial obstacles to fully participating in the economy. Maybe they use their winnings to buy a car to get to work, to put down a deposit on a home, or to simply stop wasting time in welfare queues and spend that time looking for a job.

To study the social effects of income, Guido Imbens, Donald Rubin, and Bruce Sacerdote surveyed lottery winners. What did they find? How does the survey of families receiving money from Cherokee casinos support their results?

Meanwhile, a study of lottery winners in Sweden showed that mental health did improve slightly after winning (Cesarini et al., 2016) while labor supply did indeed drop for winners (Cesarini et al., 2017).

Another study (Costello et al., 2003) concerned the lives of Cherokee children who had experienced a windfall in income thanks to legalized gambling on Native American reservations. Casino payouts in North Carolina lifted 14 percent of Cherokee families out of poverty. Among those families, children's behavioral problems decreased, largely as a result of the additional time that parents now had to supervise their children. Perhaps the negative income tax researchers were asking the wrong question 40 years ago; they should have focused on the children rather than the parents who received the checks.

With mounting evidence that income may indeed help children more than Mayer's study showed, some new income experiments are taking place. Finland, for instance, randomly provided about 2,000 of its unemployed citizens with a guaranteed basic income for two years in hopes that it can reproduce findings that nonemployed lottery winners work more after winning (Henley, 2018). Another study in the United States is providing 1,000 randomly chosen poor mothers of infants with $333 per month for the first 40 months of the child's life, while a control group will receive a token $20 per month. The researchers will conduct extensive screening of these children from cognitive testing to brain imaging to bloodwork to determine if there is a positive effect of relieving some of the family's economic stress (Duncan, 2016).

This new spate of experiments is very exciting to progressive activists who are pushing for a universal basic income (UBI). This is the same idea as the negative income tax, reborn in an era of automation and rising

At a 2016 rally for universal basic income in Switzerland, protesters wore robot costumes. Some estimates suggest that within just a few decades, artificial intelligence and robot automation could feasibly replace half of all human workers.

inequality. Leftists see providing everyone with a guaranteed income as a way to fight poverty and inequality while an increasing number of right-wing thinkers such as Charles Murray (2016) advocate for a basic income for a different reason: Doing so would allow the government to scrap all forms of income redistribution such as Medicare, Social Security, and all forms of welfare, accomplishing the same goals as the welfare state without its complex apparatus. Advocating for a similar policy caused Democratic candidate George McGovern to lose in a landslide to Richard Nixon in the 1972 presidential election. While UBI is not likely to become a policy reality any time soon (Andrew Yang's campaign notwithstanding), it is no longer a political nonstarter as it was for decades after the original negative income tax experiment.

THE WAR ON POVERTY TODAY

Today Marlin does not drink, smoke, or use drugs. He gets up early each morning to report to his temporary agency for employment. (He makes $7.25 minimum wage, although the agency probably charges his actual employer, a public housing project where he does maintenance work, twice that amount.) This is really his last chance to go straight; if he is convicted of a felony again, he will likely be eligible for Social Security the next time he is released.

Over dinner at White Castle, I asked Marlin whether he believed that extra money when he was growing up would have made a difference in his life. "My mother would have just drunk the money away," he confessed, scoring one point for the right. Then what would have made a difference? I asked. He thought for a moment, leaning back in the plastic booth we occupied, lacing his fingers behind his neck. "The issue is not money, the issue is time," he explained. "It ain't just a ghetto thing; kids all across America are being raised by Nintendo and TV 'cause the parents have no time for them." He explained that his new girlfriend's children were in this situation as well. She worked six days a week, leaving her kids in the care of their great-grandmother, who used video games and the like to create some peace in the household.

"Everyone is working all the time," he claimed. What about welfare? I inquired. "Welfare doesn't make a difference, you still gotta work, you still gotta do everything they want." Why were Americans working so hard? "Prices are so high. And everyone thinks they need all these things—the Nintendo, et cetera—so they are always stressed about money. It's like a disease, and as I said, it ain't just a ghetto thing." I asked him if that meant raising the minimum wage and implementing other antipoverty policies that could lower economic stress would make a difference. People don't need more money, he countered, just more time: quality time with their children. Maybe the negative income tax and lottery results were not so bad after all.

Maybe increased leisure and reduced work commitment would have paid off in the long run for kids.

On my way back to Manhattan—one of the most unequal counties in the continental United States (the borough is also known as New York County)—I turned over Marlin's comments in my mind. Back at White Castle, they seemed to make sense, and Marlin appeared to be almost a prophet about the state of America. But on the train, it dawned on me that his story didn't explain why rich kids still end up likely to be rich and poor kids more often grow up to be poor. So the next day, when he made his weekly trip to the wholesale district in the city, I asked him to elaborate. He claimed that it was because poor kids are not exposed to the horizon of possibilities: why they should go to college, what good jobs are like, and what living well actually means. Surrounded only by stress and frustrated expectations that are made only worse by our society's corporate-manufactured needs, "ghetto kids just do what they are exposed to."

Marlin Card and Susan Mayer may think along the same lines. *What Money Can't Buy* was about the impact of families' own money on their kids' life chances; Mayer's subsequent research addresses how "other people's money matters." She says that we face a choice in rich societies: Do we prefer a society with lots of equality, leisure, and social cohesion or one with greater inequality, less leisure, less cohesion, and a higher level of creativity and more goods and services? She claims that no clear answer exists, not for herself, for society, or even for the poorest citizens themselves.

In a personal interview with me a few years ago, Mayer concluded that "thinking about the meaning of money in a 'radical' capitalist nation like the United States is really very complicated and frustrating because it has so little to do with basic needs. The urge to want more seems so primal, and the satisfaction from having more is so fleeting, and for most of us, no amount of understanding the essential irrationality of it makes us want less." If there is one thing that rubbing elbows with the rich has taught Mayer, it is the limits of what money can buy—at least at the top. For the rest of us, all that money of those at the top may be what matters the most, even if it isn't ours, because it structures our society and our desires in ways that we aren't even aware of. It is not just poverty but poverty in the midst of growing wealth, especially ostentatious consumerism (see Chapter 3), that really matters.

If this is true, we are moving backward as a society with respect to economic opportunity by cutting taxes on the rich. Historically, high levels of income and wealth inequality mix with economic segregation (best embodied by the gated community or the exclusive apartment building) to create a noxious potion for the poor among us. It means that those at the bottom—and perhaps even the middle—have to travel farther and farther to reach their low-wage jobs servicing the needs of the wealthy. This intersection of inequality and real estate has reached absurd dimensions in Aspen, Colorado, where tourist industry workers often drive hours in their daily commutes to the ski resort; hence economist Robert Frank's term the "Aspen effect" (2007). One of the security guards at my office wakes at 4:00 each morning to ride a bus through three states to reach his job by 8:00, so that he can own a home with a backyard and send his kids to decent schools. Of course, if time supervising children is what helps break the cycle of poverty, these daily marathons may do more harm than they are worth.

While the Aspen effect forces families to move far away from their jobs in order to live in an acceptable and affordable neighborhood, sociologist Matthew Desmond has noticed another trend hitting low-income families hard: eviction. Desmond found that median rents were rising considerably; "in some areas of the country they went up 70 percent, 90 percent" from the mid-1990s through the decade of the 2000s (Conley, 2013e). But incomes were flat, especially for those at the bottom of the pay scale, so renters were paying bigger and bigger percentages of their income just to stay in place. At the same time, public assistance programs were scaled back. The result, Desmond explained, is that "most low-income families are living unassisted in the private market and that results in lots of evictions and forced moves and . . . families paying 50, 60, even 80 percent of their income just to rent a place in some of our cities' worst neighborhoods." Not only does eviction "go on your record like a criminal charge," preventing you from getting public assistance to get a new place and allowing your next landlord to pass you over for someone who has never been evicted, but if you get evicted you are more likely to lose your job too. After spending weeks in housing court watching eviction proceedings, Desmond hypothesizes that people going through eviction proceedings lose their jobs because "eviction takes a lot of time and emotional energy," and "showing up to multiple court dates often forces you to miss work." Then the search for a new home also "forces you to miss work." As a result of all these consequences, Desmond claims that eviction is not only an effect of poverty within exploitative low-end housing markets, but also a cause of poverty. The dislocation, psychological

Cordillera, Colorado, an ultra-exclusive community for the very rich, overlooks a trailer park in Edwards, Colorado. Many of the domestic workers in Cordillera cannot find affordable housing in town and must make long commutes to their jobs.

DIGITAL.WWNORTON.COM/YOUMAYASK7

You can watch my interview with Matthew Desmond at
digital.wwnorton.com/youmayask7

trauma, disruption to schooling and work, and bad mark on one's credit record all make it harder for a given evictee to achieve a stable economic footing going forward (Desmond, 2016). This makes sense; however, there is presently a robust debate about the extent to which eviction per se has these causal effects and is not merely just another marker of a tough situation that would have been bad whether or not the eviction had been carried out (Humphries, Mader, and Tannenbaum, 2019).

To make matters more challenging for families, landlords are more likely to work something out with childless adult tenants and kick families with kids to the curb. Desmond explains that "for a lot of landlords, children are inconvenient and cause the state to come in, Child Protective Services. Teenagers can draw the attention of the police. Children can flush toys down the toilet and . . . cause property damage." Whereas social division helps keep children born into poor families living in poor neighborhoods, eviction patterns demonstrate how social mechanisms load the spring on the poverty trap (Conley, 2013e). Desmond's prize-winning book that emerged from this research, *Evicted: Poverty and Profit in the American City*, has been important in shaping the public debate over urban poverty. Desmond's most recent project, the Eviction Lab (evictionlab.org), is the first nationwide database of evictions, allowing researchers and policy makers alike to examine maps and data.

Robert Frank and Matthew Desmond are not alone in noticing the pernicious effect of economic segregation. Sociologist David Grusky shared with me a fantasy, so to speak:

If one could wave with a magic wand [and] change one thing about American society, [the] one change that would have the biggest effect, in terms of reducing poverty and inequality, [would] be to delegitimate residential segregation. And simply make it as part of the commitment that Americans take on that we should all live together, no matter how rich or poor we may be. And that segregating rich people in one neighborhood and poor people in another neighborhood is simply illegitimate. I think that one change would have major effects on . . . how much poverty and inequality we see. It also would probably be one of the most difficult changes to undertake. (Conley, 2011c)

Where we live is only the most obvious way that gross inequality puts a strain on the lives of those at the bottom, however. There is also the more subtle issue of expectations and aspirations. A society with an extremely wealthy class—especially one that is socially isolated enough to lose the long-standing American taboo against conspicuous consumption—must constantly create new needs to soak up the luxury spending power of those at the top. Of course, these "needs" filter down to the rest of us through television and other such media. Marlin now supplements his paycheck with weekly runs to Manhattan to buy knockoff designer handbags in the wholesale district, which he sells for a small profit to working-class women on Long Island. In their conditions of production and distribution, the Chinese-made handbags act as a metaphor for the effects of growing inequality and consumerism. Marlin's customers are hardworking women who intentionally spend their disposable income on the counterfeit status symbols of the rich.

How did Domino's Pizza founder Tom Monaghan defend his views on poverty?

Poverty amid Plenty

The difficulties of conceptualizing poverty amid plenty are perhaps best illustrated by a speech given by one of *Forbes*'s 400 richest Americans, Tom Monaghan (1990), who rose to great wealth from meager origins. "To me one of the most exciting things in the world is being poor," he began his lecture. To explain what he meant, Monaghan cited a study that concluded a family of four could survive on $68 per year around 1970 (equivalent to $450 today). "Now you're probably wondering how you can live on $68 a year. The first thing you do is go to the Farm Bureau and buy a hundred-pound bag of powdered milk. . . . While you're at the Farm Bureau, you buy yourself a bushel of oats or wheat or corn, and you mash that stuff up. . . . And you grow some vegetables and you get a few vitamin pills to supplement your diet. And I think that's exciting." He went on to talk about how cheaply he lived in a house trailer, calling it "the greatest living I ever did." He concluded his speech with a rhetorical appeal: "Oh gosh," Monaghan said, "I'd love to talk to all these people who say they can't get by."

We could debate exactly how cheaply someone could survive in the contemporary United States or a similarly developed country, and we could question the hypocrisy of a man worth hundreds of millions of dollars castigating the poor for their implied whining, but that would miss the deeper point Monaghan raises. Namely, what does it mean to be poor in a country where starvation and death from the elements are rare? This question inevitably leads us to the debate over absolute versus relative measures of poverty. Monaghan's reasoning is not that far afield from a long tradition of absolute poverty measurement that has based its calculations on the cost of food.

ABSOLUTE AND RELATIVE POVERTY

Since the end of the eighteenth century, many individuals and institutions have tried to come up with a perfect measure of absolute poverty, the point at which a household's income falls below the necessary level to purchase food to physically sustain its members. (Note that such a concept fits very well with Karl Marx's notion of the physical reproduction of labor.) Attempts to establish such a minimal standard started in England in 1795 when the town of Speenhamland "instituted a relief program that made up the difference between a worker's wage and the cost of bread sufficient to feed him and his family" (Stone, 1994). In 1901, Benjamin Seebohm Rowntree attempted to devise a specific measure in York, England, when he documented an income level below which the necessities to maintain a person's physical efficiency could not be afforded. The results of this study were published in *Poverty, a Study of Town Life* (1910). Rowntree's approach was institutionalized in the United Kingdom by the Parliament's Beveridge Report in 1942, which became the platform for the welfare state of the Labour Party in 1945.

The most famous American version of the food-based measurement of poverty status was Mollie Orshansky's 1963 article "Children of the Poor." To estimate the poverty line, she used a strategy not unlike that implicit in Monaghan's speech. She took the US Department of Agriculture's recommendations for the minimum amount of healthy food, estimated the cost for a variety of family types (62 in all), and multiplied this figure by a factor of three (based on the results of the Consumer Expenditure Survey in the mid-1950s, which estimated that families spent an average of 35 percent of their household budgets on food). Soon, this became the official poverty line of the United States, and it has been the definition of poverty against which researchers have most frequently suggested alternatives. Figure 10.1 shows how this official poverty rate (and total numbers of "officially" poor Americans) has varied over a period of five decades.

Orshansky has been assailed from all sides for the choices she made in estimating the poverty line in the United States. Early criticism revolved around her choice of three as the multiplier. Some critics argued that three was too high because the poor often spent more than one-third of their income on food during the 1950s and early 1960s. However, this argument appears flawed as a result of its circularity: The poor may have been spending

FIGURE 10.1 Number in Poverty versus Poverty Rate, 1960–2018

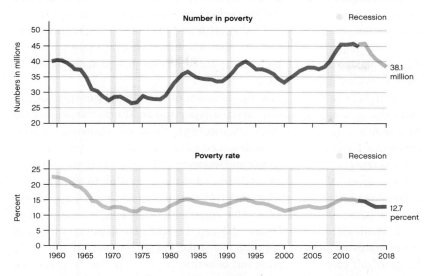

NOTE: The changes in line color reflect that in 2013 the US Census Bureau introduced redesigned income questions in its Current Population Survey, data from which was used to create this figure.

SOURCE: Semega et al., 2019.

more of their resources on food because they were poor; because food is the most basic necessity of all, we do not know what other necessities the poor may have forsaken (such as medical care or adequate shelter) while spending more than half their money to eat. Others argued that Orshansky's survey data from the 1950s overestimated the percentage of family income spent on food in the 1960s, suggesting that it had fallen to one-fourth, as indicated by the 1960–61 Consumer Expenditure Survey (Haber, 1966). The percentage of family income spent on food has steadily dropped since this period as well. Now housing makes up a much larger proportion of household budgets, and some scholars have called for housing to replace food as the basis for need calculations (Ruggles, 1990).

More recent criticisms have sought to change Orshansky's threshold by de-emphasizing food expenditures as the basis of what are considered "necessities." Specifically, some researchers argue that the range of necessities has expanded since the early 1960s to include such items as indoor plumbing (which many of the rural poor did not have in the 1950s) and telephones. Is television a necessity? Are working heat and air conditioning? How about a computer? With these concerns in mind, many analysts have argued that it is impossible to adjust the poverty threshold over long periods based on the rate of inflation; instead, the poverty measure must be reformulated from scratch every so often because what is considered a necessity changes from period to period and from society to society. The US poverty threshold has been further criticized because it does not take into account regional variation in the cost of living. Living on $8,000 a year in Mississippi is very different from trying to survive on that same income in New York City (Figure 10.2).

In response to the growing criticism of the official poverty line, in 2010 the federal government started reporting an alternative, called the Supplemental Poverty Measure. According to the Census Bureau, the Supplemental Poverty Measure is designed as "a more complex statistic" that incorporates factors such as tax and work expenditures and costs for basics such as food, clothing, and utilities, adjusted according to geographical differences in the cost of housing (US Bureau of the Census, 2017l). But because so many federal dollars that come to the state level—for education, food, Medicaid, and so on—are based on the official (old) poverty line, too many states would have opposed any tinkering with the original poverty line when it came to figuring out benefits. So the new line is merely for informational purposes.

FIGURE 10.2 Cost of Living, 2020

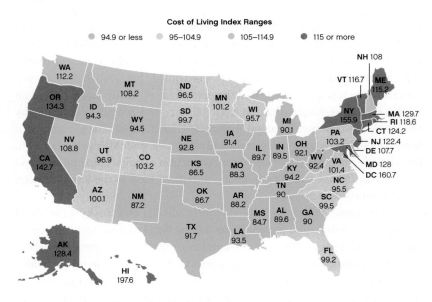

NOTE: The cost of living index compares costs between regions using data on housing, transportation, utilities, health care, and groceries. An average score is 100, so states with numbers less than 100 are affordable, and those with scores above 100 are more expensive.

SOURCE: Missouri Economic Research and Information Center, 2020.

Finally, there is the issue of assets and debts. Poverty is measured with respect to income alone. But income tells only part of the financial story for most American families. Significant variation in family wealth levels also exists. (Family wealth, often referred to as assets or net worth, equals total family debts, such as credit card debt or unpaid bills, subtracted from total salable assets, like a house or car.) This variation in net worth, over and above income levels, means that being poor can be a very different economic experience for families with the same income levels. This issue is particularly relevant to the study of race, poverty, and life chances in America. As we saw in Chapter 9, there is significant disparity in net worth between different racial groups. The median White family had a net worth of $171,000 in 2016, which is 10 times more than the median African American family's net worth of only $17,100 (Kocchar & Cilluffo, 2017). This difference cannot be explained by income or other demographic characteristics (Oliver & Shapiro, 1995). This was very evident during the recent recession as net worth dropped for everyone, but not equally. The median White family's net worth dropped 3 percent from 2005 to 2011, while African American families saw their net worth drop 46 percent, with one-third having zero or negative net worth (US Census Bureau, 2012d). So maybe additional income wouldn't have made a difference for Marlin (other than enabling his mother's drinking habit), but a nest egg might have. Because, as Marlin pointed out, lacking time to spend with your kids isn't restricted to low-income families, it's possible that this discrepancy in levels of net worth goes a long way in explaining differential outcomes in children.

There are many potential ways to integrate income and wealth into a poverty measure (such as converting wealth levels to an annuity and adding that to annual income). However, policy makers stick to the traditional income-based poverty measure. Given that many federal funds are allocated based on the proportion of a state's population that is poor, the Orshansky line has a political inertia difficult to alter. Similarly, researchers have just begun to take assets into account in explaining the impact of poverty on life chances, largely because good measures of family wealth have not been available until recent decades (as of 1984, when a number of reputable surveys started to ask about it).

All this criticism leads to the following question: Is it ever possible to arrive at an adequate measure of absolute poverty? Most scholars define necessities as those things that are required to live with dignity. Of course, if what is necessary to live with dignity in a given society is socially defined, then every measure of poverty is in some sense a relative measure; there will always be people who do not have those necessities in any market-based economy. The poor will always be with us, but to a greater or lesser degree, depending on how unequally income and wealth are distributed. This is one of the ways wealth creates poverty—by ratcheting up the social definition

RELATIVE POVERTY

RELATIVE POVERTY

a measurement of poverty based on a percentage of the median income in a given location.

of necessity. Theorists who believe that all poverty is relational have argued for the implementation of measures identifying relative poverty, the determination of poverty based on a percentage of the median income in a given location. For instance, a relative measure might consider anyone with less than one-half the median income poor (Fuchs, 1967; Rainwater, 1974). This sort of measure has become standard in the literature on international comparisons of the poverty rate because it provides an obvious yardstick across nations. However, it really measures income inequality at the bottom half of the distribution. That is, if in a given society, the 50th percentile (i.e., the median) family has $50,000 of income, half the median is $25,000. So if in the bottom half of society, more people slipped from $35,000 annual earnings to $20,000, the poverty rate would rise. Moreover, to the extent that societal wages rose so that the median (or typical) family now earned $60,000, the poverty line would rise to $30,000. Any family with less than that amount would now be considered poor. That said, changes to the income distribution *above* the 50th percentile—that is, the rich getting richer and pulling away from the middle class—would do nothing to the measure of relative poverty since what goes on in the top half does not affect the median income (of, in this case, $50,000 or $60,000). So, in a sense, a relative poverty measure is like a measure of income inequality of the bottom half.

THE EFFECTS OF POVERTY ON CHILDREN'S LIFE CHANCES

There are three basic theories about why poverty is bad for kids. First, some researchers focus on the material deprivations that low socioeconomic status induces, such as poor nutrition, lack of adequate medical care, and unsafe environments (Callan et al., 1993; Mack & Lansley, 1985; McGregor & Borooah, 1992; Ringen, 1987). Food, for example, along with water, is the most basic necessity of all. Studies of severe famine in the Netherlands during World War II found that consuming fewer than 1,000 calories per day results in dramatic reductions in pregnant women's weight gain and infants' size at birth. Research in this tradition has gone beyond basic needs such as nutrition to show that low-income households experience other forms of material deprivation, which may explain part of the effect of poverty on childhood (Mayer, 1997). For instance, some work has shown that poor children are less likely to have educational toys or books in the household, and such items are positively associated with healthy cognitive development (Duncan et al., 1994; Smith et al., 1997; Zill, 1988; Zill et al., 1991). It is hard to imagine, however, that toys and books explain a very large share of the effect of low income on children.

PARENTING STRESS HYPOTHESIS

a paradigm in which low income, unstable employment, a lack of cultural resources, and a feeling of inferiority from social class comparisons exacerbate household stress levels; this stress, in turn, leads to detrimental parenting practices such as yelling and hitting, which are not conducive to healthy child development.

A second paradigm, often called the parenting stress hypothesis, sees low income, unstable employment, a lack of cultural resources (such as reliable social networks), and a feeling of inferiority from social class comparisons as exacerbating household stress levels; this stress, in turn, leads to detrimental parenting practices such as yelling and hitting, which are not conducive to healthy child development (Conger et al., 1992, 1994; Elder et al., 1995; Hanson et al., 1997; Hashima & Amato, 1994; Lempers et al., 1989; McLeod & Shanahan, 1993; Whitbeck et al., 1991). Furthermore, both home care and day care for low-income children generally involve fewer positive interactions between the child and the caregiver and less opportunity for play as compared with children in more affluent households (Howes & Olenick, 1986; Howes & Stewart, 1987; Phillips et al., 1987). Research does suggest that parents living in poverty are more likely than parents in better conditions to display punitive behaviors such as yelling and slapping, and less likely to display love and warmth through behaviors such as cuddling and hugging (Conger et al., 1992, 1994; Elder et al., 1995). A great deal of evidence has connected such parenting practices to low IQ scores and to behavioral disorders in children (Conger et al., 1994).

What is notable about these two theories about the effects of poverty on children is how individualistic and behavioralist they are. Poverty, it seems, can either cause a family not to have enough material resources or cause the parents stress, which in turn leads to bad parenting practices. Either way, the causal arrow runs from the social condition of deprivation through the conditions of the home and the behavior of the parents and only then to the child. Parents are where the buck stops—either because they do not provide the resources their children need or because of their bad parenting practices. The bottom line is that poverty works through the family environment, so the family is ultimately responsible for mediating its impact on children. Poor heroic parents could blunt the deleterious effects by being savvy enough to provide a stimulating educational environment in the home on the cheap or by not letting financial stress get between their children and them.

A third theory asserts that it is not poverty, lack of nonmonetary resources, or relative inequality that is so detrimental to child development as much as it is the differences between poor parents and higher-income parents (Mayer, 1997). Scholars in the "no effect" camp assert that the association between socioeconomic status and child developmental outcomes is an illusion (i.e., it is false). They claim that parental characteristics, ranging from parenting styles to genetic endowments that lead to low income, less education, and low occupational prestige, also lead to detrimental developmental outcomes for offspring. The "no effect" paradigm is similar to the material deprivation and parenting stress hypotheses in that it is a causal story about parents, but it is generally considered significantly more conservative. The difference is that the material deprivation and parenting stress models optimistically believe intervening factors can be measured and therefore manipulated, whereas the "no effect" camp is less sanguine

Children play on the Lower Brule Reservation in South Dakota. In what ways can poverty be damaging to children?

on the prospects of lessening the differences between poor and nonpoor families on child outcomes.

Let's return to Marlin for a moment—or, more accurately, Marlin's mother. According to the first model, things might have turned out differently if she had been able to provide more material resources for her children: more food, clothes, and educational stimuli. According to the second model, the important factor would have been a decrease in her stress. A reduction in the pressures she faced as an unemployed single mother would have resulted in more positive interactions with Marlin and his brother, perhaps even affecting her propensities for drinking and man hunting. In the third paradigm, she was both poor and a less-than-perfect parent for the same reasons, be they genetic or behavioral. So which assessment do we believe?

Why Is the United States So Different?

America—if you can make it here, you can make it anywhere, as the song goes. The rewards for success are staggering and unparalleled in any other democracy. The net worth of Bill Gates is an estimated $104 billion, compared with the $97,300 median net worth of Americans as a whole (*Forbes*, 2020; Kocchar & Cilluffo, 2017). The average CEO at the top 350 companies in the United States received a compensation package worth $17.2 million per year in 2018 (Mishel & Wolfe, 2019). At the same time, the United States also has one of the highest poverty rates in the advanced world: 44.3 million people are living in poverty, down slightly from a high of 48.5 million in 2011. Children are particularly hard-hit: One in five American children lives in a household with income below the poverty line (Child Trends, 2019). Moreover, until the passage of the health care reform bill in 2010, many Americans had no health insurance, which was a leading cause of personal bankruptcy.

There are many ways to measure economic inequality, but they all arrive at the same answer: Economic rewards are far more lopsided here than in European countries such as social-democratic Sweden and union-driven France, and this inequality drives American poverty rates (see Chapter 7 on stratification and inequality). But the United States is also much more unequal than even our closest cousins, Great Britain and Canada. In fact, in terms of who gets what, we fall somewhere between western European countries on the one hand and developing countries such as Pakistan, Mexico, and Nigeria on the other. Of course, Americans on average have higher incomes than people in developing nations, but the way those countries' smaller pie is sliced is not that different from our own division of resources. For example, in the United States, the richest 10 percent of the population reaps incomes between 5 and 6 times greater than the poorest 10 percent. The comparable figure in Sweden is about 3.3, in the Netherlands it is about 3.3, and in Great Britain it is approximately 4.2. In Mexico, however, it is somewhere between 8 and 12, depending on which year is examined. (On another measure, called the Gini coefficient, where a higher score means more inequality, the United States scores about 0.4, between Mexico's 0.45 on the high end and Sweden's 0.27 and Germany's 0.29 on the low side.) So although we have a way to go to reach developing-world levels, the United States does not fit the model of most other industrialized nations either.

Direct comparisons of poverty rates tell a similar story: When the poverty line is set at 50 percent of the median income of a given country, a comparison of poverty rates among developed nations reveals that the United States indeed lags behind most of the developed world. In the United States, 17.8 percent of the population has incomes less than 50 percent of the median (Organisation for Economic Co-operation and Development, 2019). The next closest countries are Turkey, with a rate of 17.2 percent, and Lithuania at 17.3 percent (Figure 10.3).

A lot of explanations exist for the unique position among advanced democracies in which the United States finds itself. First, there is the issue of timing. Some countries may have transitioned to free-market capitalism

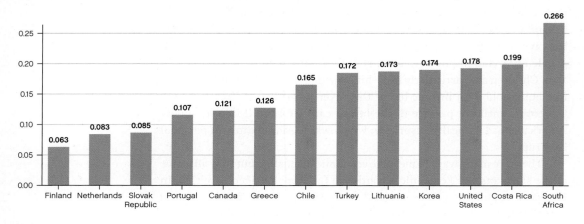

FIGURE 10.3 International Comparison of Poverty Rates among Wealthy Countries, 2019

SOURCE: Organisation for Economic Co-operation and Development, 2019b.

at a time when political institutions were better able to protect the weak through collective bargaining, welfare state transfers, and universal public services. Another explanation is institutional: The fragmented US political system, which divides power between the federal government and the states and among three branches of government, makes it difficult to develop a comprehensive safety net in the same way that European countries with strong central governments and a parliamentary system of elections can. Another explanation claims that the key aspect of "American exceptionalism" is that we have no history of feudalism (with the exception of the South before the Civil War). This seems ironic at first glance: Feudalism, a form of political and economic oppression in which serfs toiled on the land of their lords, was far more unequal than the image of early America with its citizen-farmers and bountiful land (again, with the notable exception of slavery). Given such a history of inequality, it would seem that the European countries with this sort of social history should have more disparity through the present. But feudalism also developed a culture of state paternalism, in which the serfs received protection from their lord in return for working his land. Some argue that this arrangement metamorphosed into the modern welfare state, in which citizens pay higher taxes but can confidently expect their basic economic needs to be taken care of by the government, from cradle to grave. Without such a feudal history, the American cultural tradition of individualism has acted as a hindrance to such paternalism.

Finally, there is the looming shadow of race in America. Some scholars argue that although European powers racialized "others" in the form of colonized peoples, those "others" were typically outside the country itself and far away, with no prospect of full political rights. Therefore, providing a strong safety net became a way by which European nations defined themselves in opposition to the "others" they were colonizing and to whom they were denying full political membership. In contrast, in the United States a sizable colonized population was imported. Although Black Americans were denied voting rights for much of the history of the American republic, they had begun to secure suffrage by the time the era of government redistribution had arrived in the mid-twentieth century. The result was that in order to prevent Blacks from participating fully in the American social contract, authority was shifted from the federal government to state and local authorities, and these authorities could then choose to exclude Blacks overtly or covertly. The result was a much weaker safety net, one that for a long time excluded minorities disproportionately. For example, to get Social Security through the congressional committees controlled by racist Southern Democrats, President Franklin D. Roosevelt had to agree to exclude agricultural and domestic workers from the old-age insurance system. This exception was made purposely to exclude African Americans, who were disproportionately employed in these two sectors. It was not until the following decade, when Harry S Truman addressed this gap in the safety net, that Blacks became full participants in the social insurance system. Of course, that first, Whites-only generation reaped the windfall of Social Security, receiving payouts from day one without having paid a cent into the nascent system.

None of these explanations can account for all cases. Ireland, probably the latest and most rapidly developed northern European country, displays greater inequalities than, say, the Netherlands, Denmark, and the United Kingdom. Canada does not have a feudal past, and it has a fractured, regional power structure (including semiautonomous provinces such as Québec), yet it enjoys a much more comprehensive safety net than the United States, its southern neighbor. Australia and New Zealand also lack feudal histories and have conquered racial minorities within their national borders, yet they still have much more progressive social policies than the United States. Therefore, the most probable answer is that timing, institutional structure, cultural history, and race were all necessary conditions for the unique position of the United States, but none alone was sufficient.

So maybe, ultimately, the story of poverty (in the United States) is really one of inequality. This is what David Grusky, at least, seemed to be implying with his own diagnosis when we spoke:

> I think, far too often, we give the labor market a free ride and assume that it's working perfectly and competitively. Rather [than just look at the safety net] we ought to often look at the more fundamental structural problems in [the] labor market that create such a need for a safety net. (Conley, 2011c)

Alas . . . easier said than done.

POLICY

SEEKING SWF

In the standard model of Keynesian economics, job growth is what drives the economy, and consumption, in turn, is what drives job growth. As a result, most politicians see jobs as the main avenue to economic security, the idea being that we need to create more and more jobs that pay higher and higher wages. As the economy expands, the logic goes, fewer among us will be susceptible to the problems of poverty.

But politicians are arguably misleading themselves and taxpayers when they say they can fix the poverty problem by taking short-term measures designed to boost jobs, such as scuttling trade deals or imposing tariffs, or by cutting tax rebate checks. In a globalized economy where wages are always lower somewhere else, some would argue that keeping manufacturing jobs in the United States is a losing battle.

Instead, the argument goes, we should focus on delinking economic security from the vagaries of the labor market by helping average (and even poor) Americans become part of an investor class. For example, a universal basic income (as discussed in this chapter) is one idea policy makers hope will cushion average Americans from extreme fluctuations in the labor market. Their assumption is that a minimum income would set a floor to consumption below which nobody would fall. But what if we went one step further and turned all Americans—including the poor—into global investors?

That is, what if the United States had—as a number of other rich countries already do—a sovereign wealth fund? By sovereign wealth fund (SWF), I mean a national mutual fund of stocks, bonds, and real estate holdings, including investments in private firms. The SWF would be established in hopes of realizing profits, but would also invest in public goods that are important to the long-term productivity of the US economy. In other words, the fund would bring in profits for "shareholders"—that is, American citizens—but also provide a source of badly needed investment funds for our infrastructure. The profits would, in essence, form the basis of a kind of universal basic income. (Of course, unlike a guaranteed minimal income, the size of the dividend might fluctuate year to year, depending on investment performance.)

Some Americans already have experience with such an arrangement. They are called Alaskans. The Alaska Permanent Fund was created in 1976 to manage the state oil revenue. Initially it was managed by the state of Alaska itself, but later a state-owned private corporation was formed to manage it. The fund pays out a yearly check, over $1,000 as of late, to almost all Alaskans. (Felons, new arrivals, and some other groups of residents are excluded from the bounty.) Understandably, the fund is hugely popular in the state.

Establishing a national fund based on the Alaskan model could have other salutary effects on US society aside from providing income support to the neediest Americans. It could help us rethink the difference between public and private capital, democratize long-term economic decision making (each American would own one share and thus get one vote), spread investment knowledge, and raise our dismal private savings rate. While it may sound like a leftist idea, such an approach could draw political allies from the right, because Republicans typically like anything that promotes investment. Meanwhile, an SWF could just bring the economic conditions on Wall Street and Main Street a tiny bit closer. Ready to cash your dividend check?

An Alaskan official announces the 2013 payout of the Alaska Permanent Fund dividend: $900 to each eligible Alaska resident.

Conclusion

What are we talking about when we refer to poverty? The term is used to describe villagers in the African country of Malawi struggling to live on a dollar a day when a drought leads to crop failure; it is also used to describe Americans who have little hope to realize their dreams but enjoy color televisions and indoor plumbing, and whose everyday lives involve perhaps more stress and depression than physical deprivation.

Poverty, then, is a state of absolute or relative deprivation based on economic conditions (as opposed to, say, political conditions). It has both geophysical roots, such as a high disease burden and shorter growing seasons in the tropical regions of the world, and social causes ranging from war to corruption, from segregation and ghettoization to the sometimes perverse incentives of social policies. Although poverty may be a many-faceted condition, one commonality holds true: Generally, we know it when we see it. But once we recognize its face, knowing what type of poverty it is (relative or absolute) and its root causes (social or environmental) can help us think clearly about how to tackle it without making the problem worse.

QUESTIONS FOR REVIEW

1. Poverty affected Marlin Card's life chances, although it is not completely clear how. What evidence does Marlin's life provide to support the material deprivation theory and parenting stress hypothesis? Apart from parenting, what other factors should we consider to best understand Marlin's path?

2. How does welfare help the poor? What are some characteristics of welfare that hinder work? How did the negative income tax experiment suggest that welfare creates perverse effects, and how could the results be interpreted otherwise?

3. How does the underclass theory relate to the culture of poverty? How does William Julius Wilson's argument provide a very different perspective?

4. What are the goals of work requirements for welfare (that is, workfare)? Why do these programs often fail to accomplish these goals?

5. How does the neighborhood one calls home affect a poor person's life chances? How does the Moving to Opportunity study add to our understanding of poverty?

6. How do the studies on lottery and gambling winners test the impact of income on the behavior and outcomes of the poor? How do the words of Marlin and the work of Susan Mayer shift the focus to wealth and consumerism?

7. What is the difference between absolute and relative poverty? What are some of the challenges involved in setting a poverty line and keeping this measure accurate?

8. Many policy makers have advocated for some form of universal basic income (UBI). What are the main arguments for UBI, and how do social scientists measure success?

9. What is unique about the extent of poverty in the United States compared with other countries? How might race be an explanatory factor within the United States?

KNOWN UNKNOWNS

"[T]here are known knowns; there are things we know we know. We also know there are known unknowns; that is to say we know there are some things we do not know. But there are also unknown unknowns—the ones we don't know we don't know. And if one looks throughout the history of our country and other free countries, it is the latter category that tend to be the difficult ones" (US Department of Defense, 2002).

Former US secretary of defense Donald Rumsfeld famously uttered this phrase as a flippant defense of how things were going in Iraq at the time (not well). But it has a deeper history and an appealing logic: Its central concepts were, in fact, developed by psychologists Joseph Luft and Harry Ingham in the 1950s as a way to help people understand their way of relating to others. What Rumsfeld was saying about the Iraqi situation (lack of evidence for weapons of mass destruction) could be applied to life in poverty. For many poor individuals, financial shocks are a major "known unknown" they face. Surveys show that 40 percent of Americans who encounter an unexpected $400 expense would have to sell something or borrow this money from a friend (Federal Reserve Board, 2018).

TRY IT!

Thinking about the past 12 months, and the 12 months going forward, how would you handle an unexpected expense? Say your car breaks down, or you drop your cell phone, or you fall behind on your electricity bill because a meter reading was unexpectedly high. What is the source of the income you would use to avoid financial ruin in each of these cases? Whether you can come up with the money or not, research what you might (legally) do if you could not. Here are some ideas: selling off goods you own, borrowing from payday lenders, donating plasma or other bodily tissues.

Now reflect on how these "unknown unknowns" of financial life might reinforce class stratification. How does family come into the picture, even if they're not doling out cash regularly?

Narrate a realistic scenario of events that might transpire in that worst-case scenario. What policies might we have to avoid vicious circles of poverty or financial rabbit holes—without creating incentives that could backfire (i.e., inadvertently cause people not to save any money themselves)?

SOCIOLOGY ON THE STREET

The average daily food stamp benefit is between $4 and $5, which requires calculating the exact value of each meal, even those eaten at home. Do you know how much your bowl of breakfast cereal costs? Watch the Sociology on the Street video to find out more: **digital.wwnorton.com /youmayask7**.

WANT MORE PRACTICE?

Complete the InQuizitive activity for this chapter at digital.wwnorton.com /youmayask7

11

WHAT CAUSES PEOPLE TO DIE CHANGES OVER TIME, BUT THE GROUP AT GREATEST RISK OF DYING FROM THESE AFFLICTIONS, THOSE LOW IN SOCIOECONOMIC STATUS, STAYS THE SAME.

POVERTY LINE

Animation at digital.wwnorton.com/youmayask7

Health and
Society

Like many privileged Manhattan residents, my family was lucky to escape from New York City as the number of cases of COVID-19 was on its steepest rise. It helped that we had to vacate our apartment by the end of March anyway for an upcoming move. So, we stored our belongings in a warehouse in New Jersey en route to Union Dale, Pennsylvania. Susquehanna County—about 40 miles north of Joe Biden's hometown, Scranton—was bespeckled with signs telling New Yorkers to go home. As in many places, local residents were understandably worried that people like us would spread the virus from its US epicenter. In fact, President Trump had been talking about cordoning off the greater New York metro area. We felt relieved to have gotten out "in time," but I nonetheless felt nervous driving my family in the rental van with New York license plates.

So much for the best-laid plans: Almost three weeks after our arrival, I fell ill. During the first night of pain and vomiting, I figured that I had eaten some contaminated lettuce. But when my aches and pains didn't abate after another couple of days, I worried that I might have become infected with the novel coronavirus. I called my primary care physician in New York and discovered that he had died. (I never found out whether it was coronavirus related.) So there I was, a good 40 minutes from the nearest health care. Here was my crash-course introduction to telemedicine.

I am very fortunate to know a few medical doctors. I texted a friend who is a urologist. He told me to immediately isolate myself from the rest of my family. I had figured that if I had food poisoning, it wasn't contagious, and if I had COVID-19, then it was so contagious as to be futile to try to prevent the rest of the household from catching it. I was even, at that moment the text came back from many time zones away, sharing a glass of water with my one-year-old.

On my doctor's orders, I put on a mask and spent the next month in a room alone with a fever that hovered betwxezen 102 and 105 degrees, depending on the time of day and when I had last taken Tylenol. At that time, in Pennsylvania, there was no testing available for people under 65 who were not frontline medical workers. Luckily, I had brought an oximeter with me. Based on when I experienced chills, I got good at predicting when my blood oxygen saturation was dropping into the 80s.

It turned out that I was again lucky in my medical social capital: Another doctor friend was conducting a longitudinal study on COVID-19, so he enrolled me and sent a collection kit for a mailbox test, which came back positive for me, but negative for the rest of my family members—much to our surprise. After two weeks, my fever was rising to close to 105 and my oxygen was consistently in the low 90s. "I don't give a [expletive] about your fever," my urologist friend told me over WhatsApp. "All I care about is your oxygen." He told me it was time to go to the emergency room.

At the local county hospital, I was given Tylenol, an X-ray (which confirmed pneumonia in my right lung), and another swab test. The attending physician told me they didn't admit patients unless one's oxygen saturation was below 85, so he instructed me to call my wife to pick me up.

That night my fever eased, but my oxygen did not recover. I started antibiotics prophylactically, and I saw a teledoctor through a service provided by my employer—another privilege of my social position. But after another week, I still had sharp chest pain and low oxygen; during my follow-up appointment with the same teledoctor, she told me to leave and go back to New York, where I would indeed receive treatment for an oxygen level in the low 90s. Meanwhile, my researcher friend offered to get me enrolled in a trial for remdesivir in New York. I demurred both entreaties since it was not logistically feasible for us to return to the city. After another two weeks, the feeling of broken ribs that accompanied my low oxygen slowly ebbed, day by day.

Though not widely used, telemedicine has been around since 1905. It has been vociferously championed for at least three decades as a solution to underserved urban (Ronis et al., 2017) and—especially—rural communities (Bashshur et al., 2000). It would seem as though with broadband and mobile coverage reaching saturation and 5G mobile technology imminent, the only thing holding telemedicine back was the culture of doctors, insurance companies, and regulators. The exigencies of the novel coronavirus pandemic would seem to have finally provided the tipping-point nudge for system-wide transformational change.

Indeed, in addition to being talked through my COVID-19 bout, in the last month I had my prescriptions refilled by my allergist by e-mail, my son got diagnosed with Lyme disease over Zoom (confirmed by a blood test), and my daughter had a skin condition treated remotely. The ability to interact with specialists from far away is exactly what visionaries had imagined when advocating for the expansion of telehealth services (Marchin et al., 2016).

During the pandemic federal regulators have relaxed reimbursement regulations for Medicare and Medicaid and interpreted HIPAA privacy regulations to allow for synchronous and asynchronous communication of sensitive data over electronic communications media that are not "public facing" (i.e., Facebook is not allowed). States, too, have allowed interactions that they previously deemed ineligible. But, as with many policies in our federalist system, there is incredible variation across the United States.

In most states, text message exchanges of the sort the urologist and I had would not be reimbursable. But in Pennsylvania, it turns out that even my teleconference with a doctor in New York would not legitimately be billable had it not been for a temporary suspension of in-state licensure requirements. Had I lived in Texas, though, I could consult any doctor in the nation, regardless of their licensure status in Texas. It seems time, then, to systematically think about what kind of telemedical landscape we want as a country.

One vision would allow patients to function as free agents in a national— if not global—marketplace for telecare. Like I did, a patient might speak with a urologist in another country, a dermatologist in his or her own county, and a cardiologist in a different state. While this would improve access to specialist care more than a system that allowed restrictions for providers to be licensed in the patient's state, it might also lead to the emergence of new health disparities on the patient side and concentrated market share problems on the health provider side.

I leveraged a large stock of social and cultural capital in arranging for my care, including seeking advice from close friends. Indeed, a study of Sweden found that when there was a doctor in the family, the health behaviors, health, and life expectancy of family members all improved (Chen et al., 2020). We are experiencing a moment to rethink the delivery of medicine. Must we be prepared to accept—as in the case of most domains where digital technology rears its head—that certain people will be better positioned to take advantage of the wider range of choices that the collapsing of geography provides along with the greater health inequalities that will result?

Many doctors and other medical providers have now gotten used to a new mode of service delivery, and red tape has been trimmed. Patients themselves have long desired more flexibility when it comes to the ways they interact with their providers. When the pandemic recedes, a new system of medicine will be left in its wake. This system may expand access and reduce disparities, or it may end up being one that merely exacerbates already steep gradients in health care and health. The choices of states and the national government will greatly influence which system we have.

The Rise (and Fall?) of the Medical Profession

Doctors have more power than any other professionals in America and most other societies. This, however, is a relatively recent phenomenon. Some scholars claim that doctors' power peaked in the 1980s and is now on the decline. Regardless, it might be worthwhile to examine why doctors gained so much influence over our lives in the first place.

WHY WE THINK DOCTORS ARE SPECIAL

Doctors have an enormous amount of social power, political power, and prestige—or what Pierre Bourdieu would call cultural capital. Indeed, we defer to our doctors in ways that we do not defer to other people. The respect we feel for doctors may result in part from the scarcity of doctors in our society, the fact that it takes years of education to become one, and the apparent difficulty of mastering the skills involved. For example, there are about 370 doctors per 100,000 individuals in the United States, compared with 492 lawyers, 872 accountants, and 958 college teachers (U.S. Bureau of Labor Statistics, 2020e). It generally takes 20 years of formal schooling plus an internship and residency training to become a practicing physician. Plenty of other professions require talent and many years of training, but doctors are different from investment bankers, judges, or lawyers. For starters, there are no limits on the number of law or business schools in the United States, but the number of medical schools and medical graduates is strictly regulated. This regulation allows doctors to maintain the exclusiveness of their profession and contributes to their privileged position.

One very important reason doctors occupy a unique position in modern society is that they offer a universally valued product: health and longevity (or, at least, they claim to offer it). Their power and prestige derive largely from the fact that they offer something that everybody wants—to feel better and live a long life.

If you are on a subway and someone yells for a doctor, we generally believe that if one is present, he or she has a moral obligation not to inquire about the ill passenger's health insurance status or financial means but to help that person right away. Some doctors have "MD" on their license plates, perhaps as a status symbol or because it brings them special privileges if caught speeding or parking illegally, but the title also obligates them to help in cases of emergency. We believe that doctors must not only do no harm but also do what is in the best interests of the patient. In this way, doctors appear to be answering to a high moral calling as embodied by, for instance, the Hippocratic Oath.

Greek physician Hippocrates (c. 460–377 B.C.E.).

One of the key traits of a profession (doctors included), as opposed to a job or even a career, is that the members of a given profession are oriented toward their peers, not their clients. Though doctors are serving their patients, they are equally concerned with the approval of other doctors. In fact, the sociological definition of a "quack" is a professional who violates this unstated ethic by seeking to make a client—the customer or patient—happy at the expense of the esteem of his or her peers. Your professor could make most of you students (the clients) happy by canceling the final exam and giving an A to everyone. But this would not be looked on kindly by his or her colleagues; in fact, it might get your professor bounced out of the profession.

Another reason doctors have so much social prestige is their individualized objectivity, which gives them a certain power in their relationship with clients. They are simultaneously very intimate (think about a rectal exam or psychiatry session) and personal with you but also objective and highly technical. Doctors may have knowledge of your most personal and private affairs. Your gynecologist or urologist, for example, may need to know things about your sex life that you do not tell anyone else.

This individualized objectivity may be the reason patients put so much emphasis on trust in assessing their relationships with their doctors. Sociologists David Mechanic and Sharon Meyer (2000) found that patients consider interpersonal confidence the most important factor in rating their doctors. Technical and medical competence is important, but we tend to assume that most—if not all—doctors possess these skills. While mental health patients also heavily stress the importance of confidentiality (understandably, given the stigma attached to mental illness), patients suffering from a variety of illnesses were most concerned that they be able to trust their doctors to talk to them like human beings, to show care and compassion, and to listen to them and take their concerns seriously. "Bedside manner," as we call it, matters most. If you had a serious illness, such as cancer, you would want your doctor to explain the diagnosis and treatment in terms you could understand. If you read about a new drug in the newspaper, you would want your doctor to listen to your questions and explain why the medication is or isn't appropriate for you.

Last but not least, doctors deploy specific props and scripts to assert their power. For instance, doctors set a front stage (offices with diplomas in Latin on the wall, and a large desk between the doctor and his or her patients) and a backstage (the examination room, where your paper gown exposes your backside). (See the discussion of Erving Goffman's dramaturgical theory in Chapter 4.) Have you ever arrived at a doctor's office and been seen right away? No matter if you are early, late, or right on time, you probably have to wait. We are socialized into accepting this wait as part of the drill, but it is yet another way that the power dynamic is revealed in the doctor–patient relationship. If you miss an appointment, often you will still be charged the fee, even if your doctor had plenty of work to fill up the time. But if you must wait for two hours to be seen by your dermatologist, tough luck.

The power and prestige that doctors enjoy on account of their unique circumstances translate into other benefits and privileges. In the past, doctors set their own pay rates. They essentially billed what they wanted to charge for a procedure, using as a guide what was standard. Insurance was reimbursed on a "fee for service" basis: If the doctor accepted your insurance, there was a set billable rate. If there was a co-pay of 20 percent for a $100 office visit, you would pay $20 and the insurance company had to pay the rest. In this scenario, the doctor had an incentive to say, "Take two aspirin, make an appointment with my secretary for tomorrow, and then we'll follow up with you again in two weeks and run some tests." Each time the doctor did a procedure or met with you, he or she billed you and your insurance company. And because you paid only part of the total cost, because you cared about your health, and because you trusted your doctor thanks to the asymmetry of information (assuming that he or she knew more than you did about what's best), you said, "Sure, see you then." Doctors had most of the control in this situation, which created a problem called "supplier-induced demand": Doctors created excess demand for their services.

Another form of power that doctors have, besides setting their own pay rates and controlling demand for their services, is prescription authority. There are occupational battles over who can prescribe what and who can perform which procedures.

An additional sign of doctors' power is their self-regulation. The American Medical Association (AMA) and state medical boards are their judge, jury, and jailer. A doctor who amputates the wrong leg of a patient may still be able to get a new job because there is such a (self-induced) shortage of doctors. This may seem ludicrous—in any other profession, you would be prosecuted for criminal negligence. The AMA, however, is a very strong political body. They have a monopoly over the policing of their own, and they are reluctant to take away a doctor's license.

Finally, doctors have authority in areas beyond strict medicine. Medicalization is the process by which problems or issues not traditionally seen as medical come to be framed as such. Alcoholism is a classic example. People did not formerly think of addiction as a medical problem but as a sin of excess, a moral failing, a problem of self-control. Now many accept alcoholism as a disease and talk about its medical aspects—the genetic tendencies, the biochemical aspects. We know that the disease runs in families, and researchers continue in their efforts to identify the genes that may affect one's susceptibility to alcoholism. We can treat addiction itself and even the tendency toward addictive behavior with pharmaceuticals. Even the judicial process has become medicalized, giving medical doctors legal power. Often, doctors play the critical role of expert witnesses in court cases, testifying as to whether a defendant is mentally competent to know the difference

MEDICALIZATION

the process by which problems or issues not traditionally seen as medical come to be framed as such.

between right and wrong and whether he or she is fit to stand trial. Or a doctor might attest that road rage is a syndrome with biomedical components.

Medicalization can have not only social consequences but health consequences as well. Many observers think the opioid crisis was created by overprescribing painkillers for conditions such as lower back injuries that might have been better treated with nonpharmaceutical approaches like exercise and physical therapy. One study found an 89 percent reduction in the rate of opioid prescription for patients who were prescribed physical therapy straightaway; in turn, they saved money on health care expenses and had a lower rate of hospitalization (Frogner et al., 2018).

THE RISE OF THE BIOMEDICAL CULTURE

Medical professionals currently hold a great deal of power, but it's important to realize that this hasn't always been the case. In fact, historically speaking, this is a relatively recent phenomenon. In ancient Rome, for instance, medicine was a low-level occupation. Physicians were either slaves or low-ranking freedmen or foreigners, often Turks or Arabs brought to Rome from the outlying provinces of the empire. Even in eighteenth-century England, physicians generally were at the margins of the gentry. They had higher status than in ancient Rome, but they were not considered an elite class. Surgeons had an even lower social status: The profession originally evolved from barbers, because barbers were good with straight razors and could cut people open and stitch them up. Today in the United Kingdom, surgeons are sometimes still referred to as "Mister," not "Doctor," thanks to their origins.

Ancient Roman surgical tools. Why did doctors have little prestige in ancient Rome?

More recently, in the modern Soviet Union and even after its dissolution, Russian physicians were paid relatively little, earning less than three-quarters the average industrial wage. It is no coincidence that 70 percent of doctors in Soviet Russia were women, because the percentage of women in a profession has a robust negative correlation with the profession's pay and social status.

If doctors have not always been as socially prestigious and powerful as they are in contemporary America, how did this authority come about? Health is a universally valued product, but until recently, doctors could not offer health and longevity. In fact, they were rather incompetent. They used leeches or cutting to get rid of "bad" blood

PLEASE HANG UP

Pratts HEALING OINTMENT

FOR MAN AND BEAST

WE BOTH USE IT!

CURES

HARNESS AND SADDLE GALLS.
OPEN WOUNDS, CUTS, SORES, SCRATCHES, BURNS,
EVERY BOX GUARANTEED.
GET IT HERE TO DAY!

An 1880s advertisement for a homeopathic cure.

and hoped this would cure you of the "poison" causing your illness. Some historians believe that George Washington died as the result of a blood-letting treatment for a cold that drained five pints from his body. At best, doctors sympathetically watched you die. They did not have antibiotics or vaccines. Before gaining power and prestige, doctors had to become more effective through advances in technology and knowledge. In 1816, the stethoscope was invented, allowing doctors to hear inside living beings and giving them the means to examine patients rather than merely observe them.

During the nineteenth century, doctors also promoted a system of licensing, which began to exclude other forms of medicine practiced widely at this time. One of the more prominent forms was homeopathy. Homeopathy (derived from *homeo*, meaning "same," and *patho*, meaning "poison") is guided by the notion that the "poison is the cure." It's not unlike vaccination: You are given a little bit of the poison, a little bit of the disease, in order to cure or prevent an illness. Homeopathy was a widely followed medical practice in the nineteenth century until what we now call traditional medicine became the dominant paradigm with the assistance of state licensing boards.

In addition to constraining the types of doctors who were able to practice, licensing also gave doctors more economic clout. Until the mid-nineteenth century, medicine in England and the United States was essentially considered philanthropic: If you did not pay your physician's bill, he could not sue you for payment; doctors had no legal recourse. Licensing changed this system; orthodox medical practitioners convinced state legislatures to pass laws allowing physicians to sue for payment, but only if they were licensed. This legislation led to the development of the AMA and state licensing boards and marked the beginning of the end for homeopathic doctors. These boards also constrained the number of medical degrees awarded annually, thereby restricting the number of practicing physicians so as not to create a surplus. In this way they drove up wages and guaranteed constant employment for doctors.

Another concurrent historical development was the emergence of more important roles for large institutions. Hospitals, formerly places to die, became places to heal (at least sometimes). It took a long time before death rates within hospitals declined precipitously, but at least it was no longer a sure death sentence when you walked into a hospital. By the late nineteenth century, hospitals had become important social institutions, and doctors' relationships to hospitals changed. Previously, doctors were merely employees of hospitals, but then they gained rights to admit patients to one or more hospitals—thereby obtaining a more powerful position in the relationship. Specifically, hospitals came to depend on doctors for their supply of customers, or patients; and the physician, who could easily send his or her patient to another facility, held the power.

DOCTORS' DENOUEMENT?

By 1990 or so, doctors' authority began to decline for several reasons. First, market forces had infiltrated medicine. By 1990, concerns about the rising cost of health care had become a major political issue and had led to changes in the way we pay for care, such as through health maintenance organizations (HMOs). The different types of health insurance providers are discussed later in the chapter.

Another sign of the declining authority of doctors was the rise of external regulation. No longer is the AMA the sole arbiter of what constitutes good medical practice. Medical "bills of rights" now exist. In 1998, President Bill Clinton signed into law a federal patients' bill of rights. Its main provision eliminated "drive-through deliveries" by requiring insurance companies to pay for a woman's stay in the hospital up to 48 hours after giving birth vaginally and 96 hours after a caesarean (doctors probably like this mandate, because it means more care, not less). The 1986 Emergency Medical Treatment and Active Labor Act also requires emergency rooms to treat you, at least enough to stabilize your condition, regardless of your ability to pay for services. Increasingly, emergency rooms have become money drains on hospitals, and consequently, many are being shut down.

Likewise, there are debates about whether the rise of heterodoxy, or nontraditional medicine, has challenged the authority of the traditional medical community. More and more people are exploring alternative medicines such as biofeedback, massage therapy, acupuncture, chiropractic, and herbal medicine. Doctors' monopoly on treatment is starting to decline to some extent, although a growing number of doctors have responded by incorporating these nontraditional forms of medicine into their own practices. Some of the alternative practitioners are certified; others aren't. Learning from the history of the medical profession, some try to create certification, which not only increases their legitimacy but also represents an attempt to restrict the field, allowing for greater control over prices, knowledge, and services.

Ironically, the rise of technology, which contributed to the power and prestige of the medical profession, is the fourth force that has eroded the authority of doctors. Many procedures no longer require the steady, trained hand of a doctor. A nurse practitioner can swab your throat, dip the swab

Walk-in medical clinics at many drugstore chains, such as this one at a Target store in Maryland, offer treatments for minor medical conditions and routine procedures such as vaccinations. What does this mean for the authority and prestige of doctors?

into a chemical solution, and tell in five minutes whether you have strep throat. This has led to the rise of CVS pharmacy's MinuteClinics and other integrated health service providers operating outside the traditional health care system. Many Walmart stores, for instance, offer walk-in consultations and treatments for simple issues like vaccinations and sprains. Doctors have become, in a sense, victims of their own technological innovation and success.

Developments in pharmaceuticals have given drug companies the chance to challenge the medical community too. Selling drugs used to be a matter of pharmaceutical company representatives visiting doctors' offices, flying physicians out to free "conferences" at desirable destinations, and so on. Doctors are still getting wooed by Big Pharma, but increasingly drugs are marketed directly to consumers in the hope that they will advocate for them with their medical providers—sort of how advertising for sugary cereal is aimed at kids even though the parents "officially" decide what to buy at the supermarket. The United States and New Zealand are the only countries that allow drug companies to fully advertise directly to potential patients, making claims about their products' effectiveness (Ventola, 2011). Since Merck ran the first print ad back in 1980, there has been an explosion of such direct-to-consumer advertising as the FDA has progressively eased restrictions. The result is that medical care, and the health system more generally, increasingly looks like any other big, global industry and less like a profession classically defined.

The internet has also changed the way medicine is practiced. Now you can do your own medical research online, learning about anything from pain in the lower right back to kidney stones. You can compile a list of potential causes for your symptoms and go to your doctor not as a passive patient but as an active consumer of health care, challenging and questioning his or her opinions and judgments.

Finally, declining doctor power may be related to gender: As we saw in the case of Russian doctors, when a profession becomes feminized, it tends to lose power and prestige. Back in the 1990s, the numbers of women and men graduating medical school equalized, meaning a profession that had been dominated by men has been increasingly marked by gender parity. Whether or not the uptick in female doctors has led to a decline in respect for the profession as a whole, women doctors have twice the burnout rate as male doctors and one of the highest suicide rates of any professional group—so the experience of practicing medicine differs greatly by gender (Poorman, 2018).

What Does It Mean to Be Sick?

THE SICK ROLE

Chapter 4 introduced the concept of role theory, which sees individuals taking on certain roles in society, much like actors in a movie. In the 1950s, sociologist Talcott Parsons (1951) combined role theory with medical sociology to create the concept of the sick role. According to Parsons, the sick role comes with two rights and two obligations. The sick person has the right (1) not to perform normal social roles (the degree of exemption from rights and responsibilities depends on the severity of the illness) and (2) not to be held accountable for his or her condition. The two obligations are (1) to try to get well and (2) to seek competent help and comply with doctors' orders. Those who have successfully adopted the sick role cannot be looked down on or morally judged if they do not work. But they may be the source of opprobrium if they fail to take their medicine, continue to eat fried foods after a heart attack, or smoke after a diagnosis of throat cancer.

Categorizing the sick role in such a way, however, puts the emphasis on the individual rather than on the social context and thus brings about a paradox. For example, because we know that certain behaviors are linked to specific diseases—smoking to emphysema and lung cancer, a high-fat diet to heart disease, and high sugar intake to type 2 diabetes—individuals are often seen as being at least partially responsible for their diseases, rather than unaccountable as is presumed under the second right of a sick person. Also, how many patients have the ability to assess what constitutes competent help and the resources to obtain it? If you have unlimited time and money, you might see a preeminent dermatologist about a mole on your arm. If,

SICK ROLE

concept describing the social rights and obligations of a sick individual.

Foua Yang holds a photo of her daughter Lia Lee as a child, before Lia's seizures resulted in a persistent vegetative state. Lia's parents cared for her until her death at age 30 in 2012.

however, you don't have insurance or can't take the time off from work to see a doctor, you might ignore the mole. If it turns out to be skin cancer, do you lose your rights as a sick person because you didn't fulfill your obligations?

SOCIAL CONSTRUCTION OF ILLNESS

In fact, what it means to be sick or healthy varies across time and place. *The Spirit Catches You and You Fall Down* (Fadiman, 1997) is the story of a Hmong immigrant family living in Southern California whose daughter Lia was diagnosed by her Western doctors as having epilepsy. Seizures, the main symptom of epilepsy, were viewed by her family as periods in which her soul was visiting the spirit world, a high honor in Hmong culture, one that carried a risk of failure to reunite body and soul. (It would be kind of like being able to take trips to heaven for Christians.) Author Anne Fadiman tries to give voice to both sides of the story—the doctors blame the parents for noncompliance with the prescribed medication regimen, whereas the parents blame the doctors for the medication's side effects. By examining the clash between modern Western and traditional Hmong culture, this story explores the different meanings of health and illness corresponding to the same phenomenon.

To use another example, alcoholism was not always seen as a disease, as mentioned earlier. Throughout much of history, it was seen as a moral weakness. What is seen as a personality flaw in one person (laziness) may be viewed as a legitimate medical condition in another (chronic fatigue syndrome) depending on that individual's sex, race, class background (and, therefore, access to medical care), religion, and nationality and the time period in which he or she lives.

The US Health Care System

Is health care a right or a privilege? Many other wealthy industrialized nations—the United Kingdom, the Netherlands, France, Italy, Canada—have had universal health care for decades. The United States got closer to the goal of universal health care with the passage of the Affordable Care Act (ACA) in

2010. But this law did not quite get us to universal health coverage because many states rejected a key element (Medicaid expansion) and many individuals opted out of the system altogether. The key difference between the US approach to health care and that of other nations is that we rely on the private market to provide care as well as manage the risk and finances (through insurance) for the vast majority of the population. How did we end up so different?

HEALTH CARE IN THE UNITED STATES: WHO'S GOT YOU COVERED?

The first growth spurt in the US health insurance industry occurred during the Great Depression in the 1930s. Established by the American Hospital Association, Blue Cross insurance (which covered hospital treatment), and later Blue Shield (which was aimed at nonhospital medical care), the emerging health care industry was characterized by the fee-for-service model of insurance: If you go to the doctor for a sore throat, you pay $25 for the visit and the insurance company pays for the rest—the lab work, the balance of the doctor's fees, and so on. One of the main problems with the fee-for-service model is that doctors have the incentive to overtreat (supplier-induced demand) and to see you again and again in order to bill the insurance company. This, of course, drives up medical costs for everybody. HMOs emerged as an attempt to hold down costs by paying doctors a salary based on the number of patients they take on. Under HMOs, the medical provider receives a capitation, meaning a fee per person as opposed to a fee per treatment. The patients still pay a fee, called a co-pay, each time they go to the doctor. Under this system, doctors receive (more or less) the same amount of money whether they see a patient once a year or once a week; thus the incentive for the doctor (from a strictly financial perspective) is to keep you healthy so that you require less treatment and reduce your number of visits to the doctor's office. Of course, this system creates the opposite problem: Doctors have an incentive to undertreat, because they generally don't get much extra money each time you come in.

During World War II, wage and price controls meant that employers could not easily offer raises. Thus, in lieu of more pay, many offered health insurance as a (tax-free) employee benefit. This was the origin of the employer-based system that has dominated the US market ever since. Insurance companies had to guess at how much health care a given firm's employees would consume and calibrate their premium rates (monthly charges), co-pays (patients' share of the bill), and deductibles (portion that patients have to pay all by themselves before insurance kicks in) accordingly. If they overshot their estimate, then another company could swoop in and steal the business with lower rates. If they underestimated the health care utilization of the group, then they suffered a loss. With large corporations covering thousands of employees, it's easier to guess based on the age and family composition of the workforce. But the smaller the group gets, the harder it is to accurately adjust prices and benefits to match the risk.

When we get down to an individual, not only does risk adjustment get even harder, but a new problem comes into play: adverse selection. If I am healthy, I have no incentive to get insurance. But if I am ill, or know that I will need a lot of health care resources in a given year for some other reason, then I might want to buy the best possible insurance plan that particular year. This means that when individuals have choice, they tend to sort themselves out by their own risk, which they know much better than the insurance company ever could (this is called *information asymmetry*). The result is that the individual insurance market goes into a death spiral in which only the sickest people buy insurance and prices increase, thereby further driving away potential healthy purchasers. Insurance works by spreading risk, so the health insurance market cannot function if only the sickest participate. (This is why most states require all drivers to have car insurance, not just the ones who think they may need it.)

So the bottom line, until 2014, was that if you did not get health insurance through your employer or directly from the government, then you were probably out of luck (or made the choice to fly solo). The Affordable Care Act was supposed to change all that. Even before Obamacare was passed, the government did provide health care for some of the most vulnerable groups in the population. Medicare, for example, covers most people age 65 or older and some younger people with disabilities. Medicaid is a joint federal and state program that helps cover medical costs for poor people with limited resources. Although this patchwork of programs provides medical coverage or assistance for some of society's most disadvantaged groups, the bureaucratic processes can be difficult to navigate. These programs change constantly, and qualification criteria and benefit packages may vary widely by state. Because the individuals who most need these programs, the elderly and the poor, are the least likely to have access to up-to-date technology such as the internet, it may be difficult for them to find the necessary information about what is covered, how to get reimbursed, or even where to find a doctor.

To address the multiple problems of our health insurance market—its reliance on employers, the perverse incentives that Medicaid eligibility rules might create *not* to work to qualify, the rapid rise in health care costs due in part to fee for service, and the lack of a robust individual market for those who do not get coverage through an employer—Congress passed the Affordable Care Act in 2010, which has been phased in slowly in the years since. In addition to expanding Medicaid eligibility and allowing young adults to remain on their parents' insurance through age 26, it created a mandate for all Americans to purchase insurance. Likewise, it eliminated risk adjustment—that is, variation in pricing or rejection from coverage—if it was based on preexisting medical conditions. Along with subsidies to make insurance affordable for low-income persons, this one-two punch of mandates is meant to create a robust individual market. Among the other changes introduced by the legislation, caps on the tax deductibility of employer-provided health care are meant to restrain the growth of health costs by making an additional dollar of health benefits paid by the employer the same as an additional dollar of wages tax-wise (over a certain threshold), thus reducing the incentive to provide "gold-plated" health plans that tend to encourage more (possibly wasteful) spending. Given that health care makes up 18 percent of the US economy (Centers for Medicare & Medicaid Services, 2018), the effects of these changes are not limited to health but have ripple effects on employment, retirement, economic growth, and even intergenerational family relations.

THE SOCIAL DETERMINANTS OF HEALTH AND ILLNESS

So are we all doomed if the ACA goes away and millions lose health insurance? The truth is that medical care and health care systems aren't the only factors that matter when it comes to health outcomes. In Western societies, you usually go to the doctor only when you decide that you are sick. When was the last time you woke up in the morning and said, "I feel great today! I think I'll see if the doctor has an opening to see me after lunch"?

A 2017 rally against Republican efforts to dismantle Obamacare. How was the Affordable Care Act designed to avoid perverse incentives among individuals and insurers?

The truth is that medical care and health care systems are not very important in predicting outcomes like mortality rates, life expectancy, and quality of life. Much more important, it turns out, are factors such as nutrition, clean water, lifestyle choices, and social position. In 1967, British researchers began to study the health of civil servants in what is known as the Whitehall Study. By focusing on one occupational sector, the civil service, this study controlled for the differences *between* men in different occupations and examined the differences *among* men of different social classes in similar occupations. Over an initial period of 10 years, the researchers found that men who held lower ranks and, therefore, lower status had much higher rates of common illnesses and ailments (including heart disease, diabetes, and stress) and higher mortality rates. The men in lower ranks had more risk factors, such as obesity, higher levels of stress, and low levels of physical activity. Not knowing whether this was a cause or effect of lower economic status, researchers tried to factor out prior health status and still found that men in the lowest rank were more than twice as likely as men in the highest rank to suffer from cardiovascular problems. The findings of the study were so important that the study has continued, expanding to include women and periodically looking at the impact of specific programs, such as smoking cessation, on health disparities. This study is conducted in a society where everyone has access to health care regardless of their socio-economic status (SES). None of the participants is poor or undernourished, and they all have a sufficient salary to survive. So what does the Whitehall Study tell us about the role of social factors as determinants of who gets sick?

The Whitehall Study has shown that who you are, where you live, how much you earn, and what you do for a living all play a major role in determining your health. Along with similar research, it has shown how social forces affect our bodies, our morbidity, and our general risk of mortality. Morbidity means illness in a general sense—the absence of complete health. It could mean something like having chicken pox (an acute condition) or not being able to walk very well because you have lower back pain (a chronic condition). Mortality means death, so when we refer to mortality rates in this chapter, we're talking about the likelihood of an individual or groups of individuals dying. The Whitehall scholars speculated that the social stress resulting from lower rank in the hierarchy of social class led directly to poorer outcomes for those at the bottom (through the release of stress hormones, for example) as well as indirectly (through different behavioral responses, such as overeating and smoking as a result of their social position). These assertions, however, remain controversial in the field, because some researchers argue that the Whitehall Study does not adequately address the possibility that underlying personality differences and skill sets led to both occupational and health differences, or that health directly determined the rank to which the bureaucrats rose by virtue of its effect on productivity.

Such concerns aside, today researchers have been able to show how the social environment in general—and social disparities and stressors, in particular—are associated with different rates of illness and aging among people. In an interview, Yale epidemiology professor Morgan Levine discussed with me what she found about how the social environment gets under our skin to age us in unequal ways.

MORBIDITY

illness in a general sense.

MORTALITY

death.

DIGITAL.WWNORTON.COM/YOUMAYASK7

To see my interview with Morgan Levine, go to
digital.wwnorton.com/youmayask7

Definitely health behaviors were explaining the largest proportion of the variance in our measure [of aging]. . . . I think the second biggest effect was from current socioeconomic status, measured using things like education and current wealth and income measures. Then this was followed up with lifetime stressors, so things like the death of a spouse or firing a weapon in combat or any of these kind of major life stressors. And after that, then we actually found genetics was explaining some small proportion of the variance, but definitely less than kind of these behavioral or social factors. (Conley, 2020a)

While not a disease or morbidity, per se, biological aging is a good overall measure of how long we are likely to live (and how healthy those years may be). Think of your body like a car: Even if your car runs well, if it's twenty years old, something is liable to break down on it soon. But, of course, not all twenty-year-old cars are in the same condition—some have had regular maintenance, others have been sideswiped on the highway. Human aging is a lot like that: You can't make yourself a thirty-year-old again if you're seventy. But you can be a lot healthier than most seventy-year-olds out there if you take care of yourself, are lucky enough to have pro-longevity genes, and experience a biosocial environment that does not induce chronic stress or negative health shocks. And those stressors and shocks are, as you might expect, not equally distributed across social classes. Below we examine those disparities across the life course, starting with the period before birth.

WE'RE NOT ALL BORN EQUAL: PRENATAL AND EARLY LIFE DETERMINANTS

We know that a mother's health can affect the health of her baby. Advances in technology, however, now allow the diagnosis and even the treatment of some conditions before birth. Likewise, reproductive technologies to combat infertility allow for the manipulation of genetic factors before conception. Amniocentesis, the process of inserting a needle into the uterus to extract fluid from the amniotic sack surrounding the fetus, has been used since the beginning of the 1900s. Because the fluid contains the fetus's DNA, genetic screening can be done for certain diseases before birth. This technology provides an opportunity for improving health and decreasing infant mortality, but it also raises ethical issues. If a fetus has an incurable condition like Down syndrome, should the mother abort it? What if the fetus is healthy but undesirable for some other reason? In countries such as China and India, where boys hold greater cultural value than girls, amniocentesis (and less-invasive ultrasound technology) can be used to determine the sex of the fetus early on. Particularly in rural areas where families live in poverty, if parents can give their resources to only one child, they will often choose a boy because he will likely be a better return on their investment. These considerations might lead to selective abortions of female fetuses.

Even without such procedures, more boys than girls are born worldwide, thanks to the lighter load of genetic material that male sperm carry. (The Y chromosome has hardly any genetic material compared with the X chromosome and, being lighter, tends to reach the egg more quickly.) In general, the sex ratio is usually around 1.05, meaning that for every 105 baby boys born, 100 baby girls are born. However, higher mortality rates for boys usually mean that this number evens out in adulthood and eventually flips, leaving more old women than old men. In India and China, however, the birth ratio is higher. Recent estimates put China's sex ratio at birth at 87 girls for every 100 boys (World Economic Forum, 2017). This might not seem like a big difference, but in a country with a population of 1.3 billion, this means that tens of millions of baby girls have gone "missing" since China's one-child policy was enacted in the early 1980s. This imbalance in the sex ratio leads to further social problems, including lack of marriage partners for young men, which may eventually lead to a change in the cultural valuation of women.

Another consequence of assisted reproductive technology has been the rise in the number of twins, triplets, and higher-order multiple births (Figure 11.1). This happens in two ways. When a woman has in vitro fertilization, several pre-embryos (zygotes) may be inserted into her uterus in hopes of increasing the chance of implantation, which carries the associated risk that more than one may implant. Likewise, if a woman is taking ovulation-inducing drugs, either in hope of getting pregnant or in preparation for in vitro fertilization, more than one egg may be traveling down the fallopian tubes, and two or more eggs may merge with sperm. The increase in higher-order births

Indian visitors to a New Delhi hospital stand next to a poster that reads, "Save the girl child. Finding out the gender of a fetus is a sin." Because of the rampant practice of sex-selective abortions, India has a dearth of female babies.

FIGURE 11.1 US Rate of Twin Births by Mother's Age (per 1,000 births)

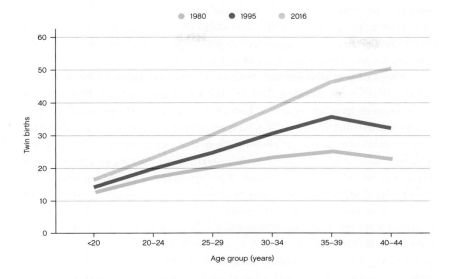

● 1980   ● 1995   ● 2016

SOURCES: Martin et al., 2015, 2018.

has raised new ethical issues as women, their partners, and their doctors must decide whether to "reduce" (i.e., selectively abort some of the embryos) because risks sharply increase for the mother and the embryos as the number of embryos increases. Another concern is that in multiple births, babies have a greater risk of low birth weight and prematurity. Babies who gestate in a crowded womb struggle to get what they need for nine months, illustrating how health inequality (and sibling rivalry) can begin even before birth.

More recently Dolores Malaspina, a professor of psychiatry at NYU Medical School, sat down with me to explain how our behaviors and social environments can have delayed health impacts by altering which parts of our genetic code are active. External factors like smoking weed, being chronically stressed out, and inhaling or eating certain things can change the way our genes are expressed. For example, Malaspina explained that while one of the risk factors for developing psychosis as a young adult is one's genetic makeup, another risk factor is smoking pot as a young adolescent, 5 to 10 years earlier. She asked my class, "Think pot is safer than alcohol for a young teenager? N. O. Alcohol, cocaine, LSD—a lot of drugs can cause [temporary] psychosis, but only one drug that we know of so far triggers *lasting* psychosis, and that's cannabis" (Conley, 2014f). Three percent of users develop lasting psychosis if they habitually smoke weed in their early teens. Malaspina pointed out that because "the brain is being resculpted and reorganized" during the teenage years, behaviors at this time can have long-term consequences. It should be added, however, that Malaspina's view is not settled fact. Absent a randomized trial, where some teens are assigned to smoke pot and others are given a placebo, it is hard to know whether individuals who are already experiencing mental health issues that were going to lead to psychosis anyway are drawn to smoking marijuana (perhaps as a form of self-medication, in fact).

Those of you who are uninterested in pot may be more interested in what Malaspina is working on now. She has found that children of older dads seem to have an increased risk of developing schizophrenia. Geneticists used to think sperm cells, which are made fresh constantly, were better able to avoid the ravages of time in a way that egg cells, which are carried in a woman's ovaries for decades from birth until they make a baby or are shed during menstruation, cannot. Now researchers like Malaspina know that fathers' age matters, too, and they are working to understand just how environment and genetics come together. For schizophrenia, Malaspina summarized what medical researchers know: "One out of a hundred people will develop schizophrenia . . . which is a type of psychotic disorder in which people have difficulty correctly interpreting stimuli. . . . The onset is usually in the late teens to early 20s for men." For people who have a family member with schizophrenia, the risk of developing it or any other psychotic disorder is higher. But, she explained, "the vast majority of people with schizophrenia have no family history at all. That means that schizophrenia is largely a sporadic disease. It appears in people without clear risk factors." In other words, once a mutation linked to schizophrenia is in the family gene pool, it can be passed on, but there are lots of cases arising from new mutations in families who have never had any members with the disease. Studying a panel of 100,000 babies as they grew into adults, Malaspina found that "the age of the father was a powerful risk factor for schizophrenia, and it accounted for a quarter of the cases in the population. So it's a very big risk factor for the disease." While this should encourage some of you to have children before you hit 40, there is a larger lesson here. Genetic disorders are not all about the genes you inherited from your ancestors—they are also about the environmental exposures your parents were subject to.

Schizophrenics with no family history of the disease are victims of either *de novo* (i.e., new) mutations within the cells that produce the father's sperm or epigenetic mutations. These are changes to the chemical switches that turn genes on or off and may be due to external or environmental factors. For schizophrenics, external factors may have affected their fathers' sperm, such that certain genes that should be dormant become active or vice versa. Despite what you might read about Pablo Picasso, Hugh Hefner, Michael Douglas, and Donald Trump having children in their sixties, sperm does, in fact, diminish in quantity and quality as men age, and the negative impacts may not even appear until the resulting children are in their

EPIGENETICS

chemical regulation of gene activity that may be switched "on" or "off" in response to environmental influence.

twenties or thirties when their dads might no longer be alive (Eskenazi et al., 2002). Malaspina's research expands a growing collection of studies that link stress of various kinds to negative impacts on health. For instance, "being born in a city will double your risks for schizophrenia and migration to a different country . . . is [also] a risk factor" for the next generation's chances of developing the disorder. Overall, it seems that "social capital may be a very protective factor" against developing what at first glance appear to be strictly genetic disorders. Our social environments, then, not

DIGITAL.WWNORTON.COM/YOUMAYASK7

To see my interview with Dolores Malaspina, go to digital.wwnorton.com/youmayask7

only may have profound impacts on our own health and well-being but also may indirectly affect that of our offspring. Kinda scary, isn't it?

POSTNATAL HEALTH INEQUALITIES

As you can imagine, if inequalities begin before birth, many more can emerge from the time the doctor slaps your behind and hands you over to your proud parents. Low birth weight has become the focus of increasing attention from the medical and academic communities and policy makers. A baby with a low birth weight weighs five pounds, eight ounces or less at birth (<2,500 grams). Low birth weight results from either inadequate growth during gestation (called intrauterine growth restriction) or a curtailed period of gestation, otherwise known as premature birth. Several factors can contribute to low birth weight, such as parental birth weight and mother's health and nutritional status, which are also associated with parental income. Once born, however, low-birth-weight babies have lower average educational attainment and SES, and a greater chance of giving birth to low-birth-weight babies themselves (Conley et al., 2003). In 2013 the rate of infants born with low birth weight was 8.17 percent. This was only 1 percent lower than in 2006, which had the highest level reported in four decades (Martin et al., 2018).

Race In the United States, Whites hold a significant advantage in health and longevity, having a life expectancy at birth of 78.9 years compared with African Americans' 75.5 in 2015 (Centers for Disease Control and Prevention, 2018b). This discrepancy is seen as both a major social problem and a sign of social inequality. David Satcher, the surgeon general during much of Bill Clinton's presidency, made the reduction of health disparities by race one of his primary goals. By 2010 and then 2020, he wanted to reduce gaps in outcomes such as hypertension, cancer, and overall mortality. But things don't even start out equal at birth. The infant mortality rate in 2017 (per 1,000 births) by race was as follows: White, 4.9; Hispanic, 5.0; Black, 11.4; Asian, 3.6; and American Indian, 9.4 (Centers for Disease Control and Prevention, 2019b; Figure 11.2). African American infants are more than twice as likely to die as their White counterparts, and compared with their middle-class White counterparts, middle-class Black women still experience high rates of low-birth-weight babies (Kashef, 2003). Asians and Pacific Islanders have the lowest infant mortality rates, probably because, although a diverse group, they do better economically, on average. Indeed, in regard to health, racial inequalities historically have played out in a variety of ways. Heart disease and cancer are most prevalent among African Americans, cirrhosis of the liver and suicide most prevalent among Native Americans. Hispanics have higher rates of diabetes and HIV/AIDS than Whites.

If we focus on health disparities between Blacks and Whites, because they are among the most extreme, what accounts for these differences? For starters, there's a high correlation between SES and race. That is, Blacks are disproportionately poor in the United States, and being poor can be very stressful, but Blacks have worse health than Whites regardless of income or education level. Middle- and upper-class African Americans experience high rates of hypertension, which is known to be linked to stress. One theory is that it is precisely the mismatch—the incongruity between what people assume their economic status to be, based on stereotypes, and what it

FIGURE 11.2 US Infant Mortality Rate, 2016

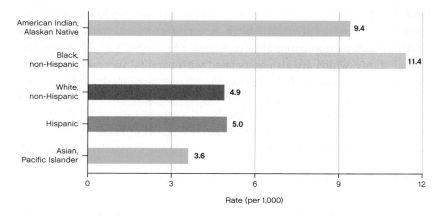

Rate (per 1,000)

SOURCE: Centers for Disease Control and Prevention, 2019b.

actually is—that elevates stress levels. Also, middle- and upper-class Blacks may face discrimination when they are perceived as "token" minorities in the workplace. Of course, high SES African Americans still live in a society rife with systemic racism—something that many Whites are now realizing to a greater extent in light of the George Floyd killing and the unrest that followed. In a recent study by Tom Laidley and myself (and other colleagues), we found that darker-skinned siblings experience higher rates of hypertension than their lighter-skinned brothers or sisters, suggesting discrimination is a major factor in contributing to stress, and in turn, high blood pressure, which itself increases risk for stroke and other problems (Laidley et al., 2019).

Although specific acts, such as a hate crime, could clearly affect someone's health, so could the gradual accumulation of more minor injustices in the form of stress and high blood pressure, not to mention racism's psychological impacts. The hypothesis of "John Henryism" is another example of how discrimination and racial symbolism may affect health. John Henry, like Paul Bunyan, is a star of American folklore. As legend has it, he was a steel-driving man, working on the railroad. With the development of the steam engine, machinery threatened to replace his manpower. John Henry told his boss he could drive the stakes into the rail through the mountain faster than the steam engine. His story was immortalized in many folk and chain-gang songs:

A stamp commemorating folk hero John Henry.

> John Henry said to his Captain,
> "A man ain't nothin' but a man,
> And before I'll let your steam drill beat me down,
> Die with the hammer in my hand,
> Die with the hammer in my hand."

The good news is that John Henry won the race and beat the steam drill. The bad news is that he died from exhaustion afterward. He remains a legend and cultural symbol of the hardworking African American man. Social psychologist Sherman James and his associates (1987), drawing on the symbolism of John Henry, suggest a link between historical and cultural factors that lead to higher rates of hypertension among Blacks. Americans value hard work and self-reliance, and these values combine with the history of slavery to make Blacks likely to take a John Henry–like approach to dealing with the psychological, social, and environmental stressors they face (Conley et al., 2003). Specifically, as John Henry battled the steam engine, many African Americans battle the negative stereotypes in American society, working extra hard to prove themselves.

Socioeconomic Status It probably won't surprise you to hear that people with higher incomes live longer, but why is that the case? Is it that health insurance and health care in the United States are so expensive? Is it diet?

What does income buy that decreases mortality? Likewise, more highly educated people enjoy longer life expectancies on average, and a number of straightforward explanations exist. Higher-educated people behave differently from people with less education. People with a college education smoke less, eat more healthily, and exercise more often. They often have more information and knowledge to work with when facing their own health choices and interactions with the health care system. But perhaps their overall better health contributed to their high levels of educational attainment. If you battled a serious illness as a child or teenager, for example, you might have missed a lot of school or not been able to attend college (Marmot & Wilkinson, 1999).

So how do we explain the correlation between SES and health? There are three main theories that attempt to explain this association. The first theory, which we might call *selection theory*, says that the relationship between lower income and higher morbidity is spurious (i.e., false or not really causal) because other factors such as genetics and biology affect both health and SES. A second theory, called the *drift explanation*, asserts that reverse causality exists—that health causes social position (as in the education example given in the previous paragraph). There is some logic behind this argument: If you don't have good health, you may not be able to work, so higher morbidity would result in lower SES.

Finally, one must consider the *social determinants* theory that social status position determines health (see Chapter 7). Being of a lower income level or SES causes higher morbidity and lower general health. What are the factors that could make this happen? Again, there are three general schools of thought for answering this question:

1. The psychosocial interpretation focuses on individuals' social class status relative to that of those around them. Feelings of inadequacy, low worth, and stigma cause people stress and wear down their bodies. If you have taken out tens of thousands of dollars in loans and work two jobs to get through college while your roommate is independently wealthy, the persistent presence of that inequality could affect your health directly by making you feel stressed, depressed, or angry, or indirectly by causing poor health choices such as smoking, using drugs, failing to exercise, and eating badly.

2. The second theory, the materialist interpretation, asserts that the differential access to a healthy life—including all monetary, psychological, and environmental risk factors—is a result of socioeconomic factors. Buying organic may be healthy, for example, but it is also expensive. So is joining a health club or obtaining top-notch medical care. Poor neighborhoods, meanwhile, are more likely to have higher concentrations of toxic chemicals.

3. The final theory seeking to explain how higher SES causes lower mortality is called the fundamental causes interpretation. This theory focuses on examining how social factors shape illness and health in order to understand the pervasive link between SES and health. The crux of the argument is this: "Because resources are differentially distributed across the socioeconomic hierarchy, people of higher social position have more resources at their disposal than those below them and are, therefore, better able to maintain good health and avoid disability and death" (Carpiano et al., 2006). Essentially, the fundamental causes hypothesis states that multiple and ever-changing mechanisms exist by which SES (and other dimensions of power) affect health. What the causes have in common, however, is the greater ability of high-status individuals to make use of new information and health resources as they become available. For example, Figure 11.3 shows that the gradient for lung cancer, which is strongly impacted by health behaviors, is much steeper than that for brain cancer, which is generally viewed as less predictable or less preventable.

If the idea of fundamental causes seems a bit abstract, historical changes can help sort out what sociologists mean. For example, by today's standards, during the 1950s and 1960s, poor people ate a healthier diet than rich people. Low-income individuals ate more whole grains, legumes, and vegetables because they cost less. Wealthier people thought it was healthy to eat red meat for its iron and milk and eggs for their protein, and they could afford to do so more often. In the 1970s, a revolution in our understanding of nutrition occurred, shifting the emphasis from meats and eggs

FIGURE 11.3 Brain and Lung Cancer Statistics

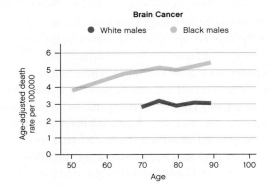

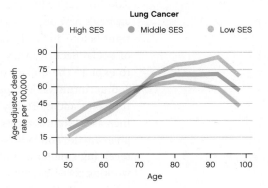

SOURCE: Phelan & Link, 2005.

to a balanced diet of fruits, vegetables, grains, and moderate amounts of meat. What was considered a healthy diet essentially flipped. The moment new health information became available, it was the high-SES individuals who were able to take advantage of it. Perhaps because they can afford to buy fresh fruits and vegetables and high-quality, low-fat meats and because they are better informed about the benefits of such food choices, wealthier people now have much better diets on average. Likewise, before the surgeon general's famous 1964 report on the dangers of smoking, there wasn't much of a class gradient in tobacco use. However, immediately upon release of that report, the SES gradient widened and has continued to do so ever since. By contrast, outcomes about which we know little, such as a brain aneurysm, show no apparent SES differences (Carpiano et al., 2006).

Changes in policy often provide "natural" experiments that social researchers can use to their advantage for teasing out cause and effect. Adriana Lleras-Muney (2005), an economist at Princeton University, used changes in state-level compulsory education laws in the early to mid-1900s to examine the impact of education on health outcomes later in life. In a nutshell, she figured, "If compulsory schooling laws forced people to get more schooling than they would have chosen otherwise, and if education increases health, then individuals who spent their teens in states that required them to go to school for more years should be relatively healthier and live longer." Such a natural experiment offers a way to gather evidence that education influences health (and not vice versa). Lleras-Muney found that an extra year of schooling decreased individuals' chances of dying by 3.6 percentage points in a given 10-year period. (Recall our discussion in Chapter 10 of the effects of poverty on children's life chances.)

Another natural experiment testing the relationship between SES and health occurred with a sudden change in Social Security policy in 1977 mandating that people born before January 1, 1917, would receive higher retirement incomes than those born after this date. The people at the Social Security Administration had to choose an arbitrary cutoff date for the enactment of the agency's new policy, so there would be no reason to believe that people born right before and right after the date are any different except in the amount of Social Security they received. Researchers used this natural experiment to explore the impact of income on elderly mortality. Their findings were counterintuitive: The people who received less Social Security lived longer. If income and mortality are negatively related, meaning that as your income increases, your chances of dying decrease, what happened here? What Stephen Snyder and William Evans (2002) found was that individuals who were receiving smaller Social Security packages compensated for the effects by working part-time longer. Because social isolation is thought to increase mortality among the elderly, staying in the labor market had a positive impact on these individuals' longevity. Something about work is beneficial—mentally, physically, or both—to one's health, provided, of course, you're not working in a coal mine or on a deep-sea fishing boat. Such natural experiments are fortunate for researchers because they show more clearly what's cause, what's effect, and under what circumstances particular causes and effects occur.

Finally, a much more recent policy experiment occurred when some states accepted the Medicaid expansion to cover poor, childless adults (as well as a raised income cutoff) while other states did not. Researchers are busy studying whether the pre- and postpolicy differences in outcomes are different in the two sets of states for the particular groups that would have benefited. Much of this research is ongoing, but at the very least, it appears that out-of-pocket medical expenses for the target population were lowered in the "treatment" states. More money, of course, is associated with better health (Goldman et al., 2018).

Marital Status Married people tend to live longer, particularly married men. But can we say that being married causes you to live longer or enjoy better health? Remember that we are not randomly assigning people to marry or remain single. There is a marriage market, and as in all markets, different groups have varying levels of success in it. Maybe healthier people do better on the marriage market, thus suggesting the true causal story is that health leads to marriage. Do you want to marry someone who suffers from a hacking tuberculosis cough and therefore cannot work and has no money? All other things being equal, you might opt for a healthier partner. Likewise, if you're very ill and spend a lot of time in the hospital or are confined to your home by a disability or chronic condition, you might have difficulty meeting people. It might be that better health leads to better marriage prospects, not the other way around.

Perhaps, though, marriage actually has a salutary effect—maybe it benefits your health. This idea certainly seems plausible. After all, when you settle down, you probably do not go out as much or engage in the risky behaviors you might have when single. Ramen noodles and soda may no longer be acceptable dinner options. Does marriage have beneficial effects, or does who gets married tend to be special in some way? There's probably some truth to both explanations.

Gender Who lives longer, women or men? Women do, at least in the United States. According to the US Department of Health and Human Services, in 2017 male life expectancy at birth was 76.1 years, but for women it was 81.1 years (Centers for Disease Control and Prevention, 2018b; Figure 11.4). Even the projected 2050 life expectancy statistics show women outliving men by five years (Centers for Disease Control and Prevention, 2015a, 2017). Many differences in mortality are linked to specific illnesses, such as heart disease and cancer, both of which are more likely to afflict men than women. In fact, heart disease is the number-one killer of both American men and women. As more women enter higher-level and consequently higher-stress

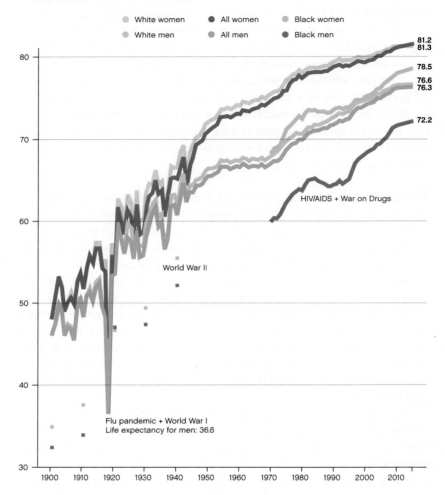

FIGURE 11.4 US Life Expectancy by Race and Gender, 1900–2017

White women · All women · Black women
White men · All men · Black men

81.2
81.3
78.5
76.6
76.3
72.2

HIV/AIDS + War on Drugs

World War II

Flu pandemic + World War I
Life expectancy for men: 36.6

SOURCES: Centers for Disease Control and Prevention, 2018b (Table 4).

jobs, their rates of hypertension, heart disease, and stroke are increasing. (See Chapter 14 for more about the impact of this change on the health of working mothers.) However, other reasons for higher mortality rates among men include the differences in health care—seeking behavior between men and women: Women are more likely to see the doctor for a persistent cough or an unexplained skin rash.

But health care differences are likely only a small part of the story. Professor Daniel Belsky of the Columbia University Medical School laid out for me in a recent interview the current state of our knowledge on sex differences in health and mortality:

One hypothesis is that much of the data on sex differences in life expectancy is an artifact of behaviors that may be disproportionately male. In the twentieth century, it might have been smoking. In the fifteenth century, it might have been getting into fights and killing other people, or sustaining damage that resulted in that kind of thing.

Another hypothesis is that, the fact that women have an extra copy of their X chromosome leads them to be protected from a range of genetic damage or defects that accelerate aging in men. A third hypothesis is that some of the hormonal differences between men and women that lead men to have bigger and stronger bodies on average, may also have a biological cost, increasing wear and tear on the system, and ultimately resulting in earlier onset of disease, disability, and death.

But the answer is that we don't really know, and because men and women live such different lives in the data that we have access to, it's very challenging to disentangle what might be an intrinsically biological process from an artifact of the different social histories of life as a man versus life as a woman. (Conley, 2020b)

Interactions between Race and Gender If Whites live longer than Blacks and women live longer than men, then how do the mortality rates of Black men compare with those of White women? Although both race and sex affect mortality rates, their individual effects pale in comparison to their interactive (i.e., multiplicative) effect. The average life expectancy at birth for White women is 81.3 years, compared with only 72.2 for Black men (Centers for Disease Control and Prevention, 2018b). That's nearly a decade. As noted earlier in the discussion of John Henryism, Black men may be at much higher risk for stress, which is linked to heart disease and stroke—the two leading killers of African Americans. Nonwhites are more likely to face racism, have low SES, and work more dangerous jobs, and the presence of several of these factors can be a deadly combination (Xu et al., 2009).

Family Structure Family structure, family size, and birth order are also determinants of mortality. Larger families have higher child mortality rates. When kids are spaced closer together, there is higher mortality. Why might this be the case? In developing countries in particular, resources key to survival (such as food) are stretched thinner in the household. If you have one pot of soup and eight mouths to feed instead of four, everyone gets half as much food, which translates into half the calories and nutrients. In our society, where food scarcity is less of an issue and accidental death is a greater cause of child mortality, supervision, or lack thereof, is the larger issue, because it's harder to supervise six children than two. The spacing of children also matters. Having three children in seven years is very different

A poor family in Musala, Kenya. How do family size and structure affect life outcomes?

from having three children in three years. Parental resources are more taxed by rapid-fire spacing than by larger gaps between births.

Likewise, according to statistics, firstborn children are more likely to die young. One reason could be that parents are less experienced: The firstborn is an experiment in which parents learn through trial and (hopefully not too much) error. Another hypothesis is that firstborns are more often unintended pregnancies. Parents tend to be younger, and the mother may have been partying, drinking, smoking, or using drugs further into the pregnancy because she did not realize she was expecting a baby; thus some of her actions early in the pregnancy may have adversely affected the health of the fetus. It is also true, however, that the effect may run in the other direction: Child mortality creates firstborns or, to be more specific, only children. We can separate firstborn children into two groups: those who have younger siblings and those who are only children (first by default). It turns out that the higher risk of death occurs in the latter group. When we say that the direction of causation runs backward (that B causes A), what we mean is that if you have a traumatic experience with your firstborn child—if the baby is severely ill or dies in infancy—you are less likely to have more children. It is not that firstborn children are at a higher risk for any real reason; rather, it is that people change their childbearing history when something bad happens to their first child. (All the firstborns reading this passage can now breathe a sigh of relief.)

AGING AND HEALTH

It doesn't take a social scientist to observe that health generally declines with advancing age. Compared to young adults, middle-aged and older adults have worse hearing, have poorer vision, experience declines in muscle mass and strength, have more brittle bones, and may experience a whole host of chronic diseases ranging from cataracts clouding their vision to painful joints caused by arthritis. To take just one example, over half of US adults over the age of 65 report living with hypertension (high blood pressure). Some afflictions of age affect men more than women (such as sleep apnea and hearing loss) while others are more common among females (arthritis and depression). Likewise, some conditions hit minorities hardest—for example, diabetes and glaucoma are more common in African American older adults than among Whites, while others are more prevalent among Whites—such as heart disease and age-related macular degeneration (AMD).

Rather than trying to ascertain the presence or absence of specific diseases or chronic conditions, many social scientists use summary measures that inform us about the overall health and functioning of aging individuals. One deceptively simple way to assess someone's health is to simply ask them to rate their own health: excellent, very good, good, fair, poor. The answer to this question predicts mortality better than many fancy approaches (Idler & Benyamini, 1997). For instance, the answer to this question predicted life expectancy much better than cutting-edge biomarkers (such as telomere length). At every age Whites are more likely than Blacks or Latinxs to report being in good to excellent health. For example, among those age 65 and over, 76 percent of non-Hispanic Whites fall into this category, while only 60 percent of African Americans and 63 percent of Latinxs do. On the other hand, self-rated health predicts mortality less well for racial minorities than it does for Whites, so the very meaning of the question and how people assess their own health varies in important ways across groups (Woo & Zajacova, 2016).

Interviewer ratings, it turns out, predicted mortality better than either self-ratings or medical doctor evaluations—at least in Taiwan (Todd & Goldman, 2013). Having health interviewers assess an individual's health takes away many of the subjective and cultural biases that may come into play when someone is asked about their own health. Interviewers consider not only the answers that patients give, but also their physical appearance, their speech and ease of movement during the conversation, and whether they manifest outward appearances of disease (such as coughing). Strangers' evaluations of the age of facial photos alone have been shown to be predictive of mortality over and above age itself (Thinggaard et al., 2009).

Another somewhat objective way to summarize health is with a measure of functioning. One index scores an individual's ability to take care of personal needs such as eating, dressing, bathing, using the toilet, walking, and getting in and out of bed and/or a chair. Each task the respondent cannot do by himself or herself is called an Activity of Daily Living (ADL) limitation. A similar scale—the Instrumental Activities of Daily Living (IADL)—summarizes a person's ability to manage more complex tasks such as grocery shopping (which is the most common limitation) or meal preparation. When we look at those age 65–74, 2.7 percent of respondents report having at least one ADL limitation and 6 percent report one IADL limitation. Jumping forward to ages 75 plus, those figures rise considerably: to 9.8 percent for ADL limitations and to 18.9 percent of people experiencing at least one IADL limitation.

These functional measures are important for assessing successful aging. According to one theory, the sweet spot of successful aging lies at the intersection of three conditions: avoidance of disease and disability, high cognitive and physical functioning, and involvement in society (Rowe & Kahn, 1997). Indeed, one theory of aging and health offered by James Fries is called "compression of morbidity" (Milbank, 2005). The idea behind the compression of morbidity is that as life expectancy increases, the burden of illness can be pushed closer and closer to death. The goal of public health in this paradigm should be to delay the onset of the first chronic infirmity. Fries's theory contrasts to a more pessimistic view that as we manage to extend life expectancy, society will be burdened with more and more folks living longer with various impairments and illnesses, creating an ever-larger burden on health care systems.

Finally, new methods are being developed to measure aging as a general bodily phenomenon at a molecular level. Scientists can now look at your cells and tell you if you appear to be older than your years or younger. I discussed these new approaches to quantifying our biological age and how they relate to social disparities with Professor Belsky, who we met above with respect to gender differences in mortality. In short, while they are rapidly improving in terms of predicting remaining life expectancy, such lab-based analyses do not currently predict that much better over and above someone's chronological age and the lower-tech measures mentioned above. Nevertheless, they do reveal health disparities and thus are very useful to researchers trying to measure the impact of unequal social exposures on our bodies.

DIGITAL.WWNORTON.COM/YOUMAYASK7

To see my interview with Daniel Belsky, go to
digital.wwnorton.com/youmayask7

HEALTH CARE FOR OLDER AMERICANS

While Americans ages 65 and over get health insurance in the form of Medicare—signed into law by President Lyndon Johnson in 1965 as part of his Great Society initiative—they still face many (growing) health-related costs. One important one regards prescription drugs. When President Bush signed into law the creation of Medicare Part D to cover outpatient prescription drugs, the plan included a "donut hole." That is, Medicare's share of the financial burden went down after a certain level of accrued costs ($3,820 in 2019) before catastrophic coverage kicked in at $5,100. The bottom line is that seniors who needed medications often shouldered significant costs. The Affordable Care Act eliminated this donut hole by 2020. However, seniors still have to pay a significant deductible (i.e., they have to pay a certain amount completely out of pocket before coverage kicks in—this was $415 in 2019) as well as a large co-pay (25 percent of costs up to the donut hole). The result is that sometimes poor seniors make hard choices between food and rent on the one hand and medications for chronic conditions on the other hand.

Despite the optimism of the "compression of morbidity" theory, there is a growing need for long-term care of the elderly thanks to increasing longevity and the fact that a particularly large birth cohort (the baby boomers) is aging. For example, in 1970 only 9.9 percent of the US population was over 65 years of age. But in 2020, that proportion had jumped to 16.8 percent. Projections are that by 2050, 20.9 percent of the population will be over 65 (West et al., 2014).

While many seniors can live independently for their entire life, others will require assistance. In fact, a majority (52 percent) of individuals turning age 65 will require long-term care at some point in their life (Nguyen, 2017). In this vein, only 3.1 percent of seniors lived in a nursing home; the rest spanned a range of housing situations—many lived independently or with family; others lived in what's called assisted living, where there is support that ranges from provision of social activities to help with ADLs. A growing trend is to receive support from health aids while "aging in place"—that is, at home. US long-term care expenditures were $30 billion in 2000; by 2015 they rose to $225 billion. The costs of assisted living or home health care are not covered by Medicare. Very few people enjoy long-term care insurance; in fact, private insurance paid only 8 percent of long-term care costs (in 2013). Meanwhile, 19 percent of costs were paid out of pocket (Reaves & Musumeci, 2015).

Unlike Medicare, Medicaid will pay for home care or nursing home care; however, you have to qualify for Medicaid, which has strict income and wealth thresholds. Thus, Americans who need such care are expected to spend down all their assets (i.e., use up retirement savings, sell their

DIGITAL.WWNORTON.COM/YOUMAYASK7

To see my interview with Corey Abramson, go to
digital.wwnorton.com/youmayask7

home, etc.) before they can apply for Medicaid. Some may argue that this is the way it should be—why should the public pay so that someone can preserve assets to pass on to their heirs? On the other hand, sometimes there is a surviving spouse that is then left with no wealth to aid with the expenses of living (since Social Security alone does not cover the cost of living for most people). In many other wealthy countries, long-term care is universally provided by the government just like other forms of health care or through a collective insurance mechanism.

Echoing this view is Corey Abramson, author of *The End Game*, and with whom I recently spoke. "We offer fewer resources compared to a lot of other developed Western nations. And I'd say fewer social resources in terms of family expectations and reciprocity than other cultures where filial piety, et cetera, is more highly valued. So I think you really are at a double disadvantage when you grow older in America, and a triple disadvantage if you're from a lower socioeconomic or a dominated racial group in that it's youth oriented, it values money. We don't have a ton of resources. It's one of the things I talk about in my book. Inequality doesn't disappear with a Social Security check. It's not enough to mitigate it. And even things like resources for senior centers, these are distributed in ways that are unequal." Abramson went on to explain that even getting to the point of experiencing the "golden years" is highly stratified. "So if you want to understand inequality, and you want to understand aging, and you want to understand their intersection, you have to look first at who gets to play. So who gets to survive to grow old? And the fact is the truly disadvantaged typically die before they ever enter a study like mine. They never get their first Medicare check, they never get their Social Security check. They essentially never make it to the endgame."

Race and the "Mortality Crossover" While Blacks are among the groups Abramson is referring to as not having as high a likelihood of getting to experience old age, it has long been thought that those who do will end up their White counterparts. Indeed, one of the big mysteries of social epidemiology is what is called the "mortality crossover effect." That is, while at every age women enjoy longer life expectancies than men (at least until age 117), the mortality advantage that Whites have over African Americans appears to narrow in later adulthood and then even flip direction. That is, before about age 75, Blacks experience higher mortality rates (i.e., risk of dying) while after that, Whites do (Wing et al., 1985). This phenomenon has been observed in US vital statistics since at least 1900—which begs the question, what's going on?

It is highly unlikely that such a dynamic reflects a reversal of fortune at age 75, whereby Whites suddenly experience (to a greater extent) the sort of discrimination and socioeconomic disadvantages that have been well documented for African Americans. Rather, the explanation most readily given by scientists is that there is mortality selection going on. That is, since more Blacks are dying at earlier ages because of the additional stresses they experience, those African Americans who do survive to their 70s are particularly tough survivors with constitutions lending themselves to living even longer.

However, some economists have recently challenged this account. They claim that the entire Black–White mortality crossover can be explained by reporting error. Namely, they show that the deaths of Black Americans are more likely to go unrecorded in the relevant databases that demographers use than the deaths of their White counterparts. The result is that those folks are assumed to still be alive and thus are included in the denominator of the population when death rates are calculated, leading to a falsely lower mortality rate than if the correct (smaller) denominator were used. This error worsens as age rises, resulting in the apparent effect observed. Dan Black and his colleagues call this source of bias the Methuselah effect, named after the Old Testament figure who is said to have lived 969 years but whose age some scholars think is a mistake resulting from a mistranslation. Such a dynamic shows the importance of digging deeply into data to understand what is going on. And what's going on in the case of race and longevity in America is much less counterintuitive than what we once believed: Namely, Blacks at all ages face higher mortality risks (Black et al., 2017).

COVID-19 AND HEALTH INEQUALITIES

While the impact of COVID-19 is global in scope, it might not surprise you to learn that the novel coronavirus has not affected every population equally. Some countries have had a much lower case rate than others. Take New Zealand: Since it is an island nation relatively far from most other population centers, the government was able to institute a tight quarantine rule for those entering the country (and restricted who entered). The result was that—as of this writing—the population has been largely spared COVID-19 (Baker et al., 2020).

In the United States, according to the COVID Racial Data Tracker Project (2020), as of July 2020 background information on race and ethnicity has been collected for about 1.5 of the 2.6 million people who have been infected

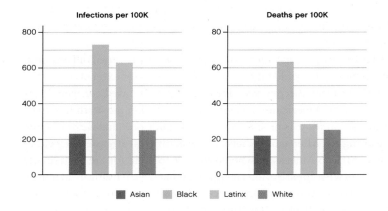

FIGURE 11.5 COVID-19 Infection and Mortality Rates by Race, 2020

SOURCE: The COVID Tracking Project, 2020.

with the virus, and about 113,000 of the 123,000 who have died from it (see Figure 11.5). African Americans in particular have suffered disproportionately, both in terms of infections and deaths. While African Americans make up about 13 percent of the US population, they make up about 20 percent of infections, and 23 percent of related deaths so far in the pandemic. Latinxs fare a bit better—18 percent of the population, 25 percent of infections, and 15 percent of deaths—but still get disproportionately sicker compared to Whites. Much of this discrepancy can likely be explained by the inequalities in general health and economic opportunity we discussed in Chapter 9.

Other reasons for the racial disparity with respect to the novel coronavirus may have to do with racial differences in household size and occupations: African Americans and Latinx people tend to work at jobs and live in places where they have more regular, close contact with others, and thus, increased chances of catching the virus. For instance, Latinxs live in households with an average of 3.25 people, compared to about about 2.37 for non-Hispanic Whites and 2.48 for African Americans (US Census Bureau, 2020b).

Meanwhile, when it comes to jobs and virus risk, Whites are also disproportionately employed in professional white-collar jobs, where opportunities for working remotely and social distancing are most prevalent. For instance, nearly 80 percent of white-collar managerial and professional jobs were held by Whites in 2019 (Bureau of Labor Statistics, 2020g). In contrast, health care support workers—nurses, home health aides, medical assistants, and so on, who are among those at greatest risk of catching the virus—are disproportionately Latinx and African American, with these two groups making up about 46 percent of the total workforce (Bureau of Labor Statistics, 2020g).

It is therefore unsurprising that African Americans and Latinxs have gotten sicker more often than Whites, as they not only are working jobs that cannot be done at home, but are often put in direct contact with people who are sick. In Washington State, where the first documented infections and deaths from COVID-19 took place in the United States, about 37 percent of infections occurred among health care workers, even though they make up only about 13 percent of total employment (Washington State Department of Health, 2020).

Not only do minority groups have a higher rate of becoming sick, but they tend to suffer worse cases (as evidenced by the higher death rate mentioned above). This is likely due to underlying risk factors. For example, African Americans (and Native Americans and Latinxs) are more likely than Whites to suffer from health problems like obesity (Singleton et al., 2016), diabetes (McBean et al., 2004), and high blood pressure (Yano et al., 2017), all of which can exacerbate the course of the disease. Add in substandard health care compared to that received by Whites, on average, and you have a recipe for a racial disparity in survivorship.

The Sociology of Mental Health

Mental illness is a tricky subject because its place in society has always been ambiguous. The label "mentally ill" was formerly reserved for individuals whose behaviors were considered bizarre or otherwise "unnatural." Asylums were used to house society's undesirables. With the work of Sigmund Freud and the advent of psychoanalysis, mental illness came to be seen, at least in the medical community, as one end of a continuum rather than one category in a dichotomy of "sane" versus "insane" persons. Diagnostic psychiatry, now the prevailing paradigm, treats mental illness much like any other illness, identifying its symptoms and prescribing treatment. Where does mental health fit into the larger health care system?

RISE OF DIAGNOSTIC PSYCHIATRY

In 1952, the American Psychiatric Association (APA) published the first edition of the *Diagnostic and Statistical Manual of Mental Disorders* (*DSM*), which described about 60 disorders. The social meanings of mental illness have always been contested, and the *DSM* is interesting because it represents the social construction of mental illness. In the nineteenth century, for example, women were frequently diagnosed as hysterical, and today the increasing diagnosis of borderline personality disorder, whose symptoms are analogous to those of hysteria, is a similar diagnosis under a different name. What the *DSM* did was standardize the canon of mental disorders and their definitions, such that a woman diagnosed with mania by one psychiatrist in Maine would (in theory) receive the same diagnosis from another psychiatrist in Texas (although it's never been that cut-and-dried, despite the APA's attempts at standardization). The second edition of the *DSM* did not make sharp distinctions between normal and abnormal behavior; rather, behaviors were considered to exist on a continuum in reaction to various life circumstances. For example, if one of your parents were killed in an automobile accident, you might be depressed, but this was still considered a normal reaction. (The second edition also included homosexuality as a psychiatric disorder, although this entry was removed in 1973.)

A major change occurred in 1980 with the publication of *DSM III*. This version was largely atheoretical, meaning that diseases were not attributed to certain causes (such as life events). In this way, it was primarily diagnostic and largely adopted a medical model (as opposed to a psychological one). You receive a diagnosis of "depressed" if you exhibit the associated symptoms for a period of two weeks or longer, much in the same way you might be diagnosed with chicken pox if you have a fever and red, itchy bumps. Unlike earlier editions, however, *DSM III* removed the social context in favor of the biomedical model. If you are depressed, it is presumed that you have a chemical imbalance. In the diagnosis criteria, no consideration is given to what life events, if any, may have triggered your feelings, although according to the manual, doctors were expected to take life factors into account.

Today the *DSM* is in its fifth edition and contains information on almost 400 distinct mental illnesses. Its use has increased, largely because of the bureaucratic requirements of the insurance industry: to get paid, mental health professionals must find a diagnosis category that "fits." In fact, medical billing is a multibillion-dollar industry expected to more than double in the next five years, despite cost-saving technologies like electronic medical records (Grand View Research, 2016). Hence the proliferation of new entries such as attention-deficit hyperactivity disorder (ADHD), generalized anxiety disorder, and premenstrual dysphoric disorder—all of which previously belonged to less medical lay categories.

The major changes in the *DSM* that took place between its second and third editions reflect both changes in the field of psychiatry and our social understanding of mental illness. Dynamic psychiatry, which focused on identifying the internal conflicts that produced a mental illness, was usurped by diagnostic psychiatry, which seeks to identify the symptoms of specific underlying diseases. As noted earlier, this change marked a radical transformation in the field of psychiatry and has, in turn, had lasting effects on the social world.

In trying to understand the current high rates of depression, for instance, sociologists Allan Horwitz and Jerome Wakefield (2007) ask whether our society is really more depressed than it used to be. Maybe it's an artifact of how we measure depression. People may be more likely to report depression now because awareness about mental illness has increased. What was formerly thought of as being "blue" or "down in the dumps" because of specific life events may now (for better or worse) be treated as a much more serious problem. Or we may have better diagnostic tools.

Depression was historically overdiagnosed in women, because the symptoms were more "female." Men's depression manifests itself differently, but this is not surprising given the different cultural scripts we have for emotion based on gender, such as yelling (male) versus crying (female), or feeling angry (male) versus feeling sad (female). Meanwhile, trans individuals tend to have very high rates of depression and suicide; this is thought to be largely due to the social stigma and bullying that they experience (Budge et al., 2013). Ditto for gay and lesbian youth (Mueller, 2015). We also know that depression and suicide are contagious (Abrutyn, 2014): Not only do the moods of those in our social network affect our own psyche, but suicides (particularly teen suicide) can spread like a virus through a school or community.

One of the larger shifts in the field of psychiatry in recent decades is the way we differentiate between sadness and depression. On its website, the National Alliance on Mental Illness notes that "the characterization of our emotional reactions to life's challenges as 'depression' is more than just a change in colloquial expression. It represents a transformation in psychiatric thinking." When multiple symptoms are present, or symptoms last for more than two weeks, or symptoms interfere with someone's daily functioning, the patient may be diagnosed as clinically depressed.

The problem with our current measurements of depression, Horwitz and Wakefield argue, is that context is largely ignored. What if you experienced symptoms of depression for longer than two weeks right after September 11, 2001? Or what if you found out that your lifelong partner had left you for someone else? That's not depression, according to Horwitz and Wakefield; that's a normal emotional reaction to life's trauma—simply the human condition. Of course, because suicidal thoughts (ideation) or impulses are the hallmark of depressed individuals, identifying and treating these individuals are serious and necessary endeavors. However, overestimating the prevalence of depression, so that those with a serious mental illness are lumped into the same category as individuals with normal sadness, may dilute the attention and resources of public health officials, policy makers, and medical practitioners.

Horwitz and Wakefield's argument aside, there are recent, more objective indicators that we are experiencing an epidemic of depression in the United States. Namely, suicide rates have been rising steadily since the end of the 1990s. Age-adjusted suicide rates have increased by 24 percent over a 15-year period (Tavernise, 2016). Drug overdoses—another "death of despair"—have also risen sharply over the same period, largely due to opioids (National Institute on Drug Abuse, 2017). The overall result is the stunning finding by economists Anne Case and Angus Deaton (2015) that overall mortality among middle-aged White Americans has increased since 1999, leading to one of the largest long-term health crises in recent history.

THE POWER OF A PILL?

Typically we think of taking a pill as a consequence of our failing health. But sometimes pills can be the cause. A letter to the editor in the January 1980 issue of the *New England Journal of Medicine* argued that pain management with narcotics rarely led to addiction (Porter & Jick, 1980), citing a study whose results supposedly supported these claims. For about a decade, this brief letter—really just a paragraph—didn't get much attention. But then Purdue Pharma started pushing the study to argue that its drug OxyContin (which was not one of the three studied) was entirely safe and should be prescribed more often to manage pain. While our present-day opioid crisis has many roots—economic dislocation, the speed of social change, and so on—the advertising of Big Pharma is certainly on the list.

Likewise with mental health. Once mental illness became medicalized, it wasn't long before pharmacological treatments overtook traditional "talk therapy." After all, once the social context is removed from the understanding of human behavior, all you need is a pill to fix the underlying organic disease, right?

Drugs can and do help people. If you have a headache, aspirin may help. Likewise, if you are clinically depressed, an antidepressant may alleviate some of your suffering. The availability of drugs may also help people seek treatment: If they felt helpless before, knowing that medication is available may inspire them to see a doctor. However, a negative side exists. Not all illnesses can be treated with drugs; some require talk therapy, which often is not covered as comprehensively by insurance companies. Drugs may be over- or misprescribed, and there may be lethal results. Some studies have shown that certain antidepressants increase suicidal thoughts and tendencies in adolescents, although much controversy surrounds these

Kathryn Orrick plays and teaches classical piano, something she couldn't do until antidepressant medications helped her out of depression. Though she agrees that the medicines should be closely monitored, especially with new patients, she credits her treatment for allowing her to live a full life.

claims. Drugs may also have the adverse social effect of increasing stigmatization, because pharmaceuticals might be seen as an indication of something seriously wrong. Prescriptions for antidepressants jumped over 400 percent from 1988 to 2008, with approximately 12.7 percent of Americans over the age of 12 taking antidepressant medication (Pratt et al., 2017).

Pharmaceutical companies can market their drugs only to treat specific diseases, so they benefit from the diagnostic model of psychiatry. If your depression stems from a traumatic childhood marked by memories of abandonment by your alcoholic parents who were primarily concerned with their own needs, costly hours of therapy might be in order. If, however, your depression is caused by a chemical imbalance in your brain, your doctor can prescribe a drug covered by your insurance company. (Of course, it may be a childhood trauma that is causing a chemical imbalance, further complicating the sometimes flimsy distinction between biology and the social environment.) As you can imagine, adopting the biomedical model in psychiatry has both benefits and drawbacks. On the one hand, recognizing that mental illnesses are diseases with biological components can alleviate some of the stigma attached to them. (We don't say that people with cancer are crazy. We say they are sick. Why shouldn't the same hold for schizophrenics?) On the other hand, we know these diseases may not be completely biological, so if we describe them as illnesses we may ignore the importance of contexts and blame the sufferers when they aren't cured by a drug.

Global Health

When we talk about the impact of SES on life expectancy in the United States, we're talking about differences of about five years on average (remember, though, that when we take into account race and sex, the difference is almost ten years). Although these differences are both real and important, they take on a whole new meaning when viewed in a global context. Ignoring differences in race, sex, and class, the United States is in 31st place (out of 183 countries with available statistics), neck and neck with countries such as Costa Rica and Cuba, for the highest life expectancy in the world (World Health Organization, 2018a; Figure 11.6). In many countries in sub-Saharan Africa—one of the most economically depressed regions in the world—life expectancy remains around 50 years. At least it started going up again after falling in the decade between 1990 and 2000 in areas that were walloped by AIDS.

What is the leading killer worldwide? Not AIDS. Cancer? Not yet. Heart disease? Diabetes? There are still plenty of regions in the world free of fast-food chains. Give up? Waterborne illness. Worldwide, about 844 million people don't have access to clean water; annually, over half a million people are estimated to die from diarrhea alone, the majority under five years of

FIGURE 11.6 Average Life Expectancy Worldwide, 2016

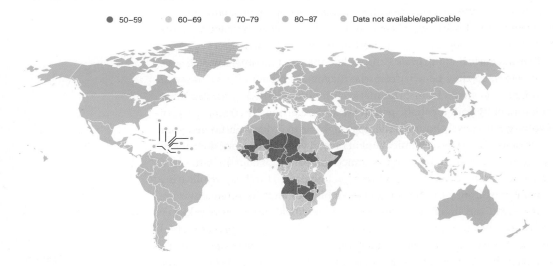

50–59   60–69   70–79   80–87   Data not available/applicable

SOURCE: World Health Organization, 2018a.

age, because of unclean water (World Health Organization, 2018b). So why is this a social issue? The technology and know-how for clean water exist. So does the money (worldwide at least). Many countries, however, don't have the funds or the infrastructure to handle these problems. As Kofi Annan, the former United Nations secretary general, said, "We shall not finally defeat AIDS, tuberculosis, malaria, or any of the other infectious diseases that plague the developing world until we have also won the battle for safe drinking water, sanitation and basic health care" (United Nations, 2001). Even ethnic conflicts and turf wars may grow out of smaller disputes over scarce resources, with clean water being a major one.

GLOBAL POVERTY AND HEALTH: CAUSE VERSUS EFFECT

Do poorer countries have more health problems because they're poor, or are they poor because they have so many health problems? Well, both. It's not a simple matter of cause and effect; unfortunately, there's an effective feedback loop. Governments, communities, and individuals in the least developed areas must expend a great deal of their energy and resources on dealing with the problems of basic survival. Girls and women in particular are limited in their opportunities for educational and economic advancement, because the burden of performing tasks such as collecting water—no small feat when the nearest well is miles away—falls disproportionately on them.

Like waterborne illness, the mosquito-borne disease malaria typically affects the least-developed areas of the world (it's the number-four killer of children younger than five worldwide). Consider the problems malaria posed for development in the Western Hemisphere. During the construction of the Panama Canal, malaria, along with yellow fever, was a major cause of death and illness for workers. In 1906, 80 percent of all the employees working on the canal were hospitalized for malaria.

In fact, the Centers for Disease Control and Prevention grew out of an agency called Malaria Control in War Areas, which served the purpose of controlling and eliminating malaria in the areas surrounding US military bases around the world. In the United States, particularly in the South, a campaign was waged during the first half of the twentieth century to drain swamps (where the parasite-carrying mosquitoes bred) and deploy window screens. By 1951, malaria was considered eradicated in the United States. In the 1950s, the World Health Organization undertook an initiative to eradicate malaria worldwide. There were notable improvements in many areas thanks to the indoor spraying of the pesticide DDT, but once programs were discontinued (largely because of concerns about DDT's environmental effects), rates rose to their previous levels in some areas, most notably sub-Saharan Africa.

No malaria-endemic region of the world has ever developed economically, claims economist Jeffrey Sachs (2001). There are lots of infectious diseases and parasites out there, so what's the big deal with malaria? This was a question I posed to him in an interview, and here's what he had to say:

> The *Anopheles* mosquito genus that carries malaria exists in a variety of species. The one that Africa has, the *Anopheles gambiae*, is different in its lethality because of the way it transmits the disease. There's this fascinating hypothesis that because Africa was simultaneously burdened by sleeping sickness, which affected cattle, spread by the tsetse fly, farmers in Africa didn't have a mixed animal crop system. So when the malaria was transmitted from chimpanzees to humans in biological time, the mosquitoes learned to bite humans in Africa. By the time malaria came to Asia and especially to India millennia later, the Vedic farming system of ancient India was a cattle-based system. So [when] you look at the mosquitoes, the *Anopheles* mosquito in Africa bites people almost exclusively. In India, about 70 percent of the bites for the dominant kind of species are on cattle. (Conley, 2009g)

"Hippo rollers," distributed by the Hippo Water Roller Project, help people carry a significant amount of water over long distances. This cuts down on the number of trips, leaving people more time to pursue education, farming, and economic activities.

Malaria can be a fatal disease in humans; before the age of antibiotics, it had a very high morbidity rate, so high it could wipe out entire villages. As Sachs has explained, the particular situation in Africa encouraged the malaria-carrying mosquitoes to target humans rather than animals. Having malaria is a real drain on productivity, especially when it turns out to be fatal.

In other words, controlling and, ideally, eliminating malaria are a prerequisite for significant economic development. Steps are being taken to help the areas of the world that struggle with the most basic of public health issues, such as high malaria infection rates. If used consistently, insecticide-treated bed nets, which cost less than $10 apiece, can save lives in malaria-infested areas. African river blindness (onchocerciasis) is a scourge similar in its devastation to malaria. However, thanks to a concerted international effort since 1974, onchocerciasis has largely been eradicated from many areas, and this example illustrates the connection between health and economic development. One group estimates that 600,000 cases of blindness have been prevented in west Africa by the worldwide campaign. Furthermore, according to some estimates, about 100,000 square miles of land are now safe for settlement because of the eradication of the disease (World Bank, 2002).

Unfortunately, we are not making similar progress on the malaria front: Not only is the malaria problem yet to be solved in many of the world's poorer regions, but it's also reemerging in parts of the world where we believed we had conquered it. Malaria, along with tuberculosis, gonorrhea, and childhood ear infections, is one of the diseases that is becoming more difficult to treat because of antibiotic-resistant strains of the disease. This problem, referred to as antimicrobial resistance, is thought to be the result of evolutionary adaptation on the part of bacteria and other infectious agents. Although antibiotics represent one of the greatest medical achievements ever made, nature is fighting back with bigger and badder antigens. Antimicrobial resistance has been exacerbated by the prescription of unnecessary antibiotics and the widespread routine practice of mixing antibiotics into animal feed to prevent herd death in the

DIGITAL.WWNORTON.COM/YOUMAYASK7

To see my interview with Jeffrey Sachs, go to
digital.wwnorton.com/youmayask7

H₂O TO GO

Considering that there are about 1 billion people in the world who still don't have access to clean drinking water, being able to buy safe drinking water is quite a luxury. Americans drank, on average, 42.1 gallons of bottled water per person in 2017, overtaking carbonated soft drinks as the most popular beverage. By volume, bottled water is often more expensive than gasoline; prices for water today range from less than $1 for a gallon jug of filtered water at the grocery store to more than $20 per gallon for high-end brands purchased in 9-ounce bottles. So why do we drink bottled water? Tastes vary by location, but generally in taste tests people can't tell the difference between tap and bottled water. Scientifically, it has not been proven

Lee Anne Walters of Flint, Michigan, heats bottled water for her sons' weekly bath in October 2015. For each bath, Walters uses 8–10 gallons of bottled water to avoid exposing her children to the Flint tap water, which is high in lead.

that bottled water is better (in fact, your dentist may recommend that you switch back to tap if you're not getting enough fluoride), and the contents of tap water are more heavily regulated than those of bottled water. Of course, there are exceptions, even in the United States, where some impoverished communities, such as Flint, Michigan, have had to drink bottled water due to contamination of their water system (by lead). To put this information in a global context, according to the International Water Management Institute, for $1.7 billion a year in addition to what's already spent on water projects, everyone on earth (including the residents of Flint) could have access to clean water. For another $9.3 billion a year, everyone could have better sanitation (a major factor in preventing illness). In 2017, Americans alone spent $18.6 billion on bottled water (International Bottled Water Association, 2018). You do the math.

unnaturally close conditions of feedlots. Failing to finish a prescribed course of antibiotics can also contribute to the development of resistant strains. International efforts are under way to identify the most dangerous antibiotic-resistant strains, but as we come up with new and improved ways to treat illnesses, we need to consider what new and improved diseases we may simultaneously create.

Vaccines are another means of preventing disease that are standard in most developed countries but often rare in poorer nations. More than 20,000 cases of polio were reported each year in the United States before the vaccine for polio was introduced in 1955. Reported cases dropped to 2,525 by 1960 and to only 61 in 1965; only 33 cases were reported in the whole world in 2018 (Landau, 2012; World Health Organization, 2019). The success of the vaccine in the United States sparked a worldwide initiative to eradicate the disease. In recent years, however, reports of polio have come from at least 15 countries that were thought to have eliminated it, including a case in Minnesota in 2009 (Centers for Disease Control and Prevention, 2012b). In 2013, approximately 50,000 Americans died from vaccine-preventable diseases (Centers for Disease Control and Prevention, 2015c). Although a vaccine for malaria does not yet exist, there is great promise for Africa from recently developed vaccines for other diseases, such as meningitis. Figure 11.7 shows the leading causes of death for young children worldwide.

THE AGE OF AIDS

When the first cases of what would later be termed acquired immunodeficiency syndrome (AIDS) were reported in 1981, it was thought to be a cancer among gay men. Several decades after the initial reports of the disease, AIDS had killed about 730,000 Americans and 32 million people worldwide (Centers for Disease Control and Prevention, 2017b; World Health Organization, 2020). AIDS affects straight and gay alike; rich and poor. However, inequalities in risk remain: Currently, men who have sex with men, and African American people (including women), have a higher risk of infection than heterosexuals, lesbians, and other races and ethnicities.

Nationally, AIDS has played a role in transforming doctor–patient relationships. AIDS took the form of a modern-day leprosy, bringing a huge stigma to those who had it. Because in its early years AIDS was most prevalent in gay communities, community groups such as ACT UP (the AIDS Coalition to Unleash Power) and the Gay Men's Health Crisis (see Chapter 18) organized to challenge stereotypes about people living with AIDS and about HIV transmission—namely, that it is transmitted only through homosexual sex. HIV is carried in bodily fluids; shared intravenous needles, unprotected sexual activity (both heterosexual and homosexual), and mother-to-infant exchange are the most frequent modes of virus transmission. Like most diseases, AIDS is more prevalent among poorer populations, especially on the global scale. Although there have been huge advances in formulating drugs that stop HIV from evolving into full-blown AIDS, in preventing HIV transmission from mother to infant, and in prolonging the life expectancy

FIGURE 11.7 Causes of Death in Children under Five, 2013

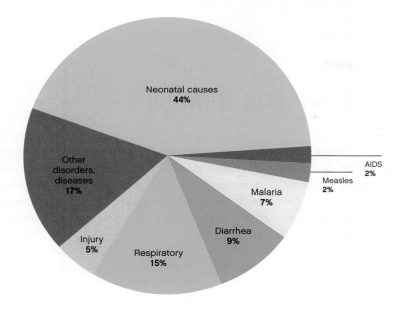

SOURCE: Liu et al., 2015.

of people with HIV/AIDS, access to these drugs is extremely limited world-wide, though access is improving. In the United States, the Ryan White Act (first passed in 1990) provided federal funds to poor Americans with AIDS to act as a last resort (when insurance was not available) to pay for treatment. Even in countries where low-cost medications are increasingly available to people with HIV, if they don't have access to proper nutrition and clean water to take the medication, it will not be effective and in fact will contribute to the problem of antiretroviral resistance to medication. Currently, the most promising strategy for combating AIDS is increasing awareness about prevention strategies such as using condoms and clean needles and, most recently, promoting male circumcision.

HOUSING FOR HEALTH

What if the best treatment for mental illness were a key? That is, literally a key to a lock, as in the lock to the door of a house or apartment. Although calling a key to a home the "best" treatment for mental illness may be going a bit overboard, the point is that for homeless people who are mentally ill and/or substance addicted, a policy called Housing First may be an important part of recovery (Henwood et al., 2012).

Housing First was pioneered by New York University psychiatrist Sam Tsemberis and a nonprofit organization called Pathways to Housing in the early 1990s. The idea is deceptively simple: Provide housing to unhoused individuals without requiring them to jump through hoops. Typical homelessness policy treats the provision of housing like a reward at the end of an obstacle course. Individuals with addiction who may be "self-medicating" depression, anxiety disorders, or even psychoses with illegal drugs and alcohol are expected to engage in psychiatric and substance-abuse treatment in order to gain access to permanent, stable housing. In practice, this carrot-on-a-stick approach means that most homeless remain on the streets or in the shelter system, because it is very tough to get treatment or stay clean when you have no sense of permanency.

By contrast, the Housing First approach provides a permanent, affordable home to homeless people regardless of whether they are in psychiatric treatment or maintaining sobriety. It may seem counterintuitive that *not* requiring individuals to seek treatment actually elevates their health, but studies confirm the transformative power of the "key" to a permanent home, at least when it comes with associated support services (Henwood et al., 2012; Padgett, 2007).

Take Denver, for example. A 2006 study found that emergency room visits were cut by more than a third and inpatient costs were down by two-thirds for "keyed" study participants (Perlman & Parvensky, 2006). Even better, incarceration was cut by more than three-fourths, and 77 percent

How might the Housing
First strategy be cheaper
in the long run?

of participants were still housed after 24 months. Instead of getting in trouble or finding housing in jail, subjects were simply able to . . . go home. A Seattle study of active alcoholics showed that the program saved taxpayers more than $4 million in just a year. Equally important for the participants was that they drank less—much less.

It should not be a surprise that something as seemingly unrelated to health care as providing a stable home would be key (bad pun) to improving the mental and physical health of a vulnerable population like the homeless. Health *care* itself is remarkably unrelated to population health. We are pretty good at curing (antibiotics) and preventing (immunization) many infectious diseases. But for chronic problems like diabetes, hypertension, and heart disease, our best practices in medical care yield mediocre results at best. Nonmedical interventions in diet, exercise, and other lifestyle adjustments turn out to be far better at getting results, especially when we target prevention. The same is true for mental illness and addiction. For a variety of reasons—including patient problems with compliance—nonmedical interventions often have the biggest payoffs (Henwood et al., 2013).

What may be a bigger surprise is that spending the money on housing and services such as counseling, which look expensive at first, actually saves money in the long run (Doran et al., 2013). We have historically taken a spend-now/save-later approach to young children's health, education, housing, and welfare. As it turns out, the same strategy works for homeless, mentally ill, and substance-abusing adults, who are typically thought of as the least "deserving" poor in contrast to children who are considered the most deserving. Thus not only is permanent, no-strings-attached housing a healthy solution for individuals and the communities where they live, but it's often the cheapest option available.

Conclusion

In this chapter, you've learned how something such as health that seems so fundamentally biological is shaped in important ways by social structure. We can decide what we eat, whether we smoke, and whether we exercise, but we can't choose what sex or race we're born, what food we can afford, and whether our health insurance company will reimburse us for our gym membership or psychotherapist. What are some of the changes that could be made to the structure of our society that would improve health for everyone? Eradicating racial disparities in wealth, power, and status might solve many problems, but unfortunately this goal is probably a long way off. What feasible short-term changes could be made? Should we tax fast-food businesses for the unhealthy merchandise they proffer in order to defray the costs that society pays for the obesity epidemic? This money could be put toward healthier school lunches or toward physical education programs. A seemingly endless list of possible questions emerges when we recognize that health and biology, on the one hand, and social life, on the other hand, are not two distinct worlds but rather intertwined systems.

QUESTIONS FOR REVIEW

1. How does the uniqueness of health as a "good" help explain the high status of doctors? How does this, in turn, help explain the discomfort around the commercialization of bodies?

2. If Housing First policies for alleviating homelessness are as successful as recent research has shown, do you think they will be widely adopted? Can you imagine how stigmas about mental illness might make it difficult to convince cities to provide housing to someone before he or she is sober?

3. What are some of the ways in which people in the United States with fewer resources are at greater risk for poor health? According to the Whitehall Study, why are certain groups at a particular disadvantage?

4. How does licensing within the medical profession relate to the status of doctors? How does the AMA contribute to the power of doctors?

5. A student gets very sick the day before an exam and (thanks to a doctor's note) is allowed to take the test later. Describe Talcott Parsons's "sick role." How do this role's rights and obligations help explain this example?

6. How could the social construction of illness help us understand hypochondria?

7. Describe the way race and stress interact to create a higher health risk for African Americans. How do gender and higher socio-economic status matter?

8. How has the way that psychologists diagnose mental illnesses changed? How does the availability of pharmacological treatments—that is, drugs—complicate things?

PRACTICE

I'LL GO TO THE GYM TOMORROW

In this chapter we learned that the meaning of "health" and "illness" vary across time and place, and how socioeconomic status and health are linked. If you are thinking about a career in health, I hope you took good notes. Indeed, the MCAT examination required of all medical students now has a section on sociology (see the MCAT correlation tables on p. xxxviii)—reflecting a growing consensus that medical professionals need to think sociologically to serve an increasingly diverse population. That starts with understanding that "healthy" is a social construction, not a fixed reality.

TRY IT!

Here's what the American Medical Association (the largest body of American physicians) and the US Department of Health and Human Services recommend for a healthy lifestyle (AMA, 2017; US Department of Health and Human Services, 2015):

HOW MANY ITEMS ON THIS CHECKLIST OF HEALTHY LIVING DO YOU ATTAIN?

- [ ] Quit smoking, and limit your exposure to secondhand smoke

- [ ] A balanced meal: over 50 percent of your calories from whole grains, fruits, and vegetables

- [ ] Avoid processed foods, foods with added sodium, or beverages with added sugars

- [ ] Consume alcohol in moderation: one drink per day for women and two drinks per day for men

☐ **Have a regular checkup with a primary-care physician, and regular dental and eye exams**

☐ **For adults ages 18–65, get at least 30 minutes of moderate aerobic exercise five days per week, or 20 minutes of vigorous exercise three times per week**

☐ **Don't eat Tide Pods***

*Seriously. In 2016 the American Medical Association released a statement against concentrated detergent packets, which have caused thousands of hospitalizations and several deaths (AMA, 2016).

THINK ABOUT IT

I'm willing to guess that none of us (including myself) meet all of these criteria. Is this an individual choice? What are some of the social reasons why we don't live up to these ideals?

SOCIOLOGY ON THE STREET

Your race and socioeconomic status affect your health in surprising ways, from stress in your daily life to the type of disease you may get. What health problems run in your family? Watch the Sociology on the Street video to find out more: **digital.wwnorton.com/youmayask7**.

WANT MORE PRACTICE?

Complete the InQuizitive activity for this chapter at digital.wwnorton.com /youmayask7

Part 3

BUILDING BLOCKS: INSTITUTIONS OF SOCIETY

Voters line up in November 2016 in Lawrenceville, Georgia. Elections are one of the many institutions that keep American society running, and are one of many vehicles for social change.

12

WE THINK OF THE FAMILY
AS A HAVEN IN A HARSH WORLD,
BUT IN FACT, INEQUALITY
BEGINS AT HOME.

ELDEST

MIDDLEBORNS

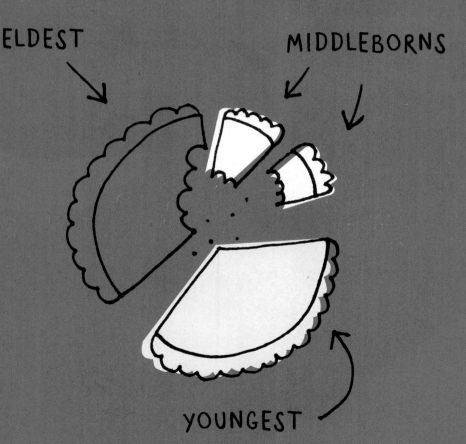

YOUNGEST

Family

The first time I had kids, I was pretty much right on time, so to speak. My eldest was born when I was 28 years old. That's about two years shy of the mean age at first birth at the time she was born, 1998. If you consider education level, then I actually had my first child six years younger than the typical man with a college degree. It may be TMI, but she was conceived the old-fashioned way (though not in the back of a Chevy, as the saying goes). When she was born premature and spent several weeks in the neonatal intensive care unit, I was panicked. While I had my mother to turn to for advice, none of my friends had kids yet. So we were really figuring it all out day to day—literally.

Fast-forward over two decades, and I just had my third child weeks shy of my fiftieth birthday. Before he was conceived, I wondered if I was making a big mistake. After all, as a social scientist I knew all about the research on age and happiness. Namely, happiness steadily declines throughout adulthood, reaching its lowest point around the mid-40s before starting a steady climb. Was it merely a coincidence that the decline corresponded to the prime years of raising kids, and the rise started when most folks were becoming empty nesters? Was I going to miss out on late adulthood happiness by pressing the fertility reset button?

Meanwhile, his conception could not have been more different from the almost-unplanned nature of my first. It took two years of in vitro fertility treatment, including two failed embryo implantation attempts, before my wife found herself with child, so to speak. Reproductively speaking, I was trying to have a child at an advanced paternal age, and the presence of certain behavioral, neurological, and psychological conditions such as ADHD, autism, and schizophrenia in offspring rises with older dads. Because this correlation is stronger in sons than in daughters, we decided to reduce these kinds of risks by testing each five-day blastocyst that we (or rather, the lab) had created to determine its sex. Those first two, failed attempts at pregnancy involved the female embryos. We were left with only frozen males to implant. We held our breath and tried. It worked.

I reassured myself by studies arguing that most of the increased risk of such conditions was not due to the aging process of older men's sperm (which do accumulate more mutations with each decade of life) but was a matter of adverse selection—to use the technical term. Namely, men who don't have their first child until 40 or 50 are different than men who manage to reproduce at, say, 30. They themselves have more genetic risk for autism and ADHD, to pick just two examples. That is, men with mental health or neurological issues are more likely to have kids late, if at all. The apparent effect of older dads was (mostly) not from the aging process, but from the logic of dating and mating—older first-time dads were more likely to have problems, even if reaching a threshold to be diagnosable.

Since I had been a first-time dad at a much younger age, I hoped my son would not be at a substantially higher risk for schizophrenia than his brother—born almost 20 years before—was. Instead, my worries (for I always worry) turned to other issues. Namely, how long would I live? As much as this third child would enjoy a much more comfortable and economically secure life than his older siblings did—given that I am more financially secure than I was at 28—he would by definition have me around for much less time than they did. I hesitated to look at the life tables provided by the Social Security Administration. It appeared that I could expect 30 more years of life, if I were an average American male. That's all he would get of me. And, I would need to stay employed—if possible—for 22 of those 30 years if I was to see him through college.

Then there are the worries about how different the world is today: My youngest niece started swiping screens before age one, and by 14 months she managed to call up her favorite Peppa Pig videos on her brothers' iPhones. Moreover, a friend recently signed up his *newborn* daughter for a Gmail account and started cc'ing her on all e-mail threads that involved her (such as brunch plans) so that she'd have a concrete record of some of her pre-verbal experiences. These were the sorts of things I needed to consider that I hadn't the first time around.

I doubt I am alone with these worries. As lifespans lengthen and age at first birth continues to climb, it turns out that I am at the leading edge of a growing group of older parents. Over 9 percent of births today are to fathers over the age of 40 and about 1 percent of births are to dads over the age of 50. Women, as well, are extending their fertility careers, with many having children well into their forties—partly thanks to the increased use of IVF. As adolescence creeps up through the twenties, such childbearing at older ages is perhaps inevitable, even if it requires an assist from technology.

I can report that while many of my worries have not abated, at least one has: Though I am exhausted and can't even believe I went through this sort of extended sleeplessness back when I needed more hours abed on account of being younger, my happiness does seem to be rising, despite (or because of) the new addition to the household. Of course, not regretting your kids is one of the strongest social norms in modern society, so you may not believe me. But I'm telling you, sociologist to sociologist, it's true. (Though you should definitely ask me again when he's a teenager asking to borrow the car keys.)

Family Forms and Changes

Why do we fall for the people we do? At first thought this might seem like a simple question. You start by envisioning the personal qualities of your lover, perhaps something about his or her physique, personality, sense of humor, or charm. If you take a step back and really try to think about it, you might admit to more practical reasons as well—physical proximity, shared language, financial security—those everyday factors vital to functioning relationships. If you take yet another step back, you face the larger question of mate selection: the phenomenon of human partnering that is patterned by history, culture, and law.

I know this is an unromantic way to view your love life, but consider the host of cultural and legal codes that prohibit you from partnering with, say, your 14-year-old first cousin. In Victorian England or a modern-day Muslim tribe, however, a man's 14-year-old first cousin might be a perfectly good match. Historically, interracial partnerships have also been prohibited. In 1961, when President Barack Obama's parents were married, it was still illegal in 22 different states for a White and a nonwhite to be married. Then in *Loving v. Virginia* (1967) the US Supreme Court unanimously struck down America's antimiscegenation laws. (See Chapter 9 for a discussion of the one-drop rule.) Similar laws, aimed at maintaining White "racial purity," existed in South Africa during apartheid as well as in Nazi Germany. In the contemporary world, ethnically mixed couples are hardly shocking, but 60 years ago in the United States they were almost unthinkable. When a culture maintains either legal or normative sanctions against people marrying outside their race, class, or caste, we call it a rule of endogamy, meaning marriage from within. To some extent, we all practice endogamy—that is, on some level people tend to hook up with similar people, because it makes for easier relations if you and your partner share a social group. In other parts of the world, such as India, historically people haven't had much of a choice: The caste system of India is based on a rigid adherence to endogamy (see Chapter 7).

In much of the contemporary Western world, exogamy, or marriage to someone outside one's social group, is legally possible, if not always

ENDOGAMY

marriage to someone within one's social group.

EXOGAMY

marriage to someone outside one's social group.

The Lovings embrace at a press conference the day after the Supreme Court ruled in their favor in *Loving v. Virginia*, June 13, 1967.

MONOGAMY

the practice of having only one sexual partner or spouse at a time.

POLYGAMY

the practice of having more than one sexual partner or spouse at a time.

POLYANDRY

the practice of having multiple husbands simultaneously.

POLYGYNY

the practice of having multiple wives simultaneously.

culturally acceptable. Consider the following unlikely pair: the African American son of a steel mill worker and the only child and sole heir of a mega-millionaire, White, chart-topping rock-and-roll star. The 1994 union of Michael Jackson and Lisa Marie Presley lasted less than two years, but it is an example of a couple who transgressed social, class, and racial groups. However, what is also telling is that by the time they met and fell for each other, they were already both celebrities and social equivalents, despite the gulf between their backgrounds. Total exogamy—when people from completely different social categories get together—is rare.

In addition to codes of endogamy and exogamy, another basic social structure governs your love life: how many partners you're expected to have. In societies that practice monogamy a person can partner with only one other. In societies that practice polygamy people have more than one sexual partner or spouse at a time. (See Chapter 8 for a more thorough discussion of a wide range of sexual practices.) This can take the form of a woman having several husbands, called polyandry, as happens in some rural areas of Asia. Or a man can take several wives, called polygyny, the most common form of polygamy, practiced in many contemporary Islamic and African cultures. Although the Mormon Church outlawed polygamy in 1890, some Mormon splinter groups, called fundamentalists, continue the practice of one man supporting several families at the same time (Lee, 2006).

If one day someone asks why you fell for your special someone, keep in mind that the answer could be quite long and sociologically involved. Cultural norms and state regulations play a fundamental, if invisible, role in your love life. These factors first set the limits as to who is even available on your romantic horizon. Once you find that person (or those persons, for you polygamists), your next move will be to form a relationship with him or her or them, probably in the shape of a family. But just how might that family look?

MALINOWSKI AND THE TRADITIONAL FAMILY

In the post–World War II era in the United States, the nuclear family—the idealized model of a male breadwinner, a female homemaker, and their dependent children—emerged as the dominant, normative, and mythical model for domestic life. It was dominant, because indeed many Americans took to it; in the 1950s, 86 percent of children lived in two-parent families, and 60 percent of children were born into homes with a male breadwinner and a female homemaker (Coontz, 2001). It was normative, because it has been hailed, then and now, as the proper form for families, the way things ought to be. Finally, the taken-for-grantedness of the nuclear family is mythical, because its existence represents not a natural, timeless, or universal approach to family arrangements but one that appeared in specific historical contexts.

In the sociological imagination, this version of the family looks less like a universal norm and more like an ideological construct, and an unusual one at that, which arose out of the unique social structural conditions of the 1950s. That is, the 1950s nuclear family model deviates from both its predecessors and its successors. Yet many of us still idealize this model and miss it terribly. By studying cross-cultural variation in family forms, we'll see that this allegedly "normal" family is not always the dominant model. By unpacking the historical development of the nuclear family model and its subsequent unraveling, we'll come to recognize that this form of family is not a universal ideal. And regardless of what kind of family ties you may deem worth forging, worth loving, and worth defending, as a sociologist your job will be to study all family forms without prejudgment.

Not only is the US nuclear family seen as the ideal family form by many, but in prior centuries, it was assumed by some scholars that the very institution of the family itself was something that had developed in Western societies and had not "yet" emerged in some other populations. However, in 1913 Bronislaw Malinowski put to rest a long-standing family debate among anthropologists about the universal existence of families. Scholars had argued that traditional tribal societies couldn't possibly have family units because of their egregious nondiscriminating sexual promiscuity. Malinowski, based on his research among Australian Aboriginals (who seemed to have sex with everyone), suggested that these natives did, in fact, form familial arrangements. They maintained a central place, the equivalent of a hearth and home, where the family gathered. And they bestowed feelings of love, affection, and care on each family member. Thus the dispute was settled: The family was accepted as a universal human institution for most of the twentieth century, and this notion continues to endure today.

Moreover, Malinowski argued that the family, in addition to being a universal phenomenon, was a necessary institution for fulfilling the task of child rearing in society. The influential structural-functional sociologist Talcott Parsons would expand on this notion in the 1950s. As we learned in Chapter 8, according to Parsons, the traditional nuclear family, consisting of a mother and father and their children, was a functional necessity in modern industrial society, because it was most compatible with fulfilling society's need for productive workers and child nurturers. And so the nuclear family reigned supreme, timeless, and universal. (Note that although the

NUCLEAR FAMILY

familial form consisting of a father, a mother, and their children.

nuclear family is a particular form of the traditional model, in this chapter we will use the two terms synonymously.)

The problem with functionalist arguments such as these is that even if one social institution seems to perform some function for society, the function is not necessarily performed only by that particular institution. A functional need is not sufficient cause for the development of an institution, especially not when other kinds of institutions can perform the function just as well. But when you have Western blinders on, as most social scientists following Malinowski did, it becomes difficult to see anything other than the kind of family life you expect to see. When properly fitted with your sociological lens, however, you can make the familiar strange, and you'll find some colorful variation among familial arrangements.

Take the Munduruku villagers of South America, for instance. They give new meaning to the hearth-and-home feature of Malinowski's universal family. Munduruku men and women live in separate houses at different ends of their village; they eat separate meals; they sleep apart. In fact, they meet up with each other only to have sex (Collier et al., 1997). Among the Na people of southwestern China (also known as the Mosuo to outsiders), who have managed to retain much of their distinctive culture despite war, Communism, and the onset of quasi-capitalism, the institution of marriage doesn't exist. The Na do not have any practice like it, nor do they put much thought into fatherhood. Children grow up with uncles rather than fathers as the primary males in the home. Sex occurs in the middle of the night, when men visit women for sexual encounters ranging in duration from one-night stands to lifelong relationships (Booth, 2017). There are no social restrictions on who can partner with whom. Property is passed down through the maternal line. Yet the Na manage just fine, reproducing from generation to generation and maintaining a stable farming economy that has recently been bolstered by Chinese tourism (people fascinated by the so-called "kingdom of women"). What are the long-term consequences of the Na's particular arrangements? It turns out that whereas in most patrilineal societies females are more risk-averse than males, among the Na, that pattern is flipped: Na girls tend to be the greater risk-takers (Liu & Zuo, 2019). Otherwise, their outcomes don't seem all that different from those in most subsistence farming societies.

If the Na take hands-off fatherhood to the extreme, women in present-day Zambia implode our notions of caring motherhood. Zambian mothers don't nurture their daughters in the way Westerners would expect. When a Zambian girl needs advice, she is expected to seek out an older female relative as a confidante in preference to her mother (Collier et al., 1997). Mothers' "essential" nature has always been defined in the West as nurturing and being connected to offspring, presumably ordained by women's biological birthing functions. However, the way motherhood is practiced in Zambian culture suggests that a mother's unconditional warmth, despite the rhetoric, is not necessarily a biological given.

Families come in all different forms. What are some of the ways that family groups can differ from culture to culture? For instance, how does an extended family in the United States (top) differ from the Na in China (middle) or Zambian families in Africa (bottom)?

THE FAMILY IN THE WESTERN WORLD TODAY

Even the modern Western family comes in a variety of forms. The typical American family today is not likely to resemble the versions so often idealized in 1950s television shows. In addition to nuclear families, one needs to count the extended family—kin networks that extend outside or beyond the nuclear family. Families with no children also exist (for instance, couples that become "empty nesters" after their children move out), as do two-wage-earner families (dual-income families), single-parent families, blended stepfamilies, and adopted families, to name just a few possibilities. Although the traditional family was the dominant model for a majority of people living in the 1950s, it never described home life for all Americans. And it's increasingly losing its edge today as families take on new shapes and sizes.

In 2019, less than 20 percent of families consisted of two married parents with children and with the husband as the sole earner (Bureau of Labor Statistics, 2020b). Only about a quarter of American households consist of a married couple with their own children, and 62 percent of households have only one or two people in them (US Census Bureau 2020o, 2020p).

In the face of soaring divorce rates, the 1950s-style way of life is indeed becoming a historical artifact. Nowadays, although the exact figure varies considerably from study to study, approximately 43 to 46 percent of all marriages end in divorce (Schoen & Canudas-Romo, 2006). This statistic doesn't seem to discourage too many people, though, because three of four divorced men and two of three divorced women try their hand at marriage again. But alas, the second time around has about the same rate of failure as the first, and those marriages are even a bit more likely to hit the skids (Coontz, 2010). It's commonly thought that divorce has skyrocketed since the 1950s, but actually the divorce rate has been steadily rising since the nineteenth century, as divorce became less and less of a social and religious taboo. Divorce rates seem to have stabilized over the past decade or so, with about 90 percent of marriages making it to the 5-year mark and 70 percent making it to 15 years; then, another 1 percent of marriages dissolve each year after that, whether by divorce or death.

But rising divorce rates in the United States have not put marriage in any danger of extinction. Eventually, about 80 percent of young adults will likely get married at some point if current projections hold, while men are more likely to remarry after a divorce (Hendi, 2019; Vespa et al., 2013).

Given the increased incidence of divorce and remarriage, families are taking on new shapes and sizes, such as single-parent and blended arrangements (Figure 12.1). As of 2013, about 15 percent of children in America lived in a blended family (Pew Research Center, 2014), which reconfigures the aftermath of divorce into step-relations. (We'll have more to say about the effect of divorce on children later.) Cohabitation, living together in an intimate relationship without formal legal or religious sanctioning, has also emerged as a socially acceptable arrangement; roughly 24 percent of never-married Americans between 25 and 34 years old live together without marriage. Within three years, though, 58 percent will be married, 19 percent will have broken up, and 23 percent will still be cohabiting (Copen et al., 2013). Many cohabiters believe that living together is an effective means of curtailing future divorce. It's the commonsense notion that living together provides a sample of what married life is like and will inform and improve the couple's future marriage. On the opposite side of the debate, conservative supporters of "family values" point to studies showing a higher divorce rate in the long term among couples who cohabit before marriage than those who don't (Rosenfeld & Roesler, 2018), or those who cohabit before engagement specifically (Rhoades et al., 2009). Conservative Christian counselors advise that "living in sin" sets up a rockier road for a marriage, but the actual reason for the higher divorce rate probably has to do more with selection bias: Most people who cohabit are open to premarital sex, which also means they are less likely to see divorce as sinful.

Single women are having their days as well. Twenty-one percent of American households with children are headed by single moms (they have children,

COHABITATION

living together in an intimate relationship without formal legal or religious sanctioning.

FIGURE 12.1 Work–Family Living Arrangements of Children, 1960 and 2015, Ages 0–14

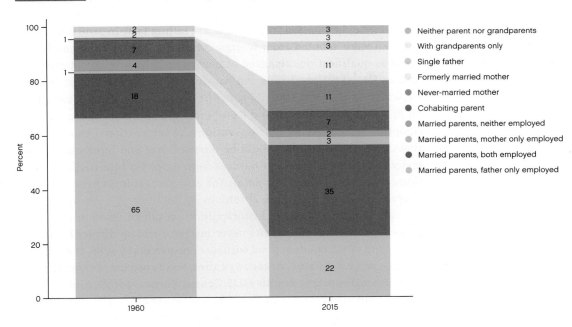

Legend:
- Neither parent nor grandparents
- With grandparents only
- Single father
- Formerly married mother
- Never-married mother
- Cohabiting parent
- Married parents, neither employed
- Married parents, mother only employed
- Married parents, both employed
- Married parents, father only employed

SOURCE: Cohen, 2017.

but are not married), and 15 percent of women remain child-free (Livingston, 2015, 2018). Women who do have children are doing so at a later age than ever before—now averaging 26 years, up from 21 in the 1970s (Martin & Osterman, 2019). However, women have been delaying marriage for even longer, tying the knot at a median of 28 years old (US Census Bureau, 2019b). The age when a woman has her first baby varies by subgroup: White professional women, on average, postpone motherhood even longer. Another interesting new twist in American families is the rapid rise in the number of twins. Between the years 1980 and 2016, the number of twin births nearly doubled, from 68,339 to 133,155 births (see Figure 11.1), and triplet and other higher-order multiple births increased by a staggering 3.1 times, from 1,337 to 4,123 (Martin et al., 2017), though this trend has stabilized and experienced slight declines over the last few years (Martin et al., 2019). This rise has taken place almost entirely among White women. As professional White women increasingly delay childbearing, they are biologically more likely to give birth to twins, and this trend is compounded by the more widespread use of fertility treatments, which increase the likelihood of a multiple birth (Martin et al., 2010). Indeed, the rate of use of assisted reproductive technology (ART) has risen rapidly. As of 2015, 1.7 percent of all live births were the result of some form of ART—a number that is sure to steadily rise over the foreseeable future (Sunderam et al., 2018).

And then there is adoption. From 2011 to 2015, approximately 0.7 percent of women 18–44 years old had ever adopted a child, while about 1.2 percent were actively pursuing adoption (Ugwu & Nugent, 2018). International adoptions, which had been climbing since the 1980s, peaked at 22,000 in 2004 and are falling fast. In 2018 only 4,059 children were adopted from foreign countries, in part because of more rigorous qualifications required of new parents by foreign countries, as well as UN-sanctioned adoption bans on countries like Guatemala (US Department of State, 2019). Meanwhile, in 2012, the Hague Convention on Protection of Children and Co-operation in Respect of Intercountry Adoption (Hague Adoption Convention), an international treaty, stated that domestic adoptions should be pursued first and foremost. Indeed, many countries that used to serve as sources for US international adoptions are now shutting their doors. For example, Ethiopia banned foreign adoptions in 2018 (Hosseini, 2018).

Single-parent families, historically the result of death or desertion, are on the rise as more parents never marry or end up divorced. In 1960, 9.1 percent of US children lived with just one parent; by 1986, that number was 23.5 percent; by 2019, it was 26 percent, and 83 percent of those children lived in single-mother families (US Census Bureau, 2019c). Single-parent families are also becoming more common worldwide; currently, approximately 14 percent of all families around the globe are headed by women (Chamie, 2016).

Keeping It in the Family: The Historical Divide between Public and Private

Given the enormous cross-cultural and even within-cultural variation among family forms, you may be wondering how and why the so-called traditional family ever came to be the standard marker of normalcy. The short answer is that the development of the family was tied to the development of modernity, state formation, and the rise of the modern economy. For starters, *traditional family* is a misleading term; this family structure is not characteristic of all tradition, just that of the 1950s. The nuclear model of stay-at-home mom and working father is itself deviant compared with American family arrangements both 50 years before it and 50 years after. It was a historically specific model in a unique era, in which many White city-dwellers moved to the suburbs, married young, and raised three or four children. It was a prosperous era, too: In the 1950s real wages grew more in any single year than they did in the 1980s as a whole. With just a high-school education, an average 30-year-old White man could earn enough at his manufacturing job to buy a median-priced home on 15 percent of his salary (Coontz, 2001). Today, with just a high-school education, an average 30-year-old man is likely to be tenuously positioned in the service sector, making about $15 an hour and probably lacking employer-provided health insurance. But it's not just money that set the 1950s apart. As Stephanie Coontz notes in *The Way We Never Were: American Families and the Nostalgia Trap* (1992), people long for the sense of simplicity, wholesomeness, and ease that 1950s families like those portrayed in popular TV shows of the time are perceived to have enjoyed.

PREMODERN FAMILIES

In the preindustrial family of the nineteenth century, each household unit operated like a small business—that is, as a miniature family economy. It was a site for both production and consumption, where work was done in the home and the home was a working unit. Families made and used their own food, clothes, and goods, and there was little if any surplus wealth.

Families tended to live near their kin and thus could get help and support from their kinship networks, strings of relationships between people

KINSHIP NETWORKS

strings of relationships between people related by blood and co-residence (i.e., marriage).

Preindustrial families, such as these settlers, operated like a small business. The home was a site for work, and the entire family was involved.

related by blood and co-residence (i.e., marriage). Preindustrial communities didn't have huge savings banks, insurance companies, payday lenders, or government agencies to help in hard times; that was the role of family. For example, a down-and-out uncle might have a failed crop of wheat one summer. He could call in an IOU from his luckier cousin across the village, borrowing some of his crop and setting off a reciprocal exchange of food, clothing, and child care. Such families would have a grapevine structure where more lateral kinship ties endured than vertical ones (usually, no more than three generations of one family were alive at a time). Communities cooperated in a noncash economy, using a barter system to swap goods. There was no significant accumulation of goods, no savings, no wealth, and not much beyond what individuals needed to survive. There was also minimal division of labor between the sexes, such that men were involved in child care, and women and children often performed the same manual labor as men. Indeed, in the preindustrial family, children were thought of as "small adults," as Philippe Ariès argued in 1962. They didn't warrant any special treatment or consideration, and childhood was hardly the nurturing period we think of today. In fact, some scholars argue that the whole notion of childhood, or children's special needs, is a relatively recent invention, as is that of motherhood as a full-time occupation. Both have emerged only since the middle of the nineteenth century and have been made possible through industrialization, the rise of the cash economy, formal schooling, and the establishment of privacy in the family.

THE EMERGENCE OF THE MALE BREADWINNER FAMILY

With the Industrial Revolution, the realms of the public and private—previously intertwined as one in the working family—split into separate spheres of work and home, as men left household production for wage work in factories. (See Chapter 14 for a brief history of capitalism and its impact on family life.) Families stopped being productive mini-economies for the barter system and instead became strictly sites for consumption. Out went household spinning and weaving, and in came the factory-made sweater. Food, clothing, furniture, decorations, appliances, cosmetics, pharmaceuticals: You name it, the family was there to consume it. Specifically, women made the choices of what and how much their families would consume.

Furthermore, "women's work"—tending the home and raising children—became relegated to the private, domestic sphere, where it went unpaid as a woman relied on a man's wages, at

This nineteenth-century painting illustrates the Victorian feminine domestic ideal. How did the Industrial Revolution transform the division of labor between men and women?

least among the middle classes. All the extra money in the new wage economy passed through the hands of women, who remained in charge of running the home and doing the shopping. Such functions might seem like a move toward women "wearing the pants" in the family, but they, in fact, provided a point of emergence for a new form of gender inequality. Women were in charge of spending the family's money, not earning it, and in our society, work for money is the most highly valued form of labor. Women's work was the unpaid management of the home, and this distinction established unequal positions for men and women in society. At the very least, a man had the chance to spend his wages before they ever reached the other members of his family.

The results of these structural changes were far-reaching. First, a gendered division of labor arose in the household, where women now were in exclusive charge of maintaining the home and rearing children. Second, as the mobility of families searching for paid labor opportunities increased, they became separated from their kinship networks. Family structures changed from grapevine forms to "beanpole" families, in which kinship ties are vertical. Because people didn't live near their siblings, aunts, and uncles, they could depend only on their children and parents who lived with them. As life expectancies increased, up to five generations may have been alive at any given time, but lateral ties (such as those existing between cousins) weakened because of the longer distances separating these kin.

The beanpole family structure is particularly taxing on women today, who, because of delayed childbirth, are likely to find that their parents need assistance just as their own children are leaving home. As a result of declining fertility and longer life expectancies, the US population is growing older, so the problem of elder care (and its disproportionate impact on women) will only get worse. In 2018 the median age in the United States was 38.2 years, with only one state—North Dakota—getting younger since 2010 (US Census Bureau, 2019d). A recent survey found that 10 percent of respondents over age 50 reported providing more than 200 hours of informal care to folks (outside their home) in the past year. Women bore most of the burden, but men did 40 percent of that care. We are in the middle as compared to other wealthy countries in this regard (Bauer, 2019). Our government's relatively low support for elder care (Medicare does not cover long-term care, for instance) is balanced out by the fact that we have one of the youngest populations in the developed world.

A third fallout of the new cash economy and the resulting split between public and private realms was the creation of the cult of domesticity, the notion that true womanhood centers on domestic responsibility and child rearing. During the first half of the twentieth century, ideas sprang up surrounding woman's true nature—ideas meant to support her newly created role as housewife. These included the notion that women, more than men, are endowed with the innate emotional qualities required to provide warmth and comfort. According to this ideology, not only are women better suited for home life, but also their domesticity comes to be seen as necessary for the survival of society. Women, so the argument goes, are needed to ensure that the home remains a safe haven in the otherwise cold seas of capitalist enterprise. As breadwinners, men struggle in the dog-eat-dog commercial world, whereas women provide the emotional shelter that anchors private life in human sentiment, emotion, care, and love.

FAMILIES AFTER WORLD WAR II

By the 1950s the model nuclear family had already come to be idealized, although it was mostly attainable only by White middle- and upper-class families (see the discussion of racial and ethnic differences in family structure later in the chapter). Most men's earnings were simply not great enough to afford a stay-at-home wife and dependent children. The gap between ideal and real narrowed as real wages (wages adjusted for inflation) increased in the 1950s, making the patriarchal tradition of a male breadwinner and a female homemaker a feasible arrangement for a greater number of families. Still, many nonwhite, non-middle-class families and individuals were excluded from the prosperity of the 1950s (see Chapter 9), and women worked outside the home throughout history, especially nonwhite women.

During the post–World War II economic boom, the manufacturing economy thrived with unionized jobs, real living wages, government housing subsidies, and job-training programs. It was a period of great optimism for good reasons: The Depression was over; America and its allies had won the war; and the United States was now dominant on the world's economic stage. Americans moved en masse to the suburbs—often to homes that required little to no down payment. Meanwhile, many women quit their jobs, if they had them, and returned to cultivating domesticity full-time; the divorce rate dropped to just over one in four marriages; and fertility rates soared during this "baby boom."

As family scholars are quick to point out, however, these trends in families were atypical. Although the divorce rate dipped in the 1950s, it had been on the rise since the end of the nineteenth century, so modern appeals to return to an age when divorce did not exist ring somewhat hollow. Furthermore, the fertility boom following World War II represented an unusual spike in family size, which had otherwise been on the decline since well before the turn of the century. What's more, the 1950s were also an era of rampant teen pregnancies: The teenage birthrate was twice as high in 1957 as in the 1990s. The difference was that pregnant teens in the postwar era had less access to abortion, and when they bore children, they more often got married. In fact, the 1950s marked the twentieth century's youngest national average for age at time of marriage—an average of 20 and 22 years old for women and men, respectively. Finally, the decline in women's workforce participation represented a dip in an otherwise upward trend, especially given women's labor power during World War II (when women were hired as temporary replacements for men serving in the armed forces).

Although the period was an anomaly in many ways, we tend to look back fondly (and sometimes bitterly) to the 1950s family as the normal and right

Textile factory workers in 1949. Why did many women leave their jobs after World War II?

way for families to be. But Stephanie Coontz found that while children's well-being and family economic security were at an all-time high toward the end of the 1960s, it was also a time of tumultuous struggle for racial and sexual equality (Coontz, 2001). What, then, do we really miss?

Family and Work: A Not-So-Subtle Revolution

Since the 1970s, American men and women have been caught up in what Kathleen Gerson (1985) calls a "subtle revolution" in our way of organizing work and home, even as we fantasize about an imagined time gone by. Women's participation in the labor force has soared, whereas fertility rates have plummeted. By the end of the 1970s, more women were in, rather than out of, the labor force for the first time. In 1950, approximately 30 percent of women worked outside the home; that number more than doubled to 60 percent by 1999 (Francis, 2005). In 2018, the labor force participation rate for women was 57.1 (Bureau of Labor Statistics, 2019f; Figure 12.2).

At the same time, birthrates have dropped, sinking from a baby boom to a baby bust. In the mid-1950s the birthrate was about 106.2 births per 1,000 women. That rate had dropped to just 62.9 in 1980 and to 59.1 as of 2018 (Martin et al., 2019). The National Center for Health Statistics reports that marriage rates since the 1960s have also declined, and many adults are postponing marriage until later in life. With the rising divorce rate, marriage is looking less and less like the stable force in women's lives that it was in the postwar era. In fact, by 2007, more Americans age 15 and older were single than married for the first time in a century. The result is that the cult of domesticity is out of the picture for most women, and daughters since the 1970s have increasingly departed from their mother's paths.

The gender revolution in work and family is probably here to stay, and with notable effects on children. Research study after research study has hinged on one basic question: Is maternal employment good, bad, or neutral for kids? There's no shortage of hypotheses. A study published in *Child Development* (Brooks-Gunn et al., 2003) suggests that having a working mother in one's early years can result in lower cognitive achievement and increased behavioral problems for a child. Yet another study published in the prestigious journal *Science* (Chase-Lansdale et al., 2003) claims the opposite: For moms with lower income levels, leaving kids in day care to enter the workforce is beneficial. Hundreds of studies fall on both sides of

FIGURE 12.2 Women in the Labor Force, 1970–2018

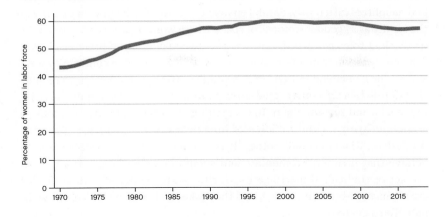

SOURCE: Bureau of Labor Statistics, 2019f.

the argument, with mothers' employment being either disastrous or advantageous to their children. Family situations are just too complex and diverse to generalize. Perhaps, then, this mishmash of results is a consequence of asking the wrong question. Maybe we should instead ask, "How does maternal employment affect children differently within the family?"

In *The Pecking Order* (2004), I found that when a mother worked while raising her children, the adult daughters and sons eventually attained jobs that were more or less equivalent and made about the same income. But in families with a stay-at-home mom, the gender gap widens. When the mother does not work and thus cannot provide a same-sex parental role model in terms of career choices, daughters fare far worse than sons, earning roughly $8,000 less a year than their brothers later in life. And without a working-mother role model, daughters are 15 percent less likely to graduate from college than their brothers (whereas in the general population, more women than men earn college degrees).

A Feminist "Rethinking of the Family"

As noted in Chapter 4, the family is the primary unit of socialization for most of us. If family life is structured by larger forces in the social order, such as wage policy and gender inequality at work, then it is also simultaneously a site for the reproduction of these relations. As we have just seen, whether or not a mother works outside the home may affect the outcomes of her sons and daughters differently. Sarah Fenstermaker Berk (1985) has characterized the family as a "gender factory" of sorts, where women and men learn to take on distinct roles paralleling the divide between public and private spheres. The family is where people first learn how to "do gender" in conformity with social rules. Sociologist Marjorie DeVault (1991) shows in *Feeding the Family* that family ties are constructed through women's acts of shopping, preparing meals, and serving them. In everything from the planning of menus to accommodating a child's dislike of lima beans, women are doing gender. As Barbara Risman (1998) notes, "It is at home that most people come to believe that men and women are and should be essentially different." In the act of traditional marriage itself, rituals are gender-stratified: Brides are given away by their fathers, and they take the last name of a husband in patrilineal custom.

The idealized cult of domesticity, although a historical and cultural anomaly among many possibilities, has had powerful and lasting effects on many women's family ideals. Feminist consciousness, raised in the 1960s, led many women to question the ideology of domesticity, finding it "stultifying, infantilizing, and exploitative" of women (Stacey, 1987). In 1963, the feminist writer Betty Friedan led the assault against the limits of being a homemaker with her classic *The Feminine Mystique*. She writes in the introduction:

> The problem lay buried, unspoken, for many years in the minds of American women. It was a strange stirring, a sense of dissatisfaction, a yearning that women suffered in the middle of the twentieth century in the United States. Each suburban housewife struggled with it alone. As she made the beds, shopped for groceries, matched slipcover material, ate peanut butter sandwiches with her children, chauffeured Cub Scouts and Brownies, lay beside her husband at night—she was afraid to ask even of herself the silent question—"Is this all?" (1997, p. 15)

Sociologists elaborated on Friedan's invocation, claiming that what really distinguishes the head of the family is power. The family, as they see it, is a battleground for the power to make collective decisions on everything from who does the laundry to what neighborhood to live in to what college fund to invest in. This is the case, argues sociologist Jessie Bernard in *The Future of Marriage* (1972), even in the comfortable living rooms of traditional nuclear families. Take, for instance, the tensions that arise from the different ways that household members spend money. In studies of welfare recipients, women have been known to spend a greater portion of their welfare benefits on children than fathers do. And in a study of Japanese American families, working wives tended to keep their earnings separate from their husbands' income, and even secret, to preserve their autonomy to spend it how they—and not their husbands—chose (Glenn, 1986).

Furthermore, money is not all the same within the family; rather, husbands', wives', and children's incomes are earmarked in distinctive ways. Women's earnings tend to be spent on extras, so-called luxury items, or otherwise nonessential expenses. Their money is devalued as "fun money." Men's earnings, on the other hand, are earmarked for essentials. When sociologist Margaret Nelson (1990) interviewed working wives, one woman explained, "What he makes there is mainly like insurance, taxes, and all that. What I make usually goes for food, clothing—whatever I find necessary . . . or just to take the kids once a week to Middlebury and blow it." So even a household's income is gendered. As Viviana Zelizer (2005) notes, the distinctions between household incomes help protect a man's status and sense of masculinity when a wife also takes on a breadwinner role in dual-income families. In this way, feminist rethinking of the family urges us not to view the family as a necessarily cohesive, unified whole but to recognize that the family is not immune from socially structured gender relations. And as gender relations change, so too do family forms. As women become less financially dependent on men, for example, more equality slowly develops in other areas of their relationships. Or does it?

Betty Friedan in 1967, advocating for the addition of an equal rights clause for women in the New York State Constitution.

When Home Is No Haven: Domestic Abuse

Family life is not always the warm, nurturing environment it appears to be on prime-time television, where moms and dads stand ready with hugs, siblings crack jokes, and grandma is strict but well intentioned. Abuse, neglect, and manipulation happen across all familial relationships: Sibling "rivalry" becomes physically aggressive, husbands and wives with powerful tempers hit and control one another, adult children plunder their elderly parents' life savings. The most frequent form of family violence is sibling on sibling (Eriksen & Jensen, 2006). But before you assign all the blame for your current low self-esteem on that time your brother walloped you upside the head with a shoe, note that the strongest two predictors of sibling-on-sibling violence are dads with short tempers and moms who get physical when it comes to punishing the kids (Eriksen & Jensen, 2006). So is it your brother's fault that he learned how to solve problems by mimicking dad's anger management strategy and piggybacking on mom's heavy hand of authority? This monkey-see, monkey-do explanation has had a long history in the study of domestic violence. Studies have found that abuse transmission is not genetic and that only about one-third of people who are abused as children go on to have a seriously neglectful or abusive relationship with their own children (Oliver, 1993). Broad social factors like poverty, single-parent households, and low levels of educational attainment are associated with higher levels of all types of domestic abuse.

When violence occurs within a couple it's often called IPV, intimate partner violence. More than one-third of women and one-quarter of men have been raped, physically attacked, and/or stalked by an intimate partner at some point in their lives (Centers for Disease Control and Prevention, 2011c). In a study of 10,018 homicides for women over 18: "Over half of all homicides (55.3%) were IPV-related; 11.2% of victims of IPV-related homicide experienced some form of violence in the month preceding their deaths, and argument and jealousy were common precipitating circumstances" (Petrosky et al., 2017).

Elder abuse is a relatively new field of study that investigates physical, verbal, and financial abuse intentionally or unintentionally perpetrated against people (usually family members) who are at least 57 years old. Estimates suggest elder abuse is not particularly widespread; one-year prevalence (that is, a statistical measure of how frequently these problems occur within a given 12-month period) was 4.6 percent for emotional abuse, 1.6 percent for physical abuse, 0.6 percent for sexual abuse, 5.1 percent for potential neglect, and 5.2 percent for current financial abuse by a family member (Acierno et al., 2010). The impact of mistreatment in intimate relationships can have serious and long-lasting financial, health, and emotional consequences for individuals, families, and communities.

The Chore Wars: Supermom Does It All

SECOND SHIFT

women's responsibility for housework and child care—everything from cooking dinner to doing laundry, bathing children, reading bedtime stories, and sewing Halloween costumes.

One of the main ways that gender is enacted within the family is with respect to the unpaid labor that needs to be done at home. In the case of housework and the chore wars, gender remains a salient social force that shapes family life. The cult of domesticity lingers on, such that even though 56.7 percent of women participated in the workforce in 2015, domestic duties, such as housework and child care, still fall disproportionately on their shoulders (Bureau of Labor Statistics, 2015a; Francis, 2005). Women return from the office to take up what Arlie Hochschild (1989) calls the second shift: Women take responsibility for housework and child care, which includes everything from cooking dinner to doing laundry, bathing children, reading bedtime stories, and sewing Halloween costumes. Despite women's gains in the public realm of work, the revolution at home has, as Hochschild described it, stalled. (Indeed, as we'll see in Chapter 14, many women view the workplace as a refuge from their harried domestic lives.)

Within a two-career household, parents are likely to spend their at-home time on separate—and unequal—tasks. One study from 1965 to 1966 found that working women averaged 3 hours each day on housework, whereas men put in a meager 17 minutes. When it comes to leisure activities, however, men surpass their working wives. Working fathers watch an hour more of television per day than working mothers. They also sleep a half hour longer (Hochschild, 2003). The resulting "leisure gap" can brew hostilities between exasperated, exhausted wives and their unresponsive husbands.

Using national studies on time use from the 1960s and 1970s, Hochschild counted the hours that women and men put in on the job in addition to their time spent on housework and child care. She determined that women worked roughly 15 hours longer each week than men (Hochschild, 2003). After 52 weeks, this added up to 780 hours more that women work than men—that's an extra month! While the gap in upaid work has shrunk since the 1960s, it has remained more or less the same over the past decade (Figure 12.3). The Pew Research Center found that as of 2016, women spent roughly 14 hours more per week on housework and child care combined (Parker & Livingston, 2018).

Recent research shows how and when this gendered division of labor arises. Before the birth of the first child, men exhibit higher total work hours than women: They tend to work more paid hours and also do a relatively equitable share of housework. But after the birth of children, the division of labor in the home changes, both because men do less of the child-care work and because, at the same time, they reduce their non-child-care housework.

FIGURE 12.3 Trends in Housework and Child Care since 1965

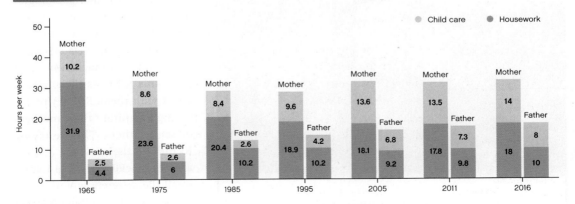

SOURCES: Pew Research Center, 2013; Parker & Livingston, 2018.

In total, before becoming parents, married men spend about three additional hours doing all forms of work (jobs and housework) compared to women—but after the birth of a child, women do about six hours more than men (Yavorsky et al., 2015).

The division of labor in the home refers to not just who does how much but also who does what. As Viviana Zelizer (2005) shows, housework tasks are patterned around gender. When men do housework, their contribution is referred to as "helping out around the house," and their wives zealously thank them. Women who have "helping" husbands in the home consider themselves extremely lucky. Many men, however, never report feeling lucky or extremely thankful when their wives do the housework. And women *run* the household; they don't simply "help out."

In addition, men are typically in charge of outdoor, stereotypically masculine activities, whereas women disproportionately do the work inside. Even cooking is broken down by gender: Men more often cook the meat for a meal when they share work in the kitchen. Men also have more control over when they help out, because they are more likely to be in charge of chores that don't require completion on a daily basis, such as changing the oil in the family car or mowing the lawn. Women are more likely to be locked into a fixed and harried housework routine: Pick up the kids from day care, cook dinner, wash the dishes, administer the bath, and put the baby to bed (Zelizer, 2005).

Yet another male advantage in the division of household labor is that men get to do more of what they like to do, while women are often stuck with the most undesirable chores, such as scrubbing toilets and ironing. The time fathers spend on domestic labor is more likely to be spent with their children, which is usually more enjoyable and satisfying than doing chores. In a recent interview with me, sociologist Jennifer Senior pointed out how much more parenting today's dads are doing: "Dads spend three times as much time with their kids today as their fathers spent with them. So they're not trying to imitate their mothers or their fathers. They're trying to imitate their wives . . . they are not slackers at all. In spite of all the differences within the house, they are really doing way more than they ever saw and ever

DIGITAL.WWNORTON.COM/YOUMAYASK7

To see an interview with Jennifer Senior, go to
digital.wwnorton.com/youmayask7

had modeled for them" (Conley, 2015b). Not only is the time that dads spend with kids more enjoyable than scrubbing pans or other household drudgery, but studies consistently also find that men who share child rearing and housework have happier marriages, better health, and longer lives (Kimmel, 2000). As best-selling author and pediatrician Dr. Spock (1998) put it, "There is no reason why fathers shouldn't be able to do these jobs as well as mothers." Furthermore, studies show that when left to their own devices, men are perfectly fine housekeepers, cooks, and primary parents (Gerson, 1993).

Neoclassical economists typically look at a member's power in the family as a direct expression of that member's utility to the family unit, and that tends to be measured in terms of his or her income. In such a formulation, money talks, and whoever earns the bacon doesn't have to cook it. This is not so for women, whose income goes only so far in increasing their power in the family. The more a wife contributes to the household income, the more her husband is likely to share, or "help out" with, the second shift. That seems to fit the bacon theory. But as soon as the wife's earnings start to overtake her husband's, he drops out of the shared domestic equation, leaving the entire second shift up to her (Bittman et al., 2003). Furthermore, when women earn more than their husbands, the perceived insult to masculinity may make for a tense home environment. Men, it seems, are not willing to let anyone else wear the proverbial pants in the household.

With all the advances in home cooking and cleaning technology over the past few decades, you might wonder why the second shift can't be handled a little more efficiently than in a whole extra month of labor a year. But as Ruth Schwartz Cowan reports in *More Work for Mother: The Ironies of Household Technology from the Open Hearth to the Microwave* (1983), all those time-saving devices like the vacuum cleaner and the washing machine have paradoxically increased the amount of time women spend on housework. As Windex, dishwashers, Swiffers, and domestic media perfectionists like Martha Stewart present sparkling everyday homes, the standards of cleanliness and household design rise, and even more housework is necessary than before. That said, as women have increased their hours in the formal labor market, the gender gap has declined in recent years: Women now do only 1.8 hours of household work for every hour a man completes, compared with the sixfold difference in the 1960s.

The entrepreneur Don Aslett, who built a business around domestic cleaning services, told one sociologist, "The whole mentality out there is that if you clean, you're a scumball" (Ehrenreich, 2001). Although not always so harshly spoken of, housework certainly is overlooked as a worthy or meaningful activity in America. For one thing, it's unpaid labor, and in a capitalist economy, it seems pretty, well, worthless. For another, it has been construed historically as women's work. A housewife, measured against modern criteria for success such as salaries, pensions, benefits, bonuses, and promotions, is just a housewife. Feminists in the 1960s argued that

↑

Many women juggle full-time jobs with caring for their children and running their home with little help from their spouses. According to Arlie Hochschild, what are the consequences of the supermom strategy?

housework should be fairly compensated, because without a woman's labor, the American workforce would not be able to keep going, an argument that is being reviewed in Italy, the United Kingdom, and the United States (Ellen, 2014; Scalise, 2014; Shulevitz, 2016). This "reproductive labor" argument stressed the value of social reproduction: All the activities and tasks that women performed daily kept their working husbands' lives running smoothly.

This movement, you've probably figured out, did not catch on immediately. In fact, it is taking more than four decades and one tragedy. Zelizer (2005) showed that women's unpaid work commanded a price tag in the distribution of monetary rewards for surviving family members of those killed in the September 11, 2001, terrorist attacks. In the aftermath of 9/11, friends and family grappled with the shock and grief of losing loved ones. Some relatives of victims filed wrongful death suits against the airlines of the hijacked planes. To curb individual lawsuits and to spare the airlines from insurmountable litigations, the US government established the September 11 Victim Compensation Fund. Attorney Kenneth Feinberg had the job of administering the $7 billion fund to settle 2,880 death claims and 2,680 personal injury claims (Chen, 2004). It was up to Feinberg to decide, among those injured and the families of those killed, who received what.

As Zelizer (2005) notes, at first the fund was distributed to surviving family members in the amount of the deceased's estimated future earnings and made no provision for compensating unpaid household work. Feminists organized and lobbied Feinberg on the issue, arguing that "ignoring the unpaid work performed by full-time workers raises sex discrimination concerns. . . . Women victims, especially mothers, are much more likely to have expended significant time on unpaid work." In the end, the Victim Compensation Fund Final Rule allowed for a case-by-case review of compensation claims on the lost economic value of household services that would have been provided by the deceased. Still, the small nod to the value of some women's valuable but unpaid domestic work has not yet translated into broader policy changes in the way housework functions in the US economy, where the government still offers no guarantee of paid maternity (or paternity) leave.

It also takes marginalization to appreciate the center, as Christopher Carrington's study of gay couples in San Francisco demonstrates. Blumstein and Schwartz (1983) have suggested that an egalitarian division of labor is much more likely to exist in the households of gay and lesbian couples. But as Carrington (1999) notes, they also pay much more care and attention to their household chores, spending about two times as long on cleaning as heterosexual couples. The explanation? Homosexual couples see housework as a means of legitimating their households; thus it is a more central, validating activity for them than it is for the typical working wife. Even as same-sex couples have become more societally accepted, their more egalitarian division of household labor has appeared to persist (Bauer, 2016; Brewster, 2015). This suggests that egalitarianism may not just be an effort to gain legitimacy but, rather, is a reflection of the attitudes of those who decide to enter into a same-sex marriage or is a result of the psychological effect of being in such a household or, perhaps, simply reflects the more equal labor market positions of such spouses.

If, as sociologists argue, the burden of the second shift falls on working mothers in dual-income families, we might expect some nasty consequences. Indeed, Hochschild found that in response to the stalled revolution, some women tried to do it all. This is the supermom strategy. She cooks, she cleans, she climbs the career ladder, all while being a devoted parent and loving partner. Supermoms, of course, don't really exist, but there is a perpetual myth that some women can do it all, and if other women can't, it's a result of some personal flaw.

Women who buy into the supermom myth burn out quickly, and typically their marriages absorb the shock. In one study, Hochschild (1989) found that married women are more likely than men to think about divorce (30 percent of married women have considered divorce versus 22 percent of men). Women are also likely to give a more comprehensive list of reasons for wanting a divorce. In her interviews of dual-income families, Hochschild encountered bitter women, fed up with doing all the work, and puzzled men, confused over their wives' hostilities or bitter themselves at begrudgingly having to help out more.

Because women still earn less than men, about $0.81 for every dollar that a man earns, a disproportionate financial shock hits women after a divorce (Hegewisch & Williams-Baron, 2017). Given the rampant threat of divorce, some women bite the second-shift bullet, just letting the hostilities simmer. Other women manage by cutting household corners where they can, allowing the dust to pile up and skimping on the children's evening story time. For them, hostilities linger beneath a growing sense of parental guilt.

By contrast, in households in which men and women genuinely share the second shift, marriages are much more likely to be stable and happy ones. Studies (e.g., that conducted by Michael S. Kimmel in 2000) have found that when men share the housework, working wives experience less stress. Barbara Risman (1998) calls these "fair families," where husbands and wives equally split the roles of breadwinner and homemaker. In fair families, couples honor an ideology of gender equality, and both men and women benefit from such an arrangement. Women win the self-respect that comes with being economically independent, and they respond by regarding marriage less as a necessity and more as a voluntary, love-based relationship. Men, by sharing the breadwinner burden, are less stressed and feel freer to find jobs they enjoy. Perhaps most important, Risman speculates about a uniqueness in these sharing couples: They are more often close friends.

Swimming and Sinking: Inequality and American Families

AFRICAN AMERICAN FAMILIES

For millions of American households, the idealized traditional family *as depicted in 1950s television* never even came close to being a lived reality. For African American families, who throughout history have combined work and family, the split between the public and private spheres has never made much sense. Neither has the ideal of exclusive, "isolationist" motherhood made sense for women lacking the resources that allow for full-time homemaking. More often, Black and poor women have come to rely on extrafamilial female networks in order to manage child-care and work responsibilities (Stack & Burton, 1994). If the average American woman has two shifts, then the typical Black American mother has three, because she is more often the primary or only breadwinner. This greater importance of women in the Black family has unfortunately been conflated with "backward" female domination or matriarchy.

Social scientists in the 1960s made heavy use of the matriarchal thesis to explain social problems in the African American community. In *The Negro Family: The Case for National Action* (1965), Daniel Patrick Moynihan found that 25 percent of Black wives outearned their husbands, versus only 18 percent of White wives. This "pathological" matriarchy, Moynihan argued, undercuts the role of the father in Black families and leads to all sorts of problems later in life, such as domestic violence, substance abuse, crime, and degeneracy. You name it, the matriarch caused it. The root of matriarchy, Moynihan asserted, dated back to the days of slavery, which reversed roles for men and women and continued to haunt African Americans up to the time of his report.

According to the Moynihan report and similar arguments, the matriarch is a stereotypically bad Black mother. She's domineering and unfeminine, always wearing the pants in the family. She's hefty and gruff. She spends so much time away from the home that she can't supervise her own kids. And when she is at home, she's too bossy and strong; thus she emasculates her man and drives him away. If only the matriarch could be a little more feminine, a little less strong, a little *Whiter*, suggested the report, the Black family could lift itself up out of poverty. The image of the matriarch makes it easier to lay the blame on African American families for their own problems—social ills such as neighborhood decay, stagnating wages, single motherhood, higher divorce rates, and lower school achievement. The matriarch is also a powerful reminder to all women of just what can go wrong when women challenge the patriarchal decree that they be submissive, dependent, and feminine. The Moynihan report's prescription for the social problems of Black people was just this: Black women should aspire to the cult of true (White) womanhood.

Scholars like W. E. B. Du Bois had argued all along, however, that African American female-headed families were the outcome, rather than the cause, of racial oppression and poverty. And in 1987 William Julius Wilson graphed a "marriageable Black male index," which highlighted the scarcity of employed, nonincarcerated Black men (fewer than 50 marriageable Black men per 100 Black women back then). In such a context, if Black women didn't work to pay the rent, put food on the table, and take care of the kids, who would? As Elaine Kamplain has pointed out, African American mothers were "damned if they worked to support their families and damned if they didn't" (Hochschild, 2003).

Many African American parents rely on extrafamilial community members to help raise children. What are some of the criticisms of the matriarchal thesis?

Matriarchy is one of many misreadings that social critics have imposed on the Black family. But when critics hold fast to the idealized concept of the nuclear family, they are likely to see any model that differs from the traditional yardstick as deviant. The sociologist's trick is to view the traditional family, in which a heterosexual couple lives together with their dependent children in a self-contained, economically independent household, as just one of many potential family forms. After all, this particular kind of family evolved from the socially constructed separation of home and work—a separation rooted in the upper classes—and the experiences of most African American families stray from that norm. In fact, asserts Patricia Hill Collins (1990), women of color have never fit this model. Collins looks at the family with a different set of lenses on—what she calls an Afrocentric worldview—which allows for alternative concepts of family and community. One instance of this worldview is more of a collective effort with strong neighborhood

support: the "it takes a village" model described in Chapter 10 on the culture of poverty.

Identifying the traditional family as a specific historical phenomenon that has rarely applied to Black families enables us to analyze the Black community's unique characteristics in a less judgmental manner. African American communities tend to have an expanded notion of kinship, as denoted by the all-encompassing use of the words *brother* and *sister*. This may have developed out of Blacks' historical experience with slavery. Because slaves were separated from their biological families at the auction block by White owners, Blacks adapted by expanding the definition of *family* from immediate bloodlines to racial ones. Under slavery, Black men and women occupied indistinct work roles, often performing the same labor side by side in plantation fields. The legacy of their shared labor was incompatible with a nuclear family, a model predicated on the differentiation between male and female spheres (Collins, 1990).

As a result of segregation throughout the twentieth century, the particular African American notions of community and family continued to endure. But after World War II, the manufacturing economy took a downturn and many Black workers, employed by shrinking industries, found themselves at risk of economic marginalization. Marital rates among Blacks have been in decline since the 1960s, and female-headed households have been on the rise among both the poor and middle classes. Kathryn Edin's ongoing research in poor African American communities has found a consistent interest in the elements that constitute family life, such as having children and getting married, although poor-quality schools, lack of jobs, and (sometimes) substance abuse make it difficult to undertake a traditional progression of dating, love, marriage, and childbearing. Childbearing often precedes marriage, but unlike common stereotypes of indifferent cads interested primarily in sex, fathers-to-be are often excited about becoming parents and tend to strengthen their commitment to the baby's mother. Unfortunately, parenting the same child (or children) may not be enough to hold these couples together until they feel financially secure enough to marry. Black children (37.4 percent) and Hispanic children (17.8 percent) were more likely to live with a single parent than non-Hispanic White children (10.9 percent) or Asian children (6.6 percent) (US Census Bureau, 2019a). This statistic reflects, in part, the high rates of unemployment and incarceration and low rates of education among Black men.

LATINX FAMILIES

According to the US Census Bureau (2020h), Latinxs are the largest minority group in America, making up 18 percent of the US population. The Census Bureau (2011c) defines Latino as "a person of Cuban, Mexican, Puerto Rican, South or Central American, or other Spanish culture or origin regardless of race." Latinxs also live all over the United States, although they have clustered on the West Coast and in the South and Midwest (Hernandez et al., 2007). Given the diverse origins and geography of Latinxs, how can we make general claims about the Latinx family? Sociologists don't all agree that such a thing exists or that a generic Latinx identity is even imaginable (Santa Ana, 2004). But there are a few common threads that run through many Latinx families. Their family ties are strong, and family is a top priority for many Latinxs—so important, in fact, that individual Latinxs often define their self-worth in terms of their family's image and accomplishments (Ho, 1987). Like African American families, Latinx families act as safety nets, and members take seriously their responsibilities to help one another, even in long chains of needy extended relations (Skogrand et al., 2004). They have a strong sense of community and allegiance to it (Hurtado, 1995). For example, so many Latinx immigrants send remittances, or money, to family members back home that remittances are now one of the largest sources of cash in the Mexican and many other Central American economies.

Traditional rules of gender and authority also loom large in Latinx culture. Women listen to their men, and children to their elders, in a clear-cut hierarchy. This should make sense to anyone who's taken a Spanish language class (or studied any other Romance language). The heavy use of titles and ranks in the everyday vocabulary shows that respect and formality are crucial (DeNeve, 1997). Most Latinx families are also shaped by a tradition of devout Catholicism. Combine high religiosity with the importance of family honor, and you soon recognize a few tendencies: high rates of marriage and relatively low rates of divorce, high rates of marriage at a young age, and a lot of babies born out of wedlock. This third outcome may seem contradictory, but think about it: If a young Latinx does have premarital sex and becomes pregnant without a marriage prospect in sight, she's less likely than her African American or White peers to have an abortion, a worse breach of Catholic culture than an out-of-wedlock birth. Add to that a tight-lipped stance on discussing sex at home, the dwindling of preventive sex education, and the difficulty (not to mention the embarrassment) teens face trying to get their hands on effective and affordable birth control, and you end up with a lot of babies born to single Latinx moms. In 2015, about 53 percent of all Latinx babies were born to unwed mothers, compared with 29.2 percent of non-Hispanic White babies (those numbers are still lower than the nearly 71 percent of African American babies born outside of marriage) (Martin et al., 2017).

FLAT BROKE WITH CHILDREN

Single mothers and poverty often go hand in hand in America, and these twin challenges plague nonwhite communities to a greater extent than White Americans. In a shrinking welfare state with widening economic gaps between the rich and the poor, single mothers are faced with tough trade-offs between mothering and work. Single mothers rely on a combination of welfare, family, lovers, luck, and creativity to make ends meet. At any given point in the past few decades, half of all mothers raising children by themselves have relied on welfare to get by. In contrast to the media myth of the "lazy welfare mother" who watches television and buys filet mignon with her food stamps, many of these mothers work hard (often off the books) and desperately want to escape poverty. Welfare critics might be surprised to read *Making Ends Meet: How Single Mothers Survive Welfare and Low-Wage Work* (1997), in which sociologists Kathryn Edin and Laura Lein find that all single mothers prefer self-reliance to welfare dependency. In fact, a majority get off the welfare rolls in two years, and hardly any stay on welfare for more than eight years.

In their study of 379 mothers across four US cities, Edin and Lein traced what happens when poor single mothers are faced with the choice between welfare and work. The word *choice* here is misleading: It implies freedom, as though these women can easily move from dependency to self-sufficiency. However, because single mothers are often unskilled or semiskilled and have less education than average, their employment options are limited to low-wage work that rarely provides benefits (the kinds of jobs listed in the paper Reagan had flashed, as mentioned in Chapter 10).

Edin and Lein found that mothers on welfare could cover about three-fifths of their expenses. In low-wage jobs, they faced a larger gap between earnings and expenses, in part to cover the costs of transportation, child-care arrangements, increased rent, and fewer food stamps. (Both the food stamp

Jenni McGlaun talks on the phone while her 15-month-old son, Jesse, plays in their Milwaukee home. McGlaun has been on and off welfare for five years. What does Kathryn Edin and Laura Lein's research on single mothers reveal about the choices these women face between welfare and work?

program and federal housing program consider income when determining benefits; even a father's child support can translate into a rent increase for a single mother.) This system makes a savings account virtually impossible for welfare recipients to maintain and is arguably the real culprit behind the trap of dependency. In fact, leaving welfare for work substantially increases these women's expenses, such that they can cover only two-thirds of those expenses on low wages alone. One working mother voiced her frustrations:

> Ask any politician to live off my budget. Live off my minimum wage job and just a little bit of food stamps—how can he do it? I bet he couldn't. I'd like him to try it for one month. Come home from work, cook dinner, wash clothes, do everything, everything, get up and go to work the next day, and then find you don't have enough money to pay for everything you need. (Edin & Lein, 1997, p. 149)

Barbara Ehrenreich, a sociologist and writer, tried to make ends meet with low-wage work in 1998. That was a year in which the Preamble Center for Public Policy estimated that the odds against a typical welfare recipient's landing a job at a living wage were about 97 to 1. Nationwide, it took an average hourly wage of $8.89 to afford a one-bedroom apartment. Currently, the federal minimum wage is $7.25, which amounts to a full-time yearly salary of $15,080. Only approximately 2.1 percent of workers paid hourly make the minimum wage or less, but about 42 percent plug away for less than $15 an hour, and Ehrenreich wanted to figure out just how they did it (Bureau of Labor Statistics, 2019a; Ehrenreich, 2001; Rodgers & Novello, 2019).

Ehrenreich traveled the country working for $6 or $7 an hour as a waitress, hotel maid, and Walmart sales clerk. At these low wages, she had to pay high rates for rent by the week (because she lacked the required one-month security deposit). She had to eat for less than $9 a day, a budget that at best included canned beans, fast food, or noodle soup microwaved at a convenience store, and she supplemented this diet by sponging junk food from charities. All the while, Ehrenreich prayed for her health to keep up (low-wage jobs are often physically taxing), gave up clothes shopping, and juggled two or more jobs. She still could not afford to live off of her wages:

> I grew up hearing over and over, to the point of tedium, that "hard work" was the secret of success: "Work hard and you'll get ahead" or "It's hard work that got us where we are." No one ever said that you could work hard—harder than you ever thought possible—and still find yourself sinking ever deeper into poverty and debt. (2001, p. 220)

Most welfare recipients live with few extras, often in neighborhoods with high poverty concentration and elevated crime rates. Yet politicians and voters alike worry about the cycle of dependency, the so-called welfare trap, and taxpayers deeply resent any person, real or perceived, who gets a free ride. Welfare critic Charles Murray, author of the conservative classic *Losing Ground* (1984), believes that welfare moms are staining the very moral fabric that holds the country together (see Chapter 10). As he sees it, all economic support should be pulled from under the feet of single mothers, and that would keep poor women and teens from having babies for whom they cannot care.

The 1996 Personal Responsibility and Work Opportunity Reconciliation Act, the national welfare reform enacted during the Clinton administration, didn't go as far as Murray would have liked, but it did make into policy the sentiment common among taxpayers that it was time for lazy welfare moms to get their act together, learn self-sufficiency, and take responsibility for themselves. But responsibility can take on several, often conflicting, meanings for mothers. Faced with either welfare or low-wage work, single mothers find that the government's definition of responsibility is narrowly defined as wage work. In *Flat Broke with Children: Women in the Age of Welfare Reform* (2003), Sharon Hays shows that many of these women are forced to take low-paying jobs with no future and little career stability. As a result, they are frequently driven to marry for financial support. All too often, Hays finds, single mothers (and their children) end up in poverty, homeless, or seeking alternatives to get by, including illicit sources of income.

Jill Lawrence is a single mother in South Dakota. Like many of the single mothers that Sharon Hays has written about in *Flat Broke with Children*, she struggles to raise her son and make ends meet on her own.

Single mothers' paid labor often requires that they sacrifice responsible parenthood. By forcing welfare moms to enter the workforce while not providing adequate child care, the government encourages women to abandon their children in an unsupervised home. To the single mothers Hays interviewed, real responsibility meant taking care of and supervising their children, looking after their health, and providing them with a safe home environment. According to Hays, for the most desperate women in America, being a responsible worker requires being an irresponsible mother. To manage this tension between being a good worker or a good mother, single mothers may shoot for the nearly impossible strategy of self-reliance, but in reality they often end up depending on cash assistance from family or boyfriends. They barter with sisters, cousins, and kindly neighbors. They also take side jobs (again hiding their income to avoid rent increases or food stamp ineligibility) or go to relief agencies, although this last option proves too humiliating for most to bear. As a last resort, some single mothers turn to criminal activity such as prostitution or drug dealing, where the earnings are high but the moral costs "rob them of the self-respect they gained from trying to be good mothers" (Edin & Lein, 1997).

The Pecking Order: Inequality Starts at Home

By now, you can see that there's no universal family form and that plenty of gender inequality exists in American families. But you might still think that, at least when it comes to the children, the home (no matter who makes up a family) is a haven of equality, altruism, and infinite love in an otherwise harsh world. In *Haven in a Heartless World* (1977), Christopher Lasch paints a rosy portrait of domestic life. To him, the home really is a haven where workers seek refuge from the cold winds of a capitalist public sphere. The family is sacred because it provides intimate privacy, managed by a caring woman who shields male workers from "the cruel world of politics and work." Building on the socially constructed split between the public and private spheres, this idea of the family as insulated from the outside world is deeply entrenched in America.

However, as you might have guessed by now, such ideas give a misleading sense of the family as a harmonious unit, its members altruistically sacrificing for one another to forge a healthy, hearty, and loving private world. As I found while researching my book *The Pecking Order* (2004), a compelling but largely invisible struggle also takes place in the home. In each American family, there exists a pecking order among siblings—a status hierarchy, if you will—that can ignite the family with competition, struggle, and resentment. Parents often abet such struggles, despite their protestations that they "love all their children equally."

Let me illustrate with the story of a future president, William Jefferson Blythe IV, born to a 23-year-old widow named Virginia. Childhood was rough for young Bill, especially after his mother married Roger Clinton, a bitter alcoholic who physically abused his wife. In 1962, when Bill was 16, Virginia finally left Roger, but by then there was another Roger Clinton in the family, Bill's younger half-brother. Although they were separated by 10 years, were only half-siblings, and ran in very different circles, the brothers were close. As Bill's political fortunes rose, Roger's prospects first stagnated and then sank. He tried his hand at a musical career, worked odd jobs, and eventually began dealing drugs. In 1984 the Arkansas state police informed then-governor Bill Clinton that his brother was a cocaine dealer under investigation. After a sting operation, which the governor did not obstruct, Roger was arrested. You might be wondering, as Clinton biographer David Maraniss (1995) has, "How could two brothers be so different: the governor and the coke dealer, the Rhodes scholar and the college dropout?" To be sure, a pair of brothers who are, respectively, a former president and an ex-con is a fairly extreme example. But the basic phenomenon of sibling differences in success that the Clintons represent is not all that unusual. In fact, in explaining economic inequality in America, sibling differences represent more than half of all the differences between individuals.

What do sibling disparities as large as these indicate? If asked to explain why one brother succeeded while the other failed miserably, most people would point to different individual characteristics, such as work ethic, responsibility, personal motivation, and discipline. To account for a sibling's failures, people again tend to cite personal reasons, such as "a bad attitude," "poor emotional or mental health," or most commonly, "lack of determination" (Conley, 2004).

Other people will grapple for an explanation by suggesting the role of birth order. The commonly held idea is that firstborns are naturally more driven and successful, if just because they are most favored by their parents. But this is still a form of individual explanation—something unique to the biology or psychology of the sibling—that fails to take into account the role of sociological factors. For example, in families with two kids, birth order doesn't matter that much. Firstborns don't have too much advantage over one younger sibling. For example, slightly less than one-fourth of US presidents were firstborns, about what we would expect from chance. Birth position matters only in the context of larger families and limited resources. When family resources are stretched thin, love really does become a pie, as they say. The children born first or last into a large family seem to fare better socioeconomically than those born in the middle. Middle kids feel the effects of a shrinking pie, as they tend to be shortchanged on resources like money for college and parental attention (Cáceres-Delpiano, 2006).

Taken as a whole, the facts about intrafamily stratification present a much darker portrait of American family life than we are accustomed to. Sure, we want to think of the home as a haven in a heartless world, but the truth is that inequality starts at home. These statistics also pose problems for media stories and politicians concerned with the erosion of the idealized nuclear family. In fact, they hint at a trade-off between economic opportunity and stable, cohesive families. The family is, in short, no shelter from the cold winds of capitalism; rather, it is part and parcel of that system.

A pecking order emerges during the course of childhood. It both reflects and determines siblings' positions in the overall status ordering that occurs within society. It is not just the will of parents or the "natural" abilities of children (or lack thereof); the pecking order is conditioned by the swirling winds of society, which in turn envelop the family. Furthermore, sibling disparities are much more common in poor families and single-parent homes than in rich, intact families. In fact, when families have limited resources, the success of one sibling often generates a negative backlash among the others. As the parents unwittingly put all their eggs—all their hopes and dreams—into just one basket, the other siblings inevitably are left out in the cold. Americans like to think that their behavior and destiny remain solely in their own hands. But the pecking order, like other aspects of the social fabric, ends up being shaped by social forces.

The Future of Families, and There Goes the Nation!

DIVORCE

Throughout this chapter we have examined the idealization of monogamous marriage as a key characteristic of American culture. Sociologist Andrew Cherlin writes in *The Marriage-Go-Round: The State of Marriage and the Family in America Today* (2009) about how the idealized conception of marriage is currently helping delay age at first marriage and otherwise shape contemporary American marital patterns. He finds a paradox. On the one hand, Americans value marriage very highly—85 to 90 percent of us will eventually get married. On the other hand, America has the highest divorce rate of any comparable Western country. How does Cherlin explain this love–hate relationship? He suggests that both the drive to get married and the desire to divorce are rooted in our collective past,

> all the way to the Colonial days when marriage was the nexus of civil society that the early settlers established. It's very important here. . . . We want to be married. At the same time though, we're very individualistic, and that has deep cultural roots too. Think about the saying "Go West, young man." Think about the rugged individual. We're individualists. And so we want to be married, but we evaluate our marriages in very personal terms. Am I getting the personal growth that I need out of my marriage? And if you think the answer is no, you feel justified in leaving. (Conley, 2009k)

Social science research over the past couple of decades has struggled to establish just how high rates of divorce alter the social fabric. Figure 12.4 illustrates the divorce rate in America since 1920. Adding a layer to the American marriage paradox, it turns out that the most politically and religiously

To see an interview with Andrew Cherlin, go to
digital.wwnorton.com/youmayask7

conservative states have the highest rates of divorce: "The states with the top ten divorce rates, eight out of ten of those voted for John McCain in the 2008 election. All ten voted for George Bush in the 2004 election" (Conley, 2009k). Cherlin explains that personal economics, not personal values, may end up contributing to rocky marriages. The states with high divorce rates are relatively poor; a sizable number of their citizens struggle to find jobs with decent wages, which compromises the ideal vision of family as a haven protected from crass financial concerns. Couples who cannot provide themselves a middle-class lifestyle may begin to question the utility of marriage in the first place. They face all of the responsibility of looking out for each other without the means to live the ideal lifestyle to which they aspire. Cherlin also notes that younger people have even more difficulty finding good jobs because they have less work experience, and this may delay their marriage plans (Conley, 2009k). Young couples may live together, even have children together, holding off on long-term personal relationships until after they have established long-term financial relationships with reliable employers.

Much of the debate about divorce follows the children of divorced parents through their educational careers and into their adult relationship choices. The moral and political debate surrounding the long-term consequences of divorce has largely treated its effects as uniform for all offspring. In *The Pecking Order* (2004), I paint a more nuanced picture, in which circumstances and context widely vary the impact of divorce on kids—even those in the same family. Everything from the timing of the divorce to a parent's hostility can influence a kid's educational attainment, future earnings, and socioeconomic success. Blanket condemnations of divorce are therefore dangerously naive, as are those who say that it's no big deal.

For example, in their best seller *The Unexpected Legacy of Divorce* (2000), Judith Wallerstein and her colleagues claim that divorce almost universally damages children's self-esteem and developmental trajectories. Based on interviews with about 50 offspring of divorced parents, they conclude that adult children of divorce suffer from higher rates of depression, endure low self-esteem, and have difficulties forming fulfilling, lasting relationships of their own.

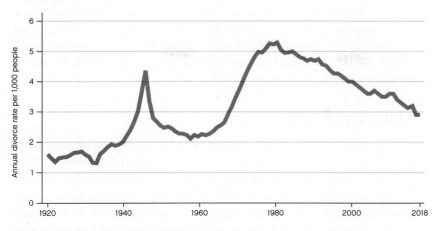

FIGURE 12.4 US Divorce Rate, 1920–2018

SOURCES: US Census Bureau, 2010c; Centers for Disease Control and Prevention, 2015f; National Center for Health Statistics, 2017; Centers for Disease Control and Prevention, 2019a.

Sociologist Linda Waite and columnist Maggie Gallagher echo this view in *The Case for Marriage: Why Married People Are Happier, Healthier, and Better Off Financially* (2000). (The title, in this case, says it all.) They claim that married parents provide better homes for their children than divorced ones because they have more money and time to spend on the children, enjoy stronger emotional bonds with them, have more social capital (connections) that will be helpful to their children's chances for success, and are physically and mentally healthier. By contrast, they say, divorced families are likely to manifest more child abuse, neglect, and delinquency, and the children will probably attain less education.

On the flip side of the debate are research findings that suggest a less calamitous future for the children of single-parent families, indicating that children from divorced households generally do not do much worse than other kids. In *For Better or for Worse: Divorce Reconsidered* (2002), psychologists E. Mavis Hetherington and John Kelly argue that the children of divorce, for the most part, do adjust well to the new reality. Under some conditions, but certainly not all, divorce produces in kids more stress and depression, and lower future socioeconomic success. Continued parental conflict and role reversals in which children "play parent," for example, make divorce potentially destructive. In other cases, however, parents who leave a high-conflict marriage probably spare their children from ongoing family feuds, hostilities, or abuse. At least one study shows that kids from high-conflict marriages that stay together may do worse than kids from high-conflict marriages that break up (Morrison & Coiro, 1999).

Too often, social science research is carelessly picked up in political debates as simple sound bites. Saying kids from divorced families fare worse than kids from intact families is one thing; saying that divorce caused those worse outcomes is quite another matter. That is, we can't really know for sure that had those parents stayed together, the kids would have been better off. We can only say that high levels of parental conflict are bad—with or without divorce in the picture.

BLENDED FAMILIES

As should be clear by this point, the dynamics involved in maintaining a family (both as a whole and in terms of the individual relationships within it) are complicated. This complexity increases drastically when two family units are integrated. As stated on **helpguide.org**, "To a child who does not belong to one, stepfamily may suggest Cinderella's family or the Brady Bunch." However, if you are part of a blended family or know someone who is (there's a good chance you do, given that one-third of the children in the United States now fall into this category), you understand that neither extreme reflects reality. As divorce becomes more common, so too does the blended family form. Two people meet, fall in love, get married, have kids—we'll call them family A. Then they decide to split. Another pair does the same (family B). Some time later, Mom A encounters Dad B, and the process repeats. The result is a blended family or stepfamily, with stepparents, stepchildren, and sometimes stepsiblings. Blended families are the result of not only divorce but also death. When either partner dies, remarriage is not uncommon. According to the 1990 US Census, 3.6 percent of grooms and 10 percent of brides had previously lost a spouse (Kreider & Ellis, 2011).

In fact, in his book, Cherlin estimates that more than a quarter of American children today experience at least two maternal partner changes, and more than 8 percent experience three or more. Some developmental psychologists worry about this dynamic, as it impacts children's ability to form trusting, stable ties with adult figures in their lives (Espejo et al., 2006). Others see children as robust and more or less adaptable to most changes that come their way.

GAY, LESBIAN, AND TRANSGENDER FAMILIES

Marriage, divorce, remarriage. Stepfamilies, blended families. Another family arrangement on the rise is same-sex couples. At present, same-sex marriages are legal in an increasing number of countries, including the United States and about half of Europe. As for gay parenting, research consistently finds that lesbian and gay parents are at least as successful as heterosexuals in producing well-adjusted, successful offspring (Stacey, 1997).

However, until recently homosexual unions faced fierce opposition. In 1996 President Clinton signed into federal law the Defense of Marriage Act (DOMA), which stipulated that federally recognized marriages had to be heterosexual and that states where gay marriage was previously illegal were not required to recognize same-sex marriages conducted in states where it was legal. But DOMA was struck down in 2013 and the Supreme Court effectively legalized same-sex marriage across the United States in 2015.

An old joke goes, "Gays and lesbians getting married—haven't they suffered enough?" That is, if homosexual couples want to marry, why not just let them do it? Opponents of gay marriage—many of whom are strongly religious, "social values" conservatives—argue that nontraditional familial arrangements will wreak social havoc. Let gays get married, so the argument goes, and you effectively destroy the family. Once the family goes, look out—the next step is chaos, no moral order. Furthermore, opponents of gay marriage claim that the purpose of a family is to procreate and raise children into functioning adults, and this is determined by biology. Because gay marriage does not produce the biological children of both parents, such people believe that it is not functional, right, or natural.

According to the Pew Research Center, views are steadily shifting. In 1996, 64 percent of Americans were opposed to gay and lesbian marriage. By 2019, those numbers had flipped: 61 percent supported gay marriage while 31 percent were opposed. Young people are the strongest supporters of same-sex marriage, with 74 percent of the millennial generation (born roughly from 1981 to 1996) supporting same-sex marriage, while 45 percent of people over 65 oppose same-sex marriage (Pew Research Center, 2019c).

Families with one or more transgender parents are another group that has challenged conservative notions of how a family "should" look.

Two married women greet their eight-year-old daughter after school in Ridgefield, Washington, in 2017. How have attitudes toward gay and lesbian families changed?

Transgender individuals lag behind gays and lesbians in terms of societal acceptance (see Chapter 8), but the trend lines are similarly toward tolerance. There is, as of yet, no reliable data on how many families include transgender parents, but best estimates put the figure at less than 1 percent.

MULTIRACIAL FAMILIES

Gays have not been the only ones who have faced obstacles to legal marriage. The technical term for interracial marriage is miscegenation, which literally means "a mixing of kinds." This term, however, is politically and historically charged and, as such, should be used with a high degree of caution. Sociologists and other social scientists generally prefer the term *exogamy* or *outmarriage*.

Considering the history of race relations in the United States (see Chapter 9), it is not surprising that the idea (and even legality) of interracial marriages and families has been cause for controversy. Although interracial marriage was never illegal at the federal level, from 1913 to 1948, 30 states enforced antimiscegenation laws. Many of these laws lasted until 1967, when the Supreme Court finally declared them unconstitutional, reversing the restrictions in 16 remaining states.

We have undoubtedly come a long way since 1967. One year after the Supreme Court ruling (1968), a Gallup poll revealed that 80 percent of Americans were opposed to Blacks and Whites getting married. By 2009 that number had dropped to 17 percent (Wang, 2012). However, attitudes toward exogamy in the United States vary greatly by location, religion, and a host of other factors. And, of course, such polls capture only expressed attitudes, subject to social desirability bias, not actual behavior (i.e., actual intermarriage rates).

American families are increasingly looking like the family pictured here. How are attitudes about multiracial families changing?

In 2015, 17 percent of new marriages were between people of different races or ethnic groups. Asian Americans had the highest rate of outmarriage at 29 percent, followed by 27 percent of Hispanics, 18 percent of Blacks, and 11 percent of Whites (Bialik, 2017). These percentages significantly change when gender is taken into account. For example, 36 percent of Asian American women marry someone outside of their race, unlike Asian American men who have only a 21 percent rate of outmarriage. Black men have a 24 percent rate of outmarriage versus Black women's rate of 12 percent.

IMMIGRANT FAMILIES

Immigrants—today arriving mostly from Latin America and Asia—face a unique set of challenges in forming and sustaining families. Aside from the difficulty of the immigration process itself, through which it can take years to reunify spouses and siblings through visa sponsorships, families who migrate to America tend to be poorer and larger, and to hold fewer educational credentials. For instance, about 9.1 percent of people born in the United States have less than a high-school degree, while the same is true for 28.8 percent of people born abroad (Ryan & Bauman, 2016). What's more, the gaps between natives and immigrants who have not obtained citizenship or who are undocumented are even larger. There are more than four times as many noncitizens who have less than a high-school degree (or equivalent) compared to those born in the United States, while those native households make about $14,000 (or about 25 percent) more in earnings (Ryan & Bauman, 2016). These socioeconomic disparities are exacerbated by the reality that an overwhelming proportion of immigrants live in expensive cities on the East and West Coasts, like Los Angeles and New York (López & Bialik, 2017). Because of these resource gaps, undocumented immigrants face a particularly daunting set of challenges in providing for their families and obtaining safe, stable, and affordable housing.

Most Americans nowadays delay forming families until they receive college degrees and earn more money precisely because of the difficulties of having children with fewer resources. Yet though we might expect immigrant families to form and stay together less often because of these challenges, the opposite is true. Immigrants tend to start families regardless of their educational attainment or income, with the poor marrying and having children at a similar rate compared to their peers with higher socioeconomic status (Qian, 2013). About a quarter of immigrants have never been married, while that's true for more than a third of native-born populations (Ryan & Bauman, 2016). And in terms of keeping the family unit intact, the gaps are similarly big—about 79 percent of foreign-born children live with married parents, compared to 64 percent of natives (US Census Bureau, 2017p).

Why do families who face greater socioeconomic, geographic, and linguistic challenges manage to form and sustain themselves more than US natives? While some propose a different set of cultural norms—for example, a greater emphasis on family ties and the necessity of social support to get ahead in America—immigration policy itself likely contributes to the structure of immigrant families. Even though the process is difficult, current immigration policy favors family-based reunification rather than education level or labor market skills (Kandel, 2018). So while the Republican Party made immigration a key issue in the 2016 election (and beyond), and sought to put an end to family-based immigration policy in particular (not to mention separating detainee families from their parents for a period), foreign-born populations actually show a greater tendency to live out the kinds of mid-twentieth-century nuclear family arrangements that many political conservatives often express a desire to return to.

POLICY

 EXPANDING MARRIAGE

When the poet Elizabeth Barrett Browning wrote, "How do I love thee? Let me count the ways," little did she know that a century and a half later the list would extend into the hundreds—at least for married couples. As of 2004, the US General Accounting Office had identified more than 1,000 legal rights and responsibilities attendant to marriage (Shah, 2004). The era of big government is clearly not over when it comes to family policy.

These rights and responsibilities range from the continuation of water rights upon the death of a spouse to the ability to take funeral leave. And that's just the federal government. States and localities have their own marriage provisions. New York State, for example, grants a spouse the right to inherit a military veteran's peddler's license. And Hawaii extends to spouses of state residents lower fees for hunting licenses. No

wonder gay and lesbian activists put such a premium on access to marriage rights. Some gay marriage advocates want all spousal rights immediately and will settle for nothing less. Others take an incremental approach, aiming to secure first the most significant domestic partner rights, such as employer benefits like health care.

But with all the divorces and blended families, it's unclear if our current legal system is best suited to the task of serving families' needs. Perhaps it is time to consider if we'd be better off by breaking down or unbundling the marriage contract into its constituent parts. Then, applying free-market principles, we could allow each citizen to assign the various rights and responsibilities now connected to marriage as he or she sees fit. In addition to employer benefits, some of the key marital rights include the ability to

Jeanne Fong (left) and Jennifer Lin, a same-sex couple from San Francisco, celebrate during a marriage equality rally in Washington, DC.

I can convince the overstretched Department of Homeland Security that my penchant for falling in love with foreign women is genuine, I can divorce and remarry as many times as I like, obtaining permanent residency for each of my failed loves along the way. Is this fair to the many Americans who can't sponsor aging grandparents or, in some cases, even parents? Or, is it even fair to the vast majority of Americans who are happy marrying other Americans and may not want to see the country fill up with all my exes?

Instead, why not give all Americans the right to sponsor one person in their lifetime—a right that they could sell, if they so desire? This would mean that if I wanted to marry a Kenyan after divorcing an Australian, I could, but I would need to purchase, perhaps on eBay, the right to confer citizenship from someone else who didn't need it. Similarly, why not let all Americans name one person (other than their lawyer, priest, or therapist) who can't be forced to testify against them in court? This zone of privacy could be transferred over the course of a lifetime, perhaps limiting such changes to once every five years.

While we are at it, how about allowing each of us to choose someone with whom we share our property, with all the tax (and liability) implications that choice would imply? We might even allow parenthood to become contractual and in multiples greater than two by letting people name individuals they want to be the co-parents to their biological children, even if that means a kid ends up with three or four parents, none of whom is married to any of the others. This would help grandparents, for instance, have the legal right to act on behalf of the grandchildren in their care.

We could go down the long list of rights and responsibilities embedded in the marriage

pass property and income back and forth tax-free, spousal privilege (i.e., the right not to testify against one's husband or wife), medical decision-making power, and the right to confer permanent residency to a foreigner, just to name a few. The mutual responsibilities of marriage include parenthood—a husband is the legal father of any child born to his wife regardless of biological paternity—and some shared legal liability under civil law. Why not allow people to parcel out each of these marital privileges?

Take my own first marriage as a case in point: My ex-wife is a foreigner who applied for citizenship, and her marriage to me made that possible. Marrying a foreigner is pretty common—7 percent of married couples in the United States are made up of a US-born spouse and a foreign-born spouse (US Census Bureau, 2013). As the law now stands, I, as a straight American man, theoretically could become a green card machine. As long as

contract. Ideally, most people would choose one person in whom to vest all these rights, but everyone would have the freedom to decide how to configure these domestic, business, legal, and intimate relationships in the eyes of the law.

Other people have proposed changing marriage by making it more flexible. Some queer activists continue to argue that the law should recognize a variety of households, from conjugal couples to groups of elderly people living collectively, as "legal families." But they have not specified the rights that should go along with such arrangements or addressed the problems and paradoxes that might arise if legal rights and responsibilities were extended to groups of more than two. Unbundling marital rights would achieve the same end without creating new inequities based on group size.

It might also take some of the vitriol out of the marriage debate. Marriage itself could stay in church (or in Las Vegas, as the case may be). And each couple could count their own ways to love.

Conclusion

By now you should be wary of any social institution that is hailed supreme because it is "more natural." You should be skeptical of any family arrangement that is deemed more functional than another, and you should hold the traditional family at a critical distance, especially considering the experiences of women, African Americans, gays and lesbians, the poor, the mainstream, and the marginalized.

Under the "postmodern family condition," as Judith Stacey (1996) calls it, clear rules no longer exist in our complex, diversified, and sometimes messy postindustrial society. Gone are the ruling days of the family structure idealized in the 1950s. Families today take on many shapes and sizes that best fit their members' needs, and they are defined not by blood ties but by the quality of relationships. Let us count the ways . . .

QUESTIONS FOR REVIEW

1. Describe the "nuclear family" and three other family forms. Does sociological research suggest that one such arrangement is necessarily the right one?

2. Think about the discussion regarding rights for same-sex couples. How do the functionalist arguments by Bronislaw Malinowski (1913) and Talcott Parsons (1951) help explain the changes (or lack thereof) in the institution of marriage?

3. How do historical cultural ideals relate to current rates of marriage and divorce in the United States? Name one reason that the likelihood of being currently married might be lower among those with low incomes.

4. Sometimes what's considered "normal" is far from what's most prevalent currently or historically. How does this statement relate to perceptions about the "traditional" family?

5. Describe how a gendered division of labor arose after the Industrial Revolution. How was this change tied to kinship networks?

6. What is the cult of domesticity? How has it changed over the last century?

7. What is the second shift, and how does it relate to a leisure gap between husbands and wives?

8. Are mothers on welfare lazy? Use the findings by Kathryn Edin and Laura Lein (1997) to help answer this question.

9. What is a pecking order, and what does the term mean for children in a family? According to this concept, does your birth position in the family or number of siblings matter to your life chances for success in school and beyond?

MAKING INVISIBLE LABOR VISIBLE

Building on the ideas introduced by Arlie Hochschild's book *The Second Shift* (1989), in recent years commentators have talked about "invisible" domestic labor—work that happens at home that is often unacknowledged and unpaid.

TRY IT!

Think about all the work a parent or caregiver did when you were growing up, and consider the economic value of that labor. Caregivers often are like an Uber driver who chauffeurs kids, acts as a health aid, or functions as a short-order cook—how much was that worth per week? Here are some estimates to get you started:

TASK	NATIONAL AVERAGE
UBER DRIVER	$4 PER 15-MINUTE RIDE
BABYSITTER / CARETAKER	$12 PER HOUR
SHORT-ORDER COOK	$5 PER MEAL
HOUSE CLEANER	$10 PER ROOM
HOMEWORK TUTOR	$20 PER HOUR

WORK PROVIDED BY PARENT OR CARETAKER	AMOUNT WORTH PER WEEK
_____	_____
_____	_____
_____	_____

For simplicity's sake, you could use minimum wage in your state for any tasks not defined above.

TOTAL AMOUNT

$ _____

THINK ABOUT IT

So, have you broken out your checkbook to pay your mother, father, or other primary caregiver for all those years of uncompensated labor on your behalf? Think about your family and others you know well: Who typically does this unpaid labor? Is it equally borne by all adults in the family? Does it break down along gender lines? Or age? Or by task (Dad is chauffeur and Mom is short-order cook, for example)? How do you feel about the social division of unpaid labor in your family—as it compares to the typical American household?

SOCIOLOGY ON THE STREET

It seems like everyone has an opinion on whether women with children—especially young children—should be in the workforce. Why is the conversation over "having it all" still mainly about mothers? Watch the Sociology on the Street video to find out more: **digital.wwnorton.com/youmayask7**.

WANT MORE PRACTICE?

Complete the InQuizitive activity for this chapter at digital.wwnorton.com /youmayask7

13

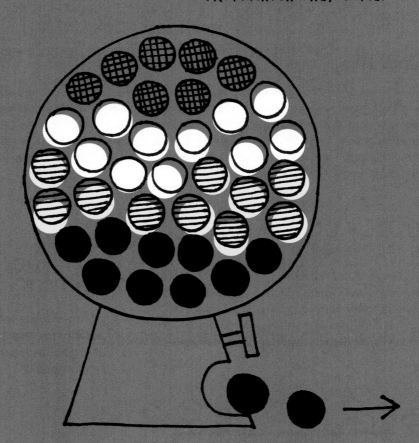

ALTHOUGH SCHOOL IS SUPPOSED TO BE THE INSTITUTION IN SOCIETY THAT PROVIDES EQUAL OPPORTUNITY, IT ENDS UP SORTING AND STRATIFYING STUDENTS BY THE BACKGROUNDS FROM WHICH THEY COME.

Animation at digital.wwnorton.com/youmayask7

Education

It probably comes as no surprise to you, reader, how expensive college is these days (see Chapter 1 for the actual figures). What may astound, however, is what Kari Smith has done to pay for her son's future education. She auctioned off her forehead as a billboard on eBay. The winning bidder would get to tattoo its advertisement across her forehead. Bidding reached $999.99 before Goldenplace.com, a Canadian internet gambling site, pressed the "buy it now" option for $10,000, preempting the auction with two days to go. (Who knows how high it might have gone?) "It feels like someone is taking a pin and just stabbing you with it," Smith told her son, Brady, seated nearby on the floor as tattoo artist Don Brouse was implementing the agreed-on design. No, Kari wasn't drunk when she got this tattoo. And she wasn't a kid, either. This was a rational plan of a 30-year-old with limited earning potential to offset the cost of education. It was perfectly legal, and an eBay spokesperson confirmed that the company's policy is to allow auctions online of pretty much anything that would be legal if transacted offline: "Basically, if it's legal offline, it's generally fine on our site," said eBay spokesman Chris Donlay. "We've seen people doing this for a number of years. I don't know that any of them have actually sold, but it's sort of interesting when people list them."

Kari is not alone in her creative financing of education. There have always been students like Kyle Taylor who pay for education through odd jobs—just usually not as fun as Kyle's job of "beer auditor" (someone who tests stores to see if they properly check IDs before selling alcohol), since he got to keep the beer he bought (Taylor, 2014). Then there is the spate of students who have used crowdfunding sites to help defray costs. An Illinois college student more than made up a $25,000 shortfall in tuition through crowdfunding on the website Gofundme.com. In her case, her mother had committed suicide and her father had lost his job, so her educational plight elicited much online empathy (Burton, 2014). Other students who have been successful in this model typically have very trying circumstances that make their plight particularly appealing to angel "investors." (In most cases the donors are providing charity, though in some cases there is a loose expectation of repayment.) Clearly, this is not a model that can be scaled up to replace our current patchwork of financial aid like Pell Grants, student loans, and work study. Or is it? The University of California has actually tried to institutionalize this approach with its Promise for Education program. Students post a "promise" they will enact if they are funded; some examples include wearing a cow suit for a week (actually suggested by the university system itself!), adopting a kitten, or putting on a marathon 24-hour magic show (O'Connor, 2013).

Even with institutional support, the University of California approach leaves many of us feeling uncomfortable. In a rich country like the United States, why do we "force" our ambitious young adults to beg or busk online? Why can't we just have free tuition for all? Of course, nothing is free. Free tuition just means tuition paid by taxpayers who may or may not benefit from the easier access to education. Free tuition for all also means that folks who could easily pay the true cost are handed a gift paid for by the public. Rather, in a capitalist system like ours, the crowdsourcing trend may reignite a long dead conservative idea: paying for education through equity rather than debt. Over 60 years ago, economist Milton Friedman argued that education would be better financed if rather than getting loans, students sold off percentages of their future earnings to investors. Rather than the English major working at a coffee shop burdened with $100,000 of debt that she cannot service, she would owe her investors (a more liberal version of this plan has the government being the "investor") a percentage of her income. That aligns incentives and uses the market (in the nongovernmental version) to drive what students should study or which schools actually provide a return on investment. It sounds pretty radical, but it can't be any worse than tattooing the space on one's forehead.

Learning to Learn or Learning to Labor? Functions of Schooling

EDUCATION

the process through which academic, social, and cultural skills are developed.

Let's start with the basics. Sociologists define education as the process through which academic, social, and cultural ideas and tools, both general and specific, are developed. First and foremost, schools are supposed to teach basic skills and impart knowledge. Thus we expect students to leave school

with at least the ability to read, write, and do arithmetic, as well as knowing who George Washington is. However, in reality, all schools do not achieve these goals. Functional illiteracy (the inability to read or write well enough to be a functioning member of society) plagues about 19 percent of the nation's population 16 to 65 years of age. Further, innumeracy, having insufficient mathematical skills to function in society, is experienced by 29 percent of the population ages 16 to 65 (US Department of Education, 2017). In 2015, only 34 percent of US eighth-graders tested were proficient in math (National Center for Education Statistics, 2019b).

Schools may also teach more specific skills that students need for the workplace. Vocational programs might focus on carpentry or mechanical skills, whereas professional schools train doctors and lawyers. In fact, the skills you obtain from vocational and postsecondary schools can be considered an investment in your future. Just as we can upgrade a computer to run faster and more efficiently, people can deliberately invest in knowledge and skills, called human capital, that make them more productive and bankable (Thurow, 1970). You can invest in human capital in a number of ways: going to college, taking a night class, or learning a trade.

How do schools train us to be good workers? What are some of the other functions of education?

SOCIALIZATION

As we saw in Chapter 4, another function of schooling is to socialize young people. Schools pass down the values, beliefs, and attitudes that are important in American society. For example, think about all the things we learn through the rules and structure of school that are valued by American culture: Bells ring to ensure that we learn how to get to places on time, we are punished for cheating to reinforce the consequences of being dishonest, and we are taught to obey authority in the form of teachers and administrators. What's especially important about universal schooling (the fact that American public schools are free and mandatory until high school) is that most students in the country go through more or less the same socialization processes. This gives them a common background that is useful when they enter the workforce or other institutions where they must function collectively. For example, consider how difficult it would be to maintain an efficient society if some schools taught students to be punctual and others didn't. At some point when these students got together, whether at college or in the workplace, these different socialization experiences would lead to inevitable conflicts. In 1968, sociologist Philip Jackson coined the term hidden curriculum to describe these nonacademic and less overt socialization functions of schooling. According to Roland Meighan (1981), "The hidden curriculum is taught by the school, not by any teacher. . . . [S]omething is coming across to the pupils which may never be spoken in the English lesson or prayed about in assembly. They are picking up an approach to living and an attitude to learning." The hidden curriculum is conveyed in many ways. Both the formal rules and regulations—be on time, don't cut class, etc.—and the informal norms of school—speak politely to teachers, for example, and respect authority—form part of the hidden curriculum that socializes children. But there are other aspects of the hidden curriculum that are, well, more hidden. Take nationalism. An important part of school in most societies is to instill a sense of patriotism on the part of youth. Since the 1950s in the United States many schools recite the Pledge of Allegiance, for example. But most socialization is much more subtle. For example, when you are studying history, language arts, or even math, you are also getting a lesson in what it means to be American, Polish, or Chinese. Professor Tamara Pavasović Trošt discussed this with me in the context of nation-building after the breakup of Yugoslavia.

Because of their ability to instill similar values in students, schools have been viewed as excellent places to integrate immigrants and other outsiders and instill dominant cultural values. Take, for example, the extreme case of the original

HIDDEN CURRICULUM

the nonacademic and less overt socialization functions of schooling.

DIGITAL.WWNORTON.COM/YOUMAYASK7

Watch more of my interview with Tamara Pavasović Trošt at
digital.wwnorton.com/youmayask7

inhabitants of the United States: Native Americans. As the country expanded westward in the 1800s, Americans racked their brains over how to best assimilate the people who populated those lands (after forced relocation, smallpox inoculation, and all-out warfare failed to eradicate tribal groups altogether). Their solution? Send them to school! Under the banner of "Kill the Indian, save the child," Americans set up boarding schools, such as the Carlisle Indian Industrial School in Pennsylvania, that took children as young as six away from their families to teach them more "civilized" ways of life. The prescribed regimen for assimilation included forbidding the children to speak their own language, placing the schools far from children's homes to prevent the continued influence of Native American culture, disparaging native practices, encouraging Christianity, and generally praising the superiority of White ways. These schools flourished for some 60 years (from 1870 to the early 1930s) before Americans started to express discontent over the education Native Americans were receiving, complaining that it was too expensive and encouraged dependency rather than self-sufficiency. Today, there are still seven federally funded boarding schools for elementary and secondary education that receive more applications than they can accommodate (US Department of the Interior, 2018). In addition, there are now tribally run schools on some reservations where students learn tribal languages and culture in small classes with other Native American students (Bear, 2008).

Initiatives for educating native populations were not specific to the United States. Between 1910 and 1970 in Australia, an estimated 100,000 Aboriginal and "half-caste" children were taken from their families and made legal wards of the state. Most were subsequently placed in British-run camps or schools with the stated purpose of culturally assimilating the kids, collectively referred to as the "stolen generation," into White society (Australian Human Rights Commission, 1997). The plight of these Aboriginal families has been dramatized in the book *Follow the Rabbit-Proof Fence* (1996; later the 2002 movie *Rabbit-Proof Fence*), written by Doris Pilkington (Nugi Garimara), the daughter of a woman who had escaped one such residential school as a young girl (along with two other girls) and walked a remarkable 1,500 miles to rejoin her family. Ten years later the heroine was taken into custody a second time—and again she escaped and survived the same journey. In 2008, the newly elected prime minister of Australia, Kevin

Boarding schools like the Carlisle Indian Industrial School were dedicated to inducing Native American children to abandon their traditional cultures.

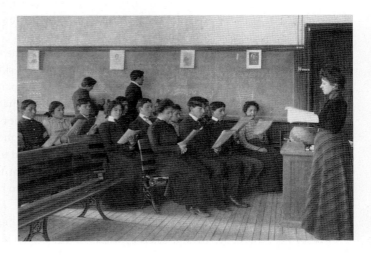

Homes Are Sought For These Children

A GROUP OF TINY HALF-CASTE AND QUADROON CHILDREN at the Darwin half-caste home. The Minister for the Interior (Mr Perkins) recently appealed to charitable organisations in Melbourne and Sydney to find homes for the children and rescue them from becoming outcasts.

I like the little girl in centre of group, but if taken by anyone else any of the others would do, as long as they are strong

Six Aboriginal girls are put up for adoption in a 1934 newspaper.

Rudd, formally apologized for these policies but stopped short of promising compensation.

Although nothing this extreme would likely take place today in the West, using school to socialize students to accept dominant cultural values is still seen by some in a sinister light. According to Marxist theorists such as Samuel Bowles and Herbert Gintis (1976), schools are unwitting pawns of the capitalist classes and teach the skills that are conducive to maintaining dominant and subordinate positions in the workforce, such as self-discipline, obedience, punctuality, and dependability. And perhaps, to a certain extent, they do. However, you might point out that not all positions require the same skills: What if your job does not require you to be subordinate or obedient? In fact, what if it requires you to hold authority over others or pursue unconventional thinking?

Some theorists answer this question by suggesting that schools first sort students according to their future jobs and then teach them the skills necessary for those positions. In the influential work *Power and Morality* (Sorokin & Lunden, 1959), Pitirim Sorokin argued that schools are sorting machines: First they test students for ability, talent, and social and moral character. Then they eliminate students who aren't up to snuff while promoting the best and brightest. Once sorted, students are taught different skills and socialized in the ways deemed most appropriate for their likely future positions. Thus if students show an aptitude for working with their hands, they may be placed in a vocational or mechanical program. Likewise, students who are intellectually exceptional may be placed in a school's gifted and talented program. Students, in their respective programs, then start learning the skills and behaviors necessary for success in their future careers.

If this were strictly the case, the sorting machine wouldn't be so bad: Schools would use students' talents, skills, and other aptitudes to place them in the programs that would best prepare them for the future. Unfortunately, however, some theorists suggest that schools don't sort students solely according to their merits; instead, they contend that schools divide students in ways that reproduce the kinds of inequalities we examined in Chapter 7. Thus, for example, schools may tend to disproportionately sort lower-class students into vocational classes that feed them into blue-collar positions. These positions essentially put them right back where they started from— the lower class.

A striking example of this sorting process was recounted by Jonathan Kozol, who toured public schools in several large American cities between

1988 and 1990 and then recounted his observations in *Savage Inequalities* (1991). In one school in New York City, he noticed that Black students were disproportionately sorted into special education classes that focused on teaching vocational skills. According to the principal, in addition to learning woodworking, the "children learn to punch in time cards at the door . . . in order to prepare them for employment." Having been sorted, these students were taught the skills that educators thought would best prepare them for their specific futures. However, the fact that these students were mostly Black and, tellingly, still in elementary school calls into question the extent to which these decisions were based solely on students' merits.

Do Schools Matter?

The school is . . . in a former roller skating rink. . . . The lobby is long and narrow. . . . There are no windows. The principal . . . tells me that the school's "capacity" is 900 but that there are 1,300 children here. The size of classes for fifth and sixth grade children in New York, she says, is "capped" at 32, but she says that the class size in the school goes "up to 34." (I later see classes, however, as large as 37.). . . . Textbooks are scarce and children have to share their social studies books. . . . The carpets are patched and sometimes taped together to conceal an open space. . . . Two first grade classes share a single room without a window, divided only by a blackboard. . . . The library is a tiny, windowless and claustrophobic room. (Kozol, 1991, pp. 85–87)

The dogwoods and magnolias on the lawn in front of P.S. 24 are in full blossom on the day I visit. . . . The school serves 825

An overcrowded school in Brooklyn (left) and students in art class at an elite Manhattan private school.

students in the kindergarten through sixth grade. . . . This is . . . a great deal smaller than the 1,300 children packed into the former skating rink; but the principal . . . still regards it as excessive for an elementary school. . . . The district can't afford librarians but P.S. 24, unlike the poorer schools of District 10, can draw on educated parent volunteers who staff the room in shifts three days a week. A parent organization also raises independent funds to buy materials, including books. . . . There is a computer in each class [except in the special education classes]. (Kozol, 1991, pp. 92, 94–95)

These two public schools are both in New York City, the first in a poor section and the second in an affluent neighborhood. As these descriptions so vividly demonstrate, all schools are not created equal, and these differences are likely to affect educational outcomes. For example, after reading the descriptions of the elementary schools above, which students do you think will do better in school? Those in the "roller skating" school, who have to share textbooks and classrooms, or those in P.S. 24, where most classrooms have their own computers? Most of us would probably guess that students in schools with more advantages get a better education than those in less adequately equipped schools.

THE COLEMAN REPORT

What if I told you that while achievement differences most likely exist between the students at these two schools, research has determined that few, if any, of the differences described actually affect educational outcomes? Such was the finding of a landmark sociological study known as the Coleman Report (Coleman et al., 1966). The study was conducted in 1964, nearly 10 years after *Brown v. Board of Education* (the US Supreme Court ruling that mandated the desegregation of schools) and at a time when public schools throughout the nation were still highly segregated. Furthermore, achievement gaps between Black and White schools remained high. Suspecting that these gaps could be explained by measurable differences between the schools Blacks and Whites attended (e.g., textbook availability and classroom size), the government commissioned a study. The results of the research were surprising even to James Coleman himself. To put it succinctly, the researchers found that differences in resources between schools didn't matter. Derived from surveys of 600,000 students in 4,000 schools and an examination of the facilities, school curricula, administration, and extracurricular activities at each school, the data indicated that school characteristics explained, if anything, only a tiny amount of the differences in educational outcomes among schools. Instead, the researchers determined that most of the differences in achievement among schools could be attributed to two factors: family background (which we'll come back to later in the chapter) and the other peers with whom students attended school (which is highly correlated with family background). Black students fared better in majority-White schools, and lower-income children did better in middle-class schools.

These findings were a bombshell in the education world. After all, American ideology tells us that schools are the place where students from all walks of life get a fair shot at obtaining a good education. And if they don't, we'd expect studies to pick up on the differences among schools that explain educational inequalities. But researchers couldn't deny the findings: Even those who reanalyzed Coleman's data arrived at similar results (e.g., Jencks et al., 1972). Schools entered an era of underappreciation, but researchers wouldn't let the issue drop. They just couldn't believe that schools, especially when they were so clearly different, didn't affect educational outcomes, so they refined their research methods and data collection tools. It did not take long for the new, improved studies to show links between students' achievement outcomes and school characteristics.

CLASS SIZE

Perhaps the most widely celebrated example of how schools affect educational achievement comes from the research conducted during Project STAR, a longitudinal, four-year study begun in 1985 by the Tennessee State Department of Education. In the study, students and teachers from kindergarten through third grade were randomly assigned to small classes (13–17 students), regular-size classes (22–26), or regular-size classes with a teacher's aide. Various researchers then examined the short- and long-term consequences of smaller class size. The results provided evidence that schools with smaller classes significantly benefited their students compared to schools with larger classes.

Specifically, the researchers found that even after returning to regular classes, students in the study assigned to smaller classes experienced significantly fewer disciplinary problems and significantly higher achievement test scores than nonparticipants (Nye et al., 1994). The researchers also determined that these benefits were long lasting. Students who were placed in the smaller classes for all four years of the study had significantly higher graduation rates (Finn et al., 2005) and were more likely to take an ACT (American College Testing) or SAT (Scholastic Aptitude Test) exam, which researchers used as a crude measure for determining whether students planned to attend college (Krueger & Whitmore, 2001). Finally, in terms of both the short- and long-term benefits, researchers found that the effects were particularly strong for minority students and those from low-income families.

PRIVATE SCHOOLS VERSUS PUBLIC SCHOOLS

Aside from Project STAR, much of the newer evidence on the importance of school effects derives from studies comparing public schools with private schools. Although some parents send their children to private schools for noneducational (e.g., religious) reasons, many do so because they believe the quality of education is higher than in public schools, and they're willing to invest money in it. In fact, the costs of some private schools rival those of an Ivy League education. Many New York City private elementary and high schools charge more than $45,000 a year, exceeding Harvard's tuition rates.

What do you get for over 40 grand a year? Columbia University sociologist Shamus Khan studied one of the most elite boarding schools in the nation, St. Paul's (his own alma mater), by accepting a teaching position there in order to conduct ethnographic research. We spoke about the findings about elite educational institutions that he reports in his book, *Privilege: The Making of an Adolescent Elite at St. Paul's School* (2010):

> [One] way to think about a place like St. Paul's is that it converts birthright into credentials. It provides [advantaged students] with a degree of legitimacy. So people who didn't go to St. Paul's can look at that kid and say, "Well, I know he came from a well-off background, but he worked really hard. He went to this amazing high school, and he went to this amazing college, and that's why he is where he is." (Conley, 2011d)

According to Khan, however, the story is slightly more complicated. He elaborates:

DIGITAL.WWNORTON.COM/YOUMAYASK7

Watch more of my interview with Shamus Khan at
digital.wwnorton.com/youmayask7

I've one big caution about thinking about them that way though: There're also lots of people who go to these institutions who aren't from families like [the typical] St. Paul's [students]. And so even if what St. Paul's does is convert the birthright of some people into credentials, that's not all [such schools] do. [They also] allow for advancement of many people at the institution who weren't born with such advantages, who do achieve a lot by going there. (Conley, 2011d)

Of course, the sociologist knows this dose of upward mobility and meritocracy is exactly what gives elite schools their "legitimating function"—otherwise they'd just be places for rich kids and known as such. Aside from whatever legitimating function they may serve, are private schools really better academically than public ones, or are wealthy parents ultimately deluding themselves and needlessly spending thousands of dollars per year in the process? Once we move beyond the benefits that Khan shows, the story is more complicated. Several studies (e.g., Bryk et al., 1993; Coleman & Hoffer, 1987; Coleman et al., 1982) have found that school sector (private versus public) is associated with educational outcomes even after students' different backgrounds are taken into account. However, the exact details of these effects are somewhat unexpected. After dividing the private institutions into Catholic and non-Catholic schools, researchers determined that Catholic schools (which are generally among the least expensive private schools) were the most successful in preparing students academically, particularly students from disadvantaged backgrounds (e.g., minority students and those from lower socioeconomic strata). For example, these studies found that Catholic school students scored the highest on achievement tests, followed by secular private school and public school students (Coleman et al., 1982), respectively. Thus private schools may have an impact but not necessarily according to how expensive they are.

How do we explain these sector differences? Are the plaid designs on some private school uniforms cognitively stimulating? According to researchers, a more plausible explanation is that certain academic and behavioral differences between private and public schools predict educational outcomes. For example, researchers determined that private school students did more homework, had a greater chance of being enrolled in academic programs, and took more college preparatory classes than public school students. Behaviorally, private school students had better attendance, became involved in fewer fights, and threatened teachers less than public school students. James S. Coleman and Thomas Hoffer (1987) also suggest that the strong effects of the Catholic schools stem from the large amounts of social capital in the community—that is, any relationship between people that can facilitate the actions of others (see Chapter 5). In the case of Catholic schools, Coleman and Hoffer (1987), as well as Anthony Bryk, Valerie Lee, and Peter Holland (1993), hypothesize that the closeness of the Catholic community reinforces among teachers, parents, and students behaviors and norms that are conducive to learning. Alternatively, it could just be that families who value education the most and are most able to get their kids into a private school are the families whose kids would succeed no matter what schools they attended; in this paradigm, schools again act as social sorting machines rather than having important effects of their own. In fact, recent evidence from private school scholarship lotteries suggests that this last explanation may indeed be the most accurate (see the Policy box later

SOCIAL CAPITAL

the information, knowledge of people, and connections that help individuals enter, gain power in, or otherwise leverage social networks.

in this chapter). Hence Khan's parents may be getting only the ideology of a better education for their money.

However, as researchers studied these differences among schools, they came across another impressive finding: Differences among students *within* schools (e.g., in achievement scores) were significantly greater (as much as four times as large) than the differences among students *between* schools (Coleman et al., 1966; Jencks et al., 1972). Let's turn now to what goes on inside a school that could explain these extreme differences.

What's Going On Inside Schools?

Given the evidence of the Coleman Report about inequalities within schools, a good idea for researchers would be to do a deep dive into one or more schools to see what's going on that produces systematic student differences. That's just what Amanda Lewis and John Diamond did to produce *Despite the Best Intentions: How Racial Inequality Thrives in Good Schools*. They picked a large integrated public high school in the Midwest and studied it quantitatively and qualitatively for five years. What they found was that differential expectations and disparities in discipline led to racial inequalities despite a veneer and rhetoric of color-blind meritocracy. A key factor in this process, they found, was White parents, who exercised privilege to successfully advocate and intervene on behalf of their offspring—be that to gain placement in an AP class or to reduce a punishment when their child was in trouble. The result, of course, was a reproduction of existing inequalities. Starting with tracking, let's take a closer look at the role within-school factors play in generating unequal outcomes.

THE SORTING MACHINE REVISITED: TRACKING

TRACKING

a way of dividing students into different classes by ability or future plans.

Earlier we talked about schools as sorting machines, placing students such that existing social structures would be reproduced. If you attended a typical comprehensive American high school, it is likely that much of this sorting was achieved through tracking, a way of dividing students into different classes by ability or future plans. School subjects might be divided by the level of ability required (high or low) or the type of preparation (academic, vocational, or general). For example, if you are college-bound, you may be sorted into honors or advanced placement (AP) college preparation classes. Dividing students into different tracks is instrumental in both preparing them for their future positions and explaining the large differences we observe among students within schools.

Tracking is intended to create a better learning environment, because students' goals are matched to their curricula. Sounds reasonable. And research has determined that tracking has significant impacts even after controlling for background characteristics. For example, Adam Gamoran and Robert Mare (1989) found that students in their school's college track had significantly higher math achievement and were more likely to graduate from high school. Furthermore, James Rosenbaum (1980) determined that tracking significantly predicted whether students attended college. Finally, Richard Arum and Yossi Shavit (1995) ascertained that students who graduated from vocational tracks were less likely to be unemployed and more likely to enter the workforce as skilled laborers. Of course, we can't know for sure whether it was the lessons learned in the respective tracks that drove these results or whether the tracking system itself is merely good at sorting students by future promise.

But tracking has a dark side. First, notice that none of the positive benefits we've reviewed involve the general track. This in-between track, preparing students for neither work nor college, seems to provide no benefits to students. Second, researchers have discovered that students from privileged backgrounds are significantly more likely to be in college tracks even after taking into account variables that should predict track placement, including achievement (Gamoran & Mare, 1989; Lucas, 1999). Furthermore, because race, ethnicity, and class are so intertwined, higher-class Whites are usually overrepresented in academic tracks, and Black, Hispanic, and lower-class students are overrepresented in noncollege tracks (O'Connor, 2009). But if privileged students aren't placed in the highest tracks based on merit, why are they so overrepresented in these classes? Qualitative research (e.g., Lareau, 2003) suggests that middle-class parents actively intervene in school matters to obtain the best advantages for their children. For

A second-grade teacher in Phoenix gives remedial help in English to students whose first language is not English. Creating separate remedial classes is an example of tracking. What are the benefits and consequences of tracking?

example, they might request that their child be placed in the highest track despite mediocre achievement because they are more likely to be college graduates and know how important the college track is for their child's future. Or, in diverse schools, these parents might want to separate their children from the minority and lower-class students in the lower tracks (Oakes, 1985).

Sociologist Stephen Morgan looked at students in private Catholic schools to see if he could tease out the relationship among academic achievement, religiosity,

DIGITAL.WWNORTON.COM/YOUMAYASK7

To see an interview with Stephen Morgan, go to
digital.wwnorton.com/youmayask7

and parental involvement. He chose Catholic schools because "what's interesting about Catholic schools in the United States is there are quite a few non-Catholic students enrolled in them, and those are the students that seem to do particularly well in Catholic school" (Conley, 2009l), even though it might seem harder for non-Catholic students to fit in with disciplinary and cultural expectations at a Catholic school, thus making it harder for them to focus on their schoolwork. Morgan attributes the success of the non-Catholic students to their parents' desire to see them succeed academically. These non-Catholic kids in Catholic schools are kids who, he says, "are particularly ambitious, and they have a belief that the Catholic schools are better in a lot of areas, and in fact they may have a more demanding curriculum" (Conley, 2009l). The evidence from non-Catholic students consistently outdoing their Catholic peers suggests that parents' goals for their children may play a large role in the kids' educational success, casting some doubt on just how much tracking actually benefits high-performing students. Maybe those in the higher track would have been equally successful had their school forgone tracking and kept all the students together.

The research conducted by Jeannie Oakes (1985) has suggested that tracking might actually be bad because there are stark differences in the quality of teaching and content of materials between tracks. This is best illustrated by the answers students gave Oakes when she asked them to identify the most important thing they had learned or done in their classes. Typical answers from students in the high tracks included the following:

> I have learned a lot about molecules and now am able to reason and figure out more things.

> Things in nature are not always what they appear to be or what seems to be happening is not what really is happening.

Responses from students in the lower track included the following:

> How to ride motorcycles and shoot trap. [I don't know what trap is either.]

To be honest, nothing.

The only thing I've learned is how to flirt with the chicks in class. This class is a big waste of time and effort.

How to blow up light bulbs. (Oakes, 1985, pp. 70–71)

We can see, then, why some have accused tracking of being an important factor in increasing or reproducing inequality (Gamoran & Mare, 1989). Although tracking gives some students educational advantages, it disproportionately awards these advantages to those who are already privileged. Minority and lower-class students are often left behind as a result, receiving inferior instruction and learning less in their classes.

Many educational systems in western Europe take tracking a step further, sorting students into different schools altogether, in some countries as early as age 10. In Germany, for example, all students are required to enter *Grundschule* (literally, "ground school") at age 6 and attend for four years. At the end of the fourth grade, teachers recommend which type of secondary schooling is most appropriate for each child based primarily on academic performance. Unlike in the United States, however, in Germany the ultimate decision lies with a student's parents. Austria, Hungary, and the Slovak Republic follow a similar tracking model. Other countries, such as Canada, Japan, Norway, and the United Kingdom, have a system more akin to the one in the United States (Hanushek & Wößmann, 2006).

A version of tracking seems to be reaching up into higher education as of late. Of course there have always been majors—English versus sociology versus physics—but there are other forms of tracking too. There is the division between two-year and four-year degrees. And in recent years there has been a movement, particularly among two-year community colleges, to institute what are called "guided pathways" (Jenkins et al., 2018). Rather than have students sample courses as if they are at an academic buffet, advisers encourage students to choose their concentration early and select all their courses toward that goal—ideally a major that opens up the most labor market or four-year college opportunities. Proponents argue that when higher education is not free, as in the United States, dabbling can leave a student with a heavy debt burden and little meaningful progress toward a degree. But while this approach is certainly better than allowing students to drift, many students cannot know what life they want until they sample a range of courses, and then there's the idea that a college education should make us broadly educated citizens, not just employable in the short run. Finally, the skills or jobs for which these pathways aim will not always be relevant in 10 years. Students may be better off learning broader, less vocationally oriented skills such as math, writing, and critical and scientific thinking. There is always, then, a tension between the dual roles of schooling as a pure education and as a job-training curriculum.

THE CLASSROOM PRESSURE COOKER

In addition to shedding light on some of the negative aspects of tracking in high schools, Oakes's (1985) study also demonstrates the importance of teacher–student and peer-to-peer dynamics in student experiences. In the United States, where schooling is not nationally standardized, individual teachers appear to matter a lot more to the intellectual dynamics of the classroom, so students in different classrooms might obtain different types of instruction that vary widely in their quality.

To be conservative, let's say that teachers spend about 5 of the 6.5 hours in a typical school day with students. This means that over the course of a 185-day school year, teachers and students have more than 900 hours of sustained contact. Philip Jackson (1968) described such an intense climate in the following way:

> There is a social intimacy [in the classrooms] . . . that is unmatched elsewhere in our society. Buses and movie theaters may be more crowded than classrooms, but people rarely stay in such densely populated settings for extended periods of time and while there, they usually are not expected to concentrate on work or to interact with each other. . . . Only in schools do thirty or more people spend several hours each day literally side by side. (p. 8)

What goes on inside will therefore play an important role in student outcomes. Let's look at the components of a classroom that affect student experiences.

First, of course, there is the teacher. We know that some teachers are more effective than others, and research backs up this notion (e.g., Murnane et al., 2005; Rockoff, 2004; Schacter & Thum, 2004). Although researchers have identified the general effects of teachers in their statistical analyses, they've had much less luck pinpointing the exact characteristics of teachers that affect student achievement. For example, some studies have found that teachers' experience is significantly related to student achievement, but only in the first few years of teaching (Hanushek et al., 1998, 2005; Murnane et al., 2005). Furthermore, although some studies (Murnane et al., 2005) have determined that teachers' own educational background is related to student achievement, others (Hanushek et al., 1998, 2005) indicate no systematic pattern between the two.

Perhaps these researchers have been unable to pinpoint characteristics of teacher quality because they are hard to quantify. For example, it is difficult to measure the routines that make a class run smoothly, the ability of teachers to quiet disruptive students, or the tendency to give extra encouragement that differentiates one teacher from another. We could also imagine that teachers who expect a lot from their students motivate them

to work harder, but of course, the problem lies in measuring these expectations. One pair of researchers succeeded in doing so through a creative research design.

In the early 1960s Robert Rosenthal and Lenore Jacobson (1968) visited an elementary school at the beginning of the academic year and administered IQ tests, which measure cognitive abilities such as verbal and numerical reasoning and knowledge. They then randomly selected one-fifth of the students and told the teachers that these students were especially bright and had great potential for growth. (Remember, though, that in reality they had been selected at random.) At the end of the school year, the researchers retested the students and found that those who had been labeled "bright" did significantly better on the new IQ test than their peers. Furthermore, teachers rated these children as being more intellectually curious and happier and needing less social approval.

What the researchers accomplished in this study was a rough quantification of how teacher expectations can affect student achievement. They confirmed that when teachers held higher expectations for certain students (and likely changed their behavior toward those children accordingly), these students responded by meeting teacher expectations. This dynamic is called the Pygmalion effect or more commonly the self-fulfilling prophecy.

Unfortunately, the power of teachers' expectations and the self-fulfilling prophecy can work both ways. Although students might benefit from high expectations, their outcomes can also be depressed by low expectations. Moreover, teachers seem to have low expectations for certain groups of students more frequently—for example, boys, minorities, and lower-income youths—even when they have the same cognitive ability as students in other groups (e.g., Clifton et al., 1986).

Researchers have found that some teachers are more effective than others. However, identifying what qualities make a good teacher has been much more difficult. What methods might a sociologist use to explain why award-winning teachers such as Clyde Hashimoto (left) and Linda Alston (right) succeed where other teachers fail?

Another way one teacher might be more effective than another is through his or her instructional methods. Some teachers may prefer more traditional teaching styles, whereas others continually try out the latest strategies for effective teaching. Take, for example, what happened daily in a particular class profiled by Amanda E. Lewis (2004). While most classes she observed spent the morning reviewing academic material, students in this teacher's class gathered in a circle to give each other compliments. However, when the class became rowdy, they were instructed to offer insults instead:

> Mr. Ortiz starts put-downs with Julio. Julio begins by telling Robin she's fat and ugly. Robin tells Thompson he's ugly. . . . Catherine tells Rebecca she doesn't like her earrings. She has to tell Darnell— Mr. Ortiz gives her several suggestions, melon head, etc. . . . Luis tells Lisa that she stinks. She tells Daniel that he dresses like a rag. He tells Rose that she farts too much. (p. 47)

Maybe the creative strategy of prompting children to share compliments and insults will benefit some of them, but it is more likely that these students will fall behind children who are studying a more traditional curriculum. In fact, as Lewis's ethnography proceeded, she reported that the same class would sometimes go days without any formal science, social studies, or math instruction.

By contrast, teaching methods supported by extensive research are called best practices. For example, after analyzing more than 700 research papers from

What are some of the best practices that Donald Langlois and Charlotte Rappe Zales identified in their research on effective teaching? Why might these teaching styles be more effective than others?

the 1980s in what is called a *meta-analysis*, Donald E. Langlois and Charlotte Rappe Zales (1992) came up with a list of the most effective teaching methods. These included such approaches as minimizing class time lost to activities other than instruction (Mr. Ortiz seems to have missed that memo), having clear expectations for acceptable behavior and consistent consequences for misbehavior, maintaining a fixed routine, and setting high standards for classwork.

Teachers are clearly an important element of classroom life, but we can't forget the many other people who are in the classroom—peers. Who attends a class and how they behave set a tone for the classroom environment. For example, a classroom might be run by one of the best teachers in the school, but if the students continually disrupt class, that teacher will have to take time away from teaching to address such problems. In fact, David Figlio (2005) determined that more behavior problems in a classroom significantly increase other students' disciplinary problems and reduce their test scores.

Recall one of the key findings of the Coleman Report: The composition of students in a school significantly affected student outcomes. Nowhere would this be more applicable than in a classroom, where contact is longer and more intense compared with schoolwide social interaction. Therefore, researchers have examined, in particular, how the academic characteristics of classmates affect their peers. For example, if low-achieving students are placed in a classroom with mostly high-achieving students, will they fall even farther behind or rise to the challenge? Research from numerous studies suggests that when students are in a classroom with others of high ability, all students profit. For example, Caroline Hoxby (2000) found that increases in peers' reading scores were successful in raising individual student scores. In another study, Ron W. Zimmer and Eugenia F. Toma (2000) determined that raising average ability in classrooms increased individual student achievement, particularly for low-ability students. Unfortunately, this effect works both ways. If you are in a classroom with mostly low-achieving students, research suggests that you will make fewer gains than you would in a classroom with more high-achieving students (Leiter, 1983).

Findings such as these have spurred the rise of mainstreaming and inclusion practices in special education. Special education is the set of instructional practices geared toward students with disabilities. Such disabilities may be cognitive (such as pervasive developmental

A group of students, including a student with Down syndrome, play a game together at Bascomb Elementary School. The Georgia school practices "mainstreaming," in which special education students are integrated into "regular" classrooms with additional teacher support. According to its proponents, what are the benefits of this approach?

delay), behavioral (such as ADHD), or physical (such as blindness). Traditional approaches to special education segregate these students from the general education students. A growing recognition that general education students learn important skills from interacting with "atypical" students and that special education students are often better served by being integrated with their full range of peers, however, has led to a push to integrate students with disabilities into regular classrooms while providing them with additional teacher support. This new approach, called *mainstreaming*, recognizes that disabled students can still gain academically from the pedagogy in a typical classroom, even if their rate of progress is different. The philosophy of inclusion claims that even if a child is not gaining academically by being taught alongside kids deemed "normal," they gain socially. Either way, such approaches recognize the critical importance of peers and peer socialization to a child's growth.

Higher Education

THE RISE AND RISE OF HIGHER EDUCATION: CREDENTIALISM

Consider this set of facts: In the United States in 1910, fewer than 3 percent of men and women over age 25 had a college degree. By 2016 this number had jumped to 32.6 percent of the population (US Census Bureau, 2018b). In a relatively short time, this country has experienced a virtual educational boom. How can we explain this dramatic increase in academic achievement?

Functionalist Perspectives According to functionalists (who believe that everything in a society exists to fulfill a function; see Chapter 1), the rise of education boils down to simple supply and demand. As industrialization took hold throughout the twentieth century, jobs became more technical and required a more educated workforce. By attaining more education, students were simply responding to employer demand.

As clear-cut as this explanation is, it is not well backed by the data. In his review of the literature, Randall Collins (1971) concludes that although the demands of industrialization did play a role in expanding the educational system, industrialization alone can't account for the extreme trends in education that we've witnessed. For example, in contrast to what we'd expect from traditional functionalist theory, Collins finds that much of what students learn in school isn't related to their future work, that necessary skills tend to be acquired on the job, and that many Americans have more education than they need for their occupations. Therefore, we must look elsewhere for a plausible explanation.

Conflict Perspectives According to the conflict theorists (who hold that conflict among competing interests is the basic, animating force of any society; see Chapter 1), in contrast, the dramatic increase in college graduation may be traced to American views on education and the expansion of the school system in the twentieth century. Since colonial times, education in the United States has been a badge of elite status (whereas in Europe, where class systems are more rigid, a fancy lineage could be a more important factor in gaining entrance into the elite). High levels of education signal to employers that you have been indoctrinated in the dominant group's values; thus education is often used as a screen for top positions. In 1910, when 24 percent of people over age 25 had completed fewer than five years of elementary school and only 14 percent had completed high school or more (Snyder & Tan, 2005), maintaining an elite status through schooling meant perhaps completing high school. However, as the American educational system expanded throughout the century, higher levels of education became universal (Figure 13.1). By 2004 only 1.5 percent of the population 25 and older had completed fewer than five years of elementary school, and 85 percent had completed high school or more (Snyder & Tan, 2005). This trend means that as education expanded, members of the elite—and those who wanted to move into the elite—had to obtain more and more education to set themselves apart from others (Collins, 1979).

FIGURE 13.1 The Rise in Educational Attainment, 1940–2018

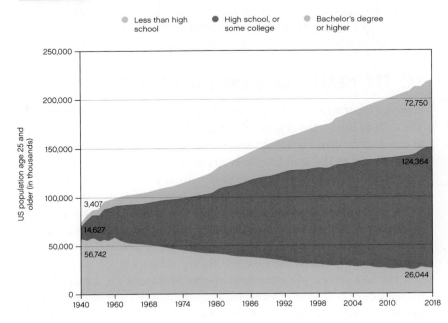

● Less than high school   ● High school, or some college   ● Bachelor's degree or higher

SOURCE: US Census Bureau, 2018b.

The conflict perspective also provides an explanation for the rise of credentialism, an overemphasis on credentials (e.g., college degrees) for signaling social status or job qualifications. When everybody attains so much education, employers tend to increase job requirements to screen out people. To do this, they rely more and more on credentials that signal both social status and area of specialty (the field in which your degree was awarded). According to Collins (1971, 1979), however, this upgrading does not reflect the increase in skills needed for particular jobs. The same jobs that 50 years ago required only a high-school diploma now require a college degree. Thus people today often are overqualified for their jobs. (In fact, countless websites now exist that give advice on how to cope with being overqualified for your job.)

The upgrading of degree requirements by employers is a cycle reinforced by students who keep getting more education to meet employer minimum requirements. (Employers increase the requirements again when too many students reach this minimum level.) So how do we break the cycle? Clearly, students can't be expected to keep increasing their educational attainment, staying in school until their forties (or can they?). Instead, trends point to people differentiating themselves academically not just through years of education but through quality of education, such as the selectivity or prestige of the college they attend. For example, Samuel R. Lucas and Aaron D. Good (2001) demonstrate that once education levels are saturated, members of the wealthier classes don't just move on to the next level of education: They also try to obtain the best education within that tier. Thus at the high-school level, which is nearly universal, higher-social-class students attend private schools at higher rates or are placed in the highest tracks at school. Likewise, as the college tier becomes more saturated, there is more competition among students to get into the most selective schools.

THE SAT: MERITOCRACY AND THE BIG TEST

In the spring of 2006, many high-school seniors' worst nightmare came true. The College Board, the organization that administers the SAT, announced that it had incorrectly scored more than 4,000 tests taken in October 2005. To add to the scandal, the errors tended toward the worst possible direction—underestimation, by anywhere from 10 to 200 points. Colleges scrambled to reassess applicants, while students who hadn't yet taken the SAT signed up for two tests in case one was scored incorrectly. But for many students, the damage was done. Although colleges reexamined the affected students' applications, some students had already made decisions about where to apply based on their incorrectly low scores.

The SAT debacle of 2006 reignited questions about a test that has been the subject of controversy for years. Questioning the merits of standardized testing and how fairly it assesses students, 731 colleges minimized the number of students who have to submit test scores (Setoodeh, 2006). Even the College Board, which administers the SAT, admits that the exam can provoke extreme anxiety, which the board attempted to alleviate in 2009 by giving students the option to send only their best scores to their chosen colleges. Still, even as more colleges gravitate away from the SAT, the test remains a pivotal part of the admissions process at most schools. Why?

According to the College Board, the SAT is a vital part of the admissions process because it helps predict a student's potential for college success above and beyond the typical measures, such as high-school grade-point average (GPA) and class rank, which may vary widely among students from different schools. In particular, the SAT was designed to predict students' grades for their freshman year of college. But does it live up to this promise? Apparently so. Research (Bowen & Bok, 1998; Zwick & Sklar, 2005) confirms that the SAT accurately predicts not only freshman year GPA but a variety of other outcomes, including class rank, likelihood of graduation, and a student's chance of obtaining an advanced degree.

If this is the case, why are critics so opposed to using these standardized tests for admissions? First, researchers note that the SAT does not, as the College Board asserts, predict college outcomes above and beyond high-school grades and class rank. For example, Rebecca Zwick and Jeffrey C. Sklar (2005) found that although the SAT was a significant predictor of freshman year GPA, one's high-school GPA was a stronger predictor. Other researchers (Crouse & Trusheim, 1988) have determined that if admissions counselors had looked only at high-school records to assess students, 84 percent of the time they would have made the same admissions decisions as when they used the SAT. In the 16 percent of cases that remained, low SAT scores were the determining factor in rejecting students, although they may not be the fairest way to eliminate candidates.

Second, even if the SAT generally predicts college outcomes pretty well, if we dig a little deeper, an intriguing pattern emerges. The SAT accurately predicts college outcomes only for White students. It doesn't do as well in predicting outcomes such as college GPA for Black and Hispanic students (Bowen & Bok, 1998; Pearson, 1993; Vars & Bowen, 1998; Zwick & Sklar, 2005).

Third, researchers question how meritocratic the SAT actually is. Do the scores reflect the abilities that *should* matter? Not necessarily. SAT scores are consistently correlated with race, ethnicity, and class. African

Amanda Hecker, a high-school senior in New Jersey, was one of the students who learned that the College Board had scored her SAT incorrectly. Why do critics question the validity of tests like the SAT for judging college admissions?

Americans and Hispanics systematically score lower than White students, and higher-class students (who, among other things, can pay for SAT preparatory classes, which do increase scores) systematically score higher than lower-class students. Unless we're willing to believe that lower-class, Black, and Hispanic students are inherently less intelligent, the SAT is biased toward certain groups of students. In fact, evidence exists that negative stereotypes of minority groups play an important role in explaining at least some of the differences in test scores—this is called stereotype threat, a particular form of test anxiety. At this point, I am compelled to point out the extreme irony of this situation. The SAT was originally created to give the child who attends local public schools the chance to show that he or she is just as "able" as the kid who went to an elite, private high school. Back in 1933, Harvard University sought to cast a wider net than the handful of elite private schools that had routinely provided most of its undergraduate population. The solution was to come up with a more "objective" standard, set by an institution external to the university itself. Thus it was in this spirit of meritocracy that the SAT was born.

Finally, much of the predictive power of the SAT stems from the correlation between the test scores and family background. When studies control for family background (meaning that they calculate how much the SAT would predict if all students came from the same background), the SAT's predictive power diminishes. That is, the SAT might appear to predict college grades, but part of that effect derives from the fact that students from families with higher incomes generally get better grades *and* higher SAT scores. In fact, researchers have found that background characteristics map onto SAT scores so well that using them to predict outcomes instead of the SAT would work equally well. For example, economist Jesse Rothstein (2004) determined that high-school GPA and school and individual demographic information predict freshman year GPA just as well as using only the high-school GPA and SAT score. Thus Rothstein points out that college admissions officers would choose the best-prepared class by explicitly admitting higher-class students from wealthier schools, rather than just using SATs as a proxy for these background characteristics. This solution would save everybody a lot of time, money, and anxiety, but of course, it would cast a dark shadow over the SAT's purported meritocratic nature.

Given all the evidence against the predictive power of the SAT and its inability to assess students fairly, we return to our original question: Why do colleges use the SAT as an admissions practice? Part of the reason may be that for colleges that receive many applications, using a numerical cutoff substantially lessens their workload. Others (Crouse & Trusheim, 1988) suggest that the longevity of the SAT is merely a testament to the ability of the College Board to sell its product. In any event, the SAT debacle of 2006 put these issues on the table and may indeed spur a reassessment of the test's importance in the college admissions process.

AFFIRMATIVE ACTION: MYTHS AND REALITY

In a study of admissions practices at elite schools, Thomas Espenshade, Chang Chung, and Joan Walling (2004) found that group A was four times as likely to be admitted as other students and that group B was three times as likely to be admitted. Not only were these groups more likely to gain admission to elite schools, but they did so despite having lower SAT scores than other applying students. Given all that we have heard about preferential admissions practices, you might assume that these preferences were given to minority students—that group A perhaps was made up of Black students, and group B Latinxs. This assumption, however, would be wrong. In this study, applicants in group A were athletes, whereas those in group B were legacies, children of alumni parents or close relatives. Both groups were disproportionately White.

As we saw in Chapter 9 on race, affirmative action refers to a set of policies that grant preferential treatment to a number of particular subgroups within the population. Affirmative action is intended to level the playing field for historically underrepresented groups, such as certain racial minorities and women (although women now make up a majority of American college students). Often, affirmative action is thought to be the only form of preferential treatment. As we have seen from the example just given, this is a myth. In reality, schools give preferential treatment based on many characteristics, not just race or ethnicity. There are preferences not only for being a legacy or an athlete but also for exhibiting leadership experience, living in a certain place such as a rural community, or even having unusual life circumstances (Fetter, 1995; Freedman, 2003; Zwick, 2002). Furthermore, in many cases, these preferences are equal to or higher than those given to African American and Hispanic students (Bowen & Bok, 1998; Espenshade et al., 2004).

Another myth is that affirmative action takes away opportunities from deserving White students. To address this myth, we should first establish a little-known fact about which institutions are affected by affirmative action. Research has found that affirmative action is an issue only at selective institutions that represent one-fifth of American colleges (Kane, 1998). Why? Because the majority of schools in the United States admit just about everyone. Economist Thomas J. Kane (1998) determined that at the least-selective colleges in his sample, being Black or Hispanic gave little to no advantage in college admissions.

Does this mean that affirmative action takes away slots in elite schools from deserving White students? Not necessarily. Kane (1998) gives the following analogy:

> Suppose that one parking space in front of a popular restaurant is for disabled drivers. Many of the non-disabled drivers who pass by the space while circling the parking lot in search of a place to park may be tempted to think that they would have an easier time

AFFIRMATIVE ACTION

a set of policies that grant preferential treatment to a number of particular subgroups within the population—typically, women and historically disadvantaged racial minorities.

finding a space if the space had not been reserved. Although eliminating the space would have only a minuscule effect on the average parking search for non-disabled drivers, the cumulative cost perceived by each passing driver is likely to exceed the true cost simply because people have a difficult time thinking about small probability events. (p. 453)

What is the actual probability of the "small-probability event," the increased chance that a White student would have in gaining admission to elite schools if affirmative action were abolished? According to Espenshade and Chung (2005), abolishing affirmative action would increase a White student's chances of acceptance by only 0.5 percent. The real gain would occur among Asian students, who are not considered part of a historically underrepresented minority group in colleges and whose grades and test scores tend to exceed those of Whites. Asians' acceptance rates would increase from 18 to 23 percent.

A third myth is that African American and Hispanic students who gain entrance to selective schools through affirmative action are underprepared and will flounder in the competitive environment. The literature here presents mixed results. On the one hand, numerous researchers have found that Black and Hispanic students whose background characteristics, SAT scores, and high-school GPAs are equivalent to those of White students have lower college GPAs (Bowen & Bok, 1998; Kane, 1998). However, these researchers also determined that the more selective the schools that Blacks and Hispanics attended, the greater their chances of graduation. Students in more selective schools were also more likely to go on to earn professional or doctoral degrees (Bowen & Bok, 1998). An important question is how minority students fare once they leave school. Here again, the contrast with athletes and legacies is informative. In *The Shape of the River* (1998), William G. Bowen and Derek Bok demonstrate that minority students admitted with lower SAT scores than their nonminority counterparts perform equally well as life marches on in a variety of contexts and measures, ranging from professional achievement to community service, but not as well in others, such as income. By contrast, student athletes, James Shulman and Bowen tell us in *The Game of Life: College Sports and Educational Values* (2002), are admitted with the lowest average SAT scores of all groups and perform worse than their higher-scoring, nonathlete counterparts in terms of educational outcomes, yet they end up earning more money. These disparities probably exist because there are many more determinants

A pair of future presidents: George H. W. Bush carries his infant son George W. Bush on his shoulders at the Yale University campus. George W. Bush would later attend Yale (like his father). Why do you think legacy students receive preferential treatment when applying for college?

of post-schooling income than the kind of education people receive or how well they perform in school—namely, the class resources of their families. Minorities in elite colleges may disproportionately come from lower-class families, and athletes may, on average, come from more advantaged families.

Despite the amount of data that refute affirmative action myths, an ongoing belief in them has contributed to the recent dismantling of many affirmative action programs. How will this affect minority students if the trend continues? Presumably, fewer African Americans and Hispanics would be admitted to selective colleges. With systematically lower SAT scores than Whites (the reasons for these test score gaps are explored in more detail in the next section), these students would be at an immediate disadvantage. According to Espenshade and Chung (2005), eliminating affirmative action would decrease Black and Hispanic acceptance rates by one-half to two-thirds. The decreased presence of minority students on these campuses would limit diversity and the attendant opportunities for interaction and dispelling of stereotypes.

INTELLIGENCE OR IQ?

Intelligence that is related to educational outcomes is generally measured using a standardized IQ test. But IQ is measured with a test, just like the SATs, and it is worth considering whether IQ tests are plagued with similar difficulties. Can we trust IQ tests to be reliable? In short, not really. First, the IQ test measures only one kind of intelligence. What about the ability to think creatively or understand complicated scientific concepts? These types of intelligence might also be relevant to academic achievement. Howard Gardner (1983) has even suggested the theory of multiple intelligences to account for such aptitudes, but we confront a roadblock when deciding how to accurately assess them.

Second, most sociologists have criticized IQ tests for being culturally biased toward those with White, middle-class knowledge. In other words, the test reflects the knowledge that the dominant group in a society deems worthy of being called intelligence. For example, in the 1960s the Stanford-Binet IQ test included a question that asked respondents to answer which of two females was prettier. The first image showed a woman with blond hair and blue eyes; the second a woman with darker skin and larger lips. Although such obviously biased cultural references have since been purged from most exams, more subtle ones may remain.

Finally, even the updated IQ tests we use don't measure innate (i.e., genetically determined) intelligence. By the time children are tested, they have interacted with their environment in ways that have affected their cognitive development. In fact, even if a test were developed that could be administered within the first few minutes after birth, it might not measure innate intelligence. It would also capture the health of the prenatal environment—did the developing baby get enough nutrients; was it exposed to toxins from the mother's bloodstream; and so on. Of course, IQ tests are generally given at later ages, when the accretion of environmental advantages or disadvantages has been proceeding for years.

ADULT LEARNING

You thought when you graduated college that you were done with school forever (notwithstanding some of you who will go on to graduate or professional schools)? Guess again. Education trends suggest that many of us will need to be training and retraining ourselves—that is, getting more education through some means—for most of our adult lives.

We are living (and working) longer than ever; meanwhile, some claim that technological change is speeding up at the workplace. Together these trends present a problem: How can older workers keep up and remain relevant? The answer, many scholars argue, lies in lifelong learning (LLL) (Laal & Salamati, 2012).

While we have not all been replaced by robots yet, there is no doubt that the demands of work continue to evolve at a rapid pace such that for many jobs, what someone learned 50 or 60 years ago in school may no longer apply. (I learned how to set lead type in a printing press in shop class; not very useful today, alas.) Just think of a secretary. While fast typing still is a key job requirement, a 60-year-old administrative assistant (the newer term for secretary) did not know how to use a word processor or a spreadsheet or listserve when he or she started four decades earlier since those essential tools did not exist back then.

Some skills can be acquired through informal means on the job—for example, having the young IT gal or guy show you the difference between "reply" and "reply all." Indeed, studies have shown that on-the-job training for older workers increases their employment prospects, wages, and productivity (Picchio & van Ours, 2013). The same is true for formal education, even when one accounts for positive selection (the fact that those workers with the best skills are the ones who seek out additional training later in life).

Yet the likelihood of such education decreases with age—right when it may be most needed. One study found that factoring out a number of variables, men in the above-50-year-old group were 38 percent less likely to be enrolled in formal training than their 25–39-year-old counterparts (the effect for women was a 16 percent drop). Even men in their forties were 14 percent less likely to receive such education (for women there was no effect of being in one's forties) (Taylor & Urwin, 2001). Given the positive effects, one obvious question is why such formal training/education is not more common for older workers.

The answer lies in the fact that usually the costs of such lifelong learning are borne by the employer. If the skills acquired then make that worker more valuable, it's more likely she will leave for another firm that poaches her with higher wages. In such a case, the firm that invested in the training doubly loses out: it not only spent the money but lost a good worker to the competition. The good news is that among older workers age 55 or above, such investment leads them to stay longer with the employer who provides such opportunities—at least in the Netherlands (Picchio & van Ours, 2013).

Meanwhile, such formal education does not merely have positive effects on the employment prospects of older individuals (or their firms). LLL also serves to keep aged folks more socially connected and, relatedly, happier. One experiment in Slovenia and Finland randomly assigned older adults (72 years old on average) to receive (or not receive) training in the use of computers. It turned out that those who got tutored on how to navigate information and communication technology reported less loneliness afterwards (Blažun et al., 2012). Meanwhile, a study in the UK showed that overall well-being was improved by music, arts, and evening classes (Jenkins, 2011). That said, more formal courses teaching specific skills often related to employment (as well as gym/exercise classes) had no discernible effect. It may be that nondemanding, yet stimulating, courses are the sweet spot for older folks—unless, of course, they want a raise.

Inequalities in Schooling

Throughout this chapter I've demonstrated that numerous inequalities in schooling exist. Minority and lower-class students are disproportionately placed in low tracks, are the subject of less-favorable teacher expectations, and consistently score lower on the SAT. However, we have yet to explore the reasons behind such inequalities. The following sections focus on some of the ways in which background characteristics, over which students themselves have no control, affect educational outcomes. Be warned that the strength of these effects is much greater than the American ideology of "equal opportunity for all" would suggest.

CLASS

As we saw in Chapter 7, social class has long been thought to socialize students into different achievement profiles and distinct schooling trajectories. Social class or socioeconomic status (SES), an individual's position in a stratified social order, is composed of any combination of parental educational attainment, parental occupational status (e.g., janitor versus doctor), family income, and family wealth. Students whose parents have higher levels of any of these four measures of class generally enjoy better educational opportunities. Higher-class students obtain more years of schooling (Conley, 2001), get better grades (Arum, 2003), are more likely to complete high school before age 19 (Conley, 1999), score higher on cognitive tests (Chase-Lansdale et al., 1997), and, as mentioned earlier, are more likely to be placed in higher tracks (Gamoran & Mare, 1989; Lucas, 1999).

SOCIAL CLASS OR SOCIOECONOMIC STATUS (SES)

an individual's position in a stratified social order.

But how do these advantages work? Clearly, teachers don't receive a list with each student's social class in order to assign grades according to this ranking. Instead, most of the effects of social class are mediated through other factors that affect educational achievement. For example, SAT scores are mediators between class and college outcomes. Class affects SAT scores, and SAT scores affect college admissions.

Let's start with some of the straightforward advantages, such as the benefits of money. If your parents have a higher income, they may be able to afford extra tutoring if you're lagging behind. They could pay for SAT prep courses (Kaplan, one of the largest test-prep services, charges about $1,000 per comprehensive course) and hand scoring ($55 for the essay section and $55 for the multiple-choice section) to ensure that the College Board doesn't screw up again. They might even enlist the services of a college consultant, who may charge tens of thousands of dollars to get you into the best college (Booth, 2015). Likewise, if your parents are wealthy, they can liquidate or borrow against stocks and bonds or mortgage their house to pay for your college education, buy another house in a better school district, or send you to a private school. The same goes for parental education. More-educated parents may feel comfortable helping their children with homework through high school, whereas less-educated parents may have difficulty with the assignments as they become more difficult. As you might imagine, these factors overlap and are cumulative—for example, parents with more income, wealth, and education can afford tutors and the best schools and provide more extensive help with homework.

The novel coronavirus pandemic has exacerbated these socioeconomic disparities. When many schools (and colleges) shut down and sent kids home to complete their studies, they were sending them to very different

A high-school student meets with a private college admissions consultant. Parents in wealthier families can devote additional resources to help position their children to succeed at school.

environments. Some college students, for example, had to share rooms with younger siblings and had no way to quietly read or video link into online classes (Casey, 2020). (Going to the library was not an option either, given the shut-down orders.) And the quality of internet connections varied by socioeconomic status as well. Among younger children, those of professionals or managers were able to go home to parents who were working remotely and could juggle their schedules to become, in essence, home schoolers. Meanwhile, students from less well-off families more often found themselves with parents who had to report to work in "essential services" and thus received less structure and support for learning at home—not to mention more economic stressors. As much as we complain that schools reproduce inequalities, they are, in general, an equalizing institution in society. Just by virtue of taking kids out of their homes and putting them in a common institution for part of the day, schools reduce inequalities stemming from family background—even if those inequalities permeate the school walls to some extent (Harris, 2020).

Cultural Capital A more subtle way that social class is related to educational outcomes is through the importance of cultural capital, the symbolic and interactional resources that people use to their advantage in various situations (Bourdeau, 1977; Lareau, 1987, 2003). Pierre Bourdieu, who coined the term, recognized three distinct types of cultural capital: embodied, objectified, and institutionalized. In the first type, the skill rests in our body—hence the term *embodied*. For example, if you learn to play the piano, that "competency" is a form of embodied cultural capital. The piano itself serves as an example of objectified cultural capital, because it requires a significant investment of time and money to acquire. Cultural capital becomes institutionalized when it is legitimated through a formal system, such as education—for example, when you are accepted into an elite music conservatory because of your piano-playing ability.

Much cultural capital, however, is not as straightforward as piano playing. Some important aspects of embodied cultural capital include the ability to deal with bureaucracies (such as the school system itself), confidence in public social settings, and even a sense of entitlement. In a school setting, many of these advantages work in concert with the rewards that schools give to students with values and expectations aligned with those of the institution. For example, teachers tend to place a high emphasis on parental involvement (e.g., volunteering in classrooms or reading to children) because it improves students' educational outcomes (Lareau, 1987). However, research has found that middle- and upper-class parents have much higher levels of involvement than lower-class parents. This is not because higher-class parents have more desire for their children to succeed but because they agree with the idea that schooling responsibilities should be shared and they may have more time to be involved. In contrast, according to Annette Lareau (2003), working-class parents more often believe that

CULTURAL CAPITAL

the symbolic and interactional resources that people use to their advantage in various situations.

educational responsibility falls solely on teachers, and thus they may not be as involved. This disparity may be compounded by the greater intimidation that lower-SES parents might experience in the face of bureaucracies (such as the educational system) and authorities (such as teachers and principals)—that is, their lower degree of cultural capital.

Numerous studies have pinpointed other ways that cultural capital from the home confers academic advantages. For example, Lareau determined that middle-class parents ask their children many questions, reason with them in the hope of persuading them to do certain things, elicit opinions, and, in general, speak more often using a wider vocabulary with their children. Conversely, lower-class families use more directives and fewer words. However, because schools value verbal ability and use middle-class speech patterns (eliciting opinions from students by following Socratic teaching methods), students accustomed to this verbal style generally enjoy advantages in school. Keep in mind that behaviors rewarded by schools are not necessarily what are "right" or "correct." Values about schooling vary according to the historical period (not long ago corporal punishment was considered a valid disciplinary tool for all students). In another period, children who quietly accepted directives and didn't share their opinions would have been considered respectful, a quality that may have been more valued by the school system at the time.

Similarly, schools tend to reward middle-class knowledge obtained outside school. Consider a game that took place in an elementary school class. The teacher gave clues about states, and students raised their hands to answer. White students dominated the game; few minority students ever raised their hands. Lewis (2004) attributed this not to differences in learning that occurred in the classroom but to the advantages that the White and middle-class students had carried over from their home life. In answering the questions, these students talked about the states as places they had visited, where relatives lived, or where parents had gone to college.

The cultural capital that derives from higher social class is also important to the interactions that parents and students have with schools. Lareau (2003) and Lewis (2004) have found that upper- and middle-class parents have more informal interactions with teachers and are much more comfortable during interactions than lower-class parents. Because middle- and upper-class parents' class positions are similar to teachers', both parties may feel more comfortable interacting with each other. It is also more likely that parents from these classes see teachers as their equals or even as inferiors, and this perception, among other factors, gives them a sense of entitlement to judge teachers and actively intervene in their children's schooling to gain advantages for them (as discussed in the earlier section on tracking). For example, Lewis (2004) writes of a mother who went to a parent–teacher conference, challenged a particular grade the teacher had given her daughter, and successfully persuaded the teacher to increase it, whereas a lower-SES parent might not have felt empowered to intervene in this manner.

RACE

Recent data continue to show that Black students underperform compared with Whites on various measures of educational achievement. Blacks score lower on cognitive achievement tests and experience higher rates of being left back, suspended, and expelled. These differences in school performance are reflected in measures of high-school and college graduation. In 2019, 87.8 percent of Blacks ages 25 and older had at least a high-school diploma (or equivalency degree), compared with 94.5 percent of Whites (Figure 13.2). During the same year only 26.1 percent of Blacks age 25 and older had at least a college degree, as opposed to 40.2 percent of Whites (US Census Bureau, 2020e). Who is to blame for these differences? Does responsibility solely lie on the shoulders of African American parents and students? Or are larger societal forces more important contributors to these gaps?

The evidence points toward societal forces. For example, school discipline is not meted out equally. A quantitative study by Edward Morris and Brea Perry found that differential punishment by race may account for one-fifth of the Black–White test score gap (Morris & Perry, 2016). Moreover, at least one study has shown that when students with the same characteristics are compared, Black students are more likely to be referred to special education than White students (Morgan et al., 2017). To address this issue,

FIGURE 13.2 Highest Degree Earned by Race and Ethnicity, 2019

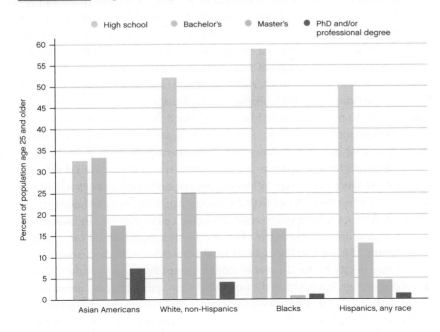

SOURCE: US Census Bureau, 2020e.

↑

At a park in Irvine, California, sixth-grader Silvestre Pineda and his peers perform a folk dance at ArtsBridge America World Dance Day, which featured traditional dances from Mexican, Chinese, European, and African cultures. What are the arguments for teaching students with an inclusive curriculum?

called *disproportionality*, Congress in 2004 reauthorized the Individuals with Disabilities Education Act, which required states to address such disparities (Green, 2017). However, since no clear thresholds were defined, states rarely did. On the other hand, some argue that minorities get fewer needed referrals to and resources from special education services—made worse by the fact that upper-income parents are more likely to advocate for disability services for their children. So the issue about disparities is a complicated one.

Economic disparities also contribute to learning differences by race. In the last section, we reviewed the importance of social class in determining educational achievements, and it is a major contributor to the Black–White achievement gap. On average, Blacks have lower levels of each of the four social class indicators mentioned earlier. One way to illustrate the class differentials between racial and ethnic groups is to compare poverty rates. In 2018, 32 percent of African American children under age 18 lived below the poverty line, compared with 25 percent of Hispanic kids and 10 and 9 percent of White and Asian American children, respectively (National Center for Education Statistics, 2020). Worse still, shifting from income poverty to wealth (net worth), we find that the typical Black family has six cents to the typical White family's dollar of wealth (Herring & Henderson, 2016). Moreover the neighborhoods that African Americans and Whites live in vary on average. For example, Patrick Sharkey showed that when a child had to take a test shortly after a shooting in his neighborhood, he performed more poorly than if the shooting took place right after the test (and thus could not affect the score). That is, whatever long-term consequences there are to growing up in a violent neighborhood, there is even a short-term effect. Given that Black children are more likely than Whites to live in poor, crime-ridden neighborhoods, this effect contributes to the test score gap. Sharkey concluded that, in Chicago, African Americans "living in the city's most violent neighborhoods spend at least one quarter of the year, or roughly 1 week out of every month, functioning at a low level because of local homicides" (Sharkey, 2010).

Adjustments in the classroom cannot completely compensate for such wide disparities, but perhaps they can help. One approach to boost achievement among all minority groups is what's called *inclusive curriculum*. An inclusive curriculum "values the culture, background and experience of all students" (Australian Catholic University, 2008) and thus tries to make course material relevant to students coming from a diverse set of backgrounds: not just by race but also by sexuality, class, disability status, and so on (Croucher & Romer, 2007). The idea is pretty straightforward: If students see themselves in the history, literature, or scientific research that they are studying, they will be more engaged and learn better.

Class Intersections When researchers have controlled for SES, many of the Black–White educational gaps are significantly narrowed; such findings attest to the importance of class differences in racial educational outcomes. For example, Christopher Jencks and Meredith Phillips (1998) found that one-third of the test score gap between young Black and White children was removed once class was controlled for. Similarly, I determined that after factoring out class differences, African Americans had a greater chance of graduating from high school, were 44 percent less likely to be held back a grade, and were equally likely to be suspended or expelled from school as White students (Conley, 1999).

More evidence for the importance of background influences in Black–White achievement gaps comes from research on summer setbacks. The idea behind this research is that during the school year it's hard to figure out how much learning is taking place in school and how much is occurring outside it (because students are exposed to both at the same time). To get around this, some researchers have compared increases in achievement that occur during the school year with those that take place during the summer. When comparing these test scores for a sample of first- and second-graders in Baltimore, Doris Entwisle and Karl Alexander found that all the students had similar growth in the achievement test scores during the school year—even those from lower-class backgrounds, which indicates that schools do matter (Alexander et al., 2001; Entwisle & Alexander, 1992). However, during the summer, upper-class children continued to make gains while the lower-class students lost ground. This suggests that the upper-class children were being exposed to educational opportunities in their homes, communities, and summer camps that encouraged learning and cognitive growth. By the time they returned to school the next fall, they were significantly ahead of their lower-class peers.

Strong evidence exists that many of the Black–White achievement gaps can be explained by class and the advantages it brings. But class can't explain all the gaps. Therefore, researchers have turned to a variety of noneconomic theories to explain what class alone can't. One prominent theory suggests that a large portion of the achievement gap can be explained by African American students' hesitancy to excel in school for fear of being accused of "acting White" (Fordham & Ogbu, 1986). According to these researchers, years of oppression (specifically, their transport to this country against their will as enslaved people and involuntary immigrants) and questions about their innate intelligence have led Blacks to doubt their own intellectual ability and associate book learning and school with being White. Not wanting to sell out, African Americans have disengaged from school or downplayed their academic achievements to avoid embracing what is seen as White behavior.

Although Signithia Fordham and John Ogbu (1986) uncovered extensive evidence of this phenomenon undermining achievement, a study by Karolyn Tyson, William Darity Jr., and Domini Castellino (2005), also conducted using ethnographic methods (researchers observing firsthand what goes on in a school; see Chapter 2), found only limited evidence to support the theory. This corroborates results from survey-based studies, which have also found little support. Instead, evidence exists that the inversion of dominant values (achievement is bad, acting out is good) is prevalent among many groups of underprivileged youth regardless of race (MacLeod, 1995; Willis, 1981). What's more, researchers have found that the association of academic achievement with acting White may be a recent phenomenon, existing only since the 1980s. The kicker is that the acting White dynamic, to the extent that it does exist, may be an ironic result of school desegregation and tracking. Because of desegregation, many Blacks find themselves in majority-White schools now. That trend combined with tracking, especially unfair tracking, means that high-achieving Blacks find themselves socially isolated in honors and advanced placement classes. The good news, Tyson and her colleagues have found, is that this does not deter Blacks from efforts to achieve once they are in a rigorous academic track. The bad news is that carrying the "burden of the race" does stop some minority students from challenging themselves in an academic setting.

Stereotypes   This last point leads to other explanations for Black–White achievement differentials that entail more social-psychological dynamics. One body of research suggests that underperformance is the result of African Americans' having internalized negative stereotypes. If you are told that you're lazy, ignorant, or stupid long enough, and treated this way, you might start to believe it. Furthermore, if you start to believe it and it affects your academic outcomes, you have acted out a self-fulfilling prophecy (recall the effects of teacher expectations examined earlier in this chapter).

A related psychological process that might contribute to Black underachievement, particularly in high-stakes testing situations, is stereotype threat, which is when members of a negatively stereotyped group are placed in a situation in which they fear they may confirm those stereotypes. For example, when Black students take the SAT, they may unconsciously worry that they will confirm negative stereotypes about African American intelligence. Support for this hypothesis comes from a series of experiments conducted by Claude Steele and Joshua Aronson (1998). Black and White Stanford undergraduates were randomly assigned to one of two groups. Both groups were given a verbal test similar to the SAT, but the first group was told it was a diagnostic test of intellectual ability, while the second group was told that it was simply a problem-solving task. After controlling for the participants' SAT scores, the researchers found that Blacks taking the so-called diagnostic test

STEREOTYPE THREAT

when members of a negatively stereotyped group are placed in a situation where they fear they may confirm those stereotypes.

scored significantly lower than the Black students taking the nondiagnostic test in a more relaxed atmosphere, and also lower than all the White students. The culprit? The activation of negative stereotypes brought about by presenting the test as a measure of intelligence. In subsequent experiments, this "activation" concept was further supported by the lower performance of Black students who were asked to check off their race on a demographic questionnaire before taking what was described as a nondiagnostic test.

The Gene Movement A final explanation for African American underachievement that refuses to die out despite masses of contrary evidence is the idea that racial differences in intelligence are genetic (see the discussion of eugenics in Chapter 9). In the 1920s, researchers found that IQ, measured with biased and unsophisticated tools, varied according to skin color. According to their measures, Whites had the highest IQ scores and Blacks the lowest. They further claimed that Black students with lighter skin scored higher than those with darker skin. (The researchers apparently tried to conduct the same study with Mexican students, but some students had spent more time out in the sun than others and their tans got in the way of measurement.) These findings were used to confirm the superiority of white skin as a marker for innate intelligence (Blanton, 2000).

In the 1960s, psychologist Arthur Jensen (1969) resuscitated this argument by claiming that the differences in IQ tests between Blacks and Whites likely resulted from genetic differences between the groups. His position was refuted by both sociological and biological evidence. Sociologists even pointed out that stigmatized minorities in all countries, even when they are of the same "race," have lower IQ test scores and lower educational and occupational outcomes. The Maori in New Zealand, for example, have lower school-retention rates and qualification levels. In 1996, nearly 50 percent of the Maori population in New Zealand had no educational qualifications at all, compared with roughly 30 percent of non-Maori. The Burakumin in Japan (see Chapter 9) have also been the targets of stigmatization and discrimination since the beginning of the seventeenth century. Although the Buraku are physically indistinguishable from the non-Buraku, a huge discrepancy exists between the educational achievements of the two groups (Ikeda, 2001). These differential outcomes disappear altogether, however, when Buraku children attend schools in the United States, where they are perceived simply as Japanese (Spencer et al., 1987).

Unfortunately, such refutations haven't stopped the racialized genetics movement. Another round of attacks on Black innate intelligence came in the form of *The Bell Curve* (1994), written by psychologist Richard J. Herrnstein and political scientist Charles Murray. In a nutshell, the authors claim that everyone is where they are because of their genes, because America is a meritocracy. If you're poor or uneducated, blame it on your genes. If you're making lots of money and have a great job, lucky you for being in a successful

gene pool. Likewise, if Blacks do worse than Whites in educational or occupational outcomes, it must be because of their genes. After the book created a stir among readers, researchers systematically negated Herrnstein and Murray's claims. For example, Claude S. Fischer and his colleagues (1996) reanalyzed all of Herrnstein and Murray's data and found that, among other things, they had underestimated the impact of SES and had used an intelligence test designed to measure what participants had learned in school, not innate intelligence. Murray once again raised these arguments in 2020 in a book entitled *Human Diversity: The Biology of Gender, Race, and Class*, where he was better armed with genetic data that did not exist when he coauthored *The Bell Curve*. The end result of Murray's sleight of hand, however, was the same: There are some genetic differences between subgroups (that track to what we call races); differences in outcomes exist as well; thus, genetic differences cause or explain the outcome differences. Whoa! Eye colors vary across populations, too, but nobody is talking about irises as an explanation for disparities in health, income, and so on. The much more likely alternative, with lots of evidence to back it up that we've already seen in this chapter, is that different groups are treated differently in society and the different treatment leads to different outcomes.

↑

A predominately Maori classroom in New Zealand. The Maori are an example of a stigmatized minority that has lower IQ test scores and lower educational and occupational outcomes. However, these outcomes vanish when these students move out of cultures that stigmatize them.

ETHNICITY

Most research on achievement gaps has focused on Black–White differences because of American history. However, there are notable differences between other minority groups and Whites as well. For example, like African Americans, Hispanics score lower on the SATs, have a higher rate of repeating grades, and are suspended or expelled at higher rates than White students. Furthermore, Hispanic students have the highest high-school dropout rate of any minority group in the nation. Some of these differences can be attributed to language difficulties, but many of the same factors that apply to Blacks apply to Hispanics. Like African Americans, Hispanics have lower social-class standings on average and are the target of numerous negative stereotypes that may depress achievement. They have also been the target of people who contend that inequalities stem from genetic differences between groups.

Asians, in contrast, have been touted in American culture as "model minorities" or the "immigrant success story." Asians first arrived in this country facing significant discrimination and oppression, and their continuing upward mobility has indeed been an impressive feat. In a relatively short time, Asians have gone from being characterized as the "yellow peril" to scoring consistently higher on tests of math ability, having higher GPAs, and going to college at higher rates than non-Asian students. How did they do it? One intriguing line of research (Portes & MacLeod, 1996) suggests that although some Asian groups are no more socioeconomically advantaged than other immigrants, their communities contain a high degree of social capital: Extremely close ties exist between adults, and they support each other's parenting rules.

IMPENDING CRISIS: THE BOY-GIRL ACHIEVEMENT GAP

"Yes, we're sorry to say, there really is a crisis," lament Michael Gurian and Kathy Stevens (2005), authors of *The Minds of Boys: Saving Our Sons from Falling Behind in School and Life*. In recent years, journalists, psychologists, and educators alike have brought attention to what they have termed the *boy crisis*. The crisis may be described as follows: Whereas 30 years ago girls lagged behind boys in educational outcomes, it seems that "girl power" mantras, Title IX (which provided equal funding to girls in classrooms and for sports), and the feminist movement have made their mark. Girls are now surpassing boys in their educational outcomes.

How true are these assertions? In recent years girls have been less likely to repeat a grade or drop out of high school. In addition, girls outperform boys in national reading and writing tests (and score roughly equal to boys in math, contrary to popular belief). They also attend college in higher numbers and are more likely to graduate (Savas, 2016). In 2019, 88.4 percent of women age 25 and older had a high-school degree as opposed to 86.6 percent of men (US Census Bureau, 2020). Furthermore, in 2016, 57.4 percent of master's degrees and 52.1 percent of doctoral degrees were earned by women (Okahana & Zhou, 2017). Note, however, that despite all of the education that women attain, it does not pay off in the workplace. As recently as 2016, women earned only 81 percent of what men with an equal education do (Bureau of Labor Statistics, 2019c). (See Chapter 8 for a more thorough discussion of wage and employment differences by gender.)

On the flip side, although boys are more likely to engage in risky behaviors and experience serious problems at school (e.g., being identified as having a learning disorder or emotional disturbance), they also make up a larger proportion of those taking calculus and science AP tests, and on average, they score higher on those tests than girls. In addition, boys score higher than girls on every AP test except foreign languages, though girls represent a larger proportion of those taking certain tests (Freeman, 2004). (The fact that a smaller, more select group of boys take such tests may contribute to their higher scores.) A male advantage is also apparent in SAT scores, with boys scoring higher than girls on the math and critical reading sections while females outperform males on the writing section.

The question remains: Is there a crisis? Boys may perform better than girls on college entrance exams, but this appears to be the only advantage they enjoy at the moment (and one that hasn't affected the exceptional rates of girls' college entrance and graduation). However, before rendering a final verdict, let's bring in one more piece of evidence. Although the media have been busy generating sensational headlines about the boy–girl achievement gap, researchers have been systematically examining trends and explanations for the differences. For example, Claudia Buchmann, Thomas A. DiPrete, and Troy A. Powell (2006) found that among students born before the mid-1960s, girls achieved as much education as boys only when both parents were college-educated. Boys, however, seemed to do equally well in school regardless of their parents' education. But for students born after the mid-1960s, the opposite pattern emerged. Girls from all backgrounds started to do better in school. At the same time, boys living with single mothers or in households where the father had a high-school education or less started doing much worse.

This suggests that headlines about the boy crisis should really read something like "Girls Catch Up, While Boys from Lower-Class Backgrounds Lose Ground." It is not so much that girls are surpassing boys in educational achievement but that they have started doing equally well at the same time that boys from lower-class backgrounds have started doing worse. The boy crisis, then, has had only a limited effect on the middle- and upper-class children whose parents have been most vocal and concerned about the trend.

ALL IN THE FAMILY

Most American parents assume that their homes are a haven from the harsh world. They like to believe that they send out each of their children into the world on an identical footing. Oh, how parents delude themselves! As discussed in Chapter 12, inequality starts at home. Growing up in the same family with the same parents is no guarantee that siblings are going to end up with similar educational outcomes.

Parents may not recognize the delicate balance that exists between the number of children they have, their spacing (e.g., three children one year apart versus three children all four years apart), and their gender composition. Yet all three factors have significant impacts on educational achievement. For example, research has consistently found that the bigger the family, the lower the children's achievement test scores and grades (Downey, 1995; Steelman & Powell, 1985). What's just as important as family size is how far apart the children are spaced. For example, Brian Powell and Lala Carr Steelman (1990) determined that students with siblings spaced closer together had lower achievement scores and grades, even after the researchers controlled for SES and previous achievement. This research also found that while an additional sibling in the family is damaging to the other children's grades, additional brothers had a particularly negative impact.

Why might the size of a family and the space between its children's ages affect achievement scores and grades?

What brings about these effects? The most prominent hypothesis, the resource dilution model, suggests simply that parental resources are finite and each additional child gets a smaller amount of them. Furthermore, if children are spaced closer together, there is more competition for the same resources at the same time. This is the case not just for economic resources but also for the amount of interaction parents and children have. Research has supported such a model, finding that the frequency of communication with parents, parents' educational expectations, the amount of money saved for college, and the presence of educational materials in the home all successfully explain the effect of family size on educational performance (Downey, 1995). Singleton children, despite common stereotypes as an at-risk group, on average outperform those children with siblings, because they enjoy a monopoly on family resources. (They also tend to come from more socioeconomically advantaged families.)

If sibling numbers and composition are important to educational achievement, what about what I've called the "pecking order" among siblings? Does the first child turn out to be a leader? Does the middle child always suffer? Although some researchers (e.g., Steelman & Powell, 1985) have found that birth order has no effects, my coauthor Rebecca Glauber and I uncovered evidence that middle children do suffer a crunch because of their family position. We determined that with the transition from two to three children, the middle child is the one who suffers from less parental monetary investment and runs a greater risk of being held back a grade—particularly if the child is a boy (Conley & Glauber, 2006). Meanwhile, Steelman and Powell (1989) found that later-born children had a better chance of getting parental financial support for college than older siblings did, perhaps because of their parents' improving financial status over the years.

RESOURCE DILUTION MODEL

hypothesis stating that parental resources are finite and that each additional child gets a smaller amount of them.

Finally, research about differences in educational achievement within families has also taken on a biological bent. Specifically, studies have examined the effect of differences in sibling birth weight on educational attainment. Whether because of health problems, slowed cognitive development, or getting bullied for their smaller size, siblings with lower birth weight have lower educational outcomes than their heftier siblings. For example, my coauthor Neil G. Bennett and I found that low birth weight significantly decreases children's chances of graduating from high school by the age of 19 (Conley & Bennett, 2000). These poor educational outcomes may be related to another disadvantage: Low-birth-weight children have a greater tendency to exhibit poor classroom behavior. Pamela Kato Klebanov, Jeanne Brooks-Gunn, and Marie McCormick (1994) found that low-birth-weight children received lower attention and higher daydreaming and hyperactivity scores from their teachers than normal-birth-weight students.

POLICY

VOUCHERS

Despite the findings of the Coleman Report and other research questioning the relevance of measurable aspects of school quality on student achievement, schools are still where the hot political debates about education are fought. One of the biggest fights centers on the question of school choice—specifically, private school vouchers. Basically, the idea behind the voucher movement is that for schooling to be equal, students should be able to choose where they want to go to school, regardless of whether they can pay for it. To make this ideology a reality, school choice proponents endorse the use of vouchers, coupons administered by the government that may be redeemed at any school, private or public. Students take the dollar amount of whatever their public school would have spent on their education and apply it toward the tuition at another school.

Supporters of school choice argue that when families are able to choose schools, everybody benefits. First, students don't have to attend subpar schools. Second, competition among schools vying for students maintains the pressure to keep educational standards high all around. For example, if students leave the public school system in significant numbers, public schools will be forced to improve. Opponents of school choice point out

Education Secretary Betsy DeVos, a staunch advocate of creating and expanding school voucher programs.

that the reality of school choice is much more complicated: Not all parents could or would send their children to different schools. (What if the closest high-quality school is two hours away?) Further, what if the schools of choice did not have room for more children? And if they started taking in all students, would their effectiveness diminish? How does choice square with the demonstrated importance of peer effects?

Despite these concerns, school choice backers were persuasive enough to convince several American cities, such as Milwaukee, Cleveland, and New York City, to test voucher programs. Therefore, some 20 years after the initial school choice debate, we can assess whether the voucher promises have come true. Unfortunately, the results of voucher programs have been mixed at best. In Milwaukee, for example, where low-income students received vouchers to the private or public schools of their choice, researchers found that after five years of the program, achievement test scores were not consistently different between those who used the vouchers and a control group of low-income public school students (Witte, 1998).

Similarly, in New York City, a lottery determined which low-income children enrolled in kindergarten through fourth grade received vouchers for three years' tuition in private schools. When this group was compared with the control (students who had applied to the voucher program but were not chosen), the effects of the vouchers varied depending on how the research question was framed (Krueger & Zhu, 2002). However, researchers generally found that the test scores of students who used vouchers didn't differ from those of other children, except for an increase in Black students' math scores in the first year of follow-up.

That didn't stopped the Trump administration from aggressively pursuing a school voucher agenda. In Education Secretary Betsy DeVos's budget requests to Congress, she repeatedly asked to cut or eliminate federal funds for such programs as after-school activities for needy children, the Special Olympics, and teacher training. These cuts, in turn, were meant to support a new initiative to spend a billion dollars to provide students with vouchers for private schools. Congress rejected such initiatives in the final budgets.

Conclusion

We've learned about the skills that schools teach as well as their role in socializing (or brainwashing, depending on your point of view) students with American values. We've also examined how differences between and within schools can affect educational outcomes. After years of being under-appreciated as a result of the findings in the Coleman Report, schools are finally receiving the attention they deserve. In fact, some research suggests that schools might do more than we realized for students, particularly for those from disadvantaged backgrounds (e.g., Alexander et al., 2001; Entwisle & Alexander, 1992). Within schools, we've looked at how tracking can inadvertently lead to reproducing inequalities, and how certain factors in classrooms are instrumental in student outcomes.

In terms of higher education, we've examined trends indicating that the rise in the number of college graduates has potentially contributed to a nation of overcredentialed workers. We've also questioned how much stock we should put in SAT scores for deciding college admissions (and if their poor predictive power weren't enough, now we have to add the possibility of future scoring mishaps to the list of problems). In addition, we've examined many of the myths about affirmative action that have led to its misrepresentation and subsequent dismantling.

Finally, we've taken a closer look at some of the background characteristics that affect educational outcomes and how they can be a powerful force in determining where you get to in life. Contrary to the American ideology of equal educational opportunity for all, schools are not the fairest places for students from disadvantaged backgrounds. This is especially unfortunate because school in America has historically been (and still is) the way for students to move up in the world.

In addition to learning what schools are all about, you should also have learned that not everything is as it seems. Scratch a little deeper and you see that the statistics paraded by the media, educators, and sometimes even sociologists may not tell the full story. For example, we've learned that the SAT might predict college GPA, but if we look more closely, it doesn't hold up to all its promises. Similarly, we've heard in the media about the impending boy crisis because of the achievement gap between boys and girls. However, after dissecting the trends, we know that girls have merely caught up with boys, whereas boys from lower-class families, not those from the middle- and upper-class families who are making all the fuss, are the students truly at risk.

I hope you've learned what sociology can do for educational policy. The most obvious example of this is the Coleman Report. The results of this study are among the most cited findings in educational literature. It also has had a significant impact on how the government has decided to address differences in educational achievement. Thus sociologists who study education don't just do it in isolation; much of what they find can be, and has been, applied to the real world.

QUESTIONS FOR REVIEW

1. What would be the risks to the individuals involved and society as a whole if education were financed through equity rather than debt?

2. Describe the school voucher system. What do preliminary findings suggest regarding the importance of which school people attend?

3. "Through the meritocratic education system, everyone has the chance to succeed in America." Do you agree with this statement? Find a theory or a research finding from this chapter that supports this assertion and another that challenges it. Do these theories or findings complicate your view of America as a meritocracy?

4. What is the "hidden curriculum" of education? In this light, how do Marxist theorists like Samuel Bowles and Herbert Gintis (1976) interpret the role of schools?

5. Why were the findings in the Coleman Report so surprising? How has research on achievement differences clarified the conclusions of the report?

6. Why do advocates push for mainstreaming special education students, and how does this approach counter the notion of tracking in schools?

7. You must complete a master's degree to get a job that your parents got with a bachelor's degree and your grandparents got with a high-school diploma. Use the work on credentialism to explain this phenomenon.

8. Why do people debate the use of SAT scores for college admission?

9. Describe the relative power of social class and genetics toward explaining inequalities in schooling.

10. How does family background—for example, cultural capital from the home (Lareau, 2003)—affect educational achievement? How do studies about family size and birth order complicate our understanding of the effect of family background?

PRACTICE

THE HIDDEN CURRICULUM OF COLLEGE

Sociologists have long recognized that schooling is not just about the three Rs: reading, 'riting, and 'rithmitic. As we saw in this chapter, Philip Jackson coined the term "hidden curriculum" (1968) to describe the nonacademic and less overt socialization functions of schooling.

TRY IT!

Think back to elementary school. What were some of the important social norms or values you learned (e.g., waiting to be called on to speak or handing work in on time or speaking English in public)? How did you learn these—was there one searing moment of embarrassment that led you to never make the same mistake again? Did you watch others make those mistakes and get scolded, or was it entirely unconscious?

SOCIAL NORM	HOW DID YOU LEARN IT?	WHEN DID YOU LEARN IT?
WAITING MY TURN TO SPEAK	TEACHER TOLD ME TO RAISE MY HAND	KINDERGARTEN

Now think about social norms you didn't learn until college:

SOCIAL NORM	HOW DID YOU LEARN IT?	WHEN DID YOU LEARN IT?
ADDRESSING PROFESSIONALS BY THEIR TITLE	MADE THE MISTAKE OF CALLING MY PROFESSOR "HEY YOU" INSTEAD OF "DR."	COLLEGE

Now think back to social norms you learned in elementary school or high school, or even the hidden curriculum of college:

SOCIAL NORM	HOW DID YOU LEARN IT?	WHEN DID YOU LEARN IT?

THINK ABOUT IT

The hidden curriculum is not always just about social rules for getting along in society. Often there is a social sorting aspect to it as well. In your experience, did school tell you who you were—that is, label you as good at math, or an artsy type, or a student-athlete? How was that message communicated: Was it by teachers or fellow students? Were you sorted into groups (such as tracks or sports teams)? Did such labels have a causal force on your life—that is, become a self-fulfilling prophesy?

SOCIOLOGY ON THE STREET

Education in America today is seen as inefficient, stratified, and flawed. But people fight over education because it is such a powerful tool. How can sociologists influence the educational system? Watch the Sociology on the Street video and find out more: **digital.wwnorton.com/youmayask7**.

WANT MORE PRACTICE?

Complete the InQuizitive activity for this chapter at digital.wwnorton.com /youmayask7

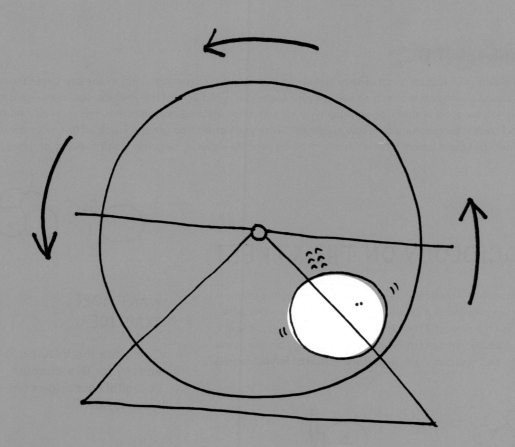

PARADOX

THE MORE ONE EARNS, THE MORE ONE CAN AFFORD LEISURE; HOWEVER, THE MORE ONE EARNS, THE MORE IT COSTS NOT TO WORK IN TERMS OF FORGONE WAGES.

Capitalism and the Economy

I bet you think you're pretty smart, don't you, sitting there in that college class. You probably think you've escaped my wrath with your higher education. I mean, you know about all the jobs that have been eliminated that used to be attainable with just a high-school degree and yet paid middle-class wages: automaker, textile worker, lumberjack, mill worker.

That's an old story, how technology has wiped out those so-called working-class careers. If a robot can't do your job better than you on the assembly line, then modern transport and logistics technologies mean that we can outsource it: Wages are lower in China (and in Bangladesh, and many other places). And, of course, it's not just the most physical jobs that have been eliminated through technological advances. Maybe you've never heard of a person called a travel agent, but I bet your parents have met a few in their lifetimes. But you are safe from losing your job to a bot (short for *robot*), what with a higher degree and all, especially one in what Richard Florida likes to call the "creative class" occupations?

Please allow me to introduce myself: I'm Emily Howell, and I'm a classical music composer. You can find some of my work here: artsites.ucsc .edu/faculty/cope/Emily-howell.htm. Or if jazz is more your style, then my buddy Shimon (gtcmt.gatech.edu/robotic-musicianship) is perfectly capable of jamming with a trio (and doesn't require free beers). Or maybe you're thinking of becoming a journalist? Or an advertising copywriter? These are both good occupations for a sociology major, for sure, but watch out, because my cousins, other creative-class bots, are moving in (see narrativescience.com or firedrop.ai).

The rap on us computers has always been that we are great for raw calculation power but useless for anything creative. When IBM's Deep Blue beat Garry Kasparov, the world chess champion, it was like an orange beating an apple. For Kasparov, chess is an art—specifically the art of strategic thinking, seeing the board as a whole, intuiting player tendencies. His opponent, the IBM machine, saw chess as a computational problem and ran every possible permutation of how the game could go, choosing the move with the highest probability of leading to a win at each juncture. So although this overwhelming firepower approach might outduel a human in a structured setting like chess, it was thought that it could not be applied to creative endeavors that were, by nature, open-ended and serendipitous.

So, you might not get rich becoming a musician, but do you think that's a job that I, the infamous bot, can never take away from you? Well, think again! (Before I do it for you . . .) "Deep learning"—an approach to artificial intelligence that tries to mimic the way a human brain works by sending information through neural nets (layers of abstraction)—is challenging all sorts of human—computer distinctions that used to be solid.

These distinctions, in fact, formed the basis of a famous thought experiment in computer science called the Turing Test, after the man who posed it, Alan Turing. The idea is that artificial intelligence can be said to have been achieved when a human can't tell the difference between another human interlocutor and a computer interacting with her (through some form of messaging app, that is). So far, nobody has been able to design an algorithm that can fool human judges into thinking it's human for long enough to win the Turing Prize. But just because we can't do the water cooler talk flawlessly, doesn't mean that we bots can't replace you college graduates. In fact, maybe you aren't so sure that I—or your professor—isn't actually a sociology bot?

Concerns about robots replacing human workers are not new for sociologists and economists; they have been studying automation and mechanization since the Industrial Revolution. To understand how we got here, perhaps we should start with a brief history of the capitalist system.

A Brief History of Capitalism

In its purest form, capitalism is an economic system in which property and goods are primarily privately owned; investments are determined by private decisions; and prices, production, and the distribution of goods are determined primarily by competition in an unfettered marketplace. Various scholars place the early stages of modern capitalism somewhere between the fifteenth and nineteenth centuries in Europe. The dates are highly disputed because many elements of capitalism existed in earlier epochs. For example, the use of money (as opposed to barter) is seen as central to capitalism, and many ancient civilizations used money in one form or another. Likewise, private property existed to different degrees in various times and places. However, capitalism as a whole, most would agree, started to develop along with the Agricultural and Industrial Revolutions in Europe.

Before capitalism in Europe, the dominant economic system was feudalism, most simply characterized by the presence of lords, vassals, serfs, and fiefs. A lord was a nobleman who owned land, and a vassal was granted the land, termed a fief, by the lord. The fief remained the property of the lord, but it was left to the vassal to reap the harvests from it. In exchange, the vassal provided military protection for the lord. Serfs, who were of peasant origin, formed the lowest class in feudal society. Serfs were bound to the land and required to give the lord a portion of their production; they were, in turn, granted protection. They differed from slaves, however, in that they were allowed to own property and could not be sold. These relationships formed the basic framework for feudalism, and arguably for the class structures that came into being in subsequent centuries on the system's demise.

During the early Tudor period in England (1485–1558), some of the open fields, often referred to as the commons (that is, they existed for the public good; anyone could graze livestock there), were "enclosed," or partitioned off. During this "enclosure movement," the lords often bounded the commons with hedges. Because this was land that had been publicly available for grazing and planting, the enclosures led to the eviction of many of the people working the land. The result was that they had little choice but to migrate to nearby cities in search of work, as one of their primary means of survival had been removed. These changes and dynamics would eventually lead to the rise of both the city and the wage system.

The evolution of capitalism was also heavily influenced by the development of technology. The history of social relations, according to Marxists, is a history of humankind's struggle to control and dominate nature through the use of technology. The technological conditions of a given epoch, in turn, determine our mode of social relationships. Around 1700, new farming technologies were introduced that directly increased food output; hence this period is commonly termed the agricultural revolution. Innovations such as the seed drill, selective breeding, and crop rotation led to an immediate increase in food abundance. As a result, the land could support more people,

↑

Fifteenth-century French peasants working the fields. What characterized work during the era of medieval feudalism?

FEUDALISM

a precapitalist economic system characterized by the presence of lords, vassals, serfs, and fiefs.

AGRICULTURAL REVOLUTION

the period around 1700 marked by the introduction of new farming technologies that increased food output in farm production.

allowing for increased population and further adding to the labor pool created by the enclosure movement.

Other changes occurred as well. For example, early colonial globalization established spice routes from colonial interests in India and the Far East and led to the development of new ways to store meat in England. Previously, livestock had to be slaughtered at the onset of winter, but new preservation methods allowed that operation to be done at any time of year. This increase in abundance, in turn, further spurred the enclosure movement, because land was now more productive and therefore more valuable.

The combination of the enclosure movement, more people, and technological improvements (which lowered the amount of labor needed per acre) led to the displacement of more and more peasants from agricultural labor. This growth of surplus peasant labor, in turn, led to mass migration to cities such as London and Manchester and to the rise of a wage-labor system. Here we can see the groundwork being laid for what we call industrial capitalism.

Of course, wage labor would not have become available unless new jobs had been created for these former peasants. At the end of the eighteenth century and the beginning of the nineteenth century, an economy once dominated by small-scale artisan labor (that is, handicrafts and subsistence farming) transitioned into one dominated by manufacturing, machinery, and unskilled factory work. This massive historical transition was also propelled by the development of new technologies. It began with the mechanization of textile industries—fabric manufacturing for clothing, rugs, upholstery, and so on. One major innovation for textile production was the power loom, a weaving machine powered by driving shafts, which made the manufacturing process much more efficient.

Another major innovation of the Industrial Revolution was the development of the steam engine, which opened up markets through its eventual

Dramatic innovations in the textile industry made the manufacturing process more efficient and corresponded with the mass migration of rural workers into cities. What were some of the social consequences of the Industrial Revolution?

use in railroads. For instance, water was often used in mining, and part of the workers' job was to remove the water in order to access the materials being extracted. Steam-powered pumps now did this, allowing workers to focus on extraction of the mineral itself.

With the rise of large-scale factory production, the influx of peasants to urban areas to find work, and the rise of a system of wage labor, along came monetization, the establishment of a legal currency. The barter system in villages allowed a peasant to trade livestock or produce, but in the context of large cities and wage labor, the need for a monetary system emerged. This led to the formation of new social institutions and organizations, such as the corporation. Corporations emerged as a way to limit the liability of investors, thus allowing corporations to attract a larger number of willing stockholders. In the United States, corporations are legally recognized persons and share many of the rights of an individual. For instance, corporations can act as legal entities by entering into contracts or owning property. The corporation can also sue (and be sued). This is where limited liability comes into the picture. Limited liability is a form of ownership that creates a division between the individual—that is, the shareholder or executive—and the business entity. It is, in this sense, a legal way to protect investors from personal responsibility for any liabilities beyond the value of the company itself. Many companies have abbreviations in their names, such as LLP (limited liability partnership) and Inc. (incorporated), or, as in South America, SA (*sociedad anónima* or "anonymous society"). Today, many of the contracts that make business possible aren't between individual people but rather between legally recognized entities in the form of corporations.

CORPORATION

a legal entity unto itself that has a legal personhood distinct from that of its members— namely, its owners and shareholders.

Theorizing the Transition to Capitalism

ADAM SMITH

Perhaps capitalism's greatest advocate was Adam Smith, the father of liberal economics. In *The Wealth of Nations* (2003), originally published in 1776, Smith wondered how societies (groups of individuals pursuing their own self-interests) manage to stay intact and not fall into the chaos of civil strife. His answer was simple: Individual self-interest in an environment of others acting similarly will lead to a situation of competition, as long as basic laws and contracts are honored. Note the difference between competition (where rules constraining the game are followed) and conflict (where no holds are barred).

For Smith, individuals have "the propensity to truck, barter, and exchange one thing for another." This drive for exchange combines with an ever-increasing division of labor to produce greater wealth for all. Smith

↑

Adam Smith.

uses the example of a pin factory. If a craftsman has to fashion each pin from scratch, snipping the wire, honing the point, attaching a head, and polishing the pin, he can make only a few dozen a day, at best. However, once the job is broken into its constitutive parts and each portion of the process assigned to a separate worker, the same craftsman can produce hundreds or perhaps even thousands of pins a day. Of course, he would now be working with others to make the pins, but dividing by the total number of man-hours, his efficiency is still orders of magnitude greater. Why so? There are two reasons: First, if the task is broken down into parts, each part can be completed more quickly; second, and perhaps more important for Smith, once people specialize in this way, they are better able to innovate. If you spent your entire work life performing a single task, you would get pretty good at it, especially compared with someone who performs that task only once in a while as part of a wider array of work. What's more, in all that time thinking about sharpening pins, you might come up with some inventions to make your life easier and to help you become the best pin sharpener in London. You might even create a machine to do your job for you. You certainly would have the incentive, because you want to drive all other pin sharpeners out of business. According to Smith, this cycle of division of labor, innovation, and trade results in the production of goods that society desires, in the proportions that it desires, and at the price it is willing to pay.

To keep this metaphorical engine running, however, money is needed to grease the gears. Smith sings the praises of monetization, or the "cash nexus" as it was dubbed by the Scottish essayist Thomas Carlyle (1971). The barter system, says Smith, was often inefficient and unwieldy. For example, let's say that I have a certain number of cows and you have a large quantity of salt. I need salt to cure my meat, and you need a cow to slaughter. How much salt would I get for a cow? However much it is, I have a fairly good notion I don't need or want that much salt. I would probably have to involve the whole village and a good bit of time to coordinate such a trade. I may have to trade my cow for a huge amount of salt and then distribute that salt to each family in the village and try to collect what I need from each of them in return. People are not going to make a trade if it's inefficient, and therefore, many trades don't occur that would be optimal in economic terms—that is, trades that would make all of us better off.

With money, however, all any trade ever requires is two partners. I *think* I know exactly how much a cow is worth. (The more widespread a market is and the better circulated the information about trading prices, the more confidence we have that we know the right price for our cow or salt.) You give me that much money, and I will buy only as much salt from you as I need. In short, money allows us to get back change. And perhaps even more important, money can store value. It gives me the ability to save efficiently. In the barter system, every sale was a purchase and vice versa. If you wanted to unload your cow, you had to take something for it, often right away. Because money stores value, the actions of buying and selling can be staggered over time and across people. Finally, money develops, or at least relies on, trust. In the barter system you know what you are getting in return when you sell something. But if I accept dollars, pesos, pounds, or euros in exchange for my cow, I am taking a leap of faith. I am trusting that the currency will be accepted wherever I go. In this sense, Smith argues, money is inherently social; it facilitates social relations between humans.

GEORG SIMMEL

The classical sociologist Georg Simmel, whose work on social groups we discussed in Chapter 5, also took a positive view of capitalism. Unlike Smith, however, Simmel (1900) didn't view money as an agent of social change. Instead, he saw the development of monetary payment systems as part of a historical evolution, the depersonalization of exchange. In a precapitalist system such as feudalism, a serf was treated more like an animal than a human being, according to Simmel. In return for his labor, the serf received in-kind payment in the form of items needed for survival—actual sustenance necessary to live and reproduce. In this sense, the payment was quite literally personal in nature. But with the arrival of capitalism, Simmel observes, payment forms evolved toward giving more and more freedom to the worker.

In the early days of capitalism, when craftsmen produced specific products from start to finish, most payment was in the form of payment per unit or piecework payment. This form of payment still exists in developed countries, although only on a smaller scale. For instance, you and a custom carpenter can agree on a design and a price for him to build some bookshelves. What happens if the wood turns out to be rotten? The craftsman is at risk. If he needs to start from scratch with a second batch of wood, he might not break even on the transaction. However, he is obligated to deliver a bookshelf that isn't rotten. Piecework payment is slightly better for the worker than in-kind payment because money carries with it a certain amount of freedom. Once a decent set of bookshelves is delivered and paid for, the carpenter can take the money and buy food or a car, or do whatever he wants with the cash. The worker remains in control of the payment he receives and therefore has vastly more freedom than under the in-kind payment scheme.

A step up from this system, for Simmel, is wage labor. Simmel argues that under the system of wage labor, people are paid in money, and furthermore, this wage is not tied to the quality of the raw materials, accidents, or other exigencies in the production process. Let's say that you work for an hourly wage for a nongovernmental organization translating reports from Spanish into English. You have been working all day on a particularly long report, and 15 minutes before your day is about to end, the hard drive crashes and all your work for the day is lost. Despite the lost report, you still get paid for the eight hours you worked under the wage labor system; it's the role of the employer to shoulder the costs of the faulty computer and the lost work. In this sense, workers under capitalism are not completely dependent on the quality of the raw materials, the technology, or the production process. The worker sells his or her labor to the employer, and it is the employer's problem if the results do not live up to expectations.

Even better than wage labor, according to Simmel, is salary. Under a salary system, workers are paid not for a direct service but for the sum total of their services. For one year of employment, you are paid a set amount of money, and that figure is what you and your employer agreed would be acceptable for an average level of performance and an average amount of work over the course of an entire year. If you have a bad day or cannot come in, you still are paid. Both sick days and vacation days are allotted. Better still than a regular salary is a civil service salary, whereby payment is not tied to the productive value of the workers at all but related to the "appropriate standard of living" for someone at that particular grade level and amount of experience.

Finally, Simmel talks about the honorarium. An honorarium is seen as distinct from the product itself. For instance, if an institution asks you to give a speech or to provide some other service, it may offer you an honorarium. The notion is that you are giving the speech or providing the service independent of the money. You may care very much about the money, but a clear sociological distinction exists between the product and the payment. You agree to provide the service, and then you act pleasantly surprised when there is some money attached to it. Likewise, the people who invited you to present the speech have to give you the honorarium just because you showed up, no matter what you end up saying. According to Simmel, a separation between the personal and the economic exists, just as there was in the development of limited liability.

Workers waiting in line for their wages. Why did Georg Simmel argue that wage labor was better than precapitalist work?

It is through these increasingly depersonalized forms of monetary payment, Simmel argues, that capitalism makes true friendship possible. By severing market relations from the personal, we now have a private sphere of pure sociability that is distinct from the economic or public sphere. Simmel argues that in precapitalist times, people traded with their neighbors and relied on each other to produce enough food and then fairly divide it up among the entire village. In this situation, business was mixed with pleasure, and people were distrustful of one another. Your friend is your business partner, and to top it off, your daughter may have married his son. But he is also your competitor.

In modern capitalist society, however, there is a strong norm against mixing business with pleasure. People keep these two worlds apart, or at least they attempt to do so. Simmel argues that it is only by maintaining a monetized, economic public sphere that we can enjoy a private sphere that truly is private, where we actively exclude market and monetary relations in order to experience pure sociability.

What would Simmel have to say about cryptocurrencies like bitcoin (see Chapter 5 opener)? Does the fact that bitcoin transactions are anonymous further the depersonalization that he champions? Or does the fact that bitcoin relies on the blockchain technology mean that we are back entangled in a web of transactions like the one in precapitalist medieval society?

KARL MARX

Unlike Smith and Simmel, Karl Marx considered capitalism both fundamentally flawed and inevitably doomed (see Chapter 1). Whereas Smith and Simmel saw the benefits of the division of labor, Marx saw alienation, which he considered the basic state of being in a capitalist society. Alienation is a condition in which people are dominated by forces of their own creation that then confront them as alien powers. Marx viewed alienation as taking four forms under capitalist production: alienation from the product, the process, other people, and oneself.

In the first sense, workers are alienated from the product that they produce. They do not know it or have complete knowledge of what they are producing. By contrast, the artisan fashions products from start to finish, from raw materials to the packaged item on the shelf. If a woman desired a new pair of shoes, she would go to the local shoemaker, who would measure her foot and choose an appropriate last (or wooden form) around which to construct the shoe. The shoemaker would then cut and fit a pattern of leather to the size of the last. In the next phase, the shoemaker would stitch the upper sole to the inner sole with thread (which he might have made himself). He would then attach the sole and a heel with some tacks. The result was a completed shoe. The point is that each craftsman was the master of his particular product, from start to finish. He knew every aspect of it, because he built it from scratch.

The situation in a modern factory is very different. The production process is now broken down among several people, sometimes several hundred, leading to greater efficiency and returns to scale, as Adam Smith celebrated. Factory work has become so specialized and workers' roles so interchangeable and devoid of skill, according to Marx, that most people working in shoemaking factories today probably do not know the entire process for making a shoe. Would they know how to spin the fabric for the shoe, dye the fabric, mold the sole, and sew it all together? It is doubtful. And we're just talking about a shoe! Imagine the process for building a car, a computer, or any of the many things around you. As a result of the same division of labor that Smith praises, capitalist workers are no longer masters of their products, in

ALIENATION

a condition in which people are dominated by forces of their own creation that then confront them as alien powers; according to Marx, the basic state of being in a capitalist society.

Marx's view. Rather, the product is the master of the worker. As Marx (1932) noted, "The object that labour produces, its product, now stands opposed to it as something alien, as a power independent of the producer."

Workers in modern capitalism are also alienated from the process of production. For instance, if the precapitalist shoemaker woke up in the morning with a hangover from the night before, he could choose to sleep in and finish his work later. He knew, in this situation, that by the end of the week he had to produce a certain number of shoes for his customers and could budget his time as he saw fit. Thus there was a certain freedom in the rhythm of work. The modern-day laborer, by contrast, has no choice but to swallow some aspirin and trudge off to the factory, fast-food restaurant, or computer terminal. This is especially true for laborers who work for subsistence wages and therefore need to work every day to survive. Think about the day laborers who stand on certain street corners in Los Angeles, San Francisco, Chicago, and many other American cities, hoping to find work that day. They do not control the process at all; it controls them. They are told when to go to work and when to go home; they are told when to leave early and when to stay late. For Marx, that is the nature of wage labor and salaried labor in the modern industrial capitalist system. Labor is, in a sense, forced by economic need, and its rhythm is controlled not by the individual producer but by some larger social force, institution, or individual. The result is alienation.

But that's not all. In addition, workers are alienated from other people, according to Marx, because capitalism turns all relations into market relations (in contrast to Simmel's belief that capitalism created a sphere separate from economic interactions). Marx (1932) notes, "What is true of man's relationship to his work, to the product of his work and to himself, is also true of his relationship to other men. . . . Each man is alienated from others. . . . [E]ach of the others is likewise alienated from human life." But what does this mean exactly? Our relationships with others become conditioned by the ethic of capitalism: profit maximization. For instance, we start using the language of worth to describe the moral qualities of individuals. Time becomes monetized in a wage labor system. Men who do not make money are viewed by others as forsaking the sale of their time on the wage labor market and thus are morally suspect.

Finally, Marx argues, we are alienated from ourselves. This is a somewhat romantic notion about what makes humans unique from other animals: We have an ability to create objects for both affective and instrumental value—objects with inherent-use value and objects that become tools to produce yet other things, respectively. (As it turns out, this ability is not uniquely human; chimpanzees and other animals also create tools and toys.) But what ultimately separates humans from other animals, according to Marx, is that humans can experience conception before execution—that is, we have the ability to create something in our minds before we fashion it in nature. Our actions aren't just hardwired like those of a bee constructing

a honeycomb; we are creative beings. (Again, recent research on animals suggests that they have notions of advance planning and time, so we are not unique in this regard either.) However, Marx sees capitalism as stifling our species-being, our natural creativity. He states that "work is *external* to the worker. . . . It is not part of his nature; consequently he does not fulfill himself in his work but denies himself" (1932).

Why would Karl Marx have argued that the factory workers making shoes on the right were more alienated from their work than the shoemaker on the left?

Marx's critique does not cast capitalism in a good light. However, Marx also suggested that these problems will sooner or later pass because, in his view, capitalism will ultimately self-destruct. Specifically, Marx argued, the capitalist system faces crises of overproduction, in which the system is so efficient that it produces an abundance of goods; the problem arises when the competition is stiff and wages are driven down so low that nobody can afford to buy these goods. For a while, in Marx's view, the system can solve such periodic occurrences by destroying some capital (through war) or by conquering new markets. But eventually, when capitalism has spread to every nook and cranny and run out of new places to invade, and when the dynamic of competition reaches its logical conclusion (one capitalist taking over all his or her competitors), then it will face the crisis that will putatively destroy it. In the *Communist Manifesto*, Marx and Friedrich Engels (1848/1998) claimed:

> The development of modern industry . . . cuts from under its feet the very foundation on which the bourgeoisie [capitalist class] produces and appropriates products. What the bourgeoisie therefore produces, above all, are its own gravediggers. Its fall and the victory of the proletariat are equally inevitable. (p. 9)

Under capitalism, Marx believed, the working class would rise against the employing (or capitalist) class and would eventually usher in a new mode of production termed socialism, in which most or all of the needs of the population are met through nonmarket methods of distribution. In socialism there is still private property and a free labor market where people get wages, but many needs—from health care to schooling to old-age support to even food and shelter—are provided by the government as a matter of right. In Marx's conception, socialism would be followed swiftly by Communism, a classless society in which the means of production are shared through state ownership and in which rewards are tied not to productivity but to need. No more private property. No more inequality in wages. But has this not happened, you counter? Marx might reply that there are still new markets to conquer in our increasingly globalized economy, and capitalists continue to compete with one another in many industries, so maybe it just hasn't happened yet.

MAX WEBER

Max Weber, whom we also met in Chapter 1, had plenty to say about how capitalism came about and why it spread in the places it did. The short version is that Weber, unlike Marx, believed that not just technology but also ideas in and of themselves generate social change. He claimed, in fact, that modern capitalism would not have arisen without the Protestant Reformation, which, according to Weber, created the necessary social conditions for capitalism by promoting theological insecurity and instilling a doctrine of predestination (the notion that only the elect will go to heaven). This religious change, combined with an advancement in accounting practices (the rise of double-entry bookkeeping), laid the groundwork for economic development. Faced with uncertainty as to whether they would be saved (go to heaven) in the afterlife, people looked to monetary fortune in this life as a sign from God that they were indeed among the lucky ones. (More on this in Chapter 16 on religion.)

Although Weber shared Marx's negative view of capitalism, his reasons were different. Weber worried that capitalism ate at the soul in a way that was somewhat different from Marx's concept of alienation. For Weber, modern industry and its associated bureaucracy and rationality create an "iron cage" from which we cannot escape. Here we can see, in Weber's own words from 1904, this chapter's paradox in action:

> In the field of highest development, in the United States, the pursuit of wealth, stripped of its religious and ethical meaning, tends to become associated with purely mundane passions, which often give it the character of sport. . . . Couldn't the old man be satisfied with his $75,000 a year and rest? No! The frontage of the store must be widened to 400 feet. Why? That beats everything, he says. In the evening when his wife and daughter read together, he wants to go to bed. Sundays he looks at the clock every five minutes to see when the day will be over—what a futile life! (2003, p. 283)

Recent Changes in Capitalism

In the time since Smith, Simmel, Marx, and Weber wrote about capitalism, world poverty has not been eliminated through the division of labor; new forms of exchange like credit default swaps and blockchain cryptocurrencies have emerged that are even more abstract than money; and capitalist-fueled development has arguably sacrificed the health of the planet for a dramatic improvement in quality of life, especially in advanced industrial and post-industrial economies. We don't directly manufacture as many goods anymore (in the United States, at least); instead, our economy is dominated by services. And we see the rise of all sorts of work arrangements in which the factory is a faint echo, and yet workers with no boss feel torn between the dual commitments of unpaid home labor and making a living in the formal world of work. Perhaps the greatest irony is that the better one does (gaining higher wages for one's commissions), the greater the pressure one feels to work, because although higher earnings can theoretically be used to "purchase" leisure in what's called the income effect by economists, the same higher wages mean that the opportunity cost of not working—the amount of earnings one is missing out on if one declines work opportunities—has also risen (creating what economists call the substitution effect). Increasingly, in a 24/7 information economy, casual workers (those not employed full-time but working on a contract-to-contract or freelance basis) choose to work more. Worries about job insecurity mean that they need to do tasks and projects whenever the work is available, but the pressures of home don't go away, particularly for women. How did we get here?

YOU'VE COME A LONG WAY, BABY (OR HAVE YOU?): WORK, GENDER, AND FAMILY

In 1914, automobile magnate Henry Ford announced a breakthrough policy at his Ford Motor Company: the $5 day. Ford's automobile factory workers were guaranteed a wage of $5 per day of work, equal to just over $128 in current dollars. The policy, designed to lower turnover rates among workers and justify faster production lines, was an effective tool thanks to its popular appeal. Male job candidates flooded the factory gates daily in hopes of being hired, and production workers thankfully conceded to the monotonous work of assembly lines (a technique of mass production that Ford played a major role in developing).

Ford, waving the banner of the family wage, or a wage paid to male workers sufficient to support a dependent wife and children, was heralded for both his generosity and his genius. Ford wrote in his autobiography: "The man does work in the shop, but his wife does the work in the home. The shop must pay them both. . . . Otherwise we have the hideous prospect of little children and

FAMILY WAGE

a wage paid to male workers sufficient to support a dependent wife and children.

'GOLD RUSH' IS STARTED BY FORD'S $5 OFFER

Thousands of Men Seek Employment in Detroit Factory.

Will Distribute $10,000,000 in Semi-Monthly Bonuses.

No Employe to Receive Less Than Five Dollars a Day.

Why did Henry Ford offer the family wage? Why might a feminist sociologist criticize this policy?

their mothers being forced out to work" (Ford & Crowther, 1973). In the context of his time, when few factory workers earned anything close to a living wage, Ford's policy was indeed arguably enlightened and progressive.

The sociological analysis of the family wage, however, reveals the ways in which work and family are connected by gender inequality, both in the workplace (as discussed in Chapter 8) and at home (Chapter 12). Advocates for the family wage in the early twentieth century asserted that every worker had the right to a "living wage," so that children and wives need not work. (This was before the enactment of child labor laws.) Implied in their definition is women's dependence on men's wages. Because women's dependence was assumed, the family wage was denied to them, thus pushing women and children into the very dependency to which they were presumed to be naturally suited. It is from policies such as these that we get our idea of the traditional family model: a male breadwinner and his female dependent. The few women who did work for Ford still earned $2.30 a day in 1915. Unmarried men and married men without dependents were also ineligible for the $5 day. Meanwhile, eligible married men had to subject themselves to Ford's "sociology department": Teams of scientists dropped by unannounced to check on workers' private lives, including everything from their health and sexual patterns, to household finances, to their drinking or gambling habits. Ford insisted that his workers, to receive the family wage, live in the "right" kind of families.

Feminist sociologists charge that the family wage is a patriarchal bargain. It is a living wage that provides a male breadwinner, but at the cost of women's autonomy and freedom. The male breadwinner–female homemaker family, firmly entrenched as an ideal by the twentieth century, disadvantaged women in several ways. First, as Alice Kessler-Harris (1990) shows, a worker's wage reveals the social value we put on his or her worth. Rather than free-market supply of and demand for an employee's skills, expectations about gender roles were primary in determining the wages earned by men and women. A man's wage was viewed as an honorable necessity; a woman's wage was just "pin money," to be used on luxuries and nonessentials (Zelizer, 2005). Rarely was a woman's wage expected to provide for her own livelihood, and never was it socially appropriate to expect a woman to support her children without the help of a father. This viewpoint justified a much lower wage for women, but it ignored the millions of unmarried, abandoned, and widowed women who worked to take care of themselves and their children. It was a particularly cruel disservice to Black women, who were eight times as likely as White women during the early twentieth century to work for wages, and more likely to live without the support of a male partner (Kessler-Harris, 1990). Figure 14.1 provides a comparison of men's and women's wages over the last half century or so.

When economists and politicians did consider single working women, they maintained that a woman's wage need meet only the barest of necessities, lest women turn away from the morality of family life, as enshrined in the cult of domesticity, and become enticed by the sinful and degrading world of work.

Never mind that lower wages might also mean the need to work more hours outside the home in order to make ends meet. One policy maker justified lower wages by appealing to women's naturally high endurance of physical discomfort: "Her physical wants are simpler. The living wage for a woman is lower than the living wage for a man because it is possible for her as a result of traditional drudgery and forced tolerance of pain and suffering to keep alive upon less" (Kessler-Harris, 1990).

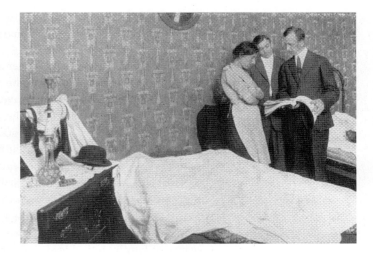

Thus the different wages for men and women reflected deeply entrenched attitudes about gender and work that became self-confirming myths and enforced women's dependence. At the most basic level, the unfair family wage pushed heavy incentives on women to marry in order to survive economically. The family wage also impelled women to stay married, even when their marriages were oppressive, rife with conflict, or simply unhappy. As Barbara Risman (1998) argues, marriage is one of the linchpins of inequality in American society:

A company sociological department adviser visits the home of a Ford Motor Company employee in 1915. The scientist uses a book of photos to give the employee's wife housekeeping advice.

> In what other institution are social roles, rights, and responsibilities based—even ideologically—on ascribed [i.e., birth] characteristics? When life options are tied to racial categories we call it

FIGURE 14.1   Male and Female Median Earnings, 1960–2018

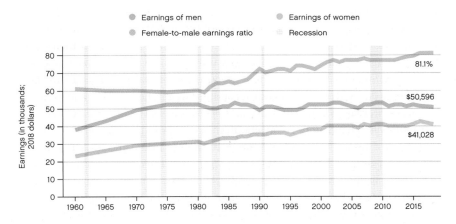

SOURCE: Hegewisch & Hartmann, 2019.

racism at best and apartheid at worst. When life options are tied to gender categories we call it marriage. (p. 36)

Surely, such an attitude no longer applies today, you're probably thinking, but the gender bias built into the family wage persists. The historical inertia of the family wage kept the average female wage at two-thirds that of the male wage through 1960. The gap has been narrowing somewhat since 1960, especially for younger workers. Women 35 years and older make 75 percent to 80 percent of what their male counterparts earn. For younger people (ages 16–24 in 2018), women earn about 91 percent of what men earn (Bureau of Labor Statistics, 2020c). Still, inequity as a result of gender continues to draw boundaries between the (male) public and (female) private spheres. It is hard to identify cause and effect when examining women's family responsibilities and their lower pay. Does lower work commitment (because of family duties) lead to lower wages? Or do lower wages make it easier for women to prioritize unpaid home labor?

As feminist economist Heidi Hartmann (1976) has argued, men still have a vested interest in maintaining their privileged position as exclusive living-wage earners. They have a material advantage over women; they benefit from women's unpaid domestic labor in the home; and their advantage further gives them a superior sense of self. Nancy Folbre (1987), another economist, has argued that not just men but also employers and capitalist owners (predominately male) stand to gain from women's weaker position in the labor market. Women, she contended, could be used as a flexible reserve army to keep the peace among White male workers. That is, by dangling the threat of cheaper women employees before male workers, employers were better able to break strikes, defy unionization, and assert control over labor. More recent research indicates that women are not "unorganizable." Whereas they were once thought to care more about their responsibilities at home than their careers and thus be uninterested or unable to invest time and effort in the unionization movement, by 2018–19, 48.2 percent of the unionized workforce consisted of women (Bureau of Labor Statistics, 2020h). Not only have union ranks grown more feminized since the 1970s, but women's participation has changed the typical bargaining framework. Unions, especially those dominated by women, now propose compensation packages in their negotiations with management that address wages, health care, and vacation time as well as paid family leave and better access to child care (Milkman, 2007). (We'll have more to say about unions later in the chapter.)

Few families today, even among the upper middle classes, can afford a full-time stay-at-home mom. Dual-income families are now the majority. Both the husband and wife were employed in 60.9 percent of married-couple families, just dad was employed in another 22.8 percent, and 8.3 percent had just mom working (Bureau of Labor Statistics, 2020b). Women with young children have also increased in numbers in the workforce. In 2015,

69.9 percent of women with children under age 17 worked, down from 77.5 percent in 2008 but still high compared with just 47.4 percent in 1975. For mothers of infants age 1 and under, only 31 percent worked in 1976. In 2014, 52 percent were employed, and 71 percent of those women were employed full-time (Bureau of Labor Statistics, 2016c). But attitudes toward mothers working full-time have recently shifted back to a more traditional perspective (at least among the moms themselves).

Although family roles have changed drastically, workplace organization has failed to keep up, and typical American parents have less disposable income now than they did in the 1960s, when a sole breadwinner could comfortably support a family of four (Warren & Warren Tyagi, 2003). Americans work longer hours than the citizens of most industrialized nations; we even put in two more weeks of work each year than our alleged "workaholic" German counterparts. What's more, until the Great Recession of 2008–9, which put a kink in the long-term trend, US work hours had been on a steady rise since the early 1960s. According to the US Bureau of Labor Statistics (2007, 2013, 2020a), in 1970 the average full-time employee worked 42.7 hours per week; in 1988 this figure rose to 43.6 (Hochschild, 1997); by 2007 it was 45.9, but then it fell to 42.5 in 2019.

For such long hours, Americans receive little vacation compared with workers in other countries. German and Spanish workers average six weeks of government-mandated paid vacation time; the British get about five. In contrast, American workers do not receive any government-mandated paid vacation days.

It's no surprise, then, that the demands of work infringe on home life. This is so even when parents experience one of the most revered and momentous events of family life—the birth of a child (Figure 14.2). A Japanese mother, after giving birth, is entitled to at least 58 weeks of paid maternity leave at full pay. Italian mothers receive more than 47.7 paid weeks. Canadian mothers, since legislation in 2002, have the right to take 51 weeks off from work after childbirth at 55 percent of their pay. Mothers in Norway get 80 percent of their salary for their child's first year. In Sweden, half of all new fathers take 6 weeks of paid paternity leave. Around the globe, 127 countries, including almost every industrialized nation, guarantee some form of paid leave for parents. The United States is not among them. In 1993, President Bill Clinton signed the much celebrated Family and Medical Leave Act, giving American workers the right to 12 weeks of leave to care for a newborn baby or attend to a family emergency. However, the leave is not necessarily paid, and it applies only to the half of the nation who work for a company of more than 50 employees. The act also doesn't apply to part-timers, most of whom are women.

Since it is pretty much up to individual companies to decide what kind of family support they will provide workers, it may come as no surprise that income predicts whether workers get paid family leave. For example, among workers who earn more than $75,000 per year, three-quarters of those who took a family or medical leave were paid at least some of their wages during

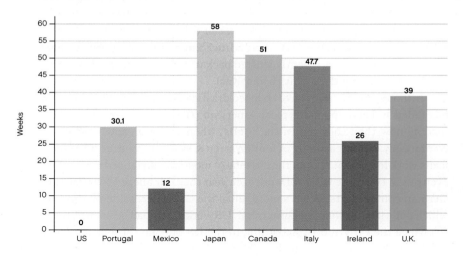

FIGURE 14.2 Weeks of Paid Leave for New Mothers

SOURCE: Organisation for Economic Co-operation and Development, 2019a.

that period. By contrast, half as many (37 percent) low-income workers, who make less than $30,000, received no pay at all when they needed to take a break from work for medical or family reasons (Horowitz et al., 2017).

Large (and growing) majorities of Americans across the political spectrum support paid family leave (Horowitz et al., 2017). Yet, curiously enough, when companies do implement family-friendly policies, workers often don't take advantage of them. In *The Time Bind: When Work Becomes Home and Home Becomes Work* (1997), Arlie Hochschild finds that people's lives increasingly center on the world of work, and as a result, families are suffering. The midwestern corporation Hochschild studied, fictitiously called "Amerco," offered generous pro-family policies, such as part-time hours and "flexplace," which allows workers to work from home. Amerco also offered flextime, so that workers could adjust their schedules, early or late, as they needed. But despite a work environment that seemed family-friendly, she found that most workers ended up working longer hours during the course of their employment. Hochschild (1997) asks, "Why don't working parents, and others too, take the opportunity available to them to reduce their hours at work?"

Her answer is surprising and differs from the economic argument about substitution effects. Working parents don't take advantage of family-friendly corporate policies, she asserts, because they prefer to avoid their homes and families. The workplace has become, in a strange departure from nineteenth-century formulations, a haven from the chaos and the emotional and physical disarray of the second shift at home. Hochschild suggests a reversal of the sacred and the profane, in which the home has fallen from grace, with its members seeking refuge and relief at the workplace. For the harried supermom, bombarded by the pressing demands of children, husband, and housework, work increasingly becomes a safe place of comfort and ease. With too much to do at home and too little time to do it, "a tired parent flees a world of unresolved quarrels and unwashed laundry for the reliable orderliness, harmony, and managed cheer of work. The emotional magnets beneath home and workplace are in the process of being reversed" (Hochschild, 1997).

If you find Hochschild's argument too narrowly focused on emotional concerns, you're not alone. In *The Time Divide: Work, Family, and Gender Inequality* (2004), sociologists Jerry Jacobs and Kathleen Gerson argue that workers do not take advantage of family-friendly policies for a number of other reasons: Under cultural and structural conditions that keep work and family divided, they are afraid of losing their jobs. Workers perceive a trade-off between family policies and opportunities for the advancement of their careers. Taking advantage of parental leave or part-time hours, working parents believe, sends a negative message to the boss that could lead to placement on the "mommy track" and a dead-end career.

Meanwhile, studies consistently show that working mothers are less depressed, have higher self-esteem, and report a greater sense of happiness than stay-at-home mothers. One study even suggests that women who work feel more valued at home than those who stay home (Hochschild, 2003). Women today share what Judith Stacey (1996) calls "post-feminist expectations" for family and work. They have "the desire to combine marriage to a communicative, egalitarian man with motherhood and a successful, engaging career." Such expectations only a few decades earlier would have sounded crazy. Although working mothers have higher self-esteem and better mental

Balancing work and family life puts a strain on most Americans. Angela drops her daughter off at her parents' house before taking her son to school and going to work at a hospital in Marshall, Missouri. She and her husband both work full-time and are up as early as 4:30 A.M. and work as late as 7:30 P.M. during the week.

health than nonworking ones, studies also show that they are more likely to feel anxious and tired. They get sick more often than their husbands. Their divorce rates have risen. The entrance of women into the workplace has increased their economic power, but in the absence of other social changes, this subtle revolution will have "stalled," in Hochschild's words.

The flip side of this story is that although the demands of work impinge on life at home, the growing cost of America's middle-class lifestyles means that many families feel they have no choice but to send both parents into the full-time workforce. Law professor turned US senator Elizabeth Warren suggests that the problem is not that Americans' greedy consumer spending habits are putting them in a financial bind but rather that they are pinched by the cost of safe housing in good school districts combined with destabilized career paths (Warren, 2007). Mortgages, property taxes, and student loan debt are fixed costs that cannot easily be trimmed if families suffer unforeseen layoffs, medical emergencies, or divorce.

THE SERVICE SECTOR

Changing gender roles and work–family tensions are two important features of the current version of capitalism, but they are by no means the only ones. Perhaps the most important recent change in the American economy is that making money no longer exclusively relies on the creation of a tangible product. The service sector, the section of the economy that provides intangible services rather than material products, has grown rapidly over the last 30 years. These services can range from restaurant work (the largest occupation for women without a college education), to health care provision, to higher education, to legal or financial advice, to computer tech support, to deep-tissue massages. The emergence of COVID-19 and related shutdowns are particularly damaging to service sector workers, who make up about 20 percent of total employment in the United States (Bureau of Labor Statistics, 2020d). Bars and restaurants—the businesses most immediately affected by shutdowns—make up about 8 percent of US employment alone. Moreover, these businesses are disproportionately smaller and pay lower wages, leaving them and their employees particularly vulnerable compared to other sectors. The unemployment rate in May 2020 among younger workers (25.3 percent among ages 16–24) and those with only a high school education (15 percent) is partly explained by their disproportionate presence in the service sector (Kochhar, 2020). Moreover, those service sector employees who managed to keep their jobs during the initial hit in spring 2020 suffered from an 8 percent wage drop on average (Gruver, 2020).

Much work in the service sector involves what Hochschild (1983) calls "emotional labor." Emotional labor is the concept that certain kinds of work require us to manage our emotions in a taxing way that exacts costs. Every time a cashier wishes you a nice day or a flight attendant plasters a smile on his or her face for the entire six-hour journey, it takes a toll on him or her. While all

We expect that our flight attendants will serve coffee with a smile, but this is a form of what Hochschild calls "emotional labor."

public life requires some self-management of feelings, service sector jobs are thought to be extreme in this regard (Grandey et al., 2005). Higher degrees of emotional labor are correlated with lower job satisfaction and higher rates of burnout; it's worth noting that the occupations with the highest demands on emotional labor—retail, hospitality, and so on—are disproportionately female.

How does the new service economy challenge old theories? Does Marx's two-class model still make sense in such an era? How are we alienated differently in the service world than in the manufacturing world? Or is the story largely the same? Service work poses challenges to Smith's and Simmel's theories as well. Does the division of labor proceed apace or slow down with conversion to a service model? And does the evolution toward depersonalized relations of payment and exchange become complicated by occupations that require face-to-face interaction with a smile and a thank-you and a receipt (or perhaps your meal is free)?

Globalization

Going hand in hand with the development of the service economy is the complicated and contested process of globalization, generally defined as a multidimensional set of social processes that create, multiply, stretch, and intensify worldwide social exchanges and interdependencies. This means that I can wake up in the morning and have a free video chat with my friend in New Delhi using Zoom, buy commodities from a Jamaican company in the afternoon, and in the evening read the Parisian newspaper *Le Figaro* online. But what are the implications of globalization for capitalism? Essentially, it means an increase in trade and economic exchanges among individuals, corporations, and states in different areas of the globe.

Such processes are, however, not entirely new. In the last flush of the great European empires, between 1890 and 1914, for instance, the relative magnitude and geographic scale of trade flow and capital were higher than they are today. However, at least four recent phenomena make the current period of globalization novel: new markets, new means of exchange, new players, and new rules.

First, new markets include financial markets where anyone with the proper equipment can participate. Second, new means of exchange, such as cellular phones, personal computers, e-mail, and the web, allow for almost instantaneous transactions. With these new forms of communication technology, a person in Buenos Aires, Argentina, can buy a commodity in Cape Town, South Africa, and sell it in Moscow, Russia, in a matter of minutes (or seconds, even). Third, there are new players. These new players are all transnational, which makes them unique to this epoch of globalization. The World Trade Organization (WTO), for example, acts as the regulation authority for trade. An increase in multinational corporations (corporations located in more than one country) and worldwide nongovernmental organizations (such as Doctors Without Borders, Oxfam, and Amnesty International) has also occurred. Fourth, new rules are at play. Although countries have always negotiated trade agreements, as of late there has been a proliferation of multilateral trade agreements, including the North American Free Trade Agreement (NAFTA) signed in the 1990s, the Central American Free Trade Agreement, which added countries to NAFTA in 2005, and the new United States—Mexico—Canada Agreement (USMCA, or "NAFTA 2") in 2020. Multilateral means that they don't result from the negotiations between two nation-states, but rather are the end result of negotiations among multiple players and thus enforce rights, impose sanctions, or encourage business at a regional or worldwide level. One thing that globalization has clearly exposed is the global divide between the haves and the have-nots. For instance, according to a 2019 Credit Suisse report, the top 1 percent of the adults worldwide hold 45 percent of the world's wealth, whereas the bottom half of the global population holds less than 1 percent of the world's wealth. In fact, it only takes $7,087 in assets to be in the top 50 percent of wealthy world citizens (Credit Suisse Research Institute, 2019). Furthermore, 821 million people (that's 1 in 9) go hungry in the world, 780 million people do not have access to clean drinking water, and 3.9 percent of children die before their fifth birthday, mostly from preventable diseases (UNICEF, 2019; Centers for Disease Control and Prevention, 2020; Roser et al., 2019). On the other hand, these global poverty rates are substantially lower than they were a generation ago, partly as a result of the increased income that globalization has brought to many.

The bottom line is that contemporary globalization tends to reduce income inequality and poverty on a worldwide scale. The differences between

China, Brazil, and the United States are shrinking. But globalization tends to exacerbate disparities within countries, where we tend to notice them. It's not so easy to sort out cause and effect when it comes to specifics, like the relationship between trade competition, automation, and wages. But some evidence from trade shocks suggests that trade does indeed eliminate domestic manufacturing jobs (Autor et al., 2013). Meanwhile, automation is known to increase productivity—thereby raising national income—but also, through its substitution effect, to depress wages. The result is a shift from labor to capital in the share of society's income (Acemoglu & Restrepo, 2018).

Although it might seem like globalization is just the direction toward which history marches, it has come in ebbs and flows. Moreover, there is nothing inevitable about globalization, as Brown University professor Nitsan Chorev points out in her book *Remaking U.S. Trade Policy: From Protectionism to Globalization* (2007), and which she discussed with me. "Globalization is not inevitable. It's not only the result of the reduction of the price of transportation, for example. Even when companies each have an interest in [expanding global trade], they had to overcome [protectionist] political barriers that were in place" (Conley, 2011e). And, of course, not all industries favor open international markets. In the United States, for instance, the steel and textile industries bitterly opposed trade liberalization. Chorev's book documents how, in the United States at least, those barriers were overcome by the pro-trade sectors— ironically, including the auto industry back when it led the world market— by shifting the locus of policy making from Congress (whose members were incentivized to protect their districts' businesses from competition even if the whole of the economy was worse off) to the executive and judicial branches (which were more immune to such pressures and, instead, had a national constituency).

Even if increasing globalization is not a law of nature, like gravity, the current wave shows no signs of abating anytime soon. So how can we manage the process so that the losers in this ongoing economic transformation do not suffer dire fates? Chorev has some thoughts here too:

DIGITAL.WWNORTON.COM/YOUMAYASK7

Watch my interview with Nitsan Chorev at
digital.wwnorton.com/youmayask7

So, the solution to the problems that globalization has brought has to be through regulation. And the question is whether the regulation should be at the national level or international. And possibly one could convincingly argue that at the moment, international regulation would be more effective. One possibility, which has been negotiated at the WTO for years now, is adding to trade negotiations agreements that protect labor and [the] environment. The U.S. government does not push enough for it. [And] developing countries resist for obvious reasons: Cheap labor is the comparative advantage, and if they lose that, then they lose the globalization struggle, right? So, you have to think of other ways. Either through the WTO, or in other means to create a better balance. (Conley, 2011e)

Indeed, a backlash against global trade agreements has become one of the most powerful political forces as of late. For example, the Trans-Pacific Partnership (TPP) was signed in 2016 by Australia, Brunei, Canada, Chile, Japan, Malaysia, Mexico, New Zealand, Peru, Singapore, Vietnam, and the United States. But President Trump withdrew the US signature when he took office in 2017, invalidating the deal (the other countries went ahead with their own agreement). Meanwhile, the Trump administration has imposed trade sanctions against China and tariffs on imports such as steel, to which China responded with equivalent tariffs on American products such as soybeans and pork. But in an interdependent world, protecting national interests is not so simple. Many US manufacturers that rely on cheap steel are crying foul. Meanwhile, farmers who rely on the Chinese market to sell their soybeans are scared about retaliation. In an interdependent world, it is not so easy to predict who gains and who loses in a trade battle.

The Reign of the Corporation

Nike, Walmart, Apple, Kraft, Microsoft. These are the engines driving our globalizing economy. Corporations are the institutions that structure economic life in every corner of the planet, displacing the roles of powerful former ruling institutions such as monarchies, religions, and perhaps even governments. As I mentioned earlier, under American law, the corporation is legally an individual. Legal scholars call it a juristic person because it has all the formalized rights, duties, and responsibilities of a person. The Latin root of the term is *corpus*, meaning "body," and a corporation is a body of people that has authority to act as an individual.

Corporate personhood came about through a series of developments starting in seventeenth-century Europe, at the beginning of the industrial age. Historically, state governments granted charters to corporations to expand trade and exploration, spawning corporate colonialism such as the massive power and spread of the Dutch and British East India companies. Under the old ways of doing things, a state provided the charter, and the corporation's duty was to carry out whatever functions the state defined. But in 1886 the US Supreme Court found that the Fourteenth Amendment, intended to protect the rights of freed slaves, also granted corporations the legal status of persons, thus establishing a distinction between corporations and their owners.

THE CORPORATE PSYCHOPATH?

From anticorporate movements like the Seattle protests of the WTO in 2000 to everyday "culture jamming," as seen in activist media such as *Adbusters* magazine (see Chapter 3), corporations are vilified for their greed, injustices, and callous ecological devastation. In the award-winning 2003 documentary *The Corporation*, the filmmakers asked: If corporations are legal persons, what kind of personality do they have? Their answer: pathological. Corporations act like psychos, claimed Federal Bureau of Investigation consultant Robert Hare in the film, because they show little regard, remorse, or guilt for harming others; they are unable to maintain long-term relationships; they lie all the time; and they fail to conform to social norms by obeying the law. That's because, like many psychopaths, corporations are solely self-interested—in their case, interested only in the relentless pursuit of profits for their shareholders.

However, as easy as it may be to stigmatize corporations, given the system in which corporations must operate, they're not necessarily pathological so much as rational. Forget the environment, forget workers' rights, forget morals and fairness. Unless these factors improve the bottom line—that is, "shareholder value"—they don't figure into corporate concerns. As the

An anticorporate advertisement from the critical magazine *Adbusters*. Why do activists compare global corporations to psychopaths?

economist Milton Friedman (1970) remarked in a now famous *New York Times Magazine* essay, "There is one and only one social responsibility of business—to use its resources and engage in activities designed to increase its profits so long as it stays within the rules of the game, which is to say, engages in open and free competition without deception or fraud."

Through the rational pursuit of profit, good people can end up doing bad things. Max Weber made this observation about modern bureaucratic organizations, of which corporations are an exemplary form (see Chapter 15). In Weber's theory, bureaucracies flourish because of their efficiency and rational means to achieve profit-driven ends. But there's a cost that comes with the increased power of the specialized bureaucracy: People become alienated from any sense of right and wrong and from a human connection, what Weber (1946) called the "parceling-out of the soul."

If profit maximization is the nature of the corporation, a problem arises when corporations turn their backs on social responsibility. This involves various types of foul play, from obstructing open competition of the free market to engaging in willful fraud and deceit. When a business is not competitive, it may take the form of a monopoly or oligopoly. A monopoly occurs when one seller of a good or service dominates the market to the exclusion of others, potentially leading to zero competition. In an oligopoly, there are only a handful of sellers. Together, these firms often have enough market power to set prices through what economists call collusion (that is, coordination), such as a cartel. Again, this means effectively zero competition, which is great for the seller firms, because they can charge whatever they like for products or services, regardless of quality. The sellers can reduce supply (including reduction of service standards) to drive up demand and/or drive down costs and reel in huge profits. But this is bad news for consumers, of course, as they will have no close substitutes and are forced to either pay high prices or forgo sometimes vital products. This is also bad news for general social welfare, because without a competitive market, vast inefficiencies arise.

Just how competitive are corporations? To do well in the game, it is in their own interests to shut out their competitors from the market. Corporations can do this in a couple of ways while skirting the line of monopoly. Take tech behemoth Google: Its key product is its search engine by the same name, which works on a proprietary ranking algorithm called PageRank. When you search on Google.com for a topic or category within which Google itself has a vested interest, it turns out that the PageRank algorithm that made the search engine so successful in the first place (compared to early competitors like AltaVista or Yahoo) is ditched in favor of a listing that puts Google's interests first. For example, if you search for an address, Google Maps comes up before MapQuest. Google shopping takes over on product searches, pushing other (often better) price comparison sites like Bizrate down. Some competitors have pushed back, and in 2017, the European Union found the company in violation of antitrust laws for skewing search results and fined Google a record $2.7 billion.

MONOPOLY

the form of business that occurs when one seller of a good or service dominates the market to the exclusion of others, potentially leading to zero competition.

OLIGOPOLY

the economic condition that exists when a handful of firms effectively control a particular market.

Another way to beat the competition is to slide into an industry through the government backdoor. This is the preferred method of dominance for the Carlyle Group, a multibillion-dollar equity firm that invests in industries such as defense, telecommunications, energy, and health care. How does it achieve mammoth success in these heavily regulated industries? Critics charge that the Carlyle Group's secret is political arbitrage, the use of insider political knowledge to earn profits. By hiring former secretaries of defense, former presidents, and former heads of government regulatory commissions in order to gain access to current officials, the Carlyle Group can influence government decisions on spending and policy in its own favor (Briody, 2003).

Corporations can also dominate the market by offering the lowest prices, thereby attracting the most buyers. To do this, they may lower production costs in a variety of creative ways, such as cutting environmental corners, weakening labor unions, and telling good old-fashioned lies. Of course, some have developed goods and services that broadly improve quality of life. Like most economists, Adam Davidson refers to this as productivity enhancing corporate activity. In an interview, he explained how economists draw broad divisions between companies based on how much value they add to society:

> Productivity enhancing means you come up with something cool that other people want and the thing you came up with is better, cheaper, faster; and people choose it. Google to me is clearly productivity enhancing. When I see that those guys are rich, it makes sense to me that they're rich. They came up with something that all of us use all the time and it makes all of our lives better. We're not forced to use it. We just use it because it's really good. . . . [T]he Google guys are worth, I don't know, twenty billion dollars, but they've brought hundreds of billions of dollars of benefit to the world. So they're taking a cut and we're all better off. (Conley, 2015c)

Even economists think some transactions in the market simply move money around—usually toward people and companies who already have capital—without increasing overall value. Davidson explained that "rent seeking is that category of things where you get rich basically by taking wealth away from others . . . where for every dollar you get, someone else doesn't have a dollar." For instance, he explained that he would be a rent seeker, "if I happened to own an apartment and I don't make it better, I don't improve

Google's PageRank algorithm prioritizes its own products. In this search for driving directions, would you choose to get directions from Google Maps (which conveniently previews the route and driving time), or would you click on a link that's further down?

PRODUCTIVITY ENHANCING

economic activities that increase the total economic value available to society.

RENT SEEKING

economic activities that aim to move value from one person or company to another without increasing value.

DIGITAL.WWNORTON.COM/YOUMAYASK7

To see my interview with Adam Davidson, go to
digital.wwnorton.com/youmayask7

it, I just own it, I just happened to buy it." Referring to the neighborhood where we both grew up that "was a total nightmare piece of crap neighborhood" 40 years ago, he pointed out that "if [our parents] had [bought an apartment building], now they could charge a higher rent without actually making it better." The lazy, opportunistic landlord is the classic example of rent seeking, but the hot question about rent seeking right now is, Is Wall Street productivity enhancing or rent seeking?

To get an insider's answer to that question, I talked to Adeel Qalbani, who worked at a hedge fund before starting a private equity firm. Qalbani explained that *Wall Street* and *finance* are terms used too broadly. While *Wall Street* used to refer to a bunch of amped-up macho people screaming and flapping their hands to signal trades in stocks of publicly traded companies, commodities, and (to a lesser degree) bonds, most of that trading activity has moved off the trading floor and onto computers. Financialization has expanded dramatically over the past years and now includes commercial banks, hedge funds, high-frequency trading, private equity firms, and a range of other boutique investment classes that use clients' money. One crucial difference is between heavily regulated commercial banks and bigger, less regulated investment banking operations. The difference, Qalbani explained, is that "commercial banks [are] where you put deposits and they make loans," while investment banks are kind of the hub of the capital markets. So if a company needs to raise money, "they can go to a commercial bank and ask for a loan, or they can go to an investment bank," where they may get access to more capital or more complex terms.

Skeptical of many financial firms' ability to participate in productivity enhancing activities, Qalbani singled out firms that invest in companies that they then try to improve or grow as most likely to be productivity enhancing. He explained that private equity is "a business about buying or investing in private companies, not in traded stocks . . . that are generally priced efficiently, particularly large cap stocks. I think there's a reasonable amount of evidence that venture capital investing, or private equity investing, or investing in new companies or private companies is much more inefficient, has far fewer people focused on it, and has more of an opportunity to kind of create value in the world" than firms that trade or invest without an aim to improve the underlying asset (Conley, 2014g). If you are confused, you are not alone. Financial journalist Gillian Tett (2010) continues to remind readers that pre-2007 financial professionals, including "most investors, regulators, and ratings agencies," were "clueless" about everything outside the mundane savings and loan banks used by consumers. We discuss the difficulty the federal government has trying to regulate the complex financial sector in the policy section that concludes the chapter.

DIGITAL.WWNORTON.COM/YOUMAYASK7

To see my interview with Adeel Qalbani, go to
digital.wwnorton.com/youmayask7

The Environment One way of keeping costs low is to maintain efficient methods of production, which often means bypassing environmental concerns. Caring about the earth's sustainability can be expensive; it requires maintaining low levels of pollution, disposing of waste in safe ways, and maybe investing in costly eco-friendly technology. But helping the environment is not always cost-prohibitive. Some companies, like Walmart, have found ways to help their bottom line and the environment by doing things like reducing packaging; Apple tries to use recyclable materials like glass and aluminum rather than nonrecyclable composites. As a general rule, though, whenever industry spreads to a developing nation, environmental damage ensues. Dumping, pollution, and toxic accidents are the costs of development when it occurs without adequate government oversight.

Even in countries with stricter environmental guidelines for industry, disasters happen. Consider the BP *Deepwater Horizon* drilling rig oil spill, the worst environmental disaster in US history. Though it was ostensibly caused by an accident, BP has long been known for its shoddy safety record. Meanwhile, the government agency charged with overseeing offshore oil drilling, the Minerals Management Service, was stacked with industry executives and hence approved BP's request to drill without a full environmental impact study. And when things blew up (literally and figuratively), BP (and government) officials were caught without a plan to stem the flow of oil in the Gulf of Mexico, and didn't have the resources to clean up the spill's aftermath. In the case of *Deepwater Horizon* (or the Exxon *Valdez* spill of 1989, for that matter), everyone pays for the accident (especially oil-coated sea creatures), but who is really to blame when our collective lifestyle and policy choices rely on, and facilitate reliance on, oil?

OFFSHORING

a business decision to
move all or part of a
company's operations
abroad to minimize costs.

UNION

an organization of workers
designed to facilitate
collective bargaining with
an employer.

UNION BUSTING

a company's assault on
its workers' union with the
hope of dissolving it.

More than 2,500
employees work in this
Haitian factory that
produces Levi's jeans and
Hanes clothing. Why do
large corporations like
Levi Strauss offshore their
manufacturing facilities?

Labor: Sweat It or Bust It Another corporate strategy to reduce production costs is to lower labor costs. One publicly unfavorable way is offshoring labor—that is, moving all or part of a company's operations abroad, to developing nations with lower pay scales and lenient labor laws. By outsourcing production to sweatshops and call centers in the developing world, large companies can manufacture their products for a fraction of what it would cost to pay even minimum wages in the United States. In the globalized economy, offshoring gives corporations based in the developed world access to a comparatively cheap and pliable workforce, largely composed of women, youth, and un-educated rural migrants in search of a better life. This strategy can, however, land companies in hot water in the form of fatal catastrophes and widespread public criticism—as did the deadly 2013 Rana Plaza factory collapse in Bangla-desh. Amid heightened public awareness, businesses are sometimes held accountable for offshore human rights violations such as starvation wages, intimidation of labor organizers, use of child labor, and inhumane working conditions. In 1991, Levi Strauss was among the first companies to adopt a corporate code of conduct regarding labor. Levi Strauss holds its contractors to good labor practices and assesses a nation's human rights record before setting up shop there. Hundreds of American companies now have similar codes. In such a scenario, power is held not by the poor laborers themselves, but by the wealthy first-world consumers who sometimes decide they are will-ing to pay a bit more in order to consume with a clear conscience.

Sometimes, however, organized labor poses a threat to corporate profits. When a group of workers gets together for collective bargaining, they form a union, which makes them better able to promote and protect their collective interests than each worker would be able to alone. When a company assaults its workers' union by, for example, refusing to negotiate or renew a union contract in the hope of breaking it up, it is called union busting. Unioniza-tion in America is protected under freedom of association, a right that is generally considered implicit in the First Amendment and that was recognized as a human right by the Right to Organize and Collective Bargaining Convention in 1949. Despite legal protection, union-ization has been on the decline in the United States since the 1950s, when 35 percent of workers in the private sector were covered by labor contracts compared with just 6.2 percent today (Bureau of Labor Statistics, 2020h). The result, according to experts at the

Economic Policy Institute, is the toll exacted from workers in the form of increasing income inequality and decreasing health and pension benefits; workers' wages have also failed to continue rising as they did during the postwar years (Eisenbrey, 2007). However, drawing a causal link between the two trends is tricky because so many other changes are occurring at the same time. Compare this set of developments with those facing our counterparts in Europe, where strong union contracts cover the majority of workers: As of 2018, 56 percent of German workers and more than 95 percent of Belgian and French workers were covered under collective bargaining agreements (Figure 14.3). Wage growth across the Atlantic has generally been better for the bottom half of employed earners, but unemployment has also been higher.

What accounts for the decline in US unionization rates? There's a common perception, especially among political conservatives, that unions are outdated, corrupt, and a drag on business. Some complain that government is inefficient, hinting that the high rate of public-sector unionization, 33.6 percent, may be to blame. It's also a widespread notion that unions hurt productivity, in theory because they impose worker rules that obstruct the free market, thereby making employees less efficient. Although this might make theoretical sense, the evidence from industrial studies is mixed. A survey of the economics literature shows that unions are associated positively with productivity in the United States across sectors, and particularly

FIGURE 14.3 Share of Workers Covered under Collective Bargaining Agreements, 2018

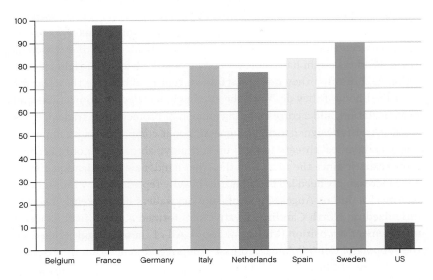

SOURCE: Organisation for Economic Co-operation and Development, 2020.

in manufacturing (Doucouliagos & Laroche, 2003). And when you look at the countries that have high rates of unionization, they also have correspondingly high rates of productivity (Eisenbrey, 2007). This is perhaps because, with collective bargaining efforts, unionized workers receive contract benefits, and contract benefits make for productive workers. After all, the better your health coverage, working conditions, and job security, the less likely you will be to worry about those things, and the more you can concentrate on doing your job well. On the other hand, it could be that the trades with enough clout to unionize tend to be those that are highly skilled and productive, making the fact that they are unionized irrelevant to their rewards.

Unions also are widely perceived as corrupt forces that the majority of workers don't want. However, according to several studies, workers today have mixed feelings about unions. In the midst of a statewide fight over unions' rights to bargain collectively in Wisconsin, 45 percent of Americans sided with Wisconsin's unions over its governor (Public Policy Polling, 2011). In the same year, a Gallup poll showed that Americans gave unions a 52 percent approval rating. Even among workers who don't necessarily favor a union, there are a considerable number who want some kind of worker representation that meets regularly with management.

Why don't workers unite if they want collective bargaining, especially given the protections of labor laws under the principle of freedom of association? According to other surveys, workers don't unionize because they are aware of management hostility to collective action (Freeman, 2007). Whether in the form of outright (and illegal) opposition such as intimidating and firing organizers or through subtler means like anti-union presentations on company time, workers get the hint that unions are not the best way to stay on their employer's good side. In fact, in one 2003 survey, workers claimed that the biggest disadvantage of having a union was worse relations between employees and management (Freeman, 2007). It is a vicious circle. Workers might have more security to speak up for their rights if they unionize, but often they never start down that road because they fear for their livelihood if they do. With the rise in global telecommunications and transportation, and a corresponding erosion of protectionist trade policies (such as tariffs designed to make domestic goods competitive with imported ones), companies' threats to pack up and move abroad have only become more realistic since the 1970s. On the other hand, new unionization efforts have increasingly been led by industries heavily represented by immigrants to America. In Los Angeles, janitors and drywallers have recently become unionized; in North Carolina, meatpackers formed a union in the face of management opposition (Milkman, 2006). All of these struggles relied on the support of Central American first- and second-generation immigrants who, recent studies have found, are at least as likely to be in unions as Whites (Rosenfeld & Kleykamp, 2009).

AN AGING ECONOMY

Back in the 1980s, many people in the United States feared that we would soon be eclipsed in economic power by Japan—then the second-largest economy and growing fast. Business books abounded covering how American managers could adopt the Japanese approach to mimic that country's success. Just-in-time manufacturing (JIT), total quality management (TQM), and life-long employment (*shushin koyo*) all became buzzwords of the executive suite.

Fast-forward to the 1990s and Japan's economy not only failed to pass us by, but even began shrinking in what would become known as the "lost decade" (or two). Though there has been some growth since then, the Japanese economic miracle of the 1960s–1980s has remained a distant dream.

Were the best sellers wrong? Was the Japanese approach to production lacking? It turns out that more important than total quality management is demography—specifically the age structure of the society (Bloom & Canning, 2004). The boom years were at least partly fueled by a big cohort in their prime work years while the ensuing secular stagnation is largely a result of the fact that Japan has the oldest population in the world (Faruqee & Mühleisen, 2003). Italy is the second oldest currently, and it's no surprise that the southern European country is right behind Japan when it comes to indicators of economic doldrums. The reasons for such effects are multiple.

First, there is the question of workers. Most studies find that labor productivity peaks between the ages of 30 and 50. However, others find what they call a Horndal effect—so named for a steel factory in Sweden that showed a positive effect of an older workforce (Malmberg et al., 2008). Of course, what is good for a particular manufacturing firm is not necessarily what's good for the economy as a whole. The debate over age and productivity will no doubt continue, especially as the nature of work keeps morphing.

Where there is less doubt, however, is in other economic effects of an older population. When a population ages (or, conversely, when it is dominated by children), there are fewer workers supporting nonworkers such as retirees, which, in turn, puts a strain on those who are producing goods and services. Such an effect is captured by the "dependency ratio"—the number of people age 14 or below and over 65 that each worker needs to "support." Japan is not the highest in the world on this measure. Indeed, many countries have youth bulges that make their ratios higher: Niger has 111 "dependents" for each 100 people of traditional working age, making it the most lopsided (World Bank, 2019a). But Japan is first when it comes to the old-age dependency ratio, where there are 46 people age 65 or older for every 100 of working age (World Bank, 2019a). Moreover, when a population ages, there is also less demand for things like education and new houses—which are drivers of economic growth (Ohtake & Shintani, 1996). And there is more demand for health care, which does not tend to have as many positive spillover effects on economic growth as other industries, especially when consumed by the elderly.

If we believe the Horndal effect that older workers are, in fact, more productive, then the solution lies in keeping workers in the labor force for longer. To do that, retirement systems may need to be reformed—for example, delaying the age at which benefits kick in and requiring older workers to keep receiving training (see section in Chapter 13 on adult learning) to remain productive. Unfortunately, though older voters dominate the polls (see policy box in Chapter 15), they tend to vote for increased retirement benefits and not extensions of their working careers. This is true even though good evidence shows that retirement is bad for one's health (Snyder & Evans, 2006) (see Chapter 11).

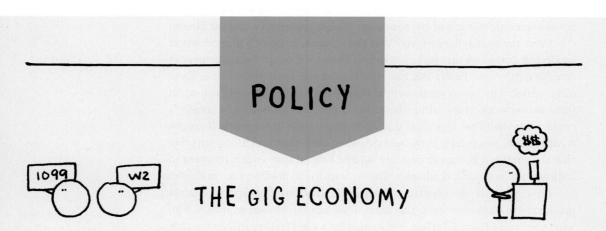

POLICY

THE GIG ECONOMY

The unemployment rate counts the number of people actively looking for work who did not work for pay in a given week. It is a useful metric, but it does not give a total picture of how the economy is doing. For example, by 2016, the unemployment rate had fallen to about half of its peak during the Great Recession; however, the labor force participation rate (the percentage of Americans over 16 years old working or looking for work) remained at near record lows. This is partly due to an aging population, and partly due to the fact that many workers had given up on the prospect of ever finding a job. And still others are on long-term disability or take early retirement. But even among the officially employed, there are many who are not working full-time but would like to. Adding these to the unemployed gives us an "underemployment rate" of about triple the raw unemployment rate.

Many of those who are underemployed are part of the growing "gig" economy. *Gig* is a term of unknown origins from the 1920s, originally applied to the jobs that jazz musicians obtained. Thus it connotes the economic uncertainty and tenuousness of the professional musician's lifestyle—along with its freedom from the traditional constraints of the rat race. The rise of web-based applications such as Uber and TaskRabbit has come to epitomize this growing sector of the labor force. Since the Great Recession, the number of 1099s (1099 refers to the tax form that independent contractors receive as opposed to a W2, which regular employees get) issued has exceeded the number of W2 forms. (We must keep in mind, however, that one person generally receives only one W2 unless they change jobs in a calendar year but can receive many 1099s from multiple payers.) Even the very use of the term

What are the advantages of working as an independent contractor for a web-based application such as Uber as part of the gig economy? What are the downsides?

gig has skyrocketed since 1980—in tandem with economic restructuring and the rise of the era of personal computing (Grose & Kallerman, 2015). Something is clearly afoot. But what are we to make of this 1099 economy? A new jazz-like freedom for the millennial generation? Or yet another sign of stagnant earnings, rising inequality, and a fraying social safety net? And what, if anything, can we do about it?

Let's start with an accounting of the downsides: First, while it is not clear whether the actual hourly pay that independent contractors receive is lower, it certainly is the case that their earnings are more unstable. The risk of slow times devolves from the company, which might pay for idle employees during slack periods, to the worker, who literally does not get any pay if there is not any work that day, week, or month. In fact, recent surveys show that nearly 70 percent of gig workers have seen their income completely disappear during the COVID-19 crisis, while 89 percent are actively looking for other work to support themselves (Moulds, 2020). Second, employees get a lot of perks that independent contractors do not. For example, employers generally pay for a good portion of health insurance when they offer their workers a plan. Even though most economists agree that perks are not really "free" from the point of view of the worker—that is, they are largely, if not completely, taken out of would-be wages—they are tax-free in many cases. In addition to health insurance, employer contributions to retirement plans, life insurance, dental insurance, commuting expenses, and so on are all taken out as pretax income. The tax code does allow individual contractors—that is, giggers—to sock away pretax income in a self-employment IRA or to deduct certain other expenses that might have been paid by their employer if they worked as an official employee of a large organization, but the onus is on the little guy. It's easy to check a box when you get hired to have money taken out of your check before you ever see it (and matched by the employer, perhaps) to save for retirement. It's hard to squirrel away that same percentage at the end of each month or year when there are many competing bills to pay in the short run—especially for gig workers whose income is sporadic. Add in all the administrative burden of managing one's own "business" of one employee (self), and it is no surprise that Uber was the defendant in a class action suit on the part of some of its California drivers, arguing that they are employees, not independent contractors. Uber won that battle, but the company has faced ongoing legal challenges about stiffing drivers over their cut on prepriced trips as well as on tips (which it originally did not allow) (Lien, 2018).

Policy makers have to be careful how much they require of employers, however. A very large "temporary" workforce is an irony arising from very strong labor laws in Europe that make it hard to fire anyone once they have passed their probationary period. One concrete example is provided by a law passed by Spain meant to be family-friendly: employees with children under seven could request reduced work hours without risk of being fired. The result? Women disproportionately utilized this new option and suffered for it: In the ensuing 10 years, women of childbearing ages were hired at a rate that was 6 percent lower than that of comparable men, and they were 37 percent less likely to be promoted and 45 percent more likely to be dismissed (for other reasons, ostensibly) (Miller, 2015).

What this means is that the gig economy may be a consequence not just of rising inequality or a less educated workforce, but of those very policies that intend to make "real" employment nicer. Capitalism is tricky that way.

Conclusion

This chapter has been a rapid tour of modern capitalism. We started with the enclosure movement, wherein the commons were divided up into private parcels of land, marking the beginning of the end of the feudal way of life. Soon after, improved agricultural technology supported many more people, leading to industrialization, urbanization, and monetization. Legal structures, such as the rise of limited liability and corporate personhood, evolved to accommodate the new relations of production. And voilà, there you have modern industrial capitalism. Some scholars, such as Smith and Simmel, saw these developments as important steps forward, leading to greater wealth and personal freedom for all; others, such as Weber and Marx, took a darker view of the rise of capitalism, pointing to alienation and the "parceling out" of the soul. Modern capitalism has, as we have seen, undergone a number of changes since the period in which these folks were writing. We have witnessed a new era of globalization, a workforce composition gender change, the emergence of a large service sector, and the rise and fall of trade unionism. Where we go from here is anyone's guess. But you now have the tools to make as educated a guess as anyone.

QUESTIONS FOR REVIEW

1. As we saw at the beginning of the chapter, robots are taking over jobs that used to be held by people. How might this trend impact the growth in income inequality? For bonus points: How does automation relate to patterns in educational attainment that you read about in the previous chapter?

2. How are guest worker programs (temporary work visas for migrants) and offshoring labor potentially related? In your own words, provide two arguments for and against guest worker programs in the United States.

3. What does Arlie Hochschild define as "emotional labor," and what are a few examples of jobs or careers where emotional labor is necessary? What are the hidden costs of these demands?

4. How has the internet and mobile phone technology changed our relationship between work and home?

5. What is capitalism? How were the enclosure movement and monetization related to the advent of capitalism?

6. How does Adam Smith, in *The Wealth of Nations*, suggest that capitalism helps keep societies together? How do monopolies deviate from Smith's ideal view of capitalism?

7. Describe the concept of alienation as described by Karl Marx and illustrate two of its forms with examples. How does Max Weber's negative view of capitalism differ from Marx's?

8. How did the $5 per day wage at the Ford Motor Company shine a light on judgments about families and the role of women in society?

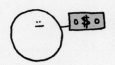

UNBANK YOURSELF!

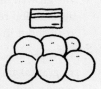

While today's economy offers many ways to pay for something—cash, credit cards, Apple Pay, bitcoin, etc.—there is a growing number of people who are "unbanked." Rather than using debit and credit cards offered by traditional banks or financial institutions, these people rely instead on alternatives such as check-cashing centers, prepaid debit cards, and payday lenders. Some of the estimated 9 million American households who live this way do it by choice—to fly below the radar—but most are shut out of mainstream financial institutions due to credit problems or lack of adequate identification or high banking fees (Federal Deposit Insurance Corporation, 2016).

TRY IT!

Money is supposed to be liquid and fungible. But today someone who is unbanked (that is, relies mainly on cash and is outside the formal financial system) cannot access some goods and services. On the other hand, someone who does not have any cash handy may be excluded from others. Make a list of goods or services that you can pay for only with cash and, conversely, ones that will not accept cash payment. Mark any items on each list that accept other forms of payment such as pre-paid debit cards, bitcoin, or PayPal.

CASH ONLY	CASH NOT ACCEPTED
HOT DOG STAND	AIRLINE TICKET
DONATIONS AT CHURCH	RENTAL CAR
BARBER SHOP	TRENDY SALAD PLACE

Think about going a single day using only cash. Then envision a day when you use only a debit card or a payment phone app such as Venmo or PayPal. Now go out and do it! Try living a day without banking (using cash only). And then try the day that plastic ruled. How well did your expectations match up with your experience?

THINK ABOUT IT

On each day of the experiment, you may have felt excluded from different institutions. How does inclusion in or exclusion from these two very different economies help create social stratification?

Was there a benefit or drawback to paying with cash versus credit in terms of taxes, anonymity, or security?

What—if anything—should we do about the unbanked in our society? Or, alternatively, should we resist the tracking inherent to electronic forms of payment?

SOCIOLOGY ON THE STREET

The rise of smartphones means that companies like Apple and Samsung are worth billions of dollars. How do companies rationalize vast pay gaps between executives and factory/retail workers? Watch the Sociology on the Street video to find out more: **digital.wwnorton.com /youmayask7**.

WANT MORE PRACTICE?

Complete the InQuizitive activity for this chapter at digital.wwnorton.com /youmayask7

15

PARADOX

AUTHORITY IS BASED ON THE IMPLICIT THREAT OF VIOLENCE, BUT THE MOMENT THAT FORCE IS USED, ALL AUTHORITY IS LOST.

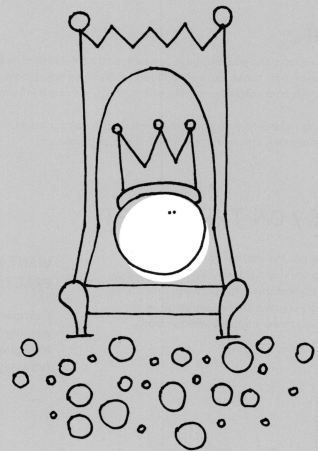

Animation at digital.wwnorton.com/youmayask7

Authority and the State

In Nathaniel Hawthorne's renowned novel *The Scarlet Letter*, Hester Prynne is made to wear an *A* on her dress for having conceived a child through an adulterous affair. (*A* stands for "adulteress.") As Hester leaves jail with her infant daughter in her arms, she endures the judgment of her fellow townsfolk who have gathered to watch her. Though the story takes place in Puritan society in 1642 Boston, the book was published in 1850. The mid-nineteenth century was a time when small-scale public punishment, such as shaming in the town square or being confined to the stocks, was on the wane, in favor of centralized punishment in the form of large-scale prisons. (See pages 242–43 for a discussion of Foucault's concept of the panopticon.) Michel Foucault pointed out that modern society moved from punishing the body (with implements like whips or the stretching rack) in the Middle Ages to punishing the soul in more recent epochs (through, for example, solitary confinement). However, even when we are talking just about punishing the soul, such sanctions can take many forms. We tend to think of public shaming as a vestige of a bygone era—of the time of Hester Prynne. But state-sanctioned shaming still exists in many jurisdictions, as Jennifer Jacquet points out in her book *Is Shame Necessary? New Uses for an Old Tool.* For instance, Ohio issues yellow license plates to drivers convicted of drunk driving. Texas sentences shoplifters to stand outside the store wearing sandwich boards declaring that they stole. California publishes the names of the biggest tax delinquents. And these are just a few of many examples in the United States.

DIGITAL.WWNORTON.COM/YOUMAYASK7

To see an interview with Jennifer Jacquet, go to
digital.wwnorton.com/youmayask7

The idea of punishing misdeeds this way makes many of us uncomfortable. But why? In her interview with me, Jacquet made the case that shaming can be an effective public policy tool to regulate behavior. But only under certain conditions. For example, a majority of the population must comply with the norm in order for shaming to work on those who don't comply. Take the example of voting: "The majority of the people don't vote in presidential elections," Jacquet said. "So it's really hard to reach for shaming in that instance where it's not a majority behavior and most of us are kind of culpable" (Conley, 2015d). Second, shaming requires a clear guilty party to target. "Global poverty is terrible," Jacquet continued. "We should use social exposure. But on who? Against who? It's really hard if you don't have clear signs of *responsibility*—and clear aspects of *reputation*—of who to go after."

In her own experiments, Jacquet found that shame (and its opposite, honor) worked very well in solving collective action problems. That is, when we all have to chip in for some common good where there is a possibility of shirking or what social scientists call "free riding," whether that is on a group project, not polluting, saving energy, voting, and so on, shame and honor are the most effective forces to ensure that we all pull our weight (and enjoy a virtuous, upward spiral where everyone is better off rather than a vicious, downward, death spiral). After all, most of our behavior is not formally regulated anyway but rather internally guided through norms and values and—failing that—through social sanctions like gossip and shunning. Some estimates suggest that two-thirds of all conversation is gossip about third parties, and of that, over three-quarters is negative.

But shaming among friends is one thing. Making it official state policy is another. The legal philosopher Martha Nussbaum argues against shaming sanctions because, among other reasons, the state should not be in the business of taking away the dignity of its citizens. Another concern, one raised by Jacquet herself, is that the reputation-destroying effects of shaming are hard to recover from: "Once you have obtained this bad reputation, is there any way of getting a good reputation back?" Jacquet asked. "How long does it take and how? Are we creating, in other words, a sort of class of shamed people that no one wants to take back into the group again?" she continued. Recall that modern social sanctions are meant to be rehabilitative and not punitive (see Chapter 6). Finally, sometimes shaming backfires. In Arizona, the DUI license plates were implemented and soon they gained a reputation as "party plates" and became a status marker among a certain segment of the population who actively sought them out. And while very few people would have any problems with shaming major corporations for malfeasance, do such institutions actually "feel" shame or merely manage their reputations?

All in all, then, shaming is like fire. It's a powerful tool. But it's one that can spread uncontrollably, like wildfire, in our globally connected online social world. Use with caution.

Students, before reading this chapter, please turn to page 816 and read the passage there. When you have finished, continue reading this section.

Types of Legitimate Authority

The ability for the state to punish individuals is one of the areas of investigation in the subdiscipline of political sociology, which studies politics—power relations among people or other social actors, be it at a governmental level or an interpersonal level or any level in between. To pass judgment on whether the state should shame individuals as punishment, we need to define the term *state*. And before we can do that, we need to talk about authority, the justifiable right, not just the ability, to exercise power. Rulers have authority if they can persuade their subordinates that their claim to power is valid.

To classify the kinds of legitimate authority or domination, sociologist Max Weber used three accounts of a ruler's "superiority and fitness to rule" (Parkin, 1982). These explanations are sometimes referred to as "claims to legitimacy," or the legitimation of authority and domination. When you, as a kid, asked to stay up past your bedtime, your mom or dad may have invoked parental authority to deny your request with a simple "because I said so" or "because I'm the parent, that's why." Generally, Weber expects rulers to legitimate their claim to authority with better explanations.

CHARISMATIC AUTHORITY

The first type of authority, charismatic authority, rests on the personal appeal of an individual leader. Have you ever met someone at school, at work, or in your group of friends who, for reasons that might have eluded you at the time, was referred to as a natural leader? This person may have

POLITICS

power relations among people or other social actors.

AUTHORITY

the justifiable right to exercise power.

CHARISMATIC AUTHORITY

authority that rests on the personal appeal of an individual leader.

had an uncanny way with people and was probably the center of attention, comfortable making decisions, responding to crises, and delivering orders with enviable panache. This "superhuman" aura and affective appeal are what Weber called charisma, specific qualities that inspire loyalty and obedience in others.

Think about presidential elections, when a candidate may be criticized for his or her insipid personality, poor sense of humor, or inadequate social grace—in other words, his or her lack of charisma. Note the ever-popular candidate charisma test: Would you rather have dinner with candidate X or candidate Y? The personal appeal of leaders has real consequences. In *Freakonomics* (2005), Steven Levitt and Stephen Dubner verify Weber's intuitions about charisma with cold, hard numbers, finding that—with some notable exceptions—no amount of campaign money will help a candidate win an election if the electorate just doesn't like him or her—what's been called the "beer test," as in which candidate would you rather have a beer with.

Because charismatic authority derives from the extraordinary attributes of a single individual, Weber anticipated that this form of legitimate authority would be particularly difficult to maintain or pass on. Imagine you are involved in a brand-new college club, for instance, with a hotshot leader who seems to be on top of everything from budget concerns to public relations. When your leader graduates, what happens to your club? Weber believed there are two options: Either you, as the club's new president, follow the hotshot's lead and try to do everything exactly as she did, or you write a constitution detailing the organization's rules and procedures. In the first case, the hotshot's charismatic authority has become traditionalized; in the latter, it has been rationalized.

Did 2016 presidential candidates Donald Trump and Hillary Clinton exhibit charismatic authority?

TRADITIONAL AUTHORITY

Traditional authority, as the name implies, rests on appeals to the past or traditions. As Weber (1968) notes, rule based on traditional authority dominates "by virtue of age-old rules and power," and leaders are "designated according to traditional rules and are obeyed because of their traditional status." Hereditary monarchies, whereby the crown passes down through a single family, are examples of traditional authority, as are the customs and ceremonies contained in the Jewish Torah. We consent to this type of legitimate domination because it is the way things have always been, the way our parents and grandparents did it, and the way we are expected to do it, too. For example, if you have ever attempted to improvise on your great-great-grandmother's cookie recipe, only to be reprimanded by your mother ("No, we have to make it the way grandma did!"), you are well acquainted with traditional authority.

Unlike charismatic authority, traditional authority does not suffer from problems of succession, but it has its own set of difficulties. Because all the decisions in a traditionalized club would be made with reference to what the former leader did in the now distant past, the club would not be very adaptable. In fact, it would be almost incapable of adapting to new circumstances unless something the first leader did or said established a clear precedent for action.

LEGAL-RATIONAL AUTHORITY

Legal-rational authority—the brand of authority that is supposedly most pervasive in modern society—is based on legal, impersonal rules. The rules rule. Even individuals in positions of authority are subject to these ubiquitous, impersonal rules (Weber, 1968). Formal roles and rules overshadow the personal attributes of individuals and the traditional ways of doing things. If you are arrested on the street by a police officer for disorderly conduct, you obey not by virtue of the officer's charm and upstanding character but because the officer reminds you that "it's the law." Likewise, the police officer does not have the authority to dispense with you as he or she pleases but has to follow a given set of rules, reading you your Miranda rights and properly documenting the entire event for his or her superiors and for the court system. At the station, the officer is responsible for filing the required paperwork and reporting the incident in accordance with the rules. In this form of authority, rules and roles transcend individuals.

Legal-rational authority is highly routinized, based on a standard, regular procedure. In the context of authority, routinization refers to the clear, rule-governed procedures used repeatedly for decision making. For example, the police officer writes down an offender's violations of the law,

TRADITIONAL AUTHORITY
authority that rests on or appeals to the past or traditions.

LEGAL-RATIONAL AUTHORITY
authority based on legal, impersonal rules; the rules rule.

ROUTINIZATION
the clear, rule-governed procedures used repeatedly for decision making.

RATIONALIZATION

a never-ending process of ordering or organizing.

BUREAUCRACY

a legal-rational organization or mode of administration that governs with reference to formal rules and roles and emphasizes meritocracy.

How is a police officer following procedures an example of legal-rational authority?

handcuffs the offender, and then transports the offender to the police station. Legal authority is also highly rationalized, or subject to ever-expanding modes of organization. That is, each step of a given process is rationalized to the extent that it is governed by considerations of efficiency. One last important aspect of legal-rational authority is that it is attached to roles, not individuals. Not just anyone has the authority to make you comply by putting your hands into metal cuffs and following orders. The police officer has that authority—but only if he or she is following proper procedure.

A bureaucracy is a legal-rational organization or mode of administration that governs with reference to formal rules and roles and emphasizes meritocracy. For example, have you ever wanted to enroll in a course that was already filled to capacity? Maybe you needed that particular course to fulfill a requirement. If so, you might have visited the registrar's office to beg for permission to enroll in that course. Once there, you probably waited in a long line only to discover that the registrar would grant you no favors because "that's the rule." You might have tried to convince her that it would be very easy to enroll you, or you might have resorted to manipulation with a good, theatrical cry or a flirtatious smile. But, alas, you will be admitted to the class only if another rule exists permitting exceptions to enrollment limits.

No matter how infuriating the registrar's "red tape" (common parlance for the morass of bureaucratic rules), it would probably never compare with the red tape of a state bureaucracy. Take the case of Rita Johnson, who was effectively killed by a state bureaucracy—not really murdered but, rather, technically murdered. In 2016, Johnson's "estate" got a notice of condolence from her credit card company for her recent passing. As it turned out, it wasn't just Discover who thought she had given up the ghost. Because of a misentered digit on a death certificate in Texas, the Social Security Administration listed her as dead. Because Johnson was dead in the eyes of the state, her health insurance was canceled and she could not legally act as the guardian of her sister, who has Down syndrome. To rejoin the living, Johnson had to enlist her elected congressional representative and one of her senators. "Everybody seems like they're trying to do the right thing, but it's like I'm in the Twilight Zone,"

Johnson said (Sawyer, 2017). She eventually received official documentation attesting to the fact that she was alive. How did this thing called bureaucracy manage to take the life of one innocent Minnesotan? As Social Security Administration officer Stewards Vang put it: "It's easy to kill somebody, but it's not easy to bring somebody back to life."

Characteristics of Bureaucracies Bureaucracies seek to make routine tasks efficient and to provide order in a disorderly world. They have several defining characteristics. First, they are usually structured hierarchically, meaning that the bureaucratic organization has many levels, and there are frequently multiple people working at each level of administration. Each successive level is typically assigned different tasks, and higher levels supervise lower levels. Each successively higher level is also granted greater decision-making control. If you must get something done through a bureaucratic organization, you may need to work with people at more than one level, often starting at the bottom and working your way up.

Second, the positions within a bureaucracy are highly specialized. Specialization, the opposite of generalization, refers to the process of giving each person specific, delimited tasks. Instead of one worker in a bureaucracy having several functions, each worker has a small and related set of specific functions. Taylorism, or scientific management, is an example of the specialization or division of labor, referring to the methods of labor management introduced by Frederick Winslow Taylor to streamline the processes of mass production. Along a figurative or literal assembly line, one worker might insert screws, the next worker might tighten the screws, and the third worker might cover the screws with plastic caps. A worker in a state bureaucracy might spend all day entering information from timesheets into a database; checking the timesheets and tallying them would be the work of other bureaucrats. Given such a system, the "deceased" Rita Johnson might never have received her proof-of-life documentation if she hadn't found the right person to contact.

A bureaucracy is also distinguished by its impersonality, the application of formal rules without regard to personal allegiances or feelings. Think back to your trip to the registrar to enroll in the full-to-capacity course. If you tried crying to convince the bureaucrat at the registrar's office that you should be allowed to enroll, it may not have worked because you appealed to the person, not the role, by using human emotion as a form of manipulation. Bureaucracies function by demanding that individual workers act only in accord with the designated tasks and responsibilities of their specific role. In fact, the authority of a given bureaucrat rests on the very fact that he or she "doesn't make the rules." The very fact that everyone has a superior all the way up the food chain is what legitimates authority at each rung. That is, of course, one of the

SPECIALIZATION

the process of breaking up work into specific, delimited tasks.

TAYLORISM

the methods of labor management, introduced by Frederick Winslow Taylor to streamline the processes of mass production, in which each worker repeatedly performs one specific task.

People wait at a California Department of Motor Vehicles office to register for a driver's license. What makes the DMV a bureaucracy?

MERITOCRACY

a society where status and mobility are based on individual attributes, ability, and achievement.

dangers of bureaucracy: the lack of personal responsibility for one's moral decisions within the framework of the organization (think of Germany's Third Reich, for instance, and the now infamous Nuremberg defense, "I was only following orders").

This also means that workers' individual quirks, personality traits, and even human empathy are relatively unimportant to their functioning within a role. Likewise, promotions to higher levels within an idealized bureaucratic hierarchy are based on achievement, not personal attributes or favoritism, thus making a bureaucracy a meritocracy. Bureaucracies are also (in theory) highly efficient. The application of practical, specialized knowledge to specific goals is a trademark of bureaucratic administration.

Of course, there is no "perfect" bureaucracy. Indeed, crying in front of the registrar may have worked, because inherent to organizations are rules to allow for exceptions to rules. So, if the registrar was a savvy and empathetic bureaucrat, she might have thought up a solution that entailed enrolling you in independent study with that same professor with the exact same course requirements. Officially, the rule about enrollment limits would have been respected, yet you could have gotten what you need, the registrar could have gotten you out of her office, and the entire legal-rational structure would not have collapsed into anarchy. Likewise, though nepotism—the favoring of relatives, especially in the allocation of jobs—is anathema to bureaucracy (and, in many cases, illegal), we have seen US presidents time and again put relatives in power. John F. Kennedy appointed his brother attorney general. Likewise, Donald Trump has given his daughter and son-in-law official positions in the White House, a fact that has troubled many observers.

Weber once said that bureaucracy was the "iron cage" of modern life. (How must Rita Johnson have felt, being alive and well but trapped by the red tape of a state bureaucracy that had categorized her as deceased?) He criticized bureaucratic administration and its effects on individuals and modern society. Weber (1946) complained about specialization, hierarchy, and meritocracy, as the world becomes "filled with nothing but those little cogs, little men clinging to little jobs and striving toward bigger ones." He referred to bureaucracy as the "parceling-out of the soul," an allusion to its specialization and bloodless efficiency. He also believed that bureaucracy was an unstoppable, totalizing machine becoming ubiquitous in the modern world—even infecting the human soul.

Obedience to Authority

What is nepotism, and why is it a problem for bureaucracies?

Earlier in the chapter, did you turn to the end of the book when instructed to do so? Why? You probably decided to obey my command because, as the author of a sociology textbook and as a college professor, I have some degree of authority. But why, although we've never met and you haven't experienced my magnetic charismatic appeal, did you obediently flip through a few hundred pages to find the correct page? The following case study shows that obedience to authority is an extraordinarily powerful mechanism of social control, capable of making perfectly rational people do otherwise unthinkable things. (Recall our discussion of social control in Chapter 6.)

THE MILGRAM EXPERIMENT

In 1961, Stanley Milgram, a psychologist at Yale University (whose work on social networks we examined in Chapter 5), devised a test, the so-called Milgram experiment, to see how far ordinary people would go to obey an authority figure. The experiment's participants, men of various backgrounds, were told that the experiment sought to test the effects of punishment on learning. As the "teacher," each participant was asked to administer an electric shock to a "learner" in another room when the learner gave an incorrect answer in a word-pairing exercise. With each wrong answer, the teacher was instructed to administer a higher-voltage electric shock to the learner. Unknown to the research subjects was the fact that the learner was not actually receiving electric shocks but was an actor employed by Milgram.

MILGRAM EXPERIMENT

an experiment devised in 1961 by Stanley Milgram, a psychologist at Yale University, to see how far ordinary people would go to obey an authority figure.

Scenes from the Milgram experiment. What does the experiment tell us about authority?

At the beginning of the experiment, the actor would set up a tape recorder with prerecorded sounds for each level of electrical shock. After an established number of wrong answers, the experiment's participants would hear the actor crying out in pain, begging the teacher to abort the test, and complaining of a serious heart condition. If the research subject expressed apprehension or refused to continue the experiment, Milgram's research team would issue a series of verbal prods, ordering him to continue. For example, the first time a participant hesitated, the researcher would say, "Please continue." After a second hesitation, the researcher would say, "It is essential that you continue." After a third hesitation, the researcher would urge, "You have no choice, you must continue." The white-coated member of the experimental team would assure the subject that the researcher would bear all responsibility. Many of the experiment's participants burst into fits of nervous laughter, expressed displeasure and anxiety, and threatened to stop the experiment. With the prodding of the Yale researchers, however, 65 percent of the research subjects went on shocking the learner to the highest voltage level, labeled "lethal."

Before the experiment, Milgram had asked a group of psychologists to estimate the percentage of research participants who would continue shocking an obviously distressed person to the maximum voltage level. The psychologists estimated that fewer than 10 percent would continue all the way up the voltage ladder. This experiment shed some light on how normal people could be complicit in war crimes like the Holocaust.

Authority, Legitimacy, and the State

POWER

the ability to carry out one's own will despite resistance.

Authority is key to our understanding of statehood; but before we define a state, we first have to talk about power. According to Weber's *Economy and Society* (1968), a social actor has power if he or she is able to "carry out his own will *despite resistance*." For instance, if you were a particularly difficult child and resisted your parents' attempt to impose a bedtime, but your resistance was futile, your parents had power. If over a cacophony of congressional support, the president vetoes a bill, the president has power. This definition of power may seem very simple and straightforward, but it is hard to pin down, because power may be based on "all conceivable qualities of a person and all conceivable combinations of circumstances" (1968), such as the power of personal persuasion through rhetorical argument or the power of love. Weber, however, gives us some tools to describe certain types of social power.

Domination is a "special case of power." Weber defines it as the "probability that a command with a given specific content will be obeyed by a given group of persons." There are two types of domination: domination by economic power and domination by authority. Domination by economic power, as defined by Weber (1968), is control "by virtue of a constellation of interests" or "by virtue of a position of monopoly." John D. Rockefeller's Standard Oil is an excellent example of domination by economic power: Until it was dissolved by the government in 1911 for violation of antitrust laws, the company was in a position to issue commands and dictate the price of oil to oil producers by virtue of its monopoly on oil refining. If the oil producers didn't like it, they were out of luck because Standard Oil was their only customer.

Domination by authority refers to a situation in which the will of the ruler influences the conduct of the ruled so they act as if the ruler's will were also their own (Weber, 1968). In other words, it is the willing obedience of the ruled to the commands of legitimate authority. Your deference to your parents and professors and your obedience to the laws of the US government are examples of domination by authority. Even though Weber acknowledges that domination by economic power is more common, he uses the term *domination* to refer only to domination by authority, of which the state is the ultimate example.

In "Politics as a Vocation" (a 1919 lecture at Munich University), Weber issued one of the most succinct and oft-cited (though contested) definitions of the state: A state, he wrote, is "a human community that (successfully) claims the *monopoly of the legitimate use of physical force* within a given territory" (2004). What exactly does this statement mean? It means that hidden under any form of domination by authority—and, by extension, any state—is the threat of violence. A perfect illustration of Weber's claim is the film *The Godfather*. The Corleone family works in a manner analogous to a state: Its members kowtow before Don Corleone because they know that if they don't do what is asked of them, they'll disappear permanently. Don Corleone doesn't have to make threats to back up his orders; rather, it is implicit that there will be consequences if his orders are not followed and that he has the power to exact physical punishment if he is crossed. (However, he is not a one-man state, as he does not quite have a monopoly on the use of physical force and it is not seen as legitimate by many.)

DOMINATION

the probability that a command with specific content will be obeyed by a given group of people.

STATE

as defined by Max Weber, "a human community that (successfully) claims the *monopoly of the legitimate use of physical force* within a given territory."

Using Weber's terminology, we would say that Don Corleone wields authority over the Corleone crime family: the ability to convince others to do as he wishes without resorting to coercion (i.e., forcing them to). Just the implicit threat of physical force suffices. But what happens if one of the Corleones demands something—money, for example—from someone who isn't in the family and thus is not fully aware of Don Corleone's authority? He will likely resort to coercion, the use of force to get these outsiders to do what he wants. In the quaint parlance of another notorious crime family, the Sopranos, you can either "play nice" or get whacked. It is in the direct use of such threats that coercion differs from authority, in which the physical ability to back up one's power is *implicitly* understood.

Within this difference lies the paradox of authority. Even though the state's (or Tony Soprano's) authority derives from the implicit threat of physical force, as soon as the state resorts to physical coercion, all its legitimate authority is lost. In other words, having to resort to violence is proof that people are not listening to you. The annals of world history corroborate Weber's theory. Take, for example, a tragic case from America's past. On May 4, 1970, a group of unarmed students at Kent State University in Ohio assembled peacefully to protest the Vietnam War. After unsuccessfully trying to disperse the crowd of protesters with tear gas, the National Guard fired at the students, killing four (two of whom were not even protesting) and wounding nine. Even though the state has a monopoly on the legitimate use of force, because it actually used that force (illegitimately, in the eyes of many), the incident sparked massive student protests across the country along with countless public debates and lawsuits, with citizens calling the government's authority into question. The state was forced to respond to the crisis. President Richard Nixon, in an effort to save the face of state authority, invited some of the Kent State students to the White House. The shootings are still sometimes referred to as the "Kent State massacre."

Likewise, though police violence against Black men in particular has long been an issue, it was the starkly naked depiction of that violence in the killing of George Floyd in Minneapolis, Minnesota, that represented the final crack in the legitimate authority for many—leading to the most massive, nationwide protests since the days of Kent State and for calls to "defund"

↑

What makes Don Corleone, Marlon Brando's character in *The Godfather*, an example of a leader who dominates by authority?

COERCION

the use of force to get others to do what you want.

PARADOX OF AUTHORITY

although the state's authority derives from the implicit threat of physical force, resorting to physical coercion strips the state of all legitimate authority.

the police. As with Kent State, the reaction to the Floyd case did not come out of nowhere. The legitimacy of municipal police's use of force had been an issue for years. For example, though not the first group to protest police violence against minority communities, the Black Lives Matter movement has been around since 2013. If it were not for a number of well-known cases that eroded the authority of city police forces (and the Minneapolis police in particular), the Floyd case might not have generated the seismic reaction that it did. The question remains whether the delegitimization of some police forces spills over into a loss of authority for the government as a whole.

THE INTERNATIONAL SYSTEM OF STATES

Weber takes it for granted that all functional states exercise a monopoly on the legitimate use of force within a given territory. But many fragile states do not or have not exercised such a monopoly in recent times. In these countries, rebel or insurrectionist groups are in constant armed conflict with their respective governments. For instance, during much of the Syrian civil war, vast swaths of its territory were controlled by the Islamic State, a radical militant group that had proclaimed itself as a legitimate government. At its peak the Islamic State, which was unrecognized by other countries because of its terrorist activity, held large tracts of territory in Iraq and Syria, though the Syrian government based in the capital city of Damascus has reasserted control over most of its territory. Such a disintegration of a monopoly can even affect relations with other states. For example, in July 2006, Hezbollah,

Mary Ann Vecchio kneels by the body of fellow student Jeffrey Miller during the May 4, 1970, antiwar demonstration at Kent State University. How does the Kent State massacre illustrate the paradox of authority?

THE CASE OF SOMALILAND

One afternoon in the summer of 2005, I was sitting in an office in Addis Ababa waiting to meet with the prime minister of Ethiopia, Meles Zenawi, as part of a UN delegation. Our meeting concerned the implementation of the UN Millennium Development Goals. While in the waiting room, I began chatting with a woman who was also waiting for a meeting with Prime Minister Zenawi. She introduced herself as the foreign minister of Somaliland. I had thought that I was pretty well versed in African geography by that point and recalled Somaliland only as the archaic, colonial name of present-day Somalia. "Excuse me?" I asked. "Don't you mean Somalia?" She handed me a pamphlet, explaining that she represented the government of Somaliland, a breakaway province in the north, bordering southern Ethiopia and Djibouti (a small port city-state).

Then it all made sense: I had never heard of Somaliland because it was literally not on the map—that is, although it declared independence from Somalia in 1991, it was not recognized by any other nation and therefore did not exist in the international system of nation-states. (It still doesn't.) The people were, no doubt, working hard to gain recognition; hence the foreign minister's visit to Ethiopia, the picture of their flag, and so on. But until they are recognized by other states and international institutions such as the UN, Somaliland remains merely a "self-proclaimed" nation-state.

What was most ironic, I later learned, was that at that time only Somaliland, the northernmost of

the three regions of Somalia, had a functional internal system of government in which a single entity had a monopoly over the legitimate use of force. In Mogadishu—the ostensible capital of all Somalia—violence was rampant, and people had to bribe warlords merely to survive. There was no legitimacy and no functional state, but in the international system, this nonstate supposedly covered the entire geographic territory of Somalia, including the area that Somaliland claimed as its own. Mogadishu today is still a violent city, but the previous president of Somalia, Sheikh Sharif Sheikh Ahmed, was recognized by the Obama administration (along with neighboring countries Uganda and Burundi and the rest of the African Union) as the legitimate ruler of Somalia even

A market in Somaliland. What role does the international system play in legitimizing state authority?

though the Bush administration was at one point contemplating what steps could be taken to rid Somalia of Sheikh Sharif because he was thought to be allied with al-Qaida (Anderon, 2009).

But back in 2005, the foreign minister of Somaliland was still hopeful that her visit might persuade her western neighbor to recognize her administration as the legitimate authority in Somalia. Somaliland did not gain independence or legitimate rule, but is relatively calm compared with the southern portion of Somalia, where the moderate government of Sheikh Sharif was fighting the Islamist militant group Shabab, which now controls the area. Within the international community, an unwritten rule exists that neighboring states must first recognize a new state's autonomy before more distant ones will do so. This convention is guided by the assumption that abutting nations are the most likely to be affected by the political upheaval caused by the emergence of a new state. For Somaliland, Ethiopia remains key, because its recognition of the new government could influence other countries to follow suit. In the case of Somalia, recognition of Sheikh Sharif's legitimacy by the African Union as well as Western states like the United States means not only legitimacy on paper and in diplomatic circles but also a reliable supply of arms and military power. The African Union stationed thousands of troops in Mogadishu; the United States sent 40 tons of arms.

Perhaps Weber focused too much on the internal workings of the state apparatus, to the neglect of external forces. For a state to have the critical monopoly on legitimate violence, it must have the consent of not only those within its territory but also important external actors. After all, what good is legitimacy among the Somalilanders if foreign tanks are going to roll in and flatten the entire region? Although it might make more sense to start from scratch and redraw the entire political map of Africa (not to mention the Middle East) with better

Berbera Point, Somaliland.

motives at heart than when it was originally divided (Gambia, for example, was created in the middle of Senegal just to preserve an English route up the Gambia River), the inertia of the international state system prevents that from occurring. Competition over natural resources, different postcolonial interests, people of the same ethnicity in neighboring countries, and religious and ideological divisions all make it difficult to rationalize and correct territorial errors made in the past. In other words, political boundaries create stakes and interests, and once boundaries are in place, they take on a logic and force of their own.

an Islamist rebel group and political party in Lebanon (and a group that played a large role in the Syrian war), began an armed conflict with the neighboring state of Israel without the sanction of the "official" Lebanese government. Hezbollah's military conflicts with Israel and territorial claims within southern Lebanon led the Lebanese prime minister to describe the rebel group as a "state within a state."

Hezbollah, by its use of military might against Israel, challenges Weber's definition of statehood. If a state by definition maintains a monopoly on the (legitimate) use of force within a territory, how do we reconcile the cases in which local authorities clearly do not exercise the requisite monopolies? The answer forces us to reach beyond Weber's terse formulation for an alternative, broader account of statehood.

Weber, being a German political theorist who lived in the late nineteenth and early twentieth centuries, no doubt had past and present European states in mind and used these states as templates for his conception of statehood. But the history of Europe is not the same as the history of the African and Asian continents. In fact, there are important differences in the historical trajectories of these continents, which Weber may have discounted or just plain missed. European states developed in a long series of fights over territorial boundaries, such as the Austro-Prussian War of 1866 and the Balkan Wars of 1912–13. European states came to exercise territorial monopolies on the use of force through a long history of conflict that coalesced into the borders we recognize today.

After all the war and other violence, the current European countries emerged as bona fide states (with striking exceptions, such as the republics of the former Soviet Union and the former Yugoslavia). The relations among

INTERNATIONAL STATE SYSTEM

a system in which each state is recognized as territorially sovereign by fellow states.

these European states led to the development of the international state system, through which each state is recognized as territorially sovereign by fellow states. Each state tacitly agrees to mind its own business when it comes to the internal affairs of other sovereign countries as long as borders are respected (and human rights atrocities are not being committed). This is the principle of noninterference. (Again, there are notable exceptions to this agreement, such as the Bush administration's doctrine of preemptive war that was put into practice during the invasion of Iraq in 2003.)

Africa is likewise composed of territorially sovereign states. These states, however, are not necessarily the products of centuries of bloody internal land disputes, as in Europe, but instead are the products of the international state system and legitimating institutions such as the United Nations (UN), which have transformed the very definition of statehood. Africa also has a history of European colonialism—the story of outside invaders controlling the lands and people of the African continent. After gaining independence from their European colonizers, each of these African states became a full-fledged member of the international system of states with all the attendant rights and obligations of participating in the system. However, their borders

Fighters for the Islamic State, a radical militant group that has proclaimed itself a legitimate government, perform a military parade in Syria, 2014. Is the Islamic State an example of a territorially sovereign state?

were often set up by European colonial powers that were in a proxy struggle with each other on the African continent. These borders often ignored local context. For example, many African nations contain multiple ancestral populations (i.e., nations), while other borders arbitrarily split up an ethnic group. These states, meanwhile, had no guarantee of a monopoly on force within their territory because they often had been arbitrarily produced through the international system of states without ever really satisfying Weber's fundamental criterion of statehood. Sudan, Lebanon, Congo, and Sierra Leone are all states—if only because once an institution is set up, it has its own force of inertia. For example, once oil-rich southern Nigeria was connected to oil-poor northern Nigeria, it was certainly in the interests of the northern Nigerians to maintain the integrity of the nation-state, even if the religious and ethnic makeups of the two regions vary greatly. Likewise, even without such stark divisions, it is in the interests of political elites to control as much territory as possible. That said, the violent civil wars in places such as Iraq or Somalia today do not necessarily reflect a process similar to the one that largely occurred in Europe centuries ago. That's because they did not just erupt internally but have been stoked by repeated foreign intervention by European powers and the United States.

NEW STATE FUNCTIONS: THE WELFARE STATE

The state's role in developing social policies—policies developed to meet social needs—has prompted scholars to reconsider the definition of statehood. After the period of rapid industrialization that began in the late eighteenth century and culminated in the beginning of the twentieth century, many states began adopting variants of social insurance and pension programs such as disability, old age, and unemployment benefits (Skocpol & Amenta, 1986). The growth in these types of benefits continued in most advanced industrial nations throughout the twentieth century, especially following World War II, buffered by the logic of Keynesian economics. (John Maynard Keynes, a prominent British economist, postulated that government intervention in the form of social expenditures could pull the economy out of a recession by stimulating demand for products and services.) Perhaps, then, starting with the postwar years, it is more accurate to think of states as "organizations that extract resources through taxation *and* attempt to extend coercive control and political authority over particular territories and the people residing in them" (Skocpol & Amenta, 1986). Notice that this definition still includes a reference to coercion and political authority (i.e., Weber's monopoly on legitimate force), but now states are concerned with another function—social provisions—and may rightly be called welfare states. A welfare state is a system in which the state is responsible for the well-being of its citizens. In practice, this usually entails providing a number of key necessities, such as food, health care, and housing, outside the economic marketplace. (See Chapter 10 for more on welfare and the welfare state in the realm of health care.)

Why and how did the welfare state develop? One theory, sometimes called the logic of industrialism thesis, holds that nations develop social welfare benefits to satisfy the social needs created by industrialization. In this view, the state intervenes to take care of people who are not needed in the labor market: children, people with disabilities, and the elderly. Simply, "economic growth is the ultimate cause of welfare state development" (Wilensky, 1974). When a society's members all work constantly just to feed themselves, there is little surplus to serve as insurance or as alms for unproductive citizens. However, once a given community has some surplus, it can afford to insure against downturns and to take care of the sick, elderly, and people with disabilities. Social Security, for example, helps meet the needs of aging citizens who no longer work. Because modern industry generally doesn't depend on the labor of senior citizens, the state intervenes to help make sure these retirees have enough money for food, clothing, and shelter.

A second view of the development of the welfare state, called neo-Marxist theory, starts with the question of how democracy and capitalism can coexist. This theory is concerned with explaining the contradictions between formal legal equality and social class inequality. Specifically, when private property is held by a small section of the population, the democratic impulse (i.e., the wishes of the masses) might be to confiscate that property.

WELFARE STATE

a system in which the state is responsible for the well-being of its citizens.

Workers from the Tennessee Valley Authority (TVA) install a turbine housing at the Cherokee Dam in Jefferson City, Tennessee. Why did economist John Maynard Keynes and President Franklin D. Roosevelt initiate New Deal projects like the TVA during the 1930s?

To resolve this tension and maintain private property rights, the welfare state emerges. In this manner, the welfare state is seen as the mediator of class conflict, "granting concessions to both capitalists and workers" (Quadagno, 1987) to ensure the long-term health of society. To serve the interests of the rich owners of the means of production, the welfare state "buys off" the workers by providing necessities and a degree of economic security. For example, many Marxist scholars have pointed to the New Deal as an example of the state acting as a class mediator. During the New Deal, industry was forced to grant concessions to labor—shorter working hours, better working conditions, and union recognition, for instance—in order to maintain existing class relationships (i.e., to avoid a more radical revolution during the Great Depression that might have led to the abolition of private property through Communism).

Third, state-centered approaches emphasize the role of state bureaucrats in formulating welfare state policies. Statist theories tie the development of the welfare state not to economic or political factors but to government bureaucrats who design policies based on perceived social conditions, because bringing home the pork enhances their power in society. Theda Skocpol and Edwin Amenta (1986), two prominent exponents of the state-centered approach, argue that in some cases, the state may act autonomously to formulate social policy—meaning that state bureaucrats are solely or primarily responsible for creating or modifying social policy.

CITIZENSHIP RIGHTS

the rights guaranteed to each law-abiding citizen in a nation-state.

CIVIL RIGHTS

the rights guaranteeing a citizen's personal freedom from interference, including freedom of speech and the right to travel freely.

POLITICAL RIGHTS

the rights guaranteeing a citizen's ability to participate in politics, including the right to vote and the right to hold an elected office.

President Bill Clinton signs welfare reform legislation in 1996.

For example, consider how a city might go about constructing housing units for low-income families. Assuming that the city council has already allocated funds to the project, control of the project would then probably be transferred to city planners for implementation. The city planners, as state bureaucrats fairly insulated from the whims of politicians or economic elites, run the project by designing the housing units, choosing their location, and rationing the project's budget. State bureaucrats may also play a role in drafting the budgets for other projects, providing further social policy recommendations and influencing the outcomes of policy proposals.

A fourth strand in studies of the welfare state concerns the types of social provisions offered by the state and to whom these provisions are granted. Specifically, what is a citizen's relationship to the state? The people living within a state, excluding noncitizens and felons, have certain rights called citizenship rights. Sociologist T. H. Marshall has defined three broad types of citizenship rights: civil rights, political rights, and social rights. Civil rights guarantee a citizen's personal freedom from interference, including freedom of speech and the right to travel freely. Political rights guarantee a citizen's rights to participate in politics, including the right to vote and the right to hold an elected office. And social rights guarantee a citizen's protection by the state, including "protection from the free market in the areas of housing, employment, health, and education" (Hasenfeld et al., 1987). Marshall recognized that an inherent contradiction exists between civil rights, which guarantee freedom from state interference, and social rights, which make it the state's responsibility to interfere in the lives of citizens.

Social rights to public assistance may be of two broad types. The first type is the right to contributory programs, such as Social Security benefits in the United States. To be eligible for these programs, "citizens earn their rights through tax contributions" (Hasenfeld et al., 1987). Rights to means-tested programs, such as Temporary Assistance for Needy Families and food stamps, are contingent on proof of insufficient financial resources. Rights to means-tested programs are subject to changes in how states define the concept of the "deserving poor." For example, in

1996, President Bill Clinton signed the Personal Responsibility and Work Opportunity Reconciliation Act, which drastically shortened the maximum allowable time during which citizens could claim welfare benefits and introduced multiple compliance requirements, such as mandatory employment searches and job training (see Chapter 10). Because of these changes, the "deserving poor" no longer included those who weren't disabled yet were chronically unemployed.

Radical Power and Persuasion

Recall that Weber defined power as an actor's capacity to "carry out his own will *despite resistance*." Thus Weber implies that where there is power, there must be resistance. But why should that be the case? Are we to believe that whenever and wherever power is at work, it presupposes (or elicits) resistance? Steven Lukes asks a similar question in *Power: A Radical View* (2005) and suggests that power may be "at its most effective when least observable"; in such a situation, it may not generate resistance at all.

Lukes describes power as three-dimensional. The first dimension of power is visible when different agendas clash, conflict results, and one side prevails. For example, when you were a child and your parents insisted that you go to bed, you may have thrown temper tantrums, perhaps threatening to run away if they didn't allow you to watch more television. Your parents wanted you to go to bed because they preferred that you get a good night's rest. Your preference was for more television and less parental involvement. Your divergent preferences generated a conflict—perhaps in the form of shouting and a resultant spanking or time-out.

The second dimension of power is more complicated and occurs when the power is so formidable that no conflict results from competing interests because one side is convinced it's a losing battle. Let's say that one night, instead of throwing a temper tantrum before being put to bed, you went to bed without a fight. Once you were tucked in with the lights turned out and your parents were safely back in the living room, you hurled your stuffed bear at your bedroom door in protest. You and your parents still had divergent preferences, but in this scenario you didn't bother to throw a temper tantrum because you knew your parents would ultimately make the decision to put you to bed.

Lukes's novel contribution to the study of power is what he calls power's third dimension. It is the power not only to persevere despite overt or veiled resistance but to "prevent such conflict from arising in the first place."

Conflict may be averted through "influencing, shaping, or determining" desires, wants, and preferences. In this scenario, still using our bedtime example, not only do you go to bed when your parents want you to and refrain from abusing any stuffed animals, but you actively want to go to bed at the appointed hour. Why? Lukes would say that your parents have manipulated your preferences. You don't fight with them at bedtime because you now believe that going to bed early is what *you* want to do.

Obviously, Lukes isn't talking about parents' power over children's bedtimes when he writes about three-dimensional power. His concern is with larger social groups, specifically with how "potential issues are kept out of politics" through means that do not generate conflict because they shape the desires of social actors. These desires may be shaped by familiar social forces such as processes of socialization (see Chapter 4) or by means of information control through the mass media (see Chapter 3).

One way to wield invisible power is by shaping the choice set. My sister, a staunch opponent of capital punishment, related a story dating back to the time period when she resided in Arizona, a state that had used capital punishment for as long as she had lived there. One year an initiative to switch from electrocution to lethal injection as the method of execution appeared on the election ballot. She was conflicted about how to vote. She departed from the voting booth troubled by the very choice she had faced. Why couldn't there be a referendum on execution itself? The answer lies in the fact that the choices had already been established by political actors. At that time in Arizona, if capital punishment itself had appeared on the ballot, it probably would have survived. But the power to frame the terms of the debate is one of the most important and invisible forms of power.

One reason that our choices are constrained is that it is impossible to decide among all alternatives at any given time. Even in democracies, choices tend to come down to yes-or-no, left-or-right votes. When more than two choices are offered, results can often become indeterminate and suboptimal for all. The economist Kenneth Arrow won the Nobel Prize for proving this "impossibility theorem," which states that there is no system of voting that will consistently yield the top choice of the most voters when there are more than two alternatives. It turns out that when faced with more than two options, no foolproof way of voting exists that is resistant to strategic voting (voters not voting in line with their underlying preferences in order to effect a desired outcome). Let's say you and your friends are trying to decide which movie to see. If there were only two movie screens, then you could just vote as a group. But imagine that a triplex comes to town. You would like to see *Get Out*, but only slightly more than *Black Panther*, which seems somewhat popular with the rest of the group. What you really want to avoid is seeing *La La Land*, and you know that many of your friends do want to see that movie. So instead of voting for *Get Out*, you vote for *Black Panther* in the hope of defeating *La La*

Land. Black Panther could win in the end, even if it wasn't anyone's first choice. There are many ways to narrow down choices, but none of them guarantees that the will of the majority rules, so the importance of power lies in its ability to narrow the choice set and socialize desires, thereby generating consent. What's most unsettling about the entire process is that such a reduction of choices seems to be unavoidable to keep things moving along.

In a real-world example, John Gaventa, in *Power and Powerlessness* (1980), describes his investigation of the synergistic effects of power's three dimensions on the lives of coal miners in the Clear Fork Valley in central Appalachia. Many of the community's miners were desperately poor, working in unsafe mines and living in dilapidated company housing. Between 1960 and 1970, 34 percent of the area's residents lived without piped water and 60 percent did not have flush toilets. The workers often suffered from black lung disease and were left with "gnarled limbs from accidents." The coal company owned the miners' homes, controlled the local stores, and even monopolized health services. The company deducted "rent, services, goods purchased at the store, medical bills, even funeral expenses" directly from miners' wages, with the result that "misbehavior in the job could cause the loss of a home; failure to shop at the company store (where prices were often higher) could mean the loss of work; disobedience of a single rule could mean eviction from the game altogether."

Given such dire conditions, the miners might be expected to revolt, or at least strike, against the all-powerful mining corporation. But in a quintessential example of how the manipulation of needs, desires, and aspirations may cut against the apparently objective interests of social actors, the

A shanty in Clear Fork, Tennessee, that coal miner Carl Miller, his wife, and their seven children called home in 1963.

workers were prone to express loyalty, even affection, for their employers. Gaventa found that through the interrelated effects of power's three dimensions, conflict was squelched as preferences and desires were shaped through the local newspaper and other information outlets, as well as the education of the miners' children in the company-run school. On the other hand, we cannot know for sure that the miners and their families were not just acting rationally in a cold-eyed assessment of their objective alternatives. That is, they may have known that the mining corporation was manipulating them, but judged working there the best available option and thought little of their ability to alter the situation. There is no alternate social universe where we can see what would have happened if they had enjoyed other sources of information (i.e., an independent press) and had, in turn, engaged in mass revolt. The best we can do as social scientists is to find another similar community—perhaps one with an independent newspaper and school system—that pursued a different path and see if the workers there revolted, and if they were, indeed, better off in the end.

POWER AND INTERNATIONAL RELATIONS

Other recent work on power has focused on international relations. Relations between states differ in important ways from relations within states. Does the paradox of state authority, in which a state's legitimate authority is contingent on not using force to secure obedience, hold true when one state is trying to influence the behavior of another state? Traditionally, scholars have highlighted the importance of "hard power," or the use of military or economic force to influence behavior, in international politics. During World War II the Allied Powers used military force (a lot of it) to influence the behavior of Germany, Japan, and Italy. The United States chose a similar strategy in 2003, when it attempted to exact political change in Iraq by overthrowing Saddam Hussein's Baathist regime and trying to squelch the resulting insurgency. In the international arena, where states struggle to influence other state actors, coercive power seems to be the rule instead of the exception.

Joseph Nye, a scholar at Harvard's Kennedy School of Government (as well as a former assistant secretary of defense), has proposed that the exclusive use of hard power in international politics is out-of-date. For one thing, states are now increasingly economically dependent on one another thanks to globalization, and this means that the use of force to influence the behavior of other states has become more costly. In 1945, we dropped an atomic bomb on the Japanese cities of Hiroshima and Nagasaki. Today Japan is consistently one of our top trading partners (not to mention the exporter of cultural products such as anime and manga). If the United States opted to use force against Japan to influence its decisions or internal politics, it would risk losing valuable import and export markets.

Instead, Nye is a proponent of what he calls soft power. Soft or co-optive power is "getting others to want what you want" through "attraction rather than coercion or payments" (Ichihara, 2006; Nye, 1990). The idea behind soft power is similar to that behind Weber's concept of legitimate authority: Cultural myths or legitimizations can help persuade people (or entire nations) to obey. Nye hypothesizes that "if a state can make its power seem legitimate in the eyes of others, it will encounter less resistance to its wishes." So, for example, Hollywood movies might be an important soft power resource for America, just as anime is an important soft power resource for Japan. Hollywood films are often popular abroad simply because they're extravagant and entertaining, but at the same time they can be vehicles for some of the United States' favorite ideologies, such as free trade or democratic political institutions. In either case, attraction is used to influence external state actors.

Take the Middle East as a case study in hard versus soft power. Citizens of Gaza use smugglers to bring Kentucky Fried Chicken (KFC) through a tunnel from the closest franchise in Egypt (DPA, 2013). This desire for greasy American fast food is a perfect example of Nye's concept of soft power. It is not culinary excellence that attracts Gazans to KFC, but the attractiveness of the wider American culture it embodies. Following the US invasion of Iraq, sales of Coca-Cola, Whoppers, and Big Macs decreased, but they are now recovering.

Violent urban warfare during World War II (left) is an example of a hard power strategy. The cultural influence of soft power resources is seen in a billboard advertising Kentucky Fried Chicken in Damascus (right). How are these approaches different? Which is more effective?

SOFT POWER

power attained through the use of cultural attractiveness rather than the threat of coercive action (hard power).

DICTATORSHIP OR DEMOCRACY? STATES OF NATURE AND SOCIAL CONTRACTS

What are the origins of the state, and how have those origins shaped the types of government we have? In *Leviathan* (1981), Thomas Hobbes suggests that in the absence of an agreed-on authority figure (a state), life would

The 1651 frontispiece of Thomas Hobbes's *Leviathan*.

be hideously chaotic and violent. The natural state of humanity is not peaceful; rather, individuals would seek to better themselves at the expense of all others. Every person would be an enemy to all other persons—it would be a war of all against all, to use Hobbes's phrasing. To achieve peace and avoid death, humans enter into a social contract and submit to an overarching sovereign authority (the "leviathan," or sea monster) charged with ensuring peace by threatening death for deviant behavior. This leviathan is not an external force that comes in to quell the war of all against all and to exact obedience, but a force composed of and created by the citizens themselves.

John Locke thought Hobbes was slightly off the mark. In his *Second Treatise of Government* (1980), Locke says that before the emergence of a sovereign authority, individuals lived in a happy, conflict-free state of nature as equals. Each person had the executive power to punish offenses committed by wayward individuals (see the discussion of informal social norms in Chapter 6). Locke believed that the sovereign state emerged not because life without it was a disaster but because individuals needed help adjudicating discord and, in particular, conflicts over personal property. For Locke, then, submitting to a centralized authority was not a matter of life or death but a matter of money.

Although they have some common features (namely, the idea of the state arising out of the self-interests of the citizenry), the two theories have different implications for social life and the role of the state. According to Hobbes, we need a strong, central authority in order to live in peace and harmony with our neighbors. Human interaction is, by nature, rife with conflict and fear. According to Locke, the state of nature is primarily peaceful, as natural law regulates interpersonal relations without the interference of a cumbersome sovereign authority. The two conceptions of what it means to be in a state of nature dictate the proper and rightful functions of the sovereign authority. They may, in fact, help us understand the origins of democracy and dictatorship.

In the world today, some states are organized as a democracy, a system of government wherein power theoretically lies with the people, and therefore citizens are allowed to vote in elections, speak freely, and participate as legal equals in social life. Other states are a dictatorship, a form of government that restricts the right to political participation to a small group or even to a single individual. Such states may limit suffrage, censor information to the public, and arrange the brutal "disappearances" of non-submissive subordinates. To Weber, the differences between democracy and dictatorship are irrelevant to statehood; bona fide states and forms of domination differ only by the types of ideas the regimes produce about their own legitimacy. They are merely different breeds of the same underlying animal.

Resisting Weber, however, many scholars have tried to explain why some states end up as democracies and others become dictatorships. Barrington Moore's classic *Social Origins of Dictatorship and Democracy* (1993) sets out to answer this question by investigating the history of several nations, including France, Great Britain, Japan, the United States, China, and India. Moore hypothesizes that the fate of each nation is determined by the struggle between social classes. Specifically, for democracy to emerge, the bourgeoisie (those who own businesses) must be strong enough to attenuate the control of the landowning feudal lords. If the bourgeoisie, in the form of traders and merchants, is strong enough, a revolution takes place. The bourgeois revolution "attacks obstacles to a democratic version of capitalism that have been inherited from the past" (Moore, 1993). Moore thus believes that the emergence of modern capitalism is important to the development of political democracy.

The economists Daron Acemoglu and James Robinson update Moore's thesis in their similarly titled book *Economic Origins of Dictatorship and Democracy* (2006). Like Moore, they build a model explaining the variations in forms of government. They ask the same kind of questions (Why are some states more democratic than others, and how did they get that way?) but produce a different answer using game theory, the study of the decisions actors make in situations where there is uncertainty and where their success depends on the strategies of others. A game can be any situation where the outcome for one or more actors depends on the choices of another actor or actors.

Have you ever tried to guess when the bathroom will be free for your morning shower? Your decision to get up at 8:00 or 8:15 A.M. depends on the information you have about the actions of your roommates. If you wake up at 8:00, you lose 15 minutes of sleep but are fairly confident that your roommates will still be snoring away. If you sleep in until 8:15, you gain 15 minutes of shut-eye but risk losing the bathroom to one of your roommates. Your decision changes based on the anticipated actions of your roommates (the other game players), who may be making the very same calculations. Games can be anything from roommates fighting for control of the bathroom, to chess and checkers, to the maneuverings of state actors.

DICTATORSHIP

a form of government that restricts the right to political participation to a small group or even to a single individual.

GAME THEORY

the study of strategic decisions made under conditions of uncertainty and interdependence.

Acemoglu and Robinson use game theory to understand how some states wind up more democratic than other states. Pretend that each state is the site of an ongoing game between two players: the elite player and the mass citizenship player. The elites are, of course, the rulers, the oppressors, the pillagers of small and unarmed villages. The mass citizenship player is the conglomeration of ordinary people who want, for instance, greater representation within their respective governments and the right to vote on specific social policies. One day, all the ordinary people join together and revolt against the elite. The elites, fearing for their lives and, more pressingly, desiring to protect their privileged social positions, need to respond. Do they give in to the demands of the rabble-rousers?

Consider the possibilities (the "strategies" in game theory talk) of each player. The ordinary people want democratic reforms. They are moderately armed and are threatening to revolt. But they are also aware that they don't have the military resources or time to sustain a revolution forever. The elites, on the other hand, are scared and will say anything to avoid the rebellion and get what they want now, but will promptly (and conveniently) forget what they promised when the crisis has passed. So although the elites will promise democratic concessions when faced with imminent danger to life, limb, and social position, they have no good reason to give the ordinary people what they want after the threat of an uprising has dwindled and life has returned to normal. Thus the ordinary people must find a way to transform "temporary opportunity into permanent advantage," and the elites must make their promises credible.

There are two basic outcomes, or solutions, to the game. The elites may promise to lower the ordinary people's taxes and give each of them a free car. However, in a few years the elites are back to exploiting the poor and oppressed population as tax rates creep up again. Alternatively, if the mass citizenry resists the temptations of a temporary concession, it may use the threat of a revolution to demand change to the political institutions of the state, such as the right to vote or the establishment of a parliament. If the citizens can use their temporary opportunity—their credible threat of revolution—to induce a change in the existing political institutions, then the country is on the path to democratization, according to Acemoglu and Robinson. The ordinary people have used their fleeting advantage to change the underlying distribution of political power. Democracy is just one possible outcome of a strategic game played by competing social groups.

COLLECTIVE ACTION PROBLEM

the difficulty in organizing large groups because of the tendency of some individuals to freeload or slack off.

To play the democratization game and make coherent demands of the elite, however, the ordinary people must first overcome a collective action problem. The theory of collective action, pioneered by Mancur Olson in *The Logic of Collective Action* (1965), asserts that it is more difficult to organize larger groups than smaller ones. (We'll take a closer look at collective action and social movements in Chapter 18.) For example, in most social systems, the ordinary people far outnumber the elite. Let's say that there are 3,000 ordinary people, and all of them agree that the present system of governance is abysmal, and they would like to change it. Here's the catch: A revolution takes work, and every ordinary person wants to reap its benefits but would rather not expend the time, energy, and resources necessary to coordinate it. If 3,000 ordinary people exist in the society, each individual represents only 1/3,000 or 0.033 percent of the total team effort. If each individual reasons that he or she is a very small and insignificant share of the total team effort, and it would be better to conserve precious time, energy, and resources and let someone else do the risky revolutionary work, then the mass of ordinary people is unlikely to come together as a team and secure concessions from the elite faction, especially when the price of failure is high (perhaps beheading) and when resources are few (i.e., most folks are just trying to scrape by and avoid starvation).

Small groups, like the elite players, are much better equipped to get what they want. Let's say the elite faction is composed of five wealthy families. These wealthy families know each other fairly well, not only through business organizations but also by virtue of vacationing in shared destinations like the Alps or perhaps by sending their children to the same elite boarding schools. If five families make up the elite, each family counts as one-fifth or 20 percent of the total team effort. Because the elites have much more to lose through the inaction of just one family, each member reasons that his or her family's effort is very significant to the team's eventual victory and decides to spend the time, energy, and resources on coordinating their efforts. In addition, because all the members of a small group usually know each other, the social consequences of inaction are much greater—they risk being chastised by their associates and friends if they choose not to participate. (Among the ordinary people, each individual is less likely to know the other team members and therefore does not suffer the same social consequences of inaction.)

Sociologist Robb Willer has augmented the finding that small groups are better able to succeed in meeting their coordination goals by looking at collective action from a different angle, the altruism angle. When people share a goal that can be achieved only if everyone participates, doing one's share might be seen as being altruistic—an act that is beneficial to a collective group even if it isn't directly beneficial to the actor—especially if it means you have to give up doing something that would have been beneficial to you. For instance, an altruistic act might be pitching in to fold and distribute pamphlets promoting suicide prevention. Willer describes how context matters when it comes to altruistic behavior: "One of the biggest factors that influences how generously people behave is whether or not the opportunity to gain reputation in the eyes of others is available. People behave much more generously when people are watching, . . . and the trouble with invisible men [when people are unwatched]" is that they "behave much

ALTRUISM

an action that benefits a group but does not directly benefit the individual performing the action.

DIGITAL.WWNORTON.COM/YOUMAYASK7

To see an interview with Robb Willer, go to
digital.wwnorton.com/youmayask7

more selfishly." In other words, "there's sort of two main forces that lead people to behave generously: either self-interest, primarily in the desires for enhanced reputation, or sincere altruistic desires to benefit others" (Conley, 2013f).

When the group is small, especially when the membership contains elites with access to social and reputational capital, there is a higher likelihood that individuals will act altruistically to promote the goals of that group. All the chronic altruists will pitch in, but those whose altruism is tied to building their own reputations will also contribute because their behavior will be noticed (it is hard to hide in a small group) and rewarded (elites have more access to social and cultural resources). In a big group of ordinary people, individuals are more likely to worry that their contributions will go unnoticed and that even if their work is recognized, it will not receive valuable reputational boosts because the group has little social capital in the first place. When "people are vigilantly monitored . . . they're more likely to behave in pro-social ways . . . and support social institutions," so one answer to the collective action problem might be enhanced surveillance, especially by the highest-status members of the group. But this strategy has some problems too.

Robert Michels (1915), in his study of political parties, concluded that even if they win the game and secure democratic governance, all organizations, no matter how democratic in principle, face coordination problems. True democracy means that each citizen is essentially a legislator. However, as the scale of democracy expands, high levels of mass participation become unsustainable. Direct deliberative democracy, like a town hall meeting, is pretty difficult to pull off when the populace grows beyond a few hundred citizens. In large and complex organizations (like a state), the power structure inevitably begins to resemble an oligarchy, a form of government in which power lies with a small group of leaders. Michels called this inevitability "the iron law of oligarchy."

For example, let's say the ordinary people overcome their initial collective action problems, win the right to vote, and organize into a political party. How do you think this political party, which represents thousands of citizens, would be run? The answer, it turns out, takes us back to Weber. Once democracy prevails, simple coordination problems necessitate the creation of a bureaucracy to efficiently manage the political party. As we already know, a bureaucracy has certain immutable characteristics. For one, the decision-making process is both rationalized, meaning it is governed by calculations of efficiency, and routinized, meaning that the same rule-governed procedure is used over and over. A bureaucracy is also structured hierarchically, which guarantees that the ultimate decision-making control is in the hands of a few elites at the top of the pyramid. So much for democratic control of the state. The ordinary people have earned a new relation of domination: life in the iron cage.

WHO RULES IN THE UNITED STATES?

If you have grown up in the United States, by now you have interacted with the state on many levels, starting the day you were born and issued a birth certificate. Bringing our discussion out of the hypothetical and into the real world, where does the United States fit within our newly acquired understanding of collective action and democratic representation? Who rules in the United States?

In the United States, national-level legal authority is split among three branches of government, a system intended to maximize legitimacy by ensuring that each branch is "checked and balanced" by the other two. The executive branch is led by the president, who is also the head of state (meaning the official representative of government to other states). The legislative branch is composed of the House of Representatives and the Senate, which together make up the US Congress. The US Supreme Court and lower federal courts are the judicial branch. Elected officials select members of the judicial branch; the president and all senators and representatives are chosen in regularly held elections. The federal government, to the extent allowed by the US Constitution, takes precedence over state and local governments. That said, the United States is a fairly decentralized (i.e., federalist) state in many respects, and individual states make and enforce many of the laws with which we are familiar.

Knowing who officially makes the decisions, however, may say fairly little about how choices are actually made. For that, we need to understand how officials gain office and which voices are heard once officials assume power. Since the Civil War, American electoral politics have almost always been organized into a two-party system, whereby two political parties have such a monopoly on voters that any other party has a difficult time garnering enough votes to win an election (with some notable exceptions, usually at

POLITICAL PARTY

an organization that seeks to gain power in a government, generally by backing candidates for office who subscribe (to the extent possible) to the organization's political ideals.

the state or local level). A political party is an organization that seeks to gain power in a government, generally by backing candidates for office who subscribe to the organization's ideals. The United States' two major parties, Democratic and Republican, tend to be fairly broad in the scope of interests they represent, although the Democratic Party is traditionally thought of as "left" or liberal, whereas the Republican Party represents the "right" or conservatives. Broadly, the Democrats seek a secular government with a relatively high level of economic and social intervention, and the Republicans seek a smaller, laissez-faire government and the upholding of religious ideals through state regulation of morality. In practice, however, both Democrats and Republicans often hold some combination of the two parties' stereotypical convictions, and many competing ideologies exist within each party.

INTEREST GROUP

an organization that seeks to gain power in government and influence policy without campaigning for direct election or appointment to office.

Political parties are not the only organizations that try to affect policy in support of their goals. An interest group is an organization that seeks to gain power in government without campaigning for direct election or being appointed to office. Rather, such groups use a variety of other paths to influence policy, such as persuading elected officials to advocate for the group's agenda or working through the existing regulatory bureaucracy or the legal system. Examples of interest groups include trade unions representing the workers in particular job categories, corporations lobbying to win a government contract, and single-issue groups seeking to affect a particular policy (such as AIPAC, the American Israel Public Affairs Committee, which seeks to influence US policy toward Israel). Interest groups represent yet another approach to making collective action work for a group of people with similar political goals.

Fordham Law School professor Zephyr Teachout ran for governor of the state of New York in 2014 on a platform opposed not to a specific special interest group, but to an entire system of campaign financing that leads politicians to spend too much time raising money from individual donors, corporations, and interest groups. Is Teachout trying to micromanage politicians' calendars, or is there a deeper problem? In an interview with me she explained:

DIGITAL.WWNORTON.COM/YOUMAYASK7

To see an interview with Zephyr Teachout, go to
digital.wwnorton.com/youmayask7

I advocate for public financing for elections because the private financing system really leads to a form of corruption. Most people who are in Congress now spend between *thirty and seventy percent* of their time raising money. Think about that. How many hours a week is that? That's every day. Forty years ago, it was two weeks a year. It's a radical change in how much of people's jobs is raising money. What it means is they, themselves, may or may not be corrupted by that, but they're spending their entire time, their alignment is with people, with the wealthiest 1 percent or the [top] fraction of 1 percent. (Conley, 2015e)

Teachout raised less than a million dollars in her run for governor of New York but garnered a substantial number of votes in the Democratic primary. Her opponent in the primary and the eventual winner, the incumbent governor, Andrew Cuomo (D), raised $23.4 million in his previous race for the same seat (Wall, 2012). Is paying for campaigns taking too much time and giving undue influence to those who can afford to write big checks?

Beyond Strawberry and Vanilla: Political Participation in Modern Democracies

Despite the extension of political rights in modern democracies, the United States has a voting rate struggling to consistently hit 60 percent in presidential elections and only reaching about 40 percent in nonpresidential elections. News anchors and political pundits often pour verbal shame on the American public for a decline in voting rates. But are the rates really declining? When political scientists set out to get to the bottom of the question, they realized that while most polls look at the total voting-age population, it would be more accurate to look only at the people who are actually eligible to vote. It is important to note that convicted felons are unable to vote; noncitizen permanent residents cannot vote either. So while it is true that the voting rate of the total population has fallen, it is not true that the voting rate of the eligible population has changed much (Figure 15.1). People don't vote like they used to not because they are too busy (or lazy) to get to the polls on election day but because they are prohibited from voting (McDonald & Popkin, 2001).

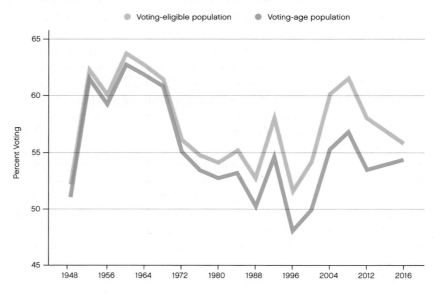

FIGURE 15.1 Presidential Turnout Rates, 1948–2016

● Voting-eligible population   ● Voting-age population

Percent Voting

SOURCE: McDonald, 2018.

Social scientists Jeff Manza and Christopher Uggen even suggest that if convicted felons—the vast majority of whom are not in prison—were able to vote, many races (including some presidential elections) would turn out differently (Manza & Uggen, 2006). However, political participation is not limited to voting in elections but rather includes a wide range of activities, from voting to working on a candidate's political campaign to marching in the streets. Succinctly, political participation is any "activity that has the intent or effect of influencing government action" (Verba et al., 2004).

Why does political participation matter? For many, democracy is the promise of a voice in governance. Political participation is important, then, because it is the sum of that voice. Through political participation, citizens "inform governing elites of their needs and preferences." Participation matters "both for its own sake and for its role in bringing about equality in the other valued goods—life, liberty, and property—that are affected by government policies" (Verba et al., 2004). In short, no participation means no voice.

So who participates and who doesn't? Sociologists have consistently found striking disparities in rates and types of participation across social groups, as reflected in the numbers of people who register to vote. In keeping with these findings, voter turnout is much lower among the poor (those with incomes below or close to the family poverty line) than among the financially well-off (those with family incomes over $75,000) (Verba et al., 2004). For

POLITICAL PARTICIPATION

an activity that has the intent or effect of influencing government action.

other forms of political participation, such as working for or donating to a candidate's campaign, the participation gap is even wider between income groups. In monetary contributions to political campaigns, "the average donation from an affluent respondent is *fourteen times* the average contribution from a poor one" (Verba et al., 2004). If we break down the population by socioeconomic status, a measure that includes both educational level and income, we find that political participation steadily declines as we go down the scale. Groups at the top of the socioeconomic scale nearly always participate more, whereas those on the bottom consistently participate less. Finally, research has found that citizens receiving means-tested benefits are the least likely to be politically active. Ironically, these citizens perhaps have the most to lose by not participating, because they are vulnerable to the changing political and policy definitions of what constitutes a social right and who is defined as belonging to the "deserving poor."

Largely prompted by the rapid decrease in political participation from the mid-1960s through the close of the twentieth century, academic inquiries into citizens' nonparticipation have produced a variety of explanations. The *civic voluntarism model* points to three components to explain political participation (or nonparticipation): political orientation, resources, and mobilization efforts. The first participatory factor, *political orientation*, is simply the strength of an individual's political commitments. If a citizen is strongly antiabortion, antigun, or pro something else, he or she is more likely to visit the polls or join a political campaign than another citizen who is apathetic about such political issues. *Resources* include money to donate to parties or causes, as well as civic skills such as leadership, communications, and organizational abilities that "make it easier to get involved and enhance an individual's effectiveness as a participant" (Verba et al., 2004). If a citizen is interested in politics and also has the necessary resources, *mobilization efforts* by political parties or nonpartisan groups can boost her political participation. These include mass mailings, phone calls, or door-to-door canvassing to encourage eligible citizens to vote or get involved in some other meaningful way. In summary, the *civic voluntarism* model suggests that individuals have certain preexisting attributes, such as civic skills and political orientations, that predispose them to participation or nonparticipation. Mobilization efforts can increase participation only among the willing and able.

Frances Fox Piven and Richard Cloward reject the notion that political nonparticipation can be traced to individual-level characteristics such as political orientation. In *Why Americans Don't Vote* (1988), Piven and Cloward hold the American party system, and political elites in particular, responsible for Americans' low rate of political participation. They attribute "apathy and lack of political skill," the two individual-level components of the *civic voluntarism* model, to "party strategies and political culture . . . sustained by legal and procedural barriers to electoral participation" (Piven &

↑

What factors do Frances Fox Piven and Richard Cloward believe cause political nonparticipation?

Cloward, 1988). Such barriers have historically included "literacy tests, stricter naturalization procedures, and burdensome voter registration procedures." These obstacles prevent certain people from voting altogether and increase the time and effort required of those who remain eligible. "Voter rights" sounds like a dry bit of constitutional law that typically engages a few corporate lawyers and judges here and there. But Piven took up voting rights as a grassroots issue during the Reagan years (1981–89) after she revisited something she already knew, which is that the electoral system in the United States "over represents the better off and under represents the worse off." She recruited a team to go out in the community and "do mass registration of poor people, voter registration of poor people at the agencies where they received services." But there was trouble: "We quickly learned from our groundwork with our organizers, that they were just signing up for it, they weren't actually doing it. It was a real free rider problem."

Piven thought the organizations serving the poor would logically want more of their constituents to get out and vote if for no other reason than to help these groups secure more government funding. But it turned out organizations were more interested in fighting for the interests of their wealthy board members. So then Piven's voter registration team "tried to get mayors, Black mayors especially, to do voter registration in municipal agencies," so that voting would be "part of the infrastructure of the election system, not dependent on volunteers whose interest was sparked by a particular campaign or by the availability of a foundation grant." But even this fight was "rough going" (Conley, 2009m). For both parties the goal was to keep the electorate stable, not to bring in large numbers of minorities and poor people. So yet again, Piven's team set out to recruit a new group of decision makers. This time they went after the political allegiance of federal lawmakers and interest groups by forming what came to be known as the Motor Voter Coalition to fight for a bill tying voter registration in federal elections to the issuance or renewal of drivers' licenses or to application for certain social services. Piven describes how the National Voter Registration Act (commonly known as Motor Voter) became law one year after Republican president George H. W. Bush vetoed it in 1992.

During his campaign Bill Clinton promised Rock the Vote, one of the groups in the coalition, that he would support the bill. When he was elected and took office, there was a little window of opportunity because by '94 we [the Democrats] no longer had the House of Representatives. The bill went through. There were compromises required at the last minute. We got calls from Washington very late at night about we had to drop some program, you couldn't have welfare, because we needed six in order to end the filibuster, we needed six Republican senators, and at the very last minute we dropped unemployment insurance because we reasoned that most of the unemployed would have driver's licenses. At any rate, the bill went through. (Conley, 2009m)

Victory at last! Or then again, no. Piven sighs, saying, "Once the Democrats lost office, the implementation collapsed."

Today, some states have made it easier to vote with same-day registration, early voting, and other innovations. However, others are trying to restrict access to the ballot under the guise of eliminating voter fraud, by implementing strict ID requirements and periodically purging voter rolls. This is arguably done for political reasons, as those least able to comply with strict barriers to voting are more likely to vote for left-wing parties. The bottom line is that the United States still lags behind other industrialized nations in turnout. For example, whereas some European countries have chosen to schedule elections on weekends, elections in the United States take place on weekdays, making it difficult for many working people to get to the polls. (Puerto Rico, a US territory, makes election day a holiday and consequently enjoys higher voting rates.) In an interview following Barack Obama's election, Piven noted that "voting is not a silver bullet, but it's one of the aspects of our political system that can be democratized, and we should protect it and expand voting rights to everyone" (Conley, 2009m). She went on to argue that access to voting rights is necessary but insufficient; political engagement after election day is required to force change in systems stymied by the significant inertia of the status quo.

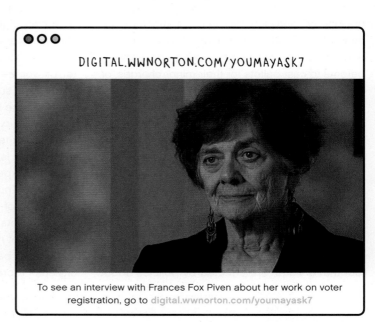

DIGITAL.WWNORTON.COM/YOUMAYASK7

To see an interview with Frances Fox Piven about her work on voter registration, go to digital.wwnorton.com/youmayask7

POLICY

 AGE AND VOTING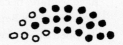

Regardless of who won the 2020 election, there was one group that was bound to lose either way: US children. That's because Americans under the age of 18 form the largest disenfranchised group in the country, even though their futures stand to lose (or gain) the most in this (and every) election. If any other bloc of 75 million American citizens were similarly disenfranchised, we'd see major street protests. But children are ill-equipped to march in the streets (especially those in strollers), and their parents are too harried to mount a social movement on their behalf. But that doesn't mean we shouldn't reform the electoral system to ameliorate the inherent antiyouth bias in our democracy. We could do this with one or more of three different approaches: by lowering the voting age, allowing parents to cast ballots for their minor charges, or prorating each of our votes by our life expectancy.

The argument back in 1971, when the twenty-sixth Amendment lowered the voting age to 18, was fairly straightforward: Through the military draft, we were asking—nay, demanding—the ultimate sacrifice of our nation's young adults. Did we trust 19-year-olds to pull triggers but not voting levers? Military conscription of a population that couldn't vote on the policy to which they were subjected seemed wrong. But while the draft has gone the way of Nixon and bell bottoms, the fact that children are affected by policies about

which they have no voice still holds sway. Entitlement reform, for example, affects a 14-year-old to a much greater extent than it does a 70-year-old. So does climate policy. And payroll tax rates. And just about every other political choice we face.

One solution to this disenfranchisement problem is to follow the logic of the twenty-sixth Amendment by lowering the voting age to, say, 14. After all, many religious traditions think of 13 as the age of transition to adulthood (think confirmation or bar mitzvah). And many states allow 14-year-olds to work and/or drive farm machinery. Teen workers do pay taxes, after all. In fact, research by Brown University sociologist Emily Rauscher shows that states that provide more freedom and responsibility to teenagers tend to spur—for better or worse—more adult behavior among that population, such as earlier family formation and entry into the labor force.

That said, even if we lowered the voting age to the early teens, such a reform still would not address the lack of representation for very young kids, who experience the highest poverty rates of any group. Thus, a different solution to this generational tug-of-war might involve allowing parents to cast ballots on the part of their dependent offspring. Right now, as a parent, my incentives are split at the ballot box. I have one vote but two citizens I represent. Do I vote in my own interest for a tax cut or higher Medicare spending? Or do I sacrifice my vote for the sake of my infant child—voting for candidates who will raise my taxes to pay for greater education investments, for instance?

While giving me two votes instead of one might not solve that problem since I could, in fact, squander my kid's ballot on my own selfish preferences, at least it means that someone who should have my child's best interests at heart will have an opportunity to voice that interest at the ballot box (i.e., me). And research finds that children do indeed influence their parents' political preferences. Of course, we can't have both parents casting votes on behalf of their kids—double counting—so we would have to come up with a system where the registration of each kid is tied uniquely to a single guardian. Legislation along these lines has been introduced in places like Japan, where people want to empower the few kids they have left there thanks to declining fertility rates and a growing elderly population.

Whether or not we somehow enfranchise children or their parents, we might also want to consider prorating voting power by age. Why should a 94-year-old who is expected to be around for another year or two get the same say on the long-term problems of the nation as I do at 50? We don't live in a traditional tribal society where the village elders get to make the decisions for the rest of us, except that, in essence, we do. Imagine the electoral map if we received one vote for each year below, say, 120 (as a putative maximum human lifespan). Or if we got one vote for each year of predicted life expectancy we enjoyed (a 25-year-old would get about 55 votes while a 75-year-old would get 12)—unadjusted for race, sex, or education level.

We could, of course, combine any of these reforms: lower the voting age and prorate our ballots by age and allow parents to cast prorated votes for their very young children too short to pull the lever themselves.

Before you cry that this is some blatantly Democratic partisan power play, consider that Utah—the nation's most reliably Republican state—would surge in importance. In fact, all five of the youngest states are red: besides Utah, these include Texas, Idaho, Georgia, and Alaska. Meanwhile, who knew that liberal Vermont was the eldest state in the nation? Florida, meanwhile, would be cut down to electoral size. And Hispanics—thanks to their high birthrates—would become even more important than they already are to the future of US politics.

Voting rates among young adults are currently the lowest of any age group. One way of interpreting that datum is to say that they don't really value the right provided by the twenty-sixth Amendment, so why should we bend over backward to extend that privilege further down the age ladder? But another way to think about it is that we need to encourage these people to go to the polls. What better way to incentivize them than to hand them the electoral car keys? Besides, research shows that voting is habit-forming, so the more chances to get someone to vote early, the better the chance of igniting a lifelong sense of civic duty.

Yes, young 'uns might make mistakes. But how much more could they screw up America's political process than we older adults have already, all by ourselves? No matter who won Tuesday's election, the winner will not be representing a majority of US citizens. There are other alarming forms of disenfranchisement ranging from felons' loss of suffrage, to state laws that make it difficult to vote, to the backlog in citizenship applications that delays would-be Americans from casting their first ballots. However, none of these affects US policy more than the nonrepresentation of youth at the polls. I'm ready to let teenagers vote, are you?

Conclusion

In this chapter we have examined power, domination, authority, bureaucracy, states, organizations, and political institutions. We have seen how Weber conceptualized authority as well as the bureaucratic organizations and the process of rationalization that continue to shape our daily lives. We have also examined some fundamental problems of modern-day political life, such as collective action problems and the iron law of oligarchy, which paint a somewhat pessimistic picture for the future of democracy and the cherished notion that everyone should have a voice in governance. Finally, as political sociologists, we are left to ponder how we might make democracy work better and how the most vulnerable members of society might be given a voice despite iron cages and oligarchies.

QUESTIONS FOR REVIEW

1. What is a "state" and how does the example of Somaliland clarify this definition?

2. Voter turnout in the United States is relatively low. Compare the *civic voluntarism* model and the position of Frances Fox Piven and Richard Cloward in explaining this phenomenon. How do the results from the National Voter Registration Act add to our understanding of voter turnout?

3. What is the difference between coercion and authority? Use an example to demonstrate this difference.

4. Choose a historical figure whose authority stemmed from his or her charisma. Describe why this person's authority was charismatic and how this form of legitimate authority changed over time (for example, describe whether it was traditionalized or rationalized).

5. Describe the concept of *domination* and its two types. How does this concept help us understand the results of the Milgram experiment?

6. What is a welfare state? Describe two theories that explain the development of the welfare state. Do these theories help us understand the way authority is maintained?

7. How are dictatorships and democracies different? How are the citizenship rights of the population (as defined by T. H. Marshall) different under these two kinds of political regimes?

8. In a democratic society, why is it possible for a small group of elites to get what it wants at the expense of the larger population? In your answer, consider the work on collective action and the sometimes selfish roots of altruism.

9. Provide examples of when public shaming might be a useful policy.

PRACTICE

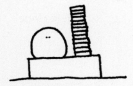

GET SH*T DONE

As we have learned in this chapter, authority can stem from tradition, from charisma, or from formalized rules and structures. While Weber thought the general arc of history was toward legal-rational authority, every community has a mix of these three kinds of legitimate authority. An important political skill is to know which sources of power to draw upon to get what you need done.

TRY IT!

Pick an issue in your local community, anything from a dangerous intersection with a missing stop sign to long wait times at the Department of Motor Vehicles.

First go through the relevant bureaucracy. If it's a pothole in a road, is it a state road or a county road? Who administers the county roads? Once you figure that out, contact the appropriate authority.

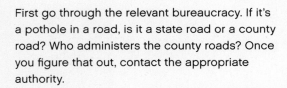

Then try direct democracy. Contact your elected official and see what he or she can do. This might be your city councilperson, your county or local commissioner, your state representative, or even your congressperson. You might try writing via a contact web page online or using social media or even sending a good old-fashioned handwritten note on—gasp—paper!

Which approach got a better response? Are elected officials in your area charismatic and powerful enough to fix problems and spark change? Or was the specialized legal-rational knowledge embedded in government bureaucracies more effective? If neither, what do you do next?

SOCIOLOGY ON THE STREET

If you experienced a civic problem, how easy would it be for you to fix it? How might socioeconomic factors affect your ability to reach people in power or even cause political change? Watch the Sociology on the Street video to find out more: **digital.wwnorton.com/youmayask7**.

WANT MORE PRACTICE?

Complete the InQuizitive activity for this chapter at digital.wwnorton.com /youmayask7

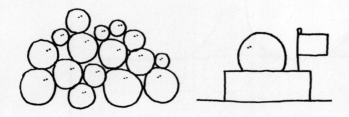

16

THE RELIGIONS THAT DEMAND
THE MOST FROM THEIR MEMBERS
OFTEN GROW THE FASTEST, BUT AS
RELIGIONS BECOME LARGE
AND SUCCESSFUL, THEY TEND TO
BECOME LESS STRICT.

Religion

We were late to dinner and I was nervous. It was not just that I was meeting new people—it was that one of those new people was Reverend Billy, a famous "preacher." I had never dined with a religious figure before, and I worried about making a faux pas. Reverend Billy turned out to be quite relaxed and, indeed, the life of the party. The next week, we showed up for the services at his church: the Church of Stop Shopping. The theater where it was being held was packed and hot. As the Stop Shopping choir sang, the crowd clapped and chanted. Then came Billy's sermon. He railed against the sin of consumerism. Though the message hewed to the lines of a more Spartan, ascetic denomination like Dutch Calvinism or German Lutheranism, the delivery was all Black Baptist. (Billy is White, the choir was equal parts Black and White, and the congregants came from all races.) He called out; we responded. As he built to his crescendo, tying the blight of consumerism in America to militarism, sweat poured off his brow.

After the service, he greeted parishioners like any other minister. The attendees filed out with a sense of solidarity; an intention to be better, more moral human beings; and a resolve to do something to improve the world. That week, pacifist Billy had called for us all to participate in a march to protest the impending invasion of Iraq. (This was 2003.) All in all, the Church of Stop Shopping achieved—for me at least—much of what most religions strive to elicit: a feeling of transcendence, of being part of something bigger than oneself; moral guidance; and an ethical education for my young children.

Reverend Billy started out preaching his anticonsumerist message in New York City's Times Square in 1999, and his popularity has exploded since then. Though it has a staff of almost 50 and a congregation of thousands, his church lacks a set location. Instead, it follows the revivalist tradition of Pentecostal preachers who set up tents in the early years of the twentieth century and spread the gospel of Christ like wildfire across North America and beyond. Like some other politically activist, evangelical preachers, Reverend

Reverend Billy leads a chant during a climate change rally outside Trump Tower in New York City in 2017.

Billy has led social actions. But his moral issues don't concern individual betrayal or behavior in the bedroom. Rather, he focuses his energies on corporate sins against the environment and labor. For example, the Church of Stop Shopping has worked to pressure Victoria's Secret to stop using lumber from virgin forest to make the paper for its catalogs, to make Starbucks give Ethiopian coffee growers better treatment, and to force JPMorgan Chase to divest from its investments in "mountaintop removal" mining in Appalachia. And in 2018, members of the church mounted a banner in the 30-foot globe outside Trump International Hotel and Tower that read: "Love No Border: Stop the Deportations."

But the Stop Shopping Church is different from other organized religions in one key way: Stop Shopping is not, in fact, a religion, and Reverend Billy is actually an actor. He got the idea for his church while working as a house manager at a theater in the Hell's Kitchen neighborhood (near Times Square) that was actually also an Episcopal church, Saint Clement's. The Reverend Sidney Lanier, who was vicar there, encouraged Bill Talen (Reverend Billy) to study radical theology, despite his suspicion of the conservative Protestant faith of his childhood in Dutch-Calvinist Minnesota. Out of this odd combination of church and theater was born the character of Reverend Billy.

Talen claims that his purpose is not to parody Christian preachers but instead to put the "the 'odd' back in God." He calls his church "postreligious." But its existence opens up important sociological questions about what makes a religion. After all, the Church of Stop Shopping has so many aspects of religion. For instance, there are church holidays, the most important of which is Black Friday, when adherents are expected not to purchase anything and are encouraged instead to protest the consumerism of that day. There are moral guidelines for living. There is a regular community of practitioners who are bound together in both ethical beliefs and weekly services. There are even feelings of transcendence—the rising "above" the material world—reported by attendees. The only thing missing is the word *god*.

But perhaps Stop Shopping is not as postreligious as Reverend Billy might think. The fastest-growing religious affiliation in America today (particularly among youth) is "none." These "nones"—which make up about a quarter of the population, up from only a tenth in 1980 (Smith & Cooperman, 2016)—are not necessarily atheists. In fact, only about 37 percent definitively state that they do not believe in God (Pew Research Center, 2018b). The rest are "not sure," or they may be spiritual believers but don't ascribe to a particular organized religion. They may, for example, borrow some doctrine from the Catholicism of their father and add to it the kosher laws of their Jewish grandmother. Or they may invent a form of spiritual practice from scratch, combining meditation, drug-induced hallucination, personal superstitions, and a daily mitzvah (good deed).

As we will see, one of the main social functions of religions is to unite members of a community around a common totem, making its followers feel part of something bigger than any one individual. In light of this, though Reverend Billy does not invoke God, his church may be more "religious"—at least in its sociological if not theological consequences—than many of the more individualized forms of spirituality that are cropping up like mushrooms across America.

What Is Religion?

In the broadest terms possible, religion is the way people make sense of their world by reference to supernatural or spiritual forces; it consists of the shared stories that guide how they live (McGuire, 2007). Our definition of religion is quite similar to the definition we used for culture in Chapter 3—"the sum of the social categories and concepts we embrace in addition to beliefs, behaviors (except instinctual ones), and practices"—though this is admittedly more comprehensive than religion. The point is that religion and culture overlap. More specifically, religion is a system of beliefs, traditions, and practices regarding sacred things. These beliefs keep us in line with expected behaviors, so religion serves as a kind of script for our actions, programming us to be able to distinguish right from wrong. The sacred realm refers to holy things that are put to special use for the worship of gods or supreme beings, things kept separate from the profane or everyday realm. The sacred realm is unknowable and mystical, so it inspires us with feelings of awe and wonder.

RELIGION

a system of beliefs, traditions, and practices around sacred things; a set of shared "stories" that guide belief and action.

SACRED

holy things endowed with special status and often used for worship and kept separate from the profane; the sacred realm is unknowable and mystical, so it inspires us with feelings of awe and wonder.

PROFANE

the things of mundane, everyday life.

The religious-sacred versus secular-profane alignment is too simple, however. For example, some religions break down the dichotomy between the sacred and the profane due to their views of *immanence*—that is, the notion that God is everywhere and in everything in the material world. Some strains of Buddhism and Jewish Hasidism ascribe to this notion, for example. Meanwhile, many secular totems achieve sacred status in societies. Think of the reverence that many Americans have for the US flag, or the Constitution as a sacred text. When the sacred (secular or religious) is combined with the profane, it results in discomfort and offense. Examples of such mixing include commerce in religious places, swearing in a house of worship, and the presence of holy texts in toilets.

This last one is no joke. In 2005, *Newsweek* broke the story that American prison guards at Guantánamo Bay had flushed a Qur'an, a sacred Muslim text, down the toilet as part of interrogation tactics. The story was later retracted, but not before sparking anti-American protests and riots throughout the Islamic world (Seelye, 2005). Given some of the previous shocking scenes of torture and abuse in detainee camps, the alleged desecration of the Qur'an may have at first seemed like small potatoes. But defacing the holy book is especially shocking to Muslims, explained one Pakistani man to *Newsweek* reporters: "We can understand torturing prisoners, no matter how repulsive. . . . But insulting the Qur'an is like deliberately torturing all Muslims. This we cannot tolerate" (Thomas, 2005). How can symbolic violence be more painful than physical violence? What makes the Muslim's Qur'an, the Christian's Bible, or the Jew's Torah so sacred?

Sacred things derive their power from the collective investment of the religious community. An affront to someone's religious symbols is therefore an insult to his or her whole social world, belief systems, and customs. This is a point the functionalist sociologist Émile Durkheim made—one that we'll come back to. But let's start with a brief introduction to the different belief systems around the world.

Religion takes three major forms: theism, the worship of a god or gods, as in Christianity, Islam, and Hinduism; ethicalism, the adherence to certain principles to lead a moral life, as in Buddhism and Taoism; and animism, the belief that spirits are part of the natural world, as in totemism.

Christianity is the most prevalent world religion: 31.2 percent of people globally, approximately 2.3 billion, identify themselves as Christian (Hackett & McClendon, 2017; Figure 16.1). The share of Christians in the world has remained flat, but the global composition of Christendom is changing. Once centered in Europe and North America, Christianity—both Protestantism and Catholicism—is experiencing a steep decline in Europe and the United States. In 1910, two-thirds of Christians lived in Europe, for example. By 2050 that share is expected to be 16% (Masci, 2015). Meanwhile, that same year, almost four in ten Christians are expected to be in sub-Saharan Africa.

THEISM

the worship of a god or gods, as in Christianity, Islam, and Hinduism.

ETHICALISM

the adherence to certain principles to lead a moral life, as in Buddhism and Taoism.

ANIMISM

the belief that spirits are part of the natural world, as in totemism.

Christians are united by their belief that Jesus Christ was the son of God, born from a virgin named Mary, and was sent to earth for the forgiveness of the sins of the world. They also believe that Christ will come once again to judge humanity and mark the end of time. Christianity is split among multiple denominations. Denominations are sets of congregations—groups of people who gather together, especially for worship—that share the same faith and are governed under one administrative umbrella. The largest Christian groups worldwide are Catholics (50.1 percent), Protestants of various denominations (36.7 percent), and Orthodox (11.9 percent), plus a slew of smaller groups like New Thought, Christian Scientists, and Quakers (Pew Forum on Religion and Public Life, 2011). Catholics follow the Roman Catholic Church and its head, the bishop of Rome, currently Pope Francis. Protestants broke from the Catholic Church during the sixteenth century because they were upset with the decadence of the church and the extortion of money from parishioners that was supposedly necessary for moving the souls of their departed relatives from purgatory on to heaven.

Muslims follow Islam, the world's second-largest religion, representing 24.1 percent of the world's population, approximately 1.8 billion people (Hackett & McClendon, 2017). Its teachings center on the authority of the Qur'an, the direct word of God (Allah) as revealed to the prophet Muhammad in the seventh century. The Muslim population in the United States has grown since the 1960s because of immigration from Middle Eastern and South Asian countries such as Indonesia, India, Pakistan, and Bangladesh (Sheler, 2001). Estimates of the number of Muslims in the United States vary considerably. One recent study found that only 1.1 percent of Americans (3.45 million people) are Muslim, but projected that their small numbers will double by 2050, and will outnumber Jews by 2040 (Mohamed, 2018). All Muslim believers are united in their adherence to the five pillars of Islam: faith, prayer, charity, fasting, and Hajj (pilgrimage to Mecca). Adherence to Islam, rather than any organizational membership or mosque attendance, defines one as a Muslim. In fact, in Arabic (the language of the Qur'an), there is no word for religion. Muslims are taught that all behavior, belief, or acts of any sort are a reflection of their "deen," or living the teachings of Islam.

Why do religions set aside certain objects, actions, or places as sacred? Whether it's praying in Mecca, receiving communion, or paying homage to the Buddha, what might be the social function of distinguishing the sacred from the profane?

DENOMINATION

a big group of congregations that share the same faith and are governed under one administrative umbrella.

CONGREGATION

a group of people who gather together, especially for worship.

That said, as in many other religions, political divisions exist within Islam, principally among the Sunnis and Shiites. Sunni Muslims, by far the largest denomination of Islam, believe that the first four caliphs or leaders to succeed the Prophet Muhammad were legitimate spiritual leaders. Shiites believe that only Ali, the son-in-law of Muhammad, is the rightful and legitimate successor. Muslims are also split by their austerity of belief and practice. Those who follow liberal Islam—which includes believing in democracy, free expression, and gender equality—try to reconcile modern secularism with Islam. Secularism is the general movement away from religiosity and spiritual belief toward a rational, scientific orientation, a trend observed in Muslim and Christian industrialized nations alike. There is plenty of debate about how faith can be reconciled with modernity, science, and democracy, and liberal Muslims try to achieve such a reconciliation. At the opposite end of the spectrum are Islamists, a small minority, who reject secularism and democracy; in the extreme, they may use terrorist means to further their religious goals.

Hindus make up the next-largest group, 15.1 percent of the world's population, primarily in India (Hackett & McClendon, 2017). Hinduism is a type of polytheism, the worship of many gods. There are countless gods according to Hindus, and all of them work to control nature, reproduction, crops, and other facets of life. A central tenet of Hinduism is the belief in reincarnation—the idea that each of us is born and reborn over and over again in a cycle that ends in salvation only by following the traditional rules of caste, decency, and prayer. Christians and Muslims believe that having

SECULARISM

a general movement away from religiosity and spiritual belief toward a rational, scientific orientation; a trend adopted by industrialized nations in the form of separation of church and state.

FIGURE 16.1 Percentages of Religious Adherents Worldwide, 2016

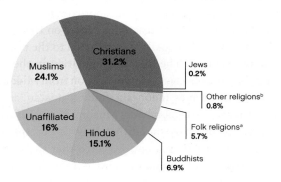

[a] Includes followers of African traditional religions, Chinese folk religions, Native American religions, and Australian Aboriginal religions.

[b] Includes Bahá'ís, Jains, Sikhs, Shintcists, Taoists, followers of Tenrikyo, Whoians, Zoroastrians, and many other faiths.

SOURCE: Hackett & McClendon, 2017.

faith in God will help them withstand the trials of life. Although Hindus do not believe in faith, they do believe in a principle called karma. Karma literally means "act," but karma also includes thoughts and speech. Hindus believe that every person and element of the natural world has a role to fulfill. Proper fulfillment of that role will result in alignment with the rest of the world; improper fulfillment of that role results in a misalignment. The net value of an individual's actions or karma is carried with that person and shapes his or her fate in the future.

Buddhism is the most prevalent form of ethicalism, in which moral principles are the sacred sources of belief. About 6.9 percent of the world's population are Buddhist, primarily in Asia (Hackett & McClendon, 2017). Like Hindus, Buddhists adhere to a belief in karma. Furthermore, they hold four noble truths: that all existence is suffering, that the cause of suffering is desire, that nirvana—a release of the soul from the body and karmic baggage—can be achieved only through giving up our cravings; and that this is achieved by following the Noble Eightfold Path of right living (with eight facets).

Judaism is the world's eleventh-largest organized religion, with an estimated 14 million adherents, representing approximately 0.2 percent of the world's population. About 1.9 percent of the US population profess to be Jewish. The Jewish faith, like Christianity and Islam, is not monolithic, meaning that it doesn't have just one form. Judaism's major denominations are Orthodox, Conservative (Masorti), Reform, and the 20 percent who self-identify as nonreligious Jews. On the Orthodox side, the emphasis is on tradition and strict adherence to Jewish law and custom, including the segregation of the sexes during worship. Conservative Jews generally adhere to many of the traditional daily and weekly practices—like observing Shabbat every Friday evening—but absorb more aspects of the predominant culture, including gender equality. Reform Judaism is even more relaxed, with the express aim of reconciling modernity and the Jewish faith. All denominations are united by a shared belief in God and the teachings of the Torah, God's revelations to the prophet Moses.

Finally, about 16 percent of the world's population and 24 percent of Americans are nonreligious, including agnostics and atheists (Cox & Jones, 2017; Hackett & McClendon, 2017). This group makes up the third-largest "religious" category in the world, but they are still far outnumbered by religious adherents worldwide. The nonreligious hold a wide range of beliefs, such as atheism, agnosticism, and humanism. Atheists believe that no supernatural being exists. Agnostics may believe in God (or be unsure), but feel that theological claims are not provable or that specific religions are unnecessary for their own practices of spirituality. Meanwhile, humanists embrace an ethical philosophy that prioritizes social justice with teachings from a range of sources, including religious teachings, science, and philosophy. Although the content of religious systems varies across cultures, the fact of religion is fairly stable and universal. How do sociologists make sense of such an omnipresent social fact?

Theory: Marx, Weber, and Durkheim

KARL MARX

A Hindu man prostrate at the feet of members of the Brahman caste during Dandajayatra, a festival dedicated to the Hindu deity Shiva.

In studying religion, Karl Marx used a conflict theoretical approach (see Chapter 1), the basis of his social theory called dialectic materialism, which is the struggle between contradictory, interacting forces that eventually results not in victory for one of the forces, but in the creation of a third force that replaces the two opposing forces. For Marx, a major force of change throughout history was conflict. It was rooted in the tension between the owners of the means of production and the propertyless workers in society. This conflict was at the heart of all social facts of life: education, family, art, and religion. In his *Contribution to the Critique of Hegel's Philosophy of Right*, Marx (1978) famously remarked that religion is the "opiate of the masses." To Marx, religion is a clever means of stratification, of allocating rewards such that some people benefit handsomely from the fruits of society while many others suffer. Religious convictions, he claimed, hold sway over people with promises of happiness in the afterlife, keeping them duped into remaining exploited workers in oppressive, alienating factory jobs. The myth of salvation keeps men toiling in manufacture, scraping by on unfair wages with the hope of finding happiness in the afterlife, while the boss grows rich on their backs. Marx agreed with critiques of religion at the time that sought to remind the world that "man makes religion; religion does not make the man." His colleague Friedrich Engels (1878) explained, "All religion . . . is nothing but the fantastic reflection in men's minds of those external forces which control their daily lives." Marx's critique of religion was part of his broader agenda to expose the "illusory happiness of men." If only workers could see the real truth, they would overthrow their oppressors and demand real happiness with honest and just working conditions.

Marx's conflict theory of religion links two ideas that might seem at odds: inequality and faith. Because religion comes with a set of norms about how the world works, faith can keep the downtrodden in their places so long as religious norms make it seem just. Historically, there's something to conflict theory. Take India as an example, where religion justified the oppressive caste system for thousands of years (see Chapter 7). Castes are ranked statuses based on birth that determined life chances for Indians, everything from what type of education they received to what jobs they could hold and whom they might marry. Until an awareness movement in the 1990s, the caste system was believed to be the natural way of the world, ordained by the gods. To take another example, in Europe through the nineteenth century, Christianity was used as a justification to exploit what were considered barbarous and uncivilized groups of people around the world. The real motivation behind imperialism, of course, was economic—to pillage natural resources and profit from slave labor—but doing so in the name of Christ made it seem okay, even commendable, for hundreds of years.

Scholars have challenged many aspects of Marxist theory, especially its failure to take religion seriously. How can faith, something experienced by the overwhelming majority of the world, be reduced to a function of class oppression?

MAX WEBER

Max Weber took up the challenge by showing religious ideas as independent forces in their own right. In Weber's view, the best way to figure out what drives social action is to put oneself in another person's shoes and imagine that person's intentions and meanings. By emphasizing *Verstehen* (German for "understanding"), Weber gives credence to the power of ideas (see Chapter 1). Ideas are so powerful, Weber insists in *The Protestant Ethic and the Spirit of Capitalism* (2003), that when enough people hold dear a certain set of beliefs, the course of history is forever altered.

The Protestant Ethic starts with the idea that the Western world has changed since the 1850s, relative to the traditional societies that existed before. Rationality is the driving force for action in the modern world, as opposed to tradition or habit, which was the reason people did things in the past. How, Weber wonders, did this modern world come into being?

To answer this question, he begins with the observation that different regions of Europe that counted greater or lesser proportions of Protestants in their populations had correspondingly different rates of capitalist activity. In predominantly Protestant areas such as central Germany, people tended to own more capital. Protestant Germany also was one of the most economically successful regions of Europe, and workers were more likely to be highly educated and skilled, often employed in large industrial and commercial companies.

How were Max Weber's interpretations of capitalist axioms similar to the advice given by Benjamin Franklin in *Poor Richard's Almanack*?

What was occurring in central Germany that wasn't happening in, say, northern Germany, which was predominantly Catholic? What motivated all this capitalist activity in central Germany? With these questions in mind, Weber visited America in 1904, touring the country for three months. Here he had the chance to observe a flourishing capitalistic economy and to read advice found in the popular writings of Benjamin Franklin, written in the eighteenth century. Some key statements that came from Franklin's writings include "Time is money," "Credit is money," "Money begets money," and "A penny saved is a penny earned." These maxims have become common sense in mainstream American culture, but in an earlier ethic where poverty was a virtue, this would have sounded like simple, dishonorable greed. In a capitalist society, however, Franklin's principles of thrift were praiseworthy for any man of honor. They included the duty to increase individual wealth, the moral duty to fulfill a calling and make money through a vocation, the validation of moneymaking as an end in itself, and the utilitarianism of values (i.e., virtues are only virtuous if they are useful to the individual). In Franklin's new philosophy, Weber identified what he called the "spirit of capitalism." This spirit, he notes, sets forth a peculiar restraint: You work very hard, but you cannot enjoy the fruits of your labor. Accumulating piles of money for the mere sake of having piles of money seems irrational. How has greed become the ideal virtue of the honest man? How did people suddenly accept the idea of labor as an end in itself if it's not in their self-interest?

As we saw in Chapter 14, according to Weber, Protestantism was a necessary condition for the emergence of capitalism. Specifically, Calvinist teachings shaped the kind of personalities needed for capitalism to develop. The early Protestant sects, especially Calvinism, believed that each person had a calling, which entailed fulfilling one's duty to God through day-to-day work in disciplined, rational labor. A person could fulfill his or her calling by choosing a vocation and then methodically completing its associated work for God's glory. Salvation entailed rigorous self-discipline, the rational application of one's labor.

Another key idea of the new Protestant faiths was predestination, the notion that only the elect are chosen by God for salvation. But the trick is that you don't know if you've been chosen or not. The best you can do is look for signs in this life of what awaits you in the next life. One such sign is success: If you're successful in this life, it's reasonable to assume you will be successful in the afterlife. Another sign is that you live a self-disciplined and simple lifestyle free from pleasures of the flesh and other luxuries. In other words, if you are successful in fulfilling your calling and you do not enjoy it, then all signs are looking good for your afterlife.

If Protestants want to be successful but can't enjoy their success, then a good Protestant is a rich one. As good Protestants sought profit, not pleasures, a new era characterized by rationalization, asceticism, and individualism began. Protestants were encouraged to earn, save, accumulate, and give to others, and as an unintended consequence, the system of capitalism took off. Thus one of the unforeseen effects of early Protestant teachings, claimed Weber, was the capitalist system.

How did the idea of predestination embraced by Dutch Protestants help early capitalism take root in western Europe?

Weber and Marx present two very different theoretical approaches. Marx saw a causal chain moving from the economic base to the cultural and religious superstructure, in which religion is part of an ideology stemming from class interests. Weber offers a more complicated story, where ideas and beliefs are not mere reflections of a class base. To Weber (2003), the causal connection works both ways, creating an "elective affinity" between the economic and the cultural: "It is not, of course, the intention here to set a one-sided spiritualistic analysis of the causes of culture and history in place of an equally one-sided 'materialistic' analysis. *Both are equally possible*" (p. 125, emphasis added). If the history of our society can be envisioned

as a train, moving along through eras of invention, war, disaster, and enlightenment, ideas are, in his words, the "switchmen" of the tracks. They hold the potential, when believed in enough and by the right people at the right time, to change the course of history in unexpected, counterintuitive ways.

Once the capitalist system took root, the Protestant ethic that had allowed it to spread began to fade away, dropping out of the new economic system. Capitalism, Weber believed, was able to sustain itself without the religious meanings crucial to its early development. In Ben Franklin's maxims, this spirit of capitalism already thrived without the religious undertones. The pursuit of money has become an end in itself, and the world has been overtaken by efficiency and rationalism. The English minister Richard Baxter claimed in 1681 that the desire for material goods should lie over people's shoulders "like a lightweight coat that could be thrown off at any time" (Weber, 2003, p. 123). But, in Weber's terms, this desire has become in the modern rational world a "steel-hard casing" or an "iron cage," in which we are forever trapped, chasing after gain for the sake of gaining, caught in a rat race of increasing coldness, calculation, and disenchantment.

Weber thought the modern world had been deserted by the gods and remade into a clinical, predictable, and demystified place. Indeed, Protestantism is a modern faith that stands removed from the ancient elements of the sacred: mystery, miracle, and magic. In a roundabout way, Weber ends up sounding like Marx in predicting that the cold, impersonal winds of capitalism would intrude on all aspects of personal and spiritual life, erasing inefficient feelings such as religious devotion.

Weber's ideas have not gone uncontested. Daniel Chirot (1985), for instance, argues that Protestantism was not the only or the most important driving force behind the spread of capitalism. He finds that because of geography—climate, agriculture, natural barriers against invasion—certain parts of Europe were more apt to nurture capitalist enterprises than others.

ÉMILE DURKHEIM

Émile Durkheim's functionalist approach (see Chapter 1) finds both purpose and power in modern religious belief. He tackled first the question of what religion is by studying totemism among Australian Aboriginal societies, which he wrote about in *Elementary Forms of the Religious Life* (1917). Durkheim argued that he researched totemism not to experience the "sheer pleasure of recounting the bizarre and the eccentric" but to comprehend a more general religious nature, which he considered a "fundamental and permanent aspect of humanity."

The sociologist's task, according to Durkheim, is not to determine which religions are "true" and which are "false." Rather, the sociologist must treat every religion as real and find out what commonalities they share. He noted that it is a "fundamental postulate of sociology that a human institution cannot rest upon error and falsehood." Durkheim, in fact, came to argue that our very categories of thought—notions of time, space, cause, and effect—are created in and from religion.

Indeed, Durkheim believed that the "skeleton of thought" that every human must possess in order to function in the world is a product of religious thought. This insight led him to theorize that religion is an "eminently social thing." Its "representations are collective representations that express collective realities." As such, the sociologist must approach a rite like a rain dance or genital mutilation and "know how to reach beneath the symbol to grasp the reality it represents and that gives the symbol its true meaning." (Recall our discussion of cultural relativism in Chapter 3.) Be they wood carvings, chants, drawings, or holy days, our sacred symbols are not just the result of some wild mythological imaginations spawned under the deceptive guise of language. How could all of humanity be strung along for centuries under some kind of elaborate trickery? Durkheim gives people more credit than that. For him, sacred things acquire power because their owners have collectively invested them with it:

↑

Why did Durkheim study Australian Aboriginal societies in the early twentieth century? What did he see as the social function of religion?

> The Arunta [a member of an Aboriginal tribe] who has properly rubbed himself with his *churinga* [a sacred stone or wooden object] feels stronger; he is stronger. The soldier who falls defending his flag certainly does not believe he has sacrificed himself to a piece of cloth. Such things happen because social thought, with its imperative authority, has a power that individual thought cannot possibly have. (1917/1995, p. 229)

Religious force is a feeling that the collectivity inspires in its individual members, which then is projected outside the individual and objectified as an external force. The power of the sacred is not felt as coercion; rather, "[e]ach individual carries the whole in himself. It is part of him, so when he yields to its promptings, he does not think he is yielding to coercion but instead doing what his own nature tells him to do." When people conform to the rules of their religion, they are in effect yielding to the moral authority of society.

Social Solidarity Durkheim further argued that religions perform social functions. Specifically, religion perpetuates social unity or solidarity by strengthening the collective conscience—the shared beliefs and ideas, ways of thinking and knowing. Religion strengthens the bonds of people not only to their gods but also to their society, because God is a representation of society. Religious thought becomes not just the sum of individual parts but a distinctive whole that cannot be reduced to its parts. Social solidarity in modern societies is a force that has become larger than individuals, acting on and constraining them—although without them, the force would not exist.

One indication that religious participation strengthens social solidarity comes from deviance studies, in which research has shown that actively religious people are less likely to commit crimes. (See our discussion of social control and deviance in Chapter 6.) In theory, when you are busy raising money for church charity, you don't have time to be exposed to criminal activities, nor would you want your religious peer group to find out about your illegitimate behavior. Furthermore, some have argued that the fear of divine punishment, called the "hellfire effect," is likely to keep you in line—though this is not the sort of thing you can easily test with an experiment. Since there is no way to randomize people to be religious or nonreligious, it could be that religion has no effect and that any observed correlation is thanks to rule-seeking people drawn to religion because they are attracted by clear moral proscriptions and social order.

There is also evidence suggestive of a positive effect of religion-induced social solidarity on individuals' well-being. In one study, for example, religious attendance and affiliation are inversely correlated with alcohol, tobacco, and substance use and therefore with the risks of developing chronic diseases (Koenig et al., 1994). On average, people who are religiously involved "live slightly longer lives and experience slightly lower levels of depressive symptoms" than people who are less religious (McCullough & Smith, 2003). Of course, we cannot know for sure if religion actually causes these positive outcomes or whether something about particular individuals predisposes them both to be religious and to live healthy lifestyles. Perhaps folks who are religious gain intrinsic enjoyment from following rules, predisposing them to gain positive feelings both from religion and from following the surgeon general's recommendations for a healthy lifestyle. Or, alternatively, perhaps the difference stems from a dynamic by which secular Americans fare worse in terms of health and well-being because of the stress they experience from being one of the most distrusted demographic groups in American society (Edgell et al., 2006; Zuckerman, 2009) and the fact that, as a result, they enjoy fewer social resources (Kasselstrand et al., 2017).

Meanwhile, if we look at demography, we see trends that fly in the face of the faith-health association. Namely, millennials—those born roughly from 1981 to 1996 who came of age along with the internet—are the least religious generation of adults in recorded US history. A full 40 percent reported being unaffiliated religiously, up 13 percentage points in 10 years (Pew Research Center, 2019b). (Most are spiritual but do not ascribe to organized religion. Only a minority of this 40 percent are atheist or agnostic.) Meanwhile, millennials are the most healthful generation as well—and not just because they are on the younger side. Some have even called them the "wellness generation." Millennials exercise more than prior generations did at their age, smoke less, and eat more healthily (Nermoe, 2018). Even though they were hit by the Great Recession and then the COVID-19 pandemic, and thus have less income than prior generations, they spend more money on health and fitness than other generations. Of course, the folks who are dropping organized religion in this group may not be the same people taking up fitness. But the dual trends suggest that the association between religion and health may be short-lived.

Secularization or Speculation?

In the 1960s, the future of religion in America was in doubt. Social scientists of the day, touting secularization theory, predicted a future American social scene in which religious influence would be diminished. The waning power of religious ideas was associated with a 400-year-old worldwide trend of modernization and is evident in the separation of religion from institutions such as the state, economy, and family. It involves the rising importance of the everyday (the profane) and the diminishing significance of the sacred. It is equally visible in the shift of marriage counseling from the priest to the therapist and in the popularity of the crucifix as a fashion accessory. Secularization affects the organization of society—less church control over state policy, for example. It also means that religion weighs less and less upon our consciousness.

Secularization was of interest to social scientists and theologians alike during the 1960s; many considered it not just a neutral parallel trend to modernization but a distinct force with which to be reckoned. Peter Berger (1967) considered secularization the result of a larger sociostructural crisis in religion caused by pluralism, the presence and engaged coexistence of numerous distinct groups in one society. Pluralism has widely been considered detrimental to religion. With diverse religions, so the argument goes, various churches offer their own answers to life's deep questions, often discrediting others' views. The result, fears Berger, is a "crisis of credibility," a loss of religious legitimacy and plausibility. Pluralism threatens to rip apart a unified faith's sacred canopy, a term Berger used to describe the entire set of religious norms, symbols, and beliefs that convey the feeling that life is worth living, reality is meaningful and ordered, and all is not just random chaos. When the sacred canopy rips and gives way to conflicting ideas about how the world works, Berger feared, we end up with religious disintegration, psychological malaise, and chaos. If every church claims to have the right answers and each doctrine seems plausible, how can you know which church to join and what to believe? Pluralism presents modern individuals with an

PLURALISM

the presence and engaged coexistence of numerous distinct groups in one society.

SACRED CANOPY

Peter Berger's term to describe the entire set of religious norms, symbols, and beliefs that express the most important thing in life—namely, the feeling that life is worth living and that reality is meaningful and ordered, not just random chaos.

unprecedented crisis: to figure out for themselves life's greater meaning (Berger, 1967). Faced with that daily challenge, why even get out of bed?

Despite many attempts, the mission to unite Christians has repeatedly failed. The reason, Roger Finke and Rodney Stark argue in *The Churching of America, 1776–1990* (1992), is that pluralism is a natural state of the unregulated religious sphere. Because different people look for different things in a religion—say, worldliness or otherworldliness, strictness or permissiveness—a plethora of churches naturally arises to satisfy people's religious tastes. Even states that mandate faiths for their citizens, as medieval and Renaissance Europe did, still end up with a considerable number of heretics and dissenters as well as religious indifference.

RELIGIOUS PLURALISM IN THE UNITED STATES

The United States is both highly religious and pluralistic, standing out among other industrialized and wealthy nations in this regard (Inglehart & Baker, 2000). About 74 percent of Americans claim a religious affiliation, although identifying, believing, and participating can mean quite different things (Pew Research Center, 2019b). People from 14 countries were asked about the strength of their belief in God. Researchers found that people from Europe tend to have weaker beliefs than those from the Americas, Asia, and Australia, though Japanese people are more like Europeans (Figure 16.2).

FIGURE 16.2 Percentage of National Populations Who Strongly Believe in God

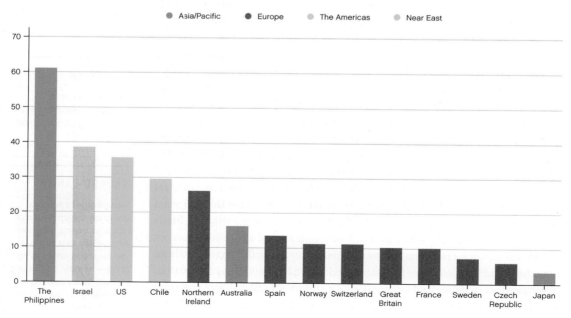

SOURCE: Smith, 2012.

In its level of religiosity, the United States is closer to some poor developing nations than to other wealthy democratic states. According to a 2017 Pew Research study, 80 percent of Americans believe in God, though this figure drops to 17 percent for the 26 percent who are not religiously affiliated (Pew Research Center, 2018a). Overall, 72 percent of Americans believe in heaven but only 58 percent believe in hell (Murphy, 2015). About 31 percent think the Bible is the literal word of God while 27 percent believe it is the nonliteral word of God (Geiger, 2017). American faith has tended to be more broad than deep, such that "of those Americans who say the Bible is either the actual or the inspired Word of God, only half can name the first book in the Bible" (Chaves, 2002).

The United States also stands out as a highly pluralistic religious society; more than 280 denominations and 300,000 congregations exist, not to mention the continuous flux of new movements (Ammerman, 2005). Protestants outnumber Catholics, although since 1900 Protestantism has shrunk from a following of 80 percent of Americans to only 43 percent (Pew Research Center, 2019). Figure 16.3 provides a visual representation of the major American faiths.

According to a 2015 survey by the Pew Forum on Religion and Public Life, in 2014, 25.4 percent of the US population were evangelical protestants (Lipka, 2015). Evangelicals can be members of any denomination, but the term is typically reserved for groups distinguished by four main beliefs: the Bible is without error, salvation comes only through belief in Jesus Christ, personal conversion is the only path to salvation (the "born again" experience), and others must also be converted. Evangelicals try to proselytize—to win people over—by engaging with wider society.

Fundamentalists also follow the Bible as a literal text but do not necessarily try to spread the gospel to the same extent that evangelicals do. The term *conservative Protestant* is often used to refer to evangelicals and fundamentalists, as well as Pentecostals, a nonmainstream group that believes in otherworldly phenomena, such as speaking in tongues, that they view as evidence of the miracle of receiving the Holy Ghost.

Taken together, conservative Protestants, mainline Protestants (denominations that do not interpret the Bible literally, such as Methodists, Lutherans, and Episcopalians), Catholics, and Orthodox Christians account for about 71 percent of all Americans. The remaining 29 percent who are non-Christians—Buddhists, Hindus, Jews, Jains, Muslims, Sikhs, Bahá'ís, Confucians, Pagans, Shintoists, Taoists, Zoroastrians, and religious non-affiliates, among others—coexist in a pluralist United States.

Pluralism is more than diversity; it is the active engagement across faiths to build a common sense of community. Historically, newcomer faiths were greeted with suspicion and hostility, and Catholics, Mormons, Jews, and other minority religious adherents were all subject to social exclusion, harassment, and even church arson and violence. If not excluded, people of minority

EVANGELICALS

members of any Christian denomination distinguished by four main beliefs: the Bible is without error, salvation comes only through belief in Jesus Christ, personal conversion is the only path to salvation (the "born again" experience), and others must also be converted. They proselytize by engaging with wider society.

FUNDAMENTALISTS

religious adherents who follow a scripture (such as the Bible or Qur'an) using a literal interpretation of its meaning.

FIGURE 16.3 One Nation, Many Faiths

Protestant
46.5%

Catholic
20.8%

Each symbol represents 1% of the US population.

SOURCE: Pew Research Center, 2015a.

faiths were encouraged to assimilate to majority Anglo-Protestantism (Eck, 2006). More recently, however, pluralism, understood as engagement with and respect for other faiths, has become a social ideal.

That's not to say that religious difference is always a smooth matter of respect and communication. Jen'nan Read is a sociologist who writes about Muslims in America and has taken on "probably the most complicated topic in the Muslim community and outside of it because it's so misunderstood," which is the veil or hijab (Conley, 2009i). She found that Muslim women in America who wear the veil tend to be highly educated and choose to veil themselves in spite of their families' disapproval. They wear it "for their own individual identity, and for their own feelings of being American. Because part of being American for them is the freedom to choose, to wear this even if their families don't want them to" (Conley, 2009i). But America is not always as accepting of their choice as they might like. In Cape Henlopen, Delaware, for instance, a Muslim family sued their daughter's school district on the grounds that a fourth-grade teacher had initiated a campaign of harassment against the young Muslim student. The teacher allegedly taught class lessons on the evils of the Qur'an and associated the Muslim student with terrorists. Fellow students began ridiculing her at school as the "loser Muslim," and eventually she had to transfer to another school district (Spiegel, 2006). Following an investigation by the US Department of Justice (2007), the school district now requires programs promoting religious tolerance and offers special training to teachers. Since September 11, 2001, reports of the harassment and bullying of

According to Jen'nan Read, why is the hijab so misunderstood?

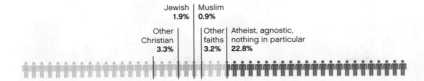

Jewish
1.9%

Muslim
0.9%

Other
Christian
3.3%

Other
faiths
3.2%

Atheist, agnostic,
nothing in particular
22.8%

Sikhs and Muslims, by fellow students and teachers alike, have continued to rise. These instances show the failures of pluralism and fly in the face of religious tolerance, a basic ideal of the Constitution.

RELIGIOUS ATTENDANCE IN THE UNITED STATES

Identification with a religious denomination is currently high in America, and Finke and Stark (1992), in *The Churching of America,* find that religious participation has increased over the course of our history, based on growing rates of church membership. They find, for instance, that church membership was only 10 percent in 1789, rising to 22 percent by 1890 and reaching 60 percent during the 1960s. Of course, the nature of churchgoing has changed as well, evolving from elite social clubs in the eighteenth century to today's informal communal gatherings.

According to Gerhard Lenski (1961), *associational involvement* refers to the frequency of religious service attendance, whereas *communal involvement* refers to how many of your primary group interactions are restricted to followers of your own faith—how isolated or enmeshed you are in the religious community. Associational and communal involvement varies by faith. For instance, Jews have weak associational involvement but strong communal ties. Catholics have strong associational involvement but weak communal ties. Both are weak for White Protestants; both are strong for Black Protestants.

Today, around 35 percent of Americans report going to the service of a religious organization nearly every week or more (Pew Research Center, 2015b). However, it's difficult to rely on the word of the average survey respondent, because Americans tend to overreport church attendance, a common problem social scientists call "social desirability bias." (Recall our discussion of survey research in Chapter 2.) When researchers have counted congregants at actual services and compared those counts to self-reports of attendance, they have found that the self-reports were 10 to 30 percent higher than observational data (Fischer & Hout, 2006). Whether from guilt, embarrassment, or a desire to look good in front of social scientists, people

Why might mosque attendance be a poor indicator of how involved someone is in their religious community?

tend to bend the truth on surveys when questions have a moral undertone. When researchers simply ask a random sample if they attend service once a month, they find that 60 percent do. But when study participants keep journals of their daily whereabouts, researchers find that rates of attendance are significantly lower (Hadaway et al., 1993; Figure 16.4).

Service attendance, in fact, seems to be declining. Time-use records have shown that weekly attendance has dipped in the last 30 years, from 40 percent going to church once a week in 1965 to only 25 to 35 percent in 1994, a figure that was about the same in 2014 (Chaves, 2002; Pew Research Center, 2015b). This is not unique to the United States. In more than 20 advanced industrial countries, churchgoing is on the decline. (The opposite is happening in former Communist countries, where people attend church in greater numbers, perhaps to make up for lost time under Communism.)

FIGURE 16.4 Reported Attendance at Religious Services among US Population

SOURCE: Pew Research Center, 2015b.

Even if only 36 percent of Americans attend services weekly (Pew Research Center, 2015b), religious service attendance far outnumbers involvement in other voluntary organizations. In addition to their time, Americans donate considerable amounts of money to religious organizations.

Given this muddled picture of a diverse religious nation, is all the concern over secularization warranted? Are there signs that pluralism is eroding faith? Given Weber's prediction that the gods would flee in the face of rationalized economy and Marx's warning that modernization would wipe out all mystical thinking, why do people continue to hold religious beliefs in modern society? Secularization theory in the 1960s foretold the end of religion's importance in not just the social world but also our individual psyches. Religious commitment, the theorists told us, was waning, and the church was in a crisis. Indeed, great differentiation exists among faiths in America, and service attendance does not match followers' proclaimed conviction or even perhaps their best intentions. Overall, however, religion has proved a sturdy force. In 1997, Peter Berger backed away from his old claims, telling an interviewer in *Christian Century*:

> I think what I and most other sociologists of religion wrote in the 1960s about secularization was a mistake. Our underlying argument was that secularization and modernity go hand in hand. With more modernization comes more secularization. It wasn't a crazy theory. There was some evidence for it. But I think it's basically wrong. Most of the world today is certainly not secular. It's very religious. ("Epistemological Modesty," 1997, p. 972)

Although American engagement in formal religious life may have declined since the 1960s, Americans retain their beliefs in the supernatural. The otherworldly *Harry Potter* and *Game of Thrones* franchises have grossed millions; advances in space travel inspire awe of the mysterious cosmos; even the decoding of DNA sequences is further proof of "intelligent design" to some believers. For all of our scientific explanations and discoveries, modern people still turn to religion because some experiences—bafflement, suffering, and wonder—forever remain a part of the human condition (Chaves, 2002).

Indeed, both men and women tend to become more religious with age. Rodney Stark and William S. Bainbridge (1987) believe this happens because of the increased need for social support systems as well as the heightened search for answers to life's big questions. This increased religiousness is correlated with increased levels of altruism and feelings of purposefulness in life's everyday activities, which may help people age more gracefully (Dillon & Wink, 2003). However, while what Stark and Bainbridge describe may be true on an individual level (in the United States), when we look across societies, we find that those countries with older populations tend to be the least religious. Think Japan. The key missing link? Low fertility among more secular countries.

At the Micro Level: Is It a Great Big Delusion?

Right around 2007, the pages of prominent book reviews and more than a fair share of bloggers became involved in a heated debate over faith. The ruckus surrounded a few books by atheist academics that had been published back to back—namely, *The God Delusion* by Richard Dawkins (2006), an Oxford University evolutionary biologist; *God Is Not Great: How Religion Poisons Everything* by Christopher Hitchens (2007), a left-leaning public intellectual; and *Letter to a Christian Nation* by Sam Harris (2006), an American neuroscience student.

These best-selling authors take aim at religious belief as being factually inaccurate, irrational, and dangerous, and they use faith in science to try to disprove the existence of supernatural intelligence. They were vehemently criticized on a number of points, especially for not taking religious belief seriously. One reviewer noted that Dawkins simply dismissed belief as "base superstition" and that he equated followers with fundamentalists (Orr, 2007). What about religion's power to console people, to give guidance and strength, to give purpose and answers to these looming questions: Why am I here? What is the meaning of life? What comes after death?

Instead of criticizing religion in general, which is Dawkins's mission, sociologists of religion are more interested in another set of questions: Why

Richard Dawkins poses in front of an ad campaign that he and the British Humanist Association posted on 800 buses around Great Britain.

do people value their religious beliefs? How do they experience their faith in a way that makes them truly believe in something that an Oxford scientist has dismissed as factually inaccurate? To answer this set of questions, we turn to microsociology, an approach that examines everyday human interactions, practices, and beliefs on the small scale (see Chapter 1).

Religious experience, as the psychologist William James (1982) defined it, involves "feelings, acts, and experiences of individual men in their solitude, so far as they apprehend themselves to stand in relation to whatever they may consider the divine." To the people who experience them, these feelings, acts, and experiences are very real, physical, and powerful. Achieving spiritual awakening (*Bodhi*) for a Buddhist or deep meditation (*dhyāna*) for a Hindu can alter how he or she perceives the world. In one interview study, a woman discussed an out-of-body experience in which she was "whooshed" up into an astral plane to meet Jesus: "It's not a person, it's not a body, it's like a being of light. . . . And I feel like I've died and gone to heaven. I'm like ahh. And this deep booming, booming male voice says, 'Welcome home, Cathy,' and I start to sob" (Bender, 2007). Is this a fairly predictable neurological response to the lack of oxygen, as rational science critics would claim? To judge the authenticity of religious experience is not the job of sociology, says sociologist Nancy Ammerman (2005), echoing Durkheim; the job of sociologists is to better understand the meaning and uses of religion in people's lives. For example, Meredith McGuire (2007) focuses on how religion is physically felt in the body. It is through "embodied practices"—touches, postures, gestures, and movements—that religion becomes constituted by some followers as authentic and real, according to McGuire. Even something as simple as breathing can be a religious practice, as in pranayama yoga, where slow and deliberate breaths are part of connecting to spirituality (McGuire, 2007). Dancing is a common embodied practice of religions, and by sharing rhythmic dance moves, a community of worshipers can express their connection to one another and to their spirituality. Inasmuch as breathing and dancing reflect spiritual experiences, they also reproduce it, strengthening believers' bonds to their faith with each breath or clap of the hands (McGuire, 2007).

Sociologists may also study the way that people reconcile religion and rationality. For example, creationism as laid out in the book of Genesis in the Bible seems fundamentally at

How might sociologists study religious experiences like transcendental meditation?

odds with theories of evolution. But people don't always accept literal interpretations of religion wholesale, as sociologist Kelly Besecke (2007) determined in her study of American Christians. Besecke found that people practice reflexive spirituality—that is, they look to religion for meaning, wisdom, and profound thought and feeling rather than for absolute truths about how the world works. The reflexive spiritualists Besecke studied were also tired of swallowing the whole scientific story. They believed in logic and reasoning to help them get to the bottom of some of life's challenges but didn't trust science to provide them with transcendent truths, symbolic meanings, or inspirational metaphors. For reflexive spiritualists, the tensions between fact and faith become less compelling, and religion remains a sensible avenue for finding meaning in life.

The Power of Religion: Social Movements

The Reverend Simeon Jocelyn of New Haven, speaking in 1834 before a meeting of the American Anti-Slavery Society, condemned slavery as the nation's moral failing. "Resolved," he said, "that the American church is stained with the blood of 'the souls of poor innocents,' and holds the keys of the great prison of oppression; that while she enslaves, she is herself enslaved" (quoted in Young, 2002). Jocelyn, like most evangelicals of the day, was riding on a new crest of social action. The antislavery and temperance (antialcohol) campaigns were among the first major social movements in the United States. (See Chapter 18 for a broader discussion of social movements.)

The American landscape in the 1830s was in turmoil. In a time of rapid market expansion, when new canal and road networks offered unprecedented possibility for mobility, people were plucked from traditional life and plunged into urban, industrial, and sometimes remote places, such as the West. The US population jumped from 3.8 million in 1790 to 12.8 million in 1830 (Young, 2002). Yet despite rapid growth, America of the early 1800s still lacked national institutions. The centralized post office had been established, making interregional communication possible, but no political institution existed that could put it to use for enacting sweeping social change. Such a context created difficulties for the abolitionist and temperance campaigns as they tried to disseminate their messages. It was nearly impossible to mobilize the kind of powerful political network that would persuade people to do anything about slavery and alcohol. Instead, they deployed religion.

Although the country enjoyed a limited national governmental apparatus, without lobbyists, political action committees, or interest group think tanks, there were a readily available and sturdy evangelical ethos, a shared culture, and a blossoming network of religious organizations. In particular, the churches of elites, such as Presbyterians and Congregationalists (to which about one-third of all regular churchgoers belonged), shared a spirit of "organized benevolence," the idea that God held high expectations for the new country. It was their mission to become the keepers of the new Promised Land, to protect it against national sins like slavery and alcohol. Meanwhile, other growing groups, such as the Methodists and Baptists, promoted the personal confession of sin, which soon grew into public spectacles. Public confessions and conversions became a widespread recruitment vehicle, bringing mass numbers to American churches. In 1780 perhaps 400 Baptist congregations and a handful of Methodist congregations existed; by 1820 these churches numbered 5,400 congregations (Gaustad, 1962).

These two elements, public confession and national sin, converged in no time into a public confession against the sins of the nation, or what sociologist Michael Young (2002) calls "confessional protest." In the face of particular sins like drinking and slavery, this religious infrastructure allowed the temperance and antislavery movements to resonate with the masses. In 1829 the American Temperance Society had just 200 branches, mostly clustered in Connecticut, Massachusetts, and New York; by 1834 there were more than 8,000 branches with 1.5 million members. The antislavery movement also boomed. For instance, the Anti-Slavery Society, which started in 1833 with the goal of "the abolition of slavery by the spirit of repentance," grew from 75 auxiliaries to 1,340 by 1838. Its messages were disseminated in large part by women, who dominated the rosters of both the temperance

Attendees at camp meetings, such as this Methodist revival in 1839, led many of the antislavery and temperance movements before the Civil War.

and the antislavery societies. Because women lacked formal political power, the societies became socially acceptable places for them to exert influence outside the home.

These movements picked up momentum as mass spectacles of confession and conversion spread throughout the country. During public confessions in upstate New York, spirits merchants poured their stock into the streets, prompting hundreds of audience members to swear off booze. It was announced at one temperance convention in Boston, in 1836, that the entire nation was guilty if its citizens indulged a sin like drinking:

> That in the support of the wholesome laws of God and our country, we here pledge ourselves never to swerve from our purposes and efforts, while the monster intemperance is allowed to spread its withering influence abroad in our land. (Young, 2002, p. 681)

Martin Luther King Jr. preaching at his church. What was religion's role in the US civil rights movement?

Similarly, in abolitionist meetings, slave owners and merchants renounced slavery as part of becoming born again.

It wasn't an easy road for members of these new movements, particularly the abolitionists, who were met with mob riots, threats, harassment, hurled eggs, stones, and in one case even bullets (Young, 2002). But they persevered, grew in number, and eventually won—a victory made possible not through state or national political institutions, the typical vehicles for enacting social change today, but through religion.

The significance of piety—dutiful adherence to religious doctrine in mind and body—in America lies not in religion's popularity but rather in its capacity to mold our social world. Religion and politics have mingled in many profound ways since the nineteenth century. Consider the civil rights movement led by the Reverend Dr. Martin Luther King Jr., who has been immortalized in our national history with near sainthood status. (In its obituary of April 5, 1968, the *New York Times* exalted the Nobel Peace Prize winner as "a veritable hero," a "prophet," and the "voice of anguish.") We tend to put a lot of stock in the power of charismatic individuals such as King. However, even a leader as oratorically gifted and politically astute as he was needed the right set of circumstances. Those circumstances, it turns out, had already been put in place by a powerful force: religion. In

The Origins of the Civil Rights Movement, Aldon Morris (1984) contends that King's power was the result of a strong organizational base that was already in place in the 1960s in the Black community, and its centerpiece was the church. Theorists of "resource mobilization" have argued that religion played a central role in the civil rights movement by providing organizational and symbolic resources, preparing African Americans and binding them into dense social networks, building coalitions, opening communication, and providing within-community funding. King was effective because he was backed by the Southern Christian Leadership Conference and the Student Non-violent Coordinating Committee, both mobilized through the Black church. In fact, argues David Garrow (1968), King was in the right place at exactly the moment when the movement needed an educated, inspiring spokesman.

Religion can be a means of gaining political momentum, strengthening group cohesion, and expressing group culture. It can work to the advantage of marginalized communities such as African Americans, but the reverse is also true: Religion can dismiss, oppress, or marginalize certain groups. For example, right-wing hate groups rely heavily on religiosity, citing the biblical determination of difference and inequality between races. White suprem-acists of the Kingdom Identity Ministries in Arkansas, for example, claim that the real difference between Whites and Blacks is preordained by the divine; and the Knights of the Fiery Cross, otherwise known as the Ku Klux Klan, define themselves as "religious warriors," justifying their anti-Black terrorist tactics in the name of God and religious values. After the Civil War, Reconstruction-era Klan members spread their message with exuber-ance and theatricality; many Klansmen committed their "holy" atrocities in squirrel-skin masks, masquerade costumes, and even women's dresses, incorporating the conventions of minstrelsy and the circus to get their mes-sage across (Parsons, 2005).

Spiritual conviction and religious organizations have been integral in shaping the social landscape—for better or for worse. Even when not put to use by competing groups as they jockey for social power, religion proves a powerful force in the day-to-day shaping of individual consciousness.

Religion and the Social Landscape

Just as religion shapes social institutions like government and social move-ments, so too does it operate on small-scale perceptions and choices in everyday spheres, such as family life, voting choices, lifestyles, and racial attitudes. Sometimes implicitly, at other times glaringly, faith is related to family structure, gender, social status, age, and educational attainment.

FAMILIES

In general, religion is seen to be associated with family. For example, religious individuals tend to have more children than their nonreligious counterparts and divorce less often (Hayford & Morgan, 2008; Sherkat, 1998). A survey found that nonreligious women intend to have 2.1 children, but women who attend religious services almost every week plan to have an average of 2.62 children (Payne, 2013). Differences in child-rearing styles do exist among faiths. Conservative Protestants are more likely than Catholics to embrace corporal punishment and hierarchical and authoritarian relationships between parents and children, but they also yell less frequently at their kids and give them more affection than other parents (Wilcox, 1999). Religious fathers spend more time one-on-one with their children and hug and praise them more often than fathers without a strong religious affiliation (Wilcox, 2004). That said, Nancy Nason-Clark (2000) has found that rates of domestic violence are no different in religious communities when contrasted with secular ones.

Evangelical Protestants, such as those belonging to the Southern Baptist Convention, tend to embrace a traditional patriarchal family structure in which the wife submits to her provider husband (see Chapter 12). This family structure appears to work fairly well for many, as evangelical Protestants report high levels of marital happiness and accord, though it may be harder for members of religious families to admit the existence of domestic abuse. Nason-Clark has found that rates of abuse within religious families are about the same as rates in the general US population but that there is a greater stigma attached to family discord in religious families, making it more difficult for them to report abuse. When they do report abuse, they may turn to clergy members who are not specifically trained to handle domestic abuse and who are invested in promoting family unity. On the other hand, some religious abuse victims find their attempts to seek help from people outside the religious community are unsatisfying because they do not draw on their faith or church doctrine to make sense of what happened to the victims, to comfort them, or to give them strength to heal (Nason-Clark, 2000).

RACE

In 1963, the Reverend Dr. Martin Luther King Jr. said in an interview, "We must face the fact that in America, the church is still the most segregated major institution in America. At 11:00 on Sunday morning when we stand and sing and Christ has no east or west, we stand at the most segregated hour in this nation." Is Sunday morning still the most segregated hour in America? Pretty much. While workplaces and neighborhoods have become more mixed, ongoing research has found that only 10 percent of churches are racially mixed, meaning that no single race makes up more than 80 percent of the congregation (Scheitle & Dougherty, 2010). Catholic churches are more likely to be mixed, owing in part to Hispanic migration. Only 2 to 3 percent of Protestant churches are racially mixed (Dart, 2001).

The Black church has long played an important role in the larger Black community—Martin Luther King Jr. was both a religious and a political leader. Of course, religious organizations are just like other organizations in that they have to adapt to and cope with the external pressures of social change. The Black church's role in Black communities has been tempered by the changing social conditions of African Americans. Some scholars have argued that Black and White churches operate in similar ways today— primarily as providers of mental health and psychological well-being. But others have argued that the Black church does more than provide spiritual fixes (Chaves & Higgins, 1992). Historically, the church has played a more central role in the secular lives of Black congregations than in those of White congregations. This has resulted from three conditions. First, African Americans share a legacy of racial discrimination, violence, and injustice. Second, no other secular institution has ever organized and helped the Black community as much as the church. Third, the Black community has substantial social needs that necessitate an effective social helping hand. (See our discussion of racism and Black–White inequality in Chapter 9.)

Religion has often been called a "free space" for African American churchgoers (Sherkat & Ellison, 1999), providing a psychological and social haven in the face of marginalization and hostility. In areas of life where other institutions may leave gaps, the Black church provides a source of collective self-help, political activism, social networking, and community involvement. The Black church remains a salient force in fighting for civil rights and easing poverty (Chaves & Higgins, 1992).

The Black church was also at the forefront of the trend to liven up Sunday services with rousing music and even dance. Here again, we see that there are links between the Black church and the wider Black community. Gospel music that started in the church filtered out and continues to influence R&B musical styles. Furthermore, whereas dancing acquired a bad name in some Christian churches, because it was seen as a gateway to sinful behavior or as a sin in itself, since the late nineteenth century some Black Southern Baptist churches have incorporated dance into worship. What was once called praise dancing and has now influenced liturgical dance (neither of which is still restricted to Black churches) involves physical interpretations of songs and scripture. There is now a national Gospelfest, sponsored by McDonald's, in which praise groups from various churches compete in a spiritual dance-off.

GENDER

Patterns of religious activity and affiliation also arise according to gender. Women are more active in religious organizations than men, either because they are socialized to be the more virtuous of the sexes or because they feel

A Gospelfest performance in Newark, New Jersey. The annual festival features choirs, steppers, and praise dancers.

a greater need for the kind of social and financial support the church offers (Figure 16.5). There is a women's group in nearly one of every three congregations but a men's group in just one of four (Ammerman, 2005). These women's groups, once called "ladies' aid" organizations, exist to help women experience spiritual growth as well as to lend a hand to congregation members in hard times, providing them with jobs, services, and food. They have been on the decline since women's mass entry into the labor force starting in the 1970s.

Conservative Protestant and Mormon women participate less in the labor force because traditional religious beliefs go hand in hand with more traditional beliefs about gender (see Chapter 8). Jennifer Glass and Jerry Jacobs (2005) show that evangelically reared women are less interested in their careers and more interested in their families, and get married and bear children earlier than other women do. Some sociologists interpret such findings as evidence that these conservative faiths breed gender inequality.

CLASS

A person's socioeconomic status is also linked to religion (see Chapter 7). Hindus, Jews, and Buddhists, along with atheists and agnostics, tend to be the most highly educated, while members of evangelical Protestant churches and historically Black churches have less education (Pew Forum on Religion and Public Life, 2015b). Interestingly, while people with more education have less attachment to some of the more traditional religious beliefs, higher education spurs increased participation in religious organizations (Iannaccone, 1997). Highly educated individuals are more likely to explore less traditional faiths and belief structures and/or to participate in religious organizations

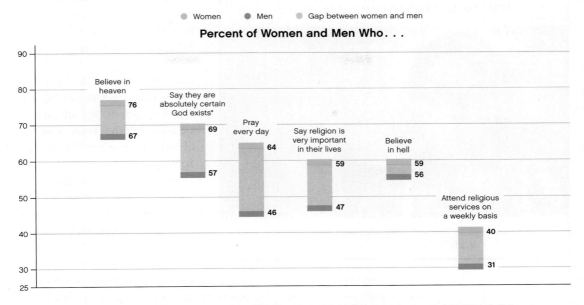

FIGURE 16.5 Religious Activity by Gender, 2014

● Women   ● Men   ● Gap between women and men

Percent of Women and Men Who. . .

Believe in heaven: 76 / 67

Say they are absolutely certain God exists*: 69 / 57

Pray every day: 64 / 46

Say religion is very important in their lives: 59 / 47

Believe in hell: 59 / 56

Attend religious services on a weekly basis: 40 / 31

*Question wording: Do you believe in God or a universal spirit? [IF BELIEVE IN GOD, ASK]: How certain are you about this belief? Are you absolutely certain, fairly certain, not too certain, or not at all certain? [IF BELIEVE IN GOD, ASK]: Which comes closest to your view of God? God is a person with whom people can have a relationship or God is an impersonal force?

SOURCE: Pew Research Center, 2015b.

for the civic rewards of belonging. On college campuses, faculty members in the natural, physical, and engineering sciences are much more likely to belong to a church and to express religious commitment than are social scientists or those in law or the humanities (Steinberg, 1974). Higher-income earners donate more to religious organizations, but they also score lower on church participation than lower-income earners (in effect, offsetting their absence with larger donations to the collection plate). And people whose education level exceeds that of their religious peer group are likely to switch to a different, higher-brow group (Sherkat, 1991).

Historically, America has been dominated by Protestants, particularly Episcopalians, Presbyterians, and Congregationalists (called the United Church of Christ since 1957). So important and powerful was this trend that its influence was referred to as the "Episcopalianization of the whole upper class" (Baltzell, 1958). The reason, sociologists contend, is that Protestants were here first, so they had the upper hand in shaping social policies and institutions in line with their values and to their own advantage, making it hard for incoming religious groups such as Jews and Catholics to get a foothold in cultural and political arenas. Protestants have lost some ground over the last few decades (Davidson et al., 1995), but they are still overrepresented

DIGITAL.WWNORTON.COM/YOUMAYASK7

To see my interview with Susan Crawford Sullivan, go to
digital.wwnorton.com/youmayask7

at the top of the status, class, and political hierarchy in America. In particular, Episcopalians have shown remarkable stability among the nation's powerful and cultural elites. With about 2.3 million members, the Episcopal Church in America is only the fifteenth largest, yet one in four US presidents has been a member of this institution (Goodstein, 2007).

Class background also influences the way religion is practiced by low-income people, especially people who may not live in families that look exactly like the traditional two-parent, stay-at-home-mom model associated with conservative religious communities. I talked to sociologist Susan Crawford Sullivan about the research she has been conducting with lower-class religious women. She told me how surprised she was that "religious faith played an important role in their lives," yet most of them had little or no interaction with churches, mosques, or other forms of organized religion. Why were they staying away? One reason was logistics. Crawford Sullivan said, "[A]bout half my sample was homeless, living in long-term homeless shelters," but another third "talked about stigma as a reason, feeling unwelcomed by religious communities . . . because they were poor . . . [and] didn't have money for the collection basket," and had "a feeling like the church didn't want poor, single mothers there" (Conley, 2013g). Many of the women who did not feel welcome at church made religion a part of their daily lives by praying in the bathroom at work or introducing their children to "faith practices at home," like Bible stories and religious video clips. Though outside of organized religion, they actively "drew on faith as a source of resilience . . . and survival." The sense of being part of something larger than oneself need not be formally organized to be meaningful (Conley, 2013g).

GEOGRAPHY AND POLITICS

Religious believers tend to be concentrated in certain parts of the country. Catholics are disproportionately located in the Northeast and Southwest. Lutherans tend to live in the upper Midwest. Baptists dominate the South, and Mormons are most common in Utah (Bradley et al., 1992). Political affiliations overlap with religious ones, such that regional voting patterns correlate to religious beliefs. Thirty years ago, voting behavior and party affiliation were best predicted by a person's income. Today, however, religious attitudes are the best indicators. A high rate of agreement with the statement "AIDS is God's punishment for immoral sexual behavior," for instance, may be highly correlated with a state that votes Republican in an election (Bradberry, 2016). Why the shift? According to one study (Glaeser & Ward, 2006), Republican strategists such as Steve Bannon and Karl Rove (and Ronald Reagan before them) deliberately shifted their base to religious followers. In contrast, people who are more politically liberal tend to be less religious (Baker, 2015; Glock & Stark, 1965). This pattern holds internationally too: Left-leaning liberal countries such as France and the Netherlands are relatively secular.

Selling God and Shopping for Faith: The Commercialization of Religious Life

On Easter Sunday 2006 in Atlanta, some 40,000 people gathered for a worship spectacle in the famous sports and concert arena, the Georgia Dome. With the expressed aim of "giving the Devil his due," the Resurrection Sunday service of New Birth Missionary Baptist Church was heralded as the largest Easter service in the world. Indeed, the big-budget production presented four hours of religious entertainment, including a 500-member choir, a marching band, a rock group, a flag corps, several dance troupes, and a closing performance by Patti LaBelle (who did not fail to mention the release of her new album). The only thing this Sunday service appeared to be missing was silence. New Birth, not one for shying away from profits, is known for its dazzling productions that attract huge crowds as well as "corporate sponsors, politicians, and entertainers looking for a way to get their own good word out" (Goodman, 2006a).

Religion in the United States is big business. Americans donated $125 billion to religious organizations in 2016, which constituted one-third of total charitable donations (National Philanthropic Trust, 2018). A study by the Hartford Institute for Religious Research found that the average annual income of a megachurch, which is typically a conservative Protestant church that attracts at least 2,000 worshipers per week, is $7.25 million (Fillinger, 2013). Ministers of megachurches reportedly earned more than $100,000 a year in the 1990s (Nussbaum, 2006).

MEGACHURCH

typically, a conservative Protestant church that attracts at least 2,000 worshipers per week.

The fast-growing market for Christian products is also quite lucrative. Mel Gibson's controversial film *The Passion of the Christ,* for instance, grossed over $600 million. (Apart from questions about its historical accuracy, the film was criticized as being anti-Semitic.) Since this was released in 2004, there have been a number of highly successful, religiously themed movies released, including *Hacksaw Ridge,* also directed by Mel Gibson (2016: $175 million) and *Heaven Is for Real* (2015: $101 million) (Fox News, 2017). Major studios now have faith-based divisions, such as Sony's Affirm Films. And there is a Christian alternative to Netflix called Pure Flix (Faughnder, 2016).

Meanwhile, Christian music totals $16.5 billion in sales annually. In 2002, evangelical pastor Rick Warren wrote *The Purpose-Driven Life,* which has sold more than 30 million copies—the largest sales figure for any non-fiction hardcover book ever published in the United States. Warren was subsequently chosen to deliver the invocation at President Barack Obama's historic inauguration. Christian products are estimated at $4.2 billion in annual sales. There's even a growing field of Christian public relations, which manages and markets particular "brands" of Christianity. Walmart, tapping into this trend, has expanded its stock of Christian-themed merchandise, which currently grosses more than $1 billion a year (Coolidge, 2011).

Among faith's consumers, plenty of "buy and return" activity exists. Approximately one-third of Americans switch religious affiliations, and nearly a third of those switch more than once (Roof, 1989). According to survey data, there is growth among conservative Protestant sects, Jehovah's Witnesses, and Mormons, whereas moderate and liberal Protestant churches are losing numbers (Sherkat & Ellison, 1999). Religion shopping is

Every Sunday tens of thousands of congregants flock to Lakewood Church, a Houston-area megachurch whose pastor, Joel Osteen, is also author of several *New York Times* best-selling books.

especially high among teens. In a 2002–3 survey of 13- to 17-year-olds, the National Study of Youth and Religion found that 16 percent of respondents participated in more than one congregation at a time. About 4 percent attend youth groups outside their congregations. Taking a consumerist approach to faith, teens report feeling more authentically connected to their religion after exploring the market for themselves (Banerjee, 2005).

Although it may make some people uncomfortable to use economic language to discuss faith, viewing religious choice through this lens of "the market" makes religious pluralism seem less like a crisis—as the old secularization theory held—and more like a strength (Sherkat & Ellison, 1999). Such a "rational choice," or economic, perspective on religion sees congregations as franchises and ministers as entrepreneurial salespeople. The churchgoer is a consumer who spends his or her time and money on religion in exchange for supernatural compensators (Stark & Bainbridge, 1985)—or promises of future rewards, such as salvation or eternity in heaven. Shopping the church market for the best promises of salvation and answers about the meaning of life is no simple task, for there are inherent risks and uncertainty about the worth of these "goods." It's up to the ministers and religious leaders to market them to you in an attractive way so as to draw you in.

Because each faith offers a different spin on the meaning of life, death, and the afterlife, the more religious diversity a society has, the less credible any one particular faith is. Secularization theory held that pluralism would undermine religion for this reason. In contrast, rational choice scholars such as Stark and Finke (2000) borrowed an idea from the eighteenth-century economist Adam Smith that competition makes for better goods (see Chapter 14). In a highly pluralistic society such as the United States, where churches compete with one another to sustain a congregation, the quality of religion is better than what would exist under a state-controlled religious monopoly, as in Catholic medieval Europe (Finke & Stark, 1992). Competition makes all religions shape up and maintain high quality in order to attract consumers; therefore, pluralism results in high overall levels of religiosity. Thus this long history of freedom and choice in the religious "marketplace" may be one explanation for America's high levels of religiosity, compared with countries such as England and Sweden (Stark & Finke, 2000). If the good news is that religious pluralism offers a range of choices among faiths, the bad news, some critics contend, is that religion is being marketed—which is ostensibly a profane act. Saddleback Church in Lake Forest, California, the church presided over by pastor and best-selling author Rick Warren, has been compared to megacorporations such as Google or Starbucks. Warren's church has become a brand; he even hires a public relations agent to manage it (Saroyan, 2006).

Just how does one go about selling God? Here are a few lessons from American religious entrepreneurship.

SUPERNATURAL COMPENSATORS
promises of future rewards, such as salvation or eternity in heaven.

LESSON 1: IF YOU CAN'T BEAT 'EM, JOIN 'EM

Youth groups appeal to teens by featuring rock bands, and incorporating teen lingo (one T-shirt slogan reads, "Jesus is my homeboy") and frank, open prayer that connects to issues of everyday life. Increasingly, churches are offering secular activities such as health clinics, gyms, sports fields, and marriage and substance abuse counseling; in one Houston church, there's even a McDonald's (James, 2003). Many churches have stripped away the traditional dogma, revamping sermons with dramatic skit performances and setting hymns to rock or pop beats to cater to young crowds. It seems to be working to lure at least some of the "unchurched generation" back into the fold. Hillsong NYC is the fastest-growing congregation in New York City, attracting 6,000 attendees to services every Sunday that are run by its swaggering, leather-jacket-wearing, skinny-jeans-toting, Evangelical preacher, Carl Lentz, who shares the good word from under a disco ball (Wyler, 2014). The message: Relent and give the video game generation what they want.

LESSON 2: BIGGER IS BETTER

Witness the megachurch phenomenon that spread through many middle-class suburbs beginning in the mid-1990s. The average megachurch Sunday worship attendance is 4,586. Sixty percent of these churches are in the American Sunbelt, mostly in California, Texas, Florida, and Georgia. Megachurch congregations run the gamut from Southern Baptist to liberal Protestant, though 54 percent of them are nondenominational (Bird & Thumma, 2011).

Attendees sway to the music at a service at Hillsong NYC.

Willow Creek Community Church of Illinois, which draws around 20,000 people a week across seven locations, had an annual budget of about $27.44 million in 2011. The House of Hope megachurch complex of Salem Baptist Church is a 10,000-seat, $50 million project built in 2005 to accommodate 22,000 members. And Warren, author of the best seller mentioned previously, has 80,000 members in five churches (Ferran, 2009).

Megachurch ministries take their cues from business management practices, luring suburbanites with a theatrical experience complete with lighting rigs, electric bands playing contemporary music, dramatic skits, and sermons that draw lessons from daily living (Niebuhr, 1995). They stress family values above religious traditions and are known for being flexible and creative. At first glance, these don't even look like churches; they seem more like community centers or even colleges (Goldberger, 1995). Some churches, seeking venues with adequate parking, have moved into old warehouses, armories, and even sporting venues. With their ordinary facades, megachurches drive home the point that religion is an integral and relevant part of routine suburban living.

Megachurches are also appearing in Black communities, particularly suburban, middle-class ones. In one of the country's most affluent African American communities, Prince George's County in Maryland, the Ebenezer African Methodist Episcopal megachurch thrives. It even has valet parking and white-gloved ushers for its 12,000 members in its $18 million building ("Black Megachurches Surge," 1996).

Megachurches have filled a niche among urban and ethnic populations too. Take, for example, the Promise Church in Queens, New York, which is home to a mostly Korean American Pentecostal congregation. It has more than 3,000 members, making it the largest of the four Korean megachurches in the city (Knafo, 2005). Featuring big-production plays, it hopes to win over young Korean Americans, who have largely abandoned Christianity in the last few years. The trend, known among Koreans as the "silent exodus," is a result of many prosperous Koreans moving out of Queens. The church was once the core source of social support and services, but as Korean businesses flourish, the church has withered. Enter megachurches like Promise, which offer pop cultural allure to win back worshipers.

LESSON 3: SPEED PLEASES

Many churches feature several quick services in one day—sometimes because the parking and seating just cannot accommodate the entire congregation. These events often get right down to the point, addressing frank issues and problems of daily living in 50 minutes or less with just enough time for one group of parishioners to file out while the next worshipers are filing in. But perhaps the epitome of speed is the so-called drive-through church. For its Memorial Day service in 2005, the Metropolitan Church of the Quad Cities in Iowa offered one that took just a few minutes (Baker, 2005).

LESSON 4: SEX SELLS

Except for the Song of Solomon, the Bible simply is not very sexy. According to Bible publisher Thomas Nelson, Inc., which has been issuing Bibles for more than 200 years, the number-one reason teens don't read the Bible is because it is "too big and freaky looking." To spice things up, some publishers have combined youth pop culture with the traditional Bible to engender a new genre of the New Testament: the Biblezine. Throughout the glossy pages of *Revolve* for girls, scripture appeared next to color photographs and advice columns addressing boy problems, fashion questions, and the complications of friendship (Haskell, 2004). Meanwhile, *Refuel*, for boys, featured articles about rock music, sports, and sexuality, and the cover featured headlines such as "How to Attract Godly Girls" and "What Is 'Radical Faith?'" This Biblezine has innovatively marketed the scripture as if it were a hot new video game, as something that is easily mastered, with immediate payoff.

Like other traditional media, Biblezines have pretty much bit the dust in recent years. (One exception is *Brio* magazine, which was revived in 2017 [McCammon, 2017].) They have largely been replaced by Facebook groups,

Publishers designed Biblezines such as *Revolve* and *Refuel* to appeal to young Christians by emulating popular magazines. They even included fashion tips, quizzes, bios, and community basics. Why are some people critical of these new kinds of Bibles?

Twitter feeds, and other new media that pitch at youth with the same angle. Some skeptics ask what happens to religion's deep meanings and sense of greatness when they are subsumed by marketing (Haskell, 2004). Despite these concerns, faith and marketing have long been intertwined. In 1925, Bruce Barton portrayed Jesus as the original businessman in his best seller *The Man Nobody Knows*. The 1970 rock opera *Jesus Christ Superstar* became a Tony Award—winning musical, and later a film, though it was condemned by religious groups at the time. Today, there's a Christian Tattoo Association, founded in the mid-1990s, with hundreds of Christian punk and goth members across the country.

The Paradox of Popularity

In his popular book *The Social Sources of Denominationalism* (1929), H. Richard Niebuhr set out to explain why so many religious groupings exist under one faith, Christianity. He concluded that the reason for so many different denominations was that people had a diversity of needs, and indeed, in a highly pluralistic society such as America, there is something for everyone. But among the sea of choices, some churches fare better than others. Some come and go, catching barely any notice, whereas others ride a wave of success followed by an inevitable crash, only to then wash away. Others endure. To track the reasons behind the various successes and failures of churches, sociologists look not at the merits of any one faith but instead at the social patterns of religious organizations in general.

THE SECT-CHURCH CYCLE

Sociologists classify religious organizations as churches, sects, or cults. Churches are religious bodies that coexist in a relatively low state of tension with their social surroundings (Finke & Stark, 1992). They have mainstream, "safe" beliefs and practices relative to those of the general population. Because they are world-affirming more often than world-criticizing, they peacefully coexist (or at least try to) with the secular world, so they are low-tension organizations.

Sects or sectarian groups, by contrast, are high-tension bodies that don't fit so well within the existing social environment (Finke & Stark, 1992). These organizations are usually most attractive to society's least privileged—outcasts, minorities, or the poor—because they downplay worldly pleasure by stressing otherworldly promises. Sects can be an appealing alternative

CHURCHES

religious bodies that coexist in a relatively low state of tension with their social surroundings. They have mainstream, "safe" beliefs and practices relative to those of the general population.

SECTS OR SECTARIAN GROUPS

high-tension organizations that don't fit well within the existing social environment. They are usually most attractive to society's least privileged—outcasts, minorities, or the poor—because they downplay worldly pleasure by stressing otherworldly promises.

to engagement in secular life, because sectarian groups typically limit their contact with the outside world, keeping mainstream culture at a distance for fear of contamination. Material things don't matter as much as the supernatural world, which each sect purports to understand better than any other religious body.

Sects usually start out by splintering off from an existing church, typically when church leaders become too involved in secular issues in some members' eyes. To distance themselves from what they see as worldly concerns and corruption, members may form their own sect. Over time, if the sect picks up a significant following, it almost inevitably transforms into its own church, ultimately becoming part of the mainstream. As this happens, a new splinter group, made up of new "true" radicals, may become discontented and branch off to form their own sect. Thus the cycle continues.

This pattern is clear among Protestant denominations, which over the centuries have modernized their doctrines, embraced mainstream values, and thus lost much of their distinctiveness; they then often go into decline (Finke & Stark, 1992). With increased popularity, mainline faiths simply become too watered down, and intense religiosity decreases. For example, the United Methodist Church (2016) has more than 12.5 million members worldwide, and although this number has grown over the last decade because of increased membership in Africa and Asia, the percentage of US adults who claim Methodist affiliation has shrunk from 5.1 percent in 2007 to 3.6 percent in 2014 (Pew Research Center, 2015b). In the founding year of the United States, 1776, the Methodists were a tiny religious society with only 65 churches throughout the colonies and 4,921 members. By 1850 they dominated the nation with 13,302 congregations and more than 2.6 million members. In *Southern Cross: The Beginnings of the Bible Belt* (1997), historian Christine Leigh Heyrman describes early Methodists as a radical bunch. They supported gender equality and the abolition of slavery, so it's no surprise that they faced difficulty drawing crowds in the South. To cement their initial popularity, Methodists shed some of their less popular beliefs and practices (such as extreme celibacy and the occasional castration of a minister). As they built seminaries, began paying full-time ministers, and developed a less radical, more systematic theology, they increasingly appealed to the mainstream and as a result soon became the most popular church. Meanwhile, sectarian splinter groups such as the Free Methodists and Holiness Churches broke off to bring the faith back to its old-time roots (Finke & Stark, 1992).

A cult, on the other hand, is a religious movement that makes some new claim about the supernatural and therefore does not as easily fit within the sect–church cycle. A famous example was Heaven's Gate, formed in 1973 by two previously mainline Protestants, Marshall Herff Applewhite Jr. and

CULT

religious movement that makes some new claim about the supernatural and therefore does not easily fit within the sect–church cycle.

Bonnie Nettles. Known as "the Two," they spread the word that civilization was doomed. Furthermore, they claimed that only the disciplined few could be saved by way of a spacecraft to be sent by God. In 1997, 39 members of the group, trying to reach God's UFO behind the Hale-Bopp comet, committed mass suicide in California. Outrageously otherworldly as they were, Heaven's Gate was not successful in generating a mass following, but a few better-known cults have been enormously successful, such as those started by Jesus, Bud-

Heaven's Gate leader Marshall Herff Applewhite Jr. What distinguishes a cult such as Heaven's Gate from a sect or a church?

dha, Joseph Smith, and Muhammad. All religions begin as cults, and their leaders offer new insights, claiming that they are the word of God. Because they're so novel, cults are often high-tension movements that antagonize their social world and/or are antagonized by it. From the examples above, it should be clear that some cults evolve into low-tension organizations, whereas others destroy themselves with their own zealotry.

The sect–church cycle is currently playing out for evangelicals, the conservative Protestant congregations that blossomed in the South and have been growing steadily over the last two centuries (as compared to liberal Protestant congregations), while mainline Protestant churches have more recently seen declines in membership. In 2011, the United Methodist Church lost 72,000 members, a 1 percent drop. In 2011 and 2012, the Presbyterian Church lost a total of 165,000 members, an 8.5 percent drop. Meanwhile, Jehovah's Witnesses had the highest overall growth, increasing their membership by 4.37 percent (Yeakley, 2011). Despite this growth, evangelicals are currently faced with the pressures of the sect–church cycle as they increasingly fracture on political issues. To make matters more unstable, one of the most prominent leaders of the evangelical movement, the Reverend Billy Graham, has died, and the movement is struggling to define its identity. John C. Green, who studies religion, characterizes evangelicals as belonging to one of three camps: traditionalists, centrists, and modernists. Traditionalists and centrists each account for 40 to 50 percent of evangelicals; modernists make up the remaining minority (Luo, 2006).

As you can see, there is tension between traditionalists and centrists. In these fissures, a new style of church has arrived on the evangelical scene. "Emerging" or "postmodern" churches, also called "alt-worship," have

Contemporary evangelicals can be divided into several different camps. What distinguishes modernists from centrists or traditionalists? How do they appeal to different groups?

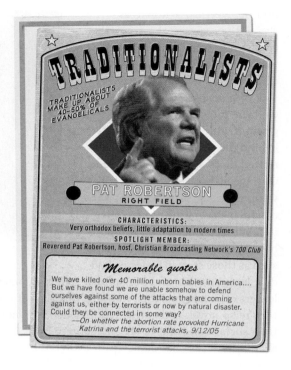

tapped into a generation of religious dropouts, those with little or no formal attachment to the church. The disillusionment of these dropouts has arisen as part of a backlash against the enormous success of megafaiths. According to Pastor Lee Rabe of Threads, an emerging church in Kalamazoo, Michigan, alt-worshipers want a church that provides an intense experience yet also makes sense within their daily lives, with theological relaxations such as reading the Bible as a narrative (i.e., as not necessarily unerring) and a deemphasis on individual salvation in favor of holistic world recovery (Luo, 2006). Emerging churches can be found in school gyms and storefronts, and some scholars predict that these small-scale sites will be the next big trend in evangelical worship (Leland, 2004).

Evangelicalism, since its very beginning, has been accustomed to friction. In the late 1940s the National Association of Evangelicals was founded with the goal of moving away from the strict fundamentalism that has always been intermingled with the evangelical Protestant tradition. The movement was initially intended to be a middle ground between what was seen as theological liberalism in mainline Protestantism and cultural separatism among fundamentalists (Luo, 2006). If evangelicalism was a middle road then, it is faced with forks and fissures of its own today.

CENTRISTS

CENTRISTS MAKE UP ABOUT 40–50% OF EVANGELICALS

RICK WARREN
CENTER FIELD

Characteristics:
Conservative beliefs, more mainstream political stance

Spotlight Member:
Reverend Rick Warren of Saddleback Church
in Orange County, California

What Rick's got to say...

Because I think the church is called to not just talk,
but to share, to love, to help tackle these issues like
poverty, and illiteracy and disease.
—On CNN's *Larry King Live*, 3/22/05

Modernists
(or liberal evangelicals)
make up less than 10%
of evangelicals

MODERNISTS

CAMERON STRANG
LEFT FIELD

CHARACTERISTICS:	SPOTLIGHT MEMBER:
Less strict adherence to orthodoxy, more diverse beliefs and practices	Alt-evangelical Cameron Strang, founder of the Christian book and magazine company Relevant Media

HIS STANCE ON RELIGION:
We don't want to show up on Sunday, sing two hymns, hear a sermon
and go home. The Bible says we're supposed to die for this thing.
If I'm going to do that, this has to be worth something. Our
generation wants a tangible experience of God who is there.
—On the emergent church movement, in the *New York Times*, 5/16/04

WHY ARE CONSERVATIVE CHURCHES GROWING?

How has evangelicalism cornered an increasing amount of the religious market? The secret to evangelicalism's success may lie in the strictness of its doctrine. Dean M. Kelley, an executive of the National Council of Churches, proposed this "strict church thesis" in his controversial *Why Conservative Churches Are Growing* (1972). Kelley claimed that conservative sects were outpacing mainline churches precisely because of their strictness: "Strong organizations are strict. . . . The stricter the stronger" (Finke & Stark, 1992). Rational choice theorists such as Finke and Stark have taken up Kelley's thesis to argue that when a religious body has a lot of low-commitment members, it will lose its highly committed members because of the problem of free riders (a more formal term for shirkers). Nobody likes free riders; they reap all the benefits of belonging without the costs of participating. Besides being just plain irksome, free riders can affect group morale and cause all the hardworking members to slack off as well, creating a snowball effect of freeloading until no one bothers any longer to do the work of running an organization.

To avoid free riders, Stark and Finke argue, a religious body has to charge a high entry fee (2000). This "strict church" thesis has been the source of much debate, but to anyone who has played on a sports team, it should make sense. If just anyone could show up on game day to play, the sports team would no doubt be swamped with freeloading jocks. But if you impose high costs like mandatory practice sessions and fund-raisers, you will weed out the casual athletes from the committed ones and end up with a more devoted, and probably more effective, team. Exclusivity generates strength for organizations, including religious bodies. As a result of exclusivity, conservative denominations and sectarian groups are also better able to mobilize their resources for social action such as fund-raising or political campaigning (Iannaccone et al., 1995).

It may seem paradoxical that stricter religious institutions are more likely to grow than easier faiths. After all, strictness is not something people necessarily seek from their religion. But people who have strong religious beliefs tend to build stronger congregations and stronger religious communities: the stronger the community, the better it works. The stronger the religious organization, the more it demands of you, the more you are likely to value it, and thus the greater chance you'll stick with it. Less restrictive churches, such as most mainline Protestant denominations, may be more reasonable in the amount of time and dedication they ask of you, but the trade-off is that you may value them less and defect more easily. Furthermore, because sectarian groups claim to hold the one and only religious truth, their devoted members get more out of their exclusive access to the truth than they do from being connected to and accepted in the wider secular world. Who needs a 401(k) individual retirement account when he or she is part of God's in-group?

An important caveat is that not all strict faiths are growing, nor can we expect, say, radical Orthodox Jewish sects to boom in the next few years just because they demand a lot of time and effort from their constituents. In fact, some Orthodox Jewish synagogues may not accept non-Jewish converts and many others require potential converts to live as observant Orthodox Jews for at least one year before they will consider performing a conversion ceremony. All voluntary organizations have to find their niche, claim Stark and Finke (2000), and the market niche for radical faiths is relatively small compared with that for mainline or moderately conservative faiths. Although sectarian or fundamentalist groups may experience rapid growth, they are ultimately limited by how many people will find those niches attractive in the first place.

The thesis indeed fits with historical trends of the success of conservative, or strict, religious groups, such as Islamists. Islam is the world's second-largest religion, after Christianity. As a large religion, it too faces fractures and separatist movements from within. One movement that has gained the most attention in US media and politics is Islamic fundamentalism, which—in common terminology—also refers to the political ideology of Islamism. Islamists call for the authority of Islamic law—known as shar'ia (often literal translations from the Qur'an)—over secular law. They also are more likely to support political violence in the name of holy war (jihad). Unfortunately, many mainstream Muslims are wrongly identified as Islamists, when in fact most Muslims oppose Islamists and their goals. Sociologist Jen'nan Read urges us to remember that "just like Christians in the United States, they're a diverse population. We've got very secular Arab Muslims who are basically Muslim in name only, attend the mosque maybe once a year or never. And then we've got very devout Muslims who are very religious and uphold the five pillars of Islam. Just like Christians, there is a difference between being a devout Christian and being an extremist. There is also a difference between being a devout Muslim and being an extremist" (Conley, 2009i). Read goes on to lament that devout Muslims and extremists became lumped together after 9/11. Americans have a tendency to think of all practicing Muslims as extremists, which can lead to bigotry, profiling, and harassment.

Because of their extreme beliefs and practices, Islamists face the same dilemmas as other radical religious movements. Should they water down their message to attract popular support? Or should they maintain a pure, radical vision among a small following (Kurzman, 2002)? Already, Islam is split along political lines (such as the Sunni/Shia dichotomy). However, some commentators speculate that the US-led wars in Iraq and Afghanistan have increased the popularity of Islamism, at least in the short run. More generally, the war on terror has increased, paradoxically, global identification with terrorists by opening up a niche for political Islamism to define itself against the power of the United States. Even within the United States, a study by the Pew Research Center found that while about a quarter of those raised Muslim leave the faith, an equal number of new converts are attracted, leading to a net wash (whereas Christianity loses more believers than it gains) (Mohamed & Sciupac, 2018).

The process of secularization that comes with a religion's successes does not weaken religiosity in general. On the contrary, with every church's falter, split, and demise, some sort of religious revival follows (Stark & Bainbridge, 1985, 1987). Likewise, as the fortunes of individual organizations fall, new ones rise in their place, and religion moves forward.

POLICY

 # TEACHING THE BIBLE IN SCHOOL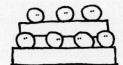

Perhaps the most significant push to expand religious influence in the contemporary United States is the inclusion of creationism in public school curricula by way of the intelligent design movement. Intelligent design posits that biological life is too complex to have happened randomly, so it could only be the work of a higher being (Goodstein, 2005). The idea has its roots in creationism, the belief that humans and the universe were created by a supreme being. (In 1987, the US Supreme Court ruled it unconstitutional to teach creationism in public schools.) In Pennsylvania in 2004, some parents of students in the town of Dover filed a lawsuit against the school board, which had voted that students must listen to a statement at the start of biology class explaining that evolution was a "flawed" theory and that an alternative existed, intelligent design (Goodstein, 2005). In December 2005, federal judge John E. Jones III determined that intelligent design was a "religious alternative masquerading as a scientific theory" and barred its instruction in the public schools. Dover is still recovering from the media hype and its stereotyping as a zone of "cultural warfare between liberal atheists and Bible-thumping fundamentalists" (Gately, 2005).

Negotiating the separation of church and state is an inherently tricky business in a highly religious, individualistic, and pluralistic country such as the United States, compared with a country with a relatively low level of religiosity and a high level of centralized authority such as France. To settle disputes about the appropriateness of religious icons in school, in 2004 the French government banned all students from wearing any religious garb or conspicuous symbols in its public schools. Students found in violation—those wearing Islamic veils, Jewish skullcaps, large Christian crosses, or Sikh turbans, for example—would be expelled. Although supported by many, such severe separation of church and state, which was seen as an attempt to uphold France's republican ideal of secularism to the extreme, has been criticized as biased by some, because its unofficial targets were seen to be female Muslim students who wore scarves and veils (Sciolino, 2004). But the reaction was nowhere near that which would ensue if such a policy were enacted in the United States.

Lawsuits and media hype abound in distinguishing between the constitutionally legitimate and the heartfelt. Tensions can be felt in football locker rooms, where pregame prayer is the norm for many top college players. Marcus Borden, a high-school football coach in East Brunswick, New Jersey, fueled a controversy when he resigned in 2005 after being ordered by the district to stop the practice of pregame prayer (Drape, 2005). In 2006, the Georgia state legislature passed a bill requiring the Bible to be taught in public schools.

A photo of Charles Darwin sticks out of the snow in Dover, Pennsylvania. Parents of high-school students in this small, rural town successfully sued the school board for trying to introduce intelligent design into the science curriculum.

Already about 1,000 public high schools nationwide use the Bible in their curriculum, which the Supreme Court allows so long as it is taught as literature and not as fact. Georgia was the first state to use the Bible as a teaching textbook, although in 2005, a federal judge ordered the state to remove stickers from one district's science textbooks that called evolution into question (Goodman, 2006b).

Finally, even though the Supreme Court ruled in 1987 (*Edwards v. Aguillard*) that the teaching of creation science alongside evolution violated the separation of church and state by bringing a supernatural being into the curriculum, that doesn't stop legislators from pushing bills that would be in violation of that ruling if they became law. In 2019, Indiana representative Dennis Kruse introduced a bill requiring schools to teach "alternative" theories of the origin of life, including creation science (National Center for Science Education, 2019). The Supreme Court may be powerful, but it is not powerful enough to stop entrepreneurial legislators from trying to score points by appealing to the political power of religion. Surely the 2019 bill won't be the last.

Conclusion

The force of religious beliefs can move social mountains. Ideas, beliefs, and convictions are, to echo Weber, the switchmen of the train tracks of history. They are powerful resources used to mobilize calls to social action, like the civil rights movement. They anchor our outlook on the world, acting as the toolkit we deploy to make sense of our daily life. It is not up to the sociologist to deem these beliefs valid or untrue; rather, it is our task to understand their origins and effects in the social world. This inquiry has led us to unlikely places: from the temperance movement of the 1830s to the organizational backbone of the Reverend Dr. Martin Luther King Jr.'s call for racial justice in the 1960s; from the glossy pages of a Biblezine to the local coffeehouse filled with talk of rock and roll and gospel music. Religion has remained a powerful, constant backdrop in our society and often plays a starring role in social life.

QUESTIONS FOR REVIEW

1. How do Reverend Billy and the Church of Stop Shopping demonstrate the relationship between religion and social movements? How is religion like a social movement? What are the main differences between religious practitioners and social activists?

2. How does the inclusion of creationism and the Bible in school curricula shed light on the delicate balance between church and state?

3. What is the "sect–church cycle"? With this in mind, describe how we can understand religion as an engine of social change. How do the abolitionist and civil rights movements illustrate this point?

4. Explain how Karl Marx and Max Weber differ in the way they link religion and the economy.

5. According to Weber, what do Calvinism and predestination have to do with the emergence of capitalism? How has this theory been challenged?

6. Although it's unclear why religious people tend to live longer and experience fewer symptoms of depression, how could Peter Berger's concept of the "sacred canopy" help explain this trend?

7. This chapter provided an overview of numerous religions. Describe why it is more sociologically significant to study the power of religion and how it is linked to other parts of society than, say, which religion is "right." Use the microsociological findings from this chapter to support your answer.

8. Why are religious attitudes such a strong predictor of voting behavior and political affiliation? How does this link relate to the geography of the United States?

9. After questioning her religious beliefs and learning about other faiths, an individual changes religious affiliations. How does the theory of secularization explain or fail to explain this change?

10. What is the difference between the "sacred" and the "profane"? Come up with an example in which a table is sacred and another where it is profane. What does this mean about the way we interpret religion and the way religion helps us interpret the social world?

PRACTICE

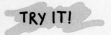 THE CULT OF YOU

Whether you practice a formal religion or are a strict atheist, I'm guessing you have a set of personal rituals you follow for good luck in your daily life. By definition, these superstitions aren't rational. They may come from a deeply rooted cultural tradition, such as knocking on wood, which, in Celtic culture, originally was meant to rouse the druids from the trees for protection from evil spirits. Another common example is saying "Bless you" when you sneeze, which some say started during the time of the bubonic plague. You even may have made up superstitions of your own.

TRY IT!

WHAT ARE YOUR SUPERSTITIONS? HERE ARE MINE:

ALWAYS PICK UP A COIN THAT'S HEADS UP

ALWAYS FLIP OVER A COIN THAT'S TAILS UP

DO EVERYTHING IN MULTIPLES OF TWO IF AT ALL POSSIBLE (E.G., I EITHER TAKE TWO OR FOUR SIPS FROM THE WATER FOUNTAIN, BUT NEVER THREE)

KNOCK ON WOOD IF I SAY SOMETHING I WANT TO HAPPEN

SAY "SMOLLA, SMOLLA" TO WARD OFF THE EVIL EYE

What are the personal and/or historical origins of your superstitious practices? Doing things in even numbers is completely my own neurosis, but "smolla, smolla" is my family's corruption of a phrase from Yiddish tradition.

THINK ABOUT IT

Have you managed to spread your superstitions to others? (My sister's aversion to strawberries has now been taken up by at least a dozen other people.) Where do your superstitious practices fall on the spectrum of strict religions—how easy would it be for someone to join the "cult of you"?

SOCIOLOGY ON THE STREET

It is difficult to "make the familiar strange" with strongly held beliefs such as religious practices and values. How might someone try to apply the sociological imagination to his or her own religion? Watch the Sociology on the Street video to find out more: **digital.wwnorton.com/youmayask7**.

WANT MORE PRACTICE?

Complete the InQuizitive activity for this chapter at digital.wwnorton.com /youmayask7

PARADOX

SOCIETY INVENTS TECHNOLOGIES TO MINIMIZE DANGERS FROM NATURE, BUT THOSE SAME INVENTIONS CREATE NEW RISKS TO BE MANAGED.

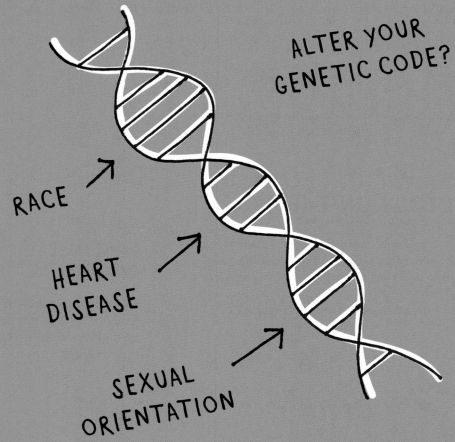

ALTER YOUR GENETIC CODE?

RACE →

HEART DISEASE →

SEXUAL ORIENTATION →

Animation at digital.wwnorton.com/youmayask7

Science, the Environment, and Society

When you think of movie star Angelina Jolie, what comes to mind? Her trademark look that includes more than a dozen tattoos? The vial of her second husband's blood she kept around her neck while they were married? Perhaps the sibling kiss during the Academy Awards? Or her very public divorce from Brad Pitt? While certainly all of these aspects of her life have received oodles of press, her most lasting contribution to history may lie in her role as a science—not a sex—symbol.

In 2013, Jolie took the courageous step of publicly revealing that she'd undergone a bilateral preventive mastectomy after finding out she had certain genetic mutations that predisposed her to breast cancer. Many observers think that her lead will inspire many women to get tested for the *BRCA* alleles that increase the risk for premenopausal breast and ovarian cancer. This will be particularly true if the cost of the screening drops significantly, which looks likely. That's because around the same time Jolie revealed her medical odyssey in an essay in the *New York Times*, the US Supreme Court struck down the patent for the very test Jolie had used to make her treatment decision.

The justices unanimously ruled that the patent on the genetic tests for the so-called breast cancer genes, *BRCA1* and *BRCA2*, was not valid because the innovation on which it was based failed the "product of nature" test.

That is, discovering an exact sequence of DNA—specifically, the mutations in the two genes that predispose an individual to greater cancer risk—does not constitute a new creation in and of itself. The tools to check the DNA sequence of a patient are already widely available. The company merely used them to discover risky variants of the two genes, which are, of course, naturally occurring.

Putting aside the issue of patenting something that was naturally occurring, we might ask: What if many more women with the risky versions of the *BRCA* genes follow Jolie's lead and undergo preventive mastectomies? For a moment, imagine all women with the *BRCA* mutations did so. Then having the "bad" DNA sequences would predict lower risk of breast cancer but higher risk of undergoing preventive surgery. This case demonstrates a different reason for not patenting human genetic sequences: The effects of genes are fluid and subject to change thanks in part to evolving social practices. It is this very process of social response to information and the resultant changing risk pattern that provides another reason to dismiss the intellectual property claim.

This phenomenon of changing scientific "facts" is not unique to genetics, but rather applies to all science that deals with humans. Effects come and go as they are absorbed by the adaptive system we call society.

My favorite example of social adaption comes from a paper by an economist, Edward Saunders, who found that, everything else equal, there was a slight uptick in the price of stocks on the New York Stock Exchange when it was sunny in Manhattan (where the trading floor is located), with a corresponding negative effect when it was cloudy or rainy in the Big Apple. Now what did this intrepid young social scientist do? Instead of forming a new private equity fund called "Helios Capital" or "Apollo Investments" to arbitrage the finding and get filthy rich, he published a paper about the phenomenon in the *American Economic Review*. The moment Wall Street found out about it, every analyst worth her salt put New York City weather into her statistical model and—*poof!*—the effect was gone thanks to the wonders of data and the free market. I hope Saunders at least got tenure.

In a similar manner, before long the gene for breast cancer may be associated with lower odds of developing the disease thanks to the steps women with the now-dangerous alleles take to mitigate their risk. In the not-so-distant future, *BRCA1* mutations may predict mastectomies, not breast cancer.

Like the analysts on Wall Street who incorporated Manhattan weather into their mathematical models, once we know about our "innate" tendencies, we can do something about them. And this even includes biological associations like cancer risk. So before the US Patent and Trademark Office grants any more intellectual property rights that rely on humans not changing their behavior in response to the "invention," they better think twice—because Americans (and their celebrities) certainly will.

Science and Society

The *BRCA* gene mutation is a good example of the ways that scientific innovations and technological advances affect society. Sociologists of science are interested in the ways scientific communities study the objects of their research, in the way science changes how we live and interact with each other, and in the unexpected social consequences of scientific discoveries. What sociologists of science do is no different from what other sociologists do: They make the familiar strange, show hidden social structures, and connect the seemingly individual and personal to larger social and historical forces. It's just that science itself (including the social sciences and sociology itself) forms the object of study. The traditions in this field range broadly from ethnographic observation of how scientists make decisions and how users adopt (and adapt to) new technologies all the way to theoretical work that questions the very notion of a scientific "fact." Sociology of science emerges from training a sociological lens on the history and philosophy of science.

THOMAS KUHN AND THE STRUCTURE OF SCIENTIFIC REVOLUTIONS

The goal of science (including social science) is to learn new things about the world. Botanists and zoologists seek new information about plants and animals. Astronomers try to discover new things about the solar system. Sociologists try to learn new things about society. But how does new information come about? How does the process of scientific discovery translate into new information about the natural and social world? According to the scientist (and scientific historian) Thomas Kuhn, scientific discovery doesn't proceed along a linear path (a straight line) or simply accumulate little by little; rather, Kuhn (1962) believes, periods of "normal science" are ruptured every so often by scientific revolutions that shift the paradigm of a given science. But what is normal science, and what is a paradigm? And how do scientific revolutions happen?

According to Kuhn, a paradigm is the framework within which scientists operate. Cell biologists share a certain paradigm with other cell biologists. The equipment they use to study cells is the same, as is their understanding of how different parts of the cell (the cytoplasm, ribosomes, or mitochondria) operate. All mainstream cell biologists agree that ribosomes make protein in a cell and that electron microscopes are good instruments to study cells. They all share the knowledge that there are two methods by which cells reproduce themselves—meiosis and mitosis, depending on the type of cell.

In each scientific field, scientists adhere to a particular set of paradigms to guide their research. The big bang, for instance, is a paradigm about

PARADIGM

the framework within which scientists operate.

the origins of the universe. Likewise, Charles Darwin's theory of evolution has become an accepted paradigm in biology. The helical structure of DNA famously described by James Watson and Francis Crick in 1953 has provided a paradigm for examining the human genome. Researchers working on the Human Genome Project adhere to this paradigm of the double helix discovered by Watson and Crick.

Now that we've defined a paradigm, what is normal science? If you were a cell biologist, you would probably work in a laboratory with other scientists. When you conducted experiments and obtained results, you would be conducting what Kuhn calls normal science: science that's conducted within an existing paradigm. Although you might learn new information about the process of meiosis or the protein-creating capabilities of ribosomes, you wouldn't be overturning existing knowledge of meiosis or ribosomes. Rather, you would gradually add to it through the process of scientific discovery. You might clarify part of the existing paradigm or gather evidence to lend stronger support to the paradigm. This, Kuhn claims, is normal science.

During the practice of normal science, anomalies arise that don't fit neatly into the existing paradigm. Researchers may make discoveries that don't conform to their current assumptions about cell biology. When enough anomalies accrue to challenge the existing paradigm, showing that it is incomplete or inadequate to explain all observed phenomena, Kuhn calls this point a paradigm shift or scientific revolution. Keep in mind that such scientific revolutions are infrequent. When they do occur, they turn existing ways of thinking about science on their heads—think of Copernicus and the shift from earth-centered to sun-centered thinking. Thus scientific revolutions represent major breaks in periods of normal science and are responsible for important scientific advancements.

IS SCIENCE A SOCIAL AND POLITICAL ENDEAVOR?

The scientific process as presented by Thomas Kuhn should occur outside the boundaries of the day-to-day world, so that social concerns and political interests don't enter into it. This is the traditional view of science: It is a value-neutral endeavor conducted by objective researchers. Although scientific researchers have particular moral, political, and religious beliefs, scientific method requires that they leave those "biases" at the laboratory door, because the process of discovering new knowledge requires scientists to remain uninfluenced by their personal views and political pressures. This is called the normative view of science, or the way science ought to be conducted.

As a sociologist, you should recognize that this traditional view of science isn't entirely accurate. Science is constantly influenced by political and social factors. Such biases are manifested through the type of research

NORMAL SCIENCE

science conducted within an existing paradigm, as defined by Thomas Kuhn.

PARADIGM SHIFT OR SCIENTIFIC REVOLUTION

when enough scientific anomalies accrue to challenge the existing paradigm, showing that it is incomplete or inadequate to explain all observed phenomena.

NORMATIVE VIEW OF SCIENCE

the notion that science should not be affected by the personal beliefs or values of scientists but rather should follow objective rules of evidence.

Copernicus's sun-centered system (above) replaced the Ptolemaic earth-centered model (left) in 1543.

that scientists decide to pursue. Why do some physicists study nuclear fusion, whereas others study thermodynamics? Why do some sociologists study patterns of international migration, whereas others study types of postmodern families? Why do some biologists research a vaccine for HIV/AIDS, whereas others try to find a cure for baldness? One answer is simply that different researchers are interested in different topics. One sociologist might believe that patterns of international migration are interesting and important, whereas another might be particularly interested in changing family patterns: Both sociologists' research topics are affected by their values and interests.

An alternative explanation, however, is that researchers select topics, in part, based on the funding available for their research. This is easy to see in the wake of the COVID-19 pandemic. In the first few months after infections started to spread from Wuhan, China, to the rest of the world, the global scientific community kicked into high gear. In the three-month period between January and May 2020, over 23,000 papers on some aspect of COVID-19 were published and the number was "doubling every 20 days—among the biggest explosions of scientific literature ever" (Brainard, 2020). Part of this explosion of research is due to the desire of scientists to help in a time of crisis. But there has also been an incredible infusion of federal research dollars into this timely subject area—$8.9 billion just for R&D in the first half of 2020, to be exact (Legislative Analyst's Office, 2020). Moreover, the financial prize of being the company that brings successful testing and, more importantly, vaccines and cures to market is immense.

In this way, nonscientists often make decisions that affect the course of science. One example is President George W. Bush's involvement in the debate about embryonic stem cell research. Scientists agree that embryonic stem cell research may unlock the cures to major diseases, including Parkinson's disease and Alzheimer's disease. In 2001, President Bush decided to allow federal funding for existing embryonic stem cell lines, but he stipulated that the funds couldn't be used to develop new stem cells from existing human embryos. Bush (2001) announced his decision via a radio announcement:

> As a result of private research, more than 60 genetically diverse stem cell lines already exist. . . . I have concluded that we should allow federal funds to be used for research on these existing stem cell lines, where the life and death decision has already been made. . . . This allows us to explore the promise and potential of stem cell research without crossing a fundamental moral line, by providing taxpayer funding that would sanction or encourage further destruction of human embryos that have at least the potential for life.

Bush is no scientist, but his position as president of the United States empowered him to make decisions about funding for science. Limiting the availability of federal funding for stem cell research was clearly a political and moral decision. Politically, he sought to placate conservative religious groups. Morally, he sought to promote his personal beliefs about life and death and right and wrong. By limiting the availability of federal funding to the existing lines of embryonic stem cells, President Bush limited the possibility of scientific research. President Barack Obama subsequently rescinded the Bush policy, although opponents of stem cell research continue

George W. Bush announces his decision to limit funding for embryonic stem cell research while surrounded by families whose children were born from frozen embryos.

to challenge its legality. Many analysts have expected President Trump to revert back to the Bush policy (or in some other way change the Obama stance); however, so far that has not come to pass. As this example demonstrates, the process and possibility of scientific discovery can be driven by political considerations.

Another example of science following the dictates of politics is the Manhattan Project. During World War II, some US leaders feared that the Nazis were developing atomic weapons. Therefore, in 1942 the United States started research on the development of an atomic weapon under the leadership of the US Army Corps of Engineers. Led by General Leslie R. Groves and physicist J. Robert Oppenheimer, the Manhattan Project was the code name given to the team of research scientists at work on developing atomic weapons for the United States. Although the details of the scientific pursuits are complicated (and probably better explained by a physicist than a sociologist), it is clear that the Manhattan Project was created for political and social reasons. The decision to pursue nuclear technologies and the rapid pace of research were both influenced by international geopolitical circumstances.

THE PURSUIT OF TRUTH AND THE BOUNDARIES OF SCIENCE

All science claims to promote knowledge, but sometimes different sources of knowledge reveal different things. Imagine that on your morning walk to your introductory earth science class, you encounter a man giving a loud public speech in the local park. Intrigued, you listen to the soapbox orator rant about the dangers of global warming, which he reports is occurring at unprecedented rates. You continue to class, unconvinced by his arguments. Arriving a few minutes early, you start to read the morning newspaper and find an article about a report by government scientists stating that global warming is, in fact, a myth. According to the report, little change in atmospheric temperatures has occurred over the century. As you finish the article, your professor arrives and introduces today's topic: global warming. Already primed, you pay careful attention. According to your professor, a world-renowned climatologist, global warming is occurring at alarming rates, melting ice caps, raising ocean temperatures, and threatening the global ecosystem. As you leave the lecture, you begin to wonder whom you should believe about global warming: the soapbox orator, the government scientists, or your professor. Who is telling the truth? Who is presenting the facts?

Science holds a privileged place in our society in relation to knowledge and truth. We are taught to accept scientific findings as fact and to trust the knowledge gained through scientific research. As the sociologist Thomas Gieryn (1999) writes, "If 'science' says so, we are more often than not inclined to believe it or act on it—and to prefer it over claims lacking this epistemic seal of approval." You'd be more likely to believe your professor than the soapbox orator, right? That's because your professor has the credibility of a scientist, whereas the soapbox orator does not. Throughout your life, you've probably been taught to trust scientists and to be wary of people screaming in local parks. But the government report was also written by scientists. When faced with different stories by different scientists, how do we decide who is more credible? As Gieryn (1999) notes, the claims of science, scientists, and scientific discovery aren't nearly as clear-cut as you might think.

Let's take a closer look at the real example from Dover, Pennsylvania, that we examined in a religious context in Chapter 16. In 2004, the Dover school board instituted a policy requiring ninth-grade science teachers to read their students a statement challenging Darwin's theory of evolution. The theory claims that organisms evolve through a natural, competitive process that allows the specific, genetically based traits that are best adapted to local conditions to survive and reproduce at the expense of those organisms that are genetically less adapted to the particular conditions they face. Darwin calls this process of competition within the species natural selection, and very few scientists disagree with Darwin's theory.

The statement prepared by the Dover school board, however, was as follows:

> The Pennsylvania Academic Standards require students to learn about Darwin's theory of evolution and eventually to take a standardized test of which evolution is a part.
>
> Because Darwin's theory is a theory, it continues to be tested as new evidence is discovered. The theory is not a fact. Gaps in the theory exist for which there is no evidence. A theory is defined as a well-tested explanation that unifies a broad range of observations.
>
> Intelligent design is an explanation of the origin of life that differs from Darwin's view. The reference book, "Of Pandas and People," is available for students who might be interested in gaining an understanding of what intelligent design actually involves.
>
> With respect to any theory, students are encouraged to keep an open mind. The school leaves the discussion of the origins of life to individual students and their families. As [Dover is] a standards-driven district, class instruction focuses upon preparing students to achieve proficiency on standards-based assessments. (*Kitzmiller v. Dover Area School District*, 2005)

The statement introduces an alternative theory, called intelligent design, to explain the origin and evolution of species. Proponents of intelligent design claim that life is too complex to have evolved through natural selection. Rather, they propose that an "intelligent designer" had a hand in creating and selecting various species.

The debate about intelligent design offers a real-life example about the boundaries of science (Gieryn, 1999). Proponents of intelligent design, backed by a tenured professor of biochemistry at Lehigh University named Michael Behe, claim that it is a legitimate scientific theory. Opponents argue that the strong empirical support for Darwin's theory of evolution and the near-universal dismissal of intelligent design in the scientific community delegitimize it as a credible alternative to natural selection. The human eye, for instance, is "designed" in quite a suboptimal way with blood vessels and nerves covering the light-sensitive cells. The retina is, in essence, inside out—resulting in the blind spot—owing to the path dependency of evolution. In fact, many biologists argue that if you don't accept natural selection, a domino effect would occur and much of what we know in biology would crumble, because the model of natural selection forms a foundation for other knowledge.

In the case of the Dover school board, a group of parents sued the board, claiming that the attempts to offer intelligent design as an alternative theory were akin to introducing religion into the classroom—a violation of the First Amendment. In December 2005, the US district court sided with the parents and forbade the teaching of intelligent design in science classes. Meanwhile, the main proponents of intelligent design instruction on the school board were voted out of office in the 2005 local elections.

The intelligent design debate demonstrates the type of boundary work being done to create a distinction between legitimate and nonlegitimate science within a specific scientific discipline. When sociologists such as Gieryn (1999) refer to boundary work, they mean "instances in which . . . divisions between fields of knowledge are created, advocated, attacked, or reinforced." In this case, biologists are debating the boundaries of legitimate theories of evolution. Another kind of boundary work occurs between different scientific disciplines. In this boundary work, scientists in different disciplines reach different answers to the same scientific questions. Urban planners, nutritionists, and biologists might all be researching the causes of obesity in America (the same scientific question), but they may arrive at different answers because they're working through different frameworks.

As an urban planner, you might examine forms of urban sprawl and the car-dependent city. Certain trends, such as cities becoming less pedestrian-friendly and people being more reliant on the automobile, might help explain obesity for an urban planner. As a nutritionist, you'd probably research the caloric intake of obese Americans. You might also research the types of food eaten by different people and the dietary patterns that cause obesity. As a biologist, you might think that the key to unlocking the obesity mystery lies in people's genetics and biochemistry. You'd search for a gene for obesity or

BOUNDARY WORK

work done to maintain the border between legitimate and nonlegitimate science within a specific scientific discipline or between legitimate disciplines.

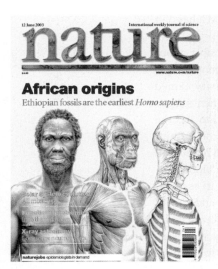

12 June 2003 — International weekly journal of science

nature

www.nature.com/nature

African origins

Ethiopian fossils are the earliest *Homo sapiens*

naturejobs epidemiologists in demand

Scientists perform boundary work when they engage in debates about the legitimacy of scientific theory. For instance, most scientists would consider the research on evolution in the journal *Nature* legitimate science, but they would not accept the alternate theories promoted by the Creation Museum in Petersburg, Kentucky (pictured above on the right).

a genetic condition that makes people prone to being obese. Urban planners, nutritionists, and biologists approach the question of obesity from their respective disciplines and reach different answers. Sometimes these are complementary, but other times they conflict.

THE LABORATORY AS A SITE FOR KNOWLEDGE

In 1979, anthropologists Bruno Latour and Steve Woolgar published *Laboratory Life*, an account of the process of scientific discovery in the laboratory. The researchers spent two years conducting ethnographic research on Nobel Prize—winning physician Jonas Salk's laboratory. As uninvolved observers, they watched scientists conduct experiments, review papers, and interact with one another in this setting. Latour and Woolgar argue that ethnographic approaches had never before been used to look at reclusive (and exclusive) scientific laboratories, largely because science holds such a privileged place in Western society. Nonetheless, they called Western scientists a "tribe" worthy of study by anthropologists and decried the lack of information about how this tribe of scientists behaved (1979).

The scientific laboratory is the primary site in which many scientific data are collected, researched, and analyzed. If you are a social scientist, your laboratory, so to speak, is the real world. If you want to understand how homeless people live, you're likely to conduct ethnography in a homeless shelter. You might also use data collected from surveys (like the US Census) or through face-to-face interviews. Most natural scientists, in contrast, tend to extract elements from the natural world and bring them into their laboratory. Although some scientists do work or gather samples in the outside world, they usually return to their laboratories to analyze those samples. Biologists, for example, examine cells under the microscopes in their labs, whereas chemists might model the structure of proteins in computational laboratories. The laboratory therefore plays an important part in the scientific process.

Inside laboratories, Latour and Woolgar argue, there exists a unique process of scientific discovery—with its own language, its own system of promotion, and its own hierarchy. Their research traces the construction of scientific fact. Scientific facts don't just pop up from experiments. Instead, scientists debate research findings, discuss their results, and work through disagreements. Some findings make it out of the laboratory and into print; others don't. Latour and Woolgar pay particularly close attention to the circumstances of the laboratory. For example, power struggles within the hierarchy of the lab may determine which results or explanations of data receive more attention.

Jonas Salk in his lab in Pittsburgh, Pennsylvania. What conclusions did Bruno Latour and Steve Woolgar make about the scientific process based on their observations of Salk?

Latour and Woolgar's work on the social construction of scientific facts has been widely criticized in the scientific community. These critics argue that their claims undermine the purity of scientific pursuit and thereby weaken scientific claims to truth. In *Fashionable Nonsense* (1999), the physicists Alan Sokal and Jean Bricmont took Latour, specifically, to task over a particular claim about the death of Pharaoh Ramses II around 1213 B.C.E. Historians claim that Ramses died of tuberculosis, but Latour points out that tuberculosis wasn't discovered until 1882. If tuberculosis didn't exist as a scientific fact until 3,000 years after Ramses's death, Latour argues, how could it be considered the cause of his death? What allows Latour to make this argument is his notion that scientific facts are "created," not discovered. Most scientists dismiss this provocative claim as nonsense: Just because tuberculosis hadn't been discovered yet doesn't mean it didn't kill Ramses. Scientific facts, they argue, are not made but rather preexist in objective reality waiting to be discovered by truth-seeking researchers.

These debates, often called the "science wars," have been taken up by philosopher Ian Hacking in *The Social Construction of What?* (1999). Hacking tries to mediate between constructionists such as Latour and scientists such as Sokal. He pushes for a middle ground, arguing that there's

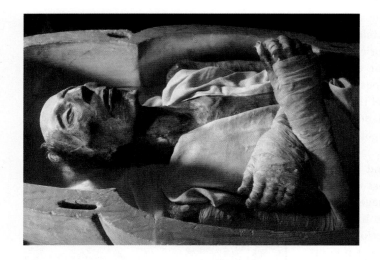

something legitimate in both social constructivism and scientific truth. On the one hand, cultural norms and social situations influence both what is discovered and how the discovery process proceeds. To argue that social norms aren't relevant is to ignore the realities of the social world. On the other hand, as Barbara Herrnstein Smith (2009) points out, the scientific models of the way the world works are taken as fact because they often enable us to predict, shape, and intervene in the world more reliably than other ways of thinking.

How did Ramses II become a flash point in the "science wars" between Bruno Latour and other scientists 3,000 years after he died?

MATTHEW EFFECT

a term used by sociologists to describe the notion that certain scientific results get more notoriety and influence based on the existing prestige of the researchers involved.

THE MATTHEW EFFECT

One example of how social life influences science that Ian Hacking (and physical scientists) might be comfortable acknowledging is the Matthew effect, a term Robert Merton coined in 1968. The term refers to a passage in the book of Matthew in the Christian Bible that reads, "For to everyone who has, more shall be given, and he will have an abundance; but from the one who does not have, even what he does have shall be taken away." Sociologists deploy the Matthew effect as a metaphor to describe how prestige is earned and rewards are distributed in the scientific community. In this context, the first half of the quotation means that prestige brings more prestige. A well-known scientist is more likely to be credited with a particular scientific discovery than lesser-known colleagues, even if they worked as a team to produce that knowledge. Scientists who have won major awards or written highly regarded books will be showered with further praise. The opposite holds true as well: Scientists without great prestige will have difficulty earning it. Graduate students often produce much of the work for which their professors become famous, running the chemistry experiments or reporting on the daily progress of plant growth and development, but the fame associated with scientific discovery is bestowed on the professor. What's more, a finding published by a famous scientist is more likely to influence the future course of research than one published by a lesser-known figure. Sociologist John Evans (2002) has found, in a study of debates over human genetic engineering, that more prestigious, senior authors were cited more often than junior researchers. Evans tried to factor out the quality of the work but, of course, it is impossible to exactly measure something like quality.

Agriculture and the Environment

The process of natural or physical science may be a subject of sociological study in itself, but sociologists also research the effects of the social world and the natural world on each other. Studies have examined how the environment affects and is affected by social institutions, how computer science is changing social relations, and how agricultural technologies affect human population growth. These are just a few examples of a potentially endless list of intersections between social science and natural science. Let's start with the sociology of the environment by way of example.

GLOBAL WARMING AND CLIMATE CHANGE

Al Gore, the former vice president and presidential candidate, has been one of the most visible crusaders raising awareness about climate change. In 2006, Gore starred in a film titled *An Inconvenient Truth*, which documented the impact of human activity on global temperatures through a process called the greenhouse effect. According to this film, the effects of global warming are devastating. It is responsible for the increase in the number of deadly hurricanes, such as Hurricane Katrina. Global warming is shifting ice caps and melting glaciers, thereby increasing sea levels and threatening human communities living in coastal areas. Because of rising atmospheric temperatures, heat waves are becoming more intense, and tropical diseases are migrating to new areas. Malaria, a tropical disease, has been found in new places where the mosquitoes that carry the disease previously had been unable to live. Hundreds of species of animals and plants are responding to increasing temperatures by moving closer and closer to the North and South Poles.

So, what exactly is global warming? Carbon dioxide (CO_2) and other greenhouse gases such as nitrous oxide, fluorinated gases, and methane (CH_4) are trapped in the atmosphere, naturally warming the temperature of the earth. This process enables the planet to remain at a temperature comfortable for human habitation. In recent years, however, scientists have observed

GLOBAL WARMING

rising atmospheric concentrations of carbon dioxide and other greenhouse gases, resulting in higher global average temperatures.

A sign indicating the location of the North Pole for tourists is surrounded by melting ice.

FIGURE 17.1 Variations in Earth's Surface Temperature over 140 Years

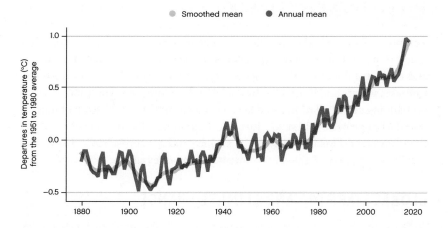

SOURCE: NASA, 2020.

rising atmospheric concentrations of these gases as well as higher average global temperatures. The growth rate of emissions was close to 1 percent annually in the 1990s and grew to an average 3 percent annually in the last decade. In 2009, the economic recession caused a 1.4 percent drop. Yet just one year later the highest increase in emissions since the Industrial Revolution was recorded: 5.9 percent. In 2017, China was responsible for 28 percent of global greenhouse gas emissions, more than any other country, though the per capita rate for individual Chinese people is still lower than the emissions rate for the average American, and indeed does not even make the top ten by that measure (Union of Concerned Scientists, 2020). Global warming refers to the rising atmospheric temperatures that result from having more greenhouse gases in the atmosphere (Figure 17.1).

Little disagreement exists in the scientific community about the exact causes of global warming. The vast majority of scientists acknowledge that the roots of global warming can be traced back to human activities. In particular, deforestation and the burning of coal, natural gas, and oil have caused atmospheric temperatures to creep upward. The burning of fossil fuels releases CO_2 and other greenhouse gases into the atmosphere. CO_2 emissions from fossil fuel combustion related to generating electricity and driving vehicles are a primary cause of global warming. The UN Intergovernmental Panel on Climate Change estimates that 2.5 percent of global warming results from airplanes, and this figure could rise to 25 percent by 2050 (Graver et al., 2019). Traffic in major cities also accounts for a significant portion of climate change. Drivers around the world waste millions of gallons of gasoline idling in traffic, adding CO_2 to the atmosphere. After CO_2

emissions from burning fossil fuels, scientists estimate that deforestation is the second-largest contributor to rising temperatures. As environmental activists have long argued, deforestation contributes to global warming in two ways: First, the burning of the forest releases CO_2 into the atmosphere, and second, the deforested trees are no longer around to absorb atmospheric carbon.

Just as the causes of climate change can be traced back to human societies, climate change will strongly affect human societies, too. Extreme weather patterns, such as prolonged heat waves and increasing numbers of hurricanes, portend drastic consequences for society. Sociologists have an interest in these topics. For example, in *Heat Wave: A Social Autopsy of Disaster in Chicago* (2002), Eric Klinenberg studied many of the effects of Chicago's 1995 heat wave on city residents. Through his research, he discovered that although the heat wave was certainly catastrophic, resulting in the deaths of 739 individuals (the human toll made it one of the worst disasters in the United States up to that point), the way that events played out had far more to do with social forces than natural ones. Specifically, most of the fatalities occurred among elderly, African American, and poor residents and were largely the result of social isolation.

Klinenberg now studies global warming more directly and has joined the scientific community in warning that global warming will create prolonged heat waves like the one he studied as well as more frequent and severe weather events of all kinds, further exacerbating socioeconomic stratification, whereby certain groups of people are affected much more severely than others (see Chapter 7). Furthermore, researchers believe that global warming will affect agricultural production by changing regional temperatures and altering rainfall patterns, thereby forcing farmers to adjust to changing environmental conditions. As ocean levels rise, human societies may experience

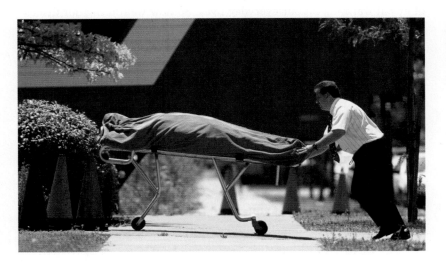

Because so many people died during the 1995 Chicago heat wave, the city government brought in refrigerated trucks to store the bodies.

a massive migration away from shorelines and islands. Populations forced from coastal communities and isolated islands because of rising water levels could cause a significant refugee crisis worldwide. Although this list isn't exhaustive, you can begin to understand some of the social challenges that human societies will face as global temperatures continue to rise.

Solutions to the challenges posed by climate change generally fall into three camps: efforts to slow greenhouse gas emission and associated climatological effects, attempts to reverse global warming through geoengineering, and approaches to mitigate the effects of climate change. In the first group fall voluntary and nonvoluntary efforts to reduce CO_2 and methane emissions by, for example, taxing carbon, promoting clean energy, banning wasteful uses, or reforesting. Under the Paris Agreement, 195 countries agreed to pursue a variety of strategies (and report back) in order to limit the global temperature rise to less than 2°C as compared to the preindustrialized period. President Trump has pulled the United States out of the agreement, which will formally take effect after a one-year waiting period in November 2020. Meanwhile, some technological optimists think we can solve the problem through geoengineering. One idea in this vein is to seed the upper atmosphere with sulfate aerosols to reflect the sun's light. Finally, others are pursuing ways to lessen the negative impact of a warmer earth by, for instance, developing a system of locks to keep rising sea levels at bay. Of course, such options are available only to the richest communities, which are not the ones likely to be the most affected.

ORGANIC FOODS AND GENETICALLY MODIFIED ORGANISMS

As changing atmospheric temperatures affect human societies globally, their impact remains abstract. It may be difficult for us to pinpoint the effects of global warming on our everyday lives. So now we'll bring our discussion closer to home: your local supermarket. Imagine you're standing in the produce section trying to decide which apples to purchase, but the options are numerous and the decision becomes too complicated. Do you buy Fuji apples flown in from New Zealand? Or maybe you prefer Empire apples from upstate New York? There are two types of Granny Smith apples, both from Washington State. One is labeled organic; the other is not. As you continue through the grocery store, you arrive at the dairy coolers and recall a story you heard on National Public Radio about a protein hormone called rBST that is injected into cows. After listening to the radio segment, you decided that you didn't want to purchase products manufactured from hormone-injected cows, so you scour the dairy section, reading the fine print, in search of rBST-free products. Before heading to the checkout counter, you remember that you're supposed to pick up some cornmeal to bake cornbread for the

What kind of apples do you buy? Organic? Local? Which one is more affordable? Which one is better for you or the environment? How can sociology help you answer these questions at the grocery store?

Mexican-themed fiesta you and your roommate are hosting. As you grab the least expensive box of cornmeal, you notice a label informing you that the product in your hand "may contain genetically modified ingredients." Although it's the cheapest, you struggle to decide if you should purchase this brand and consume a lab experiment. Exhausted, you finally reach the checkout counter. Who knew grocery shopping could be so difficult? Let's take a closer look at the scenarios you encountered in your (hypothetical) grocery store trip in relation to the environment and society.

Organic Foods In recent years, supermarkets throughout the country have begun stocking "organic" foods, and entire stores dedicated to organic products are becoming commonplace. In Seattle, the Puget Consumers' Co-op is one of the city's largest organic grocery stores, actively partnering with local organic farms to bring fresh produce to consumers. Even in your local chain grocery store, there's probably a section in the produce aisle dedicated to organic foods. You may have a notion that organic is better, but what exactly does *organic* mean? Is it about the production of food, or is it part of a certain lifestyle? Is *organic* a scientific term or a cultural one?

For Michael Pollan, the author of *The Omnivore's Dilemma: A Natural History of Four Meals* (2006), the debate over organic foods is more than a question of agricultural production. It's both a political and a moral statement—even a quasi-religious statement. Pollan investigated food production at different levels. He notes that growing demand for organic foods prompted the National Organic Program of the US Department of

Michael Pollan.

Agriculture (USDA) to release guidelines for commercial use of the word *organic* in 2002. Pollan examines the production of four meals, from fast-food megachains to straight-from-the-dirt salad. Like the book *Fast Food Nation* by Eric Schlosser (2001) and the documentary *Super Size Me* by Morgan Spurlock (2004), Pollan's work highlights the horrors of commercial slaughterhouses and the chemical components of mass-produced food. But by looking at the in-between stages, including food labeled "organic" purchased from one nationwide organic food store chain, Pollan shows that an organic label isn't simply a question of being chemical-free and straight from the land. In 2009, novelist Jonathan Safran Foer turned to nonfiction to write about the ethics of eating animals—in terms of animal suffering as well as the much greater environmental impact of consuming calories from animal sources rather than plant sources. Both Pollan and Foer have reached best-seller status—eating well is high on our collective consciousness.

Organic foods are pesticide-free and don't contain genetically modified ingredients. Organic farms follow a strict set of guidelines outlined by the USDA. Some products are certified organic, meaning that they contain at least 95 percent organic ingredients, whereas other products are labeled "made with organic ingredients," meaning that at least 70 percent of their ingredients are certified organic. Sometimes, meat and poultry aren't labeled organic even though they come from free-range animals raised without growth hormones or antibiotics. That's because maintaining an organic farm (with USDA certification) is expensive. Small farms often operate at a disadvantage—with smaller profits they may not be able to afford to comply with the costly certification requirements. Although megafarms in the Midwest might be certified organic, they still truck their produce across the country to put it in grocery stores—a process that isn't particularly friendly to the environment.

Eating organic has become a way of life, as well as a political statement about farming, food production, and consumerism. People often assume that organic also means healthier for the environment, the human consumer, and the animals (in the case of dairy and meat). Sometimes, they assume that organic produce comes from small local farms, not megafarms owned by parent companies like General Mills, which owns Annie's Homegrown Foods, and DanoneWave, a conglomerate that owns brands including Horizon Organic and Earthbound Farm. As organic becomes more and more popular, a number of social issues will come to the fore: First, big agrobusiness has the political clout to affect the US Food and Drug Administration's definition of *organic* (and it has been lobbying as of late for a relaxation of the standards for this label) and the money to undergo the process of certification. So organic farming may be another way that stratification occurs between big and small farms; it's yet another force putting the squeeze on family farms. Likewise, on the consumer end, the availability of organic products may add to health stratification by income. Specifically, organic products are almost always more expensive than nonorganic ones, offering wealthier and more educated customers a health opportunity that may not be available as readily to those with limited resources. There is hardly a technological advance that does not play out unequally across existing social divisions in society.

Genetically Modified Foods Although organic foods have hit the grocery store shelves without much controversy, another product has been filling supermarket aisles amid some debate. Genetically modified foods (made with genetically modified organisms, GMOs) have been finding their way to grocery store shelves and dinner tables, creating increasing controversy about their environmental and health effects. GMOs are products whose genetic structures have been altered. In producing these changes, scientists have been able to make specific changes to various seeds and crops. By all accounts, GMOs are one of the most significant advances in agricultural technology over the last decade. But why, you might ask, would farmers want to alter the genetic makeup of their crops? What are the benefits of genetically modified crops, and what are the dangers?

According to proponents of GMOs, altering the genetic structure of particular crops has the potential to produce higher yields (Qaim & Zilberman, 2003). With higher yields, genetically modified crops could help make American farms (which are heavily subsidized by the government) more profitable and lower food prices for consumers. Genetically modified crops may also have better resistance to insects, diseases, and other problems, further improving yields (and perhaps quality). By modifying the genetic structure of crops and seeds in this way, farmers can avoid using pesticides and herbicides that might be toxic to humans. Rather, the plant's genetic structure would make it "naturally" resistant (maybe by tasting nasty to those pests). Also, genetic modifications may decrease the maturation time of crops or keep them riper and fresher longer in the stores, thereby reducing waste.

A poster advertising Spurlock's 2004 documentary *Super Size Me.*

Genetically modified crops have also been hailed as the panacea for development woes around the world. In July 2000, *Time* magazine ran a cover with the words "This Rice Could Save a Million Kids a Year." The accompanying story was about Ingo Potrykus, a professor of plant sciences at the Federal Institute of Technology in Zurich, Switzerland, and the inventor of golden rice, which could help solve key health and nutritional problems for children in developing countries (Nash, 2000). By inserting a particular bacterial gene into the genetic structure of rice, Potrykus and his colleagues worked to create rice with high levels of vitamin A. Their goal was to combat vitamin A deficiency, a condition that causes blindness in millions of children around the world. Because rice is a staple in many

Ingo Potrykus's genetically modified golden rice might prevent health problems for millions of poor children. Why is it controversial?

RISK SOCIETY

a society that both produces and is concerned with mitigating risks, especially manufactured risks (ones that result from human activity).

children's diets worldwide (particularly in Asia), Potrykus and others believe that genetically modified rice containing more vitamin A could be an answer to this debilitating condition. In Potrykus's vision, farmers in developing countries could substitute a genetically modified crop for their traditional one.

Genetic modification is not without its problems, however. Opponents of genetically modified crops point to two primary risks: risks to the environment and risks to human health. Scientists know very little about how changes in the genetic structure of one organism may affect its relationship with other organisms and the ecosystem as a whole. For instance, one type of genetically modified corn in Canada was toxic to a particular caterpillar. Through the modification of the genetic structure of corn to keep away this predator, the Canadian corn crop has flourished. However, we don't know the consequences of reducing the population of caterpillars by cutting off a primary food source for them. Will the birds that eat the caterpillars die out? What would the ripple effects of that be? Given the interconnectedness of ecological systems, it is hard to predict the outcome of an intervention at one point in the food chain. What's more, some researchers have argued that the Canadian corn modifications have also been harmful to the monarch butterfly, a cherished species that doesn't damage corn crops.

Opponents of genetically modified food also claim that the results are simply unnatural (think fish genes turning up in tomatoes) and that we simply don't know enough about this technology to ensure safety for human consumers (Bakshi, 2003). They fear that genetically modified foods may have unanticipated long-term, adverse health effects or that they may even cause new illnesses. That said, proponents argue that farmers have been genetically modifying food organisms for centuries already—first through selective breeding (apples have been cultivated over generations from a native fruit called a hawthorn) and more recently by the exposure of seeds to X-rays to induce random mutations in the hope that some will yield benefits.

As with organic farming, the debates about the risks and rewards offered by genetically modified foods involve both natural science and social science. One framework for understanding them is Ulrich Beck's concept of the risk society. Beck (1992) argues that risks can be grouped into two categories: external risks and manufactured risks. External risks derive from nature—hurricanes, floods, earthquakes, and the like—and have been a part of human history since long before the first machine was ever invented. However, with modernity come manufactured risks, which result from human activity. These run the gamut from large-scale nuclear events (such as the meltdown at Japan's Fukushima Daiichi nuclear plant in 2011) to the personal risks of riding a motorcycle at 100 miles per hour. A risk society produces manufactured risks (like those from GMOs) but also tries to mitigate them. Meanwhile, both external and manufactured risks are unequally distributed by socioeconomic status and other dimensions of power. Risk considerations sometimes inform how we make social decisions: For example, should we really rebuild New Orleans as it was before Hurricane Katrina? Should we have constructed the Freedom Tower at Ground Zero as tall as the towers of the World Trade Center were? Should we attempt to preserve the "American way of life" by continuing to burn fossil fuels at our current rate, regardless of the irreparable harm it may do to the planet?

Charles Perrow, for one, would say no. In *The Next Catastrophe* (2007), he argues that disasters resulting from manufactured risks (as well as external risks) are an inevitable part of modern life. Although we cannot eliminate them, we can reduce their impact. Perhaps, he argues, it doesn't really make sense to have a city with a large population in a hurricane-prone area at an altitude below sea level. And maybe it doesn't make sense to build a huge tower piercing the sky when there is so much air traffic that will need to skirt by it. Perrow argues that by dispersing risks—like storing hazardous materials in smaller quantities across wider areas—we can make disasters less disastrous, even as they remain inevitable. Perrow's analysis illuminates Beck's concept of risk society: Social scientists (and society as a whole) struggle to minimize risk even as human technology produces more of it with each new discovery.

THE GREEN REVOLUTION

The green revolution is another example that may shed light on the risk society concept. The umbrella term *green revolution* refers broadly to two agricultural trends: first, the introduction of high-yield crop varietals in developing countries, and second, improvements in agricultural technologies, including irrigation systems, fertilizers, and pesticides. In 1945, the Rockefeller Foundation and the Mexican government established the Cooperative Wheat Research and Production Program (later CIMMYT, the International Maize and Wheat Improvement Center) to improve Mexico's agricultural output, especially its wheat yields. Norman Borlaug, who was instrumental to this effort, won the 1970 Nobel Peace Prize for his role.

By the mid-1960s, these same technologies were developed for use in other regions of the world, with help from many nongovernmental organizations and financing from the World Bank. In Asia, the International Rice Research Institute developed high-yield varieties of paddy rice. By the late 1990s, almost half of East Asian crops were planted with such high-yield varieties; more than two-thirds of South Asian farming is done with these seeds. The corresponding figure for sub-Saharan Africa is a mere 11 percent. Each extension of the green revolution technologies, from their home bases in Japan and the United States to Mexico, India, East Asia, Latin America, and Africa, has depended on local research to adapt high-yield technologies to local crops, pests, and farm systems (for example, rain-fed versus irrigated). Africa has been a late beneficiary of the green revolution because of its distinctive mix of crops and its very high dependence on rain-fed agriculture (whereas the first generation of high-yield varieties depended on irrigation).

The green revolution is widely credited with increasing agricultural productivity in countries throughout the developing world. Along with the introduction of fertilizers and pesticides, as well as the increased use of irrigation systems, new high-yield seeds have increased the quantity of food production. Through the green revolution, food production has kept pace with population growth. Meanwhile, as incomes have increased thanks to greater agricultural productivity, population growth has slowed (Conley et al., 2007). Likewise, because the new technologies require greater skills to realize their full benefit—coordinating irrigation with fertilizer inputs and so on—they have increased the value of formal schooling in many rural areas, particularly for women (Rosenzweig, 1982).

The green revolution has also rearranged the economic units of production. Because the costs of irrigation systems and fertilizer are sometimes prohibitively expensive for individual farms and households, new collectives and cooperatives have emerged to bring together household farmers. The results, therefore, not only have been agricultural and scientific but also have reshaped the social organization of farming. The green revolution has reduced the number of individual, family-owned farms and made farming a collective, community endeavor.

The green revolution is not without its critics, however. Because of its focus on boosting caloric output through the intensified production of staple foods such as wheat and rice, farmers are often encouraged to switch from local, indigenous crops to other high-yield crops distributed by the movement's proponents. The result, according to Vandana Shiva (1992a, 1992b, 2002), an Indian scientist and anti–green revolution activist, is the sacrifice of micronutrients attained only through variety in a diet. In this way, she argues, the green revolution has depleted biodiversity in many areas. And because they are relying on fewer crops, farmers are more susceptible to disease or predators destroying their fields.

Likewise, argues Shiva, the green revolution seed varieties emphasize higher yields but require a great deal of water. Although this switch to water-reliant varieties of wheat and paddy rice has been responsible for an increase in production, it has simultaneously created new environmental problems by overextending India's water supply and its reliance on irrigated as opposed to rain-fed agriculture. Writing for *YES! Magazine*, Shiva (2004) gave the following example:

> In the Deccan area of south India, sorghum was traditionally intercropped with pulses and oilseeds to reduce evaporation. The Green Revolution replaced this indigenous agriculture with monocultures.

Dwarf varieties replaced tall ones, chemical fertilizers took the place of organic ones, and irrigation displaced rain-fed cropping. As a result, soils were deprived of vital organic material, and soil moisture droughts became recurrent.

Moreover, these new models of production have focused on the market-based distribution of water resources, at the expense of the traditional water management techniques of local communities. Shiva points to situations in which Indian women have to walk farther and farther to find water. She also argues that the use of fertilizers and pesticides has ruined local soils, depleting natural, organic ingredients. These results, she argues, should raise long-term concerns about the sustainability of the green revolution's agricultural techniques. Although Shiva doesn't dispute that the green revolution has increased agricultural output and household incomes, her criticisms raise questions about the costs of such changes as well as their sustainability—economic, cultural, and environmental.

Biotechnology and the Human Genome

Since launching the Human Genome Project in 1990, scientists have sought to understand the role of the building blocks of DNA, which consists of four nucleotide bases: adenine (A), thymine (T), cytosine (C), and guanine (G). At the start of the Human Genome Project, scientists believed that there were 90,000 genes in human DNA. After 13 years of research, however, they discovered that only about 20,000 human genes exist. The Human Genome Project has enabled scientists to crack the genetic code, helping us understand everything from disease to race.

This may sound like the realm of biological science, not sociology. Unraveling the mysteries of the genetic code is probably better left to medical scientists, right? As with the innovations in agricultural production, though, each new piece of scientific information raises important sociological questions. Now that scientists have discovered genes that influence the risk of obesity, for instance, should we screen children for the obesity genotype? If so, what kinds of social stigma might they face throughout their childhood? Scientists have also located genes that affect one's risk of Alzheimer's disease. Should people know, long before the condition manifests itself, that they're carrying a genotype that increases their chances of eventually suffering from this debilitating disease?

When scientists embarked on the Human Genome Project, their goal was to identify all of the genes in human DNA. Their project became one of the first major scientific endeavors to acknowledge and address (with funding) the ethical, legal, and social issues (ELSI) that arose from the process of scientific discovery. You'll find that newspapers increasingly print stories about genomic discoveries: the genes associated with breast cancer risk; the genes for sexual orientation, depression, and alcoholism; the genes related to violent tendencies, assertiveness, worry, and sickle-cell anemia, to name just a few. All of these discoveries raise sociological issues about the use of the information. For example, should we allow fertility clinics to screen embryos for genetic risk of developing diabetes? Sure, why not. Major depression? Guess so. What about skin tone, IQ, or sexual orientation? Wait a minute.

Other social concerns have arisen from the Human Genome Project, including privacy, stratification, and stigmatization. The first concern involves privacy and access to data. Your genetic structure might reveal information about your susceptibility to disease or about particular personal characteristics. Who should have access to this information? What if scientists discover a gene that makes people more prone to criminal behavior? Should the government have this information so they can track these people more closely? What if scientists discover a gene for learning disabilities? Should this information be given to schools? In time, you can imagine a market for genetic information emerging, just like the existing market for your credit history. If scientists find that your genetic code, like your credit history, reveals something about your behavior patterns, should they be able to sell this information commercially?

Law enforcement agencies have increasingly relied on DNA fingerprinting to solve cases and prosecute crimes. There are, of course, many high-profile cases of exoneration of people for crimes they did not commit, thanks to DNA evidence—even of people on death row. And there are cases where killers, rapists, and others are caught by the biological samples they leave behind on the crime scene. But to have a match, someone's DNA has to be in a database, meaning that person had a prior encounter with law enforcement or willingly contributed genetic information to a service that cooperates with police agencies. Or does it? It turns out that genetic information is special in that if my brother is in a database, that's good enough to find me, even if I never consented to have my genetic information shared. Familial location of suspects was made famous by the capture of the serial killer Joseph DeAngelo, dubbed the Golden State Killer, via distant relatives' DNA. But this familial web means that individuals who are related to people more likely to be in law enforcement genetic databases are more likely to be caught than those who do not have such relatives. That is, DNA does not treat everyone equally under the law. Defenders of such databases reply that to avoid these problems, all you have to do is not commit a crime in the first place. The fact that some people are more likely to be found through a match with their relatives' DNA than are other people is no reason to scrap a system that helps victims obtain justice.

GATTACA: GENETICS AND THE FUTURE OF SOCIETY

The 1997 movie *Gattaca* presents a future divided between "those born of nature, and those engineered by science." In the futuristic world of *Gattaca*, embryos are genetically pre-screened before implantation for their probable likelihood of developing various diseases and disabilities as well as their predicted life expectancy. Ethan Hawke plays Vincent Freeman, a "natural" person (conceived the old-fashioned way) born with a high genetic propensity for heart disease and a predicted life expectancy of only 34 years. Freeman's genetic profile—combined with "genoism," illegal but commonly practiced discrimination based on one's genetic code—prevents him from gaining admission to a training program for astronauts, but Freeman overcomes that obstacle by stealing someone else's identity, which he uses to pass a series of genetic tests required for his inclusion on a mission to Saturn.

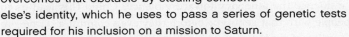

Although *Gattaca* is fictitious, some of the implications for genetic testing seem much more real today than they were when *Gattaca* was produced more than two decades ago. In 1997, the Human Genome Project was under way, but the sequencing of the human genome hadn't yet been completed. Scientists didn't know what type of knowledge they'd gain from the human genome, nor had they considered all the ethical issues involved in sequencing it. *Gattaca* presents us with an extreme scenario—a society in which children are screened at birth for genetic mutations and where only those prenatally engineered for success are given a chance—but it also challenges us to consider some of the ways that genetic knowledge and testing might be used.

A second sociological concern resulting from the Human Genome Project is that knowledge of the genetic architecture of important traits may increase stratification in society if we begin to label people as intelligent/unintelligent, beautiful/ugly, or healthy/unhealthy based on their genetic code. The Pygmalion study (discussed in Chapter 13) showed stigma's power to create its own reality, as such labels become self-fulfilling prophecies: When people

Joseph DeAngelo, aka, "the Golden State Killer," was caught by law enforcement via a distant relative's DNA.

expect a certain outcome, they tend to act in ways that bring about that outcome (otherwise known as the W. I. Thomas principle). What if we discover genes that influence the tendency toward violence? Could this lead us to lock away people with that genotype before they even commit a crime—in an extreme version of predictive policing? In a more realistic scenario, many observers worry about the concentration of wealth, power, and control that may result from the rush to patent our genetic code for private purposes.

Indeed, researchers like Daniel Belsky of Columbia University are among a small but growing group of social and behavioral scientists who are directly studying how genes affect classic sociological outcomes like social mobility and how the effects of DNA vary by social context. We call this new field "sociogenomics." In a recent interview with me, Belsky described some of his findings with respect to genes and social mobility. Specifically, he said, "People with more education-associated alleles [genes] are more likely to climb the social ladder relative to where they started in life." Can we predict

DIGITAL.WWNORTON.COM/YOUMAYASK7

To see my interview with Daniel Belsky, go to digital.wwnorton.com/youmayask7 what class in which someone will end up based on their DNA? At first glance, this finding seems like a challenge to sociology. But it turns out that how and when genes matter for climbing the social ladder is greatly affected by social environments. For example, Belsky explains that "after we account for where you started," the relationship between genes and outcomes is much weaker. More interesting is the fact that how much your genes matter depends on the social class of your parents.

A final concern revolves around the prospect of genetically altering humans. Today, fertility clinics routinely test embryos for major chromosomal diseases like Down syndrome (trisomy 21) or single-gene diseases like Huntington's. The technology already exists, however, to test for genetic propensities for eye color, height, body mass index (obesity risk), and even educational attainment. Should we allow prospective parents—à la the 1997 movie *Gattaca*—to select the "best" embryo based on the genetic prediction algorithms (best on whatever trait they value)? What about single parents going to a sperm or ova bank? The rise of gene-editing technology called CRISPR—though not yet ready for prime time—raises even more questions: Should prospective parents be allowed not just to select but *change* the genomes of their potential offspring?

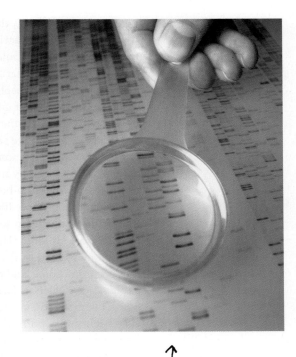

↑
A scientist scans sections of DNA for subsequent computer analysis. What are the possible social consequences of decoding the human genome?

Sociologists have long thought about the social implications of human enhancement—from prosthetic limbs to plastic surgery to performance drugs—for inequality, the family, and even the self. But some argue that gene editing, since it would alter not just an individual but all of his or her descendants, is another ball game altogether.

The perils of CRISPR become clear when we think of the ongoing search for "gay genes." Should we allow parents to select on this gene—or edit it? In 2005, scientists reported evidence of a link between homosexuality and particular genetic markers in the journal *Human Genetics* (Mustanski et al., 2005). By comparing the genetic structures of two gay brothers with those of two other brothers, only one of whom was gay, researchers located part of the genetic structure that they believe is a factor in determining homosexuality. More recent work with ever larger samples of subjects has found more genetic markers that correlate with sexual orientation (Ganna et al., 2019). This should not be surprising in one respect since it has long been known from twin and adoption studies that human variation in sexual orientation is explained in almost equal parts by genetic differences and environmental ones. (Interestingly, there have been many more genetic discoveries for sexual orientation in men than in women.)

But in another way, the existence of genetic variants that predispose one toward same-sex attraction poses a big question mark given the forces of natural selection: How and why would a gene that leads to reduced reproduction survive in a population? One answer is that gay uncles (and aunts) help raise their nieces and nephews and provide family solidarity. However, much evidence suggests that gays are no more involved with their families than are heterosexuals. Further, the idea of group selection—that some individuals make reproductive sacrifices for the sake of the wider community—is not widely accepted among biologists. A better explanation is what's called antagonistic pleiotropy in technical terms. That is, what if the same genes that caused women to be more fertile also, as an unintended by-product, caused men to be more likely to be gay? Indeed, a trio of Italian researchers found that the women with gay men in their immediate families tended to have more children than those whose immediate families included only straight men. Further, it was only on the maternal side, where men get their lone X chromosome, and not on the paternal side. This helps rule out social explanations (such as large families causing homosexuality). However, it doesn't completely rule out a nongenetic explanation, because the mother's side might have more social influence than the dad's side (particularly in Italy, where the study was done).

The biological roots of sexual orientation need not be limited to genes. Prenatal hormones may also play a role. For example, research by Anthony F. Bogaert has also identified a positive relationship between the number of older biological brothers a boy has and his chance of being gay, which could be the result of the mother's immune system's "remembering" her previous male pregnancies and altering the hormonal environment in utero for subsequent male fetuses (Blanchard & Bogaert, 1996; Bogaert, 2006). And what about lesbianism? Research indicates that increased exposure to testosterone in utero causes a number of physiological changes in female fetuses, some of which have been linked to homosexuality (Martin & Nguyen, 2004; Rahman et al., 2003).

The identification of a biological mechanism could cause further stigmatization of homosexuals in society if they are deemed to be "innately" different from heterosexuals. (See our discussion of homosexuality in Chapter 8 on gender.) Alternatively, as some gay activists hope, such a finding could promote tolerance by demonstrating that homosexuality is not a lifestyle or moral choice but a natural attribute like height or eye color. These discoveries also brush the cobwebs off old nature—nurture debates in the scientific community: Is homosexuality a product of nature (biological pathways triggered during development) or nurture (the social environment in which children are raised)? And what if there are people who did not experience the biological pathways scientists have recently discovered but still identify themselves as homosexual? What about firstborn sons who are gay? Will they be stigmatized as being "fake" gays?

RACE AND GENETICS

As scientists continue to unravel the mystery of the human genome, some researchers are searching for information about the genetic basis of race. Race is a socially ambiguous concept (see Chapter 9)—the line between who's Black and who's White, for instance, isn't clearly defined and has changed over the course of American history. But what if scientists locate a gene for racial difference buried in our genetic code? Would that clarify our understanding of race? Culling the human genome for clues about the scientific basis of race has reopened the question of whether race is a social or scientific concept.

As it turns out, if race categories were meant primarily to capture differences in genetics, they are doing an abysmal job. The genetic distance between some groups within Africa is as great as the genetic distance between many "racially divergent" groups in the rest of the world. The genetic distance between East Asians and Europeans is shorter than the divergence between Hadza in north-central Tanzania and the Fulani shepherds of West Africa (who live in present-day Mali, Niger, Burkina Faso, and Guinea). So much for Black, White, Asian, and other.

Henry Louis Gates Jr. is one of the million plus people who have taken a DNA test to determine their ancestry.

Armed with this knowledge, many investigators in the biological sciences have replaced the term *race* with the term *continental ancestry*. This in part reflects a rejection of race as a biological classification. Every so-called race has the same protein-coding genes, and there is no clear genetic line that subdivides the human species. Another reason for using the term *continental ancestry* is improved precision for locating historical and geographic origins when we look at the genome. Thus continental ancestry allows for more genetically accurate descriptors. For example, President Barack Obama was not just the first socially "Black" president. He was also the first (as far as we know) who has mixed European and African ancestry.

Meanwhile, the search to understand race and ancestry by digging into our genetic code has spawned an entire industry, with companies like 23andme.com and Ancestry.com competing to help individuals trace their ancestral history (see Chapter 9). After you send your check to one of these companies, it will mail you a simple form and a genetic testing kit. Just spit (a lot) into a tube to collect cells, fill out some paperwork, mail back, and wait to learn your ancestry as revealed by your DNA.

Harvard professor Henry Louis Gates Jr. hosted a 2006 PBS documentary in which he, along with several other African American celebrities, publicly took such a DNA test to trace his personal lineage through the genes on his Y chromosome. Because the history of slavery in the United States was truncated, many African Americans have been unable to trace their heritage back to a particular African country: Records of slaves' origins weren't always complete or even maintained. Furthermore, to blunt the potential for revolutionary action on the part of slaves who shared a common language and sense of solidarity, slave owners purposefully erased Africans' tribal and national heritage by dispersing and remixing groups arriving on the shores of the New World. Genetic testing may thus help many African Americans re-create their currently unknown genealogical history. Having matched the DNA of various African American celebrities with various populations throughout Africa, scientists such as Rick Kittles, an associate professor at the University of Illinois at Chicago and the founder of the African Ancestry network, claim to be able to trace the lineage of African Americans back to their specific African roots. Of course, this technology for tracing ancestral roots is fraught with debate. Are the DNA samples from African populations collected in a database sufficiently exhaustive to be able to trace someone's roots reliably to a particular place? What does it mean for someone to find out his or her genetic ancestry (or at least part of it), and what are the benefits and the risks? You might learn that your ancestors came from the area of West Africa now called Nigeria, but you probably couldn't pinpoint their origins much more specifically than that. Africa is, after all, a continent with more than 50 nations and 1,000 languages as well as a long history of internal migration.

As Charles Rotimi, a Nigerian geneticist living in the United States, points out, this technology can be a double-edged sword. Many people are concerned about confidentiality and accuracy. The tests can be faulty, and they require scientists to have access to people's genetic data. Other critics are simply unsure about the usefulness of such information. Rotimi gives the example of finding out that your ancestors were slave owners. What can you do with this knowledge? There could be unintended social, economic, or psychological consequences for you.

What's more, scientists have little basis to compare different racial groups. They don't have an exhaustive sample of all racial and ethnic groups in the world. Although your genetic information may be a close match to a sample in a database, it might be even closer to a population that's not included in the database. In addition, no definitive genetic markers for race exist. There's no single gene that separates people into different races, so that you're Black if you have it and White if you don't. Instead, scientists look for groups of similar outward traits in populations that society labels as one race or another.

Another PBS documentary, *The Lost Tribes of Israel* (2000), attempted to test the ancestral claims of the Lemba people of southern Africa, practicing

Jews who claim to be direct descendants of Abraham, Isaac, and Jacob. Although some historians claim that the Lemba adopted their Jewish heritage through the work of missionaries centuries ago, the Lemba maintain they are one of the Lost Tribes of Israel. They claim that their Jewish heritage can be traced directly back to the ancient populations that occupied the geographic area of modern-day Palestine and Israel. To test this genetic relationship to the earliest Jews, scientists obtained DNA samples from the Cohanim, a small group of Jews who are said to have descended directly from Aaron, the brother of Moses. They compared samples of DNA from self-described Cohanim to samples of non-Cohanim or lay Jews in Israel to determine the genetic differences between the direct descendants of Aaron and other Jews. The scientists identified a distinctive set of genetic markers found in 50 percent of the Cohanim and seen in about 10 percent of lay Jews.

↑

Members of the Lemba community at the Rusape Jewish Tabernacle during a Rosh Hashanah service.

If the Lemba people possessed this set of genetic markers unique to Jewish populations, researchers believed, their claims of being one of the Lost Tribes of Israel would be validated. The same scientific team then collected DNA samples from Bantu (African), Yemeni (Arab), and Sephardic and Ashkenazic Jews (including Cohanim from both communities) to compare the degree of similarity that existed between each of these groups. Tests of DNA from the Lemba people revealed that the tribe shared a series of genetic markers (called the Cohen Modal Haplotype) with the Cohanim at a rate that closely matched that of the lay Jews. In one particular clan of the Lemba known as the Buba, the Cohanim genetic marker was found in more than 50 percent of males (PBS, 2000). For many scientists, this confirmed that the Lemba were direct descendants of the original Israelites rather than Africans converted by missionaries long ago. Although the research may have helped set the historical record straight, it raised a handful of other sociological questions about the intersections of race, ethnicity, religion, and geography.

Alondra Nelson has been asking tough questions about how genetic testing has pushed social scientists to refine their mantra that race is a social construction. Is race *either* a social construction *or* a biological one? Nelson responds:

> For social scientists, the coding of the human genome and the quick change in science around questions of race and ancestry really forced us to go back to the drawing board and think carefully about what

POLICY

FRANKENFOOD VERSUS CRISPR VERSUS ABORTION POLITICS

At no time is the intersection of science with politics more visible than when new technologies hit the public domain. Back in the 1970s, people worried that microwave ovens would radiate their children. We kids were also warned not to sit too close to the television for fear of what the glowing phosphorous screen would do to our retinas. In the 1990s and 2000s, concerns about a potential link between brain cancer and cell phones prompted a number of studies. The same was true for a theory about a link between vaccines (and/or the mercury-based preservatives in many of them) and rising rates of autism diagnosis. This last issue, which was driven by a constituency of concerned and angry parents, prompted not one but multiple studies by the National Academy of Sciences (an apolitical body of elite scientists charged by Congress with assessing the scientific evidence on certain issues and delivering a consensus report). The vaccine worries even prompted Congress to pass legislation—but alas, it was not the kind of law that parents would have hoped for. As part of the PATRIOT Act, House majority leader Dick Armey slipped in a provision that protected Eli Lilly, a pharmaceutical company, from any lawsuits on account of thimerosal, the preservative in its vaccines.

Why do some technologies seem to evoke debate and even fierce political battles, while others—take the internet or flat-screen televisions, for example—slip comfortably into our lives with little backlash? An interesting comparison in this regard is the relatively quiet reception that genetically modified food has received in the United States as compared with the concern and protests it has unleashed in Europe. Why the difference?

At first glance, we might simply say that we Americans tend to embrace new technologies more wholeheartedly. After all, aren't we a more future-oriented, newer country that embraces ingenuity and entrepreneurship? But that would ignore the fact that we actually lag behind our European counterparts with respect to the adoption of many new technologies, such as nuclear power, cell phones, broadband, and high-speed rail, to name a few examples. Or we might argue that Europe simply has a more robust civil society—more geared to collective action and resistance than our individualistic American culture is. The answer, at least in the view of sociologist of science John Evans, lies, ironically, in the more religious nature of the United States as compared with that of Europe. This answer is ironic in that we might at first think a more secular society such as those found in western Europe would be more ready to embrace *biological* science and technology. "Well, in actuality from what I've studied of religious people in the United States, the idea of modifying plants, animals, and things is considered to be nonproblematic," he explained to me during our conversation. "One of my interviewees might say to me, 'Well, God has already given us that task to do.' Therefore, it doesn't particularly bother people to modify food forms" (Conley, 2009o). If we already have dominion over

nature as God's children, altering a few food plants to be insect-resistant or to pack in more nutrients is merely us fulfilling our divine role. In Europe, meanwhile, religion didn't really come into the picture, and the underlying frame of debate was about environmental concerns. However, if we try to mess with the human form through CRISPR gene editing, for example, that's an entirely different story, warned Evans, since that does trigger religious objections. Indeed, while pronuclear transfer (so-called three-parent fertility to address mitochondrial diseases) is legal in the United Kingdom, it remains banned in the United States. Evans also emphasizes the role of professionalized bureaucrats. The more the debate is co-opted by professionals in the technocratic language of government agencies, like the US Food and Drug Administration or the National Academy of Sciences, the less it becomes about moral, value-laden questions and the more it is about instrumental rationality (efficient means to ends). No longer do we ask if we should modify foods through genetic engineering, but rather—as Max Weber would have predicted—bureaucracy asks what is the safest, most cost-effective way to do so.

This last point doesn't explain the difference in GMO response across the Atlantic, as both the United States and Europe have large bureaucracies to deal with agricultural technologies, but it does provide some advice for those who would hope to depolarize some hot-button debates—say, gun safety or abortion: Create a federal agency to deal with the issue while somehow simultaneously turning down the volume on the debate going on outside the professional, scientific community (good luck with that!). "In the United Kingdom the abortion question was always tied in with essentially medical practice and part of the National Health Service," Evans explained. "Because abortion was always defined as part of medicine, it never had the same heat associated with it, whereas in the United States it was sort of semi-shunned by the medical profession, not brought into that framework, and remained in the public sphere as this divisive debate" (Conley, 2009o). So although we may continue to enjoy our Frankenfood with little indigestion, don't expect the abortion (or gun control) debates to go away anytime soon.

DIGITAL.WWNORTON.COM/YOUMAYASK7

To see my interview with Alondra Nelson about her research on genetic testing, go to digital.wwnorton.com/youmayask7

we mean when we state that "race is a social construct." That statement is still true. What social scientists have not done so well over the last two decades or so, perhaps, is looked at the way in which biology becomes part of that process. So, it's not to say that race is social or biological. I would still suggest that race is a social construct and I think the ways that people negotiate the genetic genealogy tests really proves this point. They get the information, these hard genetic facts, and then these facts enter this whole process about "Who am I? Who was my family before? Does this change who I think my family is now?" And so that suggests that the biological is drawn into social understandings and practices of race and ethnicity. (Conley, 2009n)

She goes on to note that the hard facts of genetics often impact the less-well-defined operations of family life. There are the obvious difficulties that could arise if genetic testing revealed the person whom you thought to be your biological father was actually not. There are also more subtle impacts of genetic testing on families. When one member of a family has DNA entered into a criminal database, that DNA submission is also exposing the genetic backgrounds of other family members who might then be at a higher risk of being apprehended by the criminal justice system. This shift toward DNA evidence disproportionately impacts poorer families who are more likely to encounter the criminal justice system in the first place and less likely to be able to afford high-quality lawyers to dispute these findings. And as Nelson points out, the sword doesn't cut the other way, because "courts are denying to people who are incarcerated the right to use DNA evidence to prove their innocence" (Conley, 2009n).

Conclusion

From genetics to nutrition to technology, scientific study is embedded in a social and political context. Progress in so-called natural science has strong implications for our social world and vice versa. As sociologists, we are interested in the effects that one has on the other. Important questions include how new technologies break down or reinforce existing social distinctions. More important, what can we do about it? However, in addition to posing these empirical inquiries, we must also follow a more fundamental line of questioning. How do we know that we know? Are facts created, as Bruno Latour would suggest, or already in existence, just waiting to be discovered? Is the boundary between the natural and the social breaking down? As in the pursuit of science itself, in the study of science, the most important part of the entire endeavor is to ask the tough questions.

QUESTIONS FOR REVIEW

1. How do findings from climate scientists and research in Eric Klinenberg's *Heat Wave* demonstrate the relationship between the environment and society? What concerns and courses of action do these examples provide?

2. Describe the Human Genome Project and the green revolution. Using these examples, explain how policies that could yield desirable results sometimes have unintended negative consequences.

3. With new scientific discoveries and technologies come new questions and often new risks. How does Ulrich Beck describe "risk" and how does Charles Perrow's response direct us for the future?

4. According to Thomas Kuhn, what is a paradigm? Use Charles Darwin's theory of evolution to illustrate how paradigms affect the way scientists do research, and describe a hypothetical paradigm shift.

5. Research is not conducted in a social vacuum. Can you provide two examples, one of them from this chapter, to show how scientific inquiry typically differs from the "traditional" view of science, including the way we choose what to study?

6. How do Thomas Gieryn's writings on the authority of science help us understand the concerns related to possible findings of the Human Genome Project? What is the potential link between science and stigmatization?

7. Why are sociologists interested in studying "the environment"? As an example, how would sociological attention to organic food result in a more profound understanding of inequality?

8. The editors at an academic journal decide what gets published (and therefore, what is "good" science). In this sense, how would the editors of a prestigious sociology journal be doing "boundary work" within their discipline and across others?

PRACTICE

SUSTAINABLE CHOICES

These days sustainability is all the rage. Electric and hybrid cars, composting, and upcycling are all recent examples of the same trend: small changes in consumption that add up to something bigger. These small acts are meaningful: Everyone's doing their part for a greener planet. Right?

While sociologists since C. Wright Mills have always applauded efforts to see the connections between our personal troubles (like how long our commute is) and historical issues (like global warming), focusing on individual actions as a solution to climate change may also obscure larger societal or even global forces that play a bigger role in "saving the earth," so to speak. Some of the macro-level factors that greatly influence how much greenhouse gas we emit include population density, level of economic development, and access to renewables—like how much sunlight a country gets or whether it's situated atop natural geysers, like Iceland is. It also, importantly, includes weather patterns: Countries like Canada with one or more extreme seasons generally use a lot more fuel to keep running.

TRY IT!

Come up with a list of the ways that your actions lead to greenhouse gas emissions, especially CO_2. Are there changes you could make in your lifestyle that could reduce your personal carbon footprint? I'll go first:

YOUR BEHAVIOR	WAYS TO REDUCE?
FLYING TO CHICAGO FOR A WORKSHOP	SKYPE IN
HIGH USE OF AC IN THE SUMMER	INSTALL SOLAR PANELS FOR POWER AT HOME
TOSSING LEFTOVERS IN THE TRASH	URBAN COMPOSTING
VEGETARIAN DIET & TAKEOUT	GO VEGAN! AND COOK AT HOME

Here are the five countries that, according to the World Bank, emitted the least CO_2 per capita in 2014.

METRIC TONS OF CO_2 EMITTED PER CAPITA		
	BURUNDI	0.0
	SOMALIA	0.0
	CHAD	0.1
	DEMOCRATIC REPUBLIC OF THE CONGO	0.1
SOURCE: World Bank, 2018.	CENTRAL AFRICAN REPUBLIC	0.1

Pick one of these countries and research the lifestyle of the average citizen. Do these countries emit less CO_2 because of personal choices the occupants are making? What societal-led factors might be at play?

Here are the countries that score highest on the Yale Center for Environment and Society's "Environmental Performance Index." This index takes into account greenhouse gas emissions, but also many other factors, such as air and water quality, sanitation, and biodiversity. Why do you think these countries rank higher on the list than the lowest CO_2 emitters listed above?

#1 SWITZERLAND	#2 FRANCE	#3 DENMARK	#4 MALTA	#5 SWEDEN

SOURCE: Environmental Performance Index, 2018.

SOCIOLOGY ON THE STREET

We constantly throw things away because they are used up, broken, or no longer wanted. But where does all this stuff go? Watch the Sociology on the Street video to find out more: **digital.wwnorton.com/youmayask7**.

WANT MORE PRACTICE?

Complete the InQuizitive activity for this chapter at digital.wwnorton.com /youmayask7

PARADOX

18

WHAT MAKES YOU AN INDIVIDUAL IS YOUR AFFILIATION WITH MULTIPLE GROUP IDENTITIES.

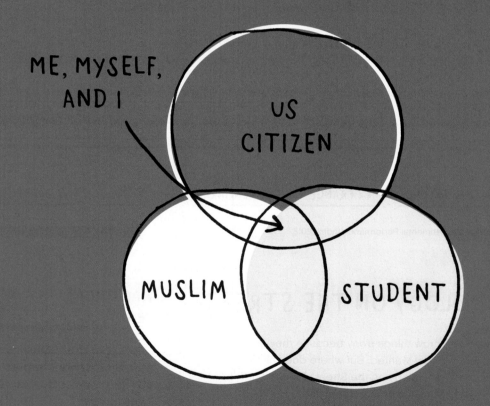

ME, MYSELF, AND I

US CITIZEN

MUSLIM

STUDENT

Animation at digital.wwnorton.com/youmayask7

Collective Action, Social Movements, and Social Change

I first met Andy Bichlbaum and Mike Bonanno almost two decades ago when they came to speak at Yale University on "21st Century Investing Strategies." As it turned out, the title was a tad misleading, as they actually showed slides of the Barbie Liberation Organization, which they had sponsored to switch the voice boxes of about 300 GI Joe and Barbie dolls and then restock them on store shelves. They also spoke about their antic disruption of the upcoming 2000 presidential campaign. I would quickly get used to—and in fact embrace—their deceptive ways. Andy and Mike aren't even their real names, so let's call them the Yes Men, which is how they are now known.

Their activism reinvented the tradition of political satire pioneered by Jonathan Swift in the eighteenth century. Over coffee after the lecture, we talked about their latest project: the co-optation of the Bush campaign website. I, in turn, told them about my idea for corporate criminal liability to go along with legal corporate personhood (bestowed by the Fourteenth Amendment to the Constitution—the very same amendment that guaranteed equal protection to former slaves after the Civil War—and reaffirmed by the US Supreme Court's controversial *Citizens United* decision). I further explained that each shareholder would have to serve time in jail proportionate to his or her ownership stake, for crimes such as 10,000 counts of criminal manslaughter in the case of the Union Carbide chemical disaster in Bhopal, India. They loved it, apparently; before I realized anything was afoot, I was asked to speak at a law school on account of my role as a "Bush adviser on corporate crime."

After a little digging around, I found that I had been made a consultant to the presidential candidate on his corporate "tough love" stance—at least in the Yes Men's alternate universe. I panicked, asking them to expunge my name and university affiliation. And yes, I declined the law school invitation—something that Andy and Mike never do. But the damage was done without my assistance. The Bush folks pursued a cease and desist order against them, and in a public statement, Bush claimed that the website had gone too far in attacking him and that "there ought to be limits to freedom." Although that ended my brief stint as a "culture jamming" hacktivist (see Chapter 3), the duo went on to impersonate the US Chamber of Commerce, the leadership of the World Trade Organization (WTO), and a host of other government and corporate officials. They even temporarily drove billions of dollars of stock value off the Dow Chemical Company (which had acquired Union Carbide) by claiming on the BBC World Service television news that Dow was taking responsibility for the Bhopal disaster and would remunerate the affected families. The Yes Men went on to make two movies documenting their stunts, and they still seek social change through impersonation and satire with web and other new-media tools that Jonathan Swift couldn't have dreamed of back in his day. I smiled a bit when I opened the "special edition" of the *New York Times* that they handed out on July 4, 2009. In the business section, "Carlton Donally" was the author of an article describing Senator John McCain's bold new plan to humanize corporations and get tough on corporate crime. Sometimes, you get swept up in a social movement whether you like it or not.

Today they are still at it, taking on the latest issues of the day with their trademark techniques of impersonation and Swiftian irony. In a chat with Andy one summer afternoon, I mentioned that gun control used to be a Republican issue. In fact, as governor of California, Ronald Reagan wanted to impose stricter regulations. Why? Because back then there was a fear—especially in that state—of the armed Black Panther Party. Wouldn't it change gun politics, I asked, if we had a modern-day Black Panther Party that patrolled White neighborhoods while openly carrying weapons? Lo and behold, a year or so later, I noticed this strange "NRA sponsored" website/organization, "Share the Safety" (**sharethesafety.org**). The site reads: "You know how important it is to protect your family. But you may not know that some of America's poorest citizens cannot afford to arm themselves against those who would limit their freedoms. That's why the National Rifle Association is proud to partner with Smith & Wesson to Share the Safety." The "program" buys a gun for someone in an "at-risk," violent neighborhood when you buy a gun, co-opting the logic of many charities and rolling it into the NRA arguments to produce a powerful critique. The Yes Men strike again.

Collective Action: What Is It Good For?

When you arrive at your sociology class, you probably sit in one of the chairs designated for students and take out your notebook. You perform these actions because you've been socialized as a student (as discussed in Chapter 4). If you were to arrive late, sit on the floor (assuming there are still seats available), or talk loudly during the lecture, this behavior would be called deviant (see Chapter 6). But what if every student sat on the floor? And as soon as the professor started to lecture, every student began to talk loudly? In that case, you would be engaged in collective action.

Have you ever been involved in a protest march? Have you ever sent a letter or an e-mail to your congressional representatives? Have you ever signed a petition or attended a political rally? If so, you've been involved in collective action. This chapter introduces the interrelated concepts of collective action, social movements, and social change. We will examine the process through which collective action becomes a social movement and the way social movements promote social change. This chapter also delineates the broader premodern, modern, and postmodern periods of social transformation.

As mentioned, for your behavior to count as collective action, you must act as part of a group and against the expected social norms of the situation. The type of behavior that counts as collective action also depends on both the number of people participating and the location of the behavior, however. If you started to speak in tongues in the middle of your sociology class, that behavior would probably be viewed as deviance. But if the entire class started to speak in tongues in the middle of the lecture, that could be called collective action. The same behavior in a Pentecostal church, however, where it is normal to speak in tongues, wouldn't violate social expectations. Speaking in tongues at a Lutheran or an Episcopalian service, on the other hand, would again be considered deviance (or collective action, if you did it as part of a group).

There are two main types of collective action: crowd collective action and mass collective action (Granovetter, 1978). In crowd

COLLECTIVE ACTION

action that takes place in groups and diverges from the social norms of the situation.

University of California students march to protest sweatshops that manufacture college apparel. Why is this an example of crowd collective action?

collective action, you must be face-to-face with the other members of your group. Collective action can also occur when people aren't physically together. Imagine the National Rifle Association asking all of its members to write letters to their senators protesting a particular law; such an initiative might produce tens of thousands of letters. This letter-writing campaign counts as collective action too, but because the people writing letters live in different towns and cities, it is known as mass collective action. If all these letter writers travel to Washington, D.C., to march on the Capitol, then mass collective action becomes crowd collective action.

THEORIES OF COLLECTIVE ACTION

How does collective action come about? How do individuals decide to get together and violate social norms? Do they plan it on private Facebook groups or huddle in underground rooms late at night to plan their collective actions? Or does it happen spontaneously? Does collective action just erupt when certain people come together? How do they come to think of themselves as connected in some way?

CONVERGENCE THEORY

theory of collective action stating that collective action happens when people with similar ideas and tendencies gather in the same place.

Convergence Theory One theory of collective action, convergence theory, states that collective action happens when people with similar ideas and tendencies gather in the same place (Cantril, 1941). It doesn't necessarily require planning. The setting isn't particularly important, except that it attracts like-minded people. One example of convergent collective action is the riots that sometimes follow an English soccer (or, as the Brits call it, football) match. Who goes to football matches? Mostly zealous fans who are antagonistic toward their opponents (and who may have consumed a couple of pints of beer before and during the match). They probably don't plan to riot at the end of the game, but the convergence of like-minded (and drunk) people causes this collective action.

The main problem with convergence theory is that it's often reduced to the sum of its parts. If collective action results from drunken English football fans coming together, then why isn't there a riot every time they come together? Sometimes they go home peacefully. Sometimes a fight or two break out. Other times enough people get angry that a rancorous riot erupts. Convergence theory doesn't explain the inconsistency of group action.

CONTAGION THEORY

theory of collective action claiming that collective action arises because of people's tendency to conform to the behavior of others with whom they are in close contact.

Contagion Theory A second theory of collective action, called contagion theory, claims that collective action arises because of people's tendency to conform to the behavior of others with whom they are in close contact (LeBon, 2002). The mechanism by which movements grow is similar to the spread of a disease—adherents spread their enthusiasm infectiously among close contacts, who then become infected themselves, and so it goes. If you're peacefully protesting the city's decision to bulldoze your apartment building and suddenly the protester next to you starts chanting, "Two-Four-Six-Eight, We Will Not Negotiate," you'll be more likely to start chanting, too. Before long, every protester will be imitating the others, chanting slogans to save the apartment building. You might never have thought that you'd chant in a public protest, but the actions of other people influenced your behavior. If you've never been involved in a public protest, imagine yourself at a rock concert. As a particular song starts playing, some people begin to jump up and down. Soon, everyone is jumping up and down, imitating nearby concertgoers. Or if you're in the stands at an (American) football game and the fans start the "wave," when the wave comes around to your section of the stadium, you might feel as if you have little choice but to stand and wave your arms like everyone else. Contagion theory suggests that the behavior of other people in groups is contagious, especially under the encouraging influence of a charismatic leader.

Greek soccer players cower behind riot police for protection from objects and flares thrown by fans after a championship game. How is a football (soccer) riot an example of convergent collective action?

Although contagion theory helps explain how collective action spreads from one person throughout the entire group, it downplays individual agency (or, as we call it in everyday life, free will) and treats individuals as mindless sheep, thoughtlessly following the actions of their neighbors. Also, like convergence theory, it doesn't explain inconsistency. Why do some members of a group choose to chant, while others resist? Contagion theory doesn't explain why some situations are more conducive to collective action and why some people are more prone to imitating their neighbors than others.

Emergent Norm Theory The third theory of collective action, emergent norm theory (Turner & Killian, 1987), emphasizes the influence of "keynoters" in promoting new behavioral norms, especially in unusual situations for which already established norms are inadequate. Keynoters are not the same as leaders. They don't have to stand on podiums, shouting into megaphones. They can just be people whose actions become, either intentionally or not, the behavior copied by an entire group. Also, keynoters don't necessarily have to be the people in charge but can be anyone from whom other people take cues in a given context. If you have to evacuate an airplane using the emergency exits, one of your fellow passengers might start directing people out of the plane in an orderly manner. Even though she wasn't formally elected or appointed as the leader, people are taking cues from her in this situation, which is highly unusual for most passengers. Now, imagine

EMERGENT NORM THEORY

theory of collective action emphasizing the influence of keynoters in promoting new behavioral norms.

you're in a battalion of 800 soldiers, marching forward toward enemy lines. All of a sudden, a couple of soldiers in front start to scream and run back, which is uncharacteristic among troops who are trained not to defect. You're not sure what, if anything, has happened up ahead, but you, too, start running backward. Better safe than sorry, right? Those soldiers are the keynoters, and their actions influence everyone's behavior as a new norm emerges on the battlefield. It isn't just that your neighbor is running, so you run too—that would be an illustration of contagion theory. Rather, it's that a novel situation has arisen in which collective behavior is determined, perhaps unwittingly, when the group copies the behavior of an individual or small group of individuals, possibly for no other reason than that these folks were the first to be forced to react. The handful of keynoters within the group may be recognizable leaders, but more often than not they're just members of the group whose behavior sets the standard.

Like contagion theory and convergence theory, emergent norm theory doesn't explain collective action perfectly (Aguirre et al., 1998). It doesn't always explain why particular people emerge as leaders. In some cases, like the soldiers in the battalion, it is fairly obvious, but in other situations why someone becomes a leader may not be so clear. In the airplane example, how did one woman emerge as the keynoter? Was it because she sat closest to the exit? Maybe the emergent leader had a particularly calm demeanor in the face of danger. Emergent norm theory says that new norms for behavior will emerge, but it doesn't suggest why particular people set the terms for this new behavior. The theory also doesn't explain why some actions emerge as norms within the group, whereas other actions don't. In the example of the battalion of soldiers, why did running away become the emergent norm? Why didn't the soldiers stay and fight, rather than turn away from their enemies? And why didn't the battalion take its cues from the other members in the front of the squad who continued marching forward? Emergent norm theory doesn't explain why one behavior rather than another emerges in collective action. It simply suggests that, in group situations, certain people in the crowd set the behavioral pattern that emerges as the norm for the group.

Value-Added Theory Neil Smelser (1962) borrowed the term *value-added* from economics to explain how social movements increase in value in a series of progressive stages. Value-added theory establishes six conditions that are required for a movement to coalesce and achieve a successful outcome. First, there must be a social strain present that existing power holders are unable or unwilling to alleviate. In New York in the 1970s an increasing number of pets were fouling the sidewalk with poop. This was a problem city leaders found rather trivial compared with all of the other troubles besetting the city. But pedestrians felt otherwise and they wanted action. The second requirement for a successful movement under the value-added theory is that folks

VALUE-ADDED THEORY

theory of collective action claiming that certain conditions are required for a social movement to coalesce and achieve a successful outcome.

must be able to agree on a definition of the problem. There was trouble early on in the movement for pooper-scooper legislation because only some people felt that the problem was a lack of public decency on the part of dog owners, who should be made to pick up after their pooches. Others (mostly dog owners themselves) felt it was a lack of commitment on the part of the Department of Sanitation and asked for more street sweeping. The third condition for value-added movements is that the folks must be free to act on their grievance. Awareness is nice, but the ability to act is critical. In the case of the aggrieved New Yorkers, severe budgetary constraints made it impossible to increase the duties of the Sanitation Department, which curtailed the activism of those who were lobbying for sidewalk cleaners to scoop up the mess. Fourth, there must be a spark that ignites the controversy. In the case of New Yorkers lobbying for a pooper-scooper law, they found their controversial episode when a young child was infected with a parasite found in dog poop. Too bad for the sick baby, but great for the movement, which could now "prove" that public dog poop threatened the eyesight of babies citywide. The fifth requirement is mobilization for action: People need to gather together in an organized fashion. For the pooper-scooper law activists, already established mothers' groups took up the cause and later united with neighborhood groups on the issue of dog droppings. The sixth requirement necessary in the value-added theory is the failure of social control by established power holders. In the case of the poop-scoop controversy, riots did not break out in the streets. In 1978, lawmakers maintained social control by passing a law requiring dog owners to scoop the poop or face a fine (Brandow, 2008). Had the law failed to pass, the steps of City Hall might have been lit up with flaming paper bags full of dog doo. (See Chapter 6 for more on social control.)

IDENTITY AND COLLECTIVE ACTION

In Chapter 5, we examined the relationship of individuals and groups and explored the way individual behavior is influenced by group behavior and vice versa. We also looked at network theory, examining how social networks develop and expand throughout society. In this section, we will build on individual–group interaction to examine the effect of collective action on the creation of individual identities.

Identity is simply a definition of who you are. How do you identify yourself? You might start by telling people that you're a student and stating the name of your school. If they ask for more details about you, you might tell them your religion or maybe your race. If they continue asking for information, what other things could you use to identify yourself? The neighborhood where you live? Your political affiliations? Your sexual orientation? Your favorite baseball team? As we said in the chapter-opening paradox, what makes you an individual is your affiliation with multiple group identities.

Perhaps you're a White Catholic student at a particular university who lives in a particular neighborhood, is a Democrat, is straight, and is a Texas Rangers fan. To identify yourself, you have to refer to various group affiliations. In this case, you're associated with a group of Rangers fans, a group of students at a university, a group of people who are Catholic, and so on. Each of these groups contributes to your identity as an individual. If you add enough questions to this list (What high school did you attend? What sport do you play at your university? To what extracurricular clubs do you belong?), you'll soon realize that you are probably the only person in the world who has that particular set of group affiliations. Your uniqueness as an individual comes from the collection of groups to which you belong.

Sharing a group affiliation with another person helps us develop emotional attachments to that person. If two people are members of Students Against Destructive Decisions, their identity as members of that group instantly gives them a connection. If nothing else, each person knows that the other believes strongly in stopping drunk driving and other risky behavior. Both may have experienced a life-altering tragedy that brought them to the group. This shared affiliation gives them an emotional connection from which to build their relationship.

Think about your best friend. Where did you meet him or her? Did you meet in a class at school or maybe on a sports team? Perhaps you met at a youth group or in your neighborhood? Unless you met randomly on the street and struck up a conversation, you probably met him or her in a context in which you already shared an affiliation, which became the basis of your current friendship. Thus our collective associations (such as church groups, baseball teams, and high-school clubs) become the foundation on which we form emotional relationships with other people.

If you work the night shift at McDonald's, you might identify yourself as a fast-food employee or as someone who works late at night. You probably didn't start working at McDonald's because you identified as a fast-food employee; rather, you identify as a fast-food employee because you started to work at McDonald's. But you may have volunteered for the late shift because you already self-identified as a night owl. As you can see from these examples, not only does your identity determine the groups to which you belong but the groups to which you belong also determine your identity. This back-and-forth process of identity and group association is an important part of collective action. If you grew up in a Jewish family and throughout your life have self-identified as Jewish, this is a stable, or static, aspect of your identity. But if in your early twenties you embrace a new religion and start to practice it, your religious identity will have changed, or become dynamic.

In addition to having both static and dynamic identities, you also have multiple identities because you belong to multiple groups. Although you think the Texas Rangers are the greatest team in baseball, you're more than just a Rangers fan. One of the difficulties of having multiple identities is that they can conflict with one another. If you identify as a Catholic but are also part of a pro-choice organization, you might find these identities difficult to resolve. As a result, one of the paradoxes of identity and collective action is that the lines between your multiple identities are often ambiguous and poorly defined. (Chapter 4 gives more information about role strain and role conflict for individuals in groups.)

Social Movements

Collective action describes an event or a particular behavior. A march to protect a woman's right to make reproductive choices and a group of students spontaneously taking over a campus office to protest sweatshop labor are examples of collective action. But when this behavior becomes purposeful, organized, and institutionalized, collective action turns into a social movement. Social movements are not ritualized. They don't simply happen every year, like a Memorial Day parade or the New Year's Eve celebration in Times Square. Such rituals don't aim to change something about society; rather, they seek to celebrate a tradition of some sort.

SOCIAL MOVEMENT

collective behavior that is purposeful and organized (but not ritualized) and that seeks to challenge or change one or more aspects of society through institutional and extra-institutional means.

Thus, according to David Meyer in his book *The Politics of Protest* (2007), social movements are "collective and sustained efforts that challenge existing or potential laws, policies, norms, or authorities, making use of extra-institutional as well as institutional political tactics" (p. 10). What this means is that social movements always have a goal, whether it's something concrete, like repealing a specific law, or more abstract, like the acceptance of same-sex couples. Social movements are organized and intentional and are more than a one-off event: Protest activity must be sustained over time. Such movements can work both within and outside the rules of relevant institutions (e.g., protesters might call their elected representatives but also hold a sit-in at a town hall meeting). But sometimes it is hard to know where social movements begin and end, given that what appears to be spontaneous protest activity is usually somewhat organized, and protest events that seem to be singular happenings are often part of larger social campaigns.

Social movements attempt to achieve their aims through conflict and action directed at particular opponents, not just through consensus and compromise. The participants in a social movement share a collective identity, but though they organize meetings and coordinate action, the tie that binds participants together in a social movement is a shared commitment to social change. In the initial stages of social movements, individuals generally participate primarily through informal social networks. As the movement develops, the institutions grow more formal and structured. Even in later phases, the movement is united through a common commitment to social or political change. But as Doug McAdam, a sociologist who has spent years examining social movements, pointed out in an interview for this book, "I still believe that social movement scholarship tends to be movement centric [so it focuses on movements], and invariably we overrate the causal significance or agency of those movements. Organized collective action is necessary, but not sufficient to generate a successful movement. . . . Some new threat or perceived opportunity in the broader social environment is a crucial component" (Conley, 2009p). Keep that in mind as you read through the following theories social scientists have developed to explain how social movements emerge and take shape.

TYPES OF SOCIAL MOVEMENTS

Social movements come in different shapes and sizes. Four main types exist: alternative, redemptive, reformative, and revolutionary (Table 18.1). They are distinguished by the people whose behavior they seek to change and the extent of societal change they hope to achieve.

ALTERNATIVE SOCIAL MOVEMENTS

social movements that seek the most limited societal change and often target a narrow group of people.

Alternative Social Movements Alternative social movements seek the most limited societal change; they often target a narrow group of people (Nicholas, 1973). They are usually issue oriented, focusing on a singular concern and seeking to change individuals' behaviors in relation to that issue. #NeverAgain is such a social movement. Founded in the aftermath of the Parkland, Florida, high-school shooting in February 2018, it is a student-initiated movement to pressure politicians to back stricter laws to prevent gun violence in general and school shootings in particular. Among other actions, it sponsored national school walkouts later that year. Although #NeverAgain has garnered national attention, it is a good example of Doug McAdams's point that energy isn't enough. There have been many school shootings in the years that followed Parkland, but the institutional resistance to gun law changes within a divided federal government (and many states) means that the meaningful legislation #NeverAgain sought has stalled in Congress.

TABLE 18.1 Types of Social Movements

	LIMITED SOCIAL CHANGE	RADICAL SOCIAL CHANGE
Target particular subgroups	Alternative	Redemptive
Target entire society	Reformative	Revolutionary

Following a mass shooting at a high school in Parkland, Florida, demonstrators advocate for gun control at a "March for Our Lives" protest in Seattle.

Another example is Mothers Against Drunk Driving (MADD), one of the most successful alternative social movements in recent history. MADD's success stems largely from the fact that it targets a relatively small group of people (people who drink and drive) and seeks a specific behavioral change (getting people to stop drinking and driving), and there is not a powerful constituency that is directly opposed to it (as the National Rifle Association [NRA] is against tighter gun laws). MADD was founded by a mother, Candy Lightner, whose daughter Cari had been killed by a drunk driver. Lightner founded MADD in her deceased daughter's bedroom, where she started to gather information about other victims of drunk driving. The organization expanded rapidly; many families of drunk-driving victims contacted MADD to become involved in the campaign. Within the narrow scope of the group's efforts, MADD is largely responsible for the concept of the "designated driver," which has helped reduce alcohol-related motor vehicle fatalities in the United States. Among its political successes, MADD was instrumental in raising the drinking age to 21 and lowering the legal blood alcohol content to 0.08 percent across the country.

Redemptive Social Movements Like alternative social movements, redemptive social movements target specific groups; however, they advocate for more radical change in behavior. If you go to a specific organization—say, Covenant House—after you have run away from home and lived on the streets addicted to drugs, you're joining a redemptive social movement. Covenant House attempts to do more than change one particular behavior (such as drug use); it tries to help you reorganize your entire life. The social workers at Covenant House might help new residents find employment and

REDEMPTIVE SOCIAL MOVEMENTS

social movements that target specific groups but advocate for more radical change in behavior.

How is a redemptive social movement as embodied by an organization such as Covenant House different from alternative movements? In this picture, Covenant House volunteers serve meals to homeless, runaway, and at-risk young adults.

open a bank account. They might then provide them with drug addiction counseling and bring together people with similar concerns to talk through their problems. At Covenant House, you'd be put on a fixed schedule. You'd probably wake up at a particular time, eat breakfast at a certain hour, and leave for work at the same time each day. This structured routine is aimed at reforming all your daily practices, not just a single behavior. What makes Covenant House different from a bread-and-butter nonprofit serving a community's needs or, say, a prison (or other total institution that controls all aspects of its residents' lives) is that it is an organization that seeks change through social organizing. For example, it sponsors a fund-raiser called "Sleep Out" in which volunteers spend a night outside, "so homeless kids don't have to" (Covenant House, n.d.). This type of redemptive social movement seeks to return people to the normal routine of day-to-day society. Redemptive social movements such as Covenant House are often, although not always, affiliated with a religious group.

REFORMATIVE SOCIAL MOVEMENTS

social movements that advocate for limited social change across an entire society.

Reformative Social Movements Reformative social movements advocate for limited social change across an entire society (DellaCava et al., 2004). You might think that America, for the most part, is doing fairly well but would be a better place if everyone ate organic vegetables and biked to work. You may be able to join a group in your community like Critical Mass, which advocates for more bicycle-friendly commuting. Critical Mass started with a group of bicyclists in Portland, Oregon, in 1992 who wanted to make cities safer for bicyclists (Maus, 2012). Since then chapters have started in many other cities, even as the earliest ones in Minneapolis and Portland

Cyclists take part in a Critical Mass rally. What makes a movement such as Critical Mass reformative?

have closed shop because thousands of miles of safe bike lanes have been introduced in those cities. That is, Critical Mass no longer needs to meet for monthly consciousness-raising rides in some cities because its original mission has been accomplished. Consciousness has been raised. Bike lanes and bike parking have been installed. Biking still isn't safe in many other cities, however, so Critical Mass still pushes for change. The COVID-19 pandemic has opened up a critical window of political opportunity to reimagine urban transportation. Critical Mass and other like-minded groups (like Transportation Alternatives) are trying to make the most of the moment to push for even greater changes—like banning cars from Manhattan in New York City. Critical Mass is not limited to small groups of bikers in a couple of liberal cities; rather, it aims to change the transportation behavior of most of the Western world one city at a time. The scope of change the group seeks is relatively minor (although its members might not agree). The group is not calling for a new system of government or an enormous change in people's approach to social interaction. The scope of its proposed change is limited to adding a safer, more convenient bicycle commuting option, but members target many cities.

Another movement that falls under the category of reformative social movements is the slow food movement, whose proponents believe that it is healthier for individuals, communities, and the environment if more people eat locally grown food. Instead of importing cherries from Argentina, avocados from Mexico, and apples from New Zealand, the movement believes, it is healthier to eat food grown in one's own geographic region. The movement seeks to change a behavior across all of society, but the scope of that change is limited. The movement doesn't want to revolutionize our land ownership system or overthrow the government; it just wants people to be more thoughtful about the implications of their eating behavior for the environment, community well-being, and personal health. However, both Critical Mass and the slow food movement may believe that if we alter one aspect of our daily behavior, the ripples through our social structures will be so huge as to result in revolutionary change (and they may be right).

REVOLUTIONARY
SOCIAL MOVEMENTS

social movements that advocate the radical reorganization of society.

Revolutionary Social Movements Revolutionary social movements are the final category of social movements. They advocate the radical reorganization of society (Goodwin, 2006). One example of a revolutionary social movement was the one led by the Weather Underground during the Vietnam War. This group of students, a radical splinter group of Students for a Democratic Society, wanted to overthrow the American government through armed attacks. The Weather Underground bombed several government buildings (after issuing evacuation warnings), took part in jailbreaks and riots, and expressed solidarity with the Vietnamese, who were experiencing the impact of US military force. They believed that only revolutionary means, not political parties or processes, could bring about change. After the Vietnam War ended, most of the Weathermen surrendered or were apprehended by the authorities, without having succeeded in their goals (Varon, 2004).

A more successful revolutionary movement took place in South Africa, where a coalition of political and labor groups, the United Democratic Front (UDF), sought to overthrow the apartheid government. The apartheid system in South Africa classified South Africans based on four "racial" categories: White, colored, Indian, and Black. The government passed laws treating each racial group separately—and unequally. Blacks weren't allowed to enter cities without government-issued passes and were forced to live in separate homelands. The antiapartheid movement sought to change these racist laws, and in the early 1980s, it coalesced around the UDF. After the primary antiapartheid political party, the African National Congress (ANC), had been banned, the UDF quickly became the main antiapartheid organization. It incorporated Black, Indian, and colored South Africans into a single movement aiming to overthrow the apartheid system. When the ANC was recognized as legal in South Africa, it took over the antiapartheid struggle, and the UDF faded into the background. This revolutionary social movement succeeded in ending the apartheid system. South Africa held its first democratic elections in 1994, electing as president the Nobel Peace Prize–winning Nelson Mandela, who had spent many years in prison as a political detainee under the apartheid regime.

I'VE BEEN FRAMED!

Thousands of social movements exist throughout society at the local, national, and global levels. There are historical social movements that have achieved their goals, such as the antiapartheid movement in South Africa, and recent social movements that have just started advocating for social change, such as the slow food movement. In such a competitive landscape for social change, social movements that succeed are ones that manage to achieve what David Snow and coauthors (1986) call "frame alignment": "By frame alignment, we refer to the linkage of individual and SMO [social movement organization] interpretive orientations, such that some set of individual interests, values and beliefs and SMO activities, goals, and ideology are congruent and complementary." Put more simply, frame alignment is getting people to see an issue through a lens that refracts it in the light you want them to see it in. If you are a pro-choice activist, you want to align abortion within the frame of women's health and control over their bodies. If you are a pro-life activist, then you want to align the debate within the frame of unborn personhood and fetal rights.

Meanwhile, a frame is not just an "argument" for or against some issue. In the conceptualization of Erving Goffman, a frame is a schema by which we organize our lives and see the world. "By rendering events or occurrences meaningful, frames function to organize experience and guide action, whether individual or collective" (Snow et al., 1986). Thus alignment between individuals' worldviews (frame) and those of activists must take place for social movements to coalesce. That is, a successful social movement gets many people to see its issue (or even the world!) through the movement's preferred lens.

Put yet another way, a frame can be thought of as an entire way of seeing on a particular issue. For example, mask wearing can be seen through a public health frame or through a frame about personal freedom. Abortion rights can be seen through the frame of reproductive choice or termination of unborn life. Often social movements try to align their goals within existing frames through frame "bridging," "amplification," and "extension": For example, transgender rights was a case of extending an existing civil rights frame to a new group (Lindstedt, 2017; Snow et al., 2014). Meanwhile, amplification may involve trying to take an existing frame and making it the dominant one. An example of this might be how climate change activists use a health frame to motivate interest in stopping global warming. Higher temperatures mean more ground level ozone and nitrous oxides, which, in turn, are bad for our bodies. But mostly climate change is not yet seen through a personal health lens. Since health is a very important frame for many people, trying to amplify the health-related aspects of climate change may yet prove to be a successful political strategy. Bridging, meanwhile, involves bringing a different frame into a new domain: the way, for example, Trump tried to portray immigration on the southern border as a violent crime emergency.

But sometimes, social movements need to engage in frame "transformation," wherein they attempt to blow up an existing frame to provide a completely new way of looking at the world (or a particular issue). For instance, after the George Floyd killing, Black Lives Matter and related activist groups tried to radically transform the frame through which law enforcement was viewed, calling for a defunding and dismantling of the police, rather than "amplification" of any extant frame of law and order (say, community policing) or the "bridging" of another institutional frame to policing. They tried to shift the frame to one of the police as agents of White supremacy. #BlackLivesMatter emerged in 2013 after George Zimmerman, a White man, was acquitted in the shooting of Trayvon Martin, a Black teenager. The movement gained national notoriety, however, after the deaths of two more Black men: the shooting of Michael Brown by a police officer in Ferguson, Missouri, and the strangling death of Eric Garner by a New York City cop. Activists pointed to these deaths as examples of a broader system of violence and institutional racism and coined the tagline and hashtag *Black Lives Matter* to decry how the criminal justice system devalues Black peoples' lives. The social media success was paralleled by many street protests and other actions. BLM is heralded as a new form of civil rights movement in a number of ways. First, it was (loosely) led by a group rather than a single charismatic individual such as Martin Luther King or Jesse Jackson. Second, it rejected traditional institutions for Black social movement organizing—namely, the church and the Democratic Party. Third, it eschewed "respectability politics"—namely, efforts to show one's goals and values are compatible with those of the broader society (think gay activists fighting for marriage rights or the right to serve in the military rather than, say, pressing for straights to accept alternative lifestyles that may be more common among nonheterosexuals). This choice is due to the view that mainstream society's values—to the extent that they are upholding a system of White supremacy through, for example, police violence—are not to be emulated or assimilated into.

Despite its success in becoming a household name, for seven years BLM accomplished little in the way of concrete legislative changes. Stop and Frisk as a policy had been abandoned by New York City and some other police departments; bodycams became common for officers to wear; but chokeholds were still legal, and civil immunity (i.e., inability to sue police in civil court for their actions) remained a bedrock of the criminal justice system—just to name a couple of reforms that were sought. Then George Floyd was killed by a Minneapolis police officer kneeling on his neck as bystanders filmed the scene and citizens pled with the cop to relent. Not only did Minneapolis explode in response, but the largest demonstrations since the days of the Vietnam War were seen across America. Observers say that many White US residents finally tipped over, becoming sympathetic with the plight of African Americans. Demands for reform morphed into demands to wholly dismantle police departments and reenvision our approaches to law and order.

While BLM is certainly focused on the main issue of racialized police violence, its loose structure has allowed its goals to broaden out to issues

A memorial in honor of George Floyd in Minneapolis created by community artists. Based on what you've learned about social movement theory, what kind of social movement is Black Lives Matter?

of criminal justice reform (such as mass incarceration or broken windows policing) and even to racial inequality more generally. BLM bills itself as an inclusive movement that is concerned with the lives of the undocumented, the disabled, women, sexual minorities, and other marginalized groups. In fact, the spark from the anti-police racism protests can be said to have lit the fire that has led to concrete reforms in other areas of social life, if not wholesale shifts in societal racial attitudes. For example, it would be hard to imagine that the Washington Redskins football team would have abandoned that name when they did if it were not for the protests that started about police violence.

As much success as BLM is having after George Floyd, all social movements inspire countermovements. For BLM, that countermovement came first in the form of Blue Lives Matter (a movement to defend police officers) and All Lives Matter (which tries to deny that there is something specific about the Black experience that merits its own movement). President Trump has been a big cheerleader for such countermovements. He critiqued professional athletes who knelt in protest during the national anthem; in his stump speeches, he has railed against "radical organizations" like BLM; and when asked by CBS News why Blacks are still being killed by law enforcement, he said, "So are White people. So are White people. What a terrible question to ask. So are White people" (Segers, 2020).

Meanwhile, Trump himself engendered another social movement: the Resistance. Starting during his campaign for the presidency, the so-called Resistance really picked up when he was elected. The marquee event happened the day after his inauguration, when the Women's March took place in cities around the world. This protest marked the single largest one-day march in history. About 2 million people attended in Washington, D.C., alone. Other actions have followed, including the first protest in outer space (by the Autonomous Space Agency Network) on April 12, 2017.

The Resistance achieved such a great turnout for its Women's March partly because participants were motivated by a wide range of grievances. Prior research had often pointed to a tension between intersectional identities (i.e., the unique social location of a gay Latinx woman or a straight Black man): How can a diverse set of actors be mobilized in a way in which everyone is highly motivated while not having to subjugate some aspects of his or her identity (say, race or sexual orientation) to others (say, gender or class position) in order to coalesce around a set of demands and strategies?

Interviewing a sample of the Women's March participants, sociologist Dana Fisher and colleagues (2017) found that each came with her own specific agenda that tied to her identity. For example, Latinx marchers tended to be more concerned about immigrant rights, while White women focused on reproductive freedom. "One has only to review the expansive list of the organizational partners for the Women's March to see how it aimed to mobilize people whose interests lie at the intersections of race, class, gender, sexual orientation, legal status, and other categories of identity, along with less identity-based sympathizers," they write. "Although we find that individuals were often motivated by issues related to their own social identities, we also find that individuals reported being motivated by reasons that extended beyond their social identities" (Fisher et al., 2017).

What did Dana Fisher and her colleagues learn about attendance at the Women's March?

This early success of the Women's March has been parlayed into concrete actions to change the US political landscape by recruitment of new candidates to challenge officeholders. The group Run for Something has helped get a record number of female candidates to run for everything from local school boards to the US Congress, and, perhaps, indirectly influenced Joe Biden to pick Kamala Harris as his running mate, the first Black woman and the first person of Indian descent to be nominated for vice president by a major party in US political history. By engaging in both street-level protest and traditional electoral politics, the Resistance can hope to achieve broad political change while remaining inclusive and not focused on a single issue. Maybe the key is having a larger-than-life mutual enemy, such as Donald Trump, who provides a common frame.

In many ways, the Resistance has learned the lessons of two other recent movements: the Tea Party and Occupy Wall Street. Both could be considered revolutionary social movements, although, of course, the way they wanted to transform society differed dramatically. The Tea Partiers sought to radically reduce the role of government in American society by slashing regulations and cutting taxes back to a bare minimum and/or by imposing socially conservative laws, such as antiabortion statutes. However, unlike most revolutionary movements, many Tea Party organizations were seeded with money from very wealthy, politically active conservatives (most notably, the industrialist Koch brothers). As such, this movement has sometimes been called "Astroturf," as in false grassroots, though there is no question that the passage of the Affordable Care Act health insurance reform law (aka Obamacare) precipitated a political uprising of sorts.

The Occupy Wall Street movement (OWS)—also known as the 99-percenters—protested rising economic inequality. During the period in which they literally "occupied Wall Street" by camping out in Zuccotti Park in lower Manhattan, the participants went out of their way to make decisions through a deliberative process with no leadership cadre. This was, in fact, one of the reasons they never coalesced around a single message of change, though most 99-percenters would agree that marginal tax rates on the wealthy (the 1 percent) should be raised to address the needs of society and, independent of the revenue rationale, to lower inequality.

The Tea Party focused more on the electoral process (and led the 2010 Republican "wave" election), while OWS showed more disdain for traditional politics, finding it corrupted by the big money it was protesting. Thus many consider the Tea Party more successful than OWS in achieving its goals; however, this may be an oversimplification because OWS became the springboard for many other progressive political movements, including the Resistance.

Stephen Duncombe, NYU professor and director of the Center for Artistic Activism, points out that OWS's lack of organization was a big part of its failure to become a lasting social movement. In an interview he asked me to "think of Occupy as a burst. One of the problems with this sort of media spectacle activism is that often the idea of media exposure ends up being the goal as opposed to what it really is: a means to an end. That is, it's great to be on the media because you get a wider dispersal of your message, but not if you don't have a really good message" (Conley, 2015f). Just as important as having a clear message is having, as he put it, "an organization that can mobilize those passions and put them into some sort of effective political machinery . . . because creative activism can never stand alone." Duncombe explained why he thought of some activist exploits as "ether activism" by pointing to the way consumer goods companies use advertising, a commercially oriented form of awareness raising. Advertising and the attention-grabbing characteristic of some activism may not be all that different, but, as he notes, "the advertising industry doesn't get you all excited about a product and then say, 'Oh, by the way, we're not sure where you can buy it. We're not sure if the product exists. You go find that product yourself.' They are part of a much larger organization of production, of distribution, and of sales. All of that has to be factored in to any form of activism as well. We tend to remember the moments—those bursts—but underneath any sustainable change is all of this organizational structure which takes those bursts, those emotions, and channels them into some sort of effective social change. I think the biggest problem is 'ether activism.' It looks great up here but it doesn't seem to bring any lasting significance down below."

DIGITAL.WWNORTON.COM/YOUMAYASK7

To see an interview with Stephen Duncombe, go to digital.wwnorton.com/youmayask7

Both the Tea Party and Occupy movements faced a choice: If they defined key issues on which they sought change, then they would lose some of their revolutionary appeal and become targeted, reformative social movements. The risk of such a narrowing is both success and failure. If, for example, OWS focused on raising taxes on the rich to redistribute revenue to the poor and built a structure to channel and organize its efforts, likely by first selecting a leadership group, then those who joined because there were no leaders or explicit policy objectives would have quit. Moreover, if the 99-percenters were successful in altering tax policy, then their raison d'être would have disappeared, just like what happened with the Critical Mass biker activists in Portland and Minneapolis. But remaining devoid of concrete goals also posed challenges in the form of fatigue, frustration, and ineffectualness in getting *anything* changed. Why join a movement that isn't moving?

MODELS OF SOCIAL MOVEMENTS: HOW DO THEY ARISE?

The timing of the emergence of #BlackLivesMatter illustrates many aspects of social movement theory, considering it is not as if police mistreatment of African Americans were a new phenomenon in the United States. However, the ubiquitous presence of cell phone video footage has made its reality much more incontrovertibly and viscerally documented—as evidenced by the George Floyd killing. But technological change can't be the whole story, either: Back in 1992, riots broke out when Los Angeles police officers were not convicted of misdoing despite graphic video footage of them beating Rodney King during his arrest. Yet a sustained social movement failed to emerge from the collective action that took place. What changed in two decades? Did the election of the first African American president shift the frame? Did Occupy Wall Street set the stage for a progressive movement? Or, perhaps, did the Tea Party cause a backlash? Or was it merely the result of pandemic-related shelter-in-place orders; that is, were people just boiling over with frustration and anxiety from the social, economic, and health impacts of the COVID-19 pandemic, and was George Floyd the spark that lit the fire of real change? That is, was it pure timing?

To explain the rise and sustenance of social movements, social scientists have developed several models. The earliest one is now known as the classical model and is based on a concept of structural weakness in society. This structural weakness results in the psychological disruption of individuals. When this disruption reaches a certain threshold, it gives rise to a social movement. Thus social movements are a collective response to structural strain that has a psychological effect on individuals. In this model, political goals or achievements do not play a large role in the formation of movements.

There are several variations of this basic account. That is, strain can arise from different sources, depending on the specific model. For example, society itself may create tension by engendering social isolation, which causes alienation and anxiety, thereby resulting in the form of discontent that leads to collective action and social movements. (Recall our discussion of capitalism and Marxism in Chapter 14.) Strain can also come from status inconsistency or when the rank orderings in society are somehow contradictory (e.g., when the new merchant class has economic power but not political

CLASSICAL MODEL

model of social movements based on a concept of structural weakness in society that results in psychological disruption of individuals.

clout). The result within the individual is what psychologists call cognitive dissonance; this condition, in turn, may spur people to take action.

There are several problems with the classical model. How do we know what magnitude and type of systemic strain will give rise to a movement? Critics of this theory point out that strains of various types and impacts are always present in societies (McAdam, 1982). The theory cannot account for social movements arising in some circumstances and not in others. Another criticism is aimed at the way individuals are pathologized by this theory. In addition, the model completely removes the desire to attain specific, rational political goals while overemphasizing psychological tensions.

Social scientists subsequently tried to work through the weaknesses of the classical model by demonstrating that social movements are collective phenomena rather than symptoms of individual discontent. These revisions led to the resource-mobilization theory, which emphasizes political context and goals (McCarthy & Zald, 1973, 1977) but also states that social movements are unlikely to emerge without the necessary resources—or, if they do, are unlikely to succeed. Discontent and the availability of resources are the key factors that determine whether a social movement will coalesce. According to the entrepreneurial version of this model, actors (individuals or organizations) make a rational cost–benefit calculation about the relative costs and potential benefits in joining a social movement. If enough actors decide that it is a good bet, the movement will be more likely to succeed. But all actors are not equal; some bring more resources (money, time, moral arguments, organizational skills, power, and so on) to the table (Edwards & McCarthy, 2004). If well-resourced individuals do not commit, then the movement is not as likely to coalesce. From this perspective, it seems that the powerful or elite members of society have a greater chance of leading or contributing in other ways to a movement because they control more resources.

Many theorists take issue with this account, because successful social movements, like the antiapartheid movement in South Africa, are often led by those who are relatively powerless and have few monetary resources. Usually, these are the people who have the most at stake in the success of the movement and in change. Theorists also point out that the involvement of the elite classes in a movement often results in its decline and eventual demise. If a movement becomes dependent on external sponsors, organizations within the movement can be easily co-opted by elite groups in cases of conflicting demands. Movements may have indigenous organizational strength (e.g., the local churches and student organizations that nurtured the civil rights movement, as discussed in Chapter 16). It is not clear whether resource-mobilization theory includes this type of resource. Furthermore, what constitutes the grievances that lead to insurgencies is unclear.

RESOURCE-MOBILIZATION THEORY

model of social movements that emphasizes political context and goals but also states that social movements are unlikely to emerge without the necessary resources.

Hundreds of students gather for a rally with the Reverend Dr. Martin Luther King Jr. (right) at the St. James Baptist Church in Birmingham, Alabama. Why were students and congregations key to the success of the civil rights movement?

The most dominant theory of social movements is the political process model, which focuses on the structure of political opportunities (McAdam, 1982). As Doug McAdam spoke of in our interview (see p. 812), social movements do not succeed or fail in a vacuum. When political conditions are favorable to a particular challenger, the chances are better for the success of a social movement led by this challenger. This model combines variables internal and external to the movement (e.g., indigenous organizational strength is internal to the movement, whereas the political context, such as the presence of political opportunities, is external). Three sets of conditions influence the development of insurgency according to this model: the expansion of political opportunities, indigenous organizational strength, and certain shared cognitions (e.g., beliefs about injustice suffered and a sense of self-empowerment) among a movement's proponents. Whether the movement is sustainable over time also depends on the responses of other groups in society. Some criticisms of this model point to its structural bias (it focuses on political or economic structures) that downplays cultural or emotional components, which can sometimes play a major role (Morris, 2004). For example, some work has emphasized how intersectional identities (e.g., being a Black woman) form the bases for social movements that aim to change cultural norms first and foremost rather than policies and politics (Armstrong & Bernstein, 2008; Melucci, 1989).

No one model can predict movement outcomes in all cases. Why a movement succeeds or fails is not just about the resources available or how many political opportunities open up for movement participants. Some

POLITICAL PROCESS MODEL

model of social movements that focuses on the structure of political opportunities. When these are favorable to a particular challenger, the chances are better for the success of a social movement led by this challenger.

Was the temperance movement a success? In the short term the prohibitionists achieved their goal, but what were the long-term consequences?

actors are better able to make use of the available resources and opportunities than others. Strategic thinking enables certain actors to make more of a situation than others who do not have such skills (Ganz, 2004). Moreover, what constitutes a favorable outcome for a movement is not always clear. A movement could win enormous gains but then lose them all over time. An example of this is the temperance movement in the United States, which achieved its ostensible goal of turning America into a dry nation, but only for about 13 years. Today few people would advocate prohibition, and many people suggest that, over the long term, prohibition resulted in a more irresponsible drinking culture in the United States (Gusfield, 1986).

What's more, sociologist Edwin Amenta (2006) claims that the success or failure of a movement cannot always be so easily measured. Amenta uses the Townsend Plan movement as an example. Conceived in the early 1930s during the austere years of the Great Depression, this movement organized about 2 million elderly Americans into Townsend Clubs to place an unprecedented and expensive demand on the government. They all wanted pensions. By 1935, when President Franklin D. Roosevelt proposed Social Security legislation to Congress, the force of the Townsend movement was palpable. The claims of the Townsend Plan's proponents were finally recognized by the welfare state. What seemed to be an impossible request at the outset actually created conditions for later success.

EMERGENCE

the first stage of a social movement, occurring when the social problem being addressed is first identified.

THREE STAGES OF SOCIAL MOVEMENTS

Social movements are generally thought to evolve through three stages, assuming they survive long enough: emergence, coalescence, and routinization. The first stage, emergence, occurs when the social problem being addressed is first identified. As bicyclists realized that Americans' reliance on automobiles to commute to work was unhealthy for the environment, they began to raise awareness of this social phenomenon. The problems of pollution and traffic congestion moved to the forefront, and bicycle commuting emerged as a transportation alternative. Likewise, in the early 1980s, a new deadly disease emerged among gay men in the United States. The disease would later be known as HIV/AIDS, but in the early stages, people didn't know what it was—they just knew that there was something wrong within this particular community. Consciousness about this disease arose among a small population, and its members began raising awareness more broadly. In this early stage of social movements, a handful of people expend great effort merely to draw attention to a particular social issue that is otherwise not in the public consciousness.

In the second stage, coalescence, resources are mobilized (i.e., concrete action is taken) around the problems outlined in the first stage. Through advocacy and education, more and more people become aware of the social problem. They organize meetings, start donating money, and begin lobbying elected political officials. New York bicycle advocates formed an organization called Transportation Alternatives and started encouraging their friends and coworkers to ride their bikes to work. They lobbied the city council for better laws and infrastructure to promote bicycle safety. Similarly, in 1981 advocates for HIV/AIDS awareness formalized an organization that started as a telephone hotline, the Gay Men's Health Crisis, and began distributing information to medical professionals and at-risk populations.

COALESCENCE

the second stage of a social movement, in which resources are mobilized (i.e., concrete action is taken) around the problems outlined in the first stage.

Members of the World Wildlife Fund (WWF) demonstrate at the World Water Forum in Mexico City. Why might sociologists define the WWF as an institutionalized social movement?

EMERGENCE, COALESCENCE, AND ROUTINIZATION IN THE HIV/AIDS MOVEMENT

In 1981, doctors began to identify a new disease among an otherwise healthy population of homosexual men. They didn't know what was causing the disease's symptoms or how to treat it, but they were able to identify that something was amiss within this subpopulation. Doctors initially called the disease "gay-related immune deficiency" or GRID. As awareness and fear mounted throughout the gay community in New York City, a group of 80 concerned men gathered in the apartment of writer Larry Kramer. They mobilized their social contacts and used the media to sound the alarm. Before long, the Centers for Disease Control and Prevention declared GRID an epidemic, and the gay community further mobilized to promote awareness of the disease and raise money for research. During this early period, the social movement that would later become the AIDS awareness movement in the United States was emerging from a small apartment in New York City.

As rates of infection grew, people rallied together to promote awareness of the disease and spread information about it. In 1981, concerned activists founded the Gay Men's Health Crisis (GMHC), around which the movement coalesced. The GMHC established an office on West 22nd Street in New York City and held its first fund-raiser in 1982. It began publishing a newsletter that was distributed to more than 50,000 doctors, hospitals, clinics, and libraries throughout the country. During this period, gay-related

Crowds visit the AIDS Memorial Quilt in Washington, D.C.

immune deficiency was renamed acquired immunodeficiency syndrome, or AIDS. With the establishment of a formal organization, the AIDS awareness movement coalesced into a defined social movement.

The activities of GMHC continued to grow. It funded the first AIDS discrimination lawsuit in 1983 and, two years later, organized the first international AIDS conference in Atlanta, Georgia. The following year, GMHC organized the first AIDS Walk—now an annual fund-raising event throughout the United States. Organizers also created the NAMES Project AIDS Memorial

A Gay Men's Health Crisis march during a 1985 gay pride parade in New York City.

Quilt to memorialize individuals who have died from the disease. On December 1, 1988, GMHC promoted the first AIDS Day, and the federal government eventually passed laws to stop AIDS-related discrimination. President Bill Clinton was the first politician to run for national office with an explicit HIV/AIDS policy, illustrating his recognition of the serious threat the disease posed. In 2003, New York City's mayor, Michael Bloomberg, appointed a citywide coordinator of AIDS policy.

Although GMHC coalesced into a formal, organized social movement, the usual tensions inherent in a burgeoning social movement took root. One major challenge GMHC faces is broadening the focus of its work. Although the AIDS crisis started in a community of mostly White gay men in New York, its reach has spread to other communities. GMHC has been challenged to respond to the needs of communities of color,

especially African American men, as well as those of infected women. In the mid-1990s, tensions erupted within GMHC about its ability to serve growing African American populations in need of HIV/AIDS awareness education, counseling, and testing. When the media mogul David Geffen donated $2.5 million to GMHC, its board of directors decided to use the money to open a facility in Chelsea, a predominately White neighborhood in Manhattan with a large gay population. Three African American GMHC board members—Richard Dudley, Doug Robinson, and Billy Jones—walked out of a GMHC meeting in a highly publicized protest of the organization's refusal to consider expanding facilities into neighborhoods of color. Rather than expand to include women and straight men infected with HIV, the organization recently launched a campaign to curtail the use of methamphetamine, a drug used disproportionately by men who have sex with men.

Because the formalization of organizations requires extensive resources, including money from donors and time commitments from members, some social movements simply fade away at this second stage. Social movement researchers disagree on the best ways to predict which social movements will make it through the second phase. Sometimes organizations achieve their objectives before becoming formalized. If a social movement begins to form on a college campus to encourage divestment from a particular country and the university decides to divest, then the social movement might disappear before it takes on a formal organizational structure. Other social movements fade away because of a lack of support. Imagine a social movement with the goal of getting every person in a city to work on Saturdays. That social movement would probably disappear quickly, because few people would support it. In the process of formalizing their organization, participants in social movements might adopt new goals and abandon old ones. If you begin a social movement to halt the construction of a building, you may broaden your goals to improve zoning laws, building regulations, or development rights in your entire city.

The final stage in the formation of social movements is called routinization or institutionalization. In this stage, the social movement is institutionalized, and a formal structure develops to promote the cause. The organization may hire an executive director, a press secretary, and field organizers, for instance. It usually sets up a headquarters from which to organize its activities and coordinate its efforts. Social movements that have reached this final phase include NARAL (National Abortion Rights Action League) Pro-Choice America, a group that defends abortion rights, and Operation Rescue, an antiabortion organization. As each movement became effective and expanded its membership base, it became institutionalized.

SOCIAL MOVEMENT ORGANIZATIONS

After social movements have been institutionalized, social movement organizations develop to recruit new members and coordinate participation. These groups also help raise money, clarify goals, and structure participation in the movement.

One type of social movement organization, a professional movement organization, has a full-time leadership staff dedicated to the movement and a large membership base that plays a minor role in the organization. The professional leaders speak on behalf of their constituency and often attempt to influence public policy through lobbying efforts. For example, NARAL Pro-Choice America is an influential professional organization that evolved from a single mother's desire to effect change as a result of her own experience. It was founded as the National Association for the Repeal of Abortion Laws in 1969. In 1975, after the Supreme Court had preempted state law by declaring the right to abortion a part of the implicit constitutional right to privacy, the organization moved to Washington, D.C., to focus on national

---

ROUTINIZATION OR INSTITUTIONALIZATION

the final stage of a social movement, in which it is institutionalized and a formal structure develops to promote the cause.

SOCIAL MOVEMENT ORGANIZATION

a group developed to recruit new members and coordinate participation in a particular social movement; these groups also often raise money, clarify goals, and structure participation in the movement.

lobbying efforts in Congress. The organization is currently run by its president, Ilyse Hogue, and employs a full-time staff dedicated to organizing, lobbying, and communicating with its membership. The membership of NARAL Pro-Choice America plays a minor role in the organization other than financing personnel and activities. On occasion, however, members are called on to sign petitions, join marches, and contact their legislators about particular pro-choice issues.

Another type of social movement organization is called a participatory movement organization. In these organizations, unlike professional movement organizations, the rank-and-file membership is directly involved. (Recall our discussion of organizations as social networks in Chapter 5.) Participatory movement organizations can be further divided into two subgroups: mass protest organizations and grassroots organizations. A mass protest organization advocates for social change through protest and demonstration. Although it lacks the organizational structure of a professional movement organization, it relies on high levels of member participation to achieve its goals. The protesters involved in global justice and antiglobalization movements have often been associated with mass protest organizations. Rather than attempt to effect social change through organized political channels or political lobbying, participants in global justice movements take to the streets to promote their cause.

Critical Mass, the cyclist organization discussed earlier in the chapter, is another example of a mass protest organization. Once a month, hundreds of members of Critical Mass meet and ride their bikes through urban areas. Their goal is to disrupt traffic flow as a form of protest against the car-centered culture in cities. They aren't highly organized—they don't have an executive director or an official website. Instead, they rely on bloggers, tweeters, word of mouth, and high levels of on-the-ground participation: To disrupt the flow of traffic, hundreds of cyclists must participate. If only 15 cyclists participated, they wouldn't be very effective at drawing attention to their cause.

Other mass protests form in response to particular events. When President Trump signed his executive order banning visitors from seven predominately Muslim countries in 2017, thousands of protesters converged on various airports across the nation to denounce the policy. To develop into a mass protest, individuals simply needed to agree on a meeting location—airports were an obvious one. There wasn't a particular group that sponsored, organized, and arranged these protests but rather a loose network of activists who coordinated their efforts. Similarly, many protests against Arizona's draconian crackdown on illegal immigrants popped up in cities across the nation when the law passed in 2010. Although some professional organizations helped coordinate the protests, their success required large numbers of participants but very little organizational structure.

A grassroots organization also relies on high levels of community-based membership participation to promote social change. Like a mass protest

GRASSROOTS ORGANIZATION

a type of social movement organization that relies on high levels of community-based membership participation to promote social change. It lacks a hierarchical structure and works through existing political structures.

organization, it lacks the hierarchical structure of a professional movement organization. Unlike a mass protest organization, however, such a group works through existing political structures to promote social change. Grassroots organizations are often involved in letter-writing campaigns and local political organizing to achieve their goals. They tend to focus on local issues and concerns, coordinating ideologically committed members through informal networks.

Grassroots social movements often develop around specific projects in specific places. A common example of such a movement is NIMBYism (Not In My Back Yard), when local communities oppose the placement of undesirable facilities in their neighborhoods. Such facilities range from power plants and low-income housing to prisons and drug treatment centers. In Harpswell, Maine, a group of concerned residents protested an attempt by ConocoPhillips to construct a liquefied natural gas (LNG) terminal off the coast of central Maine. The community believed that the LNG plant would ruin the quality of the natural environment, as well as damage the delicate local economy based on the lobster industry. There wasn't a formal organization to protest the terminal's construction, but the residents of Harpswell organized on their own to protect their environment and lifestyle. The citizens of Harpswell produced materials protesting the LNG terminal and started a petition drive. They contacted television stations and local officials. Their organization was spontaneous, and their approach wasn't radical. Nonetheless, they succeeded in stopping the construction of the LNG terminal, demonstrating the powerful potential of grassroots social movements.

In Florida, NIMBY forces opposed the establishment of oil pipelines and drilling that might damage sea-bottom marine habitats. But NIMBYism can

Citizens in Harpswell, Maine, protest the construction of a liquefied natural gas terminal. Can you think of an example of a NIMBY movement in your area?

often be hypocritical and selfish. For example, in Cape Cod in 2001, community dissent delayed the construction of a large wind farm in Nantucket Sound. Some members of the community made claims of ecological damage, but mostly they were unhappy about the farm's likely obstruction of their very expensive views. (The protesters included the Wampanoag Indian tribe, which claimed that the wind turbines would violate their rights by interfering with their views of the sunrise in sacred ceremonies.) The Massachusetts electorate generally votes in favor of wind power, but many Cape Cod residents opposed it when they would bear the aesthetic cost personally. Likewise, most Americans recognize the need for jails and homeless shelters, but they don't want to live next to them. When each locality pursues its own interests, sometimes the greater good is lost in the shuffle and the results are suboptimal from the perspective of society as a whole.

SOCIAL MOVEMENTS AND SOCIAL CHANGE

The aim of all social movements is to change society. Of course, change happens whether social movements cause it or not. The past hundred years in the United States provide several good examples of social evolution. The beginning of the twentieth century was a time of high immigration to American urban centers. Garment factories in major cities like New York and San Francisco employed many new immigrants, whereas today the factories have moved abroad where salaries are lower. One hundred years ago, most of the immigrants to New York City came from Europe, but today most of the immigrants are from Latin America and Asia.

Fifty years later, in the years following World War II, the American suburb started to develop rapidly. These were also the years of the baby boom, in which many families had larger numbers of children. (This blip in

Compare these families from 1908, 1972, and today. How has life changed over the last 100 years?

birthrates 50 years ago has had huge implications for society today.) This was also the time when the civil rights movement emerged. And in 1965, the door to immigration was opened once again, remaking the demographics of the country.

Our society has changed drastically even since the early 1980s, when the United States was still engaged in the Cold War with the now-defunct Soviet Union. Very few households had personal computers, and the internet hadn't been invented yet. The car phone, a precursor to the cell phone, was introduced so people could make calls while on the road. As these examples show, society has changed in innumerable ways in the last 100, 50, or even just 25 years.

Some changes in society affect the demographic structures of cities, states, and nations. According to the 1900 Census, for instance, the average American household had 4.60 people. By 1970, the average American household size had declined to 3.14 people. In 2016, the average household size was recorded as 2.69 people (US Census Bureau, 2018a). This dramatic fall in the size of the average household in the United States represents a major change in society over the past century. Of course, the change in household size wasn't the direct result of a social movement. Although many social movements did affect family size indirectly, such as the women's rights movement and the movement to promote birth control and legalize abortion, there wasn't a letter-writing campaign or a major protest march calling for fewer children to be born.

Other social changes have political implications. Fifty years ago, African Americans faced widespread discrimination and segregation in public facilities across some parts of the country. Since the civil rights movement of the 1950s and 1960s, legalized, overt discrimination has largely been eliminated, although other forms of discrimination remain. The civil rights movement was one of America's largest social movements, and one that effected major social change and has echoes into the present.

In an interview, Andy Bichlbaum of the activist group the Yes Men explained how he provided activist consulting services to a local group of Black rights activists who were angry about police racial profiling in New York. Bichlbaum worked with them to transform their anger and frustration into a clever, media-grabbing spoof partnership program between the NYPD and McDonald's for free Happy Meals.

> The police were stopping and frisking people, mainly in neighborhoods like the Bronx for no reason at all, just as a matter of course, and finding very little [contraband] ever. Basically just racial profiling. So an activist group came to us, and we did this brainstorm with them and a number of students and batted around ideas for what we could do about this and how we could get some mainstream media attention.
>
> We came up with a bunch of ideas, but the one idea that we actually put into effect was the one that caused the biggest cringe from the organizer. She said, "No, we can't do that." That was proof it was a good idea. The idea was a McDonald's website that offered vouchers for freebies as a partnership with the New York Police Department. It gave vouchers to people who were stopped and frisked and released without charge.
>
> If this happened to you, you would write down the officer's badge number, your ethnicity, of course, date and time of stop, and all that. If it happened three times, you would get a free Happy Meal. This was so offensive and weird, and there was this fake corporate video that we made for McDonald's explaining this wonderful program, with the voucher and pictures, and then, actually, the people who did it went into a McDonald's with a voucher, filmed themselves secretly, tried to get the free Happy Meal, and they got it. (Conley, 2014h)

The NYPD has reconsidered their stop-and-frisk policies, though it is impossible to measure the impact of this McDonald's spoof on the NYPD's policy change when we think of much larger movements such as #BlackLivesMatter. According to Bichlbaum, "We know that public outrage works, and protest works, people fighting works, rioting sometimes works . . . because we have

To see an interview with Andy Bichlbaum, go to
digital.wwnorton.com/youmayask7

the evidence that it works. . . . [For example,] we don't have slavery [anymore] . . . but what the steps are that you take to get there are a bit fuzzy." This "fuzziness" is one reason we continue to study social movements—to better understand how they work and what kind of impact they have.

When sociologists talk about social change, they are referring to transformations in social institutions, political organizations, and cultural norms across time. Some changes are planned; others are not. The civil rights movement was a planned, organized attempt to improve the way African Americans were treated in the United States. Hoping to implement social change, leaders and rank-and-file members of the movement organized events, planned sit-ins, and lobbied politicians. Smaller changes in society, such as changes in clothing fashion or hairstyles, are usually unplanned and simply happen.

Social change can be major or minor. In the eyes of different folks, it can be either important or trivial. Most people would agree that the strides made by African Americans in the civil rights movement represented an important social change, transforming social and political relations in the United States. On the other hand, the dwindling popularity of a particular brand of clothing is a trivial change, having little effect on people's lives. Also, some social changes affect everyone in society, whereas others are limited to a specific group of people. Laws about putting your feet on the seats in New York City subway cars affect the residents there but probably have minimal effect on the residents of Seattle, Washington. Other social changes, such as changes in the federal tax code, may affect everyone in the United States.

Premodern, Modern, and Postmodern Societies

Whereas social movements and collective action both respond to and create societal changes across short periods of time, the terms *premodern, modern,* and *postmodern* refer to social change across longer periods. Unlike specific social movements, which may span 10, 30, or 50 years, these terms express more

fundamental societal reorganizations across broader historical periods, and may not even refer to specific periods of time. Rather, they are meant to indicate particular ways of understanding, framing, and conceptualizing society.

PREMODERN SOCIETIES

Premodern societies are what used to be called "primitive" societies: Individuals live in small groups such as tribes or villages, there is a low degree of literacy, there is not much division of labor, and technology is relatively undeveloped. According to the sociologist Georg Simmel, such premodern societies are characterized by concentric circles of social affiliation (Figure 18.1). The social positions of individuals were primarily *ascribed* by elements over which they had no control, like what families and towns they were born into as well as their gender and racial backgrounds. In this type of community, I am in the middle of my social world. Around me is my family; one circle beyond my family is my village; one circle beyond my village is my kingdom, perhaps. Each group is embedded—or set within—the groups around it: All the people in my family live in my village; all the people in my village belong to my kingdom. Because Simmel was concerned with social networks and affiliation, this model of concentric circles was useful to him for describing premodern social relations and the period of premodernity.

In premodern societies, individuals are the source of authoritative knowledge. Villages may have a spiritual leader, who passes knowledge along from the gods to the people. Tradition is very important in premodern society; customs passed down through the generations help guide everyday life. Without science or technology, premodern societies rely largely on myths to explain the world around them. These myths or stories are also passed down through generations. Basically, any society that has not industrialized or urbanized is living in a premodern mode, but in today's interconnected world, it is difficult to find an entire society that is premodern—although some tribal cultures deep in the rain forest of South America or located in other remote rural areas still distant from the rest of the world might fill the bill.

MODERNITY

The term modernity is used in many fields, including art history, literature, and sociology, with little agreement about what it means. One relatively uncontested notion,

PREMODERNITY

social relations characterized by concentric circles of social affiliation, a low degree of division of labor, relatively undeveloped technology, and traditional social norms.

MODERNITY

social relations characterized by rationality, bureaucratization, and objectivity as well as individually created by nonconcentric, but overlapping, group affiliations.

FIGURE 18.1 Premodern Society: Concentric, Ascriptive Associations

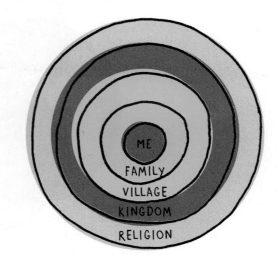

ME
FAMILY
VILLAGE
KINGDOM
RELIGION

however, is that the modern way of life replaced the premodern period with the rise of science and objectivity. Although it is impossible to pinpoint an exact transition from premodernity to modernity in the West, some scholars point to the early fifteenth century, the beginning of the Renaissance, as the origin of modernity; others use the Enlightenment, and still others point to the Industrial Revolution as the key moment. No matter when it started, modernism has generally been characterized as an era of rationality, bureaucratization, and objectivity. As scientific knowledge gained prominence throughout society, it competed with religion as the primary method of knowing, culminating in the eighteenth-century Enlightenment. New political structures developed, with the rise of the modern nation-state and the process of urbanization. Technological advances revolutionized agricultural production and forms of mass communication. Increased industrialization and the specialization of labor revolutionized economic production.

For Simmel, modernity is characterized by the birth of the individual through a web of group affiliations (see Chapter 5). No longer does everyone in my family live in my village and everyone in my village share the same religion. As noted in our discussion of identity earlier in this chapter, each person is a unique combination of overlapping group affiliations (Figure 18.2). This happens by necessity when a society urbanizes, because city-dwellers

FIGURE 18.2 Modern Society: Overlapping, Voluntary Associations

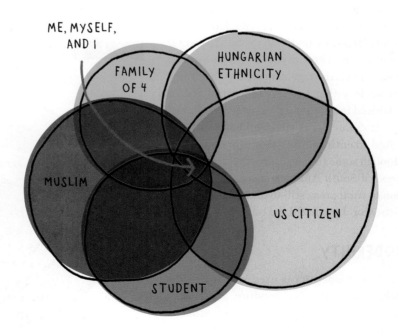

often come from various parts of the country and live side by side although they do not have a common background or set of group affiliations.

According to sociologist Max Weber, modernity emerged from the Protestant Reformation, which introduced concepts of rationality and bureaucracy. It established a legal-rational system as the basis for authority in society, and it concretized structures of bureaucracy throughout society (see Chapters 15 and 16). This rational, logical system extended to literature, architecture, and art. The rise of the novel in literature, for example, reflected these forces by imposing a logical, linear flow on the narrative. The modern affinity for linearity and order extends to public space as well. It was the modern era that saw the rise of urban planning as embodied by Pierre Charles L'Enfant's layout of Washington, D.C., and Georges-Eugène Haussmann's planning of Paris. As these examples suggest, modernity refers to a mode of social organization, not just a period of time. A common theme in modernity is the notion of progress, itself a rational, linear notion of advancement in a single direction of betterment. And central to progress is humankind's management of nature through technological innovation.

Since the 1960s, many scholars have claimed that the modern period is drawing to a close. Some point to the demolition of the Pruitt-Igoe Houses in St. Louis, a symbol of modernity, as the end of the modern period. They were one of St. Louis's largest public housing projects. According to many critics, they also demonstrated that the modern, bureaucratic approach to public housing that concentrated low-income communities in high-rise public projects had failed. In 1972, the city of St. Louis decided to demolish the 33 buildings. The towering brick structures (characteristic of modern architecture) and the planned community of the projects (representative of the modernist faith in rational, organized government solutions to social problems) came to destruction at the hands of the St. Louis Housing Authority.

POSTMODERNISM

Since the 1980s, many academics have claimed that we have entered a period of postmodernity. In the modern and premodern periods, people believed that society was always progressing forward and each new invention was built on previous inventions. History was driven by clashes between opposing forces—such as communism and capitalism—and always ended with one side emerging victorious. Society progressed along the victorious path toward some ultimate end point that was presumed to be better than what preceded it.

Postmodernity, in contrast, has been characterized by a questioning of this linear progression. The grand struggles (like communism versus

POSTMODERNITY

social relations characterized by a questioning of the notion of progress and history, the replacement of narrative with pastiche, and multiple, perhaps even conflicting, identities resulting from disjointed affiliations.

An aerial view of the Pruitt-Igoe housing project in St. Louis (left) and the exterior of the Centre Georges Pompidou in Paris (right). How does Pruitt-Igoe embody the modern period? What makes the Pompidou an example of postmodernism?

capitalism) that defined the modern period have been abandoned. In their place have arisen ideas about multiculturalism and the blending of different narratives. Some people have said that the postmodern condition is embodied by the concept of *pastiche*, taking a little bit from one culture and a little bit from another to form a sort of collage.

Like modernity, postmodernity is not a specific time period but a form of societal (dis)organization. In many ways, the postmodern period is a reaction against the modern period. Postmodern critics often suggest that science and logic, the cornerstones of modernist thinking, have failed to answer important questions and have been abandoned. You may have encountered postmodern art and architecture, which don't follow the formal rigidities of modern art and architecture. Rather, they experiment with new mediums, new techniques, and new forms. Rap music, with its tradition of sampling rather than of sole authorship, is the archetypal postmodern music genre. Architect Philip Johnson's Sony Building in New York City (completed in 1984) is often cited as a good example of postmodern architecture, because it uses a prominent ornamental feature borrowed from past architectural styles at the top of the building that modernist architects would have rejected as unnecessary decoration. A different postmodern strategy of revealing the inner workings of a building by placing them on the outside so they might be read as decorative may be seen in the Centre Georges Pompidou in Paris, constructed in the 1970s.

Simmel's group affiliation model if adapted to postmodernity might look like a series of nonconcentric, nonoverlapping, and sometimes even contradictory identities and affiliations (Figure 18.3). The individual seems to have disintegrated into fragments and multiple, postmodern selves.

FIGURE 18.3 Postmodern Society: Paradoxical, Decentered
Affiliations; No Self

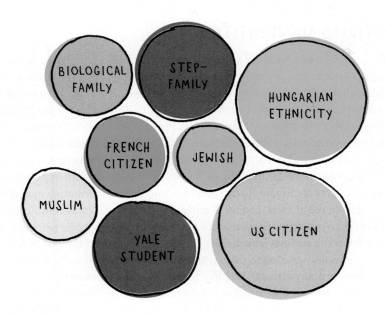

The Causes of Social Change

What drives social change, be it over 20 years or two millennia? What, besides social movements, that is? The short answer is that social change can result from technological innovation, the emergence of new ideas, changes in cultural identities, and conflict between social actors.

TECHNOLOGY AND INNOVATION

Technological innovation has been a major contributor to social change. The invention of computers and the internet has brought about major changes in society. People can live in Milan, Italy, and hold a telephone conference with a company in San Francisco, California. Managers carrying smartphones can communicate with their employees or clients 24 hours a day. People can work from home, so their homes may be farther away from their offices. Companies can locate their headquarters outside cities, where costs may be cheaper, because technology allows them to communicate instantaneously. Technology has a huge influence on the organization of social and economic life.

NEW IDEAS AND IDENTITIES

The emergence of new ideas and information has also contributed to social change. For example, in recent years, researchers have presented studies suggesting that routine consumption of blueberries lowers a person's risk of developing type 2 diabetes (Muraki et al., 2013). This information has changed some people's behavior and therefore has brought about social change. Likewise, new information about the dangers of pollution, climate change, and global warming is altering people's driving behavior, increasing the demand for hybrid cars in the United States. As fully electric cars gain in popularity and the dangers of climate change become clearer, this information may serve as a major source of social change. Finally, for many years it was commonplace in East Asian countries to wear masks in densely packed public settings; the threat from the coronavirus disease, however, has caused the public health benefits of mask wearing to diffuse to non-Asian societies as well, evincing a behavior in many cities that is likely to outlast the pandemic.

These examples all involve information flowing from experts to the general public, who then make changes for themselves or their families. But change can also arise without the help of professional experts like scientists or politicians. Changes in the cultural identities of groups of people need not be the result of findings from research studies or political movements. The secularization of some Jewish communities in America has not been the result of a top-down plan within the Jewish community or any other expert opinion. Intermarriage rates between Jews and non-Jews have slowly ticked up as Judaism has come to be seen increasingly as both an ethnicity and a religion, allowing nonreligious Jews to maintain a Jewish identity without strict adherence to religious doctrine.

Many social changes occurred in the wake of World War II, such as the founding of the United Nations, the Marshall Plan, and the conflict that resulted in the creation of Israel.

SOCIAL CHANGE AND CONFLICT

Other social changes are the result of conflict. The division of Germany in the aftermath of World War II was a direct result of the conflict itself. East and West Germany developed very differently during the postwar period, largely because of the political systems implemented at the end of the conflict. World War II was also responsible for the Cold War, the establishment of the state of Israel, and the founding of the United Nations, just to mention a few of the enduring legacies of the global reorganization after the war. When ideas or institutions clash, new patterns of social organization emerge from their resolution. This version of history was originally championed by German philosopher Georg Wilhelm Friedrich Hegel (1770–1831), who, in his theory of dialectics, argued that conflict was the motor of history. Each idea (or thesis) has an opposite (or antithesis). The thesis and the antithesis come into conflict, eventually resulting in their resolution (or synthesis). The synthesis, however, becomes a new thesis, which then evinces a new antithesis and eventually necessitates a new synthesis. This process of conflict and resolution, according to Hegel, is how history proceeds.

POLICY

DOES ACTIVISM ACTUALLY WORK?

The women's protest the day after President Trump was inaugurated represented the largest single-day protest in US history. Yet the sea of pink "Pussyhats" (a hat with cat ears meant to reclaim the term in response to Trump's boast in 2005 of grabbing women's genitals) seemed to have no impact in Washington, with Trump pursuing policies in direct opposition to the goals of the marchers on LGBTQ+ issues, health care, immigration, and so on.

One way of interpreting the failure of the Women's March to affect Trump's behavior in office is that no protest affects him. Another is that it failed strategically. Street marches may be social movements' equivalent of heavy armor and infantry, which have been supplanted by high-tech weaponry that supposedly requires fewer troops. That is, rather than taking to the public square, perhaps protesters are increasingly taking to the new commons: the internet.

Indeed, activists have been using the internet to mobilize new forms of social movements. From straightforward petitioning drives (like those found on the clearinghouse site change.org) to more innovative apps (like #NeverTrump, which enabled voters in hotly contested states who wished to vote for Jill Stein in the 2016 election but who also didn't want to tip their state into the Trump column to trade their votes with Clinton voters in a state where the election wasn't hotly contested), social movements have taken the internet by storm.

But how effective are these new online social movements? Perhaps they work only when combined with traditional street protests—as in the Arab Spring that was organized via Facebook and Twitter but resulted in the physical occupation of Tahrir Square in the Egyptian capital and the eventual ouster of President Hosni Mubarak. Or do online social movements mostly deserve their derogatory nickname "slacktivism"? How do they compare to traditional approaches to organizing, raising money, and effecting change?

On the one hand, online social movements profit from a relatively inexpensive form of organization and action. E-mailing members is cheaper than sending letters, and maintaining websites is certainly cheaper than maintaining offices. On the other hand, politicians and policy makers can easily ignore online social movements. They know that e-mail is cheap and easy, and therefore they value it less. In the 2016 elections, presidential candidate Bernie Sanders capitalized on the internet to raise money for his campaign by amassing small donations while rejecting money from large donors. While other candidates were holding fund-raising dinners and traveling across the country to raise money from major donors, Sanders relied on hundreds of thousands of small contributions made through the click of a button on his website. In fact, the average contribution made to the Sanders campaign through the internet was $29. Sanders's road had been paved by another would-be Democratic nominee for president, Howard Dean. In 2004, Dean raised millions of dollars and, using the website meetup.com, mobilized more than 25,000 supporters to attend monthly meetings in about 225 cities across the country. Now the internet is a primary way national politicians raise money.

Sociologist Doug McAdam points out that though the "information wants to be free" ethos of the internet makes it easy for nascent social movements to disseminate their messages quite broadly, the connections between e-friends may not be as sticky as the connections between members of face-to-face organizations. McAdam noted that "successful movements, movements

DIGITAL.WWNORTON.COM/YOUMAYASK7

To see my conversation with Doug McAdam about social movements, visit digital.wwnorton.com/youmayask7

that take off very quickly, emerge within established communities, and essentially the members of that community are threatened with the loss of member benefits for failure to go along. It's not clear that the electronic communities have the same capacity to monitor people's compliance with the new line of action. In an information sense, there's no question that these new technologies disseminate information, create all sorts of opportunities for new and original framings" (Conley, 2009p). But electronically based movements may not be able to take advantage of existing interpersonal relationships to mobilize behavioral change. If some long-lost friend of yours on Facebook sends out a mass e-mail about how she has decided to donate money to save Arctic seals, you are more likely to know about her choice and become aware of the plight of the seals than you would have been pre-internet, but you may not feel compelled to do much. Yet if your roommate decides to go 100 percent organic and gives you a dirty look and a lecture every time you fill the refrigerator with conventional products, you may be more likely to make changes in your behavior just to maintain the otherwise good vibes in your relationship.

Says Yes Man Bichlbaum, in an e-mail interview: "It's clear that traditional forms of protest are still the most powerful. It's always hard to measure the effects of such things, but we know that people taking to the streets helped shut down the [WTO's] Seattle Ministerial [meeting], forced [British prime minister] Tony Blair to stop pretending he was representing the majority, etc.—lots of signs that it works." So in the end, the largest payoffs may be in the linkage of the internet to live protest marches. After all, the Women's March represented the largest worldwide protests ever recorded. And although they had been coordinated by many internet activists, they still required people to show up, shout, beat drums, and in some cases risk arrest. It happened that they did not achieve their goal, but maybe they were just beginning.

Conclusion

Social movements have changed the landscape of US history. In the near future, the influence of movements may grow in scope. The increasing use of technology has brought together participants from all corners of the world. When protests were being organized against racialized police violence, complete strangers got in touch and coordinated their efforts over the internet and social media. In addition, social change that resulted from previous movements—namely, the civil rights and women's movements—means that new categories of people have the opportunity to participate in new movements. On the other hand, as movements grow, do they weaken? That is, are we more likely to click on a link and less likely to take to the streets? Are the emotional satisfaction and sense of identity that we draw from social movements thinner as such movements broaden? To understand movements, let's return to the paradox at the beginning of the chapter. Affiliation with multiple group identities is central to an individual identity. Identity and its emotional impulses both result from and form the basis of collective action. An important type of collective action, directed at social change, is a social movement. Organizations of movement activists are crucial to social movements and the resulting social change.

One of the important points in this chapter is that movements are not individual efforts, and they take place when people are resourceful, not just when they have resources. Movement culture, solidarity among participants, and indigenous organizations go a long way in nurturing a movement. Although social change may be a product of social movements, immediate social change does not prove conclusively that a movement is successful, because the change may be temporary (for instance, the temperance movement). In contrast, a movement that does not produce immediate social change cannot necessarily be termed a failure. Another irony is that a successful social movement often puts itself out of business (think of the woman suffrage movement). And because this is the final chapter, you get this irony as a bonus paradox:

BONUS PARADOX

A SUCCESSFUL SOCIAL MOVEMENT SHOULD END UP DESTROYING ITSELF, BECAUSE IT WILL HAVE SOLVED THE PROBLEM THAT MOTIVATED ITS VERY EXISTENCE.

The same is true for textbooks, so congratulations, sociologists, my job is done!

QUESTIONS FOR REVIEW

1. Pick a social movement discussed in the chapter to research on the internet. Does it illustrate the three stages of social movements? Moreover, of the various types of social movement organizations, to which does it best correspond and why?

2. How has activism changed since the advent of the internet? How has the line blurred between legally allowed activism and illegal behavior?

3. How are individuals' affiliations linked to identity? How has this relationship likely changed from premodern to modern to post-modern times?

4. What is the difference between collective action and behavior that is simply deviant? Describe this contrast through examples of both crowd collective action and mass collective action.

5. A group of students suddenly marches out of the classroom shortly after their professor makes an inappropriate comment. Voters send an e-mail through an antiwar organization's website to their local representative. Half of the population watches the season finale of a popular television show. How do the examples above demonstrate the difference between collective action, a social movement, and behavior that corresponds to neither?

6. How does the resource-mobilization theory build on a weakness of the classical model in the effort to theorize on the way social movements arise?

7. How is Alexis de Tocqueville's theory about America as a "land of joiners" (see Chapter 5) consistent with the existence of various grassroots organizations?

8. Use an example from this chapter to describe some of the possible links between technology and innovation, social movements, and social change. How do information and the way it is circulated affect social movements and, in turn, social change?

AIN'T GONNA TAKE IT NO MORE

As we've seen in this chapter, social change can come about in many ways, from specific change like voting rights to societal change like how we treat minorities in the workplace. Most social movements emerge when people who care enough about an issue decide to do something about it.

TRY IT!

What is your number one pet peeve? What really gets your goat? I don't mean how your annoying younger brother chews with his mouth open or leaves his towel on the bathroom floor at home. I mean something about your community or society as a whole. (I can't give examples, because inevitably one person's grievance is another's sacred cow.) If you had the time and inclination to try to change this, how would you go about it?

WHAT'S THE ISSUE?

_____

_____

_____

WHO WOULD IT AFFECT?

_____

_____

_____

HOW WOULD YOU FIX IT?

_____

_____

_____

THINK ABOUT IT

Are there already folks out there trying to change what you would like to see changed as well? Do their strategies align with what you suggested above? Is there a movement trying to accomplish the exact opposite?

When would either side go home in defeat or declare victory—or is this an issue that you think will always remain contentious? If so, why?

SOCIOLOGY ON THE STREET

This may be hard to believe, but your parents were once your own age. What beliefs, dreams, and problems did they have? How are these similar to and different from your own? Watch the Sociology on the Street video to find out more: **digital.wwnorton.com/youmayask7**.

WANT MORE PRACTICE?

Complete the InQuizitive activity for this chapter at digital.wwnorton.com /youmayask7

Thank you, readers of Chapter 15, for turning, as instructed, to this page. Why did you do it? That is, why did you follow instructions? You may have been curious, as when you turn to the last page of a novel to see how it ends. That would be an emotional or affective reason. But as much as I would like to think that this textbook is as exciting as a mystery novel, you probably were not dying of curiosity about the surprise ending of this chapter. It is more likely that you were just following orders. But you don't follow all orders indiscriminately, do you? You followed this order (or request—after all, I was careful to say please) because this book, or the voice of the author, has some sort of legitimate authority. Feel free to return to Chapter 15, where you left off. A systematic explanation of authority and legitimacy awaits you.

Glossary

A

absolute poverty the point at which a household's income falls below the necessary level to purchase food to physically sustain its members.

achieved status a status into which one enters; voluntary status.

affirmative action a set of policies that grant preferential treatment to a number of particular subgroups within the population—typically, women and historically disadvantaged racial minorities.

agricultural revolution the period around 1700 marked by the introduction of new farming technologies that increased food output in farm production.

alienation a condition in which people are dominated by forces of their own creation that then confront them as alien powers; according to Marx, the basic state of being in a capitalist society.

alternative social movements social movements that seek the most limited societal change and often target a narrow group of people.

altruism an action that benefits a group but does not directly benefit the individual performing the action.

altruistic suicide suicide that occurs when one experiences too much social integration.

androgynous neither masculine nor feminine.

animism the belief that spirits are part of the natural world, as in totemism.

anomic suicide suicide that occurs as a result of insufficient social regulation.

anomie a sense of aimlessness or despair that arises when we can no longer reasonably expect life to be predictable; too little social regulation; normlessness.

ascribed status a status into which one is born; involuntary status.

authority the justifiable right to exercise power.

B

bisexual an individual who is sexually attracted to both genders/sexes.

boundary work work done to maintain the border between legitimate and nonlegitimate science within a specific scientific discipline or between legitimate disciplines.

bourgeois society a society of commerce (modern capitalist society, for example) in which the maximization of profit is the primary business incentive.

bourgeoisie the capitalist class.

broken windows theory of deviance theory explaining how social cues impact whether individuals act deviantly—specifically, whether local, informal social norms allow deviant acts.

bureaucracy a legal-rational organization or mode of administration that governs with reference to formal rules and role and emphasizes meritocracy.

C

capitalism an economic system in which property and goods are primarily privately owned; investments are determined by private decisions; and prices, production, and the distribution of goods are determined primarily by competition in an unfettered marketplace.

case study an intensive investigation of one particular unit of analysis in order to describe it or uncover its mechanisms.

caste system a religion-based system of stratification characterized by no social mobility.

causal relationship the idea that one factor influences another through a chain of events; such a dynamic is different from two factors being merely associated or correlated, in which case they may appear to vary together but that could be due to chance or a third factor causing both.

causality the notion that a change in one factor results in a corresponding change in another.

charismatic authority authority that rests on the personal appeal of an individual leader.

churches religious bodies that coexist in a relatively low state of tension with their social surroundings. They have mainstream, "safe" beliefs and practices relative to those of the general population.

cisgender describes people whose gender corresponds to their birth sex.

citizenship rights the rights guaranteed to each law-abiding citizen in a nation-state.

civil rights the rights guaranteeing a citizen's personal freedom from interference, including freedom of speech and the right to travel freely.

class system an economically based hierarchical system characterized by cohesive oppositional groups and somewhat loose social mobility.

classical model model of social movements based on a concept of structural weakness in society that results in psychological disruption of individuals.

coalescence the second stage of a social movement, in which resources are mobilized (i.e., concrete action is taken) around the problems outlined in the first stage.

code switch to flip fluidly between two or more languages and sets of cultural norms to fit different cultural contexts.

coercion the use of force to get others to do what you want.

cohabitation living together in an intimate relationship without formal legal or religious sanctioning.

collective action action that takes place in groups and diverges from the social norms of the situation.

collective action problem the difficulty in organizing large groups because of the tendency of some individuals to freeload or slack off.

collective resistance an organized effort to change a power hierarchy on the part of a less-powerful group in a society.

color-blind racism the view that racial inequality is perpetuated by a supposedly color-blind stance that ends up reinforcing historical and contemporary inequities, disparate impact, and institutional bias by "ignoring" them in favor of a technically neutral approach.

Communism a political system in which the means of production are shared through state ownership and in which rewards are tied not to productivity but to need, supposedly leading to a classless society.

comparative research a methodology by which two or more entities (such as countries), which are similar in many dimensions but differ on one in question, are compared to learn about the dimension that differs between them.

conflict theory the idea that conflict between competing interests is the basic, animating force of social change and society in general.

conformist an individual who accepts both the goals and the strategies that are considered socially acceptable to achieve those goals.

congregation a group of people who gather together, especially for worship.

consumerism the steady acquisition of material possessions, often with the belief that happiness and fulfillment can thus be achieved.

contagion theory theory of collective action claiming that collective action arises because of people's tendency to conform to the behavior of others with whom they are in close contact.

content analysis a systematic analysis of the content rather than the structure of a communication, such as a written work, speech, or film.

contradictory class locations the idea that people can occupy locations in the class structure that fall between the two "pure" classes.

convergence theory theory of collective action stating that collective action happens when people with similar ideas and tendencies gather in the same place.

corporate crime a particular type of white-collar crime committed by the officers (CEOs and other executives) of a corporation.

corporation a legal entity unto itself that has a legal personhood distinct from that of its members—namely, its owners and shareholders.

correlation or association when two variables tend to track each other positively or negatively.

credentialism an overemphasis on credentials (e.g., college degrees) for signaling social status or qualifications for a job.

crime the violation of laws enacted by society.

cult religious movement that makes some new claim about the supernatural and therefore does not easily fit within the sect–church cycle.

cult of domesticity the notion that true womanhood centers on domestic responsibility and child rearing.

cultural capital the symbolic and interactional resources that people use to their advantage in various situations.

cultural lag the time gap between the appearance of a new technology and the words and practices that give it meaning.

cultural relativism taking into account the differences across cultures without passing judgment or value.

cultural scripts modes of behavior and understanding that are not universal or natural.

culture the sum of the social categories and concepts we embrace in addition to beliefs, behaviors (except institutional ones), and practices; everything but the natural environment around us.

culture jamming the act of turning media against themselves.

culture of poverty the argument that poor people adopt certain practices that differ from those of middle-class, "mainstream" society in order to adapt and survive in difficult economic circumstances.

culture shock doubt, confusion, or anxiety arising from immersion in an unfamiliar culture.

D

deductive approach a research approach that starts with a theory, forms a hypothesis, makes empirical observations, and then analyzes the data to confirm, reject, or modify the original theory.

democracy a system of government wherein power theoretically lies with the people; citizens are allowed to vote in elections, speak freely, and participate as legal equals in social life.

denomination a big group of congregations that share the same faith and are governed under one administrative umbrella.

dependent variable the outcome the researcher is trying to explain.

deterrence theory philosophy of criminal justice arising from the notion that crime results from a rational calculation of its costs and benefits.

dialectic a two-directional relationship, following a pattern in which an original statement or thesis is countered with an antithesis, leading to a conclusion that unites the strengths of the original position and the counterarguments.

dialectic materialism a notion of history that privileges conflict over economic, material resources as the central struggle and driver of change in society.

dictatorship a form of government that restricts the right to political participation to a small group or even to a single individual.

discrimination harmful or negative acts (not mere thoughts) against people deemed inferior on the basis of their racial category, without regard to their individual merit.

divide et impera the role of a member of a triad who intentionally drives a wedge between the other two actors in the group.

domination the probability that a command with specific content will be obeyed by a given group of people.

double consciousness a concept conceived by W. E. B. Du Bois to describe the behavioral scripts, one for moving through the world and the other incorporating the external opinions of prejudiced onlookers, which are constantly maintained by African Americans.

dramaturgical theory the view (advanced by Erving Goffman) of social life as essentially a theatrical performance, in which we are all actors on metaphorical stages, with roles, scripts, costumes, and sets.

dyad a group of two.

E

education the process through which academic, social, and cultural skills are developed.

egoistic suicide suicide that occurs when one is not well integrated into a social group.

elastic ties social connections that display the repeated interactions characteristic of strong ties while maintaining a degree of protective social distance (i.e., not knowing more than a first name, if that).

elite–mass dichotomy system a system of stratification that has a governing elite, a few leaders who broadly hold power in society.

embeddedness the degree to which social relationships are reinforced through indirect ties (i.e., friends of friends).

emergence the first stage of a social movement, occurring when the social problem being addressed is first identified.

emergent norm theory theory of collective action emphasizing the influence of keynoters in promoting new behavioral norms.

emotional labor managing emotions and their outward expression to meet the expectations of a job, especially in service sector work.

endogamy marriage to someone within one's social group.

epigenetics chemical regulation of gene activity that may be switched "on" or "off" in response to environmental influence.

equality of condition the idea that everyone should have an equal starting point.

equality of opportunity the idea that everyone has an equal chance to achieve wealth, social prestige, and power because the rules of the game, so to speak, are the same for everyone.

equality of outcome the idea that each player must end up with the same amount regardless of the fairness of the "game."

essentialist arguments explaining social phenomena in terms of natural, biological, or evolutionary inevitabilities.

estate system a politically based system of stratification characterized by limited social mobility.

ethicalism the adherence to certain principles to lead a moral life, as in Buddhism and Taoism.

ethnicity one's ethnic quality or affiliation. It is voluntary, self-defined, nonhierarchical, fluid and multiple, and based on cultural differences, not physical ones per se.

ethnocentrism the belief that one's own culture or group is superior to others, and the tendency to view all other cultures from the perspective of one's own.

ethnography a qualitative method of studying people or a social setting that uses observation, interaction, and sometimes formal interviewing to document behaviors, customs, experiences, social ties, and so on.

ethnomethodology literally "the methods of the people"; this approach to studying human interaction focuses on the ways in which we make sense of our world, convey this understanding to others, and produce a shared social order.

eugenics literally meaning "well born"; a pseudoscience that postulates that controlling the fertility of populations could influence inheritable traits passed on from generation to generation.

evangelicals members of any Christian denomination distinguished by four main beliefs: the Bible is without error, salvation comes only through belief in Jesus Christ, personal conversion is the only path to salvation (the "born again" experience), and others must also be converted. They proselytize by engaging with wider society.

exchange mobility mobility resulting from the swapping of jobs.

exogamy marriage to someone outside one's social group.

experimental methods methods that seek to alter the social landscape in a very specific way for a given sample of individuals and then track what results that change yields; they often involve comparisons to a control group that did not experience such an intervention.

extended family kin networks that extend outside or beyond the nuclear family.

F

face the esteem in which an individual is held by others.

family wage a wage paid to male workers sufficient to support a dependent wife and children.

fatalistic suicide suicide that occurs as a result of too much social regulation.

feminism a social movement to get people to understand that gender is an organizing principle in society and to address gender-based inequalities that intersect with other forms of social identity.

feminist methodology a set of systems or methods that treat women's experiences as legitimate empirical and theoretical resources, that promote social science for women (think public sociology, but for a specific half of the public), and that take into account the researcher as much as the overt subject matter.

formal social sanctions mechanisms of social control by which rules or laws prohibit deviant criminal behavior.

free rider problem the notion that when more than one person is responsible for getting something done, the incentive is for each individual to shirk responsibility and hope others will pull the extra weight.

functionalism the theory that various social institutions and processes in society exist to serve some important (or necessary) function to keep society running.

fundamentalists religious adherents who follow a scripture (such as the Bible or Qur'an) using a literal interpretation of its meaning.

G

game theory the study of strategic decisions made under conditions of uncertainty and interdependence.

gender a social position; behaviors and a set of attributes that are associated with sex identities.

gender roles sets of behavioral norms assumed to accompany one's status as male or female.

generalizability the extent to which we can claim our findings inform us about a group larger than the one we studied.

generalized other an internalized sense of the total expectations of others in a variety of settings—regardless of whether we've encountered those people or places before.

genocide the mass killing of a group of people based on racial, ethnic, or religious traits.

glass ceiling an invisible limit on women's climb up the occupational ladder.

glass escalator the accelerated promotion of men to the top of a work organization, especially in feminized jobs.

global warming rising atmospheric concentrations of carbon dioxide and other greenhouse gases, resulting in higher global average temperatures.

grassroots organization a type of social movement organization that relies on high levels of community-based membership participation to promote social change. It lacks a hierarchical structure and works through existing political structures.

H

hegemonic masculinity the condition in which men are dominant and privileged, and this dominance and privilege is invisible.

hegemony a condition by which a dominant group uses its power to elicit the voluntary "consent" of the masses.

heteronormativity the idea that heterosexuality is the default or normal sexual orientation from which other sexualities deviate.

hidden curriculum the nonacademic and less overt socialization functions of schooling.

historical methods research that collects data written from reports, newspaper articles, journals, transcripts, television programs, diaries, artwork, and other artifacts that date back to the period under study.

homosexual the social identity of a person who has sexual attraction to and/or relations with people of the same sex.

hypothesis a proposed relationship between two variables, usually with a stated direction.

I

I one's subjective sense of having consciousness, agency, action, or power.

ideology a system of concepts and relationships; an understanding of cause and effect.

income money received by a person for work, from transfers (gifts, inheritances, or government assistance), or from returns on investments.

independent variable a measured factor that the researcher believes has a causal impact on the dependent variable.

inductive approach a research approach that starts with empirical observations and then works to form a theory.

informal social sanctions the usually unexpressed but widely known rules of group membership; the unspoken rules of social life.

in-group another term for the powerful group, most often the majority.

innovator social deviant who accepts socially acceptable goals but rejects socially acceptable means to achieve them.

institutional racism institutions and social dynamics that may seem race-neutral but actually disadvantage minority groups.

interest group an organization that seeks to gain power in government and influence policy without campaigning for direct election or appointment to office.

international state system a system in which each state is recognized as territorially sovereign by fellow states.

interpretive sociology a type of scholarship in which researchers imagine themselves experiencing the life positions of the social actors they want to understand rather than treating those people as objects to be examined.

intersectionality the idea that it is critical to understand the interplay between social identities such as race, class, gender, ability status, and sexual orientation, even though many social systems and institutions (such as the law) try to treat each category on its own.

isomorphism a constraining process that forces one unit in a population to resemble other units that face the same set of environmental conditions.

K

kinship networks strings of relationships between people related by blood and co-residence (i.e., marriage).

L

labeling theory the belief that individuals subconsciously notice how others see or label them, and their reactions to those labels over time form the basis of their self-identity.

large group a group characterized by the presence of a formal structure that mediates interaction and, consequently, status differentiation.

legal-rational authority authority based on legal, impersonal rules; the rules rule.

M

macrosociology a branch of sociology generally concerned with social dynamics at a higher level of analysis—that is, across the breadth of society.

master status one status within a set that stands out or overrides all others.

material culture everything that is a part of our constructed, physical environment, including technology.

matrix of domination intersecting domains of oppression that create a social space of domination and, by extension, a unique position within that space based on someone's intersectional identity along the multiple dimensions of gender, age, race, class, sexuality, location, and so on.

Matthew effect a term used by sociologists to describe the notion that certain scientific results get more notoriety and influence based on the existing prestige of the researchers involved.

me the self perceived as an object by the "I"; the self as one imagines others perceive one.

mechanical or segmental solidarity social cohesion based on sameness.

media any formats, platforms, or vehicles that carry, present, or communicate information.

mediator the member of a triad who attempts to resolve conflict between the two other actors in the group.

medicalization the process by which problems or issues not traditionally seen as medical come to be framed as such.

megachurch typically, a conservative Protestant church that attracts at least 2,000 worshipers per week.

meritocracy a society where status and mobility are based on individual attributes, ability, and achievement.

microsociology a branch of sociology that seeks to understand local interactional contexts; its methods of choice are ethnographic, generally including participant observation and in-depth interviews.

middle class a term commonly used to describe those individuals with nonmanual jobs that pay significantly more than the poverty line—though this is a highly debated and expansive category, particularly in the United States, where broad swaths of the population consider themselves middle-class.

midrange theory a theory that attempts to predict how certain social institutions tend to function.

Milgram experiment an experiment devised in 1961 by Stanley Milgram, a psychologist at Yale University, to see how far ordinary people would go to obey a scientific authority figure.

miscegenation the technical term for interracial marriage, literally meaning "a mixing of kinds"; it is politically and historically charged—sociologists generally prefer the term *exogamy* or *outmarriage*.

modernity social relations characterized by rationality, bureaucratization, and objectivity as well as individually created by nonconcentric, but overlapping, group affiliations.

monogamy the practice of having only one sexual partner or spouse at a time.

monopoly the form of business that occurs when one seller of a good or service dominates the market to the exclusion of others, potentially leading to zero competition.

morbidity illness in a general sense.

mortality death.

N

narrative the sum of stories contained in a set of ties.

nativism the movement to protect and preserve indigenous land or culture from the allegedly dangerous and polluting effects of new immigrants.

natural experiment something that takes place in the world that affects people in a way that is unrelated to any other preexisting factors or their characteristics, thereby approximating random assignment to treatment or control groups.

nonmaterial culture values, beliefs, behaviors, and social norms.

normal science science conducted within an existing paradigm, as defined by Thomas Kuhn.

normative view of science the notion that science should not be affected by the personal beliefs or values of scientists but rather should follow objective rules of evidence.

norms how values tell us to behave.

nuclear family familial form consisting of a father, a mother, and their children.

O

offshoring a business decision to move all or part of a company's operations abroad to minimize costs.

oligopoly the economic condition that exists when a handful of firms effectively control a particular market.

one-drop rule the belief that "one drop" of Black blood makes a person Black, a concept that evolved from US laws forbidding miscegenation.

ontological equality the philosophical and religious notion that all people are created equal.

operationalization how a concept gets defined and measured in a given study.

organic solidarity social cohesion based on difference and interdependence of the parts.

organization any social network that is defined by a common purpose and has a boundary between its membership and the rest of the social world.

organizational culture the shared beliefs and behaviors within a social group; often used interchangeably with *corporate culture*.

organizational structure the ways in which power and authority are distributed within an organization.

other someone or something outside of oneself.

out-group another term for the stigmatized or less powerful group, the minority.

P

panopticon a circular building composed of an inner ring and an outer ring designed to serve as a prison in which the guards, housed in the inner ring, can observe the prisoners without the detainees knowing whether they are being watched.

paradigm the framework within which scientists operate.

paradigm shift or scientific revolution when enough scientific anomalies accrue to challenge the existing paradigm, showing that it is incomplete or inadequate to explain all observed phenomena.

paradox of authority although the state's authority derives from the implicit threat of physical force, resorting to physical coercion strips the state of all legitimate authority.

parenting stress hypothesis a paradigm in which low income, unstable employment, a lack of cultural resources, and a feeling of inferiority from social class comparisons exacerbate household stress levels; this stress, in turn, leads to detrimental parenting practices such as yelling and hitting, which are not conducive to healthy child development.

participant observation a qualitative research method that seeks to uncover the meanings people give their social actions by observing their behavior in practice.

party a group that is similar to a small group but is multifocal.

patriarchy a nearly universal system involving the subordination of femininity to masculinity.

perverse incentives reward structures that lead to suboptimal outcomes by stimulating counterproductive behavior; for example, it is argued that welfare—to the extent that it discourages work efforts—has perverse incentives.

pluralism the presence and engaged coexistence of numerous distinct groups in one society.

political participation an activity that has the intent or effect of influencing government action.

political party an organization that seeks to gain power in a government, generally by backing candidates for office who subscribe (to the extent possible) to the organization's political ideals.

political process model model of social movements that focuses on the structure of political opportunities. When these are favorable to a particular challenger, the chances are better for the success of a social movement led by this challenger.

political rights the rights guaranteeing a citizen's ability to participate in politics, including the right to vote and the right to hold an elected office.

politics power relations among people or other social actors.

polyandry the practice of having multiple husbands simultaneously.

polygamy the practice of having more than one sexual partner or spouse at a time.

polygyny the practice of having multiple wives simultaneously.

population an entire group of individual persons, objects, or items from which samples may be drawn.

positivism the approach to sociology that emphasizes the scientific method as an approach to studying the objectively observable behavior of individuals irrespective of the meanings those actions have for the subjects themselves.

positivist sociology the approach to sociology that emphasizes the scientific method as an approach to studying the objectively observable behavior of individuals irrespective of the meanings of those actions for the subjects themselves.

postmodernism a condition characterized by the questioning of the notion of progress and history, the replacement of narrative with pastiche (i.e., a collage of existing ideas) or imitation of other work in the service of satire or subversion, and multiple, perhaps even conflicting, identities resulting from unconnected affiliations.

postmodernity social relations characterized by a questioning of the notion of progress and history, the replacement of narrative with pastiche, and multiple, perhaps even conflicting, identities resulting from disjointed affiliations.

power the ability to carry out one's own will despite resistance.

prejudice thoughts and feelings about an ethnic or racial group, which lead to preconceived notions and judgments (often negative) about the group.

premodernity social relations characterized by concentric circles of social affiliation, a low degree of division of labor, relatively undeveloped technology, and traditional social norms.

primary deviance the first act of rule breaking that may be given a label of "deviant" and thus influence how people think about and act toward you.

primary groups social groups, such as family or friends, composed of enduring, intimate face-to-face relationships that strongly influence the attitudes and ideals of those involved.

primordialism Clifford Geertz's term to explain the strength of ethnic ties because they are fixed and deeply felt or primordial ties to one's homeland culture.

productivity enhancing economic activities that increase the total economic value available to society.

profane the things of mundane, everyday life.

proletariat the working class.

Q

qualitative methods methods that attempt to collect information about the social world that cannot be readily converted to numeric form.

quantitative methods methods that seek to obtain information about the social world that is already in or can be converted to numeric form.

R

race a group of people who share a set of characteristics—typically, but not always, physical ones—and are said to share a common bloodline.

racialization the formation of a new racial identity by drawing ideological boundaries of difference around a formerly unnoticed group of people.

rationalization a never-ending process of ordering or organizing.

rebel an individual who rejects both traditional goals and traditional means and wants to alter or destroy the social institutions from which he or she is alienated.

recidivism when an individual who has been involved with the criminal justice system reverts to criminal behavior.

redemptive social movements social movements that target specific groups but advocate for more radical change in behavior.

reference group a group that helps us understand or make sense of our position in society relative to other groups.

reflection theory the idea that culture is a projection of social structures and relationships into the public sphere, a screen onto which the film of the underlying reality of social structures of a society is projected.

reflexive spirituality a contemporary religious movement that encourages followers to look to religion for meaning, wisdom, and profound thought and feeling rather than for absolute truths on how the world works.

reflexivity analyzing and critically considering our own role in, and effect on, our research.

reformative social movements social movements that advocate for limited social change across an entire society.

relative poverty a measurement of poverty based on a percentage of the median income in a given location.

reliability the likelihood of obtaining consistent results using the same measure.

religion a system of beliefs, traditions, and practices around sacred things; a set of shared "stories" that guide belief and action.

religious experiences an individual's spiritual feelings, acts, and experiences.

rent seeking economic activities that aim to move value from one person or company to another without increasing value.

representative sample the idea that a particular slice of social observation—a sample of survey respondents, an ethnographic research site such as an organization, or a batch of social media posts—captures in an accurate way the larger set (or universe) of those phenomena that it is meant to stand in for.

research methods approaches that social scientists use for investigating the answers to questions.

resocialization the process by which one's sense of social values, beliefs, and norms are reengineered, often deliberately, through an intense social process.

resource dilution model hypothesis stating that parental resources are finite and that each additional child gets a smaller amount of them.

resource-mobilization theory model of social movements that emphasizes political context and goals but also states that social movements are unlikely to emerge without the necessary resources.

retreatist one who rejects both socially acceptable means and goals by completely retreating from, or not participating in, society.

reverse causality a situation in which the researcher believes that A results in a change in B, but B, in fact, is causing A.

risk society a society that both produces and is concerned with mitigating risks, especially manufactured risks (ones that result from human activity).

ritualist an individual who rejects socially defined goals but not the means.

role the duties and behaviors expected of someone who holds a particular status.

role conflict the tension caused by competing demands between two or more roles pertaining to different statuses.

role strain the incompatibility among roles corresponding to a single status.

routinization the clear, rule-governed procedures used repeatedly for decision making.

routinization or institutionalization the final stage of a social movement, in which it is institutionalized and a formal structure develops to promote the cause.

S

sacred holy things endowed with special status and often used for worship and kept separate from the profane; the sacred realm is unknowable and mystical, so it inspires us with feelings of awe and wonder.

sacred canopy Peter Berger's term to describe the entire set of religious norms, symbols, and beliefs that express the most important thing in life— namely, the feeling that life is worth living and that reality is meaningful and ordered, not just random chaos.

sample the subset of the population from which you are actually collecting data.

scientific method a procedure involving the formulation, testing, and modification of hypotheses based on systematic observation, measurement, and/or experiments.

scientific racism nineteenth-century theories of race that characterize a period of feverish investigation into the origins, explanations, and classifications of race.

second shift women's responsibility for housework and child care—everything from cooking dinner to doing laundry, bathing children, reading bedtime stories, and sewing Halloween costumes.

secondary deviance subsequent acts of rule breaking that occur after primary deviance and as a result of your new deviant label and people's expectations of you.

secondary groups groups marked by impersonal, instrumental relationships (those existing as a means to an end).

sects or sectarian groups high-tension organizations that don't fit well within the existing social environment. They are usually most attractive to society's least privileged—outcasts, minorities, or the poor—because they downplay worldly pleasure by stressing otherworldly promises.

secularism a general movement away from religiosity and spiritual belief toward a rational, scientific orientation; a trend adopted by industrialized nations in the form of separation of church and state.

segregation the legal or social practice of separating people on the basis of their race or ethnicity.

self the individual identity of a person as perceived by that same person.

service sector the section of the economy that involves providing intangible services.

sex the perceived biological differences that society typically uses to distinguish males from females.

sex role theory Talcott Parsons's theory that men and women perform their sex roles as breadwinners and wives/mothers, respectively, because the nuclear family is the ideal arrangement in modern societies, fulfilling the function of reproducing workers.

sexism occurs when a person's sex or gender is the basis for judgment, discrimination, or other differential treatment against that person.

sexual harassment an illegal form of discrimination revolving around sexuality that can involve everything from inappropriate jokes to sexual "barter" (where victims feel the need to comply with sexual requests for fear of losing their job) to outright sexual assault.

sexuality desire, sexual preference, and sexual identity and behavior.

sick role concept describing the social rights and obligations of a sick individual.

small group a group characterized by face-to-face interaction, a unifocal perspective, lack of formal arrangements or roles, and a certain level of equality.

social capital the information, knowledge of people or things, and connections that help individuals enter, gain power in, or otherwise leverage social networks.

social class or socioeconomic status (SES) an individual's position in a stratified social order.

social cohesion social bonds; how well people relate to each other and get along on a day-to-day basis.

social construction an entity that exists because people behave as if it exists and whose existence is perpetuated as people and social institutions act in accordance with widely agreed-on formal rules or informal norms of behavior associated with that entity.

social control mechanisms that create normative compliance in individuals.

social Darwinism the application of Darwinian ideas to society—namely, the evolutionary "survival of the fittest."

social deviance any transgression of socially established norms.

social equality a condition in which no differences in wealth, power, prestige, or status based on non-natural conventions exist.

social institution a complex group of interdependent positions that, together, perform a social role and reproduce themselves over time; also defined in a narrow sense as any institution in a society that works to shape the behavior of the groups or people within it.

social integration the extent to which you are integrated into your social group or community.

social mobility the movement between different positions within a system of social stratification in any given society.

social movement collective behavior that is purposeful and organized (but not ritualized) and that seeks to challenge or change one or more aspects of society through institutional and extra-institutional means.

social movement organization a group developed to recruit new members and coordinate participation in a particular social movement; these groups also often raise money, clarify goals, and structure participation in the movement.

social network a set of relations—essentially, a set of dyads—held together by ties between individuals.

social regulation the number of rules guiding your daily life and, more specifically, what you can reasonably expect from the world on a day-to-day basis.

social rights the rights guaranteeing a citizen's protection by the state.

socialism an economic system in which most or all of the needs of the population are met through non-market methods of distribution.

socialization the process by which individuals internalize the values, beliefs, and norms of a given society and learn to function as members of that society.

sociological imagination the ability to connect the most basic, intimate aspects of an individual's life to seemingly impersonal and remote historical forces.

sociology the study of human society

soft power power attained through the use of cultural attractiveness rather than the threat of coercive action (hard power).

specialization the process of breaking up work into specific, delimited tasks.

state as defined by Max Weber, "a human community that (successfully) claims the monopoly of the legitimate use of physical force within a given territory."

status a recognizable social position that an individual occupies.

status hierarchy system a system of stratification based on social prestige.

status set all the statuses one holds simultaneously.

status-attainment model approach that ranks individuals by socioeconomic status, including income and educational attainment, and seeks to specify the attributes characteristic of people who end up in more desirable occupations.

stereotype threat when members of a negatively stereotyped group are placed in a situation where they fear they may confirm those stereotypes.

stigma a negative social label that not only changes others' behavior toward a person but also alters that person's own self-concept and social identity.

straight-line assimilation Robert Park's 1920s universal and linear model for how immigrants assimilate: they first arrive, then settle in, and achieve full assimilation in a newly homogenous country.

strain theory Robert Merton's theory that deviance occurs when a society does not give all of its members equal ability to achieve socially acceptable goals.

stratification the hierarchical organization of a society into groups with differing levels of power, social prestige, or status and economic resources.

street crime crime committed in public and often associated with violence, gangs, and poverty.

strength of weak ties the notion that relatively weak ties often turn out to be quite valuable because they yield new information.

structural functionalism a theory in which society's many parts—institutions, norms, traditions, and so on—mesh to produce a stable, working whole that evolved over time. Best embodied by Talcott Parsons.

structural hole a gap between network clusters, or even two individuals, if those individuals (or clusters) have complementary resources.

structural mobility mobility that is inevitable from changes in the economy.

subaltern a subordinate, oppressed group of people.

subculture the distinct cultural values and behavioral patterns of a particular group in society; a group united by sets of concepts, values, symbols, and shared meaning specific to the members of that group and distinctive enough to distinguish it from others within the same culture or society.

supernatural compensators promises of future rewards, such as salvation or eternity in heaven.

survey an ordered series of questions intended to elicit information from respondents.

symbolic ethnicity a nationality, not in the sense of carrying the rights and duties of citizenship but in the sense of identifying with a past or future nationality. For later generations of White ethnics, it is something not constraining but easily expressed, with no risks of stigma and all the pleasures of feeling like an individual.

symbolic interactionism a micro-level theory in which shared meanings, orientations, and assumptions form the basic motivations behind people's actions.

T

Taylorism the methods of labor management, introduced by Frederick Winslow Taylor to streamline the processes of mass production, in which each worker repeatedly performs one specific task.

tertius gaudens the member of a triad who benefits from conflict between the other two members of the group.

theism the worship of a god or gods, as in Christianity, Islam, and Hinduism.

theory an abstracted, systematic model of how some aspect of the world works.

tie the connection between two people in a relationship that varies in strength from one relationship to the next; a story that explains our relationship with another member of our network.

total institution an institution in which one is totally immersed and that controls all the basics of day-to-day life; no barriers exist between the usual sphere of daily life, and all activity occurs in the same place and under the same single authority.

tracking a way of dividing students into different classes by ability or future plans.

traditional authority authority that rests on or appeals to the past or traditions.

transgender describes people whose gender does not correspond to their birth sex.

triad a group of three.

U

underclass the notion, building on the culture of poverty argument, that the poor not only are different from mainstream society in their inability to take advantage of what society has to offer but also are increasingly deviant and even dangerous to the rest of us.

union an organization of workers designed to facilitate collective bargaining with an employer.

union busting a company's assault on its workers' union with the hope of dissolving it.

upper class a term for the economic elite.

V

validity the extent to which an instrument measures what it is intended to measure.

value-added theory theory of collective action claiming that certain conditions are required for a social movement to coalesce and achieve a successful outcome.

values moral beliefs.

Verstehen German for "understanding." The concept of *Verstehen* comes from Max Weber and is the basis of interpretive sociology.

W

wealth a family's or individual's net worth (i.e., total assets minus total debts).

welfare state a system in which the state is responsible for the well-being of its citizens.

white coat effect the phenomenon wherein a researcher's presence affects her subjects' behavior or response, thereby disrupting the study.

white-collar crime offense committed by a professional (or professionals) against a corporation, agency, or other institution.

Bibliography

Aboim, S. (2016). *Plural masculinities: The remaking of the self in private life.* New York: Routledge.

Abrutyn, S., & Mueller, A. S. (2014). Are suicidal behaviors contagious in adolescence? Using longitudinal data to examine suicide suggestion. *American Sociological Review, 79*(2), 211–27.

Acemoglu, D., & Restrepo, P. (2018, January). Artificial intelligence, automation and work (NBER Working Paper No. 24196). National Bureau of Economic Research. Retrieved from www.nber.org/papers/w24196.

Acemoglu, D., & Robinson, J. A. (2006). *Economic origins of dictatorship and democracy.* New York: Cambridge University Press.

Acemoglu, D., et al. (2001, December). The colonial origins of comparative development: An empirical investigation. *The American Economic Review, 91*(5), 1369–401.

Acierno, R., et al. (2010). Prevalence and correlates of emotional, physical, sexual, and financial abuse and potential neglect in the United States: The National Elder Mistreatment Study. *American Journal of Public Health, 100*(2), 292–97.

Ad Council. (2018). Texting and driving prevention. Retrieved from www.psacentral.org/campaign/Texting _and_Driving_Prevention.

Adida, C. L., et al. (2010). Identifying barriers to Muslim integration in France. *Proceedings of the National Academy of Sciences USA, 107*(52), 22384–90.

Aguirre, B. E., et al. (1998). A test of the emergent norm theory of collective behavior. *Sociological Forum, 13*(2), 301–20.

Alexander, D., et al. (2019). "The Definitive Net Worth of Donald Trump's Cabinet." Retrieved from www.forbes .com/sites/michelatindera/2019/07/25/the-definitive -net-worth-of-donald-trumps-cabinet/#4c2f0e706a15.

Alexander, K., et al. (2001). Schools, achievement and equality: A seasonal perspective. *Educational Evaluation and Policy Analysis, 23*(2), 171–91.

Allen, F. A. (1981). *The decline of the rehabilitative ideal: Penal policy and social purpose.* New Haven, CT: Yale University Press.

Allen, J. T. (1973). Designing income maintenance systems: The income accounting problem (paper no. 5). *Studies in Public Welfare.* Washington, DC: Government Printing Office.

Amenta, E. (2006). *When movements matter: The Townsend Plan and the rise of Social Security.* Princeton, NJ: Princeton University Press.

American Civil Liberties Union. (2013). The war on marijuana in Black and White. Retrieved from www.aclu .org/files/assets/aclu-thewaronmarijuana-rel2.pdf.

American Time Use Survey 2018 Results. (2019, June 19). Retrieved from www.bls.gov/news.release/pdf/atus .pdf.

Ammerman, N. T. (2005). *Pillars of faith: American congregations and their partners.* Berkeley: University of California Press.

Anderson, E. (1999). *Code of the street: Decency, violence, and the moral life of the inner city.* New York: Norton.

Anderson, J. L. (2009). The most failed state: Letter from Mogadishu. *The New Yorker, 85*(41), 64.

Appiah, Kwame Anthony. (2020). The Case for Capitalizing the B in Black. *The Atlantic.* Retrieved from https://www .theatlantic.com/ideas/archive/2020/06/time-to -capitalize-blackand-white/613159/.

Ariès, P. (1965). *Centuries of childhood: A social history of family life.* New York: Vintage. (Original work published 1962.)

Armstrong, E. A., & Bernstein, M. (2008). Culture, power, and institutions: A multi-institutional politics approach to social movements. *Sociological Theory, 26*(1), 74–99.

Armstrong, E. A., et al. (2012). Accounting for women's orgasm and sexual enjoyment in college hookups and relationships. *American Sociological Review, 77*(3), 435–62.

Arnold, M. (1869). *Culture and anarchy.* London: Smith, Elder.

Arum, R. (2003). *Judging school discipline: The crisis of moral authority.* Cambridge, MA: Harvard University Press.

Arum, R., & Shavit, Y. (1995). Secondary vocational education and the transition from school to work. *Sociology of Education, 68*(3), 187–204.

Asch, S. E. (1956). Studies of independence and conformity: A minority of one against a unanimous majority. *Psychological Monographs, 70*(9, Whole No. 416).

Attanasio, O., et al. (2013). The evolution of income, consumption, and leisure inequality in the US, 1980–2010. In C. Carroll et al. (Eds.), *Improving the measure of consumer expenditures* (pp. 100–140). Chicago: University of Chicago Press.

Auletta, K. (1981, November 16). I—the underclass. *The New Yorker,* p. 63.

Australian Catholic University. (2008). Principles of inclusive curriculum. Retrieved from www.acu.edu.au

/_data/assets/pdf_file/0019/103735/Principles_of
_Inclusive_Curriculum.pdf.

Australian Human Rights Commission. (1997, April). *Bringing them home: Report of the national inquiry into the separation of Aboriginal and Torres Strait Islander children from their families.* Retrieved from www.hreoc.gov.au /social_justice/bth_report/report/index.html.

Autor, D. H., et al. (2013). The China syndrome: Local labor market effects of import competition in the United States. *American Economic Review, 103*(6), 2121–68. Retrieved from www.aeaweb.org/articles?id=10.1257/aer .103.6.2121.

Ayres, I., & Unkovic, C. (2012). Information escrows. *Michigan Law Review, 111*(2), 145. Retrieved from https://repository.law.umich.edu/mlr/vol111/iss2/1.

Babbie, E. R. (2007). *The practice of social research* (11th ed.). Belmont, CA: Wadsworth.

Bacolod, M. (2017). Skills, the gender wage gap, and cities. *Journal of Regional Science, 57*(2), 290–318.

Bailey, M. J., & Dynarski, S. M. (2011). Inequality in postsecondary education. In G. J. Duncan & R. J. Murnane (Eds.), *Whither opportunity? Rising inequality, schools, and children's life chances* (pp. 117–32). New York: Russell Sage Foundation.

Baker, D. C. (2005, May 26). Church hosts "drive-thru" Sunday services. *Quad-City Times.* Retrieved from www .qctimes.com/articles/2005/05/26/local/export93493 .txt.

Baker, J. H. (1977). Politics, paradigms, and public culture. *The Journal of American History, 84*(3), 894–99.

Baker, J. O. (2015). *American secularism: Cultural contours of nonreligious belief systems.* New York: NYU Press.

Baker, M. G., et al. (2020). Successful elimination of Covid-19 transmission in New Zealand. *The New England Journal of Medicine.* Retrieved from www.nejm .org/doi/full/10.1056/NEJMc2025203.

Bakshi, A. (2003). Potential adverse health effects of genetically modified crops, part B. *Journal of Toxicology and Environmental Health, 6*, 211–55.

Baldus, D. C., et al. (1998). Racial discrimination and the death penalty in the post-*Furman* era. *Cornell Law Review, 83*, 1638. Retrieved from www.lawschool.cornell.edu /research/cornell-law-review/upload/baldus.pdf.

Bales, K. (2016). *Blood and earth: Modern slavery, ecocide, and the secret to saving the world.* New York: Spiegel & Grau.

Baltzell, E. D. (1958). *Philadelphia gentlemen.* New York: Free Press.

Banerjee, N. (2005, December 30). Going to church to find a faith that fits. *The New York Times*, pp. 1a, 18. Retrieved from www.nytimes.com/2005/12/30/us/teenagers-mix -churches-for-faith-that-fits.html.

Banfield, E. (1970). *The unheavenly city.* Boston: Little, Brown.

Barber, K. (2016). *Styling masculinity: Gender, class, and inequality in the men's grooming industry.* Brunswick, NJ: Rutgers University Press.

Barry-Jester, A. M. (2015, June 23). Attitudes toward racism and inequality are shifting. Retrieved from https://fivethirtyeight.com/features/attitudes-toward -racism-and-inequality-are-shifting.

Barth, E. A. T., & Noel, D. L. (1972). Conceptual frameworks for the analysis of race relations: An evaluation. *Social Forces, 50*, 333–48.

Bashshur, R. L., et al. (2000). Telemedicine: A new health care delivery system. *Annual Review of Public Health, 21*(1), 613–37.

Bauer, E. (2019). Eldercare: How does the United States stack up? *Forbes.* Retrieved from www.forbes .com/sites/ebauer/2019/08/28/eldercare-how-does-the -united-states-stack-up/#425f2c96bc96.

Bauer, G. (2016). Gender roles, comparative advantages and the life course: The division of domestic labor in same-sex and different-sex couples. *European Journal of Population, 32*(1), 99–128.

Bear, C. (2008, May 13). American Indian school a far cry from the past. *Morning Edition.* National Public Radio.

Bearman, P. S., & Brückner, H. (2001). Promising the future: Virginity pledges and the transition to first intercourse. *American Journal of Sociology, 106*(4), 859–912.

Bearman, P. S., et al. (2004). Chains of affection: The structure of adolescent romantic and sexual networks. *American Journal of Sociology, 110*(1), 44–91.

Beauvoir, S. de. (1952). *The second sex.* New York: Knopf.

Beck, U. (1992). *Risk society: Towards a new modernity* (Mark Ritter, Trans.). London: Sage.

Becker, H. S. (1953, November). Becoming a marihuana user. *American Journal of Sociology, 59*, 235–43.

Becker, H. S. (1963). *Outsiders: Studies in the sociology of deviance.* New York: Free Press.

Belley, P., & Lochner, L. (2007, October). *The changing role of family income and ability in determining educational achievement* (NBER Working Paper No. 13527). National Bureau of Economic Research. Retrieved from www.nber .org/papers/w13527.

Bender, C. J. (2007). Touching the transcendent: Rethinking religious experience in the sociological study of religion. In N. Ammerman (Ed.), *Everyday religion: Observing modern religious lives* (pp. 201–19). New York: Oxford University Press. Retrieved from www.oxfordscholarship .com/oso/private/content/religion/9780195305418/p050 .html#acprof-9780195305418-chapter-11.

Benedict, R. (1934). *Patterns of culture.* New York: Mentor Books.

Berbrier, M. (2000). The victim ideology of White supremacists and White separatists in the United States. *Sociological Focus, 33*, 175–91.

Berger, P. L. (1967). *The sacred canopy: Elements of a sociological theory of religion.* Garden City, NY: Anchor Books.

Berk, R. A., et al. (2003). The legalization of abortion and subsequent youth homicide: A time series analysis. *Analyses of Social Issues and Public Policy, 3*(1), 45–64.

Berk, S. F. (1985). *The gender factory: The apportionment of work in American households.* New York: Plenum Press.

Bernard, J. S. (1972). *The future of marriage.* New York: World Publishers.

Berry, B. (1963). *Almost White.* New York: Macmillan.

Besecke, K. (2007). Beyond literalism: Reflexive spirituality and religious meaning. In N. Ammerman (Ed.), *Everyday religion: Observing modern religious lives* (pp. 169–86). New York: Oxford University Press. Retrieved from www .oxfordscholarship.com/oso/private/content/religion /9780195305418/p009.html.

Bialik, K. (2017, June 12). Key facts about race and marriage, 50 years after *Loving v. Virginia.* Pew Research Center. Retrieved from www.pewresearch.org/fact-tank/2017/06

/12/key-facts-about-race-and-marriage-50-years
-after-loving-v-virginia.

Bird, W., & Thumma, S. (2011). A new decade of megachurches. Retrieved from http://hirr.hartsem.edu /megachurch/New-Decade-of-Megachurches-2011Profile .pdf.

Birnbaum, E. (2018). Hate crimes up for the third year in a row: FBI. *The Hill*. Retrieved from https://thehill .com/policy/national-security/416418-hate-crimes-up -for-third-year-in-a-row.

Bittman, M., et al. (2003). When does gender trump money? Bargaining and time in household work. *American Journal of Sociology, 109*, 186–214.

Bixler, M. T. (1992). *Winds of freedom: The story of the Navajo code talkers of World War II*. Darien, CT: Two Bytes.

Black, D. A., et al. (2017). The Methuselah effect: The pernicious impact of unreported deaths on old-age mortality estimates. *Demography, Springer*. Population Association of America (PAA), *54*(6), 2001–24.

Black megachurches surge. (1996). *Christian Century, 113*(21), 686–87. Retrieved from www.christiancentury.org.

Blanchard, R., & Bogaert, A. F. (1996). Homosexuality in men and number of older brothers. *American Journal of Psychiatry, 153*, 27–31.

Blanton, C. K. (2000). "They cannot master abstractions, but they can often be made efficient workers": Race and class in the intelligence testing of Mexican Americans and African Americans in Texas during the 1920s. *Social Science Quarterly, 81*(4), 1014–26.

Blau, P. M., & Duncan, O. D., with collaboration of A. Tyree. (1967). *The American occupational structure*. New York: Wiley.

Blažun, H., et al. (2012). Impact of computer training courses on reduction of loneliness of older people in Finland and Slovenia. *Computers in Human Behavior, 28*(4), 1202–12. Retrieved from www.sciencedirect.com /science/article/pii/S0747563212000350?via%3Dihub#!.

Bleakley, A., et al. (2018). How patterns of learning about sexual information among adolescents are related to sexual behaviors. *Perspectives on Sexual and Reproductive Health, 50*(1), 15–23.

Bloom, D. E., & Canning, D. (2004). *Global demographic change: Dimensions and economic significance*. No. w10817. National Bureau of Economic Research. Retrieved from www.nber.org/papers/w10817.

Blum, B. (2018, June). The lifespan of a lie? *Medium*. Retrieved from http://medium.com/s/trustissues /the-lifespan-of-a-lie-d869212b1f62.

Blumer, H. (1969). *Symbolic interactionism: Perspective and method*. Englewood Cliffs, NJ: Prentice-Hall.

Blumstein, P. W., & Schwartz., P. (1983). *American couples: Money, work, and sex*. New York: Morrow.

Bobo, L. (1989). Keeping the linchpin in place: Testing the multiple sources of opposition to residential integration. *Revue Internationale de Psychologie Sociale, 2*, 306–23.

Bobo, L., et al. (1997). Laissez-faire racism: The crystallization of a kinder, gentler, antiblack ideology. In S. A. Tuch & J. K. Martin (Eds.), *Racial attitudes in the 1990s: Continuity and change* (pp. 15–42). Westport, CT: Praeger.

Bogaert, A. F. (2006). Biological versus nonbiological older brothers and men's sexual orientation. *Proceedings of the National Academy of Sciences USA, 103*(28), 10771–74.

Bogin, B. (1995). Plasticity in the growth of Mayan refugee children living in the United States. In C. G. N. Mascie-Taylor & B. Bogin (Eds.), *Human variability and plasticity* (pp. 46–74). Cambridge, UK: Cambridge University Press.

Bogle, K. A. (2008). *Hooking up: Sex, dating and relationships on campus*. New York: NYU Press.

Bonczar, T. P. (2003). Prevalence of imprisonment in the U.S. population, 1974–2001. Bureau of Justice Statistics Special Report. Retrieved from www.bjs.gov/content/pub /pdf/piusp01.pdf.

Booth, B. (2015, April 16). How much would you pay to get your kid into Harvard? CNBC. Retrieved from www.cnbc .com/2014/11/10/is-a-college-planner-really-worth-it .html.

Booth, H. (2017). The kingdom of women: The society where a man is never the boss. *The Guardian*. Retrieved from www.theguardian.com/lifeandstyle/2017/apr/01 /the-kingdom-of-women-the-tibetan-tribe-where-a -man-is-never-the-boss.

Bordo, S. (1990). Feminism, postmodernism, and gender skepticism. In L. J. Nicholson (Ed.), *Feminism /postmodernism* (pp. 133–56). New York: Routledge.

Bourdieu, P. (1977). Cultural reproduction and social reproduction. In J. Karabel & A. H. Halsey (Eds.), *Power and ideology in education* (pp. 487–511). New York: Oxford University Press.

Bowen, W. G., & Bok, D. (1998). *The shape of the river: Long-term consequences of considering race in college and university admissions*. Princeton, NJ: Princeton University Press.

Bowles, S., & Gintis, H. (1976). *Schooling in capitalist America: Educational reform and the contradictions of economic life*. New York: Basic Books.

Bozorgmehr, M., et al. (1996). Middle Easterners: A new kind of immigrant. In R. Waldinger & M. Bozorgmehr (Eds.), *Ethnic Los Angeles* (pp. 347–78). New York: Russell Sage Foundation.

Bradberry, L. A. (2016). The effect of religion on candidate preference in the 2008 and 2012 Republican presidential primaries. *PlOS One, 11*(4), e0152037. Retrieved from www .ncbi.nlm.nih.gov/pmc/articles/PMC4820110/.

Bradley, M. B., et al. (1992). *Churches and church membership in the United States, 1990*. Atlanta: Glenmary Research Center.

Brainard, J. (2020). Scientists are drowning in COVID-19 papers. Can new tools keep them afloat? *Science Mag*. Retrieved from www.sciencemag.org/news/2020/05 /scientists-are-drowning-covid-19-papers-can-new -tools-keep-them-afloat.

Brame, R., et al. (2014). Demographic patterns of cumulative arrest prevalence by ages 18 and 23. *Crime and Delinquency, 60*, 471–86.

Brandon, R. (2015, December 1). Mark Zuckerberg and Priscilla Chan to donate 99 percent of their Facebook fortune. The Verge. Retrieved from www.theverge.com /2015/12/1/9831554/mark-zuckerberg-charity-45-billion.

Brandow, M. (2008). *New York's poop scoop law: Dogs, the dirt and due process*. West Lafayette, IN: Purdue University Press.

Brewster, M. E. (2015). Lesbian women and household labor division: A systematic review of scholarly research from 2000 to 2015. *Journal of Lesbian Studies, 21*(1): 47–69.

Bridges, T., & Pascoe, C. J. (2014). Hybrid masculinities: New directions in the sociology of men and masculinities. *Sociology Compass, 8*(3), 246–58.

Briody, D. (2003). *The iron triangle: Inside the secret world of the Carlyle Group.* Hoboken, NJ: Wiley.

Brookings Institution. (2010). 2010 racial and ethnic distributions of 100 largest metropolitan and 2000–2010 change. Retrieved from www.brookings.edu/wp-content /uploads/2016/06/0831_census_race_appendixa.pdf.

Brooks-Gunn, J., et al. (2003). Maternal employment and child cognitive outcomes in the first three years of life: The NICHD study of early child care. *Child Development, 73*(4), 1052–72.

Bromwich, J. E. (2017, August 7). Minnesota governor calls mosque attack a "criminal act of terrorism." *The New York Times.* Retrieved from www.nytimes.com/2017/08/07/us /minnesota-mosque-explosion.html.

Brubaker, R. (1992). *Citizenship and nationhood in France and Germany.* Cambridge, MA: Harvard University Press.

Brückner, H., & Bearman, P. S. (2005). After the promise: The STD consequences of adolescent virginity pledges. *Journal of Adolescent Health, 36,* 271–78.

Bryk, A., et al. (1993). *Catholic schools and the common good.* Cambridge, MA: Harvard University Press.

Buchmann, C., et al. (2006). The growing female advantage in higher education: The role of family background and academic achievement. *American Sociological Review, 71*(4), 515–41.

Budge, S. L., et al. (2013). Anxiety and depression in transgender individuals: The roles of transition status, loss, support, and coping. *Journal of Consulting and Clinical Psychology, 81*(3), 545–57. Retrieved from www .ncbi.nlm.nih.gov/pubmed/23398495.

Bureau of Justice Statistics. (2014). US Correctional population declined by less than 1 percent for the second consecutive year. Retrieved from www.bjs.gov/content /pub/press/cpus13pr.cfm.

Bureau of Justice Statistics. (2019). Prisoners in 2017. Retrieved from https://www.bjs.gov/content/pub/pdf/p17.pdf.

Bureau of Labor Statistics, US Department of Labor. (2007). Working and work-related activities done by men and women in 2007. *American Time Use Survey.* Retrieved from www.bls.gov/tus/current/work.htm#a1.

Bureau of Labor Statistics, US Department of Labor. (2013). Table 19: Persons at work in agricultural and non-agricultural industries by hours of work. Retrieved from www.bls.gov/cps/cpsaat19.htm.

Bureau of Labor Statistics, US Department of Labor. (2014a). Characteristics of minimum wage workers, 2013. Retrieved from www.bls.gov/opub/reports/minimum -wage/archive/minimumwageworkers_2013.pdf.

Bureau of Labor Statistics, US Department of Labor. (2014b). Labor force characteristics by race and ethnicity, 2013. Retrieved from www.bls.gov/cps/cpsrace2013.pdf.

Bureau of Labor Statistics, US Department of Labor. (2014c). Women in the labor force: A databook. Retrieved from www.bls.gov/opub/reports/womens-databook/archive /women-in-the-labor-force-a-databook-2014.pdf.

Bureau of Labor Statistics, US Department of Labor. (2015a). Highlights of women's earnings in 2014. Retrieved from www.bls.gov/opub/reports/cps/highlights-of-womens -earnings-in-2014.pdf.

Bureau of Labor Statistics, US Department of Labor. (2015b). Table 19. Persons at work in agricultural and non-agricultural industries by hours of work. Current Population Survey. Retrieved from www.bls.gov/cps /cpsaat19.htm.

Bureau of Labor Statistics, US Department of Labor. (2016a). Labor force participation rate: Women. Retrieved from https://fred.stlouisfed.org/series/LNS11300002#0.

Bureau of Labor Statistics, US Department of Labor. (2016b). Tables 4–6. Employment characteristics of families— 2015 (News Release, USDL-16-0795). Retrieved from www.bls.gov/news.release/pdf/famee.pdf.

Bureau of Labor Statistics, US Department of Labor. (2016c). Working mothers issue brief. Retrieved from www.dol.gov/wb/resources/WB_WorkingMothers_508 _FinalJune13.pdf.

Bureau of Labor Statistics, US Department of Labor. (2017a, August). Highlights of women's earnings in 2016. Retrieved from www.bls.gov/opub/reports/womens -earnings/2016/pdf/home.pdf.

Bureau of Labor Statistics, US Department of Labor. (2017b). College enrollment and work activity of 2016 high school graduates. Economic news release. Retrieved from www .bls.gov/news.release/hsgec.nr0.htm.

Bureau of Labor Statistics, US Department of Labor. (2017c). Women in the labor force: A databook. Retrieved from www.bls.gov/opub/reports/womens-databook/2017/pdf /home.pdf.

Bureau of Labor Statistics, US Department of Labor. (2017d). Unemployment rates and earnings by educational attainment, 2016. Retrieved from www.bls.gov/emp/ep _chart_001.htm.

Bureau of Labor Statistics, US Department of Labor (2017e, April 19). Employment characteristics of families summary. Retrieved from www.bls.gov/news.release /famee.nr0.htm.

Bureau of Labor Statistics, US Department of Labor. (2017f, April 27). TED: Employment in families with children in 2016. Retrieved from www.bls.gov/opub/ted/2017 /employment-in-families-with-children-in-2016.htm.

Bureau of Labor Statistics, US Department of Labor. (2017g). May 2016 national occupational employment and wage estimates United States. Retrieved from www.bls .gov/oes/2016/may/oes_nat.htm#00-0000.

Bureau of Labor Statistics, US Department of Labor. (2018a). Average hours employed people spent working on days worked by day of week, 2017 annual averages. Retrieved from www.bls.gov/charts/american-time-use/emp-by -ftpt-job-edu-h.htm.

Bureau of Labor Statistics, US Department of Labor. (2018b). CPI inflation calculator. Retrieved from www.bls.gov /data/inflation_calculator.htm.

Bureau of Labor Statistics, US Department of Labor. (2018c, January 9). Union members—2017 [News release]. Retrieved from www.bls.gov/news.release/pdf/union2 .pdf.

Bureau of Labor Statistics, US Department of Labor. (2018d). Women in the labor force: a databook. Retrieved

from https://www.bls.gov/opub/reports/womens
-databook/2018/pdf/home.pdf.

Bureau of Labor Statistics, US Department of Labor. (2019a). BLS Reports: Characteristics of minimum wage workers, 2018. Retrieved from www.bls.gov/opub/reports /minimum-wage/2018/home.htm#:~:text=to%20BLS%20 Reports-,Characteristics%20of%20minimum%20 wage%20workers%2C%202018,wage%20of%20 %247.25%20per%20hour.

Bureau of Labor Statistics, US Department of Labor. (2019b). College enrollment and work activity of recent high school and college graduates summary. Retrieved from www.bls.gov/news.release/hsgec.nr0.htm.

Bureau of Labor Statistics, US Department of Labor. (2019c). Highlights of women's earnings in 2018. Retrieved from www.bls.gov/opub/reports/womens -earnings/2018/pdf/home.pdf.

Bureau of Labor Statistics, US Department of Labor. (2019d). Median usual weekly earnings of men and women, 2010 to 2018. *The Economics Daily*. Retrieved from www.bls .gov/opub/ted/2019/median-usual-weekly-earnings-of -men-and-women-2010-to-2018.htm.

Bureau of Labor Statistics, US Department of Labor. (2019e). Usual weekly earnings of wage and salary workers fourth quarter 2019. Retrieved from www.bls.gov/news .release/pdf/wkyeng.pdf.

Bureau of Labor Statistics, US Department of Labor. (2019f). Women in the labor force: A databook. Report 1084. Retrieved from www.bls.gov/opub/reports/womens -databook/2019/home.htm#:~:text=to%20BLS%20Reports -,Women%20in%20the%20labor%20force%3A%20a%20 databook,of%2060.0%20percent%20in%201999.

Bureau of Labor Statistics, US Department of Labor. (2020a). Average hours employed people spent working on days worked by day of week. Retrieved from www.bls .gov/charts/american-time-use/emp-by-ftpt-job-edu -h.htm.

Bureau of Labor Statistics, US Department of Labor. (2020b). Employment characteristics of families, 2019. Retrieved from www.bls.gov/news.release/pdf/famee.pdf.

Bureau of Labor Statistics, US Department of Labor. (2020c). Highlights of women's earnings in 2018. Retrieved from www.bls.gov/opub/reports/womens -earnings/2018/home.htm#:~:text=to%20BLS%20 Reports-,Highlights%20of%20women's%20 earnings%20in%202018,time%20wage%20and%20 salary%20workers.&text=Since%202004%2C%20 the%20women's%2Dto,80%20to%2083%20percent%20 range.

Bureau of Labor Statistics, US Department of Labor. (2020d). How many workers are employed in sectors directly affected by COVID-19 shutdowns, where do they work, and how much do they earn? Retrieved from www.bls .gov/opub/mlr/2020/article/covid-19-shutdowns.htm.

Bureau of Labor Statistics, US Department of Labor. (2020e). Labor force statistics from the Current Population Survey. Retrieved from https://data.bls.gov/PDQWeb/ln.

Bureau of Labor Statistics, US Department of Labor. (2020f). Labor force statistics from the Current Population Survey: Household data, not seasonally adjusted, A-36. Unemployed persons by age, sex, race, Hispanic or Latino ethnicity, marital status, and duration of employment. Retrieved from www.bls.gov/web/empsit/cpseea36.htm.

Bureau of Labor Statistics, US Department of Labor. (2020g). Labor force statistics from the Current Population Survey. Table 11, Employed persons by detailed occupation, sex, race, and Hispanic or Latino ethnicity. Retrieved from www.bls.gov/cps/cpsaat11.htm.

Bureau of Labor Statistics, US Department of Labor. (2020h). Union members—2019. Retrieved from www.bls .gov/news.release/pdf/union2.pdf.

Bureau of Labor Statistics, US Department of Labor. (n.d.). Consumer price index calculator. Retrieved from http://data.bls.gov/cgi-bin/cpicalc.pl?cost1=1&year1 =1940&year2=2015.

Burt, R. (1992). *Structural holes*. Cambridge, MA: Harvard University Press.

Burton, C. (2014). Suburban student raises $25K in 24 hours for college tuition. ABC Eyewitness News. Retrieved from http://abc7chicago.com/education/suburban-student -raises-$25k-in-24-hours-for-college-tuition/176216.

Butler, J. (2006). *Precarious life: The powers of mourning and violence*. New York: Verso Books.

Cáceres-Delpiano, J. (2006). The impacts of family size on investment in child quality. *The Journal of Human Resources*, 41(4): 738–54.

Calhoun, C. (2002). *Dictionary of the social sciences*. New York: Oxford University Press.

Callan, T., et al. (1993). Resources, deprivation and the measurement of poverty. *Journal of Social Policy*, 22, 141–72.

Cantril, H. (1941). *The psychology of social movements*. New York: Wiley.

Card, D., et al. (2008). Tipping and the dynamics of segregation. *Quarterly Journal of Economics*, 123(1), 177–218.

Carlyle, T. (1971). *Chartism*. In *Selected writings*. A. Shelston (Ed.). Harmondsworth: Penguin Books. (Original work published 1839.)

Carnevale, A. P., et al. (2014). The college payoff: Education, occupations, lifetime earnings. Washington, DC: Georgetown University, Center on Education and the Workforce. Retrieved from https://cew-7632.kxcdn.com /wp-content/uploads/2014/11/collegepayoff-complete .pdf.

Carpiano, R. M., et al. (2006). Social inequality and health: Future directions for the fundamental cause explanation for class differences in health. Paper presented at the Russell Sage Foundation conference Social Class: How Does It Work?, New York.

Carrington, C. (1999). *No place like home: Relationships and family life among lesbians and gay men*. Chicago: University of Chicago Press.

Carson, E. A. (2014). Prisoners in 2013. Washington, DC: US Department of Justice, Bureau of Justice Statistics. Retrieved from www.bjs. gov/content/pub/pdf/p13.pdf.

Case, A., & Deaton, A. (2015). Rising morbidity and mortality in midlife among White non-Hispanic Americans in the 21st century. *Proceedings of the National Academy of Sciences USA*, 112(49), 15078–83. Retrieved from www .pnas.org/content/112/49/15078.full.

Casey, N. (2020). College made them feel equal. The virus exposed how unequal their lives are. *The New York Times*. Retrieved from www.nytimes .com/2020/04/04/us/politics/coronavirus-zoom-college -classes.html.

Centers for Disease Control and Prevention. (2010). Surveillance summaries: Youth risk behavior surveillance. Retrieved from www.cdc.gov/mmwr/pdf/ss/ss5905.pdf.

Centers for Disease Control and Prevention. (2011a). National Survey of Family Growth. 2006–2010. Retrieved from www.cdc.gov/nchs/nsfg.htm.

Centers for Disease Control and Prevention. (2011b). Key statistics from the National Survey of Family Growth, Table 1. Retrieved from www.cdc.gov/nchs/nsfg/key_statistics/a.htm#adoption.

Centers for Disease Control and Prevention. (2011c). National Intimate Partner and Sexual Violence Survey: 2010 summary report. National Center for Injury Prevention and Control, Division of Violence Prevention.

Centers for Disease Control and Prevention. (2011d). Understanding intimate partner violence: Fact sheet 2011. Retrieved from www.cdc.gov/violenceprevention/pdf/ipv_factsheet-a.pdf.

Centers for Disease Control and Prevention. (2012a). Suicide: Facts at a glance. Retrieved from www.cdc.gov/violenceprevention/pdf/suicide-datasheet-a.pdf.

Centers for Disease Control and Prevention. (2012b). Reported cases and deaths from vaccine preventable diseases, United States, 1950–2011. Retrieved from www.cdc.gov/vaccines/pubs/pinkbook/downloads/appendices/g/ases&deaths.pdf.

Centers for Disease Control and Prevention. (2015a). Health, United States, 2014: With special feature on adults aged 55–64. Retrieved from www.cdc.gov/nchs/data/hus/hus14.pdf#016.

Centers for Disease Control and Prevention. (2015b). Understanding literacy & numeracy. Retrieved from www.cdc.gov/healthliteracy/learn/understandingliteracy.html.

Centers for Disease Control and Prevention. (2015c). Reported cases and deaths from vaccine preventable diseases, United States, 1950–2013. Retrieved from www.cdc.gov/vaccines/pubs/pinkbook/downloads/appendices/E/reported-cases.pdf.

Centers for Disease Control and Prevention. (2016a). 1991–2015 high school youth risk behavior survey data. Retrieved from http://nccd.cdc.gov/youthonline.

Centers for Disease Control and Prevention. (2016b). Fact sheet: Today's HIV/AIDS epidemic. Retrieved from www.cdc.gov/nchhstp/newsroom/docs/factsheets/todaysepidemic-508.pdf.

Centers for Disease Control and Prevention. (2017a). Health, United States, 2016: With chartbook on long-term trends in health. Retrieved from www.cdc.gov/nchs/data/hus/hus16.pdf#053.

Centers for Disease Control and Prevention. (2017b). Diagnoses of HIV infection in the United States and dependent areas, 2017. Table 19b. Retrieved from www.cdc.gov/hiv/pdf/library/reports/surveillance/cdc-hiv-surveillance-report-2017- vol-29.pdf.

Centers for Disease Control and Prevention. (2018a). Substance use and sexual risk behaviors among youth. Retrieved from www.cdc.gov/healthyyouth/substance-use/pdf/dash-substance-use-fact-sheet.pdf.

Centers for Disease Control and Prevention. (2018b). Table 4. Life expectancy at birth, at age 65, and at age 75, by sex, race, and Hispanic origin: United States, selected years 1900–2017. Retrieved from www.cdc.gov/nchs/data/hus/2018/004.pdf.

Centers for Disease Control and Prevention. (2018c). Youth risk behavior survey data summary & trends report 2007–2017. Retrieved from www.cdc.gov/healthyyouth/data/yrbs/pdf/trendsreport.pdf.

Centers for Disease Control and Prevention. (2019a). Provisional number of divorces and annulments and rate: United States, 2000-2018. Retrieved from https://www.cdc.gov/nchs/data/dvs/national-marriage-divorce-rates-00-18.pdf.

Centers for Disease Control and Prevention. (2019b). Reproductive health: Infant mortality, 2016. Retrieved from www.cdc.gov/reproductivehealth/maternalinfanthealth/infantmortality.htm.

Centers for Disease Control and Prevention. (2020). Global WASH (water, sanitation, and hygiene) fast facts. Retrieved from www.cdc.gov/healthywater/global/wash_statistics.html#:~:text=Worldwide%2C%20780%20million%20people%20do,world's%20population)%201%2C%203.

Centers for Medicare & Medicaid Services. (2018, January 8). National health expenditure data: Historical. Retrieved from www.cms.gov/Research-Statistics-Data-and-Systems/Statistics-Trends-and-Reports/NationalHealthExpendData/NationalHealthAccountsHistorical.html.

Central Intelligence Agency. (2020). The World Factbook. Retrieved from www.cia.gov/library/publications/the-world-factbook/rankorder/2004rank.html.

Cesarini, D., et al. (2016). Wealth, health, and child development: Evidence from administrative data on Swedish lottery players. Quarterly Journal of Economics, 131(2), 687–738. Retrieved from https://academic.oup.com/qje/article/131/2/687/2606947.

Cesarini, D., et al. (2017). The effect of wealth on individual and household labor supply: Evidence from Swedish lotteries. American Economic Review, 107(12), 3917–46.

Chamie, J. (2016, October 15). 320 million children in single-parent families. Inter Press Service. Retrieved from www.ipsnews.net/2016/10/320-million-children-in-single-parent-families.

Chandra, A., et al. (2005, December). Fertility, family planning, and reproductive health of U.S. women: Data from the 2002 National Survey of Family Growth. Vital and Health Statistics, ser. 23, no. 25. Retrieved from www.cdc.gov/nchs/data/series/sr_23/sr23_025.pdf.

Chase-Lansdale, P. L., et al. (1997). Neighborhood and family influences on the intellectual and behavioral competence of preschool and early school-age children. In J. Brooks-Gunn et al. (Eds.), Neighborhood poverty. Vol. 1 (pp. 79–118). New York: Russell Sage Foundation.

Chase-Lansdale, P. L., et al. (2003). Mothers' transitions from welfare to work and the well-being of preschoolers and adolescents. Science, 299(5612), 1548–52.

Chauncey, G. (1994). Gay New York: Gender, urban culture, and the makings of the gay male world, 1890–1940. New York: Basic Books.

Chaves, M. (2002, summer). Abiding faith. Context Magazine, 1(2).

Chaves, M., & Higgins, L. M. (1992). Comparing the community involvement of Black and White congregations. Journal for the Scientific Study of Religion, 31(4), 425–40.

Chen, D. W. (2004, November 18). $7 billion for the grief of Sept. 11. *The New York Times*. Retrieved from www.nytimes.com/2004/11/18/nyregion/7-billion-for-the-grief-of-sept-11.html.

Chen, Y., et al. (2020). *The roots of health inequality and the value of intra-family expertise*. NBER Working Paper No. 25618.

Cherlin, A. J. (2009). *The marriage-go-round: The state of marriage and the family in America today*. New York: Knopf.

Chetty, R., & Hendren, N. (2015). The impacts of neighborhoods on intergenerational mobility: Childhood exposure effects and county level estimates. Retrieved from www.equality-of-opportunity.org/images/nbhds_paper.pdf.

Chetty, R., Hendren, N., & Katz, L. F. (2015). The effects of exposure to better neighborhoods on children: New evidence from the moving to opportunity experiment. Retrieved from www.equality-of-opportunity.org/images/mto_paper.pdf.

Child Trends Data Bank (2018). Violent crime victimization: Indicators of child and youth well-being. Retrieved from https://www.childtrends.org/indicators/violent-crime-victimization.

Child Trends Data Bank. (2019). Children in poverty: Key facts about children in poverty. Retrieved from www.childtrends.org/indicators/children-in-poverty.

Chirot, D. (1985). The rise of the West. *American Sociological Review*, 50, 181–95.

Chodorow, N. (1978). *Reproduction of mothering: Psychoanalysis and the sociology of gender*. Berkeley: University of California Press.

Chorev, N. (2007). *Remaking U.S. trade policy: From protectionism to globalization*. Ithaca, NY: Cornell University Press.

Chua, A. L. (1998). Markets, democracy, and ethnicity: Toward a new paradigm for law and development. *Yale Law Journal*, 108(1), 1–107.

City of Detroit. (2019). The next step: Detroit aims to be free of residential blight by the end of 2024. Retrieved from https://detroitmi.gov/news/next-step-detroit-aims-be-free-residential-blight-end-2024.

Clark, A. (2005, January 7). Frequent flyer miles soar above sterling. *The Guardian*. Retrieved from www.theguardian.com/money/2005/jan/08/business.theairlineindustry.

Clark, G. (2014). *The son also rises: Surnames and the history of social mobility*. Princeton, NJ: Princeton University Press.

Clement, J. (2020). Internet usage penetration among adults in the US 2009–2019. *Statista*. Retrieved from www.statista.com/statistics/185700/percentage-of-adult-internet-users-in-the-united-states-since-2000.

Clifton, R. A., et al. (1986). Effects of ethnicity and sex on teachers' expectations of junior high school students. *Sociology of Education*, 59(1), 58–67.

Cloward, R., & Ohlin, L. (1960). *Delinquency and opportunity*. New York: Free Press.

Cohen, P. N. (2017). Families are changing—And staying the same. *Educational Leadership*, 75(1), 46–50. Retrieved from www.terpconnect.umd.edu/~pnc/EdLead17.pdf.

Colby, S. L., & Ortman, J. M. (2015, March). Projections of the size and composition of the U.S. population: 2014–2060. *Current Population Reports*. Retrieved from www.census.gov/content/dam/Census/library/publications/2015/demo/p25-1143.pdf.

Coleman, J., & Hoffer, T. (1987). *Public and private high schools*. New York: Basic Books.

Coleman, J., et al. (1966). *Equality of educational opportunity*. Washington, DC: US Government Printing Office.

Coleman, J., et al. (1982). *High school achievement: Public, Catholic and private schools compared*. New York: Basic Books.

College Board. (2018). Average published undergraduate charges by sector and by Carnegie classification, 2017–18. Retrieved from https://trends.collegeboard.org/college-pricing/figures-tables/average-published-undergraduate-charges-sector-2017-18.

Collier, J., et al. (1997). Is there a family? New anthropological views. In R. N. Lancaster & M. di Lionardo (Eds.), *The gender/sexuality reader: Culture, history, political economy* (pp. 71–81). New York: Routledge.

Collins, P. H. (1990). Work, family, and Black women's oppression. In *Black feminist thought: Knowledge, consciousness and the politics of empowerment* (pp. 45–68). New York: Routledge.

Collins, R. (1971). Functional and conflict theories of educational stratification. *American Sociological Review*, 36(6), 1002–19.

Collins, R. (1979). *The credential society: A historical sociology of education and stratification*. New York: Academic Press.

Conger, R., et al. (1992). A family process model of economic hardship and adjustment of early adolescent boys. *Child Development*, 63, 526–41.

Conger, R., et al. (1994). Economic stress, coercive family process and developmental problems of adolescence. *Child Development*, 65, 541–61.

Congressional Budget Office. (1977). Long-term care for the elderly and disabled. Retrieved from www.cbo.gov/publication/19669.

Conley, D. (1999). *Being Black, living in the red: Race, wealth, and social policy in America*. Berkeley: University of California Press.

Conley, D. (2001). Capital for college: Parental assets and postsecondary schooling. *Sociology of Education*, 74, 59–72.

Conley, D. (2004). *The pecking order: Which siblings succeed and why*. New York: Pantheon Books.

Conley, D. (2009a, October 8). Interview with Mitchell Duneier. New York.

Conley, D. (2009b, October 8). Interview with Duncan Watts. New York.

Conley, D. (2009c, August 8). Interview with C. J. Pascoe. 104th Annual Meeting of the American Sociological Association. San Francisco.

Conley, D. (2009d, August 8). Interview with Paula England. 104th Annual Meeting of the American Sociological Association. San Francisco.

Conley, D. (2009e, August 9). Interview with Victor Rios. 104th Annual Meeting of the American Sociological Association. San Francisco.

Conley, D. (2009f, October 8). Interview with Devah Pager. New York.

Conley, D. (2009g, October 8). Interview with Jeffrey Sachs. New York.

Conley, D. (2009h, August 9). Interview with Michael Hout. 104th Annual Meeting of the American Sociological Association. San Francisco.

Conley, D. (2009i, August 9). Interview with Jen'nan Read. 104th Annual Meeting of the American Sociological Association. San Francisco.

Conley, D. (2009j, August 9). Interview with Jennifer Lee. 104th Annual Meeting of the American Sociological Association. San Francisco.

Conley, D. (2009k, August 8). Interview with Andrew Cherlin. 104th Annual Meeting of the American Sociological Association. San Francisco.

Conley, D. (2009l, August 8). Interview with Stephen Morgan. 104th Annual Meeting of the American Sociological Association. San Francisco.

Conley, D. (2009m, August 9). Interview with Frances Fox Piven. 104th Annual Meeting of the American Sociological Association. San Francisco.

Conley, D. (2009n, October 8). Interview with Alondra Nelson. New York.

Conley, D. (2009o, August 8). Interview with John Evans. 104th Annual Meeting of the American Sociological Association. San Francisco.

Conley, D. (2009p, August 8). Interview with Doug McAdam. 104th Annual Meeting of the American Sociological Association. San Francisco.

Conley, D. (2010, January). Interview with Kate Rich. E-mail.

Conley, D. (2011a, August 21). Interview with Allison Pugh. 106th Annual Meeting of the American Sociological Association. Las Vegas, NV.

Conley, D. (2011b, August 21). Interview with Annette Lareau. 106th Annual Meeting of the American Sociological Association. Las Vegas, NV.

Conley, D. (2011c, August 21). Interview with David Grusky. 106th Annual Meeting of the American Sociological Association. Las Vegas, NV.

Conley, D. (2011d, August 21). Interview with Shamus Khan. 106th Annual Meeting of the American Sociological Association. Las Vegas, NV.

Conley, D. (2011e, August 21). Interview with Nitsan Chorev. 106th Annual Meeting of the American Sociological Association. Las Vegas, NV.

Conley, D. (2013a, August 12). Interview with Julia Adams. 108th Annual Meeting of the American Sociological Association. New York.

Conley, D. (2013b, August 12). Interview with Michael Gaddis. 108th Annual Meeting of the American Sociological Association. New York.

Conley, D. (2013c, August 12). Interview with Ashley Mears. 108th Annual Meeting of the American Sociological Association. New York.

Conley, D. (2013d, August 12). Interview with Mario Luis Small. 108th Annual Meeting of the American Sociological Association. New York.

Conley, D. (2013e, August 12). Interview with Matthew Desmond. 108th Annual Meeting of the American Sociological Association. New York.

Conley, D. (2013f, August 12). Interview with Robb Willer. 108th Annual Meeting of the American Sociological Association. New York.

Conley, D. (2013g, August 12). Interview with Susan Crawford. 108th Annual Meeting of the American Sociological Association. New York.

Conley, D. (2014a, October 1). Interview with danah boyd. New York.

Conley, D. (2014b, November 19). Interview with Shamus Khan. New York.

Conley, D. (2014c, September 17). Interview with Fadi Haddad. New York.

Conley, D. (2014d, September 24). Interview with Marc Ramirez. New York.

Conley, D. (2014e, November 5). Interview with Amos Mac. New York.

Conley, D. (2014f, November 26). Interview with Delores Malaspina. New York.

Conley, D. (2014g, October 8). Interview with Adeel Qalbani. New York.

Conley, D. (2014h, October 22). Interview with Andy Bichlbaum. New York.

Conley, D. (2015a, February 25). Interview with Asha Rangappa. New York.

Conley, D. (2015b, February 2). Interview with Jennifer Senior. New York.

Conley, D. (2015c, March 5). Interview with Adam Davidson. New York.

Conley, D. (2015d, February 4). Interview with Jennifer Jacquet. New York.

Conley, D. (2015e, April 8). Interview with Zephyr Teachout. New York.

Conley, D. (2015f, March 9). Interview with Stephen Duncombe. New York.

Conley, D. (2019a, August 10). Interview with Stacey Torres. New York.

Conley, D. (2019b, August 10). Interview with Jacqueline Stevens. New York.

Conley, D. (2019c, August 10). Interview with Kevin Lewis. New York.

Conley, D. (2019d, August 10). Interview with Corey Abramson. New York.

Conley, D. (2019e, August 10). Interview with Tamara Pavasović Trošt. New York.

Conley, D. (2020a, July 23). Interview with Morgan Levine. New York.

Conley, D. (2020b, July 23). Interview with Daniel Belsky. New York.

Conley, D. (2020c, August 11). Interview with Maria Abascal. New York.

Conley, D., & Bennett, N. G. (2000). Is biology destiny? Birth weight and life chances. *American Sociological Review, 65*(3), 458–67.

Conley, D., & Glauber, R. (2006). Parental educational investment and children's academic risk: Estimates of the impact of sibship size and birth order from exogenous variation in fertility. *Journal of Human Resources, 41*(4), 722–37.

Conley, D., & Heerwig, J. (2011). The war at home: Effects of Vietnam-era military service on postwar household stability. *American Economic Review, 101*(3), 350–54.

Conley, D., & Rauscher, E. (2013, December). The effect of daughters on partisanship and social attitudes toward women. *Sociological Forum, 28*(4), 700–718.

Conley, D., et al. (2003). *The starting gate: Birth weight and life chances.* Berkeley: University of California Press.

Conley, D., et al. (2007). *Africa's lagging demographic transition: Evidence from exogenous impacts of malaria ecology and agricultural technology* (NBER Working Paper No. 12892). National Bureau of Economic Research.

Connell, C. (2010). Doing, undoing, or redoing gender? Learning from the workplace experiences of transpeople. *Gender & Society, 24*(1), 31–55.

Connell, R. (1987). *Gender and power.* Stanford, CA: Stanford University Press.

Cookson, P. W., Jr., & Persell, C. H. (1985). *Preparing for power.* New York: Basic Books.

Cooley, C. H. (1909). *Social organization: A study of the larger mind.* New York: Scribner's.

Cooley, C. H. (1922). *Human nature and the social order.* New York: Scribner's. (Original work published 1902.)

Coolidge, C. (2011, September 16). Christian goods big seller for Wal-Mart. *ABC News.* Retrieved from http://abcnews.go.com/Business/story?id=86290&page=1#.Tt-3dXPZuoA.

Coontz, S. (Ed.). (2001). *Historical perspectives on family diversity. Shifting the center: Understanding contemporary families.* Mountain View, CA: Mayfield.

Coontz, S. (2010). How to make it work this time. *The New York Times,* Room for Debate section. Retrieved from www.nytimes.com/roomfordebate/2010/12/19/why-remarry/how-to-make-a-second-marriage-work.

Copen, C. E., et al. (2013, April 4). First premarital cohabitation in the United States: 2006–2010 National Survey of Family Growth. *National Health Statistics Reports, 64.* Retrieved from www.cdc.gov/nchs/data/nhsr/nhsr064.pdf.

Corman, H., & Mocan, N. (2005). Carrots, sticks, and broken windows. *The Journal of Law and Economics, 48*(1), 235–66.

Cornell, S. (1988). *The return of the native: American Indian political resurgence.* New York: Oxford University Press.

Cornell, S., & Hartmann, D. (1998). Fixed or fluid? Alternative views of ethnicity and race. In *Ethnicity and race: Making identities in a changing world* (pp. 39–71). Thousand Oaks, CA: Pine Forge Press.

Coser, L. A. (1957). Social conflict and the theory of social change. *British Journal of Sociology, 8*(3), 197–207.

Costello, E. J., et al. (2003). Relationships between poverty and psychopathology: A natural experiment. *Journal of the American Medical Association, 290,* 2023–29.

Council on American-Islamic Relations. (2017). Civil rights data quarter two update: Anti-Muslim bias incidents April–June 2017. Retrieved from www.cair.com/images/pdf/Civil-Rights-Data-Quarter-Two-Update-Anti-Muslim-Bias-Incidents-April--June-2017.pdf.

Covenant House. (n.d.). Sleep out to end youth homelessness. Retrieved from www.covenanthouse.org/helping-homeless/sleep-out.

Covert, B. (2011, March 8). Prepare for a possible "womancession." *National Public Radio.* Retrieved from www.npr.org/2011/03/08/134357162/the-nation-prepare-for-a-possible-womancession.

The COVID Tracking Project. (2020). COVID-19 is affecting people of color the most. We're tracking the data in real time. *The Atlantic.* Retrieved from https://covidtracking.com/race.

Cowan, R. S. (1983). *More work for mother: The ironies of household technology from the open hearth to the microwave.* New York: Basic Books.

Cox, D., & Jones, R. P. (2017). America's changing religious identity. Public Religion Research Institute. Retrieved from www.prri.org/research/american-religious-landscape-christian-religiously-unaffiliated.

Credit Suisse Research Institute. (2017, November). Global wealth databook 2017. Retrieved from http://publications.credit-suisse.com/tasks/render/file/index.cfm?fileid=FB790DB0-C175-0E07-787A2B8639253D5A.

Credit Suisse Research Institute. (2019). Global wealth report 2019. Retrieved from www.credit-suisse.com/media/assets/corporate/docs/about-us/research/publications/global-wealth-report-2019-en.pdf.

Croucher, K., & Wendelin, R. (2007). Inclusivity in teaching practice and the curriculum. *Guides for Teaching and Learning in Archaeology, 6.* Retrieved from www.heacademy.ac.uk/system/files/number6_teaching_and_learning_guide_inclusivity.pdf.

Crouse, J., & Trusheim, D. (1988). The case against the SAT. *Public Interest, 93,* 97–110.

Currie, D. H. (1999). *Girl talk: Adolescent magazines and their readers.* Toronto: University of Toronto Press.

Dahrendorft, R. (1958). Toward a theory of social conflict. *Journal of Conflict Resolution, 2*(2), 170–83.

Dart, J. (2001, February 28). Hues in the pews: Racially mixed churches an elusive goal. *Christian Century.* Retrieved from http://hirr.hartsem.edu/cong/articles_huesinthepews.html.

David, E. (2015). Purple-collar labor: Transgender workers and queer value at global call centers in the Philippines. *Gender & Society, 29*(2), 169–94.

Davidson, J. D., et al. (1995). Persistence and change in the Protestant establishment, 1930–1992. *Social Forces, 74*(1), 157–75.

Davis, F. J. (1991). *Who is Black? One nation's definition.* University Park: Pennsylvania State University Press.

Davis, G. (2015). *Contesting intersex: The dubious diagnosis.* New York: NYU Press.

Davis, G. F. (2003). American cronyism: How executive networks inflated the corporate bubble. *Contexts, 2*(3), 34–40.

Davis, K. (1940). Extreme social isolation of a child. *American Journal of Sociology, 45,* 554–65.

Davis, K., & Moore, W. E. (1945). Some principles of stratification. *American Sociological Review, 10*(2), 242–49.

Davis, L. (2011). Race, gender, and class at a crossroads: A survey of their intersection in employment, economics, and the law. *Journal of Gender, Race & Justice, 14*(2).

Dawkins, R. (2006). *The God delusion.* Boston: Houghton Mifflin.

Death Penalty Information Center. (2015). Innocence: List of people freed from death row. Retrieved from www.deathpenaltyinfo.org/innocence-list-those-freed-death-row.

Death Penalty Information Center. (2017). Execution list 2016. Retrieved from https://deathpenaltyinfo.org/execution-list-2016.

Death Penalty Information Center. (2018a). Execution list 2017. Retrieved from https://deathpenaltyinfo.org/execution-list-2017.

Death Penalty Information Center. (2018b). Facts about the death penalty. Retrieved from https://deathpenaltyinfo.org/documents/FactSheet.pdf.

Death Penalty Information Center. (2018c). Innocence and the death penalty. Retrieved from https://deathpenaltyinfo.org/innocence-and-death-penalty#race.

Death Penalty Information Center. (2020a). Executions by race and race of victim. Retrieved from https://deathpenaltyinfo.org/executions/executions-overview/executions-by-race-and-race-of-victim.

Death Penalty Information Center (2020b). Exonerations by race. Retrieved from https://deathpenaltyinfo.org/policy-issues/innocence/exonerations-by-race.

Death Penalty Information Center. (2020c). Innocence Database. Retrieved from https://deathpenaltyinfo.org/policy-issues/innocence-database.

DeLamater, J. (2012). Sexual expression in later life: A review and synthesis. *Journal of Sex Research, 49*(2–3), 125–41.

DellaCava, F. A., et al. (2004). Adoption in the U.S.: The emergence of a social movement. *Journal of Sociology and Social Welfare, 31*(4), 141–60.

DeNeve, C. (1997, winter). Hispanic presence in the workplace. *The Diversity Factor,* 14–21.

DeParle, J. (2004). *American dream: Three women, ten kids and a nation's drive to end welfare.* New York: Viking.

Desmond, M. (2016). *Evicted: Poverty and profit in the American city.* New York: Crown.

De Vos, G., & Wagatsuma, H. (1966). *Japan's invisible race: Caste in culture and personality.* Berkeley: University of California Press.

Dill, J. S., et al. (2016). Does the "glass escalator" compensate for the devaluation of care work occupations? The careers of men in low- and middle-skill health care jobs. *Gender & Society, 30*(2), 334–60.

Dillon, M., & Wink, P. (2003). Religiousness and spirituality: Trajectories and vital involvement in late adulthood. In M. Dillon (Ed.), *Handbook of the sociology of religion* (pp. 179–89). Cambridge, UK: Cambridge University Press.

DiMaggio, P. J., & Powell, W. (1983). The iron cage revisited: Institutional isomorphism and collective rationality in organizational fields. *American Sociological Review, 48,* 149.

Dinnerstein, L., et al. (1996). *Natives and strangers: A multicultural history of Americans.* New York: Oxford University Press.

Dodge, M. (2019). A black box warning: The marginalization of white-collar crime victimization. *Journal of White Collar and Corporate Crime, 1,* 24–33.

Doran, K. M., et al. (2013, December 19). Housing as health care—New York's boundary-crossing experiment. *New England Journal of Medicine, 369,* 2374–77.

Doucouliagos, C., & Laroche, P. (2003). What do unions do to productivity? A meta-analysis. *Industrial Relations, 42*(4).

Dove. (2005). *Real women have real curves.* Retrieved from www.campaignforrealbeauty.com/flat3.asp?id=2287&src=InsideCampaign_firming.

Doward, J. (2009, August 8). "Racist bias" blamed for disparity in police DNA database. *The Guardian.* Retrieved from www.theguardian.com/politics/2009/aug/09/police-dna-database-black-children.

Downey, D. B. (1995). When bigger is not better: Family size, resources, and children's educational performance. *American Sociological Review, 60*(5), 746–61.

Doyle, D. H. (1977). The social functions of voluntary associations in a nineteenth-century American town. *Social Science History, 1*(3), 333–55.

DPA. (2013, May 16). Palestinian smugglers deliver KFC to Gaza. *Haaretz.* Israel. Retrieved from www.haaretz.com/news/middle-east/palestinian-smugglers-deliver-kfc-to-gaza-1.524370.

Drape, J. (2005, October 30). Increasingly, football's playbooks call for prayers. *The New York Times.* Retrieved from www.nytimes.com/2005/10/30/sports/football/increasingly-footballs-playbooks-call-for-prayer.html.

Du Bois, W. E. B. (1903). *The souls of Black folk.* Paris: McClurg.

Duncan, G. (2016, December 19). When a basic income matters most. Economic Security Project. Retrieved from https://medium.com/economicsecproj/when-a-basic-income-matters-most-d90d093458a3.

Duncan, G., et al. (1994). Economic deprivation and early childhood development. *Child Development, 65*(2), 296–318.

Duncan, G. J., et al. (2005). Peer effects in drug use and sex among college students. *Journal of Abnormal Child Psychology, 33*(3), 375–85. Retrieved from www.gse.uci.edu/person/duncan_g/docs/11peerdrugs.pdf.

Duneier, M. (1999). *Sidewalk.* New York: Farrar Straus & Giroux.

Durante, R., et al. (2019). The political legacy of entertainment TV. *American Economic Review, 109,* 2497–530. Retrieved from https://pubs.aeaweb.org/doi/pdfplus/10.1257/aer.20150958.

Durkheim, É. (1951). *Suicide: A study in sociology* (G. Simpson & J. A. Spaulding, Trans.). New York: Free Press. (Original work published 1897.)

Durkheim, É. (1972). The forced division of labor. In A. Giddens (Ed.), *Selected writings* (p. 181). Cambridge, UK: Cambridge University Press. (Original work published 1893.)

Durkheim, É. (1995). *The elementary forms of religious life* (K. E. Fields, Intro. & Trans.). New York: Free Press. (Original work published 1917.)

Durkheim, É. (1997). *The division of labor in society* (L. A. Coser, Intro.; W. D. Halls, Trans.). New York: Free Press. (Original work published 1893.)

Duvall, M. L. (1991). *Feeding the family: The social organization of caring as gendered work.* Chicago: University of Chicago Press.

Dyer, G. (1985). *War.* New York: Crown.

Easterly, W., & Levine, R. (2002). *Tropics, germs, and crops: How endowments influence economic development* (NBER Working Paper No. W9106). National Bureau of Economic Research.

Eck, D. L. (2006). From diversity to pluralism. In *On common ground: World religions in America* [CD-ROM]. Cambridge, MA: The Pluralism Project.

Economist, The (2018a, February 3). All must have degrees: Going to university is more important than ever for young people. Retrieved from www.economist.com/news/international/21736151-financial-returns-are-falling-going-university-more-important-ever.

Economist, The. (2018b, January 10). The youth of today: Teenagers are better behaved and less hedonistic nowadays. Retrieved from www.economist.com/international/2018/01/10/teenagers-are-better-behaved-and-less-hedonistic-nowadays.

Edgell, P., et al. (2006). Atheists as "other": Moral boundaries and cultural membership in American society. *American Sociological Review, 71*(2), 211–34.

Edgerton, R. (1995). "Bowling alone": An interview with Robert Putnam about America's collapsing civic life. *American Association for Higher Education Bulletin, 48*(1).

Edin, K., & Lein, L. (1997). *Making ends meet: How single mothers survive welfare and low-wage work.* New York: Russell Sage Foundation.

Edwards, B., & McCarthy, J. D. (2004). Resources and social movement mobilization. In David A. Snow, Sarah A. Soule, and Hanspeter Kriesi (Eds.), *The Blackwell companion to social movements* (pp. 116–52). Malden, MA: Blackwell Publishing.

Ehrenreich, B. (2001). *Nickel and dimed: On (not) getting by in America.* New York: Metropolitan Books.

Ehrenreich, B., & Hochschild, A. R. (Eds.). (2004). *Global woman: Nannies, maids and sex workers in the global economy.* New York: Macmillan Holt.

Eisenberg, D., et al. (2013, November). Peer effects on risky behaviors: New evidence from college roommate assignments. *Journal of Health Economics, 33,* 126–38.

Eisenbrey, R. (2007, June 20). *Strong unions, strong productivity: Snapshot for June 20.* Economic Policy Institute. Retrieved from www.epi.org/content.cfm /webfeatures_snapshots_20070620.

Elder, G., et al. (1995). Linking family hardship to children's lives. *Child Development, 56,* 361–75.

Elders, M. J., et al. (2017, June). Re-thinking genital surgeries on intersex infants. Palm Center Report. Retrieved from www.palmcenter.org/wp-content/uploads/2017/06/Re -Thinking-Genital-Surgeries-1.pdf.

Ellen, B. (2014). Paid housework? No one'll clean up from that idea. *The Guardian.* Retrieved from www.theguardian .com/commentisfree/2014/mar/08/paying-for -housework-domestic-women-men.

Engels, F. (1878, May–July). Herrn Eugen Dühring's Umwälzung des Sozialismus in the supplement to *Vorwärts.*

Entwisle, D. R., & Alexander, K. L. (1992, February). Summer setback: Race, poverty, school composition, and mathematics achievement in the first two years of school. *American Sociological Review, 57*(1), 72–84.

Environmental Performance Index. (2018). 2018 EPI results. Retrieved from https://epi.envirocenter.yale.edu/epi -topline?country=&order=field_epi_rank_new&sort=asc.

Epistemological modesty: An interview with Peter Berger. (1997, October 29). *The Christian Century.* Retrieved from www.christiancentury.org/article /epistemological-modesty.

Epstein, C. F. (1988). *Deceptive distinctions: Sex, gender, and the social order.* New Haven, CT: Yale University Press.

Eriksen, S., & Jensen, V. (2006). All in the family? Family environment factors in sibling violence. *Journal of Family Violence, 21*(8), 497–507.

Erikson, E. H., & Erikson, J. M. (1998). *The life cycle completed: Extended version.* New York: Norton.

Erikson, K. (2005). *Wayward Puritans: A study in the sociology of deviance* (rev. ed.). Boston: Pearson/Allyn & Bacon. (Original work published 1966.)

Eskenazi, B., et al. (2002). The association of age and semen quality in healthy men. *Human Reproduction, 18*(2), 447–54.

Espejo, E. P., et al. (2006). Stress sensitization and adolescent depressive severity as a function of childhood adversity: A link to anxiety disorders. *Journal of Abnormal Child Psychology, 35,* 287–99.

Espenshade, T. J., & Chung, C. Y. (2005). The opportunity cost of admission preferences at elite universities. *Social Science Quarterly, 86*(2), 293–305.

Espenshade, T. J., et al. (2004). Admission preferences for minority students, athletes, and legacies at elite universities. *Social Science Quarterly, 85*(5), 1422–46.

Essman, E. (2007). The American people: Social classes. *Life in the USA: The complete guide for immigrants and Americans.* Retrieved from www.lifeintheusa.com /people/socialclasses.htm.

Estabrook, B. (2009, March). Politics of the plate: The price of tomatoes. *Gourmet.* Retrieved from http:// politicsoftheplate.com/wp-content/uploads/2009/11 /tomatoes.pdf.

Evans, J. (2002). *Playing God? Human genetic engineering and the rationalization of public bioethical debate.* Chicago: University of Chicago Press.

Eyerman, R. (2001). *Cultural trauma: Slavery and the formation of African American identity.* Cambridge, UK: Cambridge University Press.

Fadiman, A. (1997). *The spirit catches you and you fall down: A Hmong child, her American doctors, and the collision of two cultures.* New York: Farrar, Straus, & Giroux.

Fagan, J., et al. (2003, March 31). Reciprocal effects of crime and incarceration in New York City neighborhoods. *Fordham Urban Law Journal, 30,* 1551–602.

Falk, A. (2005, June 30). Mom sells face space for tattoo advertisement. *Deseret News.* Retrieved from www .deseretnews.com/article/600145187/Mom-sells-face -space-for-tattoo-advertisement.html?pg=all.

Farmer, P. (1999). *Infections and inequalities: The modern plagues.* Berkeley: University of California Press.

Farmer, P. (2011). *Haiti after the earthquake.* New York: PublicAffairs.

Faruqee, H., & Mühleisen, M. (2003). Population aging in Japan: Demographic shock and fiscal sustainability. *Japan and the world economy, 15*(2), 185–210.

Faughnder, R. (2016, March 26). Faith-based films are building followings at the box office. *Los Angeles Times.* Retrieved from www.latimes.com/entertainment /envelope/cotown/la-et-ct-faith-based-movies-20160325 -story.html.

Fausto-Sterling, A. (2000). *Sexing the body: Gender politics and the construction of sexuality* (1st ed.). New York: Basic Books.

Federal Bureau of Investigation. (2003). *Facts and figures 2003.* Retrieved from www.fbi.gov/libref/factsfigure/wcc.htm.

Federal Bureau of Investigation. (2014a). Financial crimes report to the public: Fiscal years 2010–2011. Retrieved from www.fbi.gov/stats-services/publications /financial-crimes-report-2010-2011.

Federal Bureau of Investigation. (2014b). Crime in the United States 2013: Property crime, tables 1 and 23. Retrieved from www.fbi.gov/about-us/cjis/ucr/crime-in-the-u.s /2013/crime-in-the-u.s.-2013/property-crime/property -crime-topic-page/propertycrimemain_final.

Federal Bureau of Investigation. (2015). 2014 crime in the United States: Table 1. Retrieved from www.fbi.gov /about-us/cjis/ucr/crime-in-the-u.s/2014/crime-in-the -u.s.-2014/tables/table-1.

Federal Bureau of Investigation. (2017). 2016 crime in the United States: Table 11. Retrieved from https://ucr.fbi.gov

/crime-in-the.u.s/2016/crime-in-the-u.s.-2016/tables
/table-11.

Federal Bureau of Investigation. (2018a). Uniform crime
report: Crime in the United States, 2018. Retrieved from
https://ucr.fbi.gov/crime-in-the-u.s/2018/crime-in-the
-u.s.-2018/topic-pages/property-crime.

Federal Bureau of Investigation. (2018b). Crime in the United
States: Table 1, volume and rate per 100,000 inhabitants,
1999–2018. Retrieved from https://ucr.fbi.gov/crime-in
-the-u.s/2018/crime-in-the-u.s.-2018/tables/table-1.

Federal Interagency Forum on Aging-Related Statistics.
(2008). *Older Americans update 2008: key indicators of
well-being.* Washington, DC: US Government Printing
Office.

Federal Reserve Bank of St. Louis. (2018, August 30).
Personal saving rate. Retrieved from https://fred
.stlouisfed.org/series/PSAVERT.

Federal Reserve Board. (2018). *Report on the economic well-
being of US households in 2017.* Retrieved from www
.federalreserve.gov/publications/files/2017-report
-economic-well-being-us-households-201805.pdf.

Ferber, A. L. (1999). *White man falling: Race, gender, and White
supremacy.* Lanham, MD: Rowman & Littlefield.

Ferran, L. (2009, December 31). Megachurch asks for nearly
$1M in 48 hours: Pastor Rick Warren of Saddleback
Church asks members for $900,000 before New Year.
Good Morning America. ABC News. Retrieved from
http://abcnews.go.com/GMA/church-asks-mil-48-hours
/story?id=9455589.

Fetter, J. H. (1995). *Questions and admissions: Reflections on
100,000 admissions decisions at Stanford.* Stanford, CA:
Stanford University Press.

Figlio, D. N. (2005). *Boys named Sue: Disruptive children and
their peers* (NBER Working Paper No. W11277). National
Bureau of Economic Research. Retrieved from http://palm
.nber.org/papers/w11277.

Figlio, D. N. (2007, September). Boys named Sue: Disruptive
children and their peers. *Education Finance and Policy, 2*(4),
376–94.

Fillinger, K. (2013). Megachurches by the numbers. *Christian
Standard.* Retrieved from http://christianstandard.com
/2013/05/megachurches-by-the-numbers.

Fink, S., et al. (2006). Mammalian monogamy is not
controlled by a single gene. *Proceedings of the National
Academy of Sciences USA, 103*(20), 10956–60. Retrieved
from www.pnas.org/content/103/29/10956.

Finke, R., & Stark, R. (1992). *The churching of America,
1776–1990: Winners and losers in our religious economy.*
New Brunswick, NJ: Rutgers University Press.

Finn, J. D., et al. (2005). Small classes in the early grades,
academic achievement, and graduating from high school.
Journal of Educational Psychology, 97(2), 214–23.

Fischer, C., & Hout, M. (2006). How Americans prayed:
Religious diversity and change. In C. Fischer & M. Hout
(Eds.), *A century of difference: How America changed in the
last one hundred years* (pp. 186–211). New York: Russell
Sage Foundation.

Fischer, C. S., et al. (1996). *Inequality by design: Cracking the
bell curve myth.* Princeton, NJ: Princeton University Press.

Fischer, P. M., et al. (1991, December). Brand logo recognition
by children aged 3 to 6 years: Mickey Mouse and Old Joe
the Camel. *Journal of the American Medical Association,
266,* 3145–48.

Fisher, D. R., et al. (2017). Intersectionality takes it to the
streets: Mobilizing across diverse interests for the
Women's March. *Science Advances, 3*(9), eaao1390.

Flora, C. (2013). *Friendfluence: The surprising ways friends make
us who we are.* New York: Anchor Books.

Foer, J. S. (2009). *Eating animals.* New York: Little, Brown.

Folbre, N. (1987). *A field guide to the U.S. economy.* New York:
Pantheon Books.

Forbes. (2018). Profile: Bill Gates. Retrieved from www.forbes
.com/profile/bill-gates.

Forbes. (2020). Profile: Bill Gates. Retrieved from https://www
.forbes.com/profile/bill-gates/#b084484689f0.

Ford, H., & Crowther, S. (1973). *My life and work, by Henry
Ford.* New York: Arno Books. (Original work published
1922.)

Fordham, S., & Ogbu, J. (1986). Black students' school
success: Coping with the "burden of acting White." *Urban
Review, 18,* 176–206.

Foss, R. J. (1994). The demise of homosexual exclusion: New
possibilities for gay and lesbian immigration. *Harvard
Civil Rights–Civil Liberties Law Review, 29,* 439–75.

Foster, D. (2006, February 19). Mind over splatter. *The New
York Times.* Retrieved from www.nytimes.com/2006/02
/19/opinion/mind-over-splatter.html.

Foucault, M. (1977). *Discipline and punish: The birth of the
prison.* New York: Pantheon Books.

Foucault, M. (1978). *The history of sexuality.* New York:
Pantheon Books.

Foucault, M. (1980). *Power/knowledge: Selected interviews and
other writings, 1972–1977.* C. Gordon (Ed.). New York:
Pantheon Books.

Fox News. (2017, May 10). Top 13 highest grossing faith films.
Retrieved from www.foxnews.com/entertainment/2017
/05/10/top-13-highest-grossing-faith-films.html.

Francis, D. R. (2005, November). Changing work behavior of
married women. *NBER Digest.* Retrieved from www.nber
.org/digest/nov05/w11230.html.

Frank, R. H. (2007). *Falling behind: How rising inequality
harms the middle class.* Berkeley: University of California
Press.

Franklin, J. H. (1980). *From slavery to freedom* (5th ed.). New
York: Knopf.

Frederick, C. (2010). A crosswalk for using pre-2000
occupational status and prestige codes with post-2000
occupation codes. Center for Demography and Ecology,
University of Wisconsin–Madison. Data files retrieved
from www.ssc.wisc.edu/cde/cdewp/OccCodes.zip.

Fredrickson, G. M. (2002). *Racism: A short history.* Princeton,
NJ: Princeton University Press.

Freedman, J. O. (2003). *Liberal education and the public interest.*
Iowa City: University of Iowa Press.

Freeman, C. E. (2004, November 19). *Trends in educational
equity of girls and women: 2004* (NCES 2005-016). US
Department of Education, National Center for Education
Statistics. Washington, DC: US Government Printing
Office. Retrieved from http://nces.ed.gov/pubsearch
/pubsinfo.asp?pubid=2005016.

Freeman, R. B. (2007, February 22). *Do workers still want
unions? More than ever* (Briefing Paper No. 182). Economic
Policy Institute, Agenda for Shared Prosperity. Retrieved
from www.sharedprosperity.org/bp182.html.

Friedan, B. (1997). *The feminine mystique.* New York: Norton.
(Original work published 1963.)

Friedman, M. (1970, September 13). A Friedman doctrine—
The social responsibility of business is to increase its
profits. *The New York Times Magazine*. Retrieved from
http://select.nytimes.com/gst/abstract.html?res=F10F11
FB3E5810718EDDAA0994D1405B808BF1D3&scp=1&sq
=The+social+responsibility+of+business+is+to+increase
+its+profits&st=p.

Frye, M. (1983). *The politics of reality: Essays in feminist theory.*
Berkeley, CA: Crossing Press.

Fryer, R. G., Jr. (2010, August 10). *Racial inequality in the 21st
century: The declining significance of discrimination* (NBER
Working Paper No. 16256). National Bureau of Economic
Research. Retrieved from www.nber.org/papers/w16256.

Fuchs, V. (1967). Redefining poverty and redistributing
income. *Public Interest, 8,* 88–95.

Gamm, G., & Putnam, R. D. (1999). The growth of voluntary
associations in America, 1840–1940. Patterns of social
capital: Stability and change in comparative perspective,
Part II. *Journal of Interdisciplinary History, 29*(4), 511–57.

Gamoran, A., & Mare, R. D. (1989). Secondary school
tracking and educational inequality: Compensation,
reinforcement or neutrality? *American Journal of Sociology,
94*(5), 1146–86.

Ganna, A., et al. (2019). Large-scale GWAS reveals insights
into the genetic architecture of same-sex sexual
behavior. *Science, 365*(6456), eaat7693.

Gans, H. (1979a). *Deciding what's news: A study of* CBS
Evening News, NBC Nightly News, Newsweek *and* Time.
New York: Vintage.

Gans, H. (1979b). Symbolic ethnicity: The future of ethnic
groups and cultures in America. *Ethnic and Racial Studies,
2,* 1–19.

Ganz, M. (2004). Why David sometimes wins:
Strategic capacity in social movements.
In J. Goodwin & J. M. Jasper (Eds.), *Rethinking social
movements: Structure, meaning, and emotion* (pp. 177–98).
Lanham, MD: Rowman & Littlefield.

Gardner, H. (1983). *Frames of mind: The theory of multiple
intelligences.* New York: Basic Books.

Garfinkel, H. (1967). *Studies in ethnomethodology.* Englewood
Cliffs, NJ: Prentice-Hall.

Garrett, J. T. (1994). Health. In M. B. Davis (Ed.), *Native
Americans in the 20th century* (pp. 233–37). New York:
Garland.

Garrow, D. (1968). *Bearing the cross: Martin Luther King, Jr. and
the Southern Christian Leadership Conference—A personal
portrait.* New York: Morrow.

Gately, G. (2005, December 31). A town in the spotlight
wants out of it. *The New York Times.* Retrieved from www
.nytimes.com/2005/12/21/education/a-town-in-the
-spotlight-wants-out-of-it.html.

Gaustad, E. (1962). *Historical atlas of American religion.* New
York: Harper & Row.

Gaventa, J. (1980). *Power and powerlessness: Quiescence and
rebellion in an Appalachian valley.* Urbana: University of
Illinois Press.

Geertz, C. (1973). *The interpretation of cultures.* New York:
Basic Books.

Geiger, A. W. (2017). 5 Facts on how Americans view the Bible
and other religious texts. Pew Research Center. Retrieved
from www.pewresearch.org/fact-tank/2017/04/14/5
-facts-on-how-americans-view-the-bible-and-other
-religious-texts/.

General Social Survey. (2012). General Social Survey 2012
cross-section and panel combined. Association of
Religion Data Archives. Retrieved from www.thearda
.com/Archive/Files/Codebooks/GSS12PAN_CB.asp.

Gerdtham, U. G., & Johannesson, M. (2001). The relationship
between happiness, health, and socio-economic factors:
Results based on Swedish microdata. *The Journal of Socio-
Economics, 30*(6): 553–57.

Gerson, K. (1985). *Hard choices: How women decide about work,
career, and motherhood.* Berkeley: University of California
Press.

Gerson, K. (1993). *No man's land: Men's changing commitments
to family and work.* New York: Basic Books.

Gibson, C., & Jung, K. (2006). Historical census statistics
on the foreign-born population of the United States:
1850 to 2000. US Census Bureau. Retrieved from www
.census.gov/population/www/documentation/twps0081
/twps0081.pdf.

Gieryn, T. F. (1999). *Cultural boundaries of science: Credibility
on the line.* Chicago: University of Chicago Press.

Gilbert, D. (1998). *The American class structure in an age of
growing inequality.* Belmont, CA: Wadsworth.

Gilligan, C. (1982). *In a different voice: Psychological theory
and women's development.* Cambridge, MA: Harvard
University Press.

Gilligan, C. (2009). *In a different voice.* Cambridge, MA:
Harvard University Press.

Glaeser, E. L., & Ward, B. A. (2006). *Myths and realities
of American political geography* (Harvard Institute
of Economic Research Discussion Paper No. 2100).
Retrieved from http://ssrn.com/abstract=874977.

Glass, J., & Jacobs, J. (2005). Childhood religious
conservatism and adult attainment among Black and
White women. *Social Forces, 84,* 555–79.

Glassner, B. (1999). *The culture of fear: Why Americans
are afraid of the wrong things.* New York: Basic
Books.

Glaze, L. E., & Kaeble, D. (2014). Correctional populations
in the United States, 2013. Bureau of Justice
Statistics. Retrieved from www.bjs.gov/index
.cfm?ty=pbdetail&iid=5177.

Glazer, N., & Moynihan, D. P. (1963). *Beyond the melting pot:
The Negroes, Puerto Ricans, Jews, Italians, and Irish of New
York City.* Cambridge, MA: MIT Press.

Glenn, E. N. (1986). *Issei, Nisei, war bride: Three generations of
Japanese American women in domestic service.* Philadelphia:
Temple University Press.

Global Slavery Index. (2016). Global slavery index 2016
report. (3rd ed.). Retrieved from www.globalslaveryindex
.org/download.

Global Slavery Index. (2020). Retrieved from www
.globalslaveryindex.org/2019/findings/executive
-summary/.

Glock, C., & Stark, R. (1965). *Religion and society in tension.*
Chicago: Rand McNally.

Glynn, A. N., & Sen, M. (2015). Identifying judicial empathy:
Does having daughters cause judges to rule for women's
issues? *American Journal of Political Science, 59*(1), 37–54.

Goffman, E. (1959). *The presentation of self in everyday life.*
New York: Doubleday.

Goffman, E. (1961). *Asylums: Essays on the social situation of
mental patients and other inmates.* New York: Doubleday
Anchor.

Goffman, E. (1963). *Stigma: Notes on the management of spoiled identity.* Englewood Cliffs, NJ: Prentice-Hall.

Goldberger, P. (1995, April 20). The gospel of church architecture, revised. *The New York Times,* pp. C1, 5. Retrieved from www.nytimes.com/1995/04/20/garden /the-gospel-of-church-architecture-revised.html?sq =+Megachurches%3A+User-friendly+architecture +&scp=1&st=cse.

Goldman, A. L., et al. (2018). Out-of-pocket spending and premium contributions after implementation of the Affordable Care Act. *JAMA Internal Medicine, 178*(3), 347–55.

Goldman, N., et al. (2017). The best predictors of survival: Do they vary by age, sex, and race? *Population and Development Review, 43*(3), 541–60.

Goodman, B. (2006a, April 17). People stand, the spirit walks: Easter at the Georgia Dome. *The New York Times.* Retrieved from www.nytimes.com/2006/04/17/us /17easter.html.

Goodman, B. (2006b, March 29). Teaching the Bible in Georgia's public schools. *The New York Times.* Retrieved from www.nytimes.com/2006/03/29/education/29bible .html.

Goodnough, A. (2020, February 14). Appeals court rejects Trump Medicaid work requirements in Arkansas. *The New York Times.* Retrieved from www.nytimes .com/2020/02/14/health/medicaid-work-requirements .html.

Goodstein, L. (2005, December 4). Intelligent design might be meeting its maker. *The New York Times.* Retrieved from www.nytimes.com/2005/12/04/weekinreview /intelligent-design-might-be-meeting-its-maker.html.

Goodstein, L. A. (2007, February 25). A divide, and maybe a divorce. *The New York Times,* p. 1. Retrieved from www .nytimes.com/2007/02/25/weekinreview/25goodstein .html.

Goodwin, J. (2006). *No other way out: States and revolutionary movements.* New York: Cambridge University Press.

Gordon, M. M. (1964). *Assimilation in American life: The role of race, religion, and national origins.* New York: Oxford University Press.

Gould, E. (2014). Why America's workers need faster wage growth—And what we can do about it. Economic Policy Institute. Retrieved from www.epi.org/publication /why-americas-workers-need-faster-wage-growth.

Gourevitch, P. (1998). *We wish to inform you that tomorrow we will be killed with our families: Stories from Rwanda.* New York: Farrar, Straus & Giroux.

Gramsci, A. (1971). *Selections from the prison notebooks.* London: Lawrence & Wishart.

Grand View Research. (2016, October 10). Medical billing outsourcing market worth $16.9 billion by 2024. *PR Newswire.* Retrieved from www.prnewswire.com/news -releases/medical-billing-outsourcing-market-worth -169-billion-by-2024-grand-view-research-inc -596501001.html.

Grandey, A., et al. (2005). Must "service with a smile" be stressful? The moderating role of personal control for American and French employees. *Journal of Applied Psychology, 90*(5), 893–904.

Granovetter, M. (1973). The strength of weak ties. *American Journal of Sociology, 78,* 1360–80.

Granovetter, M. (1974). *Getting a job: A study of contacts and careers.* Chicago: University of Chicago Press.

Granovetter, M. (1978). Threshold models of collective behavior. *American Journal of Sociology, 83*(6), 1420–43.

Grant, M. (1936). *The passing of the great race* (4th rev. ed.). New York: Scribner. (Original work published 1916.) Retrieved from www.archive.org/stream /passingofgreatra00granuoft/passingofgreatra00granuoft _djvu.txt.

Graver, B., et al. (2019). CO_2 emissions from commercial aviation, 2018. The International Council on Clean Transportation. Retrieved from https://theicct .org/sites/default/files/publications/ICCT_CO2 -commercl-aviation-2018_20190918.pdf.

Gray, K. F., & Cunnyngham, K. (2017). Trends in Supplemental Nutritional Assistance Program participation rates: Fiscal year 2010 to fiscal year 2015. Retrieved from https://fns-prod.azureedge.net/sites /default/files/ops/Trends2010-2015.pdf.

Gray, N., & Nye, P. S. (2001). American Indian and Alaska Native substance abuse: Co-morbidity and cultural issues. *American Indian and Alaska Native Mental Health Research, 10*(2), 67–84. Retrieved from www.ucdenver .edu/academics/colleges/PublicHealth/research/centers /CAIANH/journal/Documents/Volume%2010/10(2) _Gray_Substance_Abuse_67-84.pdf.

Green, E. L. (2017, December 15). DeVos delays rule on racial disparities in special education. *The New York Times.* Retrieved from www.nytimes.com/2017/12/15/us/politics /devos-obama-special-education-racial-disparities.html.

Greenhouse, S. (2013, July 27). Fighting back against wretched wages. *The New York Times.* Retrieved from www.nytimes.com/2013/07/28/sunday-review/fighting -back-against-wretched-wages.html.

Greenhouse, S. (2014, April 24). In Florida tomato fields, a penny buys progress. *The New York Times.* Retrieved from www.nytimes.com/2014/04/25/business/in-florida -tomato-fields-a-penny-buys-progress.html.

Greer, C. (2006, April). *Black ethnicity: Political attitudes, identity, and participation in New York City.* Institute for Social and Economic Research and Policy, Columbia University. Retrieved from www.iserp.columbia.edu/news/articles /black_ethnicity.html.

Grose, T., & Kallerman, P. (2015). The 1099 economy—Elusive, but diverse, and growing. *Bay Area Economy.* Retrieved from https://medium.com/@BayAreaEconomy/the-1099 -economy-elusive-but-diverse-and-growing-bcc6f65694fe #.t39kzun5w.

Grosz, E. A. (1994). *Volatile bodies: Toward a corporeal feminism.* Bloomington: Indiana University Press.

Gruver, J. (2020). Recession wages: COVID-19 questions & predictions. *Payscale.* Retrieved from www .payscale.com/data/recession-wages.

Guardian, The. (2014, June 9). Computer simulating 13-year-old boy becomes first to pass Turing test. Retrieved from www.theguardian.com/technology/2014/jun/08/super -computer-simulates-13-year-old-boy-passes-turing-test.

Gurian, M., & Stevens, K. (2005). *The minds of boys: Saving our sons from falling behind in school and life.* San Francisco: Jossey-Bass.

Gusfield, J. (1986). *Symbolic crusade: Status politics and the American temperance movement* (2nd ed.). Champaign: University of Illinois Press.

Haber, A. (1966). Poverty budgets: How much is enough? *Asia Pacific Journal of Human Resources, 1*(3), 5–22.

Hacker, J. (2006). *The great risk shift: The assault on American jobs, families, health care and retirement and how you can fight back.* New York: Oxford University Press.

Hackett, C., & McClendon, D. (2017, April 5). Christians remain world's largest religious group, but they are declining in Europe. Retrieved from www.pewresearch.org/fact-tank/2017/04/05/christians-remain-worlds-largest-religious-group-but-they-are-declining-in-europe.

Hacking, I. (1999). *The social construction of what?* Cambridge, MA: Harvard University Press.

Hadaway, K. C., et al. (1993). What the polls don't show: A close look at U.S. church attendance. *American Sociological Review, 58,* 741–52.

Haley, A. (1976). *Roots: The saga of an American family.* New York: Doubleday.

Han, J. (2006). "We are Americans too": A comparative study of the effects of 9/11 on South Asian communities. Cambridge, MA: Discrimination and National Security Initiative, Harvard University. Retrieved from www.pluralism.org/affiliates/kaur_sidhu/We_Are_Americans_Too.pdf.

Haney López, I. F. (1995). White by law. In R. Delgado (Ed.), *Critical race theory: The cutting edge* (pp. 542–50). Philadelphia: Temple University Press.

Hankins, J. D. (2014). *Working skin: Making leather, making a multicultural Japan.* Berkeley: University of California Press.

Hannaford, I. (1996). *Race: The history of an idea in the West.* Washington, DC: Woodrow Wilson Center Press.

Hanson, T. L., et al. (1997). Economic resources, parental practices and children's well-being. In G. Duncan & J. Brooks-Gunn (Eds.), *Consequences of growing up poor* (pp. 190–238). New York: Russell Sage Foundation.

Hanushek, E. A., & Wößmann, L. (2006). Does educational tracking affect performance and inequality? Differences-indifferences evidence across countries. *The Economic Journal, 116*(510), C63–76.

Hanushek, E. A., et al. (1998). *Teachers, schools, and academic achievement* (NBER Working Paper No. 6691). National Bureau of Economic Research.

Hanushek, E. A., et al. (2005). *The market for teacher quality* (NBER Working Paper No. 11154). National Bureau of Economic Research.

Harding, S. (1987). *Feminism and methodology: Social science issues.* Bloomington: Indiana University Press.

Harris, A. R., et al. (2002). Murder and medicine: The lethality of criminal assault, 1960–1999. *Homicide Studies, 6,* 128.

Harris, D. R., & Sim, J. J. (2002, August). Who is multiracial? Assessing the complexity of lived race. *American Sociological Review, 67*(4), 614–27.

Harris, E. A. (2020). "It was just too much": How remote learning is breaking parents. *The New York Times.* Retrieved from www.nytimes.com/2020/04/27/nyregion/coronavirus-homeschooling-parents.html?action=click&module=RelatedLinks&pgtype=Article.

Harris, S. (2006). *Letter to a Christian nation.* New York: Vintage.

Hartmann, H. (1976). Capitalism, patriarchy, and job segregation by sex. *Signs, 1*(2), 137–69.

Hartmann, H. (1981). The unhappy marriage of Marxism and feminism. In L. Sargent (Ed.), *Women and revolution: A discussion of the unhappy marriage between Marxism and feminism* (pp. 1–43). Boston: South End Press.

Hasenfeld, Y., et al. (1987). The welfare state, citizenship, and bureaucratic encounters. *Annual Review of Sociology, 13,* 387–415.

Hashima, P. Y., & Amato, P. R. (1994). Poverty, social support and parental behavior. *Child Development, 65,* 394–403.

Haskell, K. (2004, May 16). Revelation plus make-up advice. *The New York Times.* Retrieved from www.nytimes.com/2004/05/16/weekinreview/ideas-trends-revelation-plus-makeup-advice.html.

Hawley, A. (1968). Human ecology. In D. Sills (Ed.), *International encyclopedia of the social sciences* (pp. 327–37). New York: Macmillan.

Hayford, S. R., & Morgan, P. S. (2008). Religiosity and fertility in the United States: The role of fertility intentions. *Sociological Forces, 86*(3), 1163–88.

Hays, S. (2003). *Flat broke with children: Women in the age of welfare reform.* New York: Oxford University Press.

Heckman, J. J., et al. (2016). Returns to education: The causal effects of education on earnings, health and smoking (NBER Working Paper 2291). National Bureau of Economic Research. Retrieved from www.nber.org/papers/w22291.

Hegewisch, A., & Hartmann, H. (2019). The gender wage gap: 2018. Institute for Women's Policy Research. Retrieved from iwpr.org/wp-content/uploads/2019/03/C478_Gender-Wage-Gap-in-2018.pdf.

Hegewisch, A., & Williams-Baron, E. (2017, September 13). The gender wage gap 2016: Earnings differences by gender, race, and ethnicity. Institute for Women's Policy Research. Retrieved from https://iwpr.org/publications/gender-wage-gap-2016-earnings-differences-gender-race-ethnicity.

Heilbroner, R. L. (1999). *The worldly philosophers.* New York: Simon & Schuster.

Hendi, A. S. (2019). Proximate sources of change in trajectories of first marriage in the United States, 1960–2010. *Demography, 56,* 835–62.

Hendricks, M. (1993, November 10). Is it a boy or a girl? *Johns Hopkins Magazine.*

Henley, J. (2018, January 12). Money for nothing: Is Finland's universal basic income trial too good to be true? *The Guardian.* Retrieved from www.theguardian.com/inequality/2018/jan/12/money-for-nothing-is-finlands-universal-basic-income-trial-too-good-to-be-true.

Henwood, B. F., et al. (2012). Substance abuse recovery after experiencing homelessness and mental illness. *Journal of Dual Diagnosis, 8*(3), 238–46.

Henwood, B. F., et al. (2013, December). Permanent supportive housing: Addressing homelessness and health disparities? *American Journal of Public Health, 103*(S2), S188–92.

Herbert, W. (2011, June 7). Virginity and promiscuity: Evidence for the very first time. Association for Psychological Science. Retrieved from www.psychologicalscience.org/index.php/news/full-frontal-psychology/virginity-and-promiscuity-evidence-for-the-very-first-time.html.

Herdt, G. H. (1981). *Guardians of the flutes: Idioms of masculinity.* New York: McGraw-Hill.

Hernandez, D. J., et al. (2007, April). *Children in immigrant families in the U.S. and 50 states: National origins, language, and early education* (Research Brief Series Publication #2007–11). Albany, NY: Child Trends and the Center for Social and Demographic Analysis, SUNY.

Herring, C., & Henderson, L. (2016). Wealth inequality in Black and White: Cultural and structural sources of the racial wealth gap. *Race and Social Problems, 8*, 4–17.

Herrnstein, R. J., & Murray, C. (1994). *The bell curve: Intelligence and class structure in American life*. New York: Free Press.

Hetherington, E. M., & Kelly, J. (2002). *For better or for worse: Divorce reconsidered*. New York: Norton.

Heyrman, C. L. (1997). *Southern cross: The beginnings of the Bible Belt*. New York: Knopf.

HHS. (2020). US federal poverty guidelines used to determine financial eligibility for certain federal programs. Retrieved from https://aspe.hhs.gov/poverty -guidelines.

Hitchens, C. (2007). *God is not great: How religion poisons everything*. New York: Twelve Books.

Ho, M. K. (1987). *Family therapy with ethnic minorities*. Newbury Park, CA: Sage.

Ho, V. (2009, March 12). Native American death rates soar as most people are living longer. *Seattlepi.com*. Seattle. Retrieved from www.seattlepi.com/local/403196_tribes12 .html.

Hobbes, T. (1981). *Leviathan*. New York: Penguin Books. (Original work published 1651.)

Hochschild, A. R. (1983). *The managed heart: Commercialization of human feeling*. Berkeley: University of California Press.

Hochschild, A. R. (1989). *The second shift: Working parents and the revolution at home*. New York: Viking.

Hochschild, A. R. (1997). *The time bind: When work becomes home and home becomes work*. New York: Metropolitan Books.

Hochschild, A. R. (2003). *The commercialization of intimate life: Notes from home and work*. Berkeley: University of California Press.

Hodkinson, P. (2002). *Goth: identity, style and subculture*. New York: Berg.

hooks, b. (1984). Black women: Shaping feminist theory and feminism: A movement to end sexist oppression and the significance of the feminist movement. In *Feminist theory from margin to center* (pp. 1–17). Boston: South End Press.

Horowitz, J., et al. (2017, March 23). Americans widely support paid family and medical leave, but differ over specific policies. Pew Research Center. Retrieved from www.pewsocialtrends.org/2017/03/23/americans-widely -support-paid-family-and-medical-leave-but-differ -over-specific-policies.

Horwitz, A. V., & Wakefield, J. C. (2007). *The loss of sadness: How psychiatry transformed normal sorrow into depressive disorder*. New York: Oxford University Press.

Hosseini, B. (2018, February 3). Ethiopia bans foreign adoption. CNN. Retrieved from www.cnn.com/2018/01 /11/africa/ethiopia-foreign-adoption-ban/index.html.

Hout, M. (1983). *Mobility tables: Quantitative applications in the social sciences*. Beverly Hills, CA: Sage.

Howe, L. K. (1977). *Pink collar workers: Inside the world of women's work*. New York: Putnam.

Howes, C., & Olenick, M. (1986). Family and child influences on toddlers' compliance. *Child Development, 26*, 292–303.

Howes, C., & Stewart, P. (1987). Child's play with adults, toys, and peers: An examination of family and child care influences. *Developmental Psychology, 23*, 423–30.

Hoxby, C. (2000, August). *Peer effects in the classroom: Learning from gender and race variation* (NBER Working Paper No. 7867). National Bureau of Economic Research.

Hsin, A. (2009). Parent's time with children: Does time matter for children's cognitive achievement? *Social Indicators Research, 93*(1), 123–26.

Human Rights Watch. (2006). Building towers, cheating workers. Retrieved from www.hrw.org/sites/default/files /reports/uae1106webwcover.pdf.

Humphries, J. E., et al. (2019). Does eviction cause poverty? Quasi-experimental evidence from Cook County, IL (No. w26139). National Bureau of Economic Research.

Hurley, D. (2005, April 19). The divorce rate: It's not as high as you think. *The New York Times*. Retrieved from www.nytimes.com/2005/04/19/health/19divo .html?scp=1&sq=&st=cse.

Hurtado, A. (1995). Variations, combinations, and evolutions: Latino families in the United States. In R. E. Zambrana (Ed.), *Understanding Latino families: Scholarship, policy, and practice* (pp. 40–61). Thousand Oaks, CA: Sage.

Iannaccone, L. R. (1997). Skewness explained: A rational choice model of religious giving. *Journal of the Scientific Study of Religion, 36*, 141–57.

Iannoccone, L. R., et al. (1995). Religious resources and church growth. *Social Forces, 74*, 705–31.

Ichihara, M. (2006). Making the case for soft power. *SAIS Review, 26*(1), 197–200.

Idler, E. L. & Benyamini, Y. (1997). Self-rated health and mortality: A review of twenty-seven community studies. *Journal of Health and Social Behavior, 38*(1), 21–27.

Ikeda, H. (2001). Buraku students and cultural identity: The case of a Japanese minority. In K. Shimahara (Ed.), *Ethnicity, race, and nationality in education: A global perspective* (pp. 81–100). Mahwah, NJ: Erlbaum.

Imbens, G. W., et al. (2001). Estimating the effect of unearned income on labor earnings, savings, and consumption: Evidence from a survey of lottery players. *American Economic Review, 91*(4), 778–94.

Inglehart, R., & Baker, W. (2000, February). Modernization, cultural change and the persistence of traditional values. *American Sociological Review, 65*(1), 19–51.

International Bottled Water Association. (2013, April 25). US consumption of bottled water shows continued growth, increasing 6.2 percent in 2012; sales up 6.7 percent. Retrieved from www.bottledwater.org/us-consumption -bottled-water-shows-continued-growth-increasing -62-percent-2012-sales-67-percent.

International Bottled Water Association. (2018a). Bottled water market. Retrieved from www.bottledwater.org /economics/bottled-water-market.

International Bottled Water Association. (2018b). Bottled water: 2017 US and international developments and statistics. Retrieved from www.bottledwater.org /public/BMC2017_BWR_StatsArticle.pdf.

Intersex Society of North America. (2006). *What's wrong with the way intersex has traditionally been treated?* Retrieved from www.isna.org/faq/concealment.

Isaacs, H. (1975). *Idols of the tribe: Group identity and political change.* New York: Harper & Row.

Jackson, E. (2017, September 30). Re: Have you ever reconsidered being transgender? [Post to Quora.] Retrieved from www.quora.com/Have-you-ever-reconsidered -being-transgender.

Jackson, P. (1968). *Life in classrooms.* New York: Holt, Reinhart, & Winston.

Jacobi, T., & Schweers, D. (2017, April 11). Female Supreme Court justices are interrupted more by male justices and advocates. *Harvard Business Review.* Retrieved from https://hbr.org/2017/04/female-supreme-court-justices -are-interrupted-more-by-male-justices-and-advocates.

Jacobs, J. (1961). *The death and life of great American cities.* New York: Random House.

Jacobs, J., & Gerson, K. (2004). *The time divide: Work, family, and gender inequality.* Cambridge, MA: Harvard University Press.

Jacobson, M. F. (1998). Anglo-Saxons and others, 1840–1924. In *Whiteness of a different color: European immigrants and the alchemy of race* (pp. 39–90). Cambridge, MA: Harvard University Press.

Jacquet, J. (2016). *Is shame necessary? New uses for an old tool.* New York: Vintage Books.

James, G. (2003, June 29). Exurbia and God: Megachurches in New Jersey. *The New York Times*, pp. 1, 17. Retrieved from www.nytimes.com/2003/06/29/nyregion/exurbia-and -god-megachurches-in-new-jersey.html.

James, S. A., et al. (1987). Socioeconomic status, John Henryism, and hypertension in Blacks and Whites. *American Journal of Epidemiology, 126,* 664–73.

James, W. (1982). *The varieties of religious experience.* New York: Penguin. (Original work published 1903.)

Jencks, C., & Phillips, M. (Eds.). (1998). *The Black-White test score gap.* Washington, DC: Brookings Institution Press.

Jencks, C., et al. (1972). *Inequality: A reassessment of the effect of family and schooling in America.* New York: Basic Books.

Jenkins, A. (2011). Participation in learning and wellbeing among older adults. *International Journal of Lifelong Education, 30*(3), 403–20. Retrieved from www .tandfonline.com/doi/full/10.1080/02601370.2011 .570876.

Jenkins, D., et al. (2018, April). What we are learning about guided pathways. Community College Research Center. Retrieved from https://ccrc.tc.columbia.edu/publications /what-we-are-learning-guided-pathways.html.

Jenson, A. R. (1969). How much can we boost IQ and scholastic achievement? *Harvard Educational Review, 39,* 1–123.

Johnson, B. D., et al. (2005). The rise and decline of hard drugs, drug markets, and violence in inner city New York. In A. Blumstein (Ed.), *The crime drop in America* (pp. 164–206). Cambridge, UK: Cambridge University Press.

Johnson, E. R., et al. (2016). Extreme weight-control behaviors and suicide risk among high school students. *Journal of School Health, 86*(4), 281–87.

Johnson, L. (1998). Proposal for a nationwide war on the sources of poverty. In P. Halsall (Ed.), *Internet modern history sourcebook.* Retrieved from www.fordham.edu /halsall/mod/1964johnson-warpoverty.htm. (Original speech presented March 16, 1964.)

Johnston, D. C. (2005, June 5). Richest are leaving even the rich far behind. *The New York Times.* Retrieved from www.-nytimes.com/2005/06/05/national /class/HYPER-FINAL.html?scp=1&sq=Richest%20are %20leaving%20even%20the%20rich%20far %20behind&st=cse.

Kaeble, D., & Cowhig, M. (2018). Correctional populations in the United States, 2016. Retrieved from www.bjs .gov/index.cfm?ty=pbdetail&iid=6226.

Kaeble, D., & Glaze, L. (2016). Correctional populations in the United States, 2015. Washington, DC: US Department of Justice, Bureau of Justice Statistics. Retrieved from www.bjs.gov/content/pub/pdf/cpus15.pdf.

Kandel, W. A. (2018, February 9). U.S. family-based immigration policy. Congressional Research Service. Retrieved from https://fas.org/sgp/crs/homesec/R43145.pdf.

Kane, T. J. (1998). Racial and ethnic preferences in college admissions. In C. Jencks & M. Phillips (Eds.), *The Black- White test score gap* (pp. 431–56). Washington, DC: Brookings Institution Press.

Kanno-Youngs, Z. V. (2015, August 5). NCAA members slow to adopt transgender athlete guidelines. *USA Today.* Retrieved from www.usatoday.com/story/sports/college /2015/08/03/ncaa-transgender-athlete-guidelines -keelin-godsey-caitlyn-jenner/31055873.

Kanter, R. M. (1977). *Men and women of the corporation.* New York: Basic Books.

Kaplan, E. A. (2003, October 3–9). Black like I thought I was: Race, DNA, and a man who knows too much. *L. A. Weekly.* Retrieved from www.alternet.org/story.html?StoryID =16917.

Karen, D. (2002, July). Changes in access to higher education in the United States: 1980–1992. *Sociology of Education, 75*(3), 191–210.

Kashef, Z. (2003, February). Persistent peril: Why African American babies have the highest infant mortality rate in the developed world. *RaceWire.* Retrieved from www.arc .org/racewire/030210z_kashef.html.

Kasselstrand, I., et al. (2017). Institutional confidence in the United States: Attitudes of secular Americans. *Secularism and Nonreligion, 6,* 6.

Kelley, D. M. (1972). *Why conservative churches are growing: A study in sociology of religion.* San Francisco: Harper & Row.

Kelling, G. L., & Sousa, W. H., Jr. (2001). Do police matter? An analysis of the impact of New York City's police reforms. *Civic Report, 22.*

Kerr, E., & Powell, F. (2019, September 9). See the average college tuition in 2019–2020. *U.S. News.* Retrieved from www.usnews.com/education/best-colleges/paying-for -college/articles/paying-for-college-infographic.

Kersley, R., & Stierli, M. (2015, October 13). Global wealth in 2015: Underlying trends look good. Credit Suisse. Retrieved from www.credit-suisse.com/us/en/about -us/responsibility/news-stories/articles/news-and -expertise/2015/10/en/global-wealth-in-2015 -underlying-trends-remain-positive.html.

Kessler-Harris, A. (1990). *A woman's wage: Historical meanings and social consequences.* Lexington: University Press of Kentucky.

Khan, S. R. (2010). *Privilege: The making of an adolescent elite at St. Paul's School*. Princeton, NJ: Princeton University Press.

Khandwala, Y. S., et al. (2017). The age of fathers in the USA is rising: An analysis of 168,867,480 births from 1972 to 2015. *Human Reproduction, 32*(10), 2110–16. Retrieved from https://academic.oup.com/humrep/article/32/10/2110/4096427?searchresult=1.

Kidder, T. (2003). *Mountains beyond mountains: Healing the world: The quest of Dr. Paul Farmer*. New York: Random House.

Kilbourne, J. (1979). *Killing us softly: Advertising's image of women* [Motion picture]. Belmont, MA: Cambridge Documentary Films.

Killewald, A. (2013, August). Return to *Being Black, living in the red*: A race gap in wealth that goes beyond social origins. *Demography, 50*(4), 1177–95. Retrieved from http://link.springer.com/article/10.1007/s13524-012-0190-0.

Kim, S. (2001). Hegemony and cultural resistance. In N. J. Smelser & P. B. Baltes (Eds.), *International encyclopedia of the social & behavioral sciences*. New York: Elsevier.

Kimmel, M. S. (1996). *Manhood in America: A cultural history*. New York: Free Press.

Kimmel, M. S. (2000). *The gendered society*. New York: Oxford University Press.

Kinsey, A. C. (1948). *Sexual behavior in the human male*. Philadelphia: Saunders.

Kirkpatrick, D. (2002, June 8). Evangelical sales are converting publishers. *The New York Times*. Retrieved from www.nytimes.com/2002/06/08/books/evangelical-sales-are-converting-publishers.html.

Kitzmiller v. Dover Area School District, 400 F. Supp. 2d 707.

Klebanov, P. K., et al. (1994). Classroom behavior of very low birth weight elementary school children. *Pediatrics, 94*(5), 700–708.

Klein, N. (2000). *No logo: Taking aim at the brand bullies*. New York: Picador.

Klinenberg, E. (2002). *Heat wave: A social autopsy of disaster in Chicago*. Chicago: University of Chicago Press.

Klinenberg, E. (2013). *Going solo: The extraordinary rise and surprising appeal of living alone*. New York: Penguin.

Knafo, S. (2005, December 25). Praise the Lord and raise the curtain. *The New York Times*. Retrieved from www.nytimes.com/2005/12/25/nyregion/thecity/praise-the-lord-and-raise-the-curtain.html.

Knobel, D. T. (1986). *Paddy and the republic: Ethnicity and nationality in antebellum America*. Middletown, CT: Wesleyan University Press.

Kocchar, R. (2020). Unemployment rose higher in three months of COVID-19 than it did in two years of the great recession. Pew Research Center. Retrieved from www.pewresearch.org/fact-tank/2020/06/11/unemployment-rose-higher-in-three-months-of-covid-19-than-it-did-in-two-years-of-the-great-recession/.

Kocchar, R., & Cilluffo, A. (2017). How wealth inequality has changed in the U.S. since the great recession, by race, ethnicity, and income. Pew Research Center. Retrieved from www.pewresearch.org/fact-tank/2017/11/01/how-wealth-inequality-has-changed-in-the-u-s-since-the-great-recession-by-race-ethnicity-and-income.

Koenig, H. G., et al. (1994). Religious practices and alcoholism in a southern adult population. *Hospital Communication Psychiatry, 45*, 225–31.

Kohn, M. L., & Schooler, C. (1983). *Work and personality: An inquiry into the impact of social stratification*. Norwood, NJ: Ablex.

Kozol, J. (1991). *Savage inequalities: Children in America's schools*. New York: Crown.

Kraybill, D. B. (Ed.). (1993). *The Amish and the state*. Baltimore, MD: Johns Hopkins University Press.

Kraybill, D. B., & Nolt, S. (1995). *Amish enterprise: From plows to profits*. Baltimore, MD: Johns Hopkins University Press.

Kreider, R., & Ellis, R. (2011). Number, timing, and duration of marriages and divorces: 2009. Current population reports, US Census Bureau. Retrieved from www.census.gov/prod/2011pubs/p70-125.pdf.

Kremer, M., & Levy, D. (2008). Peer effects and alcohol use among college students. *Journal of Economic Perspectives, 22*(3), 189–206.

Krueger, A. B., & Whitmore, D. M. (2001). The effect of attending a small class in the early grades on college test-taking and middle school test results: Evidence from Project STAR. *Economic Journal, 111*(468), 1–28.

Krueger, A. B., & Zhu, P. (2002). *Another look at the New York City school voucher experiment* (NBER Working Paper No. 9418). National Bureau of Economic Research.

Krugman, P. (2005, September 16). Not the new deal. *The New York Times*. Retrieved from www.nytimes.com/2005/09/16/opinion/not-the-new-deal.html.

Kuhn, T. (1962). *The structure of scientific revolutions*. Chicago: University of Chicago Press.

Kulick, D. (1998). *Travesti: Sex, gender, and culture among Brazilian transgendered prostitutes*. Chicago: University of Chicago Press.

Kuruvil, M. C. (2006, September 3). 9/11: Five years later. Typecasting Muslims as a race. *San Francisco Chronicle*. Retrieved from www.sfgate.com/cgi-bin/article.cgi?f=/c/a/2006/09/03/MNG4FKUMR71.DTL.

Kurzman, C. (2002, December). Bin Laden and other thoroughly modern Muslims. *Contexts Magazine, 1*(4), 13–20.

Laal, M., & Salamati, P. (2012). Lifelong learning: Why do we need it? *Procedia—Social and Behavioral Sciences, 31*, 399–403. Retrieved from www.sciencedirect.com/science/article/pii/S1877042811030023.

Laidley, T., et al. (2019). New evidence of skin color bias and health outcomes using sibling difference models: A research note. *Demography, 56*(2), 753–62.

Lamont, M. (1992). *Money, morals, and manners*. Chicago: University of Chicago Press.

Landau, E. (2012, July 30). Why polio hasn't gone away yet. CNN. Retrieved from www.cnn.com/2012/07/27/health/polio-eradication-efforts/index.html.

Landsbergis, P. A., et al. (2014). Work organization, job insecurity, and occupational health disparities. *American Journal of Industrial Medicine, 57*(5), 495–515.

Langlois, D. E., & Zales, C. R. (1992). Anatomy of a top teacher. *Education Digest, 57*(5), 31–34.

Laqueur, T. (1990). *Making sex: Body and gender from the Greeks to Freud*. Cambridge, MA: Harvard University Press.

Lareau, A. (1987). Social class differences in family-school relationships: The importance of cultural capital. *Sociology of Education, 60,* 33–85.

Lareau, A. (2002). Invisible inequality: Social class and child-rearing in Black families and White families. *American Sociological Review, 67,* 747–76.

Lareau, A. (2003). *Unequal childhoods: Class, race, and family life.* Berkeley: University of California Press.

Lareau, A., et al. (2006, July). *Social class and children's time use* (working paper). College Park: University of Maryland, Department of Sociology.

Lasch, C. (1977). *Haven in a heartless world: The family besieged.* New York: Basic Books.

Lasch, C. (1991). *The true and only heaven: Progress and its critics.* New York: Norton.

Latour, B., & Woolgar, S. (1979). *Laboratory life: The social construction of scientific facts.* Los Angeles: Sage.

Lauten, E. (2018, February 19). State Rep. Steve Hurst introduces bill to teach biblical creationism alongside evolution. *Alabama Today.* Retrieved from http://altoday .com/archives/21486-state-rep-steve-hurst-introduces -bill-to-teach-biblical-creationism-alongside-evolution.

LeBon, G. (2002). *La psychologie des foules.* (*The crowd: A study of the popular mind.*) Mineola, NY: Dover. (Original work published 1895.)

Lee, B., & Conley, D. (2015). Does the gender of offspring affect parental political orientation? *Social Forces, 94*(3), 1103–27.

Lee, F. R. (2006, March 28). "Big Love": Real polygamists look at HBO polygamists and find sex. *The New York Times.* Retrieved from www.nytimes.com/2006/03/28 /arts/television/28poly.html.

Legislative Analyst's Office. (2020). Overview of federal COVID-19 research funding. Retrieved from https://lao .ca.gov/Publications/Report/4230.

Leiter, J. (1983). Classroom composition and achievement gains. *Sociology of Education, 56*(3), 126–32.

Leland, J. (2004, May 16). Alt-worship; Christian cool and the new generation gap. *The New York Times.* Retrieved from www.nytimes.com/2004/05/16/weekinreview /ideas-trends-alt-worship-christian-cool-and-the-new -generation-gap.html.

Lempers, J. D., et al. (1989). Economic hardship, parenting and distress in adolescence. *Child Development, 60,* 25–39.

Lenski, G. (1961). *The religious factor: A sociological study of religion's impact on politics, economics, and family life.* New York: Doubleday.

Leswing, K. (2015). A Yelp-sponsored study says Google is making your search results worse. *Business Insider.* Retrieved from www.businessinsider.com/a-yelp -sponsored-study-says-google-is-making-your-search -results-worse-2015-6.

Levitt, S. D. (2004). Understanding why crime fell in the 1990s: Four factors that explain the decline and six that do not. *Journal of Economic Perspectives, 18*(1), 163–90.

Levitt, S. D., & Dubner, S. J. (2005). *Freakonomics: A rogue economist explores the hidden side of everything.* New York: Morrow.

Lewis, A. E. (2004). *Race in the schoolyard: Negotiating the color line in classrooms and communities.* New Brunswick, NJ: Rutgers University Press.

Lewis, A. E., & Diamond, J. B. (2015). *Despite the best intentions: How racial inequality thrives in good schools.* New York: Oxford University Press.

Lewis, C., et al. (1992). Sex stereotyping of infants: A re-examination. *Journal of Reproductive and Infant Psychology, 10,* 53–61.

Lewis, O. (1966). The culture of poverty. *Scientific American, 215*(4), 19–25.

Lieberson, S. (1961). A societal theory of race and ethnic relations. *American Sociological Review, 26,* 902–10.

Lieberson, S., & Mikelson, K. S. (1995). Distinctive African American names: An experimental, historical, and linguistic analysis of innovation. *American Sociological Review, 60,* 928–46.

Lieberson, S., et al. (2000). The instability of androgynous names: The symbolic maintenance of gender boundaries. *American Journal of Sociology, 105*(5), 1249–87.

Lien, T. (2018, February 19). Uber class-action lawsuit over how drivers were paid gets green light from judge. *The Los Angeles Times.* Retrieved from www.latimes.com /business/technology/la-fi-tn-uber-class-action -20180219-story.html.

Lim, A. (2018, January 6). The alt-right's Asian fetish. *The New York Times.* Retrieved from https://www.nytimes .com/2018/01/06/opinion/sunday/alt-right-asian-fetish .html.

Lindstedt, N. (2017). Shifting frames: Collective action framing from a dialogic and relational perspective. *Sociology Compass, 12*(1). Retrieved from https://doi .org/10.1111/soc4.12548.

Lipka, M. (2015, May 12). 5 key findings about the changing U.S. religious landscape. Pew Research Center. Retrieved from www.pewresearch.org/fact-tank/2015/05/12 /5-key-findings-u-s-religious-landscape.

Liu, E. M., & Zuo, S. X. (2019). Measuring the impact of interaction between children of a matrilineal and a patriarchal culture on gender differences in risk aversion. *PNAS, 116*(14), 6713–19. Retrieved from www .pnas.org/content/116/14/6713.

Liu, L., et al. (2015). Global, regional, and national causes of child mortality in 2000–13, with projections to inform post-2015 priorities: An updated systematic analysis. *Lancet, 385,* 430–40, figure 2.

Liu, Z. (2015). China's carbon emissions report 2015. Harvard University Belfer Center. Retrieved from http://belfercenter.ksg.harvard.edu/publication/25417 /chinas_carbon_emissions_report_2015.html.

Livingston, G. (2015, May 7). Childlessness falls, family size grows among highly educated women. Pew Research Center. Retrieved from www.pewsocialtrends.org/2015 /05/07/childlessness.

Livingston, G. (2018, April 25). The changing profile of unmarried parents. Pew Research Center. Retrieved from www.pewsocialtrends.org/2018/04/25/the -changing-profile-of-unmarried-parents/.

Lleras-Muney, A. (2005). The relationship between education and adult mortality in the United States. *Review of Economic Studies, 72,* 189–221.

Locke, J. (1980). *Second treatise of government.* Indianapolis: Hackett. (Original work published 1690.)

López, G., & Bialik, K. (2017, May 3). Key findings about U.S. immigrants. Pew Research Center. Retrieved from www.pewresearch.org/fact-tank/2017/05/03/key-findings-about-u-s-immigrants.

Lorber, J. (1994). *Paradoxes of gender*. New Haven, CT: Yale University Press.

Lucas, S. R. (1999). *Tracking inequality: Stratification and mobility in American high schools*. New York: Teachers College Press.

Lucas, S. R., & Good, A. D. (2001). Race, class, and tournament track mobility. *Sociology of Education, 74*, 139–56.

Lui, M. (2004). Doubly divided: The racial wealth gap. In C. Collins et al. (Eds.), *The wealth inequality reader*. Cambridge, MA: Economic Affairs Bureau.

Lukes, S., & British Sociological Association. (2005). *Power: A radical view*. New York: Palgrave Macmillan. (Original work published 1974.)

Luo, M. (2006, April 16). Evangelicals debate the meaning of "evangelical." *The New York Times*, pp. 4, 5. Retrieved from www.nytimes.com/2006/04/16/weekinreview/evangelicals-debate-the-meaning-of-evangelical.html.

Mack, J., & Lansley, S. (1985). *Poor Britain*. London: Allen & Unwin.

MacKinnon, C. (1983). Feminism, Marxism, method and the state: Toward feminist jurisprudence. *Signs: Journal of Women in Culture and Society, 8*, 635.

MacLeod, J. (1995). *Ain't no makin' it: Aspirations and attainment in a low-income neighborhood*. Boulder, CO: Westview Press. (Original work published 1987.)

MacMaster, N. (2001). *Racism in Europe 1870–2000*. Basingstoke, Hampshire, UK: Palgrave.

Malinowski, B. (1913). *The family among the Australian Aborigines*. London: University of London Press.

Malmberg, B., et al. (2008). Productivity consequences of workforce aging: Stagnation or Horndal effect? *Population and Development Review, 34*, 238–56.

Maltz, M. D. (2001). *Recidivism*. Orlando, FL: Academic Press. (Original work published 1984.) Retrieved from www.uic.edu/depts/lib/forr/pdf/crimjust/recidivism.pdf.

Manza, J., & Uggen, C. (2006). *Locked out: Felon disenfranchisement and American democracy*. New York: Oxford University Press.

Maraniss, D. (1995). *First in his class: The biography of Bill Clinton*. New York: Simon & Schuster.

Marcin, J. P., et al. (2016). Addressing health disparities in rural communities using telehealth. *Pediatric Research, 79*(1), 169–76.

Marmot, M., & Wilkinson, R. G. (Eds). (1999). *Social determinants of health*. New York: Oxford University Press.

Martin, J. A., & Osterman, M. J. K. (2019). Is twin childbearing on the decline? Twin births in the United States, 2014–2018. National Center for Health Statistics, CDC: Brief No. 351, October 2019. Retrieved from www.cdc.gov/nchs/products/databriefs/db351.htm#section_3.

Martin, J. A., et al. (2010). Births: Final data for 2008. *National Vital Statistics Report, 59*(1). Retrieved from www.cdc.gov/nchs/data/nvsr/nvsr59/nvsr59_01.pdf.

Martin, J. A., et al. (2015). Births: Final data for 2013. *National Vital Statistics Reports, 64*(1). Retrieved from www.cdc.gov/nchs/data/nvsr/nvsr64/nvsr64_01.pdf.

Martin, J. A., et al. (2017). Births: Final data for 2015. *National Vital Statistics Reports, 66*(1). Retrieved from www.cdc.gov/nchs/data/nvsr/nvsr66/nvsr66_01.pdf.

Martin, J. A., et al. (2018). Births: Final data for 2016. *National Vital Statistics Reports, 67*(1). Retrieved from www.cdc.gov/nchs/data/nvsr/nvsr67/nvsr67_01.pdf.

Martin, J. A., et al. (2019). National vital statistics reports: Births, final data for 2018. Retrieved from www.cdc.gov/nchs/data/nvsr/nvsr68/nvsr68_13-508.pdf.

Martin, J. T., & Nguyen, D. H. (2004). Anthropometric analysis of homosexuals and heterosexuals: Implications for early hormone exposure. *Hormones and Behavior, 45*(1), 31–39.

Martineau, H. (1837). *Theory and practice of society in America*. London: Saunders & Otley.

Martineau, H. (1838). *How to observe morals and manners*. London: Charles Knight.

Marx, A. W. (1998). To bind up the nation's wounds: The United States after the Civil War. In *Making race and nation: A comparison of South Africa, the United States, and Brazil* (pp. 120–57). Cambridge, UK: Cambridge University Press.

Marx, K. (1932). Estranged labor. In *Economic and Philosophical Manuscripts of 1844*. Retrieved from www.marxists.org/archive/marx/works/1844/manuscripts/labour.htm. (Original work published 1844.)

Marx, K. (1978). Contribution to the critique of Hegel's philosophy of right: Introduction. In R. Tucker (Ed.), *The Marx-Engels reader* (pp. 53–65). New York: Norton. (Original work pulished 1844.)

Marx, K. (1999). Critique of the Gotha programme. *Marxists internet archive*. Retrieved from www.marxists.org/archive/marx/works/1875/gotha/index.htm. (Original work published 1890–91.)

Marx, K., & Engels, F. (1998). *The Communist manifesto*. New York: Penguin Group. (Original work published 1848.)

Masci, D. (2015). Christianity poised to continue its shift from Europe to Africa. Pew Research Center. Retrieved from www.pewresearch.org/fact-tank/2015/04/07/christianity-is-poised-to-continue-its-southward-march/.

Massey, D. S. (1995). The new immigration and ethnicity in the United States. *Population and Development Review, 21*, 631–52.

Massey, D. S., & Denton, N. A. (1993). *American apartheid: Segregation and the making of the underclass*. Cambridge, MA: Harvard University Press.

Maus, J. (2012). It's the 20th anniversary of critical mass: What it meant to Portland then and now. Bikeportland.org. Retrieved from http://bikeportland.org/2012/09/28/its-the-20th-anniversary-of-critical-mass-what-it-meant-then-and-now-in-portland-78129.

Mayer, S. (1997). *What money can't buy: Family income and children's life chances*. Cambridge, MA: Harvard University Press.

McAdam, D. (1982). *Political process and the development of Black insurgency, 1930–1970*. Chicago: University of Chicago Press.

McBean, A., et al. (2004). Differences in diabetes prevalence, incidence, and mortality among the elderly of four racial/ethnic groups: Whites, Blacks, Hispanics, and Asians. *Diabetes Care, 27*(10), 2317–24.

McCammon, S. (2017). Christian teen magazine "Brio" returns with a "Biblical worldview." NPR. Retrieved from www.npr.org/2017/04/19/524518993/christian-teen-magazine-brio-returns-with-a-biblical-worldview.

McCarthy, J. D., & Zald, M. N. (1973). *The trend of social movements in America: Professionalization and resource mobilization*. Morristown, NJ: General Learning Press.

McCarthy, J. D., & Zald, M. N. (1977). Resource mobilization and social movements: A partial theory. *American Journal of Sociology, 82*(6), 1212–41.

McCullough, M., & Smith, T. (2003). Religion and health: Depressive symptoms and mortality as case studies. In M. Dillon (Ed.), *Handbook of sociology of religion* (pp. 190–206). Cambridge, UK: Cambridge University Press.

McDonald, M. P. (2018). National turnout rates. Retrieved from www.electproject.org/home/voter-turnout/voter-turnout-data.

McDonald, M. P., & Popkin, S. L. (2001). The myth of the vanishing voter. *American Political Science Review, 95*(4), 963–74.

McGrath, L. B. (2019, January 21). Comping White. *Los Angeles Review of Books*. Retrieved from https://lareviewofbooks.org/article/comping-white?fbclid=IwAR3OXzSe2hZnaCOuAnyNNfvoZk5MLn4AJwGlii-MHi335qCj4vLOvYamlCs.

McGregor, P. P. L., & Borooah, V. K. (1992). Is low spending or low income a better indicator of whether or not a household is poor: Some results from the 1985 Family Expenditure Survey. *Journal of Social Policy, 21*(1), 53–69.

McGuire, M. (2007). Embodied practices: Negotiation and resistance. In N. Ammerman (Ed.), *Everyday religion: Observing modern religious lives* (pp. 187–200). New York: Oxford University Press.

McIntosh, P. (1988). *White privilege and male privilege: A personal account of coming to see correspondences through work in women's studies*. Wellesley, MA: Wellesley College Center for Research on Women.

McKenna, P. (2016, December 27). 2016: How Dakota pipeline protest became a Native American cry for justice. *InsideClimate News*. Retrieved from https://insideclimatenews.org/news/22122016/standing-rock-dakota-access-pipeline-native-american-protest-environmental-justice.

McLeod, J. D., & Shanahan, M. J. (1993). Poverty, parenting and children's mental health. *American Sociological Review, 58*, 351–66.

McMillan, C. (2011, July 14). State budget shortfall forces UC fee increase for 2011 [press release]. University of California Office of the President. Retrieved from http://newsroom.ucla.edu/stories/uc-regents-vote-tuition-increase-210662.

Mead, G. H. (1934). *Mind, self, and society from the standpoint of a social behaviorist*. C. W. Morris (Ed.). Chicago: University of Chicago Press.

Mead, M. (1928). *Coming of age in Samoa*. New York: Morrow.

Mechanic, D., & Meyer, S. (2000). Concepts of trust among patients with serious illness. *Social Science and Medicine, 51*(5), 657–68.

Meckler, L. (2002, July 24). Divorce, American style. Study: Certain couples more likely to split up than others. *CBS News*. Retrieved from www.cbsnews.com/stories/2002/07/24/national/main516165.shtml.

Meier, R. F. (1982). Perspectives on the concept of social control. *Annual Review of Sociology, 8*, 35–55.

Meighan, R. (1981). *A sociology of educating*. New York: Holt, Reinhart & Winston.

Melucci, A. (1989). Nomads of the present: Social movements and individual needs in contemporary society. New York: Vintage.

Merton, R. (1938). Social structure and anomie. *American Sociological Review, 3*, 672–82.

Merton, R. (1949a). Discrimination and the American creed. In R. M. MacIver (Ed.), *Discrimination and national welfare; a series of addresses and discussion* (pp. 99–126). New York: Institute for Religious and Social Studies.

Merton, R. (1949b). *Social theory and social structure*. Glencoe, IL: Free Press.

Meyer, D. S. (2007). *The politics of protest: Social movements in America*. New York: Oxford University Press.

Michels, R. (1915). *Political parties: A sociological study of the oligarchical tendencies of modern democracy* (E. Paul & C. Paul, Trans.). New York: Hearst's International Library.

Miele, F. (1995). For whom the bell curve tolls: Interview with Charles Murray. *Skeptic, 3*(2), 34–41. Retrieved from www.prometheism.net/articles/interview01.html.

Milbank, Q. (2005). The compression of morbidity. *The Milbank Quarterly, 83*(4), 801–23.

Milkie, M. A., et al. (2015). Does the amount of time mothers spend with children or adolescents matter? *Journal of Marriage and Family, 77*(2), 355–72.

Milkman, R. (2006). *LA Story: Immigrant workers and the future of the US labor movement*. New York: Russell Sage Foundation.

Milkman, R. (2007). Unions fight for work and family policies. In D. S. Cobble (Ed.), *The sex of class: Women transforming American labor* (pp. 63–80). Ithaca, NY: Cornell University Press.

Miller, C. C. (2015, May 26). When family-friendly policies backfire. *The New York Times*. Retrieved from www.nytimes.com/2015/05/26/upshot/when-family-friendly-policies-backfire.html.

Milloy, C. (2017, August 22). Want to see proof of institutional racism? Let weed open your eyes. *The Washington Post*. Retrieved from www.washingtonpost.com/local/want-to-see-proof-of-institutional-racism-let-weed-open-your-eyes/2017/08/22/099b7740-8751-11e7-a94f-3139abce39f5_story.html?utm_term=.abaaae83946b.

Mills, C. W. (1959). *The sociological imagination*. New York: Oxford University Press.

Mills, C. W. (2000). *The power elite*. New York: Oxford University Press. (Original work published 1956.)

Mishel, L., & Schieder, J. (2017). CEO pay remains high relative to the pay of typical workers and high-wage earners. Economic Policy Institute. Retrieved from www.epi.org/files/pdf/130354.pdf.

Mishel, L., & Shierholz, H. (2013, August 21). *A decade of flat wages: The key barrier to shared prosperity and a rising middle class*. Economic Policy Institute. Retrieved from www.epi.org/publication/a-decade-of-flat-wages-the-key-barrier-to-shared-prosperity-and-a-rising-middle-class.

Mishel, L., & Wolfe, J. (2019, August 14). CEO compensation has grown 940% since 1978. Economic Policy Institute. Retrieved from www.epi.org/publication/ceo-compensation-2018/.

Missouri Economic Research and Information Center. (2018). Cost of living data series: 2017 annual average. Retrieved

from www.missourieconomy.org/indicators/cost_of
_living.

Missouri Economic Research and Information Center. (2020). Cost of living data series. Retrieved from https://meric .mo.gov/data/cost-living-data-series.

Mohamed, B. (2018, January 3). New estimates show U.S. Muslim population continues to grow. Pew Research Center. Retrieved from www.pewresearch.org/fact-tank /2018/01/03/new-estimates-show-u-s-muslim -population-continues-to-grow.

Mohamed, B., & Sciupac, E. P. (2018, January 26). The share of Americans who leave Islam is offset by those who become Muslim. Pew Research Center. Retrieved from www.pewresearch.org/fact-tank/2018/01/26/the-share -of-americans-who-leave-islam-is-offset-by-those -who-become-muslim.

Monaghan, T. (1990, August). The thrill of poverty. *Harpers Magazine*, p. 22.

Montesquieu, C., Baron de. (1899). *The spirit of the laws.* (Vols. 1–2; T. Nugent et al., Trans.). New York: Colonial Press. (Original work published 1748/1750.)

Moore, B. (1993). *Social origins of dictatorship and democracy: Lord and peasant in the making of the modern world.* Boston: Beacon Press. (Original work published 1966.)

Morgan, P. L., et al. (2017). Replicated evidence of racial and ethnic disparities in disability identification in U.S. schools. *Educational Researcher, 46*(6): 305–22.

Morning, A. (2004). *The nature of race: Teaching and learning about human difference.* (Unpublished doctoral dissertation). Department of Sociology, Princeton University, Princeton, NJ.

Morris, A. (1984). *The origins of the civil rights movement.* New York: Free Press.

Morris, A. (2004). Reflections on social movement theory: Criticisms and proposals. In J. Goodwin & J. M. Jasper (Eds.), *Rethinking social movements: Structure, meaning, and emotion* (pp. 233–46). Lanham, MD: Rowman & Littlefield.

Morris, E. W., & Perry, B. L. (2016). The punishment gap: School suspension and racial disparities in achievement. *Social Problems, 63*(1), 68–86. Retrieved from www .researchgate.net/publication/289687063_The _Punishment_Gap_School_Suspension_and_Racial _Disparities_in_Achievement.

Morrison, D. R., & Coiro, M. J. (1999). Parental conflict and marital disruption: Do children benefit when high-conflict marriages are dissolved? *Journal of Marriage and the Family, 61*, 626–37.

Moulds, J. (2020). Gig workers among the hardest hit by coronavirus pandemic. Retrieved from www .weforum.org/agenda/2020/04/gig-workers-hardest-hit -coronavirus-pandemic/.

Moynihan, D. P. (1965). *The Negro family: The case for national action.* Washington, DC: Office of Policy Planning and Research, US Department of Labor.

Mueller, A. S., et al. (2015). Suicide ideation and bullying among US adolescents: Examining the intersections of sexual orientation, gender and race/ethnicity. *American Journal of Public Health, 105*(5), 980–85. Retrieved from https://ajph.aphapublications.org/doi/pdf/10.2105/AJPH .2014.302391.

Muraki, I., et al. (2013, August 29). Fruit consumption and the risk of type 2 diabetes: Results from three prospective longitudinal cohort studies. *British Medical Journal, 347.*

Murnane, R. J., et al. (2005). Learning why more learning takes place in some classrooms than others. *German Economic Review, 6*(3), 309–30.

Murphy, C. (2015). Most Americans believe in heaven . . . and hell. Pew Research Center. Retrieved from www .pewresearch.org/fact-tank/2015/11/10/most-americans -believe-in-heaven-and-hell/.

Murray, C. (1984). *Losing ground: American social policy, 1950–1980.* New York: Basic Books.

Murray, C. (2016). *In our hands: A plan to replace the welfare state.* Lanham, MD: Rowman & Littlefield.

Murray, C. (2020). *Human diversity: The biology of gender, race, and class.* London: Hachette.

Murray, S. (2009, May 9). The curse of the class of 2009. *The Wall Street Journal.* Retrieved from www.wsj .com/articles/SB124181970915002009.

Mustanski, B. S., et al. (2005, March). A genomewide scan of male sexual orientation. *Human Genetics, 116*(4), 272–78. Retrieved from http://mypage.iu.edu/~bmustans /Mustanski_etal_2005.pdf.

Nanda, S. (1999). *Neither man nor woman: The hijras of India* (2nd ed.). New York: Wadsworth.

NASA. (2018). Global temperature: Global land-ocean temperature index, temperature anomalies. Retrieved from https://climate.nasa.gov/vital-signs/global-temperature.

Nash, J. M. (2000, July 31). This rice could save a million kids a year. *Time, 156*(5). Retrieved from http://content.time .com/time/magazine/article/0,9171,997586-6,00.html.

Nason-Clark, N. (2000). Making the sacred safe: Woman abuse and communities of faith. *Sociology of Religion, 61*(4), 349–68.

Natanson, H. (2017, June 5). Harvard rescinds acceptances for at least ten students for obscene memes. *The Harvard Crimson.* Retrieved from www.thecrimson.com/article /2017/6/5/2021-offers-rescinded-memes.

National Academies of Sciences, Engineering, and Medicine. (2018). *Sexual harassment of women: Climate, culture, and consequences in academic sciences, engineering, and medicine.* Washington, DC: The National Academies Press. Retrieved from https://doi.org/10.17226/24994.

National Center for Education Statistics. (2014). Total fall enrollment in degree-granting postsecondary institutions, by attendance status, sex of student, and control of institution: Selected years, 1947 through 2024. Retrieved from https://nces.ed.gov/programs/digest/d14/tables/dt14 _303.10.asp?current=yes.

National Center for Education Statistics. (2017a). Graduation rate from first institution . . . cohort entry years, 1996 through 2009. Table 326.10. Retrieved from https://nces .ed.gov/programs/digest/d16/tables/dt16_326.10.asp?c.

National Center for Education Statistics. (2017b). Total undergraduate fall enrollment in degree-granting postsecondary institutions, by attendance status, sex of student, and control and level of institution: Selected years, 1970 through 2026. Retrieved from https://nces .ed.gov/programs/digest/d16/tables/dt16_303.70 .asp?current=yes.

National Center for Education Statistics. (2018a). The nation's report card: 2015 mathematics & reading assessments. Retrieved from www.nationsreportcard.gov /reading_math_2015/#mathematics?grade=4.

National Center for Education Statistics. (2018b, May). Characteristics of children's families. Retrieved from https://nces.ed.gov/programs/coe/indicator_cce.asp.

National Center for Education Statistics. (2018c). Total fall enrollment in degree-granting postsecondary institutions, by attendance status, sex of student, and control of institution. Retrieved from https://nces.ed.gov/programs/digest/d18/tables/dt18_303.10.asp?referrer=report.

National Center for Education Statistics. (2019a). Characteristics of children's families. Retrieved from https://nces.ed.gov/programs/coe/indicator_cce.asp.

National Center for Education Statistics. (2019b). The condition of education 2019 (NCES 1990–2019): Mathematics performance. Retrieved from https://nces.ed.gov/fastfacts/display.asp?id=514.

National Center for Education Statistics. (2019c). Undergraduate retention and graduation rates. Retrieved from https://nces.ed.gov/programs/coe/indicator_ctr.asp.

National Center for Education Statistics. (2020). Characteristics of children's families. Retrievd from https://nces.ed.gov/programs/coe/indicator_cce.asp#:~:text=The%20poverty%20rate%20for%20children%20under%20age%2018,racial%2Fethnic%20groups%20in%202018.&text=Black%2C%20American%20Indian%2FAlaska%20Native,lower%20than%20the%20national%20average.

National Center for Health Statistics. (2017). National marriage and divorce rates 2000–16. Centers for Disease Control and Prevention, National Vital Statistics System. Retrieved from www.cdc.gov/nchs/data/dvs/national_marriage_divorce_rates_00-16.pdf.

National Center for Science Education. (2019). Creation science bill in Indiana. Retrieved from https://ncse.ngo/creation-science-bill-indiana.

National Institute on Drug Abuse. (2017, September). Overdose death rates. Retrieved from www.drugabuse.gov/related-topics/trends-statistics/overdose-death-rates.

National Opinion Research Center. (2019). Changing attitudes about racial inequality. Retrieved from www.apnorc.org/PDFs/GSS%202018/APNORC_GSS_race_relations_report_2019.pdf.

National Philanthropic Trust. (2018). Charitable giving statistics. Retrieved from www.nptrust.org/philanthropic-resources/charitable-giving-statistics.

Nelson, M. K. (1990). Negotiated care: The experience of family day care providers. Philadelphia: Temple University Press.

Nermoe, K. (2018). Millenials: The "wellness generation." Retrieved from https://news.sanfordhealth.org/sanford-health-plan/millennials-wellness-generation/.

New York State Division of Parole (2007, September). New York State parole handbook (NYSPH). Retrieved from http://parole.state.ny.us/Handbook.pdf.

Nguyen, V. (2017). Fact sheet: Long-term support and services. AARP Public Policy Institute. Retrieved from www.aarp.org/content/dam/aarp/ppi/2017-01/Fact%20Sheet%20Long-Term%20Support%20and%20Services.pdf.

Nicholas, R. W. (1973). Social and political movements. Annual Review of Anthropology, 2, 63–84.

Niebuhr, G. (1995, April 18). The gospels of management. The minister as marketer: Learning from business. The New York Times, p. 1. Retrieved from www.nytimes.com/1995/04/18/us/megachurches-second-article-series-gospels-management-minister-marketer-learning.html.

Niebuhr, H. R. (1929). The social sources of denominationalism. New York: Holt.

Nissle, S., & Bshor, T. (2002). Winning the jackpot and depression: Money cannot buy happiness. International Journal of Psychiatry in Clinical Practice, 6(3), 183–86.

Nussbaum, P. (2006, January 21). A global ministry of "muscular Christianity." The Washington Post. Retrieved from www.washingtonpost.com/wp-dyn/content/article/2006/01/21/AR2006012100284_pf.html.

Nye, B. A., et al. (1994). Small is far better. Research in the Schools, 1(1), 9–20.

Nye, J. (1990). Soft power. Foreign Policy, 80, 153–71.

Oakes, J. (1985). Keeping track: How schools structure inequality. New Haven, CT: Yale University Press.

Oakley, A. (1972). Sex, gender, and society. London: Maurice Temple Smith.

O'Barr, W. (1995). Linguistic evidence: Language, power and strategy in the courtroom. San Diego, CA: Academic Press.

O'Connor, L. (2013, September 21). California universities come up with crazy crowdfunding scholarship idea. Huffington Post. Retrieved from www.huffingtonpost.com/2013/09/20/uc-promise-for-education-_n_3965021.html.

O'Connor, N. (2009, April). Hispanic origin, socio-economic status, and community college enrollment. Journal of Higher Education, 80(2), 121–45.

O'Dea, S. (2020). Smartphone penetration in the United States as share of the population, 2018–2024. Statista. Retrieved from www.statista.com/statistics/201184/percentage-of-mobile-phone-users-who-use-a-smartphone-in-the-us.

Ohtake, F., & Shintani, M. (1996). The effect of demographics on the Japanese housing market. Regional Science and Urban Economics, 26(2), 189–201.

Okahana, H., & Zhou, E. (2017). Graduate enrollment and degrees: 2006 to 2016. Council of Graduate Schools. Retrieved from http://cgsnet.org/ckfinder/userfiles/files/CGS_GED16_Report_Final.pdf.

Oliver, J. E. (1993). Intergenerational transmission of child abuse: Rates, research and clinical implications. American Journal of Psychiatry, 150, 1315–24.

Oliver, M., & Shapiro, T. (1995). Black wealth, White wealth: A new perspective on racial inequality. London: Routledge.

Olson, M. (1965). The logic of collective action. Cambridge, MA: Harvard University Press.

Orfield, G. (1996). Turning back to segregation. In G. Orfield & S. E. Eaton (Eds.), Dismantling desegregation: The quiet reversal of Brown v. Board of Education (pp. 1–22). New York: New Press.

Orfield, G., et al. (2016, May 16). Brown at 62: School segregation by race, poverty and state. Civil Rights Project/Proyecto Derechos Civiles. Retrieved from https://civilrightsproject.ucla.edu/research/k-12-education/integration-and-diversity/brown-at-62-school-segregation-by-race-poverty-and-state/Brown-at-62-final-corrected-2.pdf.

Organisation for Economic Co-operation and Development. (2017, October 26). Table PF2.1A. Summary of paid leave

entitlements available to mothers. Retrieved from www
.oecd.org/els/soc/PF2_1_Parental_leave_systems.pdf.

Organisation for Economic Co-operation and Development.
(2018a). Poverty rate (indicator). Retrieved from
https://data.oecd.org/inequality/poverty-rate.htm.

Organisation for Economic Co-operation and Development.
(2018b). Collective bargaining coverage. Retrieved from
https://stats.oecd.org/Index.aspx?DataSetCode=CBC.

Organisation for Economic Co-operation and Development.
(2019a). Parental leave systems, PF2.1. Retrieved from
www.oecd.org/els/soc/PF2_1_Parental_leave_systems.pdf.

Organisation for Economic Co-operation and Development.
(2019b). Poverty rate. Retrieved from https://data.oecd
.org/inequality/poverty-rate.htm.

Organisation for Economic Co-operation and Development.
(2020). Collective bargaining coverage. Retrieved from
https://stats.oecd.org/Index.aspx?DataSetCode=TUD.

Orr, A. H. (2007). A mission to convert. *The New York
Review of Books*, 54(1). Retrieved from www.nybooks.com
/articles/19775.

Orshansky, M. (1963). *Children of the poor* (Social Security
Bulletin). Washington, DC: US Department of Labor.

Ortner, S. (1974). Is female to male as nature to culture?
In M. Z. Rosaldo & L. Lamphere (Eds.), *Woman, culture,
and society* (pp. 67–88). Stanford, CA: Stanford University
Press.

Oswald, A. J., & Powdthavee, N. (2010). Daughters and left-
wing voting. *The Review of Economics and Statistics*, 92(2),
213–27.

Oyêwùmí, O. (1997). *The invention of women: Making an
African sense of Western gender discourses*. Minneapolis:
University of Minnesota Press.

Padgett, D. K. (2007, May). There's no place like (a) home:
ontological security among persons with serious mental
illness in the United States. *Social Science & Medicine*,
64(9), 1925–36. Retrieved from www.ncbi.nlm.nih.gov
/pubmed/17355900.

Pager, D. (2003). Blacks and ex-cons need not apply. *Contexts*,
2(4), 58–59.

Paik, A., et al. (2016). Broken promises: Abstinence pledging
and sexual and reproductive health. *Journal of Marriage
and Family*, 78(2), 546–61.

Pareto, V. (1983). *The mind and society* (A. Livingston,
Ed.; A. Bongiorno & A. Livingston, Trans.). New York:
AMS Press. (Original work published 1935.)

Pareto, V., & Finer, S. E. (1966). *Sociological writings*. New
York: Praeger Sociology.

Pariser, E. (2011). *The filter bubble: How the new personalized
web is changing what we read and how we think*. New York:
Penguin Press.

Parker, I. (2007, July 30). Our far-flung correspondents:
Swingers. *The New Yorker*. Retrieved from www
.newyorker.com/reporting/2007/07/30/070730fa_fact
_parker.

Parker, K., & Livingston, G. (2018, June 13). 7 facts about
American fathers. Pew Research Center. Retrieved
from www.pewresearch.org/fact-tank/2017/06/15
/fathers-day-facts.

Parkin, F. (1982). *Max Weber*. London: Tavistock.

Parsons, E. F. (2005). Midnight rangers: Costume and
performance in the Reconstruction-era Ku Klux Klan.
Journal of American History, 92(3), 811.

Parsons, T. (1951). *The social system*. Glencoe, IL: Free Press.

Pascoe, C. J. (2007). *Dude, you're a fag: Masculinity and
sexuality in high school*. Berkeley: University of California
Press.

Patillo, M. (2007). *Black on the block: The politics of race and
class in the city*. Chicago: University of Chicago Press.

Payne, C. (2013, August 1). Fertility forecast: Baby bust is
over, births will rise. *USA Today*. Retrieved from www
.usatoday.com/story/news/nation/2013/08/01/usa-total
-fertility-rate/2590781.

PBS. (2000, February 22). Lost tribes of Israel. *Nova*.
Retrieved from www.pbs.org/wgbh/nova/transcripts
/2706israel.html.

Pearson, B. Z. (1993). Predictive validity of the Scholastic
Aptitude Test (SAT) for Hispanic bilingual students.
Hispanic Journal of Behavioral Sciences, 15(3), 342–56.

Penner, J. E., et al. (Eds.). (1999). *Aviation and the global
atmosphere*. Cambridge, UK: Cambridge University Press.
Retrieved from www.ipcc.ch/ipccreports/sres/aviation
/index.php?idp=64.

Perkins, C. (1997). Age patterns of victims of serious violent
crime. Department of Justice, Office of Justice Programs,
Bureau of Justice Statistics. Special Report, NCJ-162031.

Perlman, J., & Parvensky, J. (2006). *Denver Housing First
Collaborative: Cost benefit analysis and program outcomes
report*. Denver: Colorado Coalition for the Homeless.
Retrieved from www.denversroadhome.org/files
/FinalDHFCCostStudy_1.pdf.

Perrow, C. (2007). *The next catastrophe: Reducing our vulnerabilities
to natural, industrial, and terrorist disasters*. Princeton, NJ:
Princeton University Press.

Petrosky, E., et al. (2017). Racial and ethnic differences
in homicides of adult women and the role of intimate
partner violence—United States, 2003–2014. *Morbidity
and Mortality Weekly Report*, 66(28), 741–46.

Pew Forum on Religion and Public Life. (2008, February). US
religious landscape survey: Religious affiliation: Diverse
and dynamic.

Pew Forum on Religion and Public Life. (2011). Global
Christianity—A report on the size and distribution of
the world's Christian population. Retrieved from www
.pewforum.org/2011/12/19/global-christianity-exec.

Pew Forum on Religion and Public Life. (2015). US public
becoming less religious. Retrieved from www.pewforum
.org/2015/11/03/u-s-public-becoming-less-religious.

Pew Research Center. (2011a). Muslim American survey.
Retrieved from www.people-press.org/2011/08/30
/section-1-a-demographic-portrait-of-muslim-americans.

Pew Research Center. (2011b, July 26). Pew Research Center's
social & demographic trends. Wealth gaps rise to record
highs between Whites, Blacks and Hispanics. Retrieved
from http://pewresearch.org/pubs/2069/housing-bubble
-subprime-mortgages-hispanics-blacks-household
-wealth-disparity.

Pew Research Center. (2011c, April 5). Multi-race Americans
and the 2010 Census. Retrieved from www.pewsocialtrends
.org/2011/04/05/multi-race-americans-and-the-2010
-census.

Pew Research Center. (2013). Modern parenthood study: Parental time use table. Retrieved from www.pewresearch.org/data-trend/society-and-demographics/parental-time-use.

Pew Research Center. (2014). Less than half of U.S. kids today live in a "traditional" family. Retrieved from www.pewresearch.org/fact-tank/2014/12/22/less-than-half-of-u-s-kids-live-in-a-traditional-family.

Pew Research Center. (2015a). Christians decline as share of US population; other faiths and the unaffiliated are growing. Retrieved from www.pewforum.org/2015/05/12/americas-changing-religious-landscape/pr_15-05-12_rls-00.

Pew Research Center. (2015b). US public becoming less religious. Retrieved from www.pewforum.org/2015/11/03/u-s-public-becoming-less-religious.

Pew Research Center. (2015c). Future immigration will change the face of America by 2065. Retrieved from http://www.pewresearch.org/fact-tank/2015/10/05/future-immigration-will-change-the-face-of-america-by-2065/.

Pew Research Center. (2017a, February 5). Internet/broadband fact sheet. Retrieved from www.pewinternet.org/fact-sheet/internet-broadband.

Pew Research Center. (2017b). Most people say they have achieved the American dream, or are on their way to achieving it. Retrieved from www.pewresearch.org/fact-tank/2017/10/31/most-think-the-american-dream-is-within-reach-for-them/ft_17-10-31_americandream_demographic.

Pew Research Center. (2017c, June 26). Support for same-sex marriage grows, even among groups that had been skeptical. Retrieved from www.people-press.org/2017/06/26/support-for-same-sex-marriage-grows-even-among-groups-that-had-been-skeptical.

Pew Research Center. (2018a). When Americans say they believe in God, what do they mean? Retrieved from www.pewforum.org/2018/04/25/when-americans-say-they-believe-in-god-what-do-they-mean/.

Pew Research Center. (2018b). Why America's "nones" don't identify with a religion. Retrieved from www.pewresearch.org/fact-tank/2018/08/08/why-americas-nones-dont-identify-with-a-religion/.

Pew Research Center. (2019a, June 12). Internet/broadband fact sheet. Retrieved from www.pewinternet.org/fact-sheet/internet-broadband.

Pew Research Center. (2019b). In US, decline of Christianity continues at rapid pace. Retrieved from www.pewforum.org/2019/10/17/in-u-s-decline-of-christianity-continues-at-rapid-pace/.

Pew Research Center. (2019c). Majority of public favors same-sex marriage, but divisions persist. Retrieved from www.pewresearch.org/politics/2019/05/14/majority-of-public-favors-same-sex-marriage-but-divisions-persist/.

Pew Research Center. (2019d, August 8). The growing partisan divide in views of higher education. Retrieved from www.pewsocialtrends.org/essay/the-growing-partisan-divide-in-views-of-higher-education/psdt_08-19-19_highered-00-08/.

Phelan, C., & Link, B. G. (2005). Controlling disease and creating disparities: A fundamental cause perspective. *Journals of Gerontology, 60B*, 30, 31.

Phillips, D., et al. (1987). Child care quality and children's social development. *Developmental Psychology, 23*, 537–43.

Phillips, M. E., et al. (2015, November 22). Transgender locker room policy eludes school district facing government sanctions under Title IX. Retrieved from www.collegeandprosportlaw.com/uncategorized/transgender-locker-room-policy-eludes-school-district-facing-government-sanctions-under-title-ix.

Picchio, M., & van Ours, J. C. (2013). Retaining through training even for older workers. *Economics of Education Review, 32*, 29–48. Retrieved from www.sciencedirect.com/science/article/abs/pii/S0272775712001100.

Pickert, K. (2014). University of California approves steep tuition hike. *Time*. Retrieved from http://time.com/3598249/university-of-california-tuition-hike/.

Pierce, J. L. (1995). *Gender trials: Emotional lives in contemporary law firms*. Berkeley: University of California Press.

Pierné, G. (2013). Hiring discrimination based on national origin and religious closeness: Results from a field experiment in the Paris area. *IZA Journal of Labor Economics, 2*(4). Retrieved from https://izajole.springeropen.com/articles/10.1186/2193-8997-2-4.

Piketty, T., et al. (2018). Distributional national accounts: Methods and estimates for the United States. *Quarterly Journal of Economics, 133*(2), 553–609.

Pilkington, D. (1996). *Follow the rabbit-proof fence*. St. Lucia, Australia: University of Queensland Press.

Pisetsky, E. M., et al. (2008). Disordered eating and substance abuse in high-school students: Results from the Youth Risk Behavior Surveillance System. *International Journal of Eating Disorders, 41*(5), 464–70.

Piven, F. F., & Cloward, R. A. (1988). *Why Americans don't vote: And why politicians want it that way*. Boston: Beacon Press.

Plan International & PerryUndem Research/Communication. (2018, September 12). The state of gender equality for US adolescents. Retrieved from www.planusa.org/docs/state-of-gender-equality-2018.pdf.

Plath, S. (1971). *The bell jar*. New York: Harper & Row. (Original work published 1963.)

Pollan, M. (2006). *The omnivore's dilemma: A natural history of four meals*. New York: Penguin Press.

Poorman, E. (2018, January 14). Why does America still have so few female doctors? *The Guardian*. Retrieved from www.theguardian.com/commentisfree/2018/jan/14/why-are-there-still-so-few-female-doctors.

Porter, J., & Jick, H. (1980). Addiction rare in patients treated with narcotics. *New England Journal of Medicine, 302*(2), 123.

Portes, A. (1969). Dilemmas of a golden exile: Integration of Cuban refugee families in Milwaukee. *American Sociological Review, 34*, 505–18.

Portes, A., & MacLeod, D. (1996). Educational progress of children of immigrants: The roles of class, ethnicity and school context. *Sociology of Education, 69*(4), 255–75.

Portes, A., & Zhou, M. (1993). The new second generation: Segmented assimilation and its variants. *Annals of the American Academy of Political and Social Science, 530*, 74–96.

Portes, A., et al. (1985). After Mariel: A survey of the resettlement experiences of 1980 Cuban refugees in Miami. *Estudios Cubanos* (Cuban Studies), *15*, 37–59.

Posner, R. A. (1992). *Sex and reason.* Cambridge, MA: Harvard University Press.

Powell, B., & Steelman, L. C. (1990). Beyond sibship size: Sibling density, sex composition, and educational outcomes. *Social Forces, 69*(1), 181–206.

Pratt, L. A., et al. (2011, October). *Antidepressant use in persons aged 12 and over: United States, 2005–2008* (National Center for Health Statistics Data Brief No. 76). Retrieved from www.cdc.gov/nchs/data/databriefs/db76.html.

Pratt, L. A., et al. (2017, August). Antidepressant use among persons aged 12 and over: United States, 2011–2014. National Center for Health Statistics Report 283. Retrieved from www.cdc.gov/nchs/data/databriefs/db283.pdf.

Public Policy Polling. (2011, March 17). Americans support unions over Walker; Sheen for president? Retrieved from www.publicpolicypolling.com/main/2011/03/americans-support-unions-over-walker-sheen-for-president.html.

Putnam, R. D. (2000). *Bowling alone: The collapse and revival of American community.* New York: Simon & Schuster.

Qaim, M., & Zilberman, D. (2003). Yield effects of genetically modified crops in developing countries. *Science, 299,* 900–902.

Qian, Z. (2013, September 11). Divergent paths of American families. US2010 Project. Retrieved from https://s4.ad.brown.edu/Projects/Diversity/Data/Report/report09112013.pdf.

Quadagno, J. (1987). Theories of the welfare state. *Annual Review of Sociology, 13,* 109–28.

Quadagno, J. (1996). *The color of welfare: How racism undermined the war on poverty.* New York: Oxford University Press.

Radway, J. (1987). *Reading the romance: Women, patriarchy, and popular literature.* Chapel Hill: University of North Carolina Press.

Rahman, Q., et al. (2003). Sexual orientation–related differences in prepulse inhibition of the human startle response. *Behavioral Neuroscience, 117*(5), 1096–102.

Rainwater, L. (1974). *What money buys: Inequality and the social meanings of income.* New York: Basic Books.

Ralli, T. (2005, September 5). Who's a looter? In storm's aftermath, pictures kick up a different kind of tempest. *The New York Times.* Retrieved from www.nytimes.com/2005/09/05/business/05caption.html.

Read, J. (2008, February). Muslims in America. Retrieved from http://contexts.org/articles/fall-2008/muslims-in-america.

Reardon, S. F. (2013, May). The widening income achievement gap. *Educational Leadership, 70*(8), 10–16. Retrieved from http://nppsd.fesdev.org/vimages/shared/vnews/stories/525d81ba96ee9/SI%20-%20The%20Widening%20Income%20Achievement%20Gap.pdf.

Reardon, S. F., et al. (2012, August 3). Race, income, and enrollment patterns in highly selective colleges, 1982–2004. Center for Education Policy Analysis, Stanford University. Retrieved from https://cepa.stanford.edu/sites/default/files/race%20income%20%26%20selective%20college%20enrollment%20august%203%202012.pdf.

Reaves, E. L., & Musumeci, M. (2015). Medicaid and long-term services and supports: A primer. KFF. Retrieved from www.kff.org/medicaid/report/medicaid-and-long-term-services-and-supports-a-primer.

Reddy, G. (2005). *With respect to sex: Negotiating hijra identity in South India.* Chicago: University of Chicago Press.

Reimer, S. (2016). It's just a very male industry: Gender and work in UK design agencies. *Gender, Place & Culture, 23*(7), 1033–46.

Reskin, B., & Roos, P. (1990). *Job queues, gender queues.* Philadelphia: Temple University Press.

Reyes, J. W. (2007). Environmental policy as social policy? The impact of childhood lead exposure on crime. *The B.E. Journal of Economic Analysis & Policy, 7*(1).

Rhoades, G. et al. (2009). The pre-engagement cohabitation effect: A replication and extension of previous findings. *Journal of Family Psychology 23*(1): 107–11.

Rich, A. (1980). Compulsory heterosexuality and lesbian existence. *Signs: Journal of Women in Culture and Society, 5,* 631–60.

Ringen, S. (1987). *The possibility of politics.* New York: Oxford University Press.

Rios, V. (2011). *Punished: Policing the lives of Black and Latino boys.* New York: NYU Press.

Risman, B. J. (1998). *Gender vertigo: American families in transition.* New Haven, CT: Yale University Press.

Roberts, S. (2010, January 5). No longer majority Black, Harlem is in transition. *The New York Times.* NY/Region section. Retrieved from www.nytimes.com/2010/01/06/nyregion/06harlem.html.

Rockoff, J. E. (2004). The impact of individual teachers on student achievement: Evidence from panel data. *The American Economic Review, 94*(2), 247–52.

Rodgers, W. M., & Novello, A. (2019). Making the economic case for a $15 minmum wage. The Century Foundation. Retrieved from https://tcf.org/content/commentary/making-economic-case-15-minimum-wage/?agreed=1.

Ronis, S. D., et al. (2017). Urban telemedicine enables equity in access to acute illness care. *Telemedicine and e-Health, 23*(2), 105–12.

Roof, W. C. (1989). Multiple religious switching. *Journal for the Scientific Study of Religion, 28,* 530–35.

Rosaldo, M. Z. (1974). Woman, culture and society: A theoretical overview. In M. Z. Rosaldo & L. Lamphere (Eds.), *Woman, culture, and society* (pp. 17–42). Stanford, CA: Stanford University Press.

Rosenbaum, J. E. (1980). Track misperceptions and frustrated college plans: An analysis of the effects of track perception in the National Longitudinal Survey. *Sociology of Education, 53*(2), 74–88.

Rosenbaum, J. E., with L. S. Rubinowitz. (2000). *Crossing the class and color lines: From public housing to White suburbia.* Chicago: University of Chicago Press.

Rosenfeld, J., & Kleykamp, M. (2009). Hispanics and organized labor. *American Sociological Review, 74*(4), 916–37.

Rosenfeld, M. J., & Roesler, K. (2018). Cohabitation experience and cohabitation's association with marital dissolution. *Journal of Marriage and Family, 81*(1): 42–58.

Rosenhan, D. L. (1973). On being sane in insane places. *Science, 179*, 25–58.

Rosenthal, R., & Jacobson, L. (1968). *Pygmalion in the classroom: Teacher expectation and pupils' intellectual development.* New York: Rinehart & Winston.

Rosenzweig, M. R. (1982). Educational subsidy, agricultural development and fertility change. *Quarterly Journal of Economics, 97*(1), 67–88.

Roser, M., et al. (2019). Child and infant mortality. Retrieved from https://ourworldindata.org/childmortality#:~:text=Globally%203.9%25%20of%20all%20children,rate%20is%20higher%20than%202.5%25.

Rothstein, J. M. (2004). College performance predictions and the SAT. *Journal of Econometrics, 121*(1–2), 297–317.

Rousseau, J.-J. (2004). A dissertation on the origin and foundation of the inequality of mankind. In *Discourse on inequality.* Whitefish, MT: Kessinger Publishing. (Original work published 1754.)

Rowe, J. W., & Kahn, R. L. (1997). Successful aging. *The Gerontologist, 37*(4), 433–40.

Rowntree, B. S. (1910). *Poverty, A study of town life.* London: Macmillan.

Rubin, G. (1975). The traffic in women: Notes on the "political economy" of sex. In R. R. Reiter (Ed.), *Toward an anthropology of women* (pp. 157–210). New York: Monthly Review Press.

Ruggles, P. (1990). *Drawing the line: Alternative poverty measures and their implications for public policy.* Washington, DC: Urban Institute Press.

Ryan, C. L., & Bauman, K. (2016, March). Educational attainment in the United States: 2015. Population characteristics. US Census Bureau. Retrieved from www.census.gov/content/dam/Census/library/publications/2016/demo/p20-578.pdf.

Sacerdote, B. (2001). Peer effects with random assignment: Results for Dartmouth roommates. *Quarterly Journal of Economics, 116.*

Sachs, J. D. (2001). *Macroeconomics and health: Investing in health for economic development.* Report of the Commission on Macroeconomics and Health. Geneva: World Health Organization.

Sadker, D., et al. (2009). *Still failing at fairness: How gender bias cheats girls and boys in school and what we can do about it.* New York: Scribner.

Sadker, M., & Sadker, D. (1994). *Failing at fairness: How America's schools cheat girls.* New York: Touchstone.

Saez, E. (2013). Striking it richer: The evolution of top incomes in the United States. University of California, Berkeley. Retrieved from http://elsa.berkeley.edu/~saez/saez-UStopincomes-2012.pdf.

Saez, E., & Zucman, G. (2016). Wealth inequality in the United States since 1913: Evidence from capitalized income tax data. *Quarterly Journal of Economics, 131*(2), 519–78.

Salai-i-Martin, X. (2002). *The disturbing "rise" of global income inequality* (NBER Working Paper No. 8904). National Bureau of Economic Research. Retrieved from www.nber.org/papers/w8904.

Salganik, M. J., et al. (2006). Experimental study of inequality and unpredictability in an artificial cultural market. *Science, 311*(5762), 854–56.

Samuels, A. (2015). Rachel Dolezal's true lies. *Vanity Fair.* Retrieved from www.vanityfair.com/news/2015/07.

Sanday, P. R. (1990). *Fraternity gang rape: Sex, brotherhood, and privilege on campus.* New York: NYU Press.

Sander, T. H., & Putnam, R. D. (2005, September 10). Sept. 11th as a civics lesson. *The Washington Post,* p. A23. Retrieved from www.washingtonpost.com/wp-dyn/content/article/2005/09/09/AR2005090901821.html.

Sander, T. H., & Putnam, R. D. (2010). Still bowling alone? The post-9/11 split. *Journal of Democracy, 21*(1), 9–16.

Santa Ana, O. (2004). Is there such a thing as Latino identity? *American Family: Journey of Dreams.* Retrieved from www.pbs.org/americanfamily/latino2.html.

Saroyan, S. (2006, April 16). Christianity, the brand. *The New York Times.* Retrieved from www.nytimes.com/2006/04/16/books/christianity-the-brand.html.

Savas, G. (2016). Gender and race differences in American college enrollment: Evidence from the education longitudinal study of 2002. *American Journal of Educational Reseach, 4*(1), 64–75.

Sawyer, K., et al. (2016). Queering the gender binary: Understanding transgender workplace experiences. In T. Kollen (Ed.), *Sexual orientation and transgender issues in organizations* (pp. 21–42). Cham, Switzerland: Springer.

Sawyer, L. (2017, January 28). Waconia woman crawls back from the "dead." *Star Tribune.* Retrieved from www.startribune.com/waconia-woman-crawls-back-from-the-dead/412049283.

Sawyer, W., & Wagner, P. (2019). Mass incarceration: The whole pie 2019. Retrieved from www.prisonpolicy.org/reports/pie2019.html.

Scalise, I. M. (2014, January 26). Lo stato riconosca a casalinghe un salario e una vera pensione. *La Repubblica.* Retrieved from www.repubblica.it/economia/2014/01/26/news/bongiorno_lo_stato_riconosca_salario_a_casalinghe-76954421.

Schackner, B. (2002, September 27). College course focuses on the wealthy minority. *Post-Gazette.* Retrieved from www.post-gazette.com/localnews/20020929wealthy6.asp.

Schacter, J., & Thum, Y. M. (2004). Paying for high- and low-quality teaching. *Economics of Education Review, 23*(4), 411–30.

Scharf, S. A., & Flom, B. A. (2010, October). Report of the fifth annual national survey on retention and promotion of women in law firms. National Association of Women Lawyers. Retrieved from www.aauw.org/learn/research/upload/NewVoicesPayEquity_NAWL.pdf.

Scheepers, P., & Van der Slik, F. (1998). Religion and attitudes on moral issues: Effects of individual, spouse and parental characteristics. *Journal for the Scientific Study of Religion,* 678–91.

Scheitle, C., & Dougherty, K. (2010). Race, diversity, and membership duration in religious congregations. *Sociological Inquiry, 80*(3), 405–23.

Scherrer, K. S., & Pfeffer, C. A. (2017). None of the above: Toward identity and community-based understandings of (a)sexualities. *Archives of Sexual Behavior, 46*(3), 643–46.

Schippers, M. (2016). *Beyond monogamy: Polyamory and the future of polyqueer sexualities.* New York: NYU Press.

Schlosser, E. (2001). *Fast food nation: The dark side of the all-American meal*. Boston: Houghton Mifflin.

Schoen, R., & Canudas-Romo, V. (2006). Timing effects on divorce: 20th century experience in the United States. *Journal of Marriage and Family, 68*(3): 749–58.

Sciolino, E. (2004, October 22). France turns to tough policy on students' religious garb. *The New York Times*. Retrieved from www.nytimes.com/2004/10/22/world /europe/france-turns-to-tough-policy-on-students -religious-garb.html.

Seelye, K. Q. (2005, May 16). *Newsweek* apologizes for report of Koran insult. *The New York Times*, p. A1. Retrieved from www.nytimes.com/2005/05/16/world/asia /newsweek-apologizes-for-report-of-koran-insult.html.

Segers, G. (2020). Asked why Black Americans are killed by police, Trump responds, "So are White people." *CBS News*. Retrieved from www.cbsnews.com/news/trump -black-americans-killed-police-so-are-white-people/.

Semega, J. L., et al. (2017). Income and poverty in the United States: 2016. Current Population Reports, US Census Bureau. Retrieved from www.census.gov/content/dam /Census/library/publications/2017/demo/P60-259.pdf.

Setoodeh, R. (2006, March 20). Troubles by the score. *Newsweek*. Retrieved from www.msnbc.msn.com/id /11788171/site/newsweek.

Shah, D. (2004). *Defense of Marriage Act: An update*. Washington, DC: US General Accounting Office.

Shaheen, J. G. (1984). *The TV Arab*. Bowling Green, OH: Bowling Green State University Popular Press.

Shapiro, D., et al. (2016). Time to degree: A national view of the time enrolled and elapsed for associate and bachelor's degree earners [signature report 11]. Herndon, VA: National Student Clearinghouse Research Center. Retrieved from https://nscresearchcenter.org/wp -content/uploads/SignatureReport11.pdf.

Sharkey, P. (2010). The acute effect of local homicides on children's cognitive performance. *PNAS, 107*(26), 11733–38. Retrieved from www.pnas .org/content/107/26/11733.

Sheff, E. (2014). The polyamorists next door: Inside multiple-partner relationships and families. Lanham, MD: Rowman & Littlefield.

Sheler, J. (2001, October 29). Muslim in America. *U.S. News & World Report*, pp. 50–52.

Sherkat, D. E. (1991). Leaving the faith: Testing theories of religious switching using survival models. *Social Science Research, 20*, 171–87.

Sherkat, D. E. (1998). Counterculture or continuity? Competing influences on baby boomers. Religious orientations and participation. *Social Forces, 76*, 1087–115.

Sherkat, D. E., & Ellison, C. G. (1999). Recent developments and current controversies in the sociology of religion. *Annual Review of Sociology, 25*, 363–94.

Shiva, V. (1992a). Recovering the real meaning of sustainability. In D. E. Cooper & J. A. Palmer (Eds.), *The environment in question: Ethics in global issues* (pp. 187–93). London: Routledge.

Shiva, V. (1992b). Women's indigenous knowledge and biodiversity conservation. In G. Sen (Ed.), *Indigenous vision* (pp. 205–14). New Delhi: Sage.

Shiva, V. (2002). *Water wars: Privatization, pollution and profit*. Cambridge, MA: South End Press.

Shiva, V. (2004). Turning scarcity into abundance. *Yes! Magazine*. Retrieved from www.yesmagazine.org/article .asp?ID=698.

Shore, B. (1998). *Culture in mind: Cognition, culture, and the problem of meaning*. New York: Oxford University Press.

Shore, L. (2017, January 3). Gal interrupted, why men interrupt women and how to avert this in the workplace. *Forbes*. Retrieved from www.forbes.com/sites/womensmedia /2017/01/03/gal-interrupted-why -men-interrupt-women-and-how-to-avert-this-in-the -workplace/#437dd01217c3.

Shulevitz, J. (2016, January 8). It's payback time for women. *The New York Times*. Retrieved from www.nytimes.com /2016/01/10/opinion/sunday/payback-time-for-women .html.

Shulman, J., & Bowen, W. G. (2002). *The game of life: College sports and educational values*. Princeton, NJ: Princeton University Press.

Silva, T. J. (2017). Bud-sex: Constructing normative masculinity among rural straight men that have sex with men. *Gender & Society, 31*(1), 51–73.

Silverglate, H. (2011). *Three felonies a day: How the feds target the innocent*. New York: Encounter Books.

Singer, N. (2017, May 13). How Google took over the classroom. *The New York Times*. Retrieved from www .nytimes.com/2017/05/13/technology/google-education -chromebooks-schools.html?mcubz=0&_r=0.

Simmel, G. (1900). *Philosophie der Geldes* (The philosophy of money). Leipzig: Duncker & Humblot.

Simmel, G. (1950). Quantitative aspects of the group. In K. Wolff (Comp. and Trans.), *The sociology of Georg Simmel* (pp. 87–180). Glencoe, IL: Free Press.

Singleton, C. R., et al. (2016). Decomposing racial disparities in obesity prevalence: Variations in retail food environment. *American Journal of Preventative Medicine, 50*(3), 365–72.

Skocpol, T. (2004). Civic transformation and inequality in the contemporary United States. In K. Neckerman (Ed.), *Social inequality* (pp. 731–69). New York: Russell Sage Foundation.

Skocpol, T., & Amenta, E. (1986). States and social policies. *Annual Review of Sociology, 12*, 131–57.

Skogrand, L., et al. (2004, July). Understanding Latino families: Implications for family education. *Family Resources*. Retrieved from http://extension.usu.edu /diversity/files/uploads/Latino02-7-05.pdf.

Smedley, A. (1999). *Race in North America: Origin and evolution of a worldview*. Boulder, CO: Westview Press.

Smelser, N. (1962). *Theory of collective behavior*. New York: Free Press.

Smith, A. (2003). *The wealth of nations*. New York: Penguin. (Original work published 1776.)

Smith, B. H. (2009). *Natural reflections: Human cognition at the nexus of science and religion*. New Haven, CT: Yale University Press.

Smith, G. A., & Cooperman, A. (2016, September 14). The factors driving the growth of religious "nones" in the U.S. Pew Research Center. Retrieved from www .pewresearch.org/fact-tank/2016/09/14/the-factors -driving-the-growth-of-religious-nones-in-the-u-s.

Smith, J. R., et al. (1997). Consequences of living in poverty for young children's cognitive and verbal ability and early school achievement. In J. G. Duncan & J. Brooks-Gunn (Eds.), *Consequences of growing up poor* (pp. 132–89). New York: Russell Sage Foundation.

Smith, T. (2012). Beliefs about God across time and countries. National Opinion Research Center (NORC), University of Chicago. Retrieved from www.norc.org /pdfs/beliefs_about_god_report.pdf.

Snapchat Business. (2019, June 25). The friendship report. Retrieved from https://forbusiness.snapchat.com/blog /the-friendship-report?mod=article_inline.

Snow, D. A., et al. (1986). Frame alignment processes, micromobilization, and movement participation. *American Sociological Review, 51*(4), 464–81.

Snow, D., et al. (2014). The emergence, development, and future of the framing perspective: 25+ years since "frame alignment." *Mobilization: An International Quarterly, 19*(1), 23–46.

Snowden, F. M. (1983). *Beyond color prejudice: The ancient view of Blacks.* Cambridge, MA: Harvard University Press.

Snyder, S., & Evans, W. (2002). *The impact of income on mortality: Evidence from the Social Security notch* (NBER Working Paper No. W9197). National Bureau of Economic Research. Retrieved from www.nber.org/papers/w9197.

Snyder, S. E., & Evans, W. N. (2006). The effect of income on mortality: Evidence from the Social Security notch. *Review of Economics and Statistics, 88*, 482–95.

Snyder, T. D., & Tan, A. G. (2005). *Digest of education statistics, 2004* (NCES 2006-005). US Department of Education, National Center for Education Statistics. Washington, DC: US Government Printing Office.

Social Security Administration. (2017). Actuarial life table. Retrieved from www.ssa.gov/oact/STATS/table4c6.html.

Sokal, A., & Bricmont, J. (1999). *Fashionable nonsense: Postmodern intellectuals' abuse of science.* London: Picador.

Sommers, C. H. (2000). *The war against boys: How misguided feminism is harming our young men.* New York: Simon & Schuster.

Sorokin, P. (1959). *Social and cultural mobility.* New York: Free Press. (Original work published 1927.)

Sorokin, P., & Lunden, W. A. (1959). *Power and morality: Who shall guard the guardians?* Boston: Porter Sargent.

Spencer, H. (1967). *The evolution of society: Selections from Herbert Spencer's* Principles of Sociology (R. L. Carneiro, Ed.). Chicago: University of Chicago Press. (Original work published 1898.)

Spencer, M. B., et al. (1987). Double stratification and psychological risk: Adaptational processes and school achievement of Black children. *Journal of Negro Education, 56*(1), 77–87.

Spiegel, A. (Producer). (2006, December 15). Shouting across the divide, act one: Which one of them is not like the other? [Radio broadcast]. *This American Life.* Retrieved from www.thisamericanlife.org/Radio_Episode .aspx?episode=322.

Spock, B. (1998). *Baby and child care.* New York: Pocket Books. (Original work published 1946.)

Spohn, C., & Holleran, D. (2002). The effects of imprisonment on recidivism rates of felony offenders: A focus on drug offenders. *Criminology, 40*(2), 329–58.

Spurlock, M. (Director). (2004). *Super size me* [Motion picture]. United States: Sony Pictures.

Spurlock, M. (Host). (2005, June 29). Muslims and America [Television series episode]. In J. Chinn et al. (Producers), *30 days.* Los Angeles, Bluebush Productions LLC.

Stacey, J. (1987). Sexism by a subtler name? Postindustrial conditions and postfeminist consciousness in the Silicon Valley. *Socialist Review, 96,* 7–28.

Stacey, J. (1996). *In the name of the family: Rethinking family values in the postmodern age.* Boston: Beacon Press.

Stacey, J. (1997). Neo-family-values campaign. In R. N. Lancaster & M. di Lionardo (Eds.), *The gender/ sexuality reader: Culture, history, political economy* (pp. 453–72). New York: Routledge.

Stacey, J. (2004). Cruising to familyland: Gay hypergamy and rainbow kinship. *Current Sociology, 52*(2), 181–97.

Stacey, J., & Thorne, B. (1985). The missing feminist revolution in sociology. *Social Problems, 32,* 301–16.

Stack, C. B. (1974). *All our kin: Strategies for survival in a Black community.* New York: Harper & Row.

Stack, C. B., & Burton, L. M. (1994). Kinscripts: Reflections on family, generation and culture. In E. N. Glenn et al. (Eds.), *Mothering: Ideology, experience, and agency* (pp. 33–44). New York: Routledge.

Stark, R., & Bainbridge, W. S. (1985). *The future of religion: Secularization, revival, and cult formation.* Berkeley: University of California Press.

Stark, R., & Bainbridge, W. S. (1987). *A theory of religion.* Toronto: Lang.

Stark, R., & Finke, R. (2000). *Acts of faith: Explaining the human side of religion.* Berkeley: University of California Press.

Steele, C. M., & Aronson, J. (1998). Stereotype threat and the test performance of academically successful African Americans. In C. Jencks & M. Phillips (Eds.), *The Black-White test score gap* (pp. 401–27). Washington, DC: Brookings Institution Press.

Steelman, L. C., & Powell, B. (1985). The social and academic consequences of birth order: Real, artifactual or both? *Journal of Marriage and the Family, 47*(1), 117–24.

Steelman, L. C., & Powell, B. (1989). Acquiring capital for college: The constraints of family configuration. *American Sociological Review, 54*(5), 844–55.

Steinberg, S. (1974). *The academic melting pot.* New York: McGraw-Hill.

Stevens, J. (2006). Pregnancy envy and the politics of compensatory masculinities. *Gender and Politics, 1,* 265–94.

Stewart, J. B. (2015, July 16). Convictions prove elusive in "London Whale" trading case. *The New York Times.* Retrieved from www.nytimes.com/2015/07/17/business /figures-in-london-whale-trading-case-escape-the -authorities-nets.html.

Stokes, B. (2017). Public divided on prospects for the next generation. Pew Research Center. Retrieved from www.pewglobal.org/2017/06/05/2-public-divided-on -prospects-for-the-next-generation.

Stone, D. A. (1994). Making the poor count. *American Prospect, 17,* 84–88.

Strom, S. (2010). Haitian quake brings more money and scrutiny to a charity. *The New York Times.* Retrieved from www.nytimes.com/2010/02/05/us/05charity.html.

Sunderam, S., et al. (2018). Assisted reproductive technology surveillance—United States, 2015. *Morbidity and Mortality Weekly Report, 67*(3), 1–28.

Super, D. A. (2018, January 15). "Work requirements" for public benefits are really just time limits. *The Los Angeles Times*. Retrieved from www.latimes.com/opinion/op-ed/la-oe-super-work-requirements-20180115-story.html.

Tavernise, S. (2016, April 22). U.S. suicide rate surges to a 30-year high. *The New York Times*. Retrieved from www.nytimes.com/2016/04/22/health/us-suicide-rate-surges-to-a-30-year-high.html.

Taylor, K. (2014, October 27). How buying beer paid me $4,000 a month for college. *Daily Finance*. Retrieved from www.dailyfinance.com/2014/10/27/how-buying-beer-paid-me-4-000-a-month-for-college.

Taylor, P., & Urwin, P. (2001). Age and participation in vocational education and training. *Work, Employment, and Society*, 15(4), 763–79. Retrieved from www.cambridge.org/core/journals/work-employment-and-society/article/age-and-participation-in-vocational-education-and-training/9AF153573EDDB7F59C2800B05512B596.

Taylor, P., et al. (2011, July 26). Wealth gaps rise to record highs between Whites, Blacks, Hispanics twenty-to-one. Pew Research Center. Retrieved from www.pewsocialtrends.org/2011/07/26/wealth-gaps-rise-to-record-highs-between-whites-blacks-hispanics.

Tett, G. (2010). Road map that opens up shadow banking. *Financial Times*. Retrieved from www.ft.com/intl/cms/s/0/1a222bf4-f33d-11df-a4fa-00144feab49a.html#axzz3x3F5SrvG.

Tharps, Lori L. (2014). The case for black with a capital b. *The New York Times*. Retrieved from https://www.nytimes.com/2014/11/19/opinion/the-case-for-black-with-a-capital-b.html.

Thinggaard, C. K., et al. (2009). Perceived age as clinically useful biomarker of ageing: Cohort study. *BMJ*, 339. Retrieved from https://doi.org/10.1136/bmj.b5262.

Thomas, E. (2005, May 23). How a fire broke out. *Newsweek*. Retrieved from www.msnbc.msn.com/id/7857407/site/newsweek.

Thomas, W. I., & Thomas, D. S. (1928). *The child in America: Behavior problems and programs*. New York: Knopf.

Thomas Nelson, Inc. (2010). *Refuel: The complete New Testament* (2nd ed.), New Century Version. Nashville, TN: Thomas Nelson.

Thurow, L. (1970). *Investment in human capital*. Belmont, CA: Wadsworth.

Time. (1941, December 22). How to tell your friends from the Japs. Retrieved from http://content.time.com/time/magazine/article/0,9171,932034,00.html.

Tinkler, J. E. (2013). How do sexual harassment policies shape gender beliefs? An exploration of the moderating effects of norm adherence and gender. *Social Science Research*, 42(5), 1269–83.

Tocqueville, A. de. (1835). *Democracy in America*. Retrieved from http://xroads.virginia.edu/~HYPER/DETOC/toc_indx.html.

Todd, M. A., & Goldman, N. (2013). Do interviewer and physician health ratings predict mortality? A comparison with self-rated health. *Epidemiology*, 24(6), 913–20.

Torres, N. G. (2017, December 19). More than 37,000 Cubans face deportation orders. *The Miami Herald*. Retrieved from www.miamiherald.com/news/nation-world/world/americas/cuba/article190571369.html.

Tourism Economics. (2016). The economic impact of tourism in Lancaster County. Retrieved from www.discoverlancaster.com/Uploads/files/TE-DLEconImpact2015-2016-05-24.pdf.

Treisman, R. (2019). FBI reports dip in hate crimes, but rise in violence. NPR. Retrieved from www.npr.org/2019/11/12/778542614/fbi-reports-dip-in-hate-crimes-but-rise-in-violence.

Triester, R. (2005, July 22). "Real beauty"—or real smart marketing? *Salon.com*. Retrieved from www.salon.com/2005/07/22/dove_2.

Truth, S. (1851). Ain't I a woman? Speech delivered at the Women's Convention in Akron, Ohio. National Park Service. Retrieved from www.nps.gov/articles/sojourner-truth.htm.

Turkewitz, J. (2018, January 4). For Native Americans, a "historic moment" on the path to power at the ballot box. *The New York Times*. Retrieved from www.nytimes.com/2018/01/04/native-american-voting-rights.html.

Turner, R., & Killian, L. M. (1987). *Collective behavior* (3rd ed.). Englewood Cliffs, NJ: Prentice-Hall.

Tyson, K., et al. (2005). It's not "a Black thing": Understanding the burden of acting White and other dilemmas of high achievement. *American Sociological Review*, 70(4), 582–605.

Ugwu, C., & Nugent, C. (2019). Adoption-related behaviors among women aged 18–44 in the United States: 2011–2015. National Center for Health Statistics, Centers for Disease Control and Prevention. Retrieved from www.cdc.gov/nchs/products/databriefs/db315.htm.

Unah, I., & Boger, J. C. (2001, April 16). *Race and the death penalty in North Carolina*. Retrieved from www.common-sense.org/pdfs/NCDeathPenaltyReport2001.pdf.

UNAIDS. (2013). *Global report: UNAIDS report on the global AIDS epidemic 2013* (pp. A1–A15). Retrieved from www.unaids.org/en/media/unaids/contentassets/documents/epidemiology/2013/gr2013/UNAIDS_Global_Report_2013_en.pdf.

UNICEF. (2017). Levels and trends in child mortality. Retrieved from www.unicef.org/publications/files/Child_Mortality_Report_2017.pdf.

UNICEF. (2019). The State of Food Security and Nutrition in the World. Retrieved from http://www.fao.org/3/I9553EN/i9553en.pdf.

Union of Concerned Scientists. (2020). Each country's share of CO_2 emissions. Retrieved from https://www.ucsusa.org/resources/each-countrys-share-co2-emissions.

United Methodist Church. (2011). 2011 state of the church: The people. Retrieved from www.umc.org/site/c.lwL4KnN1LtH/b.6765229/k.D5ED/2011_State_of_the_Church_The_People.htm.

United Methodist Church. (2016). United Methodists at-a-glance. Retrieved from www.umc.org/who-we-are/united-methodists-at-a-glance.

United Methodist Church. (2018). United Methodists at-a-glance. Retrieved from www.umc.org/news-and-media/united-methodists-at-a-glance.

United Nations. (2001, May 17). Poverty biggest enemy of health in developing world, secretary-general tells World Health Assembly [Press release]. Retrieved from www.un.org/News/Press/docs/2001/sgsm7808.doc.htm.

US Census Bureau. (1993). We the first Americans. US Department of Commerce Economics and Statistics Administration. Retrieved from www.census.gov/apsd/wepeople/we-5.pdf.

US Census Bureau. (2010a, October 19). Nation's foreign-born population nears 37 million. Retrieved from www .census.gov/newsroom/releases/archives/foreignborn _population/cb10-159.html.

US Census Bureau. (2010b). Data profile highlights, population finder fact sheet. 2006–2008 American Community Survey 3-year estimates. Retrieved from http://factfinder.census.gov/servlet/ACSSAFFFacts? _sse=on.

US Census Bureau. (2010c). 2012 statistical abstract: Income, poverty, & wealth. Retrieved from www.census.gov /compendia/statab/cats/income_expenditures_poverty _wealth.html.

US Census Bureau. (2011, May). The Hispanic population: 2010. 2010 census briefs. Retrieved from www.census.gov /prod/cen2010/briefs/c2010br-04.pdf.

US Census Bureau. (2012a). The American Indian and Alaska Native population. Retrieved from www.census.gov/prod /cen2010/briefs/c2010br-10.pdf.

US Census Bureau. (2012b). Selected population profile in the United States. 2012 American Community Survey 1-year estimates. Retrieved from http://factfinder2 .census.gov/faces/tableservices/jsf/pages/productview .xhtml?pid=ACS_12_1YR_S0201&prodType=table.

US Census Bureau. (2012c). Hispanic or Latino origin by specific origin. 2012 American Community Survey 1-year estimates. Retrieved from http://factfinder2 .census.gov/faces/tableservices/jsf/pages/productview .xhtml?pid=ACS_12_1YR_B03001&prodType=table.

US Census Bureau. (2012d). Table 4: Percent distribution of household net worth, by amount of net worth and selected characteristics: 2011. Retrieved from www .census.gov/people/wealth.

US Census Bureau. (2013). Census Bureau reports 21 percent married households have at least one foreign-born spouse. Retrieved from www.census.gov/newsroom /releases/archives/foreignborn_population/cb13-157 .html.

US Census Bureau. (2014). Asian/Pacific American Heritage Month: May 2014. Facts for features. Retrieved from www.census.gov/newsroom/facts-for-features/2014 /cb14-ff13.html.

US Census Bureau. (2016a, November 17). The majority of children live with two parents, Census Bureau reports. Retrieved from www.census.gov/newsroom/press -releases/2016/cb16-192.html.

US Census Bureau. (2016b). Household type by household size. 2011–2015 American Community Survey 5-year estimates. Retrieved from https://factfinder.census .gov/faces/tableservices/jsf/pages/productview .xhtml?src=bkmk.

US Census Bureau. (2016c). Age and sex. 2012–2016 American Community Survey 5-year estimates. Retrieved from https://factfinder.census.gov/bkmk/table/1.0/en/ACS/16 _5YR/S0101/0100000US.

US Census Bureau. (2016d). Median age of the total population—United States—states; and Puerto Rico: Total population. 2012–2016 American Community Survey 5-year estimates. Retrieved from https://factfinder.census.gov/bkmk/table /1.0/en/ACS/16_5YR/GCT0101.US01PR/0100000US.

US Census Bureau. (2016e). Hispanic or Latino origin by specific origin. 2016 American Community Survey 1-year estimates. Retrieved from https://factfinder.census.gov /bkmk/table/1.0/en/ACS/16_1YR/B03001/0100000US.

US Census Bureau. (2016f). Educational attainment. 2016 American Community Survey 1-year estimates. Retrieved from https://factfinder.census.gov/faces /tableservices/jsf/pages/productview.xhtml?pid=ACS_16 _1YR_S1501&prodType=table.

US Census Bureau. (2016g). Average household size of occupied housing units by tenure. 2016 American Community Survey 1-year estimates. Retrieved from https://factfinder.census.gov/faces/tableservices /jsf/pages/productview.xhtml?pid=ACS_16_1YR _B25010&prodType=table.

US Census Bureau. (2017a). American Indian and Alaska native alone or in combination with one or more other races. 2016 American Community Survey 1-year estimates. Retrieved from https://factfinder.census .gov/faces/tableservices/jsf/pages/productview .xhtml?pid=ACS_16_1YR_B02010&prodType=table.

US Census Bureau. (2017b). Race. 2016 American Community Survey 1-year estimates. Retrieved from https://factfinder .census.gov/faces/tableservices/jsf/pages/productview .xhtml?pid=ACS_16_1YR_B02001&prodType=table.

US Census Bureau. (2017c). Median household income in the past 12 months (in 2016 inflation-adjusted dollars) (White alone householder). 2016 American Community Survey 1-year estimates. Retrieved from https://factfinder .census.gov/faces/tableservices/jsf/pages/productview .xhtml?pid=ACS_16_1YR_B19013A&prodType=table.

US Census Bureau. (2017d). Median household income in the past 12 months (in 2016 inflation-adjusted dollars) (Black or African American alone householder). 2016 American Community Survey 1-year estimates. Retrieved from https://factfinder.census.gov/faces /tableservices/jsf/pages/productview.xhtml?pid=ACS_16 _1YR_B19013B&prodType=table.

US Census Bureau. (2017e). Hispanic or Latino origin by specific origin. 2016 American Community Survey 1-year estimates. Retrieved from https://factfinder .census.gov/faces/tableservices/jsf/pages/productview .xhtml?pid=ACS_16_1YR_B03001&prodType=table.

US Census Bureau. (2017f). Median family income in the past 12 months (in 2016 inflation-adjusted dollars) (Asian alone householder). 2016 American Community Survey 1-year estimates. Retrieved from https://factfinder .census.gov/faces/tableservices/jsf/pages/productview .xhtml?pid=ACS_16_1YR_B19113D&prodType=table.

US Census Bureau. (2017g). Place of birth for the foreign-born population in the United States. 2016 American Community Survey 1-year estimates. Retrieved from https://factfinder.census.gov/bkmk/table/1.0 /en/ACS/13_1YR/B05006/0100000US|0400000US12 |0400000US36.

US Census Bureau. (2017h). Poverty status in the past 12 months by sex by age (American Indian and Alaska native alone). 2016 American Community Survey 1-year estimates. Retrieved from https://factfinder .census.gov/faces/tableservices/jsf/pages/productview .xhtml?pid=ACS_16_1YR_B17001C&prodType=table.

US Census Bureau. (2017i). Poverty status in the past 12 months by sex by age (Asian alone). 2016 American Community Survey 1-year estimates. Retrieved from https://factfinder.census.gov/faces/tableservices/jsf

/pages/productview.xhtml?pid=ACS_16_1YR_B17001D
&prodType=table.

US Census Bureau. (2017j). Tenure (Asian alone householder). 2016 American Community Survey 1-year estimates. Retrieved from https://factfinder.census.gov/faces /tableservices/jsf/pages/productview.xhtml?pid=ACS_16 _1YR_B25003D&prodType=table.

US Census Bureau. (2017k). ACS demographic and housing estimates. 2012–2016 American Community Survey 5-year estimates. Retrieved from https://factfinder .census.gov/bkmk/table/1.0/en/ACS/16_5YR/DP05 /0100000US.

US Census Bureau. (2017l, March 16). Supplemental poverty measure. Retrieved from www.census.gov/topics /income-poverty/supplemental-poverty-measure/about .html.

US Census Bureau. (2017m). Median age at first marriage. Universe: population 15 to 54 years. 2016 American Community Survey 1-year estimates. Retrieved from https:// factfinder.census.gov/faces/tableservices /jsf/pages/productview.xhtml?pid=ACS_16_1YR _B12007&prodType=table.

US Census Bureau. (2017n). Decennial censuses, 1890 to 1940, and Current Population Survey, annual social and economic supplements, 1947 to 2017. Retrieved from www.census.gov/content/dam/Census/library /visualizations/time-series/demo/families-and -households/ms-2.pdf.

US Census Bureau. (2017o). Historical living arrangements of children. Retrieved from www.census.gov/data/tables /time-series/demo/families/children.html.

US Census Bureau. (2017p). America's families and living arrangements: 2017. Retrieved from www.census.gov /data/tables/2017/demo/families/cps-2017.html.

US Census Bureau. (2017q). Educational attainment in the United States: 2016. Retrieved from www.census.gov /data/tables/2016/demo/education-attainment/cps -detailed-tables.html.

US Census Bureau. (2018a). ACS demographic and housing estimates. Retrieved from https://data.census.gov/cedsci /table?q=total%20population&tid=ACSDP1Y2018 .DP05&t=Total%20population.

US Census Bureau. (2018b). Educational attainment: American Community Survey 1-year estimates. Retrieved from https://data.census.gov/cedsci/table?q=College %20degree&hidePreview=false&tid=ACSST1Y2018 .S1501&vintage=2018.

US Census Bureau. (2018c). Poverty status in the past 12 months. 2016 American Community Survey 1-year estimates. Retrieved from https://factfinder.census.gov /bkmk/table/1.0/en/ACS/16_1YR/S1701/0400000US27.

US Census Bureau. (2019a). America's families and living arrangements: 2019. Table A3. Retrieved from www2 .census.gov/programs-surveys/demo/tables/families /2019/cps-2019/taba3.xls.

US Census Bureau. (2019b). Historical marital status tables, Table MS-2. Retrieved from www2.census.gov/programs -surveys/demo/tables/families/time-series/marital/ms2 .xls.

US Census Bureau. (2019c). Living arrangements of children under 18 years old, 1960 to present. Retrieved from www .census.gov/data/tables/time-series/demo/families /children.html.

US Census Bureau. (2019d). Population estimates show aging across race groups differs. Release CB19-90. Retrieved from www.census.gov/newsroom/press-releases/2019 /estimates-characteristics.html.

US Census Bureau. (2020a). ACS demographic and housing estimates. Retrieved from https://data.census .gov/cedsci/table?d=ACS%205-Year%20Estimates %20Data%20Profiles&table=DP05&tid=ACSDP5Y2018 .DP05.

US Census Bureau. (2020b). America's families and living arrangements: Average number of people per household, by race and Hispanic origin, marital status, age, and education of householder, 2016. Retrieved from www2 .census.gov/programs-surveys/demo/tables/families /2016/cps-2016/tabavg1.xls.

US Census Bureau. (2020c). Comparative demographic estimates. Retrieved from https://data.census.gov/cedsci /table?g=0100000US&tid=ACSCP1Y2018.CP05&y=2018&t =Counts,%20Estimates,%20and%20Projections%3ARace %20and%20Ethnicity&hidePreview=false&cid=CP05 _2014_001E&vintage=2018.

US Census Bureau. (2020d). Demographic characteristics for occupied housing units. Retrieved from https://data .census.gov/cedsci/table?q=tenure&tid=ACSST1Y2018 .S2502&t=Owner%2FRenter%20%28Tenure%29&vintage =2018.

U.S. Census Bureau. (2020e). Educational attainment in the United States: 2019. Retrieved from https://www.census .gov/content/census/en/data/tables/2019/demo /educational-attainment/cps-detailed-tables.html

US Census Bureau. (2020f). Hispanic by country of origin. Retrieved from https://data.census.gov/cedsci /table?q=hispanic%20by%20country%20of%20ori -gin&hidePreview=false&tid=ACSDT1Y2018 .B03001&vintage=2018.

US Census Bureau. (2020g). Hispanic by region. Retrieved from https://data.census.gov/cedsci/map?q=hispanic %20by%20region&tid=ACSDP1Y2018.DP05&t=Hispanic %20or%20Latino&vintage=2018&hidePreview=false&cid =DP05_0071PE&layer=VT_2018_040_00_PY_D1&mode =selection.

US Census Bureau. (2020h). Hispanic or Latino by specific origin. Retrieved from https://data.census.gov/cedsci /table?q=hispanic%20by%20country%20of%20 origin&hidePreview=false&tid=ACSDT1Y2018 .B03001&vintage=2018.

US Census Bureau. (2020i). Median income in the past 12 months (in 2018 inflation-adjusted dollars). Retrieved from https://data.census.gov/cedsci/table?q=median %20family%20income&tid=ACSST1Y2018.S1903&t =Income%20%28Households,%20Families,%20Individuals %29%3AHousehold%20and%20Family&vintage=2018.

US Census Bureau. (2020j). People reporting ancestry. Retrieved from https://data.census.gov/cedsci /table?q=arab&tid=ACSDT1Y2018.B04006&vintage=2013.

U.S. Census Bureau. (2020k). Place of birth for the foreign-born population in the United States. Re-trieved from https://data.census.gov/cedsci/table?q=B05006&tid =ACSDT1Y2018.B05006.

US Census Bureau. (2020l). Poverty status in the past 12 months. Retrieved from https://data.census.gov /cedsci/table?q=poverty%20rate&tid=ACSST1Y2018 .S1701&t=Poverty.

US Census Bureau. (2020m). Selected characteristics of the foreign-born population by period of entry into the United States. Retrieved from https://data.census .gov/cedsci/table?q=foreign%20born%20african %20americans&hidePreview=false&tid=ACSST1Y2018 .S0502&t=Foreign%20born%3ABlack%20or %20African%20American&vintage=2018.

US Census Bureau. (2020n). Table: Detailed race. Retrieved from https://data.census.gov/cedsci/table?q =asian&hidePreview=false&tid=ACSDT1Y2010 .B02003&t=Asian&vintage=2018.

US Census Bureau. (2020o). Table F1: Family households, by type, age of own children, age of family members, and age of householder. Retrieved from www2.census.gov /programs-surveys/demo/tables/families/2019/cps -2019/tabf1-all.xls.

US Census Bureau. (2020p). Table HH-4: Households by size, 1960 to present. Retrieved from www2.census .gov/programs-surveys/demo/tables/families/time -series/households/hh4.xls.

US Census Bureau. (2020q). Table MS-2: Historical marital status tables. Retrieved from www.census.gov/data/tables /time-series/demo/families/marital.html.

US Department of Agriculture. (2018). Supplemental Nutrition Assistance Program: Participation and costs, 1969–2017. Retrieved from www.fns.usda.gov/pd /supplemental-nutrition-assistance-program-snap.

US Department of Commerce. (2009, May 15). Confirmation hearing for Robert Groves, chaired by Senator Thomas Carper (D-DE). Retrieved from www.census.gov /newsroom/releases/pdf/confirmation_transcript.pdf.

US Department of Education, National Center for Education Statistics. (2017). Program for the International Assessment of Adult Competencies (PIAAC). Retrieved from https://nces.ed.gov/surveys/piaac/current_results .asp.

US Department of Health and Human Services (2015). Dietary guidelines for Americans 2015–2020. Retrieved from http://health.gov/dietaryguidelines/2015 /guidelines.

US Department of Health and Human Services. (2016). Health, the United States, 2015: In brief. Retrieved from www.cdc.gov/nchs/data/hus/hus15_inbrief.pdf.

US Department of Health and Human Services. (2018). US federal poverty guidelines used to determine financial eligibility for certain federal programs. Retrieved from https://aspe.hhs.gov/poverty-guidelines.

US Department of the Interior, Indian Affairs. (2018). Frequently asked questions: What is the Bureau of Indian Education? Retrieved from www.bia.gov /frequently-asked-questions.

US Department of Justice, Civil Rights Division. (2007). *Enforcement and outreach following the September 11 terrorist attacks*. Retrieved from www.usdoj.gov/crt /legalinfo/discrimupdate.html.

US Department of State. (2019). Annual report on intercountry adoption. Retrieved from https://travel .state.gov/content/dam/NEWadoptionassets/pdfs /Tab%201%20Annual%20Report%20on %20Intercountry%20Adoptions.pdf.

US Department of State, Bureau of Consular Affairs. (2018). Adoption statistics. Retrieved from https://travel.state .gov/content/travel/en/Intercountry-Adoption/adopt_ref /adoption-statistics.html.

US Senate, Subcommittee on Immigration and Naturalization of the Committee on the Judiciary. (1965, February 10). Washington, DC, pp. 1–3.

Usher, N. (2014). *Making news at the* New York Times. Ann Arbor: University of Michigan Press.

Varian, H. R. (2006, May 4). Red states, blue states: New labels for long-running differences. *The New York Times*, p. 3. Retrieved from www.nytimes.com/2006/05/04 /business/04scene.html.

Varon, J. (2004). *Bringing the war home: The Weather Underground, the Red Army faction, and revolutionary violence in the sixties and seventies*. Berkeley: University of California Press.

Vars, F. E., & Bowen, W. G. (1998). Scholastic Aptitude Test scores, race, and academic performance in selective colleges and universities. In C. Jencks & M. Phillips (Eds.), *The Black-White test score gap* (pp. 457–79). Washington, DC: Brookings Institution Press.

Ventola, C. L. (2011). Direct-to-consumer pharmaceutical advertising: Therapeutic or toxic? *Pharmacy and Therapeutics, 36*(10), 669–74, 681–84.

Verba, S., et al. (2004). Political inequality: What do we know about it? In K. M. Neckerman (Ed.), *Social inequality* (pp. 635–66). New York: Sage.

Verdier, H. (2016). DTR: Define the relationship—Swipe right for Tinder's first podcast. *The Guardian*. Retrieved from www.theguardian.com/tv-and-radio/2016/dec/15 /dtr-define-the-relationship-swipe-right-for -tinders-first-podcast.

Vespa, J., et al. (2013). America's families and living arrangements: 2012. Population characteristics. US Census Bureau. Retrieved from http://www.census.gov /prod/2013pubs/p20-570.pdf.

Vestal, S. (2017, December 1). Rachel Dolezal remains unabashadly Rachel Dolezal. *The Spokesman-Review*. Retrieved from www.spokesman.com/stories/2017/dec/01 /shawn-vestal-rachel-dolezal-remains-unabashedly-ra.

Virupaksha, H. G., et al. (2016). Suicide and suicidal behavior among transgender persons. *Indian Journal of Psychological Medicine, 38*(6), 505–9.

Wade, L. (2017). *American hookup: A new culture of sex on campus*. New York: Norton.

Wall, A. (2012). Gubernatorial electons, campaign costs, and winning governors. Council of State Governments. Retrieved from http://knowledgecenter.csg.org/kc /content/gubernatorial-elections-campaign-costs -and-winning-governors.

Waite, L., & Gallagher, M. (2000). *The case for marriage: Why married people are happier, healthier, and better off financially*. New York: Doubleday.

Wallerstein, J., et al. (2000). *The unexpected legacy of divorce*. New York: Hyperion.

Wang, W. (2012, February 16). The rise of intermarriage. Pew Research Center, Social and Demographic Trends. Retrieved from www.pewsocialtrends.org/2012/02/16 /the-rise-of-intermarriage.

Wang, W. (2015, June 12). Interracial marriage: Who is "marrying out"? Pew Research Center. Retrieved from www.pewresearch.org/fact-tank/2015/06/12 /interracial-marriage-who-is-marrying-out.

Ward, J. (2015). *Not gay: Sex between straight White men.* New York: NYU Press.

Warren, E. (2007). Unsafe at any rate. *Democracy: A Journal of Ideas, 5.* Retrieved from www.democracyjournal.org/article2.php?ID=6528&limit=0&limit2=1500&page=1.

Warren, E., & Tyagi, A. W. (2003). *The two-income trap: Why middle-class mothers and fathers are going broke.* New York: Basic Books.

Warren, J. W., & Twine, F. W. (1997). White Americans, the new minority? Non-Blacks and the ever-expanding boundaries of Whiteness. *Journal of Black Studies, 28,* 200–18.

Washington, E. (2008). Female socialization: How daughters affect their legislator fathers. *American Economic Review, 98*(1), 311–32.

Washington State Department of Health. (2020). Department of Health releases new COVID-19 data tied to occupation, industry. Retrieved from www.doh.wa.gov/Newsroom/Articles/ID/1255/Department-of-Health-releases-new-COVID-19-data-tied-to-occupation-industry.

Water.org. (2014, May 18). Water facts. Retrieved from http://water.org/water-crisis/water-facts/water.

Watts, D. (2003). *Six degrees: The science of a connected age.* New York: Norton.

Weber, M. (1946). *From Max Weber: Essays in sociology.* H. H. Gerth & C. W. Mills (Eds. & Trans.). New York: Oxford University Press.

Weber, M. (1968). *Economy and society: An outline of interpretive sociology.* G. Rothe & C. Wittich (Eds.). (E. Fischoff et al., Trans.). New York: Bedminster Press. (Original work published 1922.)

Weber, M. (2003). *The Protestant ethic and the spirit of capitalism.* Oxford: Blackwell. (Original work published 1904.)

Weber, M. (2004). *The vocation lectures: Science as a vocation, politics as a vocation.* D. S. Owen et al. (Eds.). Indianapolis: Hackett.

Wegener, B. (1991). Job mobility and social ties: Social resources, prior job, and status attainment. *American Sociological Review, 56*(1), 60–71.

Welsh, B. C., & Farrington, D. P. (2004). Surveillance for crime prevention in public space: Results and policy choices in Britain and America. *Criminology and Public Policy, 3*(3), 497–526.

West, C., & Zimmerman, D. H. (1975). Sex roles, interruptions and silences in conversation. In *Language and Sex: Difference and Dominance* (pp. 105–29). Stanford, CA: Stanford University Press.

West, C., & Zimmerman, D. (1987). Doing gender. *Gender & Society, 1*(2), 125–51.

West, L. A., et al. (2014). 65+ in the United States: 2010. US Census Bureau. Retrieved from www.census.gov/content/dam/Census/library/publications/2014/demo/p23-212.pdf.

Whitbeck, L. B., et al. (1991). Family economic hardship, parental support, and adolescent self-esteem. *Social Psychology Quarterly, 54,* 353–63.

Widman, L., et al. (2016). Parent-adolescent sexual communication and adolescent safer sex behavior. *JAMA Pediatrics, 170*(1), 52–61. Retrieved from https://jamanetwork.com/journals/jamapediatrics/article-abstract/2468100.

Wilcox, W. B. (1999). *Religion and paternal involvement: Product of religious commitment or American convention?* Paper presented at the Annual Meeting of the American Sociological Association, Chicago.

Wilcox, W. B. (2004). *Soft patriarchs, new men: How Christianity shapes fathers and husbands.* Chicago: University of Chicago Press.

Wilensky, H. L. (1974). *The welfare state and equality: Structural and ideological roots of public expenditures.* Berkeley: University of California Press.

Williams, C. (1995). *Still a man's world: Men who do women's work.* Berkeley: University of California Press.

Williams, C. (2013). The glass escalator, revisited. *Gender & Society, 27*(5), 609–29.

Williams, S. (2005). Million dollar blocks. Public service announcement [Digital presentation]. Columbia University, Spatial Information Design Lab. Retrieved from www.spatialinformationdesignlab.org/movie.php?url=MEDIA/PSA_01.avi.

Willis, P. (1981). *Learning to labor: How working class kids get working class jobs.* New York: Columbia University Press. (Original work published 1977.)

Wilson, J. Q., & Kelling, G. L. (1982). Broken windows: The police and neighborhood safety. *The Atlantic Monthly, 249*(3), 29–37.

Wilson, V., & Rodgers, W. M., III. (2016, September 20). Black-White wage gaps expand with rising wage inequality. Economic Policy Institute. Retrieved from www.epi.org/publication/black-white-wage-gaps-expand-with-rising-wage-inequality.

Wilson, W. J. (1978). *The declining significance of race: Blacks and changing American institutions.* Chicago: University of Chicago Press.

Wilson, W. J. (1987). *The truly disadvantaged: The inner city, the underclass, and public policy.* Chicago: University of Chicago Press.

Wilson, W. J. (1996). *When work disappears: The world of the new urban poor.* New York: Knopf.

Winant, H. (2001). *The world is a ghetto: Race and democracy since World War II.* New York: Basic Books.

Wing, W., et al. (1985). The Black/White mortality crossover: Investigation in a community-based study. *Journal of Gerontology, 40*(1), 78–84.

Wingfield, A. H. (2009). Racializing the glass escalator: Reconsidering men's experiences with women's work. *Gender & Society, 23*(1), 5–26.

Wirth, L. (1938). Urbanism as a way of life. *American Journal of Sociology, 44*(1), 1–24.

Witte, J. F. (1998). The Milwaukee voucher experiment. *Educational Evaluation and Policy Analysis, 20*(4), 229–51.

Wolff, E. N. (2017, November 29). Has middle class wealth recovered? Table 2. Retrieved from www.aeaweb.org/conference/2018/preliminary/paper/5ZFEEf69.

Woo, H., & Zajacova, A. (2016). Predictive strength of self-rated health for mortality risk among older adults in the United States: Does it differ by race and ethnicity? *SAGE Journals, 39*(7), 879–905.

Wood, W., et al. (2002). Sources of information about dating and their perceived influence on adolescents. *Journal of Adolescent Research, 17,* 401–17.

World Bank. (2002). Global partnership to eliminate riverblindness. Retrieved from www.worldbank.org/afr/gper.

World Bank. (2018). CO_2 emissions (metric tons per capita). Retrieved from https://data.worldbank.org/indicator/EN.ATM.CO2E.PC?year_high_desc=false.

World Bank. (2019a). Indicators: Age dependency ratio (% of working-age population). Retrieved from https://data.worldbank.org/indicator/SP.POP.DPND?most_recent_value_desc=true.

World Bank. (2019b). Indicators: Age dependency ratio, old (% of working-age population). Retrieved from https://data.worldbank.org/indicator/SP.POP.DPND.OL?most_recent_value_desc=true.

World Economic Forum. (2017). The global gender gap report 2017. Retrieved from www3.weforum.org/docs/WEF_GGGR_2017.pdf.

World Food Programme. (2018). Hunger facts. Retrieved from www.wfp.org/share-a-hunger-fact.

World Health Organization. (2017). Fact sheet: Poliomyelitis. Retrieved from www.who.int/mediacentre/factsheets/fs114/en.

World Health Organization. (2018a). Life expectancy at birth (years), 2000–2016: Both sexes: 2016. Global Health Observatory (GHO) data. Retrieved from www.who.int/gho/mortality_burden_disease/life_tables/situation_trends/en.

World Health Organization. (2018b, February 7). Fact sheet: Drinking-water. Retrieved from www.who.int/mediacentre/factsheets/fs391/en.

World Health Organization. (2018c). HIV/AIDS. Global Health Observatory (GHO) data. Retrieved from www.who.int/gho/hiv/en.

World Health Organization. (2019). Poliomyelitis: Key facts. Retrieved from www.who.int/news-room/factsheets/detail/poliomyelitis.

World Health Organization. (2020). HIV/AIDS. Global Health Observatory (GHO) data. Retrieved from www.who.int/hiv/data/en.

Wuthnow, R. (1998). *Loose connections: Joining together in America's fragmented communities.* Cambridge, MA: Harvard University Press.

Wyler, G. (2014, May 6). NYC's newest megachurch is more popular than Jesus. *Vice.* Retrieved from www.vice.com/en_us/article/8gd8jp/hillsong-nyc-more-popular-than-jesus.

Xu, J., et al. (2009, August 19). Deaths: Preliminary data for 2007. Centers for Disease Control and Prevention, National Center for Health Statistics. *National Vital Statistics Reports, 58*(1). Retrieved from www.cdc.gov/nchs/data/nvsr/nvsr58/nvsr58_01.pdf.

Yano, Y., et al. (2017). Racial differences in associations of blood pressure components in young adulthood with incident cardiovascular disease by middle age. *JAMA Cardiology, 2*(4), 381–89.

Yavorsky, J. E., et al. (2015). The production of inequality: The gender division of labor across the transition to parenthood. *Journal of Marriage and the Family, 77*(3): 662–79.

Yeakley, R. (2011, February 15). Evangelical churches still growing, mainline Protestantism in decline. *Huffington Post.* Retrieved from www.huffingtonpost.com/2011/02/15/report-us-churches-contin_n_823701.html.

Young, L., & Hammock, E. (2007). On switches and knobs, microsatellites and monogamy. *Trends in Genetics, 23*(5), 209–12.

Young, L., & Wang, Z. (2004). The neurobiology of pair bonding. *Nature Neuroscience, 7*(10), 1048–54. Retrieved from www.ecfs.org/projects/pchurch/AT%20BIOLOGY/PAPERS%5CNeurobiology%20of%20Pair%20Bonding.pdf.

Young, M. P. (2002). Confessional protest: The religious birth of U.S. national social movements. *American Sociological Review, 67,* 660–88.

Zelizer, V. A. (2005). *The purchase of intimacy.* Princeton, NJ: Princeton University Press.

Zenith USA. (2018). Top 30 global media owners 2017. Retrieved from www.zenithusa.com/top-30-global-media-owners-2017.

Zernike, K. (2006, April 23). College, my way. *The New York Times.* Retrieved from www.nytimes.com/2006/04/23/education/edlife/zernike.html.

Zill, N. (1988). Behavior, achievement, and health problems among children in stepfamilies: Findings from a national survey of child health. In E. M. Hetherington & J. Arasteh (Eds.), *Impact of divorce, single parenting and stepparenting in children* (pp. 325–68). Hillsdale, NJ: Erlbaum.

Zill, N., et al. (1991). *The life circumstances and development of children in welfare families: A profile based on national survey data.* Washington, DC: Child Trends.

Zimbardo, P. (1971). *Stanford prison experiment: A simulation study of the psychology of imprisonment conducted at Stanford University.* Retrieved from www.prisonexp.org.

Zimbardo, P. (2007). *The Lucifer effect: Understanding how good people turn evil.* New York: Random House.

Zimbardo, P. (2018). Philip Zimbardo's response to recent criticisms of the Stanford Prison Experiment. Retrieved from www.prisonexp.org/response.

Zimmer, R. W., & Toma, E. F. (2000). Peer effects in private and public schools across countries. *Journal of Policy Analysis and Management, 19*(1), 75–92.

Zimmerman, D. H., & West, C. (1975). Sex roles, interruptions and silences in conversation. In B. Thorned & N. Henley (Eds.), *Language and sex: Difference and dominance* (pp. 105–29). Rowley, MA: Newbury House.

Zuckerman, P. (2009). Atheism, secularity, and well-being: How the findings of social science counter negative stereotypes and assumptions. *Sociology Compass, 3*(6), 949–71.

Zukin, S. (2003). *Point of purchase: How shopping changed American culture.* New York: Routledge.

Zwick, R. (2002). *Fair game? The use of standardized admissions tests in higher education.* New York: Routledge.

Zwick, R., & Sklar, J. C. (2005). Predicting college grades and degree completion using high school grades and SAT scores: The role of student ethnicity and first language. *American Educational Research Journal, 42*(3), 439–65.

Credits

FIGURES AND TABLES

CHAPTER 2: Figure 2.3: Used with permission of Cengage Learning, from Earl R. Babbie, *The Practice of Social Research*, 2007; permission conveyed through Copyright Clearance Center, Inc.

CHAPTER 5: Figure 5.3: Originally from "Studies of independence and conformity: A minority of one against a unanimous majority," by Asch, S. E. *Psychological Monographs* 70 (9), 1–70. doi:10.1037/h0093718. **Figures 5.5 and 5.6**: Republished with permission of University of Chicago Press, from "Chains of Affection: The Structure of Adolescent Romantic and Sexual Networks" by Peter S. Bearman, James Moody, and Katherine Stovel, *American Journal of Sociology*, Vol. 110, No. 1, July 2004, pp. 44–91, 2004; permission conveyed through Copyright Clearance Center, Inc.

CHAPTER 7: Table 7.2: From David L. Featherman and Robert Mason Hauser, *Opportunity and Change* (Academic Press, 1978). Reprinted by permission of the authors.

CHAPTER 8: Elliot Jackson, "'Have You Ever Reconsidered Being Transgender?' Answer by Elliot Jackson," Quora.com, September 30, 2017. Reprinted by permission of the author.

CHAPTER 9: Table 9.1: From Milton M. Gordon, *Assimilation in American Life: The Role of Race, Religion, and National Origins*, 1st ed. (Oxford University Press, New York). Copyright © 1964. Reprinted by permission of Oxford University Press.

CHAPTER 10: Figure 10.2: Figure: "Cost of Living Index, 2017." From the Missouri Economic Research and Information Center, 2018. Data set obtained from the Council for Community and Economic Research (C2ER). Reprinted with permission. **Figure 10.3**: Based on data from OECD (2020), "Poverty rate" (indicator), https://doi.org/10.1787/0fe1315d-en (accessed on August 3, 2020).

CHAPTER 12: Figure 12.1: Figure "Work-Family Living Arrangements of Children, 1960 & 2012" by Philip Cohen. Reprinted by permission of the author.

CHAPTER 14: Figure 14.3: OECD 2020, Collective bargaining coverage, OECD.stat, https://stats.oecd.org/Index.aspx?DataSetCode=CBC.

CHAPTER 16: Figure 16.1: "Christians remain world's largest religious group, but they are declining in Europe," Fact Tank. Pew Research Center, Washington, D.C. (April 5, 2017) https://www.pewresearch.org/fact-tank/2017/04/05/christians-remain-worlds-largest-religious-group-but-they-are-declining-in-europe/. **Figure 16.5**: "The Stronger Sex—Spiritually Speaking." Pew Research Center, Washington, D.C. (February 26, 2009) https://www.pewforum.org/2009/02/26/the-stronger-sex-spiritually-speaking/.

PHOTOS

FRONTMATTER: p. ix: AP Photo/Paul Sakuma; **p. x:** CBS/Photofest; **p. xi:** EMMANUEL DUNAND/AFP/

Getty Images; **p. xii:** Ammentorp Photography/Alamy Stock Photo; **p. xiii:** Patrick T. Fallon/Bloomberg via Getty Images; **p. xiv:** imageBROKER/Alamy Stock Photo; **p. xv:** Bettmann/Getty Images; **p. xvi:** Jim West/agefotostock; **p. xvii:** John Birdsall/Alamy Stock Photo; **p. xviii:** Laura Pedrick/The New York Times/Redux; **p. xix:** Doug Mills/The New York Times/Redux; **p. xx:** Christophe Boisvieux/Getty Images.

CHAPTER 1: pp. 2–3: Erik McGregor/Pacific Press/LightRocket via Getty Images; **p. 7:** Gjon Mili/The LIFE Picture Collection/Getty Images; **p. 9:** Miramax/Photofest; **p. 12 (left):** AP Photo/Paul Sakuma; **p. 12 (right):** Sunday Times/Moeletsi Mabe/Shutterstock; **p. 15:** Courtesy of Asha Rangappa; **p. 17 (left):** Spencer Platt/Getty Images; **p. 17 (right):** Mario Tama/Getty Images; **p. 20 (center):** GRANGER; **p. 20 (left):** SuperStock; **p. 20 (right):** Sarin Images/GRANGER; **p. 21 (left):** Private Collection/Bridgeman Images; **p. 21 (center):** GRANGER; **p. 21 (right):** Temple de la Religion de l'Humanite Paris France/Bridgeman Images; **p. 22 (left):** George Rinhart/Corbis via Getty Images; **p. 22 (right):** Bettmann/Getty Images; **p. 23 (left):** Bibliotheque Nationale Paris France/Bridgeman Images; **p. 23 (center left):** GRANGER; **p. 23 (center right):** Bentley Historical Library/The University of Michigan; **p. 23 (right):** Herbert Orth/The LIFE Picture Collection/Getty Images; **p. 24 (left):** GRANGER; **p. 24 (right):** ullstein bild/GRANGER; **p. 25 (left):** GRANGER; **p. 25 (center left):** GRANGER; **p. 25 (center right):** Sarin Images/GRANGER; **p. 25 (right):** Pictorial Parade/Getty Images; **p. 26 (top left):** From the Collections of the University of Pennsylvania Archives; **p. 26 (bottom left):** Robert W. Kelley/The LIFE Picture Collection/Getty Images; **p. 26 (center):** Fritz Goro/The LIFE Picture Collection/Getty Images; **p. 26 (right):** Sarah Lee/eyevine/Redux; **p. 27 (left):** CARL WAGNER/KRT/Newscom; **p. 27 (top center):** Courtesy of Nigel Stead/The London School of Economics; **p. 27 (mid center):** BOB PEPPING/KRT/Newscom; **p. 27 (bottom center):** American Sociological Association; **p. 27 (top right center):** Courtesy of Duncan Watts; **p. 27 (bottom right center):** Jason Jones/Lake Shore Photography; **p. 27 (right):** Amir Levy/The New York Times/Redux; **p. 31:** George Rinhart/Corbis via Getty Images; **p. 33:** Bob Krist/Getty Images; **p. 36:** Bettmann/Getty Images; **p. 38:** Fox Photos/Getty Images; **p. 39:** Courtesy of Erica Rothman/Nightlight Productions and Dalton Conley; **p. 41:** Visions of America LLC/Alamy Stock Photo.

CHAPTER 2: p. 50: Courtesy of danah boyd; **p. 54:** AP Photo/Nati Harnik; **p. 59:** Courtesy of Shamus Khan; **p. 61:** Ovie Carter; **p. 68:** AP Photo/Julie Jacobson; **p. 69:** Hansel Mieth/The LIFE Picture Collection/Getty Images; **p. 70:** Alfred Eisenstaedt/The LIFE Picture Collection/Getty Images; **p. 71:** dpa picture alliance/Alamy Stock Photo; **p. 72:** JACK GUEZ/AFP/Getty Images; **p. 73:** Courtesy of Matthew Salganik; **p. 76:** US Census Bureau.

CHAPTER 3: p. 84: Tony Roberts/Getty Images; **p. 86 (top left):** Efrain Padro/Alamy Stock Photo; **p. 86 (top right):** Orhan Cam/Shutterstock; **p. 86 (bottom left):** Werner Forman/Universal Images Group/Getty Images; **p. 86 (bottom right):** JLImages/Alamy Stock Photo; **p. 87:** GRANGER; **p. 88:** RMN-Grand Palais/Art Resource NY; **p. 90 (left):** Mitch Kezar/Getty Images; **p. 90 (center):** Atlantide Phototravel /Corbis/VCG/Getty Images; **p. 90 (right):** Rudy Sulgan/Getty Images; **p. 92:** Library of Congress; **p. 93:** Klaas Slot/Shutterstock; **p. 95 (left):** dpa picture alliance/Alamy Stock Photo; **p. 95 (right):** Christian Kober/Robert Harding World Image; **p. 98 (left):** Library of Congress; **p. 98 (right):** Weinstein Company/Courtesy Everett Collection; **p. 99 (left):** Universal History Archive/UIG via Getty Images; **p. 99 (center):** Everett Collection; **p. 99 (right):** CNN via Getty Images; **p. 100:** AP Photo/Bill Hudson; **p. 106:** Bettmann/Getty Images; **p. 107 (left):** CBS/Photofest; **p. 107 (right):** Netflix/Everett Collection; **p. 108:** Kypros/Shutterstock; **p. 109 (left):** AP Photo/Dave Martin; **p. 109 (right):** Chris Graythen/Getty Images; **p. 111:** Ruby Washington/The New York Times/Redux; **p. 113:** Courtesy of Erica Rothman Nightlight Productions and Dalton Conley; **p. 114:** Marmaduke St. John/Alamy Stock Photo; **p. 116 (all):** Adbusters; **p. 117:** Dave Lee/GC Images/Getty Images.

CHAPTER 4: p. 125: Jose Luis Pelaez/Iconica/Getty Images; **p. 127:** David Grossman/Alamy Stock Photo; **p. 129:** Steve Skjold/Alamy Stock Photo; **p. 132:** Red Images LLC/Alamy Stock Photo; **p. 134:** Courtesy of Erica Rothman Nightlight Productions and Dalton Conley; **p. 135:** Courtesy of Fadi Haddad; **p. 141:** Scott

Olson/Getty Images; **p. 143 (top left):** AP Photo/Chris Pizzello; **p. 143 (right):** John Ricard/FilmMagic/Getty Images; **p. 143 (bottom left):** EMMANUEL DUNAND/AFP/Getty Images; **p. 144:** Mark Peterson/Redux; **p. 145:** Courtesy of Erica Rothman Nightlight Productions and Dalton Conley; **p. 147 (left):** AP Photo/Patrick Semansky; **p. 147 (right):** CNAC/MNAM/Dist. RMN-Grand Palais/Art Resource NY © 2018 The Pollock-Krasner Foundation/Artists Rights Society NY; **p. 148:** Kevin Foy/Alamy Stock Photo; **p. 149 (bottom left):** STEPHANIE MCGEHEE/REUTERS/Newscom; **p. 149 (right):** ERIC VIDAL/AFP/Getty Images; **p. 149 (top left):** Michael Dwyer/Alamy Stock Photo; **p. 153:** KEVORK DJANSEZIAN/REUTERS/Newscom; **p. 156:** 20th Century Fox/Photofest; **p. 159:** Piotr Redlinski/The New York Times/Redux; **p. 160:** AP Photo/Steve Meyers.

CHAPTER 5: p. 166: Kim Hong-Ji/REUTERS/Newscom; **p. 167:** Mark Leong/Redux; **p. 169:** Dawn Villella/The New York Times/Redux; **p. 173 (left):** MBI/Alamy Stock Photo; **p. 173 (right):** PYMCA/UIG via Getty Images; **p. 174:** VARLEY/SIPA/Newscom; **p. 178:** redsnapper/Alamy Stock Photo; **p. 180:** Courtesy of Stacy Torres; **p. 181:** Courtesy of Erica Rothman Nightlight Productions and Dalton Conley; **p. 182:** Lee Celano/The New York Times/Redux; **p. 184:** Richard Perry/The New York Times/Redux; **p. 185:** Brandon Pollock/The Courier via AP; **p. 186:** AP Photo/The Ledger Independent Terry Prather; **p. 187:** AP Photo/Patriot-News Paul Chaplin; **p. 188:** Doug Pensinger/Getty Images for AFL; **p. 189:** Courtesy of Erica Rothman Nightlight Productions and Dalton Conley; **p. 190:** Ammentorp Photography/Alamy Stock Photo; **p. 198:** keith morris/Alamy Stock Photo.

CHAPTER 6: p. 204: Courtesy of Erica Rothman Nightlight Productions and Dalton Conley; **p. 206 (left):** British Library Board/Robana/Art Resource; **p. 206 (right):** Bettmann/Getty Images; **p. 207:** AP Photo/David J. Phillip; **p. 208 (left):** Bettmann/Getty Images; **p. 208 (right):** Bettmann/Getty Images; **p. 209:** Three Lions/Getty Images; **p. 210:** AP Photo/Greg Wahl-Stephens; **p. 213:** 3LH / SuperStock; **p. 216:** Pacific Press Service/GRANGER; **p. 219 (top left):** Jack Hollingsworth/Corbis; **p. 219 (top right):** Anthony-Masterson/Getty Images; **p. 219 (bottom left):** SETH WENIG/REUTERS/Newscom; **p. 219 (bottom center):** Kathy deWitt/Alamy Stock Photo; **p. 219 (bottom right):** Joseph Scherschel/The LIFE Picture Collection/Getty Images; **p. 222:** Ruth Fremson/The New York Times/Redux; **p. 223:** Allie Artists/Photofest; **p. 224:** Steve Dietls/Coup D'Etat/Sandbar/Abandon/Ifc/Kobal/Shutterstock; **p. 225:** AP Photo; **p. 228:** Courtesy of Erica Rothman Nightlight Productions and Dalton Conley; **p. 231:** TIMOTHY A. CLARY/AFP/Getty Images; **p. 237:** Courtesy of Matt Ramirez; **p. 238:** Q. Sakamaki/Redux; **p. 240:** Chronicle/Alamy Stock Photo; **p. 242:** Bettmann/Getty Images; **p. 245:** Courtesy of Jacqueline Stevens; **p. 247:** Brant Ward/San Francisco Chronicle/Polaris.

CHAPTER 7: pp. 252–53: Tuca Vieira; **p. 258:** Photo12/UIG via Getty Images; **p. 261:** AP Photo/Themba Hadebe; **p. 262:** AP Photo/Kevork Djansezian; **p. 265:** Ted Streshinsky/CORBIS/Corbis via Getty Images; **p. 266:** Ben Stechschulte/Redux; **p. 268:** WILL BURGESS/REUTERS/Newscom; **p. 270:** FAROOQ NAEEM/AFP/Getty Images; **p. 271:** AP Photo/Steve Coleman; **p. 273:** B.O'Kane/Alamy Stock Photo; **p. 277:** Patrick T. Fallon/Bloomberg via Getty Images; **p. 283:** Courtesy of Erica Rothman Nightlight Productions and Dalton Conley; **p. 286:** Courtesy of Erica Rothman Nightlight Productions and Dalton Conley; **p. 287:** Q. Sakamaki/Redux; **p. 294:** Katherine Taylor/The New York Times/Redux; **p. 295:** GRANGER.

CHAPTER 8: p. 302: Al Drago/CQ Roll Call via AP Images; **p. 308:** FO Travel/Alamy Stock Photo; **p. 309:** Courtesy of Amos Mac; **p. 311:** Marvin Joseph/The Washington Post via Getty Images; **p. 312 (left):** Erin Baiano/The New York Times/Redux; **p. 312 (right):** PYMCA/UIG via Getty Images; **p. 314:** AP Photo; **p. 316:** ClassicStock/Alamy Stock Photo; **p. 318:** Library of Congress; **p. 320:** AP Photo/Greg Smith; **p. 325:** The Advertising Archives; **p. 327:** AP Photo/Noah Berger; **p. 329:** Courtesy of Erica Rothman Nightlight Productions and Dalton Conley; **p. 331:** Ashmolean Museum University of Oxford UK/Bridgeman Images; **p. 333:** University Archives and Records Center University of Pennsylvania; **p. 334:** JASON SZENES/UPI/Newscom; **p. 335:** imageBROKER/Alamy Stock Photo; **p. 337:** Courtesy of Erica Rothman Nightlight Productions and Dalton Conley.

CHAPTER 9: p. 351: The Ohio State University Billy Ireland Cartoon Library & Museum; **p. 352:** Courtesy of Maria Abascal; **p. 356:** SPL/Science Source; **p. 357:** Hulton-Deutsch Collection/CORBIS/Corbis via Getty Images; **p. 358:** National Park Service Statue of Liberty National Monument; **p. 359:** Courtesy of Dr. Bhagat Singh Thind Spiritual Science Foundation; **p. 361:** Keith Bedford/The New York Times/Redux; **p. 362:** Simon Rawles/Alamy Stock Photo; **p. 363:** Courtesy of Erica Rothman Nightlight Productions and Dalton Conley; **p. 364:** REUTERS/Alamy Stock Photo; **p. 366:** BRAD RICKERBY/REUTERS/Newscom; **p. 368:** JONATHAN ERNST/Reuters/Newscom; **p. 370:** Mario Villafuerte; **p. 372:** Jim West/agefotostock; **p. 376:** AP Photo/The Sun Herald Sean Loftin; **p. 382 (top):** National Archives; **p. 382 (bottom):** Bettmann/Getty Images; **p. 383:** Bettmann/Getty Images; **p. 386:** Reuters/Newscom; **p. 390:** Ralph Orlowski/Getty Images; **p. 392:** Library of Congress; **p. 397:** Courtesy of Erica Rothman Nightlight Productions and Dalton Conley; **p. 398:** Courtesy of Kevin Lewis.

CHAPTER 10: p. 406: Herbert List / Magnum Photos; **p. 410:** JILL JOHNSON/KRT/Newscom; **p. 411:** Courtesy of Erica Rothman Nightlight Productions and Dalton Conley; **p. 414:** Gilles Mingasson/Liaison/Getty Images; **p. 413:** Courtesy of Erica Rothman Nightlight Productions and Dalton Conley; **p. 415:** Jeff Haynes/AFP/Getty Images; **p. 416:** Viviane Moos/CORBIS/Corbis via Getty Images; **p. 419 (left):** Tim Boyle/Getty Images; **p. 419 (right):** Scott Olson/Getty Images; **p. 421 (left):** REBECCA COOK/REUTERS/Newscom; **p. 421 (right):** CHRISTOPHER A. RECORD/KRT/Newscom; **p. 422:** ARND WIEGMANN/REUTERS/Newscom; **p. 425:** AP Photo/E Pablo Kosmicki; **p. 426:** Courtesy of Erica Rothman Nightlight Productions and Dalton Conley; **p. 427:** Peter Yates; **p. 434:** Danny Wilcox Frazier/VII/Redux; **p. 439:** AP Photo/Dan Joling.

CHAPTER 11: p. 448: Hulton Archive/Getty Images; **p. 451:** Verulamium Museum St. Albans Hertfordshire UK/Bridgeman Images; **p. 452:** GRANGER; **p. 454:** Karen Ballard/Redux; **p. 456:** ZUMA Press Inc./Alamy Stock Photo; **p. 459:** Jim West/agefotostock; **p. 462:** Pedro Ugarte/AFP/Getty Images;

p. 464: Courtesy of Delores Malaspina; **p. 467:** Blank Archives/Getty Images; **p. 474:** Andrea Kuenzig/laif/Redux; **p. 476:** Courtesy of Corey Abramson; **p. 484:** RENEE ITTNER-MCMANUS/KRT/Newscom; **p. 487:** Hippo Water Roller Project; **p. 488:** Courtesy of Erica Rothman Nightlight Productions and Dalton Conley; **p. 489:** Ryan Garza/ZUMA Press/Newscom; **p. 493:** Carmel Zucker/The New York Times/Redux.

CHAPTER 12: pp: 498–99: Bill Hughes/Bloomsburg Press Enterprise via AP; **p. 504:** Francis Miller/The LIFE Picture Collection/Getty Images; **p. 507 (top):** Jenny Acheson/Getty Images; **p. 507 (center):** Courtesy of Tami Blumenfield; **p. 507 (bottom):** Jenny Matthews/Alamy Stock Photo; **p. 512:** GRANGER; **p. 513:** Louis Edmond Pomey/Fine Art Photographic/Getty Images; **p. 515:** Bert Hardy/Getty Images; **p. 519:** Everett Collection/Newscom; **p. 522:** Courtesy of Jennifer Senior; **p. 524:** Maskot/Getty Images; **p. 527:** Ozier Muhammad/The New York Times/Redux; **p. 530:** AP Photo/Morry Gash; **p. 532:** Stephan Gladieu/Getty Images; **p. 536:** Courtesy of Erica Rothman Nightlight Productions and Dalton Conley; **p. 539:** Amanda Cowan/The Columbian via AP; **p. 540:** John Birdsall/Alamy Stock Photo; **p. 543:** Alex Wong/Getty Images.

CHAPTER 13: p. 551 (left): Hero Images/Getty Images; **p. 551 (right):** Blend Images/Getty Images; **p. 552:** Courtesy of Tamara Trost; **p. 553:** Library of Congress; **p. 554:** John van Hasselt/Sygma via Getty Images; **p. 555 (left):** Stephen Ferry/Redux; **p. 555 (right):** Mark Peterson/Corbis via Getty Images; **p. 558:** Courtesy of Erica Rothman Nightlight Productions and Dalton Conley; **p. 561:** Mark Peterman/The New York Times/Redux; **p. 562:** Courtesy of Erica Rothman Nightlight Productions and Dalton Conley; **p. 565 (left):** AP Photo/The Garden Island Dennis Fujimoto; **p. 565 (right):** AP Photo/Ed Andrieski; **p. 566:** Greg Ruffing/Redux; **p. 567:** ZUMA Press Inc./Alamy Stock Photo; **p. 571:** Laura Pedrick/The New York Times/Redux; **p. 574:** MARKA / Alamy Stock Photo; **p. 578:** Cindy Karp/The New York Times/Redux; **p. 582:** Allen J. Schaben/Los Angeles Times via Getty Images; **p. 586:** Paul A. Souders/Corbis /VCG/Getty Images; **p. 589:** Buccina Studios/Getty Images; **p. 591:** AP Photo/Carolyn Kaster.

CHAPTER 14: p. 599: GRANGER; **p. 600:** GRANGER; **p. 601:** Sarin Images/GRANGER; **p. 604:** Hulton-Deutsch Collection/CORBIS/Corbis via Getty Images; **p. 607 (left):** Walter Sanders/The LIFE Picture Collection/Getty Images; **p. 607 (right):** CRACK PALINGGI/REUTERS/Newscom; **p. 610:** The Henry Ford Museum; **p. 611:** The Henry Ford Museum; **p. 615:** Danny Wilcox Frazier/VII/Redux; **p. 617:** Robert Alexander/Getty Images; **p. 619:** Courtesy of Erica Rothman Nightlight Productions and Dalton Conley; **p. 621:** Adbusters; **p. 623:** Google; **p. 624:** Courtesy of Adam Davidson; **p. 625:** Courtesy of Adeel Qalbani; **p. 626:** Claude Richard ACCIDAT/AFP/Getty Images; **p. 631:** Lukas Coch/Epa/Shutterstock.

CHAPTER 15: p. 638: Courtesy of Jennifer Jacquet; **p. 640:** Alba Vigaray/Epa/Shutterstock; **p. 642:** Michael Nagle/Redux; **p. 644:** AP Photo/Nick Ut; **p. 645 (left):** AP Photo; **p. 645 (right):** Doug Mills/ The New York Times/Redux; **p. 646 (all):** From the film Obedience,1965 by Stanley Milgram. Renewed 1993 by Alexandra Milgram. Distributed by Alexander Street Press; **p. 648:** Silver Screen Collection/Hulton Archive/Getty Images; **p. 649:** John Filo/Getty Images; **p. 650:** Stuart Freedman/Panos Pictures; **p. 651:** Chris Sattlberger/Panos Pictures; **p. 653:** STRINGER/REUTERS/Newscom; **p. 655:** AP Photo; **p. 656:** AP Photo/J. Scott Applewhite; **p. 659:** Bettmann/Getty Images; **p. 661 (left):** Heritage Image Partnership Ltd./Alamy Stock Photo; **p. 661 (right):** AP Photo/Saleh Rifai; **p. 662:** Sarin Images/GRANGER; **p. 666:** Courtesy of Erica Rothman Nightlight Productions and Dalton Conley; **p. 668:** Courtesy of Erica Rothman Nightlight Productions and Dalton Conley; **p. 672:** Xinhua/Alamy Stock Photo; **p. 673:** Courtesy of Zephyr Teachout.

CHAPTER 16: p. 682: TIMOTHY A. CLARY/AFP/ Getty Images; **p. 685 (left):** ESB Professiona/Shutterstock; **p. 685 (center):** Pascal Deloche/Getty Images; **p. 685 (right):** PONGMANAT TASIRI/EPA/Shutterstock; **p. 688:** Christophe Boisvieux/Getty Images; **p. 690:** Herbert Orth/THE LIFE Images Collection/ Getty Images; **p. 691:** World History Archive/SuperStock; **p. 693:** Penny Tweedie/Alamy Stock Photo; **p. 698:** Peter F'rster/picture-alliance/dpa/AP Images; **p. 700:** HARRISON MCCLARY/REUTERS/Newscom;

p. 702: Leon Neal/AFP/Getty Images; **p. 703:** Joshua Lutz/Redux; **p. 705:** ART Collection/Alamy Stock Photo; **p. 706:** Donald Uhrbrock/The LIFE Images Collection/Getty Images; **p. 710:** AP Photo/Charles Sykes/ Invision; **p. 712:** Courtesy of Erica Rothman Nightlight Productions and Dalton Conley; **p. 714:** AP Photo/Jessica Kourkounis; **p. 716:** Andrew White/The New York Times/Redux; **p. 718 (left):** Revolve/Getty Images; **p. 718 (right):** KRT PHOTO VIA DALLAS MORNING NEWS/Newscom; **p. 721:** AP Photo/APTV; **p. 722:** AP Photo/Gene J. Puskar; **p. 723 (left):** AP Photo/Vincent Yu; **p. 723 (right):** JOE BURBANK/KRT/Newscom; **p. 727:** HALEY/SIPA/Newscom.

CHAPTER 17: p. 737 (left): Sheila Terry/Science Source; **p. 737 (right):** Stefano Bianchetti/CORBIS/ Corbis via Getty Images; **p. 738:** Alex Wong/Getty Images; **p. 742 (left):** Reprinted by permission from Macmillan Publishers Ltd: Nature 423 6941, June 12, 2003; **p. 742 (right):** Tom Uhlman/The New York Times/Redux; **p. 743:** Bettmann/Getty Images; **p. 744:** Patrick Landmann/Getty Images; **p. 745:** Bryan and Cherry Alexander/Science Source; **p. 747:** Ralf-Finn Hestoft/CORBIS/Corbis via Getty Images; **p. 749 (top):** JEFF HAYNES/AFP/Getty Images; **p. 750 (bottom):** Martin Klimek/ZUMAPRESS.com/Newscom; **p. 751:** Roadside Attractions/ Photofest; **p. 752:** Pallava Bagla/Corbis via Getty Images; **p. 757:** Columbia Pictures/Photofest; **p. 758 (top):** FRED GREAVES /REUTERS/Newscom; **p. 758 (bottom):** Courtesy of Daniel Belsky; **p. 759:** Sinclair Stammers/Science Source; **p. 761:** Librado Romero/ The New York Times/Redux; **p. 763:** AP Photo/Denis Farrell; **p. 766:** Courtesy of Erica Rothman Nightlight Productions and Dalton Conley; **p. 765:** Courtesy of Erica Rothman Nightlight Productions and Dalton Conley.

CHAPTER 18: p. 773: Sherry LaVars/KRT/Newscom; **p. 775:** Yiorgos Matthaios/AFP/Getty Images; **p. 781:** Mauro Pedro da Silva/Shutterstock; **p. 782:** Mario Tama/Getty Images; **p. 783:** Szilard Koszticsak/ Epa/Shutterstock; **p. 787:** CAROLINE YANG/The New York Times/Redux; **p. 788:** Natan Dvir/Polaris Images/Newscom; **p. 790:** Courtesy of Stephen Duncombe; **p. 793:** Bettmann/Getty Images; **p. 794:** Peter

Index

Bernier, François, 355
Besecke, Kelly, 704
Beveridge Report (1942), 428
Beyoncé, 143
Beyond the Melting Pot (Glazer and Moynihan), 378
Bhopal, India, chemical disaster in, 771–72
bias: and color-blind racism, 389; in criminal justice, 234, 399; and extremism, 373; and political process model, 793; and scientific method, 736; selection, 66, 509; social desirability, 341, 540, 699–700; in test construction, 395, 572, 575, 585
Bible, Christian, 684, 697, 703–4, 712, 718, 722, 726–27, 744
Biblezines, 718–19, 728
Bichlbaum, Andy, 771–72, 803–4, 813
bicycle commuting and safety, 782–83, 795, 799
Biden, Joe, 789
big bang, 735–36
Big Brothers Big Sisters program, 189
Big Sort, 402–3
biodiversity, 754, 769
bio-logic, 320–21
biologists, 741–42 743
biology compared to sociology, 41–42
biomedical culture, 451–53
bio-power, 333
biotechnology and the human genome, 732, 755–66
birdcage metaphor of gender inequality, 317–18
Birmingham, Alabama, 100, 793
birth control, 802
birth order, 268, 475, 500, 534, 589
birthrates, 516
births, out-of-wedlock, 412, 414, 416
birth weight, 590
bisexuality, 176, 331, 335, 336
Bitch (magazine), 110–11
bitcoin, 165–66, 605
"Bitcoin: A Peer-to-Peer Electronic Cash System" (Nakamoto), 165

Black, Dan, 479
Black Americans, 366–67, 369–70. *See also* African Americans
Black church, 709, 710
#Black Lives Matter movement, 399–400, 648, 786, 791, 803
Blackman, Laura, 266
Blackness, 393, 397
Black Panther Party, 772
Black Power, 117
Blair, Tony, 813
Blau, Peter M., 274, 291, 292, 293
blended families, 508, 538
blockchain technology, 165–66, 605, 609
Blood and Earth (Bales), 262
Bloomberg, Michael, 797
blue-collar workers, 275, 291, 554. *See also* working class
Blue Cross/Blue Shield, 457
Blue Lives Matter, 787
Blue Mosque, Istanbul, Turkey, 85, 86
Blum, Ben, 225
Blumenbach, Johann Friedrich, 355
Blumer, Herbert, 33–34, 220
boarding schools, 137
Boas, Franz, 91–92, 360
Bobo, Lawrence, 383
bodycams, 786
Bogaert, Anthony F., 760
Bogle, Kathleen, 190
Bok, Derek, 574
Bonanno, Mike, 771–72
Bonilla-Silva, Eduardo, 389
book editing, 326–27
Borat (film), 156
Borden, Marcus, 726
borderline personality disorder, 481–82
Bordo, Susan, 321
Borlaug, Norman, 753
bots, 103, 597–98
bottled water, 489
boundary work, 741–42
Bourdieu, Pierre, 448, 579
bourgeoisie, 272, 607, 663
bourgeois society, 265
Bowen, William G., 574
Bowles, Samuel, 554
Bowling Alone (Putnam), 184
boy crisis, 587–88

boyd, danah, 49–50, 51, 52, 197
Boy Scouts, 184
BP, 625
Brahman caste, 269
brain aneurysm and SES, 470
brain cancer, 469
Brando, Marlon, 648
Brazil, 252–53, 308, 335, 618–19
Brazilian Americans, 370
BRCA genes, 733–34, 735
breaches in social scripts, 153–56
breast cancer, genetic predisposition to, 733–34, 756
Bricmont, Jean, 743
Bridges, Tristan, 312
Brio (Biblezine), 718
Britain, 256
British Airways, 325
British Broadcasting Company (BBC), 112, 772
British East India Company, 620–21
British explorers and colonists, 367–68
British Humanist Association, 702
broken windows theory of deviance, 228–30
Brooklyn, New York City, 555
Brooks-Gunn, Jeanne, 590
Brouse, Don, 549
Brown, Michael, 786
Browning, Elizabeth Barrett, 542
browning of America, 396, 397–98
Brown v. Board of Education, 381–82, 556
Brubaker, Rogers, 71
Brunei, 620
Bryk, Anthony, 559
Buba people, 763
Buchmann, Claudia, 588
Buddhism, 684, 686, 687, 692, 703, 710, 721
Buffon, Comte de, 355, 376
Bumble app, 343
Burakumin people, 361–63, 365, 585
bureaucracies, 622, 642–45, 667, 676, 678–79, 765, 806, 807
Bureau of Indian Affairs, 368
Burgess, Tituss, 107
Burt, Ronald, 180
Burundi, 769
Bush, George H. W., 574, 672

College Work Study, 405
Collins, Patricia Hill, 319–20, 527–28
Collins, Randall, 13, 568, 570
collusion, 622
colonialism: and Africa, 176, 286–87, 652–53; and caste system, 269; corporate, 620–21; and culture, 85–86, 90; and global inequality, 285, 286–87; and in-groups, 176; and race, 354, 436–37; and reflection theory, 97–98; and slavery, 369
color-blind racism, 389–90
Columbus, Christopher, 367–68
Coming of Age in Samoa (Mead), 92
Communism: and Che Guevara, 219–20; and Cuban immigrants, 371–72; defined, 608; and equality of outcome, 267; and ideology, 91; and Marx, 24–26, 267, 608; and New Deal, 655; and religion, 700
Communist Manifesto (Marx and Engels), 607
communities: and families, 526, 527–28, 529; and incarceration, 237; and policing, 231, 237; and religion, 709; and social capital, 182; and social cohesion, 213
community colleges, 563
comparative research, 71
competition, 33
compression of morbidity, 476, 477
comps (in publishing industry), 109–10
Comte, Auguste, 20–22, 43
concepts, and language and meaning, 36, 89–90
confessional protest, 705
conflict and social change, 811
conflict theory: defined, 33, 264; of education, 569–70; and gendered division of labor, 37; of gender inequality, 317–18; of religion, 688–89
conformists, 218, 219
Confucians, 697
Congo, Democratic Republic of the, 653, 769
Congregationalists, 705, 711

congregations, 685
Conley, Dalton, *The Pecking Order*, 517, 533, 536
ConocoPhillips, 800
Conservative Jews, 687
conspicuous consumption, 298–99, 427
Constitution, US, 76–77, 667, 684, 699
construction industry, 327
Consumer Expenditure Survey, 428, 429
consumerism and consumer culture, 113, 114–15, 424, 427, 681–83, 715
contagion theory of collective action, 774–75
content analysis, 50, 71–72
continental ancestry, 761
contraceptives, 261
contradictory class locations, 272
Contribution to the Critique of Hegel's Philosophy of Right (Marx), 688
convergence theory of collective action, 774
Conyers, John, 392
Cookson, Peter W., Jr., 137
Cooley, Charles Horton, 22, 23, 24, 30, 128, 174
Coontz, Stephanie, 511, 516
Cooperative Wheat Research and Production Program, 753
Copernicus, 91, 736, 737
Coptic Christians, 257
Cordillera, Colorado, 425
core infection model (for STIs), 192
coronavirus pandemic. *See* COVID-19 pandemic
corporal punishment, 708
corporate censorship, 112
corporate crime, 232
corporate culture, 195
corporate personhood, 620–21, 632, 771–72
The Corporation (documentary film), 621
corporations, 180, 601, 618, 620–30
correlation *versus* causality, 53–56, 416
Cortés, Hernán, 87
Coser, Lewis, 33, 264

cost of living, 430
Cotillard, Marion, 98
counterfactuals, 38
countermovements, 787
Counter-Reformation, 37, 39
Covenant House, 781–82
COVID-19 pandemic: and BLM social movement, 791; and education, 578–79; and gig workers, 631; and health inequalities, 479–81; and mask wearing, 785, 810; and millennial generation, 695; and scientific research, 737; and service sector workers, 616; and telemedicine, 445–47; and urban transportation, 783
COVID Racial Data Tracker Project, 479–80
Cowan, Ruth Schwartz, 523
crack cocaine, 244, 393, 412
Cranston, Alan, 158
creationism, 703–4, 726, 727
Creation Museum, 742
creative class occupations, 597–98
creativity, 606–7
credentialism, 13–16, 568–70
The Credential Society (Collins), 13
Credit Suisse Research Institute, 618
Crenshaw, Kimberlé Williams, 319
Crick, Francis, 736
crime, 230–34; defined, 205; hate crimes, 362–63, 467; and the internet, 157; interpreting crime rate, 232–34; and racial groups in the United States, 368–69, 391; and religion, 694; and single mothers, 533; and social capital, 182; street crime, 230–31; white-collar, 231–32
crime reduction, 235–48; deterrence theory, 235–37; Goffman's total institution, 237–39; and prison, 246–47; and punishment, Foucault on, 239–43; and US criminal justice system, 243–48
criminal justice reform, 786–87

stratification, 548. *See also* college; higher education; schools

educational attainment: and divorce's impact on children, 536, 537; and domestic abuse, 520; and ethnicity, 586–87; and families, 588–90; and gender, 587–88, 593; and health, 468; and immigrant families, 541; and life expectancy, 468; and low birth weight, 465; parental, 577, 578; and race, 373, 391, 396, 528, 581; rise in, 569

Educational Testing Service, 19

Edwards, Colorado, 425

Edwards v. Aguillard (1987), 727

egoistic suicide, 214–15

Egypt, 812

Egypt, ancient, 353

Ehrenreich, Barbara, 531

8chan, 113

elastic ties, 180–81

elder abuse, 520

elder care, 514. *See also* long-term care

elections, 498–99

electric cars, 810

The Elementary Forms of the Religious Life (Durkheim), 24, 28, 692

Eli Lilly (pharmaceutical company), 764

elite–mass dichotomy system, 276–79

Ellis Island, 358, 378

El Paso, Texas, mass shooting in, 113

ELSI (ethical, legal, and social issues), 755–56

embeddedness, 177–81

embodied cultural capital, 579

embryonic stem cell research, 737–38

emergence of social movements, 794–95, 816–17

Emergency Medical Treatment and Active Labor Act (1986), 453

emergent norm theory of collective action, 775–76

emerging adulthood, 148

emerging evangelical churches, 721–22

emotional labor, 616–17

empiricists *vs.* theorists, 43

employer-based health insurance, 457–58

enclosure movement, 599, 600, 632

The End Game (Abramson), 478

endogamy, 269–70, 503

energy crisis (1973), 412

Engels, Friedrich, 607, 688

England, 96–97, 428, 451, 452, 599, 600, 715

England, Paula, 337–38

English language, 19

Enlightenment, 21, 51, 257–60, 806

entrepreneurship, 186–87

Entwisle, Doris, 583

Environmental Performance Index, 769

Environmental Protection Agency (EPA), 104

environmental sustainability, 768–69

environmental toxins and legislation, 244

environment and agriculture. *See* agriculture and the environment

environment and corporations, 625

epigenetics, 464–65

Episcopalians, 697, 711–12, 773

Epstein, Cynthia Fuchs, 312

equality of condition, 266

equality of opportunity, 264–65

equality of outcome, 267

equal opportunity, 96

equity inequality, 391–92

erectile dysfunction, 341

Erikson, Erik, 138–40

Erikson, Joan, 139

Erikson, Kai, 232–33

Espenshade, Thomas, 573, 574

essentialist arguments, 305–7, 323

Essman, Elliot, 281

estate system, 268–69

ether activism, 790

ethereum, 165, 166

ethical, legal, and social issues (ELSI), 755–56

ethicalism, 684, 687

ethics of social research, 74–75

Ethiopia, 510, 650, 651

ethnicity: in America in 2018, 394–95; and cultural practices, 29; and educational attainment, 586–87; and primordialism, 378; *versus* race, 364–67, 371, 372; and stratification, 268

ethnocentrism, 86–87, 355

ethnography, 50, 60–62, 742

ethnomethodology, 155–56, 318

eugenics, 357–59, 360

European Commission, 197–98

Europe and Europeans: and Agricultural and Industrial revolutions, 285; and belief in God, 696; and Christianity, 684, 689; genetic distance from Asians, 761; labor laws in, 632; medieval, 38, 59, 256, 268, 696, 715; and new technologies, 764–65; and racism, 390; and unions, 627

European explorers and colonists, 367–68

European immigration, 350–52

European Union, 622

evangelicals and evangelicism, 697, 708, 710, 721–23

Evans, John, 744, 764–65

Evans, Phyllis, 68

Evans, William, 470

Evicted (Desmond), 426

eviction, 425–26

Eviction Lab, 426

evolution, theory of, 51, 703–4, 736, 740–42

evolution and social change, 33

evolutionary biology, 41

exchange mobility, 291

executive branch of government, 667

Executive Order 9066, 392

exogamy, 269–70, 503–4, 540–41

experimental methods, 72–73

experimenter effects, 59–62

extended family, 508

extrafamilial female networks, 526, 527

face, 152–54

Facebook, 103, 112–13, 158, 159, 718–19, 812

Hartford Institute for Religious
Research, 713
Hartmann, Heidi, 317, 612
Harvard Business Review, 346
Harvard University, 310, 311, 572
Hashimoto, Clyde, 565
hate crimes, 362–63, 467
Haussmann, Georges-Eugène, 807
Haven in a Heartless World
(Lasch), 533
Hawaii, 542
Hawke, Ethan, 757
Hawthorne, Nathaniel, 637
Hays, Sharon, 532
Hays Code (Production Code),
105, 106
Head Start, 405, 415
health and society, 444–97; and
climate change, 785; global
health, 485–91; health care
system, US, 456–81; housing
for health, 492–93; medical
profession, 448–55; mental
health, 481–85; sick role,
455–56; social construction
of illness, 456; telemedicine
and the COVID-19 pandemic,
445–47
health care system, US, 456–81;
and aging, 474–76; COVID-
19 and health inequalities,
479–81; differential access
to, 96; health care for older
Americans, 477–79; insur-
ance, 457–59; postnatal
health inequalities, 465–81;
prenatal and early life
determinants, 461–65; and
race, 465–67, 469, 472, 473,
478–81; social determinants
of health and illness, 459–61;
and socioeconomic status,
465, 466–71, 473; stress
and health and mortality,
461, 463, 465, 466–67, 468,
471–72, 473
health insurance: Americans
lacking, 435, 455–56; for
children, 415; fee for service
model, 450; health maintenance organizations, 453; and
independent contractors, 631;
and mental health treatment,
484, 485; in the United States,

457–59. *See also* Affordable
Care Act; Medicaid; Medicare
health maintenance organizations
(HMOs), 453, 457
hearing loss, 475
heart disease, 466, 471–72, 473,
475, 493
Heat Wave (Klinenberg), 747
Heaven Is for Real (film), 714
Heaven's Gate, 720–21
Hecker, Amanda, 571
Heerwig, Jennifer A., 159
Hegel, Georg Wilhelm Friedrich,
261–63, 811
hegemonic masculinity,
310–11, 329
hegemony, 101, 108
Henry, John, 467
herbicides, 751
Herdt, Gilbert, 330–31
Herrnstein, Richard, 33, 417–18,
585–86
Hershey, Barbara, 117
heterodoxy, 453
heteronormativity, 336
heterosexuality, 176, 332
Hetherington, E. Mavis, 537
Heyrman, Christine Leigh, 720
Hezbollah, 649–52
hidden curriculum, 552, 594–95
Higgensen, Vy, 361
high blood pressure.
See hypertension
higher education, 568–77; and
adolescence, 148; adult learning, 576–77; and affirmative
action, 573–75; and credentialism, 568–70; IQ tests,
575–76; tracking in, 563.
See also college; SAT
high-school dropouts, 369, 416
high-yield crop varietals, 753–54
hijab, 363, 698
hijras, 307–8
Hillsong NYC, 716
Hinduism, 215, 269, 684, 686–87,
688, 697, 703, 710
HIPAA privacy regulations, 447
hip-hop culture, 94, 97, 312
Hippocrates, 354, 448
Hippocratic Oath, 448
Hippo Water Roller Project, 487
Hispanics: and Catholic churches,
708–9; defined, 370; diversity

among, 371, 396; and educational inequalities, 561, 582,
586; families, 528; in Harlem,
385; and infant mortality rate,
466; and outmarriage, 541;
racialization of, 379; US population by region of origin,
371; and wealth inequality,
392, 393. *See also* Latinos
(Latinx)
historical materialism, 24–25
historical methods, 70–72
historiography, 38
history compared to
sociology, 37–39
The History of Sexuality (Foucault),
332–33
The History of White People
(Painter), 375
Hitchcock, Alfred, 107
Hitchens, Christopher, 702
Hitler, Adolf, 37, 38
HIV/AIDS, 193, 466, 485, 486,
490–91, 713, 795–97
Hmong Americans and
immigrants, 373, 456
HMOs (health maintenance
organizations), 453, 457
Hobbes, Thomas, 21, 661–62
Hochschild, Arlie, 520–21, 524,
525, 546, 614–15, 616, 617
Hodkinson, Peter, 95
Hofeller, Thomas, 76
Hoffer, Thomas, 559
Hoffman, Abbie, 117
Hogue, Ilyse, 799
HOLC (Home Owners' Loan
Corporation), 385
Holiness Churches, 720
Holland, Peter, 559
Hollywood movies and soft
power, 661
Holocaust, 386–87, 646
home health care for seniors,
477–78
homelessness, 492–93, 712
homeopathy, 452
Home Owners' Loan Corporation
(HOLC), 385
homicides and IPV, 520
homicide victimization rate, 234
homophobia, 145–46
homosexuality: and AIDS, 490,
795, 796–97; in ancient

Greece, 330, 331; cultural variations in attitudes about, 330–31; defined, 332; and depression and suicide, 483; in early editions of *DSM,* 482; and fag discourse, 145–46; and families, 538–40; and genetics, 759–60; history of, 332–34; and household division of labor, 524–25; as identity, 332, 333–34; and marriage, 336, 525, 538–39, 542, 543; and media content, 106; and out-groups, 176; and social norms, 205–6, 207

honor, 638

honorariums, 604

hooks, bell, 320

hook-up culture, 190, 337–38

Horizon Organic, 750

horizontal social mobility, 289

Horndal effect, 629, 630

Horwitz, Allan, 482–83

hospitals, 452–53

Houghton, Katharine, 107

household size, 802–3

House of Hope megachurch, 717

housework, 520–26

housing: and discrimination, 384–85, 391–92, 403; and mental health, 492–93; public, 418–19, 807

Housing First, 492–93

Hout, Michael, 283–84

Howell, Emily (bot), 597–98

How to Observe Morals and Manners (Martineau), 21, 23

Hoxby, Caroline, 567

Hsin, Amy, 133

HSSD (hypoactive sexual desire disorder), 341

HUD (Department of Housing and Urban Development), 406, 418

Hull House, 23, 32

human capital, 272–73

Human Diversity (Murray), 586

Human Genetics, 759

human genome and biotechnology, 755–66

Human Genome Project, 736, 755, 756

humanism, 687–88

human nature, 126–27

Human Nature and the Social Order (Cooley), 128

human rights violations, 626

human trafficking, 262

Hungary, 563

hunger, worldwide, 618

Huntington's disease, 759

Hurricane Katrina, 108–9, 188, 745, 753

Hutu people, 385–86

hybrid cars, 810

hybrid masculinities, 312

hypertension, 466–67, 471–72, 475, 481, 493

hypoactive sexual desire disorder (HSSD), 341

hypotheses: and midrange theory, 35–36; and research cycle, 53; and scientific method, 43, 51; and sociology compared to history, 38–39; testing of, 57–58; and variables, 57

I (concept of), 128

IADL (Instrumental Activities of Daily Living), 476

IBM, 598

ICE (Immigration and Customs Enforcement), 244–45

Iceland, 768

ideas, 608, 689, 691–92, 810

identity and collective action, 770, 777–79, 813–14

ideology, 90–91, 97

Iksil, Bruno, 232

illiteracy, functional, 551

I Love Lucy (TV show), 107

Imbens, Guido, 421

immanence, 684

immigrants: children of, 131; detention of, 244–45; families of, 541–42; undocumented, 76, 541, 799; and unionization, 628; and voluntary participation, 184

immigration: from Africa and the Caribbean, 366, 369–70; and assimilation, 29, 373, 377–79; European, 350–52; family-based policy, 542; and homosexuality, 205; and nativism, 358; and pluralism, 378–80; and racism, 350–52; restrictions on, 351, 358; and social change, 801, 802; and

socialization, 131, 552; and urbanism, 29

Immigration Act of 1924, 351, 358, 360

Immigration and Customs Enforcement (ICE), 244–45

immunization, 493. *See also* vaccines and vaccinations

imperialism, 689

impossibility theorem, 658

impression management, 150–51

incarceration. *See* prison and prisoners

inclusive curriculum, 582–83

income: achievement gap, 294; and bachelor's degree, 10, 12, 14, 283–84; and elderly mortality, 470; and gambling, 421–22; gendering of, 519; and global inequality, 285, 287–88; and household division of labor, 523; and life expectancy, 467–68; and moving to opportunity, 420–241; and parenting, 422, 432–33; and poverty, 405–6, 415–17, 431; and race, 369, 373, 391, 396; and social class/SES, 271, 279–80, 282–84, 577; and status, 274; and status-attainment model, 291–92; *versus* wealth, 278

An Inconvenient Truth (Gore), 745

indentured servants, 369

independent contractors, 630–31

independent variables, 56–57, 58

Index of Occupational Status, 274

India: caste system in, 256–57, 269–70, 503, 689; and colonial globalization, 600; and global inequality, 287, 288; and green revolution technologies, 753, 754–55; Hinduism in, 686; immigration from, 685; and malaria, 487; and nonbinary gender, 307–8; and sex ratio of babies, 462; and social mobility, 256–57

Indiana, 727

Indian Bureau, 368

Indian reservations, 368–69, 434

individualism, 96, 175, 187, 215, 436, 535, 691

Jesus Christ, 685, 697, 703, 721

Jesus Christ Superstar (musical and film), 719

Jewish Hasidism, 684

Jews: in Africa, 762–63; associational and communal involvement, 699; and educational attainment, 710; and fascism, 38; Hasidic, 684; Middle Eastern, 374; percentage of US and world populations, 685, 686, 698–99; and pluralism, 697; racialization of, 359; and secularization, 810; and suicide, 215, 217–18; and Whiteness, 375; and withdrawal, 386–87

jihad, 725

Jim Crow laws, 205, 206, 207, 265, 311, 360, 380, 387

JIT (just-in-time manufacturing), 629

Job Corps, 405

Job Queues, Gender Queues (Reskin and Roos), 326

Jobs, Steve, 11–13

job searching, 178–79

Jocelyn, Simeon, 704

Joe Camel, 116

John Henryism, 467

Johnson, Lyndon B., 383, 405–6, 409, 477

Johnson, Philip, 808

Johnson, Rita, 642–43, 644

Jolie, Angelina, 733–34

Jones, Billy, 797

Jones, John E., III, 726

Joseph, Wayne, 361

journalism, 103

Journal of the American Medical Association, 116

JPMorgan Chase, 165–66, 232, 682

Judaism, 215, 687, 810. *See also* Jews

judicial branch of government, 667

just-in-time manufacturing (JIT), 629

Kalamazoo, Michigan, 722

Kamplain, Elaine, 527

Kane, Thomas J., 573–74

Kant, Immanuel, 356

Kanter, Rosabeth Moss, 327–28

Kardashian, Kim, 117

karma, 686–87

Kasparov, Gary, 598

Kelley, Dean M., 723

Kelling, George, 229–30

Kelly, John, 537

Kennedy, John F., 277, 644, 645

Kent State massacre, 648, 649

Kentucky Fried Chicken, 661

Keraki people, 331

Kerner Commission, 383

Kessler-Harris, Alice, 610

Keynes, John Maynard, 654

Keynesian economics, 438, 654

keynoters, 775–76

Khan, Shamus, 59–60, 558–59, 560

Kilbourne, Jean, 110

Killing Us Softly (film), 110

Kilroy, Patti, 159

Kimmel, Michael, 310–11

King, Billie Jean, 320

King, Martin Luther, Jr., 706–7, 708–9, 728, 793

King, Rodney, 791

Kingdom Identity Ministries, 707

Kinsey, Alfred, 334

kinship, expanded notion of, 528

kinship networks, 511–12, 513

Kittles, Rick, 762

Kitzmiller v. Dover Area School District (2005), 740

Klebanov, Pamela Kato, 590

Klein, Naomi, 113–14

Klinenberg, Eric, 185, 747

Knights of the Fiery Cross (Ku Klux Klan), 707

known unknowns, 442

Knox, Howard, 358

Koch brothers, 789

Korean Americans and immigrants, 717

Kozol, Jonathan, 554–55

Krakauer, Jon, 219

Kramer, Larry, 796

Kraybill, Donald, 186–87

Kruse, Dennis, 727

Kshatriya caste, 269

Kuhn, Thomas, 735–36

Kulick, Don, 308, 335

Kushner, Jared, 277

labeling theory, 220–27, 237

LaBelle, Patti, 713

labor: artisan, 600, 605; blue-collar, 275, 554; domestic,

invisible, 546–47; emotional, 616–17; offshoring and unionization, 626–28; physical reproduction of, 428; purple-collar, 326; reproductive, 524; specialization, 208, 806; unrest, 34; white-collar, 275, 281. *See also* division of labor

laboratories, scientific, 742–44

Laboratory Life (Latour and Woolgar), 742

labor force, women in, 516–17, 547, 587, 613–14

labor force participation, 630

Lady Gaga, 11–13

La Grande Odalisque (Ingres), 87–88

Laidley, Thomas, 133, 467

Lake Forest, California, 715

Lakewood Church, 714

L.A. Law (TV show), 107

Lamarckism, 357

Lamont, Michèle, 65–66

Lancaster County, Pennsylvania, 186–87

Langlois, Donald E., 566–67

language, 19, 89

Lanier, Sidney, 682

Laqueur, Thomas, 305

Lareau, Annette, 131–35, 579–80

large groups, 28–29, 174

Lasch, Christopher, 533

Las Vegas, Nevada, 35, 40

latent content, 72

Latin America, 220, 370, 541, 753

Latinos (Latinx): and COVID-19, 480–81; and demographic changes today, 352–53; families, 528–29; and future of race, 395–97; and health inequalities, 475, 480–81; and incarceration, 385; as racial/ethnic group in the United States, 370–72; and wealth inequality, 391. *See also* Hispanics

Latour, Bruno, 742–44

Lavater, Johann Caspar, 355–56

law enforcement. *See* police and policing

Lawrence, Jill, 532

Lawrence, John Geddes, 207

Lawrenceville, Georgia, 498–99

Lawrence v. Texas (2003), 205–6

396, 503–4, 540–41; Martineau on, 23; and negative income tax, 411; promotion of, 406; rates of, 516; same-sex, 336, 525, 538–39, 542, 543; and shared second shift, 525–26; and welfare, 412–13, 416. See also divorce

marriageable Black male index, 527

The Marriage-Go-Round (Cherlin), 535

Marshall, Missouri, 615

Marshall, T. H., 656

Marshall Plan, 810

Martin, Trayvon, 786

Martineau, Harriet, 20, 21, 22–23

Marx, Anthony, 381

Marx, Karl: and capitalism, 25–26, 271–72, 605–8, 617, 632, 692; and class, 271–72, 279; as classical sociological theorist, 23–26; Communist Manifesto, 607; Contribution to the Critique of Hegel's Philosophy of Right, 688; Critique of the Gotha Programme, 267; and dialectic materialism, 263, 264; and physical reproduction of labor, 428; and reflection theory, 97–98; and religious theory, 688–89, 691, 701; on timeline, 21, 22, 23; Weber compared to, 26–27

Marxism: and class, 271–72; and conflict theory, 33; and education, 554; and feminism, 36, 317, 331–32; and hegemony, 101; and Marx, 24; and reflection theory, 97; and technology, 599; and the welfare state, 654–55

masculinity: and doing gender, 318–19; in dual-income families, 519, 523; femininity compared to, 306–7, 313, 317; and Freud, 316; and gender inequality in the workplace, 327, 328; and gender-role socialization, 145–46; hegemonic, 310–12, 329; and homosexuality, 324–25; and intersectionality, 319–20

mask wearing, 785, 810

mass collective action, 773–74

mass communication, 32, 806

Massey, Douglas, 383

mass incarceration, 243–44. See also prison and prisoners

mass media. See media

mass migration away from coastlines, 748

mass migration into cities, 599–600

mass protest organizations, 799

mass shootings, 113, 146

mass suicide, 721

mastectomies, preventative, 733–34

master–slave dialectic, 261–62

master status, 143

masturbation, 332, 335–36, 340–41

material culture, 88

material deprivation and children, 432, 433

materialist interpretation for social determinants theory, 468

maternal employment, 516–17

maternity leave, 613–14

matriarchal thesis, 526–27

matrix of domination, 319

Matthew effect, 744

Mayer, Susan, 415–17, 424

McAdam, Doug, 779–80, 793, 812–13

MCAT examination, 496

McCain, John, 536, 772

McCandless, Christopher Johnson, 219

McCarty, Oseola, 271

McCormick, Marie, 590

McDonald's, 709, 716, 803

McGlaun, Jenni, 530

McGovern, George, 423

McGrath, Laura, 109

McGuire, Meredith, 703

McIntosh, Peggy, 375

McNamara, Robert, 277

McRobbie, Angela, 110

McVeigh, Timothy, 210

me (concept of), 128

Mead, George Herbert, 22, 24, 25, 30, 34, 128, 129, 130

Mead, Margaret, 40, 92

meaning(s): and actions, 28, 35, 220, 221; and concepts, 36;

and culture, 89–90; cycle of, 33–34; and interpretive sociology, 28, 43; and postmodernism, 34–35; and social interaction, 30, 34, 149; and symbolic interactionism, 149, 220

means-ends theory of deviance, 218

Mean Streets (film), 230

Mears, Ashley, 329–30

Mechanic, David, 449

mechanical solidarity, 207, 208, 209, 210, 211, 240

mechanization, 598, 600

media, 99–116; defined, 99; effects of, 103–5; history of, 99–101; life cycle, 102–3; and organicism, 32; political economy of, 111–16; and power, 658; race and gender politics in, 106–7; savvyness, 83–84; social norms and, 82; and stereotypes, 105–11

Mediaset, 140

mediating variables, 58

mediators, 169, 170

Medicaid, 295, 414, 415, 447, 457, 458, 471, 477–78

medical billing fraud, 232

medical clinics, walk-in, 454

medical education, 13

medicalization, 450–51, 484

medical profession, 448–55

Medicare, 447, 458, 477, 478, 514

Meetup.com, 188, 812

megachurches, 713, 714, 715, 716–17

Meighan, Roland, 552

Men and Women of the Corporation (Kanter), 327–28

meningitis, 490

menopause, 341

mental health and illness, 226–27, 481–85, 492–93. See also suicide; specific mental health issues

mental health institutions, 237–39

Merck, 454

meritocracy, 276, 644

Merton, Robert: and Matthew effect, 744; and midrange theory, 35; and prejudice and

multiracial families, 540–41

Multiracial March on Washington (1996), 396

Munduruku people, 506

murder rate, 234

Murray, Charles, 33, 412–13, 416, 417–18, 423, 532, 585–86

Murree Brewery Company, 270

Musala, Kenya, 474

music downloads, 157

Music Lab experiment, 73

Muslim Americans, 362–64, 365, 374, 685

Muslims: diversity among, 725; and faith in God, 686–87; and Islamic law, 270, 725; and pluralism, 697, 698–99; and Qur'an, 684, 685, 697, 698, 725; racialization of, 363–64; scarves and veils, 726; as share of US population, 698–99; world population of, 685, 686

Mussolini, Benito, 38

NAACP (National Association for the Advancement of Colored People), 24, 31, 380–81, 387

NAAWP (National Association for the Advancement of White People), 376

nadles, 307

NAFTA (North American Free Trade Agreement), 618

NAFTA 2. *See* United States–Mexico–Canada Agreement (USMCA)

Nakamoto, Satoshi, 165–66

names: choice of, 117–18; feminization of, 312–13; and social mobility, 255–57

NAMES Project AIDS Memorial Quilt, 796–97

Nanda, Serena, 307–8

Nantucket Sound, 801

Na people, 506, 507

Napoleonic Code, 211

NARAL (National Abortion Rights Action League) Pro-Choice America, 798–99

Nason-Clark, Nancy, 708

National Academies of Science, 325

National Academy of Sciences, 764

National Alliance on Mental Illness, 483

National Association for the Advancement of Colored People (NAACP), 24, 31, 380–81, 387

National Association for the Advancement of White People (NAAWP), 376

National Association of Evangelicals, 722

National Center for Health Statistics, 516

National College Athletic Association (NCAA), 310–11

National Council of Churches, 723

National Democratic Party in Germany, 390

National Guard, 648

nationalism, 552

National Longitudinal Study of Adolescent Health, 191, 338–39

National Organic Program of the USDA, 749–50

National Origins Act of 1924, 352

National Policy Institute, 373

National Research Council, 395

National Rifle Association, 772, 774

national sin, 705

National Study of Youth and Religion, 715

National Survey of Sexual Health and Behavior, 341

National Voter Registration Act, 672

nation-state, modern, 806

Native Americans: boarding schools for, 552–53; and health inequalities, 466, 481; and Latino racial backgrounds, 371; and legalized gambling, 422; and ownership concept, 90; and poverty, 368–69, 391, 392, 393; as racial group in the United States, 367–69

nativism, 358

natural experiments, 54

naturalization law, 351

natural selection, 357, 740, 741

Nature, 742

nature and culture, 84–85

Navajoland, 368

Navajo people, 307, 368

Nazis and Nazi Germany: and dangers of bureaucracy, 643–44; and Hitler, 38; and Manhattan Project, 739; mechanical social sanctions against collaborators, 209; and racial purity concept, 503; and racism in the US, 381; use of military force against, 660; and Whiteness, 352, 359; and withdrawal of Jews from Poland, 386–87

NCAA (National College Athletic Association), 310–11

negative income tax, 411–12, 420, 422, 423–24. *See also* universal basic income (UBI)

The Negro Family (Moynihan), 526

neighborhoods, 47

Nelson, Alondra, 763–66

Nelson, Margaret, 519

neo-Marxist theory, 654–55

nepotism, 644, 645

Netherlands, 432, 435, 437, 456, 577, 713

Nettles, Bonnie, 720–21

network analysis, 189–94

network theory, 29

net worth, 280, 291–92, 295, 391, 431. *See also* wealth

#NeverAgain, 780

#Never Trump, 812

New Birth Missionary Baptist Church, 713

New Deal, 70, 655

new immigration, 379

new institutionalism, 196–97

New Moon Girls (magazine), 110

New Orleans, Louisiana, 108, 182, 188, 753

new racism, 388–90

Newsweek, 684

New Thought Christians, 685

New York City: and AIDS crisis, 796–97; and bicycle safety and commuting, 783, 795; and BLM movement, 786; and civil inattention, 124–25; and COVID-19 pandemic, 445; crime in, 229–30; immigrants to, 801; incarcerated population in, 237; and poop

Paltrow, Gwyneth, 117
Panama Canal, 487
pandemics and symbolic
  interactionism, 149
Panel Study of Income Dynamics
  (PSID), 67
panel surveys, 67
panopticons, 242–43
Papua New Guinea, 330–31
paradigms, 735–36
paradigm shift, 736
Paradoxes of Gender (Lorber), 303
paradox of authority, 648,
  649, 660
paralegals, 328, 329
parenting strategies and
  socialization, 131–35
parenting stress hypothesis,
  432–33
Pareto, Vilfredo, 276–77
Pareto Principle (80/20 rule), 276
Paris, France, 807, 808
Paris Agreement, 748
Pariser, Eli, 103, 112
Park, Robert, 29, 360, 377, 378–79
Parkinson's disease, 738
Parkland, Florida, high-school
  shooting, 780, 781
parole, 235–36, 241
Parsons, Talcott, 23, 25, 26,
  32–33, 263, 315–16, 455, 505
participant observation, 63–65
participatory movement
  organizations, 799–800
parties, 173
Partnership for a Drug-Free
  America, 104
Pascal, Amy, 153
Pascoe, C. J., 145–46, 312
passing, 387–88
The Passion of the Christ (film), 714
pastiche, 808
paternalism, state, 436
paternity leave, 613
Pathways to Housing, 492
patients' bill of rights, 453
patriarchal family structure, 514,
  527, 610, 708
patriarchy, 313, 317–18
PATRIOT Act, 764
Patterns of Culture (Benedict), 92
Pattillo, Mary, 27, 65
The Pecking Order (Conley), 517,
  533, 536

pecking order and sibling
  differences, 533–35, 589
pedophilia, 227
peekaboo, 127, 129
peers and socialization, 137–38
peers effects in the classroom,
  567–68
penis envy, 316, 317
Pentateuch, 211
Pentecostals, 697, 717, 773
Perrow, Charles, 753
Perry, Brea, 581
Persell, Caroline Hodges, 137
Personal Responsibility and Work
  Opportunity Reconciliation
  Act (PRWORA), 414–15, 532,
  656–57
Peru, 620
perverse equality, 293
perverse incentives, 404, 413, 415,
  458, 459
pesticides, 487, 488, 750, 751, 753,
  754, 755
petit bourgeoisie, 272
Pew Forum on Religion and Public
  Life, 697
Pew Research Center, 521, 539, 725
pharmaceutical industry, 454,
  484–85
Philadelphia, Pennsylvania,
  31, 388
Philip Morris, 17–18
Phillips, Meredith, 583
phrenology, 355, 356
physical anthropology, 39
physiognomy, 355–56
Pierce, Jennifer L., 328
Pilkington, Doris, 553
Pineda, Silvestre, 582
pink-collar jobs, 326
Piper, Charles F., 69
Piven, Frances Fox, 671–73
Plainly Dressed, Paradise Town,
  Pennsylvania, 187
Plath, Sylvia, 217
Plato, 87, 88
play: gender roles in, 144, 302;
  recognition of other in,
  129–30; and social construc-
  tion of reality, 147
Pledge of Allegiance, 552
Plessy v. Ferguson (1896), 360, 380
pluralism, 378–80, 695–99, 715
Point of Purchase (Zukin), 113

Poitier, Sidney, 107
Poland, 386–87
police and policing: aggressive
  or violent, 204, 399–400,
  648–49, 785–87, 791, 813;
  and communities, 231, 237;
  and frame transformation,
  785–87; and legal-rational
  authority, 641, 642; and legitimacy of authority, 648–49;
  and social control, 213; Stop
  and Frisk policy, 786, 803
polio, 490
Polish immigrants, 378
political arbitrage, 623
political order, 276–77
political orientation, 671
political participation, 669–75
political parties, 667–68
political process model of social
  movements, 793
political rights, 656
political science compared to
  sociology, 42
political sociology, 639
politics: defined, 639; online
  activism, 185; and religion,
  712–13; and science, 736,
  737–39, 764–65; in triads,
  168–70
"Politics as a Vocation"
  (Weber), 647
The Politics of Protest (Meyer), 779
Pollan, Michael, 749–50
Pollock, Jackson, 146–47
pollution, 244, 810
polyamory, 336
polyandry, 504
polygamy, 504
polygenism, 357
polygyny, 504
polytheism, 686
pooper-scooper movement and
  law, 776–77
poor, 284–85, 671, 672. *See also*
  poverty
Poor Richard's Almanack (Franklin), 690
population and sampling,
  68–69, 76
population growth, 259–61,
  704, 754
Portland, Oregon, 782–83
Pose (TV show), 302

positivist sociology and positivism, 20, 21–22, 28, 43, 63

Posse Foundation, 266

postmodern evangelical churches, 721–22

postmodernity and postmodernism, 34–35, 320–21, 544, 807–9

Potrykus, Ingo, 751–52

poverty, 404–43; absolute and relative, 428–32, 439; before agricultural and industrial revolutions, 285; and the Black church, 709; and children, 415–18, 420, 422, 432–34, 435; culture of, 408–27; defined, 284, 428; and domestic abuse, 520; global, 618; and global health, 486–90; and incarceration, 237; paths out of, 203–5; and race, 368–69, 431, 436–37, 582; and segregation, 383; and single mothers, 529–33; and street crime, 230; in the United States compared to other countries, 434–37

Poverty, a Study of Town Life (Rowntree), 428

poverty line, 428–30, 432, 435, 444

poverty rates, 428–29, 432

Powell, Brian, 588, 589

Powell, Troy A., 588

Powell, Walter, 196–97

power, 657–69; defined, 646–47, 657; and gender inequality, 317–18, 331–32; and international relations, 660–61; and political science, 42; in research, 62–63; and sexuality, 331–32; states of nature and social contracts, 661–67; three-dimensions of, 657–60; in the United States, 667–69

Power and Morality (Sorokin), 554

Power and Powerlessness (Gaventa), 659–60

Power: A Radical View (Lukes), 657

power elite, 196

The Power Elite (Mills), 276–77

power loom, 600

pragmatist school of philosophy, 30

praise dancing, 709

pranayama yoga, 703

predestination, doctrine of, 608, 691

preindustrial families, 511–12

prejudice, 388–90

premenstrual dysphoric disorder, 482

premodern families, 511–12

premodernity and premodern societies, 207–8, 209, 211, 240, 305, 805

prenatal health inequalities, 461–65

Preparing for Power (Cookson and Persell), 137

Presbyterian Church and Presbyterians, 705, 711, 721

prescription drug costs, 477

The Presentation of Self in Everyday Life (Goffman), 26, 34, 150–51

presidential election, US (2016), 91, 103

Presley, Lisa Marie, 504

primary deviance, 226

primary groups, 174–75

primordialism, 378

Prince George's County, Maryland, 717

printing press, invention of, 99–100

prison and prisoners: abuse, 224–25, 684; and deterrence theory, 235–36; and homelessness, 492; mass incarceration, 243–44; population size, 243; and punishment, 240–43, 246–47; and race, 369, 385, 528; rape, 324; and rehabilitation, 210, 236–37, 238, 243, 246–47; and secondary deviance, 237; and suicide, 217; total institutions, 237–39

prison-industrial complex, 406

privacy and genetic data, 756

private property, 257–59, 263, 599, 607, 654–55

private schools *versus* public schools, 558–60

private school vouchers, 590–91

Privilege: The Making of an Adolescent Elite at St. Paul's School (Khan), 558

Production Code, 105, 106

productivity and aging workforce, 629, 630

productivity and unionization, 627–28

productivity enhancing activities, 623, 624–25

profane and sacred, 614–15, 683–84, 685, 695, 715

professional movement organizations, 798–99

professional schools, 551

prohibition, 794

Project STAR, 557

proletariat class, 272

Promise Church, 717

Promise for Education program, 550

pronuclear transfer, 765

prostitution, 262, 335, 533

The Protestant Ethic and the Spirit of Capitalism (Weber), 27, 689

Protestantism and Protestants: and affiliation switching, 714; associational and communal involvement, 699; and families, 708; and gender, 710; and megachurches, 713, 716; as percent of Christians worldwide, 685; and race, 709; and sect-church cycle, 720–21; as share of US population, 697, 698–99; and social class, 711–12; and suicide, 215; and Weber, 689–92. *See also specific denominations*

Protestant Reformation, 27, 354, 608, 807

Pruitt-Igoe Houses, 807, 808

PRWORA (Personal Responsibility and Work Opportunity Reconciliation Act), 414–15, 532, 656–57

PSID (Panel Study of Income Dynamics), 67

psychiatric hospitals and labeling experiment, 223–27

psychoanalytic theories of gender inequality, 316–17

psychology, compared to sociology, 41–42

psychosis and drugs, 463–64, 492

psychosocial interpretation for social determinants theory, 468

Ptolemy, 737
public confession, 705, 706
public housing, 418–19, 807
public schools *versus* private
    schools, 558–60
public shaming, 637–39
Publisher's Weekly, 109
publishing industry, 109–10
Puerto Ricans, 370, 371
Puerto Rico, 673
Puga, Malinda, 410
Puget Consumers' Co-op, 749
Pugh, Allison, 113, 114–15
Pulp Fiction (film), 8–9
pulses, 754
Punished (Rios), 204
punishment, 205–6, 207, 239–43,
    246–47, 637–39. *See also*
    social sanctions
Purdue Pharma, 484
Pure Flix, 714
Puritans, 232–33
purple-collar jobs, 326
The Purpose-Driven Life
    (Warren), 714
Pussyhats, 811
Putnam, Robert, 183, 184, 188
Pygmalion effect, 565, 757–58
Qalbani, Adeel, 624–25
Quadagno, Jill, 70
Quakers, 232, 685
qualitative methods and research,
    43, 44, 51–52, 61, 63, 69
"Quantitative Aspects of the
    Group" (Simmel), 167–68
quantitative methods and
    research, 42, 43, 44, 51, 52, 63
Queens, New York City, 717
queer people, 335–36. *See also*
    homosexuality; nonbinary
    gender/sexual identities
Qur'an, Muslim, 684, 685, 697,
    698, 725
Rabe, Lee, 722
race, 348–403; in the ancient
    world, 353–54; and crimi-
    nal justice system, 243–48;
    defined, 350; in the early
    modern world, 354–57; and
    early sociologists, 29, 30–31;
    and educational inequal-
    ities, 560, 581–86; *versus*
    ethnicity, 364–67, 371, 372;
    and eugenics, 357–59; future

of, 395–98; and genetics,
    761–66; and glass escalators,
    329; group responses to dom-
    ination, 386–88; and health,
    465–67, 469, 472, 473, 475,
    478–81; inter-group relations,
    352–53, 377–86; and life
    expectancy, 55, 465–66, 472,
    473, 478–79; and media con-
    tent, 106–7; and the mortality
    crossover, 478–79; myth of,
    350–53, 386; number of exe-
    cutions by, 248; and poverty,
    368–69, 431, 436–37, 582;
    prejudice, discrimination,
    and the new racism, 388–90;
    and property values, 393;
    racial groups in the United
    States, 367–74; realities of,
    361–64, 386; and religion,
    708–9; and socioeconomic
    status, 369, 373, 396, 466,
    582; and sociological imagi-
    nation, 349–50; and stigma,
    227–28; and stratification,
    268, 293–94; and textbooks,
    71–72; twentieth-century
    concepts of, 359–61; and US
    Census questions, 396; and
    wage gap, 325; and wealth,
    391–95, 431, 582; Whiteness,
    351, 352, 359–60, 374–77.
    See also ethnicity
race-based affirmative action, 293
race riots, 383, 387
racial conflict, 385–86
racialization, 359, 363–64, 366,
    371, 374, 379, 386
racial justice, 728. *See also* #Black
    Lives Matter movement; civil
    rights movement
racism: and citizenship rights,
    351; color-blind, 389–90; cul-
    tural, 389–90; and death pen-
    alty, 245–48; defined, 351–52;
    and ethnocentrism, 86–87;
    and exclusion of African
    Americans from safety net,
    70, 437; and global inequality,
    286; institutional, 393–95;
    and Irish immigrants, 350,
    351; in Japan, 361–62; in the
    media, 105–10; and mortality,
    473; new, 388–90; persistence

of, 389–90; and poverty, 204;
    and pseudoscience, 355–56,
    358; scientific, 355, 360;
    and social Darwinism, 357;
    and social norms, 205, 206;
    systemic, 467. *See also* White
    nationalism; White suprem-
    acy and White supremacists
radical feminists, 317
radio, 100
Radiohead, 157
Radway, Janice, 102
railroad, 37, 39
Rainbow Man, 83–84, 115, 116–18
Ramirez, Marc, 236–37
Ramses II, Pharaoh, 743, 744
Rana Plaza factory collapse, 626
Rangappa, Asha, 15–16
rape, 175–76, 330
rap music, 808
rational actor model, 42
rationality, 27, 29, 689, 703–4,
    806, 807
rationalization, 642, 667, 676, 691
Rauscher, Emily, 131, 674
rBST, 748
Read, Jen'nan, 362, 363, 698, 725
Reading the Romance (Radway), 102
Reagan, Ronald, 382, 406, 530,
    672, 713, 772
reality, social construction of, 30,
    146–59
Reardon, Sean, 294
rebels, 219–20
recidivism, 235, 237, 246
Reconstruction era, 707
Reddy, Gayatri, 307–8
redemptive social movements, 781
redistricting, 76
redlining, 385, 392, 403
reference groups, 176
reflection theory, 97–99
reflexive spirituality, 704
reflexivity, 59
reformative social movements,
    782–84
Reform Jews, 687
Refuel (Biblezine), 718
rehabilitation of prisoners, 210,
    236–37, 238, 243, 246–47
reincarnation, 686
relative poverty, 431–32, 439
reliability, 57–58

religion(s), 680–731; and biotechnology, 764–65; and capitalism, 608, 689–90; and caste system, 269, 270; Church of Stop Shopping, 681–83; commercialization of, 713–19; and Comte, 20–21; defined, 683; and deviance, 232–33; and Durkheim, 28, 684, 692–95; and families, 529, 708; as ideological framework, 91; media promotion of, 83–84, 115, 116–18; and medical practices, 92; and modernity, 806; paradox of popularity, 680, 719–25; and premodern society, 805; prevalence worldwide, 684–88; and rationality, 703–4; and secularization, 695–701; and the social landscape, 707–13; and social movements, 704–7, 727; and suicide, 215; and superstitions, 730–31; theories of, 688–95, 701

religious attendance in the United States, 699–701

religious experiences, 703

religious non-affiliates, 683, 686, 694, 697

Remaking U.S. Trade Policy (Chorev), 619–20

remedial classes in school, 561

Renaissance, 696, 806

Renoir, Pierre-Auguste, 212, 213

rent seeking activities, 623–24

reparations, 392

representative samples, 67

reproductive labor, 524

reproductive technologies, 461–63, 501–2, 510

Republic (Plato), 87

Republican Party, 76, 542, 668, 713

research, 48–81; ethics of, 74–75; methods and basics of, 51–73; research process, 64

research cycle, 52–53

residential segregation, 383–85, 391–92, 403, 418, 426–27

Resistance, 787–89

resistance and power, 657

resistance *versus* acceptance to racial oppression, 388

Reskin, Barbara, 326

resocialization, 138

resource dilution model, 589

resource mobilization, 707

resource-mobilization theory of social movements, 792

resources and political participation, 671

respectability politics, 786

retirement systems, 630

retreatists, 219

returns to schooling, 10, 11, 12

reverse causality, 56

revolutionary social movements, 784

Revolve (Biblezine), 718

Reynolds, William Bradford, 382

Rich, Adrienne, 332

Ridgefield, Washington, 539

right to be forgotten, 197–98

Right to Organize and Collective Bargaining Convention (1949), 626

right-wing hate groups, 707

Rios, Victor, 203–5

risk society, 752–53

Risman, Barbara, 518, 525–26, 611–12

ritualists, 218, 219

R. J. Reynolds, 116

Robeson, Paul, 382

Robinson, Doug, 797

Robinson, James, 663–64

Rockefeller, John D., 647

Rockefeller Foundation, 753

Rockin' Rollen, 83–84, 115, 116–18

role conflict, 142, 151, 162–63

roles, 129–30, 141–42, 151, 162–63, 172–73

role strain, 142, 162–63

role theory, 141–43, 455

romance novels, 102

romantic leftovers, 193–94

Rome, ancient, 354, 451

roommates, 158–59

Roos, Patricia, 326

Roosevelt, Franklin D., 70, 392, 437, 794

Roots (Haley), 366

Rosaldo, Michelle, 314

Rosenbaum, James, 418–19, 561

Rosenhan, David L., 223

Rosenthal, Robert, 565

Ross, Wilbur, 75–76, 277

Rothstein, Jesse, 572

Rotimi, Charles, 762

Rousseau, Jean-Jacques, 21, 86, 257–58, 263, 267

routinization, 641–42, 667

routinization of social movements, 798

Rove, Karl, 713

Rowling, J. K., 72, 98

Rowntree, Benjamin Seebohm, 428

Rubin, Donald, 421

Rubin, Gayle, 313–14

Rudd, Kevin, 553–54

Rumsfeld, Donald, 442

Run for Something, 789

Rusape Jewish Tabernacle, 763

Rwanda, 385

Ryan White Act, 491

Sacerdote, Bruce, 158, 421

Sachs, Jeffrey, 260–61, 286, 487–88

sacred and profane, 614–15, 683–84, 685, 695, 715

sacred canopy, 695–96

Saddleback Church, 715

sadness *versus* depression, 483

safety net, 413, 415, 436–37

safety net, informal, 409, 410, 529

Salai-i-Martin, Xavier, 288

salary system, 604, 606

Salem Baptist Church, 717

Salganik, Matthew, 73

Salk, Jonas, 742, 743

Sambia people, 330–31

same-sex marriage, 336, 525, 538–39, 542, 543

Samoans, 40, 92

samples and sampling, 68–69

San Clemente, California, 114

Sanders, Bernie, 185, 812

San Francisco, California, 801

sanitation, 486, 489, 769

San Quentin State Prison, 247

sanskritization, 270

São Paulo, Brazil, 252–53

Sapir-Whorf Hypothesis, 89

Satcher, David, 466

sati (suttee), 215

SAT test, 266, 292, 557, 570–75, 578, 584–85, 587

Saunders, Edward, 734

Savage Inequalities (Kozol), 554–55

Scandinavia, 38–39

scared straight programs, 246, 247

The Scarlet Letter (Hawthorne), 637

Schippers, Mimi, 336

schizophrenia, 464–65, 501, 502

Schlosser, Eric, 750

school choice, 590–91

schools: advertising in, 113–14; characteristics of, and student achievement, 555–60; desegregation of, 382, 556, 584; functions of, 550–55; primary and secondary, 18–19; segregation of, 381–83; and socialization, 135–37, 551–55, 594–95; as sorting machines (tracking), 554–55, 560–63, 584, 595; teachers and peers, influence of, 564–68. *See also* college; education

school shootings, 146, 780, 781

Schüll, Natasha Dow, 40

science, 732–69; agriculture and the environment, 745–55; biotechnology and the human genome, 732, 755–66; as ideological framework, 91; and modernity, 805–6; and politics, 736, 737–39, 764–65; and religion, 703–4; and risk, 732; and social adaptation, 733–34; and society, 735–44; sustainability, 768–69

science wars, 743–44

scientific method, 51

scientific racism, 355, 360

scientific revolutions, 735–36

Scottish Enlightenment, 258–60, 267

scrolling ticker, 99

search engines, 112, 197–98

Seattle, Washington, 411–12, 493, 749, 781, 813

secondary deviance, 226–27, 237

secondary groups, 175

Secondat, Charles de, 356

second shift, 520–26, 614

The Second Shift (Hochschild), 546

Second Treatise of Government (Locke), 662

sect-church cycle, 719–22

sects or sectarian groups, 719–20, 724

secularism, 686, 726

secularization, 695–701, 715, 725, 810

secular morality, 20

secular totems, 684

segmental solidarity, 207, 208, 209, 210, 211

segregation: and the Big Sort, 402–3; of churches, 708–9; and civil rights movement, 803; and criminal justice system, 385; and equal opportunity concept, 96; and inter-group relations, 380–85; and Jim Crow laws, 205, 206, 207, 265, 311, 360, 380, 387; and poverty, 204; residential, 383–85, 391–92, 403, 418, 426–27; of schools, 381–83; and social norms, 205, 206, 207

selection theory for SES and health correlation, 468

self, 30, 127–29

self-concept, 30, 128

self-fulfilling prophecy, 565, 584, 595, 757–58

selfishness, 42

Senior, Jennifer, 522–23

Seoul, South Korea, 166

separation of church and state, 726–27

Sephardic Jews, 763

seppuku (hara-kiri), 215, 216

September 11, 2001 (9/11), 362–63, 374, 524, 698–99, 725

September 11 Victim Compensation Fund, 524

service sector, 282, 616–17

Sesame Street (TV show), 104

sex: defined, 302–3; and feminist theory, 36; relationship with gender, 303–6. *See also* gender; sexuality

Sex, Gender, and Society (Oakley), 26, 36

sex/gender system, Rubin's, 313–15

sexism, 96, 110–11, 146, 317–18, 321

sex-reassignment surgeries, 304–5

sex recession, 340

sex role theory, 315

sex-selective abortion, 461–62

sexual assault, 342. *See also* rape

Sexual Behavior in the Human Male (Kinsey), 334

sexual harassment, 145, 322, 324–25, 328, 342–43

sexuality: adolescent, 92, 137–38, 145–46, 190–93, 337–40; and aging, 340–41; contemporary, 335–36; cultural variations in, 330–31; and daughters, 131; defined, 303; and gender inequality, 332; and gender relations, 330; in-groups and out-groups, 176; and media, 106–7; social construction of, 331–35; and social norms, 205–6

sexually transmitted diseases/infections, 190–93, 338, 339

sexual orientation, 205, 319, 332, 756, 759–60. *See also* homosexuality; sexuality

Shabab, 651

Shakespeare, William, 98–99, 147, 150, 169

shaming, public, 637–39

The Shape of the River (Bowen and Bok), 574

"Share the Safety," 772

shar'ia law, 270, 725

Sharkey, Patrick, 582

Shatner, William, 107

Shavit, Yossi, 561

Shiite Muslims, 686, 725

Shintoists, 697

Shiva, Vandana, 754–55

Shock Corridor (film), 223

Shore, Bradd, 93–94

Shudra caste, 269

Shulman, James, 574

shushin koyo (lifelong employment), 629

sibling differences and pecking order, 533–35

sibling-on-sibling violence, 519

sickle-cell anemia, 756

Sidewalk (Duneier), 61

Sierra Leone, 653

Sikhs, 358, 363, 364, 697, 698–99

silent films, 100

Simmel, Georg: and capitalism, 603–5, 606, 617, 632; as classical sociological theorist, 24,

social mobility, 255–57; and caste system, 269–70; and class system, 270–73; defined, 289; and elite-mass dichotomy system, 276; and estate system, 268–69; and genetics, 758–59; *versus* social reproduction, 288–92; and status hierarchy system, 275, 291

social movements, 779–804; alternative, 780–81; defined, 779; and frames, 784–91; models of, 791–94; organizations, 798–801; redemptive, 781; reformative, 782–84; and religion, 704–7, 728; revolutionary, 784; and social change, 801–4, 814; stages of, 794–98, 816–17; successful, 814; types of, 780–84

social networks, 17, 18–19, 176–201; and cryptocurrencies, 166; defined, 176; how to disappear from, 200–201; network analysis, 189–94; online, 50, 185, 188, 197–98; organizations, 194–97; and prep-school education, 137; right to be forgotten, 197–98; six degree theory, 181–82; social capital, 182–89; strength of weak ties, 164, 177–81

social norms, 46–47, 82, 205–6, 207, 210, 213

Social Origins of Dictatorship and Democracy (Moore), 663

social physics, 20, 21–22, 43

social regulation, 214, 216–17

social relations, 17

social reproduction, 255, 269, 288–92, 524

social rights, 656–57

social role, 17

social sanctions, 209–13, 240, 251, 638–39

social scripts, 153–56, 160

Social Security Administration, 642–43

Social Security benefits, 70, 423, 437, 470, 478, 654, 656, 794

social self, 30, 128

social solidarity, 28, 29, 693–95

The Social Sources of Denominationalism (Niebuhr), 719

social stratification. *See* stratification

social welfare benefits, 654

Society in America (Martineau), 21, 22–23

socioeconomic status (SES): and aging, 461; categories of, 279–85; defined, 279, 577; and divorce's impact on children, 536, 537; and education, 577–80; and health, 465, 466–71, 473; and immigrant families, 541; net worth distribution in the United States, 280; and political participation, 671; and race, 369, 373, 396, 466, 582; and religion, 710–12; and risk of dying, 444; and status-attainment model, 291–92. *See also* social class

sociological imagination, 2–3, 6–16, 19–20, 349–50

The Sociological Imagination (Mills), 7

sociology, 4, 5–6; compared to other disciplines, 37–42; divisions within, 43–44; interpretive, 28, 43; political, 639; positivist, 20, 21–22, 28, 43, 63; research in, 48–81; of sociology, 19–37; timeline of, 20–27

Sodhi, Balbir Singh, 363, 364

soft power, 661

Sokal, Alan, 743

Somalia, 650–51, 653, 769

Somaliland, 650–51

Sommers, Christina Hoff, 322–23

Sony, 714, 808

sorghum, 754

Sorokin, Pitirim, 289, 554

South Africa, 91, 176, 503, 784, 792

South America and South Americans, 368, 371, 506, 601, 805

South Asia, 753

South Bronx, New York, 229

Southern Baptist churches, 708, 709

Southern Christian Leadership Conference, 707

Southern Cross (Heyrman), 720

sovereign wealth fund (SWF), 438–39

Soviet Union, 91, 199, 451, 652, 802

Spain, 38, 613, 632

Spanish explorers and colonists, 367–68

spanning tree model for STIs, 192, 193

special education, 567–68, 581, 582

specialization, 208, 211, 643, 644

Special Supplemental Nutrition Program for Women, Infants, and Children (WIC), 410

specific deterrence, 235

speed networking events, 178

Spencer, Herbert, 263, 357, 373

The Spirit Catches You and You Fall Down (Fadiman), 456

spirit of capitalism, 690, 692

The Spirit of the Laws (Secondat), 356

spiritual awakening, 703

Spock, Dr., 523

spurious relationships, 55–56

Spurlock, Morgan, 750, 751

Stacey, Judith, 544, 615

Stack, Carol, 317, 346

Standard Oil, 647

Stanford-Binet IQ test, 575

Stanford Prison Experiment, 224–25, 239

The Stanford Prison Experiment (film), 224

Stanford Research Institute, 411–12

Starbucks, 682

Stark, Rodney, 696, 699, 701, 715, 723–24

Star Trek (TV show), 107

the state: and authority and legitimacy, 646–57; new functions of, 653–57; and organicism, 32, 206–7; origins of, and government, 661–67; as term, 639, 647, 652; and Weber, 27, 652, 653. *See also* authority

state paternalism, 436

states, international system of, 649–53

State University of New York, 310

Stateville Penitentiary, 242

Temporary Assistance for Needy Families, 656

Tennessee State Department of Education, 557

terrorism, 42, 362, 363, 374, 698–99, 707

tertius gaudens, 169, 170, 180

testing and institutional racism, 395

Tett, Gillian, 625

Texas, 205–6, 211, 637, 716

textile industry, 34, 600, 619

textual analysis, 102

Thatcher, Margaret, 390

theism, 684

theories: applying, 36–37; and research cycle, 52–53; and scientific method, 43, 51

The Origins of the Civil Rights Movement (Morris), 707

theorists *vs.* empiricists, 43

The Theory of the Leisure Class (Veblen), 298

Theranos, Inc., 232

theyrule.net, 195

thimerosal, 764

Thind, Bhagat Singh, 358

Third Reich, 38, 644

Thomas, W. I., 30, 757–58

Thomas Nelson, Inc., 718

Thonga people, 331

Threads (church), 722

three strikes laws, 231

Thrillist, 112

ties, 176–77

The Time Bind (Hochschild), 614

The Time Divide (Jacobs and Gerson), 615

Time magazine, 105–8, 751

Time to Talk app, 346

timid bigots, 389

Tinder app, 339, 343

Tinkler, Justine, 342

Title VII of the Civil Rights Act, 311

Title IX of the Education Amendments of 1972, 311

Tjungurrayi, Brandy, 268

Tocqueville, Alexis de, 183

Todaro, Eric, 210

tokenism, 293, 328

Tollesboro, Kentucky, 186

Toltec columns, Tula, Mexico, 85, 86

Toma, Eugenia F., 567

Torah, Jewish, 641, 684, 687

Torres, Stacy, 180–81

tort law, 210–11

torture, 224–25, 241

total institutions, 140–41, 237–39

total quality management (TQM), 629

totemism, 684, 692

Townsend Plan movement, 794

town squares, 184

TPP (Trans-Pacific Partnership), 620

TQM (total quality management), 629

tracking in schools, 560–63, 584

trade and capitalism, 602–3, 618, 619–20

traditional authority, 641

traditional family model, 504–6, 508, 511, 518, 528, 610

traditionalist evangelicals, 721–22

transcendental meditation, 703

transgender people: adolescent, 146; and bathroom/locker room issues, 301–2, 311; and civil rights frame, 785; and college sports, 310–11; defined, 308; and depression and suicide, 323, 483; and doing gender, 319; and empowerment, 343–44; and families, 539–40; and purple-collar labor, 326; and social norms, 206; *travesti,* 308, 335

Trans-Pacific Partnership (TPP), 620

Transportation Alternatives, 783, 795

trash television, 140

travesti, 308, 335

Travolta, John, 9

triadic closure, 171

triads, 167, 168–71, 193

tri-racial isolates, 359–60

Trošt, Tamara Pavasovic, 552

True Love Waits, 338

Truman, Harry S., 100, 392, 437

Trump, Donald: and countermovements, 787; and COVID-19 pandemic, 445; election of, 91, 640; and embryonic stem cell research, 739; and federal prison reform, 244; and gender identity, 311; and global trade, 620; and hate crimes, 363; and immigration, 372, 785; and modern power elite, 277; and Muslim ban, 799, 800; and nepotism, 644, 645; and online fund-raising, 185; and Paris Agreement, 748; and the Resistance, 789, 811; and school vouchers, 591; and US Census Bureau, 75–76, 77; and White nationalism, 367; and work requirements for Medicaid, 415

Trump International Hotel and Tower, 682

Truth, Sojourner, 320

Tsemberis, Sam, 492

tsetse fly, 487

tuberculosis, 486, 488, 743

Tudor period, 599

Turing, Alan, 124, 598

Turing Test, 124, 598

Tutsi people, 385–86

tween, as term, 148

Twenty-sixth Amendment, 674, 675

23andme.com, 761

twin births, 463, 510

twin studies, 126

Twitter, 718–19, 812

2 Chainz, 298

two-sex model of human bodies, 305

Tyson, Karolyn, 584

Uber, 630, 631–32

UBI. *See* universal basic income (UBI)

UDF (United Democratic Front), 784

Udry, J. Richard, 191

Uggen, Christopher, 670

UN (United Nations), 650, 652, 746, 810, 811

unbanked, 634–35

Unbreakable Kimmy Schmidt (Netflix series), 107

underclass, 285, 412–17

underemployment rate, 630

undocumented immigrants, 76, 541, 799

unemployment: and negative income tax, 411–12; and race, 369, 372, 373, 391, 528; rate of, 630; and welfare, 412

Watts, Duncan, 27, 72–73, 74, 181, 182

Wayward Puritans (Erikson), 232–33

The Way We Never Were (Coontz), 511

weak ties, strength of, 164, 177–81

wealth: and affirmative action, 294–95; *versus* income, 278; and Industrial Revolution, 285; and poverty, 424, 431–32; and race, 391–95, 431, 582; and social class/SES, 279, 577. *See also* net worth

The Wealth of Nations (Smith), 601

Weather Underground, 784

Webb, Beatrice Potter, 319

Weber, Max: and authority, 27, 661, 676, 678; and bureaucracy, 622, 667, 676, 765, 807; and capitalism, 27, 608, 632, 689–92; and class, 271, 272–73; as classical sociological theorist, 23–24, 26–28; and definition of power, 646, 657; *Economy and Society,* 24, 27, 646; and legitimate authority, types of, 639–44; and modernity, 807; "Politics as a Vocation," 647; *The Protestant Ethic and the Spirit of Capitalism,* 23, 27, 689; and religious theory, 689–92, 701, 728; and the state, 27, 652, 653, 663; and status, 273; on timeline, 22, 23, 24; *Verstehen,* 27–28, 43, 689

Weingarter, Eliot, 132–33

welfare: and children's well-being, 415–17, 519; and Moving to Opportunity, 419; and poverty, 406, 409–10; reforms, 413, 414–15, 532, 656–57; and single mothers, 530–31

welfare state, 653–57

welfare trap, 531–32

West, Candace, 143, 318

West, Kanye, 117

West, Mae, 106

West, Marion, 361

West, North, 117

West Africa, 761

Western culture, 40

What Money Can't Buy (Mayer), 415–16, 424

white coat effects, 59, 61

white-collar crime, 231–32

white-collar workers, 275, 281

White flight, 384–85, 389, 393

Whitehall Study, 459–60

White nationalism, 367, 390, 397

Whiteness, 351, 352, 359–60, 374–77, 397

White Patriot, 376

White privilege, 375–76, 390

"White Privilege" (McIntosh), 375

Whites: and conversion to Islam, 363; and COVID-19, 480–81; and demographic changes today, 352–53; and educational inequalities, 560, 561, 580, 581, 582, 583–84, 585–86; and ethnic diversity, 396; families, 528, 529; and forced assimilation of native populations, 553–54; and health inequalities, 465–66, 475, 480–81; and labeling, 221; and motherhood, 510; and naming patterns, 118; and outmarriage, 541; and residential segregation, 383–85; and symbolic ethnicity, 366; and wealth inequality, 391, 431

White supremacy and White supremacists, 373, 376–77, 707, 786

White supremacy and White supremacists, 373

Why Americans Don't Vote (Piven and Cloward), 671–72

Why Conservative Churches Are Growing (Kelley), 723

Whyte, William Foote, 25

WIC (Special Supplemental Nutrition Program for Women, Infants, and Children), 410

WikiLeaks, 103

Will and Grace (TV show), 107

Willer, Robb, 665–66

Williams, Alexander, 134

Williams, Christine, 328–29

Willow Creek Community Church, 717

Wilson, William Julius, 293–94, 413, 527

Winant, Howard, 389–90

wind farms, protests against, 801

Winfrey, Oprah, 11

Wirth, Louis, 29

Wisconsin, 211, 628

withdrawal, 386–87

Wolpe, Joseph, 333

woman question, 313, 314, 317, 319, 320–21

women: and cash economy, 512–14; in college, 321–22; and delayed marriage and motherhood, 510; execution as witches, 206, 207; green revolution benefits for, 754; and history, 38; interrupted by men, 346–47; single, 509–10; single mothers, 509–10; and suicide, 217; and textual analysis, 102; violence against, 110; and wages, 610–12; in the workforce, 284, 319, 323–30, 515, 516–17, 547, 587, 613–14. *See also* feminism; gender

Women's March, 787–89, 811, 813

women's rights, 36, 91, 802

"women's work," 513, 523

Woodsy Owl, 104

Woolgar, Steve, 742–43

workfare, 414–15

working class, 131–35, 271–72, 281–84, 285, 319–20, 579–80, 607–8. *See also* blue-collar workers

working mothers, 516–17, 520–26, 612–16

World Bank, 753, 769

World Health Organization, 304, 487

World Trade Organization (WTO), 618, 620, 621, 772, 813

World War II: and employer-based health insurance, 457; families after, 514–16; famine during, 432; and hard power, 660; and Holocaust, 386–87; and Japanese internment camps, 392; and Manhattan Project, 739; Navajo code talkers in, 7, 368; and racism, 105–8, 360; and segregation, 381–82; and social change, 7, 810, 811

World Wildlife Fund (WWF), 795